SIPRI Yearbook 2005
Armaments, Disarmament and International Security

sipri

Stockholm International Peace Research Institute

SIPRI is an independent international institute for research into problems of peace and conflict, especially those of arms control and disarmament. It was established in 1966 to commemorate Sweden's 150 years of unbroken peace.

The Institute is financed mainly by a grant proposed by the Swedish Government and subsequently approved by the Swedish Parliament. The staff and the Governing Board are international. The Institute also has an Advisory Committee as an international consultative body.

The Governing Board is not responsible for the views expressed in the publications of the Institute.

Alyson J. K. Bailes, Director, *Yearbook Editor and Publisher*
Ian Anthony, *Executive Editor*
Connie Wall, *Managing Editor*
Coordinators
Ian Anthony, Alyson J. K. Bailes, Elisabeth Sköns
Editors
D. A. Cruickshank, Jetta Gilligan Borg, Andy Mash, Connie Wall

sipri

Stockholm International Peace Research Institute
Signalistgatan 9, SE-169 70 Solna, Sweden
Cable: SIPRI
Telephone: 46 8/655 97 00
Telefax: 46 8/655 97 33
Email: sipri@sipri.org
Internet URL: http://www.sipri.org

SIPRI Yearbook 2005

Armaments, Disarmament and International Security

Stockholm International Peace Research Institute

OXFORD UNIVERSITY PRESS
2005

OXFORD
UNIVERSITY PRESS

Great Clarendon Street, Oxford OX2 6DP

Oxford University Press is a department of the University of Oxford.
It furthers the University's objective of excellence in research, scholarship,
and education by publishing worldwide in

Oxford New York

Auckland Cape Town Dar es Salaam Hong Kong Karachi
Kuala Lumpur Madrid Melbourne Mexico City Nairobi
New Delhi Shanghai Taipei Toronto

With offices in

Argentina Austria Brazil Chile Czech Republic France Greece
Guatemala Hungary Italy Japan Poland Portugal Singapore
South Korea Switzerland Thailand Turkey Ukraine Vietnam

Oxford is a registered trade mark of Oxford University Press
in the UK and in certain other countries

Published in the United States
by Oxford University Press Inc., New York

*Yearbooks before 1987 were published under the title
'World Armaments and Disarmament:
SIPRI Yearbook [year of publication]'*

British Library Cataloguing in Publication Data
Data available

Library of Congress Cataloging in Publication Data
Data available

Typeset and originated by Stockholm International Peace Research Institute
Printed and bound in Great Britain
on acid-free paper by
Biddles Ltd, King's Lynn, Norfolk

ISSN 0953–0282
ISBN 0–19–928401–6 978–0–19–928401–6

Contents

Part II. Military spending and armaments, 2004

Part III. Non-proliferation, arms control and disarmament, 2004

Annexes

Preface

The Stockholm International Peace Research Institute presents in this volume the 35th edition of the SIPRI Yearbook. It combines the continuation of SIPRI's traditional documentary and data analysis work with chapters which report and comment on developments in the fields of political and institutional security, arms control, non-proliferation and disarmament.

For the last edition of the Yearbook, reporting on events during 2003, Iraq more or less dictated itself as the leitmotif. In 2004, although the travails of the occupying forces in Iraq, the painful gestation of Iraqi democracy, and the continuing argument about the rights and wrongs of the US-led coalition's actions continued to make headline news, these topics did not colour the entire agenda in quite the same way. Even in Iraq's own region, events reminded the international public also of the seminal importance of the dispute between Israel and the Palestinians and of the dangers should another state—Iran—acquire a nuclear weapons capability. Events in Darfur, Sudan, brought the weak states/conflict nexus and the peace-building challenge freshly into focus. The tsunami disaster of 26 December 2004 brought death and suffering to foreign visitors as well as hundreds of thousands of local inhabitants, forcibly illustrating both the gravity and the literally universal impact of major natural disasters in a 'globalized' environment. Clearly, contemporary security challenges range far wider than the 'new threats' of terrorism and weapons of mass destruction, on which much of the world's attention had—perhaps too narrowly—focused since 2001.

Many of the short-term security challenges of 2004 were of a sort to underline the need for cooperative multilateral solutions, involving not just nation states and traditional forms of international organization, but also new kinds of partnership and divisions of labour with actors from other sectors (business, civil society, non-governmental organizations and so on).

Appropriately enough, the year was marked by the continuation of efforts that had started in 2003 to rebuild cooperative relationships across the Atlantic; to strengthen further the foundations of strategic unity in the European Union; to find productive ways of using the United Nations' competences, and to keep the World Trade Organization's current trade liberalization round alive. For all this, it would have required an exceptionally optimistic observer to conclude, as the year closed, that the scene was set for the sustained 're-institutionalization' of global governance. Some relationships that had seemed to be heading for stability within rule-based structures, such as Russia's relations with its Western neighbours, entered a new period of strain; while democratic regime change in Ukraine challenged assumptions about the limits of European institutional families. The problem of 'regionalizing' security in a positive way for regions like the greater Middle East, South Asia and the Far East came no nearer to a solution, despite some well-meaning experiments. The re-election of George W. Bush as US President in November was generally read as betokening a further four years in which the USA would continue to use institutional and legal frameworks, at best, instrumentally.

One reason for hope is that the advocates of law-based cooperative approaches to security problems have understood that they cannot rest on their laurels. As the European Union has committed itself to 'effective' multilateralism, supporters of the UN have engaged in major reviews of that organization's contribution to global security and development. In this Yearbook, the findings of one particularly important exercise—the High-level Panel appointed by the UN Secretary-General to look at current global security challenges and responses—are reproduced and the volume's Introduction aims to support them with reflections on some of the underlying issues. Some of the latter are taken up in more detail in the chapters of the three parts of the Yearbook that follow, coordinated respectively by myself, Elisabeth Sköns and Ian Anthony. Such themes as the unresolved tensions and shifts of institutional function within the USA–Europe and Russia–West relationships; the importance of peace-building as part of the conflict prevention and management cycle; differential rates of development in cooperative regional security; the policy and resource implications of present-day extended definitions of the meaning of security; and the challenge of finding approaches to arms control, non-proliferation and disarmament that combine respect for regulatory instruments with brisk handling of 'problem cases', seem bound to demand SIPRI's attention not just in this Yearbook but for several years ahead.

SIPRI continues to seek ways to make best use of this Yearbook and its contents as a tool of transparency. We are grateful to the sponsors and partners whose support will allow us, this year too, to produce complete translations of this Yearbook into Arabic, Chinese, Russian and Ukrainian and translations of a pocket-sized summary version into Farsi, French, German, Spanish and Swedish. (The latter short texts may be found on the SIPRI Internet site at http://www.sipri.org/contents/publications/pocket/pocket_yb.html.) All proposals for further translations and ways of reaching a wider audience with this publication will be welcome.

As always, production of this Yearbook has been a truly collective endeavour. While warmly thanking all SIPRI colleagues and outside contributors, I would like to make special mention of the invaluable work of Managing Editor Connie Wall and the team of Editors—Jetta Gilligan Borg, David Cruickshank and Andy Mash; Nenne Bodell and the SIPRI Library staff, who take the lead in producing much of the volume's reference material; Gerd Hagmeyer-Gaverus and the IT Department; Peter Rea, the indexer; and my Assistant, Cynthia Loo.

Alyson J. K. Bailes
Director of SIPRI
June 2005

Glossary

NENNE BODELL and CONNIE WALL

Abbreviations

ABM	Anti-ballistic missile
ACV	Armoured combat vehicle
AG	Australia Group
ALCM	Air-launched cruise missile
APEC	Asia–Pacific Economic Forum
APM	Anti-personnel mine
ARF	ASEAN Regional Forum
ASEAN	Association of South-East Asian Nations
ATTU	Atlantic-to-the Urals (zone)
AU	African Union
BMD	Ballistic missile defencc
BSEC	Organization of Black Sea Economic Cooperation
BTWC	Biological and Toxin Weapons Convention
BW	Biological weapon/warfare
CAR	Central African Republic
CBM	Confidence-building measure
CBW	Chemical and biological weapon/warfare
CD	Conference on Disarmament
CEI	Central European Initiative
CEMAC	Communauté Economique et Monétaire d’Afrique Centrale (Economic Community of Central African States)
CFE	Conventional Armed Forces in Europe (Treaty)
CFSP	Common Foreign and Security Policy
CICA	Conference on Interaction and Confidence-building Measures in Asia
CIS	Commonwealth of Independent States
CPA	Coalition Provisional Authority
CPA-IG	Coalition Provisional Authority Inspector General
CPC	Conflict Prevention Centre
CSBM	Confidence- and security-building measure
CSCAP	Council for Security Cooperation in the Asia Pacific
CSTO	Collective Security Treaty Organization
CTBT	Comprehensive Nuclear Test-Ban Treaty
CTBTO	Comprehensive Nuclear Test-Ban Treaty Organization
CTC	Counter-Terrorism Committee
CTR	Co-operative Threat Reduction
CW	Chemical weapon/warfare
CWC	Chemical Weapons Convention
DAC	Development Assistance Committee
DDR	Demobilization, disarmament and reintegration
DFID	Department for International Development
DPA	Department of Political Affairs

DPKO	Department of Peacekeeping Operations
DRC	Democratic Republic of the Congo
EAEC	European Atomic Energy Community (*also* Euratom)
EAPC	Euro-Atlantic Partnership Council
ECOMOG	ECOWAS Monitoring Group
ECOWAS	Economic Community of West African States
EMU	European Monetary Union
ESA	European Space Agency
ESDP	European Security and Defence Policy
ESS	European Security Strategy
EU	European Union
FP	Framework Programme
FRY	Federal Republic of Yugoslavia
FSC	Forum for Security Co-operation
FY	Financial year
FYROM	Former Yugoslav Republic of Macedonia
G8	Group of Eight
GAERC	General Affairs and External Relations Council
GCC	Gulf Cooperation Council
GDP	Gross domestic product
GLCM	Ground-launched cruise missile
GNI	Gross national income
GNP	Gross national product
GPC	General purpose criterion
HCOC	Hague Code of Conduct
HCNM	High Commissioner on National Minorities
HEU	Highly enriched uranium
IAEA	International Atomic Energy Agency
ICBM	Intercontinental ballistic missile
ICC	International Criminal Court
IGAD	Intergovernmental Authority on Development
IGC	Intergovernmental Conference
IMF	International Monetary Fund
INDA	International non-proliferation and disarmament assistance
INF	Intermediate-range Nuclear Forces (Treaty)
IRBM	Intermediate-range ballistic missile
ISG	Iraq Survey Group
JCG	Joint Consultative Group
JHA	Justice and home affairs
JSF	Joint Strike Fighter
LACM	Land-attack cruise missile
LEU	Low-enriched uranium
MANPADS	Man-portable air defence system
MDGs	Millennium Development Goals
MER	Market exchange rate
MERCOSUR	Mercado Común del Sur (Southern Common Market)
MIRV	Multiple, independently targetable re-entry vehicle
MTCR	Missile Technology Control Regime
NAM	Non-Aligned Movement
NATO	North Atlantic Treaty Organization
NBC	Nuclear, biological and chemical (weapons)
NGO	Non-governmental organization
NPT	Non-Proliferation Treaty
NRF	NATO Response Force
NSG	Nuclear Suppliers Group

OCCAR	Organisme Conjoint de Coopération en Matière d'Armement
OCHA	Office for the Coordination of Humanitarian Affairs
ODA	Official development assistance
OECD	Organisation for Economic Co-operation and Development
OIC	Organization of the Islamic Conference
OPCW	Organisation for the Prohibition of Chemical Weapons
OSCC	Open Skies Consultative Commission
OSCE	Organization for Security and Co-operation in Europe
PFP	Partnership for Peace
PPP	Purchasing power parity
PSI	Proliferation Security Initiative
R&D	Research and development
RD&E	Research, development and engineering
RDT&E	Research, development, testing and evaluation
SAARC	South Asian Association for Regional Co-operation
SADC	Southern African Development Community
SALW	Small arms and light weapons
SAM	Surface-to-air missile
SCO	Shanghai Cooperation Organization
SCSL	Special Court for Sierra Leone
SECI	Southeast European Cooperative Initiative
SLBM	Submarine-launched ballistic missile
SLCM	Sea-launched cruise missile
SOP	Statement of Interdiction Principles
SORT	Strategic Offensive Reductions Treaty
SRBM	Short-range ballistic missile
SSM	Surface-to-surface missile
SSR	Security sector reform
START	Strategic Arms Reduction Treaty
TLE	Treaty-limited equipment
UAE	United Arab Emirates
UAV	Unmanned air vehicle
UCAV	Unmanned combat air vehicle
USAID	US Agency for International Development
UN	United Nations
UNDP	UN Development Programme
UNHCR	UN High Commissioner for Refugees
UNMOVIC	UN Monitoring, Verification and Inspection Commission
UNROCA	UN Register of Conventional Arms
UNSCOM	UN Special Commission on Iraq
WA	Wassenaar Arrangement
WEAG	Western European Armaments Group
WEAO	Western European Armaments Organisation
WEU	Western European Union
WMD	Weapon(s) of mass destruction

Intergovernmental bodies and international organizations

The main organizations and export control regimes discussed in this Yearbook are described in the glossary. Members or participants are listed on pages xxvii–xxxiv. On the arms control and disarmament agreements mentioned in the glossary, see annex A in this volume.

African Union (AU)	The Constitutive Act of the African Union entered into force in 2001, formally establishing the AU. Its headquarters are in Addis Ababa, Ethiopia, and it is open for membership of all African states. In 2002 it replaced the Organization for African Unity. The AU promotes unity, security and conflict resolution, democracy, human rights, and political, social and economic integration in Africa. *See* the list of members.
Agency for the Prohibition of Nuclear Weapons in Latin America and the Caribbean (OPANAL)	Established by the 1967 Treaty of Tlatelolco to resolve, together with the IAEA, questions of compliance with the treaty. Its seat is in Mexico D.F., Mexico.
Andean Community of Nations	Established in 1969 (as the Andean Pact), the Andean Community promotes the economic and social development and integration of its member states. Its seat is in Lima, Peru. *See* the list of members.
Arab League	The League of Arab States, established in 1945, with Permanent Headquarters in Cairo, Egypt. Its principal objective is to form closer union among Arab states and foster political and economic cooperation. An agreement for collective defence and economic cooperation among the members was signed in 1950. *See* the list of members.
Association of South-East Asian Nations (ASEAN)	Established in 1967 to promote economic, social and cultural development as well as regional peace and security in South-East Asia. The seat of the Secretariat is in Jakarta, Indonesia. The ASEAN Regional Forum (ARF) was established in 1994 to address security issues. *See* the lists of the members of ASEAN and ARF.
Australia Group (AG)	Group of states, formed in 1985, which meets informally each year to monitor the proliferation of chemical and biological products and to discuss chemical and biological weapon-related items which should be subject to national regulatory measures. *See* the list of participants.
Black Sea Economic Cooperation (BSEC)	*See* Organization of the Black Sea Economic Cooperation.
Central European Initiative (CEI)	Established in 1989 to promote cooperation among members in the political and economic spheres. It provides support to its non-EU members in their process of accession to the EU. The seat of the Executive Secretariat is in Trieste, Italy. *See* the list of members.

Collective Security Treaty Organization (CSTO)	Formally established in 2003, the CSTO emanates from the 1992 Collective Security Treaty for the promotion of cooperation among the parties, mainly states in Central Asia. An objective is to provide a more efficient response to strategic problems such as terrorism and narcotics trafficking in the region. Its seat is in Moscow, Russia. *See* the list of members.
Commonwealth of Independent States (CIS)	Established in 1991 as a framework for multilateral cooperation among former Soviet republics, with headquarters in Minsk, Belarus. *See* the list of members.
Commonwealth of Nations	An organization, established in 1949, of developed and developing countries whose aim is to advance democracy, human rights, and sustainable economic and social development within its member states and beyond. Its Secretariat is in London, UK. *See* the list of members.
Comprehensive Nuclear Test-Ban Treaty Organization (CTBTO)	Established by the 1996 CTBT to resolve questions of compliance with the treaty and as a forum for consultation and cooperation among the states parties. Its seat is in Vienna, Austria.
Conference on Disarmament (CD)	A multilateral arms control negotiating body, set up in 1961 as the Eighteen-Nation Committee on Disarmament; it has been enlarged and renamed several times and has been called the Conference on Disarmament since 1984. It reports to the UN General Assembly and is based in Geneva, Switzerland. *See* the list of members under United Nations.
Conference on Interaction and Confidence-building Measures in Asia (CICA)	Initiated in 1992, and established by the 1999 Declaration on the Principles Guiding Relations among the CICA Member States, as a forum to enhance security cooperation and confidence-building measures among the member states. It also promotes economic, social and cultural cooperation. *See* the list of members.
Council for Security Cooperation in the Asia Pacific (CSCAP)	Established in 1993 as an informal, non-governmental process for regional confidence building and security cooperation through dialogue and consultation in Asia–Pacific security matters. *See* the list of member committees.
Council of Europe	Established in 1949, with its seat in Strasbourg, France, the Council is open to membership of all the European states that accept the principle of the rule of law and guarantee their citizens' human rights and fundamental freedoms. Among its organs are the European Court of Human Rights and the Council of Europe Development Bank. *See* the list of members.
Economic Community of West African States (ECOWAS)	A regional organization established in 1975, with its Executive Secretariat in Lagos, Nigeria, to promote trade and cooperation and contribute to development in West Africa. In 1981 it adopted the Protocol on Mutual Assistance in Defence Matters. The ECOWAS Monitoring Group (ECOMOG) was established in 1990 as a multinational peacekeeping/peace-enforcement force. *See* the list of members.

Euro-Atlantic Partnership Council (EAPC)	Established in 1997, the EAPC provides the overarching framework for cooperation between NATO and its PFP partners. *See* the list of members under North Atlantic Treaty Organization.
European Atomic Energy Community (Euratom, or EAEC)	Created by the 1957 Treaty Establishing the European Atomic Energy Community (Euratom Treaty) to promote the development of nuclear energy for peaceful purposes and to administer the multinational regional safeguards system covering the EU member states. Euratom is located in Brussels, Belgium. The members of Euratom are the EU member states.
European Union (EU)	Organization of European states, with its headquarters in Brussels, Belgium. The 2000 Treaty of Nice entered into force on 1 February 2003. The three EU 'pillars' are: the Community dimension, including the Single European Market, the Economic and Monetary Union (EMU) and the Euratom Treaty; the Common Foreign and Security Policy (CFSP); and cooperation in Justice and Home Affairs (JHA). The Treaty establishing a Constitution for Europe was signed by the EU heads of state or government in October 2004, but it will not enter into force until all the EU governments have ratified it, by a parliamentary vote or a referendum. *See* the list of members and *see also* European Atomic Energy Community.
Group of Eight (G8)	Group of eight (originally seven) leading industrialized nations which have met informally, at the level of heads of state or government, since the 1970s. Russia has since 1997 participated in all but the meetings on finances and is to become a full member in 2006. *See* the list of members.
Gulf Cooperation Council (GCC)	The Cooperation Council for the Arab States of the Gulf, known as the GCC and with its headquarters in Riyadh, Saudi Arabia, was created in 1981 to promote regional integration in such areas as economy, finance, trade, administration and legislation and to foster scientific and technical progress. The members also cooperate in areas of foreign policy and military and security matters. The Supreme Council is the highest GCC authority. *See* the list of members.
Intergovernmental Authority on Development (IGAD)	Established in 1996 to promote peace and stability in the Horn of Africa and to create mechanisms for conflict prevention, management and resolution. Its Secretariat is in Djibouti, Djibouti. *See* the list of members.
International Atomic Energy Agency (IAEA)	An intergovernmental organization within the UN system, with headquarters in Vienna, Austria. The IAEA is endowed by its Statute, which entered into force in 1957, to promote the peaceful uses of atomic energy and ensure that nuclear activities are not used to further any military purpose. Under the NPT and the nuclear weapon-free zone treaties, non-nuclear weapon states must accept IAEA nuclear safeguards to demonstrate the fulfilment of their obligation not to manufacture nuclear weapons. *See* the list of IAEA members under United Nations.

Hague Code of Conduct Against Ballistic Missile Proliferation (HCOC)	The 2002 HCOC is subscribed to by a group of states which recognize its principles, primarily the need to prevent and curb the proliferation of ballistic missile systems capable of delivering weapons of mass destruction and the importance of strengthening multilateral disarmament and non-proliferation mechanisms. The Austrian Ministry of Foreign Affairs, Vienna, Austria, acts as the HCOC Secretariat. *See* the list of subscribing states.
Joint Compliance and Inspection Commission (JCIC)	The forum established by the 1991 START I Treaty in which the parties exchange data, resolve questions of compliance, clarify ambiguities and discuss ways to improve implementation of the START treaties. It convenes at the request of at least one of the parties.
Joint Consultative Group (JCG)	Established by the 1990 CFE Treaty to promote the objectives and implementation of the treaty by reconciling ambiguities of interpretation and implementation.
Mercado Común del Sur (MERCOSUR)	*See* Southern Common Market.
Missile Technology Control Regime (MTCR)	An informal military-related export control regime which in 1987 produced the Guidelines for Sensitive Missile-Relevant Transfers (subsequently revised). Its goal is to limit the spread of weapons of mass destruction by controlling ballistic missile delivery systems. *See* the list of participants.
NATO–Russia Council	Established in 2002 as a mechanism for consultation, consensus building, cooperation, and joint decisions and action on security issues, focusing on areas of mutual interest identified in the 1997 NATO–Russia Founding Act on Mutual Relations, Cooperation and Security and new areas, such as terrorism, crisis management and non-proliferation.
NATO–Ukraine Commission	Established in 1997 for consultations on political and security issues, conflict prevention and resolution, non-proliferation, arms exports and technology transfers, and other subjects of common concern.
Non-Aligned Movement (NAM)	Established in 1961 as a forum for consultations and coordination of positions in the United Nations on political, economic and arms control issues among non-aligned states. *See* the list of members.
North Atlantic Treaty Organization (NATO)	Established in 1949 by the North Atlantic Treaty (Washington Treaty) as a Western defence alliance. Article 5 of the treaty defines the members' commitment to respond to an armed attack against any party to the treaty. Its institutional headquarters are in Brussels, Belgium. *See* the list of members.

Nuclear Suppliers Group (NSG)	Established in 1975 and also known as the London Club, the NSG coordinates national export controls on nuclear materials according to its Guidelines for Nuclear Transfers (London Guidelines), which contain a 'trigger list' of materials that should trigger IAEA safeguards when they are to be exported for peaceful purposes to any non-nuclear weapon state, and the Guidelines for Transfers of Nuclear-Related Dual-Use Equipment, Materials, Software and Related Technology (Warsaw Guidelines). *See* the list of participants.
Open Skies Consultative Commission (OSCC)	Established by the 1992 Open Skies Treaty to resolve questions of compliance with the treaty.
Organisation for Economic Co-operation and Development (OECD)	Established in 1961, its objectives are to promote economic and social welfare by coordinating policies among the member states. Its headquarters are in Paris, France. *See* the list of members.
Organisation for the Prohibition of Chemical Weapons (OPCW)	Established by the 1993 Chemical Weapons Convention as a body for the parties to oversee implementation of the convention and resolve questions of compliance. Its seat is in The Hague, the Netherlands.
Organisme Conjoint de Coopération en Matière d'Armement (OCCAR)	Established in 1996, with headquarters in Bonn, Germany, as a management structure for international cooperative armaments programmes between France, Germany, Italy and the UK. It is also known as the Joint Armaments Cooperation Organization (JACO).
Organization for Security and Co-operation in Europe (OSCE)	Initiated in 1973 as the Conference on Security and Co-operation in Europe (CSCE), in 1995 it was renamed the OSCE and transformed into an organization, with headquarters in Vienna, Austria, as a primary instrument for early warning, conflict prevention and crisis management. Its Forum for Security Co-operation (FSC), located in Vienna, Austria, deals with arms control and CSBMs. The OSCE comprises several institutions, all located in Europe. *See* the list of members.
Organization of American States (OAS)	Group of states in the Americas which adopted its charter in 1948, with the objective of strengthening peace and security in the western hemisphere. The General Secretariat is in Washington, DC, USA. *See* the list of members.
Organization of the Black Sea Economic Cooperation (BSEC)	Established in 1992, with its Permanent Secretariat in Istanbul, Turkey. Its aims are to ensure peace, stability and prosperity in the Black Sea region and to promote and develop economic cooperation and progress. *See* the list of members.
Organization of the Islamic Conference (OIC)	Established in 1971 by Islamic states to promote cooperation among the members and to support peace, security and the struggle of the people of Palestine and all Muslim people. Its Secretariat is in Jeddah, Saudi Arabia. *See* the list of members.
Pacific Islands Forum	A group of South Pacific states which proposed the South Pacific Nuclear Free Zone, embodied in the 1985 Treaty of Rarotonga, and contribute to monitoring implementation of the treaty. The Secretariat is in Suva, Fiji. *See* the list of members.

Partnership for Peace (PFP)	Launched in 1994, the PFP is the programme for political and military cooperation between NATO and its partner states within the framework of the EAPC. It is open to all OSCE states able to contribute to the programme. *See* the list of partner states under North Atlantic Treaty Organization.
Proliferation Security Initiative (PSI)	Based on a US initiative announced in 2003, the PSI is a multilateral forum focusing on law enforcement cooperation for the interdiction and seizure of illegal weapons of mass destruction, missile technologies and related materials when in transit on land, in the air or at sea. The PSI Statement of Interdiction Principles was issued in 2003. *See* the list of participating states.
Shanghai Cooperation Organization (SCO)	Established in 1996 and in 2001 opened for membership of all states that support its aims. The member states cooperate on confidence-building measures and regional security and in the economic sphere. The SCO Secretariat is in Beijing, China. *See* the list of members.
South Asian Association for Regional Co-operation (SAARC)	Created in 1985 as an association of states to promote political and economic regional cooperation, with its secretariat in Kathmandu, Nepal. *See* the list of members.
Southern African Development Community (SADC)	Established in 1992 to promote regional economic development and fundamental principles of sovereignty, peace and security, human rights and democracy. The Secretariat is in Gaborone, Botswana. *See* the list of members.
Southern Common Market (MERCOSUR)	Established in 1991 to achieve economic integration between the member states. In 1996 it adopted a decision that only countries with democratic, accountable institutions in place would be allowed to participate. The Common Market Council is the highest decision-making body, and the Common Market Group is the permanent executive body. The Secretariat is in Montevideo, Uruguay. *See* the list of members.
Stability Pact for South Eastern Europe	Initiated by the EU at the 1999 Conference on South Eastern Europe and subsequently placed under OSCE auspices. The aim of the Pact is to promote political and economic reforms, development and enhanced security, and facilitate the integration of South-East European countries into the Euro-Atlantic structures. Its activities are coordinated by the South Eastern Europe Regional Table and chaired by the Special Co-ordinator of the Stability Pact. The seat of the Special Co-ordinator is in Brussels, Belgium. *See* the list of partners.
Sub-Regional Consultative Commission (SRCC)	Established by the 1996 Agreement on Sub-Regional Arms Control concerning Yugoslavia (Florence Agreement) as the forum in which the parties resolve questions of compliance with the agreement.

United Nations (UN) The world intergovernmental organization with headquarters in New York, USA. It was founded in 1945 through the adoption of its Charter. The six principal UN organs are the General Assembly, the Security Council, the Economic and Social Council (ECOSOC), the Trusteeship Council, the International Court of Justice (ICJ) and the Secretariat. The UN also has a large number of specialized agencies and other autonomous bodies. *See* the list of members.

Wassenaar Arrangement (WA) The Wassenaar Arrangement on Export Controls for Conventional Arms and Dual-Use Goods and Technologies was formally established in 1996. It aims to prevent the acquisition of armaments and sensitive dual-use goods and technologies for military uses by states whose behaviour is cause for concern to the member states. *See* the list of participants.

Western European Union (WEU) Established by the 1954 Modified Brussels Treaty. The seat of the WEU is in Brussels, Belgium. WEU operational activities (the 'Petersberg tasks') were transferred to the EU in 2000. It is seated in Paris, France, and scrutinizes intergovernmental cooperation in the Western European Armaments Group (WEAG) and the Western European Armaments Organisation (WEAO). *See* the list of members.

Zangger Committee Established in 1971, the Nuclear Exporters Committee, called the Zangger Committee, is a group of nuclear supplier countries that meets informally twice a year to coordinate export controls on nuclear materials according to its regularly updated trigger list of items which, when exported, must be subject to IAEA safeguards. It complements the work of the NSG (*see* Nuclear Suppliers Group). *See* the list of participants.

Membership of intergovernmental bodies and international organizations as of 1 January 2005

The UN member states and organizations within the UN system are listed first, followed by all other organizations in alphabetical order. Note that not all members or participants of the organizations are UN member states. Membership is as of 1 January 2005. The address of an Internet site with information about each organization is provided where available.

United Nations members (191) and year of membership

<http://www.un.org>

Afghanistan, 1946
Albania, 1955
Algeria, 1962
Andorra, 1993
Angola, 1976
Antigua and Barbuda, 1981
Argentina, 1945
Armenia, 1992
Australia, 1945
Austria, 1955
Azerbaijan, 1992
Bahamas, 1973
Bahrain, 1971
Bangladesh, 1974
Barbados, 1966
Belarus, 1945
Belgium, 1945
Belize, 1981
Benin, 1960
Bhutan, 1971
Bolivia, 1945
Bosnia and Herzegovina, 1992
Botswana, 1966
Brazil, 1945
Brunei Darussalam, 1984
Bulgaria, 1955
Burkina Faso, 1960
Burundi, 1962
Cambodia, 1955
Cameroon, 1960
Canada, 1945
Cape Verde, 1975
Central African Republic, 1960
Chad, 1960
Chile, 1945
China, 1945
Colombia, 1945
Comoros, 1975
Congo, Democratic Republic of the, 1960
Congo, Republic of, 1960
Costa Rica, 1945
Côte d'Ivoire, 1960
Croatia, 1992
Cuba, 1945
Cyprus, 1960
Czech Republic, 1993
Denmark, 1945
Djibouti, 1977
Dominica, 1978
Dominican Republic, 1945
Ecuador, 1945
Egypt, 1945
El Salvador, 1945
Equatorial Guinea, 1968
Eritrea, 1993
Estonia, 1991
Ethiopia, 1945
Fiji, 1970
Finland, 1955
France, 1945
Gabon, 1960
Gambia, 1965
Georgia, 1992
Germany, 1973
Ghana, 1957
Greece, 1945
Grenada, 1974
Guatemala, 1945
Guinea, 1958
Guinea-Bissau, 1974
Guyana, 1966
Haiti, 1945
Honduras, 1945
Hungary, 1955
Iceland, 1946
India, 1945
Indonesia, 1950
Iran, 1945
Iraq, 1945
Ireland, 1955
Israel, 1949
Italy, 1955
Jamaica, 1962
Japan, 1956
Jordan, 1955
Kazakhstan, 1992
Kenya, 1963
Kiribati, 1999
Korea, Democratic People's Republic of (North Korea), 1991
Korea, Republic of (South Korea), 1991
Kuwait, 1963
Kyrgyzstan, 1992
Laos, 1955
Latvia, 1991
Lebanon, 1945
Lesotho, 1966
Liberia, 1945
Libya, 1955
Liechtenstein, 1990
Lithuania, 1991
Luxembourg, 1945
Macedonia, Former Yugoslav Republic of, 1993
Madagascar, 1960
Malawi, 1964
Malaysia, 1957
Maldives, 1965
Mali, 1960
Malta, 1964
Marshall Islands, 1991
Mauritania, 1961
Mauritius, 1968
Mexico, 1945
Micronesia, 1991
Moldova, 1992
Monaco, 1993
Mongolia, 1961
Morocco, 1956
Mozambique, 1975
Myanmar (Burma), 1948
Namibia, 1990
Nauru, 1999
Nepal, 1955
Netherlands, 1945
New Zealand, 1945
Nicaragua, 1945
Niger, 1960
Nigeria, 1960
Norway, 1945
Oman, 1971
Pakistan, 1947
Palau, 1994
Panama, 1945
Papua New Guinea, 1975

Paraguay, 1945
Peru, 1945
Philippines, 1945
Poland, 1945
Portugal, 1955
Qatar, 1971
Romania, 1955
Russia, 1945
Rwanda, 1962
Saint Kitts and Nevis, 1983
Saint Lucia, 1979
Saint Vincent and the Grenadines, 1980
Samoa, Western, 1976
San Marino, 1992
Sao Tome and Principe, 1975
Saudi Arabia, 1945
Senegal, 1960
Serbia and Montenegro, 2000
Seychelles, 1976
Sierra Leone, 1961
Singapore, 1965
Slovakia, 1993
Slovenia, 1992
Solomon Islands, 1978
Somalia, 1960
South Africa, 1945
Spain, 1955
Sri Lanka, 1955
Sudan, 1956
Suriname, 1975
Swaziland, 1968
Sweden, 1946
Switzerland, 2002
Syria, 1945
Tajikistan, 1992
Tanzania, 1961
Thailand, 1946
Timor-Leste, 2002
Togo, 1960
Tonga, 1999
Trinidad and Tobago, 1962
Tunisia, 1956
Turkey, 1945
Turkmenistan, 1992
Tuvalu, 2000
Uganda, 1962
UK, 1945
Ukraine, 1945
United Arab Emirates, 1971
Uruguay, 1945
USA, 1945
Uzbekistan, 1992
Vanuatu, 1981
Venezuela, 1945
Viet Nam, 1977
Yemen, 1947
Zambia, 1964
Zimbabwe, 1980

UN Security Council

<http://www.un.org/Docs/sc>

Permanent members (the P5): China, France, Russia, UK, USA

Non-permanent members in 2004 (elected by the UN General Assembly for two-year terms; the year in brackets is the year at the end of which the term expires): Algeria (2005), Angola (2004), Benin (2005), Brazil (2005), Chile (2004), Germany (2004), Pakistan (2004), the Philippines (2005), Romania (2005), Spain (2004)

Note: Argentina, Denmark, Greece, Japan and Tanzania were elected non-permanent members for 2005–2006.

Conference on Disarmament (CD)

<http://disarmament2.un.org/cd>

Algeria, Argentina, Australia, Austria, Bangladesh, Belarus, Belgium, Brazil, Bulgaria, Cameroon, Canada, Chile, China, Colombia, Congo (Democratic Republic of the), Cuba, Ecuador, Egypt, Ethiopia, Finland, France, Germany, Hungary, India, Indonesia, Iran, Iraq, Ireland, Israel, Italy, Japan, Kazakhstan, Kenya, Korea (North), Korea (South), Malaysia, Mexico, Mongolia, Morocco, Myanmar (Burma), Netherlands, New Zealand, Nigeria, Norway, Pakistan, Peru, Poland, Romania, Russia, Senegal, Slovakia, South Africa, Spain, Sri Lanka, Sweden, Switzerland, Syria, Tunisia, Turkey, UK, Ukraine, USA, Venezuela, Viet Nam, Zimbabwe

International Atomic Energy Agency (IAEA)

<http://www.iaea.org>

Afghanistan, Albania, Algeria, Angola, Argentina, Armenia, Australia, Austria, Azerbaijan, Bangladesh, Belarus, Belgium, Benin, Bolivia, Bosnia and Herzegovina, Botswana, Brazil, Bulgaria, Burkina Faso, Cameroon, Canada, Central African Republic, Chad, Chile, China, Colombia, Congo (Democratic Republic of the), Costa Rica, Côte d'Ivoire, Croatia, Cuba, Cyprus, Czech Republic, Denmark, Dominican Republic, Ecuador, Egypt, El Salvador, Eritrea, Estonia, Ethiopia, Finland, France, Gabon, Georgia, Germany, Ghana, Greece, Guatemala, Haiti, Holy See, Honduras, Hungary, Iceland, India, Indonesia, Iran, Iraq, Ireland, Israel, Italy, Jamaica, Japan, Jordan, Kazakhstan, Kenya, Korea (South), Kuwait, Kyrgyzstan, Latvia, Lebanon, Liberia, Libya, Liechtenstein, Lithuania, Luxembourg, Macedonia (Former Yugoslav Republic of), Madagascar, Malaysia, Mali, Malta, Marshall Islands, Mauritania, Mauritius, Mexico, Moldova, Monaco, Mongolia, Morocco, Myanmar (Burma), Namibia, Netherlands, New Zealand, Nicaragua, Niger, Nigeria, Norway, Pakistan, Panama, Paraguay, Peru, Philippines, Poland, Portugal, Qatar, Romania, Russia, Saudi Arabia, Senegal, Serbia and Montenegro, Seychelles, Sierra Leone, Singapore, Slovakia, Slovenia, South Africa, Spain, Sri Lanka, Sudan, Sweden, Switzerland, Syria, Tajikistan, Tanzania, Thailand, Togo, Tunisia,

Turkey, Uganda, UK, Ukraine, United Arab Emirates, Uruguay, USA, Uzbekistan, Venezuela, Viet Nam, Yemen, Zambia, Zimbabwe

Note: North Korea was a member of the IAEA until June 1994. Cambodia withdrew its membership as of March 2003.

African Union (AU)

<http://www.africa-union.org>

Algeria, Angola, Benin, Botswana, Burkina Faso, Burundi, Cameroon, Cape Verde, Central African Republic, Chad, Comoros, Congo (Democratic Republic of the), Congo (Republic of), Côte d'Ivoire, Djibouti, Egypt, Equatorial Guinea, Eritrea, Ethiopia, Gabon, Gambia, Ghana, Guinea, Guinea-Bissau, Kenya, Lesotho, Liberia, Libya, Madagascar, Malawi, Mali, Mauritania, Mauritius, Mozambique, Namibia, Niger, Nigeria, Rwanda, Western Sahara (Sahrawi Arab Democratic Republic, SADR), Sao Tome and Principe, Senegal, Seychelles, Sierra Leone, Somalia, South Africa, Sudan, Swaziland, Tanzania, Togo, Tunisia, Uganda, Zambia, Zimbabwe

Andean Community of Nations

<http://www.comunidadandina.org>

Bolivia, Colombia, Ecuador, Peru, Venezuela

Arab League

<http://www.arableagueonline.org/arableague/index_en.jsp>

Algeria, Bahrain, Comoros, Djibouti, Egypt, Iraq, Jordan, Kuwait, Lebanon, Libya, Mauritania, Morocco, Oman, Palestine, Qatar, Saudi Arabia, Somalia, Sudan, Syria, Tunisia, United Arab Emirates, Yemen

Association of South-East Asian Nations (ASEAN)

<http://www.aseansec.org>

Brunei Darussalam, Cambodia, Indonesia, Laos, Malaysia, Myanmar (Burma), Philippines, Singapore, Thailand, Viet Nam

ASEAN Regional Forum (ARF)

The ASEAN member states plus Australia, Canada, China, European Union, India, Japan, Korea (North), Korea (South), Mongolia, New Zealand, Pakistan, Papua New Guinea, Russia, USA

Australia Group (AG)

<http://www.australiagroup.net>

Argentina, Australia, Austria, Belgium, Bulgaria, Canada, Cyprus, Czech Republic, Denmark, Estonia, Finland, France, Germany, Greece, Hungary, Iceland, Ireland, Italy, Japan, Korea (South), Latvia, Lithuania, Luxembourg, Malta, Netherlands, New Zealand, Norway, Poland, Portugal, Romania, Slovakia, Slovenia, Spain, Sweden, Switzerland, Turkey, UK, USA

Central European Initiative (CEI)

<http://www.ceinet.org>

Albania, Austria, Belarus, Bosnia and Herzegovina, Bulgaria, Croatia, Czech Republic, Hungary, Italy, Macedonia (Former Yugoslav Republic of), Moldova, Poland, Romania, Serbia and Montenegro, Slovakia, Slovenia, Ukraine

Collective Security Treaty Organization (CSTO)

Armenia, Belarus, Kazakhstan, Kyrgyzstan, Russia, Tajikistan

Commonwealth of Independent States (CIS)

<http://www.cis.minsk.by/English/Engl_home.htm>

Armenia, Azerbaijan, Belarus, Georgia, Kazakhstan, Kyrgyzstan, Moldova, Russia, Tajikistan, Turkmenistan, Ukraine, Uzbekistan

Commonwealth of Nations

<http://www.thecommonwealth.org>

Antigua and Barbuda, Australia, Bahamas, Bangladesh, Barbados, Belize, Botswana, Brunei Darussalam, Cameroon, Canada, Cyprus, Dominica, Fiji, Gambia, Ghana, Grenada, Guyana, India, Jamaica, Kenya, Kiribati, Lesotho, Malawi, Malaysia, Maldives, Malta, Mauritius, Mozambique, Namibia, Nauru, New Zealand, Nigeria, Pakistan, Papua New Guinea, Saint Kitts and Nevis, Saint Lucia, Saint Vincent and the Grenadines, Samoa, Seychelles, Sierra Leone, Singapore, Solomon Islands, South Africa, Sri Lanka, Swaziland, Tanzania, Tonga, Trinidad and Tobago, Tuvalu, Uganda, UK, Vanuatu, Zambia

Conference on Interaction and Confidence-building Measures in Asia (CICA)

<http://www.mfa.kz/english/cica.htm>

Afghanistan, Azerbaijan, China, Egypt, India, Iran, Israel, Kazakhstan, Kyrgyzstan, Mongolia, Pakistan, Palestine, Russia, Tajikistan, Thailand, Turkey, Uzbekistan

Council for Security Cooperation in the Asia Pacific (CSCAP)

<http://www.cscap.org>

Member committees: Australia, Brunei Darussalam, Cambodia, Canada, China, CSCAP Europe, India, Indonesia, Japan, Korea (North), Korea (South), Malaysia, Mongolia, New Zealand, Papua New Guinea, Philippines, Russia, Singapore, Thailand, USA, Viet Nam

Council of Europe

<http://www.coe.int>

Albania, Andorra, Armenia, Austria, Azerbaijan, Belgium, Bosnia and Herzegovina, Bulgaria, Croatia, Cyprus, Czech Republic, Denmark, Estonia, Finland, France, Georgia, Germany, Greece, Hungary, Iceland, Ireland, Italy, Latvia, Liechtenstein, Lithuania, Luxembourg, Macedonia (Former Yugoslav Republic of), Malta, Moldova, Monaco, Netherlands, Norway, Poland, Portugal, Romania, Russia, San Marino, Serbia and Montenegro, Slovakia, Slovenia, Spain, Sweden, Switzerland, Turkey, UK, Ukraine

Economic Community of West African States (ECOWAS)

<http://www.ecowas.int>

Benin, Burkina Faso, Cape Verde, Côte d'Ivoire, Gambia, Ghana, Guinea, Guinea-Bissau, Liberia, Mali, Niger, Nigeria, Senegal, Sierra Leone, Togo

European Union (EU)

<http://europa.eu.int>

Austria, Belgium, Cyprus, Czech Republic, Denmark, Estonia, Finland, France, Germany, Greece, Hungary, Ireland, Italy, Latvia, Lithuania, Luxembourg, Malta, Netherlands, Poland, Portugal, Slovakia, Slovenia, Spain, Sweden, UK

Group of Eight (G8)

<http://www.g8.utoronto.ca>

Canada, France, Germany, Italy, Japan, Russia, UK, USA

Gulf Cooperation Council (GCC)

<http://www.gcc-sg.org>

Bahrain, Kuwait, Oman, Qatar, Saudi Arabia, United Arab Emirates

Hague Code of Conduct Against Ballistic Missile Proliferation (HCOC)

<http://www.minbuza.nl/default.asp?CMS_ITEM=MBZ460871>

Afghanistan, Albania, Argentina, Australia, Austria, Azerbaijan, Belarus, Belgium, Benin, Bosnia and Herzegovina, Bulgaria, Burkina Faso, Burundi, Cameroon, Canada, Chad, Chile, Colombia, Comores, Cook Islands, Costa Rica, Croatia, Cyprus, Czech Republic, Denmark, El Salvador, Eritrea, Estonia, Fiji, Finland, France, Gabon, Georgia, Germany, Ghana, Greece, Guinea, Guinea-Bissau, Holy See, Hungary, Iceland, Ireland, Italy, Japan, Jordan, Kenya, Kiribati, Korea (South), Latvia, Libya, Liechtenstein,

Lithuania, Luxembourg, Macedonia (Former Yugoslav Republic of), Madagascar, Malta, Marshall Islands, Mauritania, Micronesia, Monaco, Morocco, Mozambique, Netherlands, New Zealand, Nicaragua, Niger, Nigeria, Norway, Palau, Panama, Papua New Guinea, Paraguay, Peru, Philippines, Poland, Portugal, Moldova, Romania, Russia, Rwanda, Senegal, Serbia and Montenegro, Seychelles, Sierra Leone, Slovakia, Slovenia, South Africa, Spain, Sudan, Suriname, Sweden, Switzerland, Tanzania, Tajikistan, Timor-Leste, Tonga, Tunisia, Turkey, Turkmenistan, Tuvalu, Uganda, UK, Ukraine, Uruguay, USA, Uzbekistan, Vanuatu, Venezuela, Zambia

Intergovernmental Authority on Development (IGAD)

<http://www.igad.org>

Djibouti, Eritrea, Ethiopia, Kenya, Somalia, Sudan, Uganda

Missile Technology Control Regime (MTCR)

<http://www.mtcr.info>

Argentina, Australia, Austria, Belgium, Brazil, Bulgaria, Canada, Czech Republic, Denmark, Finland, France, Germany, Greece, Hungary, Iceland, Ireland, Italy, Japan, Korea (South), Luxembourg, Netherlands, New Zealand, Norway, Poland, Portugal, Russia, South Africa, Spain, Sweden, Switzerland, Turkey, UK, Ukraine, USA

Non-Aligned Movement (NAM)

<http://www.nam.gov.za>

Afghanistan, Algeria, Angola, Bahamas, Bahrain, Bangladesh, Barbados, Belarus, Belize, Benin, Bhutan, Bolivia, Botswana, Brunei Darussalam, Burkina Faso, Burundi, Cambodia, Cameroon, Cape Verde, Central African Republic, Chad, Chile, Colombia, Comoros, Congo (Democratic Republic of the), Congo (Republic of), Côte d'Ivoire, Cuba, Djibouti, Dominican Republic, Ecuador, Egypt, Equatorial Guinea, Eritrea, Ethiopia, Gabon, Gambia, Ghana, Grenada, Guatemala, Guinea, Guinea-Bissau, Guyana, Honduras, India, Indonesia, Iran, Iraq, Jamaica, Jordan, Kenya, Korea (North), Kuwait, Laos, Lebanon, Lesotho, Liberia, Libya, Madagascar, Malawi, Malaysia, Maldives, Mali, Mauritania, Mauritius, Mongolia, Morocco, Mozambique, Myanmar (Burma), Namibia, Nepal, Nicaragua, Niger, Nigeria, Oman, Pakistan, Palestine Liberation Organization, Panama, Papua New Guinea, Peru, Philippines, Qatar, Rwanda, Saint Lucia, Saint Vincent and the Grenadines, Sao Tome and Principe, Saudi Arabia, Senegal, Seychelles, Sierra Leone, Singapore, Somalia, South Africa, Sri Lanka, Sudan, Suriname, Swaziland, Syria, Tanzania, Thailand, Timor-Leste, Togo, Trinidad and Tobago, Tunisia, Turkmenistan, Uganda, United Arab Emirates, Uzbekistan, Vanuatu, Venezuela, Viet Nam, Yemen, Zambia, Zimbabwe

North Atlantic Treaty Organization (NATO)

<http://www.nato.int>

Belgium, Bulgaria, Canada, Czech Republic, Denmark, Estonia, France*, Germany, Greece, Hungary, Iceland, Italy, Latvia, Lithuania, Luxembourg, Netherlands, Norway, Poland, Portugal, Romania, Slovakia, Slovenia, Spain, Turkey, UK, USA

* France is not in the integrated military structures of NATO.

Euro-Atlantic Partnership Council (EAPC)

The NATO member states plus Albania, Armenia, Austria, Azerbaijan, Belarus, Croatia, Finland, Georgia, Ireland, Kazakhstan, Kyrgyzstan, Macedonia (Former Yugoslav Republic of), Moldova, Russia, Sweden, Switzerland, Tajikistan, Turkmenistan, Ukraine, Uzbekistan

Partnership for Peace (PFP)

Albania, Armenia, Austria, Azerbaijan, Belarus, Croatia, Czech Republic, Finland, Georgia, Hungary, Ireland, Kazakhstan, Kyrgyzstan, Macedonia (Former Yugoslav Republic of), Moldova, Poland, Russia, Sweden, Switzerland, Tajikistan, Turkmenistan, Ukraine, Uzbekistan

Nuclear Suppliers Group (NSG)

<http://www.nuclearsuppliersgroup.org>

Argentina, Australia, Austria, Belarus, Belgium, Brazil, Bulgaria, Canada, China, Cyprus, Czech Republic, Denmark, Estonia, Finland, France, Germany, Greece, Hungary, Ireland, Italy, Japan, Kazakhstan, Korea (South), Latvia, Lithuania, Luxembourg, Malta, Netherlands, New Zealand, Norway, Poland, Portugal, Romania, Russia, Slovakia, Slovenia, South Africa, Spain, Sweden, Switzerland, Turkey, UK, Ukraine, USA

Organisation for Economic Co-operation and Development (OECD)

<http://www.oecd.org>

Australia, Austria, Belgium, Canada, Czech Republic, Denmark, Finland, France, Germany, Greece, Hungary, Iceland, Ireland, Italy, Japan, Korea (South), Luxembourg, Mexico, Netherlands, New Zealand, Norway, Poland, Portugal, Slovakia, Spain, Sweden, Switzerland, Turkey, UK, USA

Organization for Security and Co-operation in Europe (OSCE)

<http://www.osce.org>

Albania, Andorra, Armenia, Austria, Azerbaijan, Belarus, Belgium, Bosnia and Herzegovina, Bulgaria, Canada, Croatia, Cyprus, Czech Republic, Denmark, Estonia, Finland, France, Georgia, Germany, Greece, Holy See, Hungary, Iceland, Ireland, Italy, Kazakhstan, Kyrgyzstan, Latvia, Liechtenstein, Lithuania, Luxembourg, Macedonia (Former Yugoslav Republic of), Malta, Moldova, Monaco, Netherlands, Norway, Poland, Portugal, Romania, Russia, San Marino, Serbia and Montenegro, Slovakia, Slovenia, Spain, Sweden, Switzerland, Tajikistan, Turkey, Turkmenistan, UK, Ukraine, USA, Uzbekistan

Organization of American States (OAS)

<http://www.oas.org>

Antigua and Barbuda, Argentina, Bahamas, Barbados, Belize, Bolivia, Brazil, Canada, Chile, Colombia, Costa Rica, Cuba*, Dominica, Dominican Republic, Ecuador, El Salvador, Grenada, Guatemala, Guyana, Haiti, Honduras, Jamaica, Mexico, Nicaragua, Panama, Paraguay, Peru, Saint Kitts and Nevis, Saint Lucia, Saint Vincent and the Grenadines, Suriname, Trinidad and Tobago, Uruguay, USA, Venezuela

* Cuba has been excluded from participation in the OAS since 1962.

Organization of the Black Sea Economic Cooperation (BSEC)

<http://www.bsec-organization.org>

Albania, Armenia, Azerbaijan, Bulgaria, Georgia, Greece, Moldova, Romania, Russia, Serbia and Montenegro, Turkey, Ukraine

Organization of the Islamic Conference (OIC)

<http://www.oic-oci.org>

Afghanistan, Albania, Algeria, Azerbaijan, Bahrain, Bangladesh, Benin, Brunei Darussalam, Burkina Faso, Cameroon, Chad, Comoros, Côte d'Ivoire, Djibouti, Egypt, Gabon, Gambia, Guinea, Guinea-Bissau, Guyana, Indonesia, Iran, Iraq, Jordan, Kazakhstan, Kuwait, Kyrgyzstan, Lebanon, Libya, Malaysia, Maldives, Mali, Mauritania, Morocco, Mozambique, Niger, Nigeria, Oman, Pakistan, Palestine, Qatar, Saudi Arabia, Senegal, Sierra Leone, Somalia, Sudan, Suriname, Syria, Tajikistan, Togo, Tunisia, Turkey, Turkmenistan, Uganda, United Arab Emirates, Uzbekistan, Yemen

Pacific Islands Forum

<http://www.forumsec.org.fj>

Australia, Cook Islands, Fiji, Kiribati, Marshall Islands, Micronesia, Nauru, New Zealand, Niue, Palau, Papua New Guinea, Samoa (Western), Solomon Islands, Tonga, Tuvalu, Vanuatu

Proliferation Security Initiative (PSI)

<http://www.state.gov/t/np/c10390.htm>

Australia, Canada, Denmark*, France, Germany, Italy, Japan, the Netherlands, Norway, Poland, Portugal, Russia, Singapore, Spain, Turkey*, UK, USA

* Denmark and Turkey are not 'core members' of the PSI.

Shanghai Cooperation Organization (SCO)

China, Kazakhstan, Kyrgyzstan, Russia, Tajikistan, Uzbekistan

South Asian Association for Regional Co-operation (SAARC)

<http://www.saarc-sec.org>

Bangladesh, Bhutan, India, Maldives, Nepal, Pakistan, Sri Lanka

Southeast European Cooperative Initiative (SECI)

<http://www.seciturk.org.tr/index_eng.html>

Albania, Bosnia and Herzegovina, Bulgaria, Croatia, Greece, Hungary, Macedonia (Former Yugoslav Republic of), Moldova, Romania, Slovenia, Turkey, Serbia and Montenegro

Southern African Development Community (SADC)

<http://www.sadc.int>

Angola, Botswana, Congo (Democratic Republic of the), Lesotho, Malawi, Mauritius, Mozambique, Namibia, Seychelles, South Africa, Swaziland, Tanzania, Zambia, Zimbabwe

Southern Common Market (Mercado Común del Sur, MERCOSUR)

<http://www.mercosur.org.uy>

Argentina, Brazil, Paraguay, Uruguay

Stability Pact for South Eastern Europe

<http://www.stabilitypact.org>

Country partners: Albania, Austria, Belgium, Bosnia and Herzegovina, Bulgaria, Canada, Croatia, Cyprus, Czech Republic, Denmark, Estonia, Finland, France, Germany, Greece, Hungary, Ireland, Italy, Japan, Latvia, Lithuania, Luxembourg, Macedonia (Former Yugoslav Republic of), Malta, Moldova, Netherlands, Norway, Poland, Portugal, Romania, Russia, Serbia and Montenegro, Slovakia, Slovenia, Spain, Sweden, Switzerland, Turkey, UK, USA

Other partners: Central European Initiative, Council of Europe (Council of Europe Development Bank), European Bank for Reconstruction and Development, European Investment Bank, European Union (Council of the European Union, European Agency for Reconstruction, European Commission, European Parliament, Office for South Eastern Europe), International Finance Corporation, International Monetary Fund, International Organization for Migration, North Atlantic Treaty Organization, Office of the High Representative in Bosnia and Herzegovina, Organisation for Economic Co-operation and Development, Organization for Security and Co-operation in Europe, Organization of the Black Sea Economic Cooperation, Southeast European Cooperative Initiative, South-East European Cooperation Process, United Nations (UN High Commissioner for Refugees, UN Mission in Kosovo), World Bank

Wassenaar Arrangement (WA)

<http://www.wassenaar.org>

Argentina, Australia, Austria, Belgium, Bulgaria, Canada, Czech Republic, Denmark, Finland, France, Germany, Greece, Hungary, Ireland, Italy, Japan, Korea (South), Luxembourg, Netherlands, New Zealand, Norway, Poland, Portugal, Romania, Russia, Slovakia, Slovenia, Spain, Sweden, Switzerland, Turkey, UK, Ukraine, USA

Western European Union (WEU)

<http://www.weu.int>

Belgium, France, Germany, Greece, Italy, Luxembourg, Netherlands, Portugal, Spain, UK

Western European Armaments Group (WEAG) and Western European Armaments Organisation (WEAO)

Austria, Belgium, Czech Republic, Denmark, Finland, France, Germany, Greece, Hungary, Italy, Luxembourg, Netherlands, Norway, Poland, Portugal, Spain, Sweden, Turkey, UK

Zangger Committee

<http://www.zanggercommittee.org/Zangger/default.htm>

Argentina, Australia, Austria, Belgium, Bulgaria, Canada, China, Czech Republic, Denmark, Finland, France, Germany, Greece, Hungary, Ireland, Italy, Japan, Korea (South), Luxembourg, Netherlands, Norway, Poland, Portugal, Romania, Russia, Slovakia, Slovenia, South Africa, Spain, Sweden, Switzerland, Turkey, UK, Ukraine, USA

Conventions

. .	Data not available or not applicable
–	Nil or a negligible figure
( )	Uncertain data
b.	Billion (thousand million)
kg	Kilogram
km	Kilometre (1000 metres)
kt	Kiloton (1000 tonnes)
m.	Million
Mt	Megaton (1 million tons)
th.	Thousand
tr.	Trillion (million million)
$	US dollars, unless otherwise indicated
€	Euros

Introduction

Global security governance: a world of change and challenge

ALYSON J. K. BAILES

I. Introduction

In the world today, good solutions have been found for practically every extant variety of security problem. The real difficulty lies in replicating, generalizing and, ideally, universalizing such solutions. At the same time, because of the march of globalization and the increasingly complex codependencies it creates, it is becoming more and more a dictate of necessity to make good security practice and experience equally global. Enhancing security for one group in the world at the expense of another, or without the others, has always been inherently discriminatory and unfair. Now it is starting to look more like a contradiction in terms.

The vision of coherent, comprehensive and even-handed global security management has never been more relevant, yet its difficulties can rarely have been so clearly exposed and so widely taken to heart as during the past decade. One difficulty is the necessity to design an enforceable system of global governance that can both serve and constrain sub-state, trans-state and traditional state players. Another is the breadth and variety of the contemporary notion of security, covering not just matters of conflict and armaments but also the need to defend against terrorism, crime, disease, natural disasters and environment damage; interruption of vital services and supplies; and, many would add, socio-economic phenomena such as poverty, exclusion, and underpopulation and overpopulation. A third problem is more historically contingent but probably has the strongest impact on day-to-day world politics: the fact that both the world's strongest power (the United States) and those most generally identified as 'problem' states (such as North Korea) have reasons to resist approaches to solving these challenges that rely on binding and universally applicable global regulation. A law-abiding world security community could not be hurt much by the defection of marginal actors. It is profoundly challenged when not only the entities causing problems but also the player with the greatest prima facie power to solve problems seem determined not to be co-opted.

These challenges have been widely discussed and documented, *inter alia* in previous SIPRI Yearbooks. This edition was prepared at a time when general issues of global security have been pushed to—and held in—the forefront of world attention, but when few thinkers can claim to have even as much confidence in the success of any given prescription as they had two or three years ago. Experience has highlighted the meagre and bitter harvest that can follow both from taking up arms against security troubles (as in Iraq) and from trying to end them quickly without violence (as in Iran or North Korea). The High-level Panel on Threats, Challenges and Change set up by the United Nations Secretary-General to reflect on these and other challenges of global governance has presented its report[1]—the synopsis of which is reproduced in the appendix to this Introduction—to an audience that knows that a better way forward is needed, but that cannot be relied on to find the imagination, energy and solidarity required to make good use of even the best of road maps.

This Introduction attempts neither to reiterate nor to second-guess the High-level Panel's reasoning. Rather, it offers some complementary reflections on the problems of establishing a global security order today and on ways to distinguish the good options from the bad for addressing these problems. Without making any claim to completeness, it deals with changes in the nature and balance of power between security actors (section II); with differences in security 'agendas'—of geographical or other origin—that add to the difficulty of finding global solutions (section III); with the pros and cons of three different generic modes of security action (section IV); and, in the concluding section, with some thoughts on the UN's own role.

II. Power and influence in the 21st century

The notion of power has become ambiguous, elusive and a subject of lively debate in recent decades. Some thinkers have elaborated the distinction between 'hard' and 'soft' power, where the first term refers mainly to military strength and the will and capability to use it coercively.[2] 'Soft' power may reside in non-military dimensions, such as cultural strength, or in legitimacy ('right' rather than 'might') and the power of example and attraction; but in general it implies getting results by persuasion and negotiation rather than by compulsion. This second kind of power has obvious limitations in an imperfect security environment where less principled actors can ignore its moral authority, exploit its weaknesses and profit from its self-restraint. The limitations of hard power have, however, also been recognized for a long time. In an analysis still to be bettered, Paul Kennedy shows how excessive reliance on it may lead a strong state to lose authority, room for manoeuvre and even the essentials of its own strength in the longer run.[3] Today, there is also high awareness of what have come to be called asymmetric threats from intrin-

[1] United Nations, 'A more secure world: our shared responsibility', Report of the High-level Panel on Threats, Challenges and Change, UN documents A/59/565, 4 Dec. 2004, and A/59/565/Corr.1, 6 Dec. 2004, URL <http://www.un.org/ga/59/documentation/list5.html>. For the synopsis and recommendations of the report see the appendix to this Introduction.

[2] See, e.g., Nye, J. S. Jr, *Bound to Lead: The Changing Nature of American Power* (Basic Books: New York, 1991); and *Soft Power: The Means to Success in World Affairs* (Public Affairs: New York, 2004).

[3] Kennedy, P., *The Rise and Fall of the Great Powers: Economic Change and Military Conflict from 1500 to 2000* (Random House: New York, 1987).

sically weak actors, such as terrorist groups who have the power to do disproportionate damage to the strong; and a fast-growing realization that trying to defeat these actors by applying power in the traditional style will often only make things worse.

Cutting across these complexities is another set of issues about the *type* of actors who hold and can wield power in international affairs. A debate developed in the early 1990s over the alleged 'death of the state', based on the view that traditional state authorities were losing control of many global processes either 'upwards', to international or supranational organizations which had taken over elements of former national competences; 'sideways', to different sectoral actors such as transnational companies or civil society organizations; or 'downwards', to sub-state and individual actors who had started doing things previously supposed to be reserved to states, such as waging war.[4] In recent years it has become clearer that, while all three of these things were indeed happening, a number of the *solutions* for sub-state, trans-state and non-state challenges can still only be found through formal international legal procedures or by types of active intervention (e.g., international peace missions) of the sort that only nation states can conduct. The present state of affairs is therefore perhaps best seen as one of increasingly diffused *power* but without, so far, a similar multiplication and reinforcement of *authority*. It is a situation that creates a mismatch between traditionally designed solutions and actual challenges and—most observers would say—also leaves the world with a certain security deficit. This is what commentators mean when they talk about the breakdown of the 'Westphalian order'[5] (the historical system of international regulation by agreement among nation states), and it is what underlies the useful concept of the 'postmodern state' that still carries unique responsibilities and potentials but has to find new ways to realize them in a fundamentally changed environment.[6]

One further point worth noting about 'power' is the essentially subjective nature of the concept in modern international life. Over the second half of the 20th century, the number and severity of interstate conflicts declined sharply, the number of intra-state conflicts is now declining more slowly, and it has become unusual for any one country to seek to resolve the latter on its own. In consequence, international players have fewer chances to test each others' power in the most extreme and direct way possible, through a contest of arms. Most of the time, countries (and other players) enjoy power and influence in proportion to their *perceived* power and influence. Once this is realized, it becomes clear that the perception of power can diverge from objective reality for many reasons. Several varieties of national behaviour can be explained as

[4] Guéhenno, J.-M., *The End of the Nation-State* (University of Minnesota Press: Minneapolis, Minn., 2000).

[5] See, e.g., Solana, J., Secretary General of NATO, 'Securing peace in Europe', Speech at the Symposium on the Political Relevance of the 1648 Peace of Westphalia, Münster, 12 Nov. 1998, URL <http://www.nato.int/docu/speech/1998/s981112a.htm>.

[6] See, e.g., Cooper, R., *The Breaking of Nations: Order and Chaos in the Twenty-first Century* (Atlantic Books: London, 2003). Cooper's work builds on terminology developed by the German philosopher Jürgen Habermas.

an attempt by the countries or regimes concerned to appear more powerful than they really are. Other actors' power may be underestimated because it is underused and under-advertised, or because of out-of-date conceptions about the kinds of power that are relevant and fungible today. If subjective distortions of this kind affect the assessment of such familiar international players as nation states and multi-state institutions, they are very much more likely to occur in relation to newer types of actor, such as transnational companies, the media or campaigning non-governmental organizations (NGOs). As a topical case, it could be argued that the power of international terrorist groups was seriously underestimated before 11 September 2001 but has quite probably been overestimated since then.

Power among states

With these caveats in mind, the present pattern of power in the *state-based* dimension of the international system can be described as combining features of both concentration and diffusion. The most obvious case of concentration lies in the military dimension, namely, the emergence of the USA as a 'single superpower'. In terms of spending on military assets, the USA now exceeds not just its traditional Soviet/Russian rival but also the collective spending of the 32 next most powerful nations, in terms of the level of military expenditure and the qualitative value of military assets.[7] Its superiority in these dimensions is rapidly growing—the increase in US military spending accounted for 75 per cent of the total world increase in 2002 and for 88 per cent in 2003.[8] At the same time, the USA represents one of the world's highest concentrations of economic power, with the world's highest national gross domestic product, which is more than one quarter of the world total.[9] Because of its key place in the world trading system, notably as a result of the role of the US dollar, it has a great influence on the way in which the economic cycle—and business confidence—develops in the global market. In the context of the debate about globalization, it has been argued that the development of world communications, media and entertainment systems, as well as trade and travel, has allowed elements of US culture and lifestyle to spread around the world in a way that was previously unknown in history and to the detriment of local traditions. The growing dominance of the English language, especially in cyberspace, can be seen as a special illustration of this.

In 2002–2003, when the USA was reacting forcefully—using military but also financial and diplomatic means—against the terrorist attacks it had suffered and the imminent dangers it perceived from Iraq, the realities of US strength tended to dominate debate. The policy options for other international

[7] US military expenditure in 2004 was $455 303 million at 2003 prices and exchange rates. The combined spending of the next 32 countries was $454 869 million at 2003 prices and exchange rates. See also table 8.3 in chapter 8 in this volume.

[8] See chapter 8 in this volume.

[9] World Bank, 'Data and statistics', Quick reference tables, URL <http://www.worldbank.org/data/quickreference/quickref.html>.

players were portrayed in terms of whether to ally with and be protected by that strength or whether to resist and look for ways to balance it. Because of the way in which the Administration of President George W. Bush chose to articulate its policies,[10] some analysts linked the prospect of increasing dominance (or even 'hegemony') of US national power with a new world order (or 'disorder') in which direct force, rather than law or institutional constraints, would play if not a ubiquitous then at least a frequently decisive role.[11]

Already, from the perspective of 2004, some of these theses look too simplistic and some of the associated fears exaggerated. Factors that appear, in the present environment, to have a limiting effect on the concentration of power in any one country's hands include: (*a*) the increasing availability of asymmetric techniques; (*b*) the generic limitations of military power; (*c*) the generic limitations of unilateral action; and (*d*) changes in political relationships and forms of organization. Each of these is discussed briefly below.

The best known example to date of an asymmetric attack was the events of 11 September 2001 in the USA. A small group of terrorists using non-military assets (hand weapons and aircraft) were able to inflict thousands of casualties and immense economic damage in the core territory of the world's single superpower.[12] As often happens in the context of terrorism, the psychological impact went far beyond the material losses. The sudden consciousness of vulnerability prompted both the president's call for an active 'global war on terrorism' and the creation of an ambitious new 'homeland security' programme with associated funding.[13] The Bush Administration concluded that only the direct and forceful elimination of its terrorist enemies (and those who harboured them) would solve the problem. As subsequent events years have shown, however, the real 'bad guys' are hard to find and kill. Attempts to do so may turn them into martyrs, alienate wider popular constituencies and thus create new ground for terrorism to spread in future. More generally, military force appears inadequate to control and transform the conditions that breed terrorism—and asymmetric resentments in general—within distant and diverse societies. Moreover, the range of asymmetric adversaries, and of the weapons available to them, seems likely to grow with the further march of globalization, of technology diffusion and of multiple codependencies (of which more is said below) within international society. The world is still searching for

[10] A new US strategy to combat asymmetric threats, if necessary by pre-emptive intervention, and to preserve the USA's military dominance was set out in the US National Security Strategy of Sep. 2002. It provides the conceptual basis notably for the non-internationally mandated invasions of Afghanistan and Iraq in 2002–2003. The White House, 'The National Security Strategy of the United States of America', Washington, DC, Sep. 2002, URL <http://www.whitehouse.gov/nsc/nss.pdf>.

[11] See, e.g., Glennon, M. J., 'Why the Security Council failed', *Foreign Affairs*, vol. 82, no. 3 (May/June 2003), pp. 16–35.

[12] See Rotfeld, A. D., 'Introduction: global security after 11 September 2001', *SIPRI Yearbook 2002: Armaments, Disarmament and International Security* (Oxford University Press: Oxford, 2002), pp. 1–18.

[13] Anthony I. *et al.*, 'The Euro-Atlantic system and global security', *SIPRI Yearbook 2003: Armaments, Disarmament and International Security* (Oxford University Press: Oxford, 2003), pp. 47–78; and Dunay, P. and Lachowski, Z., 'Euro-Atlantic organizations and relationships', *SIPRI Yearbook 2004: Armaments, Disarmament and International Security* (Oxford University Press: Oxford, 2004), pp. 31–66.

better answers to these challenges, but it seems clear that modern conditions now provide a permanent constraint at least on the *way* in which the power of the nation state can be used—and perhaps even on its inherent value.

There are other, more general limitations on the use of military power in the present environment. It can destroy enemies but cannot coerce friends. It can win a conflict but cannot build or rebuild peace afterwards. It can temporarily discipline societies but not transform them. It is at best a double-edged weapon as a conveyor of values, since the targets of the force are more likely to react to the force itself than to the good intentions and beliefs of those wielding it. On reflection, most of the great victories for progressive values in the 20th century—the reunification of Germany and Europe, the fall of the majority of Communist regimes, the end of apartheid in South Africa, the rehabilitations of Viet Nam and Cambodia, and the virtual elimination of interstate conflicts in Latin America[14]—were brought about not by direct external force but, in the last analysis, by the internal weaknesses of authoritarianism and the appeal of freer ways of being. At most, other players' military power could be said to have deterred and contained the negative forces involved so that the vectors of change could take their course. In sum, it seems not more but less correct today than in the 20th century to state that—at least in terms of ultimate effect—'power comes from the barrel of a gun'.

Military instruments seem to work better when used either in combination with others—political, economic, civilian and humanitarian—or sequentially as a first step to suppress violence so that more constructive forces can come into play. Similarly, there seem to be almost no circumstances today (except, perhaps, within its own borders) in which action by a single nation can solve a security problem for good. The transnational nature of many threats—terrorism, proliferation, crime, disease, illegal migration, violent climate and environmental change, problems of energy supply and the supply of other vital resources—self-evidently makes it necessary to tackle them in similar transnational style, ideally through the setting of universally applicable goals and common efforts. Interdependence within the global economy allows no state to guard and strengthen its social and economic welfare alone. The policy experiment made by the Bush Administration was not actually a unilateral one: in Afghanistan and Iraq, and also in Haiti, US troops acted with a number of other nations at their side. What the USA did try to do in the years after 2001 was to choose its allies freely each time and avoid being bound by the fixed membership, procedures or rules of any given institution.[15] In the event, the institutions took their 'revenge' within a remarkably short time—demonstrating how reliant even the most powerful nation has become, in reality, on attracting larger numbers of supporters and being able to draw on institutional competences. Within one month of deposing Saddam Hussein the USA was

[14] See chapter 6 in this volume.

[15] US Secretary of Defense Donald Rumsfeld stated in a speech that 'the mission must determine the coalition and not the coalition the mission'. 'Secretary Rumsfeld speaks on "21st century" transformation of US armed forces', Washington, DC, 31 Jan. 2002, URL <http://www.defenselink.mil/speeches/2002/s20020131-secdef2.html>.

seeking UN authority for regulating the questions of sanctions against Iraq and Iraqi debt. By early 2004 it was pressing the UN Secretary-General for help in designing Iraq's new political regime. By the middle of 2004 it was calling on the North Atlantic Treaty Organization (NATO) not only to take full responsibility for the peacekeeping operation in Afghanistan, but also to consider supporting military reconstruction and eventually perhaps the deployment of the Multinational Force in Iraq itself.[16]

Dependency, however, works in both directions: institutions are nothing without their member nations. Up to the present, no institution has acquired the means to coerce or punish a nation state (or similar offender) except by using other nation states as its instruments.[17] However, to stop the analysis at this point would be to miss some very important changes in the nature of modern institutional groupings compared with, for example, the alliances and treaty settlements of the 19th and early 20th centuries. The latter could never have more power than the sum of their parts. During the 20th century, in a variety of contexts and conditions, states began to experiment with granting their joint institutions, on the one hand, *legislative* and *normative* powers and, on the other hand, 'supranational' ownership and use of *resources*, including the resource of operational authority. The supreme example of the former trend is the post-1945 United Nations Organization, which from the very beginning was endowed with guardianship of certain universal values, including those of peace and security, and the right to authorize the use of force across the boundaries of traditional state sovereignty in the case of severe threat to these values. The archetype of *supranationality* is the European Union (EU), which evolved out of the European Communities, designed for common management of European coal and steel resources and a common free trading area. Today, the EU's unique system of collective governance places in the hands of a supranational executive body—the European Commission—substantial 'own resources' in cash and the right, for example, to negotiate trade and aviation agreements on behalf of all member governments. The EU also has a uniquely well-developed and permanent function of collective legislation—the ability to pass laws that are directly applicable within all members' jurisdiction and to enforce them through a supranational court. It does not, however, claim the right to exercise these powers beyond its own territory, or indeed to establish its own 'norms' for intervention.[18]

Views have differed since 2001 on whether events are promoting the further development of this new style of institutionalization, or whether—as a result

[16] See, e.g., Evans, G., 'When is it right to fight?'; and Berdal, M., 'The UN after Iraq', *Survival*, vol. 46, no. 3 (autumn 2004), pp. 58–82 and 83–102, respectively.

[17] NATO, the most strongly integrated defence organization in the world, still needs an ad hoc political decision by its members to activate their mutual aid in the event of an attack. Repeated efforts to endow the UN with 'stand-by forces' ready to move at the Secretary-General's command have foundered.

[18] The 2003 European Security Strategy does not explicitly set out the conditions for using armed force under the EU's authority; but in general it emphasizes the role of the UN as providing a superior and universal normative framework. Council of the European Union, 'A secure Europe in a better world: European Security Strategy', Brussels, 12 Dec. 2003, URL <http://ue.eu.int/ueDocs/cms_Data/docs/pressdata/EN/reports/78367. pdf>.

of institutions' perceived failure to block the latest threats and the USA's determination to tackle them in a different way—'deinstitutionalization' will be the trend of the future. The latter thesis is the harder to defend. The legislative–normative experiment is being deepened through a range of new UN enactments and conventions governing security-related behaviour at sub-state and even individual level,[19] which is logical enough given the non-state and trans-state nature of many new threats. The International Criminal Court (ICC)[20] is supported thus far by 97 of the 191 UN member states.[21] Adherence to treaties and participation in such vital functional organs as the World Trade Organization (WTO) are gradually becoming more complete, notably by the inclusion of former Communist states. The EU is extending its uniquely deep and complex *integrative* process to the whole territory of the former Western and Eastern blocs in Europe,[22] and it is creating rules and central governing authorities for its nations in new spheres such as border control and internal order, a single currency and military crisis management. It is true that a number of 'rogue' states, with non-participatory internal regimes and a fixation with their own sovereignty, have refused to join in the internationalization process,[23] and that their absence seriously vitiates some of the basic instruments of global security, such as the 1968 Treaty on the Non-Proliferation of Nuclear Weapons (Non-Proliferation Treaty, NPT). It is also true that the world's sole remaining superpower has stayed outside or withdrawn from some equally critical new global measures, including the ICC, the 1996 Comprehensive Nuclear Test-Ban Treaty (CTBT) and the 1997 Kyoto Protocol on limiting greenhouse gas emissions.[24] However, the very attention and concern which these examples attract underlines how exceptional they have become, and allows the international community's positive energies to be concentrated against them. There is not a single so-called rogue state that is not currently

[19] Most notably, UN Security Council Resolution 1373, 28 Sep. 2001, which introduced universal rules against terrorist financing; and UN Security Council Resolution 1540, 28 Apr. 2004, which did the same for unauthorized ownership and trafficking in weapons of mass destruction. UN conventions with individual-level impact have recently been signed against corruption and money laundering. The continued multiplication of agreements universally banning certain 'inhumane weapons' could be seen in the same light. UN Security Council resolutions from 1946 to 2005 are available at URL <http://www.un.org/documents/scres.htm>.

[20] Wiharta, S., 'The International Criminal Court', *SIPRI Yearbook 2003* (note 13), pp. 153–66.

[21] Guyana became the 97th country to deposit its instrument of ratification of the 1998 Rome Statute, the treaty establishing the International Criminal Court, on 24 Sep. 2004. ICC, 'States parties to the Rome Statute', URL <http://www.icc-cpi.int/asp/statesparties.html>.

[22] The EU border will extend to the edge of the Middle East if and when Turkey joins.

[23] Such states typically have very low 'indexes of globalization', i.e., openness to and penetration by international cultural, as well as economic and political, influences.

[24] The CTBT was opened for signature on 24 Sep. 1996 and will enter into force 180 days after it has been ratified by the 44 members of the Conference on Disarmament with nuclear power or research reactors on their territories. For the states which have signed and ratified the CTBT see annex A in this volume. The text of the CTBT is reproduced in *SIPRI Yearbook 1997: Armaments, Disarmament and International Security* (Oxford University Press: Oxford, 1997), pp. 414–31. The 1997 Kyoto Protocol to the 1992 United Nations Framework Convention on Climate Change will enter into force on 16 Feb. 2005, following Russia's ratification. For the Kyoto Protocol and a list of the signatories see URL <http://unfccc.int/>.

under intense outside scrutiny and pressure of some kind.[25] Perhaps most importantly, the majority of the world's regions are now seeking to form *local* multinational organizations that can provide added value in terms of conflict prevention, trade and economics, and the combating of diverse security threats. Although none has progressed as far as the EU in systemic terms—and states in most regions still have problems in accepting socially and politically intrusive common measures—the trend since 2002 in institutions such as the Association of South-East Asian Nations (ASEAN), the ASEAN Regional Forum, the Asia–Pacific Economic Forum, the Mercado Común del Sur (Southern Common Market), the African Union and various African sub-regional communities has been to raise their level of ambition and to introduce the idea of regional security management more explicitly into their agendas than before.[26] This could be interpreted not only as a symptom of stabilization and new ambitions within the regions themselves but also as a response to the way in which global evolution is driving such actors to defend their interests. Just as they join forces for the purpose of trade negotiations (notably in the WTO framework), their attempts at greater regional self-management in security can be seen as a hedge against the use of divide-and-rule tactics or violent intervention in their backyards by the USA—or any other large power. The world's worst problem regions are defined today *inter alia* by the absence of such organizations or their failure to make them work: hence the logic of the attempts made in 2003–2004 (whatever their specific weaknesses) to design a regional integration framework for the 'greater Middle East'.[27]

The power of non-state actors

As the monopoly on power by the traditional nation state has weakened, so has its monopoly on the assets and capacities associated with security transactions and processes, both 'old' and 'new'. The corporate actors of the private business sector, NGOs, other civil society groupings, cultural and religious communities and the media may all seek to influence the state in ways that can more or less be accommodated in traditional power relationships. Today, however, they also possess elements of *independent* power and influence over processes that are highly relevant for security. The case of the private sector is examined here first.[28]

[25] For discussion of a successful example of such pressure, Libya's agreement with the UK and the USA in 2003 to abandon efforts to develop weapons of mass destruction, see chapter 14 in this volume.

[26] For details and memberships of these organizations see the glossary in this volume.

[27] Other problematic regions from this viewpoint are South Asia; the former Soviet space (where the Russia-led framework of integration is rejected or at least mistrusted by some key nations and does not fully deliver the goods in practical terms); and, to a lesser extent, North-East Asia. There has been speculation over whether the Six-Party Talks to discuss the Korean peninsula's problems might turn into a more permanent security-building framework for this sub-region. See chapter 12 in this volume; and Gill, B., 'China's new security multilateralism and its implications for the Asia–Pacific region', *SIPRI Yearbook 2004* (note 13), pp. 207–30. On the greater Middle East see chapter 5 in this volume.

[28] For general and specific aspects of this interface see Bailes, A. J. K. and Frommelt, I. (eds), SIPRI, *Business and Security: Public–Private Sector Relationships in a New Security Environment* (Oxford University Press: Oxford, 2004).

Ever since the first differentiated human societies developed, warriors have relied on merchants to make or buy weapons and to create the wealth needed to finance armies. In the early 21st century, the interdependence of the private economy and of state-provided security has become far more complex and the balance of power has shifted towards corporate players in many respects. Most technologies that convey an advantage in the defence sphere are now originated as part of general science and technology development, with additional or alternative applications in the civil sector.[29] Countries such as the UK and the USA are increasingly outsourcing to private providers many of the services and resources required for security operations, not only at home and in peacetime but also in field operations overseas and sometimes even on the front line.[30] Private military and security companies provide services on their own initiative around the world, in ways that are far more diverse than the traditional role of mercenaries in combat.[31] Private capital and commerce are now recognized as having a critical role in the rebuilding and normalization of post-conflict areas.

The scale of change becomes much clearer, however, when broader dimensions of security are brought into the picture. The most familiar and debated issue is the role that transnational companies play in the globalization process. Many critics would argue that they may damage the security as well as the identity and autonomy of weaker states; that they are the main culprits in the destruction of the natural environment and exhaustion of natural resources, *inter alia* through logging and opencast mining; that they have been known to directly foment conflict or encourage repressive regimes in regions of raw material extraction;[32] that they indirectly sustain violence by engaging in or condoning the traffic in 'conflict diamonds' and other 'conflict commodities', and so on.[33] Growing awareness of these problems has inspired corrective efforts, including important efforts by business itself, to ensure that corporate actors in conflict-prone areas avoid the potential pitfalls and where possible achieve a positive and stabilizing effect.[34] When it comes to the 'new threats', the help of business is needed not only for blocking terrorist finance but also for developing, updating, applying and enforcing strategic export controls on weapons of mass destruction (WMD) and other dangerous goods and tech-

[29] Hagelin, B., 'Science- and technology-based military innovation: the United States and Europe', *SIPRI Yearbook 2004* (note 13), pp. 285–304.

[30] E.g., during the US military campaign in Iraq in 2003–2004 private security companies provided guards as well as supply and maintenance services in the front line.

[31] See Black, C., 'The security of business: a view from the security industry', eds Bailes and Frommelt (note 28), pp. 173–82; and Holmqvist, C., *Private Security Companies: The Case for Regulation*, SIPRI Policy Paper no. 9 (SIPRI: Stockholm, Jan. 2005), URL <http://www.sipri.org/contents/publications/policy_papers.html>.

[32] Batruch, C., 'Oil and conflict: Lundin Petroleum's experience in Sudan', and Adejumobi, P., 'A view from Africa', eds Bailes and Frommelt (note 28), pp. 148–60 and 242–53, respectively.

[33] See Bone, A., 'Conflict diamonds: the De Beers Group and the Kimberley Process', eds Bailes and Frommelt (note 28), pp. 129–47.

[34] Batruch (note 32); and Bailes and Frommelt (note 28), appendices 1 and 2, pp. 261–309. The appendices list organizations that provide suitable codes of conduct for business in this and other security-relevant spheres.

nologies—especially 'dual-use' items.[35] Private companies are also heavily engaged in cooperative programmes for WMD disposal.[36] Last but not least, in the important new field of *infrastructure security*, a combination of privatization and internationalization has placed most developed countries in a situation where the ownership and management of all their vital infrastructures and utilities (electricity, gas and oil, water and waste disposal, food and fuel delivery, transport networks and communications) lie in the private sector and often in foreign hands. Companies now stand in the front line in terms of protecting such systems against both natural forces and possible human attacks, and in ensuring the rapid resumption of service after emergencies.

This situation does not have to be inherently dangerous for security, since most companies have the same interest as governments in the safety and smooth functioning of their respective societies. It does, however, demand new forms of public–private sector planning and regulation, dialogue and partnership that the world has so far hardly started to design, let alone implement. Most existing rules and codes of conduct in this area are voluntary and developed by (a limited proportion of) businesses.[37] Only recently have enactments such as UN Security Council resolutions 1373 and 1540 been designed consciously to govern corporate and individual actions as well as those of state actors, and even they depend critically on national enforcement.[38] Moreover, these measures and most of the others undertaken since 11 September 2001 which affect corporate activity—such as tightened export controls and new measures to increase the security of aviation, container traffic and ports—have been imposed without prior consultation with the private sector, although they all create new burdens and costs. This lack of dialogue is anachronistic in an age of interactive and cooperative security, and also inefficient since it makes it impossible to draw on companies' own considerable experience of risk analysis and risk management. It should be a major aim of analysts and policy makers in the next few years to find better ways to enlist the world of business as a conscious, active and willing partner.[39]

In the power relationship between state and *civil society* actors, latest trends have not at first sight been favourable to the latter. It is true that terrorists and other extremists[40] have new openings for action as a result of international and internal mobility, illegal trafficking and finance, and the scope for misuse of the Internet. The peaceful majority of the world's population, however, find themselves on the receiving end both of threats from these few individuals and

[35] On export controls see chapter 17 in this volume.

[36] Notably, in the framework of the Group of Eight industrialized nations' Global Partnership. See Anthony, I., *Reducing Threats at the Source: A European Perspective on Cooperative Threat Reduction,* SIPRI Research Report no. 19 (Oxford University Press: Oxford, 2004).

[37] Bailes and Frommelt (note 34).

[38] UN Security Council Resolution 1373, 28 Sep. 2001; and UN Security Council Resolution 1540, 28 Apr. 2004. Resolution 1540 is reproduced in appendix 11A in this volume.

[39] Bailes, A. J. K., 'Business and the new security agenda: victim, accomplice or ally?', Center for Transatlantic Relations, Washington, DC, Oct. 2004, URL <http://transatlantic.sais-jhu.edu/PDF/BondiOpinionsOct2004.pdf>.

[40] E.g., those carrying out sabotage in the name of animal rights, anti-abortion, anti-globalization and environmental campaigns.

of other existential dangers involving the breakdown of modern civilized support systems. People's *dependence* on those systems is also proportionally greater than that of the predominantly rural, self-supplying and self-protecting populations of earlier days. At the political level, the developed West's shift towards an action-oriented mode of security excludes the bulk of the Western populations from participation, since an interventionist agenda creates strong pressure for professional armies and militates against democratic control inasmuch as decisions on specific operations generally lie with the executive branch. The tendency towards multilateralization and institutionalization of security activity merely compounds the difficulties for popular control. The EU's European Parliament is not allowed to intervene in European Security and Defence Policy decisions (it does not even control the major part of their financing, whereas national parliaments can at least vote on defence budgets); NATO's Parliamentary Assembly has no budgetary function; and the UN does not even have a 'parliament' equivalent in this context.[41] Analysts have warned that the new focus since 11 September 2001 on tightening internal security against terrorist threats could imperil civil society's rights on several levels—by eroding judicial norms and individual rights within the legal process, weakening data privacy rules, placing new curbs on free speech and freedom of movement, and possibly aggravating inter-cultural and inter-ethnic divides.[42]

A wider survey of global development since 1989–90, however, would convey a more complex message. The number and proportion of states following some recognized form of democracy have grown steadily over these years. Citizens' rights—and opportunities to exercise them—vary widely within such political systems, but they all imply some degree of influence for public opinion and some limit to the power of a government that forfeits public confidence. The media, meanwhile, have a growing capacity to stir up public opposition and to expose official wrongdoing. They can play a significant role in prompting security interventions, by drawing global attention in real time to civil conflicts, massacres, famines, and the like. (Institutions such as the UN and NATO have acknowledged the force of the media *inter alia* by studying the use of information as a deliberate instrument of conflict management.[43]) NGOs can exploit the same asymmetric 'force multipliers' inherent in a globalized world system that are open to the terrorists, but for generally more benign purposes such as fund-raising, lobbying, and charitable and humanitarian initiatives. They have, for example, substantially influenced the inter-

[41] For a detailed discussion of the democratic control issue in relation to intervention policies see chapter 4 in this volume

[42] See, e.g., Dalgaard-Nielsen, A., 'Civil liberties and counter-terrorism: a European point of view', Center for Transatlantic Relations, Washington, DC, 2004, URL <http://transatlantic.sais-jhu.edu/PDF/articles/Anja.pdf>; and Caparini, M., 'Security sector reform and NATO and EU enlargement', *SIPRI Yearbook 2003* (note 13), pp. 237–60.

[43] Since the Rwanda conflict—and also in the light of the experience in the Balkans—it has been increasingly understood that controlling the information available to warring factions and local populations can have a decisive effect on crisis outcomes. Media incitement to genocide can now be punished as a war crime.

governmental arms control agenda both by focusing on certain topics (e.g., in the 1990s, French nuclear testing, landmines and small arms) and by failing to exercise sustained pressure on others (e.g., the size of nuclear arsenals and missile defence).[44]

Non-governmental organizations using state-of-the-art publicity techniques can also steer the decisions of *corporate* actors to a degree that many governments might envy. Environmental lobbies have driven businesses to 'green' their image, public attitudes make it hard to market genetically modified food in Europe, and anti-sweatshop campaigning has changed the social responsibility policies of companies using labour from the developing world. NGO agitation has several times forced oil and other extractive companies to withdraw from conflict regions—and further examples could be cited. What underlies all these cases is the rise of consumer power resulting from the sheer scale of consumer spending, the growing internationalization of consumer markets and the accessibility of most developed-world consumers to media and NGO messages. For analogous reasons, 'shareholder power' has also become a significant factor in business planning and decisions. If the present debate about corporate governance is in part a reaction to and recognition of the private sector's growing power, the highly publicized recent cases where business leaders have been caught and punished—and the new government controls which this has prompted—are already helping to constrain the way in which corporate power is used. In sum, civil society actors may rarely succeed in *preventing* wrong actions, whether by governments or corporations; but they are becoming increasingly practised at *exposing* and *punishing* such actions after a lapse of time[45] and at promoting new advances in state and global legislation to stop further abuses. The outstanding, and very large, question that remains is who can and should regulate the exercise of power by civil society entities themselves.

III. Shared challenges: diverging agendas?

The world has never been free, and is never likely to be free, of diverging and sometimes clashing security interests. Differences of interest may pit state against state, but also bloc against bloc, non-state actor against non-state actor, business against business and one 'historical' or 'functional' constituency (notably in the case of belief-based groups) against another. These phenomena need not of themselves do damage to international security. Some types of difference may result in useful checks and balances, thus promoting healthy competition and helping to deter excess. Security problems do arise, both for

[44] Kile, S. N., 'Ballistic missile defence', *SIPRI Yearbook 2004* (note 13), pp. 647–58. On the nuclear arsenals as of Jan. 2005 see appendix 12A in this volume.

[45] Recent examples are the exposure by the media and parliaments of the misuse of intelligence by members of the US-led coalition that overthrew Saddam Hussein, which took a little over 1 year after the invasion, and the success of private actors in getting the US Supreme Court to rule against the detention of prisoners from the Afghanistan conflict and elsewhere at Guantánamo Bay, which took 2 years.

the parties themselves and for other stakeholders, if they are unable—for whatever reason—to manage their differences in a non-violent manner.

In the early 21st century, the major industrialized nations of the northern hemisphere (including China and Russia) no longer regard each other as strategic adversaries in any ideological, existential or permanent sense. This does not mean that there are not conflicting interests and elements of competition, even between the USA and its military allies in Europe. Some relationships such as the China–USA one are still highly ambivalent, retaining features of dispute on issues of both principle and practice. Potential 'hot spots' include those between China and the USA over Taiwan, and between Russia and the Western powers over the handling of new crises on the territory of the former Soviet Union. For all this, most analysts and policy makers would agree that open military conflict between any of these powers is unlikely in any short-term future. The chance that a conflict elsewhere in the world will draw two powers from the North into intervention on different sides is also quite remote, compared with cold war times. The growing attention to transnational and non-military security challenges has highlighted reasons for solidarity among this group of actors: they all have more to lose than gain from terrorism, would prefer not be challenged by emergent nuclear weapon powers, and benefit from stable energy flows and prices. Overall, and especially when economic transactions are brought into the picture, the trend in the major part of the northern hemisphere seems set towards greater interdependence, more widespread acceptance of joint frameworks of regulation, and the sublimation of remaining elements of competition and conflict to the political or legal level.

It is natural, therefore, to see the main opposition of interests in the world today as separating the 'North' from the 'South', or the developed from the developing group of nations. Both terminologies are of course open to manifold objections and must be used with caution. The 'South' includes nations such as Australia while geographic trouble spots such as North Korea and the notorious 'arc of conflict' from the Arab regions to Central Asia lie well north of the equator. The category of 'developing' nations contains everything from the world's smallest and poorest states to leading regional powers such as Brazil and India, which have become important centres of economic and strategic influence, technology and service provision. It is not without reason, however, that the term 'North–South' has become common parlance when addressing global challenges in the fields of trade, finance and sustainable development. Here, the interests of North and South can be seen as an interlinked circle where the acts of one party—for instance, keeping down certain commodity prices, keeping up domestic subsidies or withholding oil supplies—are liable to damage the other party in zero-sum fashion unless win–win management solutions can be found.

In the field of security, the relationship between North and South has also often taken a zero-sum form, notably during the colonial period. The use of developing countries as proxies by the Western and Eastern blocs in the cold war was a more complicated case, but this still more often hurt than helped the client states involved, given the costs, burdens and local vendettas that it drew them into. By the end of the 20th century, however, the very animus that built up over the North's impact on the South in *non-military* dimensions—ill effects of globalization, the debt issue, destruction of the environment, and so on—hinted that the zero-sum picture had become less obviously applicable on the military front. The great majority of new conflicts after 1990 were South–South, or more rarely North–North (e.g., in the Balkans and Caucasus), and almost exclusively intra-state.[46] Major powers in the North became engaged predominantly in the context of multilateral peace operations, and there were cases where former colonies actually invited the former colonial power to help them.[47] If security interests in the North and the South still diverged, therefore, it was not so much because of zero-sum feedback loops as because of diverging needs and priorities: leading the North in particular to pursue security agendas that were, at best, unrelated to requirements in the South and, at worst, unhelpful to them.[48]

Put briefly, this 'agenda gap' arises because the South is currently much worse hit than the North by phenomena at two different ends of the security spectrum: by armed conflict and other forms of physical force (lawlessness, crime, and intra-familial and gender-related violence), and by 'human security' challenges such as poverty, hunger, disease, accidents and natural disasters, exhaustion of natural resources and environmental damage—together with the forced migration to which all these factors may contribute. The world community has not failed to recognize this, in the first instance by the growing focus on conflict management in all the major security institutions after 1990, and in the second case most notably by the Millennium Declaration adopted by the UN on 8 September 2000, which set goals for the alleviation of poverty, illiteracy and other human scourges.[49] However, even before the sharp agenda shift caused by the events of 11 September 2001, there was reason to doubt whether the North was devoting sufficient energy to the task to overcome or even significantly narrow the North–South 'security gap'. The North's peace-making capacities were devoted preferentially during the 1990s to conflicts within its own area (the Balkans and, in Russia's case, conflicts on post-Soviet territory) and to cases elsewhere that directly engaged the North's own interests, such as the 1991 Gulf War. Resources for South–South conflicts of lesser strategic importance were increasingly provided by the South itself, or not at all.[50] On the human security front, statistics point to a growing

[46] All of the 19 major armed conflicts ongoing in 2004 could be defined as intra-state, involving disputes over the control of government and/or territory. See chapter 2 and appendix 2A in this volume.

[47] On the case of Sierra Leone and the UK see chapter 8 in this volume. (2 Fns added)

[48] On the negative effect this has on the security of the North see chapter 7 in this volume.

[49] United Nations, United Nations Millennium Declaration, UN General Assembly Resolution 55/2, 8 Sep. 2000, URL <http://www.un.org/millennium/declaration/ares552e.htm>.

[50] In Dec. 2004 the top 20 troop contributors to UN peacekeeping operations were all developing nations. Among the developed nations, only the UK and the USA remained on the list of the top 30 contributors. It is fair to add that funds provided by developed nations through their contributions to the UN helped to finance many developing country deployments. United Nations, Department of Peacekeeping Operations, 'Ranking of military and civilian police contributions to UN operations',

diversity of experience among actors in the South, combined with an actually widening gap between the world's richest and poorest states.[51] Progress reports on the Millennium Declaration have been a litany of under- or unfulfilled commitments—to the point where the UN Secretary-General has found it necessary to plan for a major relaunch of the millennium initiative in 2005 in combination with follow-up to the 2004 report of the High-level Panel on Threats, Challenges and Change.[52] At the same time, the growing dangers to mankind from human immunodeficiency virus (HIV), acquired immune deficiency syndrome (AIDS), other epidemic diseases such as severe acute respiratory syndrome (SARS) and—potentially—avian influenza, the destruction of natural habitats and resources, and longer-term climate change all stand to hit the world's poorer populations much harder than its richer ones, at least in the short and medium terms. Particularly sinister is the feedback loop between such dangers to human life and their impact on the world's developing economies, which threatens to widen the North–South gap in both dimensions at once. It was recently estimated that by 2025 deaths from AIDS, and the related medical costs, could slow Chinese and Indian economic growth by 33 per cent and 40 per cent, respectively, and cause the Russian economy to shrink by 40 per cent.[53]

Some security challenges, however, have been aggravated by parallel rather than divergent trends in the North and the South. The end of East–West confrontation has freed actors in the North and the South to pursue their security interests more actively *inter alia* by armed intervention, because the danger of escalation (or retaliation against the intervener's homeland) has been so greatly reduced. In developed nations, the case for 'humanitarian intervention' was pushed during the 1990s by thinkers of the Left as much as the Right. The 'peace dividend' that members of NATO and the former Warsaw Treaty

31 Dec. 2004, URL <http://www.un.org/Depts/dpko/dpko/contributors/>. See also chapter 3 in this volume.

[51] Statistics on the incidence of poverty in the world's nations, measured by the number of persons living on less than $1 or less than $2 per day, are published by the World Bank. World Bank, *World Development Indicators 2004* (World Bank: Washington, DC, 2004). The United Nations Development Programme (UNDP) monitors countries' performance under a similar 'poverty index' but also under a Human Development Index based on a combination of life expectancy and access to education, literacy and income. The UNDP report calculates that 323 million people are living on less than $1 per day in sub-Saharan Africa and 432 million in South Asia. It shows the Human Development Index as having *fallen* for the Democratic Republic of the Congo, Rwanda and Zambia in the period 1980–90, and for as many as 20 states in 1990–2002, of which 13 were in sub-Saharan Africa. UNDP, *Human Development Report 2004: Cultural Liberty in Today's Diverse World* (Oxford University Press: New York, 2004), URL <http://hdr.undp.org/reports/global/2004/>.

[52] The basis for the relaunch is expected to be the lengthy report unveiled on 17 Jan. 2005 by an expert group led by Dr Jeffrey Sachs in the framework of the Millennium Project at the UN University. This exposes the lack of progress on specific Millennium Goals adopted in 2000 and calls for a fresh effort to halve world poverty by 2015, which could require an estimated $50 billion of additional aid per year. UN Millennium Project, 'Investing in development: a practical plan to achieve the Millennium Development Goals', Overview report, 2005, URL <http://unmp.forumone.com/>.

[53] Behrman, G., 'The cost of AIDS in Asia', *Newsweek*, 19 July 2004, p. 51. The total number of people living with HIV/AIDS is currently estimated at 39.4 million. There were an estimated 4.9 million new cases of infection and 3.1 million deaths in 2004, of which 2.8 million were in the southern hemisphere. Joint UN Programme on HIV/AIDS, 'AIDS epidemic update: December 2004', URL <http://www.unaids.org/wad2004/report.html>.

Organization took in the form of defence cuts in the first part of the decade was soon succeeded by exhortations to NATO and EU members to build up their *deployable* defence capabilities again. Non-European governments have been subject to similar pressures, not only because of the diversion of sales efforts by West-based defence producers, but also because of continuing tensions and strategic competition in some regions and the interest in developing new joint capacities for local peacekeeping in others. The need which the established nuclear weapon powers apparently feel to retain (and to continue, at least qualitatively, enhancing) their nuclear capacities has been matched by—and some would say has added to—the nuclear proliferation trend in parts of the developing world. The traditional, cold war disarmament agenda has been largely squeezed out between these forces operating in both hemispheres. Significantly, new arms control initiatives in the late 1990s addressed items—such as anti-personnel mines and small arms—which the powers in the North had no strong self-interest in retaining and which, even in the South, figured more as a humanitarian scourge than as a primary determinant of conflicts won or lost.[54]

Immediately after the terrorist attacks of 11 September 2001, it was possible to hope for a new convergence between the North's and the South's semi-detached agendas. Al-Qaeda's transnational style of terrorism patently could not be tackled except by worldwide action. The revealed vulnerability of the world's single superpower could have created new fellow-feeling with the challenges faced by weaker communities. Several world leaders argued for greater efforts to tackle not just terrorism but also 'the causes of terrorism', which they saw as linked with underdevelopment, the distribution of resources, and problems of alienation and exclusion that also exist in the developed West.[55] The EU collectively warned against any over-simple labelling of the 'enemy', and in particular its identification with the international community of Islam, that would risk a descent into religious intolerance and racism.[56]

In a sequence of events which future historians may look back on as tragic, however, the particular forms of response chosen by the USA—and supported by various of its partners—produced a cumulative effect that, at least in the short term, only widened the North–South gap. The new doctrinal focus on asymmetric threats implied seeing weaker, smaller and less conventional players (including 'failed states') not as people to be helped or at worst marginalized, but as a source of deadly threat. The new readiness to use force against such threats took an inherently discriminatory form since the targets chosen

[54] These challenges for the arms control agenda are explored at more length in Bailes, A. J. K., 'Arms control: how to move from the cold war legacy to the needs of a globalized world?', Proceedings of the Bonn International Center for Conversion 10th Anniversary Symposium, Apr. 2004, URL <http://www.bicc.de>.

[55] The EU's European Security Strategy, when addressing the causes of terrorism, states that 'this phenomenon is also a part of our own society'. Council of the European Union (note 18).

[56] Council of the European Union, 'Conclusions and plan of action of the extraordinary European Council meeting on 21 September 2001', SN140/01, Brussels, URL <http://www.consilium.eu.int/uedocs/cmsUpload/140.en.pdf>.

were all non-Western ones at lower levels of development—Afghanistan, Iraq and Yemen, where the USA carried out a precision strike with the acquiescence of the local government. The freedom which the Bush Administration granted itself to act, where necessary, unilaterally and without a UN mandate, made it much harder for the broader community of states to share ownership or to import shared norms into the process. Other measures taken in the name of the 'global war on terrorism' had discriminatory effects, whether wished or incidental, either against developing-world travellers and businessmen (e.g., the USA's new visa procedures and the strengthening of West-based export control groupings) or against citizens from minority ethnic groups in developed states. The USA's increased security assistance to countries seen as combating their own 'terrorists', and its withdrawal of military aid from those who refused to sign exemptions for US personnel from the jurisdiction of the ICC,[57] risked dividing and polarizing both the states concerned and their regions.

Meanwhile, the military burdens placed on the states which joined the USA's coalitions, and the strain placed on Euro-Atlantic relations by disputes over these same issues, inevitably distracted attention from other regions' non-terrorist-related problems and aggravated the problem of getting support from the North for intervention in other conflicts.[58] In the new military peacekeeping operations launched under UN command in 2002–2004, NATO and EU members contributed only token numbers of personnel.[59] For all the talk of combating the causes of terrorism, the 5 per cent real-terms growth in the official development assistance given by members of the Organisation for Economic Co-operation and Development (OECD) Development Assistance Committee (DAC) between 2002 and 2003 was lower than the 7 per cent growth achieved between 2001 and 2002, and eight EU members showed negative growth (although mainly for technical reasons connected with the phasing of payments).[60] The USA did achieve a further real growth of 16.9 per cent in its development aid in 2003, but this included payments to Iraq,[61] while comparable or higher rates of growth in its defence-related assistance ensured that there would be no overall switch from 'harder' to 'softer' methods for

[57] Wiharta (note 20).

[58] *Vide* the difficulty experienced in persuading the USA to intervene, when invited, in Liberia, and the reluctance of most leading powers to recognize the situation in the Darfur province of Sudan in mid-2004 as constituting genocide (or to accept any other compelling justification for using their own resources there). The general issue of how to define cases for 'humanitarian intervention' is addressed below.

[59] Five new operations were launched in 2002–2004. Total personnel contributed by all NATO and EU states in 2004 were as follows: UNMISET (East Timor), 55 out of 619; UNMIL (Liberia), 810 out of 15 788; UNOCI (Côte d'Ivoire), 238 out of 6215; MINUSTAH (Haiti), 424 out of 7406; and ONUB (Burundi), 9 out of 5454. United Nations, Department of Peacekeeping Operations, 'Monthly summary of contributors of military and civilian police personnel', Dec. 2004, URL <http://www.un.org/Depts/dpko/dpko/contributors/>.

[60] OECD, Aid from DAC members, Statistics, data and indicators, 'Final ODA data for 2003', URL <http://www.oecd.org/topicstatsportal/0,2647,en_2825_495602_1_1_1_1_1,00.html>. The EU states with some measure of real decrease were Austria, Denmark, Finland, Italy, the Netherlands, Portugal, Spain and Sweden. Overall, DAC countries' aid as a proportion of their gross national income is calculated by the OECD to be lower in 2005 (0.25%) than the average for the years 1980–92 (0.33%).

[61] US payments to Iraq in 2003 were estimated at $1.9 billion. OECD (note 60).

promoting security.[62] Meanwhile, the global flow of arms transfers was higher in 2003 than any year since 1999, with developing countries such as China and India among the largest recipients.[63]

One of the most serious challenges facing any attempt, today, to relaunch movement towards a working system of world security governance is to overcome the divisive legacy of these developments. Reputable opinion polls have shown a marked shift of opinion against the USA and its policies—and to some extent against its coalition partners—even in developing countries that are traditionally tough on terrorism.[64] The reasons for the developed world to work actively to reverse this growing North–South polarization are by no means limited to charity and justice. Precisely because the asymmetric threats are real, it can make no sense for the richest countries that are most exposed to these threats to behave in a way that drives new state and non-state recruits to the terrorist cause. The deliberately induced conflicts in Afghanistan and Iraq have shown clearly enough that the use of force alone against a chaotic or deviant state risks merely increasing the chaos and planting seeds for future deviance. As some Europeans stressed in the specific context of learning lessons from 11 September 2001,[65] any conflict anywhere—even if initially unrelated to terrorism and with no anti-North agenda—creates a hole in the fabric of international order and a new environment for breeding transnational threats. There is no convincing prescription for curbing these effects that does not involve active and *voluntary* cooperation between the North's strongest security providers and the widest possible range of partners in other regions. The creation of a few—probably embattled—Western proxy states in strategic areas showed itself to be a thoroughly bad solution in cold war conditions, and is more plainly inadequate and counterproductive today. Holding other states hostage to possible unilateral attacks from the North can only motivate them

[62] The US Department of State military assistance budget rose from $24 billion in financial year (FY) 2002 to $25.4 billion in FY 2003, of which $5 billion was earmarked for terrorism-related partnerships. The Department of Defense (DOD) Foreign Military Financing budget (linked to the purchase of US defence equipment) rose from $3.6 billion in FY 2001 to $4.1 billion in FY 2003. The DOD budget for International Military Education and Training rose from $58 million in FY 2001 to $80 million in FY 2003.

[63] Hagelin, B., Bromley, M. and Wezeman, S. T., 'International arms transfers', *SIPRI Yearbook 2004* (note 13), pp. 447–74.

[64] In 2 Pew Research Center opinion polls—with findings from 2002 and 2003, and from Feb. to March 2004—the former poll reported 'favorable' feelings towards the USA declining between 2002 and 2003 from 61% to 15% in Indonesia and from 71% to 38% in Nigeria, while respondents in Indonesia, Jordan Morocco and Pakistan put Osama bin Laden among the top 3 people in whom they would have confidence to 'do the right thing regarding world affairs'. According to the 2004 results, a large majority of respondents in Jordan and Morocco thought suicide attacks against the coalition powers in Iraq were justifiable, and the percentages of respondents believing that the USA was 'overreacting' to terrorism were: Jordan 76%, Pakistan 66% and Turkey 55%. Pew Research Center, 'Views of a changing world 2003: war with Iraq further divides global public', 3 June 2003, URL <http://www.people-press.org/reports/display.php3?ReportID=185>; and 'A year after Iraq war: mistrust of America in Europe ever higher, Muslim anger persists', 16 Mar. 2004, URL <http://www.people-press.org/reports/display.php3?Report ID=206>.

[65] According to British Prime Minister Tony Blair, 'We should work hard to broker peace where conflict threatens a region's stability because we know the dangers of contagion'. Directgov, 10 Downing Street, Prime Minister's speech at the George Bush Senior Presidential Library, 7 Apr. 2002, URL <http://www.number-10.gov.uk/output/Page1712.asp>.

more strongly to defend themselves, *inter alia* by asymmetric means, and makes it harder to build the North–South trust required to achieve timely and united UN decisions when military intervention is truly needed.

On 26 December 2004, the world was given a harsh reminder of the reality of interdependence between the conditions of human existence in North and South. The huge tsunamis that struck coastal areas around the Indian Ocean killed many hundreds of tourists and an estimated 300 000 local inhabitants. The event acted, literally, as a common shock to world society: calling forth in the first instance an unprecedented outpouring of private as well as official aid, and driving policy makers of the North into some major shifts of approach to issues ranging from developing-world debt to the construction of disaster warning systems and the handling of ongoing conflicts within affected states such as Indonesia and Sri Lanka.[66] It seems not overoptimistic to hope that the consequences will improve the political climate for readdressing the broader 'millennium' agenda discussed above, and perhaps even for more universal acceptance of the UN's indispensable role, in 2005.

However, the resulting policy impulses and attitude changes will be incomplete if not accompanied by realization that the South is more than just a 'weak link' in the chain of global human security. It is not just that citizens in the North could be hit (on a much worse scale than by the tsunamis) by the South's failure to contain new disease outbreaks, mismanagement of remaining natural resources or pressures leading to sudden large-scale migration. Developing and non-Western nations also hold positive instruments of power and can place the North in a situation of 'reverse dependence', most obviously when it comes to the ownership of oil and gas and other scarce natural resources and proximity to key delivery routes. Notoriously, the USA can only maintain its current massive deficits in the national budget and in foreign trade because Asian investors, in particular, are willing to continue buying dollars.[67] China's foreign investments are growing: it bought out IBM's computer-producing business in December 2004,[68] and its oil companies (like those in several other nations in the South) are making an ambitious entry to the overseas contracts market.[69] The rise in outsourcing of commercial services from developed to developing countries makes the former increasingly dependent on the functioning of infrastructures, and on the probity and good security practices of corporate partners, in the South as well as the North. As argued above, the diffusion of key security-related technologies (for conventional as well as potential mass-destruction weapons) makes it impossible effectively to prevent their misuse without active support from developing-world producers.[70] These last few points also underline a lesson that needs greater attention

[66] On this last issue see chapter 2 in this volume.

[67] See, e.g., Munter, P., 'US rates in thrall to foreign central banks', *Financial Times* (US edn), 27 Nov. 2004, p. 11.

[68] 'Lenovo buys IBM's PC unit for $1.75 billion', *Financial Times*, 9 Dec. 2004, p. 15.

[69] Boxell, J. and Morrison, K., 'A power shift: global oil companies find new rivals snapping at their heels', *Financial Times*, 9 Dec. 2004, p. 1.

[70] Mallik, A., *Technology and Security in the 21st Century: A Demand-side Perspective*, SIPRI Research Report no. 20 (Oxford University Press: Oxford, 2004). See also chapter 11 in this volume.

in both research and policy making. Non-state as well as state actors in the developing world are now a necessary part of any comprehensive security solution. Frameworks, principles and motivations are urgently required to allow these actors to be mobilized for positive ends.[71]

IV. Modes of security action: intervention, the legislative method and integration

Among the many tendencies to oversimplification in the security debate of the past three years has been the inclination to argue for or against one mode of security action (e.g., military force) in isolation, or to argue for one mode as a preferred alternative to another. In reality, whether in the general pursuit of security, in combating new threats or in the specific field of arms control and non-proliferation, a mixture of means is the only thing that works. This section briefly discusses three different approaches that could contribute to such rational combinations (although reducing them to three is already an oversimplification): (*a*) intervention; (*b*) the legislative method; and (*c*) the historically novel method of integration.

Intervention

Intervention should not be interpreted only as the use of military force. As a generic approach it may include outside attempts at mediation and negotiation; the provision of humanitarian relief; non-military deployments (police and civilian experts); the use of economic sanctions, incentives and aid; and perhaps other, even more indirect, uses of 'carrots and sticks' to produce leverage. Intervention may be mandated by a more than national authority or not mandated at all: it may be consensual or non-consensual. What it always implies is the application of tangible or intangible resources that belong to outside actors, remain essentially under the control of those actors, and are designed to alter the given situation in a way not to be expected from the play of internal dynamics alone.

Motives to intervene are many, and the world is unlikely ever to wean itself from this method entirely. Easing human distress, including the impact of natural disasters (which are likely to increase in future), is prima facie the purest motive—although it has become linked with thorny questions about the international community's right to come to the aid of suffering populations without their own governments' consent.[72] Another common and relatively

[71] Private-sector movements for corporate responsibility (including security-related codes of conduct) have so far been strongly West- and North-dominated, and all the largest global campaigning NGOs are of developed-world *origin*. The recent initiatives (see note 19) to create universally applicable codes in the UN framework on subjects such as terrorist finance and WMD trafficking (and also money laundering and corruption) offer a regulatory framework for non-state actors in the South as well as the North, but make no, or inadequate, provision for assisting and ensuring implementation.

[72] I.e., in cases of genocide, other severe abuses of human rights, famine or other widespread death and distress caused by 'weak' or collapsing government. For earlier proposals on codifying this responsibility see International Commission on Intervention and State Sovereignty (ICISS), *The Respon-*

altruistic motive is the wish to prevent, contain and end armed conflicts and to rebuild after them. Many states would recognize the rationale for joint action to keep open international trade routes—especially at sea—and to protect international rights of passage, if necessary by de-mining. Beyond these motives of common interest lies the territory of 'extended' self-defence: full of pitfalls that have been well illustrated by events since 11 September 2001, but nevertheless based on an acknowledged right of nations under Article 51 of the UN Charter.[73]

There are, in fact, difficult issues attached to any kind of intervention, no matter how 'clean' or 'soft'. There are resource costs and rarely any prospect of profits to balance them in the short term. There are risks in inserting a new element into a situation that by definition is imperfect and unstable. It can never be known what forces and consequences the intervention will unleash, and the interveners' hopes and aims can be subverted in many ways. Humanitarian refugee camps have been exploited as bases by combatants, and negotiated settlements have led directly to a break-out of conflict elsewhere.[74] A successful intervention itself becomes part of the problem if it leads to 'aid dependence' or goes too far in relieving local actors of their political and moral responsibility.[75] A particularly crucial question for post-conflict evolution is whether the intervention has liberated local forces for positive change or whether it leaves behind a negative dynamic and a body politic lacking vital organs. Beyond these tangible indicators lie the complex issues of legality and legitimacy—which are not always the same thing. These are generally cited in relation to cases of armed and coercive intervention, but they should apply to any type of interference liable to have security consequences. Any situation where a stronger power makes use of its superior resources—or greater freedom of action—to influence a weaker one on the latter's own territory gives rise to questions of motive and fairness and of taking continuing responsibility for the results. Since even the strongest nations and institutions have only a limited exportable surplus of security, the *choice* of where and when to intervene, and where and when not to intervene, is also a delicate matter and may be, in itself, an important determinant of legitimacy.

At least four contemporary lines of soul-searching and debate provide the background to the attention which Kofi Annan's High-level Panel devoted to the intervention issue. The most prominent challenge is that of trying to construct or reconstruct a shared international understanding (in whatever form it might be recorded) on the circumstances in which coercive military intervention is justified; covering not only the familiar 'conflict' agenda but also

sibility to Protect (International Development Research Centre: Ottawa, 2001), URL <http://www.dfait-maeci.gc.ca/iciss-ciise/menu-en.asp>.

[73] The 1945 Charter of the United Nations outlaws the use of force in situations not covered by self-defence under Article 51 or collective security authorized under Chapter VII. For the UN Charter see URL <http://www.un.org/aboutun/charter/>.

[74] See Dwan, R. and Gustavsson, M., 'Major armed conflicts', *SIPRI Yearbook 2004* (note 13), pp. 113–21.

[75] For evidence of this in Bosnia and Herzegovina and in Kosovo see Caparini, M., 'Security sector reform in the Western Balkans', *SIPRI Yearbook 2004* (note 13), pp. 251–82.

situations involving or connected with the new threats of transnational terrorism and proliferation. The importance, and difficulty, of achieving rules that can convince and control both hemispheres (and all the different types of actor involved) was stressed in section II. Perhaps equally important is to recognize that the turbulence and damage caused by the introduction of new threat-linked intervention doctrines after September 2001 could be repeated in future, unless the solutions proposed now can be applied widely enough to cover even newer potential triggers for 'extended self-defence'.[76] The second and closely related set of issues refers to *who* can and should intervene: the vertical division of labour between the UN and security-capable regional organizations in Europe and elsewhere; the horizontal division between organizations coexisting in the same region (such as NATO and the EU); and the conditions under which action by a coalition or individual state may be justified and worthy of UN recognition and support.

The third set of issues concerns the current inadequacy and suboptimal use of intervention resources, where a very important question is *what kind* of resources (and what combinations of them) should be preferentially developed. Accident and design have combined over the past decade to focus the attention of developed and developing countries on deployable military capabilities, now being belatedly supplemented by measures to enhance non-military capabilities such as police and system-building expertise. Other means that might be used both as carrots and sticks—including political and economic as well as traditional diplomatic resources—have received patchier attention and even the most self-consciously multifunctional institutions such as the EU are still some way from being able to combine smoothly their military instruments with the full range of others at their disposal. This helps to explain the lag in follow-up to the talk about tackling 'causes' of terrorism, as well as the international community's long-term performance gap in conflict prevention.

Another set of issues refers to the non-state actors addressed above: whether and how to regulate the roles they play in crises, how to exploit their potential, and how to coordinate state and non-state inputs in any given case.

Legislation

The legislative method is also a very old one, used in nations for millennia and since the late 19th century increasingly in the international context. Its essence is to create explicit rules governing everyone within the sphere of application, with obvious benefits in terms of fairness, transparency and predictability, and in almost all cases also a function of restraint (rules limit the freedom of those subject to them by prescribing what must, as well as what must not, be done). These normative advantages are matched by practical ones, including the

[76] Possible motives for military strikes could be created, e.g., by conflicts over shrinking energy and other natural resources, including inhabitable or cultivable territory, or by perceived damage to a state's vital interests from migration, disease, pollution, infrastructure sabotage, cyber-sabotage, etc., initiated from the territory of another state.

value of clear benchmarks for identifying and correcting unacceptable behaviour. Since the legislative method can be used at intra-state, interstate and supranational level; can bind non-state as well as state subjects; and can take many different forms, including looser and fuzzier commitments as well as legally binding obligations, it is prima facie much better matched than forceful intervention to the challenge of dealing with today's multiplicity of security risks and security actors.

It is argued in section II above that the world today is not necessarily moving away from the legislative method, and that it would be wrong to do so. However, the method has patent limitations and raises numerous problems. First is the question of who should be bound by a particular legislative instrument. For some security purposes the adoption of shared rules by a limited group may work well, whether or not the rules are then extended to others. The present structure of arms control and proliferation-related obligations and commitments has grown up in such a way that participation in key agreements such as the NPT remains voluntary, most controls on trade in strategically sensitive goods and technologies are administered by small groups of mostly developed nations,[77] and the only constraints on major conventional weapons that have achieved their set purpose are ones entered into at local or regional level. The optimality of this pattern is now being questioned by many who argue that certain obligations (notably connected with WMD) should be universal and compulsory, and that there should be wider ownership of controls on weapon-related and dual-use technologies.[78] At the same time, however, new initiatives with an exclusive membership, largely from the North, have come into being, such as the Proliferation Security Initiative.[79] These different methods and preferences persist partly because of the lack of a solution to two further challenges, amply illustrated by the Iraq episode: how to define and judge *compliance* with legislative-type undertakings (with the necessary transparency and accuracy),[80] and how to *enforce* corrective action in the case of non-compliance. The USA and—to a lesser extent—other developed powers have—in very broad terms—tended to give priority to enforceability and enforcement over universality in regulatory solutions. It is they who have typically decided when to act coercively on perceived cases of non-compliance, and when not. States of the South are more likely to point out the objections to a situation in which a limited number of countries appoint themselves policemen, without necessarily obeying the laws in question themselves, or necessarily wielding the right truncheons to do the job.

If the use of the legislative method is to be protected and perhaps even extended in future, its proponents must address these difficulties. One chal-

[77] These groups include the Australia Group, the Nuclear Suppliers Group and the Zangger Committee, for WMD-related exports; the Wassenaar Arrangement for exports of goods and technologies related to conventional arms; and the Missile Technology Control Regime for missile-related exports. See chapter 17 and the glossary in this volume.

[78] Mallik (note 70).

[79] See chapter 18 in this volume.

[80] See chapter 13 in this volume.

lenge is to update legislative instruments at all levels to deal with new realities, including the lessons of failure to detect and correct cases of non-compliance in the past. Measures enacted at different levels and in different domains that are, in practice, bearing on the same type of security challenge need to be better linked and conflicts between them resolved. Sometimes, simplification will be a better response than elaboration. Sometimes, at least as an initial approach, looser, fuzzier and more partially applicable instruments will be what works best. Where logic calls for wider, perhaps universal, participation and application, ways will have to be found to reconcile different constituencies' interests, to promote equal ownership and to ensure that all participants entering the system are equally ready both to obey the rules and to help enforce them. Finding the right legislative instruments to cover all relevant non-state actors as well—not just in relation to conflict but in all dimensions of security—is a particularly tough but fascinating challenge.

Integration

The method of integration as applied to security challenges has much in common with the legislative approach, but as practised in the EU it goes much further. The founders of the European Communities designed them to make war impossible between their members by turning the capacities needed for war-making into a shared, interdependent and supranationally administered resource.[81] They succeeded from the outset in Western Europe, and the recent enlargement of the EU has extended the same effects to practically the whole European continent, with further applicant states already demonstrating, to various degrees, the 'contagion' of self-restraint as they vie to reach the standards for membership. Other prima facie advantages of the EU method are that: (*a*) EU competence covers virtually all spheres of governance relevant to handling the new threats; (*b*) it can create laws equally capable of governing state, private sector, civil society and even individual behaviour; and (*c*) it allows EU member states to maximize their 'export of security' by both easing their own security needs and combining their resources more effectively.

The EU is still far from realizing its full potential in this last regard, however, and its methods only secure their results at a heavy price. Governments have to surrender large parts of their sovereignty, the minority or smaller states often see their own preferences being overruled, the EU governance mechanism brings enormous process costs, and the way it works primarily through elites—with the concomitant problems of democratic participation and control[82]—risks alienating precisely those populations whose interests it should serve. In the given historical setting the EU has also grown lopsidedly, acquiring economic power ahead of political power and creating exposure to new threats for people living in its frontier-free single market long before it thought about collective policies to combat those threats. More generally,

[81] This was achieved through the European Coal and Steel Community.

[82] See chapter 4 in this volume.

Europe only achieved what it did after plumbing the depths in two terrible wars—not a sequence which imitators elsewhere will wish to follow. For this and other reasons, large questions remain over how far the full-blooded integrative approach of the EU can be extended beyond the present members and applicants, for instance in its 'new neighbour' areas of the former Soviet Union, in the Middle East and in North Africa. This has not, however, stopped independent groups of countries in other regions (as mentioned in section II above) from developing their own versions of the method. It should not stop the EU itself from striving to explore the unique security-related benefits of integration more fully, and to remedy its weaknesses notably through better internal and external coordination, better adaptation to the demands of dealing with a harsher world outside, and greater attention to problems of popular alienation and legitimacy.

V. Closing thoughts on the United Nations

The UN has properly remained at the centre of the past years' debates on security governance, and no better institution could be imagined either to have commissioned the High-level Panel report or to lead the responses to it. In terms of the analysis developed above, the UN qualifies itself to meet the security challenges of both the 20th and 21st centuries by virtue of its universal membership, its capacity and legitimacy to define norms embracing different continents and cultures, its multifunctional competences and its ability to work—notably through its agencies—with all types of non-state as well as state actors. Pragmatism should lead the world's large developed powers to recognize its merits as a way of managing interdependence, and of seeking non-zero-sum interactions between themselves and the developing world. Modesty and insight should make them see that they have need of its norms, guidance and restraint on their own account as well.

The UN has, however, never sought or possessed authority over all security-related transactions in world governance: and one of the most insidious ways of attacking it is to pretend that it does. The global regulation of commerce and the free market is in the hands of the WTO, while the Group of Eight industrialized nations often takes the lead on issues bridging the economic and security dimensions. More broadly, the UN itself (as distinct from its agencies) can very rarely fulfil a positive and active security function in the same direct way that it applies rules and sanctions for purposes of restraint. It does not have the resources in the first place and, by their very nature, the positive and interactive modes of security building (including integration) must start in a specific geographic location with interaction between one party and another. To take an example from the world of arms control, the UN may enact new rules to stop WMD materials being trafficked, and it may inspect the results of actions taken to corral and destroy such materials, but it cannot finance or carry out the collecting and destroying itself.[83]

[83] See chapter 16 in this volume.

For all these reasons and more, the true challenge of security governance in the next decades is to achieve the right *synergy* and *complementarity* between the UN and those other security-relevant processes and actors that relate to it horizontally (i.e., in other dimensions) and vertically (i.e., regional and specialized functional organizations, states and sub-state constituencies). That challenge is in itself an enormously complicated one that cannot be further analysed here. It means, however, that the ultimate benefit drawn from the recommendations of the High-level Panel will not depend only—or, perhaps in the last analysis, mainly—on things done by the UN or in the UN context. The Panel's message is addressed to everyone in the world and 'the buck stops here'.

Appendix. A More Secure World: Our Shared Responsibility, Report of the High-level Panel on Threats, Challenges and Change

Synopsis

Towards a new security consensus

The United Nations was created in 1945 above all else 'to save succeeding generations from the scourge of war'—to ensure that the horrors of the World Wars were never repeated. Sixty years later, we know all too well that the biggest security threats we face now, and in the decades ahead, go far beyond States waging aggressive war. They extend to poverty, infectious disease and environmental degradation; war and violence within States; the spread and possible use of nuclear, radiological, chemical and biological weapons; terrorism; and transnational organized crime. The threats are from non-State actors as well as States, and to human security as well as State security.

The preoccupation of the United Nations founders was with State security. When they spoke of creating a new system of collective security they meant it in the traditional military sense: a system in which States join together and pledge that aggression against one is aggression against all, and commit themselves in that event to react collectively. But they also understood well, long before the idea of human security gained currency, the indivisibility of security, economic development and human freedom. In the opening words of the Charter, the United Nations was created 'to reaffirm faith in fundamental human rights' and 'to promote social progress and better standards of life in larger freedom'.

The central challenge for the twenty-first century is to fashion a new and broader understanding, bringing together all these strands, of what collective security means—and of all the responsibilities, commitments, strategies and institutions that come with it if a collective security system is to be effective, efficient and equitable.

If there is to be a new security consensus, it must start with the understanding that the front-line actors in dealing with all the threats we face, new and old, continue to be individual sovereign States, whose role and responsibilities, and right to be respected, are fully recognized in the Charter of the United Nations. But in the twenty-first century, more than ever before, no State can stand wholly alone. Collective strategies, collective institutions and a sense of collective responsibility are indispensable.

The case for collective security today rests on three basic pillars. Today's threats recognize no national boundaries, are connected, and must be addressed at the global and regional as well as the national levels. No State, no matter how powerful, can by its own efforts alone make itself invulnerable to today's threats. And it cannot be assumed that every State will always be able, or willing, to meet its responsibility to protect its own peoples and not to harm its neighbours.

We must not underestimate the difficulty of reaching a new consensus about the meaning and responsibilities of collective security. Many will regard one or more of the threats we identify as not really being a threat to international peace and security. Some believe that HIV/AIDS is a horrible disease, but not a security threat. Or that terrorism is a threat to some States, but not all. Or that civil wars in Africa are a humanitarian tragedy, but surely not a problem for international security. Or that poverty is a problem of development, not security.

Differences of power, wealth and geography do determine what we perceive as the gravest threats to our survival and well-being. Differences of focus lead us to dismiss what others perceive as the gravest of all threats to their survival. Inequitable responses to threats further fuel division. Many people believe that what passes for collective security today is simply a system for protecting the rich and powerful. Such perceptions pose a fundamental challenge to building collective security today. Stated baldly, without mutual recognition of threats there can be no collective security. Self-help will rule, mistrust will predominate and cooperation for long-term mutual gain will elude us.

What is needed today is nothing less than a new consensus between alliances that are frayed, between wealthy nations and poor, and among peoples mired in mistrust across an apparently widening cultural abyss. The essence of that consensus is simple: we all share responsibility for each other's security. And the test of that consensus will be action.

Collective security and the challenge of prevention

Any event or process that leads to large-scale death or lessening of life chances and undermines States as the basic unit of the international system is a threat to international security. So defined, there are six clusters of threats with which the world must be concerned now and in the decades ahead:

- Economic and social threats, including poverty, infectious disease and environmental degradation
- Inter-State conflict
- Internal conflict, including civil war, genocide and other large-scale atrocities
- Nuclear, radiological, chemical and biological weapons
- Terrorism
- Transnational organized crime

In its first 60 years, the United Nations has made crucial contributions to reducing or mitigating these threats to international security. While there have been major failures and shortcomings, the record of successes and contributions is underappreciated. This gives hope that the Organization can adapt to successfully confront the new challenges of the twenty-first century.

The primary challenge for the United Nations and its members is to ensure that, of all the threats in the categories listed, those that are distant do not become imminent and those that are imminent do not actually become destructive. This requires a framework for preventive action which addresses all these threats in all the ways they resonate most in different parts of the world. Most of all, it will require leadership at the domestic and international levels to act early, decisively and collectively against all these threats—from HIV/AIDS to nuclear terrorism—before they have their most devastating effect.

In describing how to meet the challenge of prevention, we begin with development because it is the indispensable foundation for a collective security system that takes prevention seriously. It serves multiple functions. It helps combat the poverty, infectious disease and environmental degradation that kill millions and threaten human security. It is vital in helping States prevent or reverse the erosion of State capacity, which is crucial for meeting almost every class of threat. And it is part of a long-term strategy for preventing civil war and for addressing the environments in which both terrorism and organized crime flourish.

Collective security and the use of force

What happens if peaceful prevention fails? If none of the preventive measures so far described stop the descent into war and chaos? If distant threats do become imminent? Or if imminent threats become actual? Or if a non-imminent threat nonetheless becomes very real and measures short of the use of military force seem powerless to stop it?

We address here the circumstances in which effective collective security may require the backing of military force, starting with the rules of international law that must govern any decision to go to war if anarchy is not to prevail. It is necessary to distinguish between situations in which a State claims to act in self-defence; situations in which a State is posing a threat to others outside its borders; and situations in which the threat is primarily internal and the issue is the responsibility to protect a State's own people. In all cases, we believe that the Charter of the United Nations, properly understood and applied, is equal to the task: Article 51 needs neither extension nor restriction of its long-understood scope, and Chapter VII fully empowers the Security Council to deal with every kind of threat that States may confront. The task is not to find alternatives to the Security Council as a source of authority but to make it work better than it has.

That force *can* legally be used does not always mean that, as a matter of good conscience and good sense, it *should* be used. We identify a set of guidelines—five criteria of legitimacy—which we believe that the Security Council (and anyone else involved in these decisions) should always address in considering whether to authorize or apply military force. The adoption of these guidelines (seriousness of threat, proper purpose, last resort, proportional means and balance of consequences) will not produce agreed conclusions with push-button predictability, but should significantly improve the chances of reaching international consensus on what have been in recent years deeply divisive issues.

We also address here the other major issues that arise during and after violent conflict, including the needed capacities for peace enforcement, peacekeeping and peacebuilding, and the protection of civilians. A central recurring theme is the necessity for all members of the international community, developed and developing States alike, to be much more forthcoming in providing and supporting deployable military resources. Empty gestures are all too easy to make: an effective, efficient and equitable collective security system demands real commitment.

A more effective United Nations for the twenty-first century

The United Nations was never intended to be a utopian exercise. It was meant to be a collective security system that worked. The Charter of the United Nations provided the most powerful States with permanent membership on the Security Council and the veto. In exchange, they were expected to use their power for the common good and promote and obey international law. As Harry Truman, then President of the United States, noted in his speech to the final plenary session of the founding conference of the United Nations Organization, 'we all have to recognize—no matter how great our strength—that we must deny ourselves the licence to do always as we please'.

In approaching the issue of United Nations reform, it is as important today as it was in 1945 to combine power with principle. Recommendations that ignore underlying power realities will be doomed to failure or irrelevance, but recommendations that simply reflect raw distributions of power and make no effort to bolster international principles are unlikely to gain the widespread adherence required to shift international behaviour.

Proposed changes should be driven by real-world need. Change for its own sake is likely to run the well-worn course of the endless reform debates of the past decade. The litmus test is this: does a proposed change help meet the challenge posed by a virulent threat?

Throughout the work of the High-level Panel on Threats, Challenges and Change, we have looked for institutional weaknesses in current responses to threats. The following stand as the most urgently in need of remedy:

- The General Assembly has lost vitality and often fails to focus effectively on the most compelling issues of the day.
- The Security Council will need to be more proactive in the future. For this to happen, those who contribute most to the Organization financially, militarily and diplomatically should participate more in Council decision-making, and those who participate in Council decision-making should contribute more to the Organization. The Security Council needs greater credibility, legitimacy and representation to do all that we demand of it.
- There is a major institutional gap in addressing countries under stress and countries emerging from conflict. Such countries often suffer from attention, policy guidance and resource deficits.
- The Security Council has not made the most of the potential advantages of working with regional and subregional organizations.
- There must be new institutional arrangements to address the economic and social threats to international security.
- The Commission on Human Rights suffers from a legitimacy deficit that casts doubts on the overall reputation of the United Nations.
- There is a need for a more professional and better organized Secretariat that is much more capable of concerted action.

The reforms we propose will not by themselves make the United Nations more effective. In the absence of Member States reaching agreement on the security consensus contained in the present report, the United Nations will underachieve. Its institutions will still only be as strong as the energy, resources and attention devoted to them by Member States and their leaders.

Summary of recommendations

Part two
Collective security and the challenge of prevention

Poverty, infectious disease and environmental degradation

1. All States must recommit themselves to the goals of eradicating poverty, achieving sustained economic growth and promoting sustainable development.

2. The many donor countries which currently fall short of the United Nations 0.7 per cent gross national product (GNP) target for official development assistance should establish a timetable for reaching it.

3. World Trade Organization (WTO) members should strive to conclude the Doha development round of multilateral trade negotiations at the latest in 2006.

4. Lender Governments and the international financial institutions should provide highly indebted poor countries with greater debt relief, longer rescheduling and improved access to global markets.

5. Although international resources devoted to meeting the challenge of HIV/AIDS have increased from about $250 million in 1996 to about $2.8 billion in 2002, more than $10 billion annually is needed to stem the pandemic.

6. Leaders of countries affected by HIV/AIDS need to mobilize resources, commit funds and engage civil society and the private sector in disease-control efforts.

7. The Security Council, working closely with UNAIDS, should host a second special session on HIV/AIDS as a threat to international peace and security, to explore the future effects of HIV/AIDS on States and societies, generate research on the problem and identify critical steps towards a long-term strategy for diminishing the threat.

8. International donors, in partnership with national authorities and local civil society organizations, should undertake a major new global initiative to rebuild local and national public health systems throughout the developing world.

9. Members of the World Health Assembly should provide greater resources to the World Health Organization (WHO) Global Outbreak Alert and Response Network to increase its capacity to cope with potential disease outbreaks.

10. States should provide incentives for the further development of renewable energy sources and begin to phase out environmentally harmful subsidies, especially for fossil fuel use and development.

11. We urge Member States to reflect on the gap between the promise of the Kyoto Protocol and its performance, re-engage on the problem of global warming and begin new negotiations to produce a new long-term strategy for reducing global warming beyond the period covered by the Protocol (2012).

Conflict between and within States

12. The Security Council should stand ready to use the authority it has under the Rome Statute to refer cases of suspected war crimes and crimes against humanity to the International Criminal Court.

13. The United Nations should work with national authorities, international financial institutions, civil society organizations and the private sector to develop norms governing the management of natural resources for countries emerging from or at risk of conflict.

14. The United Nations should build on the experience of regional organizations in developing frameworks for minority rights and the protection of democratically elected Governments from unconstitutional overthrow.

15. Member States should expedite and conclude negotiations on legally binding agreements on the marking and tracing, as well as the brokering and transfer, of small arms and light weapons.

16. All Member States should report completely and accurately on all elements of the United Nations Register of Conventional Arms, and the Secretary-General should be asked to report annually to the General

Assembly and Security Council on any inadequacies in the reporting.

17. A training and briefing facility should be established for new or potential special representatives of the Secretary-General and other United Nations mediators.

18. The Department of Political Affairs should be given additional resources and should be restructured to provide more consistent and professional mediation support.

19. While the details of such a restructuring should be left to the Secretary-General, it should take into account the need for the United Nations to have:

(a) A field-oriented, dedicated mediation support capacity, comprised of a small team of professionals with relevant direct experience and expertise, available to all United Nations mediators;

(b) Competence on thematic issues that recur in peace negotiations, such as the sequencing of implementation steps, the design of monitoring arrangements, the sequencing of transitional arrangements and the design of national reconciliation mechanisms;

(c) Greater interaction with national mediators, regional organizations and non-governmental organizations involved in conflict resolution;

(d) Greater consultation with and involvement in peace processes of important voices from civil society, especially those of women, who are often neglected during negotiations.

20. National leaders and parties to conflict should make constructive use of the option of preventive deployment of peacekeepers.

Nuclear, radiological, chemical and biological weapons

21. The nuclear-weapon States must take several steps to restart disarmament:

(a) They must honour their commitments under Article VI of the Treaty on the Non-Proliferation of Nuclear Weapons to move towards disarmament and be ready to undertake specific measures in fulfilment of those commitments;

(b) They should reaffirm their previous commitments not to use nuclear weapons against non-nuclear-weapon States.

22. The United States and the Russian Federation, other nuclear-weapon States and States not party to the Treaty on the Non-Proliferation of Nuclear Weapons should commit to practical measures to reduce the risk of accidental nuclear war, including, where appropriate, a progressive schedule for de-alerting their strategic nuclear weapons.

23. The Security Council should explicitly pledge to take collective action in response to a nuclear attack or the threat of such attack on a non-nuclear weapon State.

24. Negotiations to resolve regional conflicts should include confidence-building measures and steps towards disarmament.

25. States not party to the Treaty on the Non-Proliferation of Nuclear Weapons should pledge a commitment to non-proliferation and disarmament, demonstrating their commitment by ratifying the Comprehensive Nuclear-Test-Ban Treaty and supporting negotiations for a fissile material cut-off treaty, both of which are open to nuclear-weapon and non-nuclear-weapon States alike. We recommend that peace efforts in the Middle East and South Asia launch nuclear disarmament talks that could lead to the establishment of nuclear-weapon-free zones in those regions similar to those established for Latin America and the Caribbean, Africa, the South Pacific and South-East Asia.

26. All chemical-weapon States should expedite the scheduled destruction of all existing chemical weapons stockpiles by the agreed target date of 2012.

27. States parties to the Biological and Toxin Weapons Convention should without delay return to negotiations for a credible verification protocol, inviting the active participation of the biotechnology industry.

28. The Board of Governors of the International Atomic Energy Agency (IAEA) should recognize the Model Additional Protocol as today's standard for IAEA safeguards, and the Security Council should be prepared to act in cases of serious concern over non-compliance with non-proliferation and safeguards standards.

29. Negotiations should be engaged without delay and carried forward to an early conclusion on an arrangement, based on the existing provisions of Articles III and IX of the IAEA statute, which would enable IAEA to act as a guarantor for the supply of fissile material to civilian nuclear users.

30. While that arrangement is being negotiated, States should, without surrendering the right under the Treaty on the Non-Proliferation of Nuclear Weapons to construct uranium enrichment and reprocessing facilities, voluntarily institute a time-limited moratorium on the construction of any further such facilities, with a commitment to the moratorium matched by a guarantee of the supply of fissile materials by the current suppliers at market rates.

31. All States should be encouraged to join the voluntary Proliferation Security Initiative.

32. A State's notice of withdrawal from the Treaty on the Non-Proliferation of Nuclear Weapons should prompt immediate verification of its compliance with the Treaty, if necessary mandated by the Security Council. The IAEA Board of Governors should resolve that, in the event of violations, all assistance provided by IAEA should be withdrawn.

33. The proposed timeline for the Global Threat Reduction Initiative to convert highly enriched uranium reactors and reduce HEU stockpiles should be halved from 10 to five years.

34. States parties to the Biological and Toxin Weapons Convention should negotiate a new bio-security protocol to classify dangerous biological agents and establish binding international standards for the export of such agents.

35. The Conference on Disarmament should move without further delay to negotiate a verifiable fissile material cut-off treaty that, on a designated schedule, ends the production of highly enriched uranium for non-weapon as well as weapons purposes.

36. The Directors-General of IAEA and the Organization for the Prohibition of Chemical Weapons (OPCW) should be invited by the Security Council to report to it twice-yearly on the status of safeguards and verification processes, as well as on any serious concerns they have which might fall short of an actual breach of the Treaty on the Non-Proliferation of Nuclear Weapons and the Chemical Weapons Convention.

37. The Security Council should consult with the WHO Director-General to establish the necessary procedures for working together in the event of a suspicious or overwhelming outbreak of infectious disease.

Terrorism

38. The United Nations, with the Secretary-General taking a leading role, should promote a comprehensive strategy against terrorism, including:

(a) Dissuasion, working to reverse the causes or facilitators of terrorism, including through promoting social and political rights, the rule of law and democratic reform; working to end occupations and address major political grievances; combating organized crime; reducing poverty and unemployment; and stopping State collapse;

(b) Efforts to counter extremism and intolerance, including through education and fostering public debate;

(c) Development of better instruments for global counter-terrorism cooperation, all within a legal framework that is respectful of civil liberties and human rights, including in the areas of law enforcement; intelligence-sharing, where possible; denial and interdiction, when required; and financial controls;

(d) Building State capacity to prevent terrorist recruitment and operations;

(e) Control of dangerous materials and public health defence.

39. Member States that have not yet done so should actively consider signing and ratifying all 12 international conventions against terrorism, and should adopt the eight Special Recommendations on Terrorist Financing issued by the Organization for Economic Cooperation and Development (OECD)-supported Financial Action Task Force on Money-Laundering and the measures recommended in its various best practices papers.

40. The Al-Qaida and Taliban Sanctions Committee should institute a process for reviewing the cases of individuals and institutions claiming to have been wrongly placed or retained on its watch lists.

41. The Security Council, after consultation with affected States, should extend the authority of the Counter-Terrorism Executive Directorate to act as a clearing house for State-to-State provision of military, police and border control assistance for the development of domestic counter-terrorism capacities.

42. To help Member States comply with their counter-terrorism obligations, the United

Nations should establish a capacity-building trust fund under the Counter-Terrorism Executive Directorate.

43. The Security Council should devise a schedule of predetermined sanctions for State non-compliance with the Council's counter-terrorism resolutions.

44. The General Assembly should rapidly complete negotiations on a comprehensive convention on terrorism, incorporating a definition of terrorism with the following elements:

(a) Recognition, in the preamble, that State use of force against civilians is regulated by the Geneva Conventions and other instruments, and, if of sufficient scale, constitutes a war crime by the persons concerned or a crime against humanity;

(b) Restatement that acts under the 12 preceding anti-terrorism conventions are terrorism, and a declaration that they are a crime under international law; and restatement that terrorism in time of armed conflict is prohibited by the Geneva Conventions and Protocols;

(c) Reference to the definitions contained in the 1999 International Convention for the Suppression of the Financing of Terrorism and Security Council resolution 1566 (2004);

(d) Description of terrorism as 'any action, in addition to actions already specified by the existing conventions on aspects of terrorism, the Geneva Conventions and Security Council resolution 1566 (2004), that is intended to cause death or serious bodily harm to civilians or non-combatants, when the purpose of such act, by its nature or context, is to intimidate a population, or to compel a Government or an international organization to do or to abstain from doing any act'.

Transnational organized crime

45. Member States that have not signed, ratified or resourced the 2000 United Nations Convention against Transnational Organized Crime and its three Protocols, and the 2003 United Nations Convention against Corruption should do so, and all Member States should support the United Nations Office on Drugs and Crime in its work in this area.

46. Member States should establish a central authority to facilitate the exchange of evidence among national judicial authorities, mutual legal assistance among prosecutorial authorities and the implementation of extradition requests.

47. A comprehensive international convention on money-laundering that addresses the issues of bank secrecy and the development of financial havens needs to be negotiated, and endorsed by the General Assembly.

48. Member States should sign and ratify the Protocol to Prevent, Suppress and Punish Trafficking in Persons, Especially Women and Children, and parties to the Protocol should take all necessary steps to effectively implement it.

49. The United Nations should establish a robust capacity-building mechanism for rule-of-law assistance.

The role of sanctions

50. The Security Council must ensure that sanctions are effectively implemented and enforced:

(a) When the Security Council imposes a sanctions regime—including arms embargoes—it should routinely establish monitoring mechanisms and provide them with the necessary authority and capacity to carry out high quality, in-depth investigations. Adequate budgetary provisions must be made to implement those mechanisms;

(b) Security Council sanctions committees should be mandated to develop improved guidelines and reporting procedures to assist States in sanctions implementation, and to improve procedures for maintaining accurate lists of individuals and entities subject to targeted sanctions;

(c) The Secretary-General should appoint a senior official with sufficient supporting resources to enable the Secretary-General to supply the Security Council with analysis of the best way to target sanctions and to assist in coordinating their implementation. This official would also assist compliance efforts; identify technical assistance needs and coordinate such assistance; and make recommendations on any adjustments necessary to enhance the effectiveness of sanctions;

(d) Donors should devote more resources to strengthening the legal, administrative, and policing and border-control capacity of Member States to implement sanctions. Capacity-building measures should include efforts to improve air-traffic interdiction in zones of conflict;

(e) The Security Council should, in instances of verified, chronic violations, impose secondary sanctions against those involved in sanctions-busting;

(f) The Secretary-General, in consultation with the Security Council, should ensure that an appropriate auditing mechanism is in place to oversee sanctions administration.

51. Sanctions committees should improve procedures for providing humanitarian exemptions and routinely conduct assessments of the humanitarian impact of sanctions. The Security Council should continue to strive to mitigate the humanitarian consequences of sanctions.

52. Where sanctions involve lists of individuals or entities, sanctions committees should establish procedures to review the cases of those claiming to have been incorrectly placed or retained on such lists.

Part three
Collective security and the use of force

Using force: rules and guidelines

53. Article 51 of the Charter of the United Nations should be neither rewritten nor reinterpreted, either to extend its long-established scope (so as to allow preventive measures to non-imminent threats) or to restrict it (so as to allow its application only to actual attacks).

54. The Security Council is fully empowered under Chapter VII of the Charter of the United Nations to address the full range of security threats with which States are concerned. The task is not to find alternatives to the Security Council as a source of authority but to make the Council work better than it has.

55. The Panel endorses the emerging norm that there is a collective international responsibility to protect, exercisable by the Security Council authorizing military intervention as a last resort, in the event of genocide and other large-scale killing, ethnic cleansing or serious violations of humanitarian law which sovereign Governments have proved powerless or unwilling to prevent.

56. In considering whether to authorize or endorse the use of military force, the Security Council should always address—whatever other considerations it may take into account—at least the following five basic criteria of legitimacy:

(a) *Seriousness of threat.* Is the threatened harm to State or human security of a kind, and sufficiently clear and serious, to justify *prima facie* the use of military force? In the case of internal threats, does it involve genocide and other large-scale killing, ethnic cleansing or serious violations of international humanitarian law, actual or imminently apprehended?

(b) *Proper purpose.* Is it clear that the primary purpose of the proposed military action is to halt or avert the threat in question, whatever other purposes or motives may be involved?

(c) *Last resort.* Has every non-military option for meeting the threat in question been explored, with reasonable grounds for believing that other measures will not succeed?

(d) *Proportional means.* Are the scale, duration and intensity of the proposed military action the minimum necessary to meet the threat in question?

(e) *Balance of consequences.* Is there a reasonable chance of the military action being successful in meeting the threat in question, with the consequences of action not likely to be worse than the consequences of inaction?

57. The above guidelines for authorizing the use of force should be embodied in declaratory resolutions of the Security Council and General Assembly.

Peace enforcement and peacekeeping capability

58. The developed States should do more to transform their existing force capacities into suitable contingents for peace operations.

59. Member States should strongly support the efforts of the Department of Peacekeeping Operations, building on the important work of the Panel on United Nations Peace Operations, to improve its use of strategic deployment stockpiles, standby arrangements, trust funds and other mechanisms in order to meet the tighter deadlines necessary for effective deployment.

60. States with advanced military capacities should establish standby high readiness, self-sufficient battalions at up to brigade level that can reinforce United Nations missions, and should place them at the disposal of the United Nations.

61. The Secretary-General should recommend and the Security Council should authorize troop strengths for peacekeeping missions that are sufficient to deter and repel hostile factions.

62. The United Nations should have a small corps of senior police officers and managers (50–100 personnel) who could undertake mission assessments and organize the start-up of police components of peace operations, and the General Assembly should authorize this capacity.

Post-conflict peacebuilding

63. Special representatives of the Secretary-General should have the authority and guidance to work with relevant parties to establish robust donor-coordinating mechanisms, as well as the resources to perform coordination functions effectively, including ensuring that the sequencing of United Nations assessments and activities is consistent with Government priorities.

64. The Security Council should mandate and the General Assembly should authorize funding for disarmament and demobilization programmes from assessed budgets for United Nations peacekeeping operations.

65. A standing fund for peacebuilding should be established at the level of at least $250 million that can be used to finance the recurrent expenditures of a nascent Government, as well as critical agency programmes in the areas of rehabilitation and reintegration.

Protecting civilians

66. All combatants must abide by the Geneva Conventions. All Member States should sign, ratify and act on all treaties relating to the protection of civilians, such as the Genocide Convention, the Geneva Conventions, the Rome Statute of the International Criminal Court and all refugee conventions.

67. The Security Council should fully implement resolution 1265 (1999) on the protection of civilians in armed conflict.

68. The Security Council, United Nations agencies and Member States should fully implement resolution 1325 (2000) on women, peace and security.

69. Member States should support and fully fund the proposed Directorate of Security and accord high priority to assisting the Secretary-General in implementing a new staff security system in 2005.

Part four
A more effective United Nations for the twenty-first century

The General Assembly

70. Members of the General Assembly should use the opportunity provided by the Millennium Review Summit in 2005 to forge a new consensus on broader and more effective collective security.

71. Member States should renew efforts to enable the General Assembly to perform its function as the main deliberative organ of the United Nations. This requires a better conceptualization and shortening of the agenda, which should reflect the contemporary challenges facing the international community. Smaller, more tightly focused committees could help to sharpen and improve resolutions that are brought to the whole Assembly.

72. Following the recommendation of the report of the Panel on Eminent Persons on United Nations–Civil Society Relations, the General Assembly should establish a better mechanism to enable systematic engagement with civil society organizations.

The Security Council

73. Reforms of the Security Council should meet the following principles:

(a) They should, in honouring Article 23 of the Charter of the United Nations, increase the involvement in decision-making of those who contribute most to the United Nations financially, militarily and diplomatically—specifically in terms of contributions to United Nations assessed budgets, participation in mandated peace operations, contributions to the voluntary activities of the United Nations in the areas of security and development, and diplomatic activities in support of United Nations objectives and mandates. Among developed countries, achieving or making substantial progress towards the internationally agreed level of 0.7 per cent of GNP for ODA should be considered an important criterion of contribution;

(b) They should bring into the decision-making process countries more representative of the broader membership, especially of the developing world;

(c) They should not impair the effectiveness of the Security Council;

(d) They should increase the democratic and accountable nature of the body.

74. A decision on the enlargement of the Council, satisfying these criteria, is now a necessity. The presentation of two clearly defined alternatives, of the kind described below as models A and B, should help to clarify—and perhaps bring to resolution—a debate which has made little progress in the last 12 years.

75. Models A and B both involve a distribution of seats as between four major regional areas, which we identify, respectively, as 'Africa', 'Asia and Pacific', 'Europe' and 'Americas'. We see these descriptions as helpful in making and implementing judgements about the composition of the Security Council, but make no recommendation about changing the composition of the current regional groups for general electoral and other United Nations purposes. Some members of the Panel, in particular our Latin American colleagues, expressed a preference for basing any distribution of seats on the current regional groups.

76. Model A provides for six new permanent seats, with no veto being created, and three new two-year term non-permanent seats, divided among the major regional areas. Model B provides for no new permanent seats, but creates a new category of eight four-year renewable-term seats and one new two-year nonpermanent (and non-renewable) seat, divided among the major regional areas.

77. In both models, having regard to Article 23 of the Charter, a method of encouraging Member States to contribute more to international peace and security would be for the General Assembly, taking into account established practices of regional consultation, to elect Security Council members by giving preference for permanent or longer-term seats to those States that are among the top three financial contributors in their relevant regional area to the regular budget, or the top three voluntary contributors from their regional area, or the top three troop contributors from their regional area to United Nations peacekeeping missions.

78. There should be a review of the composition of the Security Council in 2020, including, in this context, a review of the contribution (as defined in paragraph 249 of the main report) of permanent and non-permanent members from the point of view of the Council's effectiveness in taking collective action to prevent and remove new and old threats to international peace and security.

79. The Panel recommends that under any reform proposal, there should be no expansion of the veto.

80. A system of 'indicative voting' should be introduced, whereby members of the Security Council could call for a public indication of positions on a proposed action.

81. Processes to improve transparency and accountability in the Security Council should be incorporated and formalized in its rules of procedure.

A Peacebuilding Commission

82. The Security Council, acting under Article 29 of the Charter of the United Nations and after consultation with the Economic and Social Council, should establish a Peacebuilding Commission.

83. The core functions of the Peacebuilding Commission should be to identify countries that are under stress and risk sliding towards State collapse; to organize, in partnership with the national Government, proactive assistance in preventing that process from developing further; to assist in the planning for transitions between conflict and post-conflict peacebuilding; and in particular to marshal and sustain the efforts of the international community in post-conflict peacebuilding over whatever period may be necessary.

84. While the precise composition, procedures and reporting lines of the Peacebuilding Commission will need to be established, they should take account of the following guidelines:

(a) The Peacebuilding Commission should be reasonably small;

(b) It should meet in different configurations, to consider both general policy issues and country-by-country strategies;

(c) It should be chaired for at least one year and perhaps longer by a member approved by the Security Council;

(d) In addition to representation from the Security Council, it should include representation from the Economic and Social Council;

(e) National representatives of the country under consideration should be invited to attend;

(f) The Managing Director of the International Monetary Fund, the President of the World Bank and, when appropriate, heads of regional development banks should be represented at its meetings by appropriate senior officials;

(g) Representatives of the principal donor countries and, when appropriate, the principal troop contributors should be invited to participate in its deliberations;

(h) Representatives of regional and subregional organizations should be invited to participate in its deliberations when such organizations are actively involved in the country in question.

85. A Peacebuilding Support Office should be established in the Secretariat to give the Peacebuilding Commission appropriate Secretariat support and to ensure that the Secretary-General is able to integrate system-wide peacebuilding policies and strategies, develop best practices and provide cohesive support for field operations.

Regional organizations

86. In relation to regional organizations:

(a) Authorization from the Security Council should in all cases be sought for regional peace operations;

(b) Consultation and cooperation between the United Nations and regional organizations should be expanded and could be formalized in an agreement, covering such issues as meetings of the heads of the organizations, more frequent exchange of information and early warning, co-training of civilian and military personnel, and exchange of personnel within peace operations;

(c) In the case of African regional and subregional capacities, donor countries should commit to a 10-year process of sustained capacity-building support, within the African Union strategic framework;

(d) Regional organizations that have a capacity for conflict prevention or peacekeeping should place such capacities in the framework of the United Nations Standby Arrangements System;

(e) Member States should agree to allow the United Nations to provide equipment support from United Nations-owned sources to regional operations, as needed;

(f) The rules for the United Nations peacekeeping budget should be amended to give the United Nations the option on a case-by-case basis to finance regional operations authorized by the Security Council with assessed contributions.

The Economic and Social Council

87. The Economic and Social Council should provide normative and analytical leadership in a time of much debate about the causes of, and interconnections between, the many threats we face. To that end, the Economic and Social Council should establish a Committee on the Social and Economic Aspects of Security Threats.

88. The Economic and Social Council should provide an arena in which States measure their commitments to achieving key development objectives in an open and transparent manner.

89. The Economic and Social Council should provide a regular venue for engaging the development community at the highest level, in effect transforming itself into a 'development cooperation forum'. To that end:

(a) A new approach should be adopted within the Economic and Social Council agenda, replacing its current focus on administrative issues and programme coordination with a more focused agenda built around the major themes contained in the Millennium Declaration;

(b) A small executive committee, comprising members from each regional group, should be created in order to provide orientation and direction to the work of the Economic and Social Council and its interaction with principal organs, agencies and programmes;

(c) The annual meetings between the Economic and Social Council and the Bretton Woods institutions should be used to encourage collective action in support of the Millennium Development Goals and the Monterrey Consensus;

(d) The Economic and Social Council, with inputs from its secretariat and the United Nations Development Group, should aim to provide guidance on development cooperation to the governing boards of the United Nations funds, programmes and agencies;

(e) The Economic and Social Council should provide strong support to the efforts of the Secretary-General and the United Nations Development Group to strengthen the coherence of United Nations action at the field level and its coordination with the Bretton Woods institutions and bilateral donors.

The Commission on Human Rights

90. Membership of the Commission on Human Rights should be made universal.

91. All members of the Commission on Human Rights should designate prominent and experienced human rights figures as the heads of their delegations.

92. The Commission on Human Rights should be supported in its work by an advisory council or panel.

93. The United Nations High Commissioner for Human Rights should be called upon to prepare an annual report on the situation of human rights worldwide.

94. The Security Council and the Peacebuilding Commission should request the High Commissioner for Human Rights to report to them regularly on the implementation of all human rights-related provisions of Security Council resolutions, thus enabling focused, effective monitoring of those provisions.

The Secretariat

95. To assist the Secretary-General, an additional Deputy Secretary-General position should be created, responsible for peace and security.

96. The Secretary-General should be provided with the resources he requires to do his job properly and the authority to manage his staff and other resources as he deems best. To meet the needs identified in the present report, the Panel recommends that:

(a) Member States recommit themselves to Articles 100 and 101 of the Charter of the United Nations;

(b) Member States review the relationship between the General Assembly and the Secretariat with the aim of substantially increasing the flexibility provided to the Secretary-General in the management of his staff, subject always to his accountability to the Assembly;

(c) The Secretary-General's reform proposals of 1997 and 2002 related to human resources should now, without further delay, be fully implemented;

(d) There should be a one-time review and replacement of personnel, including through early retirement, to ensure that the Secretariat is staffed with the right people to undertake the tasks at hand, including for mediation and peacebuilding support, and for the office of the Deputy Secretary-General for peace and security. Member States should provide funding for this replacement as a cost-effective long-term investment;

(e) The Secretary-General should immediately be provided with 60 posts—less than 1 per cent of the total Secretariat capacity—for the purpose of establishing all the increased Secretariat capacity proposed in the present report.

The Charter of the United Nations

97. In addition to any amendment of Article 23 of the Charter of the United Nations required by proposed reform of the Security Council, the Panel suggests the following modest changes to the Charter:

98. Articles 53 and 107 (references to enemy States) are outdated and should be revised.

99. Chapter XIII (The Trusteeship Council) should be deleted.

100. Article 47 (The Military Staff Committee) should be deleted, as should all references to the Committee in Articles 26, 45 and 46.

101. All Member States should rededicate themselves to the purposes and principles of the Charter and to applying them in a purposeful way, matching political will with the necessary resources. Only dedicated leadership within and between States will generate

effective collective security for the twenty-first century and forge a future that is both sustainable and secure.

Source: United Nations, 'A more secure world: our shared responsibility', Report of the High-level Panel on Threats, Challenges and Change, UN documents A/59/565, 4 Dec. 2004, and A/59/565/Corr.1, 6 Dec. 2004, URL <http://www.un.org/ga/59/documentation/list5.html>. For the synopsis and recommendations of the report see the appendix to this Introduction, synopsis, pp. 11–14, and summary of recommendations, pp. 79–92.

Part I. Security and conflicts, 2004

Chapter 1. Euro-Atlantic security and institutions

Chapter 2. Major armed conflicts

Chapter 3. Multilateral peace missions: challenges of peace-building

Chapter 4. Governing the use of force under international auspices: deficits in parliamentary accountability

Chapter 5. The greater Middle East

Chapter 6. Latin America and the Caribbean: security and defence in the post-cold war era

1. Euro-Atlantic security and institutions

PÁL DUNAY and ZDZISLAW LACHOWSKI

I. Introduction

In 2004 Euro-Atlantic relations continued to be shaped by the United States' pursuit of its fight against international terrorism and by US and European Union (EU) attempts to reduce and ultimately bridge the divide created by the decision to bring about regime change in Iraq by military force. The USA began its return to multilateralism through the United Nations (UN), the North Atlantic Treaty Organization (NATO) and in relations with the EU, although not without hesitation and persistent attempts to set the agenda according to US priorities.

Both the EU and NATO, and their largest and most influential members, reached more decisively beyond their European limits in 2004. In the case of the EU, this tendency has become more pronounced because of its more active neighbourhood policy, combined with the pressure felt by all European bodies to react better to 'new' transnational threats. Competition between the two main security institutions has underlined the continuing Western dilemma between Atlantic precedence and European autonomy.

The EU and NATO enlargement processes culminated in the accession of 10 countries to the EU and 7 to NATO in 2004. In the medium-term perspective, the high point of both enlargement processes has been passed. Spreading the doctrine of 'a rule-based international order [and] effective multilateralism' continues to underpin EU policy on international security.[1] The EU has engaged with a number of countries regarding future enlargement—including Bulgaria and Romania, which have completed their accession negotiations, and Croatia and Turkey, which will begin theirs in 2005. The EU has also enhanced its efforts to create a 'ring of friends' on its borders, and NATO has started to build partnerships by reaching out to regions of strategic interest to the organization.

In those Commonwealth of Independent States (CIS) countries where the prospects for integration into the EU have remained more ambiguous, 2004 brought about a 'parting of the ways'. Developments in 2004 demonstrated that the unification of Europe as a community of values has not been completed and that democratization in many countries east of the EU and NATO areas, although routinely advocated in declarations, is neither generally accepted nor pursued by all national leaders and elites. The intra-regional divide has become pronounced both in the CIS and in the Western Balkans.

[1] Council of the European Union, 'A secure Europe in a better world: European Security Strategy', Brussels, 12 Dec. 2003, URL <http://ue.eu.int/uedocs/cms_data/docs/pressdata/EN/reports/78367.pdf>.

The fundamental changes in Georgia and Ukraine that framed the year made this highly visible. These changes mark new beginnings rather than final destinations for the countries concerned. Other neighbours of the EU have more uncertain ambitions and prospects: especially Russia, whose domestic and regional policies may complicate the pursuit of European unity. Russia has also made moves to reduce its cooperation with institutions—the Organization for Security and Co-operation in Europe (OSCE) and the Council of Europe—whose relative unimportance to Russia make such risks affordable.

This chapter addresses select issues of relevance to Euro-Atlantic security. Section II discusses the development of US policy in 2004. Section III describes developments in NATO and section IV discusses the EU. The main political developments in the CIS countries are described in section V. Section VI presents conclusions. Attempts to reform the OSCE are addressed in appendix 1A.

II. The policies of the United States

The statement by US President George W. Bush on 8 December 2004 that 'we remain a nation at war' characterizes the current US approach to international security.[2] Many countries do not share his conviction and diverging perceptions have made cooperation difficult. Three issues dominated the US security agenda: (*a*) continuing attempts to stabilize Iraq and to generate and maintain the necessary international support for the stabilization process; (*b*) further measures to strengthen homeland security after the 11 September 2001 terrorist attacks on the USA, combined with investigations into the intelligence failures that contributed to those attacks and to the rationale behind the war on Iraq; and (*c*) the presidential election, which tested the domestic political consensus on security issues in the USA.

Stabilizing Iraq: rebuilding transatlantic relations

The Iraq conflict in 2003 and the build-up to it divided the Euro-Atlantic community. The USA and its coalition partners won the war without too much difficulty but stabilizing the country afterwards posed a different challenge.[3] It became obvious that maintaining control of Iraq's territory would require capabilities other than those associated with high-intensity warfare—and more manpower than was required in the 'technology-intensive' war phase.

In 2004 the two main reasons cited for the war on Iraq were revisited—the Baathist regime's alleged connections with terrorist organizations, specifically with al-Qaeda, and its possession of weapons of mass destruction (WMD).

[2] The White house, 'President's statement on intelligence reform and Terrorism Prevention Act of 2004', Office of the Press Secretary, Washington, DC, 8 Dec. 2004, URL <http://www.whitehouse.gov/news/releases/2004/12/print/20041208-11.htm>.

[3] See Cottey, A., 'The Iraq war: the enduring controversies and challenges', *SIPRI Yearbook 2004: Armaments, Disarmament and International Security* (Oxford University Press: Oxford, 2004), pp. 67–93.

According to President Bush, 'the reason [why] I keep insisting that there was a relationship between Iraq and Saddam and al-Qaeda [is] because there was a relationship between Iraq and al-Qaeda'.[4] Analysts drew a different conclusion:

> [the] Iraqi regime no doubt had a record of support for terrorism, of which its announced incentives for Palestinian suicide bombers was an egregious . . . example. But if the primary target of the 'war on terrorism' was meant to be the 'terrorists of global reach' that could and would conduct massive attacks against the United States, then removing Saddam was a minor contribution at best. In that sense, if anything, the war in Iraq was a significant distraction from the war on terror.[5]

That international terrorists have been operating on Iraqi territory since the fall of the Saddam Hussein regime has been easier to substantiate than the allegation that Islamic terrorist groups were permitted to operate from Iraq during Saddam Hussein's rule.

As far as the presence of WMD in Iraq is concerned, international inspectors did not find WMD in Iraq before the war and they were not found there after it either.[6] British Prime Minister Tony Blair eventually conceded that the 'evidence about Saddam having actual biological and chemical weapons, as opposed to the capability to develop them, has turned out to be wrong'.[7] At the beginning of 2005, the case on Iraqi WMD was closed by the USA after nearly two years of searching in an occupied country had brought no result.[8]

If the two main factual claims behind the war on Iraq were further weakened during 2004, the general legal assessment of the war has remained unchanged—although better informed. Although the war was presented as 'pre-emptive action', in the absence of a threat of imminent attack it could at best be identified as prevention. When seeking to prevent a more remote threat, the first recourse should not normally be military measures. Despite the arbitrary change of terminology by the USA from prevention to pre-emption to legitimize the military action, the norms of international law have never supported the war on Iraq.[9]

After the end of the Iraq war the USA adapted its discourse to the changed circumstances. This was probably because of the realization that it was not in its interests for its action to be identified with a broad interpretation of pre-emption. 'Once you start down and you say, "well, preventative war is some-

[4] 'Transcript: President Bush Speaks About 9/11 Commission', *Washington Post* (Internet edn), 17 June 2004, URL <http://www.washingtonpost.com/wp-dyn/articles/A49013-2004Jun17.html>.

[5] Gordon, P. H., 'The war on terrorism', eds G. Lindstrom and B. Schmitt, *One Year On: Lessons from Iraq*, Chaillot Papers no. 68 (Institute for Security Studies: Paris, Mar. 2004), p. 161.

[6] See chapters 12 and 13 in this volume.

[7] Labour Party, 'The opportunity society', Speech by Tony Blair MP, Prime Minister and Leader of the Labour Party, Labour Party Annual Conference, Brighton Centre, 28 Sep. 2004, URL <http://www.labour.org.uk/ac2004news?ux_news_id=ac04tb>.

[8] 'Iraq's WMD: case closed', *International Herald Tribune*, 14 Jan. 2005, p. 6. On the work of the Iraq Survey Group see chapter 13 in this volume.

[9] See 'Pre-emptive action', Advice no. 39, Advisory Council on International Affairs, The Hague, July 2004, p. 5, URL <http://www.aiv-advice.nl>; and Reynolds, P., 'Choice of words matters', BBC News Online, URL <http://news.bbc.co.uk/1/hi/world/middle_east/3661976.stm>.

thing I can do because I think it could be a problem in the future", you set a new standard of international behavior. If the United States can go after Iraq when it admits it's not an imminent threat, but could be, what prevents India from going after Pakistan, Russia against Georgia, China against Taiwan?'[10] Recognizing the corrosive effect of a broad interpretation of pre-emption on the international system, the USA made efforts to limit the damage, leading US Secretary of State Colin Powell to claim that 'observers have exaggerated the centrality of pre-emption in US strategy'.[11]

In 2004 the USA's main aim seemed to be to return, or at least to pay more convincing lip service, to multilateralism. However, while it has cooperated more closely with the countries that contributed to the Iraqi stabilization effort, the opponents of war received a differentiated response. Reconciliation with Germany and Russia was considered more important than with France, which was mentioned as a source of rhetorical disease, the spread of which must be contained.[12] These differences notwithstanding, President Bush declared in November 2004, after his re-election, that he 'wants to work more closely with all of Europe'.[13] There is a growing realization in the USA that it is 'EU Europe' that has the resources, and increasingly also the complex power base, to complement US efforts in Iraq and globally.

The occupying powers sought to convince a wider range of states to assist with the stabilization of Iraq. This attempt has proved partly successful thanks to the weight and influence of the USA in international relations—as well as the attitude of many countries which realize that it would be highly irresponsible to allow Iraq to end up as a failed state. However, the improved commitment to stabilization has been clearer at the multilateral NATO and EU levels than in the actions of individual partners, demonstrating that democracies face problems when they engage in military operations that are opposed by the majority of their electorate. Many European governments found it difficult to sustain their place in the US-led military coalition in the longer run.[14] It remains to be seen whether these experiences will provoke a re-think on the value of ad hoc coalitions compared with more binding institutional frameworks for intervention.

The gradual withdrawal of the occupying forces from Iraq would not present a problem if there were stability there. Despite the handing over of sovereignty to Iraqi authorities on 28 June 2004, and elections to a National Assembly

[10] Korb, L., quoted in Stanley Foundation, US Strategies for National Security Program, 'America: more or less secure?', Transcript of a debate, 4 Oct. 2004, URL <http://www.stanleyfoundation.org/programs/sns/secure/dayton_transcript.html>.

[11] Powell, C., 'A strategy of partnerships', *Foreign Affairs*, vol. 83, no. 1 (Jan./Feb. 2004), p. 24.

[12] Daalder, I. H., The Brookings Institution, 'Troubled partnership: what's next for the United States and Europe', Brookings Institution/Hoover Institute Briefing (transcript prepared from a tape recording), 10 Nov. 2004, URL <http://www.brookings.edu/comm/events/20041110.pdf>.

[13] US Department of State, International Information Programs, 'Powell urges Europe to work with US to support democracy: Secretary of State addresses German Marshall Fund', Brussels, 8 Dec. 2004, URL <http://usinfo.state.gov/usinfo/Archive/2004/Dec/08-827028.html>.

[14] A number of countries have either declared their intention to withdraw their troops from Iraq or implemented such a decision, see below.

held on 30 January 2005,[15] security conditions remain precarious both for Iraqis and for foreign troops. The USA suffered the highest number of coalition casualties in 2004, with 894 killed and 7795 wounded.[16] Meanwhile, economic recovery is also a hostage to the broader political, legal and security conditions in Iraq. According to a December 2003 US Department of Defense (DOD) memo, competition for reconstruction contracts financed by the US Agency for International Development (USAID) was limited to 'companies from the United States, Iraq, coalition partners and force contributing nations'.[17] Under severe international pressure, the USA later modified its stance in order not to further alienate its partners, However, by late 2004 the situation appeared in a somewhat different light. In the absence of security, legal certainty and predictability, there are only a limited number of sectors where it will be possible to make a profit in the foreseeable future. Under these conditions, it is difficult to attract investors or even to prevent the departure of existing investors and contractors.[18] Reducing Iraq's national debt also requires the cooperation and agreement of the G8 countries because Iraq's six largest creditors are members of the group.[19]

The stabilization of Iraq has not been successful but the transatlantic divide that emerged during the build-up to the war there has narrowed. Powerful forces, *inter alia* in the business sector on both sides of the Atlantic, have been at work to re-establish normal working relations.[20] The sources of influence at the disposal of some European states and the USA may help bring home to the Euro-Atlantic partners their mutual indispensability to the pursuit of global stability based on the understanding that conflict management and post-conflict rehabilitation require resources beyond military power.

Homeland security and anti-terrorist programmes

The 11 September 2001 terrorist attacks on the USA were a critical watershed with lasting repercussions. Reform of US homeland security measures and of US intelligence services continued in 2004. The latter were held largely responsible for the failures that made it impossible for the USA to adequately prepare for the new security threats it faced.

Homeland security was, perhaps, the area of security management where the gap between intentions and accomplishments in the first term of the Bush

[15] Elections were also held on the same day for a Kurdish regional assembly as well as for a variety of other regional bodies and positions.

[16] 'US casualties in Iraq', Globalsecurity.org, URL <http://www.globalsecurity.org/military/ops/iraq_casualties.htm>. For details of casualties in the Iraq war see chapter 2 in this volume.

[17] Fuller, T. and Knowlton, B., 'Iraq: ban on contracts angers allies', *International Herald Tribune*, 11 Dec. 2003, pp. 1 and 6.

[18] Pelham, N., 'Mobile phone group threatens to quit Baghdad', *Financial Times*, 23 Dec. 2004.

[19] Mekay, E., 'Debt relief weighed down by IMF burden', Inter Press News Agency, 23 Nov. 2004, URL <http://www.ipsnews.net/interna.asp?idnews=26401>.

[20] See Daft, D. and Fitzgerald, N., 'Business can help bridge the transatlantic rift', *Financial Times*, 22 Jan. 2004, p. 13. The authors are co-chairs of the Transatlantic Business Dialogue.

presidency was the narrowest.[21] More than three years have elapsed since 11 September 2001 without another large-scale terrorist attack on the territory of the USA, 'yet . . . the terrorist threat to America remains'.[22] The Homeland Security Advisory System did not identify a low level of threat for a single day in 2004, oscillating most often between an elevated and a high level of threat.[23] The message is clear—the US Government is aware of the threat and is able to reassure the electorate that it can cope.

In 2004 the US Department of Homeland Security (DHS) continued to expand its activities, establishing additional institutional structures and standards, and becoming more fully operational with the opening of the Homeland Security Operations Center (HSOC). The main functions of the HSOC are to manage domestic incidents and to share information, which should increase coordination between the public and private sectors, including different levels of government.[24] The two-way channels of communication connect all 50 US states, its territories and major urban areas in real time.[25] A National Incident Management System (NIMS) has been established on the basis of the experience of the US Fire Administration. While the HSOC provides for vertical connection in the public sector, NIMS, through its Integration Center, ensures inter-agency coordination and implementation.[26] In 2004 the USA conducted the first ever federal government-wide emergency simulation exercise with the involvement of more than 40 federal agencies.[27] Although the lessons learned from this exercise have not been made public, it has reportedly provided useful experience of interoperability and interconnectivity between federal departments and agencies.

Capacity building has also continued nationally. The US Government reacted to a long-standing shortcoming by providing protection against the threat of biological attacks. The BioShield Project, signed into law on 21 July 2004, authorized $5.6 billion over 10 years 'for the government purchase and stockpile of vaccines and drugs to fight anthrax, smallpox and other potential

[21] Gaddis, J. L., 'Grand strategy in the second term', *Foreign Affairs*, vol. 84, no. 1 (Jan./Feb. 2005). p. 3.

[22] The White House, Office of the Vice President, 'Vice president's remarks at the opening of the Department of Homeland Security operations center', Washington, DC, 8 July 2004, URL <http://www.whitehouse.gov/news/releases/2004/07/20040708-20.html>.

[23] The Homeland Security Advisory System was established in Mar. 2002. It prescribes warnings at 5 different threat-condition levels corresponding to colours: low (green), guarded (blue), elevated (yellow), high (orange) and severe (red). Each level triggers an incrementally more stringent set of protective measures. Stevenson, J., International Institute for Strategic Studies, *Counter-terrorism: Containment and Beyond*, Adelphi Paper 367 (Oxford University Press: Oxford, 2004), p. 19.

[24] US Department of Homeland Security, 'Threats and protection', Fact sheet: homeland security operations center (HSOC), Washington, DC, URL <http://www.dhs.gov/dhspublic/display?theme=30&content=3813>.

[25] US Department of Homeland Security, 'Statement by Secretary Tom Ridge before the National Commission on Terrorist Attacks On the United States', Speeches and Statements, 19 May 2004 URL <http://www.dhs.gov/dhspublic/display/?content=3571&>.

[26] US Department of Homeland Security, 'DHS organization: emergency preparedness and response', Fact Sheet: National Incident Management System (NIMS), Washington, DC, URL <http://www.dhs.gov/dhspublic/display?theme=51&content=3423>.

[27] US Department of Homeland Security, 'Fact Sheet: Forward Challenge 04', Press Release, Washington, DC, URL <http://www.dhs.gov/dhspublic/display/?content=3553>.

agents of bio-terror'. It will also help expedite research and development (R&D) in this field.[28] No reference was made to earlier shortcomings, however, such as the failure to investigate the anthrax letters in 2002.[29]

The integration of the USA in the world economy makes it necessary for US homeland security measures to be enforced extra-territorially, notably through cooperation with countries that have major ports which connect the world with the USA. Before 11 September 2001, US customs officials did not inspect a container of cargo until it reached US shores. However, inspectors are now present at the 17 busiest seaports outside the USA.[30] Even though it is difficult to ascertain how effective such measures have been in addressing terrorism, there is indirect evidence that they have been effective at fighting certain criminal activities such as drug trafficking. The USA has convinced other developed nations to further improve ship and port security through multilateral frameworks. The G8 member states' justice and home affairs ministers, for example, agreed to develop an auditing checklist to enable countries 'to conduct voluntary self-audits to verify their compliance' with international codes on shipping and port security in May 2004.[31] The increased emphasis on port security and sea transport security is, however, somewhat at odds with the fact that since 11 September 2001 'about 90 per cent of the $5 billion annual investment in transportation security has gone to aviation'.[32]

The USA has made the most far-reaching changes in setting new regulations for the movement of people. Those who travel to the USA under the Visa Waiver Program are obliged to hold a machine-readable passport. If they do not have such a passport they are obliged to obtain either a visa or a one-off exemption.[33] Through this measure, the USA has encouraged the introduction of machine-readable passports worldwide. The US DHS has introduced the first biometric facial recognition standard to be used in travel documents.[34] Because of the contribution this measure has made to security, and the leading role of the USA in homeland security-related matters, the application of such measures seems likely to spread quickly. Measures that make the storage of personal data more extensive may be regarded as controversial from the pri-

[28] 'President Bush signs Project Bioshield act of 2004', The White House, Office of the Press Secretary, 21 July 2004, URL <http://www.whitehouse.gov/news/releases/2004/07/20040721-2.html>.

[29] On the 'anthrax letters' sent in the USA in 2002 see Hart, J., Kuhlau, F. and Simon, J., 'Chemical and biological weapon developments and arms control', *SIPRI Yearbook 2003: Armaments, Disarmament and International Security* (Oxford University Press: Oxford, 2003), pp. 673–75.

[30] US Department of Homeland Security, 'Secretary Tom Ridge speaks at Drexel University in Philadelphia', Speeches and Statements, 24 May 2004, Philadelphia, Pa., URL <http://www.dhs.gov/dhspublic/display?content=3588>.

[31] G8, Meeting of G8 Justice and Home Affairs Ministers, 'Communiqué', point 6, Washington, DC, 11 May 2004, URL <http://www.usdoj.gov/ag/events/g82004/documents.html>.

[32] 'Final Report of the National Commission on Terrorist Attacks upon the United States: the 9/11 Commission Report', Official Government edn, Executive Summary, URL <http://www.gpoaccess.gov/911>.

[33] US Department of Homeland Security, 'Fact sheet: machine-readable passport requirement', Washington, DC, 26 Oct. 2004, URL <http://www.dhs.gov/dhspublic/display/?content=4076>.

[34] US Department of Homeland Security, 'Department of Homeland Security adopts facial recognition standard', Press Release, Washington, DC, 28 Oct. 2004, URL <http://www.dhs.gov/dhspublic/display?content=4080>.

vacy or human rights perspective,[35] but may prove more acceptable if such measures have a positive effect on security.

The international expansion of homeland security requires cooperation by as many countries as possible, but the USA has given special priority to cooperation with Europe, and more specifically to the EU. The EU is the only actor that the USA has sought to establish a comprehensive relationship with in the broad area of homeland security. For example, (*a*) the EU and the USA in 2004 signed an agreement that calls for the 'prompt expansion of customs and border protection's Container Security Initiative throughout the European Community';[36] (*b*) the European Commission has provided funding for the transfer of airline passenger name record (PNR) data to the US DHS;[37] and (*c*) an agreement in principle was reached to use biometric features in EU passports. The latter point is an important issue because many EU citizens do not require a visa when entering the USA for a short visit. As then Secretary of Homeland Security Tom Ridge commented, 'it was up to the US and Europe to set the biometrics path for the rest of the world to follow'.[38] Originally planned for mid-2006, the introduction of biometric features is now likely to be delayed until 2007.[39]

Close transatlantic cooperation is not confined to concrete activities—it has extended to inter-institutional relations between the US DHS and EU organs.[40] Europol established a formal liaison agreement with US law-enforcement agencies in December 2001 and opened a liaison office in Washington, DC, in August 2002. Under the new transatlantic relationship, 'strategic' or 'technical' information on threats, crime patterns, risk assessments and investigative procedures can be shared. In 2004 the US DHS appointed a full-time attaché to the EU.[41] It is increasingly clear that the EU will become the primary partner of the USA across the broad array of justice and homeland security activities.

[35] Human Rights Watch, 'US Homeland Security Bill lacks rights protections', Washington, DC, 27 Sep. 2002, URL <http://hrw.org/press/2002/09/us0927.htm>.

[36] US Department of Homeland Security, 'European Community and Department of Homeland Security sign landmark agreement to improve Container Security and expand CSI', Press Release, Washington, DC, 22 Apr. 2004, URL <http://www.dhs.gov/dhspublic/interapp/press_release/press_release_0389.xml>.

[37] The White House, Secretary Ridge Statement on European Commission Decision, Statement by Homeland Security Secretary Tom Ridge on European Commission decision, US Department of Homeland Security, Washington, DC, 17 May 2004, URL <http://www.whitehouse.gov/news/releases/2004/05/20040517-9.html>.

[38] Best, J., 'US urges EU to lead the way in biometric IDs', Zdnet UK, URL <http://news.zdnet.co.uk/business/legal/0,39020651,39117495,00.htm>.

[39] US Department of Homeland Security, 'Transcript of Under Secretary Asa Hutchinson and European Union Director-General Jonathan Faull at press conference', Press Conference, Washington, DC, 19 Nov. 2004, p. 3, URL <http://www.dhs.gov/dhspublic/display/?theme=44&content=4153&>.

[40] Stevenson (note 23), p. 55.

[41] US Department of Homeland Security, 'Remarks by Secretary of Homeland Security Tom Ridge at the European Policy Centre', Speeches and Statements, Brussels, Belgium, 13 Jan. 2005, URL <http://www.dhs.gov/dhspublic/display?content=4302 >.

Despite these achievements, the funding provided for US homeland security in fiscal year 2005 increased by only $500 million on the previous year.[42] This means that US DHS activities account for approximately 10 per cent of DOD spending, making it a cost-effective contribution to the security of the USA.

The failure to predict the 11 September 2001 terrorist attacks and the incorrect assessment of the two main underlying reasons for launching a war on Iraq put the US intelligence community under the spotlight. There has been widespread criticism of the USA for politicizing intelligence on pre-war Iraqi capabilities. The Final Report of the National Commission on Terrorist Attacks upon the United States (the 9-11 Commission Report) was published on 22 July 2004.[43] Its recommendations—ordering further investigation into the allegations about Iraq's possession of WMD and reforms of the intelligence services—have been approved. The reforms were the first major reorganization of the US Government since the establishment of the US DHS.[44]

Information provided by the US intelligence services provides grounds for major operational decisions. The USA has huge strategic assets at its disposal and is better positioned than any other country to turn its political decisions into military action. Many countries follow US assessments and policy judgements derived from US intelligence, and most do not have the means to double-check such information using national resources. The huge US intelligence machinery has apparently underperformed at key moments, and the impact has been exacerbated by the reliance of decision makers on intelligence information when taking major strategic decisions. The Commission concluded that 'terrorism was not the overriding national security concern' for the USA until 11 September 2001, and it identified certain shortcomings in the fields of policy, capabilities and management. According to the report, there was a policy of belittling the terrorist threat that led to a lack of imagination when taking action to counter it.[45] The Commission concluded that capabilities remained oriented towards cold war-type threats.[46] The most important weaknesses in agency capabilities were identified in the domestic arena, specifically at the Federal Bureau of Investigation (FBI). In management, there was a lack of pooling of intelligence, resources and of priority setting. The problems identified in the aftermath of the September 2001 terrorist attacks were exacerbated by inadequate intelligence relating to Iraq. While the former case was closed in 2004, the administration took care that any final assessment of

[42] US Department of Homeland Security, 'Fact sheet: Department of Homeland Security Appropriations Act of 2005', Press Release, Washington, DC, 18 Oct 2004, URL <http://www.dhs.gov/dhspublic/interapp/press_release/press_release_0541.xml>.

[43] National Commission on terrorist attacks upon the United States, *The 9/11 Commission Report: Final Report of the National Commission on Terrorist Attacks Upon the United States* (US Government Printing Office: Washington, DC, 22 July 2004), URL <http://www.gpoaccess.gov/911>.

[44] Anthony, I. *et al.*, 'The Euro-Atlantic system and global security', *SIPRI Yearbook 2003: Armaments, Disarmament and International Security* (Oxford University Press: Oxford, 2003), p. 54.

[45] National Commission on terrorist attacks upon the United States (note 43).

[46] See Clarke, R. A., *Against All Enemies: Inside America's War on Terror* (Free Press: New York, 2004).

the intelligence on Iraq's WMD was made after the presidential election in November 2004.[47]

The Commission focused on the activities of producers rather than consumers of intelligence.[48] Discussion of the mistakes made by the latter in connection with intelligence management has remained abstract and sketchy. In contrast to other democracies, the majority of US intelligence is operational and its prime consumer is the military.[49] Prior to the Iraq war, the DOD established its own Office of Special Plans to review raw intelligence and, if necessary, to challenge the interpretations made by other parts of the US intelligence community.[50] This issue was generally dodged in the debates on reform, which focused on whether or not intelligence should be coordinated by the newly established Director of National Intelligence (DNI), separate from the director of the Central Intelligence Agency (CIA). In the end, it was agreed that the DNI would serve in the Executive Office of the President,[51] which may alleviate the problems that stem from the constitutional separation of domestic and foreign intelligence. However, the DNI will play a political role and this new function and its location in the administration may exacerbate rather than eliminate the problem of the 'politicization' of intelligence. Whether these actions alone, without carrying out changes on the 'intelligence demand side', will improve capabilities sufficiently is open to doubt.[52] Among the most important lessons learned is the need to keep distance between the intelligence community and its political masters in order to maintain professional autonomy. The political sphere should assign tasks but remain careful not to pre-judge outcomes.[53]

Security policy consensus in the USA

Presidential and congressional elections took place in the USA in 2004. While the presidential campaign emphasized the differences between the two main candidates' positions rather than the similarities, it was clear at the beginning of the campaign that any new administration's agenda would be dominated by the need to stabilize Afghanistan and Iraq, and by established challenges such

[47] The Commission on the Intelligence Capabilities of the United States Regarding Weapons of Mass Destruction was established by Executive Order 13328 in Feb. 2004 and is to report by 31 Mar. 2005. See Best, R. A., 'Intelligence issues for Congress', Congressional Research Service, Issue Brief for Congress, 9 Dec. 2004, p. 10.

[48] See Betts, R. K., 'The new politics of intelligence: will reforms work this time?', *Foreign Affairs*, vol. 83, no. 3 (May/June 2004), p. 3.

[49] Odom, W. E., 'Testimony before the Senate Select Committee on Intelligence', 20 July 2004, p. 4. URL <http://intelligence.senate.gov/0407hrg/040720/witness.htm>.

[50] Borger, J., 'The spies who pushed for war', Guardian Unlimited, 17 July 2003, URL <http://www.guardian.co.uk/Iraq/Story/0,2763,999737,00.html>.

[51] See 'Summary of intelligence reform and terrorism prevention act of 2004', 6 Dec. 2004, URL <http://www.govt-aff.senate.gov/_files/ConferenceReportSummary.doc>.

[52] For other similar investigations in Australia and the UK see chapter 13 in this volume.

[53] Such concerns were formulated in the light of the intelligence failures. See Davis, I. and Persbo, A., 'After the Butler Report: time to take on the group think in Washington and London', BASIC Papers no. 46, Occasional Papers on International Security Policy, July 2004, URL <http://www.basicint.org/pubs/Papers/BP46.htm>.

as anti-terrorism and homeland security. Consequently, it was not so much security challenges as an elaboration of the actions required to address them that differentiated the candidates.

The task of stabilizing Iraq as a top priority could not separate the two candidates since President Bush had ordered the launch of the military operation and Senator John Kerry (and his vice-presidential running-mate, John Edwards) had voted in favor of the policy.[54] Kerry campaigned on the theme that the administration 'miscalculated by rushing to war without a plan for the peace'[55] and claimed that he could do better at dealing with the consequences: 'with the right kind of leadership from us NATO can be mobilized to help stabilize Iraq and the region. And if NATO comes, others will too'.[56]

In the light of the success of homeland defence, Kerry presented an alternative of fighting 'a smarter, more effective war on terror'.[57] On intelligence, he noted that the administration had 'waited three years after September 11th to start to reform our intelligence'[58] and remarked that a 'new agency and new office space won't help us infiltrate terrorist organizations operating right in our country'.[59] However, three main reform proposals—to appoint a National Intelligence Director, structure the intelligence community 'to meet the threats of today' and strengthen human intelligence—were the subject of bipartisan consensus.[60] This made it difficult to put the issue at the centre of the campaign on security.

The concrete ideas on the Democratic Party agenda that did demonstrate clear differences between the two parties included speeding up the securing of 'bomb making' nuclear material, particularly in Russia.[61] Kerry put forward several proposals on non-proliferation and export controls. His nuclear policy was also different from the Bush Administration's and was more pro-arms control. The security initiatives included one to 'free America from its dangerous dependence on Mideast oil'.[62] However, they apparently did not strike a chord with the central security concerns of the US electorate.

In sum, although there were visible differences between the positions of the two parties, they seldom represented alternatives for the future. The philosophical differences in foreign policy were apparent when Kerry emphasized

[54] US Congress, Congressional vote on Iraq resolution: 11 Oct. 2002, URL <http://www.newsbatch.com/upd-iraqresvote.gif>.

[55] 'A real difference: remarks by John Edwards', p. 2 URL <http://www.johnkerry.com/pressroom/speeches/spc_2004_0830.html>.

[56] Kerry, J. F., 'A realistic path in Iraq', *Washington Post* (Internet edn), 4 July 2004, p. B07, URL <http://www.washingtonpost.com/ac2/wp-dyn/A24762-2004Jul2?language=printer>.

[57] 'Speech to the 2004 Democratic National Convention: remarks by John Kerry', 29 July 2004, p. 2, URL <http://www.johnkerry.com/pressroom/speeches/spc_2004_0729.html>.

[58] 'A real difference', Remarks by John Edwards, p. 2, URL <http://www.johnkerry.com/pressroom/speeches/spc_2004_0830.html>.

[59] 'Excerpts from homeland security address', Remarks by John Edwards, 18 Dec. 2003, p. 2. URL <http://www.johnkerry.com/pressroom/speeches/spc_2003_1218.html>.

[60] 'A real difference' (note 58)

[61] 'New strategies to meet new threats', Remarks by John Kerry, 1 June 2004, p. 2, URL <http://www.johnkerry.com/pressroom/speeches/spc_2004_0601.html>.

[62] 'Strength and security for a new world', Remarks by John Kerry, URL <http://www.johnkerry.com/issues/national_security/>.

'belief in collective security and alliances, respect for international institutions and international law, multilateral engagement and the use of force not as a first option but truly as a last resort'.[63] In other areas, it was difficult to translate the message into concrete policies. The eventual victory of George W. Bush by a margin of 3 per cent has generally been interpreted as a popular vote for continuity and stability in security policy: but even more, for 'values' relating purely to choices in the USA's internal affairs.

III. NATO: striving to regain ground

Having experienced the most acute existential test in its history—the crisis and internal divisions over Iraq—and confronted with the prospect of progressive marginalization in transatlantic relations by its leading member, the USA, NATO looked with hope to its Istanbul Summit on 28–29 June 2004.[64] Along with efforts to reinvent itself, NATO launched new initiatives and continued existing operations outside its treaty area of activity—in Afghanistan and Iraq, in a broader Middle East partnership scheme and through deeper involvement in the Caucasus and Central Asia. The aim was to heal the transatlantic rift and to further expand NATO's global commitments so that it might appear a credible alternative to US-led 'coalitions of the willing'. The questions were whether the necessary united political resolve could be found, and whether NATO's ambitions and commitments could be matched with adequate resources.

Meanwhile, NATO gained an additional lease of life with its 'big bang' enlargement. On 29 March 2004, a second group of new Central European countries—Bulgaria, Estonia, Latvia, Lithuania, Romania, Slovakia and Slovenia—deposited their instruments of accession with the US Government. Along with NATO transformation and new operations, the question of the future of the Partnership for Peace (PFP) thereby gained in importance.[65] An indirect consequence of NATO's new out-of-area focus was the handover of its Stabilization Force (SFOR) mission in Bosnia and Herzegovina to the EU at the end of the year—an act which by no means resolved the broader questions hanging over EU–NATO 'strategic partnership'.[66] In addition, there are signs that competition is increasing between the institutions involved in the

[63] US Council on Foreign Relations, 'Making America secure again: setting the right course for foreign policy', 3 Dec. 2003, Speeches and Statements Library, Senator John Kerry, Democratic Candidate for President, URL <http://www.cfr.org/campaign2004/pub6576/john_kerry/making_America_secure_again:_the_right_course_for_foreign_policy.php>.

[64] NATO, Istanbul Summit Communiqué, Issued by the Heads of State and Government participating in the meeting of the North Atlantic Council, Press Release, 28 June 2004, URL <http://www.nato.int/docu/pr/2004/p04-096e.htm>.

[65] For members of the PFP see the glossary in this volume.

[66] The NATO Secretary General in July 2004 described the NATO–EU rapprochement as 'too limited' and called for cooperation 'across the entire spectrum of security management' as a 'strategic necessity'. NATO, 'Beyond Istanbul', Speech by NATO Secretary General Jaap de Hoop Scheffer at the European Policy Centre, Brussels, 12 July 2004, URL <http://www.nato.int/docu/speech/2004/s040712b.htm>. One formidable obstacle in this context is the Turkey–Cyprus rift. See also chapter 3 in this volume.

transatlantic dialogue,[67] despite renewed support for NATO as a 'centerpiece' of US endeavours in Europe.[68]

The chief obstacle in determining the role of NATO remains the lack of a clear, concerted long-term Euro-Atlantic strategy to replace now antiquated cold-war concepts with a more vigorous response to the threats of the 21st century—terrorism, weak or failed states and proliferation of WMD. The challenge for NATO is to overcome the growing perception that it is a 'forum for taking decisions on operations' and to regain the role of a 'central forum for political debate and decision making'.[69] In 2004 the question of whether NATO is still an organization with shared interests continued to preoccupy observers on both sides of the Atlantic.

Transformation and capabilities

The underlying principle of NATO's recent transformation has been the ambition to 'act global' in a variety of missions.[70] The reform process began with a cluster of decisions made at NATO's 2002 Prague Summit and has continued to make progress.[71] Alongside the enlargement process, NATO has continued to restructure its strategic command, improve capabilities and build up new relationships with the aim of better projecting stability and security.

In 2004 the NATO Response Force (NRF) reached initial operational capability and its multinational chemical, biological, radiological and nuclear (CBRN) defence battalion became fully operational as planned.[72] However, in the spring of 2004, the new NATO Secretary General, Jaap de Hoop Scheffer, renewed the appeal for a radical shake-up in NATO's plans and the financing of its operations. He highlighted the gap between NATO's huge armed forces

[67] German Federal Chancellor Gerhard Schröder suggested that a high-level panel consider ways for the USA to deal more directly with the EU because the relationship 'in its current form does justice neither to the Union's growing importance, nor to the new demands on trans-Atlantic cooperation'. Gerhard Schröder, Speech to the 41st Munich Conference on Security Policy, 12 Feb. 2005, URL <http://securityconference.de/konferenzen/rede.php?menu_2004_menu_konferenzen=&sprache=en&id=143&>. The visit by President Bush to the Brussels EU building in Feb. 2005 signified US recognition of the growing role played by the EU in security matters, such as arms sales to China, policy vis-à-vis Iran, etc.

[68] US International Information Programs, 'NATO lauded as "centerpiece" of US efforts in Europe', Press Release, Washington, DC, 21 Feb. 2005, URL <http://usinfo.state.gov/xarchives/display.html?p=washfile-english&y=2005&m=February&x=20050221183425lebahcb0.7710993&t=is/is-latest.html>.

[69] 'Global NATO?', Remarks by NATO Secretary General Jaap de Hoop Scheffer at the Clingendael Institute, 29 Oct. 2004, URL <http://www.nato.int/docu/speech/2004/s041029a.htm>. The doubts about NATO's relevance have been reinforced by Chancellor Schröder's observation that 'it is no longer the primary venue where transatlantic partners discuss and coordinate strategies' (note 67).

[70] Apart from the interest in the 'greater Middle East', including the southern Mediterranean and the southern perimeter of the post-Soviet space, Supreme Allied Commander in Europe General James L. Jones has suggested that NATO could direct its activities towards Africa. *Atlantic News* no. 3543 (23 Jan. 2004), p. 3; and no. 3628 (18 Nov. 2004), p. 3.

[71] For the impact of decisions in 2002–2003 see Dunay, P. and Lachowski, Z., 'Euro-Atlantic organizations and relationships', *SIPRI Yearbook 2004: Armaments, Disarmament and International Security* (Oxford University Press: Oxford, 2004), pp. 42–44.

[72] In Apr. 2004, NATO decided to back a €4 billion offer by the Transatlantic Industrial Proposed Solution (TIPS) consortium, led by EADS, to develop the Alliance Ground Surveillance (AGS) system. The AGS will by 2010 complete the only NATO-owned airborne warning and control system (AWACS).

inventory and the meagre operational contributions of its member states as well as the need to make forces smaller, more mobile and flexible.[73] At the NATO Istanbul Summit, 'usability' targets and changes to NATO's planning processes were endorsed whereby NATO member states committed themselves to being able to deploy and sustain larger proportions of their forces for NATO operations at all times and to adopt a longer-term defence planning cycle.[74] By providing greater 'predictability' (i.e., real availability of necessary capabilities) these steps are intended to help create a pool of military assets permanently available to NATO so that it does not have to assemble a force from scratch for each mission.

Afghanistan

Afghanistan has become a key priority and a test for NATO's credibility and ability to operate outside Europe.[75] Since August 2003, NATO has exercised command of the International Security Assistance Force (ISAF).[76] The aim of filling the security vacuum in Afghanistan, which exists practically everywhere outside Kabul, and of enhanced state-building efforts led ISAF to take over responsibility for and to regularize the existing and new small civil–military Provincial Reconstruction Teams (PRTs) around the country.[77] Another task for the 6500-strong NATO-led force is to demobilize, demilitarize and integrate into the new Afghan Army the numerous militias that had previously fought against the Taliban.[78]

In 2004 NATO's Afghanistan mission struggled with the familiar problems of the limited availability of assets from member nations and the related shortfalls in 'force generation' (i.e., timely provision of personnel and matériel).[79] This was the more problematic because of the impending presidential election in Afghanistan, which in the event had to be postponed from June to 9 October. At the Istanbul Summit, NATO agreed to expand ISAF by sending another 3500 troops to provide security for the election and to take over five

[73] Dempsey, J., 'Nato chief says huge shake-up is needed', *Financial Times*, 27 May 2004, p. 1.

[74] The decision refers to an idea put forward by former NATO Secretary General Robertson, whereby each state will ensure that 40% of its armed forces are usable and 8% are sustainable for overseas missions. The defence planning cycle has been extended from 6 to 10 years and will be supplemented by adjustments within the cycle from 2 to 4 years.

[75] 'Our first and immediate priority is to get Afghanistan right'. Speech by NATO Secretary General Jaap de Hoop Scheffer at the National Defense University, Washington, DC, 29 Jan. 2004, URL <http://www.nato.int/docu/speech/2004/s040129a.htm>.

[76] For the background to ISAF and PRTs see Cottey, A., 'Afghanistan and the new dynamics of intervention: counter-terrorism and nation building', *SIPRI Yearbook 2003: Armaments, Disarmament and International Security* (Oxford University Press: Oxford, 2003), pp 167–194.

[77] On 1 Jan. 2004 the German-led PRT in Kunduz was integrated into the ISAF command chain. See chapter 3 in this volume.

[78] Some of these forces work closely with US-led Operation Enduring Force, which is separate from ISAF.

[79] The issue of helicopters for ISAF is illustrative. Belgium, the Netherlands and Turkey agreed to provide them but, for bureaucratic, financial and logistical reasons, their provision was delayed for several months.

PRTs in the north of the country. On 10 February 2005 a definite decision was taken to extend PRTs to the western part of the country ('phase 2').

Greater consistency (or 'rapprochement') between the activities of ISAF and those of Operation Enduring Freedom is still an unresolved issue. Suggestions from the USA and the NATO Secretary General that the missions be merged under a single NATO command in order to improve activities aimed at countering terrorist groups met with strong Franco-German objections at an informal ministerial meeting in Poiana Brasov, Romania, in mid-October and later.[80]

Iraq

The split in NATO over Iraq continued in 2004, with the USA calling for greater NATO involvement and many European NATO member states grouped around France and Germany opposing this. The US proposals for 'active involvement' or a 'new collective role' since 2003 have envisaged a wider engagement by NATO in Iraq, possibly in the framework of a broader Middle East policy.[81] Given the potential risk of overstretch that NATO was already facing in Afghanistan, however, it was difficult to see how NATO could engage successfully in another 'hot spot'.

A particular blow was dealt to the concept of deeper NATO involvement by the decision of Spain's new Socialist Party government to withdraw from Iraq in the spring of 2004, made in accordance with a promise made during its election campaign and in the wake of the Madrid bombings in March 2004. Hungary withdrew its troops from Iraq in December 2004 because of a lack of the parliamentary support necessary to extend their stay beyond the end of the year. In the face of growing domestic opposition, Poland and the Czech Republic also planned to withdraw their troops.[82]

By mid-2004, various ideas had been put forward for more direct NATO involvement in Iraq, encouraged by UN Security Council Resolution 1546 on transferring sovereignty to the Iraqis after 30 June 2004.[83] At the Istanbul Summit, however, it became clear that the US-led coalition could not expect support for NATO military forces to be involved in Iraq itself.[84] The most that could be achieved was an agreement for NATO countries to supply training personnel—with no combat role—for the Iraqi security forces.[85]

[80] The discussion on the possible merger of the 2 missions continued at an informal meeting of the NATO defence ministers in Nice in Feb. 2005, but inconclusively. For more on suggestions regarding the merger see *Atlantic News* no. 3650 (11 Feb. 2005), p. 1.

[81] On developments in the Middle East see chapter 5 in this volume.

[82] In Dec. 2004, Poland announced that it would keep its forces in Iraq until the end of 2005. However, the number of its troops was to fall to *c.* 1700 after the elections in Jan. 2005.

[83] UN Security Council Resolution 1546, 8 June 2004.

[84] French Foreign Minister Michel Barnier considered hoisting the 'NATO flag in Iraq' counterproductive, while President Jacques Chirac warned against the 'great risks' of NATO 'meddling', including the risks of 'the Christian West confronting the Muslim East'. Stroobants, J.-P. and Tréan, C., 'Paris et Washington s'affrontent sur le rôle de l'OTAN en Iraq' [Paris and Washington confront each other over the role of NATO in Iraq], *Le Monde*, 27–28 June 2004, p. 2.

[85] NATO (note 64). Canada, France, Germany and Spain do not envisage training Iraqi forces in Iraq.

The strategic concept and the operational plan for the NATO training mission were agreed in October–November and force generation was due to be completed before elections to the National Assembly in January 2005. An advance planning team from NATO arrived in Iraq in September 2004. The first stage of training for Iraqi security forces began in Norway in early November. In early December, NATO finally agreed to increase its security-force training mission in Baghdad's fortified 'Green Zone' from some 60–300 persons, one-third of which would be instructors. The meeting was accompanied by a renewed argument over the caveats and exceptions that some NATO member states had made regarding their personnel taking part in training in Iraq.[86] On 22 February 2005 the 26 NATO states announced that they had gathered sufficient contributions for the training mission.[87]

Partnership frameworks

The process of NATO enlargement threw a sharper light on the future of the Euro-Atlantic Partnership Council (EAPC) and the PFP programme. With seven more countries leaving the PFP to become NATO members, it has undergone a 'geographical shift' further east towards the Caucasus and Central Asia.[88] In the autumn of 2004, the NATO Secretary General paid visits to the countries of both regions, and in September he appointed NATO Deputy Assistant Secretary General for Political Affairs and Security Policy Robert F. Simmons Jr as Special Representative for the Caucasus and Central Asia. In these regions, NATO has to deal with politically difficult partners, some of which are locked in crises and conflicts. More generally, it faces a challenge in balancing its aim of democratic transformation and defence institution building, on the one hand, with concern about the authoritarian profile of most of the local regimes, on the other.[89]

In the early months of 2004, the USA canvassed ideas for a NATO 'greater Middle East initiative' to encourage reform and democracy in the Arab world. The gesture was less a military than a political one, designed by the USA to help heal transatlantic divisions after Iraq and to head off the risk that competing European and US strategies would develop for the region. The USA included some European ideas and urged its NATO and EU partners to sup-

[86] Belgium, Germany, Greece, Luxembourg and Spain, as well as France, which is less concerned because it is not part of NATO's integrated military command, referred to the reservations they made in Istanbul, which mean that that they will not send military personnel to Iraq.

[87] NATO, 'NATO leaders express unity on Iraq, reaffirm values', NATO Update, 22 Feb. 2005, URL <http://www.nato.int/docu/update/2005/02-february/e0222a.htm>. NATO also pledged to establish a military training academy at Ar Rustamiya on the outskirts of Baghdad.

[88] There are 3 distinct groups left in the PFP: the Balkans, the non-aligned European countries and countries in the Caucasus and Central Asia. Albania, Croatia and the FYROM are implementing their Membership Action Plans, while Bosnia and Herzegovina, and Serbia and Montenegro are yet to meet the established conditions for PFP. Monaco, A., 'Ten years on: is there a future for the partnership after NATO enlargement?', *NATO Notes*, vol. 6, no. 1 (ISIS Europe: Brussels, Feb. 2004), pp. 5–7.

[89] Monaco (note 88), pp. 5–7. In Sep. 2004 the PFP 'Cooperative Best Effort 2004' exercise was cancelled after Azerbaijan rejected participation by Armenian officers.

port the initiative.[90] NATO's tasks would be to help rebuild Afghanistan and Iraq and to extend cooperation to the Middle East under a new version of the PFP.[91] In the event, however, the idea of expanding NATO's role in the greater Middle East initiative came to little. Disputes over Iraq, fears about overstretching NATO, lack of agreement about the plan's scope and geographic extent and, not least, reluctance in Arab capitals overshadowed the debate.[92]

In mid-March, NATO decided to extend its Operation Active Endeavour, initiated in October 2001 in the eastern Mediterranean and the Gibraltar Strait, to the entire Mediterranean Sea, and to enlist the support of PFP states as well as the countries of the Mediterranean Dialogue and 'other selected nations'.[93] Russia agreed 'in principle' to join the operation but attached conditions unacceptable to NATO. Both Russia and Turkey have opposed extending Active Endeavour exercises to the Black Sea.[94]

In the run-up to the Istanbul Summit, NATO members discussed options such as strengthening the PFP for the Caucasus and Central Asian countries, cooperation with Russia and Ukraine, a cooperation pact with the Persian Gulf states, and the consolidation of the Mediterranean Dialogue. In addition, NATO expressed a cautious interest in supporting stability and security in the Black Sea region. These discussions resulted in two, possibly complementary, decisions at the summit meeting—to launch a new Greater Middle East Istanbul Cooperation Initiative aimed initially at the Gulf Cooperation Council countries[95] and to reinforce NATO's Mediterranean Dialogue through stronger political cooperation (i.e., political dialogue, efforts to achieve interoperabil-

[90] The 3-pronged plan envisaged promoting good governance, better education and economic growth and tallied with the EU 'Barcelona process' of engaging the Mediterranean countries in a web of trade and political arrangements and improving human rights and economic accountability. Lobjakas, A., 'Middle East: US official in Europe to promote greater regional initiative', Radio Free Europe/Radio Liberty (RFE/RL), Feature article, 5 Mar. 2004; and Dempsey, J., 'US moves closer to Brussels on Middle East political reforms', *Financial Times*, 6–7 Mar. 2004, p. 3. The main US–European difference concerns the impact of the Israeli–Palestinian conflict on reforms in the Arab world.

[91] According to a group of international experts which prepared a draft scheme for promoting democracy 'NATO's new role would be to keep the Americans and Europeans together, the aggressors out and the terrorists down'. 'A joint plan to help the greater Middle East', *International Herald Tribune*, 15 Mar. 2004, p. 6. Adverse reactions in Arab capitals led to a consequent revision and dilution of the plan.

[92] See Fiorenza, N., 'A greater NATO role in the Greater Middle East?', *NATO Notes*, vol. 6, no. 1 (ISIS Europe: Brussels, Feb. 2004), pp. 1–2. US Senator Chuck Hagel suggests 5 specific areas where NATO could play a larger role in establishing security and stability: Turkey, Afghanistan, Iraq, the Mediterranean and the Israeli–Palestinian problem. 'NATO's role in bringing security to the greater Middle East', US Foreign Policy Agenda, US State Department electronic journal, 10 June 2004, URL <http://usinfo.state.gov/journals/itps/0604/ijpe/hagel.htm>. On the greater Middle East see chapter 5 in this volume.

[93] NATO's Mediterranean Dialogue was launched in 1994. It involves Algeria, Egypt, Israel, Jordan, Mauritania, Morocco and Tunisia. Thus far, it has played a modest confidence-building role. For more on the process see Dokos, Th., Hellenic Foundation for European and Foreign Policy (ELIAMEP), *NATO's Mediterranean Dialogue: Prospects and Policy Recommendations*, ELIAMEP Policy Paper no. 3 (ELIAMEP: Athens, May 2003).

[94] For more on Russian motives see Socor, V., Jamestown Foundation, 'Russians not joining NATO Operation Active Endeavour', *Eurasia Monitor*, 30 Nov 2004, URL <http://www.jamestown.org/edm/article.php?article_id=2368922>.

[95] For membership of the Gulf Cooperation Council see the glossary in this volume.

ity, defence reform and measures to combat terrorism).[96] New operational engagements for NATO and any new multilateral framework for the region along EAPC lines were conspicuous by their absence.

IV. The EU: expanding the sphere of security and defence

The EU entered 2004 with an equivocal balance sheet in its European Security and Defence Policy (ESDP) and in the Common Foreign and Security Policy (CFSP) more broadly. It had made progress in building its strategic personality with the European Security Strategy (ESS) of December 2003, which was followed up actively in the four designated areas: (*a*) 'effective multilateralism' (with a special focus on partnership with the UN); (*b*) the Middle East; (*c*) Bosnia and Herzegovina (the handover of SFOR to the EU); and, especially after the 11 March 2004 Madrid bombings, (*d*) terrorism.[97] Iran's nuclear programme and the issue of arms sales to China have become critical tests for the EU of the effective application of 'soft power' and the EU's ability to advance its CFSP.[98]

EU–NATO cooperation and defence planning helped bring an end to haggling over independent EU military planning, while the EU's new European Defence Agency (EDA) will enhance armaments cooperation between EU member states. The EU successfully completed its own 'big bang' enlargement by admitting 10 new countries as members on 1 May 2004—Cyprus, the Czech Republic, Estonia, Hungary, Latvia, Lithuania, Malta, Poland, Slovakia and Slovenia. Their admission raised fears that the new members might seek to tilt the policy balance in a pro-US direction, putting Europe's political cohesion and efficiency at risk again, but events in the latter half of the year did not bear out such predictions.

The EU carried on with its programme of projecting security and stability at its perimeter. At the end of the year, after an intense, emotive debate among its members and in the face of public disquiet in several EU countries, the EU agreed to open accession negotiations with Turkey in October 2005. Croatia was also offered the prospect of opening accession negotiations in March 2005, provided that it cooperates with the International Criminal Tribunal for the Former Yugoslavia. In December 2004, accession negotiations with Bulgaria and Romania were successfully concluded and both countries will join the EU in January 2007. Many EU diplomats and observers detected a certain 'enlargement fatigue' after all these breakthroughs, hinting that further admissions would be indefinitely postponed. This only added to the pressure for the EU to address its 'wider Europe' policy.

[96] NATO (note 64).

[97] For more on the 4 areas see Bailes, A. J. K., *The European Security Strategy: An Evolutionary History*, SIPRI Policy Paper no. 10 (SIPRI: Stockholm, Feb. 2005), URL <http://editors.sipri.se/recpubs.html>.

[98] For broader discussion of the 2 cases see chapters 12 and 10, respectively, in this volume.

The constitutional treaty was not adopted at the end of 2003 because of several sticking points unrelated to the ESDP and CFSP.[99] France and Germany began to hint once more at a 'pioneer group' aimed at closer integration. Germany's Foreign Minister, Joschka Fischer, repudiated the idea of a core Europe in February 2004 and the Irish Presidency managed to rescue the constitutional treaty by June.[100] However, the European Parliament elections in June 2004 demonstrated a widespread disillusionment with EU politics among voters, who showed both apathy and a tendency to protest against their governments and, to some extent, against the EU in general.

The European Neighbourhood Policy

In the run-up to the 2004 EU enlargement and the formation of the EU's new external borders, the EU sought to establish a policy vis-à-vis its new neighbours that—in the words of the President of the European Commission, Romano Prodi—would leave them 'sharing everything with the EU but institutions'.[101] Following the Commission Communication of March 2003, the resulting European Neighbourhood Policy (ENP) Strategy Paper of 12 May 2004 defined the objectives and principles, the geographic scope and the methods to be used in order to implement the policy.[102] The objective of the ENP is to draw countries into a closer relationship with the EU—a 'ring of friends' in accordance with the goals of the ESS—and to give them the chance to work with the EU on political, security and economic, as well as cultural and education, issues. The EU seeks to promote partners' commitment to common values such as the rule of law, good governance, respect for human rights, the promotion of good neighbourly relations, the principles of the market economy and sustainable development.

As an initial step towards implementing the ENP, individual Action Plans with three- to five-year timeframes were offered by the EU initially to Israel, Jordan, Moldova, Morocco, Tunisia, Ukraine and the Palestinian Authority.[103] In mid-2004, the General Affairs and External Relations Council (GAERC)

[99] The text of the Treaty establishing a Constitution for Europe is at URL <http://europa.eu.int/constitution/index_en.htm>.

[100] 'Interview der *Berliner Zeitung* mit Bundesaußenminister Joschka Fischer: "Klein-europäische Vorstellungen funktionieren einfach nicht mehr"' [German Foreign Minister Joschka Fischer interviewed in *Berliner Zeitung*: 'narrow visions of Europe simply do not work any more'], *Berliner Zeitung*, 28 Feb. 2004. For other views on Europe's future see 'The future of the European Union: debate', discussion corner, at the Internet site of the EU, URL <http://europa.eu.int/futurum/congov_en.htm>.

[101] 'Wider Europe: a proximity policy as the key to stability: speech by Romano Prodi, President of the European Commission, "Peace, Security and Stability International Dialogue and the Role of the EU"', Sixth ECSA-World Conference, Jean Monnet Project, Brussels, 5–6 Dec. 2002, Speech/02/619, URL <http://europa.eu.int/comm/external_relations/news/prodi/sp02_619.htm>.

[102] 'Wider Europe neighbourhood: a new framework for relations with our eastern and southern neighbours', Communication from the Commission to the Council and the European Parliament, document COM(2003) 104 final, Brussels, 11 Mar. 2003, URL <http://www.europa.eu.int/comm/world/enp/document_en.htm>; and European Neighbourhood Policy Strategy Paper, Communication from the Commission, document COM(2004) 373 final, Brussels, 12 May 2004, URL <http://www.europa.eu.int/comm/world/enp/document_en.htm>.

[103] Belarus and all the Mediterranean countries, including Libya, can become beneficiaries of the ENP if they meet the necessary conditions.

decided to extend the ENP to the southern Caucasus to include Armenia, Azerbaijan and Georgia. Egypt and Lebanon are the next countries in line.[104] Israel signed its Action Plan on 14 December 2004. Moldova and Ukraine signed their Action Plans in February 2005.[105] It is expected that the three South Caucasus countries, together with Egypt and Lebanon, should sign their Action Plans by the end of 2005.

During the presidential election crisis in Ukraine in November–December 2004, Poland pushed for the renegotiation of Ukraine's ENP Action Plan in order to offer Ukraine a 'European perspective' and accord the country special status—if the re-run election was democratic and transparent. The Polish proposal was not agreed but EU member states asked CFSP High Representative Javier Solana and Commissioner for External Relations Benita Ferrero-Waldner to produce alternative mechanisms to improve the EU–Ukraine relationship.

The Treaty establishing a Constitution for Europe

The Irish Presidency restarted talks on the Treaty establishing a Constitution for Europe six weeks after they broke down at the December 2003 Council of the European Union (Council) meeting in Brussels, but soon ran into obstacles. Some 20 major disputes remained,[106] the fiercest being over voting weights, but also including arguments about the size of the European Commission and British determination to retain national vetoes in key policy areas (tax, foreign and defence policy, social security and the EU budget). In early March, Germany signalled its willingness to achieve a compromise on voting rights. The two main proponents of the 'triple majority' voting system, Poland and Spain, also made conciliatory gestures, which enabled the Irish Presidency to restart treaty negotiations with the aim of a final deal by June.[107] When the British Government announced that it would hold a referendum on ratifying the constitution, this caused another clash—with France and Germany threat-

[104] 'Communication from the Commission to the Council on the Commission proposals for Action Plans under the European Neighbourhood Policy (ENP)', EU Commission document COM(2004) 795 final, Brussels, 9 Dec. 2004, URL <http://www.europa.eu.int/comm/world/enp/document_en.htm>. Israel, Jordan, Moldova, Morocco, Tunisia, Ukraine and the Palestinian Authority were the first of the EU's neighbours to agree Action Plans, on 9 Dec. 2004

[105] 'The European Commission's Delegation to Ukraine, Moldova and Belarus: GAERC conclusions on Ukraine', The European Union in the world: delegations, URL <http://www.delukr.cec.eu.int/site/page34190.html>. The 'improved' Action Plan for Ukraine includes support for its bid to join the WTO, recognition as a market economy and extra funds.

[106] These included such issues as a reference to Christianity in the preamble, the Charter of Fundamental Rights, the rotating EU presidency, the European Parliament's co-decision with regard to the EU budget, the scope of EU integration versus national parliaments and the unanimity rule in EU trade policy covering services and foreign direct investment.

[107] Parker, G., Minder, R. and Dempsey, J., 'EU leaders signal fresh unity as summit ends', *Financial Times*, 27–28 Mar. 2004, p. 2. Spain's change of government in March 2004 led to a softening of its stance on voting weights. Poland reluctantly agreed to compromise for fear of being left isolated. As a result, under the new voting system, which will enter into force in 2009, a measure will pass if it is supported by 55% of member states, provided these states represent 65% of the total EU population. The compromise, however, is accompanied by 'safeguards' and blocking mechanisms, or higher thresholds, in some sensitive policy areas.

ening the UK with marginalization or even possible expulsion from the EU should it fail to ratify the constitution.[108] All this only fuelled the growing scepticism among the European public and the enthusiasm of opponents in the member states for holding a referendum elsewhere. More generally, the treaty remained a bone of contention between the Euro-sceptics striving to reduce it to a 'tidying-up exercise' and the Euro-philes pursuing a more ambitious project, as well as between those who consider the constitutional treaty too 'liberal' and those who see it as too 'socialist'.[109]

Nevertheless, under Irish leadership the member states managed to agree on 18 June 2004 to a text that constitutes a pragmatic compromise attempt to improve the efficiency and flexibility of the EU after its enlargement to 25 members. In the foreign affairs and security areas, the innovations with regard to an 'EU minister for foreign affairs', giving the EU a clearer political 'personality'; an EU 'external action service', composed of representatives of the Council and the Commission and seconded national diplomats; and a longer-term Presidency of the Council are potentially significant.[110] The text agreed in June did not introduce further changes in the ESDP dimension compared with the situation at the end of 2003.

The Treaty establishing a Constitution for Europe was signed by the EU leaders in Rome on 29 October 2004. Attention has since shifted to its uncertain prospects of surviving the coming ratification process, which involves at least 9 national referendums.[111]

European security and defence

More than five years after the ESDP was launched, building the security and defence dimension of the EU is still at an early stage, with member states cautiously exploring common responsibilities adequate to the broad spectrum of their security needs. EU experience is limited and still vulnerable to political processes and circumstances both inside and outside the EU.

The shock of the 11 March 2004 bomb attack in Madrid led the EU to adopt a new Declaration on Combating Terrorism on 25 March, reiterating and polit-

[108] Parker, G., 'Paris and Berlin raise the stakes over failure to ratify constitution', *Financial Times*, 13 May 2004, p. 2. By the end of 2004 9 member states had announced their intention to hold referendums in their countries.

[109] 'The ultra-liberal socialist constitution', *The Economist*, 18–24 Sep. 2004, p. 42.

[110] Centre for European Reform (CER), 'The CER guide to the EU's constitutional treaty' CER, London, URL <http://www.cer.org.uk/>.

[111] According to the treaty, the deadline for ratification is 1 Nov. 2006. Hungary, Lithuania and Slovenia have already completed ratification through their parliaments and Spain held a successful referendum on 20 Feb. 2005. Referendums will be held in the Czech Republic, Denmark, France, Ireland, Luxembourg, the Netherlands, Poland, Portugal and the UK. For the latest position on the ratification processs see URL <http://europa.eu.int/constitution/referendum_en.htm>. British public opinion has thus far been the most steadfastly opposed to the constitutional treaty. Joining the other mainstream French political parties in early Dec. 2004, the French Socialist Party voted in favour of endorsing the constitutional treaty. A similar pro-European shift has been observed in the new member states. 'Now that they have tasted the EU's attractions, central Europeans are much less likely than once seemed possible to revolt against the draft EU constitution'. 'Reaping the European Union harvest', *The Economist*, 8–14 Jan. 2005, p. 29.

ically reinforcing existing commitments and also introducing a new mutual pledge of 'solidarity' in the event of terrorist attacks, a pledge which was originally contained in the constitutional treaty.[112] The position of an EU counter-terrorism coordinator was established. In December the Council further updated the EU Plan of Action to Combat Terrorism agreed in June 2004.[113]

After two successful ESDP military crisis management operations, and the launching of police missions in Bosnia and Herzegovina and the FYROM, the EU started its largest military mission in Bosnia and Herzegovina in December 2004 following the NATO SFOR.[114] The EU-led Operation ALTHEA aims to deter hostilities and to support the peace-building process and existing EU civilian activities.[115] It is supported by NATO assets and advice under the 'Berlin Plus' arrangements.[116] Its main operational task, and challenge, is to strongly link the military and civilian components of the EU's activities in the field. In the civilian field, the EU launched the Rule of Law Mission EUJUST-THEMIS in Georgia on 16 July 2004 and planned to launch a police mission in Kinshasa, Democratic Republic of the Congo, in early 2005.[117]

With regard to EU–NATO cooperation, conceptual work on the EU's civilian–military planning cell and possible elements of the NATO liaison team at the EU Military Staff, as agreed at the end of 2003, was not completed in 2004. The problem of bridging the gap between the civilian and military dimensions of the ESDP persists, making it difficult to achieve an integrated and comprehensive approach to planning and implementing EU interventions.[118]

Following the endorsement in June 2004 of an Action Plan for the Civilian Aspects of the ESDP, the establishment of appropriate operational planning and mission-support capabilities in the Council Secretariat was urged to give the EU the ability to plan and conduct several civilian crisis management mis-

[112] Council of the European Union, 'European Council Conclusions: Declaration on Combating Terrorism', European Council, Brussels, 25 Mar. 2004 URL <http://ue.eu.int/cms3_fo/showPage.asp?id=632&lang=EN&mode=g>. The solidarity clause is contained in Article I.43 of the constitutional treaty (amplified by Article III.329).

[113] Council of the European Union, 'EU Plan of Action to Combat Terrorism: Update', Brussels, 14 Dec 2004. For a review of achievements in 2004 and prospects for 2005 see Council of the European Union, 'Brief Note on counter-terrorism', Brussels, 16 Dec. 2004. Both documents are available at URL <http://ue.eu.int/cms3_fo/showPage.asp?id=631&lang=EN&mode=g>.

[114] The military crisis management operations were Concordia in the Former Yugoslav Republic of Macedonia and Artemis in the Democratic Republic of the Congo, both of which ended in 2003.

[115] Council of the European, Council Decision on the launching of the European Union military operation in Bosnia and Herzegovina, document1402/04, Brussels, 23 Nov. 2004.

[116] While the EU has taken over responsibility for peacekeeping operations, NATO maintains a headquarters in Sarajevo to assist Bosnia and Herzegovina with defence reform. It also carries out some operational tasks in coordination with the EU, including counter-terrorism and assistance with apprehending persons indicted for war crimes.

[117] Other EU non-military operations include the police missions in Bosnia and Herzegovina (EUPM) and the Former Yugoslav Republic of Macedonia (EUPOL Proxima)

[118] Centre for the Study of Global Governance, *A Human Security Doctrine for Europe: The Barcelona Report of the Study Group on Europe's Security Capabilities*, Presented to EU High Representative for Common Foreign and Security Policy Javier Solana, Barcelona, 15 Sep 2004 (Centre for the Study of Global Governance: London School of Economics, 2004), URL <http://www.lse.ac.uk/Depts/global/StudyGroup/StudyGroup.htm>.

sions at once. A Civilian Capabilities Commitment Conference and a Military Capabilities Commitment Conference were held in November 2004 with the aim of identifying capabilities in the 10 new member states. The EU plans to develop a 2008 Civilian Headline Goal allowing it to further define and build its civilian capabilities. An important initiative was taken by five EU states to establish a European Gendarmerie Force with paramilitary capabilities suitable for more demanding scenarios and able to deploy rapidly to maintain public security and public order.[119]

Military capabilities

The EU continues to face the basic challenge of overcoming national particularities and policy differences in order to achieve more effective and more substantial defence expenditure, to remedy capability shortfalls and to develop armaments cooperation. In implementing the military aspects of the 2003 ESS, the EU focused in 2004 on three major issues: the Headline Goal 2010, the EDA and EU battle groups. The last two innovations were developed in the draft constitutional treaty but are being put into effect before treaty ratification.

The Headline Goal 2010, adopted on 14 June 2004, provides for a 'qualitative' strengthening of crisis management and defence capabilities through interoperability, including civilian and civil–military aspects, deployability and sustainability to enable EU member states by 2010 to respond with 'rapid and decisive action' across the expanded spectrum of crisis management operations—the Petersberg tasks,[120] as well as 'joint disarmament operations', support for third countries in combating terrorism and security sector reform—as envisaged by the ESS.[121] To evaluate progress, the Headline Goal sets 'milestones' and standards for the period up to 2010 that will require changes and adaptations in various fields of the 2001 European Capability Action Plan and the EDA. However, the Headline Goal 2010 does not mark a breakthrough in delivering capabilities and still fails to clarify some of the outstanding ambiguities of its predecessor, the 1999 Helsinki Headline Goal.[122]

The *European Defence Agency* was formally set up in July 2004 with the aim of improving European defence capabilities, encouraging and bringing about more efficient management of multinational arms cooperation, developing and integrating Europe's defence markets, and coordinating R&D. The agency will not purchase equipment or manage procurement programmes. Instead, it is intended to act as both a 'conscience' and a 'catalyst' for resolv-

[119] Ministerial Declaration, Civilian Capability Commitment Conference, Brussels, 22 Nov. 2004. An embryonic capability for these purposes was established at the end of 2004. The European Gendarmerie Force comprises units from France, Italy, the Netherlands, Portugal and Spain.

[120] The Petersberg tasks were agreed in 1992 to strengthen the operational role of the WEU. They were later incorporated in the 1997 Treaty of Amsterdam. They include humanitarian intervention and evacuation operations, peacekeeping and crisis management—including peace making.

[121] Council of the European Union, Headline Goal 2010, ESDP Presidency Conclusions, document 10547/04, Annex 1, Brussels, 15 June 2004.

[122] Quille, G., 'Implementing the defence aspects of the European Security Strategy: the Headline Goal 2010', *European Security Review* no. 23 (July 2004), pp. 5–7.

ing capability shortfall problems.[123] Its establishment was marked by controversies about such issues as the purpose of the EDA, its relation to other stakeholders such as the Organization for Joint Armament Cooperation (Organisation Conjoint de Cooperation en matiere d'Armement, OCCAR), how to spend its €20 million budget and how far to intervene in the procurement strategies of member states. The British and French visions of the EDA's long-term role clash. France tends to see the EDA as an engine to create a European defence manufacturing base, supported by more spending on R&D and a stronger 'buy European' culture. The UK puts more stress on more modest projects geared directly to improving operational capabilities. Another challenge is the extent to which the leading industrial countries will be willing to share advanced and classified technologies with other members. The EDA is to become fully operational in 2005.[124]

The concept of *battle groups*, as part of the EU's rapid response capacity, took shape in 2003–2004. These are not meant to replace the 60 000-strong European Rapid Reaction Force based on the 1999 Headline Goal, but the latter nonetheless seems to have been quietly shelved. The new units demonstrate a major reassessment of the demands of the new threats and crisis situations, and a more realistic effort to improve EU military capabilities.[125] The smaller, highly mobile and flexible battle groups will be employable across the full range of the Petersberg tasks and those identified in the ESS, especially in 'tasks of combat forces in crisis management' (i.e., the high end of the scale).[126] Their missions would be 'appropriate for, but not limited to, use in failed or failing states'.[127] France and the UK, which jointly initiated the idea of battle groups, see them as a forerunner to the 'structured cooperation' in defence matters foreseen in the constitutional treaty.[128] In contrast to the

[123] EU Military Capability Commitment Conference, Declaration on European Military Capabilities, Brussels, 22 Nov. 2004.

[124] For more on the EDA, including its work programme for 2005, see 'Agency in the field of defence capabilities development, research, acquisition and armaments', URL <http://ue.eu.int/cms3_fo/showPage.asp?id=277&lang=EN&mode=g>.

[125] Despite being declared 'operational' in 2003, the European Rapid Reaction Force is still plagued by a lack of capabilities regarding strategic airlift, communications and logistics. The 1500-strong battle groups are to be capable of being deployed within 5 days, sustainable for 30 days (extendable to 120 days), and may operate under a UN mandate. For the period 2005–2007 (when it will achieve initial operational capability) the EU is to be able to undertake at least 1 battle group-sized rapid response operation. In its full operational capability period from 2007, the EU is to be able to carry out 2 concurrent single battle group-sized rapid response operations. By Nov. 2004, member states had agreed to commit forces to 13 battle groups. EU Military Capability Commitment Conference (note 123).

[126] The critical issue remains long-range transport. In 2003 the EU adopted the 'Global approach on deployability' to improve strategic transport in support of EU-led operations, and battle groups in particular.

[127] Dempsey, J. and Blitz, J., 'France and Britain to create joint battle groups', *Financial Times*, 10 Feb. 2004, p. 1.

[128] Articles I-41(6) and III-312 of the constitutional treaty envisage the establishment of *permanent structured cooperation* for the EU members 'whose military capabilities fulfil higher criteria and which have made more binding commitments to one another with a view to the most demanding tasks' under the protocol on permanent structured cooperation. The criteria, linked to the concept of battle groups, the EDA and the Headline Goal 2010, involve high operational readiness, participation in the development of major joint or European equipment programmes and increased cooperation to meet agreed objectives concerning 'the level of investment expenditure on defence equipment'. For detailed analysis see Missi-

initial concept set out by the two countries, multinationality was later accepted as desirable in order to allow involvement by smaller nations with niche capabilities such as medical assistance or water purification. Member states also agreed that the battle groups would be 'complementary and mutually reinforcing' or compatible with the NATO Response Force.

V. The CIS countries: peaceful revolutions and stability

Until 2003, the 12 former Soviet states that make up the membership of the CIS shared a common history.[129] People there continued to live under different degrees of authoritarian rule, or at best in very inchoate democracies, more than a decade after the break-up of the Soviet Union. The year 2004 brought the most significant break to date in this pattern, with the peaceful revolutions in Georgia and Ukraine demonstrating that democratization, or at least the desire for it, had gained ground within the former Soviet area. The systemic divide was widened by the fact that, in both countries, the revolutions were linked with elections and reflected the disenchantment of a large part of the population with electoral fraud. The 'post-Soviet' political *uravnilovka* ('levelling') of the area has thus come to an end. In 2004 developments in another post-Soviet state, communist-governed Moldova, indicated a growing impatience with Russia's continued support for secessionists in the Trans-Dniester region and a reorientation to the West. A new dividing line is now superimposed on the old divides that were based on the distance from the central actor of the region, Russia, and the presence or absence of unresolved conflicts, which invariably involved Russia to some degree. The new line not only separates leaders pursuing democratic experiments from those who are not, but also those who have no personal political roots in the Soviet Union from those who have.[130] The old and new dividing lines are not identical, and the new one between incipient democratic and authoritarian regimes is arguably becoming the more significant.

Nothing better illustrates the widespread constraints on democracy in the CIS countries than the fact that thus far no election has been held in the region that could be assessed by the international community as free and fair. The elections assessed least critically were those that legalized change brought about by popular revolution—the Georgian extraordinary presidential elections of 4 January 2004 and the rerun of the second round of the Ukrainian presidential elections on 26 December 2004.[131] In contrast, a referendum in

roli, A., 'Mind the steps: the constitutional treaty and beyond', Gnesotto, N. (ed), *EU Security and Defence Policy: the First Five Years, 1999–2004* (EU Institute for Security Studies: Paris, 2004), pp. 149–153.

[129] For the members of the CIS see the glossary in this volume.

[130] President of Belarus Aleksandr Lukashenko played no political role in the Soviet times but is not among those who pursue a democratic path for his country. The same points apply to President of Azerbaijan Ilham Aliyev and, until his resignation in early 2005, President of Kyrgyzstan Askar Akayev.

[131] 'In contrast to the 2 November 2003 parliamentary elections that were characterized by systematic and widespread fraud, the authorities generally displayed the collective political will to conduct a more genuine democratic election process'. OSCE, Office for Democratic Institutions and Human Rights

Belarus and parliamentary elections in Uzbekistan were met with a more critical international response.[132]

Russia

The Russian Federation continued to face similar security challenges in 2004 to those of previous years, the most direct being what it regards as terrorist activity on its own territory. Such activity is not confined to Chechnya but has spread increasingly to the provinces bordering Chechnya, as well as to Moscow itself. The reaction of the Russian Government to terrorism as an aspect of the conflict in Chechnya is complex. Russia has been largely unsuccessful in solving the underlying conflict but also lacks a clear concept of what a 'solution' could entail.[133] In practice, the Russian authorities seem satisfied when there are no extensive hostilities between Russian military forces and insurgents. To marginalize the importance of the unresolved issues, the Russian authorities claim that Chechen-related violence has Islamic fundamentalism as its root cause rather than representing a regional insurgency. This approach also allows Moscow to portray the Chechen conflict as part of the global fight against terrorism. In order to reduce public dissatisfaction in the rest of the country, Russia has stopped sending conscripts to Chechnya. It has completed the transition of the 42nd Motorized Rifle Division to a contract service,[134] and the conscripts serving with Ministry of Interior troops will also be phased out by the end of 2005.[135] Certain terrorism-related events have meanwhile helped to spur a new wave of Russian administrative reform, including the more direct subordination of regional governors to the central

(ODIHR), Georgia: Extraordinary Presidential Election, 4 Jan. 2004, OSCE/ODIHR Election Observation Mission Report, p. 1, URL <http://www.osce.org/documents/html/pdftohtml/2183_en.pdf.html>. According to the Election Observation Mission, 'The conduct of the 26 December election process brought Ukraine substantially closer to meeting OSCE election commitments and Council of Europe and other European standards. . . . Campaign conditions were markedly more equal in contrast to previous polls.' International Election Observation Mission, Presidential Election (Repeated second round), Ukraine, 26 Dec. 2004, Statement of preliminary findings and conclusions, p. 1, URL <http://www.osce.org/documents/html/pdftohtml/4007_en.pdf.html>.

[132] In the case of Belarus, the Election Observation Mission declined to assess the referendum that lifted the constitutional limitation on a president serving more that two terms. OSCE, Office for Democratic Institutions and Human Rights (ODIHR), Republic of Belarus, Parliamentary Elections, 17 Oct. 2004, OSCE/ODIHR Election Observation Mission, Final Report, ODIHR.GAL/100/04, 9 Dec. 2004, p. 1. URL <http://www.osce.org/documents/html/pdftohtml/3951_en.pdf.html>. Parliamentary elections were held in Uzbekistan on 26 Dec. 2004, the same day as the repeated second round of the Ukrainian Presidential Elections. Fewer than 30 observers were able to monitor them. OSCE, ODIHR, Republic of Uzbekistan Parliamentary Elections, 26 December 2004, OSCE/ODIHR Limited Election Observation Mission report, URL, <http://www.osce.org/documents/html/pdftohtml/4355_en.pdf.html>: and Lewis, D. and Stroehlein, A., 'The inevitability of change in Uzbekistan', *Financial Times*, 21 Dec. 2004 p. 15.

[133] See chapter 2 in this volume. Attempts by Russia to 'insulate' the conflict are a source of its intractability.

[134] Ivanov, S. B., 'Security in the Middle East', Speech at the 41st Munich Conference on Security Policy, 12 Feb. 2005, URL <http://www.securityconference.de/konferenzen/rede.php?menu_2005=&menu_konferenzen&jahr= 2005&sprache=en&>.

[135] See The Kremlin, Press conference by President Vladimir Putin, Moscow, 23 Dec. 2004, p. 9. URL <http://www.ln.mid.ru/brp_4.nsf/e78a48070f128a7b43256999005bcbb3/4fb0f1f9c0d53683c3256f740024dec4?OpenDocument>.

authorities—developments that many outside observers regard, with some concern, as part of an ongoing centralization process.

Russia also perceives security challenges in a number of political developments in its immediate and wider neighbourhood, including the changes of political course in Georgia and Ukraine and a possible further enlargement of NATO. Its comments on these issues in 2004 took on an increasingly sharp tone, reminiscent of complaints in the early 1990s about European developments being 'directed against' or 'excluding' Russia.[136] Although Russia's tone on the EU and its enlargement has remained relatively soft, the implied return to a more zero-sum view of Russian and Western interests has sharpened the policy dilemma facing the EU in particular. Russia is an important source of energy and a key player both in the neighbourhood stabilization and the 'effective multilateralism' strategies now espoused by the EU. However, it manifestly does not meet EU standards on internal democracy, a fully functioning market economy or responsible external behaviour. At the same time, some EU members' particular awareness of the tactical and strategic advantages of partnership with Russia has led to a certain toning down of the critical elements of previously agreed EU positions, most notably on Chechnya. The dilemma for the EU is aggravated not only by a more confrontational Russian approach but also by shifts in the pattern of economic power and leverage. Although more than half its exports are directed to the enlarged EU, Russia is no longer financially dependent on EU cooperation. High oil prices have built up Russia's gold and currency reserves to a level exceeding the size of its state foreign debt and approaching $120 billion. Russia had a record trade surplus of $80 billion in 2004.[137] As a German analyst put it, 'Russia needs neither the USA nor the EU'.[138] There may be a difference, however, between needing something to survive and needing it in order to progress and maintain comparative advantages in the longer run.[139] Despite high oil prices on the world market, economic growth in Russia slowed in 2004 to approximately 5.5 per cent.[140]

Overall, the Russian Government believes that the Euro-Atlantic environment is changing increasingly to its disadvantage. It is concerned that the main Western institutions, NATO and the EU, are increasingly 'on the offensive', unifying the continent around norms, values and often policies about which the Russian Government is hesitant at best. Rather than challenging values and norms, it questions the policies. This is, understandably, more pronounced in

[136] Russia has made several complaints to this effect. It is sufficient to mention its comments concerning the 'anti-Russian' behaviour of Finland in late-2004 and the criticism addressed to Polish President Kwasniewski concerning his comment about 'A Russia without Ukraine is better than a Russia with Ukraine'. The Kremlin (note 135). See also appendix 1A.

[137] The Kremlin (note 135).

[138] Rahr, A., 'Zapad predpochitaet derzhat' Moskvu na rasstoyanii' [The West prefers to keep Russia at a distance], *Nezavisimaya gazeta*, 1 Mar. 2004, URL <http://www.ng.ru/printed/courier/2004-03-01/9west.html>.

[139] A number of failures have demonstrated this ranging from the failed EU-Russian summit on Ukraine and the failure of the 2 to agree on a common security area.

[140] 'GDP growth slows down to 5.5% in 2004', News from Russia, Pravda Online, 24 Feb. 2004, URL <http://newsfromrussia.com/main/2004/02/24/52455.html>.

the case of NATO, its 'partner adversary',[141] than the EU—although the debates about the four EU–Russian 'common spaces' have also demonstrated increasing Russian misgivings about the EU as another force for Western-style European 'unification'.[142]

Domestic political processes caused increasing concern in 2004 about Russia's record on human rights, curtailment of the freedom of the media, further centralization of state institutions and the subordination of those institutions to the executive branch. It is a reflection of the seriousness of these concerns as felt in the West that a prestigious non-governmental organization (NGO) downgraded Russia to 'not free', from its earlier 'partly free' status.[143] Poor Russian performance in these areas highlights its differences from the states in a process of democratic change referred to above, and risks encouraging those other regimes that share similar authoritarian goals and sometimes pursue them far more aggressively and brutally than Russia.

Georgia

Georgia completed the first phase of its transition between its 'rose revolution' of November 2003 and the presidential elections of January 2004, but the new administration, under the leadership of President Mikhail Saakashvili, still faces enormous tasks, including the reform of governance, security and the economy. It can at least count on increased external support and assistance, with the USA—both government organizations and NGOs—in the lead. The EU included the three states of the South Caucasus region for the first time as full and equal partners in its new neighbourhood policy in June 2004 and launched a new type of ESDP 'mission' in the form of the EUJUST-THEMIS team mandated to help build law and justice systems in Georgia.[144]

The new leadership of Georgia put territorial integrity at the forefront of its strategy: 'we must and will restore Georgia's full territorial integrity using peaceful means'.[145] The goal was understandable given the seriousness of the 'frozen' conflicts in Abkhazia and South Ossetia, which have effectively blocked central control of these territories for 15 years and 13 years, respectively, and have been factors for instability in Georgian–Russian relations and

[141] For a semi-official view see Kelin, A., Rossiya–NATO: K novomu etapu sotrudnichestva? [Russia–NATO: towards a new phase of cooperation?], *Mezhdunarodnaya zhizn'* no. 11/12 (2004), pp. 79–90.

[142] The 4 common spaces are economic co-operation; freedom, security and justice; external security; and research, education and culture. See URL <http://www.europa.eu.int/comm/external_relations/russia/intro/ip05_216.htm>.

[143] Freedom House, 'Russia downgraded to "not free"', Press Release, New York, 20 Dec. 2004, URL <http://www.freedomhouse.org/media/pressrel/122004.htm>.

[144] Council of the European Union, Joint Action 2004/523/CFSP, 28 June 2004. The European Union Mission in Georgia: EUJUST-THEMIS, *Official Journal of the European Union*, L 228 (28 June 2004), URL <http://europa.eu.int/eur-lex/pri/en/oj/dat/2004/l_228/l_22820040629en00210024.pdf>.

[145] Council on Foreign Relations, Transcript of the Russell Leffingwell Lecture, Mikhail Saakashvili, President, Republic of Georgia, New York, 26 Feb. 2004, p. 6, URL <http://www.cfr.org/pub6815/david_remnick_mikhail_saakashvili/the_russell_c_leffingwell_lecture_with_mikhail_saakashvili_php>.

for regional security generally.[146] It was also a calculated gamble to exploit the worldwide attention and sympathy, and the hopes of mustering a stronger domestic consensus, generated by the arrival of the Saakashvili regime. The Georgian leadership took a prudently graduated approach, starting with the more recent breakaway attempt by the province of Adzharia. Despite some signs of Russian interference, the first test was successful and Adzharia was firmly reintegrated into Georgia. A simple repetition of the model could not be expected to solve the different and much tougher cases of Abkhazia and South Ossetia—both adjacent to, and de facto controlled by, Russia—although the formula used in Adzharia of guaranteeing 'the highest possible degree of autonomy' is certainly relevant.[147] In the event, the first attempt by the Georgian authorities to solve the South Ossetia conflict by a similar combination of the threat of force and innovative use of diplomacy broke down, and the *status quo ante* had to be restored. A new ceasefire was agreed in November 2004, which still holds as of March 2005. The road to complete control by Georgia of its own territory is clearly a long one, and this fact must also complicate the execution of other governance- and security-related reforms in the country.

Ukraine

Ukraine's size and location have made it a state of strategic importance for Europe since it achieved independence. It has often been seen as a bridge between an enlarging community of European states and the CIS, primarily Russia. However, these visions did not lead to any particularly intensive engagement of Ukraine in European processes and institutions before 2004, partly because of the mismatch between the country's potential role and its internal conditions, and partly because of Ukrainian President Leonid Kuchma's convoluted strategy of trimming between Western aspirations and Eastern commitments. Domestic stability prevailed in Ukraine at the cost of certain authoritarian tendencies, regular violations of the rule of law,[148] regular violations of human rights,[149] high levels of corruption and slow economic development.[150] In 1999, the EU's leaders had identified Ukraine as 'a source

[146] For Russia's role in both conflicts see Lynch, D., *Engaging Eurasia's Separatist States: Unresolved Conflicts and De Facto States* (United States Institute of Peace: Washington, DC, 2004).

[147] International Crisis Group (ICG), *Saakashvili's Ajara success: Repeatable Elsewhere in Georgia?*, ICG Europe Briefing, no. 34 (ICG: Tbilisi/Brussels, 18 Aug. 2004), URL <http://www.icg.org/home/index.cfm?id=2907&l=1>.

[148] The OSCE International Election Observation Mission in its report on the Presidential Election of 31 Oct. 2004 noted that the election 'did not meet a considerable number of OSCE, Council of Europe and other European standards for democratic elections'. International Election Observation Mission, Presidential Election, Ukraine 31 Oct. 2004, Statement of preliminary findings and conclusions, p. 1, URL <http://www.osce.org/documents/html/pdftohtml/3771_en.pdf.html>.

[149] The Parliamentary Assembly of the Council of Europe has regularly criticized the human rights situation, with an emphasis on violations of the freedom of the press.

[150] The Transparency International Corruption Perception Index ranked Ukraine 122nd among 145 countries observed. This places Ukraine in the mid-range of CIS countries, with 5 ranked higher, 4 lower and 2 (Kazakhstan and Kyrgyzstan) at the same level. Transparency International, Corruption Perception Index 2004, URL <http://www.transparency.org/cpi/2004/cpi2004.en.html#cpi2004>.

of regional stability, despite its domestic difficulties and diversities'.[151] By 2002, the EU's CFSP High Representative was driven to remark that 'Ukraine is not playing by the rules but playing with the rules. We would like one day to embrace your country, but we have to know what kind of country you are'.[152] Awareness of the gap between the nation's potential and actual standing also had its consequences within Ukraine, including political apathy and disillusionment.

In 2004 it was made known that President Kuchma was not standing for re-election. In the run-up to the election for his successor, Kuchma made several moves that indicated his willingness to pay a heavy price in foreign policy terms in order to obtain Russian consent to a smooth handover of power to a successor nominated by him. Pro-Western Defence Minister Yevgeniy Marchuk was dismissed and the strategic goal of gaining full membership of the EU and NATO was removed from Ukraine's new defence doctrine, to be replaced by language on 'Euro-Atlantic integration'.

Since its independence, Ukraine has been a state with strong presidential powers—'a presidential republic'.[153] The prospect of top–down change thus attracted growing attention not just from Ukraine's own people but in the world at large. The first two rounds of the presidential election held in October and November 2004 were widely regarded as fraudulent and were followed by mass demonstrations in the Ukrainian capital city, Kyiv. Following appeals by the losing candidate and the involvement of several figures from abroad,[154] Ukraine's Supreme Court on 3 December instructed the Central Election Committee to organize a re-run of the second round. This took place, under strengthened international monitoring, on 26 December 2004 and ended with the victory of the opposition candidate, Viktor Yushchenko. Both in the November round, when Viktor Yanukovich was declared the winner, and in Yushchenko's victory on 26 December, the vote was closely balanced and divided along regional lines. Eastern and south-eastern Ukraine, where many of the population are Russian-speaking, voted for Yanukovich—echoing the clear support given to him by President Putin. Western Ukraine and the north of the country voted overwhelmingly for the Western-oriented Yushchenko. Although fears expressed in the heat of the crisis about the imminent break-up of Ukraine were not realized, these results underline that the creation of a new unity within the country is an urgent task for the new president.

[151] Council of the European Union, 'European Council Conclusions: Declaration on the Common Strategy on Ukraine', European Council document 99/259, Helsinki, 11 Dec. 1999.

[152] Interfax, 16 Oct. 2002. Quoted in Kuzio, T., *EU and Ukraine: a Turning Point in 2004?*, European Union Institute for Security Studies (EU ISS) Occasional Papers, no. 47 (EU ISS: Paris, Nov. 2003), p. 11.

[153] International Election Observation Mission (note 148), p. 3.

[154] EU High Representative for the CFSP Javier Solana, President of Poland Aleksandr Kwasniewski and President of Lithuania Valdas Adamkus played particularly active roles. In contrast with the 'rose revolution' in Georgia in 2003, it was the EU that took a leading role in influencing events outside Ukraine.

Western and pro-Western leaders have welcomed the change in Ukraine.[155] Having sided with Yanukovich in the election campaign, Russia initially tried to belittle the importance of the change and to play down its own role in opposing it. However, observers in Russia and abroad have underlined the seriousness of President Putin's motives for trying to ensure Yanukovich's installation and the consequences for Russia of his failure. According to one commentator, Putin 'tried to show the West that Russia still has all the instruments to defend its legitimate sphere of influence'.[156] In the event, the outcome could be seen not only 'as an anti-constitutional turnover but also as a large-scale geopolitical special operation of revolutionary regime change in a CIS country allied with Russia. It can be seen as the most serious crisis in Russia's relations with the west in recent years'.[157] Western sources have largely refrained from triumphalist interpretations and have focused instead on the pro-democracy aspects of the change and Ukraine's continuing challenges. A certain note of caution has also been dictated by uncertainty about how much the Western institutions can actually offer 'the new Ukraine' and how quickly. However, at least one line of analysis interprets events in Ukraine as part of a wider pattern.

> The operation—engineering democracy through the ballot box and civil disobedience—is now so slick that the methods have matured into a template for winning other people's elections . . . the campaign is an American creation, a sophisticated and brilliantly conceived exercise in Western branding and mass marketing that, in four countries in four years, has been used to try to salvage rigged elections and topple unsavoury regimes.[158]

While Ukraine is by no means immune from future instability and potential violence, there are some positive lessons to be drawn from the transformation. It is important to note that the authorities in Ukraine refused to use force against the demonstrators and also resisted the use of force by others.[159] Other actors, including the Russian leadership, reacted pragmatically and the Russian Government has—at least for the time being—shown a willingness to establish working relations with the newly elected Ukrainian President.[160] In

[155] Solana, J., 'Yushchenko offers a new opportunity for the EU', *International Herald Tribune*, 6 Jan. 2005, p. 6; and Saakashvili, M., 'Europe's third wave of liberation', *Financial Times*, 20 Dec. 2004, p. 15.

[156] Peel, Q., 'Putin is a victim of his own errors', *Financial Times*, 16 Dec. 2004, p. 17.

[157] Nikonov, V., 'Strategiya Putina' [Putin's strategy], *Rossiyskaya gazeta*, 22 Dec. 2004, URL <http://www.rg.ru/2004/12/22/putin-strategia.html>.

[158] Traynor, I., 'US campaign behind the turmoil in Kiev', *The Guardian*, 26 Nov. 2004, URL <http://www.guardian.co.uk/international/story/0,1360080,00.html>. The article mentions Belarus, the former Yugoslavia, Georgia and Ukraine as other countries where such attempts have been made, successfully in 3 out of 4 cases.

[159] 'This is Kuchma's one big positive contribution'. Wagstyl, S., Freeland, C. and Warner, T., 'Ukraine president spurned Yanukovich pressure to use troops to quell protesters', *Financial Times*, 14 Dec. 2004, p. 2.

[160] The Ukrainian President visited Moscow immediately after his inauguration and then visited a number of European institutions.

the first major act of post-election Ukrainian politics the losing party contributed to a demonstration of national unity.[161]

Ukraine has meanwhile begun a major realignment of its political relations. The role played by EU member states and other EU representatives in seeking a peaceful resolution to the weeks of crisis inevitably brought the question of Ukraine's relations with the EU, which thus far have failed to satisfy Kyiv's aspirations, to the forefront. At the same time, Yushchenko has shown a realistic understanding that Ukraine's road to full EU membership, even following the 'orange revolution', will be long. A serious investigation by the Kyiv authorities into what reaching EU standards and norms would actually entail is bound to have a sobering effect. However, the EU, not least because of its new members' views, will find it much harder to ignore Ukraine or to judge relations with Ukraine only through their effect on EU relations with Moscow. Yushchenko has comparatively played down the importance and urgency of changing Ukraine's relationship with NATO.

In December 2004, when the pre-election Ukrainian establishment realized that power might shift to the new forces supporting Yushchenko, constitutional changes were proposed to weaken presidential power and increase the role of parliament and the government. Whatever their motives, these changes will have a lasting effect in reducing the danger of an over-concentration of power in the hands of the president. Experience suggests that such balanced parliamentary democracies carry less risk of becoming authoritarian. This could thus prove to be one of the more important and lasting consequences of the 'orange revolution', as well as an example for other CIS countries.

The latter have, naturally, followed the changes taking place in Ukraine with great interest. Most authoritarian leaders in the CIS have been concerned that similar processes may take place in their countries. In some cases, foreign NGOs have been the target of 'preventive measures' and had to close their offices. In other cases, opposition parties have been banned on the grounds of 'political extremism'.[162] It remains to be seen whether these measures will stave off political change or sharpen the internal and external tensions that will eventually precipitate it—a question that may also apply to Russia.

VI. Conclusions

In recent years, the Euro-Atlantic security agenda has been dominated by splits between states in the western part of the Euro-Atlantic area. Although the problems that have heightened these tensions since September 2001 have not been resolved, some major underlying trends are now bringing about cooperation between the players. The USA and the EU may differ on the urgency of seeking political changes in select parts of the world and on the admissible means, with the USA placing greater faith in military means and in

[161] The new Ukrainian Government under Prime Minister Yulia Tymoshenko was unanimously approved by all parties in the national parliament (Verkhovna Rada). Warner, T., 'Tymoshenko wins unanimous vote as Ukrainian PM', *Financial Times*, 5–6 Feb. 2005, p. 4.

[162] Karajanov, Z., 'Kazakh leadership fears upheaval', *Times of Central Asia*, 13 Jan. 2005, p. 5.

forced transformations generally. However, both the USA and EU member states recognize that partnership between them is a precondition for their effective contribution to global stability and the spread of democracy—and indeed for their own safety in certain dimensions, such as non-proliferation and combating transnational terrorism. The deep-seated and doctrinal nature of transatlantic differences notwithstanding, pragmatic cooperation between the EU and the USA may return to something like 'default' status in the years to come.

At the same time, a new divide seems to be emerging along the eastern boundaries of Europe. The leaderships of a number of countries outside the present bounds of the EU and NATO enlargement processes are increasingly resentful of the spread of democracy and regard it as a challenge to the long-term survival of their regimes. This does not translate into a direct threat to European security of the kind familiar from the cold war. However, there is a risk that hampering democracy and depriving peoples of the prospect of prosperity will make internal dynamics more unstable and eventual changes more violent—with consequences that will spread at least temporarily beyond the frontiers of the states concerned. The risk to regional security, in this scenario, would come not from the traditional regimes' strength but from their underlying weakness, and not from the likelihood of their explosion so much as their implosion.

Russia is an important case in point, both externally and domestically. The enlargement processes and neighbourhood schemes, potentially reinforcing each other, are restricting Russia's room for manoeuvre and forcing the Putin Administration into a painful reassessment of its former *modus vivendi* with the West. It increasingly seems to regard these developments, paired with changes outside its control in the CIS region, as a threat to Russian vital interests and to Russia itself. The paradox, however, is that the longer-term effect of Western 'encroachment' can only be to bring other CIS countries gradually closer to Russia's own relatively more advanced level of democratization, the deficiencies of its model notwithstanding. A Russia that proceeds with reform—albeit for its own reasons—could expect to remain 'first among equals' in this situation, both in Western eyes and within its own region. A backsliding and increasingly autocratic Russia would not. In a further paradox, therefore, President Putin's centralization drive may soon give rise in Russia's provinces to fears *for* the government rather than fears *of* it.

Turkey, another powerful actor-in-the-making, is set to embark on a long journey of EU accession that may help further reduce the number of potentially violent conflicts in Europe. However, it also poses a challenge by bringing 'EU Europe' closer to the volatile and unstable Middle East.

Appendix 1A. The Organization for Security and Co-operation in Europe: constant adaptation but enduring problems

PÁL DUNAY

I. Introduction

Despite landmark political changes that have affected both its environment and its relevance, the Organization for Security and Co-operation in Europe (OSCE), like its predecessor the Conference on Security and Co-operation in Europe (CSCE), has proved to be a highly adaptable institution.[1] The current drive for reform, launched as an analytical debate,[2] taken up by some participating states,[3] and most recently also advocated by the organization proper,[4] has been made urgent by a more recent decline in the importance and a gradual marginalization of the OSCE. The enlargements of the European Union (EU) and the North Atlantic Treaty Organization (NATO) have been a major contributory factor to this marginalization.[5] Of the five key features that used to distinguish the CSCE/OSCE—comprehensive participation from the Euro-Atlantic states, legitimacy when addressing domestic issues, a focus on the whole conflict cycle, a home for otherwise isolated nations, and a relatively weak and non-constraining institutional structure—none any longer provides a unique advantage in the European context. Although the OSCE is still the only Euro-Atlantic institution with comprehensive participation, the EU and NATO have made major efforts to create partnership networks and eliminate sharp contrasts between their members and other states. This has offered a hedge against isolation for those non-NATO and non-EU members that want it. These same organizations have extended their role in the domestic dimensions of security, partly because the

[1] Several books and studies provide an assessment of the OSCE. The *OSCE Yearbook*, published since 1995 by the Institute for Peace Research and Security Policy, Hamburg; and the *Helsinki Monitor* are the best sources. Two monographs give insightful overviews of different aspects of OSCE activity: Ghébali, V.-Y., *L'OSCE dans l'Europe post-communiste 1990–1996: Vers une identité paneuropéenne de sécurité* [The OSCE in post-Communist Europe 1990–1996: towards a pan-European security identity] (Bruylant: Brussels, 1996); and Lachowski, Z., *Confidence- and Security-Building Measures in the New Europe*, SIPRI Research Report no. 18 (Oxford University Press: Oxford, 2004).

[2] Such expert opinions have appeared in the *OSCE Yearbook* since 1997. See in particular Kubis, J., 'The OSCE today and tomorrow', and Matveev, A., 'The OSCE identity crisis', *OSCE Yearbook 1999*, Institut für Friedensforschung und Sicherheitspolitik an der Universität Hamburg (Nomos Verlag: Baden-Baden, 2000), pp. 31–39 and 59–78, respectively; and Everts, D. W., 'The future of the OSCE', Rotfeld, A. D., 'Does the OSCE have a future', and Boden, D., 'Whither the OSCE?', *OSCE Yearbook 2003*, pp. 23–30, 31–42 and 43–49, respectively.

[3] The Russian Federation played a prominent role in this respect. For some of its earlier reform proposals see Dunay, P. and Lachowski, Z., 'Euro-Atlantic organizations and relationships', *SIPRI Yearbook 2004: Armaments, Disarmament and International Security* (Oxford University Press: Oxford, 2004), pp. 54–58.

[4] A reform of the OSCE management structure has been under way for the past 3 years.

[5] If applicant countries are included, more than half of the OSCE participating states are committed to Europe's most important integration frameworks.

difference between domestic and international aspects of security has become increasingly blurred, and have also been actively engaged in addressing different phases of conflict. The OSCE's relatively weak institutional structure has been based on a rotating Chairmanship since 1991—following the adoption of the supplementary document to the 1990 Charter of Paris for a New Europe.[6] Permanent elements were added later, to the point where it is possible to speak of a proliferation of institutions,[7] but the OSCE's lack of a strong permanent political executive has continued to limit its continuity and visibility. The need to address these problems is increasingly recognized by the OSCE.

II. OSCE reform proposals in 2004

When the OSCE addresses certain security issues, it often faces either a situation in which the issues are already on the agenda of more powerful institutions—to which OSCE participating states attribute more importance—and the OSCE 'loses out', or the issue identified by the OSCE increases in importance and the topic 'gravitates' to the agenda of other, more powerful institutions. This pattern occurs in the international arena but also has domestic roots. Political establishments, when they have a choice because of parallel competences, regularly choose to work through the most powerful institutions. Powerful institutions may also have stronger advocates in national administrations, which may contribute to such a gravitation effect.

Political demands for reform, notably from the states formed from the territory of the Soviet Union, were formulated on three occasions in 2004. In July, Armenia, Belarus, Kazakhstan, Kyrgyzstan, Moldova, Russia, Tajikistan, Ukraine and Uzbekistan—an unexpectedly large caucus—adopted a harshly critical position on the OSCE.[8] They started out from the imbalance between the organization's three original dimensions (security, economic and human) and concluded that priorities had shifted in favour of the OSCE's 'peculiar interpretation' of the human dimension,[9] with a special emphasis on monitoring human rights and building democratic institutions in the areas of the Commonwealth of Independent States (CIS) and the former Yugoslavia. The caucus argued that this imbalance: (*a*) upsets the relationship between the three dimensions; (*b*) has intensified the attention paid to some countries

[6] The 1990 Charter of Paris for a New Europe; and Supplementary document to give effect to certain provisions contained in the Charter of Paris for a new Europe, both available at URL <http://www.osce.org/docs/English/1990-1999/summits/paris90e.htm>. See also the glossary in this volume.

[7] The following main institutions have been added to the OSCE structure since 1992: a Secretary General, a High Commissioner on National Minorities, the Office for Democratic Institutions and Human Rights, a Representative on Freedom of the Media and a Special Representative in Combating Trafficking in Human Beings. There is reason to conclude that the institutions established earlier have had a more noticeable effect on the CSCE/OSCE than those established more recently.

[8] Statement by CIS Member Countries on the State of Affairs in the OSCE, Press Release, Moscow, 3 July 2004, Unofficial translation, 9 July 2004, URL <http://www.great-britain.mid.ru/pr_rel/pres16-04.htm>. According to one observer, the declaration drafted by Russia did not represent the views of all the CIS countries. Moldova attached a reservation calling on the OSCE to do more to mediate conflicts. Some signatories reportedly signed 'out of solidarity' and others assured OSCE representatives that they were trying to be constructive. Barry, R. L., 'The OSCE at a turning point', Basic Notes, Occasional Papers on International Policy, 7 Sep. 2004, URL <http://www.basicint.org/pubs/Notes/2004OSCETurningPoint.htm>.

[9] Lavrov, S., 'Reform will enhance the OSCE's relevance', *Financial Times*, 29 Nov. 2004, p. 13.

while ignoring the problems of others—thereby creating double standards;[10] and (*c*) compromises some fundamental principles of the 1975 Helsinki Final Act—notably non-intervention in internal affairs and respect for the sovereignty of states.[11]

Since the end of the cold war, only rare references have been made in the OSCE context to non-interference. Most participating states have recognized the ability of the OSCE to go further into internal affairs, beyond the boundaries of domestic jurisdiction, as one of its comparative advantages in international politics. It has recently been argued that the non-intervention principle no longer applies to the OSCE, although this is not a view shared by most participating states.[12]

In an effort to address criticisms, Bulgarian Foreign Minister Solomon Passy, the OSCE Chairman-in-Office for 2004, set out his own proposals for a transformation of the OSCE. He outlined a number of elements, including 'bringing it closer to the people and our constituencies', allocating more resources to activities in Central Asia and the Caucasus, and relocating some OSCE meetings to the area of the former Soviet Union.[13] The Chairman-in-Office sent a letter to this effect to the 54 foreign ministers of the OSCE participating states.[14]

In the so-called Astana Document of September 2004,[15] eight CIS member states went further by presenting proposals amounting to a change of the whole OSCE agenda. They called for more attention to be paid to the politico-military aspects of security and for a shift in the focus of the human dimension to address 'freedom of movement and contacts between people, improving the conditions for tourism, expanding ties in the area of education and science, and exchanging and disseminating cultural values between all the participating states'. The CIS group also proposed that the OSCE partners should move away from the practice of restricting OSCE field activities to monitoring the political situation in other countries.

One motive for seeking to shift the focus of the human dimension in this way can be readily understood. Many CIS countries have doubtful democratic credentials and would like to have less attention paid to their record on human rights and elections. Belarus, Kazakhstan, Kyrgyzstan, Ukraine and Uzbekistan each had impending elections or referendums in the months following the Astana appeal. Nonetheless, in seeking to focus more implicitly on the consequences of EU enlargement for 'new neighbours', the CIS countries identified a real issue. The common visa policy of an enlarged EU limits the free movement of citizens from other visa-obligated countries.

[10] I.e., too much attention on the former Soviet Union and the former Yugoslavia and too little attention on West European states with unresolved domestic security challenges such as Spain and the Basque region, France and Corsica, and the United Kingdom and Northern Ireland.

[11] The 1975 Helsinki Final Act. See the glossary in this volume and URL <http://www.osce.org/docs/english/summite.htm>.

[12] Bloed, A., 'CIS presidents attack the functioning of the OSCE', *Helsinki Monitor,* vol. 15, no 3, (2004), p. 220.

[13] Speech by Dr Solomon Passy, OSCE Chairman-in-Office, at the 13th Annual Session of the OSCE Parliamentary Assembly, CIO.GAL/63/04, 5 July 2004, Edinburgh, pp. 3–4, URL <http://www.osce.org/cio/bulgaria/documents/>.

[14] The letter, dated 22 July 2004, was not published but is known to have repeated the ideas already outlined by the Chairman-in-Office to the OSCE Parliamentary Assembly in July 2004. It refers in vague terms to an enhanced role for both the Secretary General and the Chairman-in-Office. The OSCE briefly reported on the letter on 9 Aug. 2004. OSCE, 'OSCE chairman believes time ripe for transforming organization to meet changed political realities', Press Release, 9 Aug. 2004, URL <http://www.osce.org/news/show_news.php?id=4277>.

[15] Ministry of Foreign Affairs of the Russian Federation, Appeal of the CIS Member States to the OSCE Partners, Astana, 15 Sep. 2004, Information and Press Department, URL <http://www.ln.mid.ru/brp_4nsf/>. The 8 states were Armenia, Belarus, Kazakhstan, Kyrgyzstan, Russia, Tajikistan, Ukraine and Uzbekistan.

However, this is an issue that the OSCE, as an all-Europe institution, should address *in addition to*, not instead of, other aspects of the human dimension.

In his response to the Astana appeal, the OSCE Chairman-in-Office informed the 12 heads of state of his support for a number of their proposals, such as convening the OSCE Economic Forum in Central Asia, holding the Human Dimension Implementation Meeting in one of the countries of the Caucasus and, in the light of discontinued or reduced activities in the Western Balkans, allocating increased budgetary resources to activities and projects in Central Asia and the Caucasus.[16]

A heated exchange of views took place between Russia and a number of participating states at the Sofia OSCE Ministerial Council of 6–7 December 2004. Russia reiterated its position concerning 'imbalances and double standards' that were eroding the comparative advantages of the OSCE, and criticized the OSCE's election-related activity in particular.[17] Clearly keen to avoid cases in which monitors' reports affected the perceived legitimacy of elections and the control of the authorities who held them, Russia and its partners called for the OSCE's electoral work to concentrate on broad normative issues rather than concrete cases.[18]

The West was united in responding that the aim of achieving a better balance between the three dimensions 'can only mean that more efforts should be put into each of them'.[19] US Secretary of State Colin Powell expressed the view that the USA is 'open to increasing the OSCE's activities to promote security and economic development, but not at the expense of the OSCE's core democracy and human rights work'.[20] The OSCE's prime focus on the humanitarian dimension notwithstanding, the facts do not support the view that the organization has neglected the other two dimensions—as witnessed by its continuing efforts to resolve 'frozen' conflicts such as those in Georgia and Moldova, and Armenia and Azerbaijan; and initiatives on anti-terrorism and counter-proliferation. The OSCE's police reform and training programme in Kyrgyzstan, alongside parallel EU efforts, is another initiative in the field of politico-military security. Moreover, the OSCE, with its comprehensive concept of security and limited resources, must at any given time look for the most pressing European security problems. When human rights and the efficiency of common efforts against crime, terrorism, smuggling and corruption are suffering in some states and regions from shortcomings related to a democratic deficit, the OSCE can hardly overlook this—OSCE participating states have subscribed steadily to increasing democracy since the adoption of the Charter of Paris.

With regard to alleged double standards, Russia's contention that the OSCE has neglected some similar phenomena in countries further to the west fails to take

[16] Address by Solomon Passy, Chairman-in-Office of the OSCE and Minister of Foreign Affairs of the Republic of Bulgaria, to the CIS Summit, Astana,15 Sep. 2004, p. 2.

[17] Ministry of Foreign Affairs of the Russian Federation, Statement by Russian Minister of Foreign Affairs Sergey Lavrov at the 12th Meeting of the OSCE Ministerial Council, Sofia, 7 Dec. 2004, URL <http://www.1n.mid.ru/brp_4.nsf>.

[18] Statement by the Delegation of the Russian Federation, OSCE Ministerial Council, Sofia, 2004, OSCE document MC(12)JOUR/2, Annex 9, 7 Dec. 2004, reproduced in 2nd Day of the Twelfth Meeting of the Ministerial Council, 3rd Plenary session (closed), available at URL <http://www.osce.org/docs/english/mincone.htm>.

[19] Statement by the European Union, OSCE Ministerial Council, Sofia, 2004, OSCE document MC(12)JOUR/2, Annex 5, 7 Dec. 2004, reproduced in 2nd Day of the Twelfth Meeting of the Ministerial Council, 3rd Plenary session (closed), available at URL <http://www.osce.org/docs/english/mincone.htm>.

[20] OSCE and US Department of State, Remarks by Secretary of State Colin L. Powell to the Ministerial Meeting of the Organization for Security and Cooperation in Europe, Office of the Spokesman, Sofia, OSCE document MC.DEL/52/04, 7 Dec. 2004.

account of the respective countries' willingness and capacity to address the challenges correctly. Some countries, still struggling to reinforce independent statehood and institutions, objectively need external support to foster democratization in terms of skills, resources and perhaps also the will for change. Where the claim concerning double standards does deserve further consideration is the way in which OSCE participating states (and their non-governmental sectors) attempt to provide such support. Election monitoring often tends towards finger-pointing. There is a thin line between fostering political processes and democracy, and intrusion that may be perceived as humiliating. Moreover, the support offered may very well be contrary to the interests of the ruling elites in those countries and hence may meet strong opposition. The OSCE, as an organization of cooperative security, should pay more attention to the style in which it contributes to change in Europe.

Several CIS countries appear to have embarked on a political course that aims to constrain transparency in their political affairs. Russia, still a major independent player in European politics and thus not over-dependent on the OSCE, is leading this political course partly for its own sake and partly as a way to consolidate consensus and leadership within the CIS. Other participating states have been happy to go along as a way of hiding damaging backsliding in their transformation and democratization processes, and no doubt to avoid a repeat of the events in Georgia and Ukraine. Russian diplomacy is playing a calculated game in the OSCE. It subscribes to the Western agenda on a number of issues, most prominently on fighting terrorism, but in return expects the West largely to respect Moscow's *droit de regard* over its internal politics and regional development. Western acceptance of this 'bargain' may help current regimes in the CIS, but at the expense of the interests of their populations in the long run. Returning to the principles of cooperative security must not mean turning a blind eye to the curtailment of democracy and transformation in several CIS countries.

At the December Ministerial Council, Russia referred to the Moscow and Astana proposals put forward by CIS member states as if these were already part of the OSCE *acquis*.[21] Russia insisted on a comprehensive reform of OSCE structures that would focus on 'specialized institutions, field activities and financing system[s]'.[22] To guard against being swamped by the majority in the OSCE still opposed to its ideas, it reiterated that 'Russia regards consensus as the underlying principle of OSCE activities and a mechanism without alternative [*bezalternativnyi*] for decision making in the Organization'.[23] Applying OSCE-style consensus to an issue in effect gives any unwilling participating state a power of veto.

Russia picked on the institution most closely identified with activities that are unpopular with many CIS member states—the Office for Democratic Institutions and Human Rights—which has responsibility *inter alia* for election monitoring and remains one of the few OSCE instruments able to operate outside Russian control. The CIS countries also argued that decisions related to OSCE field missions—from appointing the heads of mission to extending their duration or remit—should be based on the consensus rule, which could only weaken the OSCE's present room for

[21] Statement by the Delegation of the Russian Federation (note 18), p. 2.

[22] Statement by the Delegation of the Russian Federation (note 18), point 5.

[23] 'Zayavleniye delegatsii Rossiyi na zasedaniyi Postoyannovo soveta OBSE po voprosu o konsesuse' [Statement by the Russian Delegation at the OSCE Permanent Council session on the question of consensus], 15 Mar. 2004, p. 1 (in Russian), URL <http://www.ln.mid.ru/brp_4.nsf/>.

manoeuvre and may result in a 'UN-ization' of such missions.[24] The CIS initiatives of July and September 2004 also sought to integrate extra-budgetary resources into the OSCE budget process. This would mean that resources provided by Western states could no longer be assigned according to Western political priorities. Implementation of these ideas would change the OSCE fundamentally.

Russia put forward two further ideas for discussion by OSCE participating states: (*a*) a 'high-level seminar on military doctrines and defence policy in the OSCE area', especially in the context of NATO's recent enlargement; and (*b*) a conference to 'discuss problems such as the development of international cooperation in the energy sector, the strengthening of overall security in relation to energy supplies and deliveries, and the promotion of efficient energy-saving measures'.[25] The former proposal makes sense to the extent that the military doctrines and strategies of the participating states have changed significantly, notably in response to the new emphasis on terrorism, since the last such seminar was held. Energy security is also an area where Russia can demonstrate its important contribution. Russia has expressed its disappointment that its proposals have not been approved, because of what it describes as 'artificial linkages and an unworthy political haggle'.[26]

The December 2004 OSCE Ministerial Council ended without a political declaration, although an unprecedented 21 decisions were agreed. This is the third time that an OSCE Ministerial Council meeting has failed to agree a political declaration.[27] Two decisions are directly relevant to the future of the OSCE as an organization. The first modifies the role of the OSCE Secretary General—strengthening it while retaining the primacy of the Chairman-in-Office. The Secretary General, the OSCE's chief administrative officer, has already taken on certain political and support functions and will now be responsible for providing expert, material, technical, and other support and advice to the Chairman-in-Office. The Secretary General will be able to make public statements on behalf of the organization and may also support the process of political dialogue and negotiations among participating states and 'bring to the attention of the decision-making bodies . . . any matter relevant to his or her mandate'.[28] It is too soon to judge what the consequences will be, but it should be noted that a similar provision in the UN Charter gives the UN Secretary-General a major political role.[29] The second decision established a panel, composed of a maximum of 'seven eminent persons with knowledge of the OSCE . . . including from participating states hosting field presences', to make recommendations on strengthening the effectiveness of the OSCE.[30] It will present its report by 30 June 2005.

[24] Appointing heads of missions by consensus would actually go beyond practice at the UN, where they are appointed by the Secretary-General of the organization.

[25] Statement by the Delegation of the Russian Federation (note 18), pp. 1, 3.

[26] Statement by the Delegation of the Russian Federation (note 18), p. 2.

[27] The previous 2 occasions were Vienna in Nov. 2000 and Maastricht in 2003.

[28] OSCE, MC Decision no. 15/04, Role of the OSCE Secretary General, MC.DEC/15/04, point 4, 7 Dec. 2004, reproduced in 2nd Day of the Twelfth Meeting of the Ministerial Council, 3rd Plenary Session (closed), available at URL <http://www.osce.org/docs/english/mincone.htm>.

[29] Charter of the United Nations, Article 99, URL <http://www.un.org/aboutun/charter/>.

[30] OSCE, MC Decision no. 16/04, Establishment of a Panel of Eminent Persons on Stengthening the Effectiveness of the OSCE, MC.DEC/16/04, 7 Dec. 2004, reproduced in 2nd Day of the Twelfth Meeting of the Ministerial Council, 3rd Plenary session (closed), available at URL <http://www.osce.org/docs/english/mincone.htm>.

III. Conclusions

The OSCE's lack of adaptation to the post-cold war European institutional structure has not been the most important factor in its relative decline. A more basic problem is that, during this period, either the OSCE's agenda has not been important enough to increase its relevance or important issues have been taken over by other organizations that can deal with them more effectively. Consequently, the OSCE security agenda is progressively being emptied of its content. This has been the case with several recent agenda topics, such as trafficking in human beings and controlling the proliferation of man-portable air defence systems (MANPADS), that have since been appropriated by more powerful institutions. There is no reason to assume that the pattern will not be repeated in future. Some issues, primarily in the humanitarian dimension, seem best suited to the OSCE—but it would require a conscious decision by participating states to prevent them from being 'relocated'. The OSCE has initiated organizational reforms, but without moving towards a more comprehensive review or reform of policy.

A further problem is that states that have recently adopted a highly critical stance with regard to the OSCE, and those which are pressing for reform of the organization, seem to be doing so more as a matter of expediency than of principle. Consequently, the changes made, or planned, thus far could be 'too little too late'. The OSCE's struggle for a larger role is not over, but the organization could be on the verge of becoming a forum for exchanging views on a broad range of international security matters and not much more. If outgoing OSCE Secretary General Jan Kubis is correct when he says that 'What is going on in the OSCE is . . . worth watching because it is a barometer of the political atmosphere in Europe today', there is no particular reason for optimism.[31]

[31] Quoted by Dombey, D. and Jack, A., 'Concern rises in US and EU over Russia's growing hostility to OSCE', *Financial Times*, 11 Nov. 2004.

2. Major armed conflicts

RENATA DWAN and CAROLINE HOLMQVIST

I. Introduction

The discussion of major armed conflicts in the *SIPRI Yearbook 2004* focused on the dominance of intra-state armed conflict in the contemporary international system.[1] This trend was even more apparent in 2004, when every one of the 19 major armed conflicts that were active during the year was classified as intra-state. Only three of these—the conflict against al-Qaeda, the conflict in Iraq and the conflict in Darfur, Sudan—are less than 10 years old. These figures may appear at odds with a contemporary international security climate that is preoccupied with perceived 'new' security threats such as international terrorism and the spread of weapons of mass destruction. However, in a globalized world, intra-state conflicts are increasingly becoming international in nature and in effects. The complexity and diversity of these conflicts make the distinction between the 'internal' and the 'external' particularly complicated and call into question the basis on which conflicts are classified and addressed.

This chapter therefore concentrates for the second year running on intra-state conflict. Section II looks at the internationalization of these conflicts and how this affects the perceptions as well as the handling of conflict. Section III addresses a number of contemporary features of intra-state conflict that complicate traditional approaches to their analysis and management: the diversity of warring parties and multiple grievances; the evolving tactics in conflict and their consequences for civilians; and the shifting location and containment of intra-state conflict. These themes are illustrated by synopses of a number of the major armed conflicts that were active in 2004. The international dominance of the war in Iraq, and the special circumstances regarding its origin and prosecution, merit a separate discussion in section IV, and section V presents the conclusions.

II. Internationalized intra-state conflicts

The data on major armed conflicts for 2004 presented by the Uppsala Conflict Data Project (UCDP) in appendix 2A show that this is the first year of the entire data series for which no interstate conflict was reported.[2] Two interstate

[1] See Dwan, R. and Gustavsson, M., 'Major armed conflicts', *SIPRI Yearbook 2004: Armaments, Disarmament and International Security* (Oxford University Press: Oxford, 2004), pp. 95–147.

[2] The UCDP has contributed data on major armed conflicts for publication in the SIPRI Yearbook annually since the late 1980s; for the first published data in the series see Wilson, G. K. and

conflicts that were registered for 2003 do not appear in the table for 2004. The conflict between the United States and its allies and the Government of Iraq, which began in March 2003, ended formally on 1 May 2003 when US President George W. Bush declared the end of major combat operations. The conflict in Iraq in 2004 was an internal, intra-state war (see section IV). In the second, long-standing, interstate conflict registered for 2003—between India and Pakistan—the 23 November 2003 negotiated ceasefire on the disputed Line of Control (LOC) that divides Indian- and Pakistani-administered Kashmir held throughout 2004. Although fighting between India and Kashmiri separatists continued, and although the Indian Government claimed that terrorists were continuing to cross the LOC from Pakistan, the improved security situation led India to withdraw several thousand troops from Kashmir in November 2004. Formal peace talks between India and Pakistan, which began in February, made little progress on the Kashmir dispute but facilitated perceptible improvement in the relations between these two nuclear weapon powers.[3]

The prevalence of intra-state conflict has been widely noted as one of the most distinguishing features of the late 20th century. The distinction between 'intra-state' and 'interstate' as a way of categorizing and studying contemporary armed conflicts becomes irrelevant if all extant major armed conflicts are classified as intra-state. This classification arguably also stretches the term 'intra-state' to an extent that it is no longer a helpful analytical concept. The only apparent common feature of the 19 intra-state conflicts listed in appendix 2A is that they are being fought by one or more states against one or more non-state groups. Beyond that, it is the diversity of intra-state conflicts that is most striking. Both conflicts involving the USA—the conflict in Afghanistan fought against al-Qaeda and the conflict in Iraq against various Iraqi insurgent groups—began as interstate conflicts with US-led attacks on the state in question, and both were rooted in the United States' post-11 September 2001 'global war on terrorism'. These conflicts involve other states fighting alongside the USA in multinational (non-standing) coalitions against disparate non-state groups. In both cases fighting has continued after the military victory of the USA and its allies and the collapse of the government in question: the subsequent interim governments of Afghanistan and Iraq are now warring parties on the side of the USA.[4] These complex international conflicts resist neat intra-/interstate labelling.[5] Moreover, despite their shared origins and

Wallensteen, P., 'Major armed conflicts in 1987', *SIPRI Yearbook 1988: World Armaments and Disarmament* (Oxford University Press: Oxford, 1988), pp. 285–98. The data for 2004 are presented in appendix 2A in this volume.

[3] Lakshman, K., 'J&K: A violent peace', *South Asia Intelligence Review*, Weekly Assessments & Briefings, vol. 3, no. 26 (10 Jan. 2005), URL <http://www.satp.org>; and 'Rivals discuss "ceasefire breach"', BBC News Online, 19 Jan. 2005, URL <http://news.bbc.co.uk/2/4186547.stm>. On the Indian and Pakistani nuclear forces see appendix 12A in this volume.

[4] The conflict between the Government of Afghanistan and Taliban rebels, classified as intra-state with foreign involvement, has not reached 1000 battle-related deaths and is therefore not included in the data in appendix 2A.

[5] Some analysts have defined conflicts between states and non-state groups outside the territory of the state as 'extra-systemic armed conflict'. Strand, H., Wihelmsen, L. and Gleditsch, N. P. (International

protagonists, their comparability is limited. The conflict against al-Qaeda appears to be more a contest over the structure and governance of the international system, in which states are defending the system of states against challenges posed by transnational, non-state, political protest movements (al-Qaeda) and the parties that support them (the Taliban in Afghanistan). In contrast, some analysts saw the interstate war in Iraq in 2003 as a rejection of the international multilateral order by the USA and its allies.[6] The current conflict in Iraq is seen by many as an imperial or anti-colonial war, closer to the wars of national liberation that were fought in the late 19th century and much of the 20th century in Africa, Asia and the Middle East.[7]

The intra-/interstate distinction is also challenged by the international dimensions of conflicts fought by a government party on its own state territory. Some analysts have sought to define internationalized internal conflicts as those in which third-party state military intervention takes place.[8] However, this categorization fails to take into account non-military forms of intervention and the very different ways in which an internal conflict can affect and be affected by external factors. In an increasingly globalized world, it is questionable whether any internal conflict can be devoid of international dimensions.[9] All conflicts, in this context, are 'international', even if they are not interstate wars.

A particularly stark example of the complexity of internationalized internal armed conflict is the long-standing conflict between the Government of Israel, the Palestinian Authority (PA) and various militant Islamic groups, which intensified in August 2000 after the collapse of the Oslo Peace Process and the launch of the second Intifada. The conflict continued to have a significant regional dimension as regards its conduct—Israel launched air strikes on Hezbollah targets in southern Lebanon on a number of occasions during 2004—and as regards relations between countries in the region. Israel rejected Syrian overtures to renew the Middle East peace negotiations that were broken off in 2000, despite efforts by the United Nations to revive talks on the return to Syria of the Israeli-occupied Golan Heights. Israel argued that Syria's move was an effort to improve its relations with the USA rather than with Israel and

Peace Research Institute) in collaboration with Wallensteen, P., Sollenberg, M. and Erikson, M., (Department of Peace and Conflict Research, Uppsala University) and Buhaug, H. and Rød, J. K. (Department of Sociology and Political Science/Department of Geomatics, Norwegian University of Science and Technology), 'Armed Conflict Database Codebook', Version 2.1, 11 Mar. 2004, URL <http://www.pcr.uu.se/research/UCDP/>.

6 Cockayne, J. with Samii, C., *The Iraq Crisis and World Order: Structural and Normative Challenges*, International Peace Academy (IPA), United Nations University and King Prajadipok's Institute, Workshop Report (IPA: New York, Dec. 2004), URL <http://www.ipacademy.org/Publications/Publications.htm>.

7 See, e.g., Barkawi, T., 'On the pedagogy of "small wars"', *International Affairs*, vol. 80, no. 1 (2004), pp. 19–37.

8 Strand, Wihelmsen and Gleditsch *et al.* (note 5), p. 11.

9 Council of the European Union, 'A secure Europe in a better world: European Security Strategy', Brussels, 12 Dec. 2003, URL <http://ue.eu.int/uedocs/cms_data/docs/pressdata/EN/reports/78367.pdf>; United Nations, A more secure world: our shared responsibility, Report of the High-level Panel on Threats, Challenges and Change, UN document A/59/565, 4 Dec. 2004, URL <http://www.un.org/ga/59/documentation/list5.html>; and the Introduction in this volume.

that no progress was possible until Syria had made conciliatory gestures such as expelling Palestinian militants and stopping all assistance to Hezbollah, which Israel describes as 'Iran's forward military arm'.[10] Continued international efforts to resume Israeli–Palestinian peace talks through the individual engagement of members of 'the Quartet'—the USA, the UN, the European Union and Russia—failed to bring any breakthrough in 2004.[11]

The actions of the government of Ariel Sharon were particularly influenced by the policies of the USA towards the wider Middle East and the 'global war on terrorism'. Israel, supported by the USA, maintained its refusal to negotiate with the President of the PA, Yasser Arafat, on the grounds that he was not able to halt Palestinian terrorist attacks on Israeli targets.[12] Israel's policy was part of a comprehensive counter-terrorist strategy focused on the occupied territories of the West Bank and the Gaza Strip, which included Israeli Army raids on Palestinian towns in search of Palestinian militants, targeted assassinations of alleged militant leaders and the construction of a 365-km barrier intended to prevent Palestinian incursions into Israel.[13] The USA supported the construction of the barrier as a 'temporary' measure to protect Israel against terrorism.[14] Although the policy led to a significant drop in suicide bombings in Israel, the number of suicide bomber recruits appeared to rise. Moreover, many argued that Israel's policies were creating divisions within Palestinian society and increasing popular support for extremist militant groups such as Hamas and the Islamic Jihad.[15]

[10] Morris, H., 'Israelis reluctant to grasp Syria's new olive branch', *Financial Times*, 10–11 Jan. 2004, p. 5; Myre, G., 'Israeli jets hit Lebanon after attack on vehicle', *International Herald Tribune*, 21 Jan. 2004, p. 5; and Khalaf, R., 'UN urges revival of frozen Israel–Syria peace negotiations', *Financial Times*, 21 Feb. 2004, p. 3.

[11] Devi, S., 'Israeli troops kill eight as US envoys try to revive talks', *Financial Times*, 29 Jan. 2004, p. 6; Keinon, H., 'Israel wants to scuttle EU road-map changes', *Jerusalem Post* (Internet edn), 1 Mar. 2004, in 'Israel feels new EU plan "to supplement" road map lets Palestinians "off the hook"', Foreign Broadcast Information Service, *Daily Report–Near East and South Asia (FBIS-NES)*, FBIS-NES-2004-0301, 2 Mar. 2004; 'EU announces plan to end Israeli–Palestinian conflict', Madrid RNE Radio 1, 11 Oct. 2004, in *Daily Report–West Europe (FBIS-WEU)*, FBIS-WEU-2004-1011, 12 Oct. 2004; and 'Russia wants Israel, Palestinians to hold direct talks', Moscow Interfax, 6 Aug. 2004, in *Daily Report–Central Eurasia (FBIS–SOV)*, FBIS-SOV-2004-0806, 9 Aug. 2004.

[12] In the years preceding his death Arafat was a virtual captive in the PA Headquarters in the West Bank town of Ramallah, blockaded by Israeli tanks since mid-2002. On developments in the greater Middle East region see chapter 5 in this volume.

[13] Myre, G., 'Leader of Hamas is killed in missile attack in Gaza', *New York Times*, 18 Apr. 2004, p. 1; and 'Israel assassinates Al-Aqsa martyrs brigades Janin chief, two other Palestinians', Voice of Israel Network B (Jerusalem), 13 Sep. 2004, in FBIS-NES-2004-0913, 14 Sep. 2004.

[14] In July 2004 the International Court of Justice handed down its advisory opinion on the legality of the security fence, declaring that a major portion of the fence was on Palestinian land in the West Bank and therefore illegal. 'Israel and Palestine: talking again (but not to each other)', *The Economist*, 3 July 2004, p. 35; and Crouch, G. and Myre, G., 'Major portion of Israeli fence is ruled illegal', *New York Times*, 10 July 2004, p. 1.

[15] Middle East Media Research Institute (MEMRI), 'Palestinian human rights group report on international violence in the Palestinian Authority areas', *MEMRI Inquiry and Analysis Series*, no. 174 (9 May. 2004); 'Israel and Palestine: who's winning the fight?', *The Economist*, 3 July 2004, p. 36; Dudkevitch, M., 'Terrorists recruiting more women, minors—Shin Bet', *Jerusalem Post*, 22 Sep. 2004, in FBIS-NES-2004-0922, 23 Sep. 2004; International Crisis Group (ICG), 'Who governs the West Bank?: Palestinian administration under Israeli occupation', Middle East Report no. 32 (28 Sep. 2004), URL <http://www.icg.org/home/index.cfm?id=3034&l=1>; and Israel Security Agency, '2004 terrorism

Sharon's plan to pull back Israeli forces and an estimated 7500 Israeli settlers from the Gaza Strip, while keeping some West Bank settlements as part of any future peace accord with the Palestinians, was seen as particularly controversial both within and outside Israel.[16] For many Palestinians and Arab leaders, it constituted a fundamental departure from internationally agreed positions on a future Palestinian state as outlined in the 'road map' backed by the Quartet. In May 2004, the Quartet gave its qualified endorsement to the Gaza withdrawal plan.[17]

The death of Arafat on 11 November 2004, after 35 years as head of the Palestine Liberation Organization (PLO), and the election in January 2005 of the moderate Mahmoud Abbas as President of the PA appeared to offer a unique opportunity for a revival of the peace process. The incoming US Administration declared that the peace process would be a priority of the second term of President Bush, while the British Prime Minister, Tony Blair, announced that a conference on Palestinian reform would be held in London in early 2005 and Egypt committed itself to cooperation with Israel on the withdrawal from Gaza.[18] Whether renewed efforts can revive the Israeli–Palestinian peace process depends, in no small part, on the extent to which a coordinated international approach to the conflict can be reforged. Disengaging the 'international' from the 'domestic' in such intra-state conflicts is impossible.

Many analysts are now trying to analyse the term 'internal conflict' in ways other than according to the international or domestic dimensions of conflicts. They have examined *inter alia* the distinctions between civil war and insurgency, between armed conflict and criminalized violence, and between internal armed conflict and terrorism.[19] Such approaches demonstrate that conflict does not easily lend itself to categorization and comparison. Understanding intra-state conflict may require closer attention to the features and details of individual conflicts and greater caution towards using comparative labels and deriving generic recommendations.

data', *IMRA Newsletter* (Independent Media Review Analysis, Israel), 5 Jan. 2005, URL <http://www.kokhavivpublications.com/2005/israel/01/0501052131.html>.

[16] Sharon faced significant domestic opposition to the Gaza disengagement plan from within his own Likud Party as well as from the Israeli settler lobby, both of which demanded a national referendum on the issue.

[17] Bumiller, E., 'In major shift, Bush endorses Sharon plan and backs keeping some Israeli settlements', *New York Times*, 15 Apr. 2004, p. 6; MacFarquhar, N. and Blumenthal, R., 'Palestinians and other Arabs assail Bush for stand on Israel', *New York Times*, 15 Apr. 2004, p. 6; and Weisman, S., 'Gaza pullout is endorsed, with proviso, by envoys', *New York Times*, 5 May 2004, p. 11.

[18] Morris, H., 'In spite of the violence of the past four years, there is extraordinary consensus', *Financial Times*, 4 Jan. 2005, p. 9.

[19] See, e.g., Fearon J. and Laitin, D., 'Ethnicity, insurgency and civil war', *American Political Science Review*, vol. 97, no. 1 (Feb. 2003); Gutiérrez Sanín, F., 'Criminal rebels?: a discussion of war and criminality from the Colombian experience', Crisis States Programme, London School of Economics and Political Science, Working Papers no. 27, Apr. 2003, URL <http://www.crisisstates.com/Publications/wp/wp27.htm>; and *Journal of Peace Research*, Special Issue on Duration and Termination of Civil War, vol. 41, no. 3 (May 2004).

III. Features of contemporary intra-state conflicts

In explaining how contemporary armed conflicts resist neat internal/external, intra-/interstate classification, many have sought to draw attention to the way in which today's intra-state conflicts are different from the wars of national liberation or classic interstate wars of the past.[20] A number of features of contemporary intra-state conflict are highlighted: the diversity of the warring parties and their grievances; the interplay between conflict tactics and the role of civilians in conflict; and the shifting location of conflicts. While it is debatable how 'new' each of these features really is, collectively they complicate both the understanding and the management of contemporary intra-state conflict. It is important to bear in mind that the features highlighted in many cases reinforce and feed into one another or are particularly salient at different stages of a long-standing conflict.[21] Most conflicts exhibit more than one of the features in question.

Diversity of warring parties and multiple grievances

The diversity of warring parties and the grievances that they may reflect is one of the most complicating features of intra-state conflict. Most of the current interstate conflicts include more than one rebel group, and in cases such as India and Iraq it is difficult even to identify and describe all the insurgent groups. Moreover, it should be noted that the conflicts listed in table 2A.3 are only those defined as 'major' (see appendix 2B): Indonesia, for example, is negotiating at least two ongoing 'minor' conflicts in addition to the conflict in Aceh. In some cases, multiple rebel groups may reflect the ethnic divisions of a country. Such groups may share the same general grievance or incompatibility—opposition to the government—but differ in the specific nature of that opposition and how they express it in armed conflict. In cases such as the conflicts in Burundi, Colombia and Darfur, Sudan, diverse rebels groups fight independently against the government party and only rarely coordinate their armed opposition. Where rebel parties coordinate their political and military strategies they may prove a more potent threat to the government. The setting up of the National Democratic Alliance (NDA) in Sudan in 1989, an umbrella organization for several opposition parties in the south, is an example of this.

Prolonged conflict may also lead to the proliferation of warring parties as rebel groups splinter into different factions, external parties intervene and new grievances develop out of the conflict.[22] In Colombia, for example, the rise of

[20] See, e.g., Kaldor, M., *New and Old Wars: Organized Violence in a Global Era* (Polity Press: Cambridge, 1999); and Duffield, M., *Global Governance and the New Wars: The Merging of Development and Security* (Zed Books: London, 2001).

[21] The protracted nature of many intra-state conflicts, and its consequences for conflict management, are discussed in detail in Dwan and Gustavsson (note 1), pp. 95–121.

[22] E.g., in Liberia, the fighting reported in 2004 was between the Movement for Democracy in Liberia and the Liberians United for Reconciliation and Democracy rebel groups rather than between the government and rebel opposition.

the right-wing paramilitary organization Autodéfensas Unidas de Colombia (AUC, or the United Self-Defence Forces of Colombia) was a consequence of the long-standing conflict between the government and the rebel groups Fuerzas Armadas Revolucionarias de Colombia (FARC, or the Revolutionary Armed Forces of Colombia) and Ejército de Liberación Nationale (ELN, or the National Liberation Army). However, multiple parties are not only associated with non-state opposition. Government forces can be boosted by the engagement of foreign state and non-state actors, including private security companies.[23] Government parties may also make use of local militia groups either indirectly, as in the case of the Janjaweed in Darfur, Sudan, or directly, as in the case of Nepal, where the government is creating local militia groups to counter attacks by Maoist rebel groups.[24]

Multiple warring parties make for, and are made by, multiple grievances. Table 2A.3, in appendix 2A, lists two general types of incompatibility: over government and over territory. However, these say little about why groups seek control over one or the other (or both) and why they are willing to risk their lives to do so. Self-determination continues to be an important motivation for some groups to seek control over government (regional autonomy) or territory (secession). For much of the past decade, research has played down the extent to which ethnic or religious differences per se are the motivating drivers for groups to seek control over government or territory. Instead, analysts have highlighted the access to and distribution of wealth, land and natural resource in societies, which may or may not be determined along dominant and minority ethnic or religious group lines, as the driving forces in internal wars.[25] Moreover, the longer a conflict continues, the greater the likelihood of new grievances emerging as consequences of death and suffering.

Another distinction to be drawn is that between stated grievances and 'real' agendas. Much of the work explaining prolonged conflict has focused on the profit motivations of rebel groups, particularly in resource-rich countries. As Paul Collier, the leading proponent of this research, has noted, 'to get started, rebellion needs grievance, whereas to be sustained, it needs greed'.[26] In some cases, particularly where multiple warring parties are present, even the stated incompatibility is unclear: in the case of Iraq, for instance, it is difficult to identify, much less distinguish between, the motivations for many of the multiple insurgent attacks—the creation of an Islamic state or the removal of US

[23] For a detailed discussion of the private military and security industry and its impact on various security contexts see Holmqvist, C., *Private Security Companies: The Case for Regulation*, SIPRI Policy Paper no. 9 (SIPRI: Stockholm, Jan. 2005), URL <http://www.sipri.org/contents/publications/Policypaper9.html>.

[24] 'Fleeing the horsemen that kill for Khartoum', *The Economist*, 15 May 2004, p. 22; and ICG, 'Nepal: dangerous plans for village militias', ICG Asia Briefing, no. 30, 17 Feb. 2004, URL <http://www.crisisweb.org>.

[25] See, e.g., Nafziger, E. W., Stewart, F. and Väyrynen, R. (eds), *War, Hunger and Displacement: The Origins of Humanitarian Emergencies*, vol. 1, *Analysis* (Oxford University Press: Oxford, 2000).

[26] Collier, P., 'Rebellion as a quasi-criminal activity', *Journal of Peace Research*, vol. 44, no. 6 (Dec. 2000), p. 852. For further discussion see Gutierrez, F. G., 'Criminal rebels?: a discussion of war and criminality from the Colombian experience', Crisis States Programme, Working Paper no. 27 (Apr. 2003), URL <http://www.crisisstates.com/Publications/wp/wp27.htm>.

forces, or criminal gain, or local rivalries and vendettas. In cases of weak or collapsed states, such as Somalia, the presence of multiple warring parties is less representative of competing political agendas than a symptom of the absence of any political arena in which competition over power, resources and territory can be regulated. The reality of most conflicts is more complex and more mundane than the categorization by political incompatibilities may initially suggest. Rebel groups, and their individual members, may be motivated by a range of factors operating at the same time: local as well as national, personal as well as political, ideological as well as profit-based. This sometimes leads to the fragmentation of rebel groups and inter-rebel hostility.

The presence of multiple parties and multiple grievances may have a significant impact on the shape and course of a conflict. It tends to protract conflict by weakening the ability of any one party to attain outright military victory, creating multiple centres of violence within a country and provoking competition between groups, usually reflected in an increased intensity of violence. The multiplicity of actors and grievances poses particular challenges for conflict resolution efforts—whether in grappling with several essentially separate conflicts at once, as in the cases of Colombia and Sudan, or in attempting to negotiate an overall framework for peaceful resolution of conflict, as in the case of Burundi.

Burundi

The conflict in Burundi began in 1991 and has claimed approximately 200 000 lives and involved several different rebel groups. The 2000 Arusha Peace and Reconciliation Agreement for Burundi stipulated 2004 as the final year of the transition, and prospects for peace initially appeared to be good. The 16 November 2003 power-sharing agreement between the transitional government and its most significant rebel opponent, the Conseil national pour la défense de la démocratie–Forces pour la défense de la démocratie (CNDD–FDD, or the National Council for the Defence of Democracy–Forces for the Defence of Democracy) halted fighting in 16 of Burundi's 17 provinces. The agreement stipulated the integration of CNDD–FDD fighters into the transitional government forces (Forces Armeés Burundaises, FAB, or the Burundian Armed Forces), leaving only one rebel group, the Palipehutu–FNL (Parti pour la libération du peuple Hutu–Forces nationales de libération, or the Party for the Liberation of the Hutu People–Forces for National Liberation) outside the peace process.[27]

Optimism about implementation of the November 2003 agreement proved hasty, however. Failure to discipline cooperation between the government and the CNDD–FDD and to proceed with disarmament during the year hampered

[27] 'Over 90 former rebels surrender to African mission forces', Burundi Press Agency (Bujumbura), 20 Jan. 2004, in FBIS-AFR-2004-0120, 21 Jan. 2004. For more detail see ICG, 'End of the transition in Burundi: the home stretch', ICG Africa Report no. 81, 5 July 2004, URL <http://www.icg.org/home/index.cfm?id=2841&l=1>.

the consolidation of peace in the country.[28] After military successes awarded the CNDD–FDD with a boost in political support, it withdrew from the government in May, stating that it was not adequately represented, and factionalism within the CNDD–FDD further complicated the implementation and consolidation of the peace agreement. Meanwhile, the conflict between the transitional government and the Palipehutu–FNL showed few signs of de-escalation. Under the leadership of Agathon Rwasa, a faction of the Palipehutu–FNL condemned the November 2003 agreement and has continued armed attacks against the government and maintained its refusal to negotiate with the transitional government.[29] Fighting between the government and the FNL in the first half of 2004 displaced approximately 30 000 people.[30]

Confusion over rebel identities and affiliations in the conflict was further illustrated in the massacre of 160 Congolese Tutsi refugees at a UN-run camp in Gatumba, Burundi, on 13 August 2004. The FNL claimed responsibility for the massacre on the following day, but both eyewitnesses and officials from the Burundian and Rwandan governments claimed that Rwandan Hutu Interahamwe rebels based in the Democratic Republic of the Congo (DRC) were involved. Human Rights Watch, an internationally respected non-governmental organization (NGO), has disputed the involvement of Congolese and Rwandan groups. There was no conclusive word on the identity of the perpetrators, and a UN report recommended the continuation of investigations by the Burundian Government and the International Criminal Court (ICC).[31]

Negotiations on power sharing held in August between the government and various Burundian groups illustrated the intricate balance that needs to be struck between different actors in order for the peace process to continue.[32] The holding of a referendum on Burundi's new constitution, a precondition for general elections, was delayed for the third time in December, and no new date was specified, thus breaking the timetable set in the Arusha Agreement.[33] The need to find the correct modus operandi for engaging the FNL (punishment for the crimes committed in Gatumba versus continued attempts to hold

[28] HRW, 'Burundi: suffering in silence: civilians in continuing combat in Bujumbura Rural', HRW Briefing Paper, June 2004, p. 2, URL <http://www.hrw.org/backgrounder/africa/burundi/2004/>; and 'The timetable slips', *Africa Confidential*, vol. 45, no. 20 (8 Oct. 2004), p. 6.

[29] Agence France-Presse, 'Eight die in two attacks by FNL rebels in Burundian capital', ReliefWeb, 17 Dec. 2003, URL <http://reliefweb.int>.

[30] United Nations, Report of the Secretary-General on Burundi, UN document S/2004/210, 16 Mar. 2004, p. 3; 'UN urged to send Burundi force', BBC News Online, 20 Mar. 2004, URL <http://news.bbc.co.uk/1/3553275.stm>; and Agence France-Presse, 'Rebels and army clash in Burundi, ending truce', 23 Apr. 2004, URL <http://www.globalpolicy.org/security/sanction/burundi/2004/0423clash.htm>.

[31] IRIN-CEA, 'UN investigators unable to identify perpetrators of August killings', IRIN-CEA Weekly Round-up 250, 23–29 Oct. 2004.

[32] In line with the Arusha Agreement, the 'Pretoria compromise' was predicated on ethnically defined power sharing and set to guarantee minimum representation to the Tutsi minority. 'Burundi: the timetable slips', *Africa Confidential*, vol. 45, no. 20 (8 Oct. 2004), p. 5.

[33] 'New delay to Burundi referendum', BBC News Online, 14 Dec. 2004, URL <http://news.bbc.co.uk/1/4095961.stm>. For an elaboration on the effects of postponing elections see ICG, 'Elections in Burundi: the peace wager', Africa Briefing no. 20, 9 Dec. 2004, URL <http://www.icg.org/home/index.cfm?id=3159&l=1>.

peace negotiations with the group) and its supporters in the peace process will be an important factor in the consolidation of peace in Burundi.[34]

Colombia

In the conflict between the Colombian Government and the FARC and ELN rebel groups, more than 70 000 people have been killed since the early 1960s. While neither of the rebel groups has relinquished its Marxist ideologically based political opposition, analysts generally agree that the political content of the conflict has been increasingly de-emphasized in favour of the warring parties' pursuit of economic agendas, mainly through drug trafficking and kidnappings.[35]

The Colombian conflict is complicated by the role played by the AUC, dominant among the several paramilitary forces that have emerged in opposition to both the government and the rebel groups, and big players in the drugs trade.[36] Negotiations between the government of Álvaro Uribe Vélez and the AUC led to a ceasefire in July 2003. On 13 May 2004, the Ralito II Agreement was signed, establishing a neutral 'zone of location' for the paramilitaries.[37] Disarmament of the AUC started in earnest in November 2004 and was intended to reach 3000 (of an estimated total of 20 000) combatants before the end of the year, but progress was slow.[38] Although curbing the AUC is an important step forward, international endorsement has been tempered by allegations of government–AUC collusion and side-by-side fighting against the rebels.[39]

President Uribe's hard-line 'democratic security policy' aimed to uproot the insurgents militarily, deny them illegal sources of income, and boost the police

34 Further fighting between Pailpehutu-FNL and government soldiers was reported in the Musaga zone in south-eastern Bujumbura in Dec. 'Four rebels, one soldier killed during fighting in Burundi', Burundi Press Agency (Bujumbura), 28 Dec. 2004, in FBIS-AFR-2004-1228, 29 Dec. 2004.

35 Some analysts interpret the fact that armed groups seek not only to seize control of territory but also to establish basic forms of government as an indication that political grievances are returning to the forefront. 'Study finds Colombian armed groups have different motives, modes of operation', *El Espectador* (Bogota), 4 Apr. 2004, in Foreign Broadcast Information Service, *Daily Report–Latin America (FBIS-LAT)*, 'Geography of the conflict', FBIS-LAT-2004-0818, 19 Aug. 2004.

36 The AUC was officially formed in 1997 but has roots dating back almost 30 years. One estimate claims that 40% of Colombian territory is under FARC or AUC domination and the 2 groups together account for 70% of the drugs leaving the country. McDermott, J., 'FARC and the paramilitaries take over Colombia's drugs trade', *Jane's Intelligence Review*, vol. 16, no. 7 (July 2004), p. 28.

37 ICG, 'Demobilising the paramilitaries in Colombia: an achievable goal?', Latin America Report no. 8 (5 Aug. 2004), URL <http://www.icg.org/home/index.cfm?id=2901&l=1>; and 'Paramilitary peace process back from brink', Latin American Andean Report, RA-04-04 (6 Apr. 2004), pp. 6–8.

38 All 20 000 paramilitary fighters are to be disarmed by the end of 2006. '450 Colombian paramilitary fighters turn in weapons', Agence France-Presse (Paris), 25 Nov. 2004, in 'First 450 paramilitary fighters in Colombia turn in their weapons', FBIS-LAT-2004-1126, 29 Nov. 2004. The Organization of American States (OAS) agreed on 25 Jan. 2004 to help monitor the disarmament. 'Colombia: OAS ought not to be limited to verifying, legitimizing demobilization', *El Espectador* (Bogota), 1 Feb. 2004, in 'The OAS verification', FBIS-LAT-2004-0201, 4 Feb. 2004.

39 'Government taking flack over paramilitaries', *Latin American Andean Report*, RA-04-02, 3 Feb. 2004, p. 10. For a detailed account of this peace process see ICG, 'Colombia: negotiating with the paramilitaries', Latin America Report no. 5 (16 Sep. 2003), URL <http://www.icg.org/home/index.cfm?id=2302&l=1>.

and military. Under 'Plan Patriota', announced in May 2004 and involving the mobilization of 14 000–17 000 government troops, major military offensives were launched against FARC.[40] Government operations, targeting especially the southern and central regions, where FARC has maintained a stronghold for decades, yielded some success.[41] According to an army commander, 1500 'members of illegal organisations' were killed and close to 6000 captured in the first eight months of 2004.[42] The government's success in occupying several of FARC's 'strategic corridors' also curbed the mobility of the rebels.[43] Rebel leaders were specifically targeted during the year, resulting in the arrest of the most senior FARC leader ever to be captured, Simón Trindad, in January; the surrender of Herando Buitrago, another prominent FARC leader, in November; and the capture of José Ramirez, a senior ELN commander notoriously involved in the kidnapping business, in December.[44]

FARC kept up its retaliation, however, including cross-border raids into Ecuador and Venezuela.[45] Major fighting between FARC and the AUC, killing 200, took place in the Choco region, bordering Panama, in August.[46] Although informal talks were held between the government and FARC, they faltered on the rebel group's insistence on 'humanitarian exchange' (i.e., the release of imprisoned rebels in exchange for military and political hostages held by FARC) and the demand for a demilitarized zone.[47] Although the government appeared to take a more conciliatory position towards the ELN, there was no real move towards negotiations.[48]

[40] ICG, 'Hostages for prisoners: a way to peace in Colombia?', ICG Latin America Briefing no. 4, 8 Mar. 2004, p. 5; 'New campaign against the FARC', *Latin American Andean Report*, RA-04-05, 4 May 2004, p. 10; and 'War in Colombia demands greater involvement, says US military study', *Latin American Security and Strategic Review*, SSR-04-05, May 2004, pp. 1–3.

[41] 'Armed conflict enters key phase', *Latin American Andean Group Report*, RA-04-06, 8 June 2004, p. 5.

[42] 'No "decapitation" bid, but no let-up either', *Latin American Weekly Report*, WR-04-34, 31 Aug. 2004, p. 8. See also 'Colombian army commander presents results of democratic security policy', *El País* (Cali), 8 June 2004, in 'Democratic security policy continues to yield results', FBIS-LAT-2004-0608, 9 June 2004.

[43] Decker, Z. B., 'The FARC in the Uribe era', *El Espectador* (Bogota), 10 Oct. 2004, in 'Analyst contends FARC losing battle to Colombian Government', FBIS-LAT-2004-1010, 12 Oct. 2004.

[44] 'First FARC "head" falls, in Quito', *Latin American Weekly Report*, WR-04-02, 13 Jan. 2004; 'Paramilitaries to start demobilising, FARC leader surrenders', *Latin American Weekly Report*, WR-04-46, 23 Nov. 2004, p. 4; and McDermott, J., 'Colombia captures top kidnapper', BBC News Online, 12 Dec. 2004, URL <http://news.bbc.co.uk/2/4089379.stm>.

[45] 'FARC guerrillas hit back, hard', *Latin American Weekly Report*, WR-04-09, 2 Mar. 2004, p. 6; 'Cross-border FARC raid highlights vulnerability', *Latin American Weekly Report*, WR-04-05, 3 Feb. 2004, p. 4; and 'Confirmed: FARC operates across the border', *Latin American Weekly Report*, WR-04-11, 16 Mar. 2004, p. 11.

[46] 'Colombia: 200 reported killed in FARC–AUC battles in Choco region', ACAN-EFE (Panama City), 18 Aug. 2004, in 'Fighting escalates between rebels, militias in Colombia', FBIS-LAT-2004-0818, 19 Aug. 2004.

[47] 'Colombia: article doubts prisoner swap could lead to peace process', *El Espectador* (Bogota), 22 Aug. 2004, in 'Doubts and certainties of humanitarian proposal', FBIS-LAT-2004-0822, 25 Aug. 2004.

[48] 'Re-election bids advance, peace talks falter', *Latin American Weekly Report*, WR-04-25, 29 June 2004, p. 7. For analysis of the relationship between FARC and the ELN see 'Colombian analysts: FARC–ELN unity "unthinkable"', *El País* (Cali) (Internet edn), 17 Oct. 2004, in 'Issue of the week: FARC and ELN, so near and yet so far', FBIS-LAT-2004-1017, 19 Oct. 2004.

The forceful approach on the part of the Colombian Government remained controversial, and government troops, paramilitaries and rebel parties alike were accused of violence directed against civilians, particularly the indigenous population.[49] The grave humanitarian situation caused by the conflict is reflected in the fact that Colombia is third only to Sudan and the DRC in terms of the number of displaced persons, and drug-related crime continues to be the most common cause of death after cancer.[50] Nevertheless, Uribe's domestic approval ratings remained solid, and neighbouring leaders have expressed their approval of the drugs trade clamp-down.[51] US President Bush showed his approval by promising to continue aid after the formal end of 'Plan Colombia' in September 2005.[52]

Sudan

Sudan's National Islamic Front (NIF) Government and the main rebel group in the south, the Sudan People's Liberation Movement/Army (SPLM/A), at war for over 21 years, made painstaking progress towards peace in 2004. Sudan's second conflict, waged in the country's western region of Darfur between the government and two rebel groups—the Sudan Liberation Movement/Army (SLM/A) and the Justice and Equality Movement (JEM)—began in February 2003 and reached alarming levels by the end of 2004, with over 70 000 people killed and up to 2 million forcibly displaced.[53] Although the UN humanitarian coordinator for Sudan in March 2004 labelled Darfur the 'world's greatest humanitarian catastrophe', the divisions of the international community over potential military intervention in the region were reflected in an inconclusive debate over whether the events in Darfur could be classified as genocide.[54]

[49] 'Human rights in Colombia priority for European Parliament', *El Espectador* (Bogota), 7 Feb. 2004, in 'Human rights, priority for European Parliament before Uribe', FBIS-LAT-2004-0207, 10 Feb. 2004; and 'FARC in "selective" hits on Indian leaders', *Latin American Weekly Report*, WR-04-45, 16 Nov. 2004, p. 7.

[50] Reuters, 'Crisis facing Colombians is called worst in hemisphere', *New York Times*, 11 May 2004, p. 8; and 'Country profile: Colombia', BBC News Online, 26 Nov. 2004, URL <http://news.bbc.co.uk/1/1212798.stm>.

[51] Uribe's approval rate was 67 per cent in Nov. 2004. 'Uribe's popularity on the wane', *Latin American Andean Group Report*, RA-04-11, 2 Nov. 2004, p. 8; 'Uribe keeps Bush and Chávez onside', *Latin American Andean Group Report*, RA-04-12, 30 Nov. 2004, p. 10; and 'Guatemala: president thanks Colombia for bilateral cooperation against narcotics', ACAN-EFE (Panama City), 18 Nov. 2004, in 'Guatemala's Berger thanks Colombia for drug help', FBIS-LAT-2004-1118, 18 Nov. 2004.

[52] US Department of State, 'FY 2006 International Affairs (Function 150) Budget Request: foreign operations, export financing, and related programs (foreign operations)' (Department of State, Washington, DC, 2005), URL <http://www.state.gov/m/rm/rls/iab/2006/html/41795.htm>. See also chapter 8 in this volume.

[53] US Department of State, *Documenting Atrocities in Darfur* (US Department of State: Washington, DC, Sep. 2004), URL <http://www.state.gov/g/drl/rls/36028.htm>; and HRW, 'Targeting the Fur: mass killings in Darfur', HRW Briefing Paper, 21 Jan. 2005, URL <http://hrw.org/backgrounder/africa/darfur0105/>. Reliable figures are difficult to obtain, however, and some estimates are considerably higher. See, e.g., Save Darfur, 'Violence and suffering in Sudan's Darfur region', n.d., URL <http://www.savedarfur.org/>, which estimates at least 200 000 dead.

[54] 'UN envoy calls west Sudan's crisis world's worst', UN Wire, 19 Mar. 2004, URL <http://www.unwire.org/UNWire/20040319/449_14196.asp>. US Secretary of State Colin Powell referred to the situation in Darfur as 'genocide' in Sep. 2004. An investigation into war crimes and crimes against

Testifying to the importance of sustained and comprehensive peace processes, negotiations between the Sudanese Government and the SPLM/A—mediated by the Intergovernmental Authority on Development (IGAD)—finally resulted in the signing of the Comprehensive Peace Agreement on 9 January 2005.[55] Most importantly, the agreement stipulated the equal sharing of oil revenues (largely derived from the south), proportionate sharing of civil service posts and the right of the south to vote on secession after an interim period of autonomy of six years. Negotiations between the NIF Government and the rebel groups in Darfur were less successful. Talks restarted in March 2004, mediated by a representative of the Government of Chad. An agreement was signed in N'Djamena, Chad, by a representative of the Sudanese Government and leaders of both the SLM/A and the JEM on 8 April, but its effectiveness was limited.[56]

The negotiations on Darfur were complicated by the diversity of actors in the region (and periodic hostility between them) as well as a questionable commitment on the part of the Sudanese Government to bringing the violence to an end. The government-affiliated Janjaweed militias were pivotal players in the conflict but were not represented in any formal peace negotiations. Sudan's policy of publicly distancing itself from the Janjaweed yet using them in effect as a powerful proxy aggravated the situation,[57] in particular as air raids by the government paved the way for direct attacks on civilians by the Janjaweed.[58] Some of the most egregious violence, involving raids on villages, looting, raping and pillaging, took place at the hands of the Janjaweed and was primarily targeted at civilians rather than SLM/A or JEM forces.[59] The African Mission in Sudan (AMIS), deployed to Darfur in July, faced difficulties owing to the continued fighting in the region.[60]

humanity committed in Darfur was launched by the UN Secretary-General in Oct. in response to UN Security Council Resolution 1564, 18 Sep. 2004, and was expected to report its findings in early 2005. Action against genocide—defined as a specific intent to destroy, in whole or in part, a national, ethnic or religious group—is required under the 1951 Convention on the Prevention and Punishment of the Crime of Genocide; the convention is reproduced at URL <http://www.unhchr.ch/html/menu3/b/p_genoci.htm>.

[55] Landmark agreements had been reached in 2004, including the Agreement on Wealth Sharing during the Pre-Interim and Interim Period of 7 Jan. and 3 protocols of 26 May between the government and the SPLM: on power sharing (outlining a system for a separate southern administration); on the resolution of conflict in Southern Kordofan/Nuba Mountains and Blue Nile States; and on the resolution of the conflict in Abyei Area. See the Nairobi Declaration on the Final Phase of Peace in the Sudan, State House, Nairobi, 5 June 2004, at URL <http://www.usip.org/library/pa/sudan/pa_sudan.html>. For a description of earlier stages of the peace process see Dwan and Gustavsson (note 1), pp. 119–21.

[56] For the Humanitarian Ceasefire Agreement, known as the N'Djamena Agreement, see URL <http://www.unsudanig.org/emergencies/darfur/reports/index.jsp>. See also Middle East News Agency (MENA) (Cairo), 29 Dec. 2004 in 'Sudan: government thwarts attack on west Darfur, kills 21 rebels', FBIS-NES-2004-1229, 30 Dec. 2004.

[57] The Sudanese Government was required to disarm the Janjaweed militias by UN Security Council Resolution 1556, 30 July 2004. 'Fleeing the horsemen that kill for Khartoum', *The Economist*, 15 May 2004, p. 22.

[58] Wallis, W., 'Darfur's darkest chapter (part two)', *Financial Times Weekend Magazine*, 21 Aug. 2004, p. 1.

[59] Lacey, M., 'In Sudan, militiamen on horses uproot a million', *New York Times*, 4 May 2004, p. 1.

[60] For further details on AMIS see appendix 3A in this volume.

Talks continued, under the mediation of the African Union (AU), in Abuja, Nigeria, in the autumn and reached some agreement, but they broke down again in December after a government offensive directed at civilians and SLM/A targets in southern Darfur.[61] Although the SLM/A and the JEM initially cooperated as a single delegation in negotiations with the government, sporadic clashes between members of the two rebel groups complicated efforts to put up a united front against the government.[62] In addition, already at the outset of the 2004 round of talks on Darfur, individuals who did not consider themselves represented by either the SLM/A or the JEM expressed their dissatisfaction at being excluded. In October it was reported that two active groups had broken away from the JEM.[63] One group, the National Movement for Reformation and Development (NMRD), estimated to command 1000–3000 fighters, was involved in clashes with both government troops and the JEM during the autumn. In December the government decided to pursue separate talks with the NMRD.[64]

While grievances over economic governance and marginalization by the central government were expressed both in the south of Sudan and in Darfur, there was no effort to explicitly link the peace processes, either by the Sudanese Government or by external mediators. Concerns were raised during the autumn that the NIF Government was unscrupulously exploiting international goodwill over prospects for a final settlement with the SPLM/A and deliberately prolonging talks so as to have a free hand in Darfur.[65] In more positive manifestations of linkage, however, analysts have argued that the January 2005 Comprehensive Peace Agreement between the SPLM/A and the government could set a precedent for conflict resolution in Darfur.[66]

Conflict tactics and their consequences for civilians

In conflict analysis, a distinction is often made between conventional warfare between states and internal conflicts in which at least one party is a non-state

[61] 'The chairman of the African Union Commission welcomes the agreement reached by the Sudanese parties of the humanitarian situation in Darfur', African Union Press Release, 1 Sep. 2004, URL <http://www.africa-union.org/DARFUR/homedar.htm>; Agence France-Presse (Paris), 10 Nov. 2004, in 'Sudan: African Union welcomes breakthrough in Darfur talks', FBIS-AFR-2004-1110, 11 Nov. 2004; Integrated Regional Information Network for Horn of Africa (IRIN-HOA), 'Continuing violence reported in south Darfur', IRIN-HOA Weekly Round-up 218, 6–12 Nov. 2004; and Middle East News Agency (MENA) (Cairo), 19 Dec. 2004, in 'MENA: AU mediation chief says Abuja talks on Sudan stalled', FBIS-NES-2004-1219, 20 Dec. 2004.

[62] Agence France-Presse (Paris), 4 Nov. 2004, 'Sudan: clashes between Darfur rebel groups leave 20 dead', in FBIS-AFR-2004-1104, 5 Nov. 2004.

[63] Sengupta, S., 'New guerilla factions arise in Sudan ahead of peace talks', *New York Times*, 25 Oct. 2004, p. 4; and United Nations, Report of the Secretary-General on the Sudan pursuant to paragraph 15 of Security Council Resolution 1564 (2004), UN document S/2004/881, paras 6, 13 and 16.

[64] 'Sudan seeks talks with new group', BBC News Online, 5 Dec. 2004, URL <http://news. bbc.co.uk/2/4070941.stm>.

[65] ICG, 'Sudan's dual crises: refocusing on IGAD', Africa Briefing no. 19, 5 Oct. 2004, pp. 1–3, URL <http://www.icg.org/home/index.cfm?id=3043&l=1>.

[66] 'An overdue peace: the southern Sudan deal should be a model for Darfur', *Financial Times* (US edn), 10 Jan. 2005, p. 12.

actor. In the former, conflict is seen to involve large, organized and well-disciplined national forces, backed up by advanced technology, and parties which observe the international laws of war and international humanitarian law. Internal conflict, on the other hand, is seen to be characterized by small, diverse and often ill-disciplined groups relying on small arms and light weapons to fight a mobile war against one or more enemies.[67] A contrast is also drawn in the relationship between the warring parties and the civilian population in these different types of conflict, with the non-state rebel groups being seen to interact far more closely with the civilian population than with regular government forces. Rebel groups are seen to implicate civilians in conflict through their reliance on civilian support, shelter and resources, even if they are secured through brutal and coercive means. At the same time, rebels are seen as deliberately attacking civilians as part of a tactic of aiming at weaker and less-protected targets. Tactics such as suicide bombings, hostage takings and seizure of public buildings also ensure rebel groups significant media attention and can highlight their cause at home and abroad, as Chechen tactics demonstrated throughout 2004. In this context, it is becoming increasingly difficult to distinguish between asymmetric tactics and acts of terrorism.[68]

However, despite disparities in training, level of professionalism and strength both between different governments and between regular and non-government forces, the conflict tactics employed by both are seen as becoming increasingly similar, particularly in their effect on civilians. The 'Western way of warfare', which developed in the 1990s as a result of the so-called Revolution in Military Affairs and made states rely increasingly on technological advantage to pursue military advantage, has been challenged in the context of recent conflicts.[69] 'Low-risk' warfare, exercised primarily by the USA, in which fighters far removed from the battlefield rely on precision bombing and targeted attacks involving little risk to either themselves or civilian populations, has been largely discounted for two reasons. First, it has proven ineffective in purely military terms to ensure the defeat of smaller and less well-armed forces employing 'lightning' attacks, ambushes and bombs, before disappearing into familiar rural terrain or, increasingly, blending into urban civilian populations. The experience of the USA and its allies in Afghanistan and, more recently, in Iraq testifies to the impotency of overwhelming technological warfare superiority. Second, risk-free warfare has proven a chimera in contexts where a large part of the conflict is about 'winning the peace' and securing public support. In this context, the government party cannot prosecute the conflict from afar but must engage with the public. This has forced intervening states, particularly Western states, to make operational and

[67] See, e.g., Kaldor (note 20).

[68] For further discussion see Stepanova, E., *Anti-terrorism and Peace-building During and After Conflict*, SIPRI Policy Paper no. 2 (SIPRI: Stockholm, June 2003), URL <http://www.sipri.org/contents/publications/recent.html>.

[69] For a discussion of how military superiority and 'low-risk' war is not easily translated into political results see Rasmussen, M. V., 'The revolution in military affairs and the boomerang effect', Danish Institute for International Studies (DIIS), DIIS report no. 6 (2004), URL <http://www.diis.dk/sw8623.asp>; and Coker, C., *Humane Warfare* (Routledge: New York, 2001).

doctrinal changes, placing greater emphasis on infiltration and the use of special forces so as to better combat rebel groups and deprive them of cover and support among the civilian population.[70] This development turns the concept of asymmetry on its head, as tactics used by the USA and the UK in Afghanistan and Iraq resemble those normally associated with weaker parties in conflict.[71]

While the government party is perceived to have an interest, as well as a duty, to ensure the support and protection of the population in an intra-state conflict, counter-insurgency tactics can result in higher casualties, both military and civilian, at the hands of government parties. Government parties may deliberately target civilians in conflict in much the same way as rebel groups do. The reasons for this include the inability to strike targets directly, the association of the population or a sector of it with 'the enemy', the calculated shock value of civilian deaths, material incentives, as well as the fragmentation of warring parties and lack of discipline.[72] This may reflect the tactical or military weakness of the government party itself, as is evident in the Sudanese Government's aiding and abetting of the Janjaweed militias in Darfur. However, material incentives and lack of discipline of government or irregular forces also play a role, particularly in those conflicts where natural resources and 'predation' play an important role.[73]

The movement of fighting into cities further exposes civilians to conflict.[74] Urban warfare is in part a function of changing demographic patterns but may also signal the growing strength of a rebel group, as the incursions of the Nepalese Maoist parties into the capital, Kathmandu, in 2004 indicated. Moreover, attacks on urban areas and targets guarantee rebel groups increased international and domestic media attention.

The killing, wounding, raping and pillaging of civilians are permanent features of armed conflict.[75] Even where the civilian population is not deliberately targeted, the effects of prolonged intra-state conflict on the health, welfare and development of individuals are catastrophic. Although the consequences of

[70] Shortages in human intelligence is increasingly recognized as the Achilles heel of US' counter-insurgency in Iraq. Tomes, R., 'Relearning counterinsurgency warfare', *Parameters*, US Army War College Quarterly, vol. 34, no. 1 (spring 2004).

[71] O'Neill, C., 'Terrorism, insurgency and the military response from South Armagh to Falluja', *RUSI Journal*, vol. 149, no. 5 (2004), pp. 22-25.

[72] See, e.g., Humphreys, M. and Weinstein, J., 'Handling and manhandling civilians in civil war: determinants of the strategies of warring factions', Aug. 2004, Unpublished manuscript, available at URL <http://www.prio.no/cscw/pdf/micro/techniqes/handling_civilians.pdf>; and Valentino, B., Huth, P. and Balch-Lindsay, D., '"Draining the sea": mass killing and guerrilla warfare', *International Organization*, vol. 58, no. 2 (spring 2004), pp. 375–407.

[73] See, e.g., Malaquais, A., 'Diamonds are a guerilla's best friend: the impact of illicit wealth on insurgency strategy', *Third World Quarterly*, vol. 22, no. 3 (2004), pp. 311–25; and Azam, J. P. and Hoeffler, A., 'Violence against civilians in civil wars: looting or terror?', *Journal of Peace Research*, vol. 39, no. 4 (2004), pp. 461–85.

[74] For a detailed discussion of urban and rural insurgencies see Marks, T. A., 'Urban insurgency', *Small Wars and Insurgencies*, vol. 14, no. 3 (autumn 2003), pp. 100-157.

[75] Efforts at tracking the incidence of rape in conflict contexts and its use as a deliberate tactic have recently been initiated. See, e.g., Amnesty International, Women and War Project, 'Rape as a weapon of war', URL <http://web.amnesty.org/actforwomen/conflict-1-eng>.

intra-state conflict for civilians are increasingly highlighted in the media, international policy discussions and academic research, analysis and directed action are impeded by the difficulty of tabulating direct and indirect non-combatant fatalities in conflict.[76] This is an important area for future research.

Nepal

The Communist Party of Nepal (Maoist)—CPN(M)—has fought against the government and the king since 1996, with the stated aim of establishing a communist state in Nepal and abolishing the monarchy. Since the CPN(M) walk-out from negotiations with the government in August 2003, breaking an eight-month ceasefire, heavy fighting has continued virtually unabated. In November 2004 it was estimated that close to 11 000 people had died as a result of the conflict, 2700 of whom since August 2003.[77] Nepal is one of the world's 10 poorest countries, and land issues are central to popular grievances and support for the rebels.[78]

The increasing ferocity of the conflict reflected a shift in tactics on both sides. The guerrilla tactics of the rebels included bombings and intimidations as a means of increasing support for the CPN(M) as well as the forcible recruitment of fighters. In January 2004, 192 students and teachers from villages in western Nepal were abducted by rebels and reportedly sent to military training camps; a further 300 students were kidnapped in the mid-western Rolpa district in February.[79] In the single largest seizure, rebels abducted over 1000 people from villages in Nepal's western Bajura district on 30 March.[80] Abductions continued during the year and, whereas independent analysts estimate the rebels' total mobilization capacity at 15 000 fighters, CPN(M) leader Pushpa Kamal Dahal, also known as Prachanda, stated that 100 000 people were undergoing guerrilla warfare training.[81] The government's response of arming local civilians in militia groups known as Rural

[76] United Nations (note 9); and UN Millennium Project 2005, 'Investing in Development: A practical plan to achieve the Millennium Development Goals, Overview', Jan. 2005, URL <http://unmp.forumone.com/>. The work undertaken by the Human Security Centre of the Liu Institute for Global Issues, University of British Colombia, with partners to produce the first annual Human Security Report, in 2005—a compilation of new statistics on the human costs of armed conflict—is an important first step in this direction. Liu Institute for Global Issues, University of British Colombia, 'Human Security Centre', URL <http://www.humansecuritycentre.org/>; and Uppsala Conflict Data Programme, 'Human Security Project', URL <http://www.pcr.uu.se/research/UCDP/>.

[77] Agence France-Presse, 'Nepal army has secured 2,000 villages, out of 4,000', 19 Nov. 2004, URL <http://www.reliefweb.int>.

[78] Waldman, A., 'Maoist guerrilla insurgency wreaks havoc, and change, in Nepal', *Financial Times*, 6 Feb. 2004, p. 4.

[79] Deutsche Presse Agentur, 'Maoists explode bomb near capital, traffic blocked in western Nepal', 10 Dec. 2004, URL <http://www.reliefweb.int>; Agence France-Presse, 'Maoists kidnap 192 students and teachers in western Nepal', 1 Feb. 2004, URL <http://www.reliefweb.int>; and Agence France-Presse, 'Nepal's Maoists abduct more than 300 school students', 20 Feb. 2004, URL <http://www.reliefweb.int>.

[80] Deutsche Presse Agentur, 'Maoists abducted over 1,000 villagers in west Nepal', 1 Apr. 2004, URL <http://www.reliefweb.int>.

[81] Agence France-Presse, 'Maoist rebels in Nepal want to talk only with king', 2 Sep. 2004, URL <http://www.reliefweb.int>.

Volunteer Security Groups and Peace Committees fragmented the counter-insurgency.[82]

In testimony to the rebels' capacity to mount credible threats through intimidation rather than sheer strike capacity, the CPN(M) for the first time blockaded routes into Kathmandu between 17 and 24 August and launched attacks in the city centre.[83] Clashes between the army and rebels in the western parts of the country in December, killing 23 rebels and 20 police and soldiers, indicated that the armed insurgency did not wane in 2004.[84]

The conflict in Nepal is complicated by the power struggle between the rebels, the political parties in parliament and King Gyanendra, who has exercised executive powers, including control over the military, since October 2003.[85] The resignation of the royalist prime minister, Surya Bahadur Thapa, in May 2004 and the appointment of the new prime minister, Sher Bahadur Deuba, by the king led to further marginalization of the government in the conflict. The CPN(M) rejected offers of talks with Deuba and demanded direct talks with the king. The rebels also made international mediation and the removal of their labelling as terrorists by the Nepalese authorities a condition for any peace talks.[86] The political situation in Nepal came to a crisis in February 2005 when King Gyanendra assumed direct power by declaring a state of civil emergency and dismissing the government.[87]

Uganda

The conflict between the Lord's Resistance Army (LRA) rebel group and the Ugandan Government under President Yoweri Museveni continued to pose a grave threat to the Ugandan population in 2004, largely outside the international media spotlight.[88] The conflict, carried out in the north of Uganda since 1988, has seen alarming levels of child soldier recruitment: one source estimated that close to 90 per cent of the LRA fighters are minors.[89] Children also answer for a particularly large proportion of Uganda's 1.5 million

[82] ICG, 'Nepal: Dangerous plans for village militias', ICG Asia Briefing no. 30, 17 Feb. 2004, URL <http://www.icg.org/home/index.cfm?id=2520&l=1>.

[83] Agence France-Presse, 'Rebels cut off routes to capital in first ever blockade', 18 Aug. 2004, URL <http://www.reliefweb.int>; and Morrison, D., 'Unusual blockade ends in Nepal', *Christian Science Monitor*, 25 Aug. 2004, URL <http://www.reliefweb.int>.

[84] 'Bloodshed rises in western Nepal', BBC News Online, 16 Dec. 2004, URL <http://news.bbc.co.uk/1/4100457.stm>.

[85] 'Nepal Maoists insist on republic', BBC News Online, 13 Feb. 2004, URL <http://news.bbc.co.uk/1/hi/world/south_asia/3487267.stm>; and Man Singh, K., 'Nepal's Maoist rebels reject PM's deadline for peace talks', Agence France-Presse, 28 Nov. 2004, URL <http://www. reliefweb.int>.

[86] Man Singh, K., 'Nepal's Maoist rebels reject PM's deadline for peace talks', Agence France-Presse, 28 Nov. 2004, URL <http://www.reliefweb.int>.

[87] 'Nepal gripped by political crisis', BBC News Online, 1 Feb. 2005, URL <http://news.bbc.co.uk/1/4227517.stm>.

[88] Jan Egeland, UN Undersecretary for Humanitarian Affairs, has repeatedly criticized the lack of attention given to the Ugandan conflict. See Wallis, W., 'Uganda vows to avenge massacre by rebels', *Financial Times*, 24 Feb. 2004, p. 4.

[89] UN Department of Public Affairs, 'Uganda: child soldiers at centre of mounting humanitarian crisis', 19 Dec. 2004, URL <http://www.un.org/events/tenstories/story.asp?storyID=100>.

displaced persons.[90] Despite the LRA's stated aim of fighting for the establishment of a Christian regime in Uganda, analysts generally agree that the lack of clarity of the rebel group's agenda makes a politically negotiated settlement of the conflict difficult, if not impossible.[91] Nevertheless, deep divisions in Ugandan society and the marginalization of the population of Acholiland (simultaneously the base for LRA recruitment and the target of LRA attacks) in the north of the country point to the grievances in the conflict.

The government's sustained campaign against the LRA resulted in the reported killing of over 200 rebels between January and March 2004.[92] The offensive of the Ugandan national army—the Ugandan People's Defence Force (UPDF)—picked up pace again in September, and the LRA was thought to be considerably weakened as a result.[93] The government, confident that a military 'solution' to the conflict was near, rejected a ceasefire offer by the LRA in September.[94] However, a ceasefire in Acholiland was agreed on 15 November and later extended to cover southern Sudan.[95] Talks were held on two occasions near the end of the year between LRA representatives and government negotiators, raising the potential for a negotiated end to the conflict.[96]

Substantial setbacks for the LRA at the hands of UPDF forces throughout the year provided little respite for the civilian population, however. Attacks on refugee camps in Uganda's northern region followed the usual LRA hit-and-run pattern, with the gruesome massacre of over 300 internally displaced persons in the Barlonyo camp, Lira district, on 21 February.[97] Similar attacks in May left several dozen civilians dead and sent thousands fleeing.[98] On 29 July the ICC began investigations into abuses of civilians by both the LRA and

[90] ICG, 'Northern Uganda: understanding and solving the conflict', Africa Report no. 77, 14 Apr. 2004, URL <http://www.icg.org/home/index.cfm?id=2588&l=1>.

[91] ICG (note 90), pp. 5–6.

[92] 'Uganda: army reportedly kills 27 LRA rebels in engagements on 9 January', *New Vision* (Kampala), 12 Jan. 2004, in FBIS-AFR-2004-0112, 13 Jan. 2004; 'Ugandan Army says it killed 58 northern rebels last week', *New Vision* (Kampala), 16 Jan. 2004, in FBIS-AFR-2004-0116, 20 Jan. 2004; 'Ugandan army reportedly kills 62 LRA rebels in north', *New Vision* (Kampala), 20 Feb. 2004, in FBIS-AFR-2004-0220, 23 Feb. 2004; and 'Ugandan Army targets LRA rebels', BBC News Online, 21 Mar. 2004, URL <http://news.bbc.co.uk/1/3555471.stm>.

[93] 'Ugandan forces "kill 25 rebels"', BBC News Online, 19 Sep. 2004, URL <http://news.bbc.co.uk/1/3670944.stm>.

[94] 'Ugandan Army says LRA rebels surrendering', *New Vision* (Kampala), 16 Sep. 2004, in FBIS-AFR-2004-0916, 17 Sep. 2004; and 'Ugandan Army rejects LRA rebels' cease-fire offer', *Sunday Vision* (Kampala), 19 Sep. 2004, in FBIS-AFR-2004-0919, 20 Sep. 2004.

[95] 'Uganda extends cease-fire zone into southern Sudan', *New Vision* (Kampala), 15 Dec. 2004, in FBIS-AFR-2004-1215, 16 Dec. 2004.

[96] 'Ugandan authorities, rebels hold peace talks in "undisclosed location"', *New Vision* (Kampala), 20 Nov. 2004, in FBIS-AFR-2004-1120, 20 Nov. 2004; and 'Ugandan mediator meets rebel LRA commanders over peace', *New Vision* (Kampala), 30 Dec. 2004, in FBIS-AFR-2004-1230, 31 Dec. 2004.

[97] IRIN-CEA, 'Rebels kill 52 in dawn attack on Lira IDPs camp', IRIN-CEA Weekly Round-up 212, 31 Jan.–6 Feb. 2004; United Nations Office for the Coordination of Humanitarian Affairs, 'Humanitarian update Uganda Mar 2004', vol. 6, no. 3 (31 Mar. 2004), URL <http://www.reliefweb.int>; and 'Uganda rebel leader orders fighters step up attacks on displacement camps', *New Vision* (Kampala), 29 May 2004, in FBIS-AFR-2004-0530, 31 May 2004.

[98] 'The LRA fights on', *Africa Confidential*, vol. 45, no. 11 (28 May 2004), p. 3.

Ugandan government forces.[99] Reports of at least 40 000 'night commuters'—women and children leaving their homes in rural areas of northern Uganda to seek refuge for the night in the bigger towns of Gulu and Kitgum for fear of LRA abductions—indicate the continued victimization of children in the Ugandan conflict.[100]

Having rejected the AU's offer of help in March, in September the Ugandan Government appealed for UN assistance for reconstruction.[101] Reconstruction and development of northern Uganda are especially important for protection of the population from LRA attacks. In the interim, the problems of dealing with an armed group which appears to have 'no policies, no specific demands and no mercy' and which relies on children to do its work continue to make the conflict in Uganda particularly difficult to address.[102]

The shifting location and containment of intra-state conflicts

One of the obvious classic features of intra-state conflict is that it takes place within the borders of a state. The fact that the members of all the contending groups typically have to continue to coexist within the same borders after the conclusion of civil war is often cited as an explanation for why many intra-state conflicts are protracted and intense.[103]

Within the context of an intra-state conflict, however, the location of the fighting may vary considerably, with different consequences for prosecution and resolution of the conflict. A number of intra-state conflicts, often intense, are highly local. They are usually pursued in remote areas within a country, where they raise very little international attention or even awareness. Fighting in Darfur in western Sudan, for example, raged throughout 2003 but came to the attention of the international media only in early 2004.[104] The containment of some intra-state conflicts may be a function of a range of factors, such as the nature of the grievance of the rebel group, its size and capacity, the level of economic and technical development of the country, as well as the geographical location and terrain of the conflict.[105] Where the source of the conflict

[99] 'Uganda: International Criminal Court investigates massacres in north', *Jeune Afrique–l'Intelligent* (Paris), 1 Aug. 2004, in 'Uganda: massacres under examination', FBIS-AFR-2004-0809, 10 Aug. 2004; and IRIN-CEA, 'Uganda: Security forces accused of torturing suspects', IRIN-CEA Weekly Round-up 249, 16–22 Oct. 2004.

[100] Egeland, J, 'A Ugandan tragedy', ReliefWeb, 10 Nov. 2004, URL <http://wwww.reliefweb.org>.

[101] 'Ugandan president rejects calls for AU force to quell rebels in north', *New Vision* (Kampala), 5 Mar. 2004, in FBIS-AFR-2004-0305, 8 Mar. 2004; and 'Uganda appeals for UN's help in reconstructing war-torn northern region', *New Vision* (Kampala), 30 Sep. 2004, in FBIS-AFR-2004-0930, 1 Oct. 2004.

[102] 'Double war', *Africa Confidential*, vol. 45, no. 5 (5 Mar. 2004), p. 2.

[103] Licklider, R., 'The consequences of negotiated settlements in civil wars, 1945–93', *American Political Science Review*, vol. 89, no. 3 (1995), pp. 681–90.

[104] Dwan and Gustavsson (note 1), p. 121.

[105] Recent analyses have examined the nature of terrain (e.g., forest or mountain) as a factor explaining the duration of civil wars. See, e.g., DeRouen, K. and Sobek, D., 'The dynamics of civil war duration and outcome', *Journal of Peace Research*, Special Issue on Duration and Termination of Civil War, vol. 41, no. 3 (May 2004), pp. 303–20.

grievance is local or the rebel group is weak, an intra-state conflict may be isolated domestically as well as internationally. One example of this is the long-standing conflict between the Karen ethnic group and Myanmar's military junta in the region near the border with Thailand. The internal containment of an intra-state conflict is also a function of the political and military capacity of the government. The Indonesian Government's effective closure of the province of Aceh in 2003 was a clear example of this, broken only by the forces of nature in the form of the 26 December 2004 tsunami.

In some cases, even where fighting is contained in one geographical location, the effects of the intra-state conflict can be felt nationwide. This is particularly the case where the conflict has been previously prosecuted on a wider scale. Ongoing fighting in the eastern provinces of the DRC in 2004, for example, complicated post-conflict reconstruction and conflict resolution elsewhere in the country. A third variant of the location dimension of intra-state conflict is its potential to shift across a state without necessarily increasing in terms of escalation or intensity. This may occur when a rebel group is driven out of the local area or when one or more of the warring parties seek new sources of civilian support or finance or, more often, when a warring party seeks to draw national and international attention to its cause.

In the post-cold war environment, attention arguably focused more on the regional, international and transnational dimensions of internal conflict than on shifting national dimensions. The spread of internal conflicts beyond national borders was seen as an increasing feature of international politics, in part because of the growing interdependence and integration of states and in part because of the broadening of the concept of security to include economic, environmental and societal factors, none of which can be easily confined within the borders of a nation state.[106] The early debate on conflict spillover focused on the spread of conflict to immediate neighbouring states, most graphically illustrated by the long-standing conflict between ethnic Tutsi and Hutu groups in the Great Lakes region of Central Africa and the prevalence of ethnic conflict in the former Yugoslavia in the early 1990s.

As seen in 2004, however, it is the relative lack of regional spillover of intra-state conflicts that is most striking. Long-standing intra-state conflicts in, for example, Algeria, Colombia, Myanmar, Sudan, Turkey and, more recently, Iraq have not (as yet) led to a cross-border war. The location of these intra-state conflicts varies substantially, with some isolated in a particular region (e.g., the conflict in Turkey) and others under way throughout the country (Colombia and Iraq). The absence of the spread of intra-state conflict beyond national borders does not mean that neighbouring regions have been unaffected by intra-state conflict: cross-border movements of refugees, smuggling of arms and natural resources, rebel organizations' use of bases in neighbouring countries for cross-border infiltrations, and attacks and incur-

[106] Brown, M. (ed.), *The International Dimensions of Internal Conflict* (MIT Press: Cambridge, Mass., 1996); and Buzan, B., 'The logic of regional security in the post-cold war world' in Hettne, B. *et al.* (eds), *The New Regionalism and the Future of Security and Development* (Macmillan: Basingstoke, 2000).

sions by government forces into neighbouring countries in pursuit of rebels (either with or without the agreement of the neighbouring governments) create severe pressure on contiguous states. West Africa is a particularly potent example of the destabilizing effects of the spillover of refugees, rebels, arms and government forces to neighbouring countries (Guinea, Guinea-Bissau and Côte d'Ivoire) from the intra-state conflicts in Liberia and Sierra Leone.[107] The phenomenon of intra-state conflicts that are and remain contained in various ways, and with various effects, however, raises interesting research questions regarding the factors that influence the geographical scope of intra-state conflict.

More recently, attention has focused on international, as opposed to solely regional, spillover of intra-state conflict. In the past few years this debate has been fuelled by the perceived rise of global transnational terrorist threats. Internationalization is seen by many as an inevitable consequence of globalization and its effect on markets and communications, which have provided rebel groups with the means to pursue armed conflict and a global platform to make their case. The rise of political Islam is perceived to bring an additional element to this internationalization—a shared grievance and a common goal between diverse rebel groups. The US-led war against al-Qaeda is premised on this perception of a conflict without a single territorial location in terms of grievance, the parties involved or the potential of its impact.

Ironically, the perspective of the global war on terrorism and its logic of internationalized motivation have led to increased emphasis on the isolation of intra-state conflicts. Outside actors as well as domestic governments are increasingly pursuing or supporting strategies to contain and isolate intra-state conflicts perceived to have 'global' motivations or grievances. Such an approach almost inevitably aligns international support with the perspective of the government party to the intra-state conflict. In so doing it has, arguably, reduced international pressure and engagement for a negotiated end to a number of conflicts. Two of the most obvious examples of the effect of the global war on terrorism on the pursuit of a policy of international isolation of intra-state conflict in 2004 were the conflicts in Chechnya and in Aceh. The interplay between the location of a conflict and its national, regional and international dimensions is another example of the diversity and complexity of intra-state conflict and demonstrates, yet again, the difficulty of classification and generalization.

The Democratic Republic of the Congo

The conflict in the DRC ended formally on 16 December 2002 with the signing of the Global and Inclusive Agreement on Transition in the Democratic

[107] For more detail on the conflicts in West Africa see, e.g., Adebajo, A., *Building Peace in West Africa*, International Peace Academy Occasional Papers series (Lynne Rienner: Boulder, Colo., 2002); and Ero, C. and Temin, J., 'Sources of conflict in West Africa', eds C. L. Sriram and Z. Nielsen, *Exploring Subregional Conflict: Opportunities for Conflict Prevention* (Lynne Rienner: Boulder, Colo., 2004).

Republic of the Congo.[108] This agreement was enabled by prior agreements in 2002 between the DRC Government and neighbouring Rwanda and Uganda, which had provided support to rebel groups during the war.[109] Despite the establishment of a transitional power-sharing government in July 2003 under President Joseph Kabila, and the initiated disarmament and integration of former rebel groups into the new transitional government forces—Forces armées du peuple congolais (FAPC, or the Armed Forces of the Congolese People)—post-conflict efforts in 2004 were largely lost on the country's eastern provinces.[110] The Ituri and North and South Kivu provinces' legacy of volatility is attributable both to their porous borders with Burundi, Rwanda and Uganda and to local factors, such as land scarcity and persistent interethnic tension over the control of gold and diamond mines in the area.

Efforts at regional pacification were thwarted by tensions in Ituri province between the militias of the minority Hema and majority Lendu ethnic groups, combined with resistance to the UN Organization Mission in the Democratic Republic of the Congo (MONUC) and FAPC forces.[111] Sporadic attacks against MONUC were launched throughout 2004 by both the Union des patriotes congolais (UPC, or the Union of Congolese Patriots), predominantly Hema, and the Front nationaliste intégrationniste (FNI, or the Front for National Integration), a Lendu armed faction.[112] In South Kivu, anti-FAPC sentiments culminated in the mutiny of dissident former officers of the Rassemblement congolais pour la democratie–Goma (RCD, or Congolese Rally for Democracy–Goma) against the FAPC regional commander and the seizure of Bukavu, the province capital, between 2 and 9 June, sending close

[108] The agreement was signed in Pretoria, South Africa, by the parties of the Inter-Congolese Dialogue—the DRC Government, the Congolese Rally for Democracy, the Movement for the Liberation of the Congo, the political opposition, civil society, the Congolese Rally for Democracy/Liberation Movement, the Congolese Rally for Democracy/National, and the Mai-Mai. The agreement is available at URL <http://www.iss.co.za/AF/profiles/DRCongo/cdreader/bin/6global.pdf>.

[109] The agreements between the DRC Government and Rwanda and Uganda are available at URL <http://www.usip.org/library/pa/drc_rwanda/drc_rwanda_pa07302002.html> and URL <http://www.usip.org/library/pa/drc_uganda/drc_uganda_09062002.html>, respectively.

[110] In Dec. 2004 the International Rescue Committee put the total number of war-related deaths in the DRC since 1998 at 3.8 million, making this conflict the world's deadliest conflict since World War II. White, D., 'Over 31,000 a month "are dying in Congo war"', *Financial Times*, 9 Dec 2004, p. 5. In late Mar. there was also fighting in the capital Kinshasa for the first time since the peace agreement of 2002. '"Coup attempt" in DRC capital', BBC News Online, 28 Mar. 2004, URL <http://news.bbc.co.uk/1/3576139.stm>.

[111] Agence France-Presse (Paris), 12 Apr. 2004, in 'DRC: UN "grapples" with problems of armed militia groups in northeast', *Daily Report–Sub-Saharan Africa (FBIS-AFR)*, FBIS-AFR-2004-0412, 13 Apr. 2004. Arrangements for regional governance include the establishment of the Ituri Interim Administration (IIA) in Apr. 2003. For a detailed discussion of the situation in Ituri see ICG, 'Maintaining momentum in the Congo: the Ituri problem', ICG Africa Report no. 84, 26 Aug. 2004, p. 12.

[112] Agence France-Presse, 25 Feb. 2004, 'DRC: UN troops respond to attack by UPC militiamen in Ituri', in FBIS-AFR-2004-0225, 25 Feb. 2004; and Kabamba, Y., 'DRC: Ten militiamen killed in Ituri following clashes with peacekeepers in Kombokabu', ReliefWeb, 10 May 2004, URL <http://www.reliefweb.int>. In Dec. 2003 the UPC split into 2 groups: UPC–Thomas Lubanga and UPC–Floribert Kisembo, although UPC–Kisembo is a minor armed group. For a discussion of the armed groups active in Ituri see Boshoff, H. and Vircoulon, T., 'Democratic Republic of Congo: update on Ituri', *African Security Review*, vol. 13, no. 2 (2004), pp. 64–68, URL <http://www.iss.org.za/pubs/ASR/13No2/Contentpdf.html>.

to 30 000 people fleeing. Further fighting between dissident RCD–Goma forces and government forces continued in North Kivu in December.[113]

The presence of the Forces démocratiques de libération du Rwanda (FDLR, or the Democratic Forces for the Liberation of Rwanda) in the DRC since the 1994 Rwandan genocide demonstrates the conflation of local and regional tensions in eastern DRC.[114] It is estimated that 8000–10 000 Rwandan Hutu rebels remain in the DRC, continuing their strategy of launching periodic attacks into Rwanda.[115] In April 2004, MONUC officials reported the presence in the DRC of Rwandan national troops—Forces de défense Rwandaises (FDR)—although Rwandan authorities denied this.[116] Despite warnings from the UN that military incursions by Rwanda into DRC territory would undermine regional efforts at stabilization, FDR troops entered the DRC on 1 December, in an alarming repetition of events in 1996 and 1998, when Rwandan troops' pursuit of Hutu rebels in eastern DRC was instrumental in fuelling the subsequent wars. By mid-December 2004 it was reported that 1000 people a day were dying in the DRC as a result of the conflict and that only 880 of an estimated 15 000 fighters in Ituri had voluntarily disarmed.[117]

Russia (Chechnya)

The second war between the Russian Government and the breakaway Chechen Republic began in 1999. It has claimed an estimated 70 000–80 000 lives and resulted in hundreds of thousands of Chechen refugees.[118] The Chechen conflict has been characterized by Russian authorities as an internal anti-terrorist

[113] The clashing groups were reported to be local Mai-Mai militias and former RCD–Goma soldiers. Tshibangu, T., MONUC, 'Weekly retrospective for October 31st to November 6th, 2004', 9 Nov. 2004, URL <http://www.monuc.org/NewsPrint.aspx?NewsID=4210>; and Lewis, D., 'Renegade fighters gain ground in eastern Congo–UN', Reuters, Goma, DRC, 20 Dec. 2004.

[114] The conflict between the DRC Government and RCD–Goma is not listed in table 2A.3, although it previously reached the threshold of 1000 battle-related deaths. This is because the parties now fighting in the conflict are RCD dissidents, a new group which has not, on its own, reached 1000 battle-related deaths. The conflict between the Rwandan Government and the FDLR does appear in the table, however, as it is a conflict between 2 warring parties that previously resulted in 1000 battle-related deaths. For further discussion see appendix 2B. United States Agency for International Development (USAID), 'Democratic Republic of the Congo: complex emergency', Situation Report no. 3, 3 May 2004, URL <http://www.usaid.gov>.

[115] Balint-Kurti, D., 'Rwandan invasion evidence proves elusive', Associated Press Online, 5 Dec. 2004, URL <http://www.highbeam.com/library/doc0.asp?docid=1P1:103111283&refid=hbr_flinks1>.

[116] 'Killers next door?', *The Economist*, 1 May 2004, p. 44. A Joint Verification Mechanism to address border security was established by the Rwandan and DRC governments in Sep., but with little effect. Integrated Regional Information Network for Central and Eastern Africa (IRIN-CEA), 'DRC–Rwanda: Kigali, Kinshasa agree to border verification mechanism', IRIN-CEA Weekly Round-up 245, 18–25 Sep. 2004.

[117] Doyle, M., 'DRC conflict "kills 1,000 a day"', BBC News Online, 9 Dec. 2004, URL <http://news.bbc.co.uk/1/4080867.stm>; and Agence France-Presse (Paris), 'UN troops in DRC destroy three camps of armed militia group in Ituri region', 27 Dec. 2004, in FBIS-AFR-2004-1229, 30 Dec. 2004.

[118] Shah, A., 'Crisis in Chechnya', Global Issues, Sep. 2004, URL <http://www.globalissues.org/Geopolitics/Chechnya.asp>. According to another estimate, at least 10% of the Chechen population have been killed and around 50% have been forced to flee their homes at some point. Cornell, S. E., 'Chechnya: terrorists take centre stage', *RUSI/Jane's Homeland Security and Resilience Monitor*, vol. 3, no. 8 (Oct. 2004).

operation and has seen little foreign engagement and no formal negotiations.[119] Russian President Vladimir Putin came to power on the back of a promise to defeat the Chechen rebels, and the war, as well as the prestige invested in that effort, continues to shape his presidency. The complex links between the Chechen conflict, the Northern Caucasus region and the wider international stage were alarmingly demonstrated in 2004.

The most significant event of 2004 in the Chechen Republic itself was the 9 May bomb attack in the capital, Grozny, killing up to 30 people, among them Moscow-backed Chechen President Akhmad Kadyrov.[120] The attack, for which the Chechen rebel leader Shamil Basayev later claimed responsibility, was a blow to Russia's strategy of 'normalization' in Chechnya.[121] A new pro-Moscow president, Alu Alkhanov, was elected on 29 August by a huge majority.[122] International observers were not permitted to observe the election, and the conduct and outcome were widely contested.[123]

The spread of the Chechen conflict to locations external to the republic, which began in 1999 with a series of bombings in Moscow, allegedly carried out by Chechen rebels, continued in 2004.[124] Chechen rebels were widely thought to be the instigators of the 6 February bombing of a Moscow underground train, which killed 39 people, as well as a wave of attacks around the time of the Chechen elections in August.[125] Chechen rebels were also blamed for the explosion of two civilian aircraft on 24 August shortly after they had taken off from Moscow airport, killing close to 100 people. Rebel leader and former Chechen President Aslan Maskhadov consistently denied any involvement in the attacks, which some analysts see as indicative of his lack of effective control over the Chechen rebel forces.[126] The most devastating attack took place in the North Caucasus region, however, when 1200 school-

[119] The conflict in Chechnya in 1994–96 formally ended with the signing of a comprehensive ceasefire agreement, the Khasavyurt Accords, on 26 Aug. 1996, and was followed by a peace agreement in 1997. Although the Khasavyurt agreement formalized the withdrawal of Russian troops, it did not address the core issue of the future legal status of Chechnya. For more detail, see Evangelista, M., *The Chechen Wars: Will Russia Go the Way of the Soviet Union?* (Brookings Institution Press: Washington, DC, 2002).

[120] 'Chechen president killed by bomb', BBC News Online, 9 May 2004, URL <http://news.bbc.co.uk/1/3697715.stm>.

[121] 'A gaping hole', *The Economist*, 15 May 2004, p. 25.

[122] The official figure was nearly 74%. 'New Chechen president sworn in', BBC News Online, 5 Oct. 2004, URL <http://news.bbc.co.uk/2/3715602.stm>.

[123] 'International community slams Chechen ballot as undemocratic as more details surface of rigging', Radio Free Europe/Radio Liberty, *RFE/RL Newsline*, vol. 8, no. 166, part 1 (31 Aug. 2004).

[124] 'Russia to seal off Chechnya', BBC News Online, 14 Sep. 1999, URL <http://news.bbc.co.uk/1/446689.stm>; and 'Rebels seize Moscow theatre', BBC News Online, 23 Oct. 2002, URL <http://news.bbc.co.uk/1/2354753.stm>.

[125] Myers, S. L., '39 die in Moscow as bomb goes off on subway train', *New York Times*, 7 Feb. 2004, p. 1; Uzzell, L., 'No evidence required: Chechens blamed for subway bombing', *Chechnya Weekly*, vol. 5, no. 6 (11 Feb. 2004), URL <http://www.jamestown.org/publications_details.php?volume_id=396&&issue_id=2908>; and 'Moscow "suicide blast" kills ten', BBC News Online, 31 Aug. 2004, URL <http://news.bbc.co.uk/1/ 3615970.stm>.

[126] 'Double air disaster hits Russia', BBC News Online, 25 Aug. 2004, URL <http://news.bbc.co.uk/1/3596354.stm>; 'Planes blown up by "terrorists"', BBC News Online, 30 Aug. 2004, URL <http://news.bbc.co.uk/1/3612150.stm>; and Smith, S., 'Viewpoint: top Chechen commanders', BBC News Online, 9 Sep. 2004, URL <http://news.bbc.co.uk/1/3642532.stm>.

children, teachers and other adults were taken hostage in a school in Beslan, in the Republic of North Ossetia, on 1 September. When Russian troops stormed the school to end the siege on 3 September, over 330 people were killed.[127] The exact nature of the links between the Beslan school siege and the Chechen conflict was disputed: Russia blamed international terrorists with links to Maskhadov, but Chechen rebel leader Shamil Basayev eventually claimed responsibility for the siege. It later emerged that several of the perpetrators were Ingush rather than Chechen.[128]

Some analysts inferred that the violence outside Chechnya was less exemplary of Chechen rebels' strike capacity than of the failure of the Russian Government's uncompromising policy towards the North Caucasus region as a whole and the 'irrevocable spread' of the Chechen conflict in the region.[129] Chechens have frequently crossed into the adjacent republics of Dagestan, Ingushetia and North Ossetia, occasionally colluding with local rebel forces.[130] The 21 June 2004 raids against official buildings in Ingushetia, including the region's ministry of interior, killing at least 44 and wounding 60, were the biggest armed operations in the province since the second Chechen war erupted in 1999.[131] Repeated attacks and mine explosions in November 2004 killed over 40 Russian troops.[132] Concerns about the stability of the North Caucasus region extended also to Georgia, which Russia accuses of failing to take a sufficiently active stance against the Chechen rebels and whose own separatist conflict in South Ossetia also flared up in 2004.[133]

Despite earlier promises of withdrawal, the number of Russian troops on Chechen territory remains at over 80 000.[134] Ten years of violence and grave human rights abuses against civilians at the hands of Chechen rebel groups, the Russian Federal Security Service and, more recently, the Kadyrovtsy militia have left the Chechen population physically, economically and socially

[127] Liss, A., 'Pains lingers on in Beslan', BBC News Online, 2 Oct. 2004, URL <http://news.bbc.co.uk/1/3710294.stm>.

[128] 'Excerpts: Basayev claims Beslan', BBC News Online, 17 Sep. 2004, URL <http://news.bbc.co.uk/1/3665136.stm>; and Mulvey, S., 'Analysis: the hostage takers', BBC News Online, 6 Sep. 2004, URL <http://news.bbc.co.uk/1/3627586.stm>.

[129] Cornell, S. E., 'Chechnya: terrorists take centre stage', *RUSI/Jane's Homeland Security and Resilience Monitor*, vol. 3, no. 8 (Oct. 2004); and Blank, S., 'Lessons of an endless war', *RUSI/Jane's Homeland Security and Resilience Monitor*, vol. 3, no. 9 (Nov. 2004).

[130] Riskin, A., '"Erasure of borders" between Chechnya and Ingushetia', *Nezavisimaya Gazeta* (Moscow), 19 Apr. 2004, in 'Russia: Conflict seen spreading from Chechnya to Ingushetia', FBIS-SOV-2004-0419, 20 Apr. 2004.

[131] Reuters (Moscow), 'Putin calls for rebels to be hunted down', *Financial Times* (Online edn), 22 June 2004; and Jack, A., 'Fifty die as Chechen rebels mount raids in Ingushetia', *Financial Times*, 23 June 2004, p. 2. For further discussion see 'Is Russia planning a war in Ingushetia?', *RFE/RL Caucasus Report*, vol. 7, no. 16 (22 Apr. 2004).

[132] 'Over 40 Russians killed in clashes on 24–29 November—Chechen rebel web site', BBC Monitoring Service, 30 Nov. 2004.

[133] Buechsensechutz, U., 'A stability pact for the Caucasus?', *RFE/RL Newsline*, vol. 8, no. 179, Part 2 (20 Sep. 2004); and Barateli, O., 'Chechen rebels' arms cache found in Pankisi gorge', ITAR-TASS (Moscow), 19 Apr. 2004, in FBIS-SOV-96-240, 20 Apr. 2004.

[134] 'Russia to boost Chechnya forces', BBC News Online, 11 May 2004, URL <http://news.bbc.co.uk/1/3703755.stm>.

devastated.[135] The continued difficulty for international aid agencies to gain access and Putin's reluctance to engage the international community in conflict resolution efforts testify to the detrimental effects of localizing or containing conflicts.[136] At the same time, Putin continues to present the Chechen conflict as part of the global war on terrorism, contributing to the conflict's international resonance.

Indonesia (Aceh)

The conflict between Gerakan Aceh Merdeka (GAM, or the Free Aceh Movement) and the Indonesian Government dates back to 1976 and has claimed more than 15 000 lives.[137] GAM continues to demand independent statehood for the Aceh province in north-western Sumatra and its approximately 4 million inhabitants.

Although it is resource-rich, the Aceh province has suffered from poor economic governance and endemic corruption which, in combination with continuing insecurity, have spurred GAM grievances and channelled young people into the rebel movement.[138] The conflict is localized in grievance and geography: its remoteness allowed the Aceh province to be almost completely sealed off from the outside world by the Indonesian Government. Although the containment of the Aceh conflict has played a role in preventing spillover tendencies common to many intra-state conflicts, it has also limited efforts at resolution and international engagement.[139]

The declaration of a military emergency in Aceh and the imposition of martial law in the region in May 2003 marked the start of a new military offensive by 40 000 Indonesian troops in the province. According to Indonesian military officials, 2100 presumed rebels have been captured and around 2000 killed since the start of the offensive.[140] Reports of gross human rights abuses by

[135] Joint statement by Amnesty International, Human Rights Watch, the Medical Foundation for the Care of Victims of Torture, and Memorial, 'The situation in Chechnya and Ingushetia deteriorates: new evidence of enforced disappearances, rape, torture, and extrajudicial executions', Human Rights News, 8 Apr. 2004, URL <http://www.hrw.org/english/docs/2004/04/07/russia8408.htm>.

[136] 'Growing instability keeps aid out of Chechnya', *Chechen Times*, 30 Sep. 2004, URL <http://www.chechentimes.org/en/press/?id=22067>.

[137] Unidjaja; F. D., 'Indonesia extends state of civil emergency in Aceh', *Jakarta Post*, 13 Nov. 2004, in Foreign Broadcast Information Service, *Daily Report–East Asia (FBIS-EAS)*, FBIS-EAS-2004-1113, 15 Nov. 2004.

[138] Schultze, K., 'Comment: how polls offer the prospect of peace in Aceh', *Financial Times*, 3 Aug. 2004, p. 13.

[139] Agence France-Presse (Hong Kong), 'Indonesian military further curbs foreign media visits to Aceh', 25 Mar. 2004, Foreign Broadcast Information Service and World News Connection, 26 Mar. 2004; and Jones, S., 'Will Indonesia seize its chance?', BBC News Online, 8 Jan. 2004, URL <http://news.bbc. co.uk/1/4157393.stm>.

[140] Agence France-Presse (Hong Kong), 'Indonesia "warmly welcomes" arrest of Aceh separatist leaders in Stockholm', 15 June 2004, in FBIS-EAS-2004-0615, 16 June 2004; and Roosa, J., 'Aceh's dual disasters: the tsunami and military rule', *Green Left Weekly* (Internet edn), 19 Jan. 2005, URL <http://www.greenleft.org.au/back/2005/611/611p14.htm>. There is disagreement over whether those killed were civilians or rebels. For this reason, the conflict in Aceh does not appear in table 2A.3, in appendix 2A.

both sides of the conflict emerged in 2004.[141] Martial law was lifted on 19 May 2004 and replaced by a state of civil emergency, but Indonesian security forces maintained a significant presence in the area. The change in status was generally interpreted as a largely tactical move to shore up sympathies for the government rather than any significant shift in policy towards the GAM insurgents.[142] The September elections for the Indonesian presidency resulted in the victory of Susilo Bambang Yudhoyono over the incumbent president, Megawati Sukarnoputri, but did not result in an alternative agenda for Aceh, and the poor accountability of security forces continued to affect developments in the region.[143]

When the tsunami struck on 26 December 2004, the Aceh province was the worst affected in the region, and the provincial capital, Banda Aceh, was virtually wiped out. The unfathomable human costs brought the remote Aceh province, and consequently the conflict, onto the international front stage and opened up the province to international assistance, including military relief and aid agencies, and to journalists. The declaration of a ceasefire by GAM in the immediate aftermath of the tsunami offered optimistic prospects, but continued violence on both sides in the midst of the relief effort strained the situation.[144] However, accessibility for international actors to the region was soon curbed as the Indonesian Government, after pressure by the military, imposed travel restrictions on aid workers, insisted on military escorts for relief workers and set a deadline of 26 March 2005 for foreign troops participating in the relief effort to leave Aceh.[145] The tension between the civilian government and the powerful military establishment in Indonesia continued to have an impact on the handling of the Aceh conflict.

IV. Iraq

The war in Iraq, unlike almost all the major armed conflicts that were active in 2004, did not originate as an intra-state conflict. It began on 20 March 2003 when forces from the USA, the UK and Australia attacked and invaded Iraq.

[141] For detailed information see Human Rights Watch (HRW), 'Aceh at war: torture, ill-treatment and unfair trials', *Human Rights Watch Report*, vol. 16, no. 1 (28 Sep. 2004), URL <http://hrw.org/reports/2004/indonesia0904/>.

[142] Donnan, S., 'Critics question Indonesia's motives for abandoning martial law in Aceh', *Financial Times* (Internet edn), 20 May 2004. The state of civil emergency was extended indefinitely in Nov. Harvey, R., 'Civilian rule returns to Aceh', BBC News Online, 24 May 2004, URL <http://news.bbc.co.uk/1/3735391.stm>; and Unidjaja, F. D., 'Indonesia extends state of civil emergency in Aceh', *Jakarta Post*, 13 Nov. 2004, in FBIS-EAS-2004-1113, 15 Nov. 2004.

[143] 'Yudhoyono visits strife-torn Aceh', BBC News Online, 26 Nov. 2004, URL <http://news.bbc.co.uk/1/4043969.stm>. For a detailed account of the need for and problems of security sector reform in Indonesia see ICG, 'Indonesia: rethinking internal security strategy', ICG Asia Report no. 90, 20 Dec. 2004, URL <http://www.icg.org/home/index.cfm?id=3190&l=1>.

[144] 'Tensions flare in quake countries', BBC News Online, 7 Jan. 2004, URL <http://news.bbc.co.uk/1/4153769.stm>; and Agence France-Presse (Hong Kong), 'Aceh rebel leaders blame Indonesia for not keeping cease-fire', 28 Dec. 2004, in FBIS-EAS-2004-1228, 29 Dec. 2004.

[145] 'Aceh ceasefire talks edge closer', BBC News Online, 13 Jan. 2004, URL <http://news.bbc.co.uk/1/4172061.stm>; and Donnan, S. and Ibison, D., 'Foreign troops given deadline to leave Aceh', *Financial Times*, 13 Jan. 2004, p. 11.

Operation Iraqi Freedom, as the USA called the invasion, formally ended on 1 May 2003, when President Bush declared the end of major combat operations and the victory of the USA and its allies.[146] The recognition by the UN Security Council of the USA and the UK as occupying powers under unified command on 22 May 2003 established these states temporarily as 'the Authority' in Iraq, responsible for the administration of the territory of Iraq and the promotion of the welfare of the Iraqi population.[147] This meant that the USA and its allies became, effectively, the state party in the internal conflict that ensued with a wide range of often unidentified non-state groups. The transfer of sovereignty from the Coalition Provisional Authority (CPA), under the leadership of L. Paul Bremer III, to an Iraqi interim government led by Ayad Allawi on 28 June 2004 formally ended the occupation. In so doing, it established the interim government as the state party in the continuing intra-state conflict, assisted by the USA and its allies, now designated as the Multinational Force (MNF) 'with the authority to take all necessary measures to contribute to the maintenance of security and stability in Iraq'.[148]

Notwithstanding developments at the political level, violence continued unabated in Iraq in 2004. In terms of fatalities, the costs were significant. Between 20 March and 1 May 2003, 138 US troops were killed. From May 2003 to the end of December 2004, 1191 US soldiers were killed.[149] Figures for civilian deaths in Iraq cannot be verified, but estimates range from 15 038–17 240 (7350 of which occurred during the 20 March–1 May 2003 phase of the conflict) to 98 000, of which 60 000 are the result of violence.[150] Attacks on Iraqi targets, particularly government officials, political figures and security forces, escalated in the run-up to the national election on 30 January 2005. By the end of 2004 Iraq, in a reversal of the classic spillover of conflict from intra- to interstate, raised the prospect of an international conflict creating a civil war.

Despite its different origin and trajectory and the difficulty it presents for classification, the conflict in Iraq displayed many of the features common to armed conflicts elsewhere in the world. The diversity of combatant parties, the use of guerrilla warfare tactics and acts of terrorism that deliberately targeted and killed civilians, and the local focus of conflict zones characterized the conflict in 2004. These features compounded existing difficulties facing the USA and its allies, and subsequently the interim government of Iraq, as to how

[146] For the origins, conduct and immediate aftermath of the Iraq war see Cottey, A., 'The Iraq war: the enduring controversies and challenges', *SIPRI Yearbook 2004* (note 1), pp. 67–93.

[147] UN Security Council Resolution 1483, 22 May 2003.

[148] UN Security Council Resolution 1546, 8 June 2004.

[149] These death figures are from O'Hanlon, M. E. and Albuquerque, Lins de A., Brookings Institution, Saban Center for Middle East Policy, 'Iraq Index: tracking reconstruction and security in post-Saddam Iraq', 3 Jan. 2005, URL <http://www.brookings.edu/iraqindex>.

[150] The minimum figure is derived from numbers reported by the media as of 5 Jan. 2004, collected in the Iraq Body Count Database. 'Iraq Body Count', URL <http://www.iraqbodycount.net>. The maximum figure is derived from a medical research survey on mortality in Iraq during the 14.6-month period before and the 17.8-month period after the invasion. Roberts, L. *et al.*, 'Mortality before and after the 2003 invasion of Iraq: cluster sample survey', *The Lancet*, vol. 364, no. 9448 (29 Oct. 2004), pp. 1857–64, URL <http://image.thelancet.com/extras/04art10342web.pdf>.

to define and pursue the conflict. One of the most serious challenges was defining the rebel parties. For most of 2003 and early 2004, the USA characterized attacks on the occupying forces as the work of remaining elements of the former Baathist regime of Saddam Hussein. This was fuelled, in part, by the fact that much of the violence was concentrated in the so-called Sunni Triangle, the area in central Iraq dominated by Sunni Arabs, who account for around 20 per cent of the Iraqi population and formed the bedrock of support for Saddam Hussein. The capital of this resistance is the city of Falluja, 48 km west of Baghdad. With the capture of Saddam Hussein by US forces on 13 December 2003 and of 46 of the USA's list of 55 most wanted Iraqis by March 2004, the perception that former elements of the Baath regime were responsible for mounting violence became harder to sustain.[151]

Double suicide bomb attacks on the two main political parties in the northern Kurdish region on 1 February 2004, then the most stable region in Iraq, appeared to signal a new element in the geographical scope as well as the tactics of the conflict. US officials claimed that the suicide attacks were the work of foreign Islamic militants and identified Abu Musab al-Zarqawi, a Jordanian militant with alleged links to al-Qaeda and to a Kurdish militant group, Ansar al-Islam, as responsible for the attacks. The US Department of Defense had already declared the group the principal 'terrorist adversary' of the US forces in Iraq in October 2003.[152] The USA claimed that Zarqawi was the main organizer of the group and that he was behind the August 2003 bombing of the UN headquarters in Baghdad.[153] On 8 February 2004 US officials published the text of a letter purportedly written by Zarqawi to the al-Qaeda leadership requesting help to launch a civil war in Iraq, and they offered a bounty of $10 million for his capture (subsequently increased to $25 million in July).[154] The Bush Administration, against the domestic backdrop of a presidential election campaign, continued to emphasize foreign Islamic militants, in cooperation with former Baathists, as the source of the violence in the central and northern areas of Iraq.[155] The USA was particularly critical of Syria, alleging that it failed to adequately protect the 640-km Iraq–Syria border against insurgent crossings and suggesting that the Syrian Government was providing shelter and support to former supporters of Saddam Hussein

[151] As of Dec. 2004, only 8 of the 55 most wanted Iraqis had not been captured. O'Hanlon and Albuquerque (note 149), p. 16.

[152] Zarqawi came to prominence as head of the Jamaat al-Tawhid wa'l-Jihad (Monotheism and Holy War) Sunni organization that was formed in Jordan in the 1990s with the aim of overthrowing the country's Hashemite monarchy. Blanche, E., 'Ansar al-Islam bolsters European network', *Jane's Intelligence Review*, vol. 16, no. 10 (Oct. 2004), pp. 18–21.

[153] Wong, E., 'Bombs underline divisions in Iraq', *International Herald Tribune*, 2 Feb. 2004, p. 1; and 'Iraq and the Kurds: the urge to stay apart may grow', *The Economist*, 7 Feb. 2004, pp. 41–42. For more on this bombing incident see Cottey (note 146).

[154] Huband, M., 'US doubles bounty on Islamic militant suspected of setting Shia against Sunni', *Financial Times*, 12 Feb. 2004, p. 6.

[155] Koch, A., 'Iraq: Bush bypasses detail', *Jane's Defence Weekly*, 2 June 2004, p. 25.

engaged in fighting the USA in Iraq.[156] Although the conflict in Iraq evidently attracted Islamic extremists, the small number of foreigners among those detained by the US forces in Iraq challenged the assumption that foreign Islamic extremists were the principal source of violent opposition to the occupation.[157]

In early April 2004, violence extended beyond the Sunni Triangle to urban centres dominated by Shia Arabs, who constitute 60–65 per cent of the Iraqi population.[158] The main Shia opposition was led by a young militant cleric, Muqtada al-Sadr, who drew on a strong following among poor Shia townships in Baghdad as well as in southern cities and towns to recruit a private militia force, the Al-Mahdi Army of around 3000 men. Al-Sadr draws much of his support as a son of Grand Ayatollah Muhammad Sadiq al-Sadr who, until his assassination by agents of Saddam Hussein in February 1999, was Iraq's most senior and venerated cleric.[159] Al-Sadr's supporters began an uprising in the Shia slums of Baghdad, which quickly spread to the Shia holy city of Najaf and the southern city of Basra, after occupation authorities shut down a newspaper published by al-Sadr and announced their intention to arrest the firebrand cleric in connection with the killing of a rival cleric in 2003.[160] In a pattern that was repeated in 2004, insurgents overran public buildings and police stations in an effort to seize control of towns. The USA responded on 4 April by launching its biggest assault since the formal end of the war in May 2003 on Sadr City, with more than 1000 US troops involved in retaking control of government buildings and police stations. In Basra, where Al-Mahdi militia occupied the main government building on 5 April, British military forces managed to defuse the crisis by negotiating with the militia to return control of the building to the CPA. Suicide attacks targeting Iraqi police buildings and killing around 70 in Basra two weeks later, however, put an end to hopes that the southern city would return to the relative stability it had hitherto enjoyed.[161]

The April 2004 Shia uprising was significant for a number of reasons. First, it put to rest any residual hope that opposition to the occupying forces came from only one sector of the Iraqi population and forced recognition that the insurgency was as much a nationalist movement of protest against foreign occupation as a Sunni rebellion. This was reflected increasingly in the tactics used by insurgents in 2004. Attacks against the forces of the USA and its allies

[156] MacFarquhar, N., 'At tense Syria–Iraq border, American forces are batting insurgents every day', *New York Times*, 26 Oct. 2004, p. 11; and Jehl, D., 'US said to weigh sanctions on Syria over Iraqi network', *New York Times*, 5 Jan. 2005, p. 1.

[157] Burns, J. F., 'Act of hatred, hints of doubt', *New York Times*, 1 Apr. 2004, p. 1.

[158] On the background of Shiite political movements see Samii, A. W., 'Shia political alternatives in postwar Iraq', *Middle East Policy*, vol. 5, no. 2 (summer 2003), pp. 93–101.

[159] See, e.g., Terrill, W. A., *The United States and Iraq's Shi'ite Clergy: Partners or Adversaries?* (Strategic Studies Institute (SSI), US Army War College: Carlisle, Pa., Feb. 2004), URL <http://www.carlisle.army.mil/ssi/>.

[160] Gettleman, J. and Jehl, D., 'Up to 12 marines die in raid on their base as fierce fighting spreads to 6 Iraqi cities', *New York Times*, 7 Apr. 2004, p. 1.

[161] 'Iraq: a wider war, a wider worry', *The Economist*, 10 Apr. 2004, pp. 35–36; and Fisher, I., 'Attacks on Basra extend violence to a calm region', *New York Times*, 22 Apr. 2004, p. 1.

extended to foreign private contractors and aid workers as well as to Iraqi nationals seen to be cooperating with the occupation. From April, the kidnapping of foreigners became an increasing feature of the conflict.[162] Around 145 foreign nationals were kidnapped during 2004, of whom at least 30 were killed, in many cases through a beheading filmed for subsequent broadcast via television or the Internet.[163] Such terror tactics succeeded in dissuading a number of coalition partners from continued military participation in the occupation, out of security and cost concerns as well as domestic public opposition to the war.[164] The violence was particularly damaging for the work of Western NGOs and aid agencies: by the end of 2004, only a handful of foreign non-governmental actors were active on the ground in Iraq.

A second significance of the Shia uprising was that it demonstrated the failure of the occupation to deliver quick benefits to those Iraqis who had hoped to gain most from the US-led invasion. Although the USA had appropriated $24 billion for post-war reconstruction in Iraq by April 2004, as of November only $5.2 billion of this had been disbursed.[165] This delay was a reflection of the failure of the USA and its allies to adequately plan for the implementation of post-conflict reconstruction.[166] Some argued that reconstruction was also hampered by the CPA's reluctance to put in place autonomous local Iraqi government structures to address local needs and its reliance on subcontracting to the private sector.[167] Over the course of 2004, however, reconstruction progress became hostage to increased insecurity in Iraq. Violence impeded the delivery of relief aid, while the targeting of Iraq's oil infrastructure threatened the Iraqi administration's dominant source of revenue. The fact that many Iraqi contractors were threatened or intimidated into not seeking contracts or employment offered by US forces and occupation authorities compounded the lack of economic regeneration: in December 2004 Iraq had an estimated unemployment rate of over 50 per cent.[168]

Economic difficulties were exacerbated by the high rate of crime and local violence. A significant part of the violence in Iraq in 2004 was criminal in intent and often local in origin. Many middle-class Iraqis were kidnapped, usually for ransom payments. Local rivalries, sustained in part by Iraq's complex system of tribal identities and affiliations, were dangerously facilitated by the widespread availability of arms throughout the country. Iraqi frustration at the perceived failure of the occupation forces to provide security against criminal violence as well as regeneration helped fuel allegations of US 'evil

[162] 'Rebuilding Iraq: without peace, reconstruction stalls', *The Economist*, 15 May 2004, pp. 37–38.

[163] O'Hanlon and Albuquerque (note 149), p. 11.

[164] The countries which withdrew troops from the coalition during 2004 include the Dominican Republic, Honduras, Nicaragua, Norway, the Philippines and Spain; Hungary, New Zealand and the Netherlands announced that they would withdraw troops in early 2005.

[165] O'Hanlon and Albuquerque (note 149); and chapter 8 in this volume.

[166] Catan, T., 'Audit hits at coalition spending of oil revenues', *Financial Times*, 16 July 2004, p. 4.

[167] On the role of private security companies in Iraq see Holmqvist (note 23); and on peace-building see chapter 3 in this volume. See also Diamond, L., 'What went wrong in Iraq?', *Foreign Affairs*, vol. 83, no. 5 (Sep./Oct. 2004), pp. 34–57.

[168] Mills, G., 'Four scenarios for Iraq', *RUSI Journal*, vol. 149, no. 6 (Dec. 2004), pp. 20–27.

intentions' regarding Iraq. The scandal concerning the abuses committed by US military police and intelligence officers in Abu Ghraib prison, which came to international attention in April 2004 with the presentation on US television of photographs of US personnel abusing Iraqi detainees, only served to confirm the opinion of a growing number of Iraqis of the humiliation and threat which the US occupation represented.[169]

Third, the April 2004 Shia uprising illustrated that a strategy of defeating insurgency through the massive use of force in urban environments risked turning more Iraqis against the occupation and threatened to become a rallying point around which Iraqis—Kurd, Sunni or Shia—might unite in common cause. A US assault and the two-week siege on Sunni-dominated Falluja grimly illustrated the damage of such operations on efforts to win public support: the assault killed hundreds, injured civilians were blocked inside the city, and displaced families were prevented from returning to their homes. The alternative was to pull the occupation forces back from the city and leave the provision of security in Falluja in the hands of a new local force of former Iraqi soldiers.[170] This policy was tacitly applied in other parts of the country: by May, Sunni and Shia militia forces were in effective control of cities in the central and southern parts of the country, such as Falluja, Samarra, Karbala, Nasiriya, Kufa and Najaf. Most large political movements in Iraq dispose of sizeable militia groups, including the two main political parties in the Kurdish north (Peshmarga), the secular Iraqi National Congress led by former exile Ahmed Chalabi and the Shia organization, the Supreme Council for the Islamic Revolution in Iraq (Badr Brigade).[171]

Fourth, the CPA's strategy to provide security in Iraq through the raising of Iraqi military and police forces was challenged by the speed with which Iraqi police and security forces crumbled in the face of the uprising. Recruits to the new Iraqi armed forces and police services were targeted throughout 2004 in multiple violent bomb attacks and shootings. Close to 3000 Iraqi police and security forces were estimated in February 2004 to have died since May 2003, and attacks continued throughout 2004.[172] Inevitable fear, combined with the

[169] *Article 15-6 Investigation of the 800th Military Police Brigade* (Taguba Report), URL <http://www.npr.org/iraq/2004/prison_abuse_report.pdf>; *AR 15-6 Investigation of the Abu Ghraib Detention Facility and 205th Military Intelligence Brigade* (Fay Report), Aug. 2004, URL <http://www.news.findlaw.com/hdocs/docs/dod/fay82504rpt.pdf>; Schlesinger, J. R. *et al.*, *Final Report of the Independent Panel to Review DoD Detention Operations*, Aug. 2004, URL <www.defenselink.mil/news/Aug2004/d20040824finalreport.pdf>; and Danner, M., 'Abu Ghraib: the hidden story', *New York Review of Books*, 7 Oct. 2004, pp. 44–50.

[170] 'Iraq: is it war, or peace?', *The Economist*, 24 Apr. 2004, pp. 41–42; Burns, J, 'US pummels rebel positions as fierce clash shakes Falluja', *New York Times*, 28 Apr. 2004, p. 8; and Kifner J. and Fisher, I., 'US weights Falluja pullback, leaving patrols to Iraq troops', *New York Times*, 30 Apr. 2004, p. 1.

[171] For a list of the political, religious and ethnic groups after the fall of Saddam Hussein and prior to the election campaign of 2004 see Cottey (note 146), p. 88.

[172] O'Hanlon and Albuquerque (note 149), p. 6; Pelham, N., 'Second car bomb kills 47 at army recruiting post in Iraq', *Financial Times*, 12 Feb. 2004, p. 6; and Banerjee, N., 'Attacks raise doubts on Iraqi security force's readiness', *International Herald Tribune*, 17 Feb. 2004, p. 8. Two of the worst attacks were carried out in the second half of 2004. Wong, E., 'Ambush kills 50 Iraq soldiers execution style', *New York Times*, 25 Oct. 2004, p. 1; and 'Militants massacre 21 Iraq police', BBC News Online, 7 Nov. 2004, URL <http://news.bbc.co.uk/1/3989671.stm>.

limited training received by recruits and, in some cases, sympathy with the insurgents, led to poor performance by and a lack of authority of the new Iraqi security forces. This came to a head in April 2004, when Iraqi army units refused to participate in the US offensive against insurgents in Falluja.[173] At the end of April, Bremer reversed the former policy of 'debaathification' and moved to recruit former Iraqi soldiers and police as part of an expanded US recruitment and training drive.[174] The drive for more Iraqi personnel, however, had to be balanced against the risk it presented for insurgents' infiltration into Iraqi security forces—a factor seen as responsible for a number of the most violent attacks on US and Iraqi forces in the second half of 2004. Disappointing performance, widespread desertion and the lack of leadership by the new Iraqi Army, police forces and National Guard, and the related escalating attacks they faced, continued to be a concern for the US military and a central theme in discussions of a US exit strategy.[175]

Increased violence against the occupation forces underscored the political imperative of restoring Iraqi sovereignty quickly while, at the same time, complicating the design and implementation of the transfer of power. This process centred on the drafting of an interim constitution—the Transitional Administrative Law—by the CPA and on the setting out of the scope and structure of a transitional administration by the CPA-appointed 25-member Iraqi Governing Council (IGC). Regional autonomy was a particularly sensitive issue, with Kurdish representatives seeking to maintain the autonomous status they had gained as a result of the 1991 Gulf War, while many Shias opposed any provision for minorities to exercise a veto on majority opinion.[176] This issue demonstrated the fragility of Iraq as a unified state and will be a central issue when Iraqis come to draft a permanent constitution.

The timing and means of election of an interim government proved the most serious obstacle to designing the handover. The US proposal for a system of regional caucuses was vehemently opposed by Iraq's most senior and influential Shia cleric, Grand Ayatollah Ali Sistani. Sistani insisted that a permanent constitution could not be drawn up by unelected actors and demanded that direct elections be held before the transfer of sovereignty in June.[177] The only compromise Sistani was willing to accept was the opinion of UN election specialists on the timing of elections. A UN fact-finding team, led by Lakhdar Brahimi, Special Adviser to the Secretary-General, travelled to Iraq at the

[173] The limited training offered to Iraqi police forces consists of a 6-week course administered primarily by the USA and its allies at a training centre in Jordan. Ripley, T., 'Retrain, remodel, rebuild', *Janes's Defence Weekly*, 8 Dec. 2004, pp. 25–29.

[174] The shift in policy was announced by Bremer in a speech delivered on 23 Apr. 2004. Coalition Provisional Authority, 'Iraq turns the page', 23 Apr. 2004, URL <http://www.cpa-iraq.org/transcripts/20040423_page_turn.html>.

[175] Sanger, D. and Stevenson, R., 'Bush says Iraqis aren't yet able to quell rebels', *New York Times*, 21 Dec. 2004, p. 1; and Schmitt, E., 'US may add advisers to aid Iraq's military', *New York Times*, 4 Jan. 2005, p. 1.

[176] Greenstock, J., 'Iraq: what must be done now', *The Economist*, 8 May 2004, pp. 24–26.

[177] Pickering, T. R., Schlesinger, J. R. and Schwartz, E., *Iraq: One Year After*, Report of an Independent Task Force on Post-Conflict Iraq, Council on Foreign Relations, New York, Mar. 2004, URL <http://www.cfr.org/pub6847/thomas_r_pickering_james_r_schlesinger_eric_schwartz/publications_about.php>.

request of the USA to examine the issue. They reported that it was impossible to hold free and fair elections before the end of 2004.[178] Agreement was finally reached that direct elections would take place before 31 January 2005, allowing the interim constitution to be signed on 8 March 2004.[179]

Further UN assistance was required to help form an interim government that was acceptable to Iraq's main political groups, based on the May 2004 proposals of Brahimi for an expanded IGC with a president, two vice-presidents, a prime minister and deputy prime minister, and 30 ministers broadly reflecting Iraq's ethnic composition.[180] From an international perspective, the most controversial aspect of the transfer of sovereignty concerned the post-handover relationship between the Iraqi interim government and the MNF. The USA insisted that an Iraqi government could not have a veto over the deployment of the MNF. Compromise at the UN Security Council was reached only on 8 June, when Iraqi Interim Prime Minister Allawi and US Secretary of State Colin Powell provided separate written assurances that the MNF would consult with the Iraqi Government on security matters, including consultation on offensive operations.[181]

The handover of sovereignty had little effect on the violence. Although the new Iraqi Administration attempted to assert its authority and launch popular policies—such as the reinstatement of the death penalty, a general amnesty for violent crimes against the pre-June 2004 administration and the incorporation of former Baathists into the administration—its political, financial and security dependence on the MNF meant that it had little legitimacy in the eyes of many Iraqis.[182] In August the new government faced its first big test, when intense fighting broke out in Najaf between forces of al-Sadr and US and Iraqi troops. The fighting was quelled by an uneasy ceasefire after widespread Shia public protests.[183] Attacks on US forces in the second half of 2004 rose to their highest level since the start of the war, with an average of 87 per day: in Sep-

[178] Turner, M., 'UN to send mission to assess early elections in Iraq', *Financial Times*, 28 Jan. 2004, p. 7; and The political transition in Iraq: report of the fact-finding mission, Report of the UN Secretary-General to the President of the UN Security Council, UN document 04.24611, 23 Feb. 2004, URL <http://www.un.org/News/dh/iraq/rpt-fact-finding-mission.pdf>.

[179] 'Iraqis agree on new constitution', BBC News Online, 8 Mar. 2004, URL <http://news.bbc.co.uk/1/3541875.stm>.

[180] Jehl, D. and Hoge, W., 'US relies on UN to solve problems of power transfer', *New York Times*, 10 Apr. 2004, p. 6; Schweid, B., 'White House welcomes Brahimi's plan', *Guardian Online*, 16 Apr. 2004, URL <http://www.guardian.co.uk/uslatest/story/0,1282-3983330,00.html>; Raphaeli, N., 'The new leaders of Iraq (1): interim President Sheikh Ghazi Al-Yawer', *Middle East Media Research Institute (MEMRI), Inquiry and Analysis Series*, no. 178 (10 June 2004); and 'The new leaders of Iraq (2): interim Prime Minister Iyad Hashem Allawi and the interim government', Middle East Media Research Institute (MEMRI), *Inquiry and Analysis Series*, no. 182 (18 June 2004).

[181] Text of letters from the prime minister of the interim government of Iraq Dr. Ayad Allawi and the United States Secretary of State Colin L. Powell to the President of the Council, 5 June 2004, Annex to UN Security Council Resolution 1546, 8 June 2004.

[182] 'Iraq: a fresh start', *The Economist*, 19 June 2004, pp. 43–44; 'Iraq: what sort of handover?', *The Economist*, 3 July 2004, pp. 36–37; and Turner, M. and Khalaf, R., 'Baghdad tackles the disaffected with carrot and stick', *Financial Times*, 16 July 2004, p. 4.

[183] Tavernise, S. and Burns, J., 'US officers say two-day battle kills 300 Iraqis', *New York Times*, 7 Aug. 2004, p. 1; and 'Iraq: bad days in Najaf', *The Economist*, 14 Aug. 2004, pp. 29–30.

tember not a single one of Iraq's 18 provinces went without an attack.[184] US military officials reported that insurgents were showing increasing sophistication and reach in their attacks. US and Iraqi estimates of the number of insurgents differed significantly, with the USA claiming around 25 000 fighters and Iraqi intelligence services putting the number at 200 000, of whom 40 000 were claimed to be core activists.[185] The lack of unity and coordinated direction of Iraqi insurgents was the single most important factor enabling the US and Iraqi forces to retain some remaining degree of control in the country, even as the disparity of insurgents complicated efforts to counter them.[186]

The political imperative to hold national elections on schedule on 30 January 2005 led the MNF and the Iraqi Administration to pursue a variety of sometimes competing strategies to stem the violence and enable the election preparations to proceed. In October 2004 the Iraqi Government launched a weapons buy-out programme, initially aimed at Sadrist militias in Baghdad but subsequently extended.[187] By 7 November, five days after the re-election of US President Bush, the strategy changed with the declaration of a 60-day state of emergency and the launch of a massive assault on Falluja by US troops, supported by Iraqi troops.[188] Air bombardment, door-to-door searches and closing the city to humanitarian agencies were intended to flush out insurgents and prevent their escape. However, these measures ran the risk of high civilian casualties and political fallout when the main Sunni Arab group represented in the Iraqi interim government withdrew its support.[189] Fears of a Sunni boycott of the election led Allawi to seek a compromise with Sunni leaders and to describe the Falluja siege as an attempt to separate foreign terrorists from insurgents.[190] Of over 2000 men detained during the Falluja fighting, however, fewer than 30 were non-Iraqi.[191]

Moderate Sunni groups warned of the growing alienation of the Sunni minority and urged the postponement of elections until security improved.

[184] Tavernise, S., 'Scores are dead after violence spreads in Iraq', *New York Times*, 13 Sep. 2004, p. 1; and Glanz J and Shanker T., 'Iraq study sees rebels' attacks as widespread', *New York Times*, 29 Sep. 2004, p. 1.

[185] Reynolds, P., 'Blistering attacks threaten Iraq election', BBC News Online, 10 Jan. 2005, URL <http://news.bbc.co.uk/1/4145585.stm>; and Fayad, M., 'Iraqi intelligence service chief interviewed on terrorism, related issues', *Al-Sharq Al-Awsat*, 5 Jan. 2005, URL <http://www.fas.org/irp/world/iraq/ash20050105.html>.

[186] 'Iraq: the struggle for order' *The Economist*, 25 Sep. 2004, pp. 49–50; Metz, S., 'Insurgency and counterinsurgency in Iraq', *Washington Quarterly*, vol. 27 no. 1 (winter 2003/2004), pp. 25–36; and Woolner, D., 'Iraq morass; limited exit strategy', *Asia–Pacific Defence Reporter*, vol. 30, no. 7 (Sep. 2004), pp. 20–23.

[187] Oppel, R. and Filkins, D., 'Iraqi officials plan to extend buying of arms', *New York Times*, 18 Oct. 2004, p. 1.

[188] Negus, S., 'US warplanes attack rebel-held city of Falluja', *Financial Times* (Online edn), 7 Nov. 2004; and Lawrence, Q., 'US forces begin battering Falluja', BBC News Online, 8 Nov. 2004, URL <http://news.bbc.co.uk/2/3991197.stm>.

[189] 'Iraq: who's winning, really?', *The Economist*, 20 Nov. 2004, pp. 41–42.

[190] Reed, J., 'Allawi has talks with backers of Saddam's old regime', *Financial Times*, 20 Dec. 2004, p. 2.

[191] 'Iraq: when deadly force bumps into hearts and minds', *The Economist*, 1 Jan. 2005, pp. 31–33.

This was rejected by the interim government as well as by Shia political leaders, notwithstanding the onslaught of suicide and car bombs as well as targeted attacks on electoral workers, police and security forces and prominent Shia figures that followed the start of the election campaign on 15 December 2004.[192] The MNF also urged for the elections to proceed as planned: the USA increased its force presence in Iraq to 150 000, surpassing the wartime height of 148 000 troops, in an effort to facilitate election security.[193] The violence put severe constraints on the election process. No public election rallies were held and many on the lists of candidates put forward were identified only by their number on the election ballot. Voter registration rules were relaxed in the most violent areas of the country to permit Iraqis to register to vote on the same day as the election, and Allawi acknowledged that some pockets of Iraq would be too dangerous for voting.[194] Extraordinary security measures were taken to guard polling stations, with most cities closed to traffic and the location of polling stations made known only at the very last moment.

In January 2005, the higher than expected turnout of mainly Shia and Kurdish voters in the first pluralist election in Iraq in 50 years was seen as an important vindication of the strategy of the USA and its allies. Iraq's Electoral Commission estimated that around 60 per cent of registered voters—around 8 million of Iraq's population of 28 million—had taken part in the election for the 274-seat transitional National Assembly.[195] However, this inevitably produced results that were heavily skewed towards Shiite and Kurdish lists, with the Shiite religious list, the United Iraqi Alliance, winning a little over 48 per cent of the vote.[196] It further alienated the Sunni population from the political process under way in Iraq. This raised real challenges for the drafting of a permanent constitution for Iraq, the primary task of the National Assembly. Meanwhile, continued high levels of violence throughout Iraq in early 2005 suggested that the election would have little effect on ending the insurgency. The severe stretch which the continuation of violence presented for both the MNF and the Iraqi armed forces made the implementation of a comprehensive counter-insurgency strategy even more difficult. The US commander of the MNF in Iraq, General George Casey, admitted as such, noting, 'Our broad intent is to keep pressure on the insurgents . . . This is not about winning

[192] Burns, J. and Worth, R., 'As Iraqi campaign begins, a bomb kills 9 in Karbala', *New York Times*, 16 Dec. 2004, p. 24; Burns, J., 'At least 64 dead as rebels strike in 3 Iraqi cities', *New York Times*, 20 Dec. 2004, p. 1; Oppel, R., 'Explosion at big American base in Mosul kills 22', *New York Times*, 22 Dec. 2004, p. 1; 'Governor of Baghdad assassinated', BBC News Online, 4 Jan. 2005, URL <http://news.bbc.co.uk/2/4144511.stm>; and Oppel, R. and Al-Ansary, K., 'Insurgents kill senior official in Iraqi police', *New York Times*, 11 Jan. 2005, p. 1.

[193] 'US to raise troop levels in Iraq', BBC News Online, 2 Dec. 2004, URL <http://news.bbc.co.uk/2/4060545.htm>. The lowest figure for US troops in 2004 was 115 000 (Feb. 2004). O'Hanlon and Albuquerque (note 149). Other coalition troops totalled 24 000.

[194] Filkins, D. and Sanger, D., 'Amid tensions, Iraqi leader affirms Jan. 30 vote plan', *New York Times*, 6 Jan. 2005, p. 10; and Filkins, D., 'Allawi calls pockets of Iraq too perilous for voters', *New York Times*, 12 Jan. 2005, p. 1.

[195] McDonald, N. and al-Taee, A., 'Turnout better than expected in spite of bombings', *Financial Times*, 31 Jan. 2005, p. 2.

[196] Negus, S., 'Shia coalition wins 48% of Iraq vote to end the Sunni domination', *Financial Times*, 14 Feb. 2005, p. 1.

hearts and minds; we're not going to do that here in Iraq'.[197] The continued post-election violence also raised large question marks over the timing of the withdrawal of MNF troops from Iraq.[198] In January 2005 the US Department of Defense ordered a comprehensive review of the US strategy on Iraq.[199]

V. Conclusions

The major armed conflicts that were active in 2004 demonstrated that, despite the absence of conflict between states, many parts of the world remain neither peaceful nor secure. If intra-state conflict now represents a greater threat to international peace and security, the conflicts in 2004 testified to the complex and diverse forms that intra-state conflict takes. A substantial number of these conflicts had international dimensions in terms of motivations, warring parties, location, funding and resolution efforts, but many were noteworthy for their 'localized' nature—'small' wars with very big costs. This suggests the need for greater nuancing and sub-division of the broad category of 'intra-state' conflict. Moreover, while greater attention to the interconnection of the international community and the conflicts within it is welcome, it is also important not to overstate the 'global' dimension of intra-state conflict.[200] Continued policy and research attention must be devoted to the local and 'micro' factors at work and to how local factors interact with international and global forces and actors.

A second conclusion relates to the specific conflicts that were active in 2004. Many of the conflicts that continue to produce the greatest number of deaths, casualties and suffering are wars of long duration. Far from soliciting more attention, their long-standing recurrence and perennial nature tend to make them disappear from the international stage. Although the current international emphasis on the prevention of violent conflict is a positive development, it is worth considering whether the real emphasis of policy and research should be directed at addressing, in a sustained way, resolution of the world's longest-standing major armed conflicts.

[197] Quoted in 'Iraq: when deadly force bumps into hearts and minds', *The Economist*, 1 Jan. 2005, p. 33.

[198] Spiegel, P., 'US sees coalition allies step up pace of pull-out', *Financial Times*, 27 Jan. 2005, p. 2.

[199] Spiegel, P., 'US looking at rethink of its strategy in Iraq', *Financial Times*, 11 Jan. 2005, p. 3.

[200] See also chapter 7 in this volume.

Appendix 2A. Patterns of major armed conflicts, 1990–2004

LOTTA HARBOM and PETER WALLENSTEEN*

I. Global patterns[1]

In 2004, 19 major armed conflicts were active in 17 locations throughout the world. Both the number of conflicts and the number of locations were lower than in 2003, when there were 20 conflicts in 18 locations. The figure for the number of conflicts in 2004 is the lowest of the post-cold war period 1990–2004, recorded in only one other year of the period, 1997. The total number of conflicts was substantially higher in the first half of the 1990s, ranging from 27 to 31, with 1991 the peak year. The figure dropped in 1996 and 1997, but the total number of conflicts increased substantially to 26 in 1998. The trend since 1999 has been one of a slow but steady decline in both the number of major armed conflicts and the number of locations.

No interstate conflict was recorded for 2004. A low number of interstate conflicts is not a new phenomenon, however. In the 15-year period 1990–2004, only four of the 57 active conflicts were fought between states: Eritrea–Ethiopia (1998–2000); India–Pakistan (1990–92 and 1996–2003); Iraq–Kuwait (1991); and Iraq versus the USA, the UK and Australia (2003). The remaining 53 conflicts were fought within states and concerned either control over government (29 conflicts) or control of territory (24 conflicts).[2] Conflicts over government outnumbered conflicts over territory in all years of the post-cold war period, apart from 1993.

In 2004, external states contributed regular troops to three internal conflicts: the Rwandan conflict, where Burundi contributed troops on the side of the Rwandan Government; the conflict between the USA and al-Qaeda, in which a number of states contributed troops to a multinational coalition supporting the US Government;[3] and

[1] Note that the Uppsala Conflict Data Program has substantially revised its series of data on major armed conflicts. The data presented in tables 2A.1–2A.3 have been retroactively adjusted to reflect the revisions. For further discussion see appendix 2B.

[2] Note that in 2004 the incompatibility in one of the 2 conflicts in Sudan—that between the government and the Sudan People's Liberation Movement/Army in the south of Sudan—is coded as both government and territory. In these statistics and in table 2A.1, however, it is entered only as a conflict over territory so that the numbers add up to the correct total figures.

[3] For background to the conflict between the USA and al-Qaeda and the complex issues affecting its coding in the database see Eriksson, M., Sollenberg, M. and Wallensteen, P., 'Patterns of major armed conflicts, 1990–2001', *SIPRI Yearbook 2002: Armaments, Disarmament and International Security* (Oxford University Press: Oxford, 2002), pp. 67–68.

* Uppsala Conflict Data Program (UCDP), Department of Peace and Conflict Research, Uppsala University. For table 2A.3, Ylva Blondel was responsible for the conflict location Algeria, Kristine Eck for the USA, Hanne Fjelde for India, Erika Forsberg for the Philippines, Helena Grusell for Colombia and Peru, Joop de Haan for Nepal and Turkey, Lotta Harbom for Uganda, Lisa Hultman for Sudan, Stina Högbladh for Burundi and Rwanda, Joakim Kreutz for Iraq, Myanmar and Russia, Desirée Nilsson for Liberia, Daniel Strandow for Israel, and Isak Svensson for Sri Lanka.

Table 2A.1. Regional distribution, number and types of armed conflicts, 1990–2004

	1990		1991		1992		1993		1994		1995		1996		1997		1998		1999		2000		2001		2002		2003		2004[a]	
Region	G	T	G	T	G	T	G	T	G	T	G	T	G	T	G	T	G	T	G	T	G	T	G	T	G	T	G	T	G	T
Africa	6	3	7	3	5	1	5	1	6	1	5	1	3	1	4	1	9	2	9	2	7	2	7	1	6	1	5	1	5	1
Americas	5	0	4	0	3	0	3	0	3	0	3	0	3	0	2	0	2	0	2	0	2	0	3	0	3	0	3	0	3	0
Asia	4	8	3	7	4	7	4	6	4	5	4	6	4	5	3	5	3	5	2	5	2	5	2	5	2	5	2	5	2	4
Europe	0	0	0	1	0	2	0	4	0	4	0	2	0	1	0	0	0	1	0	2	0	1	0	1	0	1	0	1	0	1
Middle East	1	3	3	3	2	3	2	4	2	4	2	4	2	4	2	2	2	2	1	2	2	2	1	2	0	2	1	2	1	2
Total G & T	**16**	**14**	**17**	**14**	**14**	**13**	**14**	**15**	**15**	**14**	**14**	**13**	**12**	**11**	**11**	**8**	**16**	**10**	**14**	**11**	**13**	**10**	**13**	**9**	**11**	**9**	**11**	**9**	**11**	**8**
Total conflicts	**30**		**31**		**27**		**29**		**29**		**27**		**23**		**19**		**26**		**25**		**23**		**22**		**20**		**20**		**19**	

G = government and T = territory, the 2 types of incompatibility.

[a] The incompatibility in 1 of the 2 conflicts in Sudan in 2004—that between the Sudanese Government and the Sudan People's Liberation Movement/Army in southern Sudan—is listed in table 2A.3 as both government and territory. In this column, however, the conflict is entered for Africa as only over territory.

Table 2A.2. Regional distribution of locations with at least one major armed conflict, 1990–2004

Region	1990	1991	1992	1993	1994	1995	1996	1997	1998	1999	2000	2001	2002	2003	2004
Africa	8	9	6	6	7	6	4	5	11	11	9	8	7	5	5
Americas	5	4	3	3	3	3	3	2	2	2	2	3	3	3	3
Asia	8	8	9	8	8	8	9	8	8	7	6	6	6	6	5
Europe	0	1	2	3	3	2	1	0	1	2	1	1	1	1	1
Middle East	4	4	4	4	5	4	4	4	4	3	4	3	2	3	3
Total	**25**	**26**	**24**	**24**	**26**	**23**	**21**	**19**	**26**	**25**	**22**	**21**	**19**	**18**	**17**

Source: The Uppsala Conflict Data Program.

the conflict in Iraq where, as of 28 June 2004, a US-led coalition contributed troops to the Iraqi interim government.[4]

II. Regional patterns

Of the 19 major armed conflicts that were active in 2004, the majority were in Africa and Asia, with six conflicts in each region. There were three conflicts in the Americas and in the Middle East, and one conflict in Europe. The regional distribution of major armed conflicts and locations over the period 1990–2004 is illustrated in tables 2A.1 and 2A.2, respectively. Figure 2A.1 shows the regional distribution and total number of conflicts for each year in this period.

Africa has constituted one of the main arenas for major armed conflicts throughout the post-cold war period. Since 1990, 19 conflicts have occurred in 17 locations in this region, only one of which was interstate—the conflict between Eritrea and Ethiopia.[5] In 2004 the conflict in Rwanda recurred after one year of inactivity. However, because the conflict in Liberia became inactive, there was no change from 2003 in the total number of armed conflicts in the region. This continued the positive trend of almost yearly decreases in the number of armed conflicts in Africa since 2000. The vast majority (15) of the 18 intra-state conflicts in Africa in the period 1990–2004 concerned governmental power. This is an important observation, since conflicts in Africa are often described in terms of opposition between ethnic groups, even across national borders. On the whole, neither governments nor opponents challenge existing frontiers, but rather contest the direction and use of governmental power.

It is notable that several of the conflicts in Africa are highly regionalized. In Central Africa, the intra-state conflicts in Burundi, the Democratic Republic of the Congo (DRC) and Rwanda have been interlinked since the mid-1990s. The same is true of some of the conflicts in West Africa, where there are clear linkages between the conflicts in Côte d'Ivoire, Guinea, Liberia and Sierra Leone.[6]

For *the Americas* (including North, Central and South America as well as the Caribbean), six major armed conflicts were registered for the period 1990–2004.[7] The number decreased steadily from the peak in the first year of the period, when there were five active conflicts, until 1997–2000, when only two conflicts were registered. Since 2001 the number has remained stable, with the same three active conflicts each year. Two of these conflicts, Colombia and Peru, have been active throughout the

[4] For more information on the states contributing troops to the conflict between the USA and al-Qaeda and to the conflict between Iraq and the USA, the UK and Australia, see table 2A.3.

[5] The 19 major armed conflicts recorded for Africa for the period 1990–2004 are Algeria, Angola, Burundi, Chad, the Democratic Republic of the Congo (formerly Zaire), the Republic of Congo, Ethiopia, Ethiopia (Eritrea), Eritrea–Ethiopia, Guinea-Bissau, Liberia, Morocco (Western Sahara), Mozambique, Rwanda, Sierra Leone, Somalia, Sudan (southern Sudan), Sudan and Uganda. Note that throughout this appendix when only the name of a country is given, this indicates that the conflict is over government. When the conflict is over territory, the name of the contested territory appears after the country, in parentheses.

[6] Note that the conflicts in Côte d'Ivoire and Guinea have not reached the threshold of 1000 battle-related deaths in any calendar year and are therefore not included in the tables in this appendix.

[7] The 6 major armed conflicts recorded for the Americas in 1990–2004 are Colombia, El Salvador, Guatemala, Nicaragua, Peru and the USA (the conflict between the US Government and al-Qaeda).

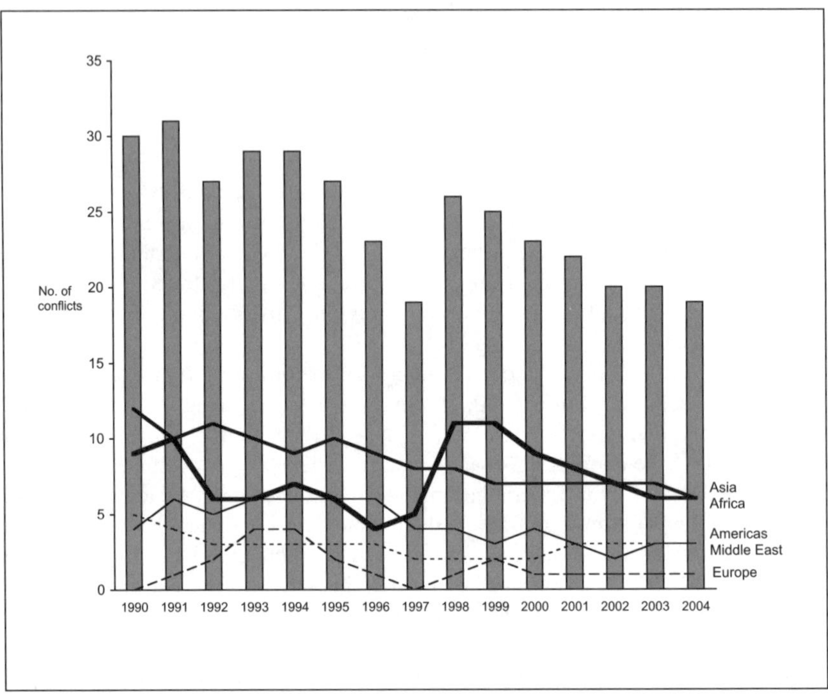

Figure 2A.1. Regional distribution and total number of major armed conflicts, 1990–2004

entire period.[8] All six armed conflicts registered for the region have been intra-state conflicts, fought over governmental power.

Asia has been the scene of 15 major armed conflicts in the period 1990–2004.[9] While Africa has seen the highest total number of conflicts for the period, on an annual basis most of the active conflicts have been in Asia. From 1990 to 1996 the number of conflicts in Asia fluctuated between 9 and 12, but since 1997 the number has slowly declined to six in 2004. Four of the conflicts recorded for 2004—India (Kashmir), Myanmar (Karen), Sri Lanka (Eelam) and the Philippines—were active in all 15 years of the period. One conflict in the region was fought between states—India and Pakistan. Of the 14 intra-state conflicts in Asia, only six concerned governmental power, with the remaining eight concerning territory.

In *Europe*, seven major armed conflicts were recorded for the post-cold war period.[10] Apart from the two years 1993 and 1994, Europe has been the region that on

[8] The third conflict in this category is that fought between the USA and al-Qaeda.

[9] The 15 major armed conflicts recorded for Asia in 1990–2004 are Afghanistan, Cambodia, India (Kashmir), India (Punjab), India–Pakistan, Indonesia (East Timor), Myanmar (Kachin), Myanmar (Karen), Myanmar (Shan), Nepal, the Philippines, the Philippines (Mindanao), Sri Lanka, Sri Lanka (Eelam) and Tajikistan.

[10] The 7 major armed conflicts in Europe in 1990–2004 are Azerbaijan (Nagorno-Karabakh), Bosnia and Herzegovina (Republika Srpska), Bosnia and Herzegovina (Herceg-Bosna), Georgia (Abkhazia), Russia (Chechnya), the Socialist Federal Republic of Yugoslavia (Croatia) and the Federal Republic of Yugoslavia (Kosovo).

an annual basis has experienced the lowest number of major armed conflicts. After an increase in the number of conflicts between 1990 (zero) and 1993–94 (four in each year), brought about mainly by the onset of the conflicts in the Balkans, the number again dropped to zero in 1997. Since 2000, the only active conflict in Europe has been that between the Government of Russia and the Republic of Chechnya. The seven conflicts fought in Europe over the 15-year period have all been intra-state conflicts. In contrast to the situation in other regions, they were all fought over territory.

In *the Middle East*, a total of 10 major armed conflicts were registered for the period 1990–2004.[11] The lowest number of conflicts in the region was recorded in 2002, when two conflicts were active. The number then increased to three in 2003 and remained at that level in 2004. Two of the conflicts that were active in 2004, Turkey and Israel, have been active for almost the entire period. Two interstate conflicts in the period since 1990 were in the Middle East: the conflict between Iraq and Kuwait; and the conflict between Iraq and the US-led coalition. There were eight intra-state conflicts in the Middle East: four fought over government and as many over territory.

III. Changes in the table of conflicts for 2004

Conflicts added to the table in 2004

Three conflicts were entered in the table for 2004: in Rwanda, Iraq and Uganda. In Rwanda, fighting again flared up between the government and the Forces démocratiques de libération du Rwanda (FDLR, or Democratic Forces for the Liberation of Rwanda), a rebel group made up of former members of the Forces armées rwandaises (FAR, or Armed Forces of Rwanda) and the Interahamwe militia. The conflict dates back to the mid-1990s and is linked to the 1994 genocide in the country. No fighting was recorded for 2003 between the government and the FDLR, for the first time since 1996. Elections were held in Rwanda in 2003 and the FDLR attempted to attract support within the country in an effort to re-join the political life of the country. However, this failed, and in April 2004 the FDLR again made an incursion into the country, attacking civilians. This led the government to initiate an offensive in the border areas. No negotiations were held in the conflict, as the Rwandan Government continues to refuse to talk to those whom they call *génocidaires*.

A new, intra-state conflict was registered for Iraq in 2004. After the US-led coalition seized control of Baghdad in the spring of 2003, ending the interstate war between Iraq and the USA, the UK and Australia (see below), numerous loosely organized groups began an armed struggle against the new Iraqi regime.[12] However,

[11] The 10 major armed conflicts in Middle East in 1990–2004 are Iran; Iran (Kurdistan); Iraq; Iraq (Kurdistan); Iraq–Kuwait; Iraq–USA, UK and Australia; Israel; Lebanon; Turkey (Kurdistan); and Yemen.

[12] For more detail see Cottey, A., 'The Iraq war: the enduring controversies and challenges', *SIPRI Yearbook 2004: Armaments, Disarmament and International Security* (Oxford University Press: Oxford, 2004), pp. 67–94; and chapter 2, section IV.

the threshold of 1000 battle-related deaths was not crossed until 2004.[13] During the year Iraq remained unstable, with clashes and bombings occurring on a daily basis. Sovereignty was transferred from the occupation forces to the Iraqi interim government on 28 June. The US-led coalition forces remained in the country and continued to support the new Iraqi regime, making up the vast majority of the troops on the government side in the conflict.

The third conflict entered in the table for 2004 is Uganda. This conflict was not entered in the data series published in the SIPRI Yearbook after the early 1990s. However, new information clearly links the Ugandan Christian Democratic Army (UCDA), fighting the regime in the 1990s, to the present rebel group, the Lord's Resistance Army (LRA). What was previously regarded as a new group was actually the same group of people, under the same leader, but acting under a new name. Since the UCDA party crossed the 1000 battle-related deaths threshold in 1991, tables 2A.1 and 2A.2 have been revised to include the conflict, with the LRA as a party, for all years in which the conflict was active, that is, 1991 and 1994–2004.

Conflicts removed from the table in 2004

Four conflicts were removed from the table: two interstate conflicts, and two intra-state conflicts.

No fighting was recorded for 2004 in the interstate conflict between India and Pakistan over the territory of Kashmir. Apart from a lull in the fighting in the three years 1993–95, this is the only year of the 15-year period in which the conflict was inactive. The declaration of a ceasefire by Pakistan along the disputed Line of Control on 26 November 2003 was accompanied by a thaw in relations between the two countries, and the ceasefire held throughout 2004. However, despite the stated intention of both sides to pursue negotiations, no substantial progress was made.

On 1 May 2003 the US-led coalition declared a victory and the end of 'major military combat operations' in the war against the Iraqi regime, bringing an end to the interstate conflict that began in 2003. However, in 2004 the USA and its allies were involved in the intra-state armed conflict in Iraq, where they became the main military supporters of the Iraqi interim government. In effect, of course, the USA continued to be a major actor in the conflict, although its role has formally shifted.

The conflict between the Liberian Government and the Liberians United for Reconciliation and Democracy, which began in 1999 and crossed the threshold of 1000 battle-related deaths in 2003, did not result in any battle-related deaths in 2004. A peace agreement was signed in August 2003, and the UN Mission in Liberia (UNMIL) was deployed in October. A transitional power-sharing government was sworn in in late 2003 and stayed in power throughout 2004. UNMIL remained in the country as the largest UN peacekeeping presence in the world. However, despite positive developments, the country was far from stable, with large-scale riots occurring on a number of occasions.

[13] The death toll in the wars in Iraq has given rise to a debate on the impact of war on civilian populations. An article in a medical journal estimated that the total number of 'excess' deaths (i.e., deaths of civilians above the normal mortality rate, not specifically battle-related deaths) since Mar. 2003 could be in the vicinity of 98 000. Roberts, L. *et al.*, 'Mortality before and after the 2003 invasion of Iraq: cluster sample survey', *The Lancet,* vol. 364, no. 9448 (29 Oct. 2004), pp. 1857–64, URL <http://image.thelancet.com/extras/04art10342web.pdf>. See also chapter 2, note 150.

The fourth conflict that was removed from the table is in the Indonesian province of Aceh, where a separatist rebel group, Gerakan Aceh Merdeka (Free Aceh Movement), has been fighting the government since the 1970s. This conflict has been intermittently included in the table since 1990, when it was first recorded as a major armed conflict. However, as more detailed information has become available, it has become apparent that the conflict has not resulted in more than 1000 battle-related deaths between the warring parties in any one calendar year. In 1990 the death toll in the province was very high, but the vast majority of casualties were civilians who were killed by government forces, as opposed to battle-related deaths. Thus, the conflict was removed from the table for 2004 (table 2A.3), and tables 2A.1 and 2A.2 were revised accordingly.

Changes in intensity of conflict

A majority of the major armed conflicts that were active in 2004—11 of the 19 conflicts—showed an increase in intensity over 2003.[14] In five of these conflicts—Rwanda, Sudan (southern Sudan), Uganda, USA–al-Qaeda and Russia—the battle-related deaths increased by more than 50 per cent. The conflict in Rwanda was re-entered in the table after a year in which there were no battle-related deaths. In Uganda, the conflict between the government and the LRA escalated markedly in 2004. Improved relations between Uganda and Sudan enabled the Ugandan Government forces for the third year running to pursue the rebels across the border into southern Sudan, previously used by the rebels as a sanctuary. In Sudan, the protracted conflict between the Sudanese Government and the Sudan People's Liberation Movement/Army (SPLM/A) in the south of the country resulted in a higher death toll in 2004 than in 2003.[15] However, negotiations continued throughout 2004, and on 31 December a comprehensive peace agreement was finally reached, after eight years of peace talks. The conflict between the USA and al-Qaeda escalated in 2004, but still remained at a relatively low overall level of intensity. The USA is supported by a multinational coalition in the conflict, and in 2004 all the fighting was carried out by one of the states contributing troops to the coalition—Pakistan. Finally, in Russia, the intensity of the conflict between the Russian Government and the Chechen rebels increased significantly in 2004. The fighting spread well beyond the borders of Chechenya, featuring increasingly large, bold operations by the rebels.

Six conflicts exhibited a decrease in intensity in 2004 compared to 2003—Algeria, Burundi, the Philippines (Mindanao), Sri Lanka (Eelam), India (Kashmir) and Myanmar (Karen)—the first four of which by more than 50 per cent. In Algeria, the government authorities had by 2004 clearly gained the upper hand in the conflict against the Groupe islamique armé (GIA, or the Armed Islamic Group) and the rebels had largely lost their operational capabilities in the country. In November 2004 GIA leader Nourredine Boudiafi was captured by the Algerian authorities, resulting in the dismantling of a number of rebel cells. In Burundi, the decrease in intensity is explained by the fact that only one rebel group remained active in 2004. In November

[14] The 11 higher-intensity conflicts are Colombia, Israel, Nepal, the Philippines, Russia, Rwanda, Sudan (southern Sudan), Sudan, Turkey (Kurdistan), Uganda and the USA.

[15] It is not uncommon for violence to escalate just prior to a final settlement. For further discussion see Dwan, R. and Gustavsson, M., 'Major armed conflicts', *SIPRI Yearbook 2004: Armaments, Disarmament and International Security* (Oxford University Press: Oxford, 2004), p. 109.

2003, the Conseil national pour la défense de la démocratie–Forces pour la défense de la démocratie (National Council for the Defence of Democracy–Forces for the Defence of Democracy) signed a peace agreement with the Burundi Government, leaving the Rwasa faction of the Parti pour la libération du peuple Hutu–Forces nationales de libération (Palipehutu–FNL, or the Party for the Liberation of the Hutu People–Forces for National Liberation) as the sole active rebel group. In the Philippines, there was a marked decrease in intensity in the conflict between the government and the Moro Islamic Liberation Front over the Mindanao island territory. A ceasefire that had been signed in 2003 held throughout 2004, with reports of only sporadic violations. In Sri Lanka, the ceasefire accord was largely respected throughout 2004, with no reports of fighting between the parties. Rather, the violence that did occur was a small number of suicide bombings and assassinations. In India, in the intra-state conflict between the government and the Kashmiri insurgents, fighting continued unabated.[16]

One conflict showed no change in intensity from 2003, the conflict in Peru.

In 6 of the 19 active major armed conflicts in 2004 there were more than 1000 battle-related deaths during the year: India (Kashmir), Iraq, Nepal, Russia (Chechnya), Sudan and Uganda. In Nepal, the Communist Party of Nepal (Maoist) rebel group continued its violent struggle against the Nepalese Government. A ceasefire that was initiated in October lasted for only a little over a week, and no substantial negotiations were held between the parties. In Sudan, large-scale fighting continued between the Sudanese Government and the Sudan Liberation Movement/Army and the Justice and Equality Movement. This conflict received particular attention in 2004, with the United Nations imposing an arms embargo on the government-aligned Janjaweed militia, to prevent the humanitarian conditions from deteriorating. The ethnic cleansing has caused massive flows of refugees both within the Darfur region and across the border with Chad.[17]

The four major armed conflicts conflicts that resulted in the lowest number of battle-related deaths in 2004 were Algeria, Myanmar (Karen), Peru and Sri Lanka (Eelam). In the conflict in Myanmar, the unofficial ceasefire agreed in 2003 became an official ceasefire in early 2004, and negotiations were carried out between the government and the Karen National Union (KNU) during the year. Only sporadic violations of the ceasefire occurred. In the conflict in Peru between the government and Sendero Luminoso, the intensity continued to be very low for the fifth year running. The rebels have been reduced to a mere fraction of their former strength and managed to carry out only a small number of attacks during 2004.[18]

[16] On the conflict in Myanmar see the discussion below.

[17] On the remaining 4 high-intensity conflicts see the discussion above.

[18] On Algeria and Sri Lanka (Eelam) see the discussion above.

Table 2A.3. Table of conflict locations with at least one major armed conflict in 2004

Location	Incompat-ibility[a]	Yr formed/ yr stated/ yr joined/ yr entered[b]	Warring parties[c]	Total deaths[d] (incl. 2004)	Deaths in 2004[e]	Change from 2003[f]
Africa						
Algeria	Govt	1982/ 1992/1992/ 1993	Govt of Algeria vs GIA	40 000– 100 000	<25	– –
GIA: Groupe islamique armé (Armed Islamic Group)						
Burundi	Govt	1991/ 1991/1991/ . .	Govt of Burundi vs Palipehutu–FNL	>6 800	<400	– –
Palipehutu–FNL: Parti pour la libération du peuple Hutu–Forces nationales de libération (Party for the Liberation of the Hutu People–Forces for National Liberation)						
Rwanda	Govt	1997/ 1997/1997/ 1998	Govt of Rwanda vs FDLR*	>2 900	25–100	+ +
FDLR: Forces démocratiques de liberation du Rwanda (Democratic Forces for the Liberation of Rwanda) * Note that the FDLR was previously called the ALiR. The group is also referred to as ex-FAR and Interahame in the news media.						
Sudan	Govt/Terr.	1983/ 1983/1983/ 1983	Govt of Sudan vs SPLM/A*	>55 000	>200	+ +
	Govt	2003/ 2003/2003/ 2003	vs SLM/A vs JEM	<5 300	<3 000	+
SPLM/A: Sudan People's Liberation Movement/Army SLM/A: Sudan Liberation Movement/Army JEM: Justice and Equality Movement * Note that the SPLM/A was previously coded under the National Democratic Alliance (NDA) but has increasingly been operating independently of the NDA. The SPLM/A has therefore been coded as an independent organization since 2003. This conflict is listed here as being over both government and territory because the aims of the SPLM/A have progressively shifted from control of government to control of territory.						
Uganda	Govt	1987/ 1987/1988/ 1991	Govt of Uganda vs LRA*	<8 700	>1 600	+ +
LRA: Lord's Resistance Army * Note that in the early years of its existence the LRA used a number of different names, notably the Ugandan Christian Democratic Army (UCDA).						

<table>
<tr><th>Location</th><th>Incompat-ibility[a]</th><th>Yr formed/ yr stated/ yr joined/ yr entered[b]</th><th>Warring parties[c]</th><th>Total deaths[d] (incl. 2004)</th><th>Deaths in 2004[e]</th><th>Change from 2003[f]</th></tr>
<tr><td colspan="7">Americas</td></tr>
<tr><td>Colombia</td><td>Govt</td><td>1964/ 1966/1966/ . .</td><td>Govt of Colombia vs FARC</td><td>>41 000*</td><td>>700</td><td>+</td></tr>
<tr><td></td><td></td><td>1964/1965/ . .</td><td>vs ELN</td><td></td><td></td><td></td></tr>
<tr><td colspan="7">FARC: Fuerzas Armadas Revolucionarias de Colombia (Revolutionary Armed Forces of Colombia)
ELN: Ejército de Liberación Nationale (National Liberation Army)
* This figure includes deaths involving other parties than those listed above in the fighting since 1964, although a vast majority of the deaths can be attributed to FARC and, to a lesser extent, the ELN.</td></tr>
<tr><td>Peru</td><td>Govt</td><td>1980/ 1980/1980/ 1981</td><td>Govt of Peru vs Sendero Luminoso</td><td>>28 000</td><td><25</td><td>0</td></tr>
<tr><td colspan="7">Sendero Luminoso: Shining Path</td></tr>
<tr><td>USA</td><td>Govt</td><td>2001/ 2001/2001/ 2001</td><td>Govt of USA, Multinational coalition* vs al-Qaeda</td><td>>3 700</td><td><300</td><td>+ +</td></tr>
<tr><td colspan="7">* The following countries contributed combat troops to the multinational coalition: Australia, Belgium, Canada, the Czech Republic, France, Germany, Italy, Pakistan, Poland, Portugal, Romania, Slovakia, Spain and the UK. For background and the origins of this intra-state conflict see SIPRI Yearbook 2002, pages 67–68.</td></tr>
<tr><td colspan="7">Asia</td></tr>
<tr><td>India</td><td>Terr.</td><td>1977/ 1977/1984/ 1990</td><td>Govt of India vs Kashmir insurgents</td><td>>27 000</td><td><1 100</td><td>–</td></tr>
<tr><td>Myanmar</td><td>Terr.</td><td>1948/ 1948/1948/ 1948</td><td>Govt of Myanmar vs KNU</td><td>>20 000</td><td><25</td><td>–</td></tr>
<tr><td colspan="7">KNU: Karen National Union</td></tr>
<tr><td>Nepal</td><td>Govt</td><td>1996/ 1996/1996/ 2002</td><td>Govt of Nepal vs CPN(M)</td><td><6 400</td><td><1 600</td><td>+</td></tr>
<tr><td colspan="7">CPN(M): Communist Party of Nepal (Maoist)</td></tr>
</table>

<table>
<tr><th>Location</th><th>Incompat-
ibility[a]</th><th>Yr formed/
yr stated/
yr joined/
yr entered[b]</th><th>Warring
parties[c]</th><th>Total deaths[d]
(incl. 2004)</th><th>Deaths
in 2004[e]</th><th>Change
from
2003[f]</th></tr>
<tr><td>Philippines</td><td>Govt</td><td>1968/
1968/1969/
1982</td><td>Govt of the
Philippines
vs CPP*</td><td>20 000–
27 000</td><td><300</td><td>+</td></tr>
<tr><td></td><td>Terr.</td><td>1968/
1981/1986/
2000</td><td>vs MILF</td><td>>37 500</td><td>25–100</td><td>– –</td></tr>
<tr><td colspan="7">CPP: Communist Party of the Philippines
MILF: Moro Islamic Liberation Front
* Note that the CPP was previously listed as the New People’s Army (NPA), the name of the armed wing of the CPP.</td></tr>
<tr><td>Sri Lanka</td><td>Terr.</td><td>1976
1976/1975/
1989</td><td>Govt of Sri Lanka
vs LTTE</td><td>60 000</td><td><25</td><td>– –</td></tr>
<tr><td colspan="7">LTTE: Liberation Tigers of Tamil Eelam</td></tr>
<tr><td colspan="7">Europe</td></tr>
<tr><td>Russia</td><td>Terr.</td><td>1991/
1991/1991/
1995</td><td>Govt of Russia
vs Republic of
Chechnya</td><td>40 000–
70 000</td><td>>1 100</td><td>+ +</td></tr>
<tr><td colspan="7">Middle East</td></tr>
<tr><td>Iraq</td><td>Govt</td><td>2003/
2003/2003/
2004</td><td>Govt of Iraq,
Multinational
coalition*
vs Iraqi insurgents**</td><td>>7 700</td><td>>7 000</td><td>n.a.</td></tr>
<tr><td colspan="7">* The US-led multinational coalition in Iraq included combat troops from Albania, Australia, Azerbaijan, Bulgaria, the Czech Republic, Denmark, Dominican Republic, El Salvador, Estonia, Georgia, Honduras, Italy, Kazakhstan, Latvia, Lithuania, Macedonia (Former Yugoslav Republic of), Moldova, Mongolia, Netherlands, New Zealand, Nicaragua, Norway, the Philippines, Poland, Portugal, Romania, Slovakia, Spain, Thailand, Tonga, the UK, Ukraine and the USA.
** These included the Jaish-i-Mahdi (Al-Mahdi Army), the Jamaat al-Tawhid wa’l-Jihad (Monotheism and Holy War) and the Jaish Ansar Al-Sunna (Army of Ansar Al-Sunna).</td></tr>
<tr><td>Israel</td><td>Terr.</td><td>1964/
1964/1964/
. .</td><td>Govt of Israel
vs Palestinian
organizations*</td><td><14 100</td><td><500</td><td>+</td></tr>
<tr><td colspan="7">* These included the Al-Aqsa Martyrs Brigades, Fatah (Movement for the National Liberation of Palestine), Hamas (Islamic Resistance Movement), Palestinian Islamic Jihad and the Popular Front for the Liberation of Palestine.</td></tr>
</table>

Location	Incompat- ibility[a]	Yr formed/ yr stated/ yr joined/ yr entered[b]	Warring parties[c]	Total deaths[d] (incl. 2004)	Deaths in 2004[e]	Change from 2003[f]
Turkey	Terr.	1974/ 1974/1984/ 1992	Govt of Turkey vs KONGRA-GEL*	<30 100	<200	+

KONGRA-GEL: Conference of the People's Congress of Kurdistan

* In Nov. 2003 the Kurdish Freedom and Democracy Congress (KADEK, previously known as the PKK) changed its name to the Conference of the People's Congress of Kurdistan (KONGRA-GEL).

The following notes apply to table 2A.3. Note that, although some countries are also the location of minor armed conflicts, the table lists only the major armed conflicts in those countries. For the definitions, methods and sources used see appendix 2B.

The conflicts in table 2A.3 are listed by location, in alphabetical order, within 5 geographical regions: Africa—excluding Egypt; the Americas—including North, Central and South America and the Caribbean; Asia—including Oceania, Australia and New Zealand; Europe—including the Caucasus; and the Middle East—Egypt, Iran, Iraq, Israel, Jordan, Kuwait, Lebanon, Syria, Turkey and the states of the Arabian peninsula.

[a] The stated general incompatible positions—'Govt' and 'Terr.'—refer to contested incompatibilities concerning *government* (type of political system or a change of central government or its composition) and *territory* (control of territory, secession or autonomy), respectively. Each location may have 1 or more incompatibilities over territory, if the disputed territories are different entities. There can be only 1 incompatibility over government in each location as, by definition, there can be only 1 government in each location. (Note, however, that the conflict between the Government of Sudan and the Sudan People's Liberation Movement/Army (SPLM/A) constitutes a special case in 2004: it is coded as being over both government and territory to reflect the fact that the goals of the SPLM/A have shifted over the years.)

[b] 'Year formed' is the year in which the original party in a major armed conflict—in conflicts where several parties have fought over the same incompatibility—first stated the incompatibility. 'Year stated' is the year in which *the active group* stated its incompatibility. 'Year joined' is the year in which the use of armed force began in the conflict between the active warring parties. 'Year entered' is the year in which the fighting between the government and the warring party for the first time reached the threshold of 1000 battle-related deaths in a single calendar year and was therefore entered in the database. In connection with the major data revision carried out by the UCDP (see appendix 2B), it became evident that the years listed in the tables for the early and mid-1990s sometimes referred to the start of the entire conflict and sometimes referred to the year in which the active group had stated its incompatibility. Although these years are often the same, there are also instances in which they are not. Therefore, in order to code this variable more stringently, 'Year formed' now refers to the start of the armed conflict itself, while the other 3 years listed in the table ('Year stated', 'Year joined' and 'Year entered') refer to the active warring party.

[c] An opposition organization is any non-governmental group which has publicly announced a name for the group as well as its political goals and has used armed force to achieve its goals. Only those parties and alliances which were active during 2004 are listed in this column. Alliances are indicated by a comma between the names of warring parties.

[d] The figures for total battle-related deaths refer to those deaths caused by the warring parties which can be directly connected to the incompatibility since the start of the conflict. This

figure thus relates to the 'Year formed' variable. In the instance of intra-state conflicts, it should be noted that the figures include only battle-related deaths that can be attributed to fighting between the government and parties which were at some point listed in the table (i.e., groups that have crossed the threshold of 1000 battle-related deaths in a year). Information which covers a calendar year is necessarily more tentative for the last months of the year. Experience has also shown that the reliability of figures improves over time; they are therefore revised each year.

[e] Numbers over 100 are as far as possible rounded to the nearest hundred. Thus, figures ranging between 101 and 150 are presented as >100, while figures ranging between 151 and 199 are presented as <200. Figures between 1 and 24 are presented as <25, while those between 25 and 100 are presented as 25–100.

[f] The 'change from 2003' is measured as the increase or decrease in the number of battle-related deaths in 2004 compared with the number of battle-related deaths in 2003. Although the symbols are based on data that cannot be considered totally reliable, they represent the following changes:

++ increase in battle deaths of >50%

\+ increase in battle deaths of >10–50%

0 stable rate of battle deaths (± 10%)

– decrease in battle deaths of >10–50%

– – decrease in battle deaths of >50%

n.a. not applicable, since the major armed conflict was not recorded for 2003.

Appendix 2B. Definitions, sources and methods for the conflict data

UPPSALA CONFLICT DATA PROGRAM

This appendix clarifies the definitions and methods used in the compilation of data on major armed conflicts, and explains the treatment of the sources consulted. The armed conflict records presented in appendix 2A are compiled by the Uppsala Conflict Data Program (UCDP), at the Department of Peace and Conflict Research, Uppsala University.[1]

I. Definitions

The UCDP defines a major armed conflict as a contested incompatibility concerning government and/or territory over which the use of armed force between the military forces of two parties, of which at least one is the government of a state, has resulted in at least 1000 battle-related deaths in a single calendar year.[2] The separate elements are defined as follows:

1. *Incompatibility that concerns government and/or territory*. This refers to the stated generally incompatible positions of the parties to the conflict. An *incompatibility that concerns government* refers to incompatible positions regarding the state's type of political system or the composition of the government. It may also involve an aim to replace the current government. An *incompatibility that concerns territory* refers to incompatible positions regarding the status of a territory and may involve demands for secession or autonomy (intra-state conflict) or aims to change the state in control of a certain territory (interstate conflict).

2. *Use of armed force*. This refers to the use of armed force by the military forces of the parties to the conflict in order to promote the parties' general position in the conflict. Arms are defined as any material means of combat, including anything from manufactured weapons to sticks, stones, fire, water, and so on.

3. *Party*. This refers to the government of a state or an opposition organization or alliance of opposition organizations. The *government of a state* is the party which is generally regarded as being in central control, even by those organizations seeking to seize power. If this criterion is not applicable, the party controlling the capital of the state is regarded as the government. In most cases these two criteria coincide. An *opposition organization* is any non-governmental group which has announced a name for the group as well as its political goals and which has used armed force to achieve them. It should be noted that opposition organizations operating from bases in neighbouring states are listed as parties to the conflict in the location (country) where the

[1] See the UCDP Internet site at URL <http://www.pcr.uu.se/research/ucdp>.

[2] This definition of major armed conflicts differs slightly from that used by the UCDP in *SIPRI Yearbooks 1988–1999* (Oxford University Press: Oxford, 1988–99). The requirement that a conflict must cause at least 1000 battle-related deaths in a single year, rather than over the entire course of the conflict, ensures that only conflicts which reach a high level of intensity, as measured by battle-related deaths, are included. Tables 2A.1 and 2A.2 have been retroactively revised accordingly.

government is challenged. Apart from these primary parties to the conflict, one other type of actor may be included in the table: a state or a multinational organization that supports one of the primary parties with regular troops. In order to be listed in the table, this secondary party must share the position of one of the warring parties. In contrast, a traditional peacekeeping operation is not considered to be a party to the conflict but is rather seen as an impartial part of a consensual peace process.

4. *State.* A state is an internationally recognized sovereign government controlling a specific territory or an internationally non-recognized government controlling a specific territory whose sovereignty is not disputed by an internationally recognized sovereign state which previously controlled the territory in question.

5. *Battle-related deaths.* This refers to the deaths caused by the warring parties that can be directly related to combat over the contested incompatibility. Once a conflict has reached the threshold of 1000 battle-related deaths in a year, it continues to appear in the annual table of major armed conflicts until the contested incompatibility has been resolved or until there is no recorded use of armed force resulting in at least one battle-related death between the same parties and concerning the same incompatibility during a year. The same conflict may re-appear in subsequent years if there is renewed use of armed force between the same warring parties, resulting in at least one battle-related death and concerning the same incompatibility. The focus is thus not on political violence per se but on incompatibilities that are contested by the use of armed force. Thus, the UCDP registers one major type of political violence—battle-related deaths—which serves as a measure of the magnitude of a conflict. Other types of political violence are excluded: for example, the unilateral use of armed force (e.g., massacres); unorganized or spontaneous public violence (e.g., communal violence); and violence that is not directed at the state (e.g., rebel groups fighting each other) These categories of political violence are thus expressions of phenomena that are distinct from armed conflict as defined here.

II. Sources

The data presented in appendix 2A are based on information taken from a wide selection of publicly available sources, printed as well as electronic. The sources include news agencies, newspapers, academic journals, research reports, and documents from international and multinational organizations and non-governmental organizations (NGOs). In order to collect information on the aims and goals of the parties to the conflict, documents of the warring parties (governments and opposition organizations) and, for example, the Internet sites of rebel groups are often consulted.

Independent news sources, carefully selected over a number of years, constitute the basis of the data_collection. The Factiva news database (previously known as the Reuters Business Briefing) is indispensable for the collection of general news reports. It contains 8000 sources in 22 languages from 118 countries and thus provides sources from all three crucial levels of the news media: international (e.g., Reuters and Agence France-Presse), regional and local. However, it is worth noting that the availability of the regional and national news sources varies. This means that for some countries several sources are consulted, whereas for other countries and regions only a few high-quality region- or country-specific sources are used. Since 2003, more efficient automated software has been used when extracting sources, serving *inter alia* to raise the comparability of the material.

The UCDP regularly scrutinizes and revises the selection and combination of sources in order to maintain a high level of reliability and comparability between regions and countries. One important priority is to arrive at a balanced combination of sources of different origin with a view to avoiding bias.

The reliability of the sources is judged by using the expertise within the UCDP together with advice from a global network of experts (academics and policy makers). Both the independence of the source and the transparency of its origins are crucial. The latter is important because most sources are secondary, which means that the primary source also needs to be analysed in order to establish the reliability of a report. Each source is judged in relation to the context in which it is published. The potential interest of either the primary or secondary source to misrepresent an event is taken into account, as is the general climate and extent of media censorship. Reports from NGOs and international organizations are particularly useful in this effort, to complement media reporting and facilitate cross-checking.

The criterion that a source should be independent does not, of course, apply to those sources that are consulted precisely because they *are* biased, such as government documents or rebel groups' Internet sites. The UCDP is aware of the high level of scrutiny required and makes great effort to ensure the authenticity of the material used.

III. Methods

The data on major armed conflicts are compiled by calendar year. They include data on conflict location, type of incompatibility, onset of the armed conflict, warring parties, total number of battle-related deaths, number of battle-related deaths in a given year and change in battle-related deaths from the previous year.[3]

The data on battle-related deaths is given the most attention in the coding process. Information on, for example, the date, news source, primary source, location and death toll is recorded for every event. Ideally, these individual events and figures are corroborated by two or more independent sources. The figures are then aggregated for the entire year of each conflict. The aggregated figures are compared to total figures given in official documents, in special reports or in the news media. Regional experts, such as researchers, diplomats and journalists, are often consulted during the data collection process. Their contribution is mainly clarification of the contexts in which the events occur, thus facilitating proper interpretation of the reporting in published sources.

Because very little precise information is publicly available on death figures in armed conflicts, the numbers presented by the UCDP are best viewed as estimates. Rather than always providing exact numbers, ranges are sometimes given. The UCDP is generally conservative when estimating the number of battle-related deaths. Experience shows that, as more in-depth information on an armed conflict becomes available, the conservative, event-based estimates are more often correct than the less conservative estimates that are widely cited in the news media. If no figures are available or if the numbers given are unreliable, the UCDP does not provide a figure. Figures are revised retroactively each year as new information becomes available.

[3] See also the notes for table 2A.3 in appendix 2A.

Finally, a comment is warranted on a major data revision initiative: from the autumn of 2002 to the spring of 2004 the UCDP established an Internet-based database on armed conflicts covering the period 1989–2003.[4] In addition to data on conflict activity, the database contains information on a number of other variables, such as negotiations, peace agreements and third-party involvement in conflicts. This major review of the data collection resulted in revisions of some UCDP data, and the tables in appendix 2A have been retrospectively revised accordingly.

[4] The database is publicly available at URL <http://www.pcr.uu.se/database>.

3. Multilateral peace missions: challenges of peace-building

RENATA DWAN and SHARON WIHARTA

I. Introduction

A total of 11 new multilateral peace missions were launched in 2004. With the exception of the African Mission in Sudan (AMIS) and the United Nations Advance Mission in Sudan (UNAMIS), all of these missions followed a previous international or regional peace operation and addressed, albeit in different contexts and phases, peacekeeping and peace-building in internal conflict. Seven of the 11 new missions were carried out by regional organizations: two by the African Union (AU)—AMIS and the Military Observer Mission to the Comoros (MIOC); two by the European Union (EU)—the EU Rule of Law Mission to Georgia (EUJUST THEMIS) and the EU Military Operation in Bosnia and Herzegovina (ALTHEA); one by NATO—the NATO Training Implementation Mission in Iraq (NTIM-I); and two by the Organization of American States (OAS)—the OAS Special Mission for Strengthening Democracy in Haiti and the Mission to Support the Peace Process in Colombia (MAPP/OEA, Misión para Apoyar el Proceso de Paz en Colombia). The remaining four new missions—the UN Operation in Côte d'Ivoire (UNOCI), the UN Stabilization Mission in Haiti (MINUSTAH, Mission des Nations Unies pour la Stabilisation en Haiti) and the UN Operation in Burundi (ONUB, Opération des Nations Unies au Burundi)—were UN operations.[1] A total of 35 operations were carried out by regional organizations and UN-sanctioned non-standing coalitions of states, with a total of 225 385 military and civilian personnel deployed.[2]

It is against this backdrop that the High-level Panel on Threats, Challenges and Change presented its report to UN Secretary-General Kofi Annan in December 2004. The initial purpose of the panel, convened at the invitation of the Secretary-General in the wake of the US-led war in Iraq in 2003, was not to address UN peace operations but, as its report pointed out, 'peacemaking, peacekeeping and post-conflict peacebuilding in civil wars have become the operational face of the United Nations in international peace and security'.[3]

[1] ALTHEA took over from NATO's Stabilization Force, and UNOCI followed the closure of the Economic Community of West African States Mission in Côte d'Ivoire.

[2] Of this number, 173 000 personnel were deployed to the Multinational Force in Iraq, which constitutes 77% of the total number of personnel deployed.

[3] United Nations, 'A more secure world: our shared responsibility', Report of the High-level Panel on Threats, Challenges and Change, UN documents A/59/565, 4 Dec. 2004, and A/59/565/Corr.1, 6 Dec. 2004, URL <http://www.un.org/ga/59/documentation/list5.html>, para. 84. The synopsis and summary of recommendations of the report are reproduced in the appendix to the Introduction in this volume.

Table 3.1. Number of peace missions conducted by the United Nations, regional organizations and non-standing coalitions worldwide, 1995–2004

	1995	1996	1997	1998	1999	2000	2001	2002	2003	2004
UN peace missions (DPKO- and DPA-administered)	26	24	23	21	24	22	18	20	18	21
Peace missions conducted or led by regional organizations or alliances	16	18	22	26	30	25	26	21	26	29
Peace missions led by non-standing coalitions	6	4	7	8	7	7	7	7	8	6
Total	**48**	**46**	**52**	**55**	**61**	**54**	**51**	**48**	**52**	**56**

DPKO = UN Department of Peacekeeping Operations; DPA = UN Department of Political Affairs.

Source: SIPRI peacekeeping missions database.

This was reflected in the 64 000 military and civilian police personnel and 4000 civilian personnel deployed in 21 UN missions in 2004.[4] Any discussion of the future role of the UN and of how consensus on it could be built will inevitably, therefore, give substantial attention to multilateral engagement in peace efforts. In this context, the High-level Panel's report drew particular attention to the challenge of post-conflict peace-building. Peace-building is an increasingly important dimension of multilateral peace missions: for 17 of the UN missions launched since 1999, peace-building tasks are included in their mandates, while a growing number of the operations of regional organizations and non-standing coalitions of states explicitly encompass activities that meet the UN's definition of peace-building, described below.

This chapter examines the question of peace-building in the context of multilateral peace missions. Section II traces the evolution of the concept of peace-building by the UN in the 1990s, while section III identifies the challenges of magnitude and of legitimacy of the current peace-building agenda. Section IV examines four specific dimensions of this agenda that were prominent in 2004: disarmament, demobilization and reintegration (DDR); the rule of law; economic reconstruction; and elections. Section V concludes by surveying possible responses to the challenges of peace-building.

[4] The long-standing UN Verification Mission in Guatemala closed in 2004. UN, Background note on peacekeeping operations, updated 31 Dec. 2004; and UN, 'Monthly summary of military and CivPol personnel deployed in current United Nations operations as of 31 Dec. 2004', 17 Jan. 2005, both at URL <http://www.un.org/depts/dpko/dpko/home.stml>.

II. The evolution of peace-building in multilateral peace missions

Peace-building is a post-cold war concept and practice. The term first appeared in the 1992 report An Agenda for Peace, in which UN Secretary-General Boutros Boutros-Ghali defined it broadly as 'action to identify and support structures which tend to strengthen and solidify peace to avoid a relapse into conflict'.[5] The introduction of peace-building as a legitimate area for UN attention reflected post-cold war optimism about the potential for international collective action to resolve violent conflict among and within states. An emerging consensus that conflict, particularly the intra-state conflicts dominating the 1990s, was inextricably linked with underdevelopment and inequality facilitated increased UN engagement in the management of peace. Peace-building went beyond physical security and reconstruction: it involved non-military instruments and addressed the political, social and economic development of a post-conflict society.

While An Agenda for Peace noted the importance of including peace-building in peace-making and peacekeeping operations so as to 'consolidate peace and advance a sense of confidence and well-being among people',[6] peace-building was initially seen as a strategy that followed, rather than accompanied, UN peace missions. It was a way of mobilizing international assistance to enable the post-conflict state to make the transition from a short-term focus on security to a longer-term focus on development. This sequential approach was exemplified by the creation of UN peace-building support offices in Liberia (1997), Guinea-Bissau (1999) and the Central African Republic (2000). All of these initiatives followed a multilateral peace operation, involved only civilian personnel and operated under a relatively broad mandate. A large part of their task was to coordinate and harmonize the activities of different UN agencies present in the country.

The increase in complex UN peace operations in the 1990s—involving significant civilian as well as military components and with mandates that included disarmament, human rights, election monitoring, refugee return and support for the rebuilding of state institutions—demonstrated the difficulty of a linear progression from peacemaking, via peacekeeping to peace-building. Many of the conflicts in which the UN and other international actors were engaged throughout the 1990s proved resistant to such an orderly sequence. Relapse into armed conflict, sporadic political violence and public disorder were persistent challenges for peace operations deploying to civil conflicts. These challenges led to increased emphasis on the need for an earlier start to peace-building activities to provide incentives to commit to peace as well as to build confidence in its potential durability among post-conflict populations.

[5] UN, An agenda for peace: preventive diplomacy, peacemaking and peace-keeping, Report of the Secretary-General pursuant to the statement adopted by the summit meeting of the Security Council on 31 January 1992, UN document A/47/277–S/24111, 17 June 1992, URL <http://www.un.org/Docs/SG/agpeace.html>.

[6] UN (note 5), para. 55.

The UN acknowledged the need for peacekeepers to engage in immediate peace-building in the 1995 Supplement to An Agenda for Peace but stressed that this was a temporary and contingent activity: a multifunctional peace operation should turn over responsibility for 'the economic, social, humanitarian and human rights activities' identified as the tasks of peace-building to the appropriate UN agencies and offices as soon as conditions permitted.[7] This caution was motivated, in part, by a recognition of the lengthy nature of peace-building and of the unsuitability of short-term peacekeeping operations drawn primarily from military personnel seconded by UN member states to take on responsibility for it. It was also a reflection of the politics surrounding international peace-building: the increased engagement of European regional organizations in the Balkans during the 1990s meant that peace-building was no longer the exclusive preserve of UN missions. Complex peace operations involved a host of different actors—UN, regional organization and state actors as well as non-governmental organizations—operating independently of each other with little coordination and often in fierce competition. The result, as the peace operations in Bosnia and Herzegovina demonstrated, made the task of peace-building even more difficult to define and implement.

The most significant test of the international commitment to identify and support structures to consolidate peace came in 1999, when the UN assumed responsibility for the post-conflict administration first of Kosovo and subsequently of East Timor. The military interventions that preceded these operations rested on the contention that the states in question (the Federal Republic of Yugoslavia and Indonesia, respectively) had failed to protect the human rights of the populations of their territories. These operations testified to a view that conflict was a consequence not only of a lack of development but also of the way in which a society was governed. The assertion of the primacy of human rights made sovereignty conditional on the extent to which the state guaranteed and protected those rights.[8] Kosovo and East Timor brought the UN into the business of state administration and governance as a temporary replacement for a state that was judged to have 'failed' in its obligations. In this context, peace-building addressed the functioning of the state. It was intended to assist the replacement of dysfunctional and illegitimate structures with durable institutions that would protect the rights of the population and sustain peace.

While the UN has so far not sought to take on additional transitional administrations, the remits of all UN peace operations launched since 1999 have explicitly included tasks addressing the reconstruction of the state, and peace-building perspectives have shaped the development of regional organi-

[7] UN, Supplement to An agenda for peace: position paper of the Secretary-General on the occasion of the fiftieth anniversary of the United Nations, UN document A/50/60–S/1995/1, 3 Jan. 1995, URL <http://www.un.org/documents/ga/docs/50/plenary/a50-60.htm>.

[8] See, e.g., Annan, K. 'Two concepts of sovereignty', *The Economist*, 18 Sep. 1999, pp. 49–50; and International Commission on Intervention and State Sovereignty (ICISS), *'The Responsibility to Protect': Report of the International Commission on Intervention and State Sovereignty* (International Development Research Centre: Ottawa, Dec. 2001), URL <http://web.idrc.ca/es/ev-9436-201-1-DO_TOPIC.html>.

zations' peace operations, particularly those of the EU. The consequences of the 11 September 2001 terrorist attacks on the USA, and the US and European identification and prioritization of 'failed states' as a security threat, have maintained momentum for the understanding of peace-building as a form of state-building.[9] In the process, this has opened the potential for peace-building to expand beyond post-conflict contexts to become a 'pre-emptive' or preventive strategy.[10] The December 2004 report of the High-level Panel, with its focus on prevention, articulated the emerging norm: 'there is a clear international obligation to assist States in developing their capacity to perform their sovereign functions effectively and responsibly'.[11]

III. The challenges of the peace-building agenda

From one perspective, peace-building could be seen as a conservative international activity, an effort to maintain the sovereign state as the cornerstone of the international system. Peace-building builds on the assumption that the state is the best framework to prevent international and domestic anarchy and conflict. The contemporary slant on this is that the state provides the best means of protecting and promoting the rights of its citizens. From another perspective, however, peace-building constitutes a radical challenge to a system built on the basis of non-interference in the state's domestic affairs. It proposes that the internal structures and functioning of a state affect international peace and security, and asserts the right, even obligation, of external actors to a role in their design and management. Moreover, it puts forward a particular state model to be implemented. Peace-building presents substantial challenges for peace operations, whether UN or non-UN, in both the magnitude of the project and its legitimacy.

Challenges of magnitude

International peace-building efforts currently under way in Afghanistan, the Democratic Republic of the Congo (DRC), Iraq, Liberia and Sierra Leone confront the legacies of decades of conflict, neglect, corruption and mismanagement. This extends beyond the functioning of the state to the entire population: for example, 15 years of war in Liberia have led to a decline in the country's literacy rate relative to the rest of the region—in 2002, 44.1 per cent of the

[9] Center for Global Development, *On the Brink: Weak States and US National Security*, Report of the Commission on Weak States and US National Security, Washington, DC, 8 June 2004, URL <http://www.cgdev.org>.

[10] Tschirgi, N., *Post-conflict Peacebuilding Revisited: Achievements, Limitations, Challenges*, Paper presented at the War-torn Societies Project (WSP) International/International Peace Academy (IPA) Peacebuilding Forum Conference, New York, 7 Oct. 2004; Council of the European Union, 'A Secure Europe in a Better World: European Security Strategy', Brussels, 12 Dec. 2003, URL <http://ue.eu.int/ueDocs/cms_Data/docs/pressdata/EN/reports/78367.pdf>; and The White House, 'The National Security Strategy of the United States of America', Washington, DC, Sep. 2002, URL <http.//www.whitehouse.gov/nsc/nss.html>.

[11] UN (note 3), p. 83.

population was illiterate, compared to 36.7 per cent in the rest of Sub-Saharan Africa. In Afghanistan, 20 per cent of children died before the age of five years in 2004. In the eastern provinces of the DRC, the number of victims of sexual violence was estimated to have increased thirtyfold in 2003. The World Health Organization estimates that 8 million people worldwide died as a result of disease in 1999 in conflict-ridden countries.[12] The extent of human suffering and the substantial humanitarian assistance response it demands distracts from as well as shapes the process of state-building. In addition, the creation of structures and order after conflict does not take place in a vacuum but has to confront informal power structures, economies and social mechanisms that emerge during and after conflict to replace or provide alternatives to formal structures. The presence of warlords and shadow economies in, for example, Afghanistan and Sierra Leone are obvious examples of the structures that need to be dismantled by a peace-building process before state-building can even begin.[13]

The magnitude of the task requires priorities in peace-building. A fair degree of consensus has emerged in the past few years on the tasks to be accomplished, and there is some agreement on the order in which they should be tackled. This order is based on the idea of a hierarchy of political goods provided by the state.[14] The first and prime function of the state is to provide security and, correspondingly, the first priority of post-conflict peace-building is to re-establish it.[15] This includes the maintenance of ceasefires between warring parties and their disarmament, the establishment of secure borders, the 'renationalization' of the use of force and the prevention of violence within the society. The second priority area is the establishment of functioning law and order within the society. The current emphasis on the importance of the rule of law for post-conflict peace-building reflects the lessons from peace operations in the past decade that economic reconstruction and social

[12] World Bank Development Data Group, 'ICT at a glance: Liberia', URL <http://www.worldbank.org/data/countrydata/countrydata.html>; United Nations Development Programme, *National Human Development Report–Afghanistan 2004: Security with a Human Face*, 21 Feb. 2005, URL <http://www.undp.org.af/nhdr_download.htm>; Pratt, M. *et al.*, *Sexual Terrorism: Rape as a Weapon of War in Eastern Democratic Republic of Congo: An Assessment of Programmatic Responses to Sexual Violence in North Kivu, South Kivu, Maniema, and Orientale Provinces*, US Agency for International Development (USAID)/Democracy, Conflict, and Humanitarian Assistance (DCHA) Assessment Report, 18 Mar. 2004, URL <http://www.peacewomen.org/resources/DRC/USAIDDCHADRC.pdf>; and Ghobarah, H. A., Huth, P. and Russett, B., 'The post-war public health effects of civil conflict', *Social Science & Medicine*, no. 59 (2004), pp. 869–84.

[13] Giustozzi, A., *Respectable Warlords? The Politics of State-Building in Post-Taleban Afghanistan*, Crisis States Programme Working Paper no. 33 (Sep. 2003); Reno, W., 'The politics of insurgency in collapsing states', *Development and Change*, vol. 33, no. 5 (Nov. 2002), pp. 837–58; and Pugh, M. and Cooper N., *War Economies in a Regional Context: Challenges of Transformation* (Lynne Rienner: Boulder, Colo., 2004), pp. 45–142.

[14] See, e.g., Center for Strategic and International Studies (CSIS) and the Association of the US Army (AUSA), *Play to Win*, Final Report of the bipartisan Commission on Post-Conflict Reconstruction, (CSIS and AUSA: Washington, DC, and Arlington, Va., 2003); Fukuyama, F., *Statebuilding: Governance and World Order in the 21st Century* (Cornell University Press: Ithaca, N.Y., 2004); and Rotberg, R. (ed.), *When States Fail: Causes and Consequences* (Princeton University Press: Princeton, N.J., 2004)

[15] UN, Report of the Panel on United Peace Operations, UN document S/2000/809, 21 Aug. 2000; and UN (note 3).

rehabilitation cannot proceed without legal and administrative structures and mechanisms in place. Bosnia and Herzegovina and Kosovo offer two clear examples of this.[16] Law and order tasks also include restorative and retributive justice to set in motion social reconciliation and confidence building.[17] The third and fourth priority areas for peace-building are social and economic reconstruction and governance and participation. Here there is less consensus on the order of priorities. It is clear that a basic degree of economic reconstruction is a prerequisite for building confidence among post-conflict societies before potentially divisive political processes are undertaken. Some, however, claim that the establishment of legitimate and effective government is a necessary basis for sustainable economic reconstruction, which may be a lengthy and destabilizing process involving painful market-oriented reforms.[18]

The domestic focus of peace-building tends to make it an introspective process. Experiences over the past decade, however, have demonstrated the importance of regional dynamics for post-conflict peace-building. The tasks of multilateral peace operations are influenced to a significant degree by the politics and actions of neighbouring states. Afghanistan's relative stability after the US-led overthrow of the Taliban in 2001, some have argued, is as much a function of a benign regional environment as of the international presence in the country.[19] The continued instability of eastern DRC, by contrast, is significantly influenced by the policies of neighbouring Rwanda.[20] However, the mandate for a multilateral peace mission, whether UN or non-UN, is usually focused on the state in question and provides the international community with little scope to engage with and in neighbouring states. In the past few years there has been some effort to redress the missing regional dimension in international peace-building efforts: in the Balkans, for instance, donor states and regional organizations have been behind a drive for regional cooperation to address shared problems such as organized crime.[21] The three UN missions in West Africa, meanwhile, have formally agreed to coordinate in a number of areas, including DDR and joint cross-border patrolling to prevent arms smuggling and the movement of combatants.[22]

[16] Crawford, C., 'Winning the peace? Identifying best practices in mature peace processes', *Lessons Learned and Best Practices from the Western Balkans*, Conference Proceedings no. 1 (Folke Bernadotte Academy: Stockholm, Oct. 2003).

[17] Wiharta, S., 'Post-conflict justice: developments in international courts', *SIPRI Yearbook 2004: Armaments, Disarmament and International Security* (Oxford University Press: Oxford, 2004), pp. 191–206.

[18] See, e.g., Paris, R., *At War's End: Building Peace After Civil Conflict* (Cambridge University Press: Cambridge, 2004); and Stewart, F. and Fitzgerald V. (eds), *War and Underdevelopment*, vol. 1, *The Economic and Social Consequences of Conflict* (Oxford University Press: Oxford, 2001).

[19] Dobbins, J. *et al.*, *America's Role in Nation-Building* (Rand: Santa Monica, Calif., 2003), p. 138; and Chesterman, S., 'Bush, the United Nations and nation-building', *Survival*, vol. 46, no.1 (spring 2004), pp. 101–16.

[20] For further details of the conflict in the DRC in 2004 see chapter 2 in this volume.

[21] See, e.g., European Commission, 'The EU's actions in support to the Stabilisation & Association Process', URL <http://europa.eu.int/comm/external_relations/see/actions/sap.htm>; the Stability Pact for South Eastern Europe, at URL <http://www.stabilitypact.org> and in the glossary in this volume; and the Southeast European Countries Initiative, URL <http://www.seciturk.org.tr/index_eng.html>.

[22] UN Security Council Resolution 1528, 27 Feb. 2004.

The magnitude of peace-building is complicated by the time frame in which it is undertaken. Peace-building attempts to compress into a few years evolutions that have taken centuries. The limited duration of most international peace operations is a particular problem for effective peace-building. If the process is too short, the risk of a return to conflict is high. Haiti's relapse into conflict in 2004, after six peace missions over the past 10 years, is the most potent illustration of the dangers of the international community departing before post-conflict state structures and processes are sufficiently stable and durable to provide public security, welfare and opportunities for development. The question of time frame is complicated by the lack of any international mechanisms to objectively assess when the structures of a state have reached a level of stability that can make peace-building self-sustaining. In the absence of such mechanisms, the end of an international peace-building operation is determined more by the political interests, priorities and financial resources of the states and organizations involved than by a comprehensive assessment of the needs of the post-conflict state.[23] Greater international awareness of the minimum time commitment required for peace-building was evident in January 2005 when, for the first time, the UN Secretary-General outlined the envisaged period of a peace operation—seven years—in the case of the planned UN peace support operation in Sudan.[24]

The magnitude of the peace-building challenge also puts demands on the personnel who make up international peace operations: 92 per cent of the current personnel in UN operations are military from less developed countries.[25] While the demands of peace-building in unstable environments require a large security presence and while many personnel from the less developed countries can relate to the operational and practical challenges of a peace-building environment, traditional military peacekeepers do not have the skills to perform peace-building tasks. Peace-building as state-building requires sizeable civilian resources and experts in civil administration, management, judicial and penal management, and financial auditing. The lack of such capacity is not confined to the UN: regional organizations and individual states are encountering similar problems in identifying, recruiting and deploying experts with careers in their own countries.[26] Even when such individuals are recruited for international service, they face significant challenges in negotiating systems of government of which they have no experience or knowledge.

[23] Dobbins *et al.* (note 19); and Chesterman, S., Ignatieff, M. and Thakur, R., *Making States Work: From State Failure to State-Building*, International Peace Academy–United Nations University project report (International Peace Academy: New York, July 2004), URL <http://www.ipacademy.org/PDF_Reports/MAKING_STATES_WORK.pdf>.

[24] UN, Report of the Secretary-General on the Sudan, UN Security Council document S/2005/57, 31 Jan. 2005, URL <http://www.un.org/Depts/dhl/da/dad.htm>.

[25] 'Western' countries account for only 5337 personnel out of the 64 720 UN peacekeepers deployed as of 31 Dec. 2004. UN, Department of Peacekeeping Operations, 'Ranking of military and civilian police contributions to UN operations', 31 Dec. 2004, URL <http://www.un.org/Depts/dpko/dpko/contributors/>.

[26] Dwan, R., 'Civilian tasks and capabilities in EU operations', eds M. Kaldor and M. Glasius, *A Human Security Doctrine for Europe: Project, Principles, Practicalities* (Routledge: London, 2005).

The scope of the peace-building challenge has an impact on cost. Peace-building is an expensive proposition and the present system for funding falls far short in terms of total amount, coherence and duration. While UN peace operations, in contrast to the ad hoc funding mechanisms of regional organizations' operations, are funded from the assessed peacekeeping budgets, substantive peace-building programmes such as DDR, elections and rule-of-law reform are entirely reliant on voluntary contributions, usually raised at ad hoc donor conferences on individual countries. Such a mechanism does not promote sustainability, produces pledges that often do not materialize and encourages rival bidding for fashionable projects.[27] Moreover, donor conferences raise funds for a country immediately after conflict at the time when it is least capable of absorbing it. Recent research by the World Bank suggests that the average period of time for which donor assistance is needed for sustainable peace-building is approximately a decade and that the optimal rate of aid 'absorption' (the capacity to manage aid) occurs only in the fourth or fifth year.[28]

Coordination in donor assistance is central.[29] Recently improved mechanisms include comprehensive post-conflict needs assessments, carried out jointly by the UN, the World Bank and the state in question to determine funding needs and longer-term reconstruction plans, as well as trust funds to manage the immediate influx of post-conflict aid.[30] A good example of such improved mechanisms was the Afghanistan Interim Administration Fund, an unearmarked fund for start-up and recurrent costs established during the transition phase preceding the convening of the December 2003 Loya Jirga (Grand Council).[31] Efforts to improve pooling of donor assistance around thematic clusters in 2004 included the Afghanistan Reconstruction Trust Fund and the International Reconstruction Trust Fund Facility for Iraq.[32]

[27] See Forman, S. and Stewart, P. (eds), *Good Intentions: Pledges of Aid for Post-conflict Recovery* (Lynne Rienner: Boulder, Colo., 2000).

[28] Collier, P. *et al.*, *Breaking the Conflict Trap: Civil War and Development Policy*, World Bank Policy Research Report, 2003, pp. 166–69.

[29] For an example of a coordinated approach between Germany, the Netherlands, Norway and the UK see Smith, D., *Towards a Strategic Framework for Peacebuilding: Getting Their Act Together*, Overview Report of the Joint Utstein Study of Peacebuilding, Evaluation Report 1/2004 (Royal Norwegian Ministry of Foreign Affairs: Oslo, Apr. 2004).

[30] See World Bank, 'Post-conflict needs assessment', URL <http://lnweb18.worldbank.org/ESSD/sdvext.nsf/67ByDocName/OperationalResourcesPost-ConflictNeedsAssessment>. Other examples of financial modalities to channel timely support and funding for post-conflict reconstruction include Consolidated Appeal Processes, the Poverty Reduction and 'Low-Income Countries Under Stress' Strategy Plans, the Consultative Group mechanism, Round Tables and agency-specific mechanisms.

[31] UN, Report of the UNDG/ECHA [UN Development Group/Executive Committee on Humanitarian Assistance] Working Group on Transition Issues, Feb. 2004. URL <http://www.peacebuild.ca/dw/documents/3330-UNDG_ECHA_WG_on_Transition_Issues__Report__-_Final_Report.doc.>.

[32] Both trust funds are jointly managed by the national government and international aid agencies. UN, Report of the Secretary-General on the situation in Afghanistan and its implications for international peace and security, UN document S/2004/230, 19 Mar. 2004; and the UNAMI Internet site, 'International Reconstruction Trust Fund Facility for Iraq', URL <http://www.uniraq.org/donors/irffi.asp>.

Legitimacy challenges

The issue of legitimacy is a serious, although less frequently addressed, challenge for peace-building. Contemporary peace-building as state-building is founded on the assumption that a particular type of state can best guarantee human rights and development, that is, one founded on democratic principles.[33] In today's globalized world, the democratic state has taken on a particular paradigm—the liberal market economy state. Large parts of the industrialized world hold this paradigm to be the most efficient and sustainable model for democratic statehood and the model for developing countries.[34] Thus, peace-building not only involves external actors in the internal workings of the state but also prescribes the direction of that transformation. This is a highly political endeavour that raises important questions of legitimacy at the international and local levels.

The international legitimacy dimension is most often raised in the debate on the right to intervene, in which the sanction of the UN, as the primary authority in the maintenance of international peace and security, is central. This has been particularly sensitive in the cases of Afghanistan and Iraq, where multilateral peace missions are a consequence of regime overthrow by US-led interventions. Peace-building pushes the debate on legitimate authority further in raising the issue of what the tasks of international interveners are in a country and what the 'responsibility to protect' implies for post-conflict peace-building. What this responsibility entails for the substantive tasks and duties of multilateral peace missions has not yet been spelled out.[35] For some states, the state-building focus of contemporary peace operations is not a part of the international responsibility: rather, it is an infringement of sovereignty and perceived to be more serving of a 'Western agenda' than of the human rights of the population in question.[36]

Competing views as to what constitutes the appropriate scope of activity of the international community during and after conflict complicate the already difficult task of coordinating multilateral peace-building. For some, regional organizations or multinational coalitions represent a better framework for peace-building. Apart from the greater probability of reaching consensus on the tasks involved, regional organizations, motivated by self-interest in stability in the immediate neighbourhood, are seen to be more likely to commit the time and resources required for peace-building and, potentially, to share common historical and cultural traditions with the post-conflict country. Such links, however, risk partisanship by regional organizations, while the

[33] See, e.g., Russett, B., *Grasping the Democratic Peace: Principles for a Post-Cold War World* (Princeton University Press: Princeton, N.J., 1993).

[34] Richmond, O. P., 'The globalization of responses to conflict and the peacebuilding consensus', *Cooperation and Conflict*, vol. 39, no. 2 (2004), pp. 129–50.

[35] See Wills, S., 'Military interventions on behalf of vulnerable populations: the legal responsibilities of states and international organizations engaged in peace support operations', *Journal of Conflict & Security Law*, vol. 9, no. 3 (winter 2004), pp. 387–418.

[36] Donini, A. *et al.*, 'The future of humanitarian action: mapping the implications of Iraq and other recent crises', *Disasters*, vol. 28, no. 2 (June 2004), pp. 190–204.

presence of a regional hegemon can further skew the impartiality on which legitimacy depends.[37]

In reality, only a few European and Euro-Atlantic organizations possess the resource capabilities to undertake peace-building. The EU's takeover of peace operations from the UN and NATO in the Balkans stands in contrast to the pattern in Africa, where large UN peace operations have replaced shorter and limited operations of ECOWAS and the AU. Nevertheless, as demonstrated by the continued increase in the number of peace operations carried out by regional organizations in 2004, regional actors provide an important resource for international peace and security management in terms of quick response, military prowess and targeted regional or specialist attention.[38] Resources alone, however, cannot replace legitimacy. This was clearly demonstrated in the significant efforts which the USA expended to secure UN sanction for and engagement in the post-war operation in Iraq, both during the US-led coalition's period as an occupying authority and in the context of its subsequent role in leading the Multinational Force after Iraq regained sovereignty. The High-level Panel reiterated the call for greater engagement of regional and sub-regional groups in peace operations as well as alliance organizations, notably NATO, while underscoring that this can only take place within the framework of the UN Charter and the purposes of the UN. It explicitly recommended that UN Security Council authorization be sought for operations carried out by regional organizations.[39]

The other, frequently neglected aspect of legitimacy is that derived from the acceptance and support of local populations and their leaders. Local legitimacy extends beyond the initial invitation or acceptance of the host state of an international presence on its territory. Rather, it is a dynamic factor that is crucial for the success of peace-building as state-building and can be gained or lost over the course of an operation. At their worst, international peace operations personnel have perpetrated the same crimes and human rights abuses on civilian populations as those carried out in conflict. The allegations of widespread rape by peacekeepers in the UN Organization Mission in the Democratic Republic of Congo (MONUC, Mission de l'Organisation des Nations Unies en République Démocratique du Congo) in 2004, as well as repeated incidences of the involvement of UN and NATO military and civilian personnel in human trafficking in the Balkans in the 1990s, testify to the way in which legitimacy can be lost as a result of actions on the part of an internationally mandated peace mission.[40] The lack of accountability of

[37] Pugh, M. and Sidhu, W. (eds), *The United Nations and Regional Security: Europe and Beyond* (Lynne Rienner: Boulder, Colo., 2003)

[38] Boulden, J. (ed.), *Dealing with Conflict in Africa: The United Nations and Regional Organizations* (Palgrave: Basingstoke, 2004); and Heldt, B. and Wallensteen, P., *Peacekeeping Operations: Global Patterns of Intervention and Success, 1948–2000*, Research Report no. 1 (Folke Bernadotte Academy: Stockholm, 2004).

[39] UN (note 3), pp. 85–86.

[40] Lacey, M., 'In Congo war, even peacekeepers add to horror', *New York Times*, 18 Dec. 2004, p. 1; and Amnesty International (AI), 'So does it mean that we have the rights?': protecting the human rights

multilateral peacekeepers to the local communities which they profess to serve remains a serious problem and one on which the High-level Panel Report remains silent.

Even in the absence of criminal activity, international peace operations and their personnel have been routinely criticized for failing to engage local populations in the transformation they seek to set in motion and in being non-responsive to local perspectives and concerns. Recent research and UN policy discussions have sought to emphasize the significance of local engagement and ownership in peace-building on grounds of legitimacy as well as on grounds of achieving practical success in peace-building.[41] What this also suggests is that the scope and pace of peace-building should be determined by the perspectives and priorities of local actors.

Identifying local partners and working closely together is not, however, a straightforward task. It necessitates going beyond wartime leaders, government and economic elites and often discredited or dysfunctional representative structures, such as parliaments, without further undermining the fragile authority of post-conflict governments. It involves consulting and engaging with actors that reflect the society's ethnic, religious, gender and social composition. It requires distinguishing between the groups and individuals willing and able to play a part in peace-building and those 'spoilers' who threaten the effort, while at the same time avoiding becoming bogged down in local feuds and rivalries.[42] It involves an open position towards approaches and initiatives coming from the local community, some of which may appear to challenge the models and priorities of international actors, while, at the same time, driving through key reforms, such as DDR, that are a prerequisite for peace-building. These are sensitive and time-consuming tasks and highly demanding for multilateral peace operations that may initially have little access to or knowledge of the country in question.

IV. Dimensions of the peace-building agenda

A number of prominent issues in 2004 highlighted how the challenges of magnitude and legitimacy intersect to make the practical tasks of peace-building difficult to address. This section examines four of these issues.

of women and girls trafficked for forced prostitution in Kosovo, AI document EUR 70/010/2004, 6 May 2004, URL <http://web.amnesty.org/library/Index/ENGEUR700102004?open&of=ENG-YUG>.

[41] See, e.g., Chopra, J. and Hohe, T., 'Participatory intervention', *Global Governance*, vol. 10 (2004), pp. 289–305; UN, Report of the Secretary-General on the rule of law and transitional justice in conflict and post-conflict societies, UN document S/2004/616, 23 Aug. 2004; and Gizelis, T. and Kosek, K. E., 'All together now: Local participation and success in peacekeeping operations', Paper presented at the American Political Studies Association annual conference, Chicago, Sep. 2004.

[42] Chopra, J. (ed.), *The Politics of Peace Maintenance* (Lynne Rienner: Boulde, Colo., 1998); and Stedman, S. J. *et al.* (eds), *Ending Civil Wars: The Implementation of Peace Agreements* (Lynne Rienner: Boulder, Colo., 2002).

Disarmament, demobilization and reintegration

Disarmament, demobilization and reintegration occupied a prominent role on the international policy agenda in 2004, after almost a decade of relative inattention. The primary reason was the recognition of the lack of success of most recent international DDR efforts and the consequences of this failure for the resumption of conflict. DDR is a crucial component of post-conflict peace-building as a prerequisite for ending violence and the re-establishment of the state's legitimate monopoly of coercive force. Iraq in 2004 testified to the perils of not engaging in systematic disarmament and demobilization: the 2003 disbanding of the Iraqi armed forces without the provision of compensation, retraining or employment for former soldiers and without any weapon collection or management programmes resulted in the presence of large numbers of unemployed trained fighters and thousands of weapons on the streets with consequent violent results.[43] Equally significant are the social and economic functions of DDR, which in many post-conflict contexts provide the principal short-term mechanisms to assist large sectors of the population to establish means and capabilities to earn a sustainable peacetime livelihood.

Seventeen current multilateral peace operations—nine UN and eight non-UN operations—have DDR tasks in their mandate. The scope and magnitude of DDR processes, however, make them difficult to strategize, coordinate, fund and implement. They face enormous structural challenges, too: unstable and violent environments, divided and bitter communities and a very real 'security dilemma' facing former fighters. In 2004, only one DDR operation was seen to have met its goals with any degree of success, the five-year programme in Sierra Leone. The programme was administered by the National Committee for Disarmament, Demobilization and Reintegration (NCDDR) and funded by over 10 international donors. It resulted in the disarmament and demobilization of over 72 000 fighters (almost 7000 of whom were child soldiers) at a cost of $36.5 million. Nonetheless, experts warned that Sierra Leone still faced substantive reintegration and reconciliation challenges with high unemployment, particularly among young men.[44]

Four criticisms of DDR programmes have been highlighted: (*a*) that they are too often politically constrained; (*b*) that international-led efforts lack adequate planning, coordination and funding; (*c*) that they fail to include all stakeholders in the society, particularly women and children; and (*d*) that they focus on the disarmament and demobilization components and neglect reintegration. The first weakness reflects the peace negotiation context in which DDR programmes are usually initiated. Although agreement to demobilize armed forces is crucial in order to persuade all sides to lay down arms, the terms of a ceasefire or peace agreement can present real dilemmas for the inclusion of a

[43] For further detail on the conflict in Iraq in 2004 see chapter 2 in this volume.

[44] Integrated Regional Information Network for West Africa (IRIN-WA), 'Disarmament and rehabilitation completed after five years', IRIN-WA Weekly 213, 31 Jan.–4 Feb. 2004. See also section IV of chapter 8 in this volume.

comprehensive DDR process from the outset. Afghanistan is a clear example of the complexities involved: the political bargains enshrined in the 2001 Bonn Agreement[45] as well as the US-led coalition's emphasis on militarily defeating the remaining al-Qaeda and Taliban forces in the country shored up, rather than undercut, the continued political and military influence of key warlords. The most obvious example of this was the militia forces loyal to the Minister of Defence of the Afghan interim government, Mohammad Qaseem Fahim, only 5 per cent of which entered the DDR programme.[46] The lack of progress in DDR in Afghanistan contributed to the deterioration of the security situation throughout the country in 2004 as fragile power-sharing arrangements between different factions broke down.[47]

The failure to initiate demobilization of armed groups is not always a function of the compromises involved in reaching a peace settlement. In the case of Iraq, the Coalition Provisional Authority (CPA) made no attempt to disarm and demobilize the main Kurdish militia groups nor the militia forces that sprang up throughout the country in the wake of the defeat of the Iraqi regime, in part because of a desire not to provoke an argument about the future political order of the country. The more violent the insurgency became, the more the occupation forces, and subsequently the interim government of Iraq, came to depend on militia groups for the maintenance of law and order in Iraqi towns and cities. In many cases, DDR involves incorporating former rebel groups into the reformed national armed forces, as in the cases of Afghanistan, Burundi and the DRC. This can make DDR hostage to progress on the government side in charting national security reform and, moreover, may compromise the status of the new security forces in the eyes of significant sectors of the population.[48]

A second weakness of DDR processes is the lack of adequate planning and coordination, linked to which is the perennial lack of funding for DDR operations. Even where agreement to disarm and demobilize formally exists, it is more often than not only partially implemented. Demobilization, in the sense of dismantling former military units, often takes place without any real disarmament, as, for example, in Haiti in both 1994 and 2004. This is in part because most DDR processes rest on voluntary disarmament and thus the international presence has to provide incentives for former combatants to give up their weapons. In most cases, this necessitates the international presence providing a safe environment in which the collection and destruction of weap-

[45] The Agreement on Provisional Arrangements in Afghanistan pending the Re-establishment of Permanent Government Institutions (Bonn Agreement) was signed under UN auspices in Bonn on 5 Dec. 2001. See UN Security Council document S/2001/1154, 5 Dec. 2001.

[46] UN, The situation in Afghanistan and its implications for international peace and security, Report of the Secretary-General, UN document S/2004/634, 12 Aug. 2004.

[47] See also Roy, O., *Afghanistan: la difficile reconstruction d'un État* [Afghanistan: the difficult reconstruction of a state], Chaillot Paper no. 73 (EU Institute for Security Studies: Paris, Dec. 2004), URL <http://www.iss-eu.org/chaillot/chai73f.html>.

[48] Examples of this include Kosovo, where the Kosovo Liberation Army was incorporated into a civilian agency, the Kosovo Protection Corps, and the Special Forces-led militia units of the Afghanistan Guard Force.

ons can be undertaken. In Afghanistan, for instance, widespread insecurity and the confinement of most of the International Security Assistance Force (ISAF) to the capital Kabul until 2003 constrained the Japanese-led DDR effort.[49] Such DDR progress as did take place focused on disarmament, primarily heavy weapon cantonment carried out by ISAF, but was undermined by the lack of a system to store arms and guard cantonment sites.[50]

Another issue is the lack of accurate knowledge about the number of irregular combatant forces and small arms and light weapons circulating in the country. This complicates DDR planning, as the experience in Liberia demonstrated in 2003–2004. The launch of the disarmament and demobilization phase by the UN Mission in Liberia (UNMIL) in December 2003 was a fiasco when more than 12 000 combatants (out of an estimated 45 000) presented themselves at the opening of a cantonment site outside the capital Monrovia, overwhelming the facilities and turning to violence when they learned that they would not immediately receive benefits.[51] The ensuing serious riots in Monrovia forced the suspension of the DDR programme until adequate preparation had taken place including 'sensitization' of combatants, the provision of information regarding numbers of combatants and their weapons to UNMIL and the establishment of cantonment sites around the country.

The disarmament components of most DDR programmes centre on the provision of monetary and other incentives to disarm. This approach can be easily abused, however, where small arms are widely available and where the payment is lucrative. The price offered for such arms in Sadr City in October 2004 by the interim government of Iraq was criticized by many as overgenerous and ultimately ineffective as a replacement weapon could be purchased at a lower price.[52] The DDR programme under way in Côte d'Ivoire offers $900 in subsistence payments spread out over 6 months for the approximately 30 000 fighters scheduled to participate and is seen as a potential good model for future DDR programmes.[53] It does demonstrate, however, the significant funds required to even launch a DDR process. This has remained a substantial problem, for example in Liberia, when at the start of a fresh DDR programme in April 2004 the UN Development Programme (UNDP) Trust Fund for DDR had received pledges of only $11.3 million of

[49] IRIN-CEA, 'ISAF must expand to areas of insecurity', IRIN-CEA Weekly Round-Up 133, 11–17 Oct. 2003; and Williamson, H., 'Berlin backs mission beyond Kabul', *Financial Times*, 25 Oct. 2003, p. 5.

[50] UN (note 46).

[51] 'Liberian soldiers hand over guns', BBC News Online, 7 Dec. 2003, URL <http://news.bbc.co.uk/1/3298955.stm>.

[52] International Crisis Group, 'What can the U.S. do in Iraq?', Middle East Report no. 34 (22 Dec. 2004).

[53] Gberie, L. and Addo, P., *Challenges of Peace Implementation in Côte d'Ivoire*, Report on an expert workshop at the Kofi Annan International Peacekeeping Training Centre with the Zentrum für Internationale Friedenseinsätze, Accra, Ghana, 31 May–2 June 2004, published as Institute for Security Studies (ISS) Monograph no. 105, Pretoria, Aug. 2004, available at URL <http://www.iss.co.za/pubs/Monographs/No105/Contents.html>.

the estimated cost of $50 million.[54] The High-level Panel Report proposed to provide DDR processes with more regular and sustainable funding through including provisions for DDR assistance programmes in the assessed budgets for UN peacekeeping operations.[55]

A third weakness of DDR programmes that is commonly identified is the focus on ex-fighters. For some groups in the community, the programmes may appear to be rewarding the perpetrators of violence and crime and must therefore be accompanied by initiatives targeted at the wider community. In that context DDR must be seen to be compatible with any truth and reconciliation process under way. In Mozambique, for example, ritual purification ceremonies run by traditional healers and involving the whole community facilitated the reintegration of former combatants.[56] Equally significant is the importance of distinguishing the different categories of combatants and, in particular, providing for the specific needs of child soldiers and women combatants. Child and women fighters are a particularly significant issue in Liberia and Sierra Leone. Swift family reunification is a crucial component in assisting child soldiers to make the transition to peace as well as specially focused education programmes. Women combatants, many of whom have been abducted for sexual services, are often neglected in programmes that concentrate on armed groups or are treated only in the context of their male partners. The social and economic reintegration of these women into society is often complex as, in addition to and as a consequence of the legacy of sexual abuse, they may be rejected by their families and communities.[57]

Ultimately, the area in which DDR has had least success is in providing for the medium-term reintegration of ex-combatants into their communities of origin or new communities. The most significant problem is the failure to provide for or generate alternative sources of employment and revenue for ex-combatants, without which the prospects for long-term peace-building are dim. Economic development programmes are also often conceived of and developed separately from the DDR process, with other priorities such as economic liberalization dominating strategy.[58] Delays in the start of economic activities and the end of disarmament and demobilization hamper the social and economic reintegration of ex-combatants and encourage their entry into criminal activities. DDR in Mozambique, in the past seen as a success, is being reassessed in the light of the growth of widespread organized crime at

[54] UN, Second progress report of the Secretary-General on the United Nations Mission in Liberia, UN document S/2004/229, 22 Mar. 2004; and Agence France-Presse (Paris), 'Liberia: UNMIL begins disarmament of ex-combatants in Gbarnga, UN envoy reacts', 14 Apr. 2004, in Foreign Broadcast Information Service, *Daily Report–Sub-Saharan Africa (FBIS-AFR)*, FBIS-AFR-2004-0415, 16 Apr. 2004.

[55] UN (note 3), p. 72.

[56] Pouligny, B., *The Politics and Anti-politics of Contemporary 'Disarmament, Demobilization and Reintegration' Programs*, Report of a seminar organized by Centre d'Études et de Recherches Internationales (CERI) and Secretariat General de la Défense Nationale (SGDN), Paris, Sep. 2004, URL <http://www.ceri-sciences-po.org>.

[57] See, e.g., de Watteville, N., *Addressing Gender Issues in Demobilization and Reintegration Programs*, African Region Working Paper Series (World Bank: Washington, DC, 2002).

[58] Pouligny (note 56).

the hands of gangs of former combatants.[59] High unemployment among ex-combatants in Haiti resulted in the rise of armed criminal gangs that in turn were used increasingly by the embattled government of President Jean-Bertrand Aristide to maintain power.[60] These examples testify to the threat to peace-building posed by high levels of criminal violence.

Behind all of these weaknesses lies the problem of coordination of DDR efforts where so many different security and development actors are involved. The High-level Panel Report suggested that the mandate and resources of all future UN peace operations should include DDR tasks. While this might go some way towards ensuring a quicker start to DDR and a degree of coordination in the field, multilateral peace operations alone have neither the capacity nor the reach to undertake extensive DDR programmes. Coordination with development actors, in particular the UNDP, the World Bank and bilateral agencies, will continue to be crucial both for funding and for planning and launching operational projects in DDR. A recent phenomenon is the growing number of private security companies involved in DDR processes, particularly in aspects of security sector reform (training of police and armed forces), an issue that raises prospects as well as challenges for the implementation of comprehensive DDR.[61]

The rule of law

The rule of law was a central theme of the international peace-building agenda in 2004, in part through the release in August of the Secretary-General's report on the rule of law and transitional justice in conflict and post-conflict societies.[62] The rule of law implies an effective justice system that is accessible, transparent, impartial, independent, efficient, and that is reinforced by the democratic application and enforcement of the law. Its establishment in a peace-building context is a multifaceted undertaking, involving the administering of justice for war crimes and transforming the justice system (judiciary, prosecution office, law and enforcement agencies, penal institutions and law associations). The Secretary-General's report underlined the importance of striking a balance between the different rule of law components and the need for careful sequencing of activities. The emerging consensus on the centrality of rule-of-law reform and the notion that it must be tackled in its entirety is drawn from the lessons of previous international engagement, where only one aspect of the rule of law was targeted or the implementation of ill-designed

59 McMullin, J., 'Reintegration of combatants: were the right lessons learned in Mozambique?', *International Peacekeeping*, vol. 11, no. 4 (2004), pp. 625–44.

60 International Crisis Group (ICG), 'Haiti's transition: hanging in the balance', Latin American/Caribbean briefing no. 7 (8 Feb. 2005), URL <http://www.icg.org/home/index.cfm?id=3255&l=1>.

61 Reuters Alert Net, 'Liberia: US hires private company to train 4,000-man army', 15 Feb 2005, URL <http://www.alertnet.org/thenews/newsdesk/IRIN/3db1c51f108f10cad0f867865f6ecfd4.htm>. For a detailed discussion of the private military and security industry and its impact on various security contexts see Holmqvist, C., *Private Security Companies: The Case for Regulation*, SIPRI Policy Paper no. 9 (SIPRI: Stockholm, Jan. 2005), URL <http://www.sipri.org/contents/publications/Policypaper9.html>.

62 UN (note 41).

assistance programmes undermined progress in other sectors.[63] For instance, the disproportionate emphasis on bringing war criminals to justice in Bosnia and Herzegovina arguably delayed international assistance with institutional legal reforms in areas such as civil law (including commercial and contractual law), which in turn has had a damaging impact on economic growth and efforts to move away from a shadow economy.[64]

Since 2003 the mandates of all the new UN peace operations—UNOCI, MINUSTAH and ONUB—explicitly address the rule of law.[65] In some non-UN operations, the rule of law is the focus of the entire mission. In January 2004 the European Union launched its first rule-of-law mission, EUJUST THEMIS, with the purpose of assisting the Georgian Government to reform the justice system, particularly the criminal justice sector; the Australian-led Regional Assistance Mission in the Solomon Islands (RAMSI) has a similar remit to assist the government in restoring law and order.[66]

Although rule-of-law reform is now a component of peace operations, neither the UN nor other international actors have so far succeeded in fleshing out the strategies and tools required for it: in this respect the Secretary-General's August report adds little specific detailing. The absence of a strategic approach has hampered reform efforts in current peace operations.[67] Progress in Afghanistan for example, has been impeded from the outset by the failure of the December 2001 Bonn Conference to give prominence to the issue. As a result, an overall strategy for the rule of law was absent in the Bonn Agreement. The implementation of a comprehensive reform programme on the ground has been further hampered by the division of responsibility for reform between different lead states.[68] In cases where the rule-of-law reform is explicitly provided for in the mission's mandate, for example, that of UNMIL, progress has been hampered by the sheer scale of the project and the need to set up a temporary skeletal legal system before embarking on a substantive overhaul of the rule of law. The emphasis in Liberia in 2004 was on the immediate functioning of the criminal courts in Monrovia, augmenting the

[63] Khouri-Padova, L., 'Haiti: lessons learned', DPKO Best Practices Unit, Discussion paper, Mar. 2004, URL <http://www.un.org/Depts/dpko/lessons/>.

[64] Williams, P. R. and Scharf, M. P., *Peace with Justice? War Crimes and Accountability in the Former Yugoslavia* (Rowman and Littlefield: Landham, Md., 2002), pp. 63–90; and Canadian International Development Agency, 'Balkans: rule of law concept paper', URL <http://www.acdi-cida.gc.ca/cidaweb/webcountry.nsf/europe_e.html>.

[65] The rule of law is also expected to be included in the mandate of the proposed multidimensional operation in Sudan in 2005. UN Security Council resolutions 1528, 27 Feb. 2004; 1542, 30 Apr. 2004; and 1545, 21 May 2004; and UN (note 24).

[66] European Union, Council Joint Action 2004/523/CFSP of 28 June 2004; and 'RAMSI–Fact Sheet', 1 Dec. 2004, URL <http://www.dfat.gov.au/geo/solomon_islands/helpemfren/ramsi.html>.

[67] UN, Third special report of the Secretary-General on the United Nations Organization Mission in the Democratic Republic of the Congo, UN document S/2004/650, 16 Aug. 2004.

[68] In Afghanistan, Germany has responsibility for police reform, Japan for DDR, Italy for rule of law and the UK for combating drugs (and law enforcement of drug control). Friborg, A. T., 'Afghanistan: lessons learned from a post-war situation', DIIS Working Paper no. 2004/5.

national police force and the rehabilitation of penal institutions.[69] At the end of 2004 the focus continued to be on securing funds to support quick impact projects (QIPs) aimed at rebuilding basic infrastructure.[70] A national Law Reform Commission to undertake a comprehensive review of the status of Liberia's judicial system is not expected to commence work until 2005.[71]

The lack of progress in identifying rule-of-law needs and strategies to address them is hampered by the lack of qualified personnel and resources within the host state. The case of Timor-Leste illustrates the implications this can have for the length of the reform effort where, after six years of significant international engagement, financial support and technical expertise, local capacity in the justice sector remains extremely weak. International advisers are still heavily depended on to perform basic line functions.[72] Strengthening institutional capacity in judiciary and law enforcement agencies requires not only legal professional training but also the development of a broad range of capacities, including organization management, financial administration and personnel training.

Reform of the rule of law is a profoundly political enterprise: at its core, it is about altering the nature of the social contract between the individual and the state.[73] If the reform process is to be legitimate and sustainable, it must build on existing judicial systems and legal traditions and reflect the culture and values of the country in question, even as it affirms international law, norms and standards. Meaningful consultations with and participation of local stakeholders to establish objectives and priorities and to assess progress are needed if substantial political and popular support is to take root.[74] Bosnia and Herzegovina provides a clear example of the legitimacy of the rule-of-law reform process being brought into question by the way in which it has been implemented by external actors. Some argue that the powers of the Office of the High Representative to introduce substantial legislation, and the way in which these powers have been used to dictate the priorities of reform, undermine the very same democratic principles which the international community claims to promote.[75] Others, however, challenge the view that rule-of-law reform must be built on local ownership, arguing that this approach merely reinforces the established legal order, one which may have

[69] United Nations, World Bank, with the National Transitional Government of Liberia (NTGL), 'Liberia: Joint Needs Assessment', UN Development Programme, Monrovia, Feb. 2004, URL <http://www.lr.undp. org>.

[70] UN, Fifth progress report of the Secretary-General on the United Nations Mission in Liberia, UN document S/2004/725, 10 Sep. 2004.

[71] United Nations, World Bank and NTGL (note 69).

[72] UN, Progress report of the Secretary-General on the United Nations Mission of Support in East Timor, UN document S/2004/888, 9 Nov. 2004.

[73] Rose-Ackerman, S., 'Establishing the rule of law', ed. Rotberg (note 11), pp. 182–221.

[74] UN (note 41), pp. 6–7.

[75] Knaus, G. and Martin, F., 'Travails of the European Raj', *Journal of Democracy*, vol. 14, no. 3 (July 2003), pp. 60–74; and Caparini, M., 'Security sector reform in the Western Balkans', *SIPRI Yearbook 2004: Armaments, Disarmament and International Security* (Oxford University Press: Oxford, 2004), pp. 251–82.

been a source of grievance in the first place.[76] This is particularly sensitive in cases where local law runs up against Western legal systems in issues such as the death penalty and humane punishment and gender equality before the law.

Economic reconstruction

Economic reconstruction is central for peace-building: in the short term to build confidence in the potential of peace and to ensure that former warring parties buy into a common state-building project. In the medium to longer term, it is crucial to address the root causes of conflict, such as poverty and economic inequity.[77] In 2004 the particular challenges of peace-building in countries that are rich in natural resources such as oil, diamonds and timber was in focus. Although resource-rich countries possess inherent potential for economic growth, competition within the society over the control and profitable exploitation of these resources can trigger a return to conflict. Peace-building thus requires the rapid assertion of the state's authority and regulation over those domestic and international actors that formerly profited from the exploitation of natural resources. In recognition of these challenges, the High-level Panel made a somewhat controversial recommendation that the UN provide assistance to weak states, especially those emerging from conflict, in the management of their natural resources.[78]

In practice, the UN, other relevant international actors and the private sector are already working with governments in, for example, Chad and Sierra Leone to design transparent accounting practices and develop schemes for equitable and socially beneficial sharing of resource revenues.[79] An expanded notion of this has been proposed for Liberia: an international trusteeship would be established for the collection of revenue from key customs services at major border crossings, including airports and seaports, and from natural resources such as timber, diamonds and gold, which would then be deposited in a central account.[80] Proposals such as that for Liberia are controversial as they arguably impinge on a state's sovereign rights to exercise control over revenue collection and raise the question of whether such an international presence would constitute occupation. Moreover, the authority of international management of natural resources was somewhat undermined in 2004 with continued investigations and probes into the CPA's alleged mismanagement of oil revenues in

[76] Jensen, E. G., and Heller, T. C. (eds), *Beyond Common Knowledge: Empirical Approaches to the Rule of Law* (Stanford University Press: Palo Alto, Calif., 2003)

[77] Collier (note 28); Collier, P. and Hoeffler, A., 'On the economic causes of war', *Oxford Economic Papers*, vol. 50, no. 4 (Oct. 1998), pp. 563–73; and Berdal, M. and Malone, D. M. (eds), *Greed and Grievance in Civil War: Economic Agendas in Civil Wars* (Lynne Rienner: Boulder, Colo., 2000).

[78] UN (note 3), para. 92.

[79] E.g., the Diamond Area Community Development Fund, the Kono Peace Diamonds Alliance, and the Chad–Cameroon Development and Pipeline Project. Nitzschke, H., 'Transforming war economies: challenges for peacemaking and peacebuilding', Report of the 725th Wilton Park Conference in association with the International Peace Academy, Sussex, 27–29 Oct. 2003, URL <http://www.wiltonpark.org.uk/web/conferences/reportwrapper.asp?confref=WP725>.

[80] ICG, 'Liberia and Sierra Leone: Rebuilding failed states', Africa Report no. 87 (8 Dec. 2004), p. 27.

Iraq.[81] The investigation into the corruption of UN officials involved in the management of the Oil-for-Food Programme in Iraq between 1996 and 2003 cast a further shadow on the notion of international resource management.[82]

The challenge of economic development is compounded by the need to eradicate shadow economies—criminal activities conducted outside of state-regulated frameworks—which provide important and, in most cases, long-established sources of income.[83] Poppy cultivation in Afghanistan is a clear example of this challenge. While opium production has a long history in the country, since the 2001 fall of the Taliban revenue generated from poppy cultivation and opium trade has risen dramatically and accounts for 40 per cent of Afghanistan's economy, which the International Monetary Fund (IMF) estimates is growing at 20–30 per cent annually.[84] Ironically, the opium trade achieves many of the development and economic objectives of the licit economy, such as employment, access to land and credit, and links between the centre and the periphery, albeit through illegitimate means.

The challenge of balancing short-term versus long-term development projects is a real one. Economic activities based on emergency relief bear no real sustainable prospects for a country but they may be vital in the initial post-conflict phase. The 2000 Report of the Panel on United Nations Peace Operations, chaired by Lakhdar Brahimi, Special Adviser to the Secretary-General, recommended that QIPs be implemented to improve the local quality of life, establish the credibility of a new UN mission and most importantly demonstrate results.[85] Since then, several missions have implemented QIPs with mixed results. Surveys in Afghanistan show that the population attached greater priority to the restoration of an accountable civil service, customs collection and payments system, and the commencement of large, multi-year infrastructure projects, than to the provision of a myriad of small-scale projects, which can be cost ineffective.[86] Large, expansive public sector programmes can be another way of bridging the gap between relief and

[81] The International Advisory and Monitoring Board, set up by the UN to monitor the Development Fund for Iraq, which holds proceeds of oil sales, issued a report in which it criticized the CPA for poor management of the Fund. Iraq Revenue Watch, 'Disorder, negligence and mismanagement: how the CPA handled Iraq reconstruction funds', Sep. 2004, URL <http://www.iraqrevenuewatch.org/>.

[82] The Oil-for-Food Programme was established in Apr. 1995 by UN Security Council Resolution 986, 14 Apr. 1995; implementation of the programme commenced in Dec. 1996 and was terminated at the end of 2003. Volcker, P. A., Goldstone, R. J. and Pieth, M., Interim Report of the Independent Inquiry Committee into the United Nations Oil-For-Food Programme, 3 Feb. 2005, URL <http://www.iic-offp.org>.

[83] Pugh and Cooper (note 13), p. 7; and Napoleoni, L., *Modern Jihad: Tracing the Dollars Behind the Terror Networks* (Pluto Press: London, 2003).

[84] Goodhand, J., 'From war economy to peace economy?: reconstruction and state building in Afghanistan', *Journal of International Affairs*, vol. 58, no.1 (fall 2004), pp. 155–74.

[85] See Report of the Panel on United Nations Peace Operations (Brahimi Report), Identical letters dated 21 August 2000 from the Secretary-General to the President of the General Assembly and the President of the Security Council, UN document A/55/305–S/2000/809, 21 Aug. 2000, URL <http://www.un.org/peace/reports/peace_operations/>; and Durch, W. J. *et al.*, *The Brahimi Report and the Future of UN Peace Operations* (Henry L. Stimson Center: Washington, DC, 2003), p. 26.

[86] Organisation for Economic Co-operation and Development (OECD), 'Senior level Forum on Development effectiveness in fragile states: harmonisation and alignment in fragile states', Draft report by the Overseas Development Institute (ODI), 17 Dec. 2004.

development. Labour-intensive infrastructure projects, such as road construction, can yield immediate and long-term benefits: they can generate a high level of employment quickly and at a relatively low cost; result in improvement of the state's infrastructure, leading to improved access for trade and industry; and facilitate the reintegration of demobilized combatants and returning refugees.[87]

The problem with large infrastructure projects is, first, that they require a substantial degree of state capacity which the post-conflicts states are unlikely to possess and, second, that they go against liberal economic orthodoxy that has been preached by international financial and development assistance actors. One potential way around this is the proposal that the private sector be brought in from the beginning to provide infrastructure services and help eliminate short-term donor-driven projects that are not sustainable or conducive to long-term economic recovery.[88] The international peace-building presence often constitutes one of those non-sustainable economic projects by creating an economic bubble in the capital city of the country. This is a function of the service industries that spring up to cater almost exclusively to the international presence. Afghanistan, again, offers an example of this dilemma, where the international community's presence has generated employment for approximately 40 000 Afghans. These individuals often have the higher education and specialized skills that are vital to state-building but instead choose the well-paying but less qualified positions that are offered by international organizations.[89]

Debt was a major issue for peace-building in 2004. Because most post-conflict countries do not have the necessary financial resources to embark on significant reconstruction programmes, the immediate normalization of relationships with the international financial institutions (IFIs) and with the Paris Club is necessary to obtain financial assistance.[90] The emergency assistance loans disbursed by the IMF often go towards repaying bridging loans from bilateral donors, which in turn are used to clear arrears to the IMF.[91]

[87] Some scholars have made comparisons between current economic reconstruction activities with the post-World War II Marshall Plan. Madlala-Routledge, N. and Liebenberg, S., 'Developmental peace-keeping: what are the advantages for Africa?', *African Security Review*, vol. 13, no. 2 (Dec. 2004); and Dunne, J. P., 'Challenges of armed conflicts to jobs and other socio-economic issues in Africa', ed. E. Date-Bah, *Jobs After War: A Critical Challenge in the Peace and Reconstruction Puzzle* (International Labour Organization: Geneva, 2003), pp. 33–51; and Chesterman, Ignatieff and Thakur (note 23), pp. 12–13.

[88] Schwartz, J. *et al.*, 'The private sector's role in the provision of infrastructure in post-conflict countries: patterns and policy options', Conflict Prevention & Reconstruction Paper no. 16 (Aug. 2004), URL <http://www.worldbank.org/conflict>.

[89] Chesterman, S., *You, the People: The United Nations, Transitional Administration, and State-Building* (Oxford University Press: Oxford, 2004), p. 201; and Goodhand (note 84).

[90] E.g., Burundi's classification by the IFIs as a 'post-conflict country' was a necessary measure to facilitate Burundi's ability to obtain loans. United Nations, Second report of the Secretary-General on the United Nations Operation in Burundi, UN document S/2004/902, 15 Nov. 2004

[91] Boyce, J. K., 'The international financial institutions: postconflict reconstruction and peacebuilding capacities', Paper prepared for the seminar on Strengthening the UN's Capacity on Civilian Crisis Management, for the UN Secretary-General's High-level Panel on Threats, Challenges and Change, Copenhagen, 8–9 June 2004.

While this mechanism enables the country in question to elicit more IMF engagement, it does little to rehabilitate the economy. Many policy makers and academics challenge this system and advocate debt relief or debt reduction to facilitate quicker economic reconstruction. In 2004 several post-conflict countries—Burundi, the DRC, Liberia, Iraq and Sierra Leone—received partial debt relief.[92] The issue of debt cancellation was particularly controversial in Iraq because a significant portion of its $137 billion debt can, arguably, be considered odious debts—loans 'obtained against the interests of the population of a state, with the full awareness of the creditor'—thus removing any obligation on the part of the new government to service the debt.[93]

Elections

Since 1989, elections have been highlighted as the principal means to legitimate the institutions and leadership of countries emerging from conflict and have been seen as a central task for UN peace operations, for example, in Cambodia and Namibia.[94] The successful holding of national elections is one of the most visible and effective means of enabling popular participation in state-building and one of the clearest signals that legitimate domestic authority has been restored. Elections are, in the words of Terence Lyons, 'one of the very few mechanisms available to provide internal and external legitimacy as a new government'.[95] For that reason alone, domestic pressures for rapid elections in a post-war context can be intense, as Kosovar Albanian demands after the NATO-led intervention in July 1999 and Shia pressure for elections in Iraq in 2004 demonstrated. In both these cases, formerly disenfranchised sectors of the society have seen post-conflict elections more as the principal means of asserting their majority status than as a step in building a durable peace. The international community, for its part, also has an interest in seeing that elections take place within a short space of time to establish a recognized sovereign authority, uphold the human rights in the name of which it may have intervened, legitimate its own presence in the country and lay the ground for its future departure.

At the same time, there are equally strong factors militating against the holding of national elections too soon after conflict and, indeed, the current

[92] E.g., the UK-led Commission for Africa was established in 2004 to address debt relief and poverty reduction in Africa. See *Our Common Interest: Report of the Commission for Africa*, Mar. 2005, URL <http://www.commissionforafrica.org>. In Dec. 2004 the US Government announced that it would cancel Liberia's debt, which amounted to $3 billion. IRIN-WA, 'Liberia: US says willing to cancel debt but warns more progress needed', IRIN-WA Weekly Round-up 254, 4–10 Dec. 2004.

[93] ICG, 'Reconstructing Iraq', Middle East Report no. 30 (2 Sep. 2004); and Boyce (note 91).

[94] See, e.g., Newman, E. and Rich, R. (eds), *The UN Role in Promoting Democracy: Between Ideals and Reality* (United Nations University Press: Tokyo, 2004); and Doyle, M. *et al.* (eds), *Keeping the Peace: Multidimensional UN Operations in Cambodia and El Salvador* (Cambridge University Press: Cambridge, 1997).

[95] Lyons, T., 'Transforming the institutions of war: postconflict elections and the reconstruction of failed states', ed. Rotberg (note 14), p. 270.

emphasis in the research debate is on the desirability of a long lead-in time.[96] The electoral process represents, in practical terms, the transfer of a dispute and the means to resolve it from the battlefield to the ballot box, through a contest over political power. A divided and traumatized society emerging from internal conflict may well be unable, in the short term, to manage this transition without endangering the entire peace process. The potential negative impact of national elections on the tentative peace process under way in Burundi prompted the postponement of national elections, originally scheduled to take place in November 2004.[97] International actors may wish to delay national elections in order to prevent a potentially divisive election process from distracting or undermining the peace-building efforts. This is all the more so where peace-building as state-building involves economic, political and military reforms that challenge the existing status quo. A pertinent example of this was Bosnia and Herzegovina, where the first post-war national elections resulted in a victory for the nationalist factions most opposed to the state-building enterprise. Another reason for international caution is the substantial military, financial and monitoring resources required to hold a nationwide election in an insecure environment, as Iraq demonstrated in 2004. Should violence mar the elections and lead to the results being contested, this could fatally undermine the progress made in peace-building made and shake whatever public confidence previously existed in the reform process.

Even without the threat of large-scale violence, conducting national elections is a complicated, laborious and expensive process, entailing substantial procedural and legal preparations over, ideally, 12–18 months.[98] In countries with a long legacy of dysfunctional government, such as Afghanistan and Liberia, basic prerequisites such as the holding of a census may lengthen the preparatory process still further. In the case of Afghanistan, the 2001 Bonn Agreement initially set an ambitious target of June 2004 for the formation of a fully representative and elected government. This depended on the holding of the Emergency Loya Jirga within six months of the Bonn Agreement to establish the Afghani interim government, followed by the development and approval of a new constitution in 2003, which set the parameters for the type of elections. It also provided for a nationwide census to be undertaken and for the registration in two phases of approximately 11.5 million voters.[99] The decision in July 2004 to hold presidential elections separately from parliamentary elections rather than simultaneously, as initially announced, and later than originally planned testified to the magnitude of the electoral challenge. Parliamentary elections were rescheduled for April 2005, while the pres-

[96] Chesterman (note 89); and Paris (note 18).

[97] 'New delay to Burundi referendum', BBC News Online, 14 Dec. 2004, URL <http://news.bbc.co.uk/1/4095961.stm>; and UN, Second report of the Secretary-General on the United Nations Operation in Burundi, UN document S/2004/902, 15 Nov. 2004.

[98] Jain, P., Remarks at the seminar Elections in Times of Conflict, International Institute for Democracy and Electoral Assistance, Stockholm, 21 Feb. 2005.

[99] ICG, 'Afghanistan: From presidential to parliamentary elections', Asia Report no. 88, 23 Nov. 2004.

idential election was reset for October 2004. Nonetheless, the painstaking three-year electoral process, which cost approximately $200 million, paid off on 9 October when a large voter turnout, a peaceful ballot and the declaration by international observers that the vote was free and fair resulted in the election of the incumbent interim president, Hamid Karzai, as president.[100]

In both Afghanistan and Iraq the grave security situation was the predominant obstacle to successful elections. National elections, in both countries, intensified this violence as the electoral process became a target of rebel groups. In Afghanistan, the extensive voter registration process got off to a slow start, the consequence of threats of violence from re-emerging Taliban forces and forces loyal to influential warlords. The offices of the electoral secretariat and UN electoral workers throughout the country were targeted by bomb attacks, kidnappings and shootings.[101] The deployment of some 80 000 Afghan troops and soldiers, 19 000 US forces and 9000 ISAF forces on election day facilitated the provision of security for the vote itself, which passed off peacefully.

In contrast, the short preparatory time for the election in Iraq complicated attempts to contain spiralling violence and undermined the entire electoral process. The decision to hold elections to an Iraqi transitional national assembly on 30 January 2005 was the result of a political compromise in March 2004 between the unofficial leader and moral authority of the Shia community, Grand Ayatollah Ali al-Sistani, and the CPA on the basis of a UN assessment that it would not be possible to hold free and fair elections by the end of the year. The 30 January date had little operational consequence in terms of electoral planning: voter registration and electoral preparations did not begin before December 2004 and in some parts of the country never took place because of the security situation.[102] Extraordinary security measures by the Multinational Force and Iraqi security forces enabled an orderly voting process on the election day itself, notwithstanding continued bomb attacks on civilian targets. The relatively good level of turnout among Shia sectors of the population (an estimated 60 per cent of registered voters) was undermined, however, by the lack of participation of the minority Sunni community in the election. This gave rise to fears that the election would only hasten the onset of increased sectarian violence within Iraq. It also cast practical and legitimacy questions over the transitional national assembly, potentially undermining it as it embarks on its primary task of drafting a permanent con-

[100] Integrated Regional Information Network for Central Asia (IRIN-CA), 'Karzai confirmed president as fraud team endorses election', IRIN-CA Weekly Round-up 188 covering the period 30 Oct.–5 Nov. 2004; and 'Observers approve Afghan election', BBC News Online, 10 Oct. 2004, <http://news.bbc.co.uk/1/3731746.stm>.

[101] UN (note 46).

[102] UN, 'The political transition in Iraq: report of the fact-finding mission', Annex to Letter dated 23 February 2004 from the Secretary-General to the President of the Security Council, UN document S/2004/140, 23 Feb. 2004; and Filkins, D., 'Rising violence and fear drive Iraq campaigners underground', *New York Times* (Internet edn), 16 Jan. 2005, URL <http://www.nytimes.com/2005/01/16/international/middleeast/16election.html>.

stitution for Iraq.[103] The Iraq experience demonstrated the essential dilemma elections present for peace-building: although a necessary condition of democracy, they are not a sufficient one and, moreover, they may conflict with the state-building enterprise to which the international community is committed.

The security, logistic and political difficulties posed by early elections have led to the more frequent establishment of interim national administrations in post-conflict contexts. This is seen as a way of balancing the demands of legitimacy with the need to maintain a basic degree of stability and, at the same time, continue the process of post-conflict transformation. Interim government processes represent a first step in creating joint consultative and decision-making processes among former combatants and provide for meaningful consultative dialogue between the international community and local stakeholders in shaping the democratization process. They can, potentially, encourage local involvement in state-building and facilitate the maturation of political participation among the population, particularly where it involves elections. The Loya Jirga processes in Afghanistan and the subsequent Transitional Administration were seen to be crucial interim steps towards the October 2004 elections. Similarly, the establishment of the National Transitional Government of Liberia in 2003 was a necessary measure as it offers a partner for the international community to engage with in developing joint peace-building strategies and projects.

Another approach that can facilitate participatory governance in lieu of national elections is to concentrate on representative and participatory local administrations. In Kosovo, municipal elections were held prior to province-wide elections because they were deemed less political and controversial since the elected officials were only responsible for the administration of local services.[104] Some have pointed to the success of British forces in southern Iraq in facilitating local city and town administrations that served as partners of the occupying forces.[105] Even if national elections are given priority, there is a strong argument to ensure that they are accompanied or soon followed by local or provincial elections because often the trickle-down effect of national elections is too slow to be concretely felt by the population. Sierra Leone's local elections in May 2004 were seen as a milestone in the extension of state authority and restoration of the system of local government and one of the most tangible demonstrations to the population that the country had turned a corner.[106]

[103] Filkins, D., 'Low voting rate risks isolation for Sunni Iraqis', *New York Times* (Internet edn), 3 Feb. 2005, URL <http://www.nytimes.com/2005/02/03/international/middleeast/03iraq.html>.

[104] Reilly, B., 'Elections, democratization and human rights', Paper presented at the UN University Global Seminar 4th Okinawa Session: From Conflict to Peace, 19–22 Dec. 2002.

[105] Diamond, L., 'What went wrong in Iraq', *Foreign Affairs*, vol. 83, no.5 (Sep./Oct. 2004).

[106] UN, Twenty-third report of the Secretary-General on the United Nations Mission in Sierra Leone, UN Security Council document S/2004/724, 9 Sep. 2004.

V. Conclusions: responding to the peace-building challenges

The continued increase in international peace-building in the face of the enormous practical and legitimacy challenges it presents raises the question of its future as a policy and practice. A variety of responses have been offered. The minimalist answer is to narrow the scope of peace-building so as to better carry out a limited range of tasks. In this perspective, international intervention should concentrate on the goal of establishing security over the medium term for local populations while 'they are sorting out on their own what kind of future for that territory makes the most long-term sense'.[107] In this vision security tasks should focus on the provision of security along the territorial borders of the state, on support for the delivery of humanitarian aid and on broad-scale public order—tasks that require the presence of a robust and well-trained international military operation willing to use force 'to forestall the possibility of anarchy'.[108] Peace-building, as well as state-building in this paradigm, is about enabling a society that is capable of functioning, not a liberal democratic state.

A more refined variation of this minimalist response is the 'light footprint' approach, most commonly associated with Special Adviser to the UN Secretary-General Brahimi and which guided the UN's response to post-conflict peace-building in Afghanistan. This approach warns of the dangers of raising the expectations of post-war populations too high by rash promises of what peace-building will bring and emphasizes that local knowledge and expertise is much more attuned to the needs of a society than international actors. Peace-building, in this perspective, should be demand- rather than supply-driven, focused on addressing basic needs rather than a comprehensive vision of statehood and operate, as much as possible, through local ownership and management.[109]

The maximal response, on the other hand, acknowledges the scope and legitimacy challenges of peace-building but points out that local ownership is a false panacea: the presence of a post-conflict peace operation is indicative of the inability of a society to govern itself. From the perspectives of both effectiveness and coherence, a period of 'benevolent autocracy' from external actors offers the best chance for successful peace-building.[110] This view, based often on a revisiting of 19th century British colonialism, acknowledges the inconsistency of Western engagement in peace-building around the world but argues that more, rather than fewer, international transitional administrations might better address the problem. Such external administrations would, in the

[107] Zisk Marten, K., *Enforcing the Peace: Learning from the Imperial Past* (Columbia University Press: New York, 2004), pp. 155–56.

[108] Zisk (note 107), p.163.

[109] Statement by Lakhdar Brahimi, Special Adviser to the Secretary-General, at the Conference on Strategies for Economic Reconstruction and Post-Conflict Management, Bertelsmann Stiftung, Berlin, 27 Oct. 2004; and Chesterman, S., 'Walking softly in Afghanistan: the future of UN statebuilding', *Survival*, vol. 44, no. 3 (autumn 2002), pp. 37–46.

[110] Chesterman (note 89); and Caplan, R., *International Governance of War-Torn Territories: Rule and Reconstruction* (Oxford University Press: Oxford, 2005).

short term and for a limited period, subordinate legitimacy concerns to efficiency in tackling the peace-building challenge and setting the state more firmly on course for a stable and durable peace.[111] Variants of this approach address how a single state or small group of like-minded states could more efficiently implement a maximal vision of peace-building than the UN.[112] While a UN sanction might be required to provide international legitimacy for such groups, local legitimacy would be built on the basis of the success of an efficient peace-building operation.

The December 2004 report of the High-level Panel tried to chart a path for the UN between the minimal and the maximal vision of peace-building and to avoid defining what the end goal of peace-building as state-building should be. It stresses the importance of the UN as the legitimator of any peace-building effort but also acknowledges that regional organizations and alliance organizations such as NATO may be best placed to implement it. It concentrates on the magnitude of peace-building and the challenges this presents for coordination, proposing the creation of a Peacebuilding Commission to work with local governments and the international community in marshalling, assisting and sustaining 'post-conflict peace-building over whatever period may be necessary'.[113]

This is a compromise position and, for all the concrete suggestions of the report of the High-level Panel, will not overcome the challenges presented by contemporary peace-building. The report seems to suggest as much in arguing that more attention should be paid to the prevention of state collapse, so as to avoid having to undertake comprehensive international post-conflict peace-building to the extent possible. Earlier and more comprehensive international prevention would certainly mitigate some of the challenges of magnitude and legitimacy presented by peace-building. In so doing, it may also call into question the dominance of the 'peace-building as liberal market economy state-building' paradigm.

In practical terms, much of the current discussion of peace-building is focused on the macro level. What current operational experiences appear to illustrate, however, is that peace-building fails most often at the micro level, in the content and delivery of specific security, rule-of-law, economic, social and political reforms. Although an improved strategic and coordinated approach is a prerequisite for meeting the challenges of peace-building, it is important that this be accompanied by substantive and careful work on the specific details of international peace-building operations. The examples identified in this chapter, like the lessons learned from past operations, testify to the uniqueness of each peace-building case. The conclusion to be drawn is that peace-building will remain a difficult, inevitable challenge for the international community.

[111] Paris (note 18).

[112] Daalder, I. H. and Lindsay, J. M., 'Our way or the highway', *Financial Times*, 5 Nov. 2004, p. 11.

[113] UN (note 3), pp. 83–84.

VI. Table of multilateral peace missions

Table 3.2 lists the 56 multilateral peace missions that were ongoing or terminated in 2004. The table lists only those operations conducted under the authority of the UN and operations conducted by regional organizations or by ad hoc coalitions of states that were sanctioned by the UN or authorized by a UN Security Council resolution, with the stated intention to: (*a*) serve as an instrument to facilitate the implementation of peace agreements already in place, (*b*) support a peace process, or (*c*) assist conflict prevention and/or peace-building efforts. SIPRI employs the UN Department of Peacekeeping Operations description of peacekeeping as a mechanism to assist conflict-ridden countries to create conditions for sustainable peace—this may include monitoring and observing ceasefire agreements; serving as confidence-building measures; protecting the delivery of humanitarian assistance; assisting with the demobilization and reintegration process; strengthening institutional capacities in the areas of judiciary and the rule of law (including penal institutions), policing, and human rights; electoral support; and economic and social development. The table thus covers a broad range of peace missions to reflect the growing complexity of mandates of peace operations and the potential for operations to change over the course of their mandate. The table does not include good offices, fact-finding or electoral assistance missions, nor does it include peace missions comprising non-resident individuals or teams of negotiators or operations not sanctioned by the UN.[114]

The missions are grouped by organization and listed chronologically within these groups. The first group, covering UN operations, is divided into two sections: 16 operations run by the Department of Peacekeeping Operations; and 5 operations that are defined as special political missions and peace-building missions. The next nine groups cover operations conducted or led by regional organizations or alliances: 3 by the AU; 1 by the Economic and Monetary Community of Central African States (CEMAC, Communauté Economique et Monétaire d'Afrique Centrale), 3 by the Commonwealth of Independent States (CIS), including 1 mission carried out by Russia under bilateral arrangements; 1 by ECOWAS; 5 by the EU; 4 by NATO; 2 by the OAS; and 10 by the Organization for Security and Co-operation in Europe (OSCE). A final group lists 6 operations led by ad hoc coalitions of states sanctioned by the UN.

Missions which were initiated in 2004, and new states participating in an existing mission, are listed in bold text; operations and individual state participation which ended in 2004 are shown in italics. Legal instruments underlying the establishment of an operation—UN Security Council resolutions or formal decisions by regional organizations—are cited in the first column. The start dates for the operations refer to actual deployment dates. Lead

[114] E.g., Malaysia, in its capacity as a mediator in the conflict in the Philippines, has deployed a team of observers to monitor the ceasefire between the Philippine Government and the Moro Islamic Liberation Front.

states (those that either have operational control or contribute the most personnel) are underlined in the table. Local support staff are not included in the figures presented in the table but, where possible, information on the number of local staff is given in the notes below the table. Mission fatalities are recorded from the beginning of the mission until the last reported date for 2004 and as a total for 2004. Where possible, information on cause of deaths is included. Unless otherwise stated all figures are as of 31 December 2004. Budget figures are given in millions of US dollars. For UN operations, unless otherwise stated, budget figures are for the financial year 1 July 2004–30 June 2005. Conversions from budgets set in other currencies are based on 30 December 2004 exchange rates.

Data on multilateral peace missions are obtained from the following categories of open source: (*a*) official information provided by the secretariat of the organization; (*b*) information from the mission on the ground, either in official publications or in responses to annual SIPRI questionnaires; and (*c*) information from national governments contributing to the mission in question. These primary sources are supplemented with secondary sources consisting of specialist journals and newspapers. The sources are given in the notes.

Table 3.2. Multilateral peace missions, 2004

Acronym/ (Legal instrument[a])	Name	Location	Start date	Countries contributing troops, military observers (mil. obs), civilian police (CivPol) and/or civilian staff in 2004	Troops/ Mil. obs/ CivPol/ Civ. staff	Deaths: To date/ In 2004	Cost ($m): 2004/ Unpaid
Operations carried out by the United Nations (21 operations): 102 countries participated in 2004					**55 909** **2 046** **6 765** **4 085**[2]	**1 957**[3] **91**	**3 870.0**[4] **2 570.0**[5]
UN peace operations (16 operations) (UN Charter, Chapters VI and VII)[1]							
UNTSO (SCR 50)[6]	UN Truce Supervision Organization	Egypt/Israel/ Lebanon/ Syria	June 1948	Argentina, Australia, Austria, Belgium, Canada, Chile, China, Denmark, Estonia, Finland, France, Ireland, Italy, Nepal, Netherlands, New Zealand, Norway, Russia, Slovakia, Slovenia, Sweden, Switzerland, USA[7]	– 153[8] – –	39 1[9]	27.7[10] –
UNMOGIP (SCR 91)[11]	UN Military Observer Group in India and Pakistan	India/Pakistan (Kashmir)	Jan. 1949	Belgium, Chile, Croatia, Denmark, Finland, Italy, Korea (South), Sweden, Uruguay[12]	– 43[13] – –	9 –[14]	7.3[15] –
UNFICYP (SCR 186)[16]	UN Peacekeeping Force in Cyprus	Cyprus	Mar. 1964	Argentina, Australia, Austria, Canada, Finland, Hungary, India, Ireland, *Korea (South)*, Netherlands, Slovakia, **UK**, **Uruguay**[17]	1 226 – 43[18] –	173 1[19]	52.0[20] 19.9[21]
UNDOF (SCR 350)[22]	UN Disengagement Observer Force	Syria (Golan Heights)	June 1974	Austria, Canada, Japan, **Nepal**, Poland, Slovakia[23]	1 018[24] – – –	40 –[25]	40.9[26] 19.9[27]

Acronym/ (Legal instrument[a])	Name	Location	Start date	Countries contributing troops, military observers (mil. obs), civilian police (CivPol) and/or civilian staff in 2004	Troops/ Mil. obs/ CivPol/ Civ. staff	Deaths: To date/ In 2004	Cost ($m): 2004/ Unpaid
UNIFIL (SCR 425 & 426)[28]	UN Interim Force in Lebanon	Lebanon	Mar. 1978	*Fiji*, France, Ghana, India, Ireland, Italy, Poland, Ukraine[29]	1 995[30] – – –	250 3[31]	92.9[32] 71.0[33]
MINURSO (SCR 690)[34]	UN Mission for the Referendum in Western Sahara	Western Sahara	Sep. 1991	Argentina, Austria, Bangladesh, China, Croatia, Egypt, El Salvador, France, Ghana, Greece, Guinea, Honduras, Hungary, *India*, Ireland, Italy, Kenya, Korea (South), Malaysia, Mongolia, Nigeria, Pakistan, Poland, Russia, Sri Lanka, Uruguay[35]	27 196 4[36] –	10 –[37]	44.0[38] 44.9[39]
UNOMIG (SCR 849 & 858)[40]	UN Observer Mission to Georgia	Georgia (Abkhazia)	Aug. 1993	Albania, Austria, Bangladesh, Czech Rep., Denmark, Egypt, France, Germany, Greece, Hungary, Indonesia, Jordan, Korea (South), Pakistan, Poland, Russia, Sweden, Switzerland, Turkey, UK, Ukraine, Uruguay, USA[41]	– 119 11[42] –	7 –[43]	33.6[44] 11.6[45]
UNMIK (SCR 1244)[46]	UN Interim Administration in Kosovo	Serbia and Montenegro (Kosovo)	June 1999	Argentina, Austria, Bangladesh, Belgium, Bolivia, Brazil, Bulgaria, Cameroon, *Canada*, Chile, **China**, Czech Rep., Denmark, Egypt, Fiji, Finland, France, Germany, Ghana, Greece, Hungary, India, Ireland, Italy, Jordan, Kenya, Kyrgyzstan, Lithuania, Malawi, Malaysia, *Mauritius*, Nepal, **Netherlands**, New Zealand, Nigeria, Norway, Pakistan, Philippines, Poland, Portugal, Romania, Russia, *Senegal*, Slovenia, Spain, Sweden, Switzerland, Tunisia, Turkey, UK, Ukraine, USA, Zambia, Zimbabwe[47]	– 37 3 509[48] –	29 5[49]	315.5[50] 105.2[51]

UNAMSIL (SCR 1270)[52]	UN Mission in Sierra Leone	Sierra Leone	Oct. 1999	Bangladesh, Bolivia, Canada, China, Croatia, Czech Rep., Denmark, Egypt, Gambia, Germany, Ghana, Guinea, India, Indonesia, Jordan, Kenya, Kyrgyzstan, **Malawi**, Malaysia, Mali, Mauritius, Namibia, Nepal, New Zealand, Nigeria, Norway, Pakistan, Russia, Senegal, Slovakia, Sri Lanka, Sweden, Tanzania, Thailand, Turkey, UK, Ukraine, Uruguay, *USA*, Zambia, Zimbabwe[53]	4 061 138 75[54] –	159 28[55]	207.3[56] 140.0[57]
MONUC (SCR 1279)[58]	UN Organization Mission in the Democratic Republic of the Congo	Democratic Republic of the Congo	Nov. 1999	Algeria, Argentina, Bangladesh, Belgium, Benin, Bolivia, Bosnia and Herzegovina, Burkina Faso, Cameroon, Canada, **Chad**, *Chile*, China, Côte d'Ivoire, Czech Rep., Denmark, Egypt, France, Ghana, Guinea, India, Indonesia, Ireland, Jordan, Kenya, Malawi, Malaysia, Mali, Mongolia, Morocco, Mozambique, Nepal, Niger, Nigeria, Pakistan, Paraguay, Peru, Poland, Portugal, Romania, Russia, Senegal, Serbia and Montenegro, South Africa, Spain, Sri Lanka, Sweden, Switzerland, Tunisia, Turkey, UK, Ukraine, Uruguay, Zambia[59]	11 903 568 175[60] –	44 21[61]	582.0[62] 239.2[63]
UNMEE (SCR 1312)[64]	UN Mission in Ethiopia and Eritrea	Ethiopia, Eritrea	July 2000	Algeria, Australia, Austria, Bangladesh, *Benin*, Bosnia and Herzegovina, Bulgaria, China, Croatia, Czech Rep., Denmark, Finland, France, Gambia, **Germany**, Ghana, Greece, India, *Iran*, Italy, Jordan, Kenya, Malaysia, Namibia, Nepal, Nigeria, Norway, Paraguay, Peru, Poland, Romania, Russia, *Slovakia*, South Africa, Spain, Sweden, Switzerland, Tanzania, Tunisia, *UK*, Ukraine, Uruguay, USA, Zambia[65]	3 705 213[66] – –	8 3[67]	198.3[68] 50.6[69]

Acronym/ (Legal instrument[a])	Name	Location	Start date	Countries contributing troops, military observers (mil. obs), civilian police (CivPol) and/or civilian staff in 2004	Troops/ Mil. obs/ CivPol/ Civ. staff	Deaths: To date/ In 2004	Cost ($m): 2004/ Unpaid
UNMISET (SCR 1410)[70]	UN Mission of Support in East Timor	Timor-Leste	May 2002	*Argentina*, Australia, Bangladesh, Bolivia, Bosnia and Herzegovina, Brazil, *Canada*, China, Denmark, Fiji, Ghana, *Ireland*, *Japan*, Jordan, *Kenya*, *Korea (South)*, Malaysia, Mozambique, Nepal, New Zealand, *Niger*, Norway, Pakistan, Philippines, Portugal, Russia, Samoa, *Serbia and Montenegro*, *Singapore*, Spain, Sri Lanka, Sweden, *Thailand*, Turkey, *UK*, Ukraine, *Uruguay*, USA, Zambia, Zimbabwe[71]	429 43 147 52[72]	13 1[73]	85.2[74] 69.3[75]
UNMIL (SCR 1509)[76]	UN Mission in Liberia	Liberia	Oct. 2003	**Argentina**, Bangladesh, Benin, Bolivia, **Bosnia and Herzegovina**, Brazil, **Bulgaria**, China, Croatia, Czech Rep., Denmark, Ecuador, Egypt, **El Salvador**, Ethiopia, **Fiji**, Finland, France, Gambia, **Germany**, Ghana, *Guinea-Bissau*, Indonesia, Ireland, **Jamaica**, Jordan, Kenya, *Korea (South)*, **Kyrgyzstan**, Malawi, Malaysia, Mali, Moldova, Namibia, Nepal, *Netherlands*, Niger, Nigeria, Norway, Pakistan, Paraguay, Peru, Philippines, Poland, **Portugal**, Romania, **Russia**, **Samoa**, Senegal, Serbia and Montenegro, South Africa, Sweden, Togo, Turkey, **Uganda**, UK, **Ukraine**, USA, **Uruguay**, Yemen, Zambia, Zimbabwe[77]	**14 501** **189** **1 098**[78] –	28 23[79]	864.8[80] 444.4[81]
UNOCI (SCR 1528)[82]	**UN Operation in Côte d'Ivoire**	**Côte d'Ivoire**	**Apr. 2004**	**Argentina, Bangladesh, Benin, Bolivia, Brazil, Burkina Faso, Cameroon, Canada, Chad, China, Congo (Rep. of), Croatia, Djibouti, Dominican Rep., Ecuador, El Salvador, France, Gambia, Ghana, Guatemala, Guinea, India, Ireland, Jordan, Kenya, Lebanon, Moldova, Morocco, Namibia, Niger, Nigeria, Pakistan, Paraguay, Peru, Philippines, Poland, Portugal, Romania, Russia, Senegal, Serbia and Montenegro, Sri Lanka, Togo, Tunisia, Uruguay, Yemen, Zambia**[83]	**5 846** **154** **215**[84] –	– –[85]	**297.0**[86] **0.4**[87]

MINUSTAH (SCR 1542)[88]	**UN Stabilization Mission in Haiti**	**Haiti**	**June 2004**	**Argentina, Benin, Bolivia, Bosnia and Herzegovina, Brazil, Burkina Faso, Cameroon, Canada, Chad, Chile, China, Croatia, Ecuador, Egypt, El Salvador, France, Ghana, Guatemala, Guinea, Jordan, Mali, Mauritius, Morocco, Nepal, Niger, Nigeria, Pakistan, Paraguay, Peru, Philippines, Portugal, Romania, Senegal, Sierra Leone, Spain, Sri Lanka, Togo, Turkey, Uruguay, USA, Zambia[89]**	**6 008** **–** **1 398[90]** **–**	**–** **–[91]**	**379.0[92]** **144.4[93]**
ONUB (SCR 1545)[94]	**UN Operation in Burundi**	**Burundi**	**June 2004**	**Bangladesh, Belgium, Benin, Bolivia, Burkina Faso, Cameroon, Chad, China, Côte d'Ivoire, Egypt, Ethiopia, Gabon, Gambia, Ghana, Guatemala, India, Jordan, Kenya, Korea (South), Madagascar, Malawi, Mali, Mozambique, Namibia, Nepal, Netherlands, Niger, Nigeria, Pakistan, Paraguay, Peru, Philippines, Portugal, Romania, Russia, Senegal, Serbia and Montenegro, South Africa, Spain, Sri Lanka, Thailand, Togo, Tunisia, Turkey, Uruguay, Yemen, Zambia[95]**	**5 190** **182** **89[96]** **–**	**5** **5[97]**	**329.7[98]** **53.6[99]**
UN special political and peace-building missions[100] (5 operations)							
MINUGUA (A/RES/ 48/267)[101]	*UN Verification Mission in Guatemala*	*Guatemala*	*Oct. 1994*	*Argentina, Barbados, Belgium, Bolivia, Canada, Chile, Dominican Republic, Ecuador, Egypt, El Salvador, France, Germany, Honduras, Italy, Mexico, Nicaragua, Peru, Russia, Spain, Ukraine, Uruguay, USA[102]*	*–* *–* *1* *11[103]*	*4* *–[104]*	*11.6[105]* *–*

Acronym/ (Legal instrument[a])	Name	Location	Start date	Countries contributing troops, military observers (mil. obs), civilian police (CivPol) and/or civilian staff in 2004	Troops/ Mil. obs/ CivPol/ Civ. staff	Deaths: To date/ In 2004	Cost ($m): 2004/ Unpaid
UNAMA (SCR 1401)[106]	UN Assistance Mission in Afghanistan	Afghanistan	Mar. 2002	*Armenia*, Australia, Austria, Bangladesh, Bosnia and Herzegovina, Brazil, *Burkina Faso*, *Burundi*, **Cameroon**, Canada, China, *Colombia*, Croatia, Denmark, El Salvador, Ethiopia, Fiji, *Finland*, France, Germany, Ghana, Guatemala, *Guyana*, *Haiti*, Honduras, India, Indonesia, Iran, Iraq, Ireland, Italy, *Jamaica*, **Japan**, Jordan, Kenya, **Korea (South)**, Kyrgyzstan, Lebanon, **Liberia**, Malaysia, Mongolia, Morocco, Myanmar, Nepal, Netherlands, New Zealand, Nigeria, Norway, Pakistan, *Peru*, Philippines, **Poland**, **Romania**, Russia, **Rwanda**, Sierra Leone, *Singapore*, *South Africa*, Spain, Sudan, Sweden, **Switzerland**, *Syrian Arab Republic*, Tajikistan, Thailand, **Trinidad and Tobago**, Tunisia, *Turkey*, **Turkmenistan**, UK, Ukraine, **Uruguay**, USA, Zimbabwe[107]	– 11 8 181[108]	– –[109]	63.6[110] –
MINUCI (SCR 1479)[111]	*United Nations Mission in Côte d'Ivoire*	*Côte d'Ivoire*	*May 2003*	*Austria, Bangladesh, Benin, Brazil, Gambia, Ghana, India, Ireland, Jordan, Kenya, Moldova, Nepal, Niger, Nigeria, Pakistan, Paraguay, Poland, Romania, Russia, Senegal, Tunisia, Uruguay*[112]	– *75* – *54*[113]	– –[114]	*7.1*[115] –
UNAMI (SCR 1500)[116]	United Nations Assistance Mission in Iraq	Iraq	Aug. 2003	*Afghanistan, Australia, Austria, Barbados, Canada, Denmark, Ethiopia, France, Germany, Ghana, India,* **Iraq**, *Jamaica,* **Jordan**, *Kenya,* **Kuwait**, *Lebanon, Macedonia, New Zealand, Philippines, Russia, Sudan, Sweden, Syria, UK, USA*[117]	3[118] – – 132[119]	15 15[120]	35.0[121] –

UNAMIS (SCR 1547)[122]	**UN Advance Mission in Sudan**	**Sudan (Darfur)**	**June 2004**	**Albania, Australia, Austria, Bangladesh, Belarus, Bhutan, Canada, Central African Rep., Croatia, Denmark, Egypt, Eritrea, Ethiopia, Fiji, France, Germany, Ghana, India, Iraq, Ireland, Jamaica, Japan, Jordan, Kenya, Lebanon, Malaysia, Morocco, Nepal, Netherlands, New Zealand, Nigeria, Norway, Pakistan, Palestine, Philippines, Poland, Romania, Russia, Rwanda, Serbia and Montenegro, Sierra Leone, Somalia, South Africa, Spain, Sri Lanka, Sweden, Tajikistan, Tanzania, Thailand, Trinidad and Tobago, Tunisia, Turkey, Uganda, UK, USA, Zimbabwe**[123]	– **24** **6** **164**[124]	– –[125]	**36.6**[126] –
Operations carried out by standing regional organizations and alliances (35 operations)							
African Union (AU) operations (3 operations)					**4 125** **440** **7** **11**	– –	**269.6** –
AMIB (AU, 3 Feb. 2003)[127]	*African Mission in Burundi*	*Burundi*	*Apr. 2003*	***Burkina Faso**, **Gabon**, Ethiopia, **Mali**, Mozambique, South Africa, **Togo**, **Tunisia***[128]	*3 335* *43*[129] – –	*1* –[130]	*43.3*[131] –
MIOC (AU, 30 Jan. 2004)[132]	***AU Military Observer Mission to the Comoros***	***Comoros***	***Mar. 2004***	***Benin, Burkina Faso, Madagascar, Mauritania, Mozambique, Senegal, South Africa, Togo***[133]	– ***41***[134] – –	– –	***0.9***[135] –
AMIS (AU, 28 May 2004)[136]	**African Mission in Sudan**	**Sudan (Darfur)**	**June 2004**	**Algeria, Chad, Congo (Rep.), Egypt, Gabon, Gambia, Ghana, Kenya, Malawi, Mali, Mauritania, Mozambique, Namibia, Nigeria, Rwanda, Senegal, South Africa, USA, Zambia**[137]	**790** **356** **7** **11**[138]	– –[139]	**225.4**[140] –

Acronym/ (Legal instrument[a])	Name	Location	Start date	Countries contributing troops, military observers (mil. obs), civilian police (CivPol) and/or civilian staff in 2004	Troops/ Mil. obs/ CivPol/ Civ. staff	Deaths: To date/ In 2004	Cost ($m): 2004/ Unpaid
Communauté Economique et Monétaire d'Afrique Centrale (CEMAC, Economic and Monetary Community of Central African States) operations (1 operation)					**380** – – –	**6** **4**	**5.6** –
– (Libreville Summit, 2 Oct. 2002)[141]	CEMAC Multinational Force in the Central African Republic	Central African Republic	Dec. 2002	Chad, Gabon, Rep. of Congo[142]	380[143] – – –	6 4[144]	5.6[145] –
Commonwealth of Independent States (CIS) operations (3 operations)					**4 185** **50** – –	– **2**	. . . .
– (Bilateral, 24 June 1992)[146]	South Ossetia Joint Force	Georgia (South Ossetia)	July 1992	Georgia, <u>Russia</u>, (South Ossetia)[147]	1 041[148] 40[149] –	(4)[150] 2[151]	. . . .
– (Bilateral, 21 July 1992)[152]	Joint Control Commission Peacekeeping Force	Moldova (Trans-Dniester)	July 1992	Moldova, Russia, (Trans-Dniester), Ukraine[153]	1 272[154] 10[155] – –	(–)[156] –[157]	–[158] –

– (CIS, 15 Oct. 1994)[159]	CIS Peacekeeping Forces in Georgia	Georgia (Abkhazia)	June 1994	Russia[160]	1 872[161] – –	96[162] –[163]	. . . .
Economic Community of Western African States (ECOWAS) operations (1 operation)					**1 300** – – –	– 4	**18.6** –
ECOMICI (SCR 1464)[164]	*ECOWAS Mission in Côte d'Ivoire*	*Côte d'Ivoire*	*Feb. 2003*	*Benin, Ghana, Niger, Senegal, Togo*[165]	*1 300*[166] – – –	*4* –[167]	*18.6*[168] –
European Union (EU) operations (5 operations)					**7 000** **96** **663** **74**	– **2**	**135.6** –
EUMM (Brioni Agree-ment)[169]	EU Monitoring Mission	Western Balkans[170]	July 1991	Austria, Belgium, Denmark, Finland, France, Germany, Greece, Ireland, Italy, *Luxembourg,* Netherlands, Norway, Portugal, Slovakia, Spain, Sweden, UK[171]	– 96[172] – –	11 –[173]	5.7[174] –
EUPM (Joint Action 2002/210/ CFSP)[175]	EU Police Mission in Bosnia and Herzegovina	Bosnia and Herzegovina	Jan. 2003	Austria, Belgium, Bulgaria, Canada, Cyprus, Czech Rep., Denmark, Estonia, Finland, France, Germany, Greece, Hungary, Iceland, Ireland, Italy, Latvia, Lithuania, Luxemburg, Netherlands, Norway, Poland, Portugal, Romania, Russia, Slovakia, Slovenia, Spain, Sweden, Switzerland, Turkey, UK, Ukraine[176]	– – 479 62[177]	3 2[178]	23.6[179] –

Acronym/ (Legal instrument[a])	Name	Location	Start date	Countries contributing troops, military observers (mil. obs), civilian police (CivPol) and/or civilian staff in 2004	Troops/ Mil. obs/ CivPol/ Civ. staff	Deaths: To date/ In 2004	Cost ($m): 2004/ Unpaid
EUPOL PROXIMA (Joint Action 2003/681/ CFSP)[180]	EU Police Mission in the Former Yugoslav Republic of Macedonia	Former Yugoslav Republic of Macedonia	Dec. 2003	Austria, Belgium, **Cyprus**, Czech Rep., Denmark, Finland, France, Germany, Greece, Hungary, Ireland, Italy, **Latvia**, Lithuania, Luxemburg, Netherlands, **Norway**, Poland, Portugal, Slovenia, Spain, Sweden, **Switzerland**, **Turkey**, UK, **Ukraine**[181]	– – 184[182] –	– –[183]	6.8[184] –
EUJUST THEMIS (Joint Action 2004/523/ CFSP)[185]	**EU Rule of Law Mission in Georgia**	**Georgia**	**July 2004**[186]	**Denmark, France, Germany, Greece, Italy, Latvia, Lithuania, Netherlands, Poland, Spain, Sweden**[187]	– – – **12**[188]	– –[189]	**2.8**[190] –
EUFOR ALTHEA (Joint Action 2004/570/ CFSP)[191]	**EU Military Operation in Bosnia and Herzegovina**	**Bosnia and Herzegovina**	**Dec. 2004**	**Albania, Argentina, Austria, Belgium, Bulgaria, Canada, Chile, Czech Rep., Estonia, Finland, France, Germany, Greece, Hungary, Ireland, Italy, Latvia, Lithuania, Luxembourg, Morocco, Netherlands, New Zealand, Norway, Poland, Portugal, Romania, Slovakia, Slovenia, Spain, Sweden, Switzerland, Turkey, UK**[192]	**7 000**[193] – – –	– –[194]	**96.8**[195] –

North Atlantic Treaty Organization (NATO) and NATO-led operations (4 operations)					**25 565** – – –	– **12**	**131.2** –
SFOR (SCR 1088)[196]	*NATO Stabilization Force*	*Bosnia and Herzegovina*	*Dec. 1996*	*Albania, Argentina, Australia, Austria, Belgium, Bulgaria, Canada,* ***Chile****, Czech Rep., Denmark,* ***Estonia****,* ***Finland****, France, Germany, Greece, Hungary, Ireland, Italy, Latvia,* ***Lithuania****,* ***Luxembourg****, Morocco, Netherlands, New Zealand, Norway, Poland, Portugal, Romania, Slovakia, Slovenia, Spain, Sweden, Turkey, UK, USA*[197]	*7 000*[198] – – –	*809* –[199]	*21.8*[200] –
KFOR (SCR 1244)[201]	NATO Kosovo Force	Serbia and Montenegro (Kosovo)	June 1999	Argentina, Austria, Azerbaijan, **Armenia**, Belgium, Bulgaria, *Canada*, Czech Rep., Denmark, Estonia, Finland, France, Georgia, Germany, Greece, Hungary, *Iceland*, Ireland, Italy, **Latvia**, Lithuania, Luxembourg, Morocco, *Netherlands*, Norway, Poland, Portugal, Romania, *Russia*, Slovakia, **Slovenia**, Spain, Sweden, Switzerland, Turkey, *UAE*, UK, Ukraine, USA[202]	18 000[203] – – –	71 5[204]	32.1[205] –
ISAF (SCR 1386)[206]	International Security Assistance Force	Afghanistan	Dec. 2001	Albania, **Austria,** Azerbaijan, Belgium, Bulgaria, Canada, Croatia, Czech Rep., Denmark, Estonia, Finland, France, Germany, Greece, **Hungary**, **Iceland**, Ireland, Italy, Latvia, Lithuania, Luxembourg, Macedonia, Netherlands, New Zealand, Norway, Poland, **Portugal**, Romania, **Slovakia**, **Slovenia**, Spain, Sweden, Switzerland, Turkey, UK, USA[207]	8 500[208] – – –	84 7[209]	73.7[210] –
NTIM-I (SCR 1546)[211]	**NATO Training Implementation Mission in Iraq**	**Iraq**	**Aug. 2004**	**Bulgaria, Canada, Denmark, Italy, Netherlands, Norway, Romania, Turkey, United Kingdom, USA**[212]	**65**[213] – – –	– –[214]	**3.6**[215] –

Acronym/ (Legal instrument[a])	Name	Location	Start date	Countries contributing troops, military observers (mil. obs), civilian police (CivPol) and/or civilian staff in 2004	Troops/ Mil. obs/ CivPol/ Civ. staff	Deaths: To date/ In 2004	Cost ($m): 2004/ Unpaid
Organization of American States (OAS) operations (2 operations)					**–** **–** **23** **29**	– –	**7.7** –
– (CP/RES. 806)[216]	**OAS Special Mission for Strengthening Democracy in Haiti**	**Haiti**	**June 2004**	**Canada**, **Colombia**, **Dominica**, **El Salvador**, **France**, **Grenada**, **Mexico**, **Uruguay**, **USA**[217]	– – **23** **18**[218]	– –[219]	**5.0**[220] –
MAPP/OEA (CP/RES. 859)[221]	**Mission to Support the Peace Process in Colombia**	**Colombia**	**Feb. 2004**	**Argentina, Costa Rica, Guatemala, Nicaragua, Norway, Peru, Sweden**[222]	– – – **11**[223]	– –[224]	**2.7** –[225]
Organization for Security and Co-operation in Europe (OSCE) operations[226] (10 operations)					**–** **144** **70** **666**	– –	**164.1** –
– (CSO 18 Sep. 1992)[227]	OSCE Spillover Mission to Skopje	Former Yugoslav Republic of Macedonia (FYROM)	Sep. 1992	Armenia, Austria, Azerbaijan, Belarus, Belgium, Bosnia and Herzegovina, Canada, Croatia, Czech Rep., Denmark, Estonia, Finland, France, Georgia, Germany, Hungary, Ireland, Italy, **Japan**, Netherlands, Norway, Poland, Portugal, Romania, Russia, Slovakia, Slovenia, Spain, Sweden, Switzerland, Tajikistan, Turkey, UK, Ukraine, USA[228]	– – 40[229] 60[230]	– –[231]	18.3[232] –

– (CSO 6 Nov. 1992)[233]	OSCE Mission to Georgia	Georgia	Dec. 1992	**Armenia**, Austria, Azerbaijan, Belarus, **Belgium**, **Bosnia and Herzegovina**, Bulgaria, Croatia, Czech Rep., *Denmark*, **Estonia**, Finland, France, Germany, **Greece**, Hungary, Ireland, **Italy,** Latvia, Lithuania, **Macedonia**, Moldova, Netherlands, Norway, Poland, Romania, Russia, Slovakia, Sweden, Switzerland, Turkey, UK, Ukraine, USA[234]	– 144[235] – 25[236]	– –[237]	28.7[238] –
– (CSO 4 Feb. 1993)[239]	OSCE Mission to Moldova	Moldova	Feb. 1993	**Belarus,** *Canada*, **France**, Germany, *Italy*, Netherlands, Norway, Poland, UK, USA[240]	– – – 11[241]	– –[242]	2.0[243] –
– (Ministerial Council, 1 Dec. 1993)[244]	OSCE Centre in Dushanbe[245]	Tajikistan	Feb. 1994	*Belarus*, Bulgaria, France, *Hungary*, Italy, Latvia, *Moldova*, Netherlands, *Norway*, **Romania**, Russia, USA[246]	– – – 16[247]	– –[248]	5.2[249] –
– (10 Aug. 1995)[250]	Personal Representative of the Chairman-in-Office on the Conflict Dealt with by the OSCE Minsk Conference	Azerbaijan (Nagorno-Karabakh)	Aug. 1995	Czech Rep., *Germany*, **Hungary**, Poland, UK, Ukraine[251]	– – – 6[252]	– –[253]	1.2[254] –
– (Ministerial Council, 18 Dec. 1995)[255]	OSCE Mission to Bosnia and Herzegovina	Bosnia and Herzegovina	Dec. 1995	Albania, *Armenia*, Austria, Azerbaijan, Belgium, Bulgaria, Canada, Czech Rep., **Denmark**, France, Georgia, Germany, Hungary, Ireland, Italy, *Japan*, Latvia, Lithuania, *Moldova*, Netherlands, Norway, Poland, *Romania*, Russia, **Slovenia**, Spain, Sweden, Switzerland, Turkey, UK, USA[256]	– – – 142[257]	– –[258]	23.8[259] –

Acronym/ (Legal instrument[a])	Name	Location	Start date	Countries contributing troops, military observers (mil. obs), civilian police (CivPol) and/or civilian staff in 2004	Troops/ Mil. obs/ CivPol/ Civ. staff	Deaths: To date/ In 2004	Cost ($m): 2004/ Unpaid
– (PC/DEC 112, 18 Apr. 1996)[260]	OSCE Mission to Croatia	Croatia	July 1996	Armenia, Austria, Belarus, Belgium, Bulgaria, Canada, **Czech Rep.**, **Denmark**, Finland, France, Georgia, **Germany**, **Greece**, Ireland, Italy, Japan, Kyrgyzstan, *Latvia*, **Lithuania**, Moldova, Netherlands, Norway, Poland, **Portugal**, Romania, Russia, Slovakia, Spain, Sweden, *Switzerland*, UK, Ukraine, USA[261]	– – – 67[262]	– –[263]	13.6[264] –
– (PC/DEC 160, 27 Mar. 1997)[265]	OSCE Presence in Albania	Albania	Apr. 1997	Austria, Belarus, **Bulgaria**, Canada, Croatia, Czech Rep., France, Finland, Germany, Hungary, Ireland, Italy, Japan, Moldova, Romania, Spain, **Sweden**, UK, USA[266]	– – – 32[267]	– –[268]	5.1[269] –
OMiK (PC/DEC 305, 1 July 1999)[270]	OSCE Mission in Kosovo	Serbia and Montenegro (Kosovo)	July 1999	Albania, Armenia, Austria, **A**zerbaijan, *Belarus*, Belgium, Bosnia and Herzegovina, Bulgaria, Canada, Croatia, Czech Rep., Denmark, Estonia, Finland, France, Georgia, Germany, Greece, Hungary, Iceland, Ireland, Italy, Kyrgyzstan, *Latvia*, Lithuania, Macedonia, Moldova, Netherlands, Norway, Poland, Portugal, Romania, Russia, **Slovakia**, Slovenia, Spain, Sweden, Switzerland, Tajikistan, Turkey, UK, Ukraine, USA, **Uzebekistan**[271]	– – – 270[272]	3 –[273]	52.9[274] –
OMiSaM (PC/DEC 401, 11 Jan. 2001)[275]	OSCE Mission to Serbia and Montenegro[276]	Serbia and Montenegro	Mar. 2001	Austria, Belgium, Bosnia and Herzegovina, **Bulgaria**, **Canada**, Estonia, France, Germany, Greece, Ireland, Italy, Kyrgyzstan, Latvia, **Liechtenstein**, Netherlands, Norway, **Portugal**, Slovakia, Sweden, Turkey, UK, USA[277]	– – 30 37[278]	– –[279]	13.3[280] –

Other operations (6 operations)[281]					**178 060** **1 691** **563** **243**	**–** **914**	**54 340.1** **–**
NNSC (Armistice Agree-ment)[282]	Neutral Nations Supervisory Commission	North Korea/ South Korea	July 1953	*Poland*, Sweden, Switzerland[283]	– 5[284] – –	– –[285]	2.1[286] –
MFO (Protocol to Treaty of Peace)[287]	Multinational Force and Observers	Egypt (Sinai)	Apr. 1982	Australia, Canada, Colombia, Fiji, France, Hungary, Italy, New Zealand, Norway, Uruguay, USA[288]	– 1 686[289] – –	48 –[290]	51.0[291] –
TIPH 2 (Hebron Protocol)[292]	Temporary International Presence in Hebron	Hebron	Jan. 1997	Denmark, Italy, Norway, Sweden, Switzerland, Turkey[293]	– – – 73[294]	2 –[295]	1.9[296] –
– (SCR 1464)[297]	Operation Licorne	Côte d'Ivoire	Feb. 2003	France[298]	5 000[299] – – –	12 12[300]	261.9[301] –
RAMSI (Biketawa Declara-tion)[302]	Regional Assistance Mission in the Solomon Islands	Solomon Islands	July 2003	Australia, Cook Islands, Fiji, Kiribati, **Nauru**, New Zealand, Papua New Guinea, Samoa, Tonga, **Tuvalu**, Vanuatu[303]	60 – 245 170[304]	– –[305]	154.1[306] –

Acronym/ (Legal instrument[a])	Name	Location	Start date	Countries contributing troops, military observers (mil. obs), civilian police (CivPol) and/or civilian staff in 2004	Troops/ Mil. obs/ CivPol/ Civ. staff	Deaths: To date/ In 2004	Cost ($m): 2004/ Unpaid
MNF-I (SCR 1511)[307]	Multinational Force in Iraq	Iraq	Oct. 2003	Albania, **Australia**, Azerbaijan, Bulgaria, Czech. Rep., Denmark, *Dominican Rep.*, El Salvador, Estonia, Georgia, *Honduras*, Hungary, Italy, **Japan**, Kazakhstan, Korea (South), Latvia, Lithuania, Macedonia, Moldova, Mongolia, Netherlands, *New Zealand*, *Nicaragua*, Norway, *Philippines*, Poland, Portugal, Romania, Slovakia, *Spain*, *Thailand*, UK, Ukraine, USA[308]	173 000[309] – 318[310] –	1 441 902[311]	53 869.1[312] –

[a] *Acronyms in the table and notes*: A/RES = UN General Assembly Resolution; CPA = Coalition Provisional Authority; CSO = OSCE Committee of Senior Officials (now the Senior Council); DDR = disarmament, demobilization and reintegration; DMZ = Demilitarized Zone; DPKO = UN Department of Peacekeeping Operations; FY = financial year; GA = UN General Assembly; MC = Ministerial Council; MOU = Memorandum of Understanding; NAC = North Atlantic Council; PC = OSCE Permanent Council; PC.DEC = OSCE Permanent Council Decision; SC = UN Security Council; SCR = UN Security Council Resolution.

[1] These operations are administered and directed by the DPKO.

[2] United Nations, DPKO, 'Monthly summary of military and CivPol personnel deployed in current United Nations operations as of 31 Dec. 2004', 17 Jan. 2005. However, the DPKO does not provide a breakdown of civilian staff.

[3] Figure as of 31 Dec. 2004, including military, observer, police and international civilian staff. Note that this figure represents the total mission fatalities for all UN missions since 1948, not only those listed below. DPKO Situation Centre, 'Fatalities by mission and incident type—as of December 31 2004', 7 Jan. 2005. UN Internet site, URL <http://www.un.org/Depts/dpko/fatalities/fatal1.htm>.

[4] Total for the costs of the 16 operations listed in the table. This total does not include the member states' prorated share of the support account for peacekeeping operations nor the costs of the UN Logistics Base at Brindisi (Italy).

[5] As of 31 Dec. 2004. United Nations, 'Background note on peacekeeping operations', 15 Jan. 2005, UN Internet site, URL <http://www.un.org/depts/dpko/dpko/home.shtml>.

[6] UNTSO was established in May 1948 to assist the Mediator and the Truce Commission in supervising the observance of the truce in Palestine after the 1948 Arab–Israeli War. The mandate was maintained during 2004.

[7] For UN operations, the underlined country represents the country with the largest number of personnel deployed to the field. United Nations (note 2).

[8] United Nations (note 2).

[9] Death owing to other causes. United Nations (note 3).

[10] UNTSO is funded through the UN's regular budget and consequently should not suffer arrears. United Nations, 'Middle East–UNTSO: Facts and figures', UN Internet site, URL <http://www.un.org/Depts/DPKO/Missions/untso/untsoF.htm>.

[11] UNMOGIP was established in Mar. 1951 to replace the UN Commission for India and Pakistan (SCR 91, 30 Mar. 1951). Its task is to supervise the ceasefire in Kashmir under the July 1949 Karachi Agreement. A positive decision by the Security Council is required to terminate the mission. UNMOGIP Internet site, URL <http://www.un.org/Depts/DPKO/Missions/unmogip.htm>.

[12] United Nations (note 2).

[13] United Nations (note 2).

[14] United Nations (note 3).

[15] UNMOGIP is funded through the UN's regular budget and consequently should not suffer arrears. United Nations, 'India and Pakistan–UNMOGIP: Facts and figures', UN Internet site, URL <http://www.un.org/Depts/DPKO/Missions/unmogip/unmogipF.htm>.

[16] UNFICYP was established by SCR 186 (4 Mar. 1964) to prevent fighting between the Greek Cypriot and Turkish Cypriot communities and to contribute to the maintenance and restoration of law and order. Since 1974 UNFICYP's mandate has included monitoring the ceasefire and maintaining a buffer zone between the 2 sides.

[17] United Nations (note 2).

[18] United Nations (note 2).

[19] Death by accident. United Nations (note 3).

[20] Figure includes a voluntary contribution amounting to one-third of the total cost from the Government of Cyprus and $6.5 million from the Government of Greece. United Nations, Report of the Secretary-General on the United Nations operation in Cyprus, UN document S/2004/925, 12 Nov. 2004, para. 15.

[21] As of 30 Sep. 2004. United Nations (note 19), para. 17.

[22] UNDOF was established after the 1973 Middle East War under the Agreement on Disengagement and SCR 350 (31 May 1974), to maintain the ceasefire between Israel and Syria and to supervise the disengagement of Israeli and Syrian forces. The mandate was extended until 30 June 2005 by SCR 1578 (15 Dec. 2004).

[23] United Nations (note 2).

[24] United Nations (note 2).

[25] United Nations (note 3).

[26] United Nations, Report of the Secretary-General on the UN Disengagement Observer Force, UN document S/2004/948, 7 Dec. 2004, para. 8.

[27] Sum outstanding as of 31 Oct. 2004. United Nations (note 26), para. 9.

[28] UNIFIL was established by SCR 425 (19 Mar. 1978), to confirm the withdrawal of Israeli forces from southern Lebanon and to assist the Government of Lebanon in ensuring the return of its effective authority in the area. The mandate was renewed until 31 July 2005 by SCR 1583 (28 Jan. 2005).

[29] United Nations (note 2).

[30] United Nations (note 2).

[31] Death by accident. United Nations (note 3).

[32] United Nations, Report of the Secretary-General on the United Nations Interim Force in Lebanon, UN document S/2004/572, 21 July 2004, para. 27.

[33] Sum outstanding as of 31 May 2004. United Nations (note 31), para. 28.

[34] MINURSO was established by SCR 690 (29 Apr. 1991) to monitor the ceasefire between the Frente Polisario and the Moroccan Government, verify the reduction of Moroccan troops in Western Sahara, and organize a free and fair referendum. The mandate was renewed until 30 Apr. 2005 by SCR 1570 (28 Oct. 2004).

[35] United Nations (note 2).

[36] United Nations (note 2).

[37] United Nations (note 3).

[38] United Nations, Financing of the United Nations Mission for the Referendum in Western Sahara, UN document A/RES/58/309, 30 July 2004.

[39] Sum outstanding as of 15 Apr. 2004. United Nations (note 38).

[40] UNOMIG was established by SCR 849 (9 July 1993) and SCR 858 (24 Aug. 1993). The mission's original mandate of verifying the ceasefire between the Georgian Government and the Abkhaz authorities was invalidated by resumed fighting in Abkhazia in Sep. 1993, and UNOMIG was given an interim mandate to maintain contacts with both sides to the conflict and with Russian military contingents and to monitor and report on the situation. Following the signing of the 1994 Agreement on a Ceasefire and Separation of Forces, UNOMIG's mandate was expanded to include monitoring and verification of the implementation of the agreement by SCR 937 (27 July 1994). The present mandate was renewed until 31 July 2005 by SCR 1582 (28 Jan. 2005).

[41] United Nations (note 2).

[42] In July 2003, SCR 1494 (30 July 2003) authorized the addition of a civilian police component of 20 officers with a view to help build local capacity to improve law and order in the Gali sector such that conditions are improved for the return of refugees and IDPS. United Nations (note 2).

[43] United Nations (note 3).

[44] United Nations, Report of the Secretary-General concerning the situation in Abkhazia, Georgia, UN document S/2005/26, 14 Jan. 2005, para. 31.

[45] Sum outstanding as of 15 Nov. 2004. United Nations (note 44), para. 33.

[46] UNMIK was established by SCR 1244 (10 June 1999). Its main tasks are: promoting the establishment of substantial autonomy and self-government in Kosovo; civilian administrative functions; maintaining law and order; promoting human rights; and ensuring the safe return of all refugees and displaced persons. A positive decision by the SC is required to terminate the mission. SCR 1244 (10 June 1999), Article 19.

[47] United Nations (note 2).

[48] United Nations (note 2).

[49] Deaths owing to hostile act(s). United Nations (note 3).

[50] United Nations, Financing of the United Nations Interim Administration Mission in Kosovo: Report of the Fifth Committee, UN document A/58/827, 10 June 2004.

[51] Sum outstanding as of 31 Mar. 2004. United Nations (note 50).

[52] UNAMSIL was established by SCR 1270 (22 Oct. 1999) following the signature of the Lomé Peace Agreement between the Sierra Leone Government and the Revolutionary United Front on 7 July 1999. In 2001 SCR 1346 (30 Mar. 2001) revised the mission's mandate to that of assisting the Sierra Leone Government's efforts to extend its authority, to restore law and order in the country, to promote the resumption of DDR activities and to assist in the anticipated elections. The present mandate was extended until 30 June 2005 by SCR 1562 (17 Sep. 2004).

[53] In 2004 the mission began its drawdown procedures. United Nations (note 2).

[54] United Nations (note 2).

[55] 17 fatalities owing to accident, 7 to illness and 4 to other causes. United Nations (note 3).

[56] United Nations, Twenty-third report of the Secretary-General on the United Nations Mission in Sierra Leone, UN document S/2004/724, 9 Sep. 2004, para. 56.

[57] Sum outstanding as of 31 July 2004. United Nations (note 56), para. 57.

[58] MONUC was established by SCR 1279 (30 Nov. 1999). SCR 1291 (24 Feb. 2000) mandated MONUC to monitor the implementation of the Ceasefire Agreement, to supervise and verify the disengagement of forces, to monitor human rights violations, and to facilitate the provision of humanitarian assistance. SCR 1493 (28 July 2003) revised the mandate to a Chapter VII mandate, which authorized the mission to use 'all necessary means' to fulfil its tasks. In 2004 SCR 1565 (1 Oct. 2004) revised the mission's mandate to deploy and maintain a presence in key areas of potential volatility, cooperate with ONUB to monitor and prevent the movement of combatants and arms across shared borders, ensure the protection of civilians and UN staff and facilities, facilitate the DDR process and assist in the successful completion of the electoral process.

[59] United Nations (note 2).
[60] United Nations (note 2).
[61] 9 fatalities owing to accident, 5 owing to hostile acts, 4 to illness and 3 owing to other causes. United Nations (note 3).
[62] United Nations, Sixteenth report of the Secretary-General on the United Nations Organization Mission in the Democratic Republic of the Congo, UN document S/2004/1034, 17 Nov. 2004, para. 69.
[63] Sum outstanding as of 30 Nov. 2004. United Nations (note 62), para. 60.
[64] UNMEE was established by SCR 1312 (31 July 2000). The mission was mandated to prepare a mechanism for verifying the cessation of hostilities, the establishment of the Military Co-ordination Commission provided for in the ceasefire agreement, and a peacekeeping deployment. The mission was later expanded with the allocation of 4200 troops and 220 military observers and tasked to monitor the ceasefire, repatriate Ethiopian troops and monitor the positions of Ethiopian and Eritrean troops outside a 25-km temporary security zone, to chair the Military Co-ordination Commission of the UN and the AU, and to assist in mine clearance. SCR 1320 (15 Sep. 2000). Delays in the demarcation process continue to necessitate the prolongation of the mandate.
[65] United Nations (note 2).
[66] United Nations (note 2).
[67] 1 fatality owing to accident and 2 to illness. United Nations (note 3).
[68] United Nations, Progress Report of the Secretary-General on Ethiopia and Eritrea, UN document S/2004/973, 16 Dec. 2004, para. 31.
[69] Sum outstanding as of 31 July 2004. United Nations (note 68).
[70] UNMISET was established by SCR 1410 (17 May 2002) as a follow-on mission to UNTAET. The tasks of the mission are to provide assistance to the administrative structures of the Timorese Government, to provide interim law enforcement while assisting in the development of a new law enforcement agency, and to contribute to the overall security of Timor-Leste.
[71] In 2004, owing to significant progress made in the handover of operational responsibilities to the Timor-Leste authorities, the mission began its drawdown procedures. United Nations (note 2).
[72] In addition, as part of a UNDP-managed assistance programme, 50 civilian advisers were attached to the mission. United Nations, Progress Report of the Secretary-General on the United Nations Mission of Support in East Timor, UN document S/2004/888, 9 Nov. 2004, para. 64; and United Nations (note 2).
[73] Death caused by illness. United Nations (note 3).
[74] United Nations, Progress Report of the Secretary-General on the United Nations Mission of Support in East Timor, UN document S/2004/888, 9 Nov. 2004, para. 60.
[75] As of 31 Oct. 2004. United Nations (note 74), para. 61.
[76] UNMIL was established by SCR 1509 (19 Sep. 2003) with UN Charter Chapter VII powers. The mission was mandated to support the implementation of the ceasefire agreement and the peace process; assist the government's efforts in national security reform, including national police training and formation of a new, restructured military; support humanitarian and human rights activities; and protect UN staff, facilities and civilians.
[77] United Nations (note 2).
[78] United Nations (note 2).
[79] 4 fatalities owing to accident, 16 to illness and 3 owing to other causes. United Nations (note 3).
[80] United Nations, Fourth progress report of the Secretary-General on the United Nations Mission in Liberia, UN document S/2004/725, 10 Sep. 2004, para. 55.
[81] United Nations (note 80), para. 56.
[82] UNOCI was established by SCR 1528 (27 Feb. 2004) with UN Charter Chapter VII powers, as a follow-on mission to MINUCI. The mission was mandated to monitor the ceasefire agreement and to prevent the movement of combatants and arms across shared borders with Liberia and Sierra Leone; to assist the interim Government of National

Reconciliation in the following activities: implementing DDR programmes, restoring state authority and the holding of elections in Oct. 2005; and facilitate the provision of humanitarian assistance. In carrying out its mandate, the mission cooperates with UNAMSIL, UNMIL and Licorne forces in Côte d'Ivoire.

[83] United Nations (note 2).

[84] As provided for in SCR 1528, the *c.* 4000 Licorne forces were deployed alongside UNOCI. United Nations (note 2).

[85] United Nations (note 3).

[86] This figure is the approved expenditure of the mission between 4 Apr. and 31 Dec. 2004. United Nations, Second report of the Secretary-General on the United Nations Operation in Côte d'Ivoire, UN document S/2004/697, 27 Aug. 2004, para. 58.

[87] United Nations (note 86), para. 59.

[88] MINUSTAH was established by SCR 1542 (30 Apr. 2004) with UN Charter Chapter VII powers. The mission was tasked to ensure a secure and stable environment to ensure the peace process is carried forward; assist the government's efforts in national security reform, including a comprehensive DDR programme, national police training and assist with the restoration and maintenance of the rule of law; support humanitarian and human rights activities; and protect UN staff, facilities and civilians.

[89] United Nations (note 2).

[90] United Nations (note 2).

[91] United Nations (note 3).

[92] United Nations, Report of the Secretary-General on the United Nations Stabilization Mission in Haiti, UN document S/2004/908, 18 Nov. 2004, para. 51.

[93] United Nations (note 92).

[94] ONUB was established by SCR 1545 (21 May 2004) with UN Charter Chapter VII powers. The mission was mandated to ensure the respect of the ceasefire agreement, to promote the re-establishment of confidence between the Burundian forces through a comprehensive DDR programme; to assist in the successful completion of the electoral process; and to protect UN staff, facilities and civilians.

[95] United Nations (note 2).

[96] United Nations (note 2).

[97] 2 fatalities owing to accident and 3 to illness. United Nations (note 3).

[98] United Nations, Second Report of the Secretary-General on the United Nations Operation in Burundi, UN document S/2004/902, 15 Nov. 2004, para. 58.

[99] United Nations (note 98), para. 59.

[100] These are UN peace operations not deployed under Chapter VI or VII of the UN Charter but which are directed and administered by the DPKO, with the exception of MINUGUA, which is administered by the UN Department of Political Affairs (DPA). This list does not include UN peace-building offices. Because the following 5 missions are mostly staffed by civilian personnel, lead states are not designated.

[101] MINUGUA (Misión de Verificación de las Naciones Unidas en Guatemala) had until 1997 been limited to verifying the 1994 Comprehensive Agreement on Human Rights and the human rights aspects of the 1995 Agreement on Identity and Rights of Indigenous Peoples. In 1997 the parties to the agreements requested that MINUGUA expand its functions to verify both agreements. A/RES/58/238 (2 Mar. 2004) authorized the final renewal of the mission's mandate and tasked the mission to focus its tasks in the areas of human rights, and demilitarization and the strengthening of civilian power. The mission closed on 31 Dec. 2004.

[102] Mercedes de Arevalo, Senior Personnel Assistant, MINUGUA, email to author, 24 Jan. 2005.

[103] The mission is supported by 30 local staff and 1 UN Volunteers (UNV) personnel. de Arevalo (note 102).

[104] de Arevalo (note 102).

[105] $11 631 400. de Arevalo (note 102).

[106] UNAMA was established by SCR 1401 (28 Mar. 2002). The mission is mandated to promote national reconciliation; to fulfil the tasks and responsibilities entrusted to the UN in the 2001 Bonn Agreement, including those related to human rights, the rule of law and gender issues; and to manage all UN humanitarian, relief, recovery and reconstruction activities in Afghanistan in coordination with the Afghan Transitional Authority. In carrying out its mandate, UNAMA cooperates with ISAF.

[107] The countries listed represent the nationalities of the international civilian staff who are recruited in their personal capacity. They are not seconded by their governments. Ariane Quentier, Senior Public Information Officer, UNAMA, email to author, 1 Feb. 2005.

[108] The mission is supported by 687 local staff. United Nations, 'Background note on United Nations political and peace-building missions', 18 Jan. 2004, UN Internet site, URL <http://www.un.org/Depts/dpko/dpko/bnote.htm>.

[109] However, 1 international UN Office for Project Services (UNOPS) personnel and 2 national UNOPS personnel died owing to a traffic accident and hostile action, respectively. Quentier (note 107).

[110] United Nations, Report of the Secretary-General, Estimates in respect of special political missions, good offices and other political initiatives authorized by the General Assembly and/or the Security Council, UN document A/59/534/Add.1, 23 Nov. 2004, p. 57.

[111] MINUCI was established by SCR 1479 (13 May 2003) to facilitate the implementation of the Linas-Marcoussis Agreement. The mission was integrated into UNOCI on 4 Apr. and subsequently closed.

[112] As of 29 Feb. 2004. MINUCI, 'Facts and figures', URL <http://www.un.org/Depts/dpko/missions/minuci/facts.html>.

[113] As of 29 Feb. 2004. The mission was supported by 55 local staff. MINUCI (note 112).

[114] United Nations (note 3).

[115] Budget for the period 1 Jan.–4 Apr 2004 and represents a portion of the mission's total budget of $29.9 million. United Nations (note 108), p. 17.

[116] UNAMI was established by SCR 1500 (July 2003) to support the efforts of the UN Secretary-General's Special Representative to fulfil his mandate to coordinate the UN's humanitarian and reconstruction efforts, promote the safe return of refugees and IDPs, and facilitate international efforts to help rebuild the local institutional capacities, as provided for by SCR 1483 (22 May 2003). In carrying out its mandate, UNAMI cooperates with MNF-I.

[117] The countries listed represent the nationalities of the international civilian staff who are recruited in their personal capacity. They are not seconded by their governments. Shiyun Sang, Peace and Security Section, Department of Public Information, United Nations, email to author, 17 Jan. 2005.

[118] These are military advisers. Sang (note 117).

[119] The mission is supported by 190 locally employed staff. Sang (note 117).

[120] United Nations (note 3).

[121] United Nations (note 110), p. 62.

[122] UNAMIS was established by SCR 1547 (11 June 2004) to monitor the ceasefire agreement of 25 Sep. 2003 in cooperation with AMIS, and to plan and prepare for the establishment of a full-fledged peace operation.

[123] Sang (note 117), email to author, 3 Mar. 2005.

[124] Sang (note 123); and United Nations, 'Background note on United Nations political and peace-building missions', 18 Jan. 2005, UN Internet site, URL <http://www.un.org/Depts/dpko/dpko/bnote.htm>.

[125] United Nations (note 3).

[126] United Nations (note 110), p. 99.

[127] AMIB was established on 3 Feb. 2003 by decision of the 7th Ordinary Session of the Central Organ of the Mechanism for Conflict Prevention, Management and Resolution at Heads of State and Government level. The mission's mandate was to monitor and verify the implementation of the 2002 and 2003 Ceasefire Agreements, to liaise

between the conflicting parties, to assist the JCC, to facilitate the DDR process and to facilitate the delivery of humanitarian assistance. AMIB was integrated in ONUB on 1 June 2004.

[128] Agoagye, F., 'The African Mission in Burundi: Lessons learned from the first African Union Peacekeeping Operation', *Conflict Trends*, no. 2 (2004).

[129] South Africa contributed 1600 soldiers, Ethiopia 858 and Mozambique 228, while the 43 observers were drawn from Brukina Faso, Gabon, Mali, Togo and Tunisia. South Africa also provided operational control of the mission. Agoagye (note 128).

[130] Salinda Biyana, First Secretary, South Africa Embassy in Stockholm, fax to author, 28 Jan. 2005.

[131] For the period 1 Jan.–31 May 2004. This figure is derived by subtracting the budget ($90 700 000) for the mission's 1st year from the total budget for the mission's entire mandated period ($134 000 000). Known individual contributions include Denmark's $1 000 000; the EU's €25 000 000; Germany's $464 920; Italy's $545 372.08; Senegal's $1132; South Africa's R 62 000 000; the UK's £2 000 000; and $300 000 from the AU's Peace Fund. Agoagye (note 128); 'Resolving conflicts', *Horn of Africa Bulletin*, vol. 1, no. 2 (Oct. 2003–Mar. 2004); Dwan, R. and Wiharta, S., 'Multilateral peace missions', *SIPRI Yearbook 2004: Armaments, Disarmament and International Security* (Oxford University Press: Oxford, 2004), pp.175–90; and Biyana (note 130).

[132] MIOC was established on 30 Jan. 2004 by decision of the 97th Ordinary Session of the Central Organ of the Mechanism for Conflict Prevention, Management and Resolution at Ambassadorial level. Central Organ/MEC/AMB/COMM.(XCVII). The mission closed on 30 May 2004.

[133] The mission was led by South Africa. El Ghassim Wane, Head, Conflict Management Division, African Union, email to author, 30 Mar. 2005; and AU, Report of the Chairperson of the Commission on the Situation in the Comoros, Peace and Security Council 6th Session, PSC/PR/3(VI), 29 Apr. 2004.

[134] Wane (note 133).

[135] Wane (note 133).

[136] AMIS was initially established by the Agreement with the Sudanese Parties on the Modalities for the Establishment of the Ceasefire Commission and the Deployment of Observers in the Darfur on 28 May 2004 as an observer mission and was endorsed by SCR 1556 (30 July 2004) with UN Charter Chapter VII powers. The mandate was expanded pursuant to a decision adopted at the 17th Meeting of the Africa Union's Peace and Security Council. The mission is currently mandated to monitor the N'Djamena ceasefire agreement, assist in confidence building between the parties and contribute to a secure environment in Darfur. African Union, Communiqué of the 17th meeting of the Peace and Security Council, AU document PSC/PR/Comm. (XVII), 20 Oct. 2004.

[137] As of 9 Jan. 2005. Rwanda provided the largest number (392) of personnel. AU, Report of the Chairperson of the Commission on the situation in the Darfur region of the Sudan, AU document PSC/AHG/4 (XXIII), 10-11 Jan. 2005.

[138] As of 9 Jan. 2005. In addition, there are 10 EU and 36 Sudanese military observers, and the mission is supported by the Darfur Integrated Task Force (DITF). The authorized strength is 3320 personnel, including 1891 troops, 450 military observers, 850 civilian police and the necessary number of civilian personnel. AU (note 137).

[139] AU (note 137).

[140] This figure includes the $3 646 379 allocated to DITF. The bulk of the mission's budget is financed by the EU (through the Africa Peace Facility), the USA the UK, Canada, the Netherlands and other contributors. AU (note 137).

[141] The CEMAC Multinational Force was established on 2 Oct. 2002 by decision of the Libreville Summit to secure the border between Chad and the CAR and to guarantee the safety of former President Patassé. Following the 15 Mar. 2003 coup, CEMAC decided at the 21 Mar. 2003 Libreville Summit to amend the mission's mandate to contribute to the overall security environment, to assist in the restructuring of CAR's armed forces and to support the transition process. Communiqué Final du Sommet des Chefs d'État et de Délégation de la Communauté Economique et Monétaire de l'Afrique Centrale, Libreville, 2 Oct. 2002; and 3rd Ordinary Session of the Executive Council, African Union, 4–8 July 2003.

[142] Brigadier General Auguste Roger Bibaye Itandas, Commander, CEMAC Multinational Force, fax to author, 30 Nov. 2004.

[143] Of this figure, 121 are from Chad, 139 from Gabon and 120 from the Republic of Congo. Bibaye Itandas (note 142).

[144] Bibaye Itandas (note 142).

[145] FCFA 3 000 000 000. FCFA 1 = $0.0018679 (SEBanken, Sweden). Bibaye Itandas (note 142).

[146] Agreement on the Principles Governing the Peaceful Settlement of the Conflict in South Ossetia, signed in Dagomys, on 24 June 1992, by Georgia and Russia. A joint Monitoring Commission with representatives of Russia, Georgia, and North and South Ossetia was established to oversee the implementation of the agreement.

[147] The participation of parties to a conflict in peace operations is typically not included in the table; however, the substantial involvement of the parties to the conflict in this operation is a distinctive feature of CIS operations and of the peace agreement which is the basis for the establishment of the operation. The official name of the Ossetian battalion is the Battalion of North Ossetian/Alania. Vladimir Barbin, Minister-Counsellor of the Embassy of Russia in Stockholm, email to author, 18 Jan. 2005.

[148] Barbin (note 147).

[149] Barbin (note 147).

[150] This figure is tallied from 2001. Prior to 2001, data could not be ascertained.

[151] Fatalities owing to hostile action. Barbin (note 147).

[152] Agreement on the Principles Governing the Peaceful Settlement of the Armed Conflict in the Trans-Dniester region, signed in Moscow on 21 July 1992 by the presidents of Moldova and Russia. A Monitoring Commission with representatives of Russia, Moldova and Trans-Dniester was established to coordinate the activities of the joint peacekeeping contingent.

[153] The participation of parties to a conflict in peace operations is typically not included in the table; however, the substantial involvement of the parties to the conflict in this operation is a distinctive feature of CIS operations and of the peace agreement which is the basis for the establishment of the operation. Email from Wenker (note 129).

[154] Russia, Moldova and Trans-Dniester contributed 334, 360 and 578 military personnel, respectively. The figures for the number of personnel from Moldova and Trans-Dniester for 2004 are not available. Barbin (note 147).

[155] Figures for 2004 are not available. Ukraine provided the military observers. Lt-Col Henk Wenker, OSCE Mission to Moldova, email to author, 11 Feb. 2004.

[156] This figure is tallied from 2001. Prior to 2001, data could not be ascertained.

[157] Barbin (note 147).

[158] There is no designated budget for the mission. Each side bears the cost of sending its respective personnel.

[159] Georgian–Abkhazian Agreement on a Cease-fire and Separation of Forces, signed in Moscow on 14 May 1994. The operation's mandate was approved by heads of states members of the CIS Council of Collective Security, 21 Oct. 1994, and endorsed by the UN through SCR 937, 21 July 1994. The period of the mission's mandate was extended indefinitely from Jan. 2004. Moscow ITAR-TASS, 17 Dec. 2003, in 'Russia peacekeepers begin planned rotation in Georgia–Abkhazia conflict zone', Foreign Broadcasting Information Service (FBIS), *Daily Report–Soviet Union (FBIS-SOV),* FBIS-SOV-3003-1217, 18 Dec. 2003.

[160] Other CIS states may participate in the mission. Moscow ITAR-TASS, 25 Dec. 2003, in 'Russian defense minister rules out use of force in Georgian–Abkhaz conflict', FBIS-SOV-2003-1225, 2 Jan. 2004.

[161] Barbin (note 147).

[162] Roman Sishuk, political officer, UNOMIG, telephone conversation with author, 4 Mar. 2004. 'Dialog luschshe groma pushek' [Dialogue is better than the thunder of cannons], *Krasnaya Zvezda*, 27 June 2003 (in Russian), URL <http://www.redstar.ru/2003/06/27_06/3_01.html>.

[163] Barbin (note 147).

[164] The SC authorized under UN Chapter VIII the establishment of ECOMICI alongside French troops to contribute to a secure environment and allow for the implementation of the Linas-Marcoussis Agreement. SCR 1464 (4 Feb. 2003). The mission's tasks included monitoring the cessation of hostilities, facilitating the free movement of persons and goods, providing security for members of the national government of reconciliation as well as humanitarian workers, and to contribute to the implementation of DDR programmes. ECOMICI was integrated into UNOCI on 4 Apr. 2004.

[165] Traore Issouf, ECOWAS, email to author, 4 Mar. 2005.

[166] Issouf (note 165).

[167] Issouf (note 165).

[168] Issouf (note 165).

[169] The mission was established by the Brioni Agreement, signed on 7 July 1991 at Brioni, Croatia, by representatives of the European Community (EC) and the 6 republics of the former Yugoslavia. MOUs were signed with the governments of Albania in 1997 and Croatia in 1998. The ECMM became the EUMM upon becoming an instrument of the EU's Common Foreign and Security Policy (CFSP), and was mandated to monitor political and security developments, borders, inter-ethnic issues and refugee returns; to contribute to the early warning mechanism of the European Council; and to contribute to confidence building and stabilization in the region. Council Joint Action of 22 Dec. 2000 on the European Union Monitoring Mission, EU document 2000/811/CFSP, 23 Dec. 2000, Introduction, para. 6 and Article 1, para. 2.

[170] The EUMM operates in Albania and in Bosnia and Herzegovina, Croatia, FYROM, Serbia and Montenegro, Kosovo and Presevo.

[171] France contributed the largest number of personnel. As of 16 Sep. 2004. Stephan Muller, Policy Unit of the General Secretariat, Council of the European Union, email to author, 10 Dec. 2004.

[172] As of 16 Sep. 2004. Muller (note 171).

[173] Muller (note 168).

[174] €4 186 482. Council Joint Action 2004/794/CFSP of 22 Nov. 2004.

[175] The EU Police Mission in Bosnia and Herzegovina was established by Council Joint Action 2002/210/CFSP of 11 Mar. 2002 to ensure sustainable policing arrangements under BiH ownership in accordance with European and international standards. The mission is tasked to monitor, mentor and inspect local police management.

[176] Germany contributed the largest number (*c.* 80–86) of police officers. Kilian Wahl, Public Information Officer, EUPM, email to author, 20 Dec. 2004.

[177] Of this figure, EU member states provided 432 officers while non-EU states provided 47. The mission is supported by 329 local staff. Wahl (note 176).

[178] 1 fatality owing to illness and the other caused by traffic accident. Wahl (note 176).

[179] €17.5 million. The figure includes salaries for the international civilian staff and local staff as well as infrastructure but does not include salaries of the international police personnel which are borne by the contributing countries. Nicolas Kerleroux, EU Council Secretariat, Directorate-General F (DG F), Press, Communication, Protocol, email to author, 27 Jan. 2005.

[180] EUPOL PROXIMA was established by Council Joint Action 2003/681/CFSP of 29 Sep. 2003 to support the development of a professional police service in FYROM in accordance with European policing standards. In carrying out its activities, the mission cooperates with the OSCE Spillover Mission to Skopje.

[181] As of 13 Dec. 2004. Germany contributed the largest number of personnel. Internet site of EUPOL PROXIMA, URL <http://www.eupol-proxima.org/sito1/people/whereweare.htm>.

[182] As of 13 Dec. 2004. Official Internet site of EUPOL PROXIMA (note 181).

[183] Francesco Bruzzesse del Pozzo, EU Council Secretariat, Directorate-General E (DG E), External Economic Relations, Common Foreign and Security Policy, Directorate IX, Police Unit, telephone conversation with author, 4 Mar. 2005.

[184] €5 000 000. Council Joint Action 2004/789/CFSP of 22 Nov. 2004.

[185] EUJUST THEMIS was established by Council Joint Action 2004/523/CFSP of 28 June 2004 to assist the Georgian Government in developing a coordinated strategy for reform of the criminal justice sector.

[186] The mission began its operational phase on 15 July 2004. This was preceded by the planning phase, which began on 1 July 2004.

[187] Sandra Paesen, EU Council Secretariat, DG E, Directorate IX; and Jolanda Bruynel, EU Council Secretariat, DG F, emails to author, 17 Dec. 2004.

[188] The mission is supported by 16 local staff. Paesen and Bruynel (note 187).

[189] Paesen and Bruynel (note 187).

[190] €2 050 000 and is allocated for the mission's mandated period, 15 July 2004–15 July 2005. €1 = $1.35 (SEBanken, Sweden). Council Joint Action 2004/523/CFSP of 28 June 2004.

[191] EUFOR ALTHEA was established by Council Joint Action 2004/570/CFSP of 12 July 2004, was endorsed and given Chapter VII Powers by UN Security Council Resolution 1551 (9 July 2004). The mission is a follow-on mission to NATO's SFOR and has a mandate to maintain a secure environment for the implementation of the 1995 Dayton Agreement, to assist in the strengthening of local capacity and to support Bosnia and Herzegovina's progress towards EU integration.

[192] The contingents are grouped into 3 task forces—MNTF North (Tuzla), MNTF Southeast (Mostar) and MNTF Northwest (Banja Luka)—for which Finland, France and the UK are the framework nations. Lt-Cdr Chris Percival, EUFOR Spokesperson, email to author, 21 Dec. 2004 and telephone conversation with author, 4 Mar. 2005.

[193] This figure includes the *c.* 500 personnel in the Integrated Police Unit. Percival (note 192); and Internet site of ALTHEA, URL <http://www.euforbih.org/sheets/fs050225a.htm>.

[194] Percival (note 192).

[195] €71 700 000. This figure refers to the common costs of the operation and does not include the salaries of the personnel, which are borne by the contributing countries. Council Joint Action 2004/570/CFSP of 12 July 2004.

[196] SFOR was established in Dec. 1996 to replace the NATO Implementation Force (IFOR), created to implement the military aspects of the 1995 Dayton Agreement. SCR 1088 (12 Dec. 1996). In 2004 NATO decided to close the mission. Although SFOR was succeeded by EUFOR ALTHEA, a small NATO military presence continues to operate in Sarajevo.

[197] SFOR contingents were grouped in 3 task forces—MNTF North (Tuzla), MNTF Southeast (Mostar) and MNTF Northwest (Banja Luka)—for which Finland, France and the UK were the framework nations. Percival (note 192).

[198] As of 30 Nov. 2004. 'NATO/EU/Bosnia–Herzegovina: everything ready for transferring authority from NATO to EU', *Atlantic News*, no. 3631 (30 Nov. 2004).

[199] Percival (note 192).

[200] €16 141 601. This figure covers only the common costs, mainly the functioning costs of NATO headquarters (civilian personnel and operations and maintenance costs) and investments in infrastructure necessary to support the operation. Contributing countries provide separate finances for their contingents. John Day, Military Budget Committee Section, NATO, email to author, 8 Mar. 2005.

[201] KFOR received its mandate from the SC on 10 June 1999. Its tasks include deterring renewed hostilities, establishing a secure environment, supporting UNMIK and monitoring borders. SCR 1244 (10 June 1999).

[202] KFOR contingents are grouped in 4 multinational brigades—MNB Centre (Lipljan), MNB Northeast (Novo Selo), MNB Southwest (Prizen), MNB East (Urosevac)—for which Finland, France, Germany and USA, respectively, are the lead nations. Colonel Yves Kermorvant, Chief Public Information Officer, KFOR, email to author, 5 Jan. 2005; and Internet site of KFOR, URL <http://www.nato.int/kfor/kfor/structure.htm>.

[203] NATO member states contributed a total of 15 000 personnel and NATO partner countries contributed 3000. Kermorvant (note 202).

[204] Kermorvant (note 202).

[205] €23 795 794. This figure covers only the common costs: mainly the functioning costs of NATO headquarters (civilian personnel and operations and maintenance costs) and investments in infrastructure necessary to support the operation. Contributing countries provide separate finances for their contingents. Kermorvant (note 202).

[206] On 20 Dec. 2001 the SC, acting under UN Charter Chapter VII, authorized a multinational force to help the Afghan Interim Authority maintain security, as envisaged in Annex I of the 2001 Bonn Agreement. UN document SC/7248, 20 Dec. 2001. In 2004, ISAF expanded its area of operations beyond Kabul to include 9 other provinces. The current mandate was extended until 12 Oct. 2005. SCR 1563 (17 Sep. 2004). Until NATO's takeover in Aug. 2003, ISAF was under the command and control of the lead nations—Germany and the Netherlands (Feb.–Aug. 2003), Turkey (June 2002–Feb. 2003) and the UK (Dec. 2001–June 2002).

[207] As of 17 Jan. 2005. Canada assumed command and leadership for ISAF until Eurocorps took over in Aug. 2004. Within Eurocorps, France and Germany are the lead nations for the Kabul Multinational Brigade (KMNB), providing *c.* 3000 soldiers each. Internet site of ISAF, URL <http://www.isaf6.eurocorps.org/structure.php#nations>.

[208] Capt. Mike Nicholson, Public Information Officer, ISAF6, email to author, 9 Jan. 2005.

[209] Nicholson (note 208).

[210] €54 610 570. This figure covers only the common costs, mainly the functioning costs for NATO headquarters (civilian personnel and operations and maintenance costs) and investments in infrastructure necessary to support the operation. Contributing countries provide separate finances for their contingents. Day (note 200).

[211] The mission was established under the authority of SCR 1546 (8 June 2004), which requests member states and other international organizations to assist the Iraqi Government's efforts in building the capacity of Iraq's security forces. The NAC agreed on 30 July 2004 to the establishment of NTIM-I.

[212] Maj. Michaela Cvanova, Supreme Headquarters Allied Powers Europe (SHAPE), Public Information Office, email to author, 28 Jan. 2005.

[213] Cvanova (note 212), 20 Jan. 2005.

[214] Cvanova (note 212).

[215] €2 696 100. This figure covers only the common costs, mainly the functioning costs of NATO headquarters (civilian personnel and operations and maintenance costs) and investments in infrastructure necessary to support the operation. Contributing countries provide separate finances for their personnel. Day (note 200).

[216] The mission was established by OAS Permanent Council decision CP/RES.806 (1303/02) on 16 Jan. 2002 to contribute to the resolution of the political crisis by *inter alia* assisting the Government of Haiti to strengthen its democratic processes and institutions. In June 2004, the OAS General Assembly, through A/RES 2058 (XXXIV-O/04) amended the mandate to include the following: assist in the holding of election, promoting and protecting human rights and assist in the professionalization of the Haitian National Police. In carrying out its mandate, the mission cooperates with MINUSTAH and CARICOM.

[217] Louise Brunet, OAS Special Mission to Haiti, email to author, 8 Mar. 2005

[218] Brunet (note 217), 24 Feb. 2005.

[219] Brunet (note 217).

[220] $5 010 965. Brunet (note 217).

[221] Misión de Apoyo al Proceso de Paz (MAPP/OEA) was established by OAS Permanent Council decision CP/RES.859 (1397/04) on 6 Feb. 2004 in support of the efforts of the Colombian Government to engage in a political dialogue with the ELN. The mission is tasked to facilitate the DDR process.

[222] Natalia Palacios, Mission to Support the Peace Process in Colombia, email to author, 11 Mar. 2005.

[223] The mission is supported by 10 civilian observers and 10 administrative staff. Palacios (note 222).

[224] Palacios (note 222).

[225] Budget for the mission is financed from contributions from: Bahamas, Colombia, the Netherlands, Sweden and the USA. Palacios (note 222).

[226] Includes OSCE long-term missions and other field activities with a peace-making or peace-building mandate but not human rights offices, election monitoring groups or liaison offices.

[227] Decision to establish the mission taken at 16th Committee of Senior Officials (CSO) meeting, *Journal* no. 3 (18 Sep. 1992), Annex 1. The mission was authorized by the FYROM Government through Articles of Understanding agreed by an exchange of letters on 7 Nov. 1992. The mission's tasks include assessing the level of stability and the possibility of conflict and unrest.

[228] Maxime Filandrov, Public Information Officer, OSCE Spillover Monitor Mission to Skopje, email to author 8 Mar. 2005.

[229] 20 are officers who work in the field (community policing) and the remaining 20 personnel are trainers or administrators within the Police Development Unit.

[230] Supported by 259 locally employed staff. Filandrov (note 228).

[231] Filandrov (note 228).

[232] €13 589 100. PC.DEC/590, 24 Dec. 2003.

[233] Decision to establish the mission taken at the 17th CSO meeting, *Journal* no. 2 (6 Nov. 1992), Annex 2. The mission was authorized by the Government of Georgia through an MOU of 23 Jan. 1993 and by South Ossetia's leaders through an exchange of letters on 1 Mar. 1993. Initially, the objective of the mission was to promote negotiations between the conflicting parties. The mandate was expanded on 29 Mar. 1994 to include monitoring of the Joint Peacekeeping Forces in South Ossetia. In Dec. 1999 this was expanded to include the monitoring of Georgia's border with Chechnya. PC.DEC/344, 15 Dec. 1999. In Dec. 2001 the mission's tasks were further expanded to include the monitoring of Georgia's border with Ingushetia. PC.DEC/450, 13 Dec. 2001. In Nov. 2002 the mandate was again expanded to observe and report on cross-border movement between Georgia and the Dagestan Republic of the Russian Federation. PC.DEC/522, 19 Dec. 2002.

[234] Martha Freeman, Spokesperson, OSCE Mission to Georgia, email to author, 22 Dec. 2004.

[235] Freeman (note 234).

[236] Of the 169 international staff, 144 serve as border monitors. The mission is supported by 104 local staff. Freeman (note 234).

[237] Freeman (note 234).

[238] €21 271 900. PC.DEC/590, 24 Dec. 2003.

[239] Decision to establish the mission taken at the 19th CSO meeting, *Journal* no. 3 (4 Feb. 1993), Annex 3. Authorized by the Government of Moldova through MOU, 7 May 1993. The mission's tasks include assisting the parties in pursuing negotiations on a lasting political settlement to the conflict as well as gathering and providing information on the situation.

[240] Trygve Kalland, OSCE Mission to Moldova, email to author, 13 Jan. 2005.

[241] In addition, there are 2 short-term verification staff and 1 contracted ammunition expert who are employed under the Voluntary Fund, which provides financial and technical assistance to Russia for the removal of troops, arms and military equipment from the region. Kalland (note 240).

[242] Kalland (note 240).

[243] €1 498 200. PC.DEC/590, 24 Dec. 2003.

[244] Decision to establish the mission taken at 4th meeting of the Ministerial Council, Rome (CSCE/4-C/Dec. 1), Decision I.4, 1 Dec. 1993. No bilateral MOU was signed. The tasks of the mission include facilitating dialogue, promoting human rights and informing the OSCE about further developments. This was expanded in 2002 to include an economic and environmental dimension.

[245] Formerly the OSCE Mission to Tajikistan. In Oct. 2002 a decision was taken to change the name of the mission to reflect the change of focus of the mission's activities.

[246] Bernard Rouault, OSCE Centre in Dushanbe, email to author, 4 Mar. 2005.

[247] The mission is supported by 65 local staff. Rouault (note 246).

[248] Rouault (note 246).

[249] €3 855 300. PC.DEC/590, 24 Dec. 2003.

[250] In Aug. 1995 the OSCE Chairman-in-Office (CIO) appointed a Personal Representative (PR) on the Conflict Dealt with by the OSCE Minsk Conference, which seeks a peaceful settlement to the Nagorno-Karabakh conflict. The PR's mandate consists of assisting the Minsk Group in planning possible peacekeeping operations, assisting the parties in confidence-building measures and in humanitarian matters, and monitoring the ceasefire between the parties. OSCE, *Annual Report 2000 on OSCE Activities (1 Nov. 1999–31 Oct. 2000)*, 24 Nov. 2000.

[251] Peter Keay, Assistant to the PR of the CIO, email to author, 1 Dec. 2004.

[252] The Personal Representative is assisted by 5 field assistants. Keay (note 251).

[253] Keay (note 251).

[254] €890 000. PC.DEC/590, 24 Dec. 2003.

[255] Decision to establish the mission taken at 5th meeting, Ministerial Council, Budapest, 8 Dec. 1995 (MC(5).DEC/1) in accordance with Annex 6 of the 1995 Dayton Agreement. The tasks of the mission include assisting the parties in regional stabilization measures and democracy building.

[256] Email from Maja Soldo, Personal Assistant to the Chief of Staff and Planning, OSCE Mission to Bosnia and Herzegovina, 2 Dec. 2004.

[257] The mission is supported by 556 local staff. Email from Soldo (note 256).

[258] Email from Soldo (note 256).

[259] €17 663 900. Email from Soldo PC.DEC/590, 24 Dec. 2003.

[260] The decision to establish the mission was taken by the PC on 18 Apr. 1996 (PC.DEC/112). Adjustment of the mandate was made by the PC on 26 June 1997 (PC.DEC/176) and 25 June 1998 (C/DEC/239). The mission's tasks include assisting and monitoring the return of refugees and displaced persons as well as the protection of national minorities.

[261] Slavka Jureta, Senior Media Assistant, Public Affairs Unit, OSCE Mission to Croatia, email to author, 28 Jan. 2005.

[262] The mission is supported by 166 local staff. Jureta (note 261).

[263] Jureta (note 261).

[264] €10 106 600. PC.DEC/590, 24 Dec. 2003.

[265] The decision to establish the mission was taken at the 108th meeting of the Permanent Council in 27 Mar. 1997 (PC/DEC/160). The current mandate was set on 11 Dec. 1997 (PC.DEC/206).

[266] Dinka Zivalj, Press and Public Information Officer, OSCE Presence in Albania, email to author, 7 Mar. 2005.

[267] The mission is supported by 92 local staff. Zivalj (note 266).

[268] Zivalj (note 266).

[269] €3 775 900. PC.DEC/590, 24 Dec. 2003.

[270] On 1 July 1999 the PC established the OSCE Mission in Kosovo to replace the transitional OSCE Kosovo Task Force, which had been established on 8 June 1999 (PC.DEC/296). The tasks of the OSCE Mission to Kosovo include training police, judicial personnel and civil administrators, and monitoring and promoting human rights. The mission is a component (Pillar III) of UNMIK.

[271] Chris Cycmanick, Information Officer, OSCE Mission in Kosovo, email to author, 9 Dec. 2004.

[272] The mission is supported by 1052 locally recruited staff members. Cycmanick (note 271).

[273] Email from Cycmanick. (note 271)

[274] €39 173 300. PC.DEC/590, 24 Dec. 2003.

[275] On 11 Jan. 2001 the PC established the OSCE Mission inthe Federal Republic of Yugoslavia with an initial mandate of 1 year. Its mandate is to provide expert assistance to the authorities of Serbia and Montenegro and civil society groups in the areas of democratization and human and minority rights, assist with the restructuring and training of law enforcement agencies and the judiciary, provide media support and facilitate the return of refugees. PC.DEC/401, 11 Jan. 2001. On 15 Nov. 2001 the Permanent Council directed the mission to open an office in Podgorica, Montenegro. PC.DEC/444, 15 Nov. 2001.

[276] Formerly the OSCE Mission to the Federal Republic of Yugoslavia. In Feb. 2003, a decision (PC.DEC/533) was taken to change the name of the country, following the adoption of the Constitutional Charter of the State Union of Serbia and Montenegro.

[277] Sandra Milosavljevic, Personnel Officer, OSCE Mission to Serbia and Montenegro, email to author, 3 Mar. 2005.

[278] The mission is supported by 148 local staff. Milosavljevic (note 277), 4 Mar. 2005.

[279] Milosavljevic (note 277).

[280] €9 860 300. PC.DEC/590, 24 Dec. 2003.

[281] These are operations carried out by non-standing coalitions of multinational states sanctioned by the UN.

[282] Agreement concerning a military armistice in Korea, signed at Panmunjom on 27 July 1953 by the Commander-in-Chief, UN Command; the Supreme Commander of the Korean People's Army; and the Commander of the Chinese People's Volunteers. Entered into force on 27 July 1953.

[283] Birgitta Delorme, Office of the Defence Attaché, Embassy of Switzerland in Stockholm, email to author, 12 Jan. 2005.

[284] Delorme (note 283).

[285] Delorme (note 283).

[286] Sum of contributions paid by Sweden (SEK 7 400 000) and Switzerland (CHF 857 000). 1 SEK = $0.1504, 1 CHF = $1.13 (SEBanken, Sweden). Irina Schoulgin, Ministry for Foreign Affairs, Sweden, email to author, 11 Feb. 2004; and Delorme (note 283).

[287] The Multinational Force and Observers (MFO) was established on 3 Aug. 1981 by the Protocol to the Treaty of Peace between Egypt and Israel, signed on 26 Mar. 1979. Deployment began on 20 Mar. 1982, following the withdrawal of Israeli forces from Sinai.

[288] MFO, Director General's Report delivered to the Trilateral Meeting, Rome, 11 Oct. 2004, p. 5.

[289] MFO (note 288).

[290] Mary Cordis, Chief of Personnel & Publications, MFO HQ, email to author, 4 Jan. 2005.

[291] Budget for the period 1 Oct. 2003–30 Sep. 2004. MFO (note 288), p. 38.

[292] The mission receives its authority from the Protocol Concerning the Redeployment in Hebron, 15 Jan. 1997, and the Agreement on the Temporary International Presence in Hebron, 21 Jan. 1997. The mandate of the mission is to provide by its presence a secure and stable environment. The mandate is renewed every 3 months pending approval from both the Palestinian and Israeli parties.

[293] Gunhild L. Forselv, Senior Press and Information Officer, TIPH, email to author, 8 Jan. 2005.

[294] Forselv (note 293).

[295] Forselv (note 293).

[296] Budget for the period 1 Feb. 2004–31 Jan. 2005. Approximate amount of the core budget; it does not include salaries, which are paid by the contributing countries. Forselv (note 293).

[297] The SC authorized under Chapter VII and in accordance with Chapter VIII the deployment of French troops alongside ECOMICI to contribute to a secure environment and allow for the implementation of the of the Linas-Marcoussis Agreement. SCR 1464 (4 Feb. 2003).

[298] Following the attack against the Licorne forces by FANCI forces and the subsequent riots in Nov. 2004, the strength of the mission was increased by 1000 soldiers. Lt. Col. Franck Lyet, Defence Attaché, Embassy of France in Stockholm, email to author, 10 Mar. 2005.

[299] Lyet (note 298).

[300] Lyet (note 298).

[301] Lyet (note 298).

[302] The Regional Assistance Mission was established under the framework of the 2000 Biketawa Declaration in which members of the Pacific Islands Forum agree to a collective response to crises usually on the request of the host government. 31st Pacific Islands Forum Comuniqué 2000, Tarawa, Kiribati, 23–30 Oct. 2000. The mission is mandated to assist the Solomon Islands Government in restoring law and order and in building up the capacity of the police force.

[303] As of 1 Dec. 2004. Office of the Special Coordinator for RAMSI, 'RAMSI—Fact Sheet', 1 Dec. 2004, URL <http://www.dfat.gov.au/geo/solomon_islands/helpemfren/ramsi.html>.

[304] As of 1 Dec. 2004. This figure includes 21 lawyers and legal advisers, 30 advisers for prisons, 100 advisers for the nation-building and development components of the operation, and 19 advisers and in-line personnel for MOF. 'RAMSI—Fact Sheet' (note 303).

[305] Nick McCaffrey, Policy Adviser, Office of the Special Coordinator, RAMSI, email to author, 2 Dec. 2004.

[306] AUS 202 million for FY 2004/2005. This figure covers both RAMSI activities and Australia's overseas development aid to Solomon Islands. AUS 1 = $0.7629 (SEBanken, Sweden). McCaffrey (note 305).

[307] The Multinational Force in Iraq was authorized by SCR 1511 (16 Oct. 2003) to contribute to the maintenance of security and stability in Iraq, including for the purpose of ensuring necessary conditions for the implementation of UNAMI's mandated tasks. The mandate of the MNF was reaffirmed by SCR 1546 (8 June 2004) following the dissolution of the Coalition Provisional Authority and the subsequent transfer of sovereignty to the Interim Government of Iraq.

[308] The MNF is divided into 3 divisions—MND Southeast, MND Central South, and Central Command Area of Responsibility—for which Poland, the UK and the USA are the lead nations. US Department of Defense, 'Iraq year in review: 2004 fact sheet', URL <http://www.defend.america.mil>, 21 Jan. 2005; and Internet site of MNF, URL <http://www.mnf-iraq.com/>.

[309] The USA contributed 148 000 soldiers and the remaining 25 000 were contributed by the rest of the coalition. The force is supported by *c.* 118 000 members of the Iraqi security forces (police, National Guard, armed forces and border patrol). O'Hanlon, M. E. and Lins de Albuquerque, A., Brookings Institution, Saban Center for Middle East Policy, 'Iraq Index: Tracking reconstruction and security in post-Saddam Iraq', URL <http://www.brookings.edu/iraqindex>, 5 Jan. 2005.

[310] This figure includes the 98 training officers operating out of the Jordanian facility. Ian Bald, Assistant Public Affairs Officer, US Embassy in Stockholm, email to author, 8 Feb. 2005.

[311] Of the 902 fatalities, 844 were US soldiers (721 owing to hostile action and 123 to other causes), 23 were British soldiers and the remaining 35 were from other countries. O'Hanlon and Lins de Albuquerque (note 309).

[312] This figure is the sum of US and British contributions; contributing countries bear the cost for their personnel. The US contribution for FY 2004 (1 Oct. 2003–30 Sep. 2004) is $52 billion, which includes the $685 million allocated to the Department of State's Mission in Iraq. The $25 billion emergency reserve fund, which was approved by Congress in Aug. 2004, is not included in this table since this amount was allocated for both Operation Iraqi Freedom and Operation Enduring Freedom in Afghanistan. Congressional Budget Office, *Estimated Costs of Continuing Operations in Iraq and Other Operations of the Global War on Terrorism*, 25 June 2004, URL <http://www.cbo.gov>. The British contribution for FY 2004/2005 (6 Apr. 2004–5 Apr. 2005) is estimated to be £975 million. £1 = $1.9170 (SEBanken, Sweden). John Hough, Directorate of Performance and Analysis 20, British Ministry of Defence, email to author, 15 Mar. 2005.

4. Governing the use of force under international auspices: deficits in parliamentary accountability

HANS BORN and HEINER HÄNGGI*

I. Introduction[1]

The war in Iraq in March–May 2003 is a clear reminder that the use of force still plays a part in current international relations. While this particular action was controversial *inter alia* because it lacked a United Nations (UN) mandate, more frequent resort to military intervention has become a trend in several international organizations. Two-thirds of all peace support operations (PSOs)[2] authorized by the UN took place in the past decade, and the North Atlantic Treaty Organization (NATO), the European Union (EU) and other regional institutions, notably in Africa, have all placed an increasing emphasis on using collective military tools for crisis management.[3]

While the use of force under international auspices has increased substantially, the same cannot be said of its democratic accountability. With decisions on the use of force increasingly being made by international organizations, even established democracies—where the control of armed forces is taken for granted—are struggling to adapt their national control mechanisms to the new situation. The role of parliamentary institutions is particularly essential to ensure the democratic accountability of national armed forces in PSOs undertaken by the EU, NATO, the UN, other organizations and ad hoc coalitions.

The discussion of PSOs by academics and practitioners has, however, so far paid little attention to the issue of democratic accountability. For example, the 2000 Brahimi Report[4] made recommendations to improve the effectiveness,

[1] This chapter draws on Born, H., 'Parliaments and the deployment of troops abroad under UN, NATO and EU auspices: a double democratic deficit?', *Sicherheit und Frienden/Security and Peace*, vol. 3 (2004), pp. 109–16; Born, H., 'The use of force under international auspices: strengthening parliamentary accountability', eds H. Born and H. Hänggi, *The 'Double Democratic Deficit': Parliamentary Accountability and the Use of Force under International Auspices* (Ashgate: Aldershot, 2004), pp. 203–15; and Hänggi, H., 'The use of force under international auspices: parliamentary accountability and "democratic deficits"', eds Born and Hänggi, pp. 3–16.

[2] The term 'peace support operations' is used here as a generic term for the full range of peacekeeping through to peace enforcement operations.

[3] For the latest statistics on EU, NATO, UN and other peace support operations see table 3.2 in this volume.

[4] United Nations, Report of the Panel on United Nations Peace Operations, UN document A/55/305, 21 Aug. 2000, known as the Brahimi Report, is available at URL <http://www.un.org/peace/reports/peace_operations/>; for a full discussion of the report see Dwan, R., 'Armed conflict prevention, management and resolution', *SIPRI Yearbook 2001: Armaments, Disarmament and International Security*

* Ingrid Beutler assisted in the preparation of this chapter.

decision-making processes, planning, staffing and management of PSOs, but democratic accountability was not taken up as a major concern in the report. The December 2004 report of the UN Secretary-General's High-level Panel on Threats, Challenges and Change devotes considerable attention to the guidelines for and legitimacy of intervention but not explicitly to making it more democratically accountable.[5] Moreover, the commemorative issue of *International Peacekeeping*, an overview of 10 years of academic publications on peacekeeping published in 2004, shows a similar lack of attention by analysts to the challenge of democratic accountability.[6]

This chapter addresses one important but under-researched aspect of security (sector) governance:[7] the role parliaments play in ensuring democratic accountability for the use of national armed forces under the aegis of international institutions. Parliamentary accountability for the use of force under international auspices is a good case in point for illuminating the internal (or national) and external (or international) dimensions of what could be termed the 'double democratic deficit' in this connection.[8]

The democratic deficit is not a new concept. In recent years, particularly in the context of anti-globalization movements, international institutions like the World Bank, the International Monetary Fund and the World Trade Organization have been criticized for their lack of accountability, representativeness and transparency. Even the EU, the only international organization in the world with a directly elected parliament, is criticized by many for its democratic deficit caused by *inter alia* the low turnout for elections to the European Parliament (EP), and the EP's limited powers especially in relation to EU foreign, security and defence policy.[9] Democratic deficits seem to be the global norm of international cooperation,[10] in which the role of parliamentarians lags well behind that of ministers, judges, diplomats and other officials.[11]

On the national level, according to Damrosch, in the past decades there has been a trend in democracies towards greater parliamentary control over 'war-

(Oxford University Press: Oxford, 2001), pp. 71–74; and Bellamy, A. and Williams, P., 'Introduction: thinking anew about peace operations', *International Peacekeeping, Special Issue on Peace Operations and Global Order*, vol. 11, no. 1 (spring 2004), pp. 17–38.

[5] United Nations, 'A more secure world: our shared responsibility', Report of the High-level Panel on Threats, Challenges and Change, UN documents A/59/565, 4 Dec. 2004, and A/59/565/Corr.1, 6 Dec. 2004, URL <http://www.un.org/ga/59/documentation/list5.html>. The synopsis and summary of recommendations of the report are reproduced in the appendix to the Introduction in this volume.

[6] Bellamy and Williams (note 4), pp. 1–15.

[7] On security sector governance see, e.g., Hänggi, H., 'Making sense of security sector governance', eds H. Hänggi and T. Winkler, *Challenges of Security Sector Governance* (LIT: Münster, 2003), pp. 3–22.

[8] For a more detailed discussion of democratic deficit and security sector governance see Hänggi (note 1), pp. 5–8.

[9] See, e.g., McGrew, A., 'Democracy beyond borders?', eds D. Held and A. McGrew, *The Global Transformation Reader: An Introduction to the Globalisation Debate* (Polity Press: Cambridge, 2002). On the democratic deficit of the EU see Harlow, C., *Accountability in the European Union* (Oxford University Press: Oxford, 2002).

[10] Clark, I., *Globalization and International Relations Theory* (Oxford University Press: Oxford, 1999), p. 147.

[11] Slaughter, A. M., *A New World Order* (Princeton University Press: Princeton, N.J., 2004).

and-peace decisions'.[12] Even so, this chapter shows that the extent of actual parliamentary accountability regarding security affairs, and more specifically international security affairs, should not be overestimated. Parliamentary oversight appears weakest as regards foreign and security policy—functions which even in the most democratic states have traditionally been reserved to the executive. This creates the first component in the double, national and international, democratic deficit in the conduct of security policy. It fits with Ian Clark's general observation on 'the reciprocal manner in which democratic deficits on the inside have been necessary accomplices of globalization'.[13]

This chapter argues that multinational PSOs are no exception. Parliamentary accountability for the use of international force is problematic at both the international and national levels—hence the expression 'double democratic deficit'. This chapter analyses the problems and offers recommendations for how this deficit could be reduced. Section II deals with accountability at the national level; section III addresses the situation in selected international institutions; and section IV suggests possible improvements at both national and international levels. The conclusions are presented in section V.

II. Deficits in parliamentary accountability at the national level

States may exercise military force abroad unilaterally, in ad hoc coalitions or in the framework of multilateral security institutions acting on their own authority or with the mandate of another institution (normally the UN). Nations and institutions that have adopted normative rules (in constitutions, treaties, etc.) for the kind of operations they are prepared to engage in have normally devoted most attention to the need for an adequate international legal mandate, followed in some cases by limits on the degree of military force they would contemplate using in a non-self-defence context. This reflects a widespread judgement that the problems of legality and legitimacy of any multilateral use of force are likely to be greater, the higher the degree of violence or coercion required and the weaker (or less explicit) the international legal authority.[14] The legitimacy gap in such cases makes the application of democratic, including parliamentary, accountability of especial interest.

In a democratic polity, the parliament is the central locus of accountability for governmental decision making concerning the use of force, whether under national or international auspices. In the current state of security governance, these parliamentary powers are exercised more or less exclusively at the national level and they vary widely from country to country, particularly in

[12] Damrosch, L. F., 'Is there a general trend in constitutional democracies toward parliamentary control over war-and-peace decisions?', *Proceedings of the 90th Annual Meeting of the American Society of International Law* (American Society of International Law: Washington, DC, 1996), pp. 36–40.

[13] Clark (note 10), p. 166.

[14] Ku, C., 'Using military force under international auspices: a mixed system of accountability', eds Born and Hänggi (note 1), pp. 33–50.

terms of the relationship between parliament and government.[15] The role of parliament is quite different in presidential, parliamentary or mixed systems of government. Beyond these constitutional differences, the role played by a parliament is contingent upon its powers, capacity and willingness to hold the government to account for its actions.[16] Bruce George, a member of the British House of Commons and former President of the Parliamentary Assembly of the Organization for Security and Co-operation in Europe (OSCE), referred in this context to a triad of 'authority', 'ability' and 'attitude'.[17]

'Authority': the formal power to hold the government accountable

Parliaments derive their powers from their constitutional and legal frameworks as well as from customary practices. Parliamentary powers can be categorized according to their standard functions, which—despite national variations—typically include legislative, budgetary, elective, representative, and scrutiny and oversight functions.[18] These functions also apply, to a greater or lesser extent, to decision making on and execution of the use of force under the auspices of international institutions (see table 4.1).

The legislative function is parliament's most traditional role but in practice may either be shared with government or eclipsed by other parliamentary powers. In the context of the use of force under international auspices, there are instances in which the parliament is asked to enact a generic law on multinational PSOs (e.g., Germany) or, as in the case of the Netherlands, succeeds in obtaining the right to authorize such operations case by case. By and large, however, the legislative function is marginal in this area.

Authorizing expenditure is one of the oldest functions of parliament, but in many democracies the 'power of the purse' has become purely nominal. More often than not, parliament can approve or reject spending proposed by the government but can neither modify it nor initiate its own expenditure proposal. In

[15] In this chapter, the term 'parliament' is preferred to 'legislature', and 'government' to (political) 'executive' because the traditional division of 'government' into legislative, executive and judicial institutions under the doctrine of 'separation of powers' is misleading. In most modern democracies, the parliament is not the only legislative power nor is it a legislative power only. Governments possess some ability to make law through devices such as decrees and orders; the enactment of law is only one of the functions of parliaments, and not necessarily their most important one. See Heywood, A., *Politics* (Palgrave Macmillan: Houndmills, 1997), pp. 294, 297–98.

[16] See Born, H. (ed.), *Parliamentary Oversight of the Security Sector: Principles, Practices and Mechanisms*, Handbook for Parliamentarians no. 5 (Geneva Centre for the Democratic Control of Armed Forces (DCAF)/Inter-Parliamentary Union (IPU): Geneva, 2003); George, B. and Morgan, J., 'A concept paper on legislatures and good governance', based on a paper prepared by Johnson, J. K. and Nakamura, R. T. for the UN Development Programme, July 1999, URL <http://magnet.undp.org/Docs/parliaments/Concept%20Paper%20 Revised%20MAGNET.htm>.

[17] George, B. and Morgan, J., 'Parliament and national security', Paper presented at the Conference on Redefining Society–Military Relations from Vancouver to Vladivostok, Birmingham, 16–18 Apr. 1999.

[18] This categorization and the description of the respective functions draw on Hague, R., Harrop, M. and Breslin, S. (eds), *Comparative Government and Politics: An Introduction*, 4th edn (Palgrave Macmillan: Houndmills, 1998), pp. 190–96; Heywood (note 15), pp. 297–300; and Brunner, G., *Vergleichende Regierungslehre* [Comparative politics], vol. 1 (UTB Schöningh: Paderbom, 1979), pp. 236–58.

the context of the use of force under international auspices, one of the strongest tools of parliament is the power to approve or reject the budgets of PSOs. Where this power does not exist, parliament may have some indirect control by way of approbation or rejection of supplementary defence budget requests, which are often triggered by unexpected PSOs.

The elective function refers to the fact that, in parliamentary systems at least, parliament makes, and sometimes breaks, governments. This applies more strongly in those systems where elections are held under proportional representation, mostly resulting in coalition governments, than in those using other electoral systems that tend to produce a one-party majority. In the context of the use of force under international auspices, this function has minimal application. It may work in a negative manner (i.e., through a no-confidence vote against the government's decision to deploy forces under international auspices or on the government's handling of the deployment). The fall of the Dutch Government as a consequence of a parliamentary report on the 1995 Srebrenica massacre presents a relatively rare example of this contingency.[19]

The representative function of parliament refers to its ideal role as a link between government and the people. In most cases, the ideal is tempered in practice by party discipline. The representative function is often limited to parliament's plenary debates on national issues, which, in the Westminster style of political systems,[20] have become one of the parliament's main, if not most important, functions. Questions of war and peace in particular lend themselves to emotional public debates; and while, in modern conditions, other vectors of influence such as non-governmental organizations and media campaigns can impact strongly on the government, the parliamentary mode of representation also remains important in such situations. Deliberations in parliament may echo popular concerns on, or disagreement with, the government's decision to deploy PSOs; they may also provide an opportunity for consensus building, particularly in instances where the level of force used is high and international authorization is lacking. Finally, they may or may not provide a means for coming to terms with a national crisis related to the use of force under international auspices.

Scrutiny or oversight of the government is one of the most important functions of parliament in modern democracies, allowing parliament to hold the government accountable for its activities. Effective scrutiny is often viewed as a means to compensate for the sidelining of parliament's traditional legislative and budgetary functions. However, most parliaments are still struggling to develop their oversight role—in competition with other societal actors and the

[19] Hoekema, J., 'Srebrenica, Dutchbat and the role of the Netherlands' Parliament', eds Born and Hänggi (note 1), pp. 73–89.

[20] In the 'Westminster-style' parliaments the powers of parliament and government are fused and government business dominates the parliamentary agenda. Norton, P. (ed.), *Parliaments and Governments in Western Europe* (Frank Cass: London, 1998), pp. 2–3; and Lijphart, A., *Patterns of Democracy: Government Forms and Performance in Thirty-Six Countries* (Yale University Press: New Haven, Ct., 1999), pp. 10–30.

Table 4.1. The range of possible powers of parliaments in overseeing international use of force

Function	Instruments
Legislative	Codification of new legal powers (e.g., authorization of the use of force)
Budgetary	Approval of expenditure on military missions ('power of the purse')
Elective	No-confidence vote in case of disagreement with government's decision to deploy forces
Representative	Facilitation of political consensus on or channelling popular disagreement with government's decision to deploy forces
Scrutiny and oversight	Information and monitoring (e.g., through the main techniques of oversight such as questioning, interpellation, emergency debates, hearings, inquiry and visits to troops abroad); consultation by government on the use of force (without binding vote); co-decision on (i.e., authorization of) the use of force (legally required or politically required; prior or *post hoc* decision)

Source: Hänggi, H., 'The use of force under international auspices: parliamentary accountability and "democratic deficits"', eds H. Born and H. Hänggi, *The 'Double Democratic Deficit': Parliamentary Accountability and the Use of Force under International Auspices* (Ashgate: Aldershot, 2004), p. 12.

investigative media—and they face particular challenges in fields that have traditionally been, or remain, the prerogative of the government such as foreign and security policy. In the context of the use of force under international auspices, parliament may seek to hold the government accountable through all the main techniques of oversight such as questioning, interpellation, emergency debates, hearings and inquiries. The techniques are all designed to extract information from the government, without which effective oversight is impossible. *Post hoc* parliamentary inquiries may also offer a major device for holding governments accountable for the use of force under international auspices. Beyond these legal means or customary practices to extract information, parliaments may also have the right to be consulted by government on its decisions regarding the use of force.

The strongest tool of parliamentary oversight by far is the constitutional or legal right to approve or reject the use of force. *Prior* authorization is an especially valuable right because once the troops are sent abroad it is difficult for a parliament to undo the government's decision—withdrawal could endanger the ongoing mission and damage the international reputation and credibility of the country. Research in a selection of 16 'old' and 'new' EU or NATO member states taking part in PSOs shows that wide variation exists between countries regarding the constitutional and legal powers of parliament to oversee PSOs (see table 4.2).[21]

[21] See also Born, H. and Urscheler, M., 'Parliamentary accountability of multinational peace support operations: a comparative perspective', eds Born and Hänggi (note 1), pp. 53–72. The research was carried out in cooperation with the NATO Parliamentary Assembly Secretariat and the parliamentary defence committees of the 16 selected countries.

The parliaments of Belgium, Canada, France, Poland, Portugal, Spain and the United Kingdom and the Congress of the United States do not have the power of prior authorization. The majority of these countries are either presidential–parliamentary democracies or parliamentary Westminster-style democracies. In presidential–parliamentary democracies such as France, Poland, Portugal and the USA,[22] the president is the commander-in-chief and has special prerogatives concerning foreign and security policy. Some of these countries are discussed in more detail below.

As far as the USA is concerned, the division of powers between the president and the Congress is unclear and continues to produce tensions. On the one hand, the US Congress has the power 'to declare war',[23] but deploying troops abroad in the context of PSOs is not the same as waging war. In 1973, after the Viet Nam War (an 'undeclared' war), Congress passed the War Powers Resolution requiring the president to consult with Congress whenever military action is contemplated and to report to Congress whenever armed forces are involved in hostilities abroad. The resolution bars any continued deployment of troops unless Congress gives its consent: if Congress does not consent within 60 days, the president must withdraw the troops within 30 days.[24] On the other hand, Article II, section 2 of the US Constitution states that the president is 'Commander in Chief of the Army and Navy of the United States', and various presidents have continued to dispute the view that the Congress is empowered to approve in advance the dispatch of troops abroad. Lori F. Damrosch shows that, in various deployments of troops abroad, the president has sometimes sought the consent of Congress (e.g., the 1991 Gulf War and in Bosnia and Herzegovina), and sometimes not (e.g., in Somalia and in Haiti), implying that it is up to the president whether prior congressional authorization for a PSO is sought or not.[25]

The French Constitution of 1958, for example, provides no procedure for prior parliamentary authorization for the deployment of forces outside France.[26] Nevertheless, international agreements, among them those involving the deployment of troops abroad, have to be submitted to the parliament.[27]

[22] Karatnycky, A. and Piano, A. (eds), *Freedom in the World: The Annual Survey of Political Rights and Civil Liberties, 2001–2002* (Rowman and Littlefield: Lanham, Md., 2002), pp. 736–37.

[23] US Constitution, Article I, section 8, clause 11.

[24] US Congress, 'Joint Resolution: Concerning the war powers of Congress and the President', Public Law 93-148, 93rd Congress, House Joint Resolution 542, 7 Nov. 1973, paras 1542–44, available at URL <http://www.yale.edu/lawweb/avalon/warpower.htm>.

[25] Damrosch, L. F., 'The interface of national constitutional systems with international law and institutions on using military forces: changing trends in executive and legislative powers', eds C. Ku and H. Jacobsen, *Democratic Accountability and the Use of Force in International Law* (Cambridge University Press: Cambridge, 2003), pp. 48–51.

[26] Lamy, F., *Le Contrôle Parlementaire des Opérations Extérieures* [Parliamentary control of external operations], Report 2237, French Parliament (Deputies), Paris, 2000.

[27] French Constitution, 1958, article 53, cited in Assembly of the WEU, *National Parliamentary Scrutiny of Intervention Abroad by Armed Forces Engaged in International Missions: The Current Position in Law*, Report submitted on behalf of the Committee for Parliamentary and Public Relations by Mrs Troncho, Rapporteur, Document A/1762, 4 Dec. 2001, p. 11.

Table 4.2. Parliamentary oversight powers concerning peace support operations

Country	Prior approval to send troops abroad	Approval of a mission's mandate	Approval of operational issues[a]	Right to visit troops abroad	Decision on the duration of the mission
Belgium	o	o	o	x	o
Canada	o	o	o	x	o
Czech Republic	x	x	o	x	x
Denmark	x	x	x	x	x
France	o	o	o	x	o
Germany	x	x	x	x	x
Hungary	x	. .	. .	. .	. .
Italy	x	. .	. .	x	. .
Netherlands	x	x	x	x	x
Norway	x	o	o	x	o
Poland	o	o	o	. .	o
Portugal	o	o	o	o	o
Spain	o	o	o	x	o
Sweden	x	x	o	x	x
UK	o	x	o	x	o
USA	o	o	o	x	x

o = no, x = yes.

[a] Operational issues include rules of engagement, command and control, and risk assessment.

Source: Born, H. and Urscheler, M., 'Parliamentary accountability of multinational peace support operations: a comparative perspective', eds H. Born and H. Hänggi, *The 'Double Democratic Deficit': Parliamentary Accountability and the Use of Force under International Auspices* (Ashgate: Aldershot, 2004).

According to a report by the French Parliamentary Defence Committee, in the 1990s, with the exception of the Gulf War, the French President did not seek prior parliamentary authorization for the deployment of troops. The French contributions in Yugoslavia—the UN Protection Force (UNPROFOR), the Implementation Force (IFOR) and the Stabilization Force (SFOR)—in Albania (Operation Alba in 1997), and in Kosovo (the Allied Force and the Kosovo Force, KFOR, since 1999) were all determined by the government without parliament having any say in the decisions.[28]

In addition to these examples of presidential–parliamentary democracies, neither the British nor the Canadian parliaments, both Westminster-type parliamentary democracies, have the power of prior authorization for PSOs. Winslow and Klep refer to the Canadian political system as an 'elected

[28] Lamy (note 26).

dictatorship'.[29] The other two countries whose parliaments lack the power of prior authorization are Belgium and Spain. It is unclear why this is the case.[30]

The parliaments of the Czech Republic, Denmark, Germany, Hungary, Italy, the Netherlands, Norway and Sweden have the power to approve or reject PSOs in advance. All these states are parliamentary democracies.[31] The Danish Constitution, for example, obliges the government to seek consent from parliament for deployments 'against a foreign state'.[32] Although formally this provision applies to the use of force against a state, in practice the government also needs approval from parliament before making any commitments concerning PSOs.[33] Under Sweden's Constitution the armed forces can only be sent abroad in accordance with a special law that sets out the grounds for such action and in accordance with Sweden's international treaties and commitments.[34] Hungary is an interesting case because its constitution requires a majority of two-thirds of the votes of the members of parliament before troops may be sent abroad, one of the few decisions requiring a qualified majority.[35] The parliamentary opposition has the opportunity to influence policy because its cooperation is necessary to reach the two-thirds majority, and in the past such votes have sometimes been swayed by domestic issues rather than the merits of the case. However, after pressure from NATO, Hungary has changed this procedure. In November 2003, the responsibility of sending troops abroad shifted from the parliament to the government in the case of consensual NATO operations. Other missions (EU, UN and ad hoc coalitions) remain in the hands of parliament and still require approval by a qualified majority.[36]

In Italy and the Netherlands, the constitution does not explicitly mention that the government has to acquire prior approval for deploying troops abroad, but it is regarded as a matter of customary practice.[37] Among all the 16 parliaments which have the power of prior authorization of PSOs, only those of Denmark, Germany and the Netherlands—and to a lesser extent the Czech Republic and Sweden—have the subsequent powers to discuss and approve the mandate, operational guidelines, budget and duration of the mission (see table 4.2). The parliaments of Italy and Norway lack these detailed

[29] Winslow, D. and Klep, C., 'The public inquiry into the Canadian peace mission in Somalia', eds Born and Hänggi (note 1).

[30] Both Spain and Belgium are monarchies and former colonial powers. The WEU Assembly suggests that parliamentary oversight of PSOs is less strict in countries with this type of political system and history. Assembly of the WEU (note 27), p. 6.

[31] Karatnycky and Piano (note 22).

[32] Constitution of the Kingdom of Denmark, 1992, Article 19.2. The Danish Constitution is available in English at URL <http://www.folketinget.dk/pdf/constitution.pdf>.

[33] Assembly of the WEU (note 27), pp. 8–9.

[34] Instrument of Government, Constitution of the Kingdom of Sweden, 1974, Chapter 10, Article 9, paras 1–3. The Swedish Constitution is available in English at URL <http://www.riksdagen.se/english/work/constitution.asp>.

[35] Constitution of the Republic of Hungary, 1949, Article 19 [3] and [6]. The Hungarian Constitution is available in English at URL <http://www.mkab.hu/en/enpage5.htm>.

[36] The authors are grateful for the information provided by Dr Ference Molnar, Deputy Director of the Institute for Strategic and Defence Studies, Budapest, Hungary.

[37] Assembly of the WEU (note 27), p. 13.

oversight powers and might be said to be in a position to give the government a 'blank cheque' once the decision is taken to deploy troops abroad.

On the basis of this analysis, four models can be distinguished with regard to parliament's involvement in the authorization of PSOs:

1. Parliament has the right of prior authorization of PSOs, including the right to discuss and influence the details of the PSO (e.g., as in Denmark, Germany and the Netherlands).

2. Parliament has the right of prior authorization but not the power to influence the detailed aspects of PSOs (including rules of engagement, duration of the mission and mandate), giving government full authority once parliament has authorized the mission (e.g., as in Italy and Norway).

3. The third group of parliaments does not have prior authorization power. Government can decide to send troops abroad on peace missions without the legal obligation to consult parliament. Nevertheless, parliament is informed about the deployments. This is the case, for example, in Canada, France, Poland, Portugal, Spain, the UK and the USA.

4. A fourth type of parliament is those parliaments which have no authorization power or right to information about future or pending PSOs. This type of parliament was not represented in those studied.

Aside from the extent to which parliaments have the power to authorize PSOs, the parliaments of all three groups often possess the power of the purse over funding for PSOs. Parliaments can use this power during debates on the annual defence budgets and debates on any additional budget requests for ongoing PSOs.[38] For example, the US Congress stopped funding for the US troops committed to the UN PSOs in Somalia in 1992–93 after the first casualties were incurred in 1993.[39] However, generally speaking, the power of the purse does not compensate for the lack of a constitutional power of prior authorization, given the difficulty of pulling back troops in mid-mission. It is also not impossible (although less common for rich Western countries) for the government to have access to alternative, non-national sources of funds to continue the deployment.

'Ability': resources, staff and expertise needed

In order to make full use of their opportunities to hold government accountable, parliamentary representatives must possess sufficient resources (and be given sufficient opportunity) to develop their own expertise. In order to be able to pass legislation, to scrutinize the budget, to engage in informed debates and to oversee governmental activities, parliaments need to work through

[38] Eekelen, W. F. van, *Democratic Control of Armed Forces: the National and International Parliamentary Dimension*, Geneva Centre for the Democratic Control of Armed Forces (DCAF) Occasional Paper no. 2 (DCAF: Geneva, Oct. 2002), URL <http://www.dcaf.ch/publications/Occasional_Papers/2.pdf>.

[39] Damrosch (note 25), p. 49.

specialized committees which have their own budget, expert and support staff as well as access to research and documentation services and external expertise provided for by civil society organizations. These needs are particularly acute in the security sector because of its closed nature. In most cases, parliaments have only small support staffs and infrastructure while the government can rely on large ministerial bureaucracies. In the context of the use of force under international auspices, lack of resources may prevent parliaments from collecting first-hand information on their own (e.g., by holding hearings and inquiries, requesting expertise from international experts or visiting troops abroad). Research on thc resources at the disposal of parliaments in 16 states shows that some parliaments are well endowed, whereas others have hardly any staff or budget (see table 4.3).[40]

All 16 countries' parliaments possess a defence committee: a prerequisite for exercising effective oversight in that policy field, and a manifestation of the institutionalized way of dealing with parliamentary oversight.[41] All these defence committees make use of external expertise provided by civil society organizations, but they differ in terms of number of members and staff as well as in the scale of the committee's budget. Of the countries examined in this chapter, the smallest committee on defence is that of Norway (10 members) and the largest committee is that of France (72 members).

The size of the committee does not have a linear impact on the effectiveness of parliamentary oversight on defence and PSOs. Too many members may transform the committee into a debating club. On the other hand, having too few members impedes the task specialization that is important for covering the security sector. In addition, party rivalry inside the committee may detract from a constructive working climate.[42]

The size of the committee staff varies from 1 staff member serving the Norwegian parliamentary defence committee to 50 staff members working for the US Senate Committee on Armed Services. Staff members usually prepare and organize committee meetings, hearings, maintain contacts with government and defence officials, collect information and help interpret government information. They are vital for effective committee work, and more staff can generally be assumed to mean more effective oversight of defence issues, including PSOs. The same is true of the size of the defence committee's budget. The larger it is, the more possibilities are available for undertaking parliamentary inquiries, organizing hearings and visits, and hiring both staff and outside expertise. The US Senate has access to the largest financial resources (€5.8 million per annum) whereas the Hungarian parliamentary defence committee has an annual budget of just €4000. Remarkably, the French Defence Committee has a lower budget than the Swedish Defence Committee, despite France's larger military forces. Of all the parliaments studied, the US

[40] Born and Urscheler (note 21).

[41] Norton (note 20), p. 196.

[42] Beyme, K. von, *Parliamentary Democracy: Democratization, Destabilization, Reconsolidation, 1789–1999* (Palgrave Macmillan: Houndmills, 2000), p. 60.

Table 4.3. Resources of national parliamentary defence committees

	Members of parliamentary defence committee	Parliamentary defence committee staff	Budget defence committee (€)	Use outside expertise
Belgium	17	1	o	x
Canada	16	3	. .	x
Czech Republic	19	4	o	x
Denmark	17	3	33 333	x
France	72	11	130 000	x
Germany	38	8	. .	x
Hungary	15	2	4 000	x
Italy	43	4	o	x
Netherlands	27	5	25 000	x
Norway	10	1	. .	x
Poland	19	4	o	x
Portugal	26	3	. .	x
Spain	40	4	o	x
Sweden	19	5	500 000	x
USA	25	50	5 800 000	x
UK	11	7	. .	x

o = These parliamentary defence committees lack their own budget but make use of the general budget of the parliament; x = parliament is able to use outside expertise.

Source: Born, H. and Urscheler, M., 'Parliamentary accountability of multinational peace support operations: a comparative perspective', eds H. Born and H. Hänggi, *The 'Double Democratic Deficit': Parliamentary Accountability and the Use of Force under International Auspices* (Ashgate: Aldershot, 2004), p. 63.

Senate Committee on Armed Services seems to be the best resourced in terms both of committee staff and budget.[43]

'Attitude': the willingness to hold the government accountable

Legal rights, resources and expertise alone do not guarantee effective parliamentary oversight of PSOs. The political willingness of parliamentarians to use the tools and mechanisms at their disposal is also a crucial prerequisite. Readiness to endorse a PSO and to accept the use of force can depend not only on the merits of the issue but also on outside pressures, such as the demand by public opinion and the media 'to do something' when civil wars occur. The conflict in the former Yugoslavia was one such example where successive levels of Western intervention were not just supported but partly driven by popular concern.[44] Parliamentarians' attitudes are also influenced by pressure

[43] The data presented on the US case do not take into account the fact that the US Senate Committee on Armed Services can avail itself of the Congressional Research Service, which employs *c.* 800 staff members, as well as the Library of Congress staff and resources.

[44] Jan Hoekema, former vice-chairman of the Dutch Parliamentary Committee on Foreign Affairs, has written that Dutch parliamentarians and government leaders were under heavy pressure from public

exerted by government. By imposing party discipline, governments may seek to limit the freedom of individual parliamentarians of the parliamentary majority to vote against proposed troop deployments. In this sense a public vote on any given PSO is not only about the PSO itself, but also a domestic political test of whether the government still enjoys broad support in parliament.

In addition to these outside pressures, the context and content of the PSO are also relevant. After the end of the cold war a 'new debate' took place on PSOs, in which support could also be found on the left and centre of the political spectrum for forceful intervention in cases with a 'humanitarian' rationale.[45] More centre–right politicians tend to favour PSOs if they serve national interests. However, after the initial enthusiasm for PSOs at the beginning of the 1990s, there has been some reaction in terms both of controversy over individual missions and of greater realism in general about the merits of military intervention as a vehicle for tackling civil wars and failed states.[46] The type of PSO also affects parliamentarians' attitudes: the larger and riskier the operation, or the more lengthy and costly it risks becoming, the deeper and more intense the debate will be.[47] Parliamentarians are more careful and perhaps even reluctant to approve 'enforcement' operations (undertaken with some coercive intent or without the consent of all the local parties) because of the greater risks of casualties among the peacekeepers.

Further research into the willingness of parliaments would need in-depth and qualitative analysis of political processes in each country, and thus falls beyond the scope of this chapter. Currently, no comparative data are available on this subject. It is assumed that among parliamentarians who support PSOs the extent of their acceptance is influenced by pressures from government, media and public opinion as well as the specificities of each PSO.

To conclude, national parliamentary accountability for the use of force under international auspices depends to a great extent on the formal and informal oversight powers vested in parliament. Timely and accurate information on the international deployment of military forces and the power to debate, authorize and review such missions appear to be the most powerful instruments of parliamentary accountability in this area. The relevance of these powers, like all parliamentary powers, is contingent on the resources and expertise at the disposal of parliaments and, last but not least, on the political will of parliamentarians to hold government accountable. Among the countries studied here, some parliaments have strong legal powers and sufficient resources at their disposal, and others do not. It is this uneven oversight practice among the parliaments of EU and NATO countries that creates the risk of a double democratic deficit.

opinion and the media to restore peace and order in Bosnia particularly in the period 1992–95. Hoekema (note 19).

[45] Everts, P., *Democracy and Military Force* (Palgrave Macmillan: Houndmills, 2002), p. 7.

[46] Jett, D. C., *Why Peacekeeping Fails?* (St Martins Press: New York, 2000).

[47] Ku (note 14), pp. 44-45.

III. Deficits in parliamentary accountability and general 'democratic' control at the international level

In examining the possible democratic deficit above the national level of decision making on PSOs, this section focuses on four of the most frequently used frameworks for mandating or launching such missions: the UN; NATO, which since the end of the cold war has increasingly shifted its focus towards mounting crisis-management operations first in Europe and now globally; the EU, which has built up a capacity for military and civilian crisis intervention since 1999; and ad hoc coalitions such as that which intervened in 2003 in Iraq.[48] The EU and NATO perhaps deserve special scrutiny since they consist entirely of states that claim democratic credentials (and in the case of new members have had to meet specific democratic criteria for accession).

Parliamentary accountability and UN-led PSOs

In the past 15 years, twice as many PSOs have been carried out as during the cold war, and the largest single number of such missions has been executed by the UN. In 2004, 16 UN PSOs were carried out, in which 64 701 military personnel, civilian police and staff were involved at a total cost of $3.87 billion.[49] UN PSOs have also become more varied in kind, ranging from monitoring missions to peace enforcement operations.

Since the UN is an intergovernmental organization, it does not have a government or parliament which is directly elected by the people. The UN derives its democratic legitimacy only via its member states, whose representatives are democratically elected at the national level, at least if those member states are democratic themselves.

The central role of the UN Security Council in decisions regarding the use of military forces—both under the UN's own direct command and in missions delegated to other organizations under a UN mandate—makes its decision-making processes important both for democratic oversight and for accountability. The design of the Security Council was influenced by League of Nations experience and to some extent aimed deliberately to achieve a concentration of power rather than true representativeness: it thus entailed, from the first, a certain loss of transparency and the exclusion from the process of many interested states. The decision-making process of the Security Council often takes place in camera, posing problems for oversight by non-participating governments, the general public and national parliaments. Article 32 of the UN Charter requires that parties to a dispute be represented and participate in the

[48] Hippel, K. von, 'NATO, EU and ad hoc coalitions-led peace support operations: the end of UN peacekeeping or pragmatic subcontracting?', *Sicherheit und Frieden/Peace and Security*, vol. 22, no. 1 (2004), pp. 7–11.

[49] United Nations, UN Peacekeeping Operations, 'Background note', 31 Dec. 2004, URL <http://www.un.org/Depts/dpko/dpko/bnote.htm>; and Dwan, R. and Wiharta, S., 'Multilateral peace missions', *SIPRI Yearbook 2004: Armaments, Disarmament and International Security* (Oxford University Press: Oxford, 2004), pp. 149–90. See also table 3.2 in this volume.

debate (without vote) in the Security Council, but troop-contributing countries do not have a similar privilege. Unless it happens to be a Security Council member, a country that contributes forces or financial resources to UN operations thus has no vote in deciding how to use them, and this issue has been of particular concern to such major troop contributors as Canada, Germany and India.[50] In 2004 over three-quarters of the military personnel involved in operations under UN command came from countries that were not Security Council members (see table 4.4). By contrast, the five permanent members (P5) of the Security Council contributed only 4.6 per cent of all civilian and military personnel of UN PSOs in 2004,[51] leading to a situation in which states contributing a tiny minority of troops have a veto power over the mandates and ensuing rules of engagement of PSOs.

Contributors that are not members of the Security Council have no say in the initial mandate and rules of engagement nor are they present if the Security Council modifies the mandate in the course of a military operation.[52] In such cases, contributor nations outside the Security Council may find themselves committed to PSOs which are not (or are no longer) in line with their own national interests or public opinion, creating the danger of a rift between the people, parliament and government of an affected country. As a partial solution to this problem, in 2001 the Security Council adopted a resolution to strengthen cooperation between troop-contributing states, the Security Council and the UN Secretariat. Among other things, the Security Council obliged itself to conduct public and private consultations, hearings and meetings with troop-contributing states.[53]

The issue of transparency also arises in cases where the Security Council authorizes the use of force by another international organization or a coalition of willing individual states. The Security Council asks states conducting the operations to report on their actions, but the frequency and detail of such reports has been variable and often perfunctory, leaving much to the discretion of the organization or states concerned.[54]

[50] Ku (note 14), p. 38. For Germany and India, being among the UN major troop contributing states is a reason for becoming a permanent member of the UN Security Council. German Embassy London, 'Permanent seat on the UN Security Council', 27 Sep. 2004, URL <http://www.german-embassy.org.uk/permanent_seat_on_the_un_secur.html; and Sri Raman, J., 'Promising seat for India', Global Policy Forum, 23 Sep. 2004, URL <http://www.globalpolicy.org/security/reform/cluster1/2004/0923promising.htm>.

[51] United Nations, 'Contributors to United Nations peacekeeping operations: monthly summary of contributors (military observers, civilian police and troops)', Dec. 2004, available at URL <http://www.un.org/Depts/dpko/dpko/contributors/>.

[52] This is not a rare occurrence. E.g., the Security Council changed the initial mandate of the UN PSOs for the UN Operation in the Congo (ONUC) in Feb. 1961, the UN Protective Force (UNPROFOR) in June 1992 and the UN PSOs in Somalia in 1992–93 (UNOSOM I, UNITAF, UNOSOM II). However, the Security Council refused to adapt the mandate of the UN Observer Mission Uganda–Rwanda (UNOMUR) in the light of the increased killing in Apr. 1994 and instead reduced the mission. Ku (note 14), pp. 38–39.

[53] UN Security Council Resolution 1353, 13 June 2001; and Born and Urscheler (note 21), p. 58.

[54] Sarooshi, D., *The United Nations and the Development of Collective Security: the Delegation by the UN Security Council of its Chapter VII Powers* (Oxford University Press: Oxford, 1999).

Table 4.4. UN Security Council and non-Security Council troop-contributing states, as of 31 December 2004

States contributing troops to UN PSOs	Number of troops contributed to UN PSOs (civilian police, military observers and troops)	Number of troops contributed to UN PSOs as % of total
Permanent Security Council member states	2 975	*4.6*
Other Security Council member states	11 768	*18.2*
Non-Security Council member states	49 977	*77.2*
Total	**64 720**	***100.0***

Source: Data derived from United Nations, 'Contributors to United Nations peacekeeping operations: monthly summary of contributors (military observers, civilian police and troops)', Dec. 2004, available at URL <http://www.un.org/Depts/dpko/dpko/contributors/>.

The UN General Assembly is not a parliament but an intergovernmental body of appointed officials. It normally only plays a limited role in respect to PSOs, but it has the right to call for a PSO as it did in its 1950 'Uniting for Peace' Resolution in the Korean War,[55] and it also adopts the general budget of the UN from which PSOs are financed. The General Assembly also often adopts declaratory statements on peacekeeping issues. Since 1965 it has had a Special Committee on Peacekeeping Operations, with membership consisting of appointed officials from as many as 100 UN member states. The Special Committee submits annual reports on peacekeeping operation issues to the General Assembly through the Special Political and Decolonization (Fourth) Committee.[56] Its size, however, makes it unwieldy and, as one of its latest reports shows, it indulges in deliberation on all imaginable aspects of peacekeeping, from the strategic to the trivial, with little prospect of enforcing its conclusions. At least, it may offer troop-contributing nations outside the Security Council some opening to reiterate their concerns and wishes.[57]

The intergovernmental nature of the UN (whose member states are not all democracies), the absence of a controlling parliamentary body and the UN's large expert staff working without democratic oversight are all factors that have led some scholars to conclude that UN decision making suffers from a major democratic deficit.[58] The UN High-level Panel did not touch on the issue of democratic deficits in global security governance, except to pay lip

[55] UN General Assembly Resolution 377, 3 Nov. 1950.

[56] United Nations, 'UN General Assembly and peacekeeping: Special Political and Decolonization (Fourth) Committee', URL <http://www.un.org/Depts/dpko/dpko/ctte/CTTEE.htm>.

[57] United Nations, Report of the Special Committee on Peacekeeping Operation and its Working Group at the 2004 Substantive Session, UN General Assembly document A/58/19, 26 Apr. 2004, available at URL <http://www.un.org/Depts/dpko/dpko/ctte/CTTEE.htm>.

[58] Scholte, J. A., 'The globalization of world politics', eds J. Baylis and S. Smith, *The Globalization of World Politics: An Introduction to International Relations* (Oxford University Press: Oxford, 2001), pp. 28–30.

service to making the Security Council more democratically accountable.[59] Genuine democratic accountability would, in fact, imply changing the UN's nature from an intergovernmental to a supranational organization composed of democratic states, a goal which is for some not desirable and for others totally unrealistic.

Democratic control of NATO-led PSOs

Recent NATO 'out of area' PSOs have been conducted in Bosnia and Herzegovina (IFOR and SFOR), Kosovo (KFOR), the Former Yugoslav Republic of Macedonia (Operations Essential Harvest and Amber Fox) and Afghanistan (International Security Assistance Force, ISAF).[60] The Kosovo intervention has attracted particular notice in debates over the legality of the use of force, given its robust nature and the absence of a direct UN mandate.[61] Such NATO actions raise questions of oversight and accountability of a quite different order from that which might have attached to the allies' use of force in their own defence under cold war circumstances.

Decision making in NATO is an intergovernmental negotiating process with special characteristics. It is regular and frequent; the Secretary General and the Secretariat have a strong position, but the USA exercises an undeniable political leadership role; it is consensus-based, requiring much effort to find a compromise between different national views and interests; it is politico-military in nature, with both parallel lines of authority and cross links between the political and military bodies; it does not depend on meetings of ministers, as the Permanent Council possesses full decision-making authority between ministerial sessions; and, finally, it has a parliamentary dimension.[62]

Decisions in NATO about PSOs have to be regarded as complex and interdependent sequences with no single key moment of decision on a given intervention. For example, with regard to the Kosovo intervention, between the autumn of 1998 and 1999 the NATO member states had to decide: whether there would be a military operation in Kosovo; which states would participate in the action; what would be the triggering conditions for military action; which state would contribute what; which state would exercise command and control over the whole operation and its specific aspects (including targeting and choice of weapons); and how to link military with diplomatic action.[63]

[59] United Nations (note 5), Point 249(d), p. 80.

[60] For a full overview of NATO PSOs see table 3.2 in this volume. See also NATO, 'NATO Handbook', chapter 5, URL <http://www.nato.int/docu/handbook/2001/>. NATO is now also conducting a military training operation in and for Iraq.

[61] For an interesting comparative study on the involvement of the US Congress and the German Bundestag in NATO's intervention in Kosovo see Damrosch L. F., 'The United States Congress, the German Bundestag and NATO's intervention in Kosovo', eds Born and Hänggi (note 1), pp. 131–46.

[62] For a further elaboration of the characteristics of NATO's decision making see Eekelen, W. van, 'Decision-making in the Atlantic Alliance and its parliamentary dimension', eds Born and Hänggi (note 1), pp. 112–15; and Gallis, P., *NATO's Decision-Making Procedure*, Congressional Research Service (CRS) Report for Congress RS 215/0 (CRS/Library of Congress: Washington, DC, 2003).

[63] See also Damrosch (note 61), p. 131.

US leadership is omnipresent and, while consensus remains necessary, the US representatives' interventions in the North Atlantic Council (NAC) generally provide the starting point and ground for debate—reflecting, not least, the large financial contribution and preponderant military contribution of the USA to NATO.[64] Among other states in the NAC, a practice has grown of not using a veto when a state is a minority of one, although there have been exceptions involving *inter alia* France, Greece and Turkey.[65] The rift between the US-led coalition and states such as France and Germany on the other hand, when NATO was called on in early 2003 to take decisions related to the imminent war in Iraq, constituted a serious breach of this consensus approach.[66]

In NATO, like any other intergovernmental organization, ultimate parliamentary control rests with national parliaments and with the extent to which they can hold national ministers to account for their collective decisions. Nevertheless, NATO decision making has an international parliamentary dimension. The NATO Parliamentary Assembly (NATO PA), created in 1955, has gradually grown in stature, thanks to the quality of its frequent reports and debates and the attention they have drawn in member countries.[67] Unlike the UN General Assembly, the NATO PA consists exclusively of delegations appointed or elected by their national parliaments in a representative manner and thus offers a fairly good reflection of public opinion in the NATO member states. After each national election, the national delegations to the NATO PA change, so the assembly's membership is continually in flux.

The NATO PA does not have co-decision powers and has no financial powers beyond its own budget.[68] Rather, it contributes to consensus building among parliamentarians of the participating countries and to the expertise they can bring to bear on decisions at home. Concerning NATO PSOs, the NATO PA can at best provide an opportunity to air and compare the views of its national members at its meetings. Since decisions about PSOs, as all others in NATO, are elaborated and taken by the NAC after strictly confidential intergovernmental negotiations, neither the NATO PA nor national parliaments can play a substantive role.

Only national parliaments can oversee the governments of the NATO member states, offering at best a degree of indirect parliamentary accountability. In contrast to the UN Security Council, all troop-contributing states that are members of NATO have the same formal opportunity to influence decision making about PSOs, even if some member states are 'more equal' than others. The way in which the NAC works behind closed doors and the confidential nature of its negotiations, however, create particular problems of transparency both for parliamentary bodies and for the public in general. Since national

[64] See Eekelen (note 62), p. 113

[65] Other countries have inserted a dissenting footnote in communiqués, without preventing their adoption, mainly in cases where their parliaments would have difficulty to approve the agreed policy.

[66] See Eekelen (note 62), p. 114

[67] See the Internet site of the NATO PA at URL <http://www.nato-pa.int/>.

[68] See Eekelen (note 62), p. 116

arrangements are so variable and the NATO PA does not have oversight powers, democratic deficits exist at both the national and the international levels.

Parliamentary accountability and EU-led PSOs

The EU is a unique institution combining intergovernmental cooperation with supranational integration. PSOs are a new but rapidly increasing field of activity for the EU, as shown by a series of military deployments from 2003 onwards. The founding documents of the European Security and Defence Policy (ESDP) making provision *inter alia* for PSOs did not, however—and probably not by accident—make any new provision for parliamentary accountability. Currently, parliamentary work at the EU level has two dimensions: the work of national parliaments and inter-parliamentary cooperation between them; and the role of the directly elected European Parliament which interacts with EU decision makers both in the European Commission and the Council of Ministers.[69] Recent research has highlighted several shortcomings in this system,[70] raising three main issues.

First, national parliaments of the EU member states have difficulty in obtaining information about the ESDP decision-making process at the European level. They have no direct access to the European institutions and must therefore rely almost exclusively on their own governments. They can only find out what other governments are doing or other parliaments are thinking by voluntary and ad hoc contacts, while the governments themselves meet and consult with each other frequently in the Council of the European Union. The EP is better informed about ESDP policy developments because it can request information either from the Presidency, the Council of Ministers or the High Representative for the Common Foreign and Security Policy (CFSP). However, it has no scrutiny powers in this area, nor power over the sending of troops on missions outside the territory of the EU.

Second, the exercise of parliamentary oversight both by the EP and by national parliaments is hampered by the hybrid and complex nature of the EU. While the ESDP is first and foremost considered an intergovernmental issue, its execution may also involve actions under the EU's 'first pillar' (e.g. civilian aspects of crisis management) or 'third pillar' (e.g. anti-terrorism cooperation).[71] Different decision-making mechanisms and institutions exist for these different ESDP instruments and the role of the executive is played variously in different contexts by the Commission, the Council and national governments. There is also scope for confusion of roles and competition on the parliamentary side between the 25 national parliaments, the European Parliament and the interim European Security and Defence Assembly (the former

[69] Gourlay, C., 'Parliamentary accountability and ESDP: the national and European level', eds. Born and Hänggi (note 1), pp. 183–202.

[70] Bono, G., 'The European Union as an international security actor: challenges for democratic accountability', eds Born and Hänggi (note 1), pp. 163–81; and Gourlay (note 69).

[71] Gourlay (note 69), p. 185–87

Western European Union (WEU) Assembly).[72] Specific decisions to engage in a military operation and deploy force in a PSO are, at all events, invariably taken by consensus in the intergovernmental 'second pillar' where the EP has no involvement in operational decision making (although it does have power to approve the CFSP budget). Authorization for governments to commit troops to PSOs is strictly the responsibility of national parliaments where they may have or may not have the relevant powers (see above). However, the EU organs do at least seem to be making more serious efforts to consult and inform the EP about ESDP generally. Currently, the Presidency and the High Representative for the CFSP as well as the Commissioner for External Relations address the EP and its Committee on Foreign Affairs (AFET) regularly, giving members of the European Parliament a chance to debate and challenge the EU executive about the EU's 2003 European Security Strategy[73] and PSOs in particular.

Third, while national parliaments can in principle hold their governments to account for decisions reached in the Council by unanimity, such oversight cannot solve the democratic deficit because of the unequal and often weak powers of different national parliaments in this area.

Ultimately, the basic challenge for parliamentary oversight here arises from the uncertainties and ambiguities of the ESDP's future. If its methods become gradually more supranational this would open up a wider role for the EP; but if it remains a permanent 'island' of intergovernmentalism in the EU, it can offer no greater opening to representative institutions than in NATO. In the meantime, national parliaments remain by and large the sole source of democratic legitimacy for EU PSOs.

Parliamentary accountability and ad hoc coalition-led PSOs

The 2003 US-led war against Iraq has, in many quarters, given ad hoc coalitions a bad name, but such coalitions can take many different forms. In contrast to the war in Iraq, various previous ad hoc coalitions operated under an explicit UN mandate.[74] Operation Desert Storm, the US-led operation to liberate Kuwait in the 1991 Gulf War, was authorized by the UN Security Council,[75] and the UN sanctioned the two Australian-led ad hoc coalitions to provide peace support for post-conflict arrangements in Papua New Guinea

[72] Wagner, W., *Für Europa sterben? Die demokratische Legitimität der Europäischen Sicherheits- und Verteidigungspolitik* [To die for Europe? The democratic legitimacy of the European Security and Defence Policy], Hessische Stiftung Friedens- und Konfliktforschung (HFSK) Report 3/2004 (HSFK: Frankfurt, 2004). pp. 22–24. The WEU Assembly chose to continue operating as an assembly for European security and defence questions after intergovernmental activity in the WEU effectively ceased in 2000. It has no formal role recognized by the organs of the EU.

[73] Council of the European Union, 'A Secure Europe in a Better World: European Security Strategy', Brussels, 12 Dec. 2003, URL <http://ue.eu.int/uedocs/cms_data/docs/2004/4/29/European%20Security%20Strategy.pdf>.

[74] Wilson, G., 'UN authorized enforcement: regional organizations versus "coalitions of the willing"', *International Peacekeeping*, vol. 10, no. 2 (summer 2003), pp. 89–106.

[75] UN Security Council Resolution 678, 29 Nov. 1990

and the Solomon Islands in 2003.[76] These examples show the possible functional range of coalition operations from traditional peace support to robust enforcement and war.

From the point of view of parliamentary accountability and democratic oversight, however, all ad hoc coalitions have serious drawbacks. First, coalitions acting outside a set institutional framework cannot by definition have an international parliamentary dimension. Parliamentary oversight or dialogue thus depends completely on the ability of national parliaments, which is a variable commodity. Second, ad hoc coalitions do not have a formalized and transparent intergovernmental layer of decision making. The mandate and command and control structures are most likely defined by the leading troop contributor, with limited or no negotiating space for the smaller troop-contributing states. Where the governments involved have little say, the role of their parliaments is bound to be even weaker. Great weight is thus laid on the mechanisms of national parliamentary accountability in the leading troop-contributing state. If these are weak or absent, the mandate and the strategy of the ad hoc coalition will be solely decided upon by that state's government. These are circumstances that can both provoke and aggravate the consequences of behaviour during operations that diverges from international norms and ignores (at least temporarily) international laws.

IV. Strengthening parliamentary accountability at the national and international levels

No consensus exists in the relevant policy and academic discourses on how to tackle the democratic deficit at the global and regional levels of governance. Robert Dahl supplies the sceptical view. He considers it unlikely that international organizations could be democratized: '[i]f democratic institutions are largely ineffective in governing the European Union, the prospects for democratizing other international systems seem even more remote'.[77] On a more optimistic note, a number of scholars and practitioners are looking for ways to address the 'democratic deficit' suffered by international institutions. From a normative perspective, three theoretical approaches or 'models' can be distinguished: liberal–democratic internationalism, which aims at reforming the current international institutions; radical communitarism, which promotes the creation of alternative structures based on transnational participatory governance according to functionalist rather than geographical patterns; and cosmopolitanism, which posits the reconstruction of global governance at all levels based on a cosmopolitan democratic law transcending national and

[76] For details of these ad hoc coalitions see Dwan and Wiharta (note 49).

[77] Dahl, R. A., *On Democracy* (Yale University Press: New Haven, Ct., 1998), p. 115. However, since Dahl made his statement, the role of the EP has been strengthened (although not necessarily in the field of security and defence policy). Adoption of the European Constitution would bring about a number of additional modest improvements in the parliamentary accountability of the EU.

other sovereignties.[78] These normative models have generated ideas on how to improve the democratic credentials of global and regional security arrangements, which may be gathered under two general headings: proposals for the gradual 'democratization' of international institutions, on the one hand; and the call for greater pluralism in terms of actors involved, on the other. The former proposals tend to focus on increasing representation, transparency and accountability in the decision making of intergovernmental bodies. Calls for greater pluralism tend to emphasize the importance of non-state actors and civil society in influencing policy and holding international bodies accountable.[79] In terms of practical reforms, the participation of civil society actors in international institutions seems to be the standard prescription for narrowing the participatory gap in global governance.[80]

The discourse on the subject of reducing the democratic deficits in international institutions tends to neglect the parliamentary dimension, although there have been some more specific proposals (e.g., for the creation of a parliamentary dimension of the UN, a strengthening of the EP and a greater involvement of national parliaments). This is striking given that parliaments are the central locus of accountability and legitimacy in democracies. In principle and despite national variations, they should oversee every element of public policy, including decisions on the deployment and use of force. What can be done or what has been done in order to reduce this deficit? Some examples can be provided that are applicable to both international assemblies and national parliaments.

On the national level, the following recommendations could strengthen the capacity of parliaments to oversee multinational PSOs.

1. *Inter-parliamentary cooperation as a step towards greater standardization of oversight practices*. Within a given group of states, parliaments could cooperate to ensure that they all have at their disposition the same information, for example, by producing joint annual reports and by having regular conferences of the chairs of the national parliamentary defence committees.

2. *Adjustment of the legal framework*. Many countries have constitutions which do not contain any provisions on parliament's role vis-à-vis sending troops abroad on PSOs. Many constitutions were drafted in the 19th or early 20th century, when such operations played a limited role, if any, and therefore deal only with parliamentary consent to the declaration of war. For example, the Dutch Parliament has recently amended the national constitution so as to strengthen its own position on the issue of sending troops abroad on PSOs.

3. *Effective rules of procedure*. Another obstacle is the confidentiality and secrecy which decision making on PSOs sometimes requires. Various parlia-

[78] McGrew, A. (note 9), pp. 405–19.

[79] See, e.g., United Nations Development Programme, *Human Development Report 2002: Deepening Democracy in a Fragmented World* (Oxford University Press: Oxford, 2002), pp. 101–22.

[80] Brühl, T. and Rittberger, V., 'From international to global governance: actors, collective decision-making, and the United Nations in the world of the twenty-first century', ed. V. Rittberger, *Global Governance and the United Nations System* (UN University: Tokyo, 2001), pp. 34–35.

ments have developed simple but practical rules of procedure in order to have access to classified information (e.g., vetting and clearance procedures for defence committee members, convening behind closed doors, making a strict distinction between public reports and classified reports, and procedures for declassifying documents after the PSOs are finished) which makes *post hoc* accountability possible.

4. *Cross-party responsibility*. Party discipline is identified as one of the major obstacles to holding government accountable. One way to overcome this obstacle might be to give the opposition parties in parliament a clear voice in the debate about deploying troops abroad. Various countries have acknowledged opposition parties' importance for a healthy and critical political climate in parliament by having a parliamentary defence committee that reflects the political diversity in parliament, by appointing a senior member of the opposition as chair of the parliamentary defence committee and by requiring a two-third's majority in parliament if troops are to be sent abroad.

At the international level, a number of options for strengthening parliamentary oversight of PSOs could be considered.

Some have proposed to tackle the problem in NATO and the UN by creating new international representative assemblies.[81] This is a far-reaching solution and for the moment perhaps not realistic. A more modest option would be to improve the functioning of the existing international assemblies by making them more representative through adding national parliamentary delegations to the assemblies (suggested for the UN), or by improving their procedures—for example, by the NATO Secretary General delivering a yearly State of the Alliance message to the NATO PA.

The EP's oversight of the ESDP could be enhanced in various ways. It should be given greater authority to scrutinize ESDP spending, to enlarge the resources available to the EP Committee on Foreign Affairs (more staff and a larger budget), to increase public access to ESDP documents and to oblige the Council of Ministers to transmit all ESDP documents to national parliaments. Following the US Congress, the EP could in theory enact 'war powers' legislation that would define the conditions and authority under which the EU could declare states of war and emergency and when troops could be sent to crises outside the EU's territory.[82] Despite the recent 'Europeanization' of the ESDP, national parliaments have retained important oversight tasks with

[81] A number of proposals have been made to create a parliamentary dimension of the UN by way of establishing a second 'People's' Assembly. Bienen, D., Rittberger, V. and Wagner, W., 'Democracy in the United Nations system: cosmopolitan and communitarian principles', eds D. Archibugi, D. Held and M. Köhler, *Re-Imaging Political Community: Studies in Cosmopolitan Democracy* (Polity Press: Cambridge, 1998), p. 297; and Held, D., *Models of Democracy*, 2nd edn (Polity Press, Cambridge, 1996), p. 358. It has also been proposed that parliamentarians be included in national delegations to the General Assembly and other UN organs. Parliamentary Assembly of the Council of Europe (PACE), 'Parliamentary scrutiny of international institutions', Resolution 1289, 25 June 2002, para. 8, URL <http://assembly.coe.int/Documents/AdoptedText/ta02/ERES1289.htm>. Apart from numerous proposals for strengthening the EP itself, there is also the idea put forward by PACE of introducing a body of representatives of national parliaments as a second chamber of the EP. PACE, Resolution 1289, para. 10.

[82] Houben, M., 'Time has come for "European War Powers' Act"', *European Voice*, 23 June 2003.

regard to national defence budgets, authority to deploy troops abroad and procurement, and in the present essentially intergovernmental phase of decision making on PSOs it is important to use these national powers to the full. Armand de Decker, former President of the WEU Assembly and former Chairman of the Belgian Senate, has urged national parliaments to take into account the European aspects of security and defence policy in their debates. The EP and the national parliaments should explore together how to make best use of the provision on inter-parliamentary cooperation on the ESDP as stipulated in the 'Protocol on the Role of National Parliaments in the EU' annexed to the EU's Constitutional Treaty.[83]

V. Conclusions

Parliamentary accountability regarding foreign and security affairs tends to be weak in most political systems. Among widely differing national practices, the lowest common denominator is apt to be at a point short of there being no parliamentary accountability at all. Even in the EU there is no 'minimum standard' of parliamentary accountability. This leads to something of a cumulative 'democratic deficit' at the national level, despite a growing number of instances in which parliaments effectively hold governments accountable for the deployment and management of national armed forces abroad.

At the international level, parliamentary accountability is largely absent when it comes to the use of force under the aegis of international organizations and ad hoc coalitions. This should not come as a surprise given the fact that, except for the EU, all relevant international organizations and ad hoc coalitions are of a purely intergovernmental character. The UN lacks a parliamentary or even an inter-parliamentary dimension. Inter-parliamentary assemblies such as the NATO PA and the interim European Security and Defence Assembly lack any of the functions that are characteristic of national parliaments. Even the role of the EP, despite its considerable resources and strong political will to check and balance the other EU organs, is at best marginal when it comes to foreign and security affairs: hence the second, international component of the 'double' democratic deficit.

Many recommendations can be made to reduce the double democratic deficit, but the primary question is how strong parliament should be and where to draw the line dividing the competences of government and parliament. From the point of view of a 'government of the people, by the people, for the people', the bottom line is that parliamentary accountability is indispensable since parliaments are the most important provider of democratic legitimacy. It is difficult to imagine that such an important—and, literally, life-and-death—issue as sending troops abroad in PSOs can be indefinitely excluded from parliamentary accountability, at both the national and international levels of security governance.

[83] de Decker, A., 'Tackling the double democratic deficit and improving accountability of ESDP', 29 Apr. 2004, available at URL <http://www.dcaf.ch/news/Democratic_Deficit/mainpage.html>.

5. The greater Middle East

ROSEMARY HOLLIS

I. Introduction

Although it is strongly interdependent with the rest of the world in the supply of energy, the greater Middle East region has been little penetrated by 'globalizing' trends, especially those that tend to emancipate the individual.[1] Most states of the region are of relatively recent creation, many borders are still disputed and interstate relations are generally of a brittle, competitive when not outright adversarial character. In 2004 the most potent conflicts in the region were over sovereignty in Iraq and between Israel and the Palestinians, although the repercussions are apparent beyond these nations' borders and they are not the only sources of instability in the region. There are tensions or unresolved border issues outstanding between Iran and Iraq, between Iran and the small Arab states in the Persian Gulf region, and between Iran and Afghanistan. Syria remains technically at war with Israel and has come under mounting pressure from the United States—as well as from France, other European states, Israel, some Arab states and the United Nations (UN)—over its presence and conduct in Lebanon.

State structures and interstate relations are called into doubt not just by such governmental disputes but by the strength of transnational elements such as tribal connections, diasporas, sects and modern terrorist movements. During 2004 almost all the countries in the region experienced some sort of terrorist incident and, whether allied to the USA or not, all the regional governments share a fear of radical Islamist militants, either associated with or inspired by al-Qaeda. Many experts have depicted the USA's long-term strategic presence in the region, and more specifically US policies in Iraq and with respect to the Palestinians, as aggravating the problem. At the strategic level, the possibility exists that Iran will develop a nuclear weapon capability and that the USA could take military action against it. As of early 2005, however, the US Administration was indicating a preference for a diplomatic solution to its differences with Iran.

Meanwhile, there has been an expansion of multilateral initiatives and engagements in the region. The North Atlantic Treaty Organization (NATO) has increased its role in both Afghanistan and Iraq and has offered to assist other states with military preparedness and performance, counter-terrorism,

[1] The greater Middle East is defined in this chapter as bounded by Turkey in the north and the Arabian Peninsula state of Yemen to the south, and stretching from Egypt, Israel and Lebanon in the west to Afghanistan in the east. In contrast to the term 'broader Middle East', as used by the United States and the Group of Eight (G8) industrialized nations, this definition does not include either Pakistan, on the one hand, or North Africa beyond Egypt, on the other.

border security and defence budgeting. The European Union (EU) launched a Strategic Partnership in 2004, offering help with economic development, security cooperation, political reform and counter-terrorism.[2] The USA is championing the cause of democratization and has re-engaged with Israel and the Palestinians in the name of a two-state solution to their conflict.

Section II of this chapter presents the general features of, and specific issues arising from, state-to-state security relations in the region. Section III examines phenomena, including core conflicts, that have a region-wide impact. The military balance in the region is discussed in section IV. Section V focuses on regionalism and cooperation and discusses the various multilateral organizations based elsewhere which have become involved in the greater Middle East. The conclusions are presented in section VI.

II. The state system and associated issues

States and identity

Following the collapse of the Ottoman Empire in World War I (1914–18), France and the United Kingdom were the principal architects of the carve-up of the Arab world into separate states and emirates, with each of them falling under the sway of one or other of these two colonial powers. New colonies were not, however, acceptable to the League of Nations, which gave the UK the newly created Mandates of Palestine (initially including modern-day Jordan) and Iraq, and France the mandatory authority for Syria (including Lebanon) on condition that they prepare these new entities for independence. In the case of Palestine the terms of the mandate required the UK to promote the establishment of a Jewish homeland while protecting the rights of the indigenous Arabs—with conflict the result.

The lines drawn on the map in the 1920s cut across established trading routes and commercial links, separated coastal ports from inland communities, and submerged pre-existing social, tribal, ethnic and sectarian identities in new national entities. Over the ensuing decades the leaders of the new states had to find ways to achieve legitimacy and distinguish themselves and their states, one from another. The Al Saud dynasty in Saudi Arabia chose to be allies and champions of the Wahhabi strand of Islam. In Syria and Iraq anti-imperialism became the rallying cry until full independence was achieved; later these regimes used Baathist pan-Arabist ideology to dress up minority rule. Egyptian President Gamal Adbul Nasser won regional influence as the leading proponent of Arab nationalism, dedicated to eliminating residual British and French influence in the region and reversing the Arab humiliation of 1948, when the establishment of the state of Israel betokened the defeat of Arab forces by the Zionist movement in Palestine.

[2] 'EU Strategic Partnership with the Mediterranean and the Middle East', *Euromed Report*, no. 78 (23 June 2004), URL <europa.eu.int/comm/external_relations/euromed/publication/2004/euromed_report_78_en.pdf>. See also the EU's Mediterranean and Middle East Policy Internet site at URL <http://europa.eu.int/comm/external_relations/med_mideast/intro/>.

If the collapse of the Ottoman Caliphate and the triumph of European imperialism was the first 20th century crisis for the Arabs, their 1948 defeat in Palestine was the second, and their subsequent failure on the battlefield in 1967 the third. It was from that moment that the appeal of Islam began slowly to encroach on secular nationalism, although the experience of fighting Soviet forces in Afghanistan in the 1980s seems to have been the incubator for the most radical Salafist ideologues,[3] many now associated with Osama bin Laden. The Soviet invasion of Afghanistan in 1979 came shortly after the fall of the Shah of Iran in a revolution which ended three decades of predominant US influence in Tehran. Iran became an Islamic republic, in this case the champion of Shia rather than Sunni Islam, and thus a rival to Saudi Wahhabism. The balance of the region's states was upset at the same time as the USA was obliged to seek new allies, bases and techniques for maintaining its strategic presence in the region—a search which arguably has culminated in, but still not been resolved by, the latest events in Iraq.

Iran and its Arab neighbours

Since agreeing the ceasefire that ended the 1980–88 Iraq–Iran War, the two countries have yet to sign a formal treaty delineating their mutual border. From an exchange of letters in 1990 between Iraqi President Saddam Hussein and Iranian President Ali Akbar Hashemi-Rafsanjani, the latter concluded that Iraq had again accepted the 1975 Algiers Accord and its related protocols and agreements, delineating the border along the *thalweg* or median line of the Shatt al-Arab waterway.[4] However, doubts persisted over the Iraqi commitment to that agreement, and the regime of Saddam Hussein was overthrown in 2003.[5] A formal agreement must thus await the constitution of a new Iraqi government with full sovereign powers. Meanwhile, there are other issues still outstanding from the 1980–88 war, including prisoners of war and reparations. In August 2004 the kidnappers of an Iranian diplomat inside Iraq threatened to punish him if Iran did not release 500 prisoners whom it captured during the war.[6] For its part, the Iranian Government has stated that it intends to pursue its claim to reparations from Iraq for damages sustained during the war.[7]

Once a fully constituted government is in place in Iraq it will also be expected to confirm the border with Kuwait announced by the UN Iraq–Kuwait Boundary Demarcation Commission in 1994. Its delineation was

[3] See 'Salafi Islam', GlobalSecurity.org, URL <http://www.globalsecurity.org/military/intro/islam-salafi.htm>.

[4] For the Algiers Accord see URL <http://www.mideastweb.org/algiersaccord.htm>. See also '*Keyhan-e Hava'I* publishes leaders letters', 26 Sep. and 3 Oct. 1990, BBC Survey of World Broadcasts, 1 Nov. 1990.

[5] Schofield, R., 'Position, function and symbol: the Shatt al-Arab dispute in perspective', eds L. G. Potter and G. G. Sick, *Iran, Iraq and the Legacies of War* (Palgrave Macmillan: New York, 2004), p. 64.

[6] Islamic Republic News Agency (IRNA), 'Iran minister, Iraq deputy premier discuss kidnapped diplomat', 29 Aug. 2004, URL <http://www.irna.com/en/>.

[7] IRNA, 'Iran will press ahead for war reparations from Iraq: says Kharrazi', 20 Oct. 2004, URL <http://www.irna.ir/irnewtest/en/news/view/line-17/0410200934184136.htm>.

vociferously opposed by many of the Iraqi opposition groups whose members have surfaced in Iraq's interim and transitional governments because the boundary restricts Iraq's access to the headwaters of the Persian Gulf by recognizing Kuwaiti sovereignty over the approach channels to the port of Umm Qasr. A trilateral agreement will thus be needed between Iran, Iraq and Kuwait in order for peaceful development and environmental cooperation to go ahead in this contentious area.[8]

Reflecting its support for Iraq in the 1980–88 war, the Gulf Cooperation Council (GCC)—founded in 1981 by Bahrain, Kuwait, Oman, Qatar, Saudi Arabia and the United Arab Emirates (UAE)—has hitherto adopted a position on the Iraq–Iran border issue that is supportive of Iraqi sovereignty over the whole of the Shatt al-Arab.[9] It remains to be seen how the GCC will respond to the need for a trilateral arrangement that reconciles Iranian, Iraqi and Kuwaiti claims. If these three states can find accommodation, presumably the GCC will acquiesce. However, if there is disagreement among the three, the GCC may side against Iran but will have to weigh the competing interests of GCC member Kuwait and its much bigger neighbour Iraq. To complicate matters, henceforward the Iraqi government will be dominated by Shia Arabs, and their ascendancy is being interpreted in other Arab capitals, not least Riyadh, as bolstering Iranian regional hegemony.

The stance of the GCC on Iran's dispute with the UAE over the lower Persian Gulf islands of Abu Musa and the Greater and Lesser Tunbs has been unequivocally in favour of the UAE. Iran rejects the GCC stance and claims sovereignty over all three islands.[10] Iran has also objected publicly to backing for the UAE claim by the Arab League.[11] GCC and Arab League solidarity with the UAE against Iran is not new and can be expected to continue. Meanwhile, an Iranian parliamentarian has suggested that the USA was behind an incident involving an Iranian fishing vessel that was intercepted by a UAE ship near Abu Musa in mid-2004.[12] The Iranian Government maintains that 'misunderstandings' over implementation of the Memorandum of Understanding signed between Iran and Sharjah (now in the UAE) in 1971 on the status of the islands should be dealt with through bilateral talks between Iran and the UAE. Such talks have been held, and in early 2005 the Iranian Foreign Ministry called for them to continue under the new presidency of the UAE (Sheikh Khalifah bin Zayed al-Nahyan succeeded his father, Shiekh Zayed bin Sultan

[8] Schofield (note 5), pp. 30–31.

[9] On the GCC (Cooperation Council for the Arab States of the Gulf) and its membership see the glossary in this volume.

[10] Voice of the Islamic Republic of Iran, 'Iran rejects Arab Inter-Parliamentary Union statement as unacceptable', BBC Monitoring, 3 Mar. 2004, (in Persian); IRNA, 'Iran Foreign Ministry says GCC statement on islands "totally unacceptable"', 21 Dec. 2004, URL <http://www.irna.com/en/>; IRNA, 'Iran dismisses latest support for UAE claims to disputed islands', BBC Monitoring, 14 Mar. 2005; and IRNA, 'Foreign Ministry spokesman says Persian Gulf islands, integral parts of Iran', BBC Monitoring, 6 Apr. 2005.

[11] IRNA, 'Iran rejects Arab League statement on disputed islands', 24 May 2004, URL <http://www.irna.com/en/>. On the League of Arab States and its membership see the glossary in this volume.

[12] Iranian Labour News Agency (ILNA), 'Iran MP says GCC statement on islands, attack on boat, "planned elsewhere"', BBC Monitoring, 7 June 2004 (in Persian).

al-Nahyan, as president in November 2004), at the same time as it objected to 'allegations' made by the UAE deputy prime minister and deputy foreign minister in a UAE daily newspaper.[13]

Developments in Iraq have also complicated the picture by reordering the relative fortunes of Iraqi Shia and Sunni Arabs and hence calling into question Iraq's traditional role as a secular/Sunni Arab bulwark against the Islamic Republic of Iran. The ramifications are already being played out in the GCC, with the Kuwaiti Government objecting to a meeting held in May 2004 between the Iranian ambassador to Kuwait and members of the Kuwaiti Shia community and Iran objecting in turn to hostile comments in the Kuwaiti press.[14] Tensions also surfaced between Iran and Qatar after the Qatari Navy engaged an Iranian fishing boat which Qatar claimed had entered its territorial waters,[15] although escalation was avoided.

On a more positive note, in February 2005 Iran and the UAE agreed to strengthen their cooperation on environmental issues, especially protection of marine life and eradication of sea pollution,[16] and called for closer cooperation on economic issues.[17] Iran has also been pursuing closer trade links with Bahrain, where the population is predominantly Shia, although the ruling family is Sunni, but at the beginning of December 2004 the Bahraini Information Minister called on Iran not to interfere in his country's domestic affairs.[18] Iran's dealings with Oman have meanwhile proceeded on a relatively cooperative basis and President Mohammad Khatami made an official visit to Muscat in October 2004 at the invitation of Sultan Qaboos.

Afghanistan and Iran

Since the USA mounted its essentially unilateralist intervention in Afghanistan in pursuit of Osama bin Laden and his Taliban hosts in 2001, Afghanistan has become a new testing ground for a combination of NATO forces, the putative multinational force unit of the EU, Eurocorps,[19] and US force structures. Both the 9000-strong NATO-led International Security Assistance Force (ISAF) in the centre and north of the country and the 18 000 US troops pursuing the Taliban remnants and al-Qaeda in the south have come in for criticism for failing to achieve their goals.[20] Towards the end of 2004 there was disagreement

[13] IRNA, 'Foreign ministry spokesman says Persian Gulf islands integral parts of Iran', BBC Monitoring, 6 Apr. 2005.

[14] IRNA, 'Kuwaiti premier's senior adviser meets Iran's envoy', BBC Monitoring, 13 May 2004.

[15] IRNA, 'Iran sends "blunt warning" to Qatar over fishing boats attack', 13 June 2004, URL <http://www.irna.com/en/>; 'Iran seizes two Qatar boats in latest Gulf dispute', Khaleej Times Online, URL <http://www.khaleejtimes.com>; and 'Iranian security forces detain 22 UAE fishermen', Radio farda.com, URL <http://www.radiofarda.com>.

[16] IRNA, 'Iran and UAE strengthen environment cooperation', BBC Monitoring, 2 Feb. 2005.

[17] IRNA, 'Iran, UAE discuss bilateral, regional ties', BBC Monitoring, 7 Feb. 2005.

[18] MENA News Agency (Cairo), 'Bahrain asks Iran not to "interfere", denies delaying GCC summit', BBC Monitoring, 1 Dec. 2004.

[19] See the Eurocorps Internet site at URL <http://www.eurocorps.org>. On the missions in Afghanistan see chapter 3 in this volume, especially table 3.2.

[20] Girardet, E., 'The west must not let Afghanistan down again', *Financial Times*, 5 Oct. 2004, p. 15; and Risen, J. and Rohde, D., 'Hunt for bin Laden is stymied in the wilds of Pakistan', *International Herald Tribune*, 14 Dec. 2004, p. 7.

in NATO over US proposals that the forces be amalgamated under NATO and thence, potentially, US command.[21] However, when they met in February 2005 NATO defence ministers did agree in principle to place all Western troops in Afghanistan under NATO command, although the modalities and timetable had still to be worked out. Expectations are that the transition will be completed by the time the UK is due to assume command of the NATO forces in Afghanistan in February 2006.[22]

At stake is more than the question of the US role in NATO. Of concern is how to combine a peacekeeping operation with a war-fighting one. A parallel problem emerged on the question of aid disbursement, when the medical charity Médecins Sans Frontières (MSF), having operated in Afghanistan for many years, decided to withdraw. MSF, like some other non-governmental organizations (NGOs), feared for both the safety of its personnel and the feasibility of its operations. The use of aid distribution by US forces as a tool for securing the cooperation of the local population undermined the ability of humanitarian workers to operate as neutral providers of care and development assistance.

The Afghan presidential elections in October 2004, organized and monitored under UN auspices, did go forward in a manner deemed sufficiently free and fair to constitute a positive development on the path to restoring internal stability. The victor, President Hamid Kharzai, curbed the power of some of the warlords who represent a challenge to central authority.[23] Yet the re-emergence of wide-scale opium production and a thriving drugs trade remains a threat to the future development of the country and security operations.[24]

Drug trafficking across the border into Iran has long been a concern for the Iranian authorities. According to Iranian Foreign Minister Kamal Kharrazi, some 4000 officials of the various Iranian counter-narcotics agencies have lost their lives in combating the problem.[25] Cooperation with the authorities in Kabul on countering the illicit trade is among the security issues that have featured in bilateral Afghan–Iranian relations. Policing their mutual border is another issue, and in March 2004 it was announced that 10 new border checkpoints had been opened as part of a plan to construct 25 in total (15 in Herat, 3 in Farah and 7 in the Nimroz provinces of Afghanistan).[26] The issue of Afghan refugees in Iran also affects Afghan–Iranian relations. Some Afghans have voiced their appreciation for Iranian assistance to refugees during the years of conflict in Afghanistan, while others criticize Iran for exploiting them

[21] Dombey, D., Koch, R. and Burnett, V., 'Differences over Afghan roles clouds Nato talks', *Financial Times*, 14 Oct. 2004, p. 7. See also chapter 1 in this volume.

[22] Spiegel, P., 'Nato gets all-clear to assume full Afghan command', *Financial Times*, 11 Feb. 2005, p. 2; and Dempsey, J., '2 Afghanistan missions to merge', *International Herald Tribune*, 11 Feb. 2005, p. 2.

[23] Associated Press, 'Warlords lose power in new Karzai cabinet', *International Herald Tribune*, 24–26 Dec. 2004., p. 5.

[24] Walsh, D., 'Karzai victory plants seeds of hope in fight to kick Afghan opium habit', *The Guardian*, 1 Jan. 2005. See also chapter 3 in this volume.

[25] Afghanistan Television (Kabul), 'Afghan president, Iranian foreign minister discuss narcotics, ties', BBC Monitoring South Asia, 7 Dec. 2004 (in Dari).

[26] Voice of the Islamic Republic of Iran (Mashhad), 'Iran to build more checkpoints along Afghan border', BBC Monitoring, 12 Mar. 2004 (in Dari).

to gain financial aid from the UN and other bodies.[27] In any case, under an agreement with the UN High Commissioner for Refugees (UNHCR), a process of repatriation is under way and the Iranian authorities are no longer willing to receive new refugees.

Iran has pledged to spend $250 million on development and construction projects in Afghanistan, including roads and a railway link. The possibility of Iranian involvement in training Afghan army officers was also discussed in early 2005. Relations at the government level appear to be more than formally correct, with Iran not only backing the basic law adopted by the Afghan Loya Jirga (Grand Council) in January 2004, but also supporting the subsequent election of President Kharzai, who made an official visit to Tehran in January 2005 at the head of a high-ranking political and economic delegation.

The Arab Gulf states

Rivalries between the member states of the GCC did not pose a significant problem in 2004 since most border disputes had been settled in recent years. However, the Qatari Government continued to cause irritation in other Arab capitals with some of its policy pronouncements, which not only embrace the US agenda for political and educational reform in the region, but also make other states look less responsive by comparison. Most irritating to other states in the region, however, is the critical news coverage of the satellite television channel Al Jazeera, which is based in Doha.

Qatar, in common with the other smaller member states of the GCC, can nevertheless still rely on its close relations with the USA to shield it from overbearing pressure from its principal critic, Saudi Arabia. This factor, together with the Saudi rulers' preoccupations with their own internal security concerns, has recently produced a shift away from the erstwhile predominance of Saudi Arabia in the internal power balance in the GCC. The question of the GCC's as yet unrealized potential to develop into a collective security structure is raised below.

Syria

Syria is still officially at war with Israel, and Syrian proposals that peace talks be resumed have been rebuffed by Israel, pending Syrian action to curb Palestinian militant groups and end the Syrian presence in Lebanon. In November 2003 Israel conducted an air attack on a site not far from Damascus, which Israel claimed housed Palestinian terrorist groups. Skirmishes continued between the Lebanese Hezbollah and Israel in the disputed border area (between Syria, Lebanon and Israel) known as Shebaa Farms. Syria—like Iran—has been repeatedly criticized by the USA, Israel and some

[27] Balkh Television (Mazar-e Sharif), 'North Afghan party official, Iranian envoy hail ties', BBC Monitoring, 23 May 2004 (in Dari); and Herat News Centre, 'Afghan agency criticises treatment of Afghan refugees by Iran', BBC Monitoring South Asia, 9 Jan. 2005 (in Dari).

European states for giving support to Hezbollah in Lebanon and to the Palestinian Islamist movements Hamas and Islamic Jihad. In May 2004 the Administration of President George W. Bush activated sanctions on Syria called for under the Syria Accountability and Lebanese Sovereignty Restoration Act, passed by the US Congress at the end of 2003.[28]

The Syrian presence in Lebanon, sanctioned by the Taif Agreement of 1989, which brought the Lebancse civil war to a close, was partially justified by Syria at the time on the basis of the Israeli occupation of the south of Lebanon.[29] Israel withdrew from Lebanon in May 2000 and UN Security Council Resolution 1559,[30] sponsored by France and the USA, called for the Syrian troops (which then numbered around 14 000) to withdraw from Lebanon, as well as the disarming of Hezbollah and Palestinian militias there, and deployment of the Lebanese Army to the border with Israel. In his State of the Union Address on 2 February 2005 US President Bush stated: 'Syria still allows its territory, and parts of Lebanon, to be used by terrorists who seek to destroy every chance of peace in the region'. He added that his administration expected the Syrian Government to 'end all support for terror and open the door to freedom'.[31] The same month the Israeli Defence Minister implicated Syria in a suicide bomb attack in Tel Aviv for which a branch of Islamic Jihad claimed responsibility.

Matters came to a head on 14 February 2005 when former Lebanese Prime Minister Rafiq Hariri was assassinated in a bomb attack in Beirut. His funeral turned into a mass protest, uniting different Lebanese factions, against Syria. Members of the Lebanese opposition to the Syrian-backed government of President Emile Lahoud accused Syria of masterminding the assassination and the USA withdrew its ambassador to Syria and joined France and the UN in calling for a full investigation.[32] Although Syria denied culpability, it removed 3000 of its troops from Lebanon almost immediately.[33] Thereafter Syria reached agreement with UN envoy Terje Roed Larsen on a timetable for full withdrawal, which was completed by the end of April 2005.[34] Meanwhile, in the face of mass demonstrations in support of Hezbollah in Lebanon, President Bush somewhat modified his previous line on the organization, calling for it to lay down arms and confine its activities to the political sphere.[35]

[28] Syria Accountability and Lebanese Sovereignty Restoration Act of 2003, 12 Dec. 2003, URL <www.fas.org/asmp/resources/govern/108th/pl_108_175.pdf>; and US Department of State, 'Sanctions on Syria: implementing the Syria Accountability and Lebanese Sovereignty Restoration Act of 2003', 11 May 2004, URL <http://www.state.gov/p/nea/rls/32396.htm>.

[29] For the Taif Agreement see URL <http://www.mideastinfo.com/documents/taif.htm>.

[30] UN Security Council Resolution 1559, 2 Sep. 2004, URL <http://www.un.org/Docs/sc/unsc_resolutions04.html>.

[31] The White House, Office of the Press Secretary, 'State of the Union Address', Washington, DC, 29 Jan. 2005, URL <http://www.whitehouse.gov/news/releases/2002/01/20020129-11.html>.

[32] 'Lebanon will work with UN', *International Herald Tribune*, 21 Feb. 2005, p. 5.

[33] Khalaf, R., 'Lebanon to move Syrian troops to ease crisis', *Financial Times*, 25 Feb. 2005, p. 5.

[34] Wallis, W. and Khalaf, R., 'Syria to pull out of Lebanon "by end of month"', *Financial Times*, 3 Apr. 2005.

[35] 'Bush: Hezbollah could enter Lebanon's political mainstream', CNN.com, 15 Mar. 2005, URL <http://www.cnn.com/2005/ALLPOLITICS/03/15/bush.hezbollah/>.

Turkey

In 2004 fears that Turkey might intervene in northern Iraq to counter the emergence of separatist tendencies in Iraqi Kurdistan proved baseless, averted by diplomatic contacts across the border. The USA abandoned all hope of involving Turkish troops in the multinational coalition in Iraq, in the face of both Kurdish and Arab opposition. Instead, 2004 witnessed an improvement in relations between Turkey and both Iran and Syria. The three countries share borders and interests, including not wanting to see Iraq fragment or Kurdish nationalism threaten their own national cohesion. In addition, the fact that the Turkish Parliament had voted against allowing the USA to use Turkey as a second front for the invasion of Iraq in March 2003[36] paved the way for improved Arab–Turkish and Iranian–Turkish relations, even if it caused some dismay in Washington. Since those events, official Turkish–US relations have recovered somewhat, although not to the level of intimacy characteristic of the cold war years. Turkey's alliance with Israel remains in place but is pursued with less enthusiasm by Turkey than was the pattern in the 1990s.

Circumstances have changed, and with the rise to power of the Justice and Development Party (AKP) Turkish democracy has brought an end to the dominance of the overtly secular elite, backed by the military. Contrary to various theories about how a government with conservative Islamic values would behave, throughout 2004 the AKP leadership lobbied enthusiastically for full membership of the EU.[37] The USA backs Turkey's EU aspirations and gave strong support to Turkey's bid to gain candidate status for EU membership. Despite nervousness and some overt opposition in Europe, this goal was achieved by December 2004, albeit subject to strict criteria for actual entry.[38]

Egypt and Jordan

Developments on the Israeli–Palestinian front[39] following the death of Yasser Arafat, Palestinian Authority (PA) President and Chairman of the Palestine Liberation Organization (PLO), in November 2004, opened a window for renewed peace moves and Egypt took that opportunity to improve its relations with Israel. Having earlier launched an initiative to withdraw Israeli settlements and troops from Gaza, Israeli Prime Minister Ariel Sharon has posited a role for Egypt in assisting the Palestinians with internal and border security as and when an Israeli withdrawal from Gaza takes place, and Egypt is taking up the challenge. Following in Jordan's footsteps, in December 2004 Egypt also signed a trilateral agreement with Israel and the USA to facilitate access to US

[36] See also chapter 1 in this volume; and Cottey, A., 'The Iraq war: the enduring controversies and challenges', *SIPRI Yearbook 2004: Armaments, Disarmament and International Security* (Oxford University Press: Oxford, 2004), pp. 67–93.

[37] Boland, V., 'European Union candidacy: "Turkey is becoming a re-religious society and trying to join a post-religious Europe"', *Financial Times*, 5 Oct. 2004, p. 13.

[38] See the discussion of EU enlargement in chapter 1 in this volume.

[39] This subject is discussed more fully in the next section.

markets for goods made, with Israeli input, in their qualified industrial zones (QIFs).[40]

In early 2005 Egypt invited Sharon and newly elected Palestinian President Mahmoud Abbas to a summit meeting in Sharm al Sheikh, also attended by Jordan. The summit produced a handshake between Sharon and Abbas and a pledge to revive the peace process.

For its part, Jordan has embarked on a major programme of administrative, political and economic reform, headed up by Marwan Muasher, former Foreign Minister and now Minister in the Royal Court. As he argues plausibly, this is needed to tackle problems of unemployment and structural dysfunction, but it will run up against vested interests and may cause popular discontent before it delivers the intended benefits.[41] Jordan's principal problem, as discussed below, remains its vulnerable location, caught between the Israeli–Palestinian conflict on the one hand and the Iraqi maelstrom on the other.

III. Region-wide and transnational challenges

Section II illustrates how a core group of issues that combine security impact with political and normative resonance—the USA's presence and policies, the unresolved Israeli–Palestinian conflict and now also the spillover from the Iraq conflict—complicate both state-to-state relations and internal security for virtually every state in the region. These issues, themselves interrelated, are further examined in this section together with the 'new threat' (not so new in the Middle East) of terrorism.

The role of the United States

The US reaction to the 1978–79 Iranian revolution and the 1979 Soviet invasion of Afghanistan was to create a military capability to intervene directly in the Persian Gulf region, having previously relied first on the UK to police the sea lanes and thence protect the free flow of oil and then, after the British withdrawal of forces 'East of Suez' in 1971, on the Shah and the Al Saud dynasty as 'proxy policemen'.[42] From these early beginnings evolved the US Central Command (CENTCOM) with an Area of Responsibility (AOR) covering Central Asia, Afghanistan, Iran, Iraq, Pakistan, Saudi Arabia and the rest of the GCC states, plus Egypt, Jordan, Lebanon, Syria, Yemen and the Horn of Africa.[43] Direct US involvement in Persian Gulf security arrangements increased during the Iraq–Iran War but took on a new order of magnitude in the 1991 Gulf War to reverse the Iraqi occupation of Kuwait.

After the Gulf War the vast majority of the US forces deployed for Operation Desert Storm left the area, but a residual presence was retained in

[40] Saleh, H., 'Trade deal helps thaw for Israel and Egypt', *Financial Times*, 15 Dec. 2004, p. 6.

[41] Abdallah, S., 'Jordan: new cabinet', *Middle East International*, no. 737 (5 Nov. 2004).

[42] Potter and Sick eds (note 5).

[43] See the CENTCOM AOR Internet site at URL <http://www.centcom.mil/aboutus/aor.htm>.

Kuwait, Saudi Arabia and other GCC states, as well as at sea (a new Fifth Fleet was created and headquartered in Bahrain). The US Air Force (with British and, for a time, French support) policed no-fly zones over southern and northern Iraq and, along with some amphibious assault forces and the US Navy, maintained a forward presence to contain both Iran and Iraq under the policy known as 'dual containment'. Defence agreements were forged with each of the GCC states, joint exercises conducted with the indigenous forces and arms supplied to enhance their capabilities. Regular exercises were also conducted with the armed forces of Egypt and Jordan, with Egypt receiving a regular disbursement of US military and civilian aid through an arrangement dating from the Egyptian–Israeli Peace Treaty of 1979.[44]

The extent of the US involvement in Gulf security arrangements in the 1990s was such that former White House official Gary Sick portrayed the USA as a regional power rather than simply an external influence.[45] Dual containment, underpinned by UN sanctions on Iraq and unilateral US sanctions on Iran, effectively determined the oil fortunes of Iran and Iraq. Iraq could not legally export oil at all (except for a UN-sanctioned dispensation for supplies to Jordan) until the oil-for-food programme was agreed in 1996,[46] while commercial companies and governments were deterred from investing in the Iranian energy sector. Saudi Arabia was the principal beneficiary, doubling its oil output in the early 1990s to make up the shortfall left by Iraq.

Antipathy to the US presence on the Arabian Peninsula, in Saudi Arabia in particular, was one of the grievances against the USA and the Al Saud family propagated by Osama bin Laden, long before the attacks on the USA of 11 September 2001. Although not directly attributed to bin Laden, there were bomb attacks on US military personnel at Al Khobar, in Ash Sharqiyah (Eastern Province), Saudi Arabia in June 1996—causing a redeployment of those forces to a new base in the desert, at Al Kharj—and also on the office of a military liaison team in Riyadh. The USS *Cole* was the target of an attack in the Yemeni port of Aden in October 2000. Meanwhile, US CENTCOM developed a posture and strategy in the Persian Gulf to protect US interests, the first of which was defined as the security of oil supplies.

The US military had become part of the landscape in the Persian Gulf and the access agreements forged with the GCC states in the 1990s provided a platform for deployments to both Afghanistan and Iraq after 11 September 2001.[47] Viewed from the region, however, the US presence can be and is interpreted as foreign intervention in support of both US interests and friendly gov-

[44] For the treaty see URL <http://www.mideastweb.org/egyptisraeltreaty.htm>.

[45] Sick, G., 'U.S. policy in the Gulf: objectives and prospects', ed. R. Hollis, *Managing New Developments in the Gulf* (Royal Institute of International Affairs: London, 2000).

[46] On the oil-for-food programme see chapter 13 in this volume.

[47] Following the invasion of Iraq in 2003, an estimated 7000 US troops and aircraft previously deployed for 'operation Southern Watch' over southern Iraq were removed from Saudi Arabia and redeployed to new headquarters in Qatar. Kirk, C., 'American troops to leave Saudi Arabia', 5 May 2003, URL <http://www.voanews.com/specialenglish/Archive>; and Saudi–US Relations Information ServiceMission complete: Operation Southern Watch forces in Saudi Arabia deactivated', 30 Aug. 2003, URL <http://www.saudi-us-relations.org/newsletter/saudi-relations-interest-8-30.html>.

ernments, and not necessarily in the interests of the people in the region. Interpreted through the prism of historical experience and the machinations of the European states in the 20th century, it is depicted as a new form of imperialism. Across the Arab world, the invasion of Iraq in 2003 was received in this light and even the governments close to the USA warned against it, for fear of the unravelling of the regional order. Whether or not the USA will retain military bases in Iraq after it withdraws from a conflict role there—and on what terms—remains an issue of keen interest to local observers in this context.

The Arab–Israeli divide and the Israeli–Palestinian conflict

On the Arab–Israeli front, the second Palestinian uprising, or intifada, against the Israeli occupation of the West Bank and Gaza Strip (captured by Israel in the 1967 Six-Day Arab–Israeli War) entered its fifth year. In the second half of 2004 there was a marked decline in the incidence of suicide attacks by Palestinians on Israelis, which Israel would claim was due to the effectiveness of its military strategy and the construction of the 'barrier' between Israel and Palestinian population centres in the West Bank. In Gaza, Palestinian militants resorted to rocket attacks across the border fence with Israel, while the Israel Defence Forces (IDF) mounted a series of operations designed to secure the border areas and demolish buildings and vegetation used as cover by Palestinian gunmen.

By the end of 2004 divisions were apparent in the Palestinian community over how best to pursue their quest for independence. The militant groups Hamas, Islamic Jihad and the Al Aqsa Martyrs Brigade had suffered many casualties from Israel's 'targeting killings' of their leaders in the West Bank and Gaza. Basic economic, social and political activity in the Palestinian community had been severely disrupted by Israeli security measures, such as internal closures and installation of checkpoints between Palestinian population centres. The Palestinian police force had virtually ceased functioning, leaving ordinary citizens at risk from lawlessness as well as the armed struggle. Meanwhile, even though sympathy for the Palestinian cause had increased across the Arab world, Arab governments offered only criticism of Israel and calls for a resumption of peace efforts.

Peacemaking

Until the death of Arafat in November 2004, the Israeli Government repeated its contention that there was no Palestinian peace partner and blamed Arafat for encouraging and permitting Palestinian terrorism. It had officially accepted the 'road map' devised in 2002 by the Quartet (the EU, Russia, the UN and the USA) and launched in 2003 as the official approach to reviving peace negotiations by EU member states, the USA and some Arab governments.[48] However, Sharon made implementation of the road map dependent on the PA halting the use of violence against Israelis, disarming and arresting militants, and dismantling 'the terror network'. In late 2003 Sharon indicated that, in the absence of a partner for peace, he was developing a unilateral initiative.

The formulation of Sharon's disengagement plan proceeded along with the accelerated construction of the barrier in 2004. In April 2004, in an exchange of letters with President Bush, Sharon secured his acceptance that in any future peace agreement Israel would not be expected to give up the main Israeli settlement blocs in the West Bank and that Palestinian refugees could not expect to exercise the 'right of return' to anywhere inside Israel.[49] The USA was also sympathetic to Israel's construction of the security barrier, irrespective of an opinion reached in 2004 by the International Court of Justice (ICJ) that the route of the barrier contravened international law.[50]

However, Arafat's death enabled the USA to argue that the main obstacle to peace had gone. Following the elections held throughout the Palestinian territories with an approximately 65 per cent turnout on 30 January 2005, Sharon declared himself ready to deal with the new Palestinian president, Mahmoud Abbas, although he stressed the first priority should be implementation of his disengagement plan.

At the London meeting between the Palestinian leadership and members of the international donor community, on 1 March 2005: 'Participants re-affirmed thcir commitment to achieving a resolution of this conflict through direct negotiations leading to the goal of two states—a safc and secure Israel and a sovereign, independent, viable, democratic and territorially contiguous Palestine, living side by side in peace and security'.[51] The participants also reaffirmed their commitment to the road map and to the achievement of a 'just, comprehensive and lasting settlement consistent with the Road Map and based on Security Council resolutions 242, 338 and 1515'. In doing so, the participants went further than the Israeli leadership had anticipated they would: Israel had portrayed the meeting as being simply about Palestinian internal reform, including restructuring of the security services, and had justified its own decision not to attend on those grounds.

Despite this new round of international efforts, implementation of the Israeli Government's disengagement initiative looked set to hold the centre stage in the summer of 2005. This could take precedence over negotiations about

[48] US Department of State, 'A performance-based roadmap to a permanent two-state solution to the Israeli–Palestinian conflict', Washington, DC, 30 Apr. 2003, URL <http://www.state.gov/r/pa/prs/ps/2003/20062.htm>.

[49] Israeli Ministry of Foreign Affairs, 'Joint Press Conference: President Bush and PM Sharon', 14 Apr. 2004, URL <http://www.mfa.gov.il/MFA/Government/Speeches+by+Israeli+leaders/2004/Bush-Sharon+Press+Conference+14-Apr-2004.htm>; and The White House, 'Statement by the President', 14 Apr. 2004, URL <www.whitehouse.gov/news/releases/2004/04>.

[50] Dwan, R. and Gustavsson, M., 'Major armed conflicts', *SIPRI Yearbook 2004* (note 36), pp. 104–106.

[51] British Foreign and Commonwealth Office, 'Conclusions of the London meeting on supporting the Palestinian Authority', 1 Mar. 2005, URL <www.fco.gov.uk/Files/kfile/LondonMeeting010305_Conclusions.pdf>.

broader, long-term issues, while Israel will in any case continue to emphasize the need for a crackdown on Palestinian militant organizations as a prerequisite for implementation of the road map. Meanwhile, Palestinian refugee groups campaigning for the right of return still reject the idea of two states, on the grounds that this will only come about through sacrificing their rights. The reinvigorated peace process will therefore have to find a way to accommodate the refugees and compensate the Arab host countries if they are to be dissuaded from rejecting or sabotaging an agreement.

There has been, in effect, a fragmentation of the Palestinian people and cause, which could presage regional instability even if direct negotiations between the Israeli and Palestinians leaderships go forward.[52] Barely half of the 8 million or so Palestinians in the region live in the West Bank and Gaza. There are about 230 000 under direct Israeli control in East Jerusalem and around 1.2 million Palestinian citizens of Israel living within the 1967 borders of the Jewish state. Up to 300 000 Palestinian refugees live in camps in Lebanon, 400 000 are registered in Syria, and over half the population of Jordan is of Palestinian origin, many of them assimilated but 1.7 million still registered as refugees awaiting a formal verdict on their status.

As Chairman of the PLO, Abbas has inherited from Arafat responsibility for the Palestinian diaspora as well as the residents of the West Bank and Gaza. By early 2005 Abbas had gained the acquiescence of militant group leaders in the West Bank and Gaza to a cessation of violence pending the resumption of negotiations with Israel. It was on the basis of this that Abbas agreed a ceasefire with Sharon at Sharm al Sheikh in February 2005. However, when this was breached, apparently by a faction of Islamic Jihad with connections in Lebanon, if not Syria, the difficulties faced by Abbas were manifest. His ability to control the factions in the West Bank and Gaza is tenuous, and his capacity to control elements in either Lebanon or Syria is even less. Abbas himself has added his voice to Israeli complaints that Hezbollah is directly assisting militants inside the occupied territories with funds and training.[53] Thus the regional dimensions of the Arab–Israeli conflict persist, even though Egypt and Jordan have formally made peace with Israel, and Syria would be unlikely to want a direct confrontation.

The USA has designated Hamas and Islamic Jihad, as well as Hezbollah, as terrorist organizations—a move which *inter alia* rules out any question of their profiting from international aid—and is demanding that Iran and Syria cease assisting all three organizations. The EU, having already designated the military wing of Hamas a terrorist organization, moved to outlaw contact with its civilian cadres as well.[54] This move could make for diplomatic difficulties

[52] Abdullah, D., Palestinian Return Centre, 'Without the right of return the peace industry has no future in Palestine', *Return Review*, vol. 9, issue 1 (Jan. 2005), URl <http://www.prc.org.uk/data/aspx/d9/889.aspx>.

[53] MacAskill, E., 'Hizbullah is involved in West Bank, says Israel', *The Guardian*, 15 Oct. 2004, p. 21.

[54] European Commission, 'Mashreq, Palestinian territories, Israel: Council conclusions on the Middle East peace process', *Bulletin of the European Union*, Bulletin EU 6-2003, URL <http://europa.eu.int/abc/doc/off/bull/en/200306/p106082.htm>; 'EU blacklists Hamas political wing', BBC News Online,

in dealings with the Palestinians if Hamas, having made substantial gains in municipal elections, attains a significant presence in the Palestinian Legislative Council following elections initially scheduled for July 2005 or thereafter.

Iraq and the regional fallout

During 2004 the USA had 110 000–140 000 military personnel deployed in Iraq. Iraq is the centrepiece of US military engagement in the greater Middle East and accounts for the vast majority of US military expenditure in the US CENTCOM AOR. The number of personnel deployed by other nationalities serving with the coalition in Iraq averaged 23 000. A further 26 000 US and coalition personnel were deployed in Kuwait.[55] No armed forces of Middle East states are deployed with the coalition in Iraq, although Jordan is training Iraqi army and security forces in Jordan, and the GCC countries continue to provide basing facilities for the USA. Official estimates of CENTCOM troops deployed in the CENTCOM AOR[56] in April 2004 put the total at 200 000–225 000. There were 10 US Aerospace Expeditionary Forces in the region (around 17 000 airmen).[57] The US Navy Fifth Fleet is headquartered at Manama, Bahrain, and as of July 2004 the US naval presence consisted of one carrier battle group and one amphibious group with a marine expeditionary unit for a total of around 17 000 naval personnel.[58]

For Islamists and Arab nationalists outside Iraq, the resistance to the US and allied presence there is a cause célèbre.[59] For the USA struggling to restore some semblance of stability and security, its opponents are variously described as 'anti-Iraqi forces', subversive foreign elements, Jihadis, Saddamists, former Baathists and insurgents. Arab intellectuals will grant the presence of Jihadists—by which they mean radical Islamists, both Iraqi and foreign—but they prefer to characterize the opponents of the US and coalition forces as 'the resistance' rather than 'an insurgency', because the former sounds legitimate and the latter not. Most Iraqis who are prepared to venture an opinion for publication speak simply of fear for their personal safety and their horror at the tactics employed both by the USA and by their Iraqi and foreign opponents.

For much of 2004 US officials maintained that the insurgency was principally the work of foreign fighters and al-Qaeda elements. They accused Iran and Syria of facilitating the passage of such volunteer fighters across their borders into Iraq. Some senior figures in the US military as well as analysts in Washington offered different assessments of the resistance. They said that the

11 Sep. 2003, URL, <http://news.bbc.co.uk/1/hi/world/middle_east/3100518.stm>; and Morris, H., 'Hamas gains in Palestinian polls', *Financial Times*, 7 May 2005.

[55] 'US forces order of battle', GlobalSecurity.org, URL <http://www.globalsecurity.org/military/ops/iraq_orbat.htm >.

[56] CENTCOM AOR (note 43).

[57] 'US forces order of battle (note 55).

[58] 'US forces order of battle' (note 55).

[59] For a narrative of events in the Iraq conflict during 2004 see chapter 2 in this volume. The failure to find weapons of mass destruction is discussed in chapter 13 in this volume.

conflict was developing into a classic guerrilla insurgency, financed by former Baathists, some from outside the country, and conducted by several thousand (some estimates claim 40 000) local Iraqis,[60] aided and abetted by a minority of foreign Jihadis.

Even if Iraq's neighbours have not been directly engaged in the struggle inside Iraq, all of them have stakes in the outcome. Turkey has long kept an eye on developments in Iraqi Kurdistan, fearing that Kurdish separatism there could infect the Kurds in south-eastern Anatolia, where the Turkish forces fought a long and bloody campaign against separatists under the banner of the Kurdistan Worker's Party (PKK, Partiya Karkeren Kurdistan).[61] Iran is the champion of Shia Islam in the region.[62] The faithful make pilgrimages to the holy sites in Najaf and Kerbala in Iraq when political relations between the two countries permit. Iraq is the birthplace of Shia Islam, and Najaf and Kerbala are traditional seats of learning, only overtaken by Qom in Iran when the clerical leaders in Iraq were repressed by Saddam Hussein and Iran took on the mantle of defender of the faith.

Family ties also link Shia on either side of the Iran–Iraq border. Grand Ayatollah Ali Sistani is himself of Iranian origin, while Muqtada al-Sadr has connections in Qom.[63] The Iraqi opposition movements, the Supreme Council for the Islamic Revolution in Iraq (SCIRI) and the Dawa Party, found safe haven in Iran during the regime of Saddam Hussein and have since returned to Iraq to take posts in the interim authority and then the transitional government. Their combined list won 48 per cent of the vote in the January 2005 election.

During the 1980s, when Iraq was at war with Iran, Jordan served as the main conduit for Iraqi trade (including arms supplies) with the outside world and enjoyed an economic boom as a result. During the 1990s, when Iraq was under international sanctions, Jordan continued to supply the Iraqi market and maintained formal relations with the regime. Meanwhile, however, Jordan repaired relations with the USA, damaged by Jordan's refusal to join the US-led coalition that liberated Kuwait from Iraqi occupation in 1991. Consequently, following the invasion of Iraq in 2003, Jordan provided facilities for the US military and has since taken on the task of training Iraqi security forces in Jordan. Many Iraqi nationals have taken refuge in Amman from the violence in Iraq. The UN, other agencies such as the US Agency for International Development, and NGOs operate their assistance programmes for Iraq out of Amman.

During 2004 Jordan's King Abdullah voiced the opinion that Iraq's needs would best be served by a strong leadership dedicated to restoring security there, ahead of elections. On a trip to Washington, DC, in December 2004, he warned the USA that elections could deliver an Iranian-style clerical regime in Iraq and accused Iran of infiltrating around a million people across the border

[60] Figure used by BBC reporters discussing Iraq on BBC Radio Four, 3 Jan. 2005.

[61] Tisdall, S., 'Poll success fuels Turkish fear of Kurdish independence', *The Guardian*, 15 Feb. 2005, p. 13; and 'U.S. agrees to meeting with Turkey over Kurds', *International Herald Tribune*, 4 Jan. 2005, p. 3.

[62] See also chapters 2 and 3 in this volume.

[63] On Muqtada al-Sadr see chapter 2 in this volume.

to inflate the Shia vote.[64] In protest, Iranian Foreign Minister Kamal Kharrazi declined to join his counterparts from countries neighbouring Iraq at a meeting in Amman to discuss their mutual concerns, although he sent a delegation.[65] King Abdullah and his ministers meanwhile sought to galvanize Iraq's Sunni and secularist Arabs to participate in the elections to bolster this facet of Iraq's identity.[66] Such statements explain why Iran depicts the competition for power in Iraq as one between anti-Iranian Arab nationalism and a more 'inclusive' system, reflecting the country's mixed sectarian and ethnic composition.

The tribal communities across south-western Iraq have branches and relatives in both Syria and Saudi Arabia. Their tribal identities transcend their mixed sectarian affiliations, yet radical Salafis have allegedly proselytized their brand of the faith among tribesmen on either side of the Iraqi–Saudi border. There has been movement back and forth across that border of people and arms, reflected in the concurrent struggles against the authorities in both Iraq and Saudi Arabia in 2003–2004. In contrast to Saudi Arabia, where the ruling family governs in part through its alliance with the Wahhabi establishment, the Baathist regime in Syria is ideologically secular and Arab nationalist. Relations between Damascus and Baghdad were hostile during the 1980s and much of the 1990s. However, following the death of Syrian President Hafez al-Assad, his son and successor, Bashar al-Assad, was able to establish links with Saddam Hussein's regime and reopen the oil pipeline from Iraq, through Syria, to the Mediterranean coast.

For a few years preceding the invasion of Iraq, Syria defied the sanctions and profited from selling more of its own oil on the market while using cheap, illicit Iraqi supplies of oil for home consumption. After the invasion, the pipeline was again closed and the Syrian economy retreated into a parlous state. Syria failed to manage the situation to advantage, alienating the USA by encouraging Iraqi resistance, before bowing to US (and British) pressure and agreeing to cooperate with the USA in policing the Syrian–Iraqi border. However, benefits have not accrued to Syria. The USA continued to complain that Syria was not doing enough and allowing Iraqi Baathists to support the insurgency from Syria. These problems are still aggravating the other sources of Syrian–US tension described in section II above, even if Lebanon has (in early 2005) become the dominant focus.

Terrorism and crises of legitimacy

Terrorism is both a long-standing feature of the enduring conflicts in the greater Middle East and a 'peacetime' phenomenon in several societies. It

[64] Wright, R. and Baker, P., 'Iraq, Jordan see threat to election from Iran: leaders warn against forming religious state', *Washington Post*, 8 Dec. 2004, p. A01, URL <http://www.washingtonpost.com/wp-dyn/articles/A43980-2004Dec7.html>.

[65] Smyth, G. and Bozorgmehr, N., 'Jordan clash a threat to Amman meeting', *Financial Times*, 5 Jan. 2005, p. 4.

[66] 'Minister says Jordan protecting Iraq's Arabism by opposing Iranian interference', BBC Monitoring Middle East, 2 Jan. 2005.

both reflects and aggravates problems of state weakness and legitimacy. It has been markedly 'transnational' in character in this region, long before the emergence of the Saudi-rooted but globally active al-Qaeda. Since May 2003 Saudi Arabia has witnessed a number of terrorist incidents directed at the Al Saud ruling family as well as a continuation of attacks on expatriate targets in the kingdom. The Yemeni authorities are engaged in a counter-terrorism campaign against elements associated with al-Qaeda. Egypt and Jordan continue to arrest and interrogate nationals accused of involvement in global terrorist activities directed against the USA and allied Arab governments. In 2003–2004 Turkey was the scene of bombings aimed at 'Western' interests, including the British consulate and an HSBC bank in Istanbul.

In Egypt, Iran, Jordan, Syria, Saudi Arabia and the rest of the GCC, demonstrations are either banned or heavily policed, if not disbanded. Government security operations across the region are raising issues of human security. Cooperation between the regional and Western governments in tracking, apprehending and detaining terrorist suspects has raised concerns in legal professional and media circles that such measures jeopardize human rights.

The net effect of so much violence, overt and subtle, has been to fuel perceptions of a regional malaise, variously diagnosed as a crisis of regime legitimacy, 'a clash of civilizations', a new phase in anti-imperialist nationalism, religious and sectarian warfare, and a struggle over access to resources, in particular oil and oil revenues, in the context of economic and cultural globalization. Clearly, different factors or combinations of factors are at work in different parts of the region, although there are linkages and themes that transcend the situation in each of the countries concerned.

For strategists in or associated with the Bush Administration, loosely designated the neo-conservatives or 'neo-cons', the problem is twofold: (*a*) religiously inspired terrorism, as manifest in the September 2001 attacks on the USA; and (*b*) a populist reaction against oppressive regimes hitherto bolstered by successive US administrations in the name of 'realism'. The cure, according to this logic, is also twofold: to demonstrate that those using terrorism will never succeed, and to democratize corrupt regimes.

In contrast, according to opinion polls in a number of the countries in the region, many Arabs feel that the overriding problem is the neo-imperialist ambitions of the USA, aided and abetted by Israel, to control the region and its oil.[67] Such thinking is informed by popular interpretations of the historical record, including the deployment of US troops and armour, at the head of an international coalition, to reverse the Iraqi occupation of Kuwait in 1991, and the absence of a similar or effective diplomatic effort to reverse the Israeli occupation of Palestinian (and other Arab) land.

Arab opinion is of course informed by Arabic satellite television coverage of US military actions in Iraq and Israeli tactics in the West Bank and Gaza. There are those in the USA who argue that such footage is pure propaganda

[67] See, e.g., *Revisiting the Arab Street: Research from Within* (Center for Strategic Studies, University of Jordan: Amman, Feb. 2005), URL <http://www.css-jordan.org/new/REVISITINGTTHEARAB STREETReport.pdf>.

and a misrepresentation of the core issues. In any case, Osama bin Laden and others associated with al-Qaeda have highlighted the suffering of the Iraqi people and the Palestinians, over the years, as evidence of their oppression at the hands of 'infidels'. These themes surfaced in bin Laden's pronouncements even before September 2001, although his main focus has been on 'collusion' between the House of Saud and the USA and on the presence of Westerners in the holy lands of Islam.

Arab intellectuals and columnists, meanwhile, are concerned that defensible Arab causes are being hijacked by radical Islamists such as bin Laden and that the use of terrorist tactics such as suicide bombings and public executions targeting civilians have reached unprecedented levels of brutality and immorality. Such interlocutors express concern that their societies are indeed in crisis, as atrocities are tolerated and Islam is tarnished by association. Yet they rail against US policies in the region at the same time as they demand an end to corrupt and dictatorial practices by their rulers.

There is an overlap between the diagnoses of the US neo-cons and those of the Arab intellectuals. Both groups point to the UN Development Programme (UNDP) Arab Human Development Reports[68] of recent years as incisive appraisals of the ills that characterize Arab societies and the remedies needed. However, where they disagree is on the role of the USA in delivering the necessary cures. A collection of public opinion polls, conducted in 2004 by a consortium of Arab institutions in Egypt, Jordan, Lebanon, Syria and the Palestinian Territories, found that respondents admire the values espoused by the USA, including democracy and human rights, but they are deeply opposed to US policies in the region, particularly in Iraq and in support of Israel.[69]

Disagreement over the drafting of a UNDP Arab Human Development Report in 2004 revealed the core elements in the contending views of the region. Reportedly, the USA objected to passages in the draft which referred to the occupation of the West Bank and Gaza and the US presence in Iraq as problems requiring remedy in the interests of reform and development in the region. Egypt apparently objected to passages critical of Egyptian government practices. The resulting furore held up publication of the 2004 report.[70]

IV. Military spending

Governments across the Middle East continue to devote significant proportions of revenue to defence. SIPRI data on military expenditure indicate that regional military spending in the Middle East has increased almost continu-

[68] United Nations Development Programme (UNDP), Regional Bureau for Arab States, 'Arab Human Development Report 2003', URL <http://www.rbas.undp.org/ahdr2.cfm?menu=9>; and UNDP, Regional Bureau for Arab States, 'Arab Human Development Report 2004', URL <http://cfapp2.undp.org/rbas/ahdr2.cfm?menu=12>.

[69] *Revisiting the Arab Street* (note 67).

[70] Fattah, H. M., 'Arab report to UN asks vast reform in Mideast', *International Herald Tribune*, 6 Apr. 2005; and Khalaf, R., 'Reforms in Arab world "are largely cosmetic"', *Financial Times*, 6 Apr. 2005.

Table 5.1. Armed forces in the greater Middle East, as of July 2004

Country	Population	Army	Navy	Air force	Total armed forces
Bahrain	724 000	8 500	1 200	1 500	**11 200**
Egypt	71 931 000	320 000	20 000	30 000	**370 000**
Iran	68 920 000	350 000	18 000	52 000	**420 000**
Iraq	25 175 000	. .	. .	. .	**35 000**[a]
Israel	6 433 000	125 000	8 000	35 000	**168 000**
Jordan	5 473 000	85 000	500	15 000	**100 500**
Kuwait	2 521 000	11 000	2 000	2 500	**15 500**
Lebanon	3 653 000	70 000	1 100	1 000	**72 100**
Oman	2 851 000	25 000	42 000	4 100	**71 100**
Qatar	610 000	8 500	1 800	2 100	**12 400**
Saudi Arabia	24 217 000	75 000	15 500	18 000	**108 500**
Syria	17 800 000	200 000	7 500	35 000	**242 500**
Turkey	71 325 000	402 000	52 750	60 100	**514 850**
UAE	2 995 000	44 000	2 500	4 000	**50 500**
Yemen	20 010 000	60 000	1 700	5 000	**66 700**

[a] Estimated required strength; Iraqi Police Service not included.

Sources: World Health Organization (WHO), *World Health Report 2005: Make Every Mother and Child Count* (WHO: Geneva, 2004), URL <http://www.who.int/whr/2005/en/>; and International Institute for Strategic Studies (IISS), *The Military Balance 2004/2005* (Oxford University Press: Oxford, 2004).

ously throughout the period 1996–2004, reaching $56.1 billion in 2004 (at constant 2003 prices and exchange rates).[71] While the biggest spenders in the region rank nowhere near the world's biggest (USA, UK, France, Japan and China are the top five, in that order), Saudi Arabia ranks 9th, Israel 12th and Turkey 14th in terms of military expenditure.[72] Table 5.1 presents data on the armed forces of 15 countries in the Middle East.

Although the region lacks any kind of negotiated restraint on conventional force levels, and thus arms races of all kinds are a permanent possibility and concern, world attention since 2001 has focused especially on acquisitions that could be relevant to weapons of mass destruction (WMD) and their means of delivery, notably missiles. In 2004 Iran developed new missile capabilities. In September a test launch of the Shahab-3 intermediate-range ballistic missile indicated that it could have exceeded its previous best range of 1000 km.[73] The test coincided with large-scale military exercises in western Iran, and was described by Iranian officials as 'an attempt to bolster deterrence against any Israeli or military strike on Iran's nuclear facilities'.[74] At the beginning of October Hashemi-Rafsanjani, Chairman of the Iranian Expediency Council,

[71] See table 8A.1 in this volume.

[72] See table 8.3 in this volume. A brief summary of military expenditure trends in the Middle East is given in chapter 8 in this volume.

[73] 'Iranian missile tests focus minds on GCC defence', *Gulf States Newsletter*, vol. 28, no. 742 (1 Oct. 2004), pp. 5–6.

[74] Ben-David, A., 'Iran unveils redesigned Shahab missile', *Jane's Defence Weekly*, vol. 41, no. 39 (29 Sep. 2004), p. 6.

said that Iran possessed missiles with a range of 2000 km.[75] Israeli commentators meanwhile claimed that the enhanced Shahab missile could be capable of carrying a nuclear warhead. Although it did not state that Iran was in possession of such a warhead, Israel openly expressed fears that Iran's civil nuclear power programme had a secret military component.

For its part, Israel proceeded with tests of its Arrow anti-ballistic missile system in 2004. Israel's missile arsenal includes the C50 Jericho II, claimed to have a range of at least 1500 km.[76] Analysts believe this missile is capable of carrying a nuclear warhead, at least 200 of which Israel is thought to possess, although Israeli government policy is neither to confirm nor deny whether this is the case.[77] Israel was also actively developing its cruise missile capabilities in 2004. In June it was reported that Israel had developed a ground-launched version of its Delilah air-launched cruise missile, reportedly with a range of over 300 km.[78] The Delilah missile is not known to have a nuclear capability. There were also unconfirmed media reports that Israel had developed a sea-based nuclear deterrent in the form of nuclear-armed modified Harpoon anti-ship missiles deployed on its German-built Dolphin class submarines.[79]

Iranian announcements on its missile programmes also indicated plans to develop a maritime cruise missile called Ra'ad, which is not known to have a nuclear capability.[80] There is speculation, however, that some Iranian claims may be for propaganda (or deterrent) purposes, rather than accurate accounts of Iranian capabilities. Even so, the EU, the International Atomic Energy Agency (IAEA), Israel and the USA harbour varying levels of suspicion about the peaceful nature of Iran's nuclear programme, which can only be reinforced by the evidence of its missile development programmes and by the rhetoric surrounding these. The story of European and US efforts to clarify and resolve the Iranian nuclear issue is told elsewhere in this yearbook.[81]

That Iran is increasing its general military advantage in relation to the GCC states seems beyond doubt.[82] The impetus for the GCC states is there to improve their air defence capabilities, although in 2004 they made no major new acquisitions in this respect, concentrating on the integration of equipment delivered under earlier contracts and on consolidation of their existing capabil-

[75] 'Iran "increases missile range"', BBC News Online, 5 Oct. 2004, URL <http://news.bbc/co.uk/1/hi/world/middle_east/3716490.stm>.

[76] 'Jericho 2', GlobalSecurity.org, URL <http://www.globalsecurity.org/wmd/world/israel/jericho-2.htm>. On Israeli nuclear forces see appendix 12A in this volume.

[77] Vause, J., 'Israel's "bomb in the basement"', CNN.com, 21 Apr. 2004, URL <http://edition.cnn.com/2004/WORLD/meast/04/21/israel.vanunu.vause/>.

[78] Ben-David, A., 'Israel develops ground-launched Delilah missile', *Jane's Defence Weekly*, vol. 41, no. 24 (16 June 2004), p. 10.

[79] 'Israel to acquire 2 more German submarines', *Maariv International* (Internet edn), 22 Dec. 2004, URL <http://www.maarivintl.com/index.cfm?fuseaction=article&articleID=12098>.

[80] Hewson, R., 'Iran ready to field maritime cruise missiles', *Jane's Defence Weekly*, vol. 41, no. 8 (25 Feb. 2004), p. 13.

[81] See chapter 12 in this volume.

[82] Blanche, E., 'Winds of change: the Gulf Co-operation Council states are adjusting to major shifts in the security environment', *Jane's Defence Weekly*, vol. 42, no. 6 (9 Feb. 2005), pp. 28–37.

ities. There was also little progress made on developing a joint defence capability or making GCC forces interoperable, although some of their systems are interoperable with those of the USA. The GCC states are not considered to have capabilities or ambitions to acquire chemical or biological weapons, although other US allies in the region, notably Israel but also Egypt, are thought to have experimental programmes as part of their defence arrangements.

Syria has long been suspected of seeking some level of chemical weapon capability, but it did initial an Association Agreement with the EU in late 2004 that included a clause renouncing WMD.[83] In January 2005 the USA indicated strong opposition to the possibility of Russia's supplying an updated version of the Scud missile to Syria, reportedly capable of 'pinpoint strikes against targets within a 300-km range, which would include all Israeli territory'.[84]

V. Regionalism and cooperation

Various multilateral organizations based elsewhere have become involved in the greater Middle East, including the EU, NATO, the Group of Eight (G8) industrialized nations, the Quartet focusing on the Israeli–Palestinian conflict, the UN and related bodies, notably the IAEA. NATO and the EU in particular have recently developed new initiatives and extended partnerships which, along with active US diplomacy and interventions, could have a transformative effect. While less robust than the initiatives instigated at the international level, within the region the Arab League has pledged to promote political reform in conjunction with the pursuit of Middle East peace. At the subregional level, the GCC continues to espouse both economic and security cooperation among its member states, and the February 2004 Agadir Agreement, signed by Jordan, Egypt, Algeria and Morocco, is designed to create a free trade area between the signatories.[85]

NATO

NATO involvement in Afghanistan and Iraq has increased. At their summit meeting in Brussels on 22 February 2005, NATO heads of state and government announced the expansion of the ISAF operation to the western part of Afghanistan and their intention to provide additional forces for the anticipated National Assembly elections. On Iraq, they issued the following statement:

[83] European Commission, 'EU and Syria mark end of negotiations for an Association Agreement', Brussels, 19 Oct. 2004, URL <http://europa.eu.int/comm/external_relations/syria/intro/ip04_1246.htm>. On the status of the agreement see European Commission, 'Association agreements', URL <http://europa.eu.int/comm/external_relations/euromed/med_ass_agreemnts.htm>.

[84] Gollust, D., 'US Opposes Russian missile sale to Syria', Voice of America, 12 Jan. 2005, URL <http://www.voanews.com/english/2005-01-12-voa52.cfm>.

[85] European Commission, 'Commissioner Patten attends signature of Agadir Agreement', Brussels, 24 Feb. 2004, URL <http://europa.eu.int/comm/external_relations/euromed/news/ip04_256.htm>.

> The Iraqi people have shown enormous courage in shaping their own future at the election booth. Reaffirming Iraq's sovereignty, unity, and territorial integrity, we are united in our commitment to support them and their newly-elected government in their effort to build an inclusive democracy and secure nation. Consistent with UNSC Resolution 1546, all 26 Allies are contributing to the NATO mission to assist in training Iraqi security forces, to hasten the day when they can take full responsibility for the stability of the country and the security of its citizens.[86]

During the visit of US Secretary of State Condoleezza Rice to NATO headquarters, and at a meeting of NATO defence ministers in Nice, in early 2005 the possibility of a role for NATO forces in implementation of a future Israeli–Palestinian peace agreement was raised. No decision was taken to prepare for such a role, but the idea was considered serious.[87]

At their summit meeting in Istanbul in July 2004, NATO members agreed to enhance their Mediterranean Dialogue Initiative (originally launched in 1994) and launch a new Istanbul Cooperation Initiative (ICI).[88] The two initiatives are distinct but complementary. Initiated with a view to building confidence through dialogue and practical cooperation with the southern Mediterranean states, the NATO Mediterranean Dialogue has been progressively adapted in keeping with NATO's own changing priorities. It is intended to deepen bilateral relations with each of the partner countries (Algeria, Egypt, Israel, Jordan, Mauritania, Morocco and Tunisia) and to increase multilateral cooperation between them and NATO on airspace management, border security, counterterrorism, defence reform, civil emergency planning, military exercises, and training and education.

Thus far, the North African partner countries have shown most interest in cooperation on border security and fighting the war on terrorism; and even though historically this was not at the forefront of NATO's own agenda, the organization is identifying ways in which it can contribute to the task. Israel is interested in the possibilities of a more extensive relationship with NATO and is even debating whether it should seek membership.[89]

The Istanbul Cooperation Initiative emerged from discussions within NATO about expanded involvement in the Middle East, with the UK and the USA apparently looking for a single overarching approach incorporating the Mediterranean Dialogue and others cautioning against diluting the latter process. The ICI was designed to reach out to Middle Eastern countries, not only in the Mediterranean but also beyond, starting with the member states of the GCC.

[86] NATO, 'Statement issued by the Heads of State and Government participating in a meeting of the North Atlantic Council in Brussels', 22 Feb. 2005, URL <www.nato.int/docu/pr/2005/p05-022e.htm>. For list of individual contributions see 'NATO nations to offer assistance in training Iraqi military', *Kansas City Star*, 21 Feb. 2005, p. A15.

[87] 'NATO role eyed in M-E peace deal', *The Australian*, URL <http://www.theAustralian.news.com.au>, 3 Feb. 2005; and Bitterlemon-international.org, Middle East Roundtable, 'NATO and the Middle East', edn 6, vol. 3 (17 Feb. 2005), URL <http://www.bitterlemons-international.org/previous.php?opt=1&id=72>.

[88] See also chapter 1 in this volume.

[89] Dempsey, J., 'Israel explores closer link to NATO, even membership', *International Herald Tribune*, 3 Mar. 2005, p. 3.

Each partner country is invited to choose the substance of bilateral dialogue and cooperation from a range of options available to them, including: (*a*) enhancing political dialogue, at ministerial/Secretary General level; (*b*) achieving interoperability, a long-term process about procedures and communications in the field; (*c*) fighting terrorism; and (*d*) defence reform, wherein NATO provides advice on best practice for upgrading armed forces capability and budgeting.[90]

In December 2004 Kuwait became the first GCC country to be officially accepted into the ICI. The way ahead will be through practical cooperation, using the tools developed in the context of NATO's Partnership for Peace (PFP),[91] and building complementarity. The focus is on preventing funds from reaching terrorist groups, building counter-insurgency capacities and combating illegal arms trafficking.[92]

Conceivably, this focus could create an unbalanced relationship. WMD and terrorism affect South–South relations and potentially threaten the NATO members, but the latter do not pose the same danger to the Southern states. NATO itself has an image problem in so far as it is perceived as a vehicle for Western 'imperialist' or US national security agendas in the region. Moreover, while NATO can provide confidence-building measures in North–South relations, it must work in conjunction with the EU, the G8 and the USA to tackle more comprehensively the economic, social and political problems that underlie the inequitable distribution of public goods and hence instability and, ultimately, terrorism.[93] Cooperation between NATO and PFP countries on combating terrorism may, moreover, because of its impact on internal security governance, cut across or even contradict the political and economic reform initiatives of the EU, the G8 and the USA.

Arab security cooperation

Plans for a joint defence capability for the GCC date back to 1983, two years after the organization was formed. At the time Iran was deemed the primary threat, but after the end of the Iraq–Iran war in 1988 there were also concerns about Iraq. In any case, in 1984 the GCC member states constituted a joint force called 'Peninsula Shield', based at Hafr al Batin military city in northern Saudi Arabia. In November 2004 the GCC drafted a plan to increase the combined force level to 12 000 by 2010, fully equipped and trained with the most advanced weapons.[94]

From the early 1990s a three-tier defence arrangement for the GCC states has been envisaged, Tier I being the local hosting of US forces, Tier II a joint

[90] NATO 'Istanbul Cooperation Initiative', Policy document, 9 July 2004, URL <www.nato.int/docu/comm/2004/06-istanbul/docu-cooperation.htm>.

[91] For the members of the NATO PFP see the glossary in this volume.

[92] Independent Media Review Analysis, 'NATO recommends ties with Gulf Arab states', 17 Feb. 2005, URL <http://www.imra.org.il/story.php3?id=24171>.

[93] For more on international security and 'global public goods' see chapter 7 in this volume.

[94] Dow Jones and Reuters, 'Persian Gulf—GCC plans restrained military growth', Daily Defense News Capsules, 2 Nov. 2004, URL <http://www.factiva.com>.

GCC capability and Tier III the self-defence capabilities of individual states. The USA has encouraged the development of Tiers I and III but has allowed Tier II to await agreement within the GCC.[95] This has been impeded by separate acquisitions policies, internal rivalries and tensions, lack of agreement on the nature of the threats faced and reliance on the USA for protection. There has been some progress on the integration of command, control, communications, computers, intelligence, surveillance and reconnaissance (C^4ISR).[96] The achievement of a more effective integration of defence remains impeded, however, by conflicting priorities and interests.

In March 2005 the member states of the Arab League adopted the Algiers Declaration, pledging closer cooperation on a range of issues, including renewing: 'our attachment to a just and comprehensive peace in the Middle East as a strategic choice to settle the Arab–Israeli conflict, highlighting in this respect the Arab peace initiative adopted by the Arab summit in Beirut in the year 2002, the resolutions of the international legality, the Madrid conference which is based on the principle of land for peace'.[97] The Declaration goes on to enumerate the Arab League's position on a number of issues, including statehood for the Palestinians, resolution of the Palestinian refugee issue in accordance with UN General Assembly Resolution 194 of 1948,[98] resolution of the Syrian–Israeli dispute over the Golan and Shebaa Farms by return to the 4 June line,[99] and support for the restoration of Iraqi sovereignty and for the efforts of the Sudanese Government to deal with the conflict in Darfur, Sudan.

The members of the Arab League did not tackle the question of WMD in the region, although they have previously discussed a nuclear weapon-free zone in the region. The Algiers Declaration was perhaps most important for its restatement of Arab solidarity and the commitment of Arab governments to the principle of reform. In this respect the initiative was a response to US and other international pressure—although Arab proponents of reform continue to complain that there is more talk than action on this.[100]

Political reform, democracy and security

In June 2004 a series of initiatives were launched to promote human rights, democracy, civil society dialogue and economic reform in the name of regional security and counter-terrorism. The USA unveiled its Broader Middle East and North Africa (BMENA) Initiative, which had been in development since President Bush announced his intention to promote reform in the region

[95] 'More than 20 years of talk, but limited progress toward GCC defence integration', *Gulf States News Letter*, vol. 28, no. 748 (22 Dec. 2004).

[96] 'More than 20 years of talk, but limited progress toward GCC defence integration' (note 95).

[97] Algerian Television, 'Arab League summit adopts "Algiers Declaration"', BBC Monitoring, 23 Mar. 2005.

[98] 'Palestine—progress report of the United Nations mediator', UN General Assembly Resolution 194, 11 Dec. 1948, URL <http://www.un.org/documents/ga/res/3/ares3.htm>.

[99] The 4 June line refers to the line of confrontation between Israel and Syria the day before the start of the June 1967 war.

[100] Khalaf, R.,'Reforms in Arab world "are largely cosmetic"', *Financial Times*, 6 Apr. 2005.

in late 2003, with an aid package of around $70 million.[101] At the 2004 G8 summit meeting in Sea Island, Georgia,[102] this powerful economic grouping finalized and adopted the Partnership for Progress and a Common Future with the Region of the Broader Middle East and North Africa.[103] Shortly thereafter the EU launched its Strategic Partnership with the Mediterranean and the Middle East.[104]

The aims of thc EU and the US/G8 initiative are broadly similar, but to be pursued in parallel rather than jointly. The US/G8 initiative pledged action in three areas: the political, the social and cultural, and the economic spheres. The objectives included state reform, good governance and modernization as ingredients of democracy; education, freedom of expression and gender equality with an emphasis on reducing illiteracy among girls and women; and job creation in the private sector, expanding trade and investment, securing property rights and the promotion of intra-regional trade. The principal vehicle for carrying forward these goals is the Forum for the Future, bringing together the G8 members and 30 partner nations of the BMENA region. The forum met for the first time in Rabat, Morocco, in December 2004. The focus was on consultation between the foreign and economic ministers from the states involved, who reviewed progress on reform to date and discussed ways to take forward some specific initiatives.[105]

The EU's Strategic Partnership is an umbrella concept designed to give direction and coherence to Europe's relations with neighbouring countries in the Mediterranean and the Middle East. The initiative encompasses the Euro-Mediterranean Partnership (EMP), launched in 1995 with the Barcelona Declaration[106] and recently enhanced with the EU European Neighbourhood Policy,[107] as well as the EU–GCC Dialogue and bilateral relations with Iran, Iraq and Yemen. As most recently formulated in the EU's European Security Strategy of December 2003, the aim of the Strategic Partnership is the promotion of 'a ring of well governed countries . . . on the borders of the Mediterranean with whom we can enjoy close and cooperative relations'.[108]

[101] US Department of State, 'Fact Sheet: Broader Middle East and North Africa Initiative', 6 Nov. 2003, URL <http://www.state.gov/e/eb/rls/fs/33380.htm>.

[102] See also chapter 17 in this volume.

[103] 'Partnership for Progress and a Common Future with the Region of the Broader Middle East and North Africa, 9 June 2004, URL <http://www.g8usa.gov/d_060904c.htm>.

[104] 'EU Strategic Partnership with the Mediterranean and the Middle East' (note 2); and the EU's Mediterranean and Middle East Policy Internet site (note 2).

[105] US Department of State, 'Forum for the Future', URL <www.state.gov/e/eb/ecosum/future/index.htm>.

[106] The Nov. 1995 Barcelona Declaration is reproduced on the Internet site of the Euro-Mediterranean Partnership at URL <http://europa.eu.int/comm/external_relations/euromed/bd.htm>.

[107] 'Communication from the Commission: European Neighbourhood Policy Strategy Paper', European Commission document no. COM(2004) 373 final, Brussels , 12 May 2004, available at URL <http://www.europa.eu.int/comm/world/enp/document_en.htm>. See also chapter 1 in this volume.

[108] Council of the European Union, 'A Secure Europe in a Better World: European Security Strategy', Brussels, 12 Dec. 2003, URL <http://ue.eu.int/uedocs/cms_data/docs/2004/4/29/European%20Security%20Strategy.pdf>; and 'EU Strategic Partnership with the Mediterranean and the Middle East: Final Report', *Euromed Report*, issue no. 78 (23 June 2004).

Partnership and dialogue are identified as the cornerstones of the strategy, building specifically on the declaration of the Arab League at its summit meeting in Tunis in May 2004, which referred to working with the international community in the interests of prosperity and development of the Arab states and peoples. The primary EU concerns are good governance, democracy, the rule of law, human rights, gender, respect for the rights of minorities, cooperation on non-proliferation, counter-terrorism, conflict prevention and resolution, and economic development.[109] Among the intended responses are: promotion of a WMD-free zone in the Middle East, addressing migration issues, ensuring security of energy supplies, and promoting sustainable development.

The EU has designated 2005 as the 'Year of the Mediterranean' and in this, the 10th anniversary year of the launch of the EMP, the intention is to reinvigorate that Partnership, which aims above all to create a Euro-Mediterranean Economic Area by 2010. While progress has been made on the economic agenda, and partnership agreements have been concluded with Algeria, Egypt, Israel, Jordan, Lebanon, Morocco, the Palestinian Authority, Syria (put on hold after the assassination of Hariri) and Tunisia, hopes that the process would promote human rights, political reform and security cooperation have not been realized. As of 2004, however, the EU has insisted that all partnership and trade and cooperation agreements with the EU include a clause pledging the signatories to the renunciation of WMD.

Overall, the EU approach to political and economic reform in the Mediterranean and the Middle East makes maximum use of the instruments of 'soft power'. The EU provides billions of dollars as aid to the EMP countries alone, dwarfing US pledges under its BMENA Initiative. However, US preparedness to use 'hard power', demonstrated in Iraq, clearly has a galvanizing effect on attitudes in the region. In his Inaugural and State of the Union addresses in early 2005, President Bush expressed renewed determination to push democratization in the region and confront 'tyranny'.[110] Although France co-sponsored UN Security Council Resolution 1559,[111] demanding that Syria withdraw its troops from Lebanon and the EU echoed that call, it was US demands to this effect that generated the most fear of the consequences if Syria failed to act.

VI. Conclusions

The state system in the greater Middle East is both fragile and unfinished. The vision of a Palestinian state alongside Israel has been endorsed by the UN, the

[109] 'EU Strategic Partnership with the Mediterranean and the Middle East' (note 108).

[110] The White House, Office of the Press Secretary, 'President sworn-in to second term', Washington, DC, 20 Jan. 2005, URL <http://www.whitehouse.gov/news/releases/2005/01/20050120-1.html>; The White House, Office of the Press Secretary, 'President holds press conference', Washington, DC, 26 Jan. 2005, URL <http://www.whitehouse.gov/news/releases/2005/01/20050126-3.html>; and The White House, Office of the Press Secretary, 'President discusses war on terror', National Defense University, Fort Lesley J. McNair, 8 Mar. 2005, URL <http://www.whitehouse.gov/news/releases/2005/03/20050308-3.html>.

[111] UN Security Council Resolution 1559 (note 30).

USA, the EU, other members of the international community, the Arab League and the protagonists themselves. What shape it will take will depend on the willingness and ability of the Israeli and Palestinian leaderships to compromise and the continuing commitment of international players to assisting them.

Iraq is being reborn as a state and whether it will hold together is not certain. In any case, the old elite has been replaced by a new one, including Shia party leaders and Kurdish nationalists. This transformation may please Iran but is not greeted with enthusiasm among Iraq's other neighbours, all dominated by secular or Sunni elites and in the case of Saudi Arabia a traditionally anti-Shia religious establishment alongside the monarchy. Even if the governments in Iraq's neighbouring states do not cooperate with the insurgency, some ideologues and opportunists among their populations will. In the midst of this maelstrom it is unclear whether the USA is bogged down or destined to prevail.

The state system is not so fragile that it is about to unravel completely. Instead, the region looks set for another round in the zero-sum competition that characterized it for much of the 20th century. The travails of some players translate into the gains of others, not least in the competition for a share of the oil market. Energy resources and military alliances with the USA provide the smaller GCC states with a significance and independence that they might otherwise have lost to more powerful regional players. Yet, by hosting the US military, they open themselves, as Saudi Arabia has done, to accusations of collusion with infidels by al-Qaeda elements and imitators. Failure to make peace between Israel and the Palestinians will keep anti-US sentiments alive among Arabs who may not wish to take up arms but who will give a sympathetic hearing to Islamists and Arab nationalists working against the current regional order.

In this context the possibility that Iran will develop a nuclear weapon capability could spell the collapse of the international strategy to contain proliferation. Pre-emptive action by the USA might avert that spectre but would trigger a backlash of hostility not only in Iran but also across the region. However, the European states are working to find a diplomatic alternative and the importance of the issue could generate more transatlantic cooperation. Realization of the benefits of a collective regional approach to security may yet combine with fear of the alternatives to temper the pursuit of short-term and ultimately self-defeating strategies and conflicting interests.

6. Latin America and the Caribbean: security and defence in the post-cold war era

MARÍA CRISTINA ROSAS

I. Introduction

In the past 20 years the 35 countries of Latin American and the Caribbean have experienced dramatic transformations.[1] Throughout the 1980s, known as the 'lost decade', the economies of most of these countries suffered a severe recession. These countries had inherited a policy of import substitution from the Great Depression of the 1930s. The crisis of the 1980s was one of the main reasons why that policy was modified and an open-economy model of deregulation and privatization was adopted—the so-called Washington Consensus.[2] At the same time, several regional economic cooperation and integration initiatives developed,[3] which increased trust and opened the way for greater, although varying, degrees of interdependence among the countries of the region. In the political arena, most of the authoritarian regimes in the region fell and were replaced by democratically elected civilian governments.

Important changes have also taken place in the security domain. In the 1980s the region experienced armed conflicts in Central America: El Salvador, 1979–92;[4] Guatemala, 1982–95; and Nicaragua, 1979–90. Other conflicts involved Argentina and the United Kingdom (the 1982 Falklands/Malvinas

[1] For the purposes of this chapter, the region Latin America and the Caribbean comprises 35 states, in the following sub-regions: *Latin America*, including *Central America*—Belize, Costa Rica, El Salvador, Guatemala, Honduras, Mexico (note that in other contexts Mexico is often included in North or South America), Nicaragua and Panama—and *South America*—Argentina, Bolivia, Brazil, Chile, Colombia, Ecuador, Guyana, Paraguay, Peru, Suriname, Uruguay and Venezuela; and *the Caribbean*—Antigua and Barbuda, Bahamas, Barbados, Dominica, the Dominican Republic, Grenada, Guatemala, Guyana, Haiti, Honduras, Jamaica, Saint Kitts and Nevis, Saint Lucia, Saint Vincent and the Grenadines, and Trinidad and Tobago. For the sake of brevity, 'Latin American' is used to denote the larger region. 'The Americas' refers to the states of the Latin America and Caribbean region plus the United States and Canada.

[2] The Washington Consensus refers to economic reforms implemented by Latin American countries and, e.g., the International Monetary Fund, the World Bank, the United States Federal Reserve, the US Congress, etc. Williamson, J., 'What Washington means by policy reform', ed. J. Williamson, *Latin American Adjustment: How Much Has Happened?* (Institute of International Economics: Washington, DC, Apr. 1990), URL <http://www.iie.com/publications/papers/williamson1102-2.htm>; and Kuczynski, P.-P. and Williamson, J. (eds), *After the Washington Consensus: Restarting Growth and Reform in Latin America* (Institute for International Economics: Washington, DC, 2003), pp. 1–19.

[3] E.g., the Southern Common Market (MERCOSUR, Mercado Común del Sur) was formed in 1991. For the member states of MERCOSUR see the glossary in this volume. In 1994 the North American Free Trade Agreement (NAFTA), which includes Mexico, Canada and the United States was established. The Association of Caribbean States (ACS) was also establshed in 1994.

[4] In the civil war 75 000 people were killed, 8000 were reported missing and almost 1 million were displaced. Instituto del Tercer Mundo, *Guía del mundo 2003–2004* [Guide to the world 2003–2004] (Instituto del Tercer Mundo: Montevideo, 2004), URL <http://www.guiadelmundo.org.uy/cd/index.html>.

War);[5] Ecuador and Peru (1981);[6] Grenada (the 1983 invasion by the United States);[7] and Panama (the 1989 US invasion).[8] These conflicts were followed by peace processes which promoted national reconciliation and diminished tensions between neighbouring states in Central and South America. Even Argentina and Chile solved most of their border disputes in the 1990s.[9] In addition, the armed forces of Latin American countries were gradually placed under civilian authority and given new responsibilities in areas such as peace-keeping operations (PKOs).

Nonetheless, the region continues to face important security challenges. For example, its income distribution is the most inequitable in the world.[10] In the past 12 years, 14 political crises occurred and at least 11 heads of state stepped down before completing their terms of office.[11] Reform of the armed forces is

[5] Goldblat, J. and Millán, V., 'The Falklands/Malvinas conflict—a spur to arms build-ups', *World Armaments and Disarmament: SIPRI Yearbook 1983* (Taylor & Francis: London, 1983), pp. 467–527.

[6] Goldblat, J. and Millán, V., 'Militarization and arms control in Latin America', *World Armaments and Disarmament: SIPRI Yearbook 1982* (Taylor & Francis: London, 1982), pp. 411–14.

[7] On 25 Oct. 1983 the US Army invaded Grenada, after a political and military crisis in which Prime Minister Maurice Bishop was killed. Supported by troops of Antigua and Barbuda, Barbados, Dominica, Jamaica, Saint Lucia, and Saint Vincent and the Grenadines, the USA carried out the invasion, arguing that it was done for 'humanitarian reasons'.

[8] Lindgren, K. *et al.*, 'Major armed conflicts in 1989', *SIPRI Yearbook 1990: World Armaments and Disarmament* (Oxford University Press: Oxford, 1990), pp. 415–16.

[9] In 1991 Argentinian President Carlos Menem and Chilean President Patricio Aylwin signed a Presidential Declaration on Borders—ending 24 border disputes, 22 of which were resolved by establishing border limits. The Laguna del Desierto border dispute was resolved by international arbitration in 1994, and the Hielos Continentales dispute was resolved in 1998. Fabián Saín, M., 'Argentina frente a la seguridad hemisférica' [Argentina in face of hemispheric security], ed. M. C. Rosas, *Seguridad hemisférica e inseguridad global: entre la cooperación interamericana y la guerra preventiva* [Hemispheric security and global insecurity: between inter-American cooperation and preventive war] (Universidad Nacional Autónoma de México/Embajada de Canadá: Mexico City, 2004), pp. 273–74.

[10] The lost decade contributed to deterioration of the standard of living. The region suffered a dramatic economic setback and poverty increased. By 1990 poverty levels were higher than in 1970. In 1980, 35% of households lived in poverty; by 1990, the figure had increased to 41%. Even in 1994, when the economic situation was improving in the region, 39% of households remained in poverty. International organizations referred to the economic situation in Latin America and the Caribbean in 1998–2002 as a 'lost half decade'. E.g., in 2002 output in the region contracted by 0.5%, and real income per capita decreased by 1.9%; 7 million more people sank into poverty. UN Economic Commission for Latin America and the Caribbean (ECLAC), *The Equity Gap: Latin America, the Caribbean and the Social Summit* (United Nations Publications: Santiago, 1997); and 'Social panorama of Latin America 2001–2002', *ECLAC Notes*, no. 25 (Nov. 2002), pp. 1–3, URL <http://www.eclac.cl/prensa/noticias/notas/6/11256/NOTAS25INGLES.pdf>.

[11] This was the case *inter alia* in Paraguay (Juan Carlos Wasmosy, president 1993–98), Peru (Alberto Fujimori, president 1990–2001), Venezuela (Hugo Chavez, president 1999–2002), Argentina (Fernando de la Rúa, president 10 Dec. 1999–21 December 2001; Federico Ramón Puerta, president, 21–23 Dec. 2001; Alfonso Rodríguez Saa, president, 23 Dec. 2001–1 Jan. 2002; Eduardo Oscar Camaño, president 1–2 Jan. 2002; and Eduardo Alberto Duhalde, president, 2 Jan. 2002–25 May 2003), Haiti (Jean-Bertrand Aristide, president for 8 months in 1991, and in 1994–96 and 2000–2004), Bolivia (Gonzalo Sánchez de Lozada, president in 1993–97 and in 2002–2003), Paraguay (Raúl Cubas Grau, president from 1998 to 1999), and Ecuador (Abdalá Bucaram Ortíz, president 1996–1997; Jamil Mahuad Witt, president 1998–2000; and Lucio Gutiérrez, president 2002–Apr. 2005). For biographies see Centre for Research, Teaching, Documentation and Dissemination of International Relations and Development (CIDOB, Centro de investigación, docencia, documentación y divulgación de Relaciones Internacionales y Desarrollo), URL <http://www.cidob.org/bios>.

incomplete, although some goals have been met.[12] As recently as 1995, Ecuador and Peru used armed force in a border dispute.[13] Political and social crises are also a source of conflict.[14]

Section II of this chapter addresses the regional and sub-regional environment, and section III covers developments in regionalism and cooperation. Section IV analyses the prospects for cooperation or conflict. Section V discusses the participation of Latin American armies in PKOs, while section VI discusses Latin American–US relations before and after 11 September 2001. The conclusions are presented in section VII.

II. The regional and sub-regional environment

Latin America extends from the Mexican–US border south to Patagonia and includes all the islands of the Caribbean. It includes countries that were formerly colonies of Portugal and Spain and some that are neither Portuguese-nor Spanish-speaking, such as the former and remaining British, Dutch, French and US dependencies.[15] From 1915–20 until today, two political and geographical factors have principally shaped the region: the growing dominance of the USA, especially but not exclusively in the Caribbean, Central America, Colombia and Mexico; and the consolidation of national borders, achieved through either diplomatic negotiations or the use of force. Prior to World War I, Cuba, the Dominican Republic, Haiti, Mexico, and all the nations in Central America and South America existed as independent states. The first country to gain independence was Haiti, in 1804, and this first

[12] An important step in reform of the armed forces is the publication of White Papers. They have been published by Argentina (on national defence) in 1999 with a revised edition in 2001; Brazil (on national defence policy) in 1996; Chile in 1997 and 2002; Colombia (on defence policy and democratic security) in 2003; Ecuador in 2002; El Salvador (on defence, security and development) in 1998; Guatemala in 2003; Peru (a proposal) in 2004; and Uruguay (rules defined for a White Paper) in 1999. In 2003 the Dominican Republic presented a defence and security White Paper for presidential approval. Bolivia, Cuba, Honduras, Mexico, Nicaragua, Paraguay and Venezuela have not produced White Papers. Nicaragua is working on a White Paper, and in Mexico the need for a White Paper has been noted. Red de Seguridad y Defensa de América Latina (RESDAL), *Atlas comparativo de la seguridad y la defensa en América Latina* [Comparative atlas of security and defence in Latin America], URL <http://www.resdal.org/atlas/atlas-definiciones.html>; and Center of Research for Development (CIDAC, Centro de Investigación para el Desarrollo), *Threats and Challenges for Mexican Security* (Center of Research for Development: Mexico City, June 2004), p. 11.

[13] Aldana, S. *Las vicisitudes de un protocolo: Reflexiones sobre la historia del problema de límites entre Perú y Ecuador* [The rocky ground of a protocol: reflections on the history of the border dispute between Peru and Ecuador], URL <http://www.cipca.org.pe/cipca/frontera/Vicisitudes_protocolo.htm>.

[14] E.g., Bolivia, one of the poorest countries in the region, possesses vast natural gas reserves that currently have to be exported through Chile. In 2003 Bolivia restated an historic claim to the Atacama corridor (ceded to Chile in 1884) in order to secure access to a port for export of its natural gas. This led to increased tension between the 2 countries.

[15] Peña, O., *Estados y territorios en América Latina y el Caribe* [States and territories in Latin America and the Caribbean] (Era: Mexico City, 1989), p. 13.

'independence cycle' in the region finished a century later, in 1903, when Panama proclaimed its independence from Colombia.[16]

The second or late 'independence cycle' affected the Caribbean states and territories of various European nations in the Americas. The major Anglophone territories were emancipated one after another starting in 1962, when Jamaica and Trinidad and Tobago obtained their independence. Suriname, a Dutch colony, gained its independence in 1975. Several territories, however, are still dependencies of European powers: the UK has five island possessions;[17] the Netherlands possesses the Dutch Antilles and Aruba; and France has three overseas territories, one of them located in South America.[18] The political status of some territories also remains disputed. These include Puerto Rico, which is associated with the USA;[19] Guantánamo Bay, which is leased by the USA but claimed by Cuba;[20] and Navassa Island, which is occupied by the USA but claimed by Haiti.

Two additional territorial disputes in the region relate to, first, parts of the Antarctic, which are claimed by several Latin American countries, and, second, the negotiations on the 1982 United Nations Convention on the Law of the Sea (UNCLOS).[21] In the course of implementing UNCLOS, disputes have occurred between the Latin American and Caribbean nations and with neighbouring and other states.

Table 6.1 lists current interstate disputes as 'major', 'minor but active' or 'latent' disputes. The issue in contention is listed for territorial or border disputes. Given the economic and political transformations experienced by Latin American countries, it is possible that even disputes which have been regarded as 'major' can now be resolved peacefully. For example, on 10 September 2002, El Salvador submitted a request to the International Court of Justice (ICJ) to review the ICJ's decision of 11 September 1992 on the maritime, territorial and insular dispute between El Salvador and Honduras. The review

[16] Peña (note 15), p. 51. The term 'independence cycle' refers to specific periods in which a group of countries became independent.

[17] The British islands in the Caribbean are Anguilla, the British Virgin Islands, the Cayman Islands, Montserrat, and Turks and Caicos. In the South Atlantic area, the UK possesses the Falklands/Malvinas Islands, South Georgia and the South Sandwich Islands.

[18] The territories are French Guiana, Guadalupe and Martinique.

[19] Puerto Rico is not an independent country or a part of the USA. However, the US President is its head of state and it elects 1 representative to the US House of Representatives. Elections are held on the island to elect its governor. Indigenous inhabitants are US citizens but cannot vote in US presidential elections.

[20] After the victory over Spain in the 1898 Spanish–American War, the USA leased in 1903 the land and water of Guantánamo Bay for use as a coaling station. When the USA ended diplomatic relations with Cuba in 1961, many Cubans sought refuge on the base; US Marines and Cuban soldiers began patrolling the fence and continue to do so. 'US Naval Station, Guanánamo Bay, Cuba', URL <http://www.nsgtmo.navy.mil/>.

[21] The UN Convention on the Law of the Sea was opened for signature at Montego Bay, Jamaica, on 10 Dec. 1982 and entered into force on 16 Nov. 1994; it is reproduced in *The Law of the Sea: United Nations Convention on the Law of the Sea* (United Nations: New York, 1983) and is available on the Internet at URL <http://www.un.org/Depts/los/index.htm>. See also chapter 18 in this volume. On related disputes in the region see Peña (note 15), pp. 129, 144–45.

was conducted, and on 18 December 2003 the ICJ found the Salvadorean claim to be groundless.[22]

Apart from 'traditional' interstate conflicts, tensions exist because of rivalries between Latin American and Caribbean countries. For example, Mexico's interaction with the USA is complex and includes such issues as undocumented migration, drug trafficking, organized crime, border security and, since September 2001, the global war on terrorism. South of the Usumacinta River (the Guatemala–Mexico border), the Central American countries face similar problems (e.g., undocumented migration, poverty, natural disasters, and organized crime, including the so-called 'maras').[23] Rivalries between these countries, however, limit the possibilities of addressing these problems collectively for the benefit of the region. In the Caribbean, the colonial heritage survives and to some degree the sub-region may still be seen as an 'imperial frontier'.[24] Cuba, the largest Caribbean state, is the only Communist country in the region, and it remains in conflict with the USA, which in turn maintains an embargo against Cuba.[25]

In South America, the Andean sub-region[26] faces challenges similar to those of Central America: drug-trafficking, guerrilla activities, terrorism, fragile democracies and poverty. The ongoing civil war in Colombia represents a special challenge as the longest running armed conflict in Latin America, and its complexity has grown over time.[27] Colombian–Venezuelan rivalry extends beyond the border demarcation issue, since both countries aspire to leadership

[22] ICJ, 'Aplicación de la revisión del fallo del 11 de septiembre de 1992 en el caso relativo a la disputa fronteriza, marítima e insular entre El Salvador y Honduras. La Corte rechaza la solicitud de revisión efectuada por El Salvador' [Application for review of the case of 11 September 1992 as regards the dispute over the sea and coastal area between El Salvador and Honduras. The Court rejects the request made by El Salvador], *La Haya*, 18 Dec. 2003, URL <http://www.icj-cij.org>.

[23] 'Maras' refers to Marabuntas (swarming ants) that are common to the Amazon jungle, where they can become plagues. In Central America, Mexico and the USA the term 'maras' is applied to gangs whose members are very young and who are identified by their tattoos, loose clothing, and the violence they employ. They use particular gestures and terms that are a mixture of English and Spanish. The maras became established in Los Angeles, Calif., and began criminal activities in El Salvador, later expanding to Honduras, Guatemala, Nicaragua and Mexico. Their numbers are growing rapidly and their current membership is *c.* 200 000. They are considered threats to the national security of the countries where they operate. García Méndez, E., 'Las maras como sombras del pasado: los niños de la calle veinte años después' [The maras as shadows of the past: street children twenty years after], 25 Apr. 2005, URL <http://www.elfaro.net/secciones/opinion/20040321/opinion4_20040321.asp>.

[24] The 'imperial frontier' concept refers to the historical presence of the USA and major European, and even Asian (e.g., China and Japan) powers in the Caribbean. Bosch, J., *De Cristobal Colón a Fidel Castro: El Caribe, frontera imperial* [From Christopher Columbus to Fidel Castro: the Caribbean, an imperial frontier] (Alfaguara: Barcelona, 1970). An excerpt from the book is available at URL <http://www.cielonaranja.com/bosch_caribe.htm>.

[25] Peters, P., *U.S.–Cuba Bilateral Relations: Cooperation at Arm's Length* (Lexington Institute: Arlington, Va., Jan. 2001), URL <http://www.lexingtoninstitute.org/pdf/CubaRelations.pdf>.

[26] The countries of the Andean sub-region are Bolivia, Colombia, Ecuador, Peru and Venezuela.

[27] On Colombia see chapters 2 and 8 in this volume.

Table 6.1. Interstate disputes involving Latin America and Caribbean countries, 2004

Countries or regions	Causes of dispute
Major disputes	
Belize–Guatemala	Border demarcation
Bolivia–Chile	Territorial dispute over access to the Pacific Ocean; exportation of Bolivian hydrocarbons
Colombia–Nicaragua	Border dispute over San Andrés and Providence Islands
Colombia–Venezuela	34 border demarcation disputes; migration; guerrillas; smuggling; drug trafficking
Costa Rica–Nicaragua	Border demarcation; migration
Dominican Republic–Haiti	Migration; border demarcation
El Salvador–Honduras	Migration; International Court of Justice decision on border demarcation
El Salvador–Honduras–Nicaragua	Maritime border demarcation in the Gulf of Fonseca; exploitation of fishing resources
Honduras–Nicaragua	Maritime border demarcation in the Atlantic Ocean; migration
Trinidad and Tobago–Venezuela	Maritime borders; natural resources
Minor but active disputes	
Chile–Peru	Implementation of the 1929 Lima Treaty
Guyana–Suriname	Dispute over the axis of the territorial sea boundary; Suriname claims a triangle of land between the New and Kutari/Koetari rivers in a dispute over the head-waters of the Courantyne River
Latent disputes	
Argentina, Australia, Chile, France, New Zealand, Norway, UK	Sovereignty claims over areas of Antarctica
Argentina–UK	Falklands/Malvinas, South Georgia and South Sandwich islands
Cuba–USA	Guantánamo Bay
Guyana–Venezuela	Venezuela claims 40% of Guyana's territory
French Guiana–Suriname	Suriname claims the area located between the Litani and Marouini rivers, both headwaters of the Lawa River
Haiti–USA	Navassa Island

Sources: Mares, D. R., 'Securing peace in the Americas in the next decade', ed. J. I. Domínguez, *The Future of Inter-American Relations* (Routledge: New York, 2000), p. 36, adapted from Rojas Aravena, F., 'Latin America: alternatives and mechanisms of prevention in situations related to territorial sovereignty', *Peace and Security in the Americas*, no. 13 (Oct. 1997), pp. 2–7; and Cheyre Espinosa, J. E., *Medidas de confianza mutua: Casos de América Latina y el Mediterráneo* [Confidence-building measures: the cases of Latin America and the Mediterranean] (Centro de Estudios e Investigaciones Militares: Santiago, 2000), pp. 31–55. On Antarctica see Goldblat, J., Peace Research Institute Oslo/SIPRI, *Arms Control: The New Guide to Negotiations and Agreements* (SAGE Publications: London, 2002), pp. 190–95. See also table 2A.3 in appendix 2A in this volume.

in the Andean sub-region. Chile, a former member of the Andean Pact,[28] is a cause of concern for both Bolivia and Peru. In addition, the remaining South American countries tend to be influenced by Brazil—the largest country in South America, which shares borders with all the South American nations except Chile and Ecuador. Together with Argentina, Brazil initiated in the middle of the 1980s an integration process that led to the establishment, in 1991, of the Southern Common Market (MERCOSUR, Mercado Común del Sur), with the participation of Paraguay and Uruguay as full members and Chile, Bolivia, Mexico and Peru as associated members.

Although Latin American countries share similar problems, they have difficulty in tackling them collectively. An example is the foreign debt burden. In the 1980s, several attempts were made to bring together major debtors like Brazil and Mexico. The UN Economic Commission for Latin America and the Caribbean (ECLAC) sponsored meetings aimed at the establishment of a 'debtors club', capable of negotiating better conditions with the 'creditors club'. However, these efforts failed, and Brazil and Mexico signed separate agreements with their creditors. The Latin American and Caribbean countries appear to lack the political will to work together on issues of mutual concern. Moreover, large and influential countries, like Brazil and Mexico, maintain a rivalry that adds to sub-regional tension.[29] The many faces of this rivalry touch different areas of interest from trade to political and security matters. For example, economic disputes between Brazil and Mexico prevent Mexico from becoming a full member of MERCOSUR.[30]

In August–September 2000, Brazil sponsored the first South American Summit, on South American identity, which was held in Brasilia.[31] The

[28] The Andean Pact (the forerunner of the Andean Community) was created on 26 May 1969, when Bolivia, Chile, Colombia, Ecuador and Peru signed the Agreement on Subregional Integration (Cartagena Agreement). Venezuela joined in 1973, and Chile withdrew in 1976.

[29] The rivalry between Brazil and Mexico can be traced to colonial times. Palacios, G., *Intimidaciones, reconciliaciones y conflictos: México y Brasil, 1822–1993* [Intimidations, reconciliations and conflicts: Mexico and Brazil, 1822–1993] (Secretaría de Relaciones Exteriores: Mexico City, 2001); and Rosas, M. C., 'México y Brasil: ¿buenos enemigos o amigos mortales?' [Mexico and Brazil: good enemies or mortal friends?], *Estudos Humanidades*, vol. 31, no. 5 (May 2004), pp. 783–814.

[30] A critical element of Brazilian–Mexican relations relates to reform of the UN Security Council, on which Brazil has long sought a permanent seat (it has participated as a non-permanent member 9 times; Mexico has done so 3 times). Mexico has focused on disarmament, drug-trafficking and international cooperation. Brazil has emphasized issues related to environment, gender, development, hunger and technology transfers. On 22 Sep. 2004, together with India, Japan and Germany, Brazil formally applied for a permanent seat on the Security Council. Mexico has argued that enlargement of the Security Council would not effect true reform. With Egypt and Pakistan, Mexico has proposed creating a new category of semi-permanent members. Rosas (note 29); 'Le Japon, le Brésil, l'Inde et l'Allemagne veulent siéger au Conseil de sécurité de l'ONU' [Japan, Brazil, India and Germany want seats in the UN Security Council], *Le Monde*, 23 Sep. 2004, URL <http://www.lemonde.fr/web/article/0,1-0@2-3220,36-380233,0.html>; and 'Debaten reforma del Consejo de Seguridad' [The debate on the reform of the Security Council], *El Universal*, 23 Sep. 2004, pp. 1, 15.

[31] The summit meeting participants were Argentina, Bolivia, Brazil, Chile, Colombia, Ecuador, Guyana, Paraguay, Peru, Suriname, Uruguay and Venezuela. Mexico was not invited to attend, but president-elect Vicente Fox sent Jorge G. Castañeda (later Minister for Foreign Affairs) as an observer. Rosas, M. C., *La economía internacional en el siglo XXI: OMC Estados Unidos y America Latina* [The

summit meeting was designed to bring together MERCOSUR, the Andean Community[32] as well as Chile, Guyana and Suriname. The second South American Summit took place on 8 December 2004, when the establishment of the South American Community was proclaimed in the Cuzco Declaration.[33] Mexico is not part of the 'new' South American Community.

III. Regionalism and cooperation

Regionalism in Latin America and the Caribbean has evolved dramatically, from preferential trade arrangements during the cold war to ambitious cooperation and integration initiatives in the post-cold war era.[34] Björn Hettne and András Inotai have developed the concept of 'new regionalism' to distinguish this transition. Several regionalization initiatives took place during the cold war. Some of these were promoted by the superpowers and subordinated the interests and room for manoeuvre of the countries involved to the needs of either the Soviet Union or the USA. New regionalism differs from previous initiatives: (*a*) it takes place in the post-cold war era; and (*b*) unlike the 'vertical' cold war initiatives that often came from 'outside' and 'above' (*inter alia* from the superpowers), it goes beyond economic goals to embrace democracy, human rights, environmental and labour concerns, and the like. New regionalism seeks to contribute to conflict resolution by increasing cooperation, trust and confidence; it is 'horizontal' and the states within the region play the leading role.[35]

In terms of regional security, however, it should be noted that one of the reasons for the greater 'autonomy' experienced by the countries of Latin America and the Caribbean in the post-cold war era is the increased indifference of the global powers to them.[36] The countries of the region clearly do not receive the attention that the USA now gives, for example, to the Middle East.

international economy in the 21st century: WTO, the USA and Latin America] (Universidad Nacional Autónoma de México: Mexico City, 2001), pp. 334–35.

[32] Bolivia, Colombia, Ecuador, Peru and Venezuela are members of the Andean Community. See the Andean Community Internet site at URL <http://www.comunidadandina.org/endex.htm>.

[33] The 12 countries (see note 31) were not represented at the highest levels. The presidents of Argentina, Ecuador, Paraguay and Uruguay did not attend the meeting. This was unfortunate for the Brazilian Government because all the MERCOSUR presidents, with the exception of Lula Da Silva, were absent. 'L'Amérique du Sud en quête d'unité' [South America in search of unity], *Le Monde*, 9 Dec. 2004, URL <http://www.lemonde.fr/web/article/0,1@2-3222,36-390157,0.html>.

[34] Regionalization and regionalism are specific concepts, usually used synonymously. Thus, in an economic sense, regionalization refers to a process where 2 or more countries in a specific geographical area grant each other preferential treatment that is not extended to third parties. Regionalism, on the other hand, refers to the way in which inter-governmental political cooperation develops to achieve economic goals. Ravenhill, J., 'Competing logics of regionalism in Asia–Pacific', *Revue d'integration européennn/Journal of European Integration,* vol. 18, nos 2–3 (1995), p. 179; and Ravenhill, J. and Bernard, M., 'Beyond procut cycles and flying geese: regionalization, hierarchy, and the industrialization of East Asia', *World Politics*, vol. 45, no. 2 (Jan. 1995), pp. 179–210.

[35] Hettne, B. and Inotai, A., *The New Regionalism: Implications for Global Development and International Security* (UN University Institute for Development Economics Research: Helsinki, 1994), pp. 1–3.

[36] Buzan, B. and Waever, O., *Regions and Powers: The Structure of International Security* (Cambridge University Press: Cambridge, 2003), pp. 17–18.

Regionalism is a global phenomenon, and virtually every country in the world participates in at least one such initiative. The Latin American and Caribbean states were not exceptions in the cold war period, and this remains the case today.[37] The most important cold war regional initiatives were the Latin American Free Trade Association (LAFTA), set up in 1960,[38] which became the Latin American Integration Association (LAIA, in Spanish Asociación Latinoamericana de Integración or ALADI) in 1981;[39] the Central American Common Market (CACM), established in 1960;[40] the Andean Group, created in 1969;[41] and the Caribbean Free Trade Association (CARIFTA), founded in 1967 and transformed into the Caribbean Community (CARICOM) in 1973.[42] Most of these initiatives were inspired by the integration process of the European Communities. However, the import substitution policies of the countries in the region kept foreign goods from reaching domestic markets. The primarily economic focus of regionalism in the cold war was related to the prevalence of authoritarian and dictatorial regimes in the region and to mistrust and rivalries, which prevented states from cooperating and increasing their economic and political links.

As noted above, the lost decade of the 1980s was accompanied by a process of democratization that paved the way for a dialogue between the new civilian governments of the Latin American countries, particularly in Central and South America. This produced several 'new regionalism' initiatives in the 1990s and the new century: MERCOSUR; the North American Free Trade Agreement (NAFTA); the Central American Integration System (SICA, Sistema de Integración Centroamericana), created in 1991;[43] the Central American Group of Four (G4), established in 1992;[44] the Association of Carib-

[37] Rodríguez y Rodríguez, S. and Guerra-Borges, A. (eds), *El desarrollo en América Latina y los procesos de integración subregional* [Development in Latin America and the processes of subregional integration] (Siglo XXI/Instituto de Investigaciones Económicas: Mexico City, 1999), pp. 76–95.

[38] LAFTA's members were Argentina, Brazil, Bolivia, Chile, Colombia, Ecuador, Mexico, Paraguay, Peru, Uruguay and Venezuela.

[39] LAIA's members are the same as those of LAFTA. In 1997 Cuba became a full member. LAFTA failed, in part, because it tended to ignore asymmetries between its members. When it was created much attention was paid to preferential trade agreements and recognition of the different levels of development of its member countries. On the history of LAFTA/LAIA see the LAIA/ALADI Internet site at URL <http://www.aladi.org>.

[40] CACM's members are Costa Rica, El Salvador, Guatemala, Honduras and Nicaragua.

[41] See note 28. The group's creation was directly linked to LAFTA's failure to deal with the asymmetries between the most and least advanced countries in the region. See Rosas (note 31), pp. 170–73.

[42] CARIFTA/CARICOM initially included only Anglophone countries or territories: Antigua and Barbuda, Bahamas, Barbados, Belize, Dominica, Grenada, Guyana, Jamaica, Montserrat, Saint Kitts and Nevis, Saint Lucia, Saint Vincent and the Grenadines, and Trinidad and Tobago. However, Suriname and Haiti subsequently became full members. See the CARICOM Internet site at URL <http://www.caricom.org>. In addition to CARIFTA/CARICOM, the East Caribbean Common Market (ECCM), created in 1968 and transformed into the Organization of Eastern Caribbean States (OECS) in 1981, includes 7 Caribbean members: Antigua and Barbuda, Dominica, Grenada, Montserrat, Saint Kitts and Nevis, Saint Lucia, and Saint Vincent and the Grenadines.

[43] SICA's members are Costa Rica, El Salvador, Guatemala, Honduras, Nicaragua and Panama. See General Secretariat of the Central American Integration System, URL <http://www.sgsica.org/>.

[44] The G4 is also known as the Northern Trade Triangle, and initially included Honduras, El Salvador and Guatemala. Nicaragua joined the group a year after its creation, in 1993.

bean States (ACS), created in 1994;[45] the Group of Three (G3), created in 1991;[46] the Andean Community,[47] the successor to the Andean Pact, which was reactivated in 1991; and the Plan Puebla-Panamá (PPP), set up in 2000 to promote development initiatives in southern Mexico and Central America in sustainable development, tourism, natural disasters, infrastructure, and so on.[48] All of these were local initiatives that aimed to go beyond tariff dismantling and limited commercial objectives. They met varying degrees of success. For example, when Paraguayan President Juan Carlos Wasmosy faced a *coup d'état* in 1996, the other MERCOSUR countries pressured and eventually convinced General Lino Oviedo not to destroy the fragile Paraguayan democracy—but this experience seems more the exception than the rule.[49]

In addition to these new regionalism initiatives, the Latin American and Caribbean countries have endorsed the negotiation of free trade agreements (FTA) bilaterally, both in and outside the region. Mexico, for instance, has signed FTAs in the region with Nicaragua, the Northern Trade Triangle, Costa Rica, Bolivia, Chile and Uruguay; and outside the region with Israel, the European Union (EU) and recently Japan. All these FTAs are considered to be 'new generation' agreements because they go beyond tariff dismantling to include trade in services, intellectual property measures, investment rules and even environmental, labour, democracy and human rights provisions.

Most of these FTAs are modelled on NAFTA, which covers areas and issues that were previously untouched by trade negotiations, and in this respect the Latin American countries could be said to be following Mexico's example with the USA. However, it remains to be seen how far the new regionalism and 'new generation' FTAs will contribute to political reconciliation and cooperation between the Latin American and Caribbean countries. Trade issues—both traditional, such as tariff dismantling and non-traditional, such as intellectual property rights—tend to be treated separately from security, political, social and cultural issues. The agreements do not give adequate attention to the link between security and development and instead are limited to commercial considerations. Even the Free Trade Area of the Americas (FTAA),[50] endorsed by the USA at the first Summit of the Amer-

[45] ACS is the most comprehensive initiative so far in the Caribbean, including not only the Caribbean islands but also continental countries with access to the Caribbean, as well as Dutch, French and British dependent territories (as associate members). Its 25 full members are Antigua and Barbuda, Bahamas, Barbados, Belize, Colombia, Costa Rica, Cuba, Dominica, Dominican Republic, El Salvador, Grenada, Guatemala, Guyana, Haiti, Honduras, Jamaica, Mexico, Nicaragua, Panama, Saint Kitts and Nevis, Saint Lucia, Saint Vincent and the Grenadines, Suriname, Trinidad and Tobago, and Venezuela.

[46] The members of the G3 are Colombia, Mexico and Venezuela.

[47] In 1991, under the Guayaquil Commitment, the Andean sub-region countries agreed on a common external tariff and the consolidation of the Andean Customs Union. See Rosas (note 31), p. 172.

[48] Inter-American Development Bank, Plan Puebla-Panamá, URL <http://www.iadb.org/ppp/ppp.asp>.

[49] At the time, it was commented that, in a hypothetical scenario where either Argentine or Brazil was at risk, neither country would have accepted the mediation efforts made by Paraguay and Uruguay. This scenario is discussed in Rosas (note 31), pp. 332–38.

[50] Then US President Bill Clinton invited all the countries in the region, except Cuba, to participate in the Summit of the Americas. The proposed FTAA includes 34 countries from the Americas; its agenda is

icas, held in Miami in December 1994, which aimed to create a continental free trade area by 2005,[51] distances itself from security, political, social and cultural considerations.[52]

IV. Cooperation or conflict

The states of the Latin America and the Caribbean region have some of the smallest defence budgets in the world and the smallest budgets relative to gross domestic product (GDP).[53] This has been the trend with a few exceptions since the first years of the post-cold war era. The accuracy of military expenditure data is, however, frequently challenged by scholars and even international institutions and governments. For instance, in November 2001 ECLAC published a study suggesting a methodology to improve the way in which military expenditure is measured in the region, in an effort to promote more stable security cooperation among Latin American countries. The cases of Argentina and Chile were considered.[54] Although ECLAC's methodology has been criticized and its findings are weakened by problems of access to data, the study highlighted some of the difficulties faced by decision makers, the armed forces, academics and other interest groups in dealing with military expenditure.[55] The most frequently encountered problems include: unclear criteria for the areas covered or excluded in military expenditure figures;[56]

based on that of NAFTA. The Internet site of the FTAA is at URL <http://www.ftaa-alca.org/alca_e.asp>.

[51] Due to divergent views mainly by Brazil and the USA on the areas that the FTAA is expected to cover, the negotiation process is currently stagnant.

[52] Curzio, L., "La seguridad hemisférica: balance y perspectivas" [Hemispheric security: balance and perspectives], ed. M. C. Rosas, *Cooperación y conflicto en las Américas: Seguridad hemisférica: un largo y sinuoso camino* [Cooperation and conflict in the Americas: hemispheric security, a long and winding road] (Universidad Nacional Autónoma de México/Center for Hemispheric Defense Studies: Mexico City, 2003), p. 87; and Rosas, M. C. and Reyes, G. E., *ALCA y OMC: América Latina frente al proteccionismo: El libre comercio en los tiempos del ántrax* [FTAA and WTO: Latin American in face of protectionism: free trade in the times of anthrax] (Universidad Nacional Autónoma de México/Sistema Económico Latinoamericano: Mexico City, 2003), pp. 29–43.

[53] Nueva Mayoría, 'América Latina y el Caribe es la región del mundo que menos gasta en defensa' [Latin America and the Caribbean is the region of the world which spends the least on defence], 16 Nov. 2004, URL <http://www.nuevamayoria.com/ES/BIBLIOTECA/resenas/041116.html>.

[54] La Comisión Económica para América Latina (CEPAL), *Metodología estandarizada común para la medición de los gastos de defensa* [Standard methodology for measurement of defence costs] (Oficina Ejecutiva de la Comisión Económica para América Latina y el Caribe: Santiago de Chile, Nov. 2001).

[55] See, e.g., Scheetz, T., 'Una evaluación del documento cepalino: metodología estandarizada común para la medición de los gastos de defensa' [An evaluation of the ECLAC document: standard methodology for meaurement of defence expenditure], *Fuerzas armadas y sociedad*, vol. 18, no. 1–2 (2004), p. 108.

[56] One of the problems of analysing Chile's military expenditure is that the budget for public security is included, which makes Chile's military expenditure appear higher than that of its neighbours. Cheyre Espinosa, J. E., *Medidas de confianza mutua: Casos de América Latina y el Mediterráneo* [Confidence-building measures: the cases of Latin American and the Mediterranean] (Centro de Estudios e Investigaciones Militares: Santiago, 2000), p. 65. There have also been political obstacles to obtaining information from the Argentinean and Chilean defence ministries.

Table 6.2. Armed forces in Latin America and the Caribbean, as of July 2004

Country[a]	Population	Army	Navy	Air force	Total armed forces
Argentina	38 428 000	41 400	17 500	12 500	**71 400**
Bolivia	8 808 000	25 000	3 500	3 000	**31 500**
Brazil	178 470 000	189 000	48 600	65 310	**302 910**
Chile	15 806 000	47 700	19 000	11 000	**77 700**
Colombia	44 222 000	178 000	22 000	7 000	**207 000**
Cuba	11 300 000	38 000	3 000	8 000	**49 000**
Dominican Republic	8 745 000	15 000	4 000	5 500	**24 500**
Ecuador	13 003 000	37 000	5 500	4 000	**46 500**
El Salvador	6 515 000	13 850	700	950	**15 500**
Guatemala[b]	12 347 000	27 000	1 500	700	**29 200**
Honduras	6 941 000	8 300	1 400	2 300	**12 000**
Mexico	103 457 000	144 000	37 000	11 770	**192 770**
Nicaragua	5 466 000	12 000	800	1 200	**14 000**
Paraguay	5 878 000	7 600	1 400	1 100	**10 100**
Peru	27 167 000	40 000	25 000	15 000	**80 000**
Uruguay	3 415 000	15 200	5 700	3 100	**24 000**
Venezuela	25 699 000	34 000	18 300	7 000	**59 300**

[a] Costa Rica and Panama do not have armed forces.

[b] Guatemala is reducing its army to 15 500.

Sources: World Health Organization (WHO), *World Health Report 2005: Make Every Mother and Child Count* (WHO: Geneva, 2004), URL <http://www.who.int/whr/2005/en/>; and International Institute for Strategic Studies (IISS), *The Military Balance 2004/2005* (Oxford University Press: Oxford, 2004).

different concepts of security and defence from country to country;[57] information access; unclear judicial frameworks; the exclusion of legislators from the debate on defence and security; confusion over the design and purpose of security and defence policies; 'securitization' of the agenda so that the armed forces are in charge of tasks not necessarily related to defence; and the inadequacy of civilian oversight.[58] The contribution of transparency and accountability to confidence building and cooperation in the field of security and defence and related areas in Latin America and the Caribbean needs to be underlined and military expenditure data are a key starting point.

Throughout the 1980s, when several armed conflicts developed especially in Central America, the defence budget as a percentage of GDP was as high as 44.1 per cent in Nicaragua (in 1986), 6.4 per cent in Honduras (1985), 4.9 per

[57] RESDAL, *Las definiciones políticas* [Political definitions], URL <http://www.resdal.org/atlas/atlas-definiciones.html>. The site compares different concepts of defence and security in some Latin American and Caribbean countries. E.g., the Dominican Republic lacks a 'security concept'.

[58] The national defence budgets of several countries in the region are listed at RESDAL, *Presupuestos nacionales y otras cifras* [National budgets and other figures], URL <http://www.resdal.org/main-transparencia.html>. See also Robles Montoya, J., *Metodología de análisis para la asignación de recursos de la defensa: presupuestos y adquisiciones* [Analytical methodology for allocation of defence resources: budgets and acquisitions], URL <http://www.resdal.org/idele-montoya.html>. See also chapter 8 in this volume.

cent in El Salvador (1986) and 3.6 per cent in Guatemala (1985).[59] In South America, Argentina spent 7.1 per cent of its GDP on defence (1981), Chile 9.6 per cent (1984), Guyana 12.4 per cent (1986), Peru 10.4 per cent (1982) and Uruguay 4 per cent (1982).[60] In sharp contrast to these figures, by the early 21st century, the country with the highest military expenditure in South America was Colombia with 4.4 per cent of GDP (in 2003), followed by Chile with 3.5 per cent (in 2003). None of the remaining Latin American countries, with the exception of Ecuador (2.4 per cent) and Cuba,[61] came close to spending 2 per cent of GDP on defence.[62]

Table 6.2 shows the number of personnel in the armies, navies and air forces of 17 Latin American and Caribbean countries. According to these figures, the aggregate armed forces of the 10 South American countries in the table, with 910 410 troops, correspond to 64 per cent of the USA's armed forces, including the Marine Corps. The largest contingent is that of Brazil (33 per cent of the region's armed force manpower), followed by Colombia (23 per cent) and Peru and Chile (9 per cent each). MERCOSUR countries, with a population almost double that of the Andean Community countries, have an average of 1.7 military personnel to every 1000 inhabitants. In the Andean Community, there are 3.5 military personnel for every 1000 inhabitants.[63] Colombia, with a population less than half that of Mexico, possesses a larger army, but the Colombian conflict demands a degree of defence expenditure and armed forces which Mexico does not need. However, the Colombian Army is still second in size to that of Brazil.

In the 1990s two contradictory trends were demonstrated in Latin America: an ostensible decrease in tension in the region as a result of disarmament and confidence-building measures (CBMs); and efforts by several governments to acquire new defence technologies. In general, Latin American arms acquisitions appear related more to modernization requirements than to threats to the security of the countries involved. Most of the military equipment possessed by the Latin American countries was designed, produced or purchased in the 1960s and 1970s, which, although seemingly outdated, is in line with

[59] These figures represent the highest military expenditure for each country in the 1980s. Hagmeyer-Gaverus, G. *et al.*, 'Tables of world military expenditure, 1979–88', *SIPRI Yearbook 1989: World Armaments and Disarmament* (Oxford University Press: Oxford, 1989), pp. 191–92.

[60] Hagmeyer-Gaverus *et al.* (note 59), pp. 191–92.

[61] According to SIPRI, in the cold war years of 1979–85 Cuba had a highly militarized society and devoted large human and material resources to defence (9.6–10.5% of GDP). There are no reliable figures on current Cuban military expenditure, but according to Pérez-López the average level of spending dropped to 5% of GDP in the 1990s. Even so, Cuba's index of armed forces per 1000 inhabitants in 1993 was still more than 5 times higher than in other Latin American countries. Hagmeyer-Gaverus *et al.* (note 59), p. 191; and Pérez López, J. F., *Cuban Military Expenditures: Concepts, Data and Burden Issues*, Paper presented at Fifth Annual Meeting of the Association for the Study of the Cuban Economy, University of Miami, Fla., 8–10 Aug. 1996, pp. 124, 140–41.

[62] See appendix 8A in this volume.

[63] Nueva Mayoría, *Balance estratégico militar de América del Sur* [Strategic military balance in South America] (Nueva Mayoría: Buenos Aires, 2004), pp. 4–5.

Table 6.3. Significant political cooperation and disarmament initiatives contributing to confidence building in Latin America and the Caribbean, 1942–2002

Name of initiative/agreement	Established	Aim/comment
Inter-American Defence Board (IADB, Junta Inter-americana de Defensa)	1942	To coordinate defence of the Americas
Inter-American Treaty of Reciprocal Assistance (Rio Treaty) (TIAR, Tratado Interamericano de Asistencia Recíproca)	1947	To ensure inter-American peace and reciprocal assistance to meet armed attack against any American state
Charter of the Organization of American States (OAS)	1948	To promote peaceful settlement of disputes and arms control; special meetings of foreign ministers of member countries may be called if a conflict or threat to peace develops in the area
American Treaty on Pacific Settlements (Bogotá Pact)	1948	To ensure settlement of disputes by pacific means
South Atlantic maritime area	1967	To proclaim a peace and cooperation zone[a]
Treaty of Tlatelolco	1968	To establish a Latin American nuclear weapon-free zone (NWFZ);[b] all Latin American and Caribbean nations, including Cuba, are parties;[c] to guarantee compliance with treaty provisions, the Agency for the Prohibition of Nuclear Weapons in Latin America (OPANAL) was established to guarantee that the region remains an NWFZ, to prohibit nuclear tests and storage of nuclear weapons in the area, and to prevent proliferation of nuclear weapons and support the use of nuclear energy for peaceful purposes[d]
Declaration of Ayacucho	1974	To control arms proliferation and ratify the non-nuclear status of the region; parties are Argentina, Bolivia, Chile, Colombia, Ecuador, Panama, Peru and Venezuela
Mendoza Commitment	1991	To eradicate chemical weapons in Argentina, Brazil, Chile and Uruguay
Cartagena Declaration	1991	To renunciate weapons of mass destruction; signed by Bolivia, Colombia, Ecuador Peru and Venezuela
Summit of the Americas	1994	To promote cooperation in the Americas in the fields of de-mining, transparency on defence expenditure, the peaceful settle-ment of disputes, etc.;[e] mechanism is not primarily focused on security matters but has generated important initiatives in this area, e.g., 1998 Declaration of Santiago

Name of initiative/agreement	Established	Aim/comment
Framework Treaty on Democratic Security in Central America	1995	To contribute to the regional security debate by introducing the 'democratic security' concept;[f] important because of the 'cooperative security' approach[g] and endorsement of disarmament and arms control in the region through 'a reasonable balance of forces';[h] agreed by El Salvador, Guatemala, Honduras, Nicaragua and 2 Central American countries that do not possess armies: Costa Rica and Panama
Treaty Establishing the Regional Security System in the Caribbean	1996	To foster cooperation on immigration environmental, smuggling, natural disaster and fishing issues;[i] established by Caribbean Anglophone countries
Inter-American Convention Against the Illicit Manufacturing of and Trafficking in Firearms, Ammunition, Explosives and Other Related Materials	1997	To regulate firearms and related materials by requiring licensing and marking of them; criminalizes illicit manufacture and trafficking; provides for information sharing and cooperation
Treaty on Maritime Boundaries between Mexico and the USA	1997	To conclude a border dispute related to the North Archipelago (Channel Islands),[j] not included in the 1848 Guadalupe Hidalgo Treaty, but which are occupied by the USA;[k] important because of the vast hydrocarbon reserves in the Gulf of Mexico area, particularly in the 'hoyos de dona',[l] which contains *c.* 43–59 billion barrels of oil
Ushuaia Declaration	1999	To establish a peace zone between MERCOSUR, Bolivia and Chile
Convention on the Prohibition of Use, Stockpiling, Production and Transfer of Anti-Personnel Mines and on their Destruction (APM, or Ottawa, Convention)[n]	1999	All but 2 countries in the Americas, Cuba and the USA,[m] have signed the convention
Inter-American Convention on Transparency in Conventional Weapons Acquisitions	1999	To establish a framework for timely notification of arms acquisitions and annual reporting on imports and exports
Lima Commitment (Andean Charter for Peace and Security and the Limitation and Control of the Expenditure on Foreign Defense)	2002	To set out principles for an Andean Community security policy and commitments to establish a peace zone and take measures to combat terrorism, limit defence spending, promote arms control and eradicate illicit arms trafficking
Amazonian Watching System (SIVAM)	2002	To safeguard Brazilian sovereignty in the light of Colombia's internal security situation, as well as the implications of Plan Colombia[o]

[a] The South Atlantic Maritime Area Coordination (CAMAS, Control del Area Marítima Atlántico Sur) was initiated in 1967 and became crucial after the 1982 Falklands/Malvinas War. Delamer, P. G. R., 'Prospects for multinational cooperation at sea in the South Atlantic', URL <http://www.centrotocqueville.com.ar/htm/htm/gdyy090101in.htm>.

[b] Cheyre Espinosa, J. E., *Medidas de confianza mutua: Casos de América Latina y el Mediterráneo* [Confidence-building measures: the cases of Latin American and the Mediterranean] (Centro de Estudios e Investigaciones Militares: Santiago, 2000), p. 84. During the cold war Argentina and Brazil decided to conduct nuclear weapon programmes. On Brazil see Rosas, M. C., *La economía política de la seguridad internacional. Sanciones, zanahorias y garrotes* [Political economy of international security: sanctions, carrots and sticks] (Universidad Nacional Autónoma de México/Sistema Económico Latinoamericano: Mexico City, 2003), p. 188. On Brazil's nuclear policies and the reasons for dismantlement see Sum, G. H., *The Brazilian Dream: A Middle Power Seeks Greatness* (Xlibris: Miami, Fla., 2000).

[c] Cuba signed the treaty on 23 Oct. 2002. Argentina, Brazil and Chile became parties in 1994. For the full list of parties to the treaty see annex A in this volume.

[d] The Treaty of Tlatelolco has inspired other non-proliferation initiatives elsewhere in the world. See the analysis by the Secretary General of the Agency for the Prohibition of Nuclear Weapons in Latin America and the Caribbean (OPANAL, Organismo para la Proscripcion de las Armas Nucleares en la America Latina y el Caribe) in Vargas Carreño, E., 'El Tratado de Tlatelolco, el desarme y la no-proliferación nuclear en América Latina y el Caribe' [The Treaty of Tlatelolco: disarmament and nuclear non-proliferation in Latin America and the Caribbean], ed. M. C. Rosas, *Seguridad hemisférica e inseguridad global: entre la cooperación interamericana y la guerra preventiva* [Hemispheric security and global insecurity: between inter-American cooperation and preventive war] (Universidad Nacional Autónoma de México/Embajada de Canadá: Mexico City, 2004) , pp. 309–22.

[e] 'Second Summit of the Americas, Declaration of Santiago', 18–19 Apr. 1998, URL <http://www.summit-americas.org/chiledec.htm>.

[f] Legler, T., '¿Víctima del terrorismo? La seguridad humana después del 11 de septiembre' [Victim of terrorism? Human security since 11 September], ed M. C. Rosas, *Cooperación y conflicto en las Américas. Seguridad hemisférica: un largo y sinuoso camino* [Cooperation and conflict in the Americas: hemispheric security, a long and winding road] (Universidad Nacional Autónoma de México/Center for Hemispheric Defense Studies: Mexico City, 2003), p. 299.

[g] Article 26g of the treaty emphasizes that 'The democratic security of each of the countries signing this Treaty is closely connected with the security of the region. Accordingly, no country shall strengthen its own security at the expense of the security of other countries'. 'Framework Treaty on Democratic Security in Central America', URL <http://www.summit-americas.org/Hemispheric%20Security/Franework3893-96.htm>.

[h] 'Framework Treaty on Democratic Security in Central America' (note g); and Jácome, F. (ed.), *Seguridad democrática en Centroamérica: Logros y limitaciones en Costa Rica, Panamá, Guatemala y El Salvador* [Democratic security in Central America: achievements and limitations in Costa Rica, Guatemala and El Salvador] (Coordinadora Regional de Investigaciones Económicas y Sociales: Caracas, 2004).

[i] The Permanent Council of the Organization of American States, Committee on Hemispheric Security, URL <http://www.oas.org/main/main.asp?sLang=E&sLink=http://www.oas.org/csh/english>, 5 Mar. 1996; and US Department of State, 'Treaty Establishing the Regional Security System', 5 Mar. 1996, URL <http://www.state.gov/t/ac/csbm/rd/4367.htm>.

[j] The archipelago comprises the islands of Anacapa, the Farallones, San Clemente, San Miguel, San Nicolas, Santa Barbara, Santa Catalina, Santa Cruz and Santa Rosa. It is located off the coast of southern California.

[k] The controversy over the archipelago is addressed in Moguel Flores, E. H., 'El Archipiélago del Norte y los Farallones: Asignaturas pendientes del Tratado de Guadalupe en la agenda de asuntos fronterizos entre México y los Estados Unidos de América' [The North

Archipelago and the Farallones: pending aspects of the Treaty of Guadalupe related to border issues between Mexico and the United Status of America], *Revista Asociación de Diplomáticos Escritores*, no. 4 (June–Aug. 2002), URL <http://diplomaticosescritores.org/NumeroActual.asp?link=4_2.htm&num=4>; and 'Treaty of Guadalupe Hidalgo', 2 Feb. 1848, URL <http://www.yale.edu/lawweb/avalon/diplomacy/mexico/guadhida.htm>.

[l] An 'hoyo de dona' is a 'discontinuous line' with eastern and western orientations. These 'hoyos' extend beyond the c. 320 km limit for both Mexico and the USA. The borders of this area were not addressed by the Treaty on Maritime Boundaries.

[m] See Rosas, M. C., 'México y Brasil: ¿buenos enemigos o amigos mortales?' [Mexico and Brazil: good enemies or mortal friends?], *Estudos Humanidades*, vol. 31, no. 5 (May 2004), pp. 783–814. Former US President Bill Clinton had promised that the USA would sign the Ottawa Convention in 2006. His successor, George W. Bush, suggested a delay that could extend to 2010. See Kucera, J., 'US changes landmine policy', *Jane's Defence Weekly*, vol. 41, no. 10 (10 Mar. 2004), p. 11.

[n] Matthew, R. A., 'Human security and the mine ban movement: introduction', ed. R. A. Matthew *et al.*, *Landmines and Human Security: International Politics and War's Hidden History* (State University of New York: Albany, N.Y., 2004), pp. 3–17.

[o] Concerns about Plan Colombia relate not only to the physical presence of US soldiers in Colombia, but also to possible incursions into neighbouring countries by Colombian drug traffickers and guerrillas seeking a better environment in which to operate.

the region's needs. Part of the military equipment is second-hand stock from European members of the North Atlantic Treaty Organization (NATO), the former Warsaw Pact, and countries such as Israel and South Africa.[64]

Despite the existence of a series of CBMs and arms control agreements on small arms and light weapons (SALW) and anti-personnel mines (APMs), Latin America lacks an equivalent to the European arms control and confidence- and security-building measures regimes (see table 6.3). This may explain why the governments of the region accede too readily to modernization requests made by the armed forces.[65] In Chile, for example, the arms procurement decision-making process occurs essentially only within the armed forces, a situation that is not expected to change in the near future.[66]

Even so, in terms of conventional weapon purchases, Latin America is a minor market compared with the Middle East and South-East Asia. Between 1998 and 2002, the Latin American country leading the list of recipients of conventional weapons was Brazil, which ranked 20th in the world, followed by Argentina at 29th, Colombia at 37th, Chile at 40th, Mexico at 47th and Peru at 57th.[67] The same applies to spending on the procurement of conven-

[64] Nueva Mayoría (note 63), pp. 37–49.

[65] Hagelin, B. *et al.*, 'International arms transfers', *SIPRI Yearbook 2003: Armaments, Disarmament and International Security* (Oxford University Press: Oxford, 2003), pp. 452–53. See also chapter 15 in this volume.

[66] Rojas Aravena, F., 'Chile', ed. R. P. Singh, SIPRI, *Arms Procurement Decision Making*, vol. 2, *Chile, Greece, Malaysia, Poland, South Africa and Taiwan* (Oxford University Press: Oxford, 2000), p. 17. The author explains that, although the Chilean president has the right to veto these decisions, he has so far chosen not to do so in most cases.

[67] Curzio (note 52), pp. 84–85.

tional arms, where the Latin American country with the highest position is also Brazil, which ranks 36th in the world.[68]

Military expenditure, the size of the armed forces and arms procurement are important considerations because civil–military relations are experiencing transformation, which may lead to crises such as the 1995 Ecuador–Peru crisis in the disputed Condor Cordillera border region.[69] Democratic control of the armed forces has not been fully achieved, and traditional border disputes and 'new' threats—like drug trafficking, organized crime and undocumented migration—have the potential to spark armed conflict. However, as suggested above, the use of force in the region has generally decreased, and the various regional CBMs appear to be taken seriously by the parties and their neighbours. The origins and rationale of such measures were as follows.

1. The disputes between the countries in Latin American and the Caribbean no longer relate to either ideological issues or conflicts between blocs.[70] Increasingly, the main security challenges for societies in the region are linked to economic crises, the prevailing unequal income distribution, poverty, environmental degradation, organized crime, corruption and the failure of existing political institutions to meet these challenges.

2. The prevailing strategic concept in military establishments is 'realist':[71] there is a state-centric perception of threats and risk with little willingness to address the 'broad concept' of security,[72] which includes notions such as human security.[73] Nonetheless, civil–military relations are moving towards the implementation of a preponderantly civilian decision-making authority on security matters.

3. Despite the asymmetries shown in table 6.2, the region's armed forces are relatively small, with limited and slow deployment capabilities.[74] Intelligence gathering about a potential 'adversary' is particularly limited.[75] The armed

[68] Hagelin *et al.* (note 65).

[69] Ortiz, R. D., 'Ampliación del horizonte estratégico y reforma militar en América Latina' [The widening of the strategic horizon in military reform in Latin America], *Fuerzas armadas y sociedad*, vol. 15, no. 1 (Jan.–Mar. 2000), p. 3.

[70] Cheyre Espinosa (note 56), p. 54.

[71] Cheyre Espinosa (note 56).

[72] The proponents of the 'realist' concept of security reject the 'broad' notion of security, arguing that it lacks clear goals and is thus difficult to translate into concrete measures. For a comparison of 'broad' and 'restricted' security see Bárcena Coqui, M., 'La reconceptualización de la seguridad: el debate contemporáneo' [Reconceptualizing of security: the contemporary debate], *Política Exterior*, no. 59 (Feb. 2000), pp. 9–31; and Garduño Valero, G. J. R., 'Epistemología y semántica de la seguridad nacional' [Epistemology and semantics of national security], ed. Rosas (note 9), pp. 65–91.

[73] The human security concept is controversial, and its translation into concrete policies has been difficult. Legler, T., '¿Víctima del terrorismo? La seguridad humana después del 11 de septiembre' [Victim of terrorism? Human security after 11 September], ed. Rosas (note 52), pp. 283–99. See also chapter 7 in this volume.

[74] Cheyre Espinosa (note 56).

[75] On the failures and limitations of the intelligence services in countries such as Argentina, Brazil, Chile, Mexico, Peru and Uruguay see Swenson, R. and Lemozy, S. C. (eds), *Profesionalismo de inteligencia en las Américas* [Professional intelligence in the Americas] (Center for Strategic Intelligence Research/Joint Military Intelligence College: Washington, DC, Aug. 2003).

forces do not possess weapons of mass destruction (WMD), and, indeed, Latin America pioneered the first nuclear weapon-free zone.[76]

4. Armed forces are typically not deployed in direct confrontation with each other, either in the region or abroad.[77]

5. Cooperative security initiatives tend to prevail and are based on the assumption that the security of one country can be guaranteed only when its neighbours are also in a 'secure environment' (win–win approach). It is considered ineffective for countries to seek to increase their security at the expense of others (zero-sum game).[78] This is the case, notably, between Colombia and Venezuela in the Andean sub-region, where it is believed that most of the challenges faced by the two countries in their relations could be solved by a cooperative approach based on continuing interdependence.[79]

6. As regards arms transfers, the most important problem is the trade in SALW.[80] The proliferation of WMD and major conventional weapons is a relatively less important issue than in other regions of the world. In fact, if not for Cuba and the USA, the Americas would be entirely committed to the prohibition and dismantling of APMs, a specific category of SALW.[81]

7. The countries of the region have an extensive set of rules, political agreements, and diplomatic mechanisms for conflict resolution. The existing CBMs are particularly important in times of crisis.

[76] See table 6.3.

[77] Cheyre Espinosa (note 56).

[78] The way in which Latin American countries deal with democratic and cooperative security initiatives is analysed in Gomariz, E., 'La doctrina de la seguridad democrática y el impacto paradigmático de la crisis global' [The doctrine of democratic security and its impact on the paradigm of the global crisis], ed. Rosas (note 9), pp. 203–12.

[79] Jiménez y Meleán, R. S., *Integración económica y fortalecimiento institucional en el nuevo perfil de las relaciones colombo-venezolanas* [Economic integration and institutional fortification in the new profile of Colombian–Venezualan relations] (Impresora Micabú: Caracas, 1999), p. 15. A more pessimistic view is presented in Bonilla, A., 'Una agenda de seguridad andina' [An agenda for Andean security], ed. Rosas (note 52), p. 239.

[80] An important step was the opening for signature, under the Organization of American States framework, of the Inter-American Convention Against the Illicit Manufacturing of and Trafficking in Firearms, Ammunitions, Explosives, and Other Related Materials, on 14 Nov. 1997. The importance of SALW in Latin America is related to the military's historical emphasis on 'internal enemies'; endemic economic crises which prevented acquisition of expensive, sophisticated weapons; US military programmes designed to strengthen internal security in the region by sponsoring production for 'domestic use'; the presence of insurgent forces, private militias and criminal organizations equipped with SALW; and the trend of privatization of security in the region. Rosas, M. C., '¿Privatización o privación de la seguridad?' [Privatization or deprivation of security?], *Metapolítica*, no. 35, vol. 8 (May/June 2004), pp. 88–97; Rosas, M. C., 'Minas terrestre anti-personal: infierno al ras del suelo' [Anti-personnel landmines: inferno on the ground], *Etcétera*, no. 233 (17 July 1997), pp. 22–25, URL <http://www.etcetera.com.mx>; and Klare, M. and Andersen, D., *A Scourge of Guns: The Diffusion of Small Arms and Light Weapons in Latin America* (Federation of American Scientists: Washington, DC, 1996), p. 90, URL <http://www.fas.org/asmp/library/publications/scourgefl.htm>. The RAND Report *Arms Trafficking and Colombia*, URL <http://www.rand.org/publications/MR/MR1468/>, analyses the black and 'grey' market sources of SALW and how illegal providers transfer, sell, acquire and ship them.

[81] The parties and signatories to the 1997 Convention on the Prohibition of Use, Stockpiling, Production and Transfer of Anti-Personnel Mines and on their Destruction are listed in annex A in this volume; see also chapter 15.

Table 6.3 shows the growing importance of treaties, declarations and commitments in the post-cold war era for ensuring non-violent outcomes in the region. The countries of the region recognize that some of these initiatives are more successful than others and that some of the institutions involved may have outlived their usefulness.[82] The Inter-American Defence Board (IADB), a mechanism created in 1942 in the context of World War II to coordinate the defence of the Americas vis-à-vis the Berlin–Rome–Tokyo axis, is such an example. After World War II the IADB became a consultant to the Organization of American States (OAS), which reciprocates by funding the IADB, but the nature of their relationship remains unclear.[83]

V. The participation of Latin American armies in peacekeeping operations

In addition to their primary aim, international peacekeeping operations may contribute positively to the democratization of the participating armed forces and their subordination to civilian rule—a trend of particular importance for Latin America, where the establishment of democracy is still an ongoing process. The military regimes of the 1960s and 1970s in the region emphasized the war against 'internal enemies' in the framework of national security doctrines,[84] and many political and human rights abuses were committed in the name of this strategy.

Today those military regimes are gone, but it is premature to speak of complete subordination of the armed forces to civilian authorities because in several domains the armed forces remain in control. There are other dimensions, however, which give cause for optimism, among them PKOs. The transformation of the armed forces from 'repressive tools' into 'peace soldiers' seems to be an increasingly popular trend in the region, as elsewhere.[85]

There has been increased Latin American participation in PKOs since 1989. Although such participation was not unknown in the cold war period,[86] at that

[82] For a comprehensive list of the security and regional cooperation arrangements in the Americas see ed. Rosas (note 52), pp. 55–61.

[83] The IADB is made up of armed forces representatives, is based in the USA and is chaired by a US officer (who reports to the US Joint Chiefs of Staff). Among its activities are de-mining and the promotion of regional CBMs at the request of the OAS General Assembly. Most CARICOM countries do not participate. Rosas, M. C., '¿Existe la seguridad hemisférica?' [Does hemispheric security exist?], ed. Rosas (note 52), p. 56. For a list of OAS members see the glossary in this volume.

[84] Cepik, M. and Antunes, P., 'Brazil's new intelligence system: an institutional assessment', *International Journal of Intelligence and Counterintelligence*, vol. 16, no. 3 (fall 2003), p. 351.

[85] Sotomayor, A. C., 'Reforming Praetorian militaries to become responsible peacekeepers', *Informational Memorandum*, no. 59 (spring 2004), pp. 7–8.

[86] E.g., in 1948, 4 Latin American soldiers were observers in the UN Truce Supervision Organization in Lebanon. Latin American forces took part in the UN Military Observer Group in India and Pakistan in 1949; in the Suez UN Emergency Force in 1956; in the UN Operation in the Congo in 1960; and in the UN Disengagement Observer Force in the Golan Heights in 1974. Childe, J., 'Peacekeeping and the inter-American system', *Military Review*, Oct. 1980, pp. 40–51; and Pala, A. L., 'The increased role of Latin American armed forces in UN peacekeeping: opportunities and challenges', *Airpower Journal*, special edn 1995, URL <http://www.airpower.maxwell.af.mil/airchronicles/apj/pala.html>.

time PKOs were not a part of the defence doctrines of the countries of the region.[87] This situation has changed dramatically since the end of the cold war. As of 31 December 2004, 12 countries in the region were contributing to 15 UN PKOs with a total of 6163 personnel, 9.5 per cent of all the personnel employed in UN PKOs worldwide.[88] Among the 20 major current national contributors of military and civilian police to UN PKOs, Uruguay ranks 9th, Brazil 14th, Argentina 16th and Chile 22nd.[89] If participation in PKOs is measured as a share of the population of each country, Uruguay is the world's largest provider of personnel to PKOs.[90] As table 6.4 illustrates, it participates in PKOs where no other Latin American country is present (e.g., in Afghanistan and Georgia).

Involvement in PKOs is not limited to UN PKOs. Following a general post-cold war trend, PKOs have been conducted under the framework of regional security organizations also in Latin America.[91] For instance, after the 1991 *coup d'état* which overthrew Haitian President Jean-Bertrand Aristide, the OAS and the UN worked together to manage the crisis, creating the OAS–UN International Civilian Mission in Haiti (MICIVIH).[92] Two years later, the Military Observer Mission Ecuador–Peru (MOMEP) was created with an equal number of observers from the four guarantor countries (Argentina, Brazil, Chile and the USA) of the 1942 Rio Protocol to help tackle the Ecuador–Peru

[87] Rosas, M. C., 'La seguridad internacional y el debate sobre la participación de México en las operaciones de mantenimiento de la paz de la Organización de las Naciones Unidas' [International security and the debate on the participation of Mexico in UN peacekeeping operations], ed. Rosas (note 9), p. 119; and Rosas, M. C. (ed.), *Las operaciones de mantenimiento de la paz de las Naciones Unidas: lecciones para México* [United Nations peacekeeping operations: lessons for Mexico], (Universidad Nacional Autónoma de México/Folke Bernadotte Academy: Stockholm, Sweden, 2005).

[88] As of 31 Dec. 2004, 102 nations, mostly developing countries, participated in UN PKOs. UN Department of Peacekeeping Operations, 'Ranking of military and civilian police contributions to UN operations', 31 Dec. 2004, URL <http://www.un.org/Depts/dpko/dpko/contributors/>. See also table 3.2 in this volume.

[89] The countries ranking higher than Uruguay were Pakistan, Bangladesh, India, Nepal, Ethiopia, Ghana, Jordan and Nigeria. The countries ranking higher than Brazil were those countries plus South Africa, Kenya, Morocco and Senegal. UN Department of Peacekeeping Operations (note 88).

[90] Pakistan, the largest contributor to UN PKOs, has a population of 145 million and contributes 8140 civilian police and troops. Uruguay, with a population of 3 415 000 (2.4% of Pakistan's population) provides 2490 civilian police and troops to PKOs (31% of Pakistan's contribution). These data refer to the total contribution to UN PKOs. UN Department of Peacekeeping Operations (note 88).

[91] Heldt, B. and Wallensteen, P., *Peacekeeping Operations: Global Patterns of Intervention and Success, 1948–2000* (Folke Bernardotte Academy: Stockholm, Sweden, 2004), p. 1. See also chapters 2 and 3 in this volume.

[92] MICIVIH (1993–2000) was a peace-building mission with no peacekeeping tasks under which the UN provided operational support. In 1995 the OAS monitored elections and the UN contributed technical assistance. Heldt and Wallensteen (note 91), p. 46; and UN Association of Great Britain and Northern Ireland, 'Regional security organisations and the challenge of peacekeeping', URL <http://www.una-uk.org/UN&C/regionalsecurity.html>.

Table 6.4. Participation of 12 Latin American and Caribbean states in United Nations peacekeeping operations, as of 31 December 2004

Country	Mission	Civilian police	Military observers	Troops	Total personnel
Argentina	MINURSO	135	5	963	**1 103**
	MINUSTAH				
	MONUC				
	UNFICYP				
	UNMIK				
	UNMIL				
	UNOCI				
	UNTSO				
Bolivia	MINUSTAH	–	19	212	**231**
	MONUC				
	ONUB				
	UNAMSIL				
	UNMIK				
	UNMIL				
	UNMISET				
	UNOCI				
Brazil	MINUSTAH	10	8	1 349	**1 367**
	UNMIK				
	UNMIL				
	UNMISET				
	UNOCI				
Chile	MINUSTAH	38	6	540	**584**
	UNMIK				
	UNMOGIP				
	UNTSO				
Dominican Republic	UNOCI	–	4	–	**4**
Ecuador	MNUSTAH	–	5	67	**72**
	UNMIL				
	UNOCI				
El Salvador	MINURSO	5	11	–	**16**
	MINUSTAH				
	UNMIL				
	UNOCI				
Honduras	MINURSO	–	12	–	**12**
Jamaica	UNMIL	10	–	–	**10**
Paraguay	MINUSTAH	–	37	9	**46**
	MONUC				
	ONUB				
	UNMEE				
	UNMIL				
	UNOCI				
Peru	MINUSTAH	–	17	209	**226**
	MONUC				
	ONUB				

Country	Mission	Civilian police	Military observers	Troops	Total personnel
	UNMEE				
	UNMIL				
	UNOCI				
Uruguay	MINURSO	22	56	2 414	**2 492**
	MINUSTAH				
	MONUC				
	ONUB				
	UNAMA				
	UNAMSIL				
	UNFICYP				
	UNMEE				
	UNMIL				
	UNMOGIP				
	UNOCI				
	UNOMIG				
Region total	**15**	**220**	**180**	**5 763**	**6 163**
Global total	**17**	**6 765**	**2 046**	**55 909**	**64 720**

MINURSO = UN Mission for the Referendum in Western Sahara; MINUSTAH = UN Stabilization Mission in Haiti; MONUC = UN Organization Mission in the Democratic Republic of the Congo; ONUB = UN Operation in Burundi; UNAMA = UN Assistance Mission in Afghanistan; UNAMSIL = UN Mission in Sierra Leone; UNFICYP = UN Peacc-keeping Force in Cyprus; UNMEE = UN Mission in Ethiopia and Eritrea; UNMIK = UN Interim Administration in Kosovo; UNMIL = UN Mission in Liberia; UNMISET = UN Mission of Support in East Timor; UNMOGIP = UN Military Observer Group in India and Pakistan; UNOCI = UN Operation in Côte d'Ivoire; UNOMIG = UN Observer Mission to Georgia; UNTSO = UN Truce Supervision Organization.

Sources: United Nations Department of Peacekeeping Operations, 'UN missions summary detailed by country', 31 Dec. 2004, URL <http://www.un.org/Depts/dpko/dpko/contributors/>; and United Nations Department of Peacekeeping Operations, 'Monthly summary of military and civilian police contribution to United Nations operations', Dec. 2004, URL <http://www.un.org/Depts/dpko/dpko/contributors/>.

border conflict.[93] Other non-UN peacekeeping efforts have included Brazil's actions under the OAS in Suriname in 1992; OAS de-mining efforts in Nicaragua, with the participation of Argentina, Brazil, Chile, Colombia, Paraguay, Peru and Uruguay; and several 'fuerzas aliadas' (allied forces) and

[93] For the Rio Protocol of Peace, Friendship, and Boundaries see URL <http://www.usip.org/pubs/peaceworks/pwks27/appndx1_27.html>. MOMEP comprised 50 personnel and was funded by Ecuador and Peru. The USA provided aerial support for reconnaissance of the demilitarized zone. Weidner, G. R., 'MOMEP's legacy: a new peace, a brighter futue', US Army School of the Americas, URL <http://carlisle-www.army.mil/usamhi/usarsa/ACADEMIC/MOMEP%27s%20Legacy.htm>; and Weidner, G. R., 'Peacekeeping in the Upper Cenepa Valley', US Army School of the Americas, URL <http://carlisle-www.army.mil/usamhi/usarsa/ACADEMIC/MOMEPNDU.HTM>.

'fuerzas unidas' (united forces) peacekeeping exercises conducted under the auspices of the USA.[94]

Currently, the most important UN peacekeeping mission in which Latin American countries participate is the UN Stabilization Mission in Haiti (MINUSTAH), which was mandated by UN Security Council Resolution 1542.[95] After the controversial ouster, on 29 February 2004, of President Jean-Bertrand Aristide, who had been re-elected in November 2000, the UN decided to support the efforts to stabilize Haiti.[96] As of December 2004, MINUSTAH comprised 7406 personnel, including 6008 troops and 1398 civilian police.[97] Nine Latin American countries contributed military personnel to MINUSTAH,[98] and five countries provided civilian police personnel.[99] MINUSTAH is primarily made up of Latin American military and civilian personnel, especially from Argentina and Brazil. Brazil leads the mission and provides the largest contingent: 1212 troops and 3 civilian police; Argentina contributes 555 troops and 5 civilian police (as of December 2004).[100]

Latin America's involvement in PKOs has been welcomed in the light of the demand for new operations and also because traditional peacekeepers such as Canada are reducing their participation.[101] The participation of the Latin American countries provides 'new blood' and their 'neutrality' may be welcomed: they have no 'imperial' ambitions in the regions in which PKOs are conducted but do have some 'cultural affinity' with the African and Latin American societies where troops are deployed. However, the relative lack of field experience and of proper equipment makes Latin American peacekeepers less capable of handling situations in which violence has not completely abated and may also increase the risk of violence during PKOs, limiting the potential contribution of these peacekeepers to peace, conflict management and national reconciliation.

Apart from the political motives for Latin America's participation in PKOs, there are economic advantages. The UN pays each participant a monthly bonus of approximately $980, and personnel in combat missions receive an

[94] These exercises are expected to develop skills relevant to PKOs. When conducted in Central America, they are called 'fuerzas aliadas'; when held in South America they are termed 'fuerzas unidas'. Washington Office for Latin America (WOLA), 'Exercise "Fuerzas aliadas"/"Fuerzas unidas" peacekeeping', Washington, DC, 14 Oct. 2003, URL <http://www.ciponline.org/facts/fapko.htm>.

[95] UN Security Council Resolution 1542, 30 Apr. 2004.

[96] Now in exile, Aristide claims that in Feb. 2004 he was kidnapped by US troops with the consent of France and taken from Haiti. González, G., Inter-Press Service, 'Haiti: Latin American-led peacekeeping operation, a "mission impossible"?', URL <www.ipsnews.net/interna.asp?idnews=26166>.

[97] See table 3.2 in this volume.

[98] The 9 countries were Argentina, Bolivia, Brazil, Chile, Ecuador, Guatemala, Paraguay, Peru and Uruguay.

[99] The 5 countries were Argentina, Brazil, Chile, El Salvador and Uruguay.

[100] For contributions by country to UN missions see UN Department of Peacekeeping Operations (note 88).

[101] As of 31 Dec. 2004 Canada was participating in 8 UN PKOs (see note 100) and in other PKOs in collaboration with its allies. See table 3.2 in this volume; and Hobson, S., 'Country briefing: Canada: readiness at a price', *Jane's Defence Weekly*, 17 Sep. 2003, pp. 22–28.

additional 25 per cent of this sum.[102] Observers receive a monthly per diem of $85–120.[103] Latin American nations have experienced severe economic crises (e.g., in Argentina and Uruguay in 2001–2002), and participation in PKOs may help ease social, political and economic tensions, especially as regards civil–military relations, and keep the military establishment satisfied.[104] According to ECLAC, Uruguay's critical economic situation in 2001 and 2002 may, for example, have played a role in stimulating the participation of Uruguayan troops in PKOs.[105] The UN encourages the participation of other Latin American countries, such as Mexico, in military PKOs.[106]

VI. Latin American–US relations before and after 11 September 2001

Historically, the USA has been the major supplier of military equipment to Latin America. The USA has justified arms sales by arguing that they contribute to the security of its allies. In 1993–96 the USA supplied 25 per cent of all arms purchased by Latin America, three times more than any other supplier.[107] During the cold war, the USA argued that arms sales were warranted as a means of supporting security doctrines in the region that aimed to prevent 'domestic subversion' by Communist-backed elements. After the 1953–59 Cuban Revolution, the US Government implemented the 1961 Foreign Assistance Act, which, in part, provided economic assistance to Latin American military forces providing that human rights and democratic standards were

[102] Pala (note 86).

[103] Pala (note 86).

[104] Rosas (note 87).

[105] La Comisión Económica para América Latina (CEPAL), *Panorama económico de América Latina y el Caribe* [Economic panorama of Latin America and the Caribbean], Comisión Económica para América Latina y el Caribe-Naciones Unidas: Santiago, 2003).

[106] Mexico has provided electoral assistance (e.g., in East Timor in 2000) and trained electoral personnel (e.g., from Iraq in 2004) in cooperation with the UN. Rosas, M. C., *Irak: el año que vivimos en peligro* [Iraq: the year of living dangerously] (Universidad Nacional Autónoma de México/Editorial Quimera: Mexico City, 2004), pp. 224–25. UN Secretary-General Kofi Annan urged Mexico to contribute military personnel to PKOs. 'L'ONU débordée par les opérations de maintien de la paix' [The UN is overstretched in peacekeeping operations], *Le Monde*, 8 Sep. 2004, URL <http://www.lemonde.fr/web/article/0,1-0@2-3220,36-378226,0.html>. Participation in PKOs requires congressional approval although recently the Mexican Congress has debated reforms to Article 76 of the Constitution, which requires such approval before the president can deploy troops abroad. The proposed reform may grant the president that authority without the need for congressional approval. In 1998 the Mexican Army provided disaster assistance in Honduras without such consent, but the May 2004 proposal that Mexico should participate in military PKOs in areas of conflict was controversial. 'Descarta Fox enviar tropes en misiones de paz' [Fox rejects the idea of sending troops on peace missions], *El Universal*, 13 May 2004, URL <http://www.eluniversal.com.mx/pls/impreso/noticia_busqueda.html?id_nota=16426&tabla=primera_h>; and 'Abre Derbez debate sobre envío de tropas' [Debate opens on troop deployments], *El Universal*, 12 May 2004, URL <http://www.eluniversal.com.mx/pls/impresonoticia_busqueda.html?id_nota=110775&tabla=nacion_h>; and Rosas (note 87), pp. 109–10, 123–26.

[107] Between 1984 and 1995, the USA was the major provider of arms and military assistance to countries in Latin America and the Caribbean. Cardamore, T., 'Arms sales to Latin America', *Foreign Policy in Focus*, vol. 2, no. 53 (Dec. 1997), p. 1, URL <http://www.fpif.org/briefs/vol2/v2n53arm_body.html>.

met.[108] This aid package was administered essentially by the US Department of State, and assistance continued despite the fact that neither democratic nor human rights were respected in several countries in the region. Following the end of the cold war, however, and after the 11 September 2001 terrorist attacks on the USA, US military assistance and arms sales to the region have experienced important changes.

The cnd of the cold war brought a reduction of the defence budgets of the USA and of most Latin American countries, leading in turn to a reduction in arms purchases. Prior to September 2001, there was no threat to international security on the scale of that experienced in the cold war. It therefore became difficult to justify the acquisition of new and sophisticated arms.

The critical domestic situation in Colombia has made it the beneficiary of the most important US military cooperation programmes in Latin America. Colombia currently receives more US military training than any other country. The Colombian Government faces internal conflicts involving guerrillas, drug lords, armed paramilitary forces, the police, and so on. The armed forces and the police battle two leftist rebel groups—the Ejército de Liberación Nacional (ELN, or National Liberation Army) and the Fuerzas Armadas Revolucionarias de Colombia (FARC, or Revolutionary Armed Forces of Colombia)—as well as the Autodefensas Unidas de Colombia (AUC, or United Self-Defence Forces of Colombia), a right-wing umbrella organization of drug traffickers and landowners, who oppose FARC and the ELN.[109]

Former Colombian President Andrés Pastrana tried to increase the involvement of the EU and the USA in Colombia's peace and reconciliation process through Plan Colombia.[110] The USA approved $1.3 billion in defence aid for the first three years of the plan's implementation: 82 per cent was to be used in support of the armed forces and the police; aid for vulnerable groups and internal displaced persons totalled 4 per cent; support for law enforcement received 2 per cent; human rights and judicial reform were given 4 per cent; promotion of alternative (i.e., non-drug-based) rural development was allocated 7 per cent; and other social programmes received 1 per cent.[111] These

[108] A description of the aid programme established by the act is available in USAID, 'About USAID: USAID history', URL <http://www.usaid.gov/about_usaid/usaidhist.html>.

[109] Krujit, D., 'Uso de, política y fuerzas armadas en América Latina y el Caribe en la post guerra fría: ¿nuevos escenarios y tendencias?' [Use of policy and armed forces in Latin America and the Caribbean after the cold war: new scenarios and trends], *Fuerzas armadas y sociedad*, vol. 17, no. 4 (Oct.–Dec. 2002), p. 54; Dwan, R. and Gustavsson, M., 'Major armed conflicts', *SIPRI Yearbook 2004: Armaments, Disarmament and International Security* (Oxford University Press: Oxford, 2004), pp. 101–103; and Borda Medina., E. *et al*, *Conflicto y seguridad democrática en Colombia: Temas críticos y propuestas* [Conflict and democratic security in Colombia: themes, criticism and proposals] (Fundación Social Friedrich Ebert in Colombia/Embajada de la República Federal de Alemania en Colombia: Bogota, 2004).

[110] US Department of State, 'Support for Plan Colombia', 14 Mar. 2001, URL <http://www.state.gov/p/wha/rt/plncol/>; and Washington Office for Latin America (WOLA), Amnesty International, US Office on Colombia, the Latin America Working Group and the Center for International Policy, 'Plan Colombia: 3 Year Anniversary Report Card, 2003', at URL <http://www.wola.org/Colombia/plan_col_report_card03.pdf>. See also chapters 2 and 8 in this volume.

[111] The budget approved for 2004 suggests that the total amount will increase to $3.67 billion. WOLA, Amnesty International, US Office on Colombia, the Latin America Working Group and the

figures confirm the militarization of the US agenda for Colombia, a trend that was reinforced after the September 2001 terrorist attacks. Indeed, in 2002 and 2003 the USA expanded the spectrum of its military assistance to Colombia beyond countering drug-trafficking.[112] In 2003 the USA helped the Colombian Army to protect an oil pipeline and to re-establish control in Arauca, near the border with Venezuela. In 2003 the USA launched a new programme, Plan Patriota, to recover territories held by FARC.[113] All these initiatives require the physical and official presence, for the first time since World War II, of US troops on South American soil.[114]

The approach taken in Colombia is being reproduced in other US-sponsored cooperation programmes in the region. As figure 6.1 shows, the USA increasingly favours military and police programmes, which have been growing relative to economic and social programmes since the end of the 1990s. Between 2002 and 2003, the number of Latin American troops trained by the USA increased by 52 per cent, making the region the major recipient worldwide of military training funded by the USA—a surprising result given the lack of any major threat to US security or US interests there.[115] Latin America and the Caribbean are of little interest for the USA in terms of a terrorist attack: the countries in the region favour cooperation with the USA, and an alliance between them and the current 'enemies' of the USA seems improbable.

The Latin American experience reflects the tendency after the 2001 terrorist attacks for the US Department of Defense to gain influence on foreign policy making at the expense of the Department of State and of a consequent greater emphasis on military solutions. The US Southern Command (SOUTHCOM) plays a prominent role in the US foreign policy agenda for the Americas, while issues such as human rights, poverty, indebtedness and environmental pollution have lost salience.[116]

Center for International Policy (note 110). This proportional allocation of aid is criticized by the EU, which believes that Colombia needs an economic and social solution not a military programme.

[112] McDermott, J., 'Washington increases assistance to Colombia', *Jane's Defence Weekly*, 4 Feb. 2004, p. 10; and Bender, B., 'Visible cracks: Colombian military units are using US training and equipment to take the country's 40 year civil war to the rebels', *Jane's Defence Weekly*, 9 July 2003, pp. 24–27.

[113] Isacson, A., Olson J. and Haugaard, L., *Diluyendo las divisiones: Tendencias de los programas militares de EEUU para América Latina* [Decreasing the divisions: tendencies of the military programmes of the US for Latin America] (Washington Office for Latin America: Washington, DC, Sep. 2004), p. 6; and Burger, K., 'USA turns up the heat on Colombian insurgents', *Jane's Defence Weekly*, 8 Jan. 2003, p. 6.

[114] Officially the presence of 800 US military advisers in Colombia has been recognized, although unofficially there seem to be at least 1400. Sennes, R. U., Onuki, J. and de Oliveira, A. J., 'La política exterior brasileña y la seguridad hemisférica' [Brazilian foreign politics and hemispheric security], ed. Rosas (note 52), p. 198.

[115] Isacson, Olson and Haugaard (note 113), p. 3. See also chapter 8 in this volume.

[116] See 'United States Southern Command', URL <http://www.southcom.mil/home/>. SOUTHCOM's conterpart, the Northern Command (NORTHCOM), was set up after Sep. 2001. It covers Canada and the USA, Cuba, Mexico and parts of the Caribbean and the Atlantic and Pacific oceans. Its focus is on US air, territorial and maritime security and natural disasters. Rosas (note 83), p. 63; and 'U.S. Northern Command', URL <http://www.northcom.mil/>.

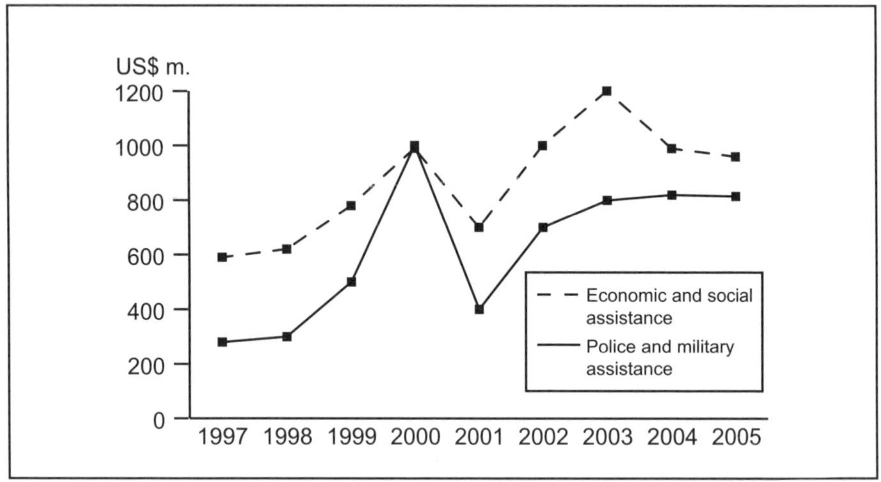

Figure 6.1. US assistance to Latin America and the Caribbean, 1997–2005

Figures are in 1997 constant dollars; figures for 2004 are estimated; and figures for 2005 are proposed.

Source: Isacson, A., Olson J. and Haugaard, L., *Diluyendo las divisiones: Tendencias de los programas militares de EEUU para América Latina* [Decreasing the divisions: tendencies of the military programmes of the US for Latin America] (Washington Office for Latin America: Washington, DC, Sep. 2004), p. 10.

The USA pursues the global 'war on terrorism' in inter-American relations with other means that do not necessarily receive major funding. Older US programmes for this purpose had limited material and human resources, and there are only two new initiatives in this area: the Anti-Terrorist Assistance (ATA) programme and a Counterterrorism Fellowship administered by the US Department of Defense. Most of ATA's funding has been used to finance anti-kidnapping programmes in Colombia. Paradoxically, the USA has reduced funding to Latin America for airport and port security and for the fight against money laundering and terrorism financing.[117]

These actions contrast with the political solidarity shown by the region after the 2001 attacks. Every country in the region condemned the attacks—even Cuba, which the US Department of State designates as a 'terrorist sponsor'.[118] Brazil even invoked the collective security provisions of the 1947 Inter-American Treaty of Reciprocal Assistance (TIAR, in Spanish Tratado Interamericano de Asistencia Recíproca).[119] As elsewhere in the world, this initial

[117] Isacson, Olson and Haugaard (note 113), p. 6.

[118] Cuban President Fidel Castro deplored the situation and condemned what he considered to be 'cowardly attacks' on the USA. International Action Center, 'Speech by Commander in Chief Fidel Castro Ruz, President of the Republic of Cuba', 22 Sep. 2001, URL <http://www.iacenter.org/fidel_on911.htm>.

[119] US Department of State, 'Inter-American Treaty of Reciprocal Assistance (Rio Treaty)', URL <http://www.state.gov/t/ac/csbm/rd/4369.htm>. Sennes, Onuki and de Oliveira express the view that the Brazilian Government made this decision in the light of strong US pressure for a formal commitment that was not acceptable to Brazil. Thus, Brazil, knowing that the TIAR was obsolete, invoked its collect-

sympathy for the USA dissipated once the USA developed its 'war on terrorism' strategy, because of the military emphasis of the strategy and the way in which it has conflicted with other important agendas. Part of the problem is rooted in the US Administration's concept of terrorism as a threat that operates everywhere and may attack anywhere at any time, making use of networks involving individuals, groups and states located anywhere.[120] This definition is wide enough, in the US view, to include Latin America and the Caribbean as an arena for the global war on terrorism.[121]

Apart from Colombia, the USA has identified several 'risk zones' where presumed terrorists operate, such as the so-called Tri-Border Region—the area where the borders of Argentina, Brazil and Paraguay meet[122]—and parts of the Caribbean. The USA considers these 'risk zones' to be 'ungoverned spaces'.[123] These assumptions are of concern to the region because of the new slant they have brought to several issues that were important in inter-American relations prior to September 2001: (*a*) in fighting drug trafficking, the 'narco-terrorist' notion is now applied not only to guerrillas but also to peasants; (*b*) illegal migrants are considered to be potential 'terrorists' and even possible sources of WMD attack; (*c*) profit from the violation of intellectual property rules is perceived as a possible source of income to finance terrorist activities; (*d*) money laundering is viewed in a similar light; and (*e*) arms trafficking is recognized as a source of aid to terrorists.[124]

Despite criticism in the region of this 'terrorization' of the agenda for inter-American relations, the states of the region have supported the USA in its pursuit of al-Qaeda. For example, they have increased border controls and passed laws to fight the financing of terrorism, making such actions a felony under their legislation. The OAS condemned the 2001 attacks. After UN Security Council Resolution 1373 was passed, representatives of the majority of Latin

ive security provisions as a 'politically friendly' gesture. Sennes, Onuki and de Oliveira (note 114), p. 200., Mexican President Vicente Fox addressed the OAS in Washington, DC, 1 week before the terrorist attacks, explaining that Mexico would withdraw from TIAR. Obviously, the call made by Brazil after the attacks forced Mexico to delay its withdrawal, which finally took place in late 2002.

[120] On such networks, 'netwars' and the challenges they pose to US and international security see Arquilla, J. and Ronsfeldt, D. (eds), *Netwars and Networks: The Future of Terror, Crime and Militancy* (RAND: Santa Monica, Calif., 2001), URL <http://www.rand.org/publications/MR/MR1382/>.

[121] Haugaard, L. *et al.*, *September's Shadow: Post-9/11 U.S.–Latin American Relations* (Washington Office for Latin America: Washington, DC, Sep. 2004), p. 2.

[122] Terrorism did not begin on 11 Sep. 2001. Argentina suffered 2 deadly attacks in 1992 and 1994. Intelligence and information gathering and exchange with neighbouring countries were thus conducted in the 1990s and remain a matter of great concern to the Tri-Border Region countries because terrorist threats have been made against them since Sep. 2001. De Lima e Silva, M. M., *9/11, Terrorism and Brazil: Facts about the Tri-Border Region* (Hispanic American Center for Economic Research: Miami, Fla., 2003), p. 2.

[123] The Tri-Border Region has long been considered a sanctuary for terrorist organizations such as Hamas and Hezbollah, which can obtain funding there. Trafficking in weapons and drugs, smuggling, money laundering and document forgery take place in the region. Nonetheless, the '3 + 1 Mechanism', an initiative endorsed by Argentina, Brazil and Paraguay plus the USA, in 2003 denied that the terrorist organizations operate in the area. Haugaard *et al.* (note 121), p. 3.

[124] Olson, J., 'Terrorism: stop inflating the concept', *Cross Currents* (Washington Office for Latin America: Washington, DC, June 2004), pp. 1, 3.

American countries appeared before the Security Council Counter-Terrorism Committee to explain the measures they had developed to fight terrorism and the legislation they had passed or were in the process of ratifying.[125]

The 2003 war against Iraq caused much criticism of the USA in the region. Chile and Mexico found themselves in a particularly difficult position as non-permanent members of the Security Council, where they consequently were exposed to strong pressure to support the USA's interpretation of Security Council Resolution 1441 as allowing the use of force in Iraq.[126] Neither state succumbed to this pressure. However, a group of Central American countries plus Colombia and the Dominican Republic joined the 'coalition of the willing' in March–April 2003, thereby providing support to the USA and helping it to legitimize the war against Iraq.

Later, in March 2004, a smaller group of Latin American countries including the Dominican Republic,[127] El Salvador, Honduras and Nicaragua[128] sent troops to Iraq, which were deployed in the area administered by Spain. The withdrawal of Spanish troops announced by Spanish Prime Minister José Luis Rodríguez Zapatero in April 2004 occurred when he took office. Honduras also announced that, once its contingent had completed its tour of duty in June 2004, the Honduran commitment would not be renewed.[129] Nicaragua withdrew its troops in February 2004, citing budget constraints, and the Dominican Republic, in the light of its forthcoming presidential elections, also withdrew its troops. The only Latin American country with troops still in Iraq is El Salvador, in spite of the death of one of its soldiers there, and the growing criticism from Salvadoreans.[130]

[125] For UN Security Council Resolution 1373, 28 Sep. 2001, see URL <http://www.un.org/Docs/scres/2001/sc2001.htm>. On the Committee see URL <http://www.un.org/Docs/sc/committees/1373/>; and Biersteker, T. J., 'Counter-terrorism measures undertaken under UN Security Council auspices', eds A. J. K. Bailes and I. Frommelt, SIPRI, *Business and Security: Public–Private Sector Relationships in a New Security Environment* (Oxford University Press: Oxford, 2004), pp. 60–63, 64–66, 73.

[126] UN Security Council Resolution 1441, 8 Nov. 2002.

[127] The contribution made by each country was symbolic: they sent 115–380 troops. 'Latinoamericanos celebran la navidad en Irak' [Latin Americans celebrate Christmas in Iraq], *El Nuevo Herald*, 25 Dec. 2003, URL <http://www.miami.com/mld/elnuevo/news/world/americas/7566627.htm>; and 'Trillo visita a las tropas españolas desplegadas en Irak' [Trillo visits the Spanish troops deployed in Iraq], IblNews, 27 Sep. 2003, URL <http://www.iblnews.com/news/print.php3?id=87880>.

[128] To explain the participation of Central American countries in Iraq, it seems that this decision was made due to the ongoing negotiations with the USA to negotiate the Central American Free Trade Agreement (CAFTA), and, especially in the cases of El Salvador and Honduras, because of the migration agreements that make it possible for Hondurans and Salvadoreans to work in the USA and send their remittances to their homelands. These remittances are the most important source of capital flows for Central America, and for Latin America in general.

[129] Honduras had been strongly criticized at home and abroad in Mar.–Apr. 2004 for its proposal that the Office of the UN High Commissioner for Human Rights in Geneva send a rapporteur to Cuba at the same time that it condemned the human rights situation in Cuba. Honduras was seemingly unwilling to make another political concession to the USA, especially given that Cuba sponsors several social programmes in Honduras. Honduran President Ricardo Maduro also needed popular support to conclude free trade negotiations with the USA. Associated Press, 'Honduras rejects 25 medical scholarships from Cuba, 18 Apr. 2005, URL <http://feeds.bignewsnetwork.com/redir.php?jid=8ec275c116227aa1&cat=d3ec65f36ba00308>.

[130] Rosas, M. C., '¡Ay! esos hermanos latinoamericanos en Irak: ¡sálvese el que pueda!' [Oh! those Latin American brothers in Iraq: Save the ones you can], *Siempre!*, 23 May 2004, p. 55.

The benefits gained by the Central American states and the Dominican Republic from these contributions are unclear. The USA did not increase military assistance to these countries, and economic assistance to El Salvador, which showed more solidarity with the USA than other countries in the region, actually dropped. The USA gave El Salvador $40.4 million in aid in 2003, and was expected to provide only $28.89 million in 2005.[131]

VII. Conclusions

The influence of the US agenda on inter-American relations is undeniable, despite the marginal importance the USA now grants to Latin America and the Caribbean in its foreign policy. Some initiatives promoted autonomously by countries in the region have, however, introduced alternative emphases into the security debate. One of these was the OAS Special Conference on Security, held on 27–28 October 2003 in Mexico City, after years of preparation and effort in the OAS framework. This conference not only recognized the contributions to the reconceptualization of security made by states such as those in Central America (democratic security), but also accepted the concept of security as multidimensional, a term embracing all the concerns that OAS member states may have about their security without exclusion or hierarchy. The 2003 OAS Declaration on Security in the Americas[132] underlined that, although the USA considers terrorism the most important threat to its security, other OAS member states have other worries: in Central America and the Caribbean natural disasters usually become threats to security; in Colombia the war on drugs is an obvious priority; organized crime and violent gangs ('maras') have expanded and affect Central America, Mexico and the USA, and so on. The states of the region have thus refused to make terrorism the only, or dominant, item on their security agenda. This approach has attracted the attention of the United Nations, which is simultaneously celebrating its 60th anniversary and facing a reform process. The war on terrorism has favoured the debate on security over the debate on development; the multidimensional profile of security suggested by the OAS can reconcile both.

Latin America and the Caribbean have not profited as much as might be expected from their generally low military expenditure, relatively peaceful environment, the existence of democratic governments and reform of the military. In many respects, the very fact that the region has become a more or less stable zone allows the major powers to shift their focus to more problematic and 'critical' areas. Nevertheless, it is very much in the interest of the USA and the international community that the region remains stable and prosperous. If the USA does not pay the necessary attention, it is a permanent task that the countries of the region must take upon themselves, but the worst-case

[131] Haugaard *et al.* (note 121), p. 5.

[132] US Department of State, Bureau of Political-Military Affairs, 'Results of the OAS Special Conference on Security', 29 Oct. 2003, URL <http://www.state.gov/t/pm/rls/fs/26001.htm>.

scenario would be one where the situation deteriorates especially owing to economic and social constraints. ECLAC, for instance, considers that few countries in the region are capable of accomplishing their millennium development goals. ECLAC analysed 18 countries of which only 7 could reduce poverty by 2015 if the economic indicators of these countries continue the trends shown in the 1990s.[133]

More worrisome is the dependence of Latin America and the Caribbean on external developments. According to ECLAC, the region witnessed a growth rate of 5.5 per cent in 2004, mostly because of the dynamism shown by the US economy and, above all, the Chinese economy.[134] Should the Chinese or US economy experience a slowdown, this would have an adverse effect on Latin America and the Caribbean.

Another challenge for Latin America and the Caribbean is domestic violence and social unrest, which are linked, in part, to the inequitable distribution of wealth and the fragility of the region's political institutions.

In this respect, the security agenda should not be divorced from the development agenda. Security and development are two sides of the same coin. As shown above, Latin America and the Caribbean countries face practically every known variety of threat in the societal–security and national–transnational areas. Yet the governments of the region have treated the trade, health, education, anti-corruption, security, judicial and political agendas independently, almost ignoring the interdependence and complementarities between them.

In reality, none of these threats and risks can be addressed in isolation, or in a single community. They demand a collective effort, which in turn means overcoming past and recent rivalries. Brazil and Mexico are key players in this equation: if they do not come to an understanding on fundamental matters, they will contribute to a kind of 'Balkanization' of the region. Political reconciliation is thus the starting point for addressing national, regional and international security agendas. In its absence, all the countries of the region will remain vulnerable to the intrusions and demands of the USA, as shown in the evolution of inter-American relations before and after the 11 September 2001 terrorist attacks.

[133] UN Economic Commission for Latin America and the Caribbean (ECLAC), *Hacia el objetivo del milenio de reducir la pobreza en América Latina y el caribe* [Toward the millennium objective of reducing poverty in Latin America and the Caribbean], (Economic Commission for Latin America and the Caribbean: Santiago, 2003), URL <http://www.eclac.cl/cgi-bin/getProd.asp?xml=/publicaciones/xml/4/12544/P12544.xml&xsl=/deype/tpl/p9f.xsl&base=/tpl/top-bottom.xsl>.

[134] ECLAC, *Balance preliminar de las economías de América Latina y el Caribe* [Preliminary balance of Latin American and Caribbean economies] (Economic Commission for Latin America and the Caribbean: Santiago, 2004), URL <http://www.eclac.cl/cgi-bin/getProd.asp?xml=/publicaciones/xml/9/20479/P20479.xml&xsl=/de/tpl/p9f.xsl&base=/tpl/top-bottom.xsl>.

Part II. Military spending and armaments, 2004

7. Financing security in a global context

ELISABETH SKÖNS

I. Introduction

With the end of the cold war, the focus in the global security environment has shifted from superpower confrontation in a bipolar environment to the sources of insecurity in the developing countries in the South.[1] In parallel there has been a gradual reconceptualization of security, particularly in the North. Apart from the war in Iraq and a few other interstate conflicts, the predominant form of armed conflict today is intra-state armed conflict in low-income countries in the South,[2] although most such conflicts also have an international dimension.[3] People in the South are also exposed to a range of other threats, risks and challenges, such as criminal violence, hunger, infectious disease, environmental degradation and other consequences of bad governance and lack of development. For the countries of the North, the reduced risk of attack by conventional armed forces in the post-cold war environment has allowed them to shift focus from external military threats to other types of threat to the functioning of their states and societies. A range of vulnerabilities in other, non-military domains are increasingly becoming part of their security agendas, leading the countries of the North to consider such concepts as economic security, information security and environmental security. This broader concept of security has been further reinforced after 11 September 2001, when the threat of transnational terrorism became more prominent.

While there is still a lack of consensus on the exact nature and scope of current threats and, in particular, on their causes and how to address them, there is an emerging common understanding of two basic elements in the new security environment. First, there is an increased perception of the ineffectiveness and growing irrelevance of military means to address many of the current security threats, with a parallel recognition of the need to apply non-military policies and policy instruments instead.

Second, there is a growing recognition of the global nature of security and thus of the need for global action to address threats to security. In particular, the North has become more receptive to the argument, which has long been

[1] The terms South and North are used here for the developing and high-income countries, respectively, following the use of these terms by international organizations such as the United Nations Conference on Trade and Development (UNCTAD). See, e.g., UNCTAD, Follow-up to UNCTAD XI: New developments in international economic relations, President's summary, UN document TD/DB/51/L.7, 14 Oct. 2004, URL <http://www.unctad.org/>.

[2] See appendix 2A in this volume.

[3] On the internationalization of intra-state conflict and the increasing irrelevance of the categorization of armed conflict as intra- and interstate, see chapter 2 in this volume.

voiced in the South, that it has a shared interest in addressing the security problems and sources of insecurity in the South.[4] Intra-state armed conflicts in the South are increasingly perceived as having actual or potential consequences not only for the neighbouring countries but also for the countries in the North, for example through drug trafficking and refugee flows. Economic and environmental security and organized crime have a strong transnational dimension. The threat of transnational terrorism has also contributed to increased awareness of global interlinkages in security.

While there is broad consensus on the diagnosis at a general level, the recommendations for cure differ. According to one view, there is a need for a new doctrine of 'cooperative imperialism' by the North to address the security threats originating in the South.[5] Another view is to regard the new threats as a common challenge to global security. Acknowledging that some of these problems can be solved only by cooperating and that the economic resources and domestic capacity of the countries of the South are insufficient for them to properly address their security problems, the logical consequence would appear to be that the countries of the North need to make a significant investment in helping to address the insecurities of the South. This is one of the rationales behind the idea of 'global public goods', public goods whose benefits cut across borders.[6] It is also reflected in the analysis of the United Nations (UN) High-level Panel on Threats, Challenges and Change, which reported its findings in December 2004.[7] Inherent in the reconceptualization of security challenges according to this view is a global reallocation of resources, from the national to the international level and from military to non-military activities.

The aim of this chapter is to discuss the implications of the reconceptualization of security for the financing of security. Since great costs are associated with the provision of security, resource allocation must constitute a fundamental basis for this reconceptualization. While it is not possible to look at all relevant resource flows because available statistics are not adapted to

[4] See, e.g., Council of the European Union, 'A secure Europe in a better world: European Security Strategy', Brussels, 12 Dec. 2003, URL <http://europa.eu.int/comm/research/security/>. Other national security and defence strategies and policies also reflect this view.

[5] Robert Cooper, a former senior British diplomat, identifies the main threats to the postmodern world (Europe and Japan) as coming from the modern and pre-modern worlds (the South). He calls for a new liberal imperialism involving a doctrine of humanitarian intervention and based on the acceptance of a need for double standards: 'Among ourselves, we operate on the basis of laws and open co-operative security. But when dealing with more old-fashioned kinds of states . . . we need to revert to the rougher methods of an earlier era—force, pre-emptive attack, deception, whatever is necessary to deal with those states who still live in the 19th century world of "every state for itself".' Cooper, R., 'The post-modern state', ed. M. Leonard, *Re-Ordering the World* (Foreign Policy Centre: London, 2002), URL <http://fpc.org.uk/publications/>, pp. 11–20; further developed in Cooper, R., *The Breaking of Nations: Order and Chaos in the Twenty-First Century* (Atlantic Books: London, 2003).

[6] Kaul, I. *et al.*, *Providing Global Public Goods: Managing Globalization*, published for the United Nations Development Programme (Oxford University Press: New York, 2003).

[7] United Nations, 'A more secure world: our shared responsibility', Report of the High-level Panel on Threats, Challenges and Change, UN documents A/59/565, 4 Dec. 2004, and A/59/565/Corr. 1, 6 Dec. 2004, URL <http://www.un.org/ga/59/documentation/list5.html>. For the synopsis of the report see the appendix to the Introduction in this volume.

this purpose, examination of some of these flows can be productive at this stage, not least in order to stimulate further research and demand for data that are better adapted to the needs of such an analysis.

This chapter continues in section II with a survey of the main threats, risks and challenges in the current security environment. The available statistics on relevant types of resource flows are examined in section III with a view to evaluating the extent to which resource allocation meets the needs of the current security threats. Section III also presents models for the international financing of common global activities to promote security. Section IV provides a summary and the conclusions.

II. Threats, risks and challenges

Changes in the actual security environment and the consequent reconceptualization of security are still ongoing. These developments are composed of different strands, which makes it difficult to summarize them briefly. This section attempts to capture some of the major elements in these changes. It gives a brief description of the post-cold war conceptualization of threats, risks and challenges, outlining the main developments in four areas: military territorial threats, terrorism, intra-state armed conflicts, and a range of broader and deeper challenges to security, including functional security and human security.

Military territorial threats

During the early post-cold war period, the reduced external military threats to state and territorial security led to a profound reduction in military expenditure in many of the major powers that had previously been involved in the East–West arms race. The security debate in the North was shaped in terms of disarmament, the peace dividend and conversion of military resources to non-military use. There was a gradual shift in focus to other security problems, in particular to the threats from weapons of mass destruction (WMD) and to intra-state armed conflict in the South and in the disintegrating European states. Threats from WMD have continued to be perceived as a major concern, but non-military policy instruments are increasingly being seen as relevant for addressing such threats.[8] Security strategies and military doctrines have been adapted in many countries in order to integrate new military and non-military tasks that address these security problems.

During the cold war, cooperation within international organizations for collective defence played an important role in territorial security; today the North Atlantic Treaty Organization (NATO) is the major remaining organization of this type. International cooperation for new military tasks is more limited. Peacekeeping within the UN framework, which began in the after-

[8] See chapter 11 in this volume.

math of World War II, has in recent year been complemented and supported by a range of peace missions carried out by other international organizations, such as NATO, the European Union (EU), the African Union (AU) and the Economic Community of West African States (ECOWAS).[9]

The concept of military intervention for humanitarian purposes emerged in the early post-cold war period in response to the massive killings in intra-state armed conflicts in several countries, including Bosnia and Herzegovina, East Timor and Rwanda. However, military intervention has so far been limited. The main exception to this rule is the USA, which has integrated out-of-area pre-emptive strikes into its national security doctrine, most recently implemented in Afghanistan and Iraq. While the objective of the war in Afghanistan was to combat terrorism, the official objective of the war in Iraq was to pre-empt an attack by WMD; when this threat was proven to be non-existent, the objective was reformulated as regime change and democratization. Australia, the United Kingdom and a range of other big and small states have also shown their readiness for military intervention, but only in US-led operations such as the war in Iraq.

While the emerging post-cold war military security environment is still far from reaching final definition, current trends indicate some paradoxes. The major military powers in the North have moved from a collectivist approach to military territorial and state security to a situation in which some countries are reverting to a unilateralist approach. Territorial defence remains an important element of national security strategies, while new military tasks in out-of-area locations have been added. The result is a fragmented notion of military security in the North, which suggests that further significant changes are to come.

Terrorism

Contemporary terrorism is predominantly transnational and has a strongly transnational economic foundation. A recent study of the economic resources involved in the financing of activities by terrorist groups and other non-state armed actors illustrates the economic scale and nature of the problems.[10] It is argued in the study that the roots of terrorism are economic rather than political or religious and that contemporary transnational terrorism has become possible as a result of three main developments since World War II: (*a*) the growth of state-sponsored terrorism, in particular during the early cold war period when both superpowers fought wars by proxy; (*b*) the privatization of terrorism during the late 1970s and early 1980s, when armed organizations made themselves independent of their sponsors and developed strategies of

[9] See chapter 3 in this volume.

[10] Napoleoni, L., *Modern Jihad: Tracing the Dollars Behind the Terror Networks* (Pluto Press: London, 2003). An even more radical view of the emerging fragmentation of the global economic system is provided by Peter Lock, who argues that the world economy is now split into 3 segments: the regular, the informal and the criminal. Lock, P., 'Gewalt als Regulation: Zur Logik der Schattenglobalisierung' [Violence as order: the dynamics of shadow globalization], eds S. Kurtenbach and P. Lock, *Kriege als (Über)Lebenswelten* [Wars as worlds of existence/survival] (Dietz-Verlag: Bonn, 2004), pp. 41–52.

self-financing; and (*c*) the globalization of terrorism in the 1990s, when the deregulation of the international financial markets made it possible for armed groups to raise money in more than one country and to operate across borders. The study maps out how different types of armed organizations have built their own economies with the support of income from illegal trade in narcotics, natural resources and people as well as from legal activities. It is claimed that what has emerged is an international economic system, run primarily by armed organizations, which is termed the 'new economy of terror', with a turnover of the magnitude of $1.5 trillion, corresponding to about 5 per cent of world gross domestic product.[11]

Consensus is emerging that military means are ineffective in fighting international terrorism. The issue is instead one of finding the proper balance between means of protection from terrorist activities and means of combating terrorism through long-term policies that address its sources. The USA's National Strategy for Combating Terrorism, adopted in February 2003, identifies four counter-terrorism goals: (*a*) defeating terrorist organizations with global reach; (*b*) denying sponsorship, support and sanctuary to terrorists; (*c*) diminishing the underlying conditions that terrorists seek to exploit; and (*d*) defending US citizens and interests.[12] It explicitly states that the strategy must also include long-term measures against the 'underlying conditions that promote the despair and the destructive visions of political change that lead people to embrace, rather than shun, terrorism'.[13] The EU's security strategy identifies a range of complex causes of global terrorism, including the pressures of modernization, cultural, social and political crises, and the alienation of young people living in foreign societies.[14]

A range of internal security instruments have been developed at the national level for the prevention of and protection against terrorist attacks. In the USA the relevant agencies for combating terrorism have been brought together in the Department of Homeland Security, established in 2003.[15] Budget allocation for homeland security in the USA has increased significantly since 11 September 2001,[16] but it is still criticized for being insufficient.[17] In particular, the relative priorities assigned to military expenditure and spending on

[11] Napoleoni (note 10).

[12] The White House, 'National Strategy for Combating Terrorism', Washington, DC, Feb. 2003, URL <http://www.whitehouse.gov/news/releases/2003/02/20030214-7.html>.

[13] The White House (note 12), p. 29.

[14] Council of the European Union (note 4), p. 3.

[15] On the Department of Homeland Security's activities in 2004 see chapter 1 in this volume.

[16] The US budget proposal for financial year (FY) 2005 included $31 billion in outlays for homeland security, more than twice the sum spent in FY 2001. Office of Management and Budget, 'Department of Homeland Security', *Budget of the United States Government: Fiscal Year 2005* (The White House: Washington, DC, 2004), URL <http://www.whitehouse.gov/omb/budget/fy2005/homeland.html>.

[17] This was the conclusion of a 2003 study by the Brookings Institution and by both Democrat and Republican members of the United States Congress. 'White House accused of shortchanging security budget', *New York Times*, 3 Feb. 2003. Others argue that nearly one-third of the Department of Homeland Security's budget goes to non-homeland security functions, while at the same time less than 60% of funding for homeland security purposes is covered by the department's budget. Berteau, D. J., 'Homeland security budgeting: can confusion produce priorities?', *ECAAR NewsNetwork*, vol. 16, no. 2 (July 2004), URL <http://www.ecaar.org/Newsletter/July2004.pdf>, pp. 1, 4–5.

homeland security are seen as being misguided. In Europe the waves of terrorist activity since the 1970s have meant that a range of measures for the prevention of terrorist attacks have been introduced.[18] European countries do not have a specific budget heading for 'homeland security'. Instead, such expenditure falls under a variety of budget headings, such as internal security, intelligence and border controls, so it is not possible to identify the amount of public spending on homeland security. Thc EU itsclf has responded to threats of terrorism with policies affecting not only the security of citizens but also the broader economic infrastructure and environmental areas.[19]

In the longer term, measures focused on domestic protection and prevention are insufficient. Furthermore, it is increasingly acknowledged that such measures have a range of adverse consequences at both the national and international levels, and that some of these may even aggravate the problems and introduce new risks. As argued in a recent survey of the problems inherent in this approach, if they go too far, many of these measures will erode domestic civil liberties and alienate minority groups, whose cooperation is crucial in the domestic counter-terrorism effort. They will also undermine Western moral authority and the West's ability to pressure others to adhere to international norms and standards, thus hindering the creation of broad international anti-terrorism coalitions.[20]

In parallel with approaches at the national level, there is broad agreement that transnational terrorism must also be combated by international means. Since 11 September 2001 a range of measures have been introduced for this purpose. The Organisation for Economic Co-operation and Development (OECD) has developed guidelines for the international community and governments on how to address linkages between terrorism and development.[21] It has a comprehensive approach: 'OECD governments need to rally actors in trade, defence, foreign affairs, finance and development agencies to work together to articulate clearly roles in combating terrorism'.[22] Four main tasks are identified: (*a*) to bolster long-term structural stability; (*b*) to dissuade disaffected groups from embracing terrorism and other forms of violent conflict; (*c*) to deny groups or individuals the means to carry out terrorism, in particular to reinforce governance; and (*d*) to promote policy coherence and complementarity. These guidelines are not uncontroversial but have raised a number of issues, including whether development policy should be directed

[18] For a detailed overview of these measures see Dalgaard-Nielsen, A., 'Civil liberties and counter-terrorism: a European point of view', Opinions series, Center for Transatlantic Relations, Paul H. Nitze School of Advanced International Studies, Johns Hopkins University, Washington, DC, 2004, URL <http://transatlantic.sais-jhu.edu/Publications/opinions/>.

[19] Burgess, N. and Spence, D., 'The European Union: new threats and problems of coherence', eds A. J. K. Bailes and I. Frommelt, SIPRI, *Business and Security: Public–Private Relationships in a New Security Environment* (Oxford University Press: Oxford, 2004), pp. 84–101.

[20] Dalgaard-Nielsen (note 18).

[21] OECD Development Assistance Committee (DAC), 'A development co-operation lens on terrorism prevention: key entry points for action', DAC Guidelines and Reference Series, Paris, 2003, URL <http://www.oecd.org/dataoecd/17/4/16085708.pdf>.

[22] OECD DAC (note 21), p. 8.

towards countries where terrorism is a problem or towards countries from which terrorists have come; whether aid to such countries creates an incentive to 'deliver terrorists'; and whether development aid should be used for purposes other than aid for the poor.[23]

Most importantly in the international context, the UN has adopted several resolutions that address international terrorism.[24] In particular, UN Security Council Resolution 1373, adopted on 28 September 2001, obliges all UN member states to enact domestic legislation that criminalizes terrorist acts and the support and financing of such acts; denies safe haven to terrorists and prohibits any other support for terrorists, such as the provision of arms; and requires prompt cooperation with other states in the implementation of such measures.[25] To monitor implementation of this resolution, the UN Security Council established the Counter-Terrorism Committee (CTC).[26] However, as argued in a recent analysis, the CTC lacks both the authority and the resources required to undertake its tasks.[27] According to its first chairman, Sir Jeremy Greenstock, the goal of the CTC is 'to help the world system to upgrade its capability to deny space, money, support, haven to terrorism, and to establish a network of information-sharing and co-operative executive action'.[28] A major obstacle to this is that many countries cannot afford to strengthen their weak border controls or do not have the capacity to police their territories effectively. For the effective implementation of Resolution 1373 these countries would need help to finance and set up counter-terrorism programmes. The failure to set up an assistance trust fund for these purposes, because the USA rejected the proposal, has so far restricted this type of assistance.

Resource allocation requires policies. While policies for national protection are comparatively easy to design, long-term policies to address the causes of international terrorism are much more difficult to develop, not least because of the lack of a commonly agreed definition of terrorism and the lack of consensus on its sources. The UN High-level Panel on Threats, Challenges and Change reported that many of the governments and civil society organizations consulted expressed fears that approaches to terrorism which focus wholly on military, police and intelligence measures risk undermining efforts to promote

[23] Canadian Council for International Co-operation (CCIC), 'A CCIC commentary on "A development co-operation lens on terrorism prevention: key entry points for action"', Ottawa, Oct. 2003, URL <http://www.ccic.ca/>. This paper also argues that the link between terrorism, poverty and failed states has not been demonstrated and that the DAC guidelines may well undermine donor approaches to preventing violent conflict by being overtaken by a Northern-driven agenda that targets significant resources to the 'war on terrorism'.

[24] For an overview see Biersteker, T. J., 'Counter-terrorism measures undertaken under UN Security Council auspices', eds Bailes and Frommelt (note 19), pp. 59–75.

[25] UN Security Council Resolution 1373, 28 Sep. 2001, URL <http://www.un.org/Docs/sc/>.

[26] On CTC activities see URL <http://www.un.org/Docs/sc/committees/1373/>.

[27] de Jonge Oudraat, C., 'Combating terrorism', *Washington Quarterly*, vol. 26, no. 4 (autumn 2003), pp. 163–76.

[28] Greenstock, J., Chairman of the UN CTC, Press briefing, New York, 19 Oct. 2001, quoted by de Jonge Oudraat (note 27), p. 169.

good governance and human rights, alienate parts of the world's population and thereby weaken the potential for collective action against terrorism.[29]

Intra-state armed conflicts

Most armed conflicts today are intra-state conflicts—although often with strong international elements—in low-income countries. In order to develop policies to reduce the incidence of armed conflict, it is necessary to understand the causes and dynamics of such conflicts. A considerable amount of research has been devoted to this subject in recent years. While there is some divergence in the findings of these research efforts and there are still major gaps in knowledge, partly because the pattern and causes of conflicts are not homogenous, it is generally believed that there is now sufficient knowledge to develop appropriate international approaches to reducing the incidence of intra-state armed conflict.[30]

This subsection provides a brief account of the main current findings on the resource-related causes of intra-state armed conflict and of the recommended policies and policy instruments emerging from this research. In order to indicate the potential benefits that might be gained from successful policies, rough estimates of the costs of intra-state armed conflict are presented.

The causes and remedies: conflict and development

In a review of recent research on the relationships between economics and armed conflict, this subject is categorized according to the five main economic factors that are considered as having an impact on the incidence of intra-state armed conflict: poverty and wealth, economic inequality, natural resources, economic policies and trade.[31] There is some disagreement on the importance of these factors and in some cases on whether the relationship is positive or negative. However, there is rather broad consensus on one point: economic growth is associated with lower levels of conflict. Consequently, policies to promote growth in developing countries are 'likely to act as agents for conflict prevention'.[32]

The two main schools of thought on the economic sources of intra-state armed conflict have developed from the research teams of Frances Stewart and Paul Collier. Stewart focuses on armed conflict in poor countries, claiming that 80 per cent of the world's poorest countries are suffering or have recently suffered from large-scale violent conflict.[33] She argues against the tendency to

[29] United Nations (note 7), paragraph 147, p. 48.

[30] Collier, P. *et al.*, *Breaking the Conflict Trap: Civil War and Development Policy*, A World Bank Policy Research Report (Oxford University Press: New York, 2003). See also chapter 2 in this volume.

[31] Humphreys, M., 'Economics and violent conflict', Program on Humanitarian Policy and Conflict Research, School of Public Health, Harvard University, Feb. 2003, URL <http://www.preventconflict.org/portal/economics/>.

[32] Humphreys (note 31), Executive summary.

[33] Stewart, F., 'Root causes of violent conflict in developing countries', *British Medical Journal*, vol. 324 (9 Feb. 2002), p. 342.

attribute armed conflict in developing countries to ethnic divisions, since it diverts attention from important underlying economic and political factors. According to Stewart, the major root causes of conflict include political, economic and social inequalities, extreme poverty, economic stagnation, poor government services, high unemployment, environmental degradation and individual economic incentives to fight.[34] In particular, horizontal inequality (i.e., inequality among groups) has been identified as the fundamental source of organized conflict.[35] Against this background, the policies recommended to reduce the likelihood of wars include the promotion of inclusive development; the reduction in inequalities between groups; the tackling of unemployment; and, via national and international control over illicit trade, the reduction in private incentives to fight.[36]

The Collier team has identified four basic types of conflict situation: (*a*) sudden economic crashes in middle-income countries; (*b*) low-income countries with stagnant or declining economies; (*c*) countries in conflict; and (*d*) countries in the first decade of post-conflict peace, about half of which will fall back into conflict.[37] Strategies for risk reduction need to differentiate between these different types of conflict. They also need to consider a range of policies, including not only development policy but also peacekeeping, domestic military spending and the design of political institutions, and to take an integrated approach when implementing these policies. According to the assessment of the Collier team, international intervention to reduce the incidence of conflict has the greatest chance of being effective in the fourth of these situations, through a combination of external military peacekeeping during the first few years following the end of a conflict and large aid programmes. In the second situation, the low-income countries, the risk of conflict would be reduced if development could be ignited, but this is likely to be difficult for historical reasons.

International responses to intra-state armed conflict are increasingly focusing on the challenges of state-building and the practice of governance.[38] This is the result of the current emphasis on the economic dynamics of conflict and the structural approach to understanding the persistence of intra-state conflict. This structural approach, which focuses on a state's lack of capacity to deliver basic security and welfare to its citizens, has led to increased attention being paid to the relationship between security and development and to the legitimacy of external intervention in state-building.[39]

The relationship between globalization and armed conflict is complex and contested. According to one view, globalization contributes to the reduction of

[34] Stewart, F. and FitzGerald, V. (eds), *War and Underdevelopment*, vol. 1, *The Economic and Social Consequences of Conflict* (Oxford University Press: Oxford, 2001).

[35] Stewart, F., 'The root causes of conflict: some conclusions', QEH Working Paper Series no. 16, Queen Elizabeth House, University of Oxford, June 1998, URL <http://www.eldis.org/>.

[36] Stewart (note 33).

[37] Collier *et al.* (note 30).

[38] Dwan, R. and Gustavsson, M., 'Major armed conflicts', *SIPRI Yearbook 2004: Armaments, Disarmament and International Security* (Oxford University Press: Oxford, 2004), pp. 95–131.

[39] Dwan and Gustavsson (note 38), pp. 100–101.

armed conflict because it is assumed that 'liberal globalization' is likely to strengthen rather than weaken states and democratic forces in the long run. This view is based on the belief that most decisions about resource allocations are best left to the market.[40] According to another view, globalization increases the risk of armed conflict because deregulation and other aspects of globalization have contributed to unemployment, poverty and unequal development;[41] it thereby 'generates conditions that are conducive to the emergence of extremist movements, instability and conflict'.[42] According to a third view, globalization is a major factor in the causation of internal armed conflict because it is the major reason for the erosion of state capability to govern, which in turn is seen as the predominant cause of internal armed conflict.[43]

The costs of intra-state armed conflict

There is a dearth of information on the costs of armed conflict since such costs are extremely difficult to estimate: first, because it is difficult to identify all the component costs, in particular the indirect ones, which as a rule are higher than the direct costs; second, because it is difficult to distinguish the impact of war from the impact of other factors; and third, because there is a lack of data. Even existing data are often unreliable; for example, the official figures on military expenditure are severely understated in countries in armed conflict.

A rough calculation to estimate the cost of some major components of armed conflict showed that the average cost of intra-state armed conflict in low-income countries during the post-cold war period amounted to at least $64.2 billion over a period of 21 years.[44] This estimate includes those economic and social items that it was possible to make estimates for within a reasonable degree of certainty, namely the increase in military expenditure, the impact of armed conflict on economic growth in both the conflict-affected

[40] de Soysa, I. and Gleditsch, N. P., 'The liberal globalist case', eds Hettne, B. and Odén, B., *Global Governance in the 21st Century: Alternative Perspectives on World Order*, Swedish Foreign Ministry Expert Group on Development Issues Study no. 2002:2 (Almkvist & Wiksell: Stockholm, 2002), URL <http://www.egdi.gov.se/>, pp. 26–73.

[41] This was the conclusion of the 1995 Global Summit in Copenhagen and has been reinforced by further research since then. See, e.g., United Nations Research Institute for Social Development (UNRISD), *Visible Hands: Taking Responsibility for Social Development* (UNRISD: Geneva, 2000), URL <http://www.unrisd.org/>; the theoretical chapters and case studies in Veltmeyer, H. (ed.), *Globalization and Antiglobalization: Dynamics of Change in the New World Order* (Ashgate: Aldershot, 2004); and the seminal findings reported in Cornia, G. A. (ed.), *Inequality, Growth, and Poverty in an Era of Liberalization and Globalization* (Oxford University Press: Oxford, 2004).

[42] Sandbrook, R. and Romano, D., 'Globalisation, extremism and violence in poor countries', *Third World Quarterly*, vol. 25, no. 6 (Sep. 2004), pp. 1007–30.

[43] Brzoska, M., '"New wars" discourse in Germany', *Journal of Peace Research*, vol. 41, no. 1 (2004), pp. 107–17.

[44] Collier, P. and Hoeffler, A., 'The challenge of reducing the global incidence of civil war', Copenhagen Consensus Challenge Paper, Apr. 2004, URL <http://www.copenhagenconsensus.com/Default.asp?ID=221>, pp. 6–10. The period of 21 years was chosen because the average length of armed conflict in low-income countries during this period was 14 years and it was assumed that the impact of war lasted 7 years after the end of conflict. See also Bohnstedt, A., 'Why civil wars are costly—and what could be done to reduce these costs', World Markets Research Centre, London, Nov. 2004, URL <http://www.pwcglobal.com/>.

country and the neighbouring countries, and the cost of health deterioration in the conflict-affected country. The impact of war on economic growth arises primarily from five main factors: (*a*) the crowding out of productive expenditure by the rise in military expenditure; (*b*) destruction of infrastructure; (*c*) looting and destruction by soldiers; (*d*) loss of private capital as a result of population flight; and (*e*) reduced constraints on criminal behaviour.[45] In addition to these factors, $10.2 billion of the estimated average cost of conflict arises from the 'conflict trap effect', a concept devised to capture the increased risk of resumed conflict in countries that have been affected by conflict.

Few intra-state major armed conflicts remain self-contained; they often have an impact on neighbouring countries and on the wider international community.[46] Roughly half of the above estimate is assigned to costs borne by neighbouring countries, which are often strongly affected, for example, by the disruption to their economic activities and by refugee flows. However, the estimate does not include the global cost of conflict because of the insurmountable difficulties of estimation. It is nevertheless argued that the global costs are very high since intra-state armed conflicts have facilitated the spread of three global social evils: drugs, HIV/AIDS and terrorism.

These regional and global costs of intra-state armed conflict point to the potential cost-effectiveness for richer countries of investing in measures that reduce the incidence of armed conflict in low-income countries. This is also the conclusion of another study, which has estimated both the external costs of armed conflict and the potential costs of prevention.[47] It concluded that the external costs of armed conflict—that is, costs incurred by countries that are not parties to the conflict—exceed the cost of potential measures to reduce the number or scale of armed conflicts, in some cases by a large factor.

Broader and deeper security challenges

With the broadening and deepening of the concept of security, traditional security agendas are being complemented with a range of additional risks and challenges.[48] The broader security agendas expand the spectrum of vulnerabilities in the functioning of state and society. The deeper security agendas shift the focus from states to individuals, under the rubric of 'human security'.

The broader security agendas give more attention to risks to life, property and the environment. These include risks to economic and environmental security and threats from organized crime, as well as the risks of disturbance to or destruction of critical infrastructure and information technology. In general, there is a stronger focus on the vulnerabilities of societies, in particular

[45] Collier, P. *et al.* (note 30).

[46] Dwan and Gustavsson (note 38), p. 96.

[47] Brown, M. E. and Rosecrance, R. N. (eds), *The Costs of Conflict: Prevention and Cure in the Global Arena* (Rowman and Littlefield: Lanham, Md., 1999).

[48] For a discussion of the broader and the deeper conception of security see Hagelin, B. and Sköns, E., 'The military sector in a changing context', *SIPRI Yearbook 2003: Armaments, Disarmament and International Security* (Oxford University Press: Oxford, 2003), pp. 281–300.

complex societies. These risks must be met by almost exclusively non-military means, mostly in the domain of internal security. Many of the policy instruments for protection and prevention in the area of broader security challenges coincide with those developed for protection from and prevention of terrorism. Thus, the USA's homeland security budget is devoted not only to anti-terrorism measures but also to a range of other threats to internal security. In Europe different types of crisis-management instrument are being developed to cope with such broader security challenges.[49] In the Nordic countries a so-called 'functional security' agenda is being developed to address security issues in the areas of critical infrastructure, information technology, nuclear, biological and chemical issues, and terrorism.[50] Some of these broader security risks have domestic sources, but many also originate abroad, and their reduction thus requires international cooperation.

Policies to address new types of threat to security are being widely discussed at the national level and, in Europe, by the EU. Rather than looking at ways to remove or diminish man-made and structural sources of insecurity, governments and regional organizations tend to think primarily in terms of their own immediate security: border controls, rescue services and domestic crisis management. This reflects a view of security that focuses on domestic or regional security and for which the solution is to seal the territory off from international threats. While such measures better reflect the new security challenges than military defence, they suffer from the limitations of only addressing the symptoms and of imposing restrictions on domestic freedom.

Human security agendas focus on the security of the individual rather than on state security. The concept of human security became widely known with the publication of the *Human Development Report 1994* of the United Nations Development Programme (UNDP).[51] It has subsequently developed in two directions, one that covers challenges to the basic needs of people, sometimes described as 'freedom from want', and another that is more narrow, focusing on the threat of force and violence to people's everyday lives, which can be described as 'freedom from fear'.[52] While the first of these encompasses issues

[49] For analysis and proposals on how to deal with broader internal security challenges within the EU see, e.g., the writings of Heather Grabbe, Centre for European Reform, London, URL <http://www.cer.org.uk/>.

[50] Holmgren, J. and Softa, J., 'The functional security agenda in the Nordic states', Threat Politics, Swedish Emergency Management Agency, 2003, URL <http://www.threat-politics.net/>; Bailes, A. J. K., 'New challenges to human security: how relevant is the "Nordic model"?', Statement at the Conference Exploring Functional Security: National Responses and Prospects for Nordic and European Collaboration, 24–25 Oct. 2002, Swedish Institute for International Affairs, Stockholm, URL <http://www.nnss.org/functionalsecurity_seminars.htm>; and Ekengren, M. (ed.), *Functional Security: A Forward Looking Approach to European and Nordic Security and Defence Policy*, Proceedings of the conference held at the Swedish National Defence College, 5–6 Dec. 2003, SI Acta B no. 30 (Försvarshögskolan: Stockholm, 2004).

[51] United Nations Development Programme, *Human Development Report 1994: New Dimensions of Human Security* (Oxford University Press: New York, 1994), URL <http://hdr.undp.org/>.

[52] Krause, K., 'Is human security "more than just a good idea"?' and Mack, A., 'The concept of human security', eds Brzoska, M. and Croll, P. J., *Promoting Security: But How and For Whom?*, Bonn International Center for Conversion (BICC) Brief no. 30 (BICC: Bonn, Oct. 2004), URL <http://www.bicc.de/publications/>, pp. 43–46, 47–50.

of economic development, the latter does not. However, that does not mean that the proponents of the more narrow version see no links between human security and human and economic development. On the contrary, they acknowledge the interconnections between security, development and governance.[53]

The UN Millennium Declaration includes goals related to both freedom from want and freedom from fear.[54] The latter class of goals is difficult to discuss in terms of resource allocation, but the goals related to freedom from want are more suitable for this. The UN established eight Millennium Development Goals (MDGs) to consolidate the development targets in the Millennium Declaration. They range from the universal provision of primary education, gender equality, reduction in child mortality and improved maternal health, to stemming the spread of HIV/AIDS and ensuring environmental sustainability, with the overarching aim of reducing extreme income poverty by half, all by the deadline of 2015. The eighth goal, a global partnership for development, comprises a set of commitments by developed countries to support these efforts through increased aid, a non-discriminatory trading system and debt relief.[55]

III. Resource allocation

Resources allocated for security purposes have traditionally meant public expenditure on military forces, that is, military expenditure. The new threats and challenges identified during the post-cold war period have implied a need for reallocation of resources from military to non-military means and from measures applied domestically to assistance to other countries to help them address their security problems and sources of insecurity. In particular, it has been argued that it would be cost-effective for the North to invest the resources needed to prevent armed conflict and promote peace and security in the South because of the negative economic impact if they abstain from doing so. For example, this is the rationale behind the global public goods initiative, originally conceived by the UNDP.[56] It is modelled on the concept of public goods in economics: goods whose benefits are not limited to a single consumer, as with private goods, but which are available to all and are thus open to a 'free ride', and for which, therefore, no single individual is prepared to pay. At the national level, public goods are paid for via a system of public budgets and taxes. Similarly, it is argued that there are global public goods that no individual country is prepared to pay for. These are defined in relation to challenges, or global public 'bads', exemplified by many of the world's main crises, from armed conflict and terrorism to climate change. These affect many indiscriminately, but they hit those with the fewest resources more

[53] Mack (note 52), p. 50.

[54] UN General Assembly Resolution 55/2, 8 Sep. 2000, URL <http://www.un.org/ga/>.

[55] United Nations, Millennium Development Goals, URL <http://www.un.org/millenniumgoals/>.

[56] Kaul *et al.* (note 6).

Table 7.1. Patterns of military expenditure and armed conflict, 2003

Country income group	Share of world military expenditure (%)	Number of major armed conflicts[a]	Total number of armed conflicts[b]
High income	*76.5*	2[c]	1
Upper middle income	*9.1*	0	0
Lower middle income	*10.3*	8	8
Low income	*4.1*	9	20
Total	***100***	**19**	**29**

Notes: [a] A major armed conflict is defined as a contested incompatibility concerning government or territory that results in the use the military forces of 2 parties, at least 1 of which is the government of a state, with at least 1000 battle-related deaths in any single year.

[b] An armed conflict is defined as above, but with at least 25 battle-related deaths in one year.

[c] This includes the USA–al-Qaeda conflict, while the figure for total armed conflicts does not. This is the result of different interpretations of the conflict in the two series.

Sources: **Military expenditure**: SIPRI Military expenditure database; **major armed conflicts**: Eriksson, M. and Wallensteen, P., 'Patterns of major armed conflicts, 1990–2003', *SIPRI Yearbook 2004: Armaments, Disarmament and International Security* (Oxford University Press: Oxford, 2004), pp. 132–143; **total armed conflicts**: Eriksson, M. and Wallensteen, P., 'Armed conflict, 1989–2003', *Journal of Peace Research*, vol. 41, no. 5 (Sep. 2004), pp. 625–36; and The Uppsala Conflict Database, Uppsala Conflict Data Program, Department of Peace and Conflict Research, Uppsala University, URL <http://www.pcr.uu.se/database/>.

severely than those with private or national means to protect themselves. Therefore, they need to be addressed by global public goods, that is, by measures to promote peace and security. The global public good initiative raises the question of which global public goods need to be jointly produced in our age of open borders and increasingly intertwined national public domains.[57] The rationale behind an approach along these or similar lines is not humanitarian charity but enlightened self-interest.[58]

This section analyses, as far as the available data allow, some patterns of resource allocation that are relevant in this context. It also presents a menu of different mechanisms that could be used for public and private international financing of measures to promote global peace and security.

Military expenditure

In spite of the reduction in external military threats to national territory since the end of the cold war, most governments still assign high priority to military strength. After a nine-year post-cold war decline in military expenditure,

[57] Kaul *et al.* (note 6), p. xvi.

[58] Müller, H., 'Farewell to unilateralism', *Internationale Politik Transatlantic Edition*, vol. 5, no. 2 (summer 2004), pp. 54–58.

world military expenditure has been rising again since 1998, and in recent years at a particularly high rate.[59]

The global pattern of armed conflict does not correspond to the pattern of military expenditure. Since poor countries can afford to spend less on military security than rich countries can, the global pattern of military expenditure corresponds roughly to the pattern of national income rather than to the pattern of conflict. There is a consequent profound mismatch between the pattern of provision of military force and the distribution of armed conflict. As table 7.1 shows, while roughly half of major armed conflicts and more than two-thirds of all armed conflicts take place in low-income countries, more than three-quarters of world military expenditure is spent by high-income countries. On a regional basis, it is only in the Middle East and Latin America that there is a correspondence between the incidence of conflict and the level of military expenditure.

This discrepancy between patterns of military expenditure and armed conflict is subject to a range of explanations. Some would argue that it is because of the high military expenditure in the North that there is a lower incidence of armed conflict and a higher degree of security in the North than in the South. According to this view, military forces prevent conflict through deterrence, their internal security roles, positive effects on nationhood and collective security in the region. Others would argue that military expenditure does not always provide military security and that, indeed, the expenditure is often made for reasons other than security: economic, industrial, technological, social and regional policy reasons. In addition, official figures on military expenditure do not always reflect the full extent of actual military expenditure, since they exclude off-budget and hidden spending.[60] This is especially true in countries in conflict or affected by conflict.

The burden of military expenditure, measured as its share of gross domestic product, is better correlated with the pattern of armed conflict. The majority of the countries with the highest known military burden are countries that are, or have recently been, involved in armed conflict or are located in regions with major security problems.[61] The regions with the highest military burden are the Middle East, North America, Central and Eastern Europe, and Africa.[62]

In comparison with military expenditure, the resources devoted to multilateral peace missions in locations of intra-state armed conflict are small. However, the full picture of expenditure on peacekeeping is not available. The UN's budget of $2.3 billion for peacekeeping, financed by national contributions, often via ministries for foreign affairs, covers only part of these resources. Military peace missions provided by the EU and NATO are funded according to the principle that 'costs lie where they fall'; that is, member

[59] See chapter 8 in this volume.

[60] Omitoogun, W., *Military Expenditure Data in Africa: A Survey of Cameroon, Ethiopia, Ghana, Kenya, Nigeria and Uganda*, SIPRI Research Report no. 17 (Oxford University Press: Oxford, 2003).

[61] Sköns, E. *et al.*, 'Military expenditure', *SIPRI Yearbook 2004* (note 38), p. 309.

[62] Sköns, E. *et al.*, 'Military expenditure', *SIPRI Yearbook 2003* (note 48), table 10.2, p. 303.

states pay directly for the missions they provide.[63] While it may be possible to identify the share of military expenditure that some countries devote to peacekeeping—both the deployment costs and the cost of equipment and training—there are no international statistics available that would allow an assessment of the global expenditure on peacekeeping.

Peace missions carried out by the AU and ECOWAS are eligible for funding from the African Peace Facility, established by the EU in 2003.[64] Access to the facility—to which the EU has allocated an initial sum of €250 million—means that, unlike its predecessor, the Organization for African Unity, the AU does not need to rely on wealthier member states to lead and finance missions or to ask for UN approval in order to obtain UN funding.

Although it is difficult to estimate the total costs of peace operations, since they are funded in a variety of ways and by a range of sources,[65] it is nevertheless evident that the funds committed to peace operations within multilateral organizations are still small in comparison with total military expenditure. The total number of military personnel in UN peace missions was only 55 909 in December 2004; the four NATO operations deployed another 25 565 military personnel; the EU operation with a military component another 7000; and other regional organizations another 10 390 military personnel.[66] Even if the full cost of sustaining a peace mission is three times the cost of deployment, spending for peace operations still constitutes a relatively small proportion of total military expenditure. The US-led military intervention in Iraq, organized and funded by the coalition countries, had 173 000 troops deployed at the end of 2004. The expenditure on the military operations in this war, not to mention the expenditure on reconstruction, is many times greater than the combined spending on peacekeeping by multilateral organizations. By the end of 2004, supplementary expenditure by the USA for military operations in Iraq had reached $126 billion.[67] The size of the war expenditure by the coalition partners Australia and the UK is also significant.[68]

[63] For overviews of the financing systems for peace missions see Missiroli, A., '€uros for ESDP: financing EU operations', Occasional Papers no. 45, European Union Institute for Security Studies, Paris, June 2003, URL <http://www.iss-eu.org/>; and Future of Peace Operations Project, 'Funding for post-conflict operations: NATO and the EU', Peace Operations Factsheet Series, Henry L. Stimson Center, Washington, DC, Mar. 2004, URL <http://www.stimson.org/fopo/?SN=FP20020610372>.

[64] European Union, 'Decision no 3/2003 of the ACP-EC Council of Ministers of 11 December 2003 on the use of resources from the long-term development envelope of the ninth EDF for the creation of a Peace Facility for Africa', *Official Journal of the European Union*, L345 (31 Dec. 2003), URL <http://europa.eu.int/eur-lex/>, pp. 108–11.

[65] Efforts to create a measure for national (monetary and personnel) contributions to peacekeeping have been made by the Center for Global Development; see URL <http://www.cgdev.org/rankingtherich/> and, in particular, O'Hanlon, M. and de Albuquerque, A. L., 'Note on the security component of the 2004 CDI', Center for Global Development, Washington, DC, Apr. 2004, URL <http://www.cgdev.org/rankingtherich/details.html>.

[66] See table 3.2 in chapter 3 in this volume. Other regional organizations that lead peace missions include the AU, the Commonwealth of Independent States, ECOWAS and the Organization of American States.

[67] Kosiak, S. M., 'Funding for defense, military operations, homeland security, and related activities since 9/11', Center for Strategic and Budgetary Assessments, Washington, DC, 18 Oct. 2004, URL <http://www.csbaonline.org/>.

[68] See chapter 8 in this volume.

In view of the scale of resources devoted to traditional military security in the North, it is reasonable to argue that it is in the enlightened self-interest of the North to reallocate some of its military expenditure to the financing of other types of security. This reallocation would acknowledge the broader and deeper security dimensions as well as the strong interdependence between sources of insecurity in the South and the security of the North

Internal security expenditure

While there are no international statistics that are specifically designed to capture expenditure related to the broader security challenges, the data provided by the International Monetary Fund (IMF) on 'public order and safety' are the most relevant data existing today, although they have a much broader scope than is desirable for this purpose.[69] The year 2000 is the most recent for which a comparison can be made between government spending on 'defence' and on 'public order and safety' for more than 20 countries.[70] Measured in this way, this comparison shows a great variation between countries in the priorities assigned to external and internal security expenditure. However, most countries spend more on defence than on public order and safety. The countries in this small sample that give higher priority to public order and safety than to defence are Germany, Italy, Kenya and the Philippines.

As regards expenditure for other broader security areas, such as economic and environmental security and the security of critical infrastructure and information technology, it is extremely hard to identify relevant data.

External support for development

Development cannot be achieved by development assistance and other external resource flows alone. Debt cancellation, the removal of barriers to trade in goods and services from low-income countries and increased technology sharing would go a long way towards promoting economic development in low-income countries.[71] Furthermore, without proper domestic economic development policies, these flows will not have any great positive impact. However, for many low-income countries external resource flows represent a significant share of the economic resources available for their economic development, so it is of interest to study these flows. Table 7.2 shows that total net resource flows from member countries of the OECD to aid-recipient countries have declined from $264 billion in 1995 to $151 billion in

[69] Public order and safety includes police services, fire protection services, law courts, prisons, and research and development on public order and safety. International Monetary Fund (IMF), *Government Finance Statistics Manual 2001* (IMF: Washington, DC, 2001), p. 76.

[70] International Monetary Fund (IMF), *Government Finance Statistics Yearbook 2003* (IMF: Washington, DC, 2003).

[71] United Nations Development Programme, *Human Development Report 2003, Millennium Development Goals: A Compact Among Nations to End Human Poverty* (Oxford University Press: New York, 2003), URL <http://hdr.undp.org/>, chapter 8, pp. 145–62.

Table 7.2. Resource flows from member states of the OECD Development Assistance Committee and multilateral agencies to aid recipients, 1995–2002

Figures are in US$ b., at current prices and exchange rates.

Type of flow	1995	1996	1997	1998	1999	2000	2001	2002[a]
Public flows[b]	93.0	77.5	80.2	97.7	90.1	73.4	71.5	61.2
ODF[c]	87.4	73.5	75.4	89.3	86.0	65.6	68.7	62.7
ODA[c]	58.9	55.8	47.8	50.6	52.1	49.6	50.9	59.1
Export credits	5.6	4.0	4.8	8.4	4.1	7.8	2.8	–1.5
Private flows	171.1	273.1	241.4	130.7	221.9	143.1	149.2	89.8
Direct investment	59.6	68.9	102.3	117.1	145.5	124.4	134.8	103.6
Grants by NGOs	6.4	5.9	6.4	7.2	8.9	9.5	10.4	12.3
Total net flow	**264.1**	**350.6**	**321.5**	**228.4**	**312.0**	**216.5**	**220.7**	**151.0**

Notes: ODA = Official development assistance; ODF = Official development finance; NGO = Non-governmental organization; OECD = Organisation for Economic Co-operation and Development.

[a] Figures for 2002 are provisional.

[b] All figures for public flows include bilateral and multilateral flows.

[c] ODF includes ODA to developing countries, official assistance to other countries and other ODF.

Source: OECD Development Assistance Committee (DAC), 'Aid from DAC members', Statistics, data and indicators, URL <http://www.oecd.org/>.

2002, in nominal terms. This is the result of reductions in both public and private flows. Official development assistance (ODA) to developing countries declined during the second half of the 1990s but has increased since 2000 in current dollars. Total public flows continued to fall as a result of reductions in non-ODA development finance. The decline in private flows is the result of cuts in international bank lending and other types of lending, while direct investment and grants by non-governmental organizations (NGOs) have been increasing in nominal terms.

Out of the total ODA flows in financial year 2001/2002, around 43 per cent addressed the MDGs specifically.[72] A World Bank study has estimated that the resources required to attain the MDGs by 2015 would correspond to an additional $40–60 billion per year in foreign aid.[73] This should not be taken to mean that, if this amount is made available, it would guarantee that the MDGs will be reached. The World Bank study emphasizes that 'if the aid goes to countries with poor policies and institutions, it is likely to be wasted'.[74] According to the August 2004 UN report on the implementation of the Millen-

[72] United Nations, Implementation of the United Nations Millennium Declaration, Report of the Secretary-General, UN document A/59/282, 27 Aug. 2004, URL <http://www.un.org/millennium goals/>, paragraph 46.

[73] Shantayanan, D., Miller, M. J. and Swanson, E. V., 'Goals for development: history, prospects and costs', Policy Research Working Paper Series no. 2819, World Bank, Washington, DC, Apr. 2002, URL <http://econ.worldbank.org/working_papers/13269/>.

[74] World Bank, 'The costs of attaining the Millennium Development Goals', Paper summarizing Shantayanan *et al.* (note 73), URL <http://www.worldbank.org/html/extdr/mdgassessment.pdf>, p. 1.

nium Declaration, progress towards the MDGs varied between countries.[75] For example, most countries in Asia and North Africa were largely on track to meet the target of halving extreme poverty by 2015 and to achieve many of the social targets, while many countries in sub-Saharan Africa and the least developed countries in other regions were far from making adequate progress on most of the goals.

Armed conflicts have a major impact on the effectiveness of development aid.[76] The international donor community now acknowledges this linkage between security and development, a perception that 'opens the way to mainstreaming security as a public policy and a governance issue' and 'invites greater public scrutiny of security policy'.[77] In April 2004 the OECD Development Assistance Committee endorsed a policy statement to that end.[78] Thus, in future it is likely that the international donor community will provide more financial resources to security-related development assistance.[79]

International financing mechanisms

Any significant increase in the support for peace and security, in particular through means that reach out to the countries most affected by insecurities, requires rethinking of the mechanisms for generating international finance for this support. There are a number of different potential approaches to the international financing of common activities, also thought of as global public goods. Table 7.3 presents a typology of financing mechanisms, grouping these into four categories based on their basic function or source of funding.

The first category, 'internalizing externalities', consists of measures to make the suppliers or recipients of support instruments finance them directly in two ways: by creating a market for them or through taxes, fees or levies. While the purchasing power of the recipients constitutes part of the problem to be solved, various forms of global taxes have been suggested. As early as the 1980s the Brandt Commission developed the idea of raising revenues from taxes on international trade (e.g., the arms trade) for development purposes.[80]

[75] United Nations (note 72), paragraph 41.

[76] Stewart and FitzGerald (note 34).

[77] OECD Development Assistance Committee (DAC), 'Security system reform and governance: policy and good practice', DAC Guidelines and Reference Series, OECD, Paris, 2004, p. 12, URL <http://www.oecd.org/>.

[78] OECD DAC (note 77).

[79] See also chapter 8 in this volume.

[80] Brandt, W. (chairman), *North–South: A Programme for Survival*, Report of the Independent Commission on International Development Issues (Pan Books: London, 1980). See also the papers presented to the United Nations Ad Hoc Expert Group Meeting on Innovations in Mobilizing Global Resources for Development, UN Headquarters, New York, 25–26 June 2001, URL <http://www.unpan.org/>; and Broadway, R., 'National taxation, fiscal federalism and global taxation', WIDER Discussion Paper no. 2003/87, World Institute for Development Economics Research (WIDER), UN University, Helsinki, Dec. 2003, URL <http://www.wider.unu.edu/>.

Table 7.3. International financing mechanisms

Category of financing mechanisms	Financing mechanism
Internalizing externalities	Market creation or strengthening Taxes, fees and levies

Private sources	Corporations: for profit
	Corporations: not for profit
	  Private foundations
	  Non-governmental organizations
	Individuals

Public sources	National: developed countries National: developing country International financial institutions International organizations and agencies
Partnerships	Combination of various sources

Source: Adapted from Sagasti, F. and Bezanson, K., *Financing and Providing Global Public Goods: Expectations and Prospects*, Development Financing 2000, Study 2001:2 (Swedish Ministry of Foreign Affairs: Stockholm, 2001), URL <http://www.egdi.gov.se/dev_financing/financing.htm>, table 3.3, p. 41.

This idea surfaced again in 2003 in a proposal by the presidents of Brazil and France.[81]

In theory it is possible to imagine the financing of activities that promote peace in other countries from private sources, for example, from private foundations and NGOs. Grant-making foundations finance practical programmes in preventing violent conflicts. Considerable resources are provided by NGOs for humanitarian activities, financed from a variety of sources such as membership dues, grants from governments and international institutions including development assistance agencies, grants from private foundations and donations from corporations and wealthy individuals. While some of the private funding schemes are of considerable size, they are still small in relation to the needs. Furthermore, it is difficult to ensure sustainability in the provision of financing from private sources.

Public finance remains the main source of funds for the provision of security, whether for military or non-military means and whether at the national or international level. Donor countries provide finance through four different mechanisms: (*a*) ODA, (*b*) debt-reduction schemes, (*c*) assistance from non-ODA agencies and ministries, and (*d*) tax incentives for private firms to encourage their support for peace and security measures. International financial institutions, such as the IMF and multilateral development banks, and international organizations, such as the UN, make significant contributions to peace and security. A large part of their income is generated from contributions from member states. Major issues include how to design the system of

[81] 'Lula proposes hunger fund', BBC News Online, 2 June 2003, URL <http://news.bbc.co.uk/2/2954990.stm>.

contributions from member states and how to design the decision-making system for the allocation of resources between different activities.

IV. Conclusions

The internationalization of security problems in the globalized context requires changes in security policies. While thinking on security problems is undergoing fundamental transformation in a variety of directions, there has been less rethinking of the required reallocation of resources for security purposes, either at national, regional or global level. Although statistics on resource allocation are not designed to enable comparisons of the different ways of promoting security, some tentative conclusions can be drawn.

The pattern of security financing is still strongly focused on traditional national military security objectives. Most obviously, a large proportion of public resources is spent on military forces for territorial security purposes, much of it by countries facing the lowest level of immediate threat. There is still a strong emphasis on financing security measures at the national level. For example, although international statistics do not allow a strict comparison, the resources allocated to international peacekeeping are small compared with military expenditure for territorial defence.

In low-income countries, armed conflict cannot be resolved exclusively by military means. Linkages between armed conflict and the lack of development in such countries are sufficiently strongly established to allow the conclusion that a range of non-military means is required in order to reduce the incidence of conflict there. The resources required for this are not available in the countries affected by conflict and little has been done to establish a resource base for addressing the development problems. Although development assistance has increased since 2000, the net resource flow to aid-recipient countries is falling, and the level is still very low in comparison with the needs.

International financing of peace and security on a fundamentally different scale than today would require new thinking and priorities in resource allocation. Furthermore, governments are likely to be neither willing nor able to invest the full amount of required resources. Thus, innovative new means of financing will probably be considered, including taxation of international flows and private sources of funding, from private industry as well as NGOs. In order to enable coherence, legality, timeliness and cost-effectiveness in the allocation of resources generated from such a diverse system of funding, new forms of governance would be needed.

A North–South shift of resources for these purposes would have to be based on the enlightened self-interest of the North. However, that would require substantially improved knowledge about how to promote security and, even more, wide dissemination of such knowledge to the broader public in the North, which in one way or the other would have to finance this investment in future security. In particular, more knowledge is needed: (*a*) of the sources of different types of insecurities, both internal and external, and of both the immediate and the more long-term structural insecurities; (*b*) of the linkages between sources of insecurity in regions which lack the resources to remedy them and the security of countries where such resources are available; and (*c*) about the relative effects of different security policy instruments. These are important areas of future research. In addition, since available statistics are not adapted to the purpose of examining priorities in resource allocation for security purposes outside the military domain or through multilateral organizations, it might be useful to begin thinking about designing new types of public expenditure categories, such as for non-military spending for the securing of peace and contributions to international activities for such purposes.

8. Military expenditure

ELISABETH SKÖNS, WUYI OMITOOGUN,
CATALINA PERDOMO and PETTER STÅLENHEIM

I. Introduction

World military expenditure in 2004 is estimated to have been $975 billion at constant (2003) prices and exchange rates or $1035 billion in current dollars. This is just 6 per cent lower in real terms than at the 1987–88 peak of cold war world military spending. As a global average, 2004 world military expenditure corresponds to $162 per capita[1] and 2.6 per cent of world gross domestic product (GDP).[2] However, there is a wide variation between regions and countries in the scale and economic burden of military spending (see section II).

The average annual rate of increase in world military expenditure over the 10-year period 1995–2004 was 2.4 per cent in real terms. This average encompasses two distinct trends: first, the post-cold war reduction in military spending which culminated in 1998; second, an increasing trend since 1998, accelerating to an annual average increase of around 6 per cent in real terms over the three-year period 2002–2004.

The major determinant of the world trend in military expenditure is the change in the USA, with its 47 per cent of the world total. United States military expenditure has increased rapidly during the period 2002–2004 as a result of massive budgetary allocations for the 'global war on terrorism', primarily for military operations in Afghanistan and Iraq. These have been funded through supplementary appropriations on top of the regular budget. The supplementary appropriations for this purpose allocated to the Department of Defense (DOD) for financial years (FYs) 2003–2005 amounted to approximately $238 billion and exceeded the combined military spending of Africa, Latin America, Asia (except Japan but including China) and the Middle East in 2004 ($214 billion in current dollars), that is, of the entire developing world. Thus, while regular military spending has also increased, in the USA as well as in several other countries and regions, the main explanation for the current level of and trend in world military spending is the spending on mili-

[1] This per capita average is based on an estimated total world population of 6378 million in 2004. United Nations Population Fund (UNFPA), *State of the World Population 2004* (UNFPA: New York, 2004), URL <http://www.unfpa.org/swp/>.

[2] This share of GDP is based on a projected figure for world GDP in 2004 of $40 108 billion at market exchange rates. International Monetary Fund (IMF), *World Economic Outlook, September 2004: The Global Demographic Transition* (IMF: Washington, DC, 2004), URL <http://www.imf.org/external/pubs/ft/weo/>, Statistical appendix, table 1, 'Summary of world output', p. 199.

tary operations abroad by the USA, and to a lesser extent by its coalition partners.[3]

High-income countries are also beginning to perceive that they have an interest in investing in the security of poorer countries. This is shown in the increased focus in their thinking on how to promote peace and security in developing countries, in the short term by means of security-related development assistance,[4] as well as in the longer term, for example, by providing for the achievement of the Millennium Development Goals.[5]

This chapter brings together the three themes discussed above: the trends and pattern displayed by SIPRI military expenditure statistics; the rising military spending in the USA; and the international financing of security in low-income countries. Section II presents the trends and pattern in military expenditure based on the SIPRI data on military expenditure provided in appendix 8A; first the regional trends; second the economic burden of military expenditure; and third the 15 major spenders in 2004. Section III considers the trends in US military expenditure, including the US defence budget for FY 2006, the costs of foreign military operations and the economic implications of the current levels of military spending. Section IV examines two cases of international financial support for security-related activities in two countries in two continents: Colombia in South America and Sierra Leone in Africa. It describes the foreign aid programmes for these two countries and analyses the different profiles and outcomes of these two programmes with a view to extracting some experience of how to promote security in developing countries that are engaged in or at risk of new or resumed armed conflict. This experience can then be applied in the development of new policies by donor countries. Conclusions are drawn in section V.

II. Regional trends and major spenders

The SIPRI military expenditure statistics reflect official military spending, as reported by governments. The tables on military expenditures in appendix 8A to this chapter include 10-year series of military expenditure for 159 countries.[6] Table 8.1 below summarizes the country data by geographical region and by group of national per capita income.

[3] The difficulty of estimating the annual distribution of expenditure resulting from the US supplementary appropriations produces uncertainties in the growth rate for the most recent year in US military expenditure and thus also for world military spending. Consequently, the downward revision in the growth of world military spending in 2003 is due to the fact that part of the 2003 supplement was actually spent in 2004. See Sköns, E. *et al.*, 'Military expenditure', *SIPRI Yearbook 2004: Armaments, Disarmament and International Security* (Oxford University Press: Oxford, 2004), p. 305.

[4] Security-related development assistance refers to various forms of aid to strengthen security in developing countries. See the Internet site of the Organisation for Economic Co-operation and Development (OECD), Development Assistance Committee (DAC), Network on Conflict, Peace and Development Co-operation, URL <http://www.oecd.org/dac/conflict/>.

[5] United Nations Millennium Project, *Investing in Development: A Practical Plan to Achieve the Millennium Development Goals* (Earthscan: New York, 2005), URL <http://unmp.forumone.com/>.

[6] Appendix 8B provides the sources and methods for the SIPRI military expenditure data. Appendix 8C provides statistics on governments' reporting of their military expenditure to SIPRI and to the

The world and regional totals are likely to be much higher than presented here, since it is known that many governments tend to underreport their spending, especially governments in developing countries and particularly those in countries engaged in armed conflict. The difference is often accounted for by off-budget income generated by the military for their own use. Second, the statistics reflect budgeted expenditure, which is sometimes exceeded by actual expenditure. Third, they reflect only government expenditure and not the spending of non-government armed forces.[7]

The total costs of wars and armed conflicts are much greater than indicated by these sums. Most armed conflicts take place in low-income countries.[8] The costs of these conflicts are largely unknown: first, because of the lack of transparency in the public expenditure accounts of most government engaged in armed conflicts; and second, because of the lack of knowledge of the costs of armed activities by non-government forces. More importantly, the expenditure on the fighting of war is only part of the cost of war. In addition, there are the economic and social costs of wars, such as the impact on human capital and economic growth in the countries in conflict as well as the external impact on countries and people who are not parties to the conflict. Although these types of cost have not been comprehensively assessed, it is nevertheless clear that they exceed by far the costs of the actual fighting of war.[9]

Regional trends

The region in which military expenditure increased most in 2004 is South Asia, where spending increased by 14.3 per cent in real terms. Other regions with strong increases in 2004 are North Africa (12 per cent) and North America (9.9 per cent). In Central America and Western Europe regional military expenditure declined in 2004 (see table 8.1).

In *Africa* military expenditure increased by 7.4 per cent in real terms in 2004. The increase in African military expenditure was owing primarily to increased spending in the major spending nations of Algeria, Morocco and South Africa, which together accounted for more than half of the regional total in 2004. The main reason for the continuing rise in their military spending was the continuation of the various programmes of modernization of their armed forces. The regional total for Africa excludes Angola because of uncertainty in the data.[10] Angola increased its military expenditure considerably in 2004, partly due to debt payments and the cost of demobilizing former UNITA rebel

United Nations. The usual appendix on data on expenditure on military personnel and equipment of the member states of the North Atlantic Treaty Organization (NATO) is not provided this year because NATO did not release these data in time for their inclusion.

[7] For the sources and methods of SIPRI military expenditure statistics see appendix 8B.

[8] In 2004 there were 19 major armed conflicts (including the war in Iraq). See chapter 2 and appendix 2A in this volume.

[9] See chapter 7 in this volume.

[10] This includes uncertainty in the estimates of military expenditure and in economic parameters more generally.

Table 8.1. World and regional military expenditure estimates, 1995–2004

Figures are in US$ b., at constant (2003) prices and exchange rates. Figures do not always add up to totals because of the conventions of rounding. Figures in italics are percentages.

Region[a]	1995	1996	1997	1998	1999	2000	2001	2002	2003	2004	Change 95–04
Africa	**8.8**	**8.5**	**8.7**	**9.3**	**10.3**	**10.8**	**11.0**	**11.6**	**11.7**	**12.6**	*+43*
North	(3.4)	3.5	3.7	3.8	3.9	4.3	4.4	4.8	4.9	5.5	*+65*
Sub-Saharan	5.5	5.0	5.0	5.5	6.3	6.5	(6.6)	6.8	6.8	(7.1)	*+29*
Americas	**367**	**347**	**347**	**340**	**341**	**353**	**358**	**398**	**446**	**488**	*+33*
North	347	328	326	319	320	332	335	375	424	466	*+34*
Central	3.2	3.3	3.4	3.3	3.5	3.6	3.7	3.5	3.4	3.2	*+2*
South	17.2	15.6	18.1	17.4	17.0	17.9	19.9	19.6	18.4	18.8	*+9*
Asia, Oceania	**136**	**141**	**138**	**135**	**137**	**147**	**151**	**151**	**(158)**	**(164)**	*+21*
Central	0.4	0.5	0.5	(0.5)	0.5	. .	(0.6)	. .	(0.6)	(0.7)	*+73*
East	113	119	115	111	112	121	124	123	(129)	(132)	*+17*
South	13.4	13.6	14.2	14.4	15.5	16.2	16.8	17.0	17.5	20.0	*+50*
Oceania	8.7	8.6	8.8	9.1	9.6	9.5	9.9	10.3	10.6	11.0	*+26*
Europe	**237**	**236**	**237**	**234**	**239**	**243**	**244**	**250**	**256**	**254**	*+7*
Central, Eastern	28.1	26.2	27.7	23.4	24.8	27.3	29.2	30.7	33.2	34.2	*+22*
Western	209	210	209	211	214	216	215	220	223	220	*+5*
Middle East	**40.1**	**39.1**	**43.0**	**46.5**	**46.0**	**51.7**	**55.3**	**52.9**	**54.4**	**56.1**	*+40*
World	**789**	**772**	**774**	**765**	**773**	**806**	**819**	**864**	**927**	**975**	*+23*
Change (%)		*–2.3*	*0.3*	*–1.2*	*1.1*	*4.2*	*1.6*	*5.4*	*7.2*	*5.3*	

( ) = Total based on country data accounting for less than 90% of the regional total; . . = Available data account for less than 60% of the regional total.

[a] For the country coverage of the regions, see appendix 8A, table 8A.1. Some countries are excluded because of lack of data or of consistent time series data. Africa excludes Angola, Benin, Equatorial Guinea and Somalia; Asia excludes Afghanistan; and the Middle East excludes Iraq and Qatar. World totals exclude all these countries.

Source: Appendix 8A, tables 8A.1 and 8A.3.

soldiers;[11] thus, if Angola were included, the increase in the regional total would have been even greater. In North Africa the 12 per cent real-terms increase in 2004 military expenditure was accompanied by increasing transparency; all countries in the region released information on their military expenditure or budgets for 2004 in one way or another.[12]

In *East Asia* the 2.7 per cent real-terms increase in 2004 military spending represented a continuation of a long-term pattern of growth—although this was interrupted in 1997 and 1998 when the Asian financial crisis forced several of the major spenders in the region to cancel or postpone large procurement projects. However, in comparison with 2003, the East Asian increase in 2004 represents a slowdown, owing primarily to the impact of the reduced rate of increase in military expenditure in China, which accounted for over one-quarter of East Asian military expenditure. In spite of the increase in military

[11] Economist Intelligence Unit (EIU), *Country Report: Angola* (EIU: London, Feb. 2004).

[12] See appendix 8C.

spending in China in 2004—by $2.3 billion, or almost 7 per cent in real terms—this is still significantly less than its average annual growth of 11.5 per cent during 1995–2003. It is also lower than the estimated 9 per cent rate of economic growth, thus leading to a further reduction in military expenditure as a share of China's GDP. China has increased its military expenditure by more than 150 per cent in real terms since 1995 and by 60 per cent since 2000. Continuing tension between North and South Korea has driven South Korea to increase its military expenditure by 4.2 per cent in 2004, giving a total increase of 15.2 per cent in real terms since 2000.

The main factor behind the strong increase in *South Asian* military expenditure in 2004 is a massive increase in India's defence budget. This increase reportedly reflects India's ambitions to play the role of a regional leader, rather than being directly connected to the ongoing tensions in the Kashmir conflict.[13] To a large extent it is also a measure to compensate the Indian Armed Forces for long-standing management problems, such as inefficient procurement processes and difficulties in the implementation of major procurement projects.[14] In Sri Lanka the government reacted to setbacks in the peace process with the Liberation Tigers of Tamil Eelam by increasing its military budget by 13.1 per cent.[15] However, as Sri Lanka spends only about 3 per cent of what India spends on its armed forces, this big increase had little impact on the regional trend.

Australian military expenditure accounts for more than 90 per cent of the regional total for *Oceania* and is thus decisive for the regional trend. The Australian defence posture is being reoriented towards a more global focus,[16] with improved capabilities to counter emerging types of threats, such as 'terrorism, concerns associated with the proliferation of weapons of mass destruction and the risk of failed states in the region'.[17] For this purpose the Australian Government is not only raising military spending but is also freeing resources through cuts in the size of its armed forces.[18]

Central America is one of the two regions where military expenditure decreased during 2004. The regional giant Mexico, which accounts for 87 per cent of total regional military expenditure, decreased its military spending by $122 million or 4.1 per cent in 2004. All other countries in the region for which data were available also decreased their military spending in 2004. Since 2000, Central American military expenditure, which historically has been devoted primarily to internal security, has decreased by more than 10 per cent in real terms, and in 2004 regional spending was at roughly the same level as in 1995.

[13] For a survey of military expenditure trends in India see Sköns *et al.* (note 3), pp. 333–34.

[14] 'India defense budget up 18 percent', *Defense News*, 19 July 2004, p. 44; and 'India steps up defence spending to buy new arms', *Air Letter*, no. 15 530 (13 July 2004), p. 5.

[15] 'Sri Lanka violence fears sour return to normality', *Financial Times*, 4 Dec. 2004.

[16] 'Australia plans to upgrade defence force', *Air Letter*, no. 15 367 (12 Nov. 2003), p. 4.

[17] Wyatt, S., 'Australia announces 10-year plan to improve military equipment', *Financial Times* (Japan edition), 5 Feb. 2004, p. 2.

[18] Ferguson, G., 'Australia cuts deep to fund future needs', *Defense News*, 17 Nov. 2003, p. 18.

Five countries in *South America* increased their military budgets in 2004, five countries reduced theirs, while no data were available for one country, Guyana. In relative terms, Paraguay was the country that decreased its military budget most in 2004, with a decrease of 14.7 per cent in real terms. Brazil and Ecuador made the largest absolute cuts in their military budgets, $401 million and $67 million, respectively. These decreases were too small to offset the enormous increases in the Chilean and Colombian military budgets, resulting in a slight increase for the region as a whole. In Chile the sharp increase in copper prices made additional resources available (in accordance with the 1958 Copper Law[19]) for its military modernization plan and for participation in international military missions.[20] The main motives behind Colombia's decision to increase spending on its armed forces are the continuing internal conflict and the government's efforts to increase the number and professionalism of military personnel.[21] During the past decade military expenditure in South America has followed a fluctuating but slowly increasing trend, largely following the trend of the major regional spender, Brazil, which accounts for 40 per cent of the regional total.

Military spending in the *Middle East* increased by 3.1 per cent in real terms in 2004, thereby continuing a long-term increase. Over the ten-year period 1995–2004 military spending in the region increased by 40 per cent in real terms with Saudi Arabia and Israel (and to a lesser extent Kuwait) being the main countries accounting for this trend. The increase in 2004 is owing primarily to a $700 million increase in the Israeli military budget and a $500 million increase in Saudi Arabia. In relative terms, Israel and Kuwait are the countries with the strongest increase in 2004, approximately 7 per cent each. The increase in Israel was in reaction to the reduction in 2003, which was fiercely opposed by Israeli military chiefs of staff at a time of continuing security crisis. The rise in 2004 is expected to continue in 2005 according to preliminary budget figures for defence and this is seen as a victory for the Israeli military establishment.[22] The Kuwaiti increase in military spending continued a trend in spending that started in 2000 and which is associated with the procurement of new equipment. The increase of 2.8 per cent in Saudi

[19] According to the Ley Reservada del Cobre (Restricted Law on Copper), law no. 13 196 of 29 Oct. 1958 (most recently modified in 1987), 10% of total revenue from copper exports is set aside to finance military acquisitions.

[20] Chilean Ministry of Finance, 'Informe presupuestario del gobierno central cuarto trimestre 2004' [Budget report of the central government fourth quarter 2004], Santiago, 10 Feb. 2004, p. III; and International Monetary Fund, 'Chile: 2004 Article IV Consultation', IMF Country Report no. 291/2004, 13 Sep. 2004, URL <http://www.imf.org/external/country/chl/>.

[21] Villmizar, A. and Espejo, G., *El Gasto en Seguridad y Defensa en Colombia: De la Contención a la Ofensiva* [Defence and security spending in Colombia: from containment to offence] (Fundación Seguridad y Democracia: Bogotá, Nov. 2004), p. 8.

[22] 'Part of defense budget hike to come from separation fence', *Rishon Leziyyon Globes*, 17 Aug. 2004, in Foreign Broadcast Information Service, *Daily Report–Near East and South Asia (FBIS-NES)*, FBIS-NES-2004-0817, 18 Aug. 2004.

Arabia in 2004 is mainly associated with the authorities' increasing focus on internal order in the aftermath of terrorist attacks in the country.[23]

European military expenditure increased slightly in both 2002 and 2003, but the combined budgeted expenditure for 2004 showed a small decline. The overall trend for these countries is strongly influenced by the spending of the five major powers in Europe—France, Germany, Italy, Russia and the United Kingdom—which together accounted for approximately 70 per cent of total European military expenditure in 2004. These five countries exhibit different trends.

France's military expenditure has been increasing at a rate of 2 per cent per year over the period 2001–2004, and is most likely to continue to grow during the remaining years of its 2003–2008 military programme law.[24] This law defines the annual budgets for investment in defence, giving priority to military equipment: in 2004 the total defence budget increased by 4.3 per cent in total, while the equipment budget increased by 9.2 per cent, reaching 46 per cent of the total.[25] While a spending freeze has been imposed on French public expenditure in order to reduce the budget deficit from 4.1 per cent of GDP (well above the 3 per cent limit set by the European Union (EU) Growth and Stability Pact),[26] the Ministry of Defence has been exempted from that freeze.[27]

Germany and Italy reduced their military spending during 2002 and 2003. Germany, which also has problems in meeting the economic targets of the Growth and Stability Pact, has taken the opposite approach to France and is extending heavy budget cuts to the military.[28] However, the German Ministry of Defence is simultaneously trying to restructure the armed forces to focus the German Army on peacekeeping, crisis management and anti-terrorist oper-

[23] For an account of military expenditure trends in the Middle East see Omitoogun, W., 'Military expenditure in the Middle East after the Iraq war', *SIPRI Yearbook 2004* (note 3), pp. 381–88.

[24] Loi de programmation militaire 2003–2008 [Military programme 2003–08 law], Loi no. 2003-73, 27 Jan. 2003, URL <http://www.legifrance.gouv.fr/>; and 'Armed forces welcome 2005 budget allocations', *Le Monde*, 3 Oct. 2004, in Foreign Broadcast Information Service, *Daily Report–Western Europe (FBIS-WEU)*, FBIS-WEU-2004-1004, 5 Oct. 2004.

[25] 'Un budget de redressement pour la France' [A correction budget for France], *Air & Cosmos*, no. 1906 (3 Oct. 2003), pp. 32–33.

[26] Council of the European Union, 'Resolution of the European Council on the Stability and Growth Pact, 17 June 1997', *Official Journal of the European Communities*, C236, 2 Aug. 1997, URL <http://europa.eu.int/eur-lex/lex/en/index.htm>, pp. 1–2; and 'Editorial: Sarkozy and the budget', *Le Monde*, 18 Apr. 2004, in 'French daily views Minister Sarkozy's approach to budget management', FBIS-WEU-2004-0419, 26 Apr. 2004.

[27] President Jacques Chirac made a commitment in 2002 that the Ministry of Defence would be a 'protected sanctuary' from spending cuts. 'Sarkozy ready for a budget battle against Mrs. Alliot–Marie', *Le Monde*, 18 Apr. 2004, in 'France's Sarkozy reportedly to include defence cuts in effort to reduce deficit', FBIS-WEU-0419, 23 Apr. 2004; and 'France to boost 2004 military spending', *Air Letter*, no. 15 532 (15 July 2004), p. 5.

[28] 'Germany unveils huge defence cuts', BBC News Online, 14 Jan. 2004, URL <http://news.bbc.co.uk/2/3395575.stm>; and Agüera, M., 'German budget deficit may spell further cuts in defense spending', *Defense News*, 24 May 2004, p. 9.

ations.[29] Since 1995, Germany has reduced its military expenditure by more than 10 per cent and since 2000 by about 6 per cent in real terms.

Despite a slight increase in the Italian defence budget for 2004, there was a substantial cut in the procurement part of the budget because of the resources required for the transformation of the Italian armed forces into an all-professional force. Furthermore, in a mid-year revision, the budget was cut by 3.8 per cent, resulting in a 3.2 per cent decrease in spending since 2003. Most of this cut was in arms procurement, leading Italy to postpone several major procurement programmes.[30]

In Russia, the 2004 budget for national defence, signed into law by the president on 27 December 2003, amounted to 411.5 billion roubles ($12 billion), an 8 per cent increase in real terms over the 2003 budget.[31] In October 2004 the budget was amended, adding another 14.7 billion roubles ($435 million) for national defence. This extra allocation was due mostly to increased budget revenues as a result of higher oil prices and was largely oriented towards paying off debts to the arms industry and the energy sector and to regulating unpaid salaries.[32] Total Russian military expenditure in 2004, including this supplement and military-related expenditure outside the official budget for national defence, amounted to 655.8 billion roubles ($19 billion), an increase over 2003 of 4.8 per cent in real terms.

The trend in the military expenditure of the UK is difficult to assess because of its change to a new accounting system for government public expenditure.[33] The higher level of spending in 2002 and 2003 is to some extent caused by the additional costs of unprogrammed military activity in Afghanistan, Bosnia and Herzegovina, Iraq and Kosovo.[34] However, this does not explain the large increase in 2003 and only partly explains the fall in budgeted expenditure for 2004. In July 2004 the British Treasury announced an increase of 1.4 per cent

[29] Williamson, H., 'Defence overhaul sets new focus for Germany', *Financial Times*, 14 Jan. 2004, p. 2; and 'German transformation adopts official agenda', *Defense News*, 25 Oct. 2004, p. 42.

[30] Kington, T., 'Italian spending increase? Not so fast', *Defense News*, 11 Oct. 2004, pp. 1, 12; and Valpolini, P., 'Italian budget set for major cut', *Jane's Defence Weekly*, 26 Jan. 2005, p. 12.

[31] Russian Ministry of Finance, Federal law of 23 December 2003, 186-FZ: on the federal budget for 2004, Moscow, Dec. 2003, URL <http://www.minfin.ru/> (in Russian).

[32] Sklyarova, I., 'Uncovered reserves', *Vremya Novostei*, no. 172 (22 Sep. 2004), p. 4, URL <http://vremya.ru/print/108014.html> (in Russian).

[33] In 2001 the British Government decided to change its accounting system from a 'cash basis' to an 'accrual basis' (or 'resource basis' in British terminology). In accrual basis accounting systems, revenue and expenditure are accounted for in the period in which they arise rather than in the period in which the associated cash transactions occur. This change, implemented in 2001 and 2003, produces a break in the military expenditure series for the UK. Following advice from the British Ministry of Defence, SIPRI has selected the expenditure series that are most consistent over time. Thus, the figures used for the SIPRI military expenditure database and presented in appendix 8A for FY 2002/2003 are for Departmental Expenditure Limits (DEL) and for the period from FY 2003/2004 onwards are Total DEL. Bennett, N., Defence Analytical Service Agency, British Ministry of Defence, Personal communications with the authors, 20 Sep. 2004 and 11 Jan. 2005.

[34] The figures used by SIPRI include the 'cost of unprogrammed operation/conflict prevention', such as the activity in Afghanistan, Bosnia and Herzegovina, Iraq and Kosovo. British Ministry of Defence, *The Government's Expenditure Plans 2004/2005–2005/2006*, Command Paper no. 6212 (The Stationery Office: London, 2004), URL <http://www.hmso.gov.uk/>, p. 24. The extent to which these costs include the total amount of contingency funds for military operations in Iraq in 2003 is unclear.

in real terms in the 2005 defence budget.[35] In the same month the defence minister, Geoff Hoon, announced a major restructuring of the British armed forces, the costs of which are to be partly compensated for by cuts in troops, bases and major weapon systems.[36]

With the exception of the new North Atlantic Treaty Organization (NATO) member states and those that aspire to NATO membership, most other countries in Europe budgeted for a reduction in military expenditure in 2004. The comparison with US military expenditure appears to have lost ground as an argument for increased European military expenditure. For example, Nick Witney, the chief executive of the European Defence Agency, established in 2004, questioned the relevance of this comparison for Europe on the basis that the USA is a 'global hyper-power', while 'the EU does not aspire to that role'.[37] According to Witney, the important target for Europe is to increase spending on research and technology in order to maintain strategic defence-industrial capability. The arguments referring to a transatlantic gap in advanced new military technology and a lack of transatlantic interoperability were also challenged in 2004. In a major study of European capabilities in command, control, communications, computers, intelligence, surveillance and reconnaissance technologies (so-called C^4ISR technologies, required for network centric capability), the conclusion was that the European countries studied have a greater commitment to the deployment of such capabilities and provide greater interoperability within NATO than is sometimes thought.[38] According to this report, the transatlantic interoperability problems are neither as extreme nor as powerful a barrier to transatlantic interoperability as is sometimes claimed. It is argued that the capabilities gap is to some degree a misperception. 'Only the United States has set for itself the twin goals of global operations and a fully network centric military force to conduct those operations. European agendas are more modest with respect to geographic reach and the creation of a fully networked force.'[39]

The economic burden of military expenditure

The share of global resources used for military purposes has increased steadily during the period 2000–2004. As a global average, the military burden, as expressed by the share of GDP spent on the military, increased from 2.3 per cent in 2001 to 2.5 per cent in 2003 (see table 8.2). This represents a rate of increase of a full 0.1 percentage point per year, a significant rate considering the large size of world GDP. Estimated world military expenditure in 2004

[35] Kemp, D., 'UK budget gets £3.7 billion boost', *Jane's Defence Weekly*, 21 July 2004, p. 15.

[36] Kemp, I., 'UK details armed forces restructure', *Jane's Defence Weekly*, 28 July 2004, p. 14.

[37] 'EDA chief: defence budget race with US is irrelevant', *EurActiv*, 21 Jan. 2005, URL <http://www.euractiv.com/Article?tcmuri=tcm:29-134450-16&type=News>.

[38] Adams, G. *et al.*, 'Bridging the gap: European C4ISR capabilities and transatlantic interoperability', Defense & Technology Papers no. 5, Center for Technology and National Security Policy, National Defence University, Washington, DC, Oct. 2004, URL <http://www.ndu.edu/ctnsp/>.

[39] Adams *et al.* (note 38), p. 8.

Table 8.2. Military expenditure per capita in 2004 and as a share of gross domestic product in 2000–2003, by region and by income group

Per capita expenditure figures are in US$, at current prices and exchange rates.

Region/income group[a] (GDP/GNI per capita)[b]	Military expenditure per capita, 2004	Military expenditure as a share of GDP (%)			
		2000	2001	2002	2003
World ($6019)	162	*2.3*	*2.3*	*2.4*	*2.5*
Region					
Africa ($775)	18	*2.2*	*2.1*	*2.1*	*2.1*
Americas ($16 599)	597	*2.7*	*2.8*	*3.0*	*3.3*
North America ($36 464)	1 453	*2.9*	*2.9*	*3.2*	*3.6*
Latin America ($3406)	47	*1.3*	*1.5*	*1.4*	*1.3*
Asia ($2651)	45	*1.6*	*1.6*	*1.6*	*1.6*
Oceania ($24 145)	516	*1.8*	*1.8*	*1.8*	*1.8*
Europe ($15 397)	351	*2.1*	*2.0*	*2.1*	*2.1*
Western Europe ($23 971)	530	*2.0*	*2.0*	*2.0*	*2.0*
Central and Eastern ($3133)	112	*2.8*	*2.9*	*2.9*	*3.0*
Middle East ($4513)	248	*7.0*	*7.5*	*6.9*	*6.7*
Income group					
Low income (≤$765)	20	*2.3*	*2.0*	*1.8*	*1.8*
Lower-middle income ($766–$3035)	46	*2.6*	*2.7*	*2.7*	*2.7*
Upper-middle income ($3036–$9385)	136	*2.5*	*2.6*	*2.4*	*2.4*
High income (≥$9386)	867	*2.2*	*2.2*	*2.4*	*2.5*

GDP = Gross domestic product; GNI = Gross national income.

[a] For the definition and coverage of regions and income groups, see appendix 8A.

[b] The figures in parentheses after regions are 2003 GDP per capita. The ranges in parentheses after income groups are 2003 GNI per capita.

Source: **Military expenditure**: appendix 8A, table 8A.1. **GDP**: International Monetary Fund, International Financial Statistics database, Dec. 2004, URL <http://www.imf.org/>. **2004 population**: United Nations Population Fund (UNFPA), *State of the World Population 2004* (UNFPA: New York, 2004), URL <http://www.unfpa.org/swp/>.

corresponds to 2.6 per cent of world GDP,[40] which suggests a continuation of this rate of increase. However, world military expenditure is very unevenly distributed, as is national output. Furthermore, the military burden also varies significantly between geographical regions and income groups.

The Middle East is the region with by far the highest military spending in proportion to GDP. However, there has been a decrease in recent years to 6.7 per cent of GDP in 2003. The region with the second highest military burden is North America, with allocations for military purposes representing 3.6 per cent of GDP in 2003, a major increase over the 2.9 per cent share in 2000. The regions with the lowest shares of GDP devoted to military expenditure are Latin America, Asia and Oceania. In these regions the burden has

[40] For GDP data see note 2.

also been roughly stable over the period 2000–2003. Africa and Europe each had an average share of 2.1 per cent of GDP spent on the military in 2003. Within Europe, the share is lower for Western Europe than for Central and Eastern Europe. Furthermore, while the share has been stable in Western Europe during the period 2000–2003, in Central and Eastern Europe it has increased from 2.8 to 3.0 per cent of GDP. This reflects the efforts of countries in the latter region to fulfil the requirements of NATO membership.

The level and trend in the share of GDP devoted to military spending also vary between countries belonging to different income groups, as defined by the World Bank (see table 8.2). Low-income countries have on average the lowest share: 1.8 per cent of GDP in 2003, which is even more noteworthy considering that this group includes many individual countries that spend an extremely high share of their GDP on the military, in particular African countries engaged in armed conflict. However, the level of military spending is severely underreported in many countries in this group. More importantly, in countries with a per capita income near or below the poverty line, even a very low share of GDP spent on the military can represent a very heavy economic burden.

As regards trends in the military burden over the period 2000–2003, there was a significant increase in the group of high-income countries and a slight increase in lower-middle-income countries, while the military burden in upper-middle- and low-income countries has decreased over this period.

Military expenditure as a share of GDP is the most common way of measuring the military burden. It captures to some extent the economic burden that the armed forces constitute at the national level. An alternative measure is military expenditure per capita, which shows both the average individual burden of the military sector and the level of provision of military funding per inhabitant, whether by country, region or other grouping.

In 2004 estimated world military expenditure corresponded to an average of $162 per capita. The region with by far the highest per capita spending on the military sector is North America at $1453. The level of per capita spending on the military sector is strongly linked to the level of income. It is much higher in high-income regions—including Western Europe and Oceania, both spending more than $500 per capita—than in low-income regions, such as Africa, which spends only $18 per person. This pattern is in many ways the reverse of the pattern of armed conflict: 20 of the 29 armed conflicts in 2003 were located in low-income countries.[41]

Major spenders

The 15 countries with the highest military spending in 2004 accounted for 82 per cent of the global total, as measured at 2003 prices and converted to US dollars at 2003 market exchange rates (see table 8.3). Hence, the remaining

[41] See table 7.1 in chapter 7 in this volume.

Table 8.3. The 15 countries with the highest military expenditure in 2004 in market exchange rate terms and purchasing power parity terms

Spending figures are in US$, at constant (2003) prices and exchange rates.

Military expenditure in MER dollar terms						Military expenditure in PPP dollar terms[a]		
				World share (%)				
Rank[b]	Country	Spending ($ b.)	Spending per capita ($)	Spending	Popul.	Rank[b]	Country	Spending ($ b.)
1	USA	455.3	1 533	*47*	*5*	1	USA	455.3
2	UK	47.4	798	*5*	*1*	2	China	[161.1]
3	France	46.2	764	*5*	*1*	3	India	81.8
4	Japan	42.4	332	*4*	*2*	4	Russia	[66.1]
5	China	[35.4]	[27]	*[4]*	*21*	5	France	51.2
Sub-total, top 5		**626.7**		***64***	***29***	**Sub-total, top 5**		**815.6**
6	Germany	33.9	411	*3*	*1*	6	UK	46.2
7	Italy	27.8	484	*3*	*1*	7	Germany	36.9
8	Russia	[19.4]	[136]	*[2]*	2	8	Japan	35.2
9	Saudi Arabia[c d]	19.3	775	*2*	*0*	9	Italy	34.5
10	Korea, South	15.5	323	*2*	*1*	10	Saudi Arabia[c]	29.1
Sub-total, top 10		**742.5**		***76***	***35***	**Sub-total, top 10**		**997.4**
11	India	15.1	14	*2*	*17*	11	Turkey	24.3
12	Israel[d]	10.7	1 627	*1*	*0*	12	Korea, South	23.1
13	Canada	10.6	336	*1*	*1*	13	Brazil	20.7
14	Turkey	10.1	140	*1*	*1*	14	Iran[c]	18.5
15	Australia[d]	10.1	507	*1*	*0*	15	Pakistan	16.1
Sub-total, top 15		**799.2**		***82***	***54***	**Sub-total, top 15**		**1 100.2**
World		**975**	**153**	***100***	***100***	**World**		..

MER = market exchange rate; PPP = purchasing power parity; [ ] = Estimated figure.

[a] The figures in PPP dollar terms are converted at PPP rates (for 2003), calculated by the World Bank, based on comparisons of gross national product.

[b] The top 15 list would probably include Myanmar if data were available.

[c] Data for Iran and Saudi Arabia include expenditure for public order and safety and are a slight overestimate.

[d] The populations of Australia, Israel and Saudi Arabia each constitute less than 0.5 per cent of the total world population.

Sources: **Military expenditure**: appendix 8A. **PPP rates**: World Bank, *World Development Report 2005: A Better Investment Climate for Everyone* (Oxford University Press: New York, 2004), URL <http://www.worldbank.org/wdr/>, table 1, Key indicators of Development, pp. 256–57, and table 5, Key indicators for other economies, p. 264. **2004 population**: United Nations Population Fund (UNFPA), *State of the World Population 2004* (UNFPA: New York, 2004), URL <http://www.unfpa.org/swp/>.

144 countries in the SIPRI military expenditure database together accounted for only 18 per cent of global military spending. The combined share of the five top spenders—the USA, the UK, France, Japan and China—was 64 per cent of the world total. The US share alone was 47 per cent of the total, while the other four countries accounted for 4–5 per cent each.

Military expenditure per capita varies considerably between the major spenders, from populous China, which spends $27 per capita, to the USA, which spends $1533 per capita. Because of their great resources, high-income countries generally have high per capita military spending, as reflected in table 8.3 by the examples of the USA, the West European countries, Saudi Arabia and South Korea. For the same reason, there is a striking asymmetry in the pattern of world military spending in comparison with the global population pattern: the top five spenders account for 64 per cent of world military expenditure for the protection of 29 per cent of the global population.

Table 8.3 also provides an alternative top 15 list of major spenders in purchasing power parity (PPP) terms in order to illustrate the problems involved in international comparisons of economic data. On the left-hand side of the table, countries are ranked according to their military spending when converted into dollars by ordinary market exchange rates (MERs), while on the right-hand side countries are ranked according to their spending converted according to PPP. In conceptual terms, the comparison based on military expenditure in MER dollar terms indicates the purchasing power on the international market, while the comparison based on military spending in PPP dollar terms indicates the relative amounts of alternative goods and services (in terms of a standardized basket of national output) that the military budget could buy on the domestic market (i.e., its 'opportunity cost').

Military expenditure data expressed in PPP dollar terms, while reflecting the non-military items that the military budget could buy on the domestic market, can exaggerate 10-fold what that budget can buy on the international market. In particular, military expenditure expressed in PPP dollar terms does not appropriately reflect the technological level of the military equipment it can buy. Furthermore, in practice there are reliability problems with some PPP rates since they are artificial: calculated on the basis of comparisons of the GDPs of the USA and the respective countries.[42]

An additional problem is that military expenditure figures are often used for international comparisons of the size, strength or even capability of the military forces. However, neither of these two series is suitable for these purposes, and in particular PPP-based figures can be highly misleading in this context. While military expenditure is a measure only of the financial resources that are allocated to the military sector, military size or capability also depends on

[42] On the relative merits and impact of using MERs and PPP rates see Sköns, E. *et al.*, 'Military expenditure', *SIPRI Yearbook 2003: Armaments, Disarmament and International Security* (Oxford University Press: Oxford, 2003), pp. 304–306; and 'Sources and methods for military expenditure data', *SIPRI Yearbook 1999: Armaments, Disarmament and International Security* (Oxford University Press: Oxford, 1999), pp. 327–33. Table 7C.1 in the latter reference shows the difference between MER-based and PPP-based military expenditure for selected countries.

several other factors, such as the level of military technology, the mix of military equipment and manpower paid for by the military budget, whether soldiers are reimbursed conscripts or salaried professionals, and a host of other factors.

As shown in table 8.3 the choice of exchange rate has a significant impact on the apparent level of military spending, in particular for China, India and Russia. This is the main reason for the difference in military spending estimates for these countries. For instance, most researchers agree on the general level of Chinese military expenditure when expressed in the local currency, the yuan. However, estimates in dollar terms differ significantly, ranging from SIPRI's MER-based estimate of $35 billion, via estimates of $56 billion by the International Institute of Strategic Studies and $50–70 billion by the US DOD,[43] to SIPRI's PPP-based estimate of $161 billion. The differences between the estimates depend largely on the type of exchange rate that has been used.

III. The United States

Since the post-cold war low point in 1999, US military expenditure has increased by 41 per cent in real terms.[44] Most of the increase occurred during the period 2001–2004, when outlays for national defence increased at an annual average rate of 10 per cent in real terms. This increase reflects the supplementary appropriations made to fund the USA's military operations in Afghanistan and Iraq, in addition to increased regular military expenditure.

The US defence budget for financial year 2006

The US defence budget request for FY 2006 (1 October 2005–30 September 2006) amounted to $419.3 billion in budget authority for the Department of Defense, an increase of 4.8 per cent in nominal terms over FY 2005.[45] Figures released for the Future Years Defense Program 2006–11 show planned budget authority increasing to $502.3 billion in FY 2011 (see table 8.4). These figures do not include funding of military operations abroad, which are not part of the regular US defence budget process but are financed instead through supplementary appropriations.

In the presentation of the budget, the continued increase in budget authority for FY 2006 and beyond was motivated by four main objectives as pledged by

[43] These 2 estimates are presented in US–China Economic and Security Review Commission, 'The national security implications of the economic relationship between the United States and China', Report to the US Congress, Washington, DC, July 2002, URL <http://www.uscc.gov/researchpapers/2000_2003/reports/anrp02.htm>, chapter 9, 'The defense budget and the military economy'.

[44] This refers to official US budget data, which differ from the NATO-supplied data used in the tables in appendix 8A.

[45] US Department of Defense (DOD), 'Fiscal 2006 Department of Defense budget is released', News Release no. 129-05, 7 Feb. 2005, URL <http://www.dod.mil/releases/2005/>. Additional DOD budget documents are available at URL <http://www.dod/mil/comptroller/defbudget/fy2006/>.

the administration of President George W. Bush: 'to defeat global terrorism, restructure America's armed forces and global defence posture, develop and field advanced war-fighting capabilities, and take good care of our forces'.[46] 'We are a nation at war', said Defense Secretary Donald Rumsfeld, and the 'budget, together with the supplemental spending proposals the President has made, provides the men and women in uniform what they need to prevail'.[47] This includes funding for the restructuring of the army and Marine Corps to increase the number and types of forces needed to fight terrorism; for making more units available for deployment to Afghanistan and Iraq; and for the Special Operations Forces to increase their personnel and give them a more prominent role in fighting terrorism. The budget also includes requests for authorities to enable the DOD to provide assistance to military or security forces in Iraq and other designated nations in fighting the 'global war on terrorism'.

Restructuring of the forces focuses on increasing the number of combat units in the ground forces: the army and the Marine Corps. It also provides new funding to return military personnel now doing 'commercial-like functions' back to combat functions. The US global defence posture is being restructured to better position US forces to strengthen coalition and partner nation relationships in order to fight terrorism and meet other challenges. The budget request highlights major investments in a number of 'capabilities essential to the transformation and future dominance of America's military forces', including in missile defence; the Future Combat Systems programme for the modernization of the army; a continued shift to a new generation of ships; acquisition of advanced combat, transport and tanker aircraft and a series of programmes in intelligence, communications and related systems, which are seen as key to predicting threats and defeating terrorism.[48]

Supplementary appropriations for military operations abroad

The US Administration has decided that military operations in Afghanistan, Iraq and other countries will not be financed through the regular defence budget but by separate supplementary appropriations. By February 2005 the total amount of supplementary appropriations requested for the 'global war on terrorism' since 11 September 2001 had reached $346 billion, of which $268 billion was for the DOD, $238 billion for the period FYs 2003–2005 (see table 8.5).[49] The total includes funding for agencies other than the DOD, such as the Department of Homeland Security and the Department of State, and for reconstruction in Afghanistan and Iraq.

[46] US DOD (note 45), p. 1.

[47] US DOD (note 45), title page.

[48] US DOD (note 45), pp. 4–6.

[49] See also Lumpkin, J. J., 'Iraq, Afghan war costs may exceed $300b', Associated Press, 16 Feb. 2005, available at URL <http://www.truthout.org/docs_2005/021605E.shtml>.

Table 8.4. US budget authority[a] for the Department of Defense,[b] financial years 2004–11

Figures are in US$ b., at current prices. Years are financial years.[c]

Budget title	2004	2005	2006	2007	2008	2009	2010	2011
Figures excluding supplementary appropriations[d]								
Military personnel	97.0	104.0	108.9	112.0	115.4	119.4	123.3	127.1
Operation and maintenance	128.1	137.0	147.8	154.1	160.8	167.3	172.1	177.4
Procurement	76.1	78.1	78.0	91.6	101.4	105.3	111.3	118.6
Research, development, testing and evaluation	64.3	68.8	69.4	66.8	66.5	72.4	68.8	59.7
Military construction	5.6	6.0	7.8	12.3	13.6	11.1	10.5	10.9
Family housing	3.8	4.1	4.2	3.9	3.0	2.7	2.7	2.7
Other	0.7	2.1	3.2	2.4	1.7	3.8	3.4	5.9
Total DOD	**375.7**	**400.1**	**419.3**	**443.1**	**462.4**	**482.0**	**492.1**	**502.3**
Figures including supplementary appropriations enacted before 8 February 2005								
Enacted supplements[e]	92.8	1.1	–	–	–	–	–	–
Total DOD[e]	**468.5**	**401.1**	**419.3**	**443.1**	**462.4**	**482.0**	**492.1**	**502.3**

DOD = Department of Defense.

[a] Budget authority is the authority to incur legally binding obligations on behalf of the government. These will result in immediate or future outlays, i.e. expenditure.

[b] DOD programmes constitute the major part of US national defence programmes. Other defence-related activities, including those of the Department of Energy, accounted for less than 0.5% of budget authority for national defence in financial year (FY) 2004. Comparable data for total military expenditure were not available at the time of writing.

[c] The US financial year runs from 1 Oct. of the previous year to 30 Sep. of the named year.

[d] These figures exclude supplementary appropriations for foreign military operations in Afghanistan and Iraq. The figures for FYs 2005–11 are from the defence budget for FY 2006 and the Future Years Defense Program for FY 2006–11, as released by the DOD on 7 Feb. 2005. The figures for FY 2004 are comparable figures released by the White House Office of Management and Budget on 8 Feb. 2005.

[e] These figures include supplementary appropriations for foreign military operations in Afghanistan and Iraq enacted before 8 Feb. 2005, as provided by the White House, Office of Management and Budget, 8 Feb. 2005.

Sources: US DOD, 'Fiscal 2006 Department of Defense budget is released', News Release no. 129-05, 7 Feb. 2005, URL <http://www.dod.mil/releases/2005/>; and Office of Management and Budget, 'Department of Defense', *Budget of the United States Government, Fiscal Year 2006* (White House: Washington, DC, 8 Feb. 2005), URL <http://www.whitehouse.gov/omb/budget>, pp. 83–95.

The FY 2005 supplementary appropriation requested on 14 February 2005 amounted to $81.9 billion 'to fund ongoing military operations in the War on Terror, reconstruction activities in Afghanistan, tsunami relief and reconstruction, and other purposes'.[50] The request included $75 billion for the DOD, $5.6 billion for international functions, including the Department of State; $0.95 billion for multi-agency tsunami relief efforts; and nearly $0.4 billion for other agencies, including the Department of Energy and the Department of Homeland Security (in particular, the US Coast Guard) for counter-terrorism efforts in support of the 'global war on terrorism'.[51] The $75 billion DOD share included $36.3 billion to fund combat operations in support of Operation Enduring Freedom in Afghanistan and Operation Iraqi Freedom during FY 2005. Other items funded by the supplement include restructuring of the army (the 'Army Modularity' plan); refurbishment and replacement of equipment used in operations in Afghanistan and Iraq; addition of armour to all convoy trucks and procurement of armoured security vehicles; additional contributions to the Afghan Security Forces Fund and the Iraq Security Forces Fund; and funding of the activities of coalition partners in direct support of US military operations, including Pakistan's counter-terrorist operations along its border with Afghanistan and for the Polish forces in Iraq.[52] Some of these funds will reportedly also be used to establish more permanent military bases in Iraq, assuming that the new Iraqi Government permits a long-term US military presence.[53]

Some of the DOD items in this supplement are not directly related to costs incurred as a result of the ongoing military operations abroad. It has therefore been argued that those should be financed through the regular DOD budget and not through supplementary appropriations.[54] This applies, for example, to the Army Modularity plan, which is a central component of the army's plans to transform its forces and would have been carried out regardless of whether US forces were engaged in military operations abroad. This practice of funding costs not directly related to military operations abroad adds to the difficulties of assessing the realism of the projected future budgets for the DOD as presented in the Future Years Defense Program (see table 8.4).[55]

The $5.6 billion requested for international affairs activities includes funding for State Department operations in Iraq; a new US embassy in Iraq; aid for critical partners in the 'global war on terrorism'; reconstruction, police support and counter-drug activities in Afghanistan; support for Palestinian efforts to build a democratic state; the humanitarian crisis in Darfur, Sudan; and for new

[50] Office of Management and Budget (OMB), 'Emergency supplemental (various agencies)', White House, Washington, DC, 14 Feb. 2005, URL <http://www.whitehouse.gov/omb/budget/amendments.htm>.

[51] OMB (note 50).

[52] OMB (note 50).

[53] Andrews, E. L., 'Bush aides say budget deficit will rise again', *New York Times*, 26 Jan. 2005.

[54] Kosiak, S., 'FY 2006 defense budget request: DOD budget remains on upward trajectory', Center for Strategic and Budgetary Assessment, Washington, DC, 4 Feb. 2005, URL <http://www.csbaonline.org/>.

[55] Kosiak (note 54).

Table 8.5. US supplementary appropriations for the 'global war on terrorism', financial years 2002–2005

Figures are in US$ b., at current prices. Figures do not always add up to totals because of the conventions of rounding.

Date of appropriation	Financial year[a]	DOD	Non-DOD	Total
September 2001	2001	13	7	20
January 2002	2002	3	17	20
August 2002	2002	14	10	24
February 2003[b]	2003	10	0	10
April 2003	2003	63	16	78
November 2003	2004	65	22	87
May 2004	2005	25	0	25
February 2005[c]	2005	75	7	82
Total		**268**	**79**	**346**

DOD = Department of Defense; Non-DOD = Agencies other than the DOD.

[a] The US financial year runs from 1 Oct. of the previous year to 30 Sep. of the named year.

[b] This additional funding was provided in the Consolidated Appropriations Act 2003.

[c] This supplement was requested on 14 Feb. 2005.

Sources: Kosiak, S., 'Funding for defense, military operations, homeland security, and related activities since 9/11', Center for Strategic and Budgetary Assessments, Washington, DC, 18 Oct. 2004, URL <http://www.csbaonline.org/>, p. 6; Office of Management and Budget, 'Budget amendment: $25 billion contingent emergency reserve fund (Department of Defense—Iraq Freedom Fund)', White House, Washington, DC, 12 May 2004, URL <http://www.whitehouse.gov/omb/budget/04amendments.htm>; and Office of Management and Budget, 'Emergency supplemental (various agencies)', White House, Washington, DC, 14 Feb. 2005, URL <http://www.whitehouse.gov/omb/budget/amendments.htm>.

international peacekeeping missions in Burundi, the Democratic Republic of the Congo, Côte d'Ivoire, Haiti and Sudan. These efforts were said to 'not only assure the delivery of critical humanitarian supplies, they also provide an important alternative to deploying U.S. forces'.[56]

The request for supplementary appropriations for FY 2006, planned for submission in early 2006, is expected to be of roughly the same magnitude as that for FY 2005.[57] According to Lieutenant General James J. Lovelace, the director of US Army operations, in January 2005 the army was operating on the assumption that the number of US troops in Iraq would remain above 100 000 throughout 2006,[58] compared with the presence of 150 000 at that time.

[56] OMB (note 50), p. 4.

[57] Kosiak (note 54); and Shanker, T. and Schmitt, E., 'Pentagon budget up: war cost is excluded', *New York Times*, 8 Feb. 2005.

[58] Andrews (note 53).

The economic and social impact of US military spending

Assessments of the economic and social impact of the significant rise in US military expenditure have evolved around two major and interrelated issues: its impact on the USA's economic growth and its impact on non-military government spending. The first issue concerns the extent to which military expenditure contributes to the budget deficit and the impact of the deficit on future economic growth. The second issue concerns whether military expenditure is crowding out non-military government expenditure or will do so in future. In addition, there is disagreement on the projections of military expenditure, caused primarily by the uncertainties about future trends in expenditure for foreign military operations.

United States expenditure (or 'outlays' in US terminology) for national defence have increased from $276 billion in FY 1999 to $454 billion in FY 2004, including expenditure deriving from the supplementary appropriations for military operations abroad (see table 8.6). During the period FYs 2005–10 national defence outlays are projected to increase from $464 billion to $502 billion. However, these projections do not include funding for a continued US military presence in Iraq and other outlays resulting from supplementary appropriations approved in 2005 and beyond; these projections thus understate actual outlays by a significant amount, at least for the earlier years.[59] The share of its GDP that the USA spends on defence has increased from 3.0 per cent in 1999 to 3.9 per cent in 2004. While this share is high, it is still much lower than at its peak level in 1985–87 during the cold war, when it exceeded 6 per cent of GDP. Similarly, outlays on national defence as a share of total government outlays have increased from 16.2 per cent in 1999 to 19.8 per cent in 2004, but are still lower than at the cold war peak of 27–28 per cent of total outlays in 1987–88.[60] The reason for concern is that the current spending hike comes in a financial context of rising budget deficits. Some groups are concerned about the deficit per se, while others are concerned that the combined policies of cutting taxes, raising military expenditure and trying to cut the deficit in half by 2009, which is the declared goal of the US Administration, will result in significant crowding out of non-military federal spending.

While the main cause of the deficit is the tax cuts enacted during 2001, 2002 and 2003, the level of military expenditure is an important contribution. Without the increase in defence spending as a share of GDP in 1999–2004, the budget deficit as a share of GDP would have been 0.9 percentage points lower. Furthermore, only one-third of federal budget expenditure is made up of dis-

[59] The figure for FY 2005 does, however, include expenditure resulting from supplements approved before 2005. The outlays resulting from the supplement proposed in Feb. 2005 are shown separately in table 8.6.

[60] Office of Management and Budget, *Historical Tables FY2006: Budget of the United States Government Fiscal Year 2006* (US Government Printing Office: Washington, DC, 2004), table 6.1, 'Composition of outlays: 1940–2009'.

Table 8.6. US military expenditure and other federal expenditure, financial years 1999–2010

Years are financial years.[a] Figures do not always add up to totals because of the conventions of rounding.

Outlay category	1999	2000	2001	2002	2003	2004	2005[b]	2006[b]	2007[b]	2008[b]	2009[b]	2010[b]	Source[c]
Outlays ($ b., at current prices)													
Total Federal outlays	1 702	1 789	1 864	2 011	2 160	2 292	2 479	2 568	2 656	2 758	2 883	3 028	Table 8.1
Discretionary[d]	572	615	649	734	826	895	965	946	935	935	953	971	Table 8.1
National defence	276	295	306	349	405	454	464	444	446	463	485	502	Table 8.1
Proposed supplement[e]							34.9	24.5	17.8	2.5	1.3	–	Table 8.1
Non-defence[f]	297	320	343	385	421	441	466	477	471	469	467	470	Table 8.1
Mandatory[g]	900	951	1 008	1 106	1 181	1 237	1 337	1 410	1 476	1 551	1 635	1 743	Table 8.1
Net interest[h]	230	223	206	171	153	160	178	211	245	272	294	314	Table 8.1
Surplus/deficit	125	236	128	–158	–378	–412	–427	–390	–312	–251	–233	–207	Table 1.1
Outlays as a share of total federal outlays (%)													
National defence	*16.2*	*16.5*	*16.4*	*17.4*	*18.7*	*19.8*	*18.7*	*17.3*	*16.8*	*16.8*	*16.8*	*16.6*	Table 8.3
Proposed supplement[e]							*1.4*	*1.0*	*0.7*	*0.1*	negl.	. .	Table 8.3
Non-defence[f]	*17.4*	*17.9*	*18.4*	*19.2*	*19.5*	*19.3*	*18.8*	*18.6*	*17.7*	*17.0*	*16.2*	*15.5*	Table 8.3
Net interest[e]	*13.5*	*12.5*	*11.1*	*8.5*	*7.1*	*7.0*	*7.2*	*8.2*	*9.2*	*9.9*	*10.2*	*10.4*	Table 8.3
Outlays as a share of gross domestic product (%)													
Total Federal outlays	*18.7*	*18.4*	*18.5*	*19.4*	*19.9*	*19.8*	*20.3*	*19.9*	*19.5*	*19.2*	*19.1*	*19.0*	Table 8.4
National defence	*3.0*	*3.0*	*3.0*	*3.4*	*3.7*	*3.9*	*3.8*	*3.4*	*3.3*	*3.2*	*3.2*	*3.2*	Table 8.4
Non-defence[f]	*3.2*	*3.3*	*3.4*	*3.7*	*3.9*	*3.8*	*3.8*	*3.7*	*3.5*	*3.3*	*3.1*	*3.0*	Table 8.4
Net interest[h]	*2.5*	*2.3*	*2.0*	*1.6*	*1.4*	*1.4*	*1.5*	*1.6*	*1.8*	*1.9*	*1.9*	*2.0*	Table 8.4
Surplus/deficit	*1.4*	*2.4*	*1.3*	*–1.5*	*–3.5*	*–3.6*	*–3.5*	*–3.0*	*–2.3*	*–1.7*	*–1.5*	*–1.3*	Table 1.2
Memoranda ($ b., at current prices)													
Federal debt	5 606	5 629	5 770	6 198	6 760	7 355	8 031	8 708	9 350	9 949	10 544	11 137	Table 7.1
Gross domestic product	9 125	9 710	10 058	10 389	10 839	11 553	12 227	12 907	13 617	14 349	15 111	15 906	Table 1.2

[a] The US financial year runs from 1 Oct. of the previous year to 30 Sep. of the named year.

[b] These figures exclude outlays from financial year 2005 supplementary appropriations and any supplements that will be required in later years for military operations in Afghanistan and Iraq.

[c] This refers to the table in the source document (see below) from which the figures were obtained.

[d] Discretionary outlays are for programmes whose budgetary resources are provided in appropriations acts. (In financial year 2004 discretionary outlays accounted for 39% of total federal outlays and national defence accounted for 50% of discretionary spending.)

[e] Proposed supplement shows the allowance for an anticipated supplementary budget request of $80 billion in 2005, expected to include $75 billion for military operations and $5 billion for non-defence. The actual supplement requested in Feb. 2005 amounted to $82 b.

[f] Non-defence discretionary programmes include mainly international affairs, science, natural resources and environment, transportation, education, health, and administration of justice.

[g] Mandatory outlays are for entitlement programmes whose budget authority is provided by laws other than appropriations acts (social security, Medicare, Medicaid and income security programmes).

[h] These are figures for interest payments on the federal debt

Source: Office of Management and Budget, *Historical Tables FY2006: Budget of the United States Government Fiscal Year 2006* (US Government Printing Office: Washington, DC, 2004).

cretionary spending, that is, programmes whose spending can be decided directly in the budgetary process. The other two-thirds is made up of so-called mandatory spending, resulting from entitlement programmes, such as social and income security programmes, whose costs are influenced by changes in the entitlement criteria; any cuts in these programmes thus require decisions to change these criteria.

The US budget has gone from a surplus of $125 billion in 1999 to a deficit of $427 billion in 2005, corresponding to 3.5 per cent of GDP. The federal debt has increased from $5.6 trillion in 1999 to $8.0 trillion in 2005, corresponding to 65.7 per cent of GDP (see table 8.6). The deficit is projected to fall to $233 billion in FY 2009, thus indicating that the policies of the current US Administration will achieve its goal of cutting the deficit in half by the end of its term. However, as required by law, this projection is based on assumptions that make it unrealistic.[61] In particular, (*a*) it is assumed that all temporary tax provisions expire as scheduled, although President Bush is committed to making them permanent; (*b*) future war cost funding is excluded; and (*c*) the projections do not include the borrowing that would be needed to establish the private investment accounts that President Bush has proposed for Social Security starting in 2009, which according to US Administration officials would add $23 billion to the deficit in 2009 and $56.5 billion in 2010.[62] An alternative, independent, projection that abandons such assumptions shows instead that the deficit will remain at 3.5 per cent of GDP over the next decade.[63]

The impact of budget deficits on economic growth is a contested issue, with views differing between schools of economic theory.[64] Alice Rivlin, former head of the US Congressional Budget Office, argues that persistent deficits of the magnitude of the current US deficit 'are likely to lower standards of living, make [the USA] dangerously dependent on the rest of the world, and pass on large fiscal burdens to future generations'.[65] The fact that other major powers, in particular China and Japan, hold significant currency reserves in dollars and can thus influence the value of the dollar—and therefore US debt repayment—has emerged as an additional source of concern during recent years.

[61] US Congressional Budget Office (CBO), *The Budget and Economic Outlook: Fiscal Years 2006 to 2015* (CBO: Washington, DC, Jan. 2005), URL <http://www.cbo.gov/ftpdoc.cfm?index=6060&type=1>.

[62] Andrews, E. L. and Rosenbaum, D. E., 'The big picture may seem rosy, but the deficit is in the details', *New York Times*, 8 Feb. 2005; and Stevenson, R. W., 'President offers budget proposal with broad cuts', *New York Times*, 8 Feb. 2005.

[63] Gale, W. G. and Orszag, P. R, 'The US budget deficit: on an unsustainable path', *New Economy* (Dec. 2004), pp. 236–42, URL <http://www.brookings.edu/views/articles/20041201orszaggale.htm>.

[64] Some critics argue that budget deficits matter because they reduce national savings and thus reduce future national income, either by leading to a rise in interest rates and reductions in domestic investment or by increasing foreign borrowing and therefore future foreign debt. Gale and Orszag (note 63). Adherents of the Keynesian school of economic theory argue that deficits do not matter because they lead to economic growth and therefore to increased tax revenues, which will lead to a reduction of the deficit in future. However, even this school argues that budgeting for long-term deficits is not sustainable.

[65] Rivlin, A. M. and Sawhill, I. V., 'How to balance the budget', Policy Brief no. 130, Brookings Institution, Washington, DC, Mar. 2004, URL <http://www.brook.edu/>, p. 1.

The efforts to cut the deficit in half have involved cuts in both non-security discretionary spending and mandatory spending. National defence accounts for roughly half of discretionary spending. The FY 2006 budget projects that all discretionary spending except that on the military and domestic security will be frozen for the next five years. Thus, military spending will expand at the cost of other discretionary programmes, such as education, health, environment, agriculture and space.[66] The budget projections also include substantial reductions in mandatory programmes such as Medicaid, which provides medical assistance for those on low incomes.[67] The share of total federal expenditure that is spent on national defence is projected to decline from 18.7 per cent in FY 2005 to 16.6 per cent in FY 2010 (but this excludes funding of military operations abroad), while the share of non-defence spending will decline from 18.8 per cent to 15.5 per cent of federal spending over the same period (see table 8.6). Considering that these falling shares will take place in the context of a decline in the federal budget as a share of GDP, this projection includes a substantial reduction in non-military spending and it is most likely that the actual reduction will be much greater when the effect of future supplements on discretionary outlays becomes known. Thus, there are reasons to question the sustainability of the current US military effort.

IV. Financing security through international assistance

Security is a prerequisite for sustainable development. Several donors of development assistance are now favourably disposed to treating the security sector as a legitimate area of support in many recipient countries, particularly those that are conflict prone.[68]

While all major donors of development assistance seem to agree on the need for security as the basis for sustainable development and accept the broad development goals underlining the agenda of security sector reform,[69] they differ in the ways in which they approach support for the security sector.[70]

[66] Stevenson (note 62).

[67] Stevenson (note 62).

[68] See, e.g., Brzoska, M., 'Development donors and the concept of security sector reform', Occasional Paper no. 4, Geneva Centre for the Democratic Control of Armed Forces, Geneva, Nov. 2003, URL <http://www.dcaf.ch/>, pp. 37–45.

[69] This is demonstrated by their adoption of the OECD guidelines on security sector reform. OECD Development Assistance Committee (DAC), 'Security system reform and governance: policy and good practice', DAC Guidelines and Reference Series, OECD, Paris, 2004, URL <http://www.oecd.org/dac/conflict/>. See also White House, 'The national security strategy of the United States of America', Washington, DC, Sep. 2002, URL <http://www.whitehouse.gov/nsc/nss.html>; US Agency for International Development, 'Conflict management: security sector reform and conflict', webpage, n.d., URL <http://www.usaid.gov/our_work/cross-cutting_programs/conflict/focus_areas/security.html>; and Colletta, N., Mendelson Forman, J., and Vanheukelom, J., 'Security, poverty reduction & sustainable development: challenges for the new millennium', Working paper, World Bank, Washington, DC, Sep. 1999, URL <http://www.worldbank.org/socialdevelopment/>.

[70] See, e.g., Samuelsson, T., 'Sweden takes a closer look at security vs development', *New Routes*, no. 1, 2004, pp. 16–17; and Maxwell, S., 'The Washington Consensus is dead! Long live the meta-narrative!', Working Paper no. 243, Overseas Development Institute, London, Jan. 2005, URL <http://www.odi.org.uk/publications/working_papers/>.

Some countries fear that extending the definition of official development assistance (ODA) to cover security-related issues may diminish the overall support for real (social and economic) development efforts since security problems abound in several aid-receiving countries. Others fear that including security in ODA may result in the cold war-style assistance, with the strategic interests of donors dictating the direction of their aid policy or with assistance skewed in favour of the military sector.

Much of the debate on this subject among donors has taken place in the Development Assistance Committee (DAC) of the Organisation for Economic Co-operation and Development (OECD). In 2004 the DAC agreed on a compromise position that, as a first step towards the expansion of the definition of ODA, allows the inclusion of certain non-controversial categories of security-related assistance in ODA. The DAC high-level meeting agreed to count as ODA such security-related activities as: (*a*) providing technical cooperation to government for the management of security expenditure, including military budgets; (*b*) improving civilian oversight and democratic control of security forces by providing assistance to civil society to enhance its capacity to scrutinize the security establishment; and (*c*) providing assistance to government and civil society organizations to support legislation designed to prevent the recruitment of child soldiers.[71] Discussion of the more controversial areas such as support for peacekeeping activities was deferred. In taking this least controversial position the DAC's greatest concern was the implication of an expansion of the definition of ODA for the credibility of the ODA statistics.

The financing of security in recipient countries is already becoming common among some members of the DAC.[72] Two ongoing support programmes for security activities in recipient countries by two members of the DAC—the USA's assistance to Colombia and the UK's support for the security sector in Sierra Leone—are examined here as examples of emerging patterns of security assistance to recipient countries. The programmes are examined within the context of the development assistance policies of the two countries and the increasing realization by developed countries that funding security in crisis-prone developing countries can be an indirect way of enhancing security at home.

[71] OECD Development Assistance Committee (DAC), 'Annex 5: ODA coverage of certain conflict, peace building and security expenditures', *DAC Statistical Reporting Directives* (OECD: Paris, 28 Apr. 2004), URL <http://www.oecd.org/dac/stats/dac/directives/>.

[72] Some donor countries, such as the Netherlands, Norway and the UK, as well as the World Bank, have developed innovative ways of dealing with the interface between peace, security and development through the creation of special accounts. For details see Randel, J. with Cordeiro, M. and Mowjee, T., 'Financing countries in protracted humanitarian crisis: an overview of new instruments and existing aid flows', eds A. Harmer and J. Macrae, *Beyond the Continuum: The Changing Role of Aid Policy in Protracted Crises*, Humanitarian Policy Group Report no. 18 (Overseas Development Institute: London, July 2004), URL <http://www.odi.org.uk/hpg/>, pp. 54–70. The EU's African Peace Facility is also an example of an attempt to support the security sector.

The USA's assistance to Colombia

Traditionally, the USA has used its foreign aid to pursue its strategic interests abroad, although it has also contributed to humanitarian assistance from time to time: in the age of global media, strategic interest and humanitarian aid may often coincide. Throughout the cold war the strategic interest of the USA was the major determining factor in the disbursement of its aid. As a result, the aid was not always directed to the countries in the greatest need.[73] This pattern of support changed briefly in the 1990s as the cold war came to an end and the development of the least developed countries came to be seen as a strategic goal in itself. However, since the September 2001 terrorist attacks on the USA, the approach to foreign assistance has returned to the traditional cold war pattern; the USA's strategic interests dictate the location and form of assistance and the recipient countries it considers most important both in terms of proximity and the fight against terrorism.

Owing to the region's strategic importance, Latin America has always been of interest to the USA. In recent years, the issues of drugs and terrorism have narrowed the focus of the USA to a few countries in the Andean region where the problems of instability and narcotic production are most prevalent. Colombia—from where over 90 per cent of the illicit drugs entering the USA originate—and other countries such as Bolivia and Peru have been the focus of US foreign assistance programmes that combat the problem of illicit drugs through eradication of their means of production.[74]

Colombia has been embroiled for decades in an armed conflict with a number of left-wing guerrilla and right-wing paramilitary groups over social and economic inequalities.[75] Attempts to resolve the conflict have met with little success. Over the years the armed groups have become involved in narcotics production and trafficking to finance their activities.

In 1999 the Colombian Government announced a national initiative known as Plan Colombia, which aimed to restart the peace process with the rebels, generate employment, intensify the war against drugs and provide alternative economic activity to drug cultivation. The plan also aimed to provide a stable justice system and to modernize the armed forces.[76] The total cost of the plan was estimated at $7.5 billion, to be financed through three main sources: $4.5 billion from the Colombian Government, $1.3 billion from the US Government and the remaining $1.7 billion from other donors.[77] The bulk of

[73] Chauvet, L. and Collier, P., 'Development effectiveness in fragile states: spillovers and turnarounds', Background paper, Senior Level Forum on Development Effectiveness in Fragile States, OECD, Paris, 13–14 Jan. 2005, URL <http://www.oecd.org/dac/lap/slffragilestates/>; and Lancaster, C., 'Redesigning foreign aid', *Foreign Affairs*, vol. 79, no. 5 (Sep./Oct. 2000).

[74] US Department of State, 'A report to Congress on United States policy towards Colombia and other related issues', Washington, DC, 3 Feb. 2003, URL <http://www.state.gov/p/wha/rls/rpt/>.

[75] See also chapters 2 and 6 in this volume for discussions of the Colombian conflict.

[76] For a summary of Plan Colombia see US Department of State, 'Plan Colombia', Fact sheet, Washington, DC, 14 Mar. 2001, URL <http://www.state.gov/p/wha/rls/fs/2001/>; and US Department of State (note 74).

[77] US Department of State, 'Support for Plan Colombia', Fact sheet, 14 Mar. 2001, URL <http://www.state.gov/p/wha/rt/plncol/>.

Table 8.7. US assistance to Colombia by programme, financial years 1998–2005

Figures are actual expenditure, in US$ m., at current prices. Years are financial years.

Type of assistance	1998	1999	2000	2001	2002	2003	2004	2005
Military assistance								
FMF	. .	. .	. .	. .	. .	17.1	98.5	99
IMET	0.9	0.9	0.9	1.0	1.2	1.2	1.7	1.7
INCLE and ACI	66	206	895	48	380	580	474	463
NADR	. .	. .	. .	. .	25	3.3	. .	4.0
Peace Corps	. .	. .	. .	. .	. .	. .	. .	. .
Peacekeeping operations	. .	. .	. .	. .	. .	. .	. .	. .
Sub-total	**67**	**207**	**896**	**49**	**406**	**602**	**574**	**568**
Economic or development assistance								
Child survival and health	. .	. .	. .	. .	. .	. .	. .	. .
Development assistance	0.02	. .	. .	. .	. .	. .	. .	. .
Economic Support Fund	. .	3.3	4.0	. .	. .	. .	. .	. .
FSA	. .	. .	. .	. .	. .	. .	. .	. .
MRA	. .	. .	. .	. .	. .	. .	. .	. .
SEED	. .	. .	. .	. .	. .	. .	. .	. .
Other	. .	. .	. .	. .	. .	. .	. .	. .
Sub-total	**0.02**	**3.3**	**4.0**	**0**	**0**	**0**	**0**	**0**
Total	**67**	**210**	**899**	**49**	**406**	**602**	**574**	**568**

FMF = Foreign military financing; IMET = International military education and training; INCLE = International narcotics control and law enforcement; ACI = Andean counter-drug initiative; NADR = Non-proliferation, anti-terrorism, de-mining and related; FSA = Freedom Support Act Undergraduate Program (FSA); MRA = Migration and refugee assistance; SEED = Supporting Entrepreneurs for Environment and Development.

Source: US Congress, 'Foreign Operations, Export Financing, and related programs appropriations', Hearings before a Subcommittee of the Committee on Appropriations, US House of Representatives, Part 1A, 'Justification of budget estimates', annual, 2000–2005, (US Government Printing Office: Washington, DC, 1999–2004).

the US assistance was to be military under the International Narcotics Control and Law Enforcement (INCLE) programme.[78] The Colombian Government supported the idea of the US assistance being mainly military as it planned major offensives against the rebel groups to regain territories under their control.

The primary objective of the US assistance programme for Colombia is the eradication of the production of illicit drugs and of terrorism through the enhancement of the counter-terrorism capability of the Colombian armed forces by providing military advice, supplying equipment and sharing intelligence. Other objectives include the defence of human rights, the promotion of

[78] Storrs, K. L. and Serafino, N. M., 'Andean Regional Initiative (ARI): FY2002 supplemental and FY2003 assistance for Colombia and neighbors', Library of Congress, Congressional Research Service, Washington, DC, 12 June 2002, URL <http://fpc.state.gov/fpc/c6943.htm>. According to the SIPRI definition of military expenditure, military assistance is counted as part of the donor country's military expenditure (see appendix 8B).

economic, social and alternative development initiatives, the reform and strengthening of the administration of justice, assistance to internally displaced persons, and the promotion of economic growth through trade.[79]

The Aerial Eradication Program (AEP) is a key component of the US and Colombian governments' strategy to eliminate the production of coca and poppy crops while they simultaneously offer compensation through the Alternative Development Program (ADP) to farmers who give up coca and poppy production. Conceptually, the AEP and ADP are therefore complementary, although in their application in Colombia they are not.

Under Plan Colombia, the country received over $895 million in US assistance in 2000, mainly for the training of its armed forces in anti-narcotics operations, the upgrade of military aviation facilities and the supply of equipment to the armed forces, especially the anti-narcotics brigade.[80] Most of the US military assistance is offered through private military companies, which train Colombian security forces and fight alongside them against the rebel groups and coca producers.[81] In addition, normal military assistance worth $0.9 million was provided in the form of military education and training for Colombian officers and $4 million was provided from the Economic Support Fund for social and economic purposes (see table 8.7).[82] After the terrorist attacks on the USA on 11 September 2001 a new approach was adopted towards Colombia, as the anti-narcotics war was re-categorized as a counter-terrorism war.[83] As a first step under the new approach all armed groups in the long-running conflict in Colombia were categorized as terrorist groups and were therefore included in the USA's list of foreign terrorist organizations.[84] As a result, the counter-narcotics assistance was broadened to include counter-terrorism as a complementary strategy. Furthermore, Plan Colombia was replaced by a new initiative known as the Andean Counter-drug Initiative (ACI) to cover all countries in the Andean region, although still with an overwhelming focus on Colombia—as suggested by the level of resources allocated to that country.[85]

[79] US Department of State (note 77).

[80] US Department of State, *Congressional Budget Justification for Foreign Operations Fiscal Year 2002* (Department of State: Washington, DC, 2001), URL <http://www.state.gov/m/rm/rls/cbj/>.

[81] Fidler, S. and Catn, T., 'Colombia: Private companies on the frontlines', *Financial Times*, 12 Aug. 2003, available at URL <http://www.corpwatch.org/article.php?id=8028>. See also 'Letter to Secretary of State Powell from Cynthia McKinney (D-Georgia), Jan Schakowsky (D-Illinois), Barbara Lee (D-California), and Pete Stark (D-California)', 15 Mar. 2001, URL <http://www.ciponline.org/colombia/031506.htm>.

[82] US Department of State, 'U.S. social, economic and development support for Plan Colombia', Fact sheet, 20 Feb. 2001, URL <http://www.state.gov/p/wha/rls/fs/2001/>.

[83] Taylor, F. X., 'The presence of international terrorist groups in the western hemisphere', Remarks before the Committee on International Relations, Subcommittee on the Western Hemisphere Committee, US House of Representatives, Washington, DC, 10 Oct. 2001, URL <http://state.gov/s/ct/rls/rm/2001/>; and US Department of State, 'Fact sheet: Secretary of State designates Foreign Terrorist Organizations (FTO's)', Washington, DC, 5 Oct. 2001, URL <http://state.gov/r/pa/prs/ps/2001/>.

[84] US Department of State (note 83).

[85] Between 2001 and 2004 Colombia received over 51 per cent of the total assistance disbursed under the ACI programme. US Congress, 'Foreign Operations, Export Financing and related programs appropriations', Hearings before a Subcommittee of the Committee on Appropriations, US House of

Table 8.8. US assistance to Colombia by source, financial years 2000–2004

Figures are in US$ m. Years are financial years.

Type of assistance	2000[a]	2001	2002	2003[b]	2004	Total
Agency[c]						
Department of State[d]	774.9	48.0	275.4	416.6	495.8	2 110.7
USAID[e]	123.5	0	104.5	122.2	122.2	472.4
Department of Defense	128.5	190.2	119.1	165.0	122.0	724.8
Total	**1 026.9**	**238.2**	**499.0**	**703.8**	**740.0**	**3 307.9**
of which non-military[f]						
Obligated	125	24	151	152	123	575
Expended	1	130	97	59	23	310

[a] Figures for 2000 include funds appropriated for Plan Colombia through the 2000 Emergency Supplemental Appropriations Act.

[b] Figures for 2003 include $93 million in foreign military financing funds appropriated in the 2003 Foreign Operations, Export Financing, and Related Appropriations Act; $34 million appropriated to the Department of State; $34 million in the 2003 Emergency Wartime Supplemental Appropriations Act; and $1 million for foreign military financing allotted from the supplementary appropriation for financial year 2003.

[c] These figures are for appropriations.

[d] These figures include $88 million in funding transferred by the Department of State to the Department of Justice for its rule-of-law programmes.

[e] In financial years 2000–2003 the Department of State transferred $375 million to USAID for alternative development, democracy and rule of law, and internally displaced persons programmes. In financial year 2004 the US Congress directly appropriated money for these programmes to USAID.

[f] The Department of State's Bureau of International Narcotics and Law Enforcement Affairs did not provide complete funding data. As a result, the table may not reflect what was actually promised (obligated) and spent (expended).

Source: US General Accounting Office (GAO), 'Drug control: U.S. non-military assistance to Colombia is beginning to show intended results, but programs are not readily sustainable', GAO Report no. GAO-04-726, Washington, DC, July 2004, URL <http://www.gao.gov/>, table 1, p. 8, and table 2, p. 9.

Between 2000 and 2004 the total US assistance (economic and security) to Colombia was $3.3 billion (see table 8.8), which made Colombia the largest recipient of US aid in the western hemisphere and the fifth largest in the world.[86] About 82 per cent of this assistance was for the military and the police (who are trained and equipped for military operations). The remaining portion of the assistance was for non-military purposes, including the ADP, the programme for internally displaced persons and the justice and democracy programmes.

Representatives, Part 1A, *Justification of Budget Estimates*, annual, 2000–2005 (US Government Printing Office: Washington, DC, 1999–2004).

[86] The first 4 countries are Iraq, Israel, Egypt and Afghanistan. See US General Accounting Office (GAO), 'U.S. non-military assistance to Colombia is beginning to show intended results, but programs are not readily sustainable', GAO Report no. GAO-04-726, Washington, DC, July 2004, URL <http://www.gao.gov/>, p. 7.

In spite of the huge military-related assistance, there is little to suggest that the intended result is being achieved or that the military operations are sustainable over the long term. First, although there was an estimated reduction of 37.5 per cent in the coca crop between 2000 and 2002 and a further 43 per cent reduction between 2002 and 2003,[87] there is little evidence that the small, modern and hi-tech cartels are being apprehended and that the overall availability of drugs is affected, as the US street price of cocaine is reported to be falling.[88] Moreover, the AEP's efforts to eliminate coca and poppy farms are wreaking havoc on small farmers by displacing them from their farmlands, while the ADP is not as effective as it should be as it reaches only about a quarter of its target recipients. Of the total US assistance received by Colombia between 2000 and 2004, only 17 per cent, or $575 million, was devoted to non-military programmes including the ADP and only $310 million was spent (see table 8.8), while the intended beneficiaries of the programme complained of the lack of compensation for their destroyed farms. It is little surprise therefore that the impact of these projects is felt by only a fraction of those targeted and the projects themselves face a number of challenges in their implementation that may result in their being unsustainable.[89] This has increased local resentment of the Colombian Government, whose principal contact with the people in rebel-controlled regions is through the AEP's destruction of their crops.[90] The programme itself has led to what is called the 'balloon effect' whereby illicit crop cultivation goes down in certain areas but goes up in others. It has led to the 'atomization of drug cultivation' across the country, with the number of departments where illicit drug cultivation takes place increasing from 21 in 2002 to 23 in 2003 (of a total of 32 departments).[91]

Second, the branding of the conflict as a war on terrorism is leading to restrictions on civil liberties and human rights abuses by the security forces in Colombia.[92] Like many countries supporting the USA's 'global war on terrorism', Colombia was encouraged to adopt an anti-terrorism law; this has greatly restricted the civil liberties of citizens and has given enormous powers

[87] US Agency for International Development (USAID), 'Colombia', *Congressional Budget Justification: FY 2005* (USAID: Washington, DC, 2004), URL <http://www.usaid.gov/policy/budget/cbj2005/lac/>, Annex IV, 'Latin America and the Caribbean'.

[88] Walsh, J. M., 'Are we there yet? Measuring progress in the U.S. war on drugs in Latin America', Drug War Monitor, Washington Office on Latin America, Dec. 2004, URL <http://www.wola.org>. See also International Crisis Group, 'War and drugs in Colombia', Latin America Report no. 11, Brussels, 27 Jan. 2005, URL <http://www.crisisgroup.org/>.

[89] US GAO (note 86).

[90] US General Accounting Office (GAO), 'Drug control: aviation program safety concerns are being addressed, but State's planning and budgeting process can be improved', GAO Report no. GAO-04-918, Washington, DC, July 2004, URL <http://www.gao.gov/>.

[91] International Crisis Group (note 88)

[92] US assistance to Colombian military and police forces is provided in accordance with Section 556 (the Leahy Amendment) of the 2000 Foreign Operations Appropriations Act (Public Law 107-115) and with Section 8098 of 2000 Department of Defense Appropriations Act (Public Law 106-79) which requires that no assistance be provided to any unit of the security forces for which the US Government has credible evidence of commission of gross violations of human rights, unless the Secretary of State is able to certify that the Colombian Government has taken effective measures to bring those responsible to justice. See US Department of State, 'Colombia: Profile', Washington, DC, Apr. 2002, URL <http://www.state.gov/outofdate/bgn/c/>.

to the security forces.[93] The anti-terrorism legislation gives the military power to arrest, to tap telephones and to carry out searches without warrants.[94] These powers have reportedly been abused by state officials. In a country where a major cause of the conflict is injustice and social inequality, giving security forces such powers is likely to only aggravate the situation.

Third is the issue of sustainability of the current military efforts and spending. To date the US Government has shown no desire to stop its assistance to Colombia. In the US budget request for FY 2006, President Bush asked for assistance for Colombia at the level of 2005 (see table 8.7) even though US assistance under Plan Colombia officially ends in September 2005.[95] In its bid to completely rout the rebel groups and complement the mainly military assistance from the USA, the Colombian Government has already increased both the size of its armed forces and the military budget. Between 2000 and 2004 its military budget increased by 44 per cent in real terms. However, with an economy saddled with a public debt that is 57 per cent of GDP, it is doubtful whether this level of resource commitment to military activities is sustainable in the long term.[96] Critics of the Colombian Government have attributed the current budget deficit of 2.5 per cent of GDP to the increase in military spending.[97] This does not bode well for the sustainability of an expanded military force and the on-going military operations, especially when the USA's assistance eventually ceases.

Although the US Government recognizes that the Colombian situation is complex, the bulk of its support has continued to be military related, perhaps reflecting its preoccupation with the military approach that has so far characterized its response to terrorism. According to the USA, this approach is necessary because the three designated terrorist groups in Colombia—through their activities financed by narcotics trafficking, extortion and kidnapping—pose the greatest threat to the ability of the Colombian Government to resolve its people's economic and social problems.[98] While the activities of the guerrilla groups undoubtedly pose a serious threat to the ability of the government to reach all parts of the country, military operations alone are not suf-

[93] Congress of the Republic of Colombia, Acto Legislativo 02 de 2003 (diciembre 18) [Act 2 of 2003 (December 18)], *Diario Oficial* (Bogotá), no. 45 406 (19 Dec. 2003), URL <http://www.secretariasenado.gov.co/leyes/acl02003.htm>. See also Human Rights Watch (HRW), 'Human rights overview: Colombia', Jan. 2004, URL <http://hrw.org/english/docs/2004/01/21/colomb6978.htm>.

[94] HRW (note 93).

[95] US Department of State, 'FY 2006 international affairs (function 150) budget request: foreign operations, export financing and related programs', Washington, DC, 7 Feb. 2005, URL <http://www.state.gov/m/rm/rls/iab/2006/html/41795.htm>.

[96] 'Tracking trends', *Latin American Weekly Report*, 28 Sep. 2004, p. 9; and 'Colombian defence ministry faces 3 trillion peso budget cut', *Cali El Pais* (Internet version, in Spanish), 13 Sep. 2004, in Foreign Broadcast Information Service, *Daily Report–Latin America (FBIS-LAT)*, FBIS-LAT-2004-0913, 13 Sep. 2004.

[97] Rueda, M. I., 'Harry Potter y el primer año de Uribe' [Harry Potter and Uribe's first year], *Revista Semana*, 14 Feb. 2005, URL <http://semana.terra.com.co/opencms/opencms/Semana/articulo.html?id=72170>.

[98] US Department of State, 'Western hemisphere', *Supporting Human Rights and Democracy: The U.S. Record 2004–2005* (Department of State: Washington, DC, Mar. 2005), URL <http://www.state.gov/g/drl/rls/shrd/2004/>, pp. 250–87. See also US Department of State (note 77).

ficient to restart the peace process nor can they address the questions of inequality, social justice and rule of law that are fundamental to the resolution of the long-running Colombian conflict.[99]

Other major donors, especially the European Union, have repeatedly emphasized the complex nature of the Colombian crisis.[100] In particular they have stressed the social and economic inequalities in Colombia and the urgent need to address these as part of the wider peace process. Thus, the EU's assistance has focused on the ADP, on strengthening the participation of civil society in the peace process, and on measures to improve respect for human rights and the rule of law.[101]

Overall, the military focus of US assistance has achieved limited results due to the neglect of, or inadequate attention to, other components of the original objectives. A more appropriate balance between security and the socio-economic issues central to the complex Colombian conflict would probably have achieved a better outcome.

The UK's assistance to Sierra Leone

As a major donor of development assistance, the United Kingdom has over the years articulated the view that development and security must be linked if the former is to have the desired impact. Central to the British Government's argument linking security, poverty and development is that uncontrolled security expenditure and ill-disciplined security forces can be a burden on and source of insecurity to the state and its people, especially the poor. This view is informed by the fact that the UK directs a large share of its development assistance to poor countries where security is often a major problem.[102] It is no surprise therefore that the UK, through its Department for International Development (DFID), has been a major advocate of the expansion of the definition of ODA to cover security-related development assistance. The connections between security and development were emphasized in both the 1997 and 2000 White Papers on international development.[103] As a result, since

[99] International Crisis Group (note 88).

[100] See, e.g., European Parliament, 'Resolution on Plan Colombia and support for the peace process in Colombia', Resolution B5-0087/2001, 18 Jan. 2001, URL <http://www.europarl.eu.int/>

[101] Patten, C., EU external relations commissioner, 'The EU commitment to Colombia', Message to EU–Colombia Forum, Bogotá, 12–13 May 2003, EU Directorate-General for External Relations, Brussels, URL <http://europa.eu.int/comm/external_relations/news/patten/sp03_241.htm>.

[102] British Department for International Development (DFID), *Departmental Report 2004* (The Stationery Office: London, 2004), URL <http://www.dfid.gov.uk/aboutdfid/performance.asp>, annex 3, p. 189. See also Baulch, B., 'Aid for the poorest? The distribution and maladministration of international development assistance', Chronic Poverty Research Centre (CPRC) Working Paper no. 35, CPRC, Manchester, Mar. 2004, URL <http://www.chronicpoverty.org/>.

[103] British DFID, *Eliminating World Poverty: A Challenge for the 21st Century*, White Paper on International Development, Command Paper no. 3789 (The Stationery Office: London, Nov. 1997); and British DFID, *Eliminating World Poverty: Making Globalization Work for the Poor*, White Paper on International Development, Command Paper no. 5006 (The Stationery Office: London, Dec. 2000)—both at URL <http://www.dfid.gov.uk/pubs/>.

Table 8.9. British assistance to Sierra Leone, financial years 2002/2003–2005/2006

Figures are in thousands of pounds sterling, at current prices. Years are financial years.

Type of assistance	2002/2003	2003/2004	2004/2005	2005/2006	Total, 2002/03–2005/06
Military assistance	14 165	14 801	17 245	17 139	**63 350**
Other assistance	33 044	33 000	40 000	40 000	**146 044**
Total	**47 209**	**47 801**	**57 245**	**57 139**	**209 394**

Sources: **Military assistance**: British Ministry of Defence, Policy and Defence Relations (South), Personal communication with the authors, 28 Jan. 2005. **Other assistance**: British Department for International Development, *Departmental Report 2004* (The Stationery Office: London, 2004), URL <http://www.dfid.gov.uk/aboutdfid/performance.asp>, annex 1, p. 170.

2000 the UK has made security sector reform a part of its development focus, especially in states in conflict and those coming out of conflict.

The main focus of British aid is Africa and poor countries of East Asia,[104] but nowhere has the UK's policy of connecting security and development been put into practice more coherently and effectively than in Sierra Leone.

After more than a decade of fighting, the civil war in Sierra Leone was officially declared to be over in January 2002. Two of the critical areas of need for the country, as for any post-conflict state, were security and post-conflict reconstruction. The country's security forces needed to be rebuilt from scratch, given their ignoble role in the civil war; without new and professional armed forces, and new security forces generally, there would be no guarantee that civil war would not start again after the departure of international peacekeepers. However, this was a process with which many donors were neither familiar nor ready to engage in given their operational limits and the lack of clearly measurable output from any investment. Above all, the process seemed to require long-term commitment, whereas donors prefer quick returns on their investments. Although many donors have experience of disarmament, demobilization and rehabilitation, very few had undertaken the complete restructuring of a country's security structures after a civil war.

In 1998 the democratically elected president of Sierra Leone, Tejan Kabbah, declared his government's desire to have professional security forces and invited the British Government to give assistance. The British Government responded through its Foreign and Commonwealth Office by allocating £10 million ($18 million) in 1999 for the design of a security sector reform initiative in Sierra Leone.[105] Another £20 million ($36 million) was earmarked

[104] British DFID, 'Aid framework 2001–2004', DFID, London, 14 Sep. 2004, URL <http://www.dfid.gov.uk/pubs/>.

[105] Ero, C. 'Sierra Leone's security complex', Working Paper no. 3, Conflict, Security and Development Group, King's College London, 2000, URL <http://www.grc-exchange.org/info_data/record.cfm?id=221>.

by the British DFID to be spent over a three-year period to implement security sector reform.[106]

After the end of the war in 2002, the Sierra Leone Government and the British Government signed a memorandum of understanding committing them to a 10-year partnership in which the British Government provides financial assistance and expertise to support the Sierra Leone Government's programme of reconstruction and poverty alleviation.[107] As a first step the British Government provided £120 million ($202 million) for the first three years of the partnership, starting in 2002.[108] In return, the Sierra Leone Government agreed to meet mutually agreed benchmarks for every supported programme before moving on to the next stage.[109] For comparison, over the four-year period 1999–2002 Sierra Leone's average annual government budget was 413 million leones ($154 million) and in 2004 its defence budget was 45.5 million leones ($17 million),[110] illustrating the magnitude of the British aid from a local perspective.

Sierra Leone's security sector was one of the key areas supported by the British Government in line with the policy outlined above. The principal British contribution has been the training of the soldiers of the new Republic of Sierra Leone Armed Forces (RSLAF)—which includes former rebel soldiers—initially through the British Military Advisory Training Team, but later through the International Military Advisory Training Team. A new building for the Ministry of Defence was constructed to replace the old one that was destroyed during the war, and British officials hold key defence administration posts within the ministry. The British Government also helped in conducting a defence review for the RSLAF to identify the needs and direction of the new armed forces.[111] In total, about £45 million ($67 million) was spent between 2002 and 2004 on training and other forms of assistance to the new RSLAF (see table 8.9). In addition to this, in June 2004 £4.5 million ($6.8 million) was promised over three years from FY 2004/2005 for a technical assistance package for new military trucks and communications equipment.[112] This brings the total of military assistance for each of the three years covered to over £17 million ($25 million). Most of the assistance to the Sierra Leone military has come through the British Ministry of Defence. Other forms of security-related assistance from the British Government to the Sierra Leone Government are listed in table 8.10 along with their costs.

[106] Ero (note 105), p. 23.

[107] Poverty reduction framework arrangement between the Government of the United Kingdom of Great Britain and Northern Ireland and the Government of the Republic of Sierra Leone, Nov. 2002, URL <http://www.dfid.gov.uk/countries/africa/sierraleone.asp>.

[108] Poverty reduction framework arrangement (note 107), paragraph 3.2.

[109] These benchmarks were updated in Apr. 2004; see Poverty reduction framework arrangement (note 107).

[110] See tables 8A.2 and 8A.3 in appendix 8A.

[111] Williams, R., 'National defence reform and the African Union', *SIPRI Yearbook 2004* (note 3), pp. 231–49.

[112] British Ministry of Defence, Policy and Defence Relations (South), Personal communication with the authors, 28 Jan. 2005.

Table 8.10. Financial support by the British Department for International Development to security-related programmes in Sierra Leone, 2000–2004

Figures are in pounds sterling, at current prices.

Programme dates	Programme title	Purpose	Commitment (£)
Jan. 2005– Nov. 2009	Safety, Security and Access to Justice	To improve safety, security and access to justice for the people of Sierra Leone, especially the poor	25 000 000
June 2000– June 2005	Sierra Leone Community Safety and Security Project	To improve safety, security and respect for people's rights by re-establishing an effective and accountable police service	25 848 000
July 2003– Mar. 2005	Sierra Leone Security Sector Programme	To establish effective and disciplined armed forces, controlled by and accountable to the democratic government of Sierra Leone, in the interests of lasting peace and stability	7 080 100
Mar. 2003– Feb. 2005	Operation Pebu[a]	To provide all members of the Sierra Leone Armed Forces with adequate personal and operational accommodation	3 900 000
Nov. 2000– Feb. 2004	Security Sector Project: Ministry of Defence headquarters	To provide the Sierra Leone Ministry of Defence with a new headquarters	1 124 000
Feb. 2000	Sierra Leone Police Force: Emergency Public Order Needs	To quickly equip and train 500 police officers in the management of public disorder and to train senior police officers in the command and control of public order	650 000
June 2000– Oct. 2000	Humanitarian assistance to the Sierra Leone Police Force	To enable the Sierra Leone Police Force to alleviate hardship suffered by police officers and their families	155 000

[a] Pebu is a Mende word meaning shelter.

Source: British Department for International Development, Personal communication with the authors, 2 Feb. 2005.

Apart from the support given to the RSLAF and the Sierra Leone Police Force, aid has been given to other critical areas of the state that require expert support: these include projects such as the Anti-Corruption Commission, the rehabilitation of the legal system, assistance to the National Electoral Commission and the country's Special Court, the strengthening of the financial management systems, civil service reform, the strengthening of the diamond industry and support for the preparation of a poverty-reduction strategy. According to available statistics, military assistance constitutes about 30 per cent of total British assistance provided (and planned) in 2002/2003–2005/2006 (see table 8.9).

The DFID uses a broad definition of the security sector.[113] According to official data, Britain provided support for this sector amounting to about £39 million ($58 million) between 2000 and 2004 (see table 8.10; this figure excludes commitments given in the table for the period 2005–2009). In spite of this strong focus on security, however, other forms of assistance have not been neglected. The focus of other donors on areas other than security complements the role of the British Government in building the capacity of the security forces.

Given the atrocities committed by both government and rebel forces during the civil war, the normative aspect of military professionalism, especially the need to respect human rights and obey the law like any other citizens, has been a major focus of the training of the new RSLAF. Respect for human rights is very important if the brutal mutilation of people that occurred during the civil war is to be avoided in the future.[114] As a result, those who committed crimes during the war have been excluded from the new force.

On the whole the British efforts appear to be achieving the desired results. This is shown by the relative peace in Sierra Leone and the gradual but steady return of the country to normalcy. While there was an initial reluctance on the part of several donors to get involved in the security sector, there was a consensus on the need to rebuild the security system in Sierra Leone as the basis for sustainable development. The memory of the badly structured and financed security forces that led to the decade-long civil war still lingers. The British support has been well complemented by other donors that have concentrated in the more traditional area of support for development cooperation, such as poverty alleviation and infrastructure building; this support has relied on the security provided by the British effort. The result is the consolidation of peace in Sierra Leone.

However, the key question remains: can the Sierra Leone Government sustain the reformed security sector after the termination of the British aid programme? Its maintenance requires sustained and, in the short to medium terms, probably increasing level of military spending. The government depends on external donors for nearly half of its annual budget and the security sector is just one of many sectors competing for resources. Finding the required level of resources to maintain the newly established system will be a tough challenge for the government. It demonstrated its commitment by increasing military expenditure by 18 per cent in 2003, but allocations fell by 6 per cent in 2004.[115] Thus, the answer to the above question remains unclear.

[113] The DFID definition of the security sector is: 'those who are, or should be, responsible for protecting the state. This includes military, paramilitary, intelligence and police services as well as those civilian structures responsible for oversight and control the security forces and for the administration of justice.' British DFID (note 102), annex 7, p. 206.

[114] For details of the atrocities committed during the war see Ero, C., 'Vigilantes, civil defence forces and militia groups: the other side of the privatisation of security in Africa', *Conflict Trends*, June 2000, URL <http://www.accord.org.za/ct/intro.htm>, pp. 25–29.

[115] See table 8A.3 in appendix 8A.

Summary

The nature of assistance provided by the US and British governments to Colombia and Sierra Leone is in both cases primarily a reflection of the objectives of their respective aid policies. How those objectives are achieved is a question of tactics. While the UK adopted a holistic approach—and may have examined the problem from the recipient's perspective given the history of the war in Sierra Leone and the reputation of its security forces and paramilitary groups for banditry and human rights violations—the US approach in Colombia is influenced primarily by the desire to stem the flow of narcotics into the USA. Overall, these two examples show both the problems and the merits of supporting security-related activities within the context of foreign assistance. In general, the outcome of a donor's involvement in the support of security abroad is highly dependent on the objectives of its intervention and on adequate understanding of the problem to be addressed.

V. Conclusions

World military spending, according to official data, is again approaching its level at the height of the cold war. The main reason for this is the high levels of military spending by the USA in recent years, reflecting its global security agenda and in particular its foreign military operations. While US military spending is still lower than during the cold war in terms of its share of GDP, the sustainability of the current levels is being increasingly questioned. In addition, in other countries there is an emerging dilemma over financial policies and military spending; for example, in some of the major EU countries that are exceeding the targets of the Growth and Stability Pact. Military spending has also been under severe criticism in certain developing countries, especially in the Middle East where military spending has assumed alarming proportions in relation to other public sector spending.

Beyond the issue of sustainability, however, is the question of the nature of security threats driving expenditure in these countries. In a globalizing world, in which security is becoming increasingly internationalized, it could be more cost-effective for high-income countries to use some of the resources that they now allocate for military purposes to help improve the security environment and promote peaceful conditions in low-income countries that are increasingly perceived as hotbeds of international insecurity. These are some of the reasons why international consensus is building around ideas to the effect that the new types of threats and challenges to security in an increasingly globalized world have to be addressed at source and that this requires global action and multilateral approaches.[116]

[116] United Nations, 'A more secure world: our shared responsibility', Report of the High-level Panel on Threats, Challenges and Change, UN documents A/59/565, 4 Dec. 2004, and A/59/565/Corr. 1, 6 Dec. 2004, URL <http://www.un.org/ga/59/documentation/list5.html> (for the synopsis of the report see the appendix to the Introduction in this volume); and United Nations, 'The relationship between dis-

A number of difficulties are associated with the design of policies for such global action, as illustrated by the two case studies on foreign assistance in this chapter. There is no doubt that security is intertwined with development, especially in conflict and post-conflict states, but attempting to address the security problem without identifying the underlying causes of insecurity can result in a negative outcome. Since the resources available for development are small, there is a need to ensure that they are used for genuine development or for security-related activities that demonstrably protect and promote development. However, consensus is needed among key actors on the modalities for supporting such security-related development programmes. The examples of US aid to Colombia and British aid to Sierra Leone show that, while development resources are already being used for security purposes, the outcome depends on the objectives and methods of the donor and on how these relate to the actual needs and conditions in the field.

There is also the question of what implications the emerging patterns of action to address security threats will have for understanding of military expenditure as an analytical concept. The general applicability of the traditional definition of military expenditure as the cost of providing security has always been limited. Given the generally comprehensive approach to security that is being taken worldwide, and the increasing blurring of the lines between external and internal security and between domestic and international dimensions of national security, the applicability of the traditional definition is about to be even more limited as states grapple with a new set of security threats. In order to obtain a comprehensive picture of the costs of addressing security problems by force—'hard security'—there is a need to supplement data on military expenditure with data on that part of internal security spending that is devoted to internal security forces, and to examine the extent to which data on expenditure on intelligence services should be integrated into security expenditure. Furthermore, access to data on military aid, which is currently very limited, needs to be improved, both on the donor side and the recipient side. A comparable series of data on the costs of providing security by means other than force—'soft security'—would serve as a useful tool for policy makers in assessing the costs and benefits of different means for providing security. A first step in that direction would be to develop an operational definition of 'soft security'.

armament and development in the current international context', Report of the Group of Government Experts on the relationship between disarmament and development, UN document A/59/119, 23 June 2004. A similar idea constitutes the rationale for the concept of 'global public goods'. See, e.g., Kaul, I. *et al.*, *Providing Global Public Goods: Managing Globalization*, published for the United Nations Development Programme (Oxford University Press: New York, 2003). See also chapter 7 in this volume.

Appendix 8A. Tables of military expenditure

PETTER STÅLENHEIM, WUYI OMITOOGUN and CATALINA PERDOMO*

Table 8A.1 presents military expenditure by region, by certain international organizations and by income group for the period 1995–2004 in US dollars at constant 2003 prices and exchange rates, and also for 2004 in current US dollars. Military expenditure by individual countries is presented in table 8A.2 in local currency and at current prices for the period 1995–2004 and in table 8A.3 in US dollars at constant 2003 prices and exchange rates for the period 1995–2004 and for 2004 in current US dollars. Table 8A.4 presents military expenditure of individual countries for the period 1995–2004 as a percentage of the country's gross domestic product. Sources and methods are explained in appendix 8B. Notes and explanations of the conventions used appear below table 8A.4.

Military expenditure data from different editions of the SIPRI Yearbook should not be combined because of data revision between editions. Revision can be significant; for example, when a better time series becomes available the entire SIPRI series is revised accordingly. Revisions in constant dollar series can also originate in significant revisions in the economic statistics of the International Monetary Fund that are used for these calculations. When data are presented in local currency but not in US dollars or as a share of GDP, this is due to a lack of economic data.

* Contribution of military expenditure data, estimates and advice are gratefully acknowledged from Lena Andersson (OSCE Mission to Bosnia and Herzegovina, Sarajevo), Kwesi Anning (Africa Security Dialogue and Research, Accra), Mesfin Binega (African Union, Addis Ababa), Julian Cooper (Centre for Russian and East European Studies, University of Biringham), David Darchiashvili (Center for Civil–Military Relations and Security Studies, Tbilisi), Dimitar Dimitrov (University of National and World Economy, Sofia), Paul Dunne (University of the West of England, Bristol), Ken Epps (Project Ploughshares, Ontario), Armen Kouyoumdjian (International Institute for Strategic Studies, Valparaiso), Luc Mampaey (Groupe de Recherche et d'Information sur la Paix et la Sécurité, Brussels), Elina Noor (Institute of Strategic and International Studies, ISIS, Kuala Lumpur), Tamara Pataraia (Caucasus Institute for Peace, Democracy and Development, Tbilisi), Reuven Pedatzur (Tel Aviv University), Jaime Polanco (Ministerio de Defensa Nacional, Bogotá), Thomas Scheetz (Lincoln University College, Buenos Aires), Nouhoum Sangare (Ministère de la Défense et des Anciens Combattants, Bamako), Ron Smith (Birkbeck College, London), Shaoguang Wang (Chinese University of Hong Kong) and Ozren Zunec (University of Zagreb).

Table 8A.1. Military expenditure by region, by international organization and by income group, in constant US dollars for 1995–2004 and current US dollars for 2004

Figures are in US$ b., at constant 2003 prices and exchange rates except in the right-most column, marked *, where they are in current US$ b. Figures do not always add up to the given totals because of the conventions of rounding.

	1995	1996	1997	1998	1999	2000	2001	2002	2003	2004	2004*
World total	**789**	**772**	**774**	**765**	**773**	**806**	**819**	**864**	**927**	**975**	**1035**
Geographical regions											
Africa	8.8	8.5	8.7	9.3	10.3	10.8	11.0	11.6	11.7	12.6	13.9
North Africa	(3.4)	3.5	3.7	3.8	3.9	4.3	4.4	4.8	4.9	5.5	6.1
Sub-Saharan Africa	5.5	5.0	5.0	5.5	6.3	6.5	(6.6)	6.8	6.8	(7.1)	(7.9)
Americas	367	347	347	340	341	353	358	398	446	488	502
North America	347	328	326	319	320	332	335	375	424	466	478
Central America	3.2	3.3	3.4	3.3	3.5	3.6	3.7	3.5	3.4	3.2	3.3
South America	17.2	15.6	18.1	17.4	17.0	17.9	19.9	19.6	18.4	18.8	20.8
Asia and Oceania	136	141	138	135	137	147	151	151	(158)	(164)	(176)
Central Asia	0.4	0.5	0.5	(0.5)	0.5	. .	(0.6)	. .	(0.6)	(0.7)	(0.8)
East Asia	113	119	115	111	112	121	124	123	(129)	(132)	(141)
South Asia	13.4	13.6	14.2	14.4	15.5	16.2	16.8	17.0	17.5	20.0	21.3
Oceania	8.7	8.6	8.8	9.1	9.6	9.5	9.9	10.3	10.6	11.0	12.9
Europe	237	236	237	234	239	243	244	250	256	254	286
Central and Eastern	28.1	26.2	27.7	23.4	24.8	27.3	29.2	30.7	33.2	34.2	39.2
Western	209	210	209	211	214	216	215	220	223	220	247
Middle East	40.1	39.1	43.0	46.5	46.0	51.7	55.3	52.9	54.4	56.1	57.7

Organizations											
ASEAN	11.7	12.2	34.9	29.9	29.7	36.2	34.2	28.8	. .	. .	. .
CIS	16.7	15.3	16.7	12.3	14.3	16.5	17.9	19.2	21.1	22.2	26.0
CIS Asia	0.4	0.5	0.5	(0.5)	0.5	. .	(0.6)	. .	(0.6)	(0.7)	(0.8)
CIS Europe	16.3	14.8	16.1	11.8	13.8	15.9	17.3	18.6	20.4	21.5	25.0
European Union	192	192	191	192	195	197	196	200	205	211	237
NATO	542	525	521	515	527	540	542	587	641	683	722
NATO Europe	195	197	195	196	207	208	207	213	216	217	239
OECD	609	609	607	602	607	622	625	672	726	765	811
OPEC	27.6	27.2	31.5	33.7	32.5	37.3	39.6	36.0	37.8	39.4	40.6
OSCE	584	564	562	553	559	576	579	626	681	721	764
Income groups (by 2003 gross national income per capita)											
Low (≤$765)	41.7	43.6	39.9	36.5	38.6	45.6	43.5	37.7	(39.3)	(42.4)	(47.0)
Lower middle ($766–$3035)	76.2	75.6	79.4	76.8	81.8	90.5	98.7	105	109	113	123
Upper middle ($3036–$9385)	35.2	34.2	39.0	41.3	40.0	42.2	44.9	42.4	43.7	44.4	46.2
High (≥$9386)	636	618	616	610	613	628	632	679	734	775	819

( ) = Total based on country data accounting for less than 90% of the regional total; . . = Available data account for less than 60% of the regional total; ASEAN = Association of Southeast Asian Nations; CIS = Commonwealth of Independent States; NATO = North Atlantic Treaty Organization; OECD = Organisation for Economic Co-operation and Development; OPEC = Organization of the Petroleum Exporting Countries; OSCE = Organization for Security and Co-operation in Europe.

The world total and the totals for regions, organizations and income groups in table 8A.1 are estimates, based on data in table 8A.3. When military expenditure data for a country are missing for a few years, estimates are made, most often on the assumption that the rate of change in that country's military expenditure is the same as that for the region to which it belongs. When no estimates can be made, countries are excluded from the totals. The countries excluded from all totals in table 8A.1 are Afghanistan, Angola, Benin, Equatorial Guinea, Iraq, Somalia and Qatar.

Totals for geographical regions add up to the world total and sub-regional totals add up to regional totals. Totals for regions and income groups cover the same groups of countries for all years, while totals for organizations cover only the member countries in the year given.

The country coverage of income groups is based on figures for 2003 gross national income (GNI) per capita as calculated by the World Bank and presented in its *World Development Report 2005: A Better Investment Climate For Everyone* (Oxford University Press: Oxford, 2004), URL <http://econ.worldbank.org/wdr/>.

Africa: Algeria, Angola, Benin, Botswana, Burkina Faso, Burundi, Cameroon, Cape Verde, Central African Republic, Chad, Congo (Republic of), Congo (Democratic Republic of, DRC), Côte d'Ivoire, Djibouti, Equatorial Guinea, Eritrea, Ethiopia, Gabon, Gambia, Ghana, Guinea, Guinea-Bissau, Kenya, Lesotho, Liberia, Libya, Madagascar, Malawi, Mali, Mauritania, Mauritius, Morocco, Mozambique, Namibia, Niger, Nigeria, Rwanda, Senegal, Seychelles, Sierra Leone, Somalia, South Africa, Sudan, Swaziland, Tanzania, Togo, Tunisia, Uganda, Zambia, Zimbabwe. *North Africa*: Algeria, Libya, Morocco, Tunisia. *Sub-Saharan Africa*: Angola, Benin, Botswana, Burkina Faso, Burundi, Cameroon, Cape Verde, Central African Republic, Chad, Congo (Republic of), Congo (Democratic Republic of, DRC), Côte d'Ivoire, Djibouti, Equatorial Guinea, Eritrea, Ethiopia, Gabon, Gambia, Ghana, Guinea, Guinea-Bissau, Kenya, Lesotho, Liberia, Madagascar, Malawi, Mali, Mauritania, Mauritius, Mozambique, Namibia, Niger, Nigeria, Rwanda, Senegal, Seychelles, Sierra Leone, Somalia, South Africa, Sudan, Swaziland, Tanzania, Togo, Uganda, Zambia, Zimbabwe.

Americas: Argentina, Belize, Bolivia, Brazil, Canada, Chile, Colombia, Costa Rica, Ecuador, El Salvador, Guatemala, Guyana, Honduras, Mexico, Nicaragua, Panama, Paraguay, Peru, Uruguay, USA, Venezuela. *North America*: Canada, USA. *Central America*: Belize, Costa Rica, El Salvador, Guatemala, Honduras, Mexico, Nicaragua, Panama. *South America*: Argentina, Bolivia, Brazil, Chile, Colombia, Ecuador, Guyana, Paraguay, Peru, Uruguay, Venezuela.

Asia and Oceania: Afghanistan, Australia, Bangladesh, Brunei, Cambodia, China, Fiji, India, Indonesia, Japan, North Korea, South Korea, Kazakhstan, New Zealand, Kyrgyzstan, Laos, Malaysia, Mongolia, Myanmar (Burma), Nepal, Pakistan, Papua New Guinea, Philippines, Singapore, Sri Lanka, Taiwan, Tajikistan, Thailand, Turkmenistan, Uzbekistan, Viet Nam. *Central Asia*: Kazakhstan, Kyrgyzstan, Tajikistan, Turkmenistan, Uzbekistan. *East Asia*: Brunei, Cambodia, China, Indonesia, Japan, North Korea, South Korea, Laos, Malaysia, Mongolia, Myanmar (Burma), Philippines, Singapore, Taiwan, Thailand, Viet Nam. *South Asia*: Afghanistan, Bangladesh, India, Nepal, Pakistan, Sri Lanka. *Oceania*: Australia, Fiji, New Zealand, Papua New Guinea.

Europe: Albania, Armenia, Austria, Azerbaijan, Belarus, Belgium, Bosnia and Herzegovina, Bulgaria, Croatia, Cyprus, Czech Republic, Denmark, Estonia, Finland, France, Georgia, Germany, Greece, Hungary, Iceland, Ireland, Italy, Latvia, Lithuania, Luxembourg, Macedonia (Former Yugoslav Republic of, FYROM), Malta, Moldova, Netherlands, Norway, Poland, Portugal, Romania, Russia, Serbia and Montenegro, Slovakia, Slovenia, Spain, Sweden, Switzerland, Turkey, UK, Ukraine. *Central and Eastern Europe*: Albania, Armenia, Azerbaijan, Belarus, Bosnia and Herzegovina, Bulgaria, Croatia, Czech Republic, Estonia, Georgia, Hungary, Latvia, Lithuania, Macedonia (Former Yugoslav Republic of, FYROM), Moldova, Poland, Romania, Russia, Serbia and Montenegro, Slovakia, Slovenia, Ukraine. *Western Europe*: Austria, Belgium, Cyprus, Denmark, Finland, France, Germany, Greece, Iceland, Ireland, Italy, Luxembourg, Malta, Netherlands, Norway, Portugal, Spain, Sweden, Switzerland, Turkey, UK.

Middle East: Bahrain, Egypt, Iran, Iraq, Israel, Jordan, Kuwait, Lebanon, Oman, Qatar, Saudi Arabia, Syria, United Arab Emirates (UAE), Yemen.

ASEAN: Brunei, Cambodia (1999–), Indonesia, Laos (1997–), Malaysia, Myanmar (Burma) (1997–), Philippines, Singapore, Thailand, Viet Nam (1995–).

CIS: Armenia, Azerbaijan, Belarus, Georgia, Kazakhstan, Kyrgyzstan, Moldova, Russia, Tajikistan, Turkmenistan, Ukraine, Uzbekistan. *CIS Europe*: Armenia, Azerbaijan, Belarus, Georgia, Moldova, Russia, Ukraine. *CIS Asia*: Kazakhstan, Kyrgyzstan, Tajikistan, Turkmenistan, Uzbekistan.

European Union: Austria (1995–), Belgium, Cyprus (2004–), Czech Republic (2004–), Denmark, Estonia (2004–), Finland (1995–), France, Germany, Greece, Hungary (2004–), Ireland, Italy, Latvia (2004–), Lithuania (2004–), Luxembourg, Malta (2004–), Netherlands, Poland (2004–), Portugal, Slovakia (2004–), Slovenia (2004–), Spain, Sweden (1995–), UK.

NATO: Belgium, Bulgaria (2004–), Canada, Czech Republic (1999–), Denmark, Estonia (2004–), France, Germany, Greece, Hungary (1999–), Iceland, Italy, Latvia (2004–), Lithuania (2004–), Luxembourg, Netherlands, Norway, Poland (1999–), Portugal, Romania (2004–), Slovakia (2004–), Slovenia (2004–), Spain, Turkey, UK, USA. *NATO Europe*: Belgium, Bulgaria (2004–), Czech Republic (1999–), Denmark, Estonia (2004–), France, Germany, Greece, Hungary (1999–), Iceland, Italy, Latvia (2004–), Lithuania (2004–), Luxembourg, Netherlands, Norway, Poland (1999–), Portugal, Romania (2004–), Slovakia (2004–), Slovenia (2004–), Spain, Turkey, UK.

OECD: Australia, Austria, Belgium, Canada, Czech Republic (1995–), Denmark, Finland, France, Germany, Greece, Hungary (1996–), Iceland, Ireland, Italy, Japan, South Korea (1996–), Luxembourg, Mexico (1994–), Netherlands, New Zealand, Norway, Poland (1996–), Portugal, Slovakia (2000–), Spain, Sweden, Switzerland, Turkey, UK, USA.

OPEC: Algeria, Gabon (–1995), Indonesia, Iran, Iraq, Kuwait, Libya, Nigeria, Qatar, Saudi Arabia, United Arab Emirates (UAE), Venezuela.

OSCE: Albania, Armenia, Austria, Azerbaijan, Belarus, Belgium, Bosnia and Herzegovina, Bulgaria, Canada, Croatia, Cyprus, Czech Republic, Denmark, Estonia, Finland, France, Georgia, Germany, Greece, Hungary, Iceland, Ireland, Italy, Kazakhstan, Kyrgyzstan, Latvia, Lithuania, Luxembourg, Macedonia (Former Yugoslav Republic of, FYROM) (1995–), Malta, Moldova, Netherlands, Norway, Poland, Portugal, Romania, Russia, Serbia and Montenegro (2000–), Slovakia, Slovenia, Spain, Sweden, Switzerland, Tajikistan, Turkey, Turkmenistan, UK, Ukraine, USA, Uzbekistan.

Low-income countries (GNI/capita ≤ $765 in 2003): Afghanistan, Angola, Bangladesh, Benin, Burkina Faso, Burundi, Cambodia, Cameroon, Central African Republic, Chad, Congo (Republic of), Congo (Democratic Republic of, DRC), Côte d'Ivoire, Equatorial Guinea, Eritrea, Ethiopia, Gambia, Ghana, Guinea, Guinea-Bissau, India, Kenya, North Korea, Kyrgyzstan, Laos, Lesotho, Liberia, Madagascar, Malawi, Mali, Mauritania, Moldova, Mongolia, Mozambique, Myanmar (Burma), Nepal, Nicaragua, Niger, Nigeria, Pakistan, Papua New Guinea, Rwanda, Senegal, Sierra Leone, Somalia, Sudan, Tajikistan, Tanzania, Togo, Uganda, Uzbekistan, Viet Nam, Yemen, Zambia, Zimbabwe.

Lower-middle-income countries (GNI/capita $766–$3035 in 2003): Albania, Algeria, Armenia, Azerbaijan, Belarus, Bolivia, Bosnia and Herzegovina, Brazil, Bulgaria, Cape Verde, China, Colombia, Djibouti, Ecuador, Egypt, El Salvador, Fiji, Georgia, Guatemala, Guyana, Honduras, Indonesia, Iran, Iraq, Jordan, Kazakhstan, Macedonia (Former Yugoslav Republic of, FYROM), Morocco, Namibia, Paraguay, Peru, Philippines, Romania, Russia, Serbia and Montenegro, South Africa, Sri Lanka, Swaziland, Syria, Thailand, Turkey, Turkmenistan, Tunisia, Ukraine.

Upper-middle-income countries (GNI/capita $3036–$9385 in 2003): Argentina, Belize, Botswana, Chile, Costa Rica, Croatia, Czech Republic, Estonia, Gabon, Hungary, Latvia, Lithuania, Lebanon, Libya, Malaysia, Mauritius, Mexico, Oman, Panama, Poland, Saudi Arabia, Seychelles, Slovakia, Uruguay, Venezuela.

High-income countries (GNI/capita ≤ $9386 in 2003): Australia, Austria, Bahrain, Belgium, Brunei, Canada, Cyprus, Denmark, Finland, France, Germany, Greece, Iceland, Ireland, Israel, Italy, Japan, South Korea, Kuwait, Luxembourg, Malta, Netherlands, New Zealand, Norway, Portugal, Qatar, Singapore, Slovenia, Spain, Sweden, Switzerland, Taiwan, United Arab Emirates (UAE), UK, USA.

Table 8A.2. Military expenditure by country, in local currency, 1995–2004

Figures are in local currency at current prices, and are for calendar years, unless stated otherwise.

Country	Currency	1995	1996	1997	1998	1999	2000	2001	2002	2003	2004
Africa											
North Africa											
Algeria[1]	m. dinars	58 847	79 519	101 126	112 248	121 597	141 576	149 468	167 000	170 764	201 929
Libya	m. dinars	. .	. .	577	675	535	556	496	575	626	740
Morocco[2]	m. dirhams	12 957	12 890	12 476	12 666	13 921	14 639	15 643	16 994	17 722	20 134
Tunisia	m. dinars	324	387	396	417	424	456	483	491	525	540
Sub-Saharan Africa											
Angola[3]	m. kwanzas	2.5	163	(391)	288	3 670	4 400	6 100	16 200	48 090	148 300
Benin	m. CFA francs	. .	. .	. .	. .	. .	. .	. .	. .	. .	. .
Botswana	m. pulas	460	467	586	808	855	974	1 055	1 325	1 482	[1 501]
Burkina Faso	m. CFA francs	18 400	19 000	22 500	23 300	25 700	26 100	27 000	33 400	31 960	35 228
Burundi	m. francs	10 517	15 408	21 800	26 300	28 500	30 500	44 200	44 200	38 500	42 000
Cameroon	m. CFA francs	56 691	59 819	69 288	80 969	89 095	87 598	91 118	101 500	109 556	116 808
Cape Verde	m. escudos	477	352	382	443	518	814	572	530	554	586
Central Afr. Rep.[4]	m. CFA francs	6 496	6 239	. .	. .	. .	. .	. .	7 445	8 729	7 979
Chad	m. CFA francs	10 000	12 681	9 700	9 500	12 900	15 200	18 200	19 300	22 700	23 800
Congo, Republic of	m. CFA francs	. .	. .	. .	. .	. .	. .	. .	. .	28 374	. .
Congo, DRC[5]	m. francs	. .	44.8	110	42.8	600	2 901	. .	. .	. .	. .
Côte d'Ivoire	b. CFA francs	. .	52.5	54.6	. .	. .	. .	. .	. .	124	. .
Djibouti	m. francs	4 481	3 712	4 019	4 042	4 053	3 979	4 045	4 500	. .	. .
Equatorial Guinea	m. CFA francs	1 721	. .	. .	. .	. .	. .	. .	. .	. .	. .
Eritrea[6]	m. nakfa	771	968	634	1 936	2 225	2 220	1 884	2 104	2 020	. .
Ethiopia[7]	m. birr	754	803	1 512	3 263	5 589	5 075	3 154	3 000	3 000	3 000
Gabon	m. CFA francs	. .	. .	. .	9 000	. .	. .	. .	. .	. .	. .
Gambia[8]	m. dalasis	27.6	38.5	42.6	43.1	40.1	42.5	44.6	44.6	45.1	45.3
Ghana[9]	m. cedis	58 823	72 644	93 148	132 812	158 060	277 269	231 740	297 800	439 200	[636 100]

Guinea	m. francs	. .	. .	48 600	55 700	76 600	80 300	171 100	185 000	. .	. .
Guinea-Bissau[10]	m. CFA francs	615	770	1 061	1 711	. .	6 786	4 533	. .	. .	. .
Kenya	m. shillings	7 668	9 756	10 327	10 381	10 684	12 614	15 349	16 844	18 676	20 158
Lesotho	m. maloti	125	122	132	154	208	212	201	206	221	218
Liberia[11]	m. dollars	. .	. .	. .	. .	. .	. .	(1 990)	(2 590)	. .	. .
Madagascar[12]	b. francs	116	201	267	275	283	320	428	. .	. .	. .
Malawi	m. kwachas	169	309	434	450	635	916	1 021	. .	. .	. .
Mali	b. CFA francs	26.9	27.1	31.3	32.2	36.0	41.4	43.8	44.7	47.3	49.4
Mauritania[13]	m. ouguiya	3 640	3 680	3 660	3 950	4 090	4 200	4 400	4 900	4 800	4 800
Mauritius	m. rupees	234	233	206	203	228	246	262	285	304	328
Mozambique	b. meticais	[302]	[407]	[485]	[585]	722	843	1 048	1 267	1 367	1 585
Namibia[14]	m. dollars	248	286	383	435	660	786	736	880	893	883
Niger	b. CFA francs	9.2	8.9	10.1	13.0	14.5	18.2	14.4	14.3	. .	. .
Nigeria[15]	m. naira	14 000	15 350	17 920	25 162	45 400	37 490	63 472	64 908	76 890	76 100
Rwanda[16]	b. francs	14.8	22.6	23.3	27.7	29.0	25.8	28.6	27.5	26.6	22.1
Senegal[17]	m. CFA francs	40 389	40 809	41 324	44 300	48 200	44 400	50 500	51 829	54 619	[55 803]
Seychelles	m. rupees	55.2	52.4	57.3	55.5	59.3	59.0	64.8	64.1	66.1	73.7
Sierra Leone	m. leones	18 898	17 119	(9 315)	. .	. .	[55 000]	37 868	33 371	42 600	45 503
Somalia	shillings	. .	. .	. .	. .	. .	. .	. .	. .	. .	. .
South Africa	m. rand	11 942	11 143	11 131	10 716	10 678	13 128	15 516	18 138	19 638	20 169
Sudan[18]	m. dinars	8 060	9 520	16 300	42 800	62 200	84 100	. .	102 000	102 000	. .
Swaziland	m. emalangeni	[120]	[130]	137	163	180	186	184	. .	. .	. .
Tanzania[19]	b. shillings	44.0	52.8	61.2	. .	. .	97.0	118	138	228	357
Togo	m. CFA francs	15 400	. .	. .	. .	. .	. .	. .	. .	16 757	16 770
Uganda[20]	b. shillings	118	135	139	181	212	203	214	255	297	324
Zambia[21]	b. kwacha	65.8	56.9	90.8	114	73.7	[58.0]	. .	. .	. .	. .
Zimbabwe[22]	m. dollars	2 214	2 742	3 441	3 710	10 068	15 361	16 208	34 403	123 100	815 000
Americas											
Central America											
Belize	th. dollars	16 106	15 932	18 790	. .	. .	. .	. .	. .	. .	
Costa Rica[23]	m. colones	. .	. .	. .	. .	. .	. .	. .	. .	. .	

Country	Currency	1995	1996	1997	1998	1999	2000	2001	2002	2003	2004
El Salvador[24]	m. US dollar	97.0	96.4	97.5	96.3	99.8	112	109	109	106	[105]
Guatemala	m. quetzals	843	784	801	875	914	1 225	1 143	1 020	950	880
Honduras[25]	m. lempiras	. .	. .	. .	. .	. .	516	646	898	919	928
Mexico[26]	m. new pesos	10 368	14 637	18 306	20 950	25 825	28 335	31 298	31 224	31 730	31 821
Nicaragua	m. córdobas	265	266	286	278	318	390	389	501	537	505
Panama[27]	m. balboas	96.6	101	118	104	112	. .	. .	. .	. .	. .
North America											
Canada[28]	m. dollars	12 457	11 511	10 831	11 716	12 360	12 314	13 191	13 379	14 064	[15 166]
USA[28]	m. dollars	278 856	271 417	276 324	274 278	280 969	301 697	312 743	356 720	[414 400]	[466 600]
South America											
Argentina	m. pesos	4 102	3 888	3 769	3 782	3 852	3 739	3 638	3 784	4 433	[4 555]
Bolivia	m. bolivianos	612	682	857	1 128	864	792	917	976	1 017	1 124
Brazil	m. reais	[13 320]	[13 301]	[17 440]	[16 960]	[16 408]	18 617	23 062	25 095	24 312	24 606
Chile[29]	b. pesos	[866]	[965]	1 114	1 249	1 367	1 502	1 615	1 765	1 743	2 216
Colombia[30]	b. pesos	[2 228]	[2 786]	3 537	4 356	5 372	5 935	7 228	8 430	[10 044]	[11 143]
Ecuador[31]	m. US dollars	475	419	499	549	249	266	384	558	641	590
Guyana	m. dollars	808	780	. .	. .	. .	. .	. .	. .	. .	. .
Paraguay	b. guaranís	. .	. .	[284]	[294]	[266]	[283]	284	296	345	310
Peru	m. new sols	2 256	2 426	2 224	2 671	2 773	3 228	3 486	2 496	2 695	2 807
Uruguay	m. pesos	[2 084]	[2 557]	[3 027]	[3 267]	3 575	4 321	4 383	4 333	4 966	[5 263]
Venezuela[32]	b. bolívares	212	306	753	716	927	1 218	1 554	1 575	1 812	2 431
Asia and Oceania											
Central Asia											
Kazakhstan[33]	b. tenge	10.8	16.3	17.9	19.0	17.2	20.4	32.5	37.7	47.5	[57.9]
Kyrgyzstan[34]	m. soms	251	699	955	912	1 309	1 864	1 733	2 055	2 408	[2 748]
Tajikistan[33]	th. somoni	713	3 977	10 713	17 562	18 723	21 496	29 577	70 700	106 500	134 000
Turkmenistan[35]	b. manat	15.1	158	440	436	582	. .	. .	. .	. .	. .
Uzbekistan[33]	m. soums	(3 355)	(6 900)	[13 700]	. .	34 860	. .	41 115	. .	53 018	. .

East Asia											
Brunei[36]	m. dollars	[425]	474	555	614	[520]	[485]	[548]	507	. .	. .
Cambodia[37]	b. riels	456	434	447	481	474	455	404	423	413	432
China, P. R.[38]	b. yuan	[105]	[126]	[131]	[149]	[165]	[182]	[215]	[251]	[274]	[305]
Indonesia	b. rupiahs	[7 158]	[8 400]	8 336	10 349	10 254	13 945	16 416	19 291	27 446	32 100
Japan[39]	b. yen	4 714	4 815	4 922	4 942	4 934	4 935	4 950	4 956	4 954	4 916
Korea, North	b. won	. .	. .	. .	(2.9)	(2.9)	(3.0)	(3.1)	(3.3)	(3.9)	(4.2)
Korea, South[41]	b. won	11 074	12 243	13 102	13 594	13 337	14 477	15 497	16 672	17 707	19 141
Laos	b. kip	. .	49.2	53.0	66.5	224	278	325	. .	. .	. .
Malaysia	m. ringgits	6 121	6 091	5 877	4 547	6 321	5 826	7 351	8 504	10 950	10 419
Mongolia	m. tugriks	9 547	11 850	14 830	16 749	18 416	26 126	25 380	26 490	. .	. .
Myanmar	b. kyats	22.3	27.7	29.8	37.3	43.7	58.8	63.9	73.1	. .	. .
Philippines	m. pesos	27 493	30 978	29 212	31 512	32 959	36 208	35 977	38 907	40 645	43 191
Singapore	m. dollars	5 206	5 782	6 618	7 475	7 616	7 466	7 721	8 108	8 240	8 528
Taiwan	b. dollars	277	288	302	299	258	243	248	226	242	251
Thailand	m. baht	94 681	100 220	98 172	86 133	74 809	71 268	75 413	76 724	77 027	[75 146]
Viet Nam	b. dong	. .	. .	. .	. .	. .	. .	. .	. .	. .	. .
South Asia											
Afghanistan	m. afghanis	. .	. .	. .	. .	. .	. .	. .	. .	. .	33 958
Bangladesh	m. taka	21 582	23 076	25 863	28 436	31 277	33 377	34 020	34 105	36 150	38 560
India[42]	b. rupees	260	291	339	387	453	490	531	553	592	728
Nepal	m. rupees	2 064	2 242	2 471	2 789	3 240	3 650	4 837	6 640	7 903	8 196
Pakistan	m. rupees	112 085	123 550	131 803	139 818	146 931	153 795	169 761	188 426	208 031	228 996
Sri Lanka[43]	b. rupees	35.2	38.1	37.1	42.5	40.1	56.9	54.2	49.2	47.0	[57.0]
Oceania											
Australia	m. dollars	9 871	10 005	10 207	10 799	11 496	11 975	12 995	14 077	14 965	15 986
Fiji	m. dollars	48.8	51.2	47.0	48.0	49.0	73.0	86.0	71.0	[70.0]	[55.0]
New Zealand	m. dollars	1 316	1 356	1 344	1 363	1 380	1 422	1 428	1 411	1 468	1 524
Papua New Guinea	m. kina	60.0	68.0	92.6	86.0	80.0	85.0	97.6	53.7	68.8	. .

Country	Currency	1995	1996	1997	1998	1999	2000	2001	2002	2003	2004
Europe											
Albania[44]	m. leks	4 719	4 777	4 442	5 067	5 891	6 519	7 638	8 220	9 279	9 643
Armenia	b. drams	21.2	21.7	31.4	33.7	36.5	36.7	36.8	36.8	44.3	[50.3]
Austria	m. euro	1 562	1 576	1 600	1 619	1 662	1 742	1 666	1 664	1 760	1 740
Azerbaijan	b. manats	248	305	353	388	436	485	532	605	[670]	[740]
Belarus[45]	m. roubles	1 933	2 266	6 079	9 834	38 740	115 250	247 012	366 489	475 410	580 280
Belgium[46]	m. euro	3 251	3 256	3 267	3 297	3 378	3 463	3 393	3 344	3 452	[3 973]
Bosnia–Herzegov.[47]	m. marks	. .	. .	. .	. .	. .	. .	. .	505	353	324
Bulgaria[48]	m. leva	[22.8]	34.5	372	512	595	677	805	859	895	930
Croatia[49]	m. kuna	9 282	7 760	7 000	7 500	6 084	4 510	4 336	4 355	4 088	3 585
Cyprus	m. pounds	91.0	141	185	169	106	118	142	100	101	107
Czech Republic[50]	m. korunas	25 070	26 817	27 582	33 570	37 210	39 807	44 842	47 308	51 982	50 507
Denmark[46]	m. kroner	17 468	17 896	18 521	19 071	19 428	19 339	21 017	21 269	21 110	21 495
Estonia[51]	m. krooni	417	499	736	843	1 083	1 329	1 640	2 028	2 376	2 582
Finland	m. euro	1 445	1 644	1 555	1 715	1 494	1 647	1 631	1 674	1 751	1 843
France[46]	m. euro	36 349	36 188	36 756	36 012	36 510	36 702	37 187	38 681	40 212	[41 822]
Georgia[52]	m. laris	. .	85.5	[57.1]	[57.1]	[52.4]	[37.2]	[49.4]	74.6	91.5	135
Germany[46]	m. euro	30 159	29 998	29 451	29 822	30 603	30 554	30 648	31 168	30 800	[30 515]
Greece[46]	m. euro	3 438	3 942	4 433	5 061	5 439	5 921	5 986	6 085	6 309	. .
Hungary	m. forints	89 397	103 132	146 820	151 215	191 485	226 041	272 424	299 448	341 310	[356 464]
Iceland	kronur	0	0	0	0	0	0	0	0	0	0
Ireland	m. euro	541	580	623	644	677	734	835	841	874	914
Italy[46]	m. euro	16 300	18 680	19 987	21 052	22 240	24 325	24 592	25 887	24 421	25 160
Latvia[53]	m. lats	23.0	21.0	22.1	24.8	33.1	42.4	54.6	91.0	108	124
Lithuania	m. litai	115	169	302	553	479	760	805	884	917	1 042
Luxembourg[46]	m. euro	104	109	119	129	132	139	179	192	205	[221]
Maced. (FYROM)	m. denars	. .	5 223	4 163	4 302	3 769	4 602	15 397	6 841	6 292	6 683
Malta[54]	th. liri	10 996	12 002	12 020	11 297	11 164	11 109	12 205	12 317	15 058	13 970

Moldova[55]	m. lei	60.0	70.7	80.5	57.0	63.0	63.3	76.7	94.7	109	113
Netherlands[46]	m. euro	5 837	5 989	6 056	6 154	6 595	6 482	6 929	7 149	7 265	[7 536]
Norway[46]	m. kroner	22 224	22 813	23 010	25 087	25 809	25 722	26 669	32 461	31 060	31 191
Poland	m. zlotys	6 595	8 313	10 075	11 687	12 242	13 239	14 032	14 580	15 888	16 751
Portugal[46]	m. euro	2 013	2 001	2 089	2 098	2 259	2 393	2 598	2 765	2 792	[2 825]
Romania	b. lei	[1 999]	[2 697]	[7 704]	[11 132]	14 648	20 310	28 644	34 911	44 639	52 303
Russia[56]	m. roubles	[63 220]	[82 485]	[105 034]	[85 574]	[167 822]	[273 106]	[365 374]	[457 640]	[567 692]	[655 787]
Serbia–Monten.[57]	m. dinars	. .	3 950	[5 406]	6 441	8 600	21 292	33 060	43 695	42 070	48 275
Slovakia[58]	m. koruny	18 708	19 665	16 792	14 009	13 532	15 760	19 051	19 947	22 965	23 173
Slovenia	m. tolars	39 664	44 666	46 434	50 030	49 958	49 518	65 903	78 552	86 346	99 700
Spain[59]	m. euro	6 483	6 560	6 750	6 756	7 092	7 599	7 972	8 414	8 587	8 729
Sweden	m. kronor	40 872	27 015	39 726	40 801	42 541	44 542	43 274	[42 854]	[43 280]	[44 156]
Switzerland[60]	m. francs	5 011	4 782	4 634	4 532	4 416	4 503	4 476	4 461	4 437	4 477
Turkey[46]	tr. liras	303	612	1 183	2 289	4 168	6 248	8 844	13 641	15 426	16 807
UK[61]	m. pounds	21 439	22 330	21 612	22 477	22 548	23 532	24 464	26 227	31 286	29 868
Ukraine[62]	m. hryvnias	1 542	2 680	3 851	3 442	3 890	6 184	5 848	6 266	7 615	8 963
Middle East											
Bahrain	m. dinars	103	109	109	111	123	121	126	126	176	180
Egypt[63]	m. pounds	7 164	7 573	7 986	8 154	8 312	9 124	9 975	10 717	11 824	[13 400]
Iran[64]	b. rials	4 457	6 499	8 540	10 624	17 757	31 113	38 310	35 362	41 774	48 209
Iraq	m. dinars	. .	. .	. .	. .	. .	. .	. .	. .	. .	. .
Israel[65]	b. new shekels	24.3	28.4	31.4	34.3	37.4	39.5	41.1	47.9	45.7	48.7
Jordan[66]	m. dinars	586	417	445	491	512	531	537	551	629	623
Kuwait	m. dinars	1 102	971	745	696	696	827	824	864	1 126	1 231
Lebanon	b. pounds	[1 210]	[1 156]	[1 044]	1 052	1 251	1 327	1 383	1 222	[1 177]	[1 232]
Oman[67]	m. rials	776	737	760	676	687	809	933	[958]	1 010	974
Qatar	m. dinars	. .	. .	. .	. .	. .	. .	. .	. .	. .	. .
Saudi Arabia[68]	b. rials	49.5	50.0	66.0	78.0	69.0	74.9	78.9	69.4	70.3	72.4
Syria	b. pounds	40.5	40.7	42.8	46.1	45.0	[49.6]	[61.4]	[62.6]	[74.4]	. .
UAE[69]	m. dirhams	8 129	[8 292]	8 629	8 712	8 790	8 688	8 796	9 139	9 236	. .
Yemen	b. riyals	32.9	39.2	51.3	52.2	61.5	76.6	91.1	130	148	156

Table 8A.3. Military expenditure by country, in constant US dollars for 1995–2004 and current US dollars for 2004

Figures are in US$ m., at constant 2003 prices and exchange rates, and are for calendar years. Figures in the right-most column, marked *, are in current US$ m.

Country	1995	1996	1997	1998	1999	2000	2001	2002	2003	2004	2004*
Africa											
North Africa											
Algeria[1]	1 118	1 273	1 531	1 620	1 709	1 984	2 009	2 213	2 206	2 523	2 804
Libya	. .	. .	371	418	323	346	339	435	484	560	565
Morocco[2]	1 553	1 501	1 437	1 420	1 550	1 600	1 699	1 796	1 851	2 056	2 258
Tunisia	318	365	361	368	364	381	369	392	408	403	432
Sub-Saharan Africa											
Angola[3]	1 438	2 237	(1 681)	597	2 186	617	355	430	645	1 320	1 779
Benin	. .	. .	. .	. .	. .	. .	. .	. .	. .	. .	. .
Botswana	174	161	186	240	236	247	251	292	299	[284]	[318]
Burkina Faso	39.0	37.9	43.9	43.3	48.3	49.2	48.5	58.7	55.0	61.1	66.3
Burundi	27.8	32.2	34.7	37.3	39.0	33.6	44.6	47.3	35.6	35.7	38.2
Cameroon	122	124	137	155	168	168	168	176	189	199	220
Cape Verde	6.4	4.5	4.5	5.0	5.6	9.0	6.1	5.5	5.7	5.9	6.6
Central African Republic[4]	13.0	12.0	. .	. .	. .	. .	. .	13.2	15.0	13.6	15.0
Chad	25.7	29.0	21.0	18.4	26.7	30.3	32.3	32.6	39.1	45.6	44.8
Congo, Republic of	. .	. .	. .	. .	. .	. .	. .	. .	48.8	. .	. .
Congo, DRC[5]	. .	69.0	56.7	17.1	62.2	50.7	. .	. .	. .	. .	. .
Côte d'Ivoire	. .	113	113	. .	. .	. .	. .	. .	213	. .	. .
Djibouti	29.8	23.9	25.2	24.8	24.4	23.4	23.4	25.8	. .	. .	. .
Equatorial Guinea	. .	. .	. .	. .	. .	. .	. .	. .	. .	. .	. .
Eritrea[6]	149	171	109	328	316	263	195	186	146	. .	. .
Ethiopia[7]	104	117	215	453	719	648	438	411	349	339	348
Gabon	. .	. .	. .	16.1	. .	. .	. .	. .	. .	. .	. .
Gambia[8]	1.5	2.1	2.2	2.2	2.0	2.1	2.0	2.0	1.7	1.5	1.5
Ghana[9]	39.6	33.4	33.5	41.6	44.1	61.8	38.8	43.5	50.6	[65.5]	[70.7]

Guinea	. .	. .	35.2	38.4	50.4	49.5	100	105	. .	. .	. .
Guinea-Bissau[10]	2.8	2.3	2.1	3.2	. .	12.0	7.8	. .	. .	. .	. .
Kenya	180	210	200	188	183	197	226	244	246	237	255
Lesotho	31.1	27.8	27.8	30.0	37.7	36.2	38.0	29.1	29.2	33.1	33.4
Liberia[11]	. .	. .	. .	. .	. .	. .	(43.7)	(49.8)	. .	. .	. .
Madagascar[12]	37.5	54.3	69.2	66.9	62.7	63.2	79.2	. .	. .	. .	. .
Malawi	9.8	13.0	16.7	13.4	13.0	14.5	13.2	. .	. .	. .	. .
Mali	54.8	51.7	59.9	59.3	67.0	77.6	78.1	75.9	81.4	88.8	92.9
Mauritania[13]	20.1	19.4	18.5	18.5	18.4	18.3	18.3	19.6	18.2	17.9	18.1
Mauritius	13.3	12.4	10.3	9.5	10.0	10.3	10.4	10.6	10.9	11.3	12.0
Mozambique	[34.4]	[31.2]	[34.7]	[41.2]	49.4	51.2	58.4	60.4	57.5	58.6	69.3
Namibia[14]	63.2	67.6	83.3	89.3	124	136	116	125	118	113	135
Niger	18.9	17.4	19.2	23.6	27.0	32.9	25.0	24.2	. .	. .	. .
Nigeria[15]	292	247	267	340	585	422	632	573	595	518	572
Rwanda[16]	40.4	57.4	52.9	59.2	63.5	54.1	58.3	54.7	49.5	37.2	38.4
Senegal[17]	78.5	77.2	77.0	81.5	88.0	80.5	88.8	89.2	94.0	[95.6]	[105]
Seychelles	12.9	12.4	13.5	12.7	12.8	12.0	12.4	12.3	12.2	13.1	13.4
Sierra Leone	21.8	16.0	(7.6)	. .	. .	[24.9]	16.8	15.3	18.1	17.0	16.9
Somalia	. .	. .	. .	. .	. .	. .	. .	. .	. .	. .	. .
South Africa	2 662	2 314	2 128	1 917	1 816	2 120	2 371	2 538	2 596	2 645	3 090
Sudan[18]	187	94.9	111	248	311	398	. .	421	391	. .	. .
Swaziland	[29.7]	[30.2]	29.6	32.6	34.0	31.3	29.2	. .	. .	. .	. .
Tanzania[19]	88.1	87.3	87.2	. .	. .	107	125	139	220	337	326
Togo	32.7	. .	. .	. .	. .	. .	. .	. .	28.8	29.3	31.5
Uganda[20]	82.6	88.3	84.6	110	122	113	117	140	151	159	178
Zambia[21]	89.0	53.8	69.0	69.5	35.5	[22.2]	. .	. .	. .	. .	. .
Zimbabwe[22]	336	343	362	296	508	497	297	262	177	260	167
Americas											
Central America											
Belize	9.0	8.4	9.8	. .	. .	. .	. .	. .	. .	. .	
Costa Rica[23]	. .	. .	. .	. .	. .	. .	. .	. .	. .	. .	

Country	1995	1996	1997	1998	1999	2000	2001	2002	2003	2004	2004*
El Salvador[24]	127	115	111	107	110	121	113	111	106	[101]	[105]
Guatemala	188	157	147	150	150	189	164	136	120	103	111
Honduras[25]	. .	. .	. .	. .	. .	37.9	43.2	55.7	53.0	49.6	51.2
Mexico[26]	2 692	2 828	2 933	2 895	3 061	3 067	3 186	3 027	2 941	2 819	2 818
Nicaragua	35.2	31.7	31.2	26.8	27.6	30.3	28.2	34.9	35.6	31.0	31.8
Panama[27]	105	109	125	110	116	. .	. .	. .	. .	. .	. .
North America											
Canada[28]	10 437	9 492	8 793	9 420	9 769	9 474	9 894	9 815	10 039	10 640	[11 595]
USA[28]	336 635	318 420	316 789	309 447	310 326	322 309	324 908	364 819	[414 400]	[455 304]	[466 600]
South America											
Argentina	1 987	1 881	1 813	1 803	1 858	1 821	1 791	1 480	1 528	[1 503]	[1 560]
Bolivia	115	114	136	167	125	110	125	132	133	141	142
Brazil	[8 249]	[7 116]	[8 726]	[8 223]	[7 587]	8 042	9 323	9 357	7 901	7 500	8 358
Chile[29]	[1 757]	[1 823]	1 984	2 115	2 240	2 371	2 461	2 625	2 521	3 178	3 619
Colombia[30]	[1 949]	[2 027]	2 173	2 255	2 508	2 537	2 862	3 138	[3 490]	[3 655]	[4 208]
Ecuador[31]	537	474	542	596	385	444	466	602	641	574	590
Guyana	6.3	5.7	. .	. .	. .	. .	. .	. .	. .	. .	. .
Paraguay	. .	. .	[77.7]	[72.1]	[61.1]	[59.6]	55.8	52.6	53.7	45.8	52.1
Peru	945	911	769	861	864	970	1 027	734	775	778	819
Uruguay	[198]	[189]	[187]	[182]	189	218	211	183	176	170	182
Venezuela[32]	1 393	1 006	1 650	1 156	1 211	1 369	1 552	1 285	1 128	1 235	1 287
Asia and Oceania											
Central Asia											
Kazakhstan[33]	190	205	191	190	159	166	245	268	318	[361]	[424]
Kyrgyzstan[34]	18.8	39.8	44.1	38.1	40.2	48.3	24.0	48.7	55.2	[57.1]	[64.2]
Tajikistan[33]	10.0	10.7	15.4	17.6	14.7	12.7	12.6	26.9	34.8	40.8	45.2
Turkmenistan[35]	116	112	169	143	155	. .	. .	. .	. .	. .	. .
Uzbekistan[33]	(71.0)	(94.9)	[110]	. .	166	. .	88.9	. .	69.2	. .	. .

East Asia											
Brunei[36]	[251]	275	316	352	[298]	[275]	[308]	292	. .	. .	. .
Cambodia[37]	160	139	138	130	123	119	106	108	104	105	108
China, P. R.[38]	[14 000]	[15 500]	[15 700]	[18 000]	[20 200]	[22 200]	[26 100]	[30 700]	[33 100]	[35 400]	[36 800]
Indonesia	[2 595]	[2 820]	2 623	2 065	1 701	2 115	2 212	2 363	3 200	3 522	3 603
Japan[39]	40 454	41 269	41 468	41 362	41 439	41 726	42 150	42 619	42 729	42 442	45 267
Korea, North[40]	. .	. .	. .	(19.5)	(19.5)	(20.0)	(20.9)	(22.0)	(26.0)	(27.9)	(27.9)
Korea, South[41]	12 501	13 175	13 494	13 026	12 672	13 450	13 839	14 487	14 860	15 488	16 588
Laos	. .	44.6	37.7	24.8	36.6	36.2	39.3	. .	. .	. .	. .
Malaysia	1 961	1 886	1 772	1 302	1 762	1 600	1 991	2 263	2 882	2 707	2 742
Mongolia	24.7	20.9	19.1	19.8	20.2	25.7	23.5	24.3	. .	. .	. .
Myanmar	25 746	27 492	22 861	18 817	18 661	25 165	22 555	16 425	. .	. .	. .
Philippines	805	832	741	729	714	752	704	739	750	756	771
Singapore	3 159	3 461	3 884	4 398	4 481	4 334	4 437	4 682	4 730	4 817	5 034
Taiwan	8 605	8 679	9 009	8 783	7 565	7 017	7 160	6 554	7 043	7 211	7 513
Thailand	2 925	2 924	2 713	2 202	1 907	1 789	1 862	1 884	1 857	[1 761]	[1 864]
Viet Nam	. .	. .	. .	. .	. .	. .	. .	. .	. .	. .	. .
South Asia											
Afghanistan	. .	. .	. .	. .	. .	. .	. .	. .	. .	611	794
Bangladesh	524	548	582	591	612	639	639	620	622	621	649
India[42]	9 042	9 286	10 091	10 178	11 364	11 821	12 357	12 342	12 698	15 059	16 028
Nepal	42.2	42.0	44.5	45.1	48.8	53.6	69.2	92.2	104	105	111
Pakistan	3 020	3 016	2 889	2 885	2 911	2 920	3 125	3 358	3 602	3 685	3 938
Sri Lanka[43]	749	699	621	651	586	784	655	542	487	[551]	[565]
Oceania											
Australia	7 779	7 684	7 820	8 203	8 606	8 581	8 921	9 382	9 705	10 085	11 720
Fiji	32.7	33.3	29.6	28.6	28.6	42.1	47.6	39.0	[36.9]	[28.3]	[31.5]
New Zealand	880	886	868	869	881	885	866	833	852	864	1 003
Papua New Guinea	41.3	42.0	55.0	44.9	36.4	33.4	35.1	17.3	19.3	. .	. .

Country	1995	1996	1997	1998	1999	2000	2001	2002	2003	2004	2004*
Europe											
Albania[44]	78.6	70.6	49.3	46.6	54.0	59.7	67.9	67.8	76.1	76.9	92.7
Armenia	58.7	50.6	64.4	63.5	68.4	69.3	67.3	66.5	76.6	[80.9]	[93.5]
Austria	2 002	1 983	1 987	1 993	2 034	2 083	1 941	1 904	1 986	1 925	2 145
Azerbaijan	61.8	63.4	71.0	78.5	96.5	105	114	126	[136]	[143]	[151]
Belarus[45]	127	97.7	160	150	150	166	220	229	232	237	269
Belgium[46]	4 216	4 137	4 085	4 083	4 137	4 136	3 954	3 834	3 896	[4 398]	[4 899]
Bosnia–Herzegovina[47]	. .	. .	. .	. .	. .	. .	. .	292	204	185	204
Bulgaria[48]	[526]	359	335	388	440	453	502	506	516	503	586
Croatia[49]	1 860	1 491	1 291	1 299	1 019	718	659	650	610	517	590
Cyprus	222	334	423	378	233	249	294	201	195	203	227
Czech Republic[50]	1 315	1 293	1 225	1 347	1 462	1 505	1 619	1 680	1 843	1 741	1 946
Denmark[46]	3 181	3 192	3 232	3 268	3 248	3 142	3 337	3 297	3 330	3 228	3 564
Estonia[51]	52.8	51.4	68.6	72.6	90.3	106	124	148	171	181	204
Finland	1 850	2 092	1 956	2 128	1 832	1 954	1 886	1 906	1 976	2 077	2 273
France[46]	46 100	44 992	45 156	43 946	44 318	43 806	43 677	44 574	45 384	[46 174]	[51 568]
Georgia[52]	. .	63.4	[39.6]	[38.2]	[29.4]	[20.1]	[25.5]	36.4	42.6	59.5	70.1
Germany[46]	37 852	37 124	35 768	35 886	36 612	36 021	35 432	35 546	34 762	[33 888]	[37 626]
Greece[46]	5 450	5 776	6 155	6 708	7 023	7 412	7 250	7 114	7 120	. .	. .
Hungary	967	903	1 086	980	1 128	1 212	1 338	1 397	1 522	[1 485]	[1 743]
Iceland	0	0	0	0	0	0	0	0	0	0	0
Ireland	786	829	878	886	916	941	1 021	983	986	1 010	1 127
Italy[46]	22 425	24 720	25 920	26 777	27 825	29 681	29 192	30 004	27 562	27 759	31 023
Latvia[53]	60.7	47.2	45.8	49.1	64.0	79.9	100	164	189	204	229
Lithuania	54.9	64.5	106	185	159	249	261	285	300	336	372
Luxembourg[46]	136	140	151	162	164	168	211	221	231	[244]	[272]
Macedonia (FYROM)	. .	96.5	76.1	78.2	69.4	84.2	284	126	116	123	134
Malta[54]	34.7	37.2	36.1	33.1	32.1	31.2	33.3	32.9	39.9	36.1	40.3

Moldova[55]	14.8	14.5	15.2	10.1	7.7	5.9	6.5	7.6	7.9	7.1	9.1
Netherlands[46]	8 104	8 151	8 067	8 038	8 429	8 080	8 262	8 237	8 199	[8 407]	[9 292]
Norway[46]	3 761	3 812	3 749	3 997	4 018	3 886	3 911	4 699	4 387	4 387	4 587
Poland	3 343	3 516	3 703	3 845	3 753	3 685	3 702	3 778	4 085	4 149	4 466
Portugal[46]	2 887	2 784	2 845	2 780	2 925	3 011	3 135	3 223	3 151	[3 115]	[3 483]
Romania	[1 367]	[1 328]	[1 489]	[1 353]	1 221	1 162	1 219	1 212	1 345	1 399	1 586
Russia[56]	[14 700]	[13 300]	[14 300]	[10 300]	[12 300]	[14 200]	[15 700]	[16 900]	[18 500]	[19 400]	[22 700]
Serbia–Montenegro[57]	. .	654	[755]	695	653	952	773	843	729	776	819
Slovakia[58]	909	903	727	568	496	516	581	589	625	585	712
Slovenia	350	359	344	343	323	294	361	400	417	465	515
Spain[59]	9 160	8 949	9 031	8 876	9 108	9 434	9 555	9 784	9 692	9 565	10 763
Sweden	5 514	3 627	5 295	5 456	5 660	5 875	5 572	[5 401]	[5 352]	[5 439]	[5 961]
Switzerland[60]	3 948	3 737	3 603	3 523	3 405	3 419	3 365	3 332	3 294	3 301	3 576
Turkey[46]	8 939	10 008	10 427	10 926	12 064	11 675	10 703	11 388	10 278	10 142	11 784
UK[61]	42 579	43 267	40 608	40 842	40 344	40 925	41 777	44 068	51 082	47 401	54 434
Ukraine[62]	1 247	1 203	1 490	1 205	1 109	1 376	1 163	1 237	1 429	1 553	1 685
Middle East											
Bahrain	267	283	272	278	312	318	336	337	468	474	478
Egypt[63]	1 653	1 630	1 644	1 616	1 598	1 708	1 826	1 909	2 021	[2 061]	[2 164]
Iran[64]	1 976	2 234	2 502	2 641	3 676	5 626	6 225	5 026	5 098	5 150	5 607
Iraq	. .	. .	. .	. .	. .	. .	. .	. .	. .	. .	. .
Israel[65]	7 809	8 202	8 320	8 620	8 935	9 330	9 606	10 594	10 035	10 738	10 830
Jordan[66]	1 004	671	694	744	771	795	789	796	887	849	879
Kuwait	4 222	3 591	2 737	2 553	2 480	2 896	2 835	2 936	3 777	4 032	4 172
Lebanon	[1 009]	[885]	[741]	715	848	903	945	821	[781]	[793]	[817]
Oman[67]	1 950	1 835	1 902	1 706	1 727	2 056	2 397	[2 477]	2 622	2 526	2 533
Qatar	. .	. .	. .	. .	. .	. .	. .	. .	. .	. .	. .
Saudi Arabia[68]	12 974	12 953	17 080	20 258	18 165	19 934	21 233	18 637	18 772	19 290	19 332
Syria	4 089	3 800	3 921	4 250	4 310	[4 939]	[5 941]	[5 998]	[6 628]	. .	. .
UAE[69]	2 696	[2 670]	2 700	2 673	2 641	2 575	2 539	2 558	2 515	. .	. .
Yemen	402	366	469	451	488	581	[618]	782	807	735	842

Table 8A.4. Military expenditure by country as a percentage of gross domestic product, 1995–2003

Country	1995	1996	1997	1998	1999	2000	2001	2002	2003
Africa									
North Africa									
Algeria[1]	2.9	3.1	3.6	4.0	3.8	3.5	3.5	3.7	3.3
Libya	. .	. .	4.1	5.3	3.8	3.2	2.9	2.4	2.0
Morocco[2]	4.6	4.0	3.9	3.7	4.0	4.1	4.1	4.3	4.2
Tunisia	1.9	2.0	1.9	1.8	1.7	1.7	1.7	1.6	1.6
Sub-Saharan Africa									
Angola[3]	17.6	19.5	(22.3)	11.3	21.4	4.8	3.1	3.7	4.7
Benin	. .	. .	. .	. .	. .	. .	. .	. .	. .
Botswana	3.8	3.3	3.3	4.0	4.0	3.9	3.7	4.2	4.1
Burkina Faso	1.4	1.3	1.4	1.3	1.4	1.4	1.3	1.5	1.3
Burundi	4.2	5.8	6.4	6.6	6.3	6.0	8.0	7.6	5.9
Cameroon	1.3	1.2	1.3	1.5	1.5	1.3	1.3	1.3	1.5
Cape Verde	1.3	0.8	0.8	0.9	0.8	1.3	0.8	0.7	0.7
Central African Republic[4]	1.2	1.2	. .	. .	. .	. .	. .	1.0	1.3
Chad	1.4	1.5	1.1	0.9	1.4	1.5	1.5	1.4	1.5
Congo, Republic of	. .	. .	. .	. .	. .	. .	. .	. .	1.4
Congo, DRC[5]	. .	1.5	1.4	0.4	1.2	0.9	. .	. .	. .
Côte d'Ivoire	. .	0.9	0.8	. .	. .	. .	. .	. .	1.5
Djibouti	5.1	4.2	4.5	4.4	4.3	4.0	4.0	4.3	. .
Equatorial Guinea	2.1	. .	. .	. .	. .	. .	. .	. .	. .
Eritrea[6]	20.8	22.0	12.8	35.3	37.6	36.4	24.8	23.9	19.4
Ethiopia[7]	2.0	1.8	3.4	6.7	10.7	9.6	6.1	5.3	4.3
Gabon	. .	. .	. .	0.3	. .	. .	. .	. .	. .
Gambia[8]	0.8	1.0	1.0	1.0	0.8	0.8	0.7	0.6	0.5
Ghana[9]	0.8	0.6	0.7	0.8	0.8	1.0	0.6	0.6	0.7

Guinea	. .	. .	1.2	1.3	1.6	1.5	2.9	2.9	. .
Guinea-Bissau[10]	0.5	0.6	0.7	1.4	. .	4.4	3.1	. .	. .
Kenya	1.6	1.8	1.7	1.5	1.4	1.6	1.7	1.7	1.7
Lesotho	3.7	3.0	2.8	3.1	3.7	3.6	3.0	2.7	2.6
Liberia[11]	. .	. .	. .	. .	. .	. .	(7.7)	(7.5)	. .
Madagascar[12]	0.9	1.2	1.5	1.3	1.2	1.2	1.4	. .	. .
Malawi	0.8	0.8	1.0	0.8	0.8	0.9	0.8	. .	. .
Mali	2.3	2.1	2.0	1.9	2.0	2.2	2.0	1.9	1.9
Mauritania[13]	2.7	2.5	2.3	2.1	2.0	1.8	1.8	1.8	1.6
Mauritius	0.3	0.3	0.2	0.2	0.2	0.2	0.2	0.2	0.2
Mozambique	[1.5]	[1.2]	[1.2]	[1.2]	1.4	1.5	1.5	1.5	1.3
Namibia[14]	1.9	1.9	2.3	2.3	3.2	3.4	2.8	2.8	2.8
Niger	1.1	0.9	0.9	1.1	1.2	1.5	1.1	1.1	. .
Nigeria[15]	0.7	0.5	0.6	0.9	1.4	0.8	1.1	1.1	1.2
Rwanda[16]	4.4	5.3	4.1	4.4	4.6	3.6	3.7	3.3	2.8
Senegal[17]	1.8	1.7	1.6	1.6	1.7	1.4	1.5	1.5	1.5
Seychelles	2.3	2.1	2.0	1.7	1.8	1.7	1.8	1.7	1.7
Sierra Leone	2.9	2.0	(1.1)	. .	. .	[4.1]	2.2	1.5	1.7
Somalia	. .	. .	. .	. .	. .	. .	. .	. .	. .
South Africa	2.2	1.8	1.6	1.5	1.3	1.5	1.6	1.6	1.6
Sudan[18]	1.7	0.9	1.0	1.8	2.4	2.9	. .	2.8	2.4
Swaziland	[2.4]	[2.3]	2.1	2.2	2.1	1.9	1.7	. .	. .
Tanzania[19]	1.5	1.4	1.3	. .	. .	1.3	1.4	1.5	2.1
Togo	2.4	. .	. .	. .	. .	. .	. .	. .	1.6
Uganda[20]	2.0	2.0	1.9	2.3	2.4	2.1	2.1	2.3	2.3
Zambia[21]	2.2	1.4	1.8	1.9	1.0	[0.6]	. .	. .	. .
Zimbabwe[22]	3.6	3.1	3.2	2.5	4.5	4.9	2.9	2.9	2.1
Americas									
Central America									
Belize	1.2	1.1	1.3	. .	. .	. .	. .	. .	. .
Costa Rica[23]	0.0	0.0	0.0	0.0	0.0	0.0	0.0	0.0	0.0

Country	1995	1996	1997	1998	1999	2000	2001	2002	2003
El Salvador[24]	1.0	0.9	0.9	0.8	0.8	0.9	0.8	0.8	0.7
Guatemala	1.0	0.8	0.7	0.7	0.7	0.8	0.7	0.6	0.5
Honduras[25]	. .	. .	. .	. .	. .	0.6	0.7	0.8	0.4
Mexico[26]	0.6	0.6	0.6	0.5	0.6	0.5	0.5	0.5	0.5
Nicaragua	1.1	0.9	0.9	0.7	0.7	0.8	0.7	0.9	0.9
Panama[27]	1.1	1.1	1.2	1.0	1.0	. .	. .	. .	. .
North America									
Canada[28]	1.5	1.4	1.2	1.3	1.3	1.2	1.2	1.2	1.2
USA[28]	3.8	3.5	3.3	3.1	3.0	3.1	3.1	3.4	[3.8]
South America									
Argentina	1.6	1.4	1.3	1.3	1.4	1.3	1.4	1.2	1.2
Bolivia	1.9	1.8	2.1	2.4	1.8	1.5	1.7	1.7	1.7
Brazil	[2.1]	[1.7]	[2.0]	[1.9]	[1.7]	1.7	1.9	1.9	1.6
Chile[29]	[3.1]	[3.1]	3.2	3.4	3.7	3.7	3.7	3.8	3.5
Colombia[30]	[2.6]	[2.8]	2.9	3.1	3.5	3.4	3.8	4.1	[4.4]
Ecuador[31]	2.4	2.0	2.1	2.4	1.5	1.7	1.8	2.3	2.4
Guyana	0.9	0.8	. .	. .	. .	. .	. .	. .	. .
Paraguay	. .	. .	[1.4]	[1.3]	[1.1]	[1.1]	1.0	0.9	0.9
Peru	1.9	1.8	1.4	1.6	1.6	1.7	1.9	1.3	1.3
Uruguay	[1.7]	[1.6]	[1.5]	[1.4]	1.5	1.8	1.8	1.7	1.6
Venezuela[32]	1.5	1.0	1.7	1.4	1.5	1.5	1.7	1.4	1.3
Asia and Oceania									
Central Asia									
Kazakhstan[33]	1.0	1.2	1.1	1.1	0.8	0.8	1.0	1.0	1.1
Kyrgyzstan[34]	1.6	3.0	3.1	2.7	2.7	2.9	2.3	2.7	2.9
Tajikistan[33]	1.1	1.3	1.7	1.7	1.4	1.2	1.2	2.1	2.2
Turkmenistan[35]	2.3	2.0	4.0	3.1	2.9	. .	. .	. .	. .
Uzbekistan[33]	(1.1)	(1.2)	[1.4]	. .	1.6	. .	0.8	. .	0.5

East Asia									
Brunei[36]	[5.7]	6.4	7.3	9.4	[7.3]	[6.5]	[7.3]	6.6	. .
Cambodia[37]	5.5	4.8	4.5	4.1	3.6	3.3	2.8	2.7	2.5
China, P. R.[38]	[1.8]	[1.8]	[1.7]	[1.9]	[2.0]	[2.0]	[2.2]	[2.4]	[2.3]
Indonesia	[1.6]	[1.6]	1.3	1.1	0.9	1.1	1.1	1.2	1.5
Japan[39]	0.9	0.9	0.9	1.0	1.0	1.0	1.0	1.0	1.0
Korea, North	. .	. .	. .	. .	. .	. .	. .	. .	. .
Korea, South[41]	2.9	2.9	2.7	2.8	2.5	2.5	2.5	2.4	2.5
Laos	. .	2.9	2.4	1.6	2.2	2.0	2.1	. .	. .
Malaysia	2.8	2.4	2.1	1.6	2.1	1.7	2.2	2.4	2.8
Mongolia	1.7	1.8	1.8	2.0	2.0	2.6	2.3	2.2	. .
Myanmar	3.7	3.5	2.7	2.3	2.0	2.1	1.7	1.2	. .
Philippines	1.4	1.4	1.2	1.2	1.1	1.1	1.0	1.0	0.9
Singapore	4.4	4.4	4.7	5.5	5.5	4.7	5.0	5.1	5.2
Taiwan	4.0	3.8	3.6	3.3	2.8	2.5	2.6	2.3	2.5
Thailand	2.3	2.2	2.1	1.9	1.6	1.4	1.5	1.4	1.3
Viet Nam	. .	. .	. .	. .	. .	. .	. .	. .	. .
South Asia									
Afghanistan	. .	. .	. .	. .	. .	. .	. .	. .	. .
Bangladesh	1.4	1.4	1.4	0.1	1.4	1.4	1.3	1.2	1.2
India[42]	2.2	2.1	2.2	2.2	2.3	2.3	2.3	2.2	2.1
Nepal	0.8	0.8	0.8	0.8	0.9	0.9	1.1	1.5	1.6
Pakistan	5.3	5.1	4.9	4.8	4.6	4.5	4.7	4.7	4.4
Sri Lanka[43]	5.3	5.0	4.2	4.2	3.6	4.5	3.9	3.1	2.7
Oceania									
Australia	2.0	1.9	1.9	1.9	1.9	1.8	1.9	1.9	1.9
Fiji	1.7	1.7	1.5	1.5	1.4	2.1	2.2	1.8	[1.6]
New Zealand	1.4	1.4	1.3	1.3	1.3	1.2	1.2	1.1	1.1
Papua New Guinea	1.0	1.0	1.3	1.1	0.9	0.9	1.0	0.5	0.6

Country	1995	1996	1997	1998	1999	2000	2001	2002	2003
Europe									
Albania[44]	1.9	1.5	1.4	1.2	1.2	1.2	1.3	1.2	1.2
Armenia	4.1	3.3	3.9	3.5	3.7	3.6	3.1	2.7	2.7
Austria	0.9	0.9	0.9	0.9	0.8	0.8	0.8	0.8	0.8
Azerbaijan	2.3	2.2	2.2	2.3	2.3	2.1	2.0	2.0	[1.9]
Belarus[45]	1.6	1.2	1.7	1.4	1.3	1.3	1.4	1.4	1.3
Belgium[46]	1.6	1.6	1.5	1.5	1.4	1.4	1.3	1.3	1.3
Bosnia and Herzegovina[47]	. .	. .	. .	. .	. .	. .	. .	4.3	2.9
Bulgaria[48]	[2.6]	2.0	2.1	2.3	2.5	2.5	2.7	2.7	2.6
Croatia[49]	9.4	7.2	5.7	5.5	4.3	3.0	2.6	2.4	2.1
Cyprus	2.3	3.4	4.2	3.6	2.1	2.1	2.4	1.6	1.5
Czech Republic[50]	1.8	1.7	1.6	1.8	2.0	1.9	1.9	2.0	2.2
Denmark[46]	1.7	1.7	1.7	1.7	1.6	1.5	1.6	1.6	1.5
Estonia[51]	1.0	0.9	1.1	1.1	1.3	1.4	1.6	1.7	1.9
Finland	1.5	1.7	1.5	1.5	1.2	1.3	1.2	1.2	1.2
France[46]	3.1	3.0	2.9	2.8	2.7	2.6	2.5	2.5	2.6
Georgia[52]	. .	2.2	[1.2]	[1.1]	[0.9]	[0.6]	[0.7]	1.0	1.1
Germany[46]	1.7	1.6	1.6	1.5	1.5	1.5	1.5	1.5	1.4
Greece[46]	4.3	4.5	4.6	4.8	4.8	4.9	4.6	4.3	4.1
Hungary	1.6	1.5	1.7	1.5	1.7	1.7	1.8	1.8	1.8
Iceland	0.0	0.0	0.0	0.0	0.0	0.0	0.0	0.0	0.0
Ireland	1.1	1.1	1.0	0.9	0.8	0.8	0.8	0.7	0.7
Italy[46]	1.8	1.9	1.9	2.0	2.0	2.1	2.0	2.1	1.9
Latvia[53]	0.9	0.7	0.6	0.6	0.8	0.9	1.1	1.6	1.7
Lithuania	0.5	0.5	0.8	1.2	1.1	1.7	1.7	1.7	1.6
Luxembourg[46]	0.8	0.8	0.8	0.8	0.7	0.7	0.8	0.9	0.9
Macedonia (FYROM)	. .	3.0	2.2	2.2	1.8	1.9	6.6	2.8	2.5
Malta[54]	1.0	1.0	0.9	0.8	0.8	0.7	0.7	0.7	0.8

Moldova[55]	0.9	0.9	0.9	0.6	0.5	0.4	0.4	0.4	0.4
Netherlands[46]	1.9	1.9	1.8	1.7	1.8	1.6	1.6	1.6	1.6
Norway[46]	2.4	2.2	2.1	2.2	2.1	1.8	1.7	2.1	2.0
Poland	2.1	2.1	2.1	2.1	1.9	1.8	1.8	1.9	2.0
Portugal[46]	2.6	2.4	2.3	2.2	2.1	2.1	2.1	2.1	2.1
Romania	[2.8]	[2.5]	[3.0]	[3.0]	2.7	2.5	2.5	2.3	2.4
Russia[56]	[4.1]	[3.8]	[4.2]	[3.1]	[3.5]	[3.7]	[4.0]	[4.2]	[4.3]
Serbia and Montenegro[57]	. .	. .	[4.8]	4.4	4.5	5.9	4.9	4.8	. .
Slovakia[58]	3.2	3.1	2.4	1.8	1.6	1.7	1.9	1.8	1.9
Slovenia	1.7	1.6	1.5	1.4	1.3	1.2	1.4	1.5	1.5
Spain[59]	1.5	1.4	1.4	1.3	1.3	1.2	1.2	1.2	1.2
Sweden	2.3	1.5	2.1	2.1	2.0	2.0	1.9	[1.8]	[1.8]
Switzerland[60]	1.3	1.3	1.2	1.2	1.1	1.1	1.1	1.0	1.0
Turkey[46]	3.9	4.1	4.1	4.4	5.4	5.0	5.0	4.9	4.9
UK[61]	3.0	2.9	2.7	2.6	2.5	2.5	2.5	2.5	2.8
Ukraine[62]	2.8	3.3	4.1	3.4	3.0	3.6	2.9	2.8	2.9
Middle East									
Bahrain	4.7	4.7	4.6	4.8	4.9	4.0	4.2	4.4	5.1
Egypt[63]	3.1	2.9	2.8	2.7	2.4	2.5	2.6	2.6	2.6
Iran[64]	2.4	2.6	2.9	3.2	4.1	5.4	5.7	3.8	3.8
Iraq	. .	. .	. .	. .	. .	. .	. .	. .	. .
Israel[65]	9.0	9.0	8.8	8.7	8.7	8.4	8.6	9.7	9.1
Jordan[66]	12.4	8.5	8.7	8.8	8.9	8.9	8.5	8.2	8.9
Kuwait	13.9	10.4	8.2	9.1	7.8	7.3	7.9	8.1	9.0
Lebanon	[6.7]	[5.7]	[4.6]	4.3	5.0	5.4	5.5	4.7	[4.3]
Oman[67]	14.6	12.5	12.5	12.5	11.4	10.6	12.2	[12.3]	12.2
Qatar	. .	. .	. .	. .	. .	. .	. .	. .	. .
Saudi Arabia[68]	9.3	8.5	10.7	14.3	11.4	10.6	11.5	9.8	8.7
Syria	7.1	5.9	5.7	5.8	5.5	[5.5]	[6.4]	[6.3]	[7.1]
UAE[69]	5.5	[5.1]	4.8	5.1	4.3	3.4	3.4	3.5	3.1
Yemen	6.4	5.3	5.8	6.2	5.2	5.0	[5.6]	7.2	7.1

( ) = Uncertain figure; [ ] = SIPRI estimate.

[1] The figures for Algeria are budget figures for recurrent expenditure only.

[2] Figures for Morocco in 2002–2003 are for the adopted budget.

[3] The figures for Angola should be seen in the context of highly uncertain economic statistics due to the impact of war on the Angolan economy. Figures are for defence, public order and security.

[4] The figures for the Central African Republic are for recurrent expenditure only.

[5] The Democratic Republic of the Congo was formerly named Zaire (1971–97).

[6] Figures for Eritrea in 1995 include expenditure for demobilization. Eritrea changed currency during the period; all figures have been converted to the most recent currency.

[7] The figure for Ethiopia in 1999 includes an allocation of 1 billion birr (US$130 million) in addition to the original defence budget. Figures for 2002–2004 are for the adopted budget.

[8] Figures for the Gambia are for recurrent expenditure only.

[9] Figures for Ghana are for the adopted budget.

[10] An armed conflict broke out in Guinea-Bissau in 1998, which led to a substantial increase in defence expenditure, especially in the financial year 2000/01. According to the IMF, the increase was financed by a credit from the banking system, as well as by promissory notes. Guinea-Bissau changed currency during the period; all figures have been converted to the most recent currency.

[11] Figures for Liberia are unreliable due to the continuing conflict in the country and problems associated with the exchange rate.

[12] Figures for Madagascar include expenditure for the gendarmerie and the National Police.

[13] Figures for Mauritania are for operating expenditure only.

[14] Figures for Namibia in 1999 refer to the budget of the Ministry of Defence only. In addition to this the 1999 budget of the Ministry of Finance includes a contingency provision of Na$104 million (US$20 million) for the Namibian military presence in the Democratic Republic of the Congo (DRC). The figure for 2002 includes a supplementary allocation of Na$78.5 million (US$11 million).

[15] Figures for Nigeria before 1999 are understated because of the use by the military of a favourable specific dollar exchange rate.

[16] Figures for Rwanda in 1997 do not include the demobilization allowance of 1.0 billion francs (US$2.3 million). The figure for 1998 is the official defence budget. According to the IMF, there are additional sources of funding for military activities, both within the budget and extra-budgetary. Alternative estimates put Rwanda's military expenditure at twice the official figure.

[17] Figures for Senegal do not include expenditure for paramilitary forces, which in 1998 amounted to 21 100 million francs (US$39 million).

[18] Sudan changed currency during the period; all figures have been converted to the most recent currency.

[19] The figures for Tanzania from 2003–2004 are for defence and security.

[20] Figures for Uganda are for recurrent expenditure only.

[21] Figures for Zambia are uncertain, especially in tables 8A.3 and 8A.4, because of very rapid inflation and several changes in the currency.

[22] The figure for Zimbabwe in 1999 includes a supplementary allocation of Zw$1800 million (US$91 million).

[23] Costa Rica has no armed forces. Expenditure for paramilitary forces, border guard, and maritime and air surveillance is less than 0.05% of GDP.

[24] El Salvador changed currency during the period; all figures have been converted to the most recent currency.

[25] Figures for Honduras do not include military pensions or arms import.

[26] Figures for Mexico do not include military pensions.

[27] The Panamanian defence forces were disbanded in 1990 and replaced by the National Guard, consisting of the national police and the air and maritime services.

[28] Figures for Canada and the USA are taken from NATO military expenditure statistics published in a number of NATO sources. Publication of the most recent data, due in 2004, was heavily delayed, so SIPRI data on military expenditure for these countries for the most recent years are based on other, mainly primary sources and may not be entirely consistent with data for earlier years. Figures are for financial years rather than for calendar years.

[29] Figures for Chile are for the adopted budget. They include direct transfers from the state-owned copper company Corporacion Nacional del Cobre (CODELCO) for military purchases. In 2004 the transfers from CODELCO increased by 143% as a consequence of the high copper price.

[30] The figure for Colombia includes in 2002–2004 a special allocation of 2.6 billion pesos from a war tax according to a decree of 12 August 2002.

[31] Ecuador changed its currency from the sucre to the US dollar on 13 Mar. 2000, at a rate of 1 dollar to 25 000 sucres. Current price figures for each year represent the dollar value of military expenditure at the market exchange rate for that year. Figures for 2002–2004 are for the adopted budget.

[32] Figures for Venezuela are for the adopted budget.

[33] For this country purchasing power parity (PPP) rates were used for conversion to constant dollars up to and including SIPRI Yearbook 2002.

[34] Figures for Kyrgyzstan are for defence, public order and safety. Up to and including SIPRI Yearbook 2002, PPP rates were used for converting local currency figures to constant dollars.

[35] The coverage of the series for Turkmenistan varies over time due to classification changes in the Turkmenistan system of public accounts. Up to and including SIPRI Yearbook 2002, PPP rates were used for converting local currency figures to constant dollars.

[36] Figures for Brunei are recurrent expenditure on the Royal Brunei Armed Forces.

[37] Figures for Cambodia are for defence and security, including the regular police force.

[38] Figures for China are for estimated total military expenditure. On the estimates in local currency and share of GDP for the period 1989–98, see Wang, S., 'The military expenditure of China, 1989–98', *SIPRI Yearbook 1999: Armaments, Disarmament and International Security* (Oxford University Press: Oxford, 1999), pp. 334–49. The estimates for the years 1999–2002 are based on the percentage change in official military expenditure and on the assumption of a gradual decrease in the commercial earnings of the People's Liberation Army.

[39] Figures for Japan are for the adopted budget. They exclude military pensions and include the Special Action Committee on Okinawa.

[40] Dollar figures for North Korea are in current dollars.

[41] The figures for South Korea do not include military pensions, arms imports or paramilitary forces.

[42] Figures for India do not include military pensions.

[43] Figures for Sri Lanka are for recurrent expenditure only. A special allocation in 2000 of Rs28 billion (US$386 million) for war-related expenditure is therefore not fully reflected in the official figure.

[44] Figures for Albania for 2001–2003 are for the adopted budget. The figure for 2004 is a projection made by the Albanian authorities. These figures do not include expenditure for paramilitary forces.

[45] Figures for Belarus exclude expenditure on military pensions and on paramilitary forces.

[46] Figures for the pre-1999 NATO member states are taken from NATO military expenditure statistics published in a number of NATO sources. Publication of the most recent data, due in 2004, was heavily delayed, so SIPRI data on military expenditure for these countries for the most recent years are based on other, mainly primary sources and may not be entirely consistent with data for earlier years.

[47] The figures for Bosnia and Herzegovina include expenditure for both the Army of the Federation of Bosnia and Herzegovina and the Army of Republika Srpska. The former is divided into 2 components, Bosniac and Croat. The local currency since Jan. 1998 has been the convertible mark, set at 1 convertible mark = 1 Deutsche Mark (= $0.577 in 2003).

[48] Figures for Bulgaria do not include expenditure for military pensions.

[49] Figures for Croatia exclude military pensions of 448 million kuna (US$71 million) for 2000, 428 million kuna (US$65 million) for 2001, 433 million kuna (US$65 million) for 2002 and 430 million kuna (US$64 million) for 2003.

[50] Figures for the Czech Republic do not include military pensions up to 1999.

[51] Figures for Estonia do not include expenditure on paramilitary forces.

[52] Figures for Georgia in 2002–2004 are for the budgeted expenditure. During the period 1997–2001 the implementation rate for the defence budget fluctuated between 56% and 90%. The budget figure for 2003 is believed to be an underestimation of actual spending due to the political turmoil during the year.

[53] Figures for Latvia do not include: (*a*) allocations for military pensions paid by Russia, which averaged 27 million lats (US$56 million) per year over the 3 years 1996–98; or (*b*) expenditure on paramilitary forces, which amounted to 98.5 million lats (US$190 million) in 1999.

[54] Figures for Malta exclude expenditure on military pensions.

[55] Figures for Moldova exclude expenditure on military pensions and paramilitary forces. Adding all military items in the budget would give total military expenditure of 360.9 million lei instead of 109 million lei in 2003 and 431.9 million lei instead of 113 million lei in 2004.

[56] For the sources and methods behind the military expenditure figures of Russia, see Cooper, J., 'The military expenditure of the USSR and the Russian Federation, 1987–97', *SIPRI Yearbook 1998: Armaments, Disarmament and International Security* (Oxford University Press: Oxford, 1998), appendix 6D, pp. 243–59. Up to and including SIPRI Yearbook 2002, PPP rates were used for Russia for converting local currency figures to constant dollars.

[57] Serbia and Montenegro was formerly named the Federal Republic of Yugoslavia (1992–2003).

[58] Figures for Slovakia do not include expenditure on pensions or paramilitary forces. Expenditure on paramilitary forces amounted to 400 million korunas (US$16 million) in 1998 and 458 million korunos (US$17 million) in 1999.

[59] Figures for Spain do not include a major part of the government expenditure on military research and development of *c.* 111.7 billion pesetas (US$880 million) in 1998, 163.1 billion pesetas (US$1260 million) in 1999 and 159.4 billion pesetas (US$1190 million) in 2000, financed by the Ministry of

Industry. The figures are taken from NATO military expenditure statistics published in a number of NATO sources. Publication of the most recent data, due in 2004, was heavily delayed, so SIPRI data on military expenditure for Spain for the most recent years are based on other, mainly primary sources and may not be entirely consistent with data for earlier years.

[60] Figures for Switzerland do not include expenditure on military pensions or paramilitary forces.

[61] The series for the UK has breaks between 2000 and 2001 and between 2003 and 2004 because the UK changed its accounting system, in two steps, from a 'cash basis' to an 'accrual basis' (or 'resource basis' in British terminology). It is not clear what impact this change had on the trend in British military expenditure. Figures are for financial year rather than for calendar year. The figures are taken from NATO military expenditure statistics published in a number of NATO sources. Publication of the most recent data, due in 2004, was heavily delayed, so SIPRI data on military expenditure for the UK for the most recent years are based on other, mainly primary sources and may not be entirely consistent with data for earlier years.

[62] Figures for Ukraine are for the adopted budget for Ministry of Defence, military pensions and paramilitary forces. Actual expenditure is reportedly 95–99% of that budgeted for the years 1996–99 and about 80–90% of that budgeted for 1995.

[63] Figures for Egypt include military aid from the USA of approximately US$1.3 billion annually.

[64] Figures for Iran include expenditure for public order and safety.

[65] Figures for Israel include military aid from the USA of *c.* US$2 billion annually.

[66] Figures for Jordan are expenditure on defence and security.

[67] Figures for Oman are for recurrent expenditure on defence and national security.

[68] Figures for Saudi Arabia are for defence and security.

[69] Figures for the UAE exclude the local military expenditure of each of its 7 constituent emirates.

Source: SIPRI military expenditure database.

Appendix 8B. Sources and methods for military expenditure data

PETTER STÅLENHEIM

I. Introduction

This appendix describes the sources and methods for the SIPRI military expenditure data provided in the tables in chapter 8 and appendix 8A, and on the SIPRI Internet site, URL <http://www.sipri.org/contents/milap/>. For a more comprehensive overview of the conceptual problems and sources of uncertainty involved in all sets of military expenditure data, the reader is referred to other sources.[1] The data in this Yearbook should not be linked with the SIPRI military expenditure series in earlier editions because data are continuously revised and updated. This is true in particular for the most recent years as data for budget allocations are replaced by data for actual expenditure. In some cases entire series are revised as new and better data become available. Consistent series for the period since 1988 are available on the SIPRI Internet site and on request from SIPRI. These series cannot always be combined with the SIPRI series for the earlier years, 1950–87, since there has been a major revision in the data for many countries for the period beginning in 1988. Changes in base years and method of currency conversion also hinder comparison between editions of the SIPRI Yearbook. In the current edition, the base year for the constant dollar series is 2003. Conversion to constant US dollars has been made by the use of market exchange rates (MERs) for all countries (for details, see section IV).

II. Purpose of the data

The main purpose of the data on military expenditure is to provide an easily identifiable measure of the scale of resources absorbed by the military. Military expenditure is an input measure, which is not directly related to the 'output' of military activities, such as military capability or military security.[2] Long-term trends in military expenditure and sudden changes in trend may be signs of a change in military output, but such interpretations should be made with caution.

Military expenditure data as measured in constant dollars (see table 8A.3) are an indicator of the trend in the volume of resources used for military activities with the purpose of allowing comparisons over time for individual countries and comparisons between countries. Military expenditure as a share of gross domestic product (see

[1] Such overviews include Brzoska, M., 'World military expenditures', eds K. Hartley and T. Sandler, *Handbook of Defense Economics*, vol. 1 (Elsevier: Amsterdam, 1995); and Ball, N., 'Measuring third world security expenditure: a research note', *World Development*, vol. 12, no. 2 (1984), pp. 157–64. For African countries see Omitoogun, W., *Military Expenditure Data in Africa: A Survey of Cameroon, Ethiopia, Ghana, Kenya, Nigeria and Uganda*, SIPRI Research Report no. 17 (Oxford University Press: Oxford, 2003).

[2] For a discussion of this see Hagelin, B. and Sköns, E., 'The military sector in a changing context', *SIPRI Yearbook 2003: Armaments, Disarmament and International Security* (Oxford University Press: Oxford, 2003), pp. 282–300.

table 8A.4) is an indicator of the proportion of national resources used for military activities, and therefore of the economic burden imposed on the national economy.

III. Coverage of the data

The military expenditure tables in appendix 8A cover 159 countries. This edition of the Yearbook covers the 10-year period 1995–2004.

Total military expenditure figures are calculated for three country groupings—by geographical region, by membership in international organizations and by income per capita. The coverage of these groupings is provided in the notes to table 8A.1.

Definition of military expenditure

The definition of military expenditure adopted by SIPRI, based on the NATO definition, is used as a guideline. Where possible, SIPRI military expenditure data include all current and capital expenditure on: (*a*) the armed forces, including peacekeeping forces; (*b*) defence ministries and other government agencies engaged in defence projects; (*c*) paramilitary forces, when judged to be trained and equipped for military operations; and (*d*) military space activities. Such expenditure should include: (*a*) military and civil personnel, including retirement pensions of military personnel and social services for personnel; (*b*) operations and maintenance; (*c*) procurement; (*d*) military research and development; and (*e*) military aid (in the military expenditure of the donor country). Civil defence and current expenditure for previous military activities, such as for veterans' benefits, demobilization, conversion and weapon destruction, are excluded.

In practice it is not possible to apply this definition for all countries, since this would require much more detailed information than is available about what is included in military budgets and about off-budget military expenditure items. In many cases SIPRI is confined to using the national data provided, regardless of definition. Priority is then given to the choice of a uniform time series for each country to achieve consistency over time, rather than to adjusting the figures for single years according to a common definition. In cases where it is impossible to use the same source and definition for all years, the percentage change between years in the deviant source is applied to the existing series in order to make the trend as correct as possible. Such figures are shown in square brackets. In the light of these difficulties, military expenditure data are not suitable for close comparison between individual countries and are more appropriately used for comparisons over time.

IV. Methods

Estimation

SIPRI data reflect the official data reported by governments. As a general rule, SIPRI assumes national data to be accurate until there is evidence to the contrary. Estimates are made primarily either when the coverage of official data does not correspond to the SIPRI definition or when there is no consistent time series available. In the first case, estimates are made on the basis of an analysis of official government budget and expenditure accounts. The most comprehensive estimates of this type, those for

China and Russia, have been presented in detail in previous Yearbooks.[3] In the second case, differing time series are linked together. In order not to introduce assumptions into the military expenditure statistics, estimates are always based on empirical evidence and never on assumptions or extrapolations. Thus, no estimates are made for countries that do not release any official data, and these countries are displayed without figures. SIPRI estimates are presented in square brackets in the tables (these are most often used when two different series are linked together). Round brackets are used when data are uncertain for other reasons, such as the reliability of the source or the economic context.

Data for the most recent years include two types of estimate, which apply to all countries. First, figures for the most recent year or years are for adopted budget, budget estimates or revised estimates, and are thus more often than not revised in subsequent years. Second, the deflator used for the last year in the series is an estimate based on part of a year or as provided by the International Monetary Fund (IMF). Unless exceptional uncertainty is involved, these estimates are not bracketed.

The world total and the totals for regions, organizations and income groups in table 8A.1 are estimates because data are not always available for all countries in all years. These estimates are most often made on the assumption that the rate of change in an individual country for which data are missing is the same as the average in the region to which it belongs. When no estimate can be made, countries are excluded from the totals.

Calculations

The SIPRI military expenditure figures are presented on a calendar-year basis, with a few exceptions. The exceptions are Canada, the UK and the USA, for which NATO statistics report data on a financial-year basis. Calendar-year data are calculated on the assumption of an even rate of expenditure throughout the financial year. The ratio of military expenditure to gross domestic product (see table 8A.4) is calculated in domestic currency at current prices and for calendar years.

The original data are provided in local currency at current prices (in table 8A.2). In order to enable comparisons between countries and over time, these are converted to US dollars at constant prices (table 8A.3). The *deflator* used for conversion from current to constant prices is the consumer price index of the country concerned. This choice of deflator is connected to the purpose of the SIPRI data—it should be an indicator of resource use on an opportunity cost basis.[4] In order to better facilitate comparison to other current economic measures, often expressed in current dollar terms, the right-most column in tables 8A.1 and 8A.3 also provides military expenditure for 2004 in current US dollars.

Beginning in SIPRI Yearbook 2003, *conversion to dollars* has been done for all countries using the average MER. Previously, data for countries in transition and for

[3] Cooper, J., 'The military expenditure of the USSR and the Russian Federation, 1987–97', *SIPRI Yearbook 1998: Armaments, Disarmament and International Security* (Oxford University Press: Oxford, 1998), pp. 243–59; and Wang, S., 'The military expenditure of China, 1989–98', *SIPRI Yearbook 1999: Armaments, Disarmament and International Security* (Oxford University Press: Oxford, 1999), pp. 334–49.

[4] A military-specific deflator would be a more appropriate choice if the objective were to measure the purchasing power in terms of the amount of military personnel, goods and services that could be bought for the monetary allocations for military purposes.

North Korea were converted by use of the purchasing power parity (PPP) conversion rate.[5] The change to using MERs instead of PPPs has resulted in a significant shift downward in the level of military expenditure for these countries. For example, at the SIPRI base year 2003, Russian military expenditure converted to dollars by use of the PPP ($66.1 million in 2004) is 3.4 times higher than in MER dollars ($19.4 million in 2004). In the most extreme cases, the use of a PPP conversion factor instead of the MER can result in a tenfold increase in the dollar value of a country's military expenditure.[6]

The PPP rate is in many ways more appropriate than the MER for international comparison of economic data, especially for countries in transition and developing countries. Taking an opportunity cost approach, the ideal approach would be to use PPP rates for all countries. However, this is not possible since currently available PPP data are still not sufficiently reliable for all countries in the SIPRI database. Furthermore, PPP data for countries that are not members of the Organisation for Economic Co-operation and Development are not regularly updated, which means that comparable PPP rates are not available for recent years. Therefore, for the sake of consistency and simplicity, MERs will be used for all countries until more reliable, regularly updated PPP data become available.[7]

The choice of base year for the constant dollar series also has a significant impact on cross-country comparisons of expenditure data because different national currencies move against the dollar in different ways. In this edition of the Yearbook, the base year has been changed to 2003, having been 2000 in previous editions. This also has an impact on the regional shares of total world military expenditure. The most extreme example is Europe, because of the relative increase of the European currencies compared to the dollar: the shift in base year from 2000 to 2003 has resulted in an increase of approximately 4 percentage points in the region's share in world military spending.

V. Limitations of the data

A number of limitations are associated with the data on military expenditure. They are of three main types: reliability, validity and comparability.

The main problems of reliability are due to the limited and varying definitions of expenditure. The coverage of official data on military expenditure varies significantly between countries and over time for the same country. In many countries, the official data cover only part of actual military expenditure. Important items can be hidden under non-military budget headings or can even be financed entirely outside the government budget. A multitude of such off-budget mechanisms are employed in

[5] The PPP dollar rate of a country's currency is defined as 'the number of units of a country's currency required to buy the same amount of goods and services in the domestic market as a U.S. dollar would buy in the United States'. World Bank, *World Development Indicators 2003* (World Bank: Washington, DC, Mar. 2003), p. 285.

[6] Table 8.3 in chapter 8 shows the impact of using PPP rates rather than MERs on the level of military expenditure in dollar terms for the 15 countries with the highest military expenditure in 2004. Table 7C.1 in *SIPRI Yearbook 1999* (note 3), appendix 7C, pp. 327–33, shows the same effect for a selection of developing countries and countries in transition.

[7] A new round of benchmark surveys of price levels used for producing PPP rates was started in 2003. The hope is that this will produce more reliable PPP rates. The issues involved in the conversion of local currency figures to dollar figures are described in *SIPRI Yearbook 1999* (note 3), appendix 7C, pp. 327–33.

practice.[8] Furthermore, in some countries actual expenditure may be very different from budgeted expenditure—it is most often higher, but in some cases it may be significantly lower. These factors limit the utility of military expenditure data.

A second reason for their limited utility is the very nature of expenditure data. The fact that they are merely input measures limits their utility as an indicator of military strength or capability. Just as military expenditure has a major impact on the military capability, so do many other factors such as the technological level of military equipment, the state of maintenance and repair, and so on. The most appropriate use of military expenditure data, even when reliably measured and reported, is therefore as an indicator of the economic resources consumed for military purposes.

For the purpose of international comparison, a third complicating factor is the method used for conversion into a common currency, usually the US dollar. As illustrated above, the choice of conversion factor makes a great difference in cross-country comparisons of military expenditure. This is a general problem in international comparisons of economic data, which is not specific to military expenditure. Nonetheless, it does represent a major limitation, which should be borne in mind when using military expenditure data converted by different types of conversion rate.

VI. Sources

The sources for military expenditure data are, in order of priority: (*a*) primary sources, that is, official data provided by national governments, either in their official publications or in response to questionnaires; (*b*) secondary sources which quote primary data; and (*c*) other secondary sources.

The first category consists of national budget documents, defence White Papers and public finance statistics as well as responses to a SIPRI questionnaire which is sent out annually to the finance and defence ministries, central banks, and national statistical offices of the countries in the SIPRI database. It also includes government responses to questionnaires about military expenditure sent out by the United Nations and the Organization for Security and Co-operation in Europe.

The second category includes international statistics, such as those of the North Atlantic Treaty Organization (NATO) and the IMF. Data for the 16 pre-1999 NATO member states are taken from NATO military expenditure statistics published in a number of NATO sources. Data for many developing countries are taken from the IMF's *Government Finance Statistics Yearbook*, which provides a defence line for most of the IMF's member countries, and from Country Reports by IMF staff. This category also includes publications of other organizations that provide proper references to the primary sources used, such as the Country Reports of the Economist Intelligence Unit.

The third category of sources consists of specialist journals and newspapers.

The main sources for economic data are the publications of the IMF: *International Financial Statistics*, *World Economic Outlook* and Country Reports by IMF staff. The source for PPP rates is the World Bank's *World Development Report*.[9]

[8] For an overview of such mechanisms see Hendrickson, D. and Ball, N., 'Off-budget military expenditure and revenue: issues and policy perspectives for donors', Conflict, Security and Development Group (CSDG) Occasional Papers no. 1, CSDG, King's College London, Jan. 2002, URL <http://www.grc-exchange.org/info_data/record.cfm?Id=295>.

[9] World Bank, *World Development Report 2005: A Better Investment Climate For Everyone* (Oxford University Press: Oxford, 2004), URL <http://econ.worldbank.org/wdr/>.

Appendix 8C. The reporting of military expenditure data

ELISABETH SKÖNS and NATASZA NAZET

I. Introduction

The United Nations (UN) 2004 report on the relationship between disarmament and development states that 'reliable data on military expenditure, arms production, arms imports and arms exports and on the means to verify them are scarce' and defines lack of transparency as one of the main obstacles to understanding the magnitude and consequences of military expenditure and levels of armament.[1] As one of its recommendations, the report calls for measures to promote security through openness, transparency and confidence.[2]

Obtaining primary and comparable data on official military expenditure has been a key project for both SIPRI and the UN Department of Disarmament Affairs (DDA). SIPRI has collected and published official data on military expenditure since 1969 and since 1993 has sent out requests to governments to report their data by filling in a standardized form.[3] Annually since 1981 the UN has requested that its member states (now 191) report their military expenditure using the UN's 'Standardized Instrument for Reporting Military Expenditures'.[4] This appendix presents the response rates by governments in these two systems of reporting in 2004 (see section II). It also presents data on the number of responses over the four-year period 2001–2004 and describes efforts made by the UN to improve reporting of military expenditure (see section III).

[1] United Nations, 'The relationship between disarmament and development in the current international context', Report of the Group of Government Experts on the relationship between disarmament and development, UN document A/59/119, 23 June 2004, URL <http://www.un.org/ga/59/documentation/list1.html>, paragraph 43, p. 16. This report is an updated version of the 1987 Final Document of the International Conference on the Relationship between Disarmament and Development from 1987 and dwells on issues such as the role of security, the costs and consequences of military expenditure, conversion, the release of resources for development, and the role of the UN and other international organizations in dealing with these issues.

[2] United Nations (note 1), paragraphs 95–97, pp. 25–26. The report urges the international community to strengthen its knowledge of the disarmament–development relationship and to build up a more secure international situation by promoting transparency and encouraging further research by UN bodies and non-governmental organizations.

[3] At first, data requests were sent only to countries for which data was most difficult to get. However, since 2002 requests have been sent to the governments of all countries included in the SIPRI military expenditure database, currently 159.

[4] For a description of the UN and SIPRI reporting systems, including two tables reproducing their respective standardized forms for reporting of military expenditure, see Sköns, E. and Nazet, N., 'The reporting of military expenditure data', *SIPRI Yearbook 2004: Armaments, Disarmament and International Security* (Oxford University Press: Oxford, 2004), pp. 376–77.

Table 8C.1. Reporting of military expenditure data to SIPRI and the United Nations, by region, 2004

Figures are numbers of countries.

Region/ sub-region	SIPRI coverage (1)	SIPRI reports (2)[a]	UN coverage (3)	UN data reports (4)[b]	UN nil reports (5)[c]	Total UN reports (6)	SIPRI + UN reports (7)[d]
Africa	50	3	52	3	(1)	4	4
America, North	2	2	2	2	(0)	2	2
America, Central	8	4	13	3	(1)	4	5
America, South	11	6	12	3	(0)	3	7
Asia, Central	5	0	5	3	(0)	3	3
Asia, East	16	5	16	6	(0)	6	7
Asia, South	6	2	6	1	(0)	1	3
Oceania	4	2	6	2	(0)	2	3
Europe, West	21	17	21	20	(1)	21	21
Europe, CEE[e]	15	15	16	15	(0)	15	16
Europe, CIS	7	2	7	5	(0)	5	5
Middle East	14	3	15	3	(0)	3	3
Small states[f]	–	–	20	2	(8)	10	2
Total	**159**	**61**	**191**	**68**	**(11)**	**79**	**81**

CEE = Central and Eastern Europe; CIS = Commonwealth of Independent States.

[a] The countries reporting to SIPRI were: Albania, Argentina, Austria, Belarus, Bosnia and Herzegovina, Brazil, Bulgaria, Cambodia, Canada, Colombia, Croatia, Cyprus, Czech Republic, Denmark, Ecuador, Estonia, Fiji, Finland, Georgia, Germany, Greece, Guatemala, Honduras, Hungary, India, Indonesia, Israel, Italy, Japan, Jordan, South Korea, Latvia, Lebanon, Lithuania, Luxembourg, Macedonia (Former Yugoslav Republic. of, FYROM), Malta, Mauritius, Mexico, Netherlands, New Zealand, Nicaragua, Norway, Pakistan, Paraguay, Poland, Portugal, Romania, Serbia and Montenegro, Seychelles, Slovakia, Slovenia, South Africa, Spain, Sweden, Switzerland, Taiwan, Turkey, UK, Uruguay and USA.

[b] The countries reporting data to the UN were: Albania, Australia, Austria, Belarus, Belgium, Bosnia and Herzegovina, Brazil, Bulgaria, Cambodia, Canada, Chile, Croatia, Cyprus, Czech Republic, Denmark, Ecuador, El Salvador, Estonia, Finland, France, Germany, Georgia, Greece, Guatemala, Hungary, Indonesia, Ireland, Israel, Italy, Jamaica, Japan, Jordan, Kazakhstan, South Korea, Kyrgyzstan, Latvia, Lebanon, Lithuania, Luxembourg, Macedonia (Former Yugoslav Republic. of, FYROM), Malaysia, Malta, Mauritius, Mexico, Moldova, Nepal, Netherlands, New Zealand, Norway, Philippines, Poland, Portugal, Romania, Russia, Senegal, Serbia and Montenegro, Seychelles, Slovakia, Slovenia, Spain, Sweden, Switzerland, Trinidad and Tobago, Turkey, Ukraine, UK, USA and Uzbekistan.

[c] The UN member states submitting nil reports were: Andorra, Costa Rica, Holy See, Iceland, Kiribati, Liechtenstein, Marshall Islands, Salomon Islands, Samoa, San Marino and Zambia.

[d] Column 7 shows the total number of countries that submitted reports with military expenditure data (excluding the nil reports). Totals may be smaller than the sums of columns 2 and 4 because the same country may appear in both columns.

[e] The row for Central and Eastern Europe excludes members of the Commonwealth of Independent States (CIS), since these are shown separately.

[f] These are very small UN member states with no or only minimal defence forces.

Sources: Submitted filled-in SIPRI questionnaires; and United Nations, 'Objective information on military matters, including transparency of military expenditures', Report of the UN Secretary-General, UN document A/59/192, 30 July 2004, URL <http://www.un.org/ga/59/documentation/list1.html>; and United Nations, 'Objective information on military matters, including transparency on military expenditures', Report of the UN Secretary-General, UN document A/59/192/Add. 1, 21 Dec. 2004, URL <http://disarmament2.un.org/cab/milex.html>.

II. Reporting of military expenditure data in 2004

In 2004 a total of 81 countries reported data on military expenditure either to the UN or to SIPRI (see table 8C.1, column 7). In addition, 11 countries submitted reports with no data (nil reports) to the UN (table 8C.1, column 5) giving a total of 92 countries who submitted reports in response to a request for military expenditure data from the UN or SIPRI in 2004. The account below focuses on the countries that actually reported data and neglects the nil reports, which, with the single exception of Zambia, were submitted by countries that have no defence forces.

The rates of response to the UN and SIPRI were almost the same. SIPRI received 61 reports with data (table 8C.1, column 2)—38 per cent of the 159 countries covered in by the SIPRI database. The UN received 68 reports with data (table 8C.1, column 4)—36 per cent of the 191 member states—and, including nil reports, a total of 79 reports (table 8C.1, column 6).

In comparison with the response rate in 2003, when a total of 83 countries reported data to either SIPRI or the UN,[5] the 81 countries reporting in 2004 represent a slight decline. The number of countries reporting to SIPRI decreased from 62 in 2003 to 61 in 2004. The number of countries reporting data to the UN increased from 64 in 2003 to 68 in 2004. Including the nil reports, the total number of reports to the UN increased from 76 in 2003 to 79 in 2004 (table 8C.2).

On a regional basis, table 8C.1 shows the following. In *Africa*, three countries—Mauritius, the Seychelles and South Africa—reported to SIPRI.[6] The UN received data reports from three countries—Mauritius, Senegal and the Seychelles. In *North America* both Canada and the USA reported to SIPRI and the UN. Four of the eight *Central American* countries reported to SIPRI—Guatemala, Honduras, Mexico and Nicaragua—while three—El Salvador, Guatemala and Mexico—reported data to the UN. In *South America* six out of the 11 countries covered reported to SIPRI—Argentina, Brazil, Colombia, Ecuador, Paraguay and Uruguay. Only Brazil, Chile and Ecuador reported data to the UN.

None of the five states of *Central Asia* reported to SIPRI, while three countries reported data to the UN—Kazakhstan, Kyrgyzstan and Uzbekistan. Five out of 16 countries in *East Asia* reported to SIPRI—Cambodia, Indonesia, Japan, South Korea and Taiwan. Six East Asian countries reported data to the UN—Cambodia, Indonesia, Japan, Malaysia, the Philippines and South Korea. In *South Asia* two countries—India and Pakistan—reported to SIPRI and one country—Nepal—to the UN. In *Oceania* Fiji and New Zealand reported to SIPRI and Australia and New Zealand reported to the UN.

[5] Sköns and Nazet (note 4), pp. 375–80.

[6] A study of the availability and quality of military expenditure data in 6 African countries is presented in Omitoogun, W., *Military Expenditure Data in Africa: A Survey of Cameroon, Ethiopia, Ghana, Kenya, Nigeria and Uganda*, SIPRI Research Report no. 17 (Oxford University Press: Oxford, 2003).

Table 8C.2. Number of countries reporting their military expenditure to the United Nation, 1981–2004[a]

Figures are numbers of countries.

	1981–98	1999	2000	2001	2002	2003	2004
Standardized reports (incl. nil reports)	≤36	35	32	61	82	66	65
Simplified reports	0	0	0	0	0	10	14
Total reports (incl. nil reports)	**≤36**	**35**	**32**	**61**	**82**	**76**	**79**

[a] The data for 1999–2003 include late submissions of data to the UN and are therefore slightly higher than those presented in previous editions of the SIPRI Yearbooks. The data for 2004 include a first batch of late submissions but, should more countries report after 31 Dec. 2004, the figures for 2004 may be revised slightly upwards.

Sources: United Nations, Department of Disarmament Affairs, Report of the Secretary-General on objective information on military matters, including transparency of military expenditures, various years, and other data available at URL <http://disarmament2.un.org/cab/milex.html>; **Data for the simplified reports**: United Nations, 'Objective information on military matters, including transparency of military expenditures', Report of the UN Secretary-General, UN document A/58/202, 1 Aug. 2003, URL <http://www.un.org/ga/58/documentation/list2.html>; and United Nations, 'Objective information on military matters, including transparency of military expenditures', Report of the UN Secretary-General, UN documents A/59/192, 30 July 2004, and A/59/192/Add.1, 21 Dec. 2004, URL <http://www.un.org/ga/59/documentation/list1.html>.

Most, although not all, governments in Europe submitted data. In *Western Europe* 17 out of 21 countries reported to SIPRI and 15 reported to the UN. In *Central and Eastern Europe* all 15 countries in the SIPRI database reported to SIPRI and 15 out of the 16 UN member states to the UN. Of the seven European member states of the Commonwealth of Independent States, two reported to SIPRI—Belarus and Georgia—and five to the UN—Belarus, Georgia, Moldova, Russia and Ukraine.

In the *Middle East* the response rate is still very low. Three countries—Israel, Jordan and Lebanon—reported to both SIPRI and the UN. However, several Middle Eastern governments have begun to provide defence budget data on their government websites.

III. Trends in reporting of military expenditure to the United Nations, 1999–2004

The response rates to the UN request for information was very low during the first two decades of the existence on the UN Reporting Instrument. During the period 1981–98 the annual number of country reports was 36 or lower (see table 8C.2). The number began to increase in 2001, but respondents still represented a minority of UN member states. In order to improve the reporting rates, the UN Department of Disarmament Affairs has since 2001 been engaged in efforts to encourage and facilitate reporting by member states. In particular, it has facilitated the holding of regional and sub-regional workshops to increase familiarity with the reporting instrument and to raise awareness regarding the transparency building process. In

May 2004, the fourth such workshop[7] was held in Nairobi, Kenya, with representatives from all countries adhering to the Nairobi Declaration, from some development assistance donor countries, from the regional offices of the UN Development Programme (UNDP) and the DDA Centre for Peace and Disarmament in Africa.[8] One particular objective of this workshop was to motivate the countries of the Great Lakes region and the Horn of Africa to participate in the UN military expenditure reporting system.

Another method of improving the response rate was the introduction of a simplified form for reporting. The standardized reporting instrument has the format of a complex matrix for reporting data in great detail. Based on the belief that this was an obstacle for many countries, in 2003 the DDA introduced an alternative, simplified reporting form with only a few cells for data entry.[9]

Judging from the trend in table 8C.2, it appears that, despite the DDA's efforts to enhance participation in the UN Standardized Instrument for Reporting Military Expenditures, there has been no significant increase in participation in recent years. The number of countries reporting to the UN was lower in 2004 (79 countries) than in 2002 (82 countries; see table 8C.2). The intended result of the introduction of the simplified reporting form seems not to have been achieved by the end of 2004. An examination of countries that have used the simplified form shows that those that had previously reported have moved from using the complex matrix to the simplified form. Thus, in order to provide increased motivation for countries to report their military expenditure to the UN, it appears that additional initiatives will be required by UN member states to support the DDA in its efforts to enhance participation.

[7] Previous workshops were held in Accra, Ghana (May 2002), Windhoek, Namibia (June 2002), and Lima, Peru (Nov. 2002).

[8] UN Information Centre in Nairobi, 'Disarmament workshop calls for international co-operation', *UN Gazeti*, no. 84 (12 May 2004), URL <http://www.unicnairobi.org/display.asp?section_id=30&story nr=85>; and United Nations, 'Disarmament workshops address issues of transparency, small arms in "Nairobi Declaration" countries', Press release no. AFR/941:DC/2924, 21 May 2004, URL <http://dis armament2.un.org/press.htm>. The Nairobi Declaration on the Problem of the Proliferation of Illicit Small Arms and Light Weapons in the Great Lakes Region and the Horn of Africa was signed in Nairobi on 15 Mar. 2000. The adhering countries are: Burundi, the Democratic Republic of the Congo, Djibouti, Eritrea, Ethiopia, Kenya, Rwanda, Sudan, Uganda and Tanzania.

[9] This simplified reporting form is reproduced in Sköns and Nazet (note 4).

9. Arms production

ELISABETH SKÖNS and EAMON SURRY

I. Introduction

The process of adaptation to the new security environment continues in the arms industry. In the United States the industry is adjusting to the new demands created by the ongoing transformation of the armed forces, the privatization of military services and the increasing importance of the homeland security sector. In Europe the emphasis is on intra-European consolidation and access to the expanding US 'market', that is, the US Government's arms procurement budget.

This chapter describes recent developments in the major arms-producing companies in Europe and North America. Section II considers data on the 100 largest arms-producing companies in the world (excluding China) in 2003.[1] Section III analyses the major acquisitions of companies with arms-producing activities in 2004 and compares company size in the arms industry and the size of some national economies. Section IV provides a brief description of the military services industry, which has expanded in the post-cold war period, in particular in the USA, and has been further reinforced by the war in Iraq. In Europe the two sectors that have undergone the least restructuring during the post-cold war period are the military vehicle and military shipbuilding industries: section V describes attempts to restructure the European military shipbuilding industry during 2004.

Section VI considers transparency in the arms sales of the major arms-producing companies and sets this in the context of other types of transparency initiative in the industry more generally. It describes a loosely defined industry that is subject to a wide variety of attempts at regulation, emphasizing that such attempts tend to be directed not specifically at arms-producing companies but at broader industrial sectors. Company responses to the demand for data on arms sales are assessed, drawing on a table of original data compiled for the SIPRI top 100 list of arms-producing companies.

Section VII provides a short summary and the conclusions of the chapter. Appendix 9A presents financial and employment data on the top 100 arms-producing companies in the world (excluding China) in 2003. Appendix 9B lists the major national and transnational acquisitions of arms-producing firms and units by North American and West European companies in 2004.

[1] Companies in China are excluded owing to a lack of data. Other countries that could possibly have companies that are large enough to appear in the top 100 list include Kazakhstan and Ukraine.

Table 9.1. Regional and national shares of arms sales for the top 100 arms-producing companies in the world excluding China, 2003 compared to 2002

Arms sales figures are in US$ b., at current prices and exchange rates. Figures do not always add up because of the conventions of rounding.

Number of companies	Region/ country	Arms sales ($ b.)[a] 2002	2003	Change in arms sales, 2002–2003 (%) Nominal[b]	Real[c]	Share of total arms sales, 2003 (%)
39	**North America**	**116.4**	**149.1**	***28***	***25***	***63.2***
38	USA	116.0	148.6	*28*	*25*	*63.0*
1	Canada	0.4	0.5	*15*	*0*	*0.2*
42	**Europe**	**58.0**	**72.0**	***24***	***5***	***30.5***
12	UK	23.7	26.9	*13*	*1*	*11.4*
9	France	13.4	17.6	*32*	*7*	*7.5*
1	Trans-European[d]	5.6	8.0	*42*	*16*	*3.4*
3	Italy	4.7	6.4	*36*	*10*	*2.7*
5	Germany	4.5	5.2	*14*	*–5*	*2.2*
6	Russia[e]	2.8	3.4	*25*	*7*	*1.5*
2	Sweden	1.4	2.1	*48*	*21*	*0.9*
2	Spain	1.1	1.3	*26*	*–1*	*0.6*
1	Switzerland	0.5	0.6	*32*	*13*	*0.3*
1	Norway	0.3	0.4	*30*	*13*	*0.2*
10	**Other OECD**	**7.3**	**7.7**	***6***	***–2***	***3.3***
7	Japan	5.9	6.1	*3*	*–4*	*2.6*
2	Korea, South[e]	1.2	1.3	*10*	*3*	*0.5*
1	Australia	0.3	0.4	*32*	*8*	*0.2*
9	**Other non-OECD**	**6.4**	**7.1**	***11***	***3***	***3.0***
4	Israel	3.2	3.5	*9*	*5*	*1.5*
3	India	2.1	2.3	*11*	*1*	*1.0*
1	Singapore	0.8	0.9	*7*	*4*	*0.4*
1	South Africa	0.3	0.5	*41*	*–5*	*0.2*
100	**Total**	**188.2**	**236.0**	***25***	***17***	***100.0***

OECD = Organisation for Economic Co-operation and Development.

[a] Arms sales include both sales for domestic procurement and export sales.

[b] This column gives the change in arms sales 2002–2003 calculated in current dollars.

[c] This column gives the change in arms sales 2002–2003 calculated in constant (2003) dollars.

[d] The company classified as trans-European is EADS, which is based in three countries—France, Germany and Spain—and registered in the Netherlands.

[e] Data for Russian and South Korean companies are uncertain.

Source: Appendix 9A, table 9A.1.

II. The SIPRI top 100 arms-producing companies

The value of the combined arms sales of the top 100 companies in the world (excluding China) in 2003 was $236 billion. Of the 100 companies, 38 are USA-based and one is Canadian and together these accounted for 63.2 per cent of arms sales by the top 100, while 42 European companies (including 6 Russian ones) accounted for 30.5 per cent of sales. Ten companies based in other member countries of the Organisation for Economic Co-operation and Development (OECD) had a 3.3 per cent share and nine companies in other non-OECD countries accounted for 3.0 per cent of arms sales by the top 100 in 2003 (see table 9.1).

In comparison with 2002, the top 100 companies in 2003 increased their combined arms sales by 25 per cent in current dollars. Because of the sharp deterioration in the value of the US dollar during 2003, the increase in real terms was much smaller: roughly 17 per cent. The decline of the dollar had a strong impact on companies located in countries other than the USA, since these companies have revenues in dollars but costs in local currency. This impact was strongest in the countries in the eurozone and in Sweden, Switzerland and Australia. Thus, much of the increase in the arms sales of European (except the United Kingdom) and Australian companies was offset by the decline in the value of the dollar, and thus in revenues in local currency.

The 38 US companies in the top 100 had the greatest increases in arms sales—28 per cent in current dollars and 25 per cent in real terms—and so their combined share of the total also increased. The 42 European companies increased their arms sales by 24 per cent in current dollars but by only 5 per cent in real terms. The combined arms sales of the 10 companies in other OECD countries increased by 6 per cent in current dollars but in real terms they fell by 2 per cent, and those of the 9 companies in non-OECD countries increased by 11 per cent in current dollars but by only 3 per cent in real terms (table 9.1).

The composition of the list has not changed much since 2002. Only four new companies entered the list in 2003 (see table 9.2), with Avio appearing as a consequence of Fiat divesting its engine manufacturing subsidiary FiatAvio to the Carlyle Group (USA) and Finmeccanica (Italy) during 2003.[2] More significantly, the Swedish electronics company Ericsson increased its arms sales by 253 per cent principally as a result of revenue from sales of the Erieye radar system to Brazil and Greece. Dyncorp lost its independent ranking in the list following its acquisition by Computer Sciences Corporation in March 2003. General Motors left the arms industry entirely when it sold its Canadian

[2] The Carlyle Group, 'The Carlyle Group and Finmeccanica: agreement for the acquisition of Fiat-Avio's aerospace business', Press release, 2 July 2003, URL <http://www.thecarlylegroup.com/eng/industry/l3-topnews-article2600.html>. Avio appears in the SIPRI top 100 list as an independent company since the SIPRI definition of an arms-producing company does not include investment companies such as the Carlyle Group.

Table 9.2. Companies that entered and exited the SIPRI top 100 list of arms-producing companies in 2003

Rank				Rank			
2003	2002	Company	Country	2003	2002	Company	Country
Entering companies				*Exiting companies*			
67	S	Avio	Italy	S	24	Dyncorp	USA
85	128	Ericsson	Sweden	147	41	General Motors	USA
92	104	Curtiss-Wright	USA	110	48	Fiat	Italy
100	105	SNPE	France	108	96	Bombardier	Canada

S = subsidiary company.

Source: The SIPRI Arms Industry Database.

subsidiary GM Canada to General Dynamics;[3] and Bombardier divested its Military Aviation Services unit to L-3 Communications' Canadian division.[4]

III. Mergers and acquisitions in 2004

The process of concentration of the arms industry has been slowing down since the late 1990s. While still significant, mega-mergers no longer dominate the pattern of acquisition. In 2003 there were six acquisitions with a deal value exceeding $1 billion.[5] In 2004 there was only one deal of this size (see appendix 9B): the acquisition by Finmeccanica of Italy of the British firm GKN's 50 per cent share in their previous joint venture, the helicopter company AgustaWestland and related assets, for €1.59 billion ($1.98 billion).[6] A major merger—between Lockheed Martin and Titan—that had been negotiated during the year fell through because of a 'government bribery probe'.[7]

Acquisition activity was more intense in the USA than in Western Europe. The large number of major acquisitions that took place in the USA was concentrated in a smaller number of companies, each making several acquisitions. The most active companies among these were L-3 Communications, a supplier of intelligence, surveillance and reconnaissance products and secure communications systems, and SAIC, a provider of information technology and systems integration.

[3] General Dynamics, 'General Dynamics completes acquisition of GM Defense', Press release, 3 Mar. 2003, URL <http://www.generaldynamics.com/news/press_releases/2003/March 3, 2003 News Release. htm>.

[4] Bombardier, 'Bombardier closes the sale of its military aviation services unit', Press release, 3 Nov. 2003, URL <http://www.bombardier.com/en/0_0/pressreleaselist.jsp>.

[5] Surry, E. and Baumann, H., 'Table of acquisitions, 2003', *SIPRI Yearbook 2004: Armaments, Disarmament and International Security* (Oxford University Press: Oxford, 2004), pp. 429–30.

[6] Finmeccanica, 'Finmeccanica: closing with GKN of the acquisition of 100% of AgustaWestland', Press release, 30 Nov. 2004, URL <http://www.finmeccanica.it/>.

[7] 'Titan extends dead-line for 2011 notes offer', *Air Letter*, 15 July 2004, p. 6.

The pattern of acquisitions in the US arms industry was strongly oriented towards two broad areas. One group of acquisitions focused on companies providing products and, primarily, services in the fields of (often space-based) communications, remote sensing and imaging in order to target the markets for network-centric solutions and unmanned air vehicles. A major example was the $725 million acquisition by ITT Industries of the Remote Sensing Systems unit of Eastman Kodak, which was targeted at the $6 billion government, science and commercial remote sensing markets.[8] The second group of acquisitions was aimed at the markets for individual protection, public safety and homeland security more generally. This indicates that current acquisitions are driven by those sections of the US defence budget with the strongest growth, partly as a result of the war in Iraq and the expansion in the homeland security sector. Overall, the current pattern of acquisitions in the US arms industry may not have a strong effect on the concentration of the industry, since it is focused on developing and strengthening new capabilities, often by acquiring companies outside the traditional arms industry.

The expectation that the expansion of these sectors will generate a new wave of acquisitions in the US arms industry has again drawn banking and investment firms into the business of brokering such deals, as in the wave of acquisitions in the late 1990s, when such firms played a major role.[9] In 2004 four major arms industry deals involved banking and investment firms: the Carlyle Group's acquisitions of a unit of Dunlop Standard for $670 million and of Stellex Aerostructures for an undisclosed sum, Veritas Capital's acquisition of Dyncorp International for $850 million,[10] and the decision by the owner of AM General, the producer of HMMWV (Humvee) armoured vehicles, to form a new joint venture with MacAndrews & Forbes Holdings to own the company.[11] In 2004 a new merchant banking firm, TCG Financial Partners, was established by William Cohen, a former US defence secretary. The aim of this company, which includes leading former defence officials such as Lord Robertson, former NATO secretary-general, and Joseph Ralson, former NATO supreme allied commander Europe, is to broker arms industry mergers.[12] This new firm is a similar venture to the Carlyle Group, which was formed in the 1990s by former US defence secretary Frank Carlucci and since then has completed 27 transactions in the aerospace and defence industries, with a combined purchase price of over $5.8 billion.[13]

[8] ITT Industries, 'ITT Industries to acquire Kodak's Remote Sensing Systems (RSS)', Press release, 2 Sep. 2004, URL <http://www.itt.com/news/>.

[9] For an analysis of the role of Wall Street in the restructuring of the US arms industry during the 1990s see Markusen, A., 'The post-cold war persistence of defense specialized firms', eds G. Susman and S. O'Keefe, *The Defense Industry in the Post-Cold War Era: Corporate Strategies and Public Policy Perspectives* (Elsevier: Oxford, 1998), pp. 121–46.

[10] 'Computer Sciences to sell DynCorp assets', Associated Press, 13 Dec. 2004, URL <http://www.forbes.com/business/businesstech/feeds/ap/2004/12/13/ap1706893.html>.

[11] AM General, 'New joint venture created to own AM General', AM General corporate news, 10 Aug. 2004, URL <http://www.amgeneral.com/corporate_news.php>.

[12] Bloomberg News, 'Banking on military firms', *Long Island Newsday*, 20 Aug. 2004.

[13] See the website of the Carlyle Group, URL <http://www.thecarlylegroup.com/>.

Table 9.3. The top 10 arms-producing companies in 2003: comparison of company sales with the national output of select countries

Figures are in US$ b., in current dollars.

Arms-producing company					Country of comparison			
					(compared with arms sales)		(compared with total sales)	
Rank	Company	Country/ region	Arms sales	Total sales	Country	GDP	Country	GDP
1	Lockheed Martin	USA	24.9	31.8	Guatemala	24.7	Slovakia	31.9
2	Boeing	USA	24.4	50.5	Tunisia	24.3	Ukraine	49.5
3	Northrop Grumman	USA	22.7	26.2	Syria	21.5	Slovenia	26.3
4	BAE Systems	UK	15.8	20.5	Angola	31.2	Bulgaria	19.9
5	Raytheon	USA	15.5	18.1	El Salvador	14.4	Serbia–Mont.	19.2
6	General Dynamics	USA	13.1	16.6	Kenya	13.8	Belarus	17.5
7	Thales	France	8.4	11.9	Zimbabwe	8.3	Uruguay	11.2
8	EADS	Europe	8.0	34.0	Ghana	7.7	Kuwait	35.4
9	United Technologies	USA	6.2	31.0	Uganda	6.2	Kazakhstan	29.7
10	Finmeccanica	Italy	5.3	9.3	DR Congo	5.6	Jordan	9.8
Subtotal top 10 companies			**144.3**	**249.9**				
Total top 100 companies			**236.0**	**992.6**	**Low-income (61) countries**			**1 101.0**

GDP = gross domestic product.

Sources: Appendix 9A; and World Bank, *World Development Report 2005: A Better Investment Climate for Everyone* (Oxford University Press: New York, 2004), table 3, pp. 260–61.

European companies have also made acquisitions in the USA, in particular the two British companies BAE Systems and Smiths, which each acquired five US companies in 2003. BAE Systems' acquisition of DigitalNet for $600 million is aimed at enhancing 'its ability to address evolving U.S. national security priorities for network centric infrastructure and information sharing between the intelligence, homeland security and warfighting communities'.[14] At the time of the acquisition, BAE Systems North America had total sales of $5 billion, had more than 26 000 employees in the USA, accounted for more than 20 per cent of BAE Systems total sales and had a 10 per cent growth in annual organic sales (i.e., excluding sales growth through acquisitions).[15]

Within Europe there were few major acquisitions in the arms industry in 2004 and all except one were domestic. One intra-European acquisition was very significant, however: the acquisition by BAE Systems of the British vehicle manufacturer Alvis. BAE Systems outbid the US tank producer General Dynamics, which had already received clearance from the European Commission to buy Alvis, one of its main competitors in Europe. The deal

[14] BAE Systems, 'BAE Systems agrees to acquire DigitalNet', Press release, 11 Sep. 2004, URL <http://www.baesystems.com/newsroom/2004/sep/110904news1.htm>.

[15] BAE Systems (note 14).

reflects BAE Systems' ambition to have a major role in the Future Rapid Effects Systems, a new British Government armoured vehicle programme.[16]

Company size

The concentration process in the arms industry since the early 1990s has resulted in some very large companies, several of which are strongly dependent on military sales. However, there is a strong national and regional variation in company size. The 38 US companies in the top 100 list had average arms sales of about $3900 million in 2003 and the 36 West European companies roughly half of this, or $1900 million. In contrast, the average arms sales of the 6 Russian companies were around $570 million, those of the companies in other OECD countries were $770 million and those of the companies in other non-OECD countries were $790 million.

During the past decade the top arms-producing companies have grown immensely in size, primarily through acquisitions. They are now comparable in economic importance to many other multinational corporations and, like them, the largest arms-producing companies have sales of a magnitude that make them major economic entities, not only in their domestic environment but also globally. The value of their arms sales exceed the gross domestic product (GDP) of most poor countries and their total sales compare to the GDP of medium-sized developed or industrializing countries (see table 9.3). A comparison for the entire group of top 100 companies shows that the value of their total sales in 2003 is roughly equal to the combined national output of all 61 low-income countries in 2003. The top 10 companies had average arms sales of $14 billion and average total sales of $25 billion, while the 61 low-income countries had an average GDP of $18 billion.

IV. The expanding military services industry

With the increasing outsourcing of services from defence ministries and armed forces to the private sector, a growing number of the top 100 companies specialize in services. This trend is most pronounced in the USA, but exists also in the West European industry. Table 9.4 shows the US companies in the SIPRI top 100 list for 2003 for which services accounted for more than 85 per cent of contracts awarded to them by the US Department of Defense (DOD) in financial year (FY) 2003. The table shows the total value of the DOD contracts awarded to them during FYs 1996–2003 according to the list of DOD top 100 companies for the respective years. Most of these companies show a gradual increase in DOD contracts awarded, and in FY 2003 the increase was particularly strong. Some of these services companies have increased their sales to the DOD as a result of the war in Iraq, but most have expanded as part of a more general trend towards the privatization of military services.

[16] 'BAE trumps rival to buy Alvis for $651 m', *Air Letter*, 7 June 2004, p. 7.

Table 9.4. US services companies: total value of US Department of Defense prime contract awards, financial years 1996–2003[a]

Figures are in US$ m., in current dollars.

Company (parent company)	Financial year[b]							
	1996	1997	1998	1999	2000	2001	200	2003
Companies specializing in research and development services								
Aerospace Corporation	156	298	339	365	334	443	473	540
Companies specializing in other services								
Anteon	. .	. .	123	220	317	324	336	509
CACI International	. .	. .	. .	177	228	249	311	454
Computer Sciences, CSC	709	704	647	712	1 165	819	808	2 531
Dyncorp (CSC)	380	535	537	566	771	909	1 359	1 663
EDS	415	359	261	238	330	223	468	772
Halliburton	574	290	286	658	595	428	484	3 921
Brown & Root Services (Halliburton)	533	. .	. .	. .	. .	. .	. .	1 542
KBR (Halliburton)	. .	. .	. .	657	594	427	484	2 170
Jacobs Engineering	140	. .	130	406	387	409	486	557
Mantech International	. .	188	. .	180	211	166	210	317
Mitri	375	304	394	417	409	441	474	456
SAIC	1 066	1 095	1 224	1 358	1 522	1 748	2 075	2 616
Titan	. .	. .	136	162	314	345	502	799
URS Corporation	. .	. .	. .	171	145	165	801	578

. . = Not included in the US Department of Defense's list of 100 companies with the largest prime contract awards (source below) for that year. These companies may have contracts smaller than those of the company with rank 100 ($205 million in financial year (FY) 2003).

[a] This table includes US companies in the SIPRI top 100 list for 2003 for which services accounted for more than 85% of contracts awarded to them by the US Department of Defense in FY 2003

[b] The US FY runs from 1 Oct. of the previous year to 30 Sep. of the named year.

Sources: US Department of Defense, '100 companies receiving the largest dollar volume of prime contract awards', annual publication, 1996–2003, URL <http://www.dior.whs.mil/peidhome/procstat/procstat.htm>.

Contractors for the war in Iraq

The war in Iraq has generated a large number of contracts for the private sector, both for the equipment used during the initial combat phase and for reconstruction work during the 'post-war period', defined as starting in May 2003 when US President George W. Bush declared that 'major combat operations in Iraq' had ended.[17] Information on contracts awarded is difficult to find. The US Government has not produced any comprehensive lists of con-

[17] Bush, G. W., Statement, USS Abraham Lincoln, 1 May 2003, URL <http://www.state.gov/p/nea/rls/rm/20203.htm>.

tracts, but some US non-governmental organizations (NGOs) have made a great effort to do so.[18] It is also difficult to find information on the extent to which awarded contracts have been implemented in actual projects.

The business generated by the war can be divided into three basic types: (*a*) DOD contracts for military equipment used both during and after the initial combat phase; (*b*) DOD contracts awarded for reconstruction work during the post-war period; and (*c*) contracts awarded for post-war reconstruction by US government departments other than the DOD, such as the departments of State, Commerce and Interior, and by the US Agency for International Development (USAID). In the first category are many major US arms-producing companies supplying aircraft, missiles, IT systems and other equipment used in the war and requiring replacement after the end of the war. It is difficult to trace the impact of the war on these companies because war replacement orders are included in larger contracts. However, it is most likely that some of the increases in arms sales of the major suppliers of such equipment are for war replacement.[19] After the 'combat phase' of the war, there has been continuing violence and thus a need for continuing supplies of military equipment. In particular, armoured vehicles have been in high demand, as shown by the increase in orders for armoured versions of HMMWV light vehicles and trucks and for armour kits for other vehicles.[20]

The contracts awarded as a consequence of the war in Iraq—and to a lesser extent those following the war in Afghanistan—will have a noticeable impact on the structure of the arms industry. The Center for Public Integrity, a US NGO that has investigated contracts awarded to US companies for post-war work in Afghanistan and Iraq, partly based on 73 requests and appeals under the US Freedom of Information Act, had identified prime contract awards with a combined value of $48.7 billion to 150 US companies by July 2004.[21] Table 9.5 shows a selection of these contracts: the US companies with the largest total value of DOD contracts for reconstruction work in Iraq. Only five of these companies are included in the SIPRI top 100 list for 2003, but several more are likely to appear in the list for 2004.[22]

Table 9.5 does not include contracts awarded by USAID or by US government departments other than the DOD. Nor does it include contracts awarded to non-US companies. Not all companies were initially eligible to bid for these

[18] Relatively comprehensive information is provided by the Center for Public Integrity, URL <http://www.publicintegrity.org/>; and the Center for Corporate Policy, URL <http://www.corporatepolicy.org/>.

[19] Center for Corporate Policy, 'War profiteers: the Center for Corporate Policy's ten worst war profiteers of 2004', URL <http://www.corporatepolicy.org/topics/topten2004list.htm>.

[20] Sher, A., 'Army orders speed up of Humvee armor production', aol.journals, 12 Dec. 2004. URL <http://journals.aol.com/sharonmc2002/McMinnMurmurs/entries/426/>.

[21] Politi, D., 'US awards $48.7 billion in contracts for postwar Afghanistan and Iraq', *Business Journal*, 9 July 2004, URL <http://www.publicintegrity.org/wow/report.aspx?aid=338>.

[22] *Defense News* already included more of these companies in its top 100 list for 2003. The reason for their inclusion could be that *Defense News* has access to different information to SIPRI, or that their definition of defence companies differs from SIPRI's definition of arms-producing companies. See 'Defense News top 100', *Defense News*, 28 June 2004, pp. 11–34; for SIPRI's definition see appendix 9A in this volume.

Table 9.5. US companies with the largest US Department of Defense contract awards for work in Iraq, 2002–June 2004

Figures are in US$ m., in current dollars. Companies are listed by total contract value.

Company (parent company)	Contracts ($ m.)	Company (parent company)	Contracts ($ m.)
KBR (Halliburton)[a]	10 832	International American Products	628
Parsons Corp.	5 286	Titan[a]	402
Fluor Corp.	3 755	Harris	165
Washington Group International	3 133	SAIC[a]	159
Shaw Group	3 051	Lucent Technologies World Services	75
Perini Corp	2 525	EOD Technology	72
Contrack International	2 325	NANA Pacific	70
Tetra Tech Inc.	1 542	Earth Tech Inc.	65
USA Environmental	1 542	Vinnell (Northrop Grumman)[a]	48
CH2M Hill	1 529	Parsons Energy	43
American International Contractors	1 500	Louis Berger Group	28
Odebrecht-Austin	1 500	AECOM	22
Zapata Engineering	1 479	Blackwater Security Consulting	21
Environmental Chemical Corp.	1 475	Motorola	16
Explosive Ordnance Technologies	1 475	Raytheon Tech. Services (Raytheon)[a]	12
Stanley Baker Hill	1 200	Ronco Consulting Corp.	12

[a] These companies were on the SIPRI top 100 list in 2003.

Source: 'Contractors: Iraq', Center for Public Integrity, Windfalls of war website, URL <http://www.publicintegrity.org/wow/>.

contracts.[23] The US Government list of countries whose companies could be awarded US primary reconstruction contracts excluded those that did not participate in the coalition effort or otherwise support it, for example, France, Germany and Russia.[24]

The huge number of large post-war reconstruction contracts has led to severe problems in the contracting process, since government oversight has been difficult. The Office of the Coalition Provisional Authority Inspector General (CPA-IG),[25] established to monitor Iraqi reconstruction work, had by the end of September 2004 managed or coordinated 113 criminal investigations and opened cases on 272 reports on fraud, waste and other problems.[26]

[23] 'Iraq contracts bar war opponents', BBC News Online, 10 Dec. 2003, URL <http://news.bbc.co.uk/2/3305501.stm>; and 'US defends ban on Iraq contracts', BBC News Online, 11 Dec. 2003, URL <http://news.bbc.co.uk/2/3308997.stm>.

[24] 'U.S. faces backlash over contracts', CNN, 11 Dec. 2003, URL <http://edition.cnn.com/2003/WORLD/meast/12/10/sprj.irq.contracts/>.

[25] According to a decision signed by President Bush on 29 Oct. 2004, the CPA-IG has been succeeded by the Special Inspector General for Iraq Reconstruction (SIGIR) since the provisional authority was dissolved on 28 June 2004. The SIGIR's mandate will last until 10 months after 80% of the money allocated to the Iraq Relief and Reconstruction Fund is committed to contracts. The SIGIR will report to the US DOD and State Department, instead of the administrator of the CPA, as was previously the case. See the website of the SIGIR, URL <http://www.cpa-ig.com/>.

[26] Weisman, J., 'Only a small part of funds to help rebuild Iraq', *Washington Post*, 1 Nov. 2004.

Independent researchers have also reported on serious mismanagement of these funds.[27] One such study described the post-war reconstruction contracting process as 'a complex and lucrative system of private enterprise, where billions of tax dollars are spent, and sometimes misspent, to support warriors and rebuild Iraq'.[28]

The company that has benefited most from post-war Iraq contracts awarded by the US DOD is KBR, a subsidiary of Halliburton (and formerly known as Kellogg, Brown and Root). With total DOD contract awards of $10 832 million for activities in Iraq (in addition to $599 million for work in post-war Afghanistan),[29] Halliburton has moved from rank 66 in the SIPRI top 100 list for 2002 to rank 12 for 2003 (see appendix 9A).[30] This company, together with a few others, has come to symbolize the deficiencies of the contracting process. Nine reports by government auditors during the period December 2003–December 2004 found widespread, systemic problems with almost every aspect of Halliburton's work in Iraq, from cost estimation and billing systems to cost control and subcontract management, and 'multiple criminal investigations into overcharging and kickbacks involving Halliburton's contracts'.[31] However, Halliburton is not alone; it simply represents the general problems with the contracting process for the war in Iraq. This process resulted in cost-plus contracts, guaranteeing a set profit on top of costs, and a rapid outsourcing of work to private companies, while at the same time the number of personnel at the DOD's Defense Contract Audit Agency was almost halved.[32]

V. The European military shipbuilding industry

Consolidation of the European military shipbuilding industry continued to be on the agenda during 2004. These efforts were focused on two initiatives: to create a naval counterpart to what EADS represents in aerospace, and to con-

[27] 'The profit motive goes to war', *Financial Times*, 17 Nov. 2004.

[28] Chatterjee, P., *Iraq, Inc.: a Profitable Occupation* (Seven Stories Press: New York, 2004); summarized in Scherr, J., 'Berkeley author investigates Iraq war Profiteers', *Berkeley Planet*, 30 Nov. 2004, URL <http://www.berkeleydaily.org/text/article.cfm?issue=11-30-04&storyID=20204>.

[29] Center for Public Integrity, 'Post-war contractors ranked by total contract value in Iraq and Afghanistan, from 2002 through July 1, 2004', URL <http://www.publicintegrity.org/wow/resources.aspx?act=total>, 'Contractors: Afghanistan', URL <http://www.publicintegrity.org/wow/bio.aspx?act=pro&fil=AF>, and 'Contractors: Iraq', URL <http://www.publicintegrity.org/wow/bio.aspx?act=pro&fil=IQ>.

[30] The success of Halliburton in the award of contracts was particularly noteworthy because of the company's strong links to the Bush Administration. US Vice-President Dick Cheney is a former chief executive officer who retired from Halliburton in 2000. The extent to which he maintained a financial interest in the company after this date is a matter of some dispute. See Chatterjee (note 28), pp. 42–44; and 'Cheney may still have Halliburton ties', CNN, 25 Sep. 2003, URL <http://money.cnn.com/2003/09/25/news/companies/cheney/>.

[31] Waxman, H. A., ranking minority member of the Committee on Government Reform, US House of Representatives, 'Fact Sheet: Halliburton's Iraq contracts now worth over $10 billion', Truthout, 9 Dec. 2004, URL <http://www.truthout.org/docs_04/121004A.shtml>. See also 'Halliburton Watch' at the website of the Center for Corporate Policy (note 18).

[32] Chaffin, J., 'Focus on Halliburton masks deeper problems with Iraq contracts', *Financial Times*, 30 Mar. 2004.

Table 9.6. Owners of major European shipyards, as of end 2004

Company (owner)	Country	Shipyard	Country
DCN (state)	France	DCN shipyards	France
ThyssenKrupp	Germany	Blohm+Voss	Germany
		Blohm+Voss Repair	Germany
		HDW Werft	Germany
		HDW-Nobiskrug	Germany
		Nordseewerke	Germany
		Hellenic Shipyards	Greece
		Kockums	Sweden
Fincantieri (state)	Italy	Riva Trigoso	Italy
Royal Schelde	Netherlands	Royal Schelde yards	Netherlands
New Izar (state, SEPI)	Spain	Izar shipyards	Spain
Babcock International	UK	Rosyth	UK
BAE Systems	UK	Barrow-in-Furness	UK
		Govan	UK
		Scotstoun	UK
Devonport Management Limited (KBR, USA)	UK	Devonport	UK
Swan Hunter	UK	Wallsend	UK
VT Group	UK	Portsmouth	UK

Sources: The SIPRI Arms Industry Files.

solidate and develop an industrial strategy for the British shipbuilding industry.

The shipyard side of the European naval shipbuilding industry is still fragmented compared to other sectors in the arms industry (see table 9.6). Other parts of the naval industry—companies that produce naval electronics (radar, sonar and combat systems) and propulsion systems and those that act as systems integrators—are more consolidated, with only a handful of companies in Europe. The significant decline in the demand for military ships since the end of the cold war and competition from a more consolidated US naval industry have created pressure for European consolidation. It is still uncertain whether recent policy developments towards increased military intervention in distant areas—involving, for example, the reorienting of the military planning of both the North Atlantic Treaty Organization and the European Union—will result in new demand for naval vessels such as large amphibious vessels for troop transport and logistical and operations support, mine countermeasures vessels and submarines.[33]

European consolidation efforts have focused on the French and German shipyards, but extend also to Italian and Spanish yards; separate efforts are being made at the national level in the UK, where the arms industry had already gone through an earlier phase of considerable consolidation. The strat-

[33] Bauer, S., SIPRI, 'Naval shipbuilding in the EU: escaping cross-border consolidation?', Unpublished manuscript, 14 May 2004.

egy proposed by the French Government to the German Government—to form a 'naval EADS' by merging the French state-owned shipbuilding company DCN and the naval activities of the French electronics company Thales with the German shipyards—has been met with a lukewarm response from the German Government and industry. Two major reasons for this are that DCN is state-owned and heavily subsidized and fear of French dominance in a merged company.[34] In late October 2004 the French defence minister announced that France would enact a law allowing Thales to buy a 49 per cent stake in DCN, but the French Government would not allow its stake to drop below 51 per cent.[35]

Consolidation of the German naval industry took a major step in 2004, when an agreement was signed to form a new German shipbuilding group under the control of ThyssenKrupp Marine Systems. It combined the shipyards of ThyssenKrupp with those of HDW, owned by the US company One Equity Partners (OEP), with the latter company receiving a 25 per cent stake in ThyssenKrupp Marine Systems. The new group combines shipyards in Germany, Greece and Sweden (see table 9.6) with total annual sales of about €2.2 billion and a workforce of 9300.[36]

Italian and Spanish shipyards are likely to be part of the European consolidation process. The Franco-Italian FREMM frigate programme may serve as a common basis for a merger between the French and Italian naval industries, both of which are state-owned, but the shipyards may be left out of this.[37] The split of the Spanish shipbuilding company Izar into two companies, one of which, 'New Izar', will comprise all military activities, may also facilitate its merger with other companies.[38]

The British naval industry also saw attempts at consolidation in 2004, in response to the British Government's efforts to build a new relationship with the naval industry that would cut costs and remove duplication.[39] The industry for its part has been concerned that a decline in large British procurement programmes could jeopardize the British shipbuilding capability. The shipyards of BAE Systems are not expected to move into profit until well into 2008 at the earliest.[40] The industry has therefore sought to persuade the government to abandon competition and instead allocate contracts in a planned manner to enable as many shipyards as possible to survive. For this purpose, BAE Systems proposed a concept that would merge its three shipyards with three

[34] 'Germany rejects French shipbuilding plan', defense-aerospace.com, citing Deutsche Welle German Radio, 15 Oct. 2004; and 'European shipbuilders think of mergers, but eye each other wearily', *Defense News*, 28 Oct. 2004.

[35] 'France to allow DCN/Thales merger', *Financial Times*, 26 Oct. 2004, p. 28.

[36] ThyssenKrupp, 'German shipyard alliance forged—ThyssenKrupp and OEP sign agreement to merge ThyssenKrupp Werften and HDW', Press release, 8 Oct. 2004, URL <http://www.thyssenkrupp.com/en/presse/art_detail.html&aid=1231>.

[37] 'Giuseppe Bono', *Defense News*, 25 Oct. 2004.

[38] 'Restructuring plan calls for separate arms of Izar', *Defense News*, 28 Dec. 2004. 'New Izar' will be known as Navantia.

[39] 'UK seeks industry change for ship plan', *Defense News*, 18 Oct. 2004, p. 6.

[40] Jameson, A., 'BAE hopes that naval review will secure shipyards' future', *The Times*, 10 Sep. 2004, URL <http://business.timesonline.co.uk/article/0,,9067-1254804,00.html>.

yards owned by Babcock International, Devonport Management Limited and the VT Group, with a combined workforce of about 10 000, and comprising most of the British warship-building capacity.[41] As of early 2005, it seemed that these plans have failed, as it was reported that the British Ministry of Defence did not see the need for a merger of producers of surface warships, 'particularly as the efficiency savings resulting from any merger were not proven'.[42]

The British Government's plans to build two new-generation aircraft carriers—the largest warships ever constructed in the UK—in coordination with France's procurement of a second aircraft carrier,[43] will have a great impact on the future of the British shipbuilding industry. The issue became highly controversial when the British Government in 2004 changed its procurement approach, from having selected BAE Systems and Thales UK to build the ships jointly, to opting to have the ships built by a broad alliance of companies, with one company taking the 'physical integrator' role.[44] This was seen as a major setback for the British companies, which had expected work on sections of the aircraft carriers to become a major activity for their shipyards for the next four years. In late December it was announced that the winner in the selection process for the physical integrator role was KBR.[45]

The future structure of the European military shipbuilding industry is closely linked to future procurement plans and to progress in European harmonization, two factors of great uncertainty.

VI. Transparency in the arms industry

While transparency in the government military sector has been on the political agenda since the 1970s and has resulted in voluntary schemes for reporting military expenditure (see appendix 8C) and international arms transfers (see chapter 10)[46] to the United Nations, no similar reporting requirements have been developed for the arms production industry. Company reporting of the military share of their sales is rare and incomplete, and reporting of the military share of their exports and research and development is almost non-existent.

'Transparency in the arms industry' is a phrase that is often used but less often defined. The terms 'transparency' and 'arms industry' can mean very different things from different perspectives, and both can have political over-

[41] Klinger, P., 'BAE will consider merging UK's naval shipyards', *The Times*, 27 Sep. 2004, URL <http://business.timesonline.co.uk/article/0,,9067-1281005,00.html>.

[42] 'UK shipyard consolidation falters', *Defense News*, 17 Jan. 2005.

[43] 'UK and France cooperate on warships', *Financial Times*, 5 June 2004, p. 8; and 'France, UK find common ground on new carriers', *Defense News*, 14 June 2004, p. 12.

[44] 'UK looks beyond military procurement methods', *Defense News*, 15 Nov. 2004, pp. 14, 18.

[45] This may have an impact on the choice of subcontractors for the British aircraft carrier programme, since KBR owns 51% of Devonport Management Limited, the owner of the Devonport shipyard. 'UK shipyard consolidation falters', *Defense News*, 17 Jan. 2005.

[46] See also Wezeman, S. T., 'The future of the United Nations Register of Conventional Arms', SIPRI Policy Paper no. 6, SIPRI, Stockholm, 2003, URL <http://www.sipri.org/>.

tones. The majority of the initiatives in this field have focused on either the broad issue of regulating multinational enterprises or the more narrow issue of combating corruption in the arms industry.[47] Often overlooked is the basic stumbling block to any kind of research in this area: the lack of publicly available information on company arms sales. This section is confined to this particular aspect of 'transparency': the extent to which companies fully and accurately report their sales, including sales for domestic procurement and for export, in the 'military', 'arms' or 'defence' sector.[48]

SIPRI makes a systematic effort to monitor developments in arms-producing companies for several reasons. These companies develop and produce military goods and services and thus provide the material basis for military activities. The analysis of companies' military-related financial and employment data provides a firm foundation for the study of armaments issues, both for policy makers and the wider public. It helps to assess broad trends in company strategies and industry development—including company dependence on arms sales and exports for their revenues and profits, and trends in employment—and to propose reasons for these. All these goals are hard to achieve, however, without consistent, regular and reliable reporting by companies of data on their revenues, profits, exports and employment arising from their supply of military equipment, research and other military services.

The demand for information

There is a clear demand for information on the arms industry from parliaments, the public and NGOs interested in disarmament and similar issues. Since the arms industry's products have a direct impact on national security, they are fundamentally different from other industrial products. The level of public interest in what kinds of military goods and services are produced and where they are sold is high.

Transparency is a condition for regulation. International initiatives on transparency and regulation in the military sector focus on arms exports,[49] leakage of arms to non-state actors and, recently, the foreign activities of private secur-

[47] On attempts at regulation of multinational enterprises see the brief history in Abrahams, D., 'Regulating corporations: a resource guide', United Nations Research Institute for Social Development, Geneva, July 2004, URL <http://www.unrisd.org/publications/>, pp. 1–5. On the issue of corruption in the arms trade see Courtney, C., 'Corruption in the official arms trade', Transparency International (UK) Policy Research Paper no. 001, Apr. 2002, URL <http://www.transparency.org/working_papers/>; and the section on transparency in chapter 10 in this volume.

[48] There is no one universally accepted definition of what these industries actually are. SIPRI defines an arms sale to be the sale of military goods and services to military customers. On the different ways in which to define the defence industry see Chu, D. and Waxman, M., 'Shaping the structure of the American defense industry', eds Susman and O'Keefe (note 9), pp. 36–39.

[49] E.g., the European Union Code of Conduct on Arms Exports. For a recent study see Bauer, S. and Bromley, M., 'The European Union Code of Conduct on Arms Exports: improving the annual report', SIPRI Policy Paper no. 8, SIPRI, Stockholm, 2004, URL <http://www.sipri.org/>.

Table 9.7. Numbers of companies reporting arms sales for 2003[a]

		Level of transparency[b]					
		Company sources			Other sources		
Country	Company sample	(*a*) Exact data	(*b*) Similar data	(*c*) Enough information	(*d*) Exact data	(*e*) Similar data	(*f*) No data
World	**150**	**41**	**33**	**12**	**33**	**25**	**6**
Australia	3	1	0	0	2	0	0
Brazil	1	1	0	0	0	0	0
Canada	2	0	1	0	0	1	0
Czech Republic	1	0	0	0	0	0	1
Denmark	1	1	0	0	0	0	0
Finland	1	1	0	0	0	0	0
France	9	6	2	1	0	0	0
Germany	8	4	0	0	3	0	1
Greece	1	0	0	0	0	0	1
India	3	1	0	0	1	1	0
Israel	5	1	1	3	0	0	0
Italy	4	0	0	0	4	0	0
Japan	17	0	0	0	0	17	0
Korea, South	4	1	0	1	1	0	1
Netherlands	2	2	0	0	0	0	0
Norway	1	1	0	0	0	0	0
Russia	10	1	0	0	9	0	0
South Africa	1	1	0	0	0	0	0
Singapore	1	1	0	0	0	0	0
Spain	3	0	1	1	1	0	0
Sweden	5	2	0	0	3	0	0
Switzerland	1	1	0	0	0	0	0
Taiwan	2	0	0	0	0	0	2
Turkey	4	0	0	0	4	0	0
UK	13	7	0	3	3	0	0
USA	47	8	28	3	2	6	0

[a] See appendix 9A for the SIPRI definition of arms sales.

[b] The levels of transparency are: (*a*) the company reports its arms sales in its normal reporting procedures, e.g., in an annual report, press release or website; (*b*) the company reports data that are similar to arms sales, e.g., sales to a defence ministry, some share of which may be for non-military applications; (*c*) the company reports sufficient information to enable a rough estimate of the company's arms sales, e.g., the defence shares of different divisions; (*d*) the company's arms sales are reported but not by the company itself in its normal reporting procedures, e.g., data are obtained by special request from SIPRI or are reported by a research institute, a trade journal or other media source—this may be with the cooperation of the company but not part of normal company reporting procedure, and is therefore considered to be at a lower level of transparency; (*e*) reports of data that are similar to arms sales are made by others than the company itself, e.g., reports by a government of the value of contracts awarded to a company in a financial year; (*f*) no data, or insufficient information to enable an estimate, were available to the standard SIPRI sources in 2003.

Source: The SIPRI Arms Industry Database and Arms Industry Files.

ity companies.[50] However, efficient disclosure and regulation in these areas require transparency also in the supply of goods and services, including by the supplier companies. Supplier transparency can be seen as the first level upon which transparency and regulation of other activities can be built. Without a solid structure of coherent and comparable reporting by suppliers of military goods and services, this basis is lost.

There have been different attempts to influence and regulate corporate transparency, some of which have focused on the arms industry but most on industry more generally. These have taken different forms, including industry self-regulation; multilateral initiatives; and what could be described as civil-society-driven corporate social responsibility initiatives. None of these initiatives legally obliges a company to report its arms sales, however. Many encourage companies to be financially transparent and to reveal the extent of their social and environmental impact, but there are no enforcement mechanisms.

The supply of information

There has been no major transparency initiative that applies specifically to the 'arms industry'. While legal frameworks generally exist that compel publicly listed companies to report financial data to their shareholders, there is no legal obligation for them to report what share of their revenue comes from arms sales. Of the three broad classes of pressure identified above, the case for compelling companies to declare their arms sales fits best into the last, the civil-society-driven corporate social responsibility initiatives.

Table 9.7 presents the reporting of arms sales data for 2003 for 150 arms-producing companies in 26 countries. The table identifies six categories of disclosure, *a* to *f*, in approximate declining order of transparency. It shows that company reporting of arms sales varies widely, both between and within countries. Of the 150 companies, only 41 can be described as having fully and completely disclosed their arms sales in a company financial document (category *a*). At the other end of the scale there were 6 companies for which no information was available on the value of their arms sales in 2003 (category *f*). Between these two extremes is a 'grey area' characterized by inconsistent reporting or reporting only of data that are similar to arms sales data.[51] Another point of interest is that some companies do not report these data in their widely distributed annual reports but choose instead to do so only in their less widely read '10-K' financial statements.[52] Twelve companies did

[50] Holmqvist, C., 'Private security companies: the case for regulation', SIPRI Policy Paper no. 9, SIPRI, Stockholm, Jan. 2005, URL <http://www.sipri.org/>.

[51] E.g., 'sales to department of defence' may not all be for military application.

[52] Each publicly traded company in the USA is required to file a 10-K report every year with the Securities and Exchange Commission (SEC). These documents frequently contain information that is not available in the company's annual report. E.g., the 10-K document filed with the SEC by CACI on 29 Sep. 2003 contained the following statement: 'We derived 63.6% of our total revenue in FY2003 . . . from contracts with agencies of the DoD.' The same information was not provided in their 2003 annual report. CACI International Inc., 'Form 10-K: Annual report under section 13 or 15(d) of the Securities

not report their arms sales but provided enough information to allow accurate estimates to be made (category *c*).

The level of transparency varies widely between the countries listed in table 9.7. Finding arms sales data for companies based in the Nordic countries presented no major problems for the present study. France and the UK also had high levels of transparency. Companies in the USA had a fair degree of transparency but often reported 'sales to the DOD' or 'sales to government' without precisely reporting their volume of arms sales. Two countries stand out as having consistently low transparency: Japan and Russia. China was not included in the study, but the level of transparency there is very low.[53]

For Japanese companies, arms production generally accounts for only a small part of their overall revenue. Japan's pacifist constitution means that the issue of arms production is politically sensitive.[54] None of the 17 Japanese companies listed in the table provided data on their arms sales or data from which estimates could be made. Instead, SIPRI relies on a list provided annually by the Japan Defense Agency. This list ranks companies by the value of contracts awarded by the agency, so the data give only an approximation of the value of arms produced by that company in a year.

Of the sample of 10 Russian companies in table 9.7, only one, Irkut, could be described as being transparent. This is of particular interest because Irkut is the only major Russian military company to have been listed on a stock exchange: 23.3 per cent of the company's shares were sold in an initial public offering on the Russian RTS Stock Exchange in March 2004.[55] At around the same time the company website was updated and information on arms sales was added to the front page.[56] The company has also started to produce annual financial statements audited to US GAAP (Generally Accepted Accounting Principles) standards. Russian state secrecy laws still limit what Irkut can disclose,[57] but it is not unreasonable to conclude that the public listing of the company may have been a factor in this increased level of transparency.[58] The other major Russian arms-producing companies are government owned and release little information.

Exchange Act of 1934 for the fiscal year ended June 30, 2003', SEC File no. 0-8401, SEC, Washington, DC, 29 Sep. 2003, URL <http://www.sec.gov/edgar/searchedgar/companysearch.html>.

[53] See note 1.

[54] Mizushima, A., 'Japan should maintain ban on arms exports', *Asahi Shimbun*, 8 Sep. 2004, URL <http://www.asahi.com/english/opinion/TKY200409080110.html>.

[55] 'Russian plane maker embraces capitalism', *New York Times*, 11 Mar. 2004, section W, p. 1. KAMAZ, a Russian producer of heavy vehicles, including trucks used by militaries, became the first incorporated company in the USSR in 1990. See the company history at URL <http://www.kamaz.net/eng/corporation/history/history/>

[56] See the Irkut website, URL <http://www.irkut.com/en/>.

[57] 'The operations of the Group related to the construction and sale of military aircraft are subject to the Law of the Russian Federation on State Secrets signed by the President of the Russian Federation on July 21, 1993.' Irkut, 'Consolidated financial statements December 31, 2003 and 2002', 27 Aug. 2004, URL <http://www.irkut.com/en/for_investors/reports/>, p. 8.

[58] Irkut announced its quarterly financial results for the first time under international accounting standards on 11 Feb. 2004, just a month before the public offering was to take place. Irkut, 'Irkut Corporation announces 9 months results under US GAAP', Press release, 11 Feb. 2004, URL <http://www.irkut.com/en/news/press_release_archives/index.php?id48=62>

The low level of transparency in arms sales: some possible explanations

The 'arms industry' is a loosely defined group of companies engaged in a wide variety of industrial sectors. It is therefore difficult to generalize about what makes some companies more transparent than others. Several factors may act in concert to encourage a company to fully and accurately disclose the nature of its business. Based on the difficulties in gathering data encountered by the SIPRI Arms Production Project, however, it is possible to make some general observations.

Ownership model

The SIPRI arms production database shows that there is a correlation between arms industry transparency (as defined in this section) and company ownership. Shareholder-owned companies are accountable to their investors, while family- or government-owned companies are not. This may partly account for the low level of transparency in Russia, as all but one of the major arms-producing companies (Irkut) are government owned. Annual reports are produced primarily for shareholders, and government-owned companies are obliged only to report to their respective governments. Companies that are not publicly listed are also under no obligation to report their arms sales.

Shareholder-owned companies frequently come under pressure from their own investors to disclose the exact nature of their business. This may be the result of shareholder activism with political motives or simply of the demands of investors to be able to better assess the extent to which their company is dependent on arms production for revenue and profit. Requests can be made at shareholder meetings for disclosure of additional data not provided in annual company statements.[59]

Industry sector

There are many examples of publicly listed companies that do not fully and accurately describe their arms sales, however, so factors other than ownership model must also be relevant. One important factor is the type of work performed by the company. Companies that produce electronics may find it particularly difficult to distinguish sales that are for military purposes. High-tech military goods may have civilian applications, and there may be import-

[59] E.g., Boeing responded to a shareholder request for information on company arms sales as follows: 'Publication of such information would put Boeing at a disadvantage in its business, may breach contractual arrangements and would not be in the best interest of the Company or the majority of its shareholders.' Boeing Company, 'Proxy statement: annual meeting of shareholders, May 1, 2000', 21 Mar. 2000, URL <http://www.boeing.com/companyoffices/financial/finreports/annual/00proxy/1074t08.pdf>, 'Proposal 3, Shareholder Proposal on Foreign Military Contracts', p. 37. Another example is a 2004 shareholder proposal made to the Textron board of directors for a report that would include 'Categories of military equipment or components, including dual use items exported for the past three years, with as much statistical information as permissible'. Textron Inc., 'Proxy statement pursuant to Section 14(a) of the Securities Exchange Act of 1934', 19 Mar. 2004, URL <http://investor.textron.com/financials/edgar.cfm>, p. 35.

ant questions of commercial sensitivity regarding proprietary technologies in such products, as well as other competition considerations.

A second important factor is the problem of definition; in other words, the question of what actually constitutes a military product. For example, a company producing radio components for military applications may not consider these as arms sales.

The 'culture of transparency'

Table 9.7 shows that some countries have particularly low levels of transparency in comparison with other parts of the world. There may be several explanations for this. Countries with only a short experience of private enterprise, such as Russia, may require additional time before pressures from shareholders and the general public result in greater transparency at the enterprise level. Equally, efforts to attract investment may prompt Russian companies to provide more details about their arms sales.[60] A lack of financial information on Chinese arms-producing companies means that China is not included in the SIPRI top 100 list.

It may also be possible to draw the conclusion that governments in regions with a precarious security environment are less inclined to allow their arms-producing companies to release data on their arms sales. This is likely to be a factor that contributes to the low level of transparency in South Korea and Taiwan. In Israel the major arms-producing companies are government owned and do not produce publicly available annual reports with detailed information on their activities.

VII. Conclusions

Arms sales by the large arms-producing companies are increasing. This is primarily the result of rising arms procurement budgets in the USA but is also caused by the concentration in the arms industry. These two trends are interlinked since concentration activities are focused on those sectors where arms procurement is expanding. Among the top 100 companies the share of services companies is increasing, owing to the privatization of services that were formerly provided by the armed services. The concentration of the arms industry in the USA and Western Europe since the early 1990s has resulted in some very large companies, comparable in size to the national output of most developing countries and even exceeding many of them.

The pattern of US acquisitions in 2004 was heavily oriented towards strengthening capabilities in the sectors that are most relevant for military transformation and homeland security. The focus on new war-fighting capabilities is clearly reflected in the US acquisitions. A large proportion of the

[60] There is a growing trend towards producing annual financial statements among Russian companies seeking to attract investment. See, e.g., Iskyan, K., 'The mighty Red Army's IPO', *Slate*, 22 Mar. 2004, URL <http://fray.slate.msn.com/id/2097499/>.

acquired US companies are companies from outside the traditional arms industry which provide sought-after technological capabilities. Thus, these acquisitions contribute to a broader defence-industrial base rather than to further concentration of the industry.

In Europe, the military vehicles and military shipbuilding industries are still fragmented between many companies in several countries. Some initiatives were taken to consolidate the European military shipbuilding industry during 2004, and continued restructuring efforts can be expected in both these sectors during the next few years.

The war in Iraq has increased the share of the arms production industry held by services companies and has reinforced the focus on new military technologies. Transparency in the contracting process for work in Iraq is limited; what transparency there is depends on NGOs trying to compile information about the size and content of these contracts and about the companies that receive them.

Only limited information is available on company arms sales worldwide. This lack of data makes it difficult to establish a firm foundation for political and public discussion of issues relating to arms production and arms sales. Pressures on companies to report their arms sales are weak and current reporting relies entirely on voluntary disclosure of information by the companies themselves. Comprehensive, regular and standardized reporting can be ensured only through internationally harmonized legal requirements for companies to report.

Appendix 9A. The 100 largest arms-producing companies, 2003

EAMON SURRY and THE SIPRI ARMS INDUSTRY NETWORK*

I. Selection criteria and sources of data

Table 9A lists the world's 100 largest arms-producing companies (excluding China), ranked by their arms sales in 2003. The table contains information on the companies' arms sales in 2002 and 2003, and their total sales, profit and employment in 2003. It includes public and private companies, but excludes manufacturing or maintenance units of the armed services. Only companies with manufacturing activities in the field of military goods and services are listed, not holding or investment companies. Chinese companies are excluded because of the lack of data. Companies from other countries might also have been included at the lower end of the list had sufficient data been available.

Publicly available information on arms sales and other financial and employment data of the arms industry worldwide are limited. The sources of data for table 9A.1 include: company annual reports and Internet sites; a SIPRI questionnaire; and corporation news published in the business sections of newspapers, military journals and by Internet news services specializing in military matters. Press releases, marketing reports, government publications of prime contract awards and country surveys were also consulted. In the absence of data from these sources, estimates have been made by SIPRI. The scope of the data and the geographical coverage are largely determined by the availability of information. All data are continuously revised and updated and may change between different editions of the SIPRI Yearbook.

The source for the dollar exchange rates is the International Monetary Fund (IMF), as provided in its *International Financial Statistics*.

II. Definitions

Arms sales. Arms sales are defined by SIPRI as sales of military goods and services to military customers, including both sales for domestic procurement and sales for export. Military goods and services are those which are designed specifically for military purposes and the technologies related to such goods and services. They exclude sales of general-purpose goods (e.g., oil, electricity, office computers, cleaning services, uniforms and boots). They include all revenue related to the sale of military equipment, that is, not only for the manufacture but also for the research and

* Participants in the network for this yearbook were: Ken Epps (Project Ploughshares, Canada), Jean-Paul Hébert (Centre Interdisciplinaire de Recherches sur la Paix et d'Etudes Stratégiques, Paris), Reuven Pedatzur (Tel Aviv University), Giovanni Gasparini (Istituto Affari Internazionali, Rome), Gülay Günlük-Senesen (Istanbul University), Paul Dunne (University of the West of England, Bristol) and Julian Cooper (Centre for Russian and East European Studies, University of Birmingham).

development, maintenance, servicing and repair of the equipment. Sales related to post-war reconstruction are defined as arms sales if the contracts are awarded by a defence ministry. This definition serves as a guideline; in practice it is difficult to apply. Nor is there any good alternative, since no generally agreed standard definition of 'arms sales' exists. The data on arms sales in table 9A.1 often reflect only what each company considers to be the defence share of their total sales. The comparability of company arms sales in table 9A.1 is therefore limited.

Total sales, profit and employment. Data on total sales, profit and employment are for entire companies, not for arms-producing divisions alone. All data are for consolidated sales, including those of national and foreign subsidiaries. The profit data represent profit after taxes. Employment data are year-end figures, except for those companies which publish only a yearly average. All data are presented on the financial year basis reported by the company in its annual report.

III. Calculations

Arms sales are sometimes estimated by SIPRI. In some cases SIPRI uses the figure for the total sales of a 'defence' division, although the division may also have some, unspecified, civil sales. When the company does not report a sales figure for a defence division or similar entity, estimates can sometimes be made based on data on contract awards, information on the company's current arms production programmes and figures provided by company officials in media or other reports.

The data for arms sales are used as an approximation of the annual value of arms production. For most companies this is realistic. The main exception is shipbuilding companies. For these companies there is a significant discrepancy between the value of annual production and annual sales because of the long lead (production) time of ships and the low production run (number). Some shipbuilding companies provide estimates of the value of their annual production. These data are then used by SIPRI for those companies.

All data are collected in local currency and at current prices. For conversion from local currencies to US dollars, SIPRI uses the IMF annual average of market exchange rates. The data in table 9A.1 and most of the tables in chapter 9 are provided in current dollars. Changes between years in these data are difficult to interpret because the change in dollar values is made up of several components: the change in arms sales, the rate of inflation and, for sales conducted in local currency, fluctuations in the exchange rate. Sales on the international arms market are often conducted in dollars. Fluctuations in exchange rates then do not have an impact on the dollar values but affect instead the value in local currency. If the value of the dollar declines, then the company's revenue in local currency falls and, if its production inputs are paid for in local currency—which most often is the case—this has a negative impact on the company's profit margins. Calculations in constant dollar terms are difficult to interpret for the same reasons. Without knowing the relative shares of arms sales derived from domestic procurement and from arms exports, it is impossible to interpret the exact meaning and implications of the arms sales data. These data should therefore be used with caution. This is particularly true for countries with strongly fluctuating exchange rates.

Table 9A.1. The 100 largest arms-producing companies (excluding China), 2003

Figures in columns 6, 7, 8 and 10 are in US$ m., at current prices and exchange rates.

1	2	3	4	5	6	7	8	9	10	11
Rank[a]					Arms sales		Total sales	Column 6 as % of	Profit	Employment
2003	2002	Company (parent company)	Country/ region	Sector[b]	2003	2002	2003	column 8	2003	2003
1	2	Lockheed Martin[c]	USA	Ac El Mi Sp	24 910	18 870	31 824	*78*	1 053	130 000
2	1	Boeing[d]	USA	Ac El Mi Sp	24 370	22 170	50 485	*48*	718	157 000
3	4	Northrop Grumman[e]	USA	Ac El Mi SA/A Sh Sp	22 720	17 800	26 206	*87*	808	122 600
4	5	BAE Systems[f]	UK	A Ac El Mi SA/A Sh	15 760	14 070	20 542	*77*	10	92 500
5	3	Raytheon	USA	El Mi	15 450	14 510	18 109	*85*	365	77 700
6	6	General Dynamics[g]	USA	A El MV Sh	13 100	9 820	16 617	*79*	1 004	67 600
7	7	Thales	France	El Mi SA/A	8 350	6 840	11 929	*70*	126	57 440
8	9	EADS[h]	Europe	Ac El Mi Sp	8 010	5 630	34 010	*24*	172	109 140
9	8	United Technologies, UTC	USA	El Eng	6 210	5 640	31 034	*20*	2 361	203 300
10	10	Finmeccanica	Italy	A Ac El MV Mi SA/A	5 290	3 720	9 339	*57*	225	46 860
11	11	L-3 Communications[i]	USA	El	4 480	3 020	5 061	*89*	278	38 700
12	66	Halliburton[j]	USA	Comp (Oth)	3 920	480	16 271	*24*	–820	101 380
13	16	Computer Sciences Corp., CSC[k]	USA	Comp (Oth)	3 780	1 980	14 768	*26*	519	90 000
14	12	SAIC	USA	Comp (Oth)	3 700	3 000	6 720	*55*	351	42 700
S	S	Pratt & Whitney (UTC)	USA	Eng	3 030	2 490	7 505	*40*	. .	. .
15	13	Rolls Royce	UK	Eng	2 970	2 850	9 224	*32*	190	35 210
S	S	MBDA (BAE Systems, UK/ EADS, Europe/ Finmeccanica, Italy)[l]	Europe	Mi	2 710	1 690	2 710	*100*	. .	10 000
16	14	Mitsubishi Heavy Industries[m]	Japan	Ac MV Mi Sh	2 430	2 780	20 472	*12*	187	59 949
17	15	General Electric	USA	Eng	2 400	2 200	134 187	*2*	15 002	305 000

18	17	Honeywell International	USA	El	2 270	1 830	23 103	*10*	1 324	108 000
S	S	KBR (Halliburton)[j]	USA	Comp (Oth)	2 170	480	9 276	*23*	–36	60 000
19	19	United Defense, UD[n]	USA	MV	2 050	1 730	2 050	*100*	141	7 300
20	18	GKN	UK	Ac	2 020	1 800	7 492	*27*	165	35 480
21	23	DCN[o]	France	Sh	1 870	1 370	1 870	*100*	46	12 780
22	30	Groupe Dassault Aviation	France	Ac	1 810	1 140	3 722	*49*	333	8 860
23	20	Rheinmetall	Germany	A El MV SA/A	1 810	1 580	5 923	*31*	–97	20 890
S	S	Rheinmetall DeTec (Rheinmetall)	Germany	A El MV SA/A	1 810	1 580	1 810	*100*	. .	. .
24	21	ITT Industries	USA	El	1 790	1 510	5 627	*32*	391	39 000
25	29	Groupe SNECMA	France	Eng	1 750	1 160	7 258	*24*	205	39 700
26	24	Saab	Sweden	Ac El Mi	1 700	1 310	2 133	*80*	92	13 320
S	–	Dyncorp (CSC)[p]	USA	Comp (Oth)	1 660	1 359	. .	. .	. .	14 000
27	32	CEA	France	Oth	1 540	1 100	3 175	*49*	–168	15 040
S	–	Brown & Root Services (Halliburton)[j]	USA	Comp (Oth)	1 540	. .	. .	. .	. .	. .
28	26	ATK	USA	SA/A	1 460	1 250	2 366	*62*	162	13 000
29	35	Sukhoi[q r]	Russia	Ac	1 420	960	1 500	*95*	. .	35 000
30	22	Textron	USA	Ac El Eng MV	1 400	1 390	9 859	*14*	259	43 000
31	41	Kawasaki Heavy Industries[m]	Japan	Ac Eng Mi Sh	1 370	880	10 008	*14*	55	29 310
32	34	Goodrich	USA	Comp (Ac)	1 320	1 020	4 383	*30*	100	20 000
33	25	Israel Aircraft Industries	Israel	Ac El Mi	1 310	1 260	1 868	*70*	15	14 350
34	31	Rockwell Collins	USA	El	1 270	1 120	2 542	*50*	258	14 500
35	28	Ordnance Factories[s]	India	A SA/A	1 210	1 180	1 426	*85*	. .	130 000
36	36	Harris	USA	El	1 170	960	2 093	*56*	60	10 300
37	37	ThyssenKrupp, TK	Germany	Sh	1 110	950	40 787	*3*	578	190 100
S	S	ThyssenKrupp Werften (TK)	Germany	Sh	1 110	950	6 153	*18*	. .	. .
38	33	Smiths	UK	El	1 100	1 100	4 296	*26*	183	32 300
39	38	QinetiQ[t]	UK	Comp (Oth)	1 090	930	1 300	*84*	64	9 000
40	45	Titan[u]	USA	Comp (Oth)	1 010	730	1 775	*57*	29	11 500
41	53	DRS Technologies[v]	USA	El	940	610	1 001	*94*	45	5 800
42	39	DaimlerChrysler, DC[w]	Germany	Eng	920	920	153 992	*1*	506	362 060

1	2	3	4	5	6	7	8	9	10	11
Rank[a]					Arms sales		Total	Column 6		
2003	2002	Company (parent company)	Country/ region	Sector[b]	2003	2002	sales 2003	as % of column 8	Profit 2003	Employment 2003
43	50	Anteon[x]	USA	Comp (Oth)	920	640	1 042	*88*	36	7 600
44	42	Elbit Systems	Israel	El	900	860	900	*100*	46	5 200
45	43	Singapore Technologies, ST	Singap.	Ac El MV SA/A Sh	890	830	7 290	*12*	58	. .
S	S	ST Engineering (ST)	Singap.	Ac El MV SA/A Sh	890	830	1 618	*55*	187	11 750
46	49	VT Group	UK	Sh	840	660	1 096	*77*	25	8 640
47	51	Groupe SAGEM[y]	France	El	830	620	3 590	*23*	135	14 680
48	48	SEPI[z]	Spain	Sh	830	700	2 370	*35*	. .	. .
49	44	GIAT Industries	France	A MV SA/A	820	730	820	*100*	–722	6 000
50	54	Mitsubishi Electric[m]	Japan	El Mi	820	590	28 548	*3*	387	98 990
51	46	Rafael	Israel	Ac Mi SA/A Oth	790	720	830	*95*	30	5 000
52	27	URS Corporation	USA	Comp (El Oth)	720	. .	3 187	*23*	58	26 000
S	S	EG&G (URS Corporation)	USA	Comp (El Oth)	720	. .	928	*78*	. .	10 000
53	56	Krauss-Maffei Wegmann	Germany	MV	710	570	710	*100*	. .	2 380
54	57	EDS[aa]	USA	Comp (Oth)	690	570	21 476	*3*	–1 698	132 000
55	60	Cobham	UK	Comp (Ac El)	680	540	1 360	*50*	30	8 990
56	59	Samsung[bb]	S. Korea	A El MV Mi Sh	670	550	. .	. .	. .	. .
57	55	Oshkosh Truck	USA	MV	660	590	1 926	*34*	76	6 100
58	62	Hindustan Aeronautics	India	Ac Mi	650	510	816	*80*	129	. .
59	74	ManTech International[cc]	USA	Comp (Oth)	640	430	702	*91*	35	5 000
60	61	Diehl	Germany	Mi SA/A	630	510	1 751	*36*	. .	10 730
61	67	RUAG	Switzerl.	A Ac Eng SA/A	620	470	907	*68*	19	5 670
62	72	Babcock International Group	UK	Sh	620	440	739	*84*	19	6 540
63	52	Korea Aerospace Industries[dd]	S. Korea	Ac	600	610	671	*89*	9	3 080
64	68	Fincantieri[ee]	Italy	Sh	570	460	2 644	*22*	102	9 490
65	85	Alvis	UK	MV Oth	570	340	570	*100*	33	2 800

66	69	Devonport Management Limited[ff]	UK	Sh	570	450	624	*92*	33	5 120
67	S	Avio[gg]	Italy	Eng	560	530	1 436	*39*	–8	4 800
68	64	Jacobs Engineering Group[hh]	USA	Comp (Oth)	560	490	4 615	*12*	128	21 100
69	73	CACI International	USA	Comp (Oth)	540	430	843	*64*	45	6 400
70	81	Engineered Support Systems	USA	El	540	380	573	*95*	43	2 950
S	S	Samsung Techwin (Samsung)	S. Korea	A El Eng MV	520	420	1 455	*36*	37	3 920
71	82	Indra	Spain	El	510	360	1 114	*46*	81	6 370
72	71	The Aerospace Corporation[ii]	USA	Comp (Oth)	510	450	581	*88*	. .	. .
S	S	US Marine Repair (UD)	USA	Comp (Sh)	510	240	545	*93*	. .	. .
73	79	NEC[m]	Japan	El	490	390	42 325	*1*	354	143 390
74	65	Aerokosmicheskoe Oborud.[r]	Russia	El	490	480	582	*84*	44	44 480
75	80	AM General Corporation[jj]	USA	MV	490	380	. .	. .	. .	. .
76	63	Irkut[r kk]	Russia	Ac	480	490	522	*92*	–14	16 346
77	76	Bharat Electronics	India	El	460	410	599	*77*	. .	. .
78	84	Israel Military Industries	Israel	A MV SA/A	460	350	514	*90*	. .	2 900
79	78	CAE[ll]	Canada	El	450	390	780	*58*	46	5 000
80	88	Denel	S. Africa	A Ac El MV Mi SA/A	450	320	587	*76*	–50	10 930
81	70	Stewart & Stevenson	USA	MV	450	450	1 176	*38*	–53	3 300
82	86	Kongsberg Gruppen	Norway	El Mi SA/A	430	330	939	*46*	18	4 180
83	75	Mitre[mm]	USA	Comp (Oth)	430	420	785	*55*	. .	. .
S	S	ADI (Transfield Group/ Thales, France)	Australia	El SA/A Sh	420	330	462	*92*	. .	2 600
84	93	EDO	USA	El	410	290	461	*89*	15	2 640
85	–	Ericsson	Sweden	El	400	110	14 561	*3*	–1	51 580
S	S	Ericsson Microwave (Ericsson)	Sweden	El	400	110	407	*97*	. .	1 990
86	87	Ufimskoe MPO[r]	Russia	Eng	390	320	407	*96*	90	20 660
S	S	MTU Aero Engines (DC)	Germany	Eng	390	430	2 144	*18*	. .	8 400
S	S	MTU Friedrichshafen (DC)	Germany	Eng	380	480	1 458	*26*	. .	6 680
87	94	Tenix	Australia	El SA/A Sh	370	280	571	*65*	. .	2 300
88	89	Ultra Electronics	UK	El	370	320	465	*80*	33	2 510

1	2	3	4	5	6	7	8	9	10	11
Rank[a]					Arms sales		Total	Column 6		
			Country/				sales	as % of	Profit	Employment
2003	2002	Company (parent company)	region	Sector[b]	2003	2002	2003	column 8	2003	2003
89	90	Cubic Corporation	USA	Comp (El Oth)	370	310	634	*58*	37	4 700
90	98	SMA	France	Comp (Ac)	360	230	360	*100*	4	. .
91	91	Moog	USA	Comp (El Mi)	360	300	755	*47*	43	4 740
92	–	Curtiss-Wright	USA	Comp (Ac)	350	210	746	*47*	52	4 660
93	77	Toshiba[m]	Japan	El Mi	340	400	48 127	*1*	249	161 000
94	99	MMPP Salyut[r]	Russia	Comp (Ac)	340	230	532	*64*	8	15 000
95	92	Komatsu[m]	Japan	MV SA/A	320	290	10 320	*3*	233	31 640
96	97	Uralvagonzavod[r]	Russia	MV	320	270	717	*44*	39	34 000
97	58	Ishikawajima-Harima HI[m]	Japan	Eng Sh	310	550	9 035	*3*	–331	8 140
98	83	Silicon Graphics[nn]	USA	Comp (Oth)	300	360	962	*31*	–130	3 710
S	S	Samsung Thales (Thales, France/ Samsung, South Korea)	S. Korea	El	300	260	300	*100*	15	1 250
99	100	Meggitt	UK	Oth	290	230	658	*45*	34	3 480
S	S	Hägglunds Vehicle (Alvis, UK)	Sweden	MV	290	150	290	*100*	. .	1 000
100	–	Groupe SNPE	France	A SA/A	280	200	885	*32*	46	5 310

Notes: This table includes companies supplying military goods and services to military customers. For definitions see the introduction to this appendix.

[a] Companies are ranked according to the value of their arms sales in 2003. Companies with the designation S in column 1 or 2 are subsidiaries. A dash (–) in column 2 indicates either that the company did not make arms sales in 2002 or that it did not rank among the 100 largest companies in 2002. Company names and structures are listed as they were on 31 Dec. 2003. Information about subsequent changes is provided in these footnotes. The 2002 ranks may differ from those published in the SIPRI Yearbook 2004 due to the continual revision of data, most often because of changes reported by the company itself and sometimes because of improved estimations. Major revisions are explained in these footnotes.

[b] Key to abbreviations: A = artillery, Ac = aircraft, El = electronics, Eng = engines, Mi = missiles, MV = military vehicles, SA/A = small arms/ammunition, Sh = ships, Sp = space and Oth = other. Comp (. . .) = components, services or anything less than final systems in the sectors within the parentheses; it is used only for companies that do not produce final systems.

[c] Data for Lockheed Martin arms sales include management fees from the US Department of Energy for the management of nuclear weapons programmes.

[d] Data for Boeing arms sales are for the Total Integrated Defense Systems unit, excluding the sales of the largely civilian Launch and Orbital Systems unit. Beginning in 2003 Boeing changed the way in which they report their market segments.

[e] Northrop Grumman completed its acquisition of TRW Inc. on 11 Dec. 2002. They provided pro forma data in their 2002 annual report.

[f] Data for BAE Systems arms sales are for total non-commercial sales, although it is known that some elements in its defence divisions are civilian in nature, and that some elements in the commercial divisions are military in nature.

[g] Data for General Dynamics' arms sales include an estimate of $300 million for the arms sales of Veridian in the first seven months of the year. Veridan was acquired by General Dynamics in Aug. 2003.

[h] EADS (European Aeronautic Defence and Space Company) is 30.2% owned by DaimlerChrysler (Germany), 30.2% by Lagardère (France) together with French financial institutions and Sogepa (a French state holding company), and 5.5% by SEPI (a Spanish state holding company; see note *z*). EADS is registered in the Netherlands.

[i] Data for L-3 Communications' arms sales include $470 million for Vertex Aerospace, which was acquired by L-3 Communications in Dec. 2003.

[j] Arms sales data for Halliburton and its subsidiaries, KBR and Brown and Root Services, represent US Department of Defense (DOD) prime contracts awarded rather than arms sales. An uncertain share of these contracts is for military applications, and revenues received from the contracts may be spread out over several years. Some of the tasks performed under these contracts would usually be considered by SIPRI to be civilian in nature. The work done by these companies at times of war, however, presents particular definitional difficulties. See the section on sources and methods.

[k] Computer Sciences Corporation is a provider of IT services and products to defence ministries. Figures for arms sales are for revenues from the US DOD, an unknown share of which is for military applications. Computer Sciences Corporation acquired Dyncorp in March 2003 and agreed in Dec. 2004 to sell that company to Veritas Capital.

[l] MBDA was established in Dec. 2001 through the merger of Matra BAe Dynamics, EADS-Aérospatiale Matra Missiles and the missile activities of Alenia Marconi Systems. The company is 37.5% owned by BAE Systems, 37.5% by EADS and 25% by Finmeccanica.

[m] For Japanese companies figures in the arms sales column represent new military contracts rather than arms sales.

[n] The Carlyle Group exited their investment in United Defense in April 2004.

[o] Data for DCN are for sales revenue rather than value of production. In the SIPRI Yearbook 2004 data were for value of production.

[p] Dyncorp was acquired by Computer Sciences Corporation in March 2003. Veritas Capital subsequently agreed to acquire Dyncorp in Dec. 2004. Arms sales represent US DOD prime contracts awarded rather than arms sales.

[q] Data for Sukhoi are from the Centre for Analysis of Strategies and Technologies. In the SIPRI Yearbook 2004 data for Sukhoi were listed under KnAAPO.

[r] This is the second year that Russian companies have been integrated into the SIPRI list of arms-producing companies. There may be other companies that should be in the list, but insufficient data are available. The situation in the Russian arms industry is still very fluid, and company names are likely to change as they are restructured. For all companies except Sukhoi and Irkut, data for total sales and profits are from Expert RA, the Russian rating agency, while data for arms sales share estimates and employment are from the Centre for Analysis of Strategies and Technologies.

[s] Data for Ordnance Factories are based on the Indian Ministry of Defence Annual Report 2003–2004. In the SIPRI Yearbook 2004 an estimate of sales was made based on available total sales data for Apr.–Dec. 2002 and arms sales share for 2001.

[t] QinetiQ was created on 1 July 2001 out of a major part of the British Ministry of Defence's Defence Evaluation and Research Agency. In Feb. 2003 the British Government sold a 33.8% share in the company to the investment company the Carlyle Group, USA. The British government retained a 62.5% share.

[u] Titan is a provider of IT services and products to defence ministries. Figures for arms sales are for total sales to the US Air Force, Army and Navy, an unknown share of which is for military applications.

[v] DRS acquired Integrated Defense Technologies in the third quarter of 2003. DRS financial data include data for Integrated Defense Technologies only from 4 Nov. 2003 until the end of the DRS financial year on 31 Mar. 2004. Integrated Defense Technologies had approximate arms sales of $300 million in 2002.

[w] Data for DaimlerChrysler arms sales are for the arms-producing activities of MTU Aero Engines and MTU Friedrichshafen but exclude DaimlerChrysler's 30.1% share in EADS. The private equity firm Kohlberg Kravis Roberts & Co. agreed in Nov. 2003 to acquire MTU Aero Engines.

[x] Anteon is a provider of IT services and products to defence ministries. Figures for arms sales are for total sales to the US DOD, an unknown share of which is for military applications.

[y] Data for SAGEM's arms sales are based on the company's reported 'aeronautics and defence' sales, and exclude their primarily civilian 'security' sales.

[z] The state-owned holding company SEPI (Sociedad Estatal de Participaciones Industriales) is the owner of Spanish shipbuilder Izar. The military shipbuilding activities of Izar were transferred to a new company, 'New Izar', also fully owned by SEPI, on 31 Dec. 2004 (the new company is now known as Navantia). Arms sales data for 2002 are uncertain.

[aa] EDS is a provider of IT services and products to defence ministries. Figures for arms sales represent total sales to defence ministries, an unknown share of which is for military applications.

[bb] Data for Samsung arms sales are for the estimated arms sales of Samsung Techwin in addition to 50% of the sales of Samsung Thales.

[cc] ManTech International is a provider of IT services and products to defence ministries. Figures for arms sales are for total sales to departments of defense and intelligence agencies, an unknown share of which is for military applications.

[dd] Korea Aerospace Industries was established in 1999 through the consolidation of Samsung Aerospace, Daewoo Heavy Industries and Hyundai Space and Aircraft Company.

[ee] Fincantieri is owned by Fintecna, which was formed in Nov. 2002 from the Institute for Industrial Reconstruction, an Italian state holding company which had been in a process of liquidation since 2000.

[ff] Devonport Management Limited is owned by KBR, a subsidiary of Halliburton, USA.

[gg] FiatAvio was acquired in July 2003 by the Carlyle Group (70%) and Finmeccanica (30%) and renamed Avio SpA.

[hh] Data for Jacobs Engineering Group arms sales represent US DOD prime contracts awarded rather than arms sales.

[ii] The Aerospace Corporation operates a Federally Funded Research and Development Center for the US DOD.

[jj] Limited financial data are publicly available for AM General. The SIPRI estimate of arms sales is based on a three-year average of US DOD prime contract awards plus a rough estimate of their exports.

[kk] Irkut was partly privatized in Mar. 2004 when 23.3% of the company was sold on the Russian stock exchange. Irkut provides detailed information about the company on its website, and all data are from their own consolidated financial statements.

[ll] Data for CAE arms sales are the total sales of their 'military' and 'marine' divisions, although it is known that an element of their 'marine' division is civilian in nature.

[mm] Mitre operates three Federally Funded Research and Development Centers for the US DOD.

[nn] Silicon Graphics is a provider of IT services and products to defence ministries.

Appendix 9B. Table of acquisitions, 2004

EAMON SURRY

Table 9B.1 lists major acquisitions in the North American and West European arms industry that were announced or completed between 1 January and 31 December 2004. It is not an exhaustive list of all acquisition activity but gives a general overview of strategically significant and financially noteworthy transactions.

Table 9B.1. Major acquisitions in the North American and West European arms industry, 2004

Figures are in US$ m., at current prices.

Buyer company (country/region)	Acquired company (country)	Seller company (country)[a]	Deal value ($ m.)[b]
Within North America (between USA-based companies unless indicated otherwise)			
Anteon	Simulation Technologies	Privately held	15
Armor Holdings	Specialty Defense	. .	92
ATK	Mission Research Corp.	. .	215
ATK	PSI Group	Privately held	165
BAE Systems N. America[c]	Alphatech	. .	88
BAE Systems N. America[c]	Commercial Electronics Unit	Boeing	. .
BAE Systems N. America[c]	DigitalNet Holdings	. .	600
BAE Systems N. America[c]	Practical Imagineering	Privately held	8
BAE Systems N. America[c]	STI Government Systems	. .	27
Bell Helicopter	Acadian Composites	Petroleum Helicopters	. .
Boeing	Frontier Systems	Privately held	. .
CACI International	Defense and Intelligence Group	American Management Systems	415
CACI International	CMS Information Services	. .	. .
Carlyle Group	Standard Aero division of Dunlop Standard Aerospace (Canada)	Doughty Hanson (UK)	670
Carlyle Group	Stellex Aerostructures	Privately held	. .
DRS Technologies	Night Vision Equipment	Privately held	43
Curtiss-Wright	Everlube Products	Morgan Advanced Ceramics	6
Curtiss-Wright	GMBU Division	Flowserve Corp.	28
Curtiss-Wright	Primagraphics	. .	21
Curtiss-Wright	Synergy Microsystems	. .	49
General Dynamics	Spectrum Astro	Privately held	. .
General Dynamics	TriPoint Global Communications	Privately held	. .
Honeywell	Vindicator Technologies	. .	. .
ITT Industries	Remote Sensing Systems unit	Eastman Kodak	725
L-3 Communications	AVISYS	. .	8
L-3 Communications	BEAMHIT	. .	40

Buyer company (country/region)	Acquired company (country)	Seller company (country)[a]	Deal value ($ m.)[b]
L-3 Communications	Brashear	. .	36
L-3 Communications	Canadian navigation systems and space sensors system division business	Northrop Grumman	65
L-3 Communications	Cincinnati Electronics	CMC Electronics	172
L-3 Communications	DP Associates	. .	. .
L-3 Communications	Electron Dynamic Devices	Boeing	. .
L-3 Communications	Marine controls division (Canada)	CAE (Canada)	225
L-3 Communications	Propulsion systems unit	General Dynamics	185
L-3 Communications	Raytheon Commercial Infrared	Raytheon	42
Lockheed Martin	Sippican Holdings	. .	. .
MacAndrews & Forbes[d]	AM General	Renco Group	. .
Pratt & Whitney	CTA	Privately held	. .
Raytheon	Photon Research Associates	Privately held	. .
SAGEM Avionics	ARNAV Systems	. .	. .
SAIC	Aquidneck Management	. .	. .
SAIC	Presearch	. .	. .
SAIC	ProcureNet Holdings	. .	. .
SAIC	Trios Associates	. .	. .
Sikorsky Aircraft Corp.	Schweizer Aircraft Corp.	Privately held	. .
Teledyne Wireless	Defence electronics business	Celeritek	33
Teledyne	Reynolds Technologies	. .	42
Triumph Group	Rolls-Royce Gear Systems	Rolls-Royce N. America	36
United Defense	Cercom	. .	.
United Defense	Kaiser Compositek	. .	9
United Defense	US Navy Ship Repair unit	Honolulu Shipyards	16
Veritas Capital	Dyncorp International	Computer Sciences Corp.	850
Within Western Europe			
BAE Systems (UK)	Alvis (UK)	. .	651
BAE Systems (UK)[e]	Aerosystems International (UK)	GKN (UK)	27
Cobham (UK)	Spectronic (Denmark)		37
Finmeccanica (Italy)[f]	AgustaWestland (Europe)	GKN (UK)	1 978
QinetiQ (UK)	HVR Consulting Services (UK)	. .	17
Thales (France)	Arisem (France)	. .	. .
ThyssenKrupp (Germany)	HDW (Germany)	One Equity Partners (USA)	286
Zodiac (France)	Evac (Finland)	Sanitec (Finland)	73
Transatlantic: West European acquisitions of companies based in Canada and the USA			
Cobham (UK)	REMEC Defense and Space (USA)	REMEC (USA)	260
Cobham (UK)	DTC Communications (USA)	. .	48
EADS (Europe)	Racal Instruments (USA)	. .	130

Buyer company (country/region)	Acquired company (country)	Seller company (country)[a]	Deal value ($ m.)[b]
Meggitt (UK)	Dunlop Aerospace Design and Manufacturing division (Canada)	Doughty Hanson (UK)	747
QinetiQ (UK)	Foster-Miller (USA)	. .	163
QinetiQ (UK)	Westar Aerospace & Defense Group (USA)	. .	130
Smiths Group (UK)	Cyrano Sciences (USA)	. .	15
Smiths Group (UK)	Dynamic Gunver (USA)	Privately held	102
Smiths Group (UK)	Integrated Aerospace (USA)	Privately held	110
Smiths Group (UK)	SensIR Technologies (USA)	Privately held	75
Smiths Group (UK)	Trak Communications (USA)	Veritas Capital (USA)	112
Ultra Electronics (UK)	DNE Systems (USA)	Alpine Group (USA)	40
Volvo Aero (Sweden)	Aero-Craft (USA)	. .	. .
Transatlantic: US and Canadian acquisitions of Western Europe-based companies			
Ceradyne (USA)	Wacker Ceramics (Germany)	. .	136
J. F. Lehman & Co. (USA)	Thales Acoustics (UK)	Thales (France)	. .
Lockheed Martin (USA)	STASYS Limited (UK)	. .	. .
MSA (USA)	Sordin (Sweden)	. .	. .

[a] '. .' in the 'seller company' column indicates that the ownership of the acquired company was not specified in the company press release. The company may have been either privately held or publicly listed.

[b] In cases where the deal value was not available in US dollars, currency conversion was made using the International Monetary Fund average exchange rate for the calendar month in which the transaction was made. Companies do not always disclose the value of transactions.

[c] BAE Systems North America is a wholly owned subsidiary of BAE Systems (UK).

[d] A new joint venture between MacAndrews & Forbes and the Renco Group was created to own AM General.

[e] BAE Systems increased its holding in Aerosystems International from 50% to 100%.

[f] Finmeccanica acquired GKN's 50% stake in their joint venture company AgustaWestland.

Source: The SIPRI arms industry files on mergers and acquisitions.

10. International arms transfers

SIEMON T. WEZEMAN and MARK BROMLEY*

I. Introduction

The SIPRI Arms Transfers Project identifies trends in international *transfers* of major conventional weapons using the SIPRI trend indicator.[1] Data for 2004 show an increase in the volume of global arms transfers over 2003. However, using five-year moving averages, the trend is one of decline between 2000 and 2004, after a slight upward trend in the late 1990s (see figure 10.1).[2]

Section II discusses the three main suppliers and the main recipients of major conventional weapons in 2000–2004. It addresses some of the major arms transfer-related issues that were important for Russia and the United States in 2004. For Russia, this includes concerns about retaining and finding markets. For the USA, relations with European clients and Taiwan and the 'global war on terrorism' are highlighted. Section III discusses international arms embargoes, including the European Union (EU) embargo on China. Section IV reports on developments in 2004 in national and international transparency in arms transfers, and section V presents the conclusions. Appendix 10A contains tables showing the volume of transfers of major conventional weapons, by recipients and suppliers, for 2000–2004. Appendix 10B lists details of the equipment that was delivered and received. Appendix 10C outlines the sources and methods used to compile the arms transfers data.

II. The suppliers and recipients

There have been few significant changes in the ranking of the major suppliers in the past five years. The biggest change is that Russia is the largest exporter in the period 2000–2004, replacing the USA, which was the largest exporter in

[1] SIPRI data on arms *transfers* refer to actual deliveries of major conventional weapons. To permit comparison between the data on deliveries of different weapons and identification of general trends, SIPRI uses a *trend-indicator value*. The SIPRI values are therefore only an indicator of the volume of international arms transfers and not of the actual financial values of such transfers. Thus they are not comparable to economic statistics such as gross domestic product or export/import figures. The method used in calculating the trend-indicator value is described in appendix 10C. A more extensive description of the methodology used, including a list of sources, is available on the project Internet site, URL <http://www.sipri.org/contents/armstrad/atmethods.html>. The figures may differ from those given in previous editions of the SIPRI Yearbook; the SIPRI arms transfers database is constantly updated as new data become available, and the trend-indicator values are revised each year.

[2] Five-year moving averages are a more stable measure of the trend in arms transfers than often erratic year-to-year figures.

* SIPRI intern Johan Björkman assisted with the preparation of this chapter.

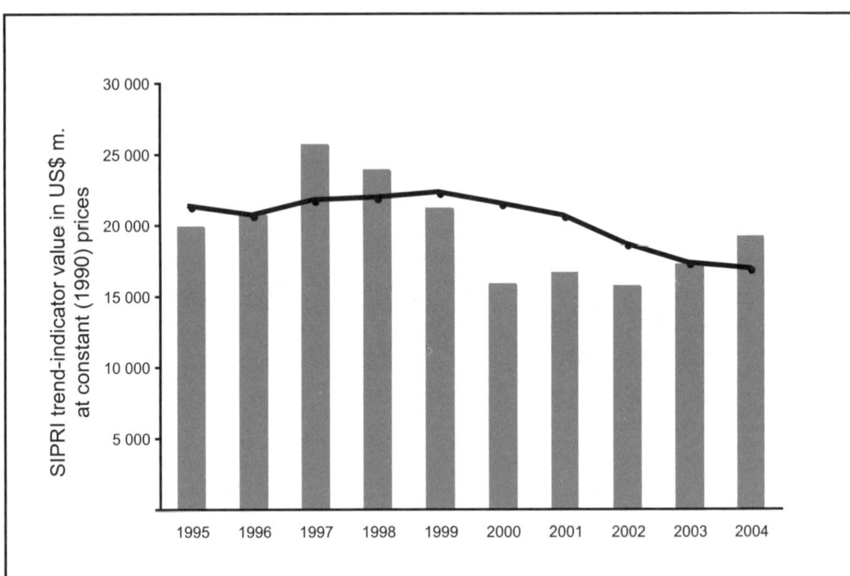

Figure 10.1. The trend in international transfers of major conventional weapons, 1995–2004

Note: The histogram shows annual totals and the line graph denotes the five-year moving average. Five-year averages are plotted at the last year of each five-year period.

the period 1999–2003. In order of size, Russia, the USA, France, Germany and the United Kingdom were the five largest suppliers of major conventional weapons in the period 2000–2004, together accounting for 81 per cent of all transfers (see table 10.1).

Russia

Russia was the largest exporter of major conventional weapons in the period 2000–2004, accounting for 32 per cent of transfers, up from second place in 1999–2003. The high level of Russian exports, measured using SIPRI trend-indicator values, is mainly the result of exports of combat aircraft and ships. In both these categories Russia exported more units in the period 2000–2004 than any other exporter, and the exported equipment was usually from new production. In general, Russia is lagging behind, in comparison with the USA and Western Europe, in the development of new generations of weapons. However, Russian arms are competitive in terms of price and often in terms of performance.[3]

Until recently, there was widespread optimism in the Russian Government and among industry officials about the future of Russian arms exports. How-

[3] E.g., the Indian Su-30 combat aircraft displayed a surprising superiority over US F-15C aircraft in an Indian–US exercise in 2004. 'Die Su-30 ist ein Exportschlager' [The Su-30 is an export success], *Soldat und Technik*, July 2004, p. 60.

ever, there are indications that a peak may have been reached.[4] Sergei Chemezov, the head of Rosoboronexport, Russia's main export agency, announced in July 2004 that, while the sales target of $4.1 billion for 2004 would be met, there would be no repeat of the record $5.1 billion volume of sales in 2003.[5] In November 2004 the head of the defence industry department of the Ministry for Economic Development and Trade, Yuri Koptev, said that the 2003 export results were unlikely to be repeated in the foreseeable future.[6] These predictions proved slightly premature when Chemezov announced in early 2005 that Russian exports for 2004 amounted to $5.7 billion. However, he acknowledged that a limit had been reached, that Russia is selling equipment that was developed in the 1970s and 1980s and for which there is no funding for development, and that Russia cannot offer 'modern military hardware'.[7]

According to a Russian source, the reasons behind Russia's impending decline in exports are the fact that China and India purchase fewer of the most expensive weapon systems—aircraft and ships—which now account for over half of Russian exports, and Russia's lack of any notable successes in selling such weapons on markets in South-East Asia and the Middle East.[8]

Russia's competitiveness is not helped by the fact that the quality of Russian weapons is lower than that of Western systems. Only about 1 per cent of Russian arms producers meet the international quality standard ISO 9000—the common standard for Western producers. Complaints from customers about the quality of Russian weapons have increased by '20 times' over the past 'several years'.[9]

In 2004 there were further signs of a Russian consolidation of arms producers in order to enable them to compete better on the export market.[10] Russian companies are reportedly joining forces, for example, to fulfil India's requirement for 125 combat aircraft—where Sukhoi and RSK-MiG formed a consortium for a joint bid.[11] RSK-MiG Director Valeriy Toryanin had earlier rejected a merger with Sukhoi. He argued that Sukhoi aircraft were too large and therefore too expensive for most buyers and that MiG would have to develop a light combat aircraft to compete with designs from China, India, the USA and Europe. Failure to do so could mean that Russia would lose up to 75 per cent of its aircraft export market after 2010. He also rejected cooperation with non-Russian companies on the grounds that MiG still had a techno-

[4] Russian optimism was not always shared by non-Russian analysts. See Hagelin, B., Bromley, M. and Wezeman, S., 'International arms transfers', *SIPRI Yearbook 2004: Armaments, Disarmament and International Security* (Oxford University Press: Oxford, 2004), pp. 453–54; and Cooper, J., 'The arms industries of the Russian Federation, Ukraine and Belarus', *SIPRI Yearbook 2004*, pp. 431–46.

[5] Nikolsky, A., 'Bureaucrats are to blame', *Vedomosti*, 7 July 2004, p. A2. These data are in US dollars not SIPRI trend-indicator values.

[6] Novosti, 'Russia's arms export earnings will decline', 5 Nov. 2004, URL <http://en.rian.ru/rian/index.cfm?prd_id=160&msg_id=5053751&startrow=1&date=2004-11-05&doalert=0>.

[7] TASS, 'Russia's Rosoberoneksport arms sales reach limit', 9 Feb. 2005.

[8] Novosti (note 6).

[9] Even complaints from the Russian armed forces have increased tenfold. 'Quality of Russian weapons deteriorating', *Moscow News*, 6 Sep. 2004, URL <http://www.mosnews.com/news/2004/06/09/weapons.shtml>.

[10] On developments before 2004 see Cooper (note 4).

[11] 'India to replace MiG-21s', *Asian Defence Journal*, Mar. 2004, p. 45.

Table 10.1. Transfers of major conventional weapons from the 10 largest suppliers to the 38 largest recipients, 2000–2004

Figures are trend-indicator values expressed in US$ m. at constant (1990) prices. Figures may not add up because of the conventions of rounding.

	Suppliers											
Recipient	Russia	USA	France	Germany	UK	Ukraine	Canada	China	Sweden	Israel	Other	Total
Africa	**2 671**	**174**	**178**	**22**	**10**	**608**	–	**80**	–	**17**	**1 370**	**5 130**
Algeria	1 064	89	–	–	–	130	–	33	–	–	263	1 579
Ethiopia	427	–	–	–	–	30	–	–	–	–	43	500
Sudan	549	–	–	–	–	–	–	–	–	–	26	575
Other	631	85	178	22	10	448	–	47	–	17	1 038	2 476
Americas	**295**	**1 343**	**536**	**296**	**1 673**	**50**	**1 167**	–	**146**	**444**	**982**	**6 932**
Brazil	–	184	472	–	4	–	16	–	80	–	132	888
Canada	–	232	1	69	1 235	–	. .	–	–	–	138	1 675
Chile	–	32	32	–	210	–	–	–	–	64	166	504
Colombia	41	429	–	–	–	–	–	–	–	–	45	515
Mexico	97	217	–	–	–	–	9	–	16	168	103	610
USA	. .	–	–	–	206	50	1 128	–	12	155	209	1 760
Other	157	249	31	227	18	–	14	–	38	57	189	980
Asia	**20 170**	**5 903**	**1 402**	**736**	**516**	**758**	**31**	**964**	**280**	**452**	**2 361**	**33 573**
China	11 112	–	33	–	–	409	–	. .	–	36	87	11 677
India	6 649	40	303	88	65	173	–	–	–	179	1 029	8 526
Indonesia	272	–	125	98	78	–	–	–	–	–	89	662
Japan	–	953	6	–	–	–	–	–	–	–	13	975
Malaysia	101	16	19	165	113	–	–	–	12	–	271	697
Pakistan	180	113	510	–	–	–	–	900	20	–	295	2 018
Singapore	–	1 094	3	–	–	–	–	–	240	105	–	1 441
South Korea	116	1 680	400	253	150	–	–	–	–	19	137	2 755
Taiwan	–	1 562	–		–	–	–	–	–	9	–	1 571
Thailand	–	324	–	132	27	–	21	28	8	1	62	603
Other	1 740	121	3	–	83	176	10	36	–	103	378	2 648

Europe	**737**	**12 596**	**1 260**	**2 925**	**675**	**234**	**112**	**–**	**678**	**301**	**2 357**	**21 875**
Denmark	–	177	10	157	33	–	36	–	30	–	48	491
Finland	–	511	21	198	–	–	–	–	88	1	–	818
Germany	–	376	–	. .	83	–	–	–	19	22	75	575
Greece	443	3 004	492	372	59	60	40	–	136	–	657	5 263
Italy	–	1 529	41	6	15	–	–	–	2	–	–	1 594
Netherlands	–	685	2	168	–	–	–	–	–	–	10	865
Norway	–	208	12	–	65	–	–	–	120	–	101	506
Poland	3	347	–	506	–	–	–	–	61	1	218	1 136
Spain	–	593	118	155	46	–	2	–	5	–	67	986
Turkey	–	1 840	399	505	34	–	–	–	–	190	330	3 298
UK	–	2 806	–	462	. .	–	29	–	68	–	30	3 395
Other	291	520	165	396	340	174	5	–	149	87	821	2 948
Middle East	**3 057**	**4 905**	**2 966**	**725**	**996**	**472**	**195**	**393**	**–**	**–**	**807**	**14 517**
Egypt	–	2 581	1	152	–	30	–	249	–	–	90	3 103
Iran	1 678	–	–	–	–	150	–	54	–	–	38	1 920
Israel	–	1 108	–	571	–	–	–	–	–	. .	–	1 678
Jordan	–	218	12	–	499	23	–	–	–	–	99	851
Saudi Arabia	–	171	1 212	–	22	–	195	–	–	–	72	1 672
United Arab Emirates	163	404	1 591	–	158	229	–	–	–	–	36	2 581
Yemen	796	–	–	–	–	40	–	–	–	–	300	1 136
Other	420	423	150	2	318	–	1	90	–	–	172	1 577
Oceania	**–**	**1 012**	**23**	**180**	**581**	**–**	**189**	**–**	**143**	**45**	**209**	**2 382**
Australia	–	937	23	180	581	–	105	–	143	45	163	2 177
Other	–	75	–	–	–	–	84	–	–	–	46	205
Other[a]	**–**	**–**	**–**	**–**	**–**	**–**	**–**	**–**	**18**	**3**	**204**	**225**
Total	**26 925**	**25 930**	**6 358**	**4 878**	**4 450**	**2 118**	**1 693**	**1 436**	**1 290**	**1 258**	**8 155**	**84 491**

Note: The SIPRI data on arms transfers refer to actual deliveries of major conventional weapons. To permit comparison between the data on such deliveries and identification of general trends, SIPRI uses a *trend-indicator value*, which is an indicator of the volume of international arms transfers and not of the actual financial values of such transfers. Trend-indicator values are not comparable to economic statistics such as gross domestic product or export figures.

[a] Includes the UN and NATO (as organizations, not as combinations of all member states) and unknown recipients.

Source: SIPRI arms transfers database.

logical edge.[12] MiG is hopeful that it can continue to play a major role in the export of combat aircraft. However, it can only offer the new MiG-AT trainer aircraft or upgraded versions of MiG-29 and MiG-31 combat aircraft.[13] Its main domestic competitor, Sukhoi, exported about 140 aircraft in 2002–2004 and accounted for around 30 per cent of total Russian arms exports in the same period.[14]

In the event, in late 2004 the Russian Government replaced Toryanin with Alexey Federov, who is also the head of Irkut, the producer of most of Sukhoi's designs and the most successful arms exporter in Russia. The move is a step to consolidate Russian aircraft producers—and possibly even to merge them into one company.[15]

Russia is increasing its efforts to diversify beyond its traditional customer base, offering competitive prices or technology transfers at higher levels than the USA and some European competitors. Several Latin American countries, notably Brazil and Venezuela, have been targeted for sales of Russian combat aircraft.[16] Several Russian companies are involved in indigenous South Korean development programmes, probably using the technology transfer issue as their main sales pitch. The Russian S-300PMU1 (SA-10d) surface-to-air missile (SAM) system is thought to be the basis of the South Korean KM-SAM system. Almaz, the Russian producer of the S-300, has received contracts worth $110 million for work on the radar and the command system for the $1.2 billion KM-SAM programme. Kolomna, another Russian missile design company, has been involved in the South Korean KP-SAM portable SAM project, providing components for the warhead in contracts worth $31 million.[17]

Russian relations with China: facing Chinese competition

In the five-year period 2000–2004, China was by far the largest recipient of major conventional weapons—accounting for 14 per cent of the global total. Russia has a near monopoly on transfers to China, supplying 95 per cent of China's imports, and China is Russia's most important market—accounting for 41 per cent of Russia's exports. This partly explains Russia's success as an exporter. There is little expectation that other suppliers will play an important role in the Chinese market in the near future (see below). However, there are also indications that Russia's position is changing. Russia's relations with China are moving in a direction that Russia tried to prevent in the early 1990s—Russia is being forced to give China access to its most advanced

[12] 'Interview [with Valeriy Toryanin]', *Jane's Defence Weekly*, 16 June 2004, p. 90.

[13] Ivanov, H., 'RSK MiG set to survive on its own', *Jane's Defence Weekly*, 5 May 2004, p. 18.

[14] 'Interview with Mikhail Pogosyan, general-director, Sukhoi company', *Asian Defence Journal*, Oct. 2003, p. 40.

[15] Ivanov, H. and Novichkov, N., 'Russia set to restructure aircraft industry', *Jane's Defence Weekly*, 6 Oct. 2004, pp. 23–25.

[16] 'Russia wants to swap fighters for Embraer jets', *Air Letter*, 20 Oct. 2004, p. 1; and 'Brazil denies Russian fighter jet-Embraer deal', *Air Letter*, 21 Oct. 2004, p. 5.

[17] Karniol, R., 'South Korea advances KM-SAM programme', *Jane's Defence Weekly*, 2 June 2004, p. 16.

weapon technologies. The original restrictions on the levels and types of technology that the Russian Government was willing to sell to China appear to have been relaxed. Russia is now selling systems to China that only a few years ago the Russian military establishment was hesitant to even discuss, for example the Klub-S (SS-N-27) anti-ship and land-attack cruise missile, an improved version of the Moskit (SS-N-22) anti-ship missile, and Tu-22M3 and Tu-95 strategic bomber aircraft.[18] In some cases, such as the Su-30MMK2 and the Su-30MKK3 combat aircraft, Russia has sold China more advanced weapons than those used by the Russian armed forces. With the possibility of more competition for the Chinese market from EU member states if the EU arms embargo is lifted (see below), the Russian Government may feel forced to authorize the export of even more sophisticated systems to China in order to retain its market share.[19]

There are also indications that China is learning from and copying imported Russian technology in order to establish a Chinese high-technology arms industry. China appears to be less interested in buying complete Russian systems than in buying Russian components for weapons developed in China. One source claims that Russia's current share of the technology transfers to China is about 30 per cent, as opposed to 70 per cent for transfers of complete systems.[20] However, China is seeking to increase its level of technology transfers to 70 per cent in its effort to become self-sufficient.[21] As an indication of how far Chinese arms production has developed, Russian arms industry sources have disclosed that China is close to mastering the complex skills required to build the AL-31 engine used in the Su-27 combat aircraft. If this is true, China will have used the Su-27 project to establish a total systems capability for advanced combat aircraft in little more than 10 years. Most observers had expected that this would take China much longer—especially in the case of tightly controlled key technologies such as engines. [22]

There are some hopes in Russia that this development may lead to joint Chinese–Russian weapon programmes and exports, including a fifth generation combat aircraft which Russian sources claim would cost over $12 billion to develop and which Russia would find difficult to finance alone.[23] However, indigenous Chinese developments based on Russian technology, with less

[18] Litovkin, D., 'Russia may be squeezed out of Chinese arms market', *Izvestiya*, 20 Jan. 2004, quoted in US–China Economic and Security Review Commission, '2004 report to Congress of the US–China Economic and Security Review Commission', 108th Congress, 2nd session, Washington, DC, June 2004, p. 193, URL <http://www.uscc.gov>, p. 199; and Novichkov, N., 'Military exercises with China to promote Russian bomber potential', *Jane's Defence Weekly*, 26 Jan. 2005, p. 17.

[19] US–China Economic and Security Review Commission (note 18), p. 199.

[20] Kogan, E. for the Jamestown Foundation, 'Russia–China aerospace cooperation', International Relations and Security Network: Security Watch, Center for Security Studies, Zurich, 6 Oct. 2004, URL <http://www.isn.ethz.ch/news/sw/details.cfm?ID=9869>.

[21] Kogan (note 20).

[22] Kogan (note 20).

[23] Jintao, J., 'Sukhoi completes delivery of fighter aircraft to China', *Jane's Defence Weekly*, 1 Sep. 2004, p. 15. This would be the equivalent of the US F-22 and F-35 aircraft.

input from Russian industry, seem more likely.[24] China has a long tradition of copying or using technology from weapons acquired from abroad. For example, the Chinese PL-11 (or FD-60), the first Chinese beyond-visual-range air-to-air missile (BVRAAM), is probably based heavily on the Italian Aspide missile delivered in the 1980s.[25]

Several recently developed Chinese weapons strongly resemble Russian weapons, some of the technology for which was reportedly transferred to China in recent years. A new Chinese infantry fighting vehicle (IFV), for example, has a turret with guns and missiles that are almost identical to that of the Russian BMP-3.[26] The turret, only recently developed in Russia and introduced in BMD-4 IFVs in 2004, appears to have been sold, along with advanced guided anti-tank missiles, to China for use on a Chinese-developed IFV.[27] In 2004 China unveiled a new conventionally powered submarine that combined the advanced hull design of the Russian Kilo Class submarine, several of which were acquired by China in the 1990s, with a Chinese fin and European technology.[28] The quality of Chinese radar systems has also improved dramatically in the past decade. Chinese airborne early-warning (AEW) radars, which were apparently developed in tandem with an order for A-50Eh airborne early-warning and control (AEW&C) aircraft from Russia, may be based on Russian technology.[29] Russian radar technology was probably also used to develop a radar for the Chinese indigenous J-10 combat aircraft. Pakistan has shown enough confidence in it to fit it in the new JF-17 combat aircraft. Previously, Pakistan had equipped combat aircraft imported from China with a non-Chinese radar.[30]

Notwithstanding these rapid developments in Chinese advanced weapons and components, Russia will still, at least in the short term, remain a major supplier of weapons to China. At least 10 major warships (8 Kilo Class submarines and 2 Sovremenny Class destroyers) and probably over 100 Su-27 and Su-30 combat aircraft are on order. In 2004 China signed an additional $980 million contract for eight advanced S-300PMU2 (SA-10e) SAM systems.[31] According to Russian sources, China is still dependent on imported technology in key areas such as aircraft radar, where China is believed to be

[24] 'Die Zusammenarbeit mit China' [Cooperation with China], *Österreichische Militärische Zeitschrift*, vol. 42, no. 2 (Mar./Apr. 2004), p. 225; and Nivokov, N., 'Growth in Russian arms exports', *Asia–Pacific Defence Reporter*, vol. 29, no. 3 (May 2003), p. 35.

[25] Hewson, R., 'Chinese missile may be for Pakistan's F-16s', *Jane's Defence Weekly*, 21 Apr. 2004, p. 15.

[26] Foss, C. F., 'China develops powerful new infantry fighting vehicle', *Jane's Defence Weekly*, 18 June 2003, p. 22.

[27] Novichkov, N., 'Russia acquires BMD-4', *Jane's Defence Weekly*, 6 Oct. 2004, p. 13; and Foss, C. F. (ed.), *Jane's Armour and Artillery 2004–2005* (Jane's Information Group: Coulsdon, 2004), p. 288.

[28] Chang, Y. and Scott, R., 'New submarine picture presents Chinese puzzle', *Jane's Defence Weekly*, 4 Aug. 2004, p. 8.

[29] Hewson, R. and Streetly, M., 'New "mainstay" AEW&C aircraft flying in China', *Jane's Defence Weekly*, 21 Apr. 2004, p. 7.

[30] 'JF-17 Thunder', *Air Forces Monthly*, no. 200 (Nov. 2004), p. 19.

[31] Pronina, L., 'Report: $900 m arms deal is close', *Moscow Times*, 20 Aug. 2004, URL <http://www.themoscowtimes.com/stories/2004/08/20/042-print.html>.

15 years behind, and aircraft engines.[32] However, in October 2004 Russian President Vladimir Putin failed to secure a guarantee from China that it would continue to buy Su-30 combat aircraft after the final deliveries are made under the existing contract, which ends in 2006.[33] In December 2004 there were reports that China had suggested an end to the licensed production of the older Su-27 version after delivery of 95 out of a planned 200 combat aircraft because it considered that the technology was becoming outdated.[34]

Russia's relations with India: facing growing international competition

In the period 2000–2004 India was the second largest recipient of major conventional weapons—accounting for 10 per cent of the global total. India is Russia's second most important arms buyer, accounting for 25 per cent of Russia's exports, and Russia is India's most important supplier—accounting for 78 per cent of India's imports in the period 2000–2004. In 2004 after 10 years of negotiations, India and Russia finally signed the contract for the sale of the Russian aircraft carrier *Admiral Gorshkov* for the price of its modernization, $675 million, and a $700 million contract for aircraft for the ship. India has probably also signed a lease with Russia worth $700 million for two nuclear-powered Akula Class submarines. A new Indian Maritime Doctrine, published in April 2004,[35] mentioned officially for the first time the need for a submarine-based Indian nuclear deterrent, and the Akula Class submarines are reportedly to form the sea-based part of the Indian nuclear triad. Russian expertise in and technology for nuclear-powered submarines, particularly propulsion technology, are reportedly helping India to produce a nuclear reactor for the Indian ATV submarine, which is under development and may also function as the sea-based part of its nuclear triad. However, because development of the Indian Sagarika nuclear-capable missile has been delayed by technical problems, it is unclear which missiles would be carried by the Akulas or the ATV.[36]

India, like China, has a policy of self-sufficiency in weapons but, unlike China, appears to be more interested in joint programmes and has shown an interest in developing such programmes with Russia. The Brahmos anti-ship missile, based on the Russian Yakhont, is now ready for operational use and is likely to be installed on all Indian surface warships. India is also interested in

[32] Hewson, R., 'China's Su-27 may fall short in capability', *Jane's Defence Weekly*, 17 Nov. 2004, p. 32.

[33] 'Russia wants to swap fighters for Embraer jets', *Air Letter*, 20 Oct. 2004, p. 1.

[34] *Air Forces Monthly*, no. 201 (Dec. 2004), p. 19. China's growing desire to assert its independence from Russia in the defence sector is mirrored to a certain extent in the civil sector, where the potential for cooperation in the areas of civil aviation and space has decreased substantially since China realized that Russia is not as reliable a partner or supplier of advanced technology as, e.g., European Airbus or US Boeing. Kogan (note 20).

[35] Bedi, R., 'A new doctrine for the navy', *Frontline*, vol. 21, no. 14 (3–16 July 2004), URL <http://www.flonnet.com/fl2114/stories/20040716002104600.htm>.

[36] Official Indian pronouncements on the ATV are ambiguous and even its existence is sometimes denied. At the same time, there are indications that it could carry nuclear weapons. Bedi, R., 'Russians help India to solve SSN snags', *Jane's Defence Weekly*, 26 May 2004, p. 16; and Bedi, R., 'India outlines vision of future nuclear navy', *Jane's Defence Weekly*, 23 June 2004, pp. 30–31.

cooperating on the R-172 long-range air-to-air missile, which is being developed in Russia. Some sources claim that development of the R-172 is already financially and technically supported by India.[37]

Russia faces serious competition in the Indian market, however. Unlike China, India has the option of acquiring weapons from almost all arms-producing countries. In 2004 Russia lost several large procurement competitions in India. India chose Israeli radar systems in a $1 billion order for three AEW aircraft, with Russia only marginally involved in modifying the aircraft, in preference to a complete Russian solution. A $1.5 billion order for 66 trainer aircraft was won by BAE Systems, the producer of the British Hawk, which was chosen over the Russian MiG-AT or Yak-130.[38] India's choice of indigenous, instead of Russian, steel for the production of the first Indian ADS aircraft carrier was reportedly linked to problems with maintaining a regular supply and to financial complications. Surprisingly, the final design chosen for the carrier is based not on the Russian Kuznetsov but on an Italian design.[39]

Indian relations with European suppliers and with the USA are improving. As a reaction to the problems that India encountered after the EU and the USA embargoed it in 1998 (many Indian weapon systems were grounded for lack of spare parts), India now insists on unrestricted support for the equipment it purchases from European countries.[40] The UK has agreed to allow such support for the Hawk trainer aircraft for a period of at least 25 years.[41] The USA now regards India as a strategic partner and is willing to allow the transfer of a wide range of military equipment. US engines have been ordered for the Tejas (formerly LCA) combat aircraft and for the Shivalik Class frigate, which was developed from a design supplied only recently by Russia. The US engines will also be used on the ADS aircraft carrier.[42] In 2003 the US company United Defense offered India self-propelled guns and since then the US Government has authorized the offer of Patriot air-defence systems, P-3 ASW aircraft and even F-16 combat aircraft.[43] India's relationship with Israel may also lead to a distancing from Russia. Russia has supplied almost all the missiles imported by India. However, India prefers Israel's Arrow ABM system to Russian systems, and the development of missiles for the Indian

[37] 'India, Russia in talks for a new missile', *Asian Defence Journal*, no. 193 (Apr. 2004), p. 89.

[38] 'Indian Phalcon deal signed' and 'India finally signs Hawk deal', *Air Forces Monthly*, no. 194 (May 2004), pp. 4 and 5, respectively.

[39] Interview with Admiral Arun Prakash, Indian Chief of Naval Staff, *Jane's Defence Weekly*, 3 Nov. 2004, p. 34.

[40] E.g., as part of a competition for 125 combat aircraft India is demanding access to the technology and the software source codes as well as guaranteed support for the aircraft. *Air Forces Monthly*, no. 202 (Jan. 2005), p. 17.

[41] Bedi, R., 'India closer to buying Hawks', *Jane's Defence Weekly*, 24 Mar. 2004, p. 6; and Hotten, R., 'Protests loom over Hawk deal with India', *The Times* (Internet edn), 20 Mar. 2004, URL <http://business.timesonline.co.uk/article/0,,8209-1044629,00.html>.

[42] Bedi, R., 'India's air defence ship gains new momentum', *Jane's Defence Weekly*, 11 Aug. 2004, p. 12.

[43] Bedi, R., 'Cost issue hampers Arjun turret project', *Jane's Defence Weekly*, 18 June 2003, p. 6; *Aviation Week & Space Technology*,13 Dec. 2004, p. 20; and 'India to replace MiG 21s', *Asian Defence Journal*, Mar. 2004, p. 45.

Navy is reportedly to be in cooperation with Israel, not with Russia.[44] Israel is rapidly becoming a major supplier of military equipment to India, second only to Russia.[45] India's ruling Congress Party announced a review of India's relationship with Israel at the end of 2004 but emphasized that it does not want to alter India's defence relationship with Israel.[46]

The United States

The USA was the second largest exporter of major conventional weapons in the period 2000–2004 with 31 per cent of total deliveries, calculated using the SIPRI trend-indicator values. There are indications that the USA will increase its arms exports, particularly because there is a large backlog of deliveries of combat aircraft. In 2004 US deliveries and discussions on future transfers were affected by the war on terrorism, Euro-Atlantic relations and China–Taiwan relations.

The global war on terrorism

The war on terrorism has led to few US arms transfers that would not otherwise have been made. Since September 2001 anti-terrorism has been cited by the US Government as the rationale for arms transfers to countries that it sees as key allies in the war on terrorism. Some of the most notable were transfers to Pakistan and Yemen, both of which were banned from receiving US weapons before September 2001. How far the war on terrorism is being used in political rhetoric to justify the supply of weapons remains unclear. Certainly, the sale to Pakistan of P-3C anti-submarine warfare (ASW) aircraft and F-16 combat aircraft does not seem appropriate for use in the war on terrorism.

US sales and proposed sales to Pakistan in 2004 included 6 C-130E transport aircraft, 8 P-3C ASW aircraft, over 100 helicopters and 2000 TOW-2 anti-tank missiles. The USA argued that these were all specifically for use in anti-terrorist operations along the border with Afghanistan where semi-autonomous groups are believed to support the remnants of the Afghan Taliban and al-Qaeda. The total value of these sales is over $1 billion.[47] In September 2004 the USA indicated that it might be willing to sell F-16 combat aircraft to Pakistan after many years of refusing such sales. The F-16s are presented as useful in fighting 'Islamist insurgents'.[48]

[44] Interview with Admiral Arun Prakash (note 39), p. 34; and Ben-David, A., 'More robust target to be used for Arrow test', *Jane's Defence Weekly*, 21 July 2004, p. 8.

[45] Blanche, E., 'Israel strengthens alliance with India', *Jane's Intelligence Review*, vol. 15, no. 10 (Oct. 2003), p. 4; and 'Sharon in Indien' [Sharon in India], *Österreichische Militärische Zeitschrift*, vol. 41, no. 6 (Nov./Dec. 2003), p. 808.

[46] Ben-David, A., 'Double jeopardy', *Jane's Defence Weekly*, 17 Nov. 2004, p. 20.

[47] US Department of Defense, Defense Security Cooperation Agency (DSCA), 'Pakistan: PHALANX close-in weapon systems', DSCA News Release, 16 Nov. 2004; and Bohari, F., 'Pakistan hopes FMS deal will herald F-16 sale', *Jane's Defence Weekly*, 24 Nov. 2004, p. 15.

[48] Baker, P., 'Bush: US to sell F-16s to Pakistan, reversal, decried by India, is coupled with fighter-jet promise to New Delhi', *Washington Post* (Internet edn), 26 Mar. 2005, p. A01, URL <http://www.

In August 2004 the USA lifted a 10-year ban on arms sales to Yemen to reward and support its efforts in fighting terrorism.[49] According to government officials in Yemen, the USA provided roughly $100 million to support the fight against terrorism, but most of this was in the form of spare parts and training.[50] However, Yemen's most recent weapon orders and acquisition plans are to be met by non-US systems, probably to avert any problems that a future US ban could bring.

Many of the USA's partners in the global war on terrorism had previously been much criticized by US officials and the US Congress for human rights violations. While scrutiny of the human rights situation seems to have been overtaken by anti-terrorism efforts, the debate over supporting the war on terrorism, on the one hand, and an emphasis on human rights, on the other, has not ended. Indonesia is regarded as a base for several 'terrorist' groups operating in Asia. However, US restrictions on arms transfers to Indonesia have not changed significantly since they were imposed in 1999 in reaction to Indonesian human rights violations in East Timor.[51] In mid-2004 an Indonesian court freed military officers who had been accused of abuses in East Timor in 1999. Coupled with a lack of Indonesian cooperation with the investigation into the murder in 2002 of two US teachers in Papua province, this led the USA to review its plans to lift its restrictions.[52] Indonesia seems to be reacting to the prolonged block on US exports by changing to other suppliers rather than changing its internal policies. Recent requirements have been met mainly by suppliers in Europe and by Russia. The Director General of Defence Strategy at the Indonesian Ministry of Defence, Major General Edi Sudrajat, announced that Indonesia would turn to 'Eastern European countries' for arms supplies because of the long-standing US military embargo.[53] There are also signs of an increased interest in supplies from China.[54]

US relations with Europe

Relations between the USA and Europe, one of the USA's traditional markets, were in some difficulty in 2004. The USA was heavily criticized for its

washingtonpost.com/wp-dyn/articles/A800-2005Mar25.html>; and Kucera, J., 'US offers to sell F-16s to Pakistan', *Jane's Defence Weekly*, 22 Sep. 2004, p. 4. The F-16 is also regarded by many as a prime candidate to carry Pakistan's nuclear weapons.

[49] Deutsche Presse-Agentur, 'US lifts ban on arms sales to Yemen', 1 Sep. 2004; and 'Sale of military gear to Yemen okd', *Los Angeles Times* (Internet edn), 2 Sep. 2004, URL <http://www.latimes.com/news/nationworld/world/la-fg-briefs2.5sep02,1,2597667,print.story>.

[50] Willems, P., 'US lifts ban on arms sales', *Yemen Times* (Internet edn) 5 Sep. 2004, URL <http://yementimes.com/article.shtml?i=770&p=front&a=4>.

[51] Some spare parts for transport aircraft were exempted after the tsunami catastrophe of late 2004 and Indonesia was in early 2005 allowed to join the US International Military Education and Training Program. US Department of State, Press Statement, 'Indonesia: Secretary Rice's decision to certify international military education and training', Washington, DC, 26 Feb. 2005, URL <http://www.state.gov/r/pa/prs/ps/2005/42752.htm >.

[52] 'Debate reignites over US aid to Indonesia', *Christian Science Monitor*, 25 Aug. 2004; and 'US–Indonesian military ties on hold', *Far Eastern Economic Review*, 30 Sep. 2004.

[53] 'Defense expo pays off for embargoed Indonesia', *Jakarta Post* (Internet edn), 29 Nov. 2004, URL <http://www.thejakartapost.com/misc/PrinterFriendly.asp>.

[54] Agence France-Press, 'China, Indonesia look for ways to boost military ties', 5 Nov. 2004.

unwillingness to approve technology transfers as part of arms sales and, more importantly, as part of cooperative weapon development programmes—and for erecting barriers to participation by European industry in joint programmes.[55]

This criticism was most pronounced in connection with the F-35 Joint Strike Fighter (JSF) combat aircraft—the major joint programme between the USA and European and other countries.[56] It is also the most expensive weapon project ever, with total development and acquisition costs of over $200 billion. Several non-US companies and governments have complained that their participation in the project is being frustrated. For instance, the Netherlands invested $800 million to become a level-two partner, and Dutch companies hope for orders worth $8–9 billion throughout the life of the programme. However, Dutch companies still have no clear information about the extent to which they will be included in the development and production of the JSF. At least one Dutch company has suggested that Lockheed Martin, the leading company in the programme, should involve them in other projects as compensation. However, this would contradict the idea that the JSF is not an offset programme but an open competition for components used in the aircraft. By mid-2004, Lockheed Martin projected that the Dutch industry's share of the programme would be $5.5 billion, considerably lower than the original estimate.[57] However, by the end of 2004 Lockheed Martin had reassured the Netherlands about its involvement—predicting an $11.2 billion share.[58] Apart from uncertainties about shares in the programme, European companies fear that they will be left out because of the US restrictions on information sharing. British and Italian companies complain that the USA is so restrictive that their involvement is rapidly becoming impossible.[59] Lockheed Martin rejects the criticism from Europe, claiming, for example, that Dutch industry participation is 'on or ahead of schedule'. However, commenting on Norway's criticism, Lockheed Martin said that everything was being done to ensure that Norwegian companies would be given their share, placing in doubt its 'best value' approach.[60]

[55] On the issue of technology transfers see Sköns, E., Bauer, S. and Surry, E., 'Arms production', *SIPRI Yearbook 2004* (note 4), section V; and appendix 17A in this volume.

[56] On the JSF programme and the 4 levels of 'membership' see Hagelin *et al.*, 'International arms transfers', *SIPRI Yearbook 2002: Armaments, Disarmament and International Security* (Oxford University Press: Oxford, 2002), pp. 395–400. Other projects, e.g., MEADS, have similar problems particularly with technology transfers. Wall, R., 'Sharing the wealth', *Aviation Week & Space Technology* (Internet edn), 28 Mar. 2004, URL <http://www.aviationnow.com/avnew/news/channel/awst_story.jsp?id=news/03294wha.xml>.

[57] Jannsen Lok, J., 'Netherlands set to win $5.5b in JSF business', *Jane's Defence Weekly*, 16 June 2004, p. 72.

[58] Janssen Lok, J., 'Dutch confident in JSF business volume', *Jane's Defence Weekly*, 26 Jan. 2005, p. 23. For an overview of the JSF Programme, and specifically Dutch participation, see the JSF section of the AMOK Internet site, URL <http://www.antenna.nl/amokmar>.

[59] Jannsen Lok, J., 'Frustration mounts among JSF partners', *Jane's Defence Weekly*, 24 Mar. 2004, pp. 16–17.

[60] Sirak, M., 'JSF partners are "on track" for long-term boom', *Jane's Defence Weekly*, 5 May 2004, p. 6.

Despite the fact that the JSF is meant to be a joint development programme, most of the sensitive technology will be US technology. There is still doubt about the level of technology transfers that the USA will be willing to allow, as well as about the exact specifications of the JSF export model.[61] The US Government is willing to ease some restrictions on technology transfer to 'US allies', but that willingness is not shared in Congress.[62] In 2004 non-US partners voiced concern on many occasions that they would receive an aircraft that they do not understand and cannot easily modify for their own needs, particularly if they do not have full access to the source codes for the software. Even Lockheed Martin admits that this is a serious problem.[63] It is not only the JSF that is troubled by US restrictions on software code transfers. In most modern weapon systems the software is more sophisticated than the hardware (or platform), and other possible US arms exports are facing the same problem.[64]

US relations with Taiwan

In its annual report to Congress on Chinese military strategy and modernization, the US Department of Defense (DOD) stated that 'Beijing's military modernization program is eroding the spatial, temporal, and distance challenges that historically inhibited using force against Taiwan'.[65] The report also stated that the China–Taiwan balance of power is shifting in China's favour.[66] There is serious concern in the USA that China, with the aid of massive imports of weapons and technology from Russia, and possibly also from the EU (see below), will for the first time be able to use force successfully against Taiwan.[67] Relations between China and Taiwan have not improved with the re-election in Taiwan of President Chen Shui-bian, who is in favour of clarifying Taiwan's status with a constitution and a declaration of independence, and with the passage in China in March 2005 of the anti-secession law.[68]

The USA is willing to provide Taiwan with advanced weapons and other military equipment, including submarines and air-defence systems, worth over $18 billion. The USA has also suggested to Taiwan that it should order a

[61] 'RAF may face JSF delays', *Air Forces Monthly*, vol. 194 (May 2004), p. 4; and Hobson, S. *et al.*, 'Not all JSF partners are reaping contract awards', *Jane's Defence Weekly*, 26 May 2004, p. 21.

[62] Alden, E., 'US threat to restrict arms sales to Europe', *Financial Times* (Internet edn), 13 May 2004, URL <http://news.ft.com/servlet/ContentServer?pagename=FT.com/StoryFT/FullStory&c=StoryFT&cid=1083180493141>.

[63] Spiegel, P., 'Aerial combat: why there are doubts for the US and its allies over this $200bn jet', *Financial Times*, 31 Jan. 2005, p. 13.

[64] 'Navy, Boeing pitch Super Hornet for potential international sales', *Inside the Navy*, 4 Oct. 2004, p. 1; and Sariibrahimoglu, L., 'Turkey to boost naval warfare capabilities', *Jane's Defence Weekly*, 8 Dec. 2004, p. 15.

[65] US Department of Defense, FY 2004 Report to Congress on PRC Military Power, Pursuant to the FY 2000 National Defense Authorization Act, May 2004, URL <http://www.defenselink.mil/pubs/d20040528PRC.pdf>

[66] US Department of Defense (note 65).

[67] Minnick, W., 'Identity crisis', Country briefing: Taiwan, *Jane's Defence Weekly*, 30 June 2004, p. 25.

[68] 'Taiwan rallies against China law', BBC News Online, 26 Mar. 2005, URL <http://news.bbc.co.uk/1/4382971.stm>.

radar-equipped reconnaissance satellite to monitor Chinese movements.[69] The USA has made clear that failure on the part of Taiwan to approve the weapon purchases would be interpreted as a weakening of Taipei's commitment to its own self-defence. This, in turn, could lead to a reassessment of US commitments to defend Taiwan. The weapon package has become a test of the readiness of Taiwan to budget for enough military equipment to hold out against a Chinese attack until US help could arrive.[70] In October 2004 the US DOD Deputy Undersecretary for Asian and Pacific Affairs, Richard Lawless, stated that if the deal was not approved by the end of the year it would 'be regarded as a signal . . . as [to] the attitude of the legislature toward the national defense of Taiwan' and that there would be 'serious repercussions'.[71]

Despite US pressure, agreement on the deal has been difficult to achieve. The Taiwanese Government has proposed a special $18 billion budget for the arms package but the Taiwanese Parliament opposes the deal.[72] Many commentators in Taiwan, including many retired military officers, warn that the plan risks forcing China and Taiwan into an arms race.[73] The Taiwanese Ministry of Defence stepped up its lobbying efforts, playing down the cost, but a decision on the plan was postponed until after the parliamentary elections in December 2004 when opposition lawmakers prevented it from being included in the pre-election parliamentary timetable.[74]

A US agreement to sell Taiwan eight conventionally powered submarines has led to specific problems related to price and, not least, the fact that the USA does not produce conventionally powered submarines. The price issue has led to heated debates in Taiwan. It is not clear how the price for the eight boats could be $12.3 billion, since similar submarines were recently sold by France and Germany for $300–450 million per boat—including support, training and armaments.[75] To some extent, the inflated price is related to Taiwanese insistence on an element of local construction to support the troubled state-owned China Shipbuilding Corporation. However, while this accounts for about $3 billion, it still leaves the submarines overpriced.[76]

Problems with finding a producer may well halt the whole plan. The USA has not produced a conventionally powered submarine since the 1950s and European submarine designers are unwilling to design or build the boats for

[69] Minnick, W., 'Challenge to update Taiwan's SIGNINT', *Jane's Intelligence Review*, vol. 16, no. 2 (Feb. 2004), p. 9.

[70] Cody, E., 'Politics puts hold on Taiwan arms purchase: $18.2 billion deal for US weapons stalled despite American warning of China threat', *Washington Post*, 10 Oct. 2004, p. 28.

[71] Cody (note 70).

[72] 'Taiwan debates US arms purchase', *Far Eastern Economic Review*, 15 July 2004, p. 11.

[73] 'Taiwan budget battle', *Defense News*, 27 Sep. 2004, p. 3; and Gluck, C., 'Arms plan sparks Taiwan protests', BBC News Online, 25 Sep. 2004, URL <http://news.bbc.co.uk/1/3689110.stm>.

[74] The Taiwanese Ministry of Defence argued *inter alia* that the price of the arms was equal to 1 cup of Taiwan's popular pearl, or bubble, tea per head of population over the next 15 years. Gluck, C., 'Arms plan sparks Taiwan protests', BBC News Online, 25 Sep. 2004, URL <http://news.bbc.co.uk/1/3689110.stm>; and 'Massive arms deal unlikely to be discussed before December polls', *China Post* (Internet edn), 3 Nov. 2004, URL <http://www.chinapost.com.tw/i_latestdetail.asp?id=23922>.

[75] See, e.g., transfers to Chile, Greece, South Korea and Malaysia in appendix 10B.

[76] 'Taiwan debates US arms purchase', *Far Eastern Economic Review*, 15 July 2004, p. 11; and 'Taiwan set to buy $15 b of US arms', *Air Letter*, 17 Sep. 2004, p. 5.

Taiwan either directly or indirectly through the USA. In 2004 the US company Northrop Grumman offered a version of the 1950s-vintage Barbel Class, the last conventionally powered submarine designed in the USA, which would have been modernized in cooperation with the German company HDW. However, the offer was not made with the support of the German Government.[77] A possible solution would be for the USA to procure second-hand submarines and modernize them. There was an interesting twist in 2004 when it was reported that the USA would support, and fund, Taiwan's procurement of submarines from Russia—of the same type that Russia is supplying to China.[78] It is not clear what the Russian reaction was, but it seems likely that any attempt by Russia to sell military equipment to Taiwan would lead to serious losses in the Chinese market.

Two indirectly related issues complicated the discussion even further. In the USA, Navy officers opposed the production of conventionally powered submarines. They argued that any production, even for export, would inevitably lead in future to the replacement of some orders for expensive nuclear-powered submarines, priced at up to $2.5 billion each, with a cheaper, conventionally powered alternative. Such a suggestion has already been made by some members of Congress and has possibly found support at the DOD.[79] Meanwhile, Israel has been lobbying for the USA to produce conventionally powered submarines for Taiwan in order to be able to buy such boats with US military aid.[80]

The European Union

After Russia and the USA, France, Germany and the UK are among the top five exporters of major conventional weapons for the five-year period 2000–2004. While decisions on arms exports are still made by national governments in each EU member state, the EU guidelines of 1991 and 1992 and, more importantly, the 1998 EU Code of Conduct on Arms Exports have gained in importance.[81] Pan-European factors and industrial integration are increasingly

[77] Minnick (note 67), p. 27; and Koch, A. and Minnick, W., 'Taiwan–USA ship deals stalled', *Jane's Defence Weekly*, 26 May 2004, p. 7.

[78] In 2001 there were reports of a possible deal involving Russian Kilo Class submarines, the same type of boats sold to China. Bishop, M. C., 'The troubles over sub deals are more political than financial', *Taipei Times* (Internet edn), 23 July 2004, p. 9, URL <http://www.taipeitimes.com/News/edit/archives/2004/07/23/2003180088>.

[79] 'US Navy nuclear advocates sabotage presidential move to aid Taiwan on submarines', *Defense & Foreign Affairs Daily*, 23 Sep. 2004; and Koch, A., 'Funding curb forces Virginia reality check', *Jane's Defence Weekly*, 26 Jan. 2005, p. 4.

[80] 'Israel lobbying for Taiwan submarine buy', Worldtribune.com, 30 Sep. 2004, URL <http://216.26.163.62/2004/ea_israel_09_28.html>.

[81] For the EU guidelines see URL <http://www.sipri.org/contents/expcon/eu_criteria.html>, and for the Code of Conduct see Council of the European Union, European Union Code of Conduct on Arms Exports, document 8675/2/98 Rev. 2, Brussels, 5 June 1998, URL <http://ue.eu.int/cms3_fo/showPage.asp?id=408&lang=en&mode=g>. For a discussion of the 1992 EU guidelines and the Code of Conduct see Bauer, S. and Bromley, M., *The European Code of Conduct on Arms Exports: Improving the Annual Report*, SIPRI Policy Paper no. 8 (SIPRI: Stockholm, Nov. 2004), URL <http://www.sipri.org/contents/publications/policy_papers.html>.

important to decision making on export licensing. The EU Code of Conduct is evolving and gaining in importance. The accession of 10 countries to the EU in 2004—including the Czech Republic, Poland and Slovakia, each of which has a significant arms industry—increases the importance of the EU as an arms exporter.[82] On the basis of the SIPRI trend-indicator values, the EU made 25 per cent of total deliveries in the period 2000–2004, making it the third largest exporter of major conventional weapons.[83]

The EU is also a major arms importer. For the period 2000–2004, the 25 countries that were EU members after 1 May 2004 accounted for 20 per cent of global imports, of which imports by EU members from non-EU suppliers accounted for 69 per cent. This picture may change because there is now a tendency for EU member states to consider European options first when looking to meet weapon requirements. This is partly because many larger European weapon systems are cooperative projects between several EU member states. European industries are still becoming more integrated, often making procurement from an EU company the equivalent of supporting domestic industry. US reluctance to share technology may increasingly become an important reason for EU member states to seek EU solutions for their weapon needs.

EU relations with Turkey

Several countries that aspire to join the EU have allowed this to influence their decisions on arms procurement. There are signs that Turkey, one of the larger arms markets globally and the fifth largest importer according to the SIPRI trend-indicator value for 2000–2004, is altering its arms procurement decisions as it moves towards EU membership. EU member states that had previously denied export licences to Turkey are now increasingly willing to grant them, and Turkey is increasingly leaning towards European suppliers in an attempt to smooth its path to membership. Turkey has declared that it would rather procure equipment from the EU than from the USA. Several large Turkish procurement projects (e.g., combat helicopters and tanks) where US equipment had been thought to be favoured were either cancelled or modified in 2004. However, this may also have been a tactic to persuade US companies to lower their prices or to persuade the US Government to allow more technology transfers.[84] Reports of a Turkish requirement for combat aircraft as 'gap-fillers' until the JSF is ready for delivery have been mentioned in this

[82] Cyprus, the Czech Republic, Estonia, Hungary, Latvia, Lithuania, Malta, Poland, Slovakia and Slovenia joined the EU on 1 May 2004. See chapter 1 in this volume.

[83] This figure includes the combined deliveries of all 25 EU member states for the period 1 Jan. 2000 to 31 Dec. 2004. Exports by the EU members states to states outside the EU account for 75% of EU deliveries.

[84] E.g., Turkey wanted the price of 12 SH-60B helicopters to be reduced from $440 million to $380–$400 million. At the same time, it made clear that its requirement for 46 transport helicopters would be opened to tender, instead of selecting the expected US S-70. Sariibrahimoglu, L., 'Price wars stall Seahawk procurement', *Jane's Defence Weekly*, 17 Nov. 2004, p. 14; Bekdil, B. and Enginsoy, U., 'Turkey leans towards Eurocopter for gunship deal', *Defense News*, 1 Nov. 2004, p. 14; and Bekdil, B., 'Tank deal awaits EU decision on Turk membership', *Defense News*, 1 Nov. 2004, p. 14.

context, although a recent decision to modernize the Turkish F-16 combat aircraft seems to have superseded any plans for such acquisitions.[85]

III. International arms embargoes

There were 23 international arms embargoes in force in 2004,[86] of which 8 were mandatory UN embargoes, 1 was a non-mandatory UN embargo and 14 were embargoes by smaller groups of states.[87] During the year, the UN embargo on Iraq was lifted and UN embargoes were established on Côte d'Ivoire and on entities and individuals in western Sudan.[88]

UN and other embargoes have not been successful at completely stopping the flow of arms to an embargoed country or group. Nor have they ended conflict in the embargoed areas. Supplier countries often make narrow interpretations of the equipment that is covered by an embargo. In other cases, the fact that embargoed countries have porous borders is misused, or the existence of the embargo is ignored for political or economic reasons. Many cases have come to light where individuals, either state employees or private business people, have been involved as sellers, brokers or smugglers of embargoed equipment.[89] These cases raise fundamental questions about the effectiveness of embargoes when enforcement is lacking.

UN embargoes

In mid-2004 a UN embargo on *Sudan* was suggested, primarily by the USA and EU member states, in reaction to atrocities carried out against non-Arab groups in the Darfur region by the Arab Janjaweed militia. The conflict has caused at least 70 000 deaths since 2003 and the Sudanese Government is accused of not acting to prevent the attacks as well as actively supporting the Janjaweed with weapons and even joining forces with them.[90] An arms embargo would be a strong political signal of disapproval but probably do

[85] Lake, J., 'Typhoon manoeuvres over Saudi Arabia', *Jane's Defence Weekly*, 16 June 2004, p. 8; Bekdil, B., 'Eurofighter group seeks market in Turkey', *Defense News*, 16 Sep. 2004; and Bekdil, B. and Enginsoy, U., 'Turkey picks F-16 upgrade over new fighters', *Defense News*, 25 Oct. 2004, p. 14.

[86] Defined here as an embargo established by an international organization or a group of states. Embargoes imposed by single states are not discussed in this chapter.

[87] These 14 include 11 EU embargoes and 1 OSCE embargo. For a full list of international arms embargoes see the SIPRI Arms Transfers Project page, URL <http://www.sipri.org/contents/armstrad/embargoes.html>.

[88] UN Security Council Resolution 1546, 8 June 2004, for Iraq; UN Security Council Resolution 1572, 15 Nov. 2004, for Côte d'Ivoire; and UN Security Council Resolution 1556, 30 July 2004, for Sudan.

[89] The UN usually establishes a sanctions committee to oversee the working of an embargo. Reports from these committees are available on the UN Internet site at URL <http://www.un.org/Docs/sc/committees/INTRO.htm>.

[90] MacKinnon, M., 'Russia's weapon sales to Sudan assailed', *Globe and Mail*, 12 Aug. 2004; and 'UN urges Darfur war crimes trials', BBC News Online, 1 Feb. 2005, URL <http://news.bbc.co.uk/2/4225353.stm>. See also chapter 2 in this volume.

little to stop the killing.[91] On 30 July the UN Security Council established an arms embargo against 'non-governmental entities and individuals, including the Janjaweed' operating in the Darfur region. The Security Council also gave the Sudanese Government 30 days to change its behaviour and threatened additional sanctions.[92] However, despite reports that the situation had not changed, the Security Council did not establish an embargo after the 30-day deadline had expired and, as of February 2005, no action had been taken. China and Russia, the two permanent members of the Security Council most opposed to sanctions against Sudan, stood to lose business, including arms sales, if an arms embargo had been established. Sudan reportedly notified Russia that it had $3 billion to spend on military hardware.[93] Days before the deadline expired, and with sanctions becoming a distinct possibility, Russia delivered 12 MiG-29 combat aircraft ahead of schedule—despite strong US protests.[94] Belarus, China and Ukraine also supplied Sudan with weapons in 2000–2004. The USA has voiced concern that some states, in particular China, might be tempted to sell weapons to Sudan in order to gain access to Sudan's oil reserves. China has a rapidly growing demand for energy and limited national oil reserves.[95]

Côte d'Ivoire became the target of a UN arms embargo on 15 November 2004. After agreements were reached on a ceasefire and a peace settlement in 2003, the Government of Côte d'Ivoire prepared for a resumption of hostilities *inter alia* by buying weapons.[96] The pattern of arms deliveries to Côte d'Ivoire is familiar from earlier conflicts in Africa—Central and East European countries, in this case Belarus and Bulgaria, and Israel, often acting through brokers, sell the hardware, which is delivered through neighbouring countries, in this case Guinea. The equipment is often operated by mercenaries, usually from the country that sold the weapons, who are under contract to small private military companies.[97] While the sales to Côte d'Ivoire were not illegal, they were clearly destabilizing. In November 2004 government aircraft, supplied by Belarus in 2003 and 2004, were used to attack French peacekeepers and rebels. This led within days to the implementation of a 13-month arms embargo by the UN Security Council.[98] The government remained defiant,

[91] The Janjaweed use mainly small arms and the reported attacks by Sudanese Government forces involve generally small numbers of simple low-tech weapons such as armed helicopters and transport aircraft used as bombers. Chamberlain, G., 'Sudanese forces "directly involved in slaughter of civilians"', *The Scotsman* (Internet edn), 4 Aug. 2004, URL <http://thescotsman.scotsman.com/international.cfm?id=891422004>.

[92] UN Security Council Resolution 1556, 30 July 2004.

[93] MacKinnon (note 90).

[94] 'RSK MiG delivers fighters to Sudan', *Jane's Defence Weekly*, 11 Aug. 2004, p. 17; and 'US protests against MiG sale to Sudan', *Jane's Defence Weekly*, 4 Aug. 2004, p. 11.

[95] Hill., J., 'US report sees 10-year window to engage China', *Jane's Intelligence Review*, vol. 16, no. 8 (Aug. 2004), p. 53.

[96] 'At war with the peacekeepers', *Africa Confidential*, 19 Nov. 2004, p. 1. See also chapter 2 in this volume; and, on private security companies, Holmqvist, C., *Private Security Companies: The Case for Regulation*, SIPRI Policy Paper no. 9 (SIPRI: Stockholm, 2005), URL <http://www.sipri.org/contents/publications/policy_papers.html>.

[97] 'At war with the peacekeepers', *Africa Confidential*, 19 Nov. 2004, p. 2.

[98] UN Security Council Resolution 1572 (note 88).

stating that new weapons, including combat aircraft, had been ordered. If this is true, the embargo was broken within days.[99]

The UN embargo on arms supplies and other military assistance against armed groups in *the Democratic Republic of the Congo* (DRC), established in July 2003, was further extended for a period of 12 months until August 2005.[100] A UN-appointed group of experts reported in July 2004 that the embargo had not stopped the flow of military supplies and assistance to several armed groups.[101] The report specifically singled out Rwanda as having violated the embargo. In the past, Rwanda has been actively involved with troops in the DRC and has made no secret of its support for any group opposed to the Interhamwe militias in the DRC. To make the embargo more effective, the report recommended the creation of a verification mechanism by *inter alia* the UN Mission in the DRC (MONUC) and the African Union (AU), and the improvement of MONUC's capacity to monitor and intercept supplies and assistance, which *inter alia* would require additional surveillance systems.[102] By the end of 2004, there was little evidence that any of these recommendations had been implemented or that MONUC's capacity to monitor borders has improved.[103]

On 8 June 2004 the UN Security Council modified the arms embargo on *Iraq*, which was imposed in August 1990 after the Iraqi invasion of Kuwait, to allow the delivery of arms and related matériel to the Iraqi Government and to the Multinational Force.[104] These modifications followed changes made in May 2003, which allowed deliveries for internal security and border protection. The embargo remains in force for supplies to other recipients such as rebel groups.[105]

In April the USA had announced that it was dropping its ban on lethal military equipment for the Iraqi military and authorized the delivery of such equipment for use by the new Iraqi military and police forces.[106] On 23 July the EU also lifted its arms embargo on Iraq.[107]

Since 1990, there have been many alleged and proven breaches of the Iraq embargo. After the US-led coalition occupied Iraq in March 2003 it was possible to gain access to documents and equipment that gave additional

[99] 'Ivory Coast Air Force wiped out', *Air Forces Monthly*, no. 202 (Jan. 2005), p. 5.

[100] UN Security Council Resolution 1552, 27 July 2004.

[101] United Nations, Letter dated 15 July 2004 from the Chairman of the Security Council Committee established pursuant to Resolution 1533 (2004) concerning the Democratic Republic of the Congo addressed to the President of the Security Council, conveying the report of the group of experts, UN document S/2004/551, 15 July 2004, URL <http://www.un.org/Docs/sc/committees/DRC/DRCselectedEng.htm>.

[102] United Nations (note 101). UN Security Council Resolution 1533 gives MONUC the mandate to enforce the embargo.

[103] See chapter 3 in this volume.

[104] Cottey, A. 'The Iraq war: the enduring controversies and challenges', *SIPRI Yearbook 2004* (note 4).

[105] UN Security Council Resolution 1546 (note 88).

[106] 'Amendment to the International Traffic in Arms Regulations: denial policy against Iraq', *Federal Register*, vol. 69, no. 69 (9 Apr. 2004), p. 18810.

[107] 'EU lifts Iraq weapons embargo', *Deutsche Welle*, 23 July 2004, URL <http://www.dw-world.de/dw/article/0,,1274516,00.html>.

insights into the way the embargo was circumvented by a host of countries, companies and individuals. The September 2004 Central Intelligence Agency (CIA) report by the Special Advisor to the Director of Central Intelligence on Iraq's weapons of mass destruction, Charles Duelfer, gives extensive details of where and how the sanctions failed.[108] Offered lucrative contracts by Iraq, a surprisingly large number of arms suppliers and government officials ignored the UN restrictions, despite the fact that Iraq was more closely watched than any other embargoed country at the time.[109] The report demonstrates the relative ease with which Iraq was able after 1990 to acquire weapons—including engines and other components for ballistic missiles, spare parts for tanks, air-surveillance and night-vision equipment and probably anti-tank missiles—from or with the assistance of the governments of Belarus, North Korea, Syria, Yemen, the former Yugoslavia and possibly Russia, as well as from corrupt government officials and private companies in Europe, Asia and the Middle East.[110] The list of suppliers in the report includes companies and private individuals from Bulgaria, Poland and Ukraine—countries that later sent troops to Iraq to join the US-led military coalition.[111] The smuggled equipment included components for ballistic missiles—systems that were under extra scrutiny by the USA and its allies and by UN missions. The report notes that Iraq was designing missile systems on the assumption that prohibited material would be readily available.[112] The fact that the equipment was generally small made it easier to smuggle.

This illicit trade increased once it became clear that little action was taken against those who circumvented the embargo, and again when US military action against Iraq became more likely. The number of deals with countries and companies that were willing to undermine UN sanctions rose from approximately 5 in 1998 to over 15 in 2000 and more than 35 in 2002.[113] However, despite the loopholes, the embargo did prove effective in so far as the purchases were in no way large enough to allow Iraq to rebuild its conventional military arsenal or to create a viable chemical-, biological- or nuclear-weapon programme.[114]

EU embargoes

In addition to the lifting of the EU embargo on Iraq, the EU also lifted its embargo on *Libya* on 11 October 2004. By that time several contracts for weapons and equipment were under discussion between Libya and British,

[108] US Central Intelligence Agency, 'Comprehensive Report of the Special Advisor to the DCI [Director of Central Intelligence] on Iraq's WMD', 30 Sep. 2004, URL <http://www.cia.gov/cia/reports/iraq_wmd_2004>.

[109] US Central Intelligence Agency (note 108), p. 93.

[110] US Central Intelligence Agency (note 108), p. 93.

[111] US Central Intelligence Agency (note 108), p. 93.

[112] US Central Intelligence Agency (note 108), p. 11.

[113] US Central Intelligence Agency (note 108), pp. 93–94.

[114] US Central Intelligence Agency (note 108), p. 3.

French, Greek and Italian companies.[115] The lifting of the embargo had been driven mainly by Greece and Italy, albeit with little or no opposition from other EU member states, in order to help Libya improve its border patrol and maritime surveillance capabilities so that it could help reduce the number of illegal immigrants entering the EU through the Mediterranean.[116]

The EU reaffirmed its arms embargo on *Sudan*,[117] which dates from March 1994, and expanded it in January 2004 to include financing and brokering of arms sales and military technical advice, assistance and support.[118] The prohibition on brokering by EU nationals came at a time when British and Central and East European nationals were reportedly heavily involved as middlemen in the supply of weapons from Ukraine to Sudan. Most of the reported transfers (150 armoured vehicles, 42 pieces of artillery, 150 man-portable defence systems, MANPADS and other weapons) were halted by the new prohibition.[119]

The EU arms embargo on China

The embargo that received the most attention in 2004 was the EU arms embargo on *China*, imposed in 1989 as a reaction to Chinese human rights violations—in particular the 1989 Tiananmen Square massacre. EU leaders discussed the possibility of lifting the embargo on several occasions in 2004. Several EU member states, notably France and Germany, argued that the time was right to lift the embargo and to increase trade and cooperation with China.[120] The embargo on China was established by the European Community (EC) and it has the status of a political declaration by the EC Council of Foreign Ministers expressing the consensus of the then EC member states, some of which had already established 'national embargoes'. Unlike later EU embargoes, which are grounded in the European Political Cooperation and are part of the EU Common Foreign and Security Policy, the declaration was not legally binding.[121] During a visit to China in December 2003, German

[115] 'Libye' [Libya], *Damoclès: la Lettre*, no. 107 (Sep. 2004), p. 2; and Kington, T., 'EU eyes coastal patrol needs in sales to Libya', *Defense News*, 11 Oct. 2004, p. 14.

[116] Kington (note 115). On 20 Sep. 2004 the USA ended its economic embargo on Libya but retained its ban on military sales.

[117] The USA also has in place trade restrictions on Sudan. However, in May 2004 the USA removed Sudan from its list of countries not cooperating with US anti-terrorism efforts, thereby opening the door for an easing of trade (including arms trade) restrictions. Lee, M., 'US moves to ease arms embargo against Sudan, hints Libya may be next', Agence France-Press, 18 May 2004.

[118] Common Position 2004/31/CFSP and Council Regulation (EC) no. 131/2004, available on the SIPRI Internet site at URL <http://www.sipri.org/contents/expcon/eu_sudan.html>.

[119] Leppard, D. and Winnett, R., 'Briton supplies arms to Sudan', *Sunday Times*, 5 Sep. 2004.

[120] Several countries proposed lifting the embargo in the 1990s. For a discussion of the history of the EU arms embargo on China see the SIPRI Internet site, at URL <http://www.sipri.org/contents/expcon/euchiemb.html>. For a complete list of EU embargoes and related EU documents see the SIPRI Internet site 'European Union approach to arms embargoes', URL <http://www.sipri.org/contents/expcon/euembargo.html>.

[121] The 10 states that joined the EU in May 2004 accepted as binding all EU decisions but not the political declarations made by the EC. The embargo on China thus applies only for 15 EU member states. See Grimmet, R. F., and Papademetriou, T., Library of Congress, Congressional Research Service (CRS), *European Union's Arms Control Regime and Arms Exports to China: Background and Legal Analysis*, CRS Report for Congress RL32785 (US Government Printing Office: Washington, DC, 1 Mar.

Chancellor Gerhard Schröder said that Germany was in favour of ending the embargo.[122] During a visit to France by Chinese President Hu Jintao in January 2004, President of France Jacques Chirac said that the embargo 'no longer corresponds with the political reality of the contemporary world' and called for it to be ended.[123]

However, a number of EU member states, including Finland, the Netherlands and the UK, argued that China had not demonstrated sufficient improvement in the area of human rights to warrant the lifting of the embargo. EU sentiment on the embargo remained divided in 2004 and a meeting of EU foreign ministers in October failed to resolve the issue. At the meeting of the Council of the European Union on 16–17 December 2004, EU leaders declared their willingness to consider lifting the embargo in 2005 but at the same time committed themselves to not increase the quality or quantity of exports of military equipment to China.[124]

Proponents of lifting the embargo argue that it would be a mainly political signal in a process of 'engaging China in dialogue', that it would tidy up an outmoded legacy of the EC and that the EU Code of Conduct on Arms Exports could be interpreted in a restrictive manner in order to prevent an increase in arms sales to China. It is possible to argue that the EU Code of Conduct has overtaken the embargo and that if the embargo were lifted the code's criteria on human rights, regional stability, the security of EU allies, and probably on the risk of diversion to third countries would still prevent major increases in the quantity and quality of exports to China. This view was expressed, for example, by British Foreign Secretary Jack Straw.[125] However, as a joint report of four select committees of the British House of Commons (the Quadripartite Committee) concluded, if the EU Code of Conduct has superseded the arms embargo on China, then it has presumably also superseded other EU arms embargoes, given that sales to any embargoed country could equally well be controlled under the EU Code of Conduct.[126]

No list of items covered by the term 'arms' was agreed when the EC imposed its embargo on China.[127] Interpretation of what is actually embargoed is left to individual EU member states, which continue to interpret the embargo in different ways. Only the UK and, to some extent, Italy have published their interpretations.[128] In 1995, the British Government clarified its

2005). For a more detailed account of the embargo on China and data on transfers of equipment from the EU to China see URL <http://www.sipri.org/contents/armstrad/atchi_taidata.html>.

[122] 'Schroeder backs sales to China of EU weapons', *Wall Street Journal*, 2 Dec. 2003.

[123] Agence France-Presse, 'Chirac renews call for end of EU arms embargo on China', 27 Jan. 2004.

[124] Council of the European Union, Presidency Conclusions, document 16238/1/04 Rev 1, Brussels, 1 Feb. 2005. Wall, R. and Taverna, M. A., 'Chinese poker: US cites fear of shifting military balance in Asia if Europe lifts Chinese arms ban', *Aviation Week & Space Technology*, 25 Oct. 2004, p. 82; and 'Swedish PM faces backlash after support for lifting China arms embargo', Agence France-Presse, 18 Dec. 2004.

[125] British House of Commons, Defence, Foreign Affairs, International Development and Trade and Industry Committees, *Strategic Export Controls: Annual Report for 2002, Licensing Policy and Parliamentary Scrutiny* (Stationery Office: London, May 2004), p. 39.

[126] British House of Commons (note 125), p. 39.

[127] For the agreed scope of later embargoes see the SIPRI Internet site (note 87).

[128] British House of Commons (note 125), p. 39.

interpretation of the arms embargo against China in response to a Parliamentary Question.[129] Italy apparently interprets the embargo as a ban on equipment designed for the maintenance of internal security. In mid-2004 Italy was in the process of ratifying a 1999 agreement on military equipment and technology cooperation with China. According to the sponsor of the bill to ratify the agreement, Marcello Pacini, it does not violate the arms embargo because 'military equipment' is defined under Italian law as naval vessels, aircraft, helicopters and related equipment, which are 'armaments pertaining to national defense and not specifically designed for internal repression or to restrict individual rights and freedoms'.[130]

The existence of the embargo has not prevented several EU member states from delivering military equipment or components to China.[131] In the 2003 annual report on the implementation of the EU Code of Conduct, for example, the Czech Republic, France, Germany, Italy and the UK reported licences for exports of goods on the EU Military List with a combined value of €416 million ($475 million).[132] While it is possible to deduce from public sources that the equipment is either mainly for civilian use or 'non-lethal', the equipment is important for the modernization of the Chinese armed forces and for the production of Chinese weapon systems such as submarines, tanks and combat aircraft. China is keen to gain greater access to key European components. China is capable of developing relatively advanced weapon platforms but has serious problems with developing engines, transmissions, avionics and electronics—and is heavily dependent on foreign technology in these fields. Russia can provide some of these components but there is wide agreement that Russian technology either is or is rapidly becoming outdated. Almost all Chinese tanks and armoured vehicles are powered by German

[129] The British Government stated that: 'Since 7 June 1995 the United Kingdom has enforced an embargo on the sale to China of "weapons, and equipment which could be used for internal repression". The EU introduced a ban on arms sales to China on 26 June 1989 but the scope of that ban has, in the absence of agreement on a common interpretation, been left for national interpretation. In the interests of clarity we have decided that hence forward the embargo will include: lethal weapons such as machine guns, large calibre weapons, bombs, torpedoes, rockets and missiles; specially designed components of the above, and ammunition; military aircraft and helicopters, vessels of war, armoured fighting vehicles and other such weapons platforms; any equipment which is likely to be used for internal repression. All applications will be considered on a case-by-case basis in the light of these criteria as well as our usual criteria governing all defence exports'.

[130] Kington, T., 'Italy ponders arms sales to China', *Defense News*, 28 June 2004, p. 6.

[131] Hill, J., 'Europe considers ending Chinese arms embargo', *Jane's Intelligence Review*, vol. 16, no. 6 (June 2004), pp. 54–55. The UK, which has complained that other EU members were less restrictive on exports to China, granted licences for military equipment worth £76.5 million ($139 million) in 2003. Lawrence, S., 'New cracks in the alliance', *Far Eastern Economic Review*, 12 Aug. 2004, pp. 24–26; and Lague, D., 'How a lifted embargo would help China', *Far Eastern Economic Review*, 12 Aug. 2004, p. 27. On EU exports to China see the SIPRI Arms Transfers Project Internet site at URL <http://www.sipri.org/contents/armstrad/atchi_taidata.html>.

[132] Council of the European Union, 'Common Military List of the European Union', *Official Journal of the European Union*, C314 (21 Dec. 2004), URL <http://europa.eu.int/eur-lex/lex/JOHtml.do?uri=OJ:C:2003:314:SOM:EN:HTML>. The value of actual deliveries from the Czech Republic and Italy was €1.7 million, only 1.3% of the value of licences granted by the 2 countries. France, Germany and the UK did not report on the value of deliveries. Council of the European Union, 'Sixth Annual Report according to Operative Provision 8 of the European Union Code of Conduct on Arms Exports', *Official Journal of the European Union*, C316 (12 Dec. 2004), p. 43, URL <http://ue.eu.int/cms3_fo/showPage.asp?id=408&lang=en&mode=g>.

engines, which are often produced under licence in China.[133] Chinese submarines are powered by French and German engines and equipped with French sonar systems.[134] China produces helicopters either under licence from France or making extensive use of French technology.[135]

The USA is putting pressure on EU member states to maintain the embargo, not primarily because of the events of 1989 but because Chinese access to European military technology, in addition to what it already receives from Russia, might help China to more rapidly improve its military performance and may partly replace its dependence on outdated Russian technology. This could lead to a destabilizing Chinese arms build-up in a region where the USA has troops and defence commitments.[136] The matter is seen as extremely sensitive in the USA, with some analysts suggesting that lifting the embargo could bring NATO close to collapse.[137] The Bush Administration has exerted constant pressure on the EU in an attempt to dissuade it from lifting the embargo, warning that such a move would be a significant obstacle to US defence cooperation with EU member states. It specifically identifies the issue of technology transfers and argues that EU military technology provided to China could be diverted to third parties or terrorists.[138]

Both houses of the US Congress have also argued against lifting the embargo. In June 2004 the influential US–China Economic and Security Review Commission warned that access to European technology would accelerate Chinese modernization and dramatically enhance Chinese military capabilities. Such a decision might also lead Russia to authorize the export of even more sophisticated systems to China in response to the increased competition.[139] The Commission recommended 'that Congress urge the president and the secretaries of State and Defense to press strongly their EU counterparts to maintain the EU arms embargo on China'.[140] In May 2004 the US House of Representatives Committee on Armed Services agreed a bill that would restrict exports of arms and other sensitive technologies to any country exporting arms to China, as well as prohibit US government agencies from doing business with any company that sells arms to China, for five years.[141]

[133] See, e.g., the various entries for Chinese tanks and armoured vehicles in *Jane's Armour and Artillery 2004–2005* (Jane's Information Group: Coulsdon, 2004).

[134] *Jane's Fighting Ships 2004–2005* (Jane's Information Group: Coulsdon, 2004).

[135] *Jane's all the World's Aircraft 2004–2005* (Jane's Information Group: Coulsdon, 2004).

[136] Lawrence, S., 'New cracks in the alliance' and Lague, D., 'How a lifted embargo would help China', *Far Eastern Economic Review*, 12 Aug. 2004, pp. 24–26 and 27; and Brookes, P., 'Keep the pressure on China', *Far Eastern Economic Review*, 26 Aug. 2004, p. 22.

[137] Hill, J., 'China, France hold joint naval exercises', *Jane's Intelligence Review*, vol. 16, no. 6 (May 2004), p. 9.

[138] 'US warns EU against arms trade with China', *International Herald Tribune* (Internet edn), 7 Oct. 2004, URL <http://www.iht.com/bin/print.php?file=542527.html>; and Sherman, J., 'US to EU: think twice about China arms trade', *Defense News*, 18 Oct. 2004, p. 3.

[139] US–China Economic and Security Review Commission (note 18), p. 193.

[140] US–China Economic and Security Review Commission (note 18), p. 22.

[141] Alden, E., 'US threat to restrict arms sales to Europe', *Financial Times* (Internet edn), 13 May 2004, URL <http://news.ft.com/servlet/ContentServer?pagename=FT.com/StoryFT/FullStory&c=StoryFT&cid=1083180493141>.

IV. Arms transfer reporting and transparency

The value of the international arms trade

The SIPRI trend-indicator value was not developed to assess the economic magnitude of national arms markets or of the global market.[142] In order to make such assessments, data are needed on the financial values of weapon sales, here called the arms trade. By aggregating data released by supplier governments on the value of their arms trade it is possible to arrive at a rough estimate of the financial value of this trade.[143] That value for 2003, the most recent year for which data are available, is estimated at $38–43 billion (see figure 10.2), which accounts for 0.5–0.6 per cent of total world trade.[144] The figure is reported as a range because certain countries produce more than one set of data on the value of their arms exports. In particular, Sweden, the UK and the USA each produce at least two sets of such data.

SIPRI's current estimate of the value of the arms trade in 1999–2003 is higher than that given in the *SIPRI Yearbook 2004*. In addition, the gap between the maximum and minimum estimates is more pronounced. In large part, this is because of revisions to the data on US arms exports contained in the 2004 US Congressional Research Service (CRS) annual report.[145] The values for US arms deliveries in 1997–2004 are substantially higher in the 2004 report compared to the figures given in previous reports. In particular, the 2003 report values US deliveries in 2002 at $10.241 billion, while the 2004 report gives a value of $23.872 billion for 2002. Similarly, the 2003 report values US deliveries in 2001 at $9.530 billion while the 2004 report

[142] See note 1.

[143] SIPRI estimates that the countries that provide data on national exports account for over 90% of the total volume of deliveries of major conventional weapons. It can be assumed that these countries together account for a roughly similar percentage of total arms exports in financial terms. By aggregating national export values it is possible to arrive at a rough estimate of the total financial value of the annual global arms trade. Because some governments present several reports with different arms export data, this estimate can only be a range including the aggregates of the lowest and the highest reported values. Figures are in US dollars at constant (2003) prices. Conversion to US dollars is made using current values and current market exchange rates (MERs). Values are then converted into constant (2003) prices using the US consumer price index (CPI). It should be noted that government arms export data are not entirely reliable or comparable and are based on different methodologies and different definitions of what constitute 'arms' and 'military equipment'. In certain cases, data are based on information supplied by industry on the value of their arms exports. In other cases they are based on the value of goods identified as military equipment that pass through customs in a given year. For some smaller countries, data on the value of arms export licences have been used because these are the only figures available. For certain countries and certain years official data are unavailable and estimates have been made on the assumption that the rate of change in an individual country for which data are missing is the same as the average in the sample as a whole. On the value of the global arms trade see the SIPRI Arms Transfers Project Internet site, URL <http://www.sipri.org/contents/armstrad/at_gov_ind_data.html>.

[144] Total world exports in 2003 amounted to $7444 billion. International Monetary Fund, International financial statistics online, URL <http://ifs.apdi.net/imf/>.

[145] Grimmett, R. F., Library of Congress, Congressional Research Service (CRS), *Conventional Arms Transfers to Developing Nations 1996–2003*, CRS Report for Congress RL32547 (US Government Printing Office: Washington, DC, 26 Aug. 2004).

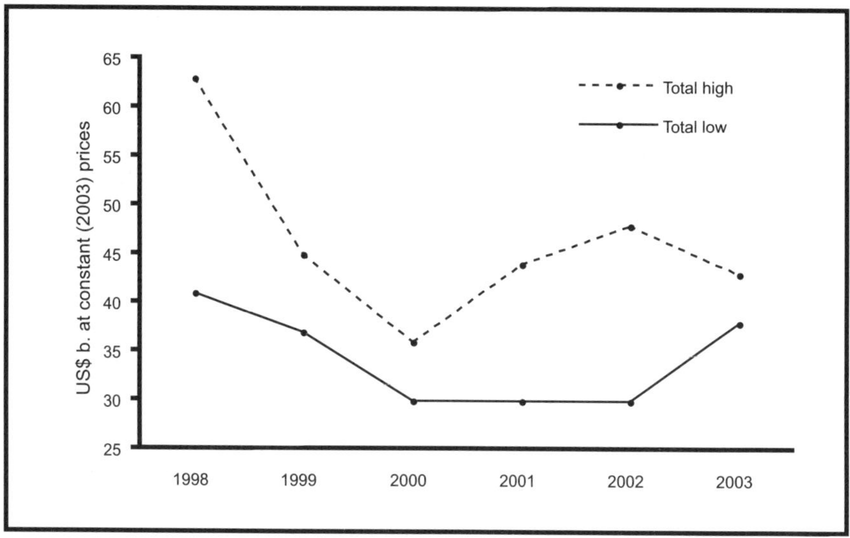

Figure 10.2. The value of the international arms trade, 1998–2003

Source: The data used to compile these figures are available at URL <http://www.sipri.org/contents/armstrad/at_gov_ind_data.html>.

gives $22.342 billion.[146] These increases are not reflected in either the values given for arms transfer agreements or the data on deliveries to the developing world in the 2004 report.

International transparency

The two main international mechanisms for public transparency on arms transfers are the UN Register of Conventional Arms (UNROCA), introduced in 1992, and the Annual Report according to Operative Provision 8 of the EU Code of Conduct on Arms Exports, which has been produced since 1999.[147]

The UN Register on Conventional Arms

The number of UNROCA participating countries increased from an all-time low of 83 in 1998 to 121 reporting data for 2002 in 2004. By January 2005,

[146] Grimmett, R. F., Library of Congress, Congressional Research Service (CRS), *Conventional Arms Transfers to Developing Nations 1995–2002*, CRS Report for Congress RL32084 (US Government Printing Office: Washington, DC, 22 Sep. 2003); and Grimmett (note 145).

[147] This section covers developments in national and international transparency tools that increase public knowledge of arms exports. Intergovernmental exchanges of information, such as those which take place under the auspices of the Organization for Security and Co-operation in Europe and the Wassenaar Arrangement, are not discussed. On the OSCE information exchanges see chapter 15 in this volume. On the Wassenaar Arrangement see chapter 17 in this volume. International transparency is also part of a proposed 'Arms Trade Treaty', which gained the support of several governments, most notably the British and Finnish, by the end of 2004. The proposed treaty is meant to control the arms trade but recognizes that this can only be achieved if there is some level of international and national transparency on arms exports and imports. For more on the discussions around this treaty see URL <http://www.controlarms.org/latest_news/steps-forward.htm>. For the text of the proposed treaty see URL <http://www.armstradetreaty.com/fccomment.html>.

112 countries had reported data for 2003. However, experience demonstrates that some countries report data much later.[148] In 2004 countries for the first time reported on artillery with a caliber of 75–100 mm and on MANPADS. Five countries clearly identified exports of artillery with a caliber of 75–100 mm. There were no reports of any imports. Four countries identified exports of MANPADS and two reported imports.[149] There has been no marked increase in the number of countries that provide information on their military inventories and their acquisitions from domestic sources. In the past three years, this total remained fairly constant at about one-third of all countries participating in the register.

The data submitted to the UNROCA are important because they are the only official data available on the arms exports and imports of many countries. However, the value of the data is difficult to assess. Many, if not most, of the reports from exporters do not match the corresponding reports from importers. One side often reports different numbers from the other and does not always include the systems reported by the other. Where both exporter and importer have submitted reports to the UNROCA for 2003, about 80 per cent of the entries do not match. Sometimes the difference is marginal but in 65 per cent of these cases one side has reported a transfer which is not reported by the other side.[150] Taking data from the UNROCA at face value is problematic and can lead to incorrect conclusions being drawn. Moreover, many importers do not seem interested in making submissions. In 2003, 26 countries identified from exporter reports as having received weapons did not submit reports.

The EU Code of Conduct on Arms Exports

In December 2004 the EU published its sixth annual report on the implementation of the EU Code of Conduct on Arms Exports.[151] The accession of 10 new member states to the EU in May 2004 had a significant impact on the volume of statistical data included in the report.[152] All 10 incoming member states have agreed to abide by the operative provisions of the code, including those related to the provision of statistical data on arms exports.[153] However, because the sixth annual report covers export licences issued and actual exports in 2003 the 10 new member states were not obliged to submit data.

[148] A complete list of participating countries and their reports for the 12-year period 1992–2003 are available at URL <http://disarmament2.un.org/cab/register.html>. Data on participation exclude the Cook Islands and Niue.

[149] This figure does not include 1 MANPADS export report which is either a mistake or an import. In cases where countries have only reported numbers of items in the categories, without describing the systems, MANPADS and artillery below 100 mm may be included in the numbers.

[150] These statistics exclude reported transfers of systems that clearly fall outside the UNROCA definitions, such as Argentina's reported imports of TOW missiles and 40-mm grenade launchers. For further analysis see the SIPRI Arms Transfer Project Internet site, URL <http://www.sipri.org/contents/armstrad/unroca.html>.

[151] Council of the European Union, 'Sixth Annual Report' (note 132).

[152] See note 82.

[153] For a discussion of the obligations of the 10 new EU member states under the EU Code of Conduct see chapter 17 in this volume; and Bauer and Bromley (note 81).

Instead, they were invited to submit figures for 2003 if they were available,[154] which eight of them did.[155]

In a further enhancement of transparency, member states agreed that 'breakdowns of licences and actual exports by [EU] Military List category (if available) should also be included in the report'.[156] Of the 25 member states, 12 submitted data on the value of licences granted or actual exports by destination, disaggregated by the 22 categories of the EU Military List. The subsequent increase in the volume of statistical data led to the adoption of a new format for the sixth annual report, which contains nearly 200 pages of statistical data, compared to fewer than 40 pages in the fifth report.

Disaggregating financial data by the categories of the EU Military List allows a better informed analysis of the types of goods licensed and exported by EU member states. However, many of the Military List categories are defined broadly, making it difficult to identify specific items or weapon systems. In addition, since the annual report is meant to be a tool for evaluating states' interpretation of the EU Code, and since the EU Code criteria are related mainly to the impact which weapons have on certain situations, a reporting system that focuses on the financial values of exports without giving details of the type or quantity of weapon exported is of relatively little use. It is worth noting that the UNROCA and the exchange of information within the OCSE, both of which share some of the aims of the EU Code, focus on the *type* and *quantity* of weapons exported, not on financial data.[157]

In 2004 the EU member states discussed making the submission of certain categories of data for the EU Code annual report compulsory. States had previously agreed that submissions should only be made if data were 'available'.[158] The sixth annual report states that consensus has been reached on providing national data on the value of licences issued. However, additional data such as the value of actual exports will only be made available by those states that are able to do so.[159] As a result, there continues to be significant variation in the quantity of statistical data submitted, with some states submitting data on all possible categories and others submitting only the minimum required. This disparity continues to reduce the comparability of national data presented in the annual report.[160]

[154] Working Party on Conventional Arms Exports (COARM), Operational conclusions of the meeting of 22 June 2004.

[155] The Czech Republic, Estonia, Hungary, Latvia, Malta, Poland, Slovakia and Slovenia submitted data for the sixth annual report on either the number of licences issued, the value of licences issued, the value of actual exports or a combination of all 3.

[156] Council of the European Union, 'Common Military List of the European Union' (note 132); and Working Party on Conventional Arms Exports (note 154).

[157] For an analysis of the data submitted for the EU annual report see Bauer and Bromley (note 81).

[158] Council of the European Union, 'Fifth Annual Report according to Operative Provision 8 of the European Union Code of Conduct on Arms Exports', *Official Journal of the European Union*, C320 (31 Dec. 2004), p. 8, URL <http://ue.eu.int/cms3_fo/showPage.asp? id=408&lang=en&mode=g>.

[159] Council of the European Union, 'Sixth Annual Report' (note 132).

[160] Bauer and Bromley (note 81).

National transparency

It had been anticipated that the total number of countries providing national annual reports on arms exports would increase after the enlargement of the EU. However, while the majority of new EU member states did submit data for its annual report, only *the Czech Republic* published a national annual report in 2004. The Czech report reproduced the data submitted to the EU annual report and contained additional information on the number and type of weapon systems imported and exported, along with a separate section on imports and exports of small arms and light weapons.[161] Among the new EU member states that failed to produce national annual reports, reasons cited include a lack of capacity and ongoing intra-governmental disputes over the competing needs of transparency and commercial confidentiality.

The number of annual reports produced by EU member states may increase as a result of a review of the EU Code of Conduct that was carried out in 2004.[162] A number of states sought to include a requirement for national annual reporting in the code review while the sixth EU annual report states that that 'the code will be significantly reinforced by including several new elements in the text [including] national reporting'.[163] Meanwhile, according to the updated User's Guide to the European Union Code of Conduct, each member state is required to 'publish a national report on its defence exports, the contents of which will be in accordance with national legislation'.[164]

Apart from the Czech Republic, no state that had not previously done so produced a national annual report in 2004. However, the level of detail of the information provided by countries that had previously produced reports continues to improve. In March 2004 *Romania* produced its second national annual report, covering exports in 2002.[165] In an improvement on the 2003 report it includes the number of licences issued to each destination, the category of goods covered and whether the licences were for a complete weapon system, repairs and loans or spare parts. The annual report on exports in 2003 published by *Germany* lists the percentage of the total value of licences granted to each country that relate to exports of what Germany defines as 'war weapons'.[166] The report also lists the value of exports of war weapons disaggregated by recipient countries. Previous German reports list only

[161] Ministry of Foreign Affairs of the Czech Republic, Export controls in the Czech Republic in 2003, Dec. 2004, URL <http://www.mzv.cz/wwwo/mzv/default.asp?id=29913&ido=10459&idj=2&amb=1>.

[162] For a discussion of the 2004 review of the EU Code of Conduct see chapter 17 in this volume.

[163] Council of the European Union, 'Sixth Annual Report' (note 132).

[164] Council of the European Union, 'User's guide to the European Union Code of Conduct on Exports of Military Equipment', Brussels, 23 Dec. 2004, p. 22, URL <http://ue.eu.int/cms3_fo/showPage.asp?id=408&lang=en&mode=g>.

[165] Romanian National Agency for Export Controls, Raport: Privind Controlexporturilor de Arme 2002 [Report on arms export controls 2002], Bucharest, Mar. 2004, URL <http://www.ancex.ro/raport_arme.php>.

[166] *Bericht der Bundesregierung über ihre Exportpolitik für konventionelle Rüstungsgüter im Jahre 2003* [Report of the Federal Republic of Germany on its export policy for conventional armaments 2003], Berlin, Dec. 2004, URL <http://www.bmwa.bund.de/bmwa/generator/Navigation/Service/bestellservice,did=51910.html>.

Germany's 10 largest recipients. The report from *Norway*, on exports in 2003, for the first time gives a description of the goods exported to each country and indicates whether the items are complete products or components.[167] In addition, the report gives the number of licence applications that were turned down and lists the intended destinations. In January 2005 the US Government Accountability Office published a report criticizing the collection and reporting of data on licences for commercial exports by the US State Department.[168]

There were several notable improvements in the provision of more timely and up-to-date statistics on arms exports in 2004. In July the UK released its first quarterly report on its arms exports, detailing licences granted from January to March 2004.[169] In November the Netherlands began publishing monthly reports on export licences granted after Dutch political parties and NGOs requested more up-to-date information. By January 2005 these monthly reports were providing information that was only three to four months old.[170] For several years Ireland published monthly reports detailing the category and destination of new export licences. However, the most recent update, covering licences issued in September 2003, was posted in January 2004 and no new information has been published since then.[171]

In 2004 the Netherlands and the UK began publishing information on the final destination of goods that will be re-exported by the recipient country, either as complete systems or as components integrated into a complete system. The Dutch monthly reports state whether an export licence refers to goods that will be re-exported to a third country and lists the country of final destination.[172] The British annual report on exports in 2003 identifies licences that have been granted for items that will be incorporated into a completed system and re-exported to a third country but does not list the country of final destination.[173] The UK's second quarterly report contains details of brokering licences, which the UK began issuing in May 2004. This information includes

[167] Norwegian Ministry of Foreign Affairs, *Eksport av forsvarsmateriell frå Norge i 2003* [Export of defence equipment from Norway in 2003], Oslo, 28 May 2004, URL <http://odin.dep.no/ud/norsk/publ/stmeld/bn. html>.

[168] US Government Accountability Office (GAO), *State Department Needs to Resolve Data Reliability Problems that Led to Inaccurate Reporting to Congress on Foreign Arms Sales*, GAO-05-156R (GAO: Washington, DC, 28 Jan. 2005). For more information see appendix 17A in this volume.

[169] British Foreign and Commonwealth Office, Official documents, 'Strategic export controls report 2004', First quarterly report, Jan.–Mar. 2004, 28 July 2004, URL <http://www.fco.gov.uk/servlet/Front?pagename=OpenMarket/Xcelerate/ShowPage&c=Page&cid=1089131553823>.

[170] Dutch Ministry of Economic Affairs, Maandrapportages afgifte vergunningen militaire goederen [Monthly reports on licences granted for exports of military products], Jan. 2005, URL <http://minez.nl/content.jsp?objectid=27352>.

[171] Irish Department of Enterprise, Trade and Employment, 'Military goods: monthly statistics concerning military export licences issues by the Irish authorities', 22 Oct. 2003, URL <http://www.entemp.ie/trade/export/statistics.htm>.

[172] Dutch Ministry of Economic Affairs (note 170).

[173] British House of Commons, Defence, Foreign Affairs, International Development, and Trade and Industry Select Committees, *Strategic Export Controls: Annual Report for 2003, Licensing Policy and Parliamentary Scrutiny* (Stationery Office: London, June 2004).

the origin of the goods, their destination and the number of licences issued, but does not give details of the type of equipment covered.[174]

V. Conclusions

The volume of transfers of major conventional weapons increased in 2003 and 2004. However, it is too soon to judge whether this is a trend or just a fluctuation linked to a rush of deliveries.

Russia has established itself as the main supplier for the five-year period 2000–2004, followed by the USA. The EU as a whole formed the third largest supplier. It is probable that Russia will not be the largest supplier of major conventional weapons in the future—even in Russia there is pessimism about its future levels of arms exports. Russia is lagging behind in military research and development, and this is starting to influence procurement decisions by China and India—the largest customers for Russian weapons.

China was by far the largest recipient of major conventional weapons in 2000–2004, followed by India. Both countries are important markets for Russia but, while Russia has a near monopoly on the Chinese market, competition on the Indian market is fierce and appears to be growing.

Arms embargoes, both global UN embargoes and regional embargoes, have been found to be ineffective. Access to Iraqi documents has demonstrated that there were many breaches of the UN embargo by government and private actors, to the extent that Iraq counted on being able to obtain certain equipment. In the EU, discussion of the lifting of the arms embargo on China led to disagreements with the USA, partly because of what seems to be a misunderstanding about the purpose and status of the embargo and about the effectiveness of the EU Code of Conduct. It is clear, however, that the EU embargo has not stopped several European countries from supplying key military technology to China.

Levels of transparency increased slightly again in 2004. At the international level, MANPADS and light artillery were added to the UNROCA. At the national level, the amount of data available in the different, mainly European, national export reports increased slightly, largely because of the accession of 10 new countries to the EU and the consequent demand for such data under the EU Code of Conduct.

[174] British Foreign and Commonwealth Office, Official documents, 'Strategic export controls report 2004', Second quarterly report, Apr.–June 2004, 28 Oct. 2004.

Appendix 10A. The volume of transfers of major conventional weapons: by recipients and suppliers, 2000–2004

SIEMON T. WEZEMAN and MARK BROMLEY

Table 10A.1. The recipients of major conventional weapons, 2000–2004

The table includes all countries/non-state actors with imports of major conventional weapons in the five-year period 2000–2004. Ranking is according to the 2000–2004 aggregate imports. Figures are SIPRI trend-indicator values expressed in US$ m. at constant (1990) prices. Figures may not add up because of the conventions of rounding.

Rank order								
2000–2004	1999–2003[a]	Recipient	2000	2001	2002	2003	2004	2000–2004
1	1	China	1 797	3 018	2 586	2 038	2 238	11 677
2	2	India	598	899	1 671	2 983	2 375	8 526
3	3	Greece	648	683	481	2 017	1 434	5 263
4	5	UK	833	1 189	594	608	171	3 395
5	4	Turkey	789	448	985	658	418	3 298
6	6	Egypt	807	778	599	521	398	3 103
7	7	South Korea	873	475	308	362	737	2 755
8	16	UAE	312	185	201	637	1 246	2 581
9	10	Australia	334	627	434	448	334	2 177
10	9	Pakistan	144	354	559	617	344	2 018
11	13	Iran	331	449	422	435	283	1 920
12	19	USA	129	164	359	575	533	1 760
13	11	Israel	320	88	267	279	724	1 678
14	18	Canada	424	458	352	101	340	1 675
15	12	Saudi Arabia	68	74	558	134	838	1 672
16	20	Italy	236	355	330	356	317	1 594
17	15	Algeria	376	501	222	198	282	1 579
18	8	Taiwan	536	411	293	101	230	1 571
19	22	Singapore	530	167	227	61	456	1 441
20	26	Yemen	158	92	537	40	309	1 136
21	27	Poland	136	68	274	402	256	1 136
22	24	Spain	264	176	215	70	261	986
23	14	Japan	174	217	180	209	195	975
24	23	Brazil	106	508	150	86	38	888
25	25	Netherlands	127	137	262	156	183	865
26	29	Jordan	132	156	123	308	132	851
27	17	Finland	513	10	16	222	57	818
28	21	Malaysia	40	24	161	195	277	697
29	30	Indonesia	153	34	83	307	85	662
30	48	Mexico	177	114	39	15	265	610
31	32	Thailand	94	122	149	133	105	603
32	53	Sudan	–	146	57	102	270	575
33	37	Germany	138	146	61	40	190	575

Rank order								
2000–2004	1999–2003[a]	Recipient	2000	2001	2002	2003	2004	2000–2004
34	38	Colombia	51	243	123	81	17	515
35	31	Norway	267	148	90	–	1	506
36	34	Chile	174	41	73	173	43	504
37	43	Ethiopia	125	–	20	193	162	500
38	51	Denmark	64	113	52	68	194	491
39	47	Viet Nam	8	72	121	27	247	475
40	35	Bangladesh	214	176	39	9	26	464
41	28	Angola	115	313	29	2	5	464
42	78	Eritrea	4	60	2	–	382	448
43	40	Syria	420	–	–	27	–	447
44	44	Bahrain	308	31	58	6	10	413
45	41	Myanmar (Burma)	1	130	198	13	65	407
46	42	Sri Lanka	236	136	12	14	6	404
47	54	Libya	–	145	–	145	74	364
48	70	Romania	20	21	16	18	276	351
49	46	Kazakhstan	147	31	83	62	27	350
50	36	Argentina	190	2	12	12	129	345
51	62	Oman	109	12	61	19	123	324
52	52	Morocco	123	5	168	–	–	296
53	45	Sweden	107	93	40	39	13	292
54	33	Switzerland	13	53	46	54	125	291
55	50	Kuwait	123	67	18	49	–	257
56	55	Venezuela	90	84	50	14	12	250
57	58	Afghanistan/NA[b]	20	204	–	–	–	224
58	63	Czech Republic	18	27	32	111	18	206
59	39	New Zealand	–	45	17	100	42	204
60	61	France	43	–	22	50	89	204
61	64	Austria	25	15	61	38	46	185
62	56	Peru	–	161	5	–	14	180
63	57	Congo (DRC)	74	57	29	–	–	160
64	60	Macedonia	11	133	–	–	–	144
65	67	Azerbaijan	3	–	140	–	–	143
66	76	Portugal	2	15	–	60	59	136
67	49	Cyprus	2	121	–	8	–	131
68	65	Belgium	30	33	29	27	12	131
 69	69	Nigeria	42	7	9	49	10	117
70	72	Côte d'Ivoire	–	–	22	66	14	102
71	73	Croatia	–	61	2	24	8	95
72	71	Ireland	–	42	21	–	25	88
73	68	Georgia	6	80	–	1	–	87
74	75	Slovenia	–	55	1	14	14	84
75	93	Namibia	–	18	11	–	53	82
76	144	Iraq	–	–	–	–	82	82
77	104	Philippines	–	7	5	8	59	79
78	130	Armenia	–	–	–	–	68	68
79	74	Uganda	6	–	22	19	19	66
80	79	Tunisia	–	11	49	–	–	60
81	96	Nepal	–	11	8	9	32	60

Rank order								
2000–2004	1999–2003[a]	Recipient	2000	2001	2002	2003	2004	2000–2004
82	83	Latvia	3	13	3	27	14	60
83	91	Lithuania	4	15	7	–	31	57
84	86	Botswana	24	12	1	8	10	55
85	82	Bahamas	54	–	–	–	–	54
86	59	North Korea	14	24	5	5	5	53
87	81	United Nations[c]	49	–	–	–	–	49
88	66	Qatar	14	12	12	10	–	48
89	84	Afghanistan	–	–	31	17	–	48
90	89	Estonia	26	–	1	15	5	47
91	77	Hungary	14	14	–	–	15	43
92	85	Laos	7	34	–	–	–	41
93	103	Ghana	1	8	1	4	27	41
94	87	South Africa	–	17	–	13	8	38
95	105	Dominican Republic	13	1	–	3	21	38
96	80	Zimbabwe	2	8	–	23	–	33
97	92	Slovakia	3	–	27	–	–	30
98	140	Ukraine	–	–	–	–	29	29
99	94	Zambia	27	–	1	–	–	28
100	95	El Salvador	–	–	18	10	–	28
101	97	Yugoslavia	–	27	–	–	–	27
102	100	Ecuador	4	–	1	–	22	27
103	98	Guinea	19	5	–	1	–	25
104	141	Turkmenistan	–	–	–	–	20	20
105	102	Bolivia	15	–	–	–	1	16
106	101	Uruguay	4	–	11	–	–	15
107	106	Chad	–	15	–	–	–	15
108	88	Rwanda	14	–	–	–	–	14
109	112	Kyrgyzstan	–	–	–	9	5	14
110	117	Bulgaria	–	–	–	2	12	14
111	108	Trinidad & Tobago	10	1	–	–	–	11
112	109	Uzbekistan	–	5	5	–	–	10
113	119	Paraguay	–	6	–	–	4	10
114	110	Mauritania	9	–	–	–	–	9
115	114	Mali	7	–	1	–	–	8
116	111	Liberia	8	–	–	–	–	8
117	116	Equatorial Guinea	–	8	–	–	–	8
118	131	Albania	–	–	1	1	6	8
119	120	Lesotho	–	6	–	–	1	7
120	121	Guyana	–	6	–	–	–	6
121	122	Benin	–	–	6	–	–	6
122	125	Burundi	–	1	4	–	–	5
124	115	Lebanon	4	–	–	–	–	4
125	126	Cameroon	–	1	3	–	–	4
126	127	Djibouti	–	1	2	–	–	3
127	118	Brunei	–	3	–	–	–	3
128	128	Swaziland	1	1	–	–	–	2
129	139	Lebanon/Hizbollah[b]	–	–	–	–	1	1
130	133	Mozambique	–	–	–	1	–	1

Rank order 2000–2004	Rank order 1999–2003[a]	Recipient	2000	2001	2002	2003	2004	2000–2004
131	129	Luxembourg	–	–	–	1	–	1
132	135	Cape Verde	1	–	–	–	–	1
133	136	Belize	1	–	–	–	–	1
134	137	Sri Lanka/LTTE[b]	–	–	–	–	–	–
135	138	Macedonia/NLA[b]	–	–	–	–	–	–
136	113	Suriname	–	–	–	–	–	–
137	132	Somalia	–	–	–	–	–	–
138	107	Sierra Leone	–	–	–	–	–	–
139	142	Panama	–	–	–	–	–	–
140	143	Malta	–	–	–	–	–	–
141	124	Jamaica	–	–	–	–	–	–
142	145	Gabon	–	–	–	–	–	–
143	134	Congo	–	–	–	–	–	–
144	99	Bosnia & Herzegovina	–	–	–	–	–	–
145	90	Belarus	–	–	–	–	–	–
146	146	Bhutan	–	–	–	–	–	–
. .	. .	Unknown country[d]	–	22	–	–	3	25
. .	. .	Unknown rebels[d]	–	–	–	–	–	–
		Total	**15 840**	**16 618**	**15 692**	**17 178**	**19 162**	**84 490**

. . = not available or not applicable.

– = between 0 and 0.5.

[a] The rank order for recipients in 1999–2003 differs from that published in the *SIPRI Yearbook 2004* (pp. 475–78) because of subsequent revision of figures for these years.

[b] Non-state actor/rebel group. NA = Northern Alliance (UFSA, United Islamic Front for the Salvation of Afghanistan); LTTE = Liberation Tigers of Tamil Eelam; NLA = National Liberation Army.

[c] Non-state actor/international organization.

[d] One or more unknown recipient(s).

Note: The SIPRI data on arms transfers relate to actual deliveries of major conventional weapons. To permit comparison between the data on such deliveries of different weapons and identification of general trends, SIPRI uses a *trend-indicator value*. The SIPRI values are only an indicator of the volume of international arms transfers and not the actual money values of such transfers, Thus they are not comparable to economic statistics such as gross domestic product or export/import figures.

Source: SIPRI arms transfers database.

Table 10A.2. The suppliers of major conventional weapons, 2000–2004

The list includes all countries/non-state actors with exports of major conventional weapons in the period 2000–2004. Ranking is according to the 2000–2004 aggregate exports. Figures are SIPRI trend-indicator values expressed in US$ m. at constant (1990) prices. Figures may not add up because of the conventions of rounding.

Rank order								
2000–2004	1999–2003[a]	Supplier	2000	2001	2002	2003	2004	2000–2004
1	2	Russia	4 016	5 516	5 541	5 655	6 197	26 925
2	1	USA	6 400	5 079	4 470	4 528	5 453	25 930
3	3	France	717	1 111	1 301	1 107	2 122	6 358
4	4	Germany	1 195	529	551	1 512	1 091	4 878
5	5	UK	1 121	1 081	670	593	985	4 450
6	6	Ukraine	326	631	255	454	452	2 118
7	9	Canada	124	78	356	591	543	1 692
8	7	China	157	349	415	390	125	1 436
9	11	Sweden	280	432	108	210	260	1 290
10	13	Israel	272	226	289	188	283	1 258
11	8	Italy	143	188	357	303	261	1 252
12	10	Netherlands	215	188	251	318	211	1 183
13	12	Belarus	261	299	54	80	50	744
14	15	Uzbekistan	–	–	85	340	170	595
15	14	Spain	50	7	149	198	75	479
16	19	Poland	49	93	43	96	86	367
17	17	Czech Republic	78	89	71	85	–	323
18	21	Norway	27	63	91	83	51	315
19	22	South Korea	6	198	–	59	50	313
20	25	Switzerland	44	32	12	33	154	275
21	20	Georgia	54	54	120	–	20	248
22	18	Slovakia	83	89	47	–	–	219
23	16	Australia	–	43	30	40	52	165
24	38	Brazil	–	–	31	–	100	131
25	27	Indonesia	–	20	60	–	50	130
26	28	Austria	25	21	79	1	1	127
27	30	South Africa	17	27	13	30	35	122
28	26	Turkey	21	2	29	47	18	117
29	29	North Korea	–	64	32	–	–	96
30	31	Kyrgyzstan	–	–	–	92	–	92
31	23	Bulgaria	2	4	32	48	–	86
32	52	Singapore	1	–	2	–	70	73
33	65	Jordan	–	–	–	–	72	72
34	33	Finland	9	12	13	17	17	68
35	32	Belgium	20	21	20	–	–	61
36	34	Libya	–	–	27	23	–	50
37	35	Lebanon	–	–	45	–	–	45
38	40	India	16	2	–	4	22	44
39	37	Denmark	22	–	6	2	6	36
40	41	Pakistan	3	–	9	9	10	31
41	24	Kazakhstan	16	9	–	–	5	30
42	64	Macedonia	–	–	–	–	29	29

Rank order 2000–2004	Rank order 1999–2003[a]	Supplier	2000	2001	2002	2003	2004	2000–2004
43	36	Romania	3	–	–	22	–	25
44	39	Egypt	–	25	–	–	–	25
45	44	Peru	–	4	5	–	5	14
46	49	Thailand	–	–	–	5	5	10
47	63	Malta	–	–	–	–	10	10
48	42	Greece	–	2	–	8	–	10
49	45	Moldova	3	5	–	–	–	8
50	47	Yugoslavia	–	7	–	–	–	7
51	48	Taiwan	–	6	–	–	–	6
52	50	Argentina	2	3	–	–	–	5
53	62	UAE	–	–	–	–	3	3
54	53	New Zealand	1	–	1	–	1	3
55	54	Lithuania	–	–	3	–	–	3
56	51	Chile	1	–	2	–	–	3
57	55	Croatia	2	–	–	–	–	2
58	56	Bosnia & Herzegovina	–	–	2	–	–	2
59	57	Bahrain	–	2	–	–	–	2
60	61	Venezuela	–	–	–	–	1	1
61	58	Uruguay	1	–	–	–	–	1
62	59	Malawi	1	–	–	–	–	1
63	66	Iran	–	–	–	–	1	1
64	60	Angola	–	–	1	–	–	1
65	43	Qatar	–	–	–	–	–	–
66	46	Malaysia	–	–	–	–	–	–
67	67	Eritrea	–	–	–	–	–	–
. .	. .	Unknown country[b]	54	5	20	–	4	83
		Total	**15 840**	**16 618**	**15 692**	**17 178**	**19 162**	**84 490**

. . = not available or not applicable.

– = between 0 and 0.5.

[a] The rank order for suppliers in 1999–2003 differs from that published in the *SIPRI Yearbook 2004* (pp. 479–80) because of subsequent revision of figures for these years.

[b] One or more unknown supplier(s).

Note: The SIPRI data on arms transfers relate to actual deliveries of major conventional weapons. To permit comparison between the data on such deliveries of different weapons and identification of general trends, SIPRI uses a *trend-indicator value.* This is an indicator of the volume of international arms transfers, not the actual money values of such transfers. These figures are thus not comparable to economic statistics such as gross domestic product or export/import figures.

Source: SIPRI arms transfers database.

Appendix 10B. Register of transfers and licensed production of major conventional weapons, 2004

SIEMON T. WEZEMAN and MARK BROMLEY

The register in table 10B.1 lists major weapons on order or under delivery, or for which the licence was bought and production was under way or completed during 2004. Sources and methods for data collection are explained in appendix 10C. Entries in table 10B.1 are arranged alphabetically, by recipient, supplier and licenser. 'Year(s) of deliveries' includes aggregates of all deliveries and licensed production since the beginning of the contract. 'Deal worth' values in the Comments column refer to real monetary values as reported in sources and not to SIPRI trend-indicator values. Conventions, abbreviations and acronyms are explained below the table. The data presented are as of March 2004. For current or previous years' data and for registers of suppliers, consult the SIPRI Arms Transfers Project via URL <http://projects.sipri.se/armstrade/atrequest.html>.

Table 10B.1. Register of transfers and licensed production of major conventional weapons, 2004, by recipients

Recipient/ supplier (S) or licenser (L)	No. ordered	Weapon designation	Weapon description	Year of order/ licence	Year(s) of deliveries	No. delivered/ produced	Comments
Afghanistan							
S: USA	78	M-113	APC	(2004)		. .	Ex-US; aid; M-113A2 version; incl 15 M-577A2 CP version
Albania							
S: Italy	7	Bell-205/UH-1D	Helicopter	(2002)	2004	7	Ex-Italian; AB-205 version; aid
Algeria							
S: Belarus	28	MiG-29S/Fulcrum-C	FGA aircraft	(1998)	1999–2004	(28)	Ex-Belarus; part of deal incl 8 MiG-29UB version delivered from Russia via Belarus
Russia	42	Mi-8/Mi-17/Hip-H	Helicopter	2002	2002–2004	(42)	Deal worth $180 m; Mi-171Sh armed version

Recipient/ supplier (S) or licenser (L)	No. ordered	Weapon designation	Weapon description	Year of order/ licence	Year(s) of deliveries	No. delivered/ produced	Comments
	22	Su-24MK/Fencer-D	Bomber aircraft	2000	2001–2004	(18)	Ex-Russian; deal worth $120 m; probably modernized before delivery; delivery 2001–2005
	3	Drum Tilt	Fire control radar	(1997)	2000	1	For modernization of 3 Koni (Mourad Rais) Class frigates
	3	Garpun/Plank Shave	Air surv radar	(1997)	2000	1	For modernization of 3 Nanuchka (Hamidou) Class corvettes
	6	Pozitiv-ME1.2	Air/sea surv radar	(1997)	2000	2	For modernization of 3 (Mourad Rais) Class frigates and 3 Nanuchka (Hamidou) Class corvettes
	(96)	SS-N-25/Kh-35 Uran	Anti-ship missile	1998	2000–2004	(24)	For modernized Nanuchka (Hamidou) Class corvettes
	(24)	TEST-71	AS/ASW torpedo	(1997)	2000	(8)	For modernized Koni (Mourad Rais) Class frigates; desig uncertain
Spain	6	C-295M	Transport aircraft	2004		. .	Deal worth €130 m ($165 m)
Angola							
S: Peru	6	EMB-312 Tucano	Trainer aircraft	2002	2004	(6)	Ex-Peruvian; deal worth $1.6–4.8 m; delivery postponed while Peruvian court investigating claims that deal undervalues aircraft and by Angolan claim for $1.2 m damages for late delivery
Argentina							
S: Netherlands	6	DA-05	Air surv radar	(1979)	1985–2004	6	For 6 MEKO-140 Type (Espora Class) frigates from Germany
	6	WM-28	Fire control radar	(1979)	1985–2004	6	For 6 MEKO-140 Type (Espora Class) frigates from Germany
USA	2	AN/TPS-43	Air surv radar	2003	2004	2	Ex-US; aid
	3	AN/TPS-43	Air surv radar	2004	2004	(3)	Ex-US; deal worth $2 m; status uncertain

L: Germany	6	MEKO-140 Type	Frigate	1979	1985–2004	6	Argentine desig Espora Class; delivery of last 2 delayed 10–15 years until 2000–2004 for lack of funding
Armenia							
S: Russia	2	Il-76M/Candid-B	Transport aircraft	2004	2004	2	Probably ex-Russian; part of Collective Security Treaty Organisation Cooperation
Australia							
S: Canada	(69)	Piranha	APC	1998	2002–2004	(66)	Part of 'Project Land-112 Phase-3' or 'ASLAV programme Phase-3' worth $180–210 m; incl 7 ambulance, 11 ARV, 14 CP, 15 radar reconnaissance and 11 repair version; Australian desigs ASLAV-PC/R/A/C/S/F; assembled in Australia; delivery 2002–2005
	(81)	Piranha/LAV-25	IFV	1998	2003–2004	(61)	Part of 'Project Land-112 Phase-3' or 'ASLAV programme Phase-3' worth $180–210 m; Australian desig ASLAV-25; assembled in Australia; delivery 2003–2005
France	22	AS-665 Tiger	Combat helicopter	2001	2004	2	'Project Air-87' worth $670 m (offsets incl production of components and production of EC-120 helicopter for Asian market); Aussie Tiger version; incl 18 assembled in Australia; delivery 2004–2008
Germany	259	Waran	APC	2002	2004	(1)	Part of 'Project Land-106 Phase-2' worth AUD500 m ($280 m); Australian M-113A1 APCs rebuilt to Waran; Australian desig M-113AS4; delivery 2004–2009
Israel	(18)	EL/M-2022	MP aircraft radar	1995	2002–2004	(18)	Part of 'Project Air-5276' worth $372–495 m for modernization of 18 P-3C ASW/MP aircraft to AP-3C Sea Sentinel version by US company
Multiple sellers	5	A330-200	Tanker/transport ac	2004		. .	'Project Air-5402' worth AUD1.4 b ($1.1 b); delivery 2007–2009

Recipient/ supplier (S) or licenser (L)	No. ordered	Weapon designation	Weapon description	Year of order/ licence	Year(s) of deliveries	No. delivered/ produced	Comments
	12	NH-90 TTH	Helicopter	(2004)		. .	'Project Air-9000/Phase-2' worth AUD1 b ($704 m); Australian desig MRH-90; delivery 2007–2008
	. .	MU-90 Impact	ASW torpedo	2001		. .	'Joint Project-2070 Djimindi Phase-2' worth €150 m; delivery from 2005
	. .	MU-90 Impact	ASW torpedo	2003		. .	'Joint Project-2070 Djimindi Phase-3' worth €150 m; assembled in Australia (incl up to 35% of components produced in Australia); delivery from 2005
South Korea	1	Delos Class	Tanker	2004	2004	1	Deal worth AUD50 m ($35 m); modified in Australia to oiler/support ship
Sweden	8	9LV	Fire control radar	(1991)	1996–2004	6	9LV453 version; for 8 MEKO-200ANZ Type (Anzac Class) frigates from Germany; incl for use with Seasparrow SAM
	8	Sea Giraffe-150	Air/sea surv radar	1991	1996–2004	6	For 8 MEKO-200ANZ Type (Anzac Class) frigates from Germany
	. .	RBS-70 Mk-2	Portable SAM	2003	2003–2004	(50)	'Project Land-19 Phase-6' worth AUD83 m ($55 m) including launchers and modernization of existing RBS-70 systems and radars; Bolide version; delivery 2003–2006
UK	61	MSTAR	Ground surv radar	1999	2002–2004	(45)	'Project NINOX' worth $32 m; incl 55 assembled in Australia; Australian desig AMSTAR
USA	4	Boeing-737-7ES	AEW&C aircraft	2000		. .	'Wedgetail' programme worth $1.6–1.8 b; Australian desig A-30; incl 2 assembled in Australia; delivery 2006–2007
	2	Boeing-737-7ES	AEW&C aircraft	2004		. .	'Wedgetail' programme worth AUD326 m ($224 m); Australian desig A-30; assembled in Australia; delivery 2008
	7	King Air-350/C-12S	Light transport ac	2002	2003–2004	(7)	10-year lease worth $170 m; owned by Australian company; for training

	8	Mk-45 127mm	Naval gun	(1989)	1996–2004	6	Mk-45 Mod-2 version; for 8 MEKO-200ANZ Type (Anzac Class) frigates from Germany
	59	M-1A1 Abrams	Tank	2004		. .	Part of 'Project Land-907' worth $420–475 m; ex-US M-1A1 rebuild to M-1A1AIM(D) version; delivery from 2007
	7	M-88A2 HERCULES	ARV	2004		. .	Ex-US; part of 'Project Land-907' worth $475 m; delivery from 2007
	8	AN/SPS-49	Air surv radar	1993	1996–2004	6	AN/SPS-49V(8) version; for 8 MEKO-200ANZ Type (Anzac Class) frigates from Germany
	4	AN/TPS-77	Air surv radar	1998	2004	(2)	'Project Air-5375' worth $68–90 m; assembled in Australia
	. .	AGM-114K Hellfire	Anti-tank missile	(2004)		. .	For Tiger combat helicopters
	(400)	AIM-120B AMRAAM	BVRAAM	(2000)	2001–2004	(300)	'Project Air-5400'; for F/A-18A combat aircraft
	(676)	Javelin	Anti-tank missile	2003		. .	'Project Land-40-1' worth $60–110 m; delivery 2005–2007
	. .	Mk-48 ADCAP	AS/ASW torpedo	(2003)		. .	'Project Sea-1429' worth AUD465 m ($280 m); for Collins Class submarines; delivery from 2006
	64	RGM-84 Harpoon	Anti-ship missile	2002	2004	(10)	Deal worth AUD170 m ($96 m); RGM-84L Harpoon Block-2 version (possibly incl some Harpoon Block-1B version); for MEKO-200ANZ Type (Anzac Class) frigates
	(576)	RIM-162 ESSM	SAM	2002	2003–2004	(150)	For MEKO-200ANZ Type (Anzac Class) and modernized Adelaide (Perry) Class frigates
	(48)	RIM-66M Standard-2	SAM	(2003)		. .	'Project Sea 1390-4b'; for modernized Adelaide (Perry) Class frigates
L: Germany	8	MEKO-200ANZ Type	Frigate	1989	1996–2004	6	Deal worth $2.7 b; Australian desig Anzac Class; delivery 1996–2006
Austria							
S: Germany	18	Eurofighter/Typhoon	FGA aircraft	2003		. .	Deal worth €1.95 b ($2.2–2.6 b; offsets worth $4.7 b incl UK order for trucks produced in Austria); delivery 2007–2009

Recipient/ supplier (S) or licenser (L)	No. ordered	Weapon designation	Weapon description	Year of order/ licence	Year(s) of deliveries	No. delivered/ produced	Comments
	20	Dingo-2	APC	2004	2004	1	Delivery 2004–2005
Switzerland	12	F-5E Tiger-2	FGA aircraft	2004	2004	(8)	Ex-Swiss; 4-year lease worth €56–75 m ($67–92 m); delivery 2004–2005
UK	3	C-130K Hercules	Transport aircraft	2002	2003–2004	3	Ex-UK; deal worth $36 m; modernized before delivery
Bahrain							
S: Malta	1	BAe-146	Transport aircraft	2004	2004	1	Deal worth $8.1 m; second-hand; sold and delivered via UK
UK	6	Hawk-100	Trainer/combat ac	2003		. .	Hawk-129 version; possibly option on 6 more; delivery 2006
USA	1	AN/TPS-59	Air surv radar	2004		. .	Deal worth $44 m; AN/TPS-59(V)3 version; delivery 2008
Bangladesh							
S: Pakistan	19	T-37B	Trainer aircraft	2003	2004	(10)	Ex-Pakistani, T-37C version
Russia	3	Mi-8/Mi-17/Hip-H	Helicopter	2004		. .	Armed Mi-171 version
UK	5	Island Class	OPV	2002	2002–2004	5	Ex-UK; Bangladeshi desig Kapatakhaya Class
Belgium							
S: Germany	220	Dingo-2	APC	(2004)		. .	'MPPV' programme worth €170 m ($222 m); option on 132 more; delivery 2005–2011
USA	(92)	AN/APG-66	Combat ac radar	1993	1996–2004	(92)	For MLU modernization of 92 F-16A combat aircraft to F-16AM (F-16C) version
Bhutan							
S: India	(1)	MPV	APC	(2003)	2004	(1)	

Recipient/supplier	No. ordered	Weapon designation	Weapon description	Year of order	Year(s) of deliveries	No. delivered	Comments
Bolivia							
S: Brazil	8	MB-326GB/AT-26	Trainer/combat ac	2004		. .	Ex-Brazilian; aid
Venezuela	8	T-34 Mentor	Trainer aircraft	2004	2004	8	Ex-Venezuelan; aid; VT-34A version
Botswana							
S: Switzerland	(45)	Piranha-3	APC	(2002)	2003–2004	(45)	Piranha-3C version
Brazil							
S: France	8	AS-532U2/AS-332L2	Helicopter	2001	2002–2004	(8)	Deal worth $160 m; assembled in Brazil
	9	Ocean Master	MP aircraft radar	(2002)		. .	Part of deal worth $326 m for modernization of 9 P-3A ASW/MP aircraft to P-3BR version; desig uncertain; delivery from 2005
	(8)	MM-40 Exocet	Anti-ship missile	(1995)	2002	(1)	For Barroso Class frigate
Italy	(46)	Grifo	Combat ac radar	2000		. .	Grifo-F version; for $285 m 'F-5BR' modernization programme of F-5E combat aircraft to F-5EM/FM version; delivery from 2005
	7	RAN-20S	Air/sea surv radar	1995	2001–2004	6	Part of deal worth $112 m; for 1 Barroso Class frigate produced in Brazil and modernization of 6 Niteroi Class frigates; delivery 2001–2006
	13	RTN-30X	Fire control radar	1995	2001–2004	12	Part of deal worth $112 m; for 1 Barroso Class frigate produced in Brazil and modernization of 6 Niteroi Class frigates; delivery 2001–2006
	(53)	SCP-01 Scipio	Aircraft radar	(2003)		. .	For modernization of 53 AMX A-1 combat aircraft
	(96)	Aspide Mk-1	BVRAAM/SAM	1996	2001–2004	(96)	Deal worth $49 m; for modernized Niteroi Class frigates
USA	9	P-3A Orion	ASW/MP aircraft	2002		. .	Ex-US; 'P-X' programme; modernized in Spain to P-3BR before delivery from 2007; 3 more for spares only
	10	S-70A/UH-60L	Helicopter	(2004)		. .	Deal worth $250 m; possibly ex-US; contract probably not yet signed

Recipient/ supplier (S) or licenser (L)	No. ordered	Weapon designation	Weapon description	Year of order/ licence	Year(s) of deliveries	No. delivered/ produced	Comments
L: Germany	1	Type-209/1400	Submarine	1995		. .	Brazilian desig Tikuna Class; 1 more planned but cancelled; delivery 2005–2006
Brunei							
S: France	(36)	MM-40 Exocet	Anti-ship missile	2000		. .	For Yarrow-95m Type frigates; MM-40 Block-2 version
Indonesia	3	CN-235MPA	MP aircraft	(1995)		. .	Status uncertain
UK	(96)	Seawolf VL	SAM	(2001)		. .	For Yarrow-95m Type frigates
	3	Yarrow-95m Type	Frigate	1998		. .	Bruneian desig Nakhoda Ragam or Brunei Class; delivery from 2006
Bulgaria							
S: Belgium	1	Wielingen Class	Frigate	2004		. .	Ex-Belgian; deal worth €23 m ($28m); transferred to Bulgaria direct after modernization for Belgium finished
France	6	AS-365/AS-565 Panther	Helicopter	2004		. .	AS-565MB Panther version; delivery from 2006
	12	AS-532UL/AS-332L1	Helicopter	2004		. .	Deal worth €120 m ($160 m; incl offsets); AS-532AL version; incl 4 for CSAR; option on 4 more; delivery from 2006
Switzerland	6	PC-9	Trainer aircraft	2003	2004	6	Part of deal worth CHF50 m ($37 m)
Canada							
S: UK	4	Upholder Class	Submarine	1998	2000–2004	4	Ex-UK; lease worth $504 m (in exchange for 8 year UK use of Canadian bases for training); Canadian desig Victoria Class
USA	28	H-92 Superhawk	ASW helicopter	2004		. .	'MHP' programme worth CAD4.2 b (incl CAD2.7 b for 20 year support and training); incl assembly and

Recipient/ supplier (S) or licenser (L)	No. ordered	Weapon designation	Weapon description	Year of order/licence	Year(s) of deliveries	No. delivered/produced	Comments
							production of components in Canada; Canadian desig Cyclone; delivery from 2008
	66	Stryker MGS	AFSV	(2004)		. .	Deal worth $459 m; delivery 2006–2009; contract not yet signed
	80	AN/APG-73	Combat ac radar	2001	2003–2004	(28)	For modernization of 80 CF-18 (F/A-18) combat aircraft to CF-18IMP version; delivery 2003–2006
	(97)	AIM-120C AMRAAM	BVRAAM	2003	2004	(97)	Deal worth $80 m
	(3 000)	BGM-71F TOW-2B	Anti-tank missile	2004		. .	Deal worth 136 m; incl 2000 TOW-2A, 600 TOW-2B and 400 anti-bunker version; status uncertain
	(288)	RIM-162 ESSM	SAM	2001	2004	(10)	For modernized Halifax Class frigates; delivery 2004–2010
	12	RIM-66M Standard-2	SAM	2002		. .	Deal worth $19 m
L: Switzerland	171	Piranha	APC	(1999)	2002–2004	(171)	Incl 71 anti-tank, 39 AEV and 47 artillery fire control version; Canadian desig Kodiak
Chile							
S: France	(8)	AS-355/555	Light helicopter	(2004)		. .	Second-hand; modernized before delivery
	(16)	MM-40 Exocet	Anti-ship missile	(2003)	2004	(16)	MM-40 Block-2 version; for modernized Boxer (Almirante Williams) Class frigate
	1	Scorpene Class	Submarine	1997		. .	'Neptune' programme worth $400–460 m incl 1 from Spain; Chilean desig O'Higgins Class; delivery 2005
Israel	. .	Derby	BVRAAM	2003		. .	For F-16C combat aircraft
	. .	Python-4	BVRAAM	2003		. .	For F-16C combat aircraft
Italy	. .	Black Shark	AS torpedo	(2003)		. .	For Scorpene (Hyatt) Class and modernized Type-209 (Thomson Class) submarines; contract not yet signed
Netherlands	200	RIM-66B Standard-1MR	SAM	2004		. .	Ex-Dutch; for Heemskerck Class frigates
	2	Doorman Class	Frigate	2004		. .	Ex-Dutch; part of deal worth $350–380 m; delivery 2005–2007

Recipient/ supplier (S) or licenser (L)	No. ordered	Weapon designation	Weapon description	Year of order/ licence	Year(s) of deliveries	No. delivered/ produced	Comments
	2	Van Heemskerck Class	Frigate	2004		. .	Ex-Dutch; part of deal worth $350–380 m; delivery 2005–2006
Spain	1	Scorpene Class	Submarine	1997		. .	'Neptune' programme worth $400–460 m incl 1 from France; Chilean desig O'Higgins Class; delivery 2005–2006
Switzerland	24	M-109A1 155mm	Self-propelled gun	2004		. .	Ex-Swiss; M-109A1 version; modernized before delivery; delivery 2005
UK	16	Protector Class	Patrol craft	(1998)	1999–2004	(16)	'Danubio' programme; produced in Chile; Chilean desig Alacalufe Class; for Coast Guard
USA	10	F-16C	FGA aircraft	2003		. .	'Caza-2000' or 'F-2000' progamme worth $660 m (not including engines; offsets 100%); F-16C Block-50/52 version; incl 4 F-16D version; delivery from 2006–2007
	(158)	M-113	APC	2001	2004	(158)	Ex-US
China							
S: Russia	(3)	A-50U Mainstay	AEW&C aircraft	(2003)		. .	No. ordered could be up to 6 (possibly incl lease of 2); ordered after Israel (under US pressure) refused delivery of ordered AEW&C aircraft; delivery possibly from 2005
	(200)	Su-27SK/Flanker-B	FGA aircraft	1996	1998–2004	(57)	Deal worth $1.5–2.5 b; assembled in China; Chinese desig J-11; delivery 1998–2007/2008; possibly only 95 ordered and plans for 105 more cancelled
	24	Su-30MK/Flanker	FGA aircraft	2003	2004	24	Deal worth $1 b; Su-30MKK2 naval attack version
	1	64N6/Tombstone	Air surv radar	2004		. .	Part of deal worth $980 m; 64N6E2 version; for use with SA-10/S-300PMU2 SAM systems; delivery 2005–2006
	(12)	MR-90/Front Dome	Fire control radar	(2002)		. .	For 2 Type-052B destroyers produced in China

		(4)	SA-10d/S-300PMU-1	SAM system	2001	2003–2004	(4)	Deal worth $400 m (partly payment for Russian debt to China)
		8	SA-10e/S-300PMU-2	SAM system	2004		. .	Part of deal worth $980 m; delivery 2005–2006
		. .	AA-11 Archer/R-73	SRAAM	(1995)	1996–2004	(1 800)	For Su-27SK and Su-30MKK combat aircraft
		. .	AA-12 Adder/R-77	BVRAAM	(2000)	2002–2004	(300)	For Su-27SK and Su-30MKK combat aircraft
		. .	AS-17/Kh-31A1	Anti-ship missile	(1997)	2003–2004	(75)	For Su-30MKK, J-8MIIM and/or JH-7 combat aircraft; possibly incl assembly /production in China
		. .	AS-17/Kh-31P1	Anti-radar missile	(1998)	2001–2004	(139)	Incl for Su-30MKK and JH-7A combat aircraft; possibly produced in China as KR-1 or YJ-91
		. .	AS-18 Kazoo/Kh-59M	ASM	(1999)	2004	(50)	Incl for Su-30MKK combat aircraft
		(297)	SA-10/48N6E2	SAM	2004		. .	Part of deal worth $980 m; for SA-10/S-300PMU2 SAM systems; delivery 2005–2006
		(264)	SA-17 Grizzly/9M317	SAM	(2001)		. .	SA-N-12/9M317 version for Type-052B and Sovremmeny Class destroyers; desig uncertain
		(212)	SA-19 Grisom/9M111	SAM	(2002)		. .	For Kashtan AD system on Sovremenny Class destroyers
		(32)	SS-N-22 Sunburn/P-80	Anti-ship missile	(2001)		. .	3M80MBE version; for Sovremenny Class destroyers
		. .	SS-N-27/3M54E1 Klub	Anti-ship missile	2002		. .	For modernized and new Kilo Class submarines; probably incl 3M14E land-attack version
		8	Kilo Class/Type-636E	Submarine	2002		. .	Deal worth $1.5–1.6 b; delivery 2005–2007
		2	Sovremenny Class	Destroyer	2002		. .	Deal worth $1–1.4 b; Type-956EM version; option on 2 more; delivery 2005–2006
	UK	(6)	Searchwater	AEW aircraft radar	1996	1999	(1)	Deal worth $62–66 m; for Y-8 AEW and MP aircraft or possibly SA-341/Z-8 helicopters and/or Chinese-developed AEW aircraft based on Il-76 transport aircraft; status uncertain
	Ukraine	(1 260)	AA-10a/b Alamo/R-27	BVRAAM	(1995)	1996–2004	(900)	For Su-27SK and Su-30MKK combat aircraft; some could be delivered from Russia
		(1 260)	AA-10c/d Alamo/R-27E	BVRAAM	(1995)	1996–2004	(900)	For Su-27SK and Su-30MKK combat aircraft; some could be delivered from Russia
L:	France	. .	AS-350/550 Fennec	Light helicopter	(1992)	1995–2004	(28)	Chinese desig Z-11; incl Z-11W armed version

Recipient/ supplier (S) or licenser (L)	No. ordered	Weapon designation	Weapon description	Year of order/ licence	Year(s) of deliveries	No. delivered/ produced	Comments
	. .	AS-365/AS-565	Helicopter	1988	1992–2004	(25)	Chinese desig Z-9A or Z-9A-100 Haitun and Z-9B/C/G; incl Z-9C ASW and WZ-9 anti-tank versions
Colombia							
S: Spain	2	C-212 Aviocar	Transport aircraft	2004	2004	(2)	Ex-Spanish; aid
USA	3	BT-67	Transport aircraft	2004	2004	(1)	Aid; for police anti-narcotics operations; possibly Colombian DC-3/C-47 transport aircraft modernized to BT-67 version in USA
	1	C-130H Hercules	Transport aircraft	(2003)	2004	1	Ex-Italian aircraft sold back to US producer and resold to Colombia
Côte d'Ivoire							
S: Belarus	(4)	Su-25/Frogfoot-A	Ground attack ac	(2003)	2003–2004	(4)	Ex-Belarus; incl 2 Su-25UB version
Croatia							
S: Poland	4	MiG-21PFM/Fishbed-F	Fighter aircraft	2002	2003–2004	(4)	Ex-Polish; aid; MiG-21UM version; modernized to MiG-21UD version in Romania before delivery
Czech Republic							
S: Italy	72	Grifo	Combat ac radar	(1998)	2000–2004	(72)	Grifo-L version; for 72 L-159A combat aircraft produced in Czech Rep.
	2	RAT-31S/L	Air surv radar	2002	2004	(1)	Part 'NATO ACCS' programme; for 'NADGE' air-surveillance network; RAT-31DL version
Russia	10	Mi-24V/Mi-35/Hind-E	Combat helicopter	2004		. .	Part of payment for $200–250 m Russian debt (part of total $751 m debt) to Czech Republic; delivery 2007

Recipient/supplier	No. ordered	Weapon designation	Weapon description	Year of order	Year(s) of delivery	No. delivered	Comments
	16	Mi-8/Mi-17/Hip-H	Helicopter	2004		. .	Part of payment for $200–250 m Russian debt (part of total $751 m debt) to Czech Republic; delivery 2007; Mi-171S version
Sweden	14	JAS-39 Gripen	FGA aircraft	2004		. .	Originally ordered by Sweden but declared surplus; 10-year lease worth $750 m (offsets 130%); JAS-39C version; incl 2 JAS-39D version; delivery 2005
	. .	RBS-70	Portable SAM	2004		. .	Deal worth SEK204 m ($29 m); delivery 2005–2007
Denmark							
S: Germany	51	Leopard-2A4	Tank	1997	2002–2004	(51)	Ex-German; deal worth $91 m; handed over 1998–2000 but modernized in Germany to Leopard-2A5DK version 2000–2004 mostly before delivery
	(70)	Waran	APC	(2001)	2003–2004	(70)	Danish M-113A1 APCs rebuilt to Waran
Netherlands	2	SMART	Air surv radar	2004		. .	For 2 LSS-FS frigates; SMART-S Mk-2 version
Sweden	2	CEROS-200	Fire control radar	(2004)		. .	For 2 FS Type frigates; incl for use with RIM-162 ESSM SAM and Millennium CIWS
Switzerland	22	Piranha-3	APC	2003		. .	Deal worth $30 m; Piranha-3C version; incl 11 ambulance version; delivery 2005
	69	Piranha-3	APC	2004		. .	Deal worth DKR650 m ($108 m; incl components worth DKR150 m produced in Denmark) incl 22 ordered in 2003; Piranha-3C version, incl CP, ambulance and reconnaissance versions; delivery 2005–2007
UK	14	EH101-400	Helicopter	2001	2004	(4)	Deal worth $329 m (offsets incl production of EH-101 components in Denmark); incl for SAR; delivery 2004–2006
	4	EH101-400	Helicopter	(2004)		. .	Deal worth $261 m; contract not yet signed
USA	3	C-130J-30 Hercules	Transport aircraft	2000	2004	3	Deal worth $328 m (incl buy-back of 3 Danish C-130H aircraft by producer); option on 1 more
	1	C-130J-30 Hercules	Transport aircraft	2004		. .	Deal worth DKR525 m ($88 m); delivery 2007

Recipient/ supplier (S) or licenser (L)	No. ordered	Weapon designation	Weapon description	Year of order/ licence	Year(s) of deliveries	No. delivered/ produced	Comments
	2	Mk-45 127mm	Naval gun	2002		. .	Ex-US; deal worth $30 m; modernized to Mod-4 version before delivery; for 2 LSS-FS Type frigates
	3	AN/APS-143(V)	MP aircraft radar	2002	2003–2004	(3)	For modification of 3 Challenger-604 transport aircraft for MP
	(60)	AIM-9X Sidewinder	SRAAM	2004		. .	
	(108)	RIM-162 ESSM	SAM	2002		. .	For LSS-FS Type frigates
Dominican Republic							
S: Brazil	10	EMB-314 Super Tucano	Trainer aircraft	(2001)		. .	Incl for anti-narcotics operations; status uncertain
USA	(11)	Bell-205/UH-1H	Helicopter	(2002)	2004	(11)	Ex-US; aid; modernized to Huey-2 before delivery
	12	Bell-206/OH-58	Light helicopter	2002	2003–2004	12	Ex-US; aid; OH-58C version
	4	Schweizer-330	Light helicopter	(2003)	2003–2004	4	Schweizer-333 version; for training
Ecuador							
S: Spain	1	CN-235MP Persuader	MP aircraft	2003	2004	1	Deal worth $24 m (partly financed by Spain)
	3	Vigilante Type	Patrol craft	2004		. .	Deal worth $32 m; designed in UK; partly financed by Spain; for Coast Guard
Egypt							
S: China	80	K-8 Karakorum-8	Trainer/combat ac	1999	2001–2004	(74)	Deal worth $345 m; K-8E version; incl 70 assembled/ produced in Egypt
Finland	. .	155-GH-52 155mm	Towed gun	(1999)	2000–2004	(16)	Deal worth $17–21 m; incl assembly/production in Egypt; Egyptian desig 155 EH-52 or E52
Netherlands	(400)	AIFV	IFV	(2004)		. .	Ex-Dutch
USA	3	C-130H Hercules	Transport aircraft	2004	2004	(3)	Ex-Danish aircraft sold back to US producer and resold to Egypt; deal worth $31 m

Recipient/ supplier	No. ordered	Weapon designation	Weapon description	Year of order/licence	Year(s) of deliveries	No. delivered/ produced	Comments
	201	M-109A1 155mm	Self-propelled gun	(2003)	2004	(25)	Ex-US; deal worth $44 m; M-109A2 and M-109 A3 version; delivery 2004–2005
	100	M-1114 ECV	APC	2003	2004	(100)	Deal worth $109 m incl 450 other (unarmoured and lightly armoured) HMMWV versions
	100	M-1A1 Abrams	Tank	2001	2004	(50)	Deal worth $590 m; assembled in Egypt; delivery 2004–2005
	125	M-1A1 Abrams	Tank	2003		. .	Deal worth $275 m; assembled in Egypt; delivery 2005–2008
	13	M-88A2 HERCULES	ARV	2001	2003–2004	13	Deal worth $73 m; assembled in Egypt
	21	M-88A2 HERCULES	ARV	2004		. .	Assembled in Egypt
	5	AN/APS-145	AEW aircraft radar	1999		. .	Deal worth $138 m (plus $36 m for installation) incl modernization of 1 ex-US E-2C; for modernization of 5 E-2C AEW&C aircraft to Hawkeye-2000 version; delivery until 2007
	6	AN/SPS-48	Air surv radar	2001		. .	Deal worth $143 m; AN/SPS-48E version; delivery by 2006
	4	Phalanx Mk-15	CIWS	2001	2004	(1)	Ex-US; deal worth $32 m (incl $31 m for modernization); modernized before delivery; incl 1 to Block-1B version; delivery 2004–2005/2006
	414	AIM-9M Sidewinder	SRAAM	2003		. .	Deal worth $38 m or $50 m; AIM-9M-2 version; delivery by 2006
	25	RGM-84L Harpoon	Anti-ship missile	2003		. .	RGM-84L-4 version; land-attack capablity removed before delivery after Israeli pressure
	. .	RIM-116A RAM	SAM	(2004)		. .	Part of deal worth $565 m; for 3 Ambassador Type FAC; contract not yet signed
	3	Ambassador Type	FAC(M)	(2004)		. .	Deal worth $565 m; Ambassador Mk-3 or King Cobra version; contract probably not yet signed
Ukraine	(5)	An-74/Coaler-B	Transport aircraft	2004	2004	(2)	An-74TK200 and/or AN-74TK300 version; incl for VIP transport
Eritrea							
S: Russia	(8)	MiG-29S/Fulcrum-C	FGA aircraft	(2001)	2001–2004	(8)	

Recipient/ supplier (S) or licenser (L)	No. ordered	Weapon designation	Weapon description	Year of order/ licence	Year(s) of deliveries	No. delivered/ produced	Comments
	10	Su-27SK/Flanker-B	FGA aircraft	2003	2004	(5)	
Estonia							
S: Finland	60	XA-180	APC	2004		. .	Ex-Finnish; deal worth EEK173 m ($14 m; not incl EEK62 m for overhaul and EEK25 m for armament); delivery 2006
Germany	(18)	FH-70	Towed gun	2003	2003–2004	(18)	Ex-German
	(160)	MILAN	Anti-tank missile	(2003)	2003–2004	(150)	Ex-German; desig uncertain
UK	7	Mamba Mk-2	APC	2004	2004	7	Ex-UK; deal worth EEK6.5 m ($0.5m)
Ethiopia							
S: Russia	(7)	Su-27SK/Flanker-B	FGA aircraft	(2002)	2003–2004	(7)	
Finland							
S: France	(10)	NH-90 TTH	Helicopter	2001	2004	1	Deal worth $350 m ($520 m incl support) for 20 from France and Italy of which 18 assembled in Finland; delivery 2004–2008
Germany	2	TRML-CS	Air/sea surv radar	2002		. .	For 2 Hamina Class FAC produced in Finland; assembled in Finland
Israel	6	Ranger	UAV	2003		. .	Deal worth $20 m; Ranger-2 version; ordered via Swiss company; delivery 2005
	. .	Spike-MR/LR	Anti-tank missile	2000		. .	Deal worth $30 m; from German Eurospike production line; Spike-2.5 or Spike-MR version
Italy	(10)	NH-90 TTH	Helicopter	2001		. .	Deal worth $350 m ($520 m incl support) for 20 from France and Italy of which 18 assembled in Finland; delivery 2005–2008
South Africa	. .	Umkhonto-1R	SAM	2002		. .	Deal worth $17 m; for Hamina and T-2000 Class FAC

Sweden	57	CV-9030	IFV	2000	2003–2004	(32)	'TA-2000' project worth $176 m (offsets incl production of components in Finland); CV-9030FIN version; delivery 2002–2005
	45	CV-9030	IFV	2004		. .	Deal worth €120 m ($145 m); CV-9030FIN version; delivery 2006–2007
	4	CEROS-200	Fire control radar	2003	2004	(1)	Deal worth SEK85 m ($10 m); for Hamina Class FAC produced in Finland
	(16)	HARD	Air surv radar	2002		. .	Part of deal worth $120 m; for ASRAD-R SAM systems
	. .	RBS-15 Mk-3	Anti-ship missile	2001	2003–2004	(10)	Deal worth $50 m incl modernization of Finnish RBS-15 missiles to Mk-3 version; Finnish desig RBS-15SF-3
	(128)	RBS-70 Mk-2	Portable SAM	2002		. .	Deal worth $30 m (part of deal worth $120 m for ASRAD-R SAM systems)
France							
S: Netherlands	4	SMART-L	Air/sea surv radar	(2001)		. .	S1850M version; for 4 Forbin (Horizon) Class destroyers produced in France; French desig DRBV-27 Astral
Sweden	4	Giraffe AMB-3D	Air surv radar	2001	2003–2004	(4)	Deal worth S34 m
USA	2	A-4N Skyhawk-2	FGA aircraft	2003	2003–2004	2	Second-hand; leased by civilian company target towing for French navy
	1	E-2C Hawkeye	AEW&C aircraft	1999	2004	1	Part of deal worth $894 m (offsets worth $440 m incl French production of components)
Germany							
S: Netherlands	8	P-3CUP Orion	ASW/MP aircraft	2004		. .	Ex-Dutch; 'MPA-2000' or 'MPA-R' programme worth €324 m ($390 m, incl €24 m for training and €29 m for spare parts); transfered to Germany direct after modernization in USA for Netherlands finished; delivery 2005–2006
	3	APAR	Multi-function radar	(1997)	2004	2	For 3 Sachsen Class (F-124 or Type-124) frigates produced in Germany; delivery 2004–2005

Recipient/ supplier (S) or licenser (L)	No. ordered	Weapon designation	Weapon description	Year of order/ licence	Year(s) of deliveries	No. delivered/ produced	Comments
	3	SMART-L	Air/sea surv radar	(1997)	2004	2	or 3 Sachsen Class (F-124 or Type-124) frigates produced in Germany; delivery 2004–2005
Sweden	75	Bv-206S	APC	2004		. .	Deal worth €62 m ($77 m); incl assembly in Germany; incl CP version
	31	Bv-206S	APC	2002	2003–2004	(31)	Deal worth $12 m; ambulance version
	. .	RBS-15 Mk-3	Anti-ship missile	(2004)		. .	For K-130 Class corvettes; incl assembly in Germany; contract not yet signed
UK	(15)	Seaspray-3000	MP aircraft radar	(1999)	2002–2004	(15)	Part of $125 m modernization of 17 Lynx Mk-88 helicopters to Super Lynx Mk-88A version
USA	6	RQ-4A Global Hawk	UAV	(2004)		. .	Deal worth €600 m ($725 m) incl sensors from European companies; for ELINT role; Euro Hawk version; delivery 2007; contract not yet signed
	(1 400)	FIM-92C Stinger	Portable SAM	1986	1998–2004	(1 400)	German desig Fliegerfaust-2; part of 'European Stinger Production Programme' involving production of components in Germany, Greece, Netherlands and Turkey and final assembly in Germany
	(144)	RIM-162 ESSM	SAM	(2002)	2004	(72)	For Sachsen Class (F-124 or Type-124) frigates
	108	RIM-66M Standard-2	SAM	2001	2003–2004	(58)	SM-2 Block-3A version; for Sachsen Class (F-124 or Type-124) frigates
Ghana							
S: Russia	4	Mi-8/Mi-17/Hip-H	Helicopter	2004	2004	4	Deal worth $55 m (financed with loan from British bank)
Greece							
S: Brazil	4	EMB-145AEW&C	AEW&C aircraft	1999	2004	(1)	Part of deal worth $476–676 m; fitted in Sweden with PS-890 Erieye radar; EMB-145H version; delivery 2004–2005; option on 2 more

Canada	2	CL-415MP	MP aircraft	1999	2004	2	CL-415GR CSAR version; deal worth $380 m incl 8 CL-415GR for fighting fires
France	4	AS-532UL/AS-332L1	Helicopter	2000	2003–2004	(4)	Deal worth $90 m (offsets 100%); AS-532A2 CSAR version
	2	AS-532UL/AS-332L1	Helicopter	2003		. .	AS-532A2 CSAR version
	15	Mirage–2000-5	FGA aircraft	2000	2004	(8)	Part of deal worth $1.4 b; option on 3 more
	(8)	Sperwer	UAV	2002	2003–2004	(8)	Deal worth €36 m ($35 m)
	10	RDY	Aircraft radar	2000		. .	Part of deal worth $1.4 b; for modernization of 10 Mirage-2000EG combat aircraft to Mirage-2000-5 version
	(50)	MICA	BVRAAM	2004		. .	
	27	MM-40 Exocet	Anti-ship missile	2000	2004	(18)	Deal worth $55 m (160% offsets); MM-40 Block-2 version; for Super Vita Class FAC
	. .	MM-40 Exocet	Anti-ship missile	(2003)		. .	MM-40 Block-2 version; for Super Vita Class FAC
	(22)	Storm Shadow/SCALP	ASM	2001	2004	(22)	Part of deal worth $1.4 b; SCALP-EG version
	(34)	Storm Shadow/SCALP	ASM	2004		. .	
Germany	114	M-109A5 155mm	Self-propelled gun	2003	2004	(114)	Ex-German; M-109A3GEA version; offsets for Greek order for 24 PzH-2000 self-propelled guns
	24	PzH-2000 155mm	Self-propelled gun	2001	2003–2004	(24)	Part of deal worth $164–228 m (offsets 120% and 114 ex-German M-109 guns); PzH-2000GR version; option on 12 more
	20	Bergepanzer-1	ARV	(2004)		. .	Ex-German; contract not yet signed
	10	BrPz-1 Biber	ABL	(2004)		. .	Ex-German; contract not yet signed
	12	Buffel	ARV	2003		. .	Part of deal worth €1.7 b ($1.9 b, offsets incl 40% direct); Buffel–2 version; delivery 2005/2006–2009
	150	Leopard-1A5	Tank	(2004)		. .	Ex-German; contract not yet signed
	183	Leopard-2A4	Tank	(2004)		. .	Ex-German; contract not yet signed
	170	Leopard-2A5	Tank	2003		. .	Part of deal worth €1.7 b ($1.9b, offsets incl 40% direct); Leopard-2HEL (Leopard-2A6EX) version; incl 140 assembled/produced in Greece; delivery 2006–2009
	28	PzH-2000 ALV	ALV	2001	2003–2004	(28)	Part of deal worth $164–228 m (offsets 120% and 114 ex-German M-109 guns); incl 24 ammunition carrier and 4 ammunition loader version

Recipient/ supplier (S) or licenser (L)	No. ordered	Weapon designation	Weapon description	Year of order/ licence	Year(s) of deliveries	No. delivered/ produced	Comments
	35	AN/APG-65	Combat ac radar	1997	2003–2004	(35)	Part of $315–336 m ‘Peace Icarus-2000’ modernization programme of 35 F-4E combat aircraft
	(350)	IRIS-T	SRAAM	(2004)		. .	Delivery possibly from 2005
	(95)	RIM-116A RAM	SAM	(2003)	2004	(48)	Deal worth $25 m incl 3 launchers; for 3 Super Vita Class FAC
	(63)	RIM-116A RAM	SAM	(2003)		. .	For 2 Super Vita Class FAC
	3	Type-214	Submarine	2000		. .	Deal worth $0.9–1.3 b (offsets 115% incl $224 m direct offsets and setting up of submarine production in Greece); incl 2 assembled/produced in Greece; Greek desig Katsonis Class; delivery 2005–2009
	1	Type-214	Submarine	2002		. .	Deal worth €700 m ($700 m) incl modernization of 3 Greek Type-209 submarines; assembled/produced in Greece; delivery 2009–2010
Italy	12	C-27J Spartan	Transport Aircraft	2003		. .	Deal worth $312 m (offsets 360%); delivery 2005–2006
	1	RAT-31S/L	Air surv radar	(2002)		. .	Part ‘NATO ACCS’ programme; for ‘NADGE’ air-surveillance network; RAT-31DL version
Multiple sellers	20	NH-90 TTH	Helicopter	2003		. .	Deal worth €657 m ($716–755 m; offsets 120%); to be delivered from France/Germany/Italy; option on 14 more; delivery 2005–2010
Netherlands	(7)	LIROD	Fire control radar	2000	2003–2004	(6)	For 3 Super Vita Class and 4 Osprey-55 Type (Pyrpolitis Class) FAC from UK and Denmark
	3	MW-08	Air surv radar	2000	2004	2	For 3 Super Vita Class FAC from UK
	2	MW-08	Air surv radar	2003		. .	For 2 Super Vita Class FAC from UK
	3	STING	Fire control radar	2000	2004	2	For 3 Super Vita Class FAC from UK
	2	STING	Fire control radar	2003		. .	For 2 Super Vita Class FAC from UK
	3	Scout	Sea surv radar	2000	2004	2	Scout Mk-2 version; for 3 Super Vita Class FAC from UK

	6	Scout	Sea surv radar	2003		. .	Scout Mk-2 version; part of deal worth $353 m for modernization of 6 Kortenaer (Elli) Class frigates
	2	Scout	Sea surv radar	2003		. .	Scout Mk-2 version; for 2 Super Vita Class FAC from UK
	(7)	Variant	Air/sea surv radar	2000	2003–2004	(6)	For 3 Super Vita Class and 4 Osprey-55 Type (Pyrpolitis Class) FAC from UK and Denmark
Russia	19	SA-15/9A331 Tor-M1	Mobile SAM system	(2002)		. .	Part of deal worth $400 m or $700 m; status uncertain
	1 100	AT-14/9M133 Kornet	Anti-tank missile	2001	2002–2004	(1 100)	Deal worth $95 m
	(323)	SA-15 Gauntlet/9M338	SAM	(2002)		. .	Part of deal worth $400 m or $700 m; status uncertain
	1	Pomornik Class	ACV/landing craft	2002		. .	Deal worth $64 m; Greek desig Kefallinia Class; delivery 2005
Sweden	(6)	ARTHUR	Arty locating radar	2002	2004	(6)	Deal worth $43–44 m
	4	PS-890 Erieye	AEW aircraft radar	1999	2004	(1)	Part of deal worth $476–676 m; for 4 EMB-145H AEW aircraft from Brazil; option on 2 more; delivery 2004–2005
USA	4	AH-64D Apache	Combat helicopter	2003		. .	Deal worth $680–703 m (offsets worth $845 m) incl 8 AH-64D without Longbow radar; option on 4 more; delivery 2007
	8	AH-64D Apache	Combat helicopter	2003		. .	Deal worth $675–703 m (offsets worth $845 m) incl 4 AH-64D with Longbow radar; option on 4 more; delivery 2007
	50	F-16C	FGA aircraft	2000	2003–2004	(50)	'Peace Xenia-3' deal worth $2.1 b; F-16CG Block-52+ version; incl 16 F-16DG version
	10	F-16C	FGA aircraft	2001	2004	10	'Peace Xenia-3' deal worth $183 m; F-16CG Block-52+ version; incl 4 F-16DG version
	2	S-70B/SH-60F Seahawk	ASW helicopter	(2003)		. .	Deal worth S107 m; S-70B-6 Aegean Hawk version
	6	AN/TPQ-37 Firefinder	Arty locating radar	(2000)	2003–2004	(6)	
	(6)	Patriot	SAM system	1999	2002–2004	(6)	Deal worth $1.13 b (offsets 120%)
	2	Phalanx Mk-15	CIWS	2002	2004	(2)	Ex-US; Phalanx Block-1A version
	(53)	AIM-120C AMRAAM	BVRAAM	2004		. .	Part of deal worth $53 m; AIM-120C-5 version; delivery by 2005
	(200)	FIM-92A Stinger	Portable SAM	2001	2003–2004	(200)	Part of deal worth $89 m
	(350)	FIM-92C Stinger	Portable SAM	1986	1998–2004	(350)	Part of 'European Stinger Production Programme' involving production of components in Germany,

Recipient/ supplier (S) or licenser (L)	No. ordered	Weapon designation	Weapon description	Year of order/ licence	Year(s) of deliveries	No. delivered/ produced	Comments
							Greece, Netherlands and Turkey and final assembly in Germany
	. .	MIM-104 PAC-3	SAM	(1999)		. .	For Patriot SAM systems
	. .	RIM-162 ESSM	SAM	(2003)		. .	For modernized Kortenaer (Elli) Class
L: Denmark	4	Osprey-55 Type	Patrol craft	1999	2003–2004	(4)	Deal worth $208 m; Greek desig Pyrpolitis Class or Hellenic-56 Type
UK	2	Super Vita type	FAC(M)	2003		. .	Deal worth €200–270 m ($227–325 m); Greek desig Rousen Class; delivery 2006–2007
	3	Super Vita type	FAC(M)	2000	2004	2	Deal worth €580 m ($580 m); Greek desig Rousen Class; delivery 2004–2005
Hungary							
S: Italy	3	RAT-31S/L	Air surv radar	2002	2004	(1)	Part 'NATO ACCS' programme; for 'NADGE' air-surveillance network; RAT-31DL version
Sweden	14	JAS-39 Gripen	FGA aircraft	2001		. .	Ex-Swedish; modernized before delivery to JAS-39EBS HU version; 10-year lease worth $924 m (offsets 110%); to be bought after lease; incl 2 JAS-39D version; delivery 2006–2007
USA	40	AIM-120C AMRAAM	BVRAAM	(2004)		. .	Deal worth $38 m; AIM-120C-5 version; for JAS-39 combat aircraft; delivery by 2007
Ukraine	1	An-26/Curl-A	Transport aircraft	(2004)	2004	1	Probably second-hand
India							
S: France	10	Mirage-2000E	FGA aircraft	2000	2004	(10)	Deal worth $312–353 m; Mirage-2000H version; incl 6 Mirage-2000TH version; Indian desig Vajra
	(36)	SM-39 Exocet	Anti-ship missile	(2004)		. .	Deal worth $150 m; for Scorpene submarines; contract not yet signed

	6	Scorpene Class	Submarine	(2004)		. .	‘Project-75’ worth $1–2.1 b; assembled/produced in India; delivery 2010–2016; contract not yet signed
Israel	(12)	Heron-2	UAV	(2004)		. .	Deal worth $200–266 m; Heron/Eagle version; contract not yet signed
	(2)	EL/M-2032	Combat ac radar	(1999)		. .	For 2 Jaguar-IM (Maritime Jaguar) combat aircraft from UK
	3	EL/M-2075 Phalcon	AEW aircraft radar	2004		. .	Part of deal worth $1.1 b (incl $350 m advance payment); for 3 A-50EhI AEW&C aircraft (aircraft delivered from Uzbekistan via Russia and fitted with radar in Israel); delivery 2007–2009
	6	EL/M-2221	Fire control radar	(2002)	2003–2004	(2)	For 3 Delhi and 3 Bangalore Class destroyers produced in India; for use with Barak SAM
	5	EL/M-2221	Fire control radar	(2003)	2004	(2)	For use with Barak SAM on 3 Brahmaputra and 2 modernized Godavari Class frigates
	2	Green Pine	Air surv radar	2002		. .	
	(144)	Barak	SAM	(2002)	2003–2004	(48)	For Delhi and Bangalore Class destroyers
	(60)	Barak	SAM	(2003)	2004	(30)	For Brahmaputra and modernized Godavari Class frigates
Italy	9	Seaguard TMX	Fire control radar	1993	2000–2004	(9)	For 3 Brahmaputra Class (Project-16A) frigates produced in India; assembled/produced in India; Indian desig Shikari
	6	Seaguard TMX	Fire control radar	(2001)		. .	For 3 Shivalik Class (Project-17) frigates produced in India; assembled/produced in India; Indian desig Shikari
	(72)	A244/S	ASW torpedo	(1993)	2000–2004	(40)	For Brahmaputra Class (Project-16A) and Shivalik (Project-17) frigates; possibly produced in India as NST-58
Netherlands	4	DA-05	Air surv radar	(1989)	1995–2004	(4)	For modernization of 1 Viraat Class aircraft carrier and for 3 Brahmaputra Class (Project-16A) frigates produced in India; incl assembly/production in India; Indian desig RAWS, RAWS-03 or PFN-513
	7	LW-08	Air surv radar	(1989)	1997–2004	(7)	For modernization of 1 Viraat Class aircraft carrier and for 3 Delhi (Project-15) Class destroyers and 3 Brahmaputra (Project-16A) Class frigates; incl

Recipient/ supplier (S) or licenser (L)	No. ordered	Weapon designation	Weapon description	Year of order/ licence	Year(s) of deliveries	No. delivered/ produced	Comments
							assembly/production in India; Indian desig RALW, RAWL-2 or PLN-517
	6	LW-08	Air surv radar	(2003)		. .	For 3 Bangalore (Project-15A) Class destroyers and 3 Shivalik Class (Project-17) frigates produced in India; assembled/produced in India; India desig RAWL or RAWL-02
	(12)	ZW-06	Sea surv radar	(1989)	1997–2004	(9)	For modernization of 1 Viraat Class aircraft carrier and for 3 Delhi Class (Project-15) destroyers and 3 Brahmaputra (Project-16A) and 3 Shivalik Class (Project-17) frigates produced in India; incl assembly/production in India; Indian desig Rashmi
Poland	80	WZT-3	ARV	2002	2002–2004	(80)	Deal worth $60–75 m; incl 40 assembled in India; Indian desig ARV-3
	228	WZT-3	ARV	2004	2004	(10)	Deal worth $202 m; assembled in India (Indian content 18–40%); deliver 2004–2007
Qatar	11	Mirage-2000-5	FGA aircraft	(2004)		. .	Ex-Qatari; status uncertain
Russia	2	Il-38/May	ASW/MP aircraft	(2002)		. .	Ex-Russian; modernized to Il-38SD version before delivery; donation to replace 2 lost; delivery possibly 2005
	(3)	Ka-27PL/Helix-A	ASW helicopter	2004		. .	Ka-28 version
	(3)	Ka-31/Helix	AEW helicopter	2004		. .	
	6	Mi-8/Mi-17/Hip-H	Helicopter	2003	2003–2004	6	For Border Guard; for use in Jammu and Kashmir; Mi-17 version
	16	MiG-29K/Fulcrum-D	FGA aircraft	2003		. .	Deal worth $700 m; for use on Gorshkov Class aircraft carrier; incl 4 MiG-29KUB version; option on 30 more; delivery 2007–2008
	140	Su-30MK/Flanker	FGA aircraft	2000	2004	1	Deal worth $3–5 b; Su-30MKI version; assembled/ produced in India; delivery until 2017–2018
	10	Su-30MK/Flanker	FGA aircraft	1998	2004	10	Su-30MKI version; ordered while still being developed

(4)	140mm RL	Naval MRL	(1992)	1997	(2)	For 2 Magar Class landing ships produced in India; desig uncertain
3	AK-100 100mm	Naval gun	(2003)		. .	For 3 Bangalore (Project-15A) Class destroyers produced in India
(12)	BM-9A52 Smerch	MRL	(2004)		. .	Contract not yet signed
310	T-90S	Tank	2001	2001–2004	(264)	Deal worth $600–700 m (incl 55% advance payment); ordered as reaction on Pakistani acquisition of 320 T-80UB tanks; incl 124 assembled in India; delivery 2001–2004/2005
4	Cross Dome	Air surv radar	(1992)	1998–2004	4	For 4 Kora (Project-25A) Class corvettes produced in India
3	Fregat/Top Plate	Air surv radar	(2001)		. .	For 3 Shivalik Class (Project-17) frigates produced in India
7	Garpun/Plank Shave	Air surv radar	(1993)	1997–2004	7	For 3 Delhi (Project-15) Class destroyers and 4 Kora Class (Project-25A) corvettes produced in India; for use with SS-N-25 missiles
9	Garpun/Plank Shave	Air surv radar	(1998)	2000–2004	(3)	For 3 Bangalore (Project-15A) Class destroyers and 3 Brahmaputra (Project-16A) and 3 Shivalik Class (Project-17) frigates produced in India; for use with SS-N-25 missiles; probably assembled/produced in India; Indian desig Aparna
3	Half Plate	Air/sea surv radar	(2003)		. .	For 3 Bangalore (Project-15A) Class destroyers produced in India
3	Kite Screech	Fire control radar	(2003)		. .	For 3 Bangalore (Project-15A) Class destroyers produced in India
(125)	Kopyo	Combat ac radar	1996	2001–2004	(88)	Part of deal worth $428–626 m for modernization of up to 125 MiG-21bis combat aircraft to MiG-21UPG (MiG-21I or MiG-21-93) version; option on 50 more; delivery 2001–2005
6	MR-123/Bass Tilt	Fire control radar	(2003)		. .	For 3 Bangalore (Project-15A) Class destroyers produced in India
6	MR-90/Front Dome	Fire control radar	(2003)		. .	For 3 Bangalore (Project-15A) Class destroyers produced in India; for use with SA-N-7 SAM

Recipient/ supplier (S) or licenser (L)	No. ordered	Weapon designation	Weapon description	Year of order/ licence	Year(s) of deliveries	No. delivered/ produced	Comments
	(19)	Zmei/Sea Dragon	MP aircraft radar	2000	2004	(2)	For modernization of 5 Il-38 ASW/MP aircraft to Il-38SD (deal worth $205 m) and some 14 Ka-28 ASW helicopters
	(1 140)	AA-10c/d Alamo/R-27E	BVRAAM	1996	1997–2004	(400)	For Su-30MKI combat aircraft
	(3 900)	AA-11 Archer/R-73	SRAAM	(1996)	1997–2004	(1 150)	For Su-30MKI, MiG-21UPG (modernized MiG-21bis) and probably for MiG-29 and modernized MiG-27ML combat aircraft
	(750)	AA-12 Adder/R-77	BVRAAM	(2000)	2002–2004	(225)	For Su-30MK, MiG-21UPG (modernized MiG-21bis) and possibly for MiG-29 and modernized MiG-27ML combat aircraft
	(1 440)	AT-16/9M120	Anti-tank missile	(2000)	2002–2004	(1 440)	For Mi-17 helicopters
	(324)	SA-11 Gadfly/9M38	SAM	(2000)		. .	For Bangalore (Project-15A) Class destroyers and Shivalik (Project-17) Class frigates; SA-N-7/9M38M1 or SA-N-12/9M317 version
	(416)	SS-N-25/Kh-35 Uran	Anti-ship missile	(1992)	1997–2004	(416)	For Delhi Class (Project-15) and modernized Kashin-2 (Rajput) Class destroyers, Brahmaputra Class (Poject-16A) frigates, Kora Class (Project-25A) corvettes and Tarantul-1 (Vibhuti) Class FAC
	(228)	SS-N-27/3M54E1 Klub	Anti-ship missile	(1998)	2001–2004	(98)	For Talwar and Shivalik (Project-17) Class frigates, Bangalore (Project-15A) Class destroyers and Kilo Class (incl modernized) submarines
	2	Akula-2 Class	Nuclear submarine	(2004)		. .	Lease worth $700 m or $1.4 b; option on 1 more; possibly to be armed with Indian nuclear weapons; contract possibly not yet signed
	1	Gorshkov Class	Aircraft-carrier	2004		. .	Ex-Russian; deal worth $625–675 m incl modernization and modification to CTOL carrier before delivery; Indian desig Vikramaditya Class; delivery 2008

		3	Talwar Class	Frigate	1997	2003–2004	3	Deal worth INR35 b ($0.8–1 b); Russian desig Project-1135.6; ordered due to problems with Indian production of major warships; delivery 2 years delayed due to financial problems of producer and technical problems with systems on the ships
	South Africa	(180)	G-6 Rhino	Self-propelled gun	(2004)		. .	Status uncertain
		(100)	T-6 155mm	Turret	(2004)		. .	For Bhim self-propelled gun (on Indian Arjun tank chassis); contract not yet signed
	UK	66	Hawk-100	Trainer/combat ac	2004		. .	'Advanced Jet Trainer' (AJT) programme worth £1.1 b ($1.7 b; incl £800 m for aircraft); incl assembly/production of 42 in India; Hawk-132 version; delivery from 2007
	USA	8	AN/TPQ-37 Firefinder	Arty locating radar	2002	2003–2004	(8)	Part of deal worth $142–190 m; orginally planned for 1998 but embargoed by USA after Indian nuclear tests in 1998; AN/TPQ-37(V)3 version
		(4)	AN/TPQ-37 Firefinder	Arty locating radar	(2003)		. .	Part of deal worth $142–190 m; AN/TPQ-37(V)3 version; delivery probably 2005–2006
	Ukraine	6	MiG-23MF/Flogger-B	Fighter aircraft	2002	2004	(6)	Ex-Ukrainian; MiG-23UB version
		(1 140)	AA-10a/b Alamo/R-27	BVRAAM	(1996)	1997–2004	(470)	For Su-30MKI combat aircraft; desig uncertain
	Uzbekistan	3	A-50EhI	AEW&C aircraft	2004		. .	Part of deal worth $1.1 b (incl $350 m advance payment); with Phalcon AEW system from Israel; ordered via Israel and Russia; delivery from Israel 2006–2009
		6	Il-78M/Midas	Tanker aircraft	2001	2003–2004	(6)	Deal worth $150 m; Il-78MK version
L:	France	(200)	SA-315B Lama	Light helicopter	1971	1977–2004	(200)	Cheetah version
		. .	MILAN	Anti-tank missile	(1981)	1984–2004	(53 500)	MILAN-2 version; incl for BMP-2 IFVs
	Germany	47	Do-228MP	MP aircraft	1983	1993–2004	(38)	Incl 11 for Coast Guard
	Russia	. .	AT-5 Spandrel/9M113	Anti-tank missile	(1988)	1992–2004	(5 800)	For BMP-2 IFVs; ordered from Soviet Union and produced under Russian licence after break-up of Soviet Union; incl 9M113M version from 2003

Recipient/ supplier (S) or licenser (L)	No. ordered	Weapon designation	Weapon description	Year of order/ licence	Year(s) of deliveries	No. delivered/ produced	Comments
UK	17	Jaguar International	FGA aircraft	1999	2003–2004	(12)	Jaguar-B version; for night-attack role; possibly incl 2 Jaguar-IM (Jaguar Maritime version); Indian desig Shamsher; delivery 2003–2005
	20	Jaguar International	FGA aircraft	(2000)		. .	Jaguar International-IS version; Indian desig Shamsher; delivery 2005–2007
Indonesia							
S: Czech Republic	(6)	RM-70 122mm	MRL	(2002)	2003–2004	(6)	Ex-Czech
France	5	TB-9 Tampico	Light aircraft	2004	2004	2	Deal worth $2.5 m; TB-10 Tobago GT version; for training; delivery 2004–2005
	1	Master-T	Air surv radar	2004		. .	
	3	Ocean Master	MP aircraft radar	2001	2002–2004	(3)	Deal worth $50 m; for 3 CN-235MPA aircraft produced in Indonesia
	(6)	Ocean Master	MP aircraft radar	1996	2000–2004	(6)	For 3 NC-212MP MP aircraft and 3 NBO-105 helicopters from Spain and Germany
Israel	. .	Heron-2	UAV	(2003)		. .	Possibly for MP; status uncertain
Netherlands	4	LIROD	Fire control radar	(1994)	2000–2004	4	Part of deal worth $42 m; for 4 PB-57 Type (Todak Class) patrol craft from Germany
	4	Variant	Air/sea surv radar	(1999)	2000–2004	4	Part of deal worth $42 m; for 4 PB-57 Type (Todak Class) patrol craft from Germany
	2	Sigma-90 Type	Frigate	(2003)		. .	Deal worth $340 m (payment spread over 3 years); delivery 2007
Poland	11	M-28 Skytruck	Light transport ac	(2004)		. .	Incl MP version
Russia	(16)	Mi-2/Hoplite	Helicopter	2002	2003–2004	(16)	
	4	Mi-8/Mi-17/Hip-H	Helicopter	2002	2004	(4)	Deal worth $22 m (loaned from Malaysian company); Mi-17 version
USA	16	AN/APG-66	Combat ac radar	1996	1999	10	For 16 Hawk-200 combat aircraft from UK; status of last 6 uncertain after being embargoed by USA

L: Germany	4	PB-57 Type	Patrol craft	1993	2000–2004	4	Deal worth $260 m; PB-57 NAV-5 version; Indonesian desig Todak Class
Spain	(3)	C-212MP Aviocar	MP aircraft	1996	2004	(3)	'On Top-2' programme; NC-212-200MP version
Iran							
S: China	. .	C-701/FL-10	Anti-ship missile	(1998)	2001–2004	(40)	For China Cat Type FAC; C-701T and possibly C-701R version; possibly assembled/produced in Iran as Noor
	. .	TL-10/FL-8	Anti-ship missile	(2002)	2004	(10)	Iranian desig Kosar; TL-10A and possibly TL-10B version; possibly incl assembly in Iran
	. .	TL-6/FL-9	Anti-ship missile	(2003)		. .	Iranian desig Nasr; possibly incl assembly in Iran
	. .	China Cat Type	FAC(M)	(2000)	2001–2004	(7)	
Russia	1 500	BMP-2	IFV	(1991)	1993–2004	(650)	Part of deal worth $2.2 b; most assembled or produced in Iran; Iranian desig could be BMT-2
	(1 000)	T-72M1	Tank	(1991)	1993–2004	(686)	Part of deal worth $2.2 b; T-72S1 version; most assembled/produced in Iran
	(15 000)	AT-4 Spigot/9M111	Anti-tank missile	(1991)	1993–2004	(8 250)	For BMP-2 and Boraq IFVs; incl assembly/ production in Iran
	. .	AT-5 Spandrel/9M113	Anti-tank missile	(1998)	1999–2004	(1000)	Probably assembled/produced in Iran; Iranian desig Towsan-1
L: China	. .	FL-6	Anti-ship missile	(2000)	2002–2004	(60)	Developed or copied by China from Italian Sea Killer anti-ship missile supplied by Iran to China; incl for use on SH-3D helicopters; Iranian desig Fajr-e Darya
Russia	. .	AT-3 Sagger/9M14M	Anti-tank missile	(1995)	1996–2004	(2 250)	Iranian desig RAAD; incl I-RAAD version
Iraq							
S: Australia	2	SB7L-360 Seeker	Light aircraft	2004	2004	2	Deal worth AUD2.8 m ($2 m); ordered via Jordan
Canada	8	CH-2000	Light aircraft	2004	2004	(4)	Deal worth $5.8 m; option on 8 more worth $6.2 m; SAMA CH-2000 version; ordered via USA; assembled in Jordan; for surveillance; delivery 2004–2005

Recipient/ supplier (S) or licenser (L)	No. ordered	Weapon designation	Weapon description	Year of order/ licence	Year(s) of deliveries	No. delivered/ produced	Comments
Germany	(20)	Tpz-1 Fuchs	APC	2004	2004	(20)	Ex-German; aid
Jordan	16	Bell-205/UH-1H	Helicopter	2004		. .	Ex-Jordanian; aid; delivery 2005
	2	C-130B Hercules	Transport aircraft	2004	2004	(2)	Ex-Jordanian; aid
	50	BTR-94	IFV	2004	2004	(50)	Ex-Jordanian; aid
	100	M-113	APC	2004	2004	(100)	Ex-Jordanian; M-113A1 version; aid
	100	Spartan	APC	2004	2004	100	Ex-Jordanian; aid
Poland	20	W-3 Sokol	Helicopter	2004		. .	Deal worth $120–132 m; incl 4 for VIP transport, 4 for SAR and 12 W-3W armed version; delivery 2005–2006
Turkey	(300)	Akrep/Scorpion	Reconnaissance veh	(2004)		. .	Desig uncertain; delivery from 2005
UAE	4	Bell-206/OH-58	Light helicopter	2004	2004	4	Ex-UAE; aid
	44	M-3 VTT	APC	2004	2004	44	Ex-UAE; aid
USA	4	C-130E Hercules	Transport aircraft	(2004)		. .	Ex-US; aid; delivery 2005
	7	Comp Air-7SL	Light aircraft	2004	2004	7	Financed by UAE
	43	ASV-150/M-1117	APC	2004	2004	(10)	Deal worth $50 m; incl 2 CP version; delivery 2004–2005
Unknown country	24	Mi-8/Mi-17/Hip-H	Helicopter	2004		. .	Second-hand; deal worth $105 m; bought via Polish company from a former Soviet republic (probably Russia or Ukraine)
Ireland							
S: Italy	4	AB-139	Helicopter	2004		. .	Delivery 2005
	2	EC-135/EC-635	Helicopter	2004		. .	Incl for training; delivery 2005
Switzerland	8	PC-9	Trainer aircraft	(2002)	2004	8	Deal worth $63 m; PC-9M version; incl for combat role
	25	Piranha-3	APC	(2002)	2004	(25)	Piranha-3H version; incl 4 CP and 1 ambulance version
USA	36	Javelin	Anti-tank missile	2003		. .	Deal worth $12.5 m

Recipient/supplier	No. ordered	Weapon designation	Weapon description	Year of order	Year(s) of deliveries	No. delivered	Comments
Israel							
S: Germany	(103)	Dingo-2	APC	(2004)		. .	Deal worth $99 m; from US production line financed by US FMF aid; contract not yet signed
USA	(9)	AH-64D Apache	Combat helicopter	2001		. .	Part of deal worth $509 m; financed by US FMF aid; Israeli desig Sharaf; delivery 2005
	6	AH-64D Apache	Combat helicopter	(2004)		. .	Deal worth $200 m; contract not yet signed
	18	Bonanza	Light aircraft	2004	2004	(5)	Deal worth $11 m; option on 6 more; delivery 2004–2005
	50	F-16I	FGA aircraft	1999	2004	(18)	'Peace Marble-5' deal worth $2.5 b (offsets 25%); financed by USA; Israeli desig Suefa; delivery 2004–2005
	52	F-16I	FGA aircraft	2001		. .	'Peace Marble-5' deal worth $2 b (incl $1.3 b for aircraft and $300 m for engines; offsets worth $800 m); Israeli desig Suefa; delivery 2006–2008
	4	Gulfstream-5	Transport aircraft	2003		. .	Deal worth $473 m incl option on 2 more; modified in Israel to AEW aircraft
	3	Gulfstream-5	Transport aircraft	2001		. .	Deal worth $174–206 m; G-550 version; modified in Israel to ELINT aircraft; Israeli desig Nachshon; delivery from 2005
	120	M-1114 ECV	APC	(2002)	2003–2004	(120)	For use in West Bank and Gaza Strip Palestinian areas
	(3)	AN/APG-78 Longbow	Combat ac radar	2001		. .	Part of deal worth $509 m; financed by US FMF aid; for modernization of 3 Israeli AH-64A helicopters to AH-64D version
	(480)	AGM-114K Hellfire	Anti-tank missile	(2000)		. .	For AH-64D helicopters
	48	AIM-120C AMRAAM	BVRAAM	2001	2003–2004	(48)	
	2 030	BGM-71 TOW	Anti-tank missile	2002	2003–2004	(2 030)	Deal worth $80 m; TOW-2A version
	(400)	BGM-71F TOW-2B	Anti-tank missile	2002	2003–2004	(400)	Part of deal worth $52 m; TOW-2A/TOW-2B version
Italy							
S: France	(139)	MO-120-RT-61 120mm	Mortar	(1998)	2000–2004	(139)	
Germany	70	PzH-2000 155mm	Self-propelled gun	2002	2003–2004	(4)	Deal worth $455–510 m; incl 68 assembled in Italy; delivery 2003–2008

Recipient/ supplier (S) or licenser (L)	No. ordered	Weapon designation	Weapon description	Year of order/ licence	Year(s) of deliveries	No. delivered/ produced	Comments
	(444)	IRIS-T	SRAAM	(2003)		. .	Delivery probably from 2005
Netherlands	2	SMART-L	Air/sea surv radar	(2001)		. .	S1850M version; for 2 Andrea Doria (Horizon) Class destroyers produced in Italy
Sweden	112	Bv-206S	APC	2003	2004	(5)	Deal worth €57 m ($68 m; offsets for Swedish NH-90 helicopter order); delivery 2004–2007
	34	Bv-206S	APC	2003		. .	Deal worth €24 m ($29 m) incl 12 Bv-206 unarmoured vehicles (offsets for Swedish NH-90 helicopter order)
UK	200	Storm Shadow/SCALP	ASM	1999	2004	(10)	Deal worth $275 m
USA	34	F-16(ADF)	FGA aircraft	2001	2003–2004	(34)	Ex-US; 'Peace Ceasar' lease worth $760 m (for total of 45000 flying hours) until Eurofighter enters service in 2010; F-16A Block-15ADF version; incl 4 F-16B version; modernized before delivery; 4 more delivered for spares only
	4	KC-767	Tanker/transport ac	2002		. .	Deal worth $619 m (offsets worth up to $1.1 b); option on 2 more; delivery 2005–2008
	(4)	RQ-1A Predator	UAV	2001	2004	(4)	Deal worth $55 m; option on 2 more
	2	AN/FPS-117	Air surv radar	2002		. .	AN/TPS-117 version
	(200)	FIM-92A Stinger	Portable SAM	2001	2003–2004	(200)	Part of deal worth $89 m for 1007 missiles for Greece, Italy and UK
L: Germany	2	Type-212	Submarine	1997		. .	Italian desig Todaro Class; option on 2 more; delivery 2005–2006
Japan							
S: France	(14)	Ocean Master	MP aircraft radar	1996		. .	For 14 US-1A Kai (US-2) MP aircraft produced in Japan; delivery from 2006–2007
	2	Ocean Master	MP aircraft radar	(2001)	2003–2004	(2)	For 2 Gulfstream-5 MP aircraft from USA
Italy	5	127mm/54	Naval gun	(1999)	2003–2004	3	For 5 Takanami Class frigates produced in Japan

Supplier	No. ordered	Weapon designation	Weapon description	Year of order	Year(s) of deliveries	No. delivered	Comments
UK	14	EH101-400	Helicopter	(2003)		. .	'MCH-X' programme worth $518 m; incl for mine-sweeping
USA	(60)	AH-64D Apache	Combat helicopter	2001		. .	'AH-X' programme; incl assembly in Japan; delivery from 2005
	(21)	BAe-125-800	Light transport ac	1995	1997–2004	(19)	'H-X' programme; RH-800 or Hawker-800 version; for SAR; Japanese desig U-125A
	2	Gulfstream-5	Transport aircraft	2001	2003–2004	(2)	Deal worth $100 m; modified in Netherlands before delivery to long-range MP aircraft; for Coast Guard; incl for use against piracy in South-East Asia
	4	KC-767	Tanker/transport ac	2003		. .	'KC-X' programme; delivery 2007–2010
	(20)	King Air-350/C-12S	Light transport ac	1997	1999–2004	(7)	Incl for reconnaissance; Japanese desig LR-2
	(90)	M-270 MLRS	MRL	1993	1995–2004	(78)	Assembled in Japan
	2	Mk-45-4 127mm	Naval gun	(2002)		. .	For 2 Improved Kongou Class destroyers produced in japan
	(13)	AN/APS-145	AEW aircraft radar	2000	2004	(3)	For modernization of E-2C AEW&C aircraft
	6	AN/SPG-62	Fire control radar	(2002)		. .	For 2 Improved Kongou Class destroyers produced in Japan; for use with Standard SAM
	2	AN/SPY-1D	Air surv radar	2002		. .	For 2 Improved Kongou Class destroyers produced in Japan
	(38)	Phalanx Mk-15	CIWS	(1993)	1996–2004	30	For 2 Improved Kongou Class destroyers, 9 Murasame Class and 5 Takanami Class frigates and 3 Oosumi Class AALS produced in Japan; incl some Block-1B version
	(400)	BGM-71F TOW-2B	Anti-tank missile	2002	2003–2004	(400)	Part of deal worth $52 m; TOW-2A/TOW-2B version
	. .	MIM-104 PAC-3	SAM	(2004)		. .	Part of $6.5–9.3 b anti-ballistic missile defence system; incl assembly/production in Japan; delivery 2006/2007–2011; contract not yet signed
	. .	RIM-162 ESSM	SAM	2004		. .	For Takanami and Murasame Class frigates
	. .	RIM-66/SM-3	SAM	(2004)		. .	SM-3 Block-1 version; for Kongou Class destroyers; part of $6.5–9.3 b anti-ballistic missile defence system; contract not yet signed
	16	RIM-66M Standard-2	SAM	(2002)	2004	(16)	Deal worth $24 m; SM-2 Block-3A version

Recipient/ supplier (S) or licenser (L)	No. ordered	Weapon designation	Weapon description	Year of order/ licence	Year(s) of deliveries	No. delivered/ produced	Comments
	(336)	RIM-7M Sea Sparrow	SAM	1993	1996–2004	(269)	For Murasame Class and Takanami Class frigates
L: France	. .	MO-120-RT-61 120mm	Mortar	1992	1993–2004	(348)	Incl for Type-96 mortar carrier produced in Japan
USA	79	CH-47D Chinook	Helicopter	1986	1988–2004	(66)	CH-47J and CH-47JA versions
	(64)	S-70/UH-60J Blackhawk	Helicopter	1988	1991–2004	(47)	
	(80)	S-70/UH-60J Blackhawk	Helicopter	1995	1998–2004	(27)	Deal worth $2.7 b; UH-60JA version
	(110)	S-70B/SH-60J Seahawk	ASW helicopter	1988	1991–2004	(103)	Incl SH-60K version
	(27)	Sea Vue	MP aircraft radar	1992	1995–2004	(25)	For 27 BAe-125-800/RH-800 (U-125A) SAR aircraft
Jordan							
S: France	6	EC-135/EC-635	Helicopter	2003	2003–2004	6	EC-635T-1 version; for border patrol; option on 7 more
Netherlands	18	MOBAT 105mm	Self-propelled gun	2003		. .	Deal worth $19 m; option on 20 more
South Africa	(200)	Ratel-20	IFV	2004	2004	(100)	Ex-South African; delivery 2004–2006
Turkey	100	AIFV-APC	APC	2003	2004	(10)	Deal worth $42 m; assembled in Jordan; delivery 2004–2006
UK	(104)	Challenger	Tank	2002	2003–2004	(104)	Ex-UK; aid (partly as reward for Jordanian support in 2003 war against Iraq); Jordanian desig Al Hussein
USA	16	F-16(ADF)	FGA aircraft	2003	2003–2004	(16)	Ex-US; 'Peace Falcon-2' or 'Jordan-2' deal; incl 1 F-16B version; aid (partly as reward for Jordanian support in 2003 war against Iraq)
	8	S-70A/UH-60L	Helicopter	2004		. .	Deal worth $220 m; UH-60L version; delivery 2006
	17	AN/APG-66	Combat ac radar	2004		. .	Part of deal worth $87 m for modernization of 17 Jordanian F-16ADF combat aircraft to F-16AM version in Turkey; delivery 2006–2009
	50	AIM-120C AMRAAM	BVRAAM	(2004)		. .	Deal worth $39 m; contract not yet signed
	(400)	BGM-71F TOW-2B	Anti-tank missile	2002	2003–2004	(400)	Part of deal worth $52 m; TOW-2A/TOW-2B version

Kazakhstan							
S: Russia	20	Mi-8/Mi-17/Hip-H	Helicopter	2004	2004	(4)	Deal worth $100 m; Mi-17 version; for anti-terrorist and anti-narcotics operations; delivery 2004–2006
	(38)	Su-27S/Flanker-B	Fighter aircraft	(1995)	1996–2003	(26)	Ex-Russian; payment for Russian debt to Kazakhstan; status uncertain
Kuwait							
S: USA	8	AH-64D Apache	Combat helicopter	2002		. .	Part of deal worth $868 m (part of larger deal worth $2.1 b); delivery 2005–2008
	1	L-88 LASS	Air surv radar	2003		. .	Deal worth $85 m
	384	AGM-114K Hellfire	Anti-tank missile	2002		. .	Part of deal worth $868 m (part of larger deal worth $2.1 b); for AH-64D helicopters; delivery 2005–2008
Kyrgyzstan							
S: Kazakhstan	2	Mi-8/Mi-17/Hip-H	Helicopter	2003	2004	2	Ex-Kazakh; deal worth $3.5 m (financed by USA); Mi-8MTV version
Latvia							
S: Russia	2	Mi-8/Mi-17/Hip-H	Helicopter	(2003)	2004	2	Mi-8MTV-1 version; incl for SAR
Sweden	. .	RBS-70	Portable SAM	2004		. .	Deal worth SEK185 m ($28 m) incl ex-Swedish launchers as aid; delivery 2006–2007
Lebanon							
S: USA	. .	R44	Helicopter	(2003)		. .	R44 Raven-2 version; for training; delivery 2005
Lebanon/Hizbollah							
S: Iran	8	Mahajer	UAV	(2004)	2004	8	Probably Mahajer-4 version; Hizbollah desig Mirsad-1

Recipient/ supplier (S) or licenser (L)	No. ordered	Weapon designation	Weapon description	Year of order/ licence	Year(s) of deliveries	No. delivered/ produced	Comments
Lesotho							
S: Australia	1	GA-8 Airvan	Light aircraft	(2003)	2004	1	
Germany	1	Bo-105L	Light helicopter	(2003)	2004	1	
Libya							
S: Ukraine	7	An-32/Cline	Transport aircraft	2004	2004	(7)	An-32M version
	(5)	An-74/Coaler-B	Transport aircraft	2004		. .	An-74TK200 and/or AN-74TK300 version; incl for VIP transport
Lithuania							
S: Germany	3	TRML-CS	Air/sea surv radar	2002	2004	3	TRML-3D/32 version
Norway	(5)	Giraffe-40	Air surv radar	2004	2004	(5)	Ex-Norwegian; part of aid worth LTL135 m ($49 m)
	21	RBS-70	Portable SAM	2004	2004	21	Ex-Norwegian; part of aid worth LTL135 m ($49 m)
USA	60	FIM-92A Stinger	Portable SAM	2002		. .	Part of deal worth $31 m; deal incl also incl 8 launchers; delivery 2006
	(75)	Javelin	Anti-tank missile	2001	2004	(75)	Deal worth $10 m; deal incl also 18 launchers
Malaysia							
S: France	6	AS-555UN Fennec	Light helicopter	2001	2003–2004	(6)	Deal worth $38 m; AS-555SN version
	40	SM-39 Exocet	Anti-ship missile	2002		. .	For Scorpene submarines; delivery 2007–2008
	1	Agosta Class	Submarine	2002		. .	Ex-French; modernized before delivery; incl for 4-year training of Malaysians in France; delivery probably 2004
	1	Scorpene Class	Submarine	2002		. .	Deal worth $947 m–$1.1 b (incl over 50% barter) incl 1 delivered by Spain; delivery 2007–2008
Germany	6	MEKO-A100 Type	Frigate	1999	2004	1	'New Generation Patrol Vessel' (NGPV) programme worth $1.4 b (incl at least 30% produced in Malaysia); assembled/produced in Malaysia;

							MEKO-100RMN version; Malaysian designaton Kedah Class; delivery 2004–2008
Indonesia	2	CN-235	Transport aircraft	2002	2004	(2)	Deal worth $34 m; possibly ex-Indonesian; incl for VIP transport
Italy	11	A-109K	Light helicopter	2003		. .	Deal worth $70–75 m (offsets incl technology transfer); A-109LUH armed version; probably incl some assembled in Malaysia
	6	Seaguard TMX	Fire control radar	(2000)	2004	1	For 6 MEKO-A100 Type (Kedah Class) frigates from Germany; desig uncertain
	(30)	Black Shark	AS torpedo	2002		. .	For Scorpene Class submarines
	(24)	Otomat Mk-2	Anti-ship missile	(2001)	2002–2004	(24)	For Laksmana (Assad) Class corvettes
Poland	3	MID-M	AEV	2003		. .	Part of deal worth $368–400 m (offsets worth $111 m); delivery 2005–2006
	5	PMC-90	ABL	2003		. .	Part of deal worth $368–400 m (offsets worth $111 m); PMC Leguan version; delivery 2005–2006
	48	PT-91	Tank	2003		. .	Part of deal worth $368–400 m (offsets worth $111 m); PT-91M version; delivery 2005–2006/2007
	6	WZT-4	ARV	2003		. .	Part of deal worth $368–400 m (offsets worth $111 m); PT-91M version; delivery 2005–2006
Russia	10	Mi-8/Mi-17/Hip-H	Helicopter	2003	2004	(5)	Deal worth $70–120 m; Mi-171Sh armed version; for CSAR
	18	Su-30MK/Flanker	FGA aircraft	2003		. .	Deal worth $900 m (incl $270 m barter; offsets incl space technology transfer and training of Malaysian astronaut); Su-30MKM version; delivery 2006–2007
	(204)	AA-12 Adder/R-77	BVRAAM	(1997)		. .	For MiG-29N combat aircraft; status uncertain
Spain	1	Scorpene Class	Submarine	2002		. .	Deal worth $947 m–$1.1 b (incl over 50% barter) incl 1 delivered by France; delivery 2008–2009
Turkey	167	AIFV-APC	APC	2000	2002–2004	(167)	Part of deal worth $278–300 m; incl ambulance, ALV, 81mm mortar carrier and CP version; incl assembly of 65 in Malaysia; Malaysian desig Adnan; option on more

Recipient/ supplier (S) or licenser (L)	No. ordered	Weapon designation	Weapon description	Year of order/ licence	Year(s) of deliveries	No. delivered/ produced	Comments
UK	15	Jernas	SAM system	2002		. .	Part of deal worth £220 m ($400 m, offsets incl production of components); delivery from 2005
	. .	Rapier Mk-2	SAM	2002		. .	Part of deal worth £220 m ($400 m, offsets incl production of components); for Jernas SAM systems
USA	6	RDR-1500	MP aircraft radar	(2001)	2003–2004	(6)	Part of deal worth $38 m; for 6 AS-555SN helicopters
Mexico							
S: Brazil	1	EMB-145AEW&C	AEW&C aircraft	2001	2004	1	Part of deal worth $230–250 m; incl for SIGINT; mainly for anti-narcotics operations
	2	EMB-145MP	MP aircraft	2001	2004	2	Part of deal worth $230–250 m; mainly for anti-narcotics operations
Denmark	4	SCANTER-2001	Sea surv radar	(2003)	2004	(2)	For 4 Oaxaca Class OPVs produced in Mexico
France	2	AS-365/AS-565 Panther	Helicopter	2003		. .	AS-565 version; option on 8 more; delivery 2005
Israel	3	E-2C Hawkeye	AEW&C aircraft	2002	2004	3	Ex-Israeli; deal worth $18 m; incl for anti-narcotics operations
	2	Aliya Class	FAC(M)	2003	2004	(2)	Ex-Israeli; deal worth $64 m or $90 m
Sweden	1	PS-890 Erieye	AEW aircraft radar	2001	2004	1	Part of deal worth $230–250 m; for 1 EMB-145 AEW&C aircraft from Brazil
Switzerland	14	F-5E Tiger-2	FGA aircraft	2004	2004	14	Ex-Swiss; deal worth $8.5 m
USA	2	Sea Vue	MP aircraft radar	2001	2004	2	Part of deal worth $230–250 m; for 2 EMB-145 MP aircraft from Brazil
	8	Sea Vue	MP aircraft radar	2002	2004	(1)	For modernization of 8 C-212 MP aircraft
Myanmar (Burma)							
S: Ukraine	. .	BTR-3U Guardian	IFV	(2003)	2003–2004	(60)	No. ordered may be up to 1000; possibly assembled in Myanmar

	(60)	AA-10c/d Alamo/R-27E	BVRAAM	(2002)	2003–2004	(60)	For MiG-29 combat aircraft
NATO							
S: Multiple sellers	(4)	A321	Transport aircraft	(2004)		. .	Part ‘NATO AGS’ programme worth $4.8 b; for modification to AGS aircraft; contract not yet signed; delivery 2010–2013
USA	(7)	RQ-4A Global Hawk	UAV	(2004)		. .	Part ‘NATO AGS’ programme worth $4.8 b; contract not yet signed; delivery 2010–2013
Namibia							
S: Brazil	6	Marinheiro Class	Tug	2003	2004	6	Ex-Brazilian; for use as OPV
Italy	1	AB-139	Helicopter	2002	2004	1	Deal worth $8 m
Nepal							
S: India	2	Druhv/ALH	Helicopter	(2003)	2004	2	Deal worth $12–18 m (incl 70% as aid); armed version
	1	Druhv/ALH	Helicopter	2004		. .	Aid; probably armed version
	10	SA-315B Lama	Light helicopter	(2001)	2003–2004	(10)	Lancer armed version; for police; for use against Maoist rebels
	100	MPV	APC	(2003)	2004	(100)	Aid (Nepal pays 33% of costs)
Poland	1	M-28 Skytruck	Light transport ac	2003	2004	1	Deal worth $2.5 m
Russia	1	Mi-8/Mi-17/Hip-H	Helicopter	2004	2004	1	Deal worthe $4 m; Mi-17 version
UK	2	BN-2A/B Islander	Light transport ac	2003	2004	2	Ex-UK; aid on condition not to be used in offensive or armed role
Netherlands							
S: Germany	57	PzH-2000 155mm	Self-propelled gun	2002	2004	(4)	Deal worth $420 m (offsets 100%; incl 18 to be sold immediately after delivery to Netherlands); delivery 2004–2009
	3	TRS-3D	Air/sea surv radar	2004		. .	‘FGBADS Phase-1’ programme worth €35 m ($44 m); TRS-3D/32 version; delivery 2007
Israel	2 400	Spike-MR/LR	Anti-tank missile	2001		. .	Deal worth $150–225 m; Spike-MR version

Recipient/ supplier (S) or licenser (L)	No. ordered	Weapon designation	Weapon description	Year of order/ licence	Year(s) of deliveries	No. delivered/ produced	Comments
Italy	12	NH-90 NFH	ASW helicopter	2000		. .	Originally 20 NFH version ordered but changed to 12 NFH and 8 TTH version
	8	NH-90 TTH	Helicopter	(2004)		. .	
	4	127mm/54	Naval gun	1996	2002–2004	3	Ex-Canadian guns sold back to producer; modernized before delivery; for 4 De Zeven Provincien Class destroyers produced in Netherlands
Sweden	184	CV-9035	IFV	2004		. .	Deal worth €749–891 m ($939–992 m; offsets 100%); CV-9035 Mk-3 or CV-9035NL version; incl 34 CP version; delivery 2007–2010
UK	1	C-130K Hercules	Transport aircraft	2004		. .	Ex-UK; deal worth €17.6 m ($22 m) incl modernization
USA	1	DC-10-40	Transport aircraft	2004	2004	1	Second-hand; DC-10-30CF version
	24	AN/APG-78 Longbow	Combat ac radar	(2004)		. .	For modernization of 24 AH-64D helicopters; contract not yet signed
	(32)	MIM-104 PAC-3	SAM	2004		. .	Delivery 2005
	(240)	RIM-162 ESSM	SAM	2002	2003–2004	(125)	For De Zeven Provincien Class destroyers
	(164)	RIM-66M Standard-2	SAM	(2002)	2003–2004	(123)	For De Zeven Provincien Class destroyers
New Zealand							
S: Australia	2	Tenix-1600 Type	OPV	2004		. .	Part of ‘Project Protector’ worth NZ$500 m ($317 m); designed by UK company; partly produced in New Zealand and assembled in Australia; delivery 2007
	4	Tenix-340 Type	Patrol craft	2004		. .	Part of ‘Project Protector’ worth NZ$500 m ($317 m); produced in New Zealand; delivery 2007–2008
Canada	105	Piranha/LAV-25	IFV	2001	2003–2004	(105)	Deal worth $241–388 m (offsets worth $3 m); New Zealand desig NZLAV
Netherlands	2	PAGE	Air surv radar	2004		. .	For use with Mistral SAM; delivery 2006

	1	MRV Type	AALS	2004		. .	Part of 'Project Protector' worth NZ$500 m ($317 m); ordered via Australian company; delivery 2006
USA	(164)	Javelin	Anti-tank missile	2003		. .	part of 'Project Crossbow' worth NZD27 m ($18 m); incl 24 launchers; delivery 2006
Nigeria							
S: Italy	4	A-109K	Light helicopter	(2002)	2004	4	A-109E Power version
North Korea							
L: Russia	. .	AT-4 Spigot/9M111	Anti-tank missile	(1987)	1992–2004	(3 250)	Ordered from Soviet Union and produced under Russian licence after break-up of Soviet Union
	. .	SA-16 Gimlet/Igla-1	Portable SAM	(1989)	1992–2004	(1 250)	Probably ordered from Soviet Union and produced under Russian licence after break-up of Soviet Union
Norway							
S: Finland	2	XA-200	APC	2002	2004	(2)	XA-203M CP version
France	6	MRR-3D	Air surv radar	2003		. .	MRR-3D(NG) version; for 6 Skjold Class FAC produced in Norway; delivery 2006–2009
Germany	150	IRIS-T	SRAAM	(2003)		. .	Delivery 2005–2007
Multiple sellers	6	NH-90 NFH	ASW helicopter	2001		. .	Part of deal worth $425 m; for Coast Guard; ordered from France, Germany and Italy; from Finnish production line; delivery 2005–2008
	8	NH-90 TTH	Helicopter	2001		. .	Part of deal worth $425 m; for Coast Guard; for SAR; ordered from France, Germany and Italy; from Finnish production line; option on 10 more; delivery 2005–2008/2009
Spain	5	Mod. F-100 Class	Frigate	2000		. .	Part of deal worth $1.5 b (offsets 100% in 10 years incl NASAMS SAM system and Penguin missiles for Spain); incl 3 assembled/produced in Norway;

Recipient/ supplier (S) or licenser (L)	No. ordered	Weapon designation	Weapon description	Year of order/ licence	Year(s) of deliveries	No. delivered/ produced	Comments
							Norwegian desig Nansen Class; delivery 2005–2009
Sweden	6	CEROS-200	Fire control radar	2004		. .	Deal worth SEK155 m ($16 m); for 6 Skjold Class FAC produced in Norway; delivery 2006–2009
USA	5	AN/SPY-1F	Air surv radar	2000		. .	Part of deal worth $500 m; part of AEGIS combat system for 5 Mod. F-100 (Nansen) Class frigates from Spain
	526	Javelin	Anti-tank missile	2004		. .	Deal worth $86 m incl 90 launchers (offsets incl production of components in Norway); delivery 2006–2007
	(240)	RIM-162 ESSM	SAM	(2000)		. .	For Mod. F-100 (Nansen) Class frigates
Oman							
S: France	(81)	VBL	Reconnaissance veh	2000	2001–2004	(81)	Incl some fitted with ALBI Mistral SAM launcher
Multiple sellers	20	NH-90 TTH	Helicopter	2004		. .	Deal worth €600–800 m ($720–960 m); incl for SAR; delivery from 2008
UK	16	Super Lynx	ASW helicopter	2002	2004	(8)	Super Lynx-300 Mk-120 version
USA	12	F-16C	FGA aircraft	2002		. .	Deal worth $224 m (part of deal worth $1.1 b); F-16C/D Block-50 version; delivery 2005–2006
	14	LANTIRN	Combat ac radar	2002		. .	Part of deal worth $1.1 b; for F-16C combat aircraft
	80	AGM-65D Maverick	ASM	(2002)		. .	Part of deal worth $1.1 b; AGM-65D/E version; for F-16C combat aircraft
	50	AIM-120C AMRAAM	BVRAAM	2002		. .	Part of deal worth $1.1 b; for F-16C combat aircraft
	100	AIM-9M Sidewinder	SRAAM	2002		. .	Part of deal worth $1.1 b; AIM-9M-8/9 version; for F-16C combat aircraft
	(100)	Javelin	Anti-tank missile	2004		. .	Deal worth $15–20 m
	20	RGM-84 Harpoon	Anti-ship missile	2003		. .	Deal worth $22 m (part of deal worth $1.1 b); AGM-84D version; for F-16C combat aircraft

Pakistan							
S: China	(150)	JF-17	FGA aircraft	1999		. .	Developed for Pakistan; incl production of components and assembly in Pakistan; delivery from 2006
	(4)	Z-9C/AS-565	ASW helicopter	(2004)		. .	Contract not yet signed
	2	Type-347G	Fire control radar	(2003)	2004	1	For 2 Jalalat Class FAC produced in Pakistan
	(16)	C-802/CSS-N-8 Saccade	Anti-ship missile	(2003)	2004	(8)	For Jalalat Class FAC
	. .	PL-12/SD-10	BVRAAM	(2004)		. .	For JF-17 and possibly modernized Mirage-3/5 combat aircraft; contract not yet signed
	4	Jiangwei Class	Frigate	(2004)		. .	Deal worth $500–750 m; contract not yet signed
France	40	Mirage-5	FGA aircraft	1996	1998–2004	(40)	Ex-French; 'Blue Flash-6' deal worth $120 m; modernized before delivery; incl 6 Mirage-3D version
	(96)	F-17P	AS torpedo	(1996)	1999–2004	(72)	F-17P Mod-2 version; for Agosta-90B Type (Khalid Class) submarines
	(24)	SM-39 Exocet	Anti-ship missile	1994	1999–2004	(21)	Deal worth $100 m; for Agosta-90B Type (Khalid Class) submarines
	3	Agosta-90B Type	Submarine	1994	1999–2003	2	Deal worth $750 m (+ $200 m for modernization of Pakistan Naval Dockyard to build submarines); incl 2 assembled in Pakistan; incl 1 with air-independent propulsion system; Pakistani desig Khalid Class; delivery 1999–2006
Indonesia	3	CN-235	Transport aircraft	2002	2004	3	Part of deal worth $49–52 m; CN-235-220 version; 1 more delivered for VIP transport
Italy	(135)	Grifo	Combat ac radar	1995	2000–2004	(135)	Grifo-7 version; for modernization of some 35 Mirage-3 and 100 F-7P combat aircraft; assembled/produced in Pakistan
	(57)	Grifo	Combat ac radar	(2002)	2004	(10)	Grifo-7PG version; for 57 F-7MG (F-7PG) combat aircraft from China; assembled/produced in Pakistan
Russia	12	Mi-8/Mi-17/Hip-H	Helicopter	(2003)	2004	(12)	Part of deal worth $51 m; 1 more delivered for VIP transport; ordered via UK company
Sweden	. .	RBS-70	Portable SAM	(1985)	1988–2004	(425)	Assembled in Pakistan

Recipient/ supplier (S) or licenser (L)	No. ordered	Weapon designation	Weapon description	Year of order/ licence	Year(s) of deliveries	No. delivered/ produced	Comments
	(24)	Type-43	ASW torpedo	1994	1999–2004	(24)	Type-43X2 version; for modernized Tariq (Amazon) Class frigates
USA	40	Bell-205/UH-1H	Helicopter	(2004)		. .	Ex-US; status uncertain
	40	Bell-209/AH-1F	Combat helicopter	(2004)		. .	Ex-US; possibly all or some for spares only; status uncertain
	26	Bell-412EP	Helicopter	2004	2004	(20)	Deal worth $230 m; from Canadian production line; for use in 'war on terrorism'; incl some for police; delivery 2004–2005
	6	C-130E Hercules	Transport aircraft	2004	2004	(1)	Ex-Australian aircraft sold back to US producer and resold to Pakistan; deal worth $64 m; modernized before delivery; 1 more delivered for spares only; delivery 2004–2005
	8	P-3C Orion	ASW/MP aircraft	(2004)		. .	Ex-US; deal worth $970 m; modernized before delivery; contract not yet signed
	6	AN/TPS-77	Air surv radar	(2004)		. .	Deal worth $100 m; contract not yet signed
	(6)	L-88 LASS	Air surv radar	(2003)		. .	Deal worth $155 m; for Afghan border patrol; contract possibly not yet signed
	6	Phalanx Mk-15	CIWS	(2004)		. .	Deal worth $155 m incl modernization of 6 Pakistani Phalanx; contract not yet signed
	2 014	BGM-71 TOW	Anti-tank missile	(2004)		. .	Deal worth $82 m; TOW-2A version; for AH-1 helicopters; contract not yet signed
L: China	. .	QW-1 Vanguard	Portable SAM	(1993)	1994–2004	(850)	Pakistani desig Anza-2
	. .	Red Arrow-8	Anti-tank missile	1989	1990–2004	(15 100)	Pakistani desig Baktar Shikan
Sweden	(150)	MFI-17 Supporter	Trainer aircraft	(2001)	2001–2004	(46)	Super Mushshak version
Paraguay							
S: Spain	1	C-212 Aviocar	Transport aircraft	2003	2004	1	C-212-400 version

Recipient/supplier	No. ordered	Weapon designation	Weapon description	Year of order	Year(s) of delivery	No. delivered	Comments
Peru							
S: Italy	2	Lupo Class	Frigate	(2004)		. .	Ex-Italian; deal worth $30 m; modernized before delivery; delivery 2005
USA	16	Bell-205/UH-1H	Helicopter	(2003)	2004	8	Ex-US; aid for police anti-narcotics operations; modernized to Huey-2 version before delivery; delivery 2004–2005
Philippines							
S: Singapore	(7)	Bell-205/UH-1H	Helicopter	2003	2004	(7)	Ex-Singaporean; part of deal worth $12 m; modernized before delivery
Thailand	8	OV-10 Bronco	Ground attack ac	2003	2003–2004	8	Ex-Thai; aid; OV-10C version
Turkey	(2)	AIFV-APC	APC	(2002)	2003–2004	(2)	ARV version
USA	20	Bell-205/UH-1H	Helicopter	2003	2004	(15)	Ex-US; part of $30 m aid; 10 more delivered for spares only; delivery 2004–2005
	(7)	Bell-205/UH-1H	Helicopter	2003	2004	(7)	Second-hand; part of deal worth $12 m; bought and delivered via Singapore; modernized in Singapore before delivery
	10	Bell-205/UH-1H	Helicopter	2003		. .	Deal worth $8 m; delivery 2005–2006
	4	C-130K Hercules	Transport aircraft	(2002)		. .	Ex-UK aircraft sold back to US producer; deal worth $41 m; modernized before delivery; incl for MP
	48	M-113	APC	(2003)		. .	Ex-US; aid
	1	Cyclone Class	Patrol craft	(2001)	2004	1	Ex-US; aid; Philippine desig Alvares Class
Unknown country	(6)	Bell-205/UH-1H	Helicopter	2003	2004	(4)	Second-hand; part of deal worth $12 m; bought and delivered via Singapore; modernized in Singapore before delivery
Poland							
S: Finland	313	AMV	IFV	2003	2004	(3)	Part of 'Suhak' programme worth PLN4.9 b ($1.3–1.6 b; incl $308 m for turrets from Italy; offsets 133%); delivery 2004–2013

Recipient/ supplier (S) or licenser (L)	No. ordered	Weapon designation	Weapon description	Year of order/ licence	Year(s) of deliveries	No. delivered/ produced	Comments
	377	AMV	APC	2003	2004	(6)	Part of 'Suhak' programme worth PLN4.9 b ($1.3–1.6 b; offsets 133%); incl 32 reconnaissance version; Polish desig Rosomak; most assembled and produced in Poland; delivery 2004–2013
Germany	(14)	MiG-29S/Fulcrum-C	FGA aircraft	2002	2003–2004	(14)	Ex-German; aid; MiG-29G version; incl MiG-29GT version; some 8 more delivered for spares only
	(100)	AA-10a/b Alamo/R-27	BVRAAM	2002	2003–2004	(100)	Ex-German; aid; for MiG-29 combat aircraft
	(400)	AA-11 Archer/R-73	SRAAM	2002	2003–2004	(400)	Ex-German; aid; for MiG-29 combat aircraft
	(150)	AA-8 Aphid/R-60	SRAAM	2002	2003–2004	(150)	Ex-German; aid; for MiG-29 combat aircraft
	2	MEKO-A100 Type	Frigate	2001		. .	Polish desig Project-621 Gawron-2 Type; assembled/produced in Poland; option on 2–5 more; delivery 2005–2006
Israel	(2 675)	Spike-MR/LR	Anti-tank missile	2003	2004	20	Deal worth PLN1.49b ($397–450 m) incl 264 launchers (offsets worth $826 m incl production of components and assembly in Poland); Spike-LR version; delivery 2004–2013
Italy	3	RAT-31S/L	Air surv radar	(2002)		. .	Deal worth $38 or $90 m; part of 'NATO ACCS' programme; for 'NADGE' air-surveillance network; RAT-31DL version; delivery 2006–2007
Multiple sellers	. .	MU-90 Impact	ASW torpedo	(2002)		. .	Deal worth €30 m; incl for Mi-14PL and SH-2G helicopters and MEKO-A100 Type and Perry (Pulaski) Class frigates; ordered from Germany, Italy or France
Netherlands	3	STING	Fire control radar	2001	2004	(1)	For modernization of 3 Orkan Class corvettes
Norway	(34)	Mk-37	AS torpedo	2002	2002–2004	(34)	Ex-Norwegian; part of aid worth $168 m; for Kobben Class submarines
	(30)	Type-613	AS torpedo	2002	2002–2004	(30)	Ex-Norwegian; part of aid worth $168 m; for Kobben Class submarines
	4	Type-207/Kobben Class	Submarine	2002	2002–2004	4	Ex-Norwegian; part of aid worth $168 m; 1 more delivered for spares only

Russia	(200)	AT-9/9M120 Vikhr	Anti-tank missile	(2004)		. .	For modernized Mi-24PL helicopters
Spain	8	C-295M	Transport aircraft	2001	2003–2004	5	Deal worth $212 m (offsets 100%); option on 4 more; delivery 2003–2005
Sweden	(128)	Eagle-1	Fire control radar	(2001)	2004	(1)	For Loara AAV(G) produced in Poland
	3	Giraffe AMB-3D	Air surv radar	2001	2004	(1)	Sea Giraffe AMB version; for modernization of 3 Orkan Class corvettes
	(60)	RBS-15 Mk-3	Anti-ship missile	(2001)	2004	(5)	For 3 Orkan Class corvettes and probably for 2 MEKO-A100 Type frigates
UK	(78)	AS-90 turret	Turret	(2004)		. .	For use on Polish chassis as Chrobry or Krab self-propelled gun; incl assembly/production in Poland; contract not yet signed
USA	5	C-130K Hercules	Transport aircraft	(2003)		. .	Ex-UK aircraft returned to US producer and transferred to Poland as FMF aid worth $72 m; incl 1 C-130H-30 version; modernized before delivery; delivery 2005–2006
	48	F-16C	FGA aircraft	2003		. .	'Peace Sky-1' deal worth $3.5 b ($4.7 b incl interest; offsets $6 b or $12.5 b); delivery 2007–2008
	(30)	Shadow-600	UAV	(2004)		. .	Financed by US FMF aid; desig uncertain; contract not yet signed; delivery 2006
	13	MSTAR	Ground surv radar	2003	2003–2004	(13)	Deal worth $5.6 m; AN/PPS-5C version
	11	MSTAR	Ground surv radar	2004		. .	Deal worth $2.7 m; delivery 2005
	360	AGM-65G Maverick	ASM	2004		. .	Deal worth $78 m; AGM-64G2 version; delivery by 2007
	384	AIM-120C AMRAAM	BVRAAM	2003		. .	AIM-120C-5 version
	178	AIM-9X Sidewinder	SRAAM	2004		. .	For F-16C combat aircraft
	. .	RIM-162 ESSM	SAM	(2003)		. .	For MEKO-A100 Type frigates; contract not yet signed
L: Russia	12	An-28TD Bryza-1TD	Light transport ac	2001	2001–2004	(12)	

Recipient/ supplier (S) or licenser (L)	No. ordered	Weapon designation	Weapon description	Year of order/ licence	Year(s) of deliveries	No. delivered/ produced	Comments
Portugal							
S: Austria	260	Pandur-2	APC	2004		. .	Deal worth €344 m ($456 m); incl assembly in Portugal; incl ambulance, ARC, CP and anti-tank versions; delivery from 2006
France	12	EC-120B Colibri	Light helicopter	2003	2004	(6)	
Germany	2	Type-214	Submarine	2004		. .	Deal worth €846 m ($970 m; offsets 100%); Type-209PN version; option on 1 more; delivery 2009–2010
Italy	12	EH101-400	Helicopter	2001	2004	(3)	Deal worth $287–315 m (incl 2 financed by EU for fishery protection); incl for SAR; delivery 2004–2005/2006
Netherlands	3	P-3C Orion Update-2.5	ASW/MP aircraft	2004		. .	Ex-Dutch; part of deal worth €70 m or €223 m ($85 m or $265 m)
	2	P-3CUP Orion	ASW/MP aircraft	2004		. .	Ex-Dutch; part of deal worth €70 m or €223 m ($85 m or $265 m); transfered to Portugal direct after modernization in USA for Netherlands finished
Spain	1	S763-LANZA	Air surv radar	2004		. .	Deal worth €18 m ($22 m); option on 3 more
USA	20	F-16C	FGA aircraft	1998	2003–2004	(3)	'Peace Atlantis-2' deal worth $268 m (incl aircraft as aid); ex-US F-16OCU version modernized to F-16AM (F-16C) in Portugal with US components; incl 4 F-16B version; 5 more delivered for spares only; delivery 2003–2006
	12	AIM-120C AMRAAM	BVRAAM	(2002)		. .	
	(96)	MIM-72F Chaparral	SAM	(2004)		. .	Ex-US; aid; MIM-72G version; status uncertain

Recipient/supplier	No. ordered	Weapon designation	Weapon description	Year of order	Year(s) of deliveries	No. delivered	Comments
Romania							
S: France	(100)	R-550 Magic-2	SRAAM	(1996)	2003–2004	(100)	For MiG-21 Lancer (modernized MiG-21MF) and possibly for MiG-29 combat aircraft; probably incl assembly/ production in Romania
Germany	36	Gepard	AAV(G)	1998	2004	(6)	Ex-German; aid worth $37 m; modernized before delivery; 7 more delivered for spares only
Israel	(960)	Spike-ER	Anti-tank missile	(1998)	1999–2004	(960)	For modernized SA-330 (IAR-330) helicopters
	. .	Spike-MR/LR	Anti-tank missile	(2003)		. .	For modernized MLI-84 IFVs; contract not yet signed
UK	2	Boxer Class	Frigate	2003	2004	1	Ex-UK; deal worth £116 m ($187 m; offsets 80–90%); modernized before delivery; Romanian desig Regele Ferdinand Class; delivery 2004–2005
USA	1	C-130H Hercules	Transport aircraft	2004		. .	Ex-Italian aircraft sold back to US producer; aid; modernized before delivery; delivery 2005
	21	AN/TPS-73 MMSR	Air surv radar	2003	2004	(3)	Delivery 2004–2008
Russia							
S: Uzbekistan	(2)	Il-76M/Candid-B	Transport aircraft	(2004)		. .	Il-76MF version; delivery 2005–2006
Saudi Arabia							
S: France	(72)	ASTER-15 SAAM	SAM	(1997)	2002–2004	(72)	For F-3000S Type (Al Riyadh Class) frigates
	(24)	F-17P	AS torpedo	(1997)	2002–2004	(24)	For F-3000S Type (Al Riyadh Class) frigates
	(48)	MM-40 Exocet	Anti-ship missile	1994	2000–2004	(48)	For F-3000S Type (Al Riyadh Class) frigates; MM-40 Block-2 version
	3	F-3000S Type	Frigate	1994	2002–2004	(3)	Part of 'Sawari-2' deal worth $3.4 b (offsets 35%); also designated Modified La Fayette Type; Saudi desig Al Riyadh Class
Pakistan	20	MFI-17 Supporter	Trainer aircraft	(2003)	2004	(20)	Deal worth $34 m; Super Mushshak version
USA	500	AIM-120C AMRAAM	BVRAAM	2000	2003–2004	(156)	Deal worth $475 m; for F-15 combat aircraft

Recipient/ supplier (S) or licenser (L)	No. ordered	Weapon designation	Weapon description	Year of order/ licence	Year(s) of deliveries	No. delivered/ produced	Comments
Singapore							
S: Denmark	6	SCANTER-2001	Sea surv radar	(2002)		. .	For 6 La Fayette (Formidable) Class frigates from France
France	(144)	ASTER-15 SAAM	SAM	(2001)		. .	Part of 'Project Delta' worth $1.6 b; for La Fayette Class frigates
	6	La Fayette Class	Frigate	2000		. .	Deal worth $750 m (part of 'Project Delta' worth $1.6 b); incl 5 assembled/produced in Singapore; Singapore desig Formidable Class; delivery 2007–2009
Israel	(600)	Python-4	BVRAAM	(1997)	1997–2004	(600)	For F-5S and F-16 combat aircraft
	. .	Spike-MR/LR	Anti-tank missile	1999	2001–2003	(600)	Probably Spike-LR version; assembled in Singapore
USA	12	AH-64D Apache	Combat helicopter	2001		. .	'Peace Vanguard' deal worth $617 m; delivery by 2005; stationed in USA until 2006
	20	F-16C	FGA aircraft	(2000)	2004	(15)	'Peace Carvin-4' deal; F-16D Block-52 version
	6	S-70B/SH-60B Seahawk	ASW helicopter	(2004)		. .	SH-70(N) version; delivery 2008–2010
	(192)	AGM-114K Hellfire	Anti-tank missile	(2001)		. .	For AH-64D helicopters
	50	AIM-120C AMRAAM	BVRAAM	2004		. .	Deal worth $25 m; AIM-120C5 version
Slovenia							
S: France	2	AS-532UL/AS-332L1	Helicopter	2002	2004	2	Deal worth $35 m; AS-532AL version; incl for SAR
L: Austria	36	Pandur	APC	2003	2004	(8)	Slovenian desig Valuk
South Africa							
S: France	4	MRR-3D	Air surv radar	(2000)		. .	For 4 MEKO-A200 Type frigates from Germany
	(64)	MM-40 Exocet	Anti-ship missile	2000		. .	For MEKO-A200 Type frigates
Germany	4	MEKO-A200 Type	Frigate	(2000)		. .	Deal worth $0.8–1.12 b (offsets $3.2 b incl $403 m for arms industry); South African desig Amatola Class; delivery 2005–2006

	3	Type-209/1400	Submarine	1999		. .	Deal worth $600–795 m (offsets 375–430%); Type-209/1400MOD version; delivery 2005–2007
Italy	30	A-109K	Light helicopter	1999	2003–2004	(8)	Deal worth $240 m (offsets $977 m incl $191 m for arms industry; incl production of A-109 and A-119 in South Africa for export); A-109LUH version; incl 25 assembled in South Africa; option on 10 more; delivery 2003–2007
Multiple sellers	(8)	A400M	Transport aircraft	(2004)		. .	Deal worth €750 m ($1 b); contract not yet signed; delivery 2010–2014
Netherlands	2	PAGE	Air surv radar	2003		. .	Part of 'Ground Based Air Defence System (GBADS) Phase-1' programme worth $117 m
Sweden	9	JAS-39 Gripen	FGA aircraft	1999		. .	Part of deal worth $1.2 b (offsets $8.7 b incl $1.5 b for arms industry); JAS-39B version; for delivery 2007–2009; option on 19 more
UK	12	Hawk-100	Trainer/combat ac	2002		. .	Hawk-100LIFT/Hawk-120 version; assembled in South Africa; delivery 2006
	12	Hawk-100	Trainer/combat ac	1999		. .	Part of deal worth $1.2 b (offsets $8.7 b incl $1.5 b for arms industry); incl 11 assembled in South Africa; Hawk-100LIFT/Hawk-120 version; delivery 2005
	4	Super Lynx	ASW helicopter	2003		. .	Deal worth $107 m ($173 m offsets incl $88 m for arms industry); option on 2 more; delivery 2007
	(72)	Starstreak	Portable SAM	2003		. .	Deal worth $13 m (part of 'Ground Based Air Defence System (GBADS) Phase-1' programme worth $117 m)
USA	4	AN/APS-143(V)	MP aircraft radar	2003		. .	For 4 Super Lynx helicopters
South Korea							
S: France	(48)	Crotale-NG	SAM system	(1997)	1999–2004	(46)	Part of Chun Ma (or Pegasus) AAV(M); for use with Korean developed SAM
Germany	3	Type-214	Submarine	2000		. .	'KSS-2' programme worth $1.1 b (incl $711 m import from Germany); assembled/produced in South Korea; delivery 2007–2009

Recipient/ supplier (S) or licenser (L)	No. ordered	Weapon designation	Weapon description	Year of order/ licence	Year(s) of deliveries	No. delivered/ produced	Comments
Netherlands	3	Goalkeeper	CIWS	1999	2003–2004	2	For 3 KDX-2 Type frigates produced in South Korea
	5	Goalkeeper	CIWS	2003		. .	Deal worth $54 m; for 1 LPX Type AALS and 3 KDX-3 Class frigates produced in South Korea
	3	MW-08	Air surv radar	1999	2003–2004	2	For 3 KDX-2 Type frigates produced in South Korea; assembled/produced in South Korea
	1	MW-08	Air surv radar	(2003)		. .	For 1 LPX Type AALS produced in South Korea; assembled/produced in South Korea
	6	STIR	Fire control radar	1999	2003–2004	4	For 3 KDX-2 Type frigates produced in South Korea; STIR-240 version; assembled/produced in South Korea
Russia	(23)	Il-103	Light aircraft	2002	2004	(8)	Deal worth $9 m (incl $4.5 m payment of Russian debt to South Korea); part of 'Bul-Gom' deal worth $534 m (incl $267 m payment of Russian debt to South Korea); for training; delivery 2004–2006
	7	Ka-32A/Helix-C	Helicopter	2002	2003–2004	(7)	Part of 'Bul-Gom' deal worth $534 m (incl $267 m payment of Russian debt to South Korea)
	30	BMP-3	IFV	2002		. .	Part of 'Bul-Gom' deal worth $534 m (incl $267 m payment of Russian debt to South Korea); delivery by 2006
	10	T-80U	Tank	2002		. .	Part of 'Bul-Gom' deal worth $534 m (incl $267 m payment of Russian debt to South Korea); delivery by 2006
	. .	AT-13 Saxhorn/9M131	Anti-tank missile	2002	2003–2004	(2 000)	Part of 'Bul-Gom' deal worth $534 m (incl $267 m payment of Russian debt to South Korea); delivery 2003–2006
Sweden	. .	CEROS-200	Fire control radar	2003		. .	Deal worth SEK114 m ($14 m); for PKX Type FAC; produced in South Korea incl assembly/production in South Korea; delivery from 2006–2007

USA	40	F-15K	Fighter/bomber ac	2002		. .	‘F-X’ programme worth $4.4 b (offsets 65–83% incl all production of AH-64 combat helicopter fuselages); F-15K version; delivery 2005–2008
	8	P-3B Orion	ASW/MP aircraft	(2004)		. .	Ex-US; deal worth $636 m; modernized before delivery; 1 more for spares only; delivery by 2007
	29	M-270 MLRS	MRL	2002	2002–2004	(29)	Deal worth $498 m
	3	Mk-45 127mm	Naval gun	1999	2003–2004	2	Deal worth $22 m; Mk-45 Mod-4 version; for 3 KDX-2 Type frigates produced in South Korea; assembled in South Korea
	67	LVTP-7A1/AAV-7A1	APC	2000	2001–2004	(46)	Deal worth $99–120 m; South Korean desig Korean Armoured Amphibious Vehicle (KAAV); assembled/produced in South Korea; delivery 2001–2006
	(44)	AN/APG-67	Combat ac radar	(2003)		. .	AN/APG-67(V)4 version; for 44 T-50 LIFT (South Korean desig A-50) trainer/oombat aircraft produced in South Korea; contract possibly not yet signed
	3	AN/SPS-49	Air surv radar	(1999)	2003–2004	2	For 3 KDX-2 Type frigates produced in South Korea; AN/SPS-49(V)5 version
	3	AN/SPY-1D	Air surv radar	(2002)		. .	For 3 KDX-3 Type destroyers produced in South Korea
	3	AN/TPS-77	Air surv radar	2002	2004	(3)	Deal worth $39 m
	. .	Tiger Eyes	Combat ac radar	2002		. .	Deal worth $164 m; for F-15K combat aircraft; delivery 2004–2005
	(45)	AGM-84H SLAM-ER	ASM	(2003)		. .	Deal worth $70 m; for F-15K combat aircraft
	147	AIM-120C AMRAAM	BVRAAM	2002	2004	(147)	Part of deal worth $110 m; for F-15K combat aircraft
	. .	AIM-9X Sidewinder	SRAAM	2002		. .	Part of deal worth $110 m; for F-15K combat aircraft
	111	MGM-140A1 ATACMS	SSM	2001	2004	(111)	Deal worth $81 m
	(150)	Mk-46 Mod-5 NEARTIP	ASW torpedo	(1995)	1998–2004	(140)	For KDX-1 Type (Kwanggaeto the Great Class) and for ASROC ASW missiles on KDX-2 Type destroyers
	(72)	RGM-84 Harpoon	Anti-ship missile	(1994)	1998–2004	(72)	UGM-84 version; for Type-209 (Chang Bogo Class) submarines
	64	RIM-116A RAM	SAM	2001	2003–2004	(43)	For KDX-2 Type frigates

Recipient/ supplier (S) or licenser (L)	No. ordered	Weapon designation	Weapon description	Year of order/ licence	Year(s) of deliveries	No. delivered/ produced	Comments
	. .	RIM-116A RAM	SAM	(2004)		. .	For KDX-3 Class destroyers
	. .	RIM-66/SM-3	SAM	(2004)		. .	For KDX-3 Class destroyers; contract not yet signed
	110	RIM-66M Standard-2	SAM	2000	2003–2004	(74)	Deal worth $159 m; for KDX-2 Type frigates
L: USA	20	F-16C	FGA aircraft	2000	2003–2004	(20)	'Korean Fighter Programme-2 (KFP-2)' worth $663 m; Block-52 version; incl 5 F-16D version; for use as reconnaissance aircraft; South Korean desig KF-16
Spain							
S: France	3	AS-665 Tiger	Combat helicopter	(2003)		. .	HAP version; lease until delivery of AS-665 HAD version; incl for training
	. .	Mistral	Portable SAM	(2003)		. .	For AS-665 Tiger helicopters
Germany	16	Buffel	ARV	1998	2003–2004	(4)	Part of deal worth €1.9 b ($2.2 b; offsets 80%); incl 12 assembled/produced in Spain
	30	Leopard-2A5	Tank	1998	2003–2004	(30)	Part of deal worth €1.9 b ($2.2 b; offsets 80%); Leopard-2A5E version
	(40)	DM2A4	AS torpedo	2004		. .	For Scorpene (S-80) Class submarines; contract not yet signed
	(700)	IRIS-T	SRAAM	(2004)		. .	Delivery possibly from 2005
	(350)	Taurus KEPD-350	ASM	2004		. .	Contract probably not yet signed
Italy	62	B-1 Centauro	Armoured car	2002	2004	(10)	Deal worth €219 m ($185 m); Spanish desig VRC-105; delivery 2004–2006
	4	RAN-12L/X	Air/sea surv radar	(1996)	2002–2004	3	For 4 De Bazán (F-100) Class frigates produced in Spain
Multiple sellers	24	AS-665 Tiger	Combat helicopter	2003		. .	Deal worth $1.5–1.9 b; HAD version ordered from France and Germany; delivery from 2007
	. .	TRIGAT-LR	Anti-tank missile	(2003)		. .	For AS-665 Tiger helicopters; ordered from France and Germany; delivery 2007

Norway	(20)	Penguin-2	Anti-ship missile	(2000)	2004	(5)	Deal worth $26 m (offsets for Norwegian order for 5 frigates); Penguin-2 Mod-7 version; for S-70/SH-60B helicopters; option on more
Sweden	20	Bv-206S	APC	2000	2002–2004	(20)	Incl 10 ordered in 2001 for SEK41 m ($4.5 m); option on up to 30 more
Switzerland	18	Piranha-3	APC	2001	2003–2004	(18)	Piranha-3C version; incl CP and ambulance version
USA	4	Mk-45 127mm	Naval gun	1999	2002–2004	3	Ex-US; modernized before delivery; for 4 De Bazán (F-100) Class frigates produced in Spain
	4	AN/MPQ-64	Air surv radar	(2000)	2004	(1)	Ordered via Norway as part of 4 NASAMS SAM systems
	8	AN/SPG-62	Fire control radar	(1996)	2002–2004	6	AN/SPG-62 Mk-99 version; for use with Standard and ESSM SAMs on 4 De Bazán (F-100) Class frigates produced in Spain
	4	AN/SPY-1F	Air surv radar	1996	2002–2004	3	Deal worth $750 m; part of AEGIS combat system for De Bazán (F-100) Class frigates produced in Spain
	. .	AGM-114K Hellfire	Anti-tank missile	(2003)		. .	For SH-60B helicopters; contract not yet signed
	. .	AIM-120A AMRAAM	SAM	(2000)	2004	(25)	For NASAMS SAM systems ordered from Norway
	31	AIM-120C AMRAAM	BVRAAM	(2002)	2004	(25)	Deal worth $21 m; for F/A-18 combat aircraft
	(400)	BGM-71F TOW-2B	Anti-tank missile	2002	2003–2004	(400)	Part of deal worth $52 m; TOW-2A/TOW-2B version
	226	Javelin	Anti-tank missile	(2001)		. .	Deal worth $25 m incl 12 launchers; status uncertain
	(384)	RIM-162 ESSM	SAM	(2003)		. .	For De Bazán (F-100) Class frigates; contract possibly not yet signed
	29	RIM-66M Standard-2	SAM	(2002)	2004	(29)	Deal worth $29 m; SM-2 Block-3A version; for De Bazán (F-100) Class frigates
L: Germany	189	Leopard-2A5+	Tank	1998		. .	Part of deal worth €1.9 b ($2.2 b; offsets 80%); Leopard-2A5E version; delivery 2005–2008
Sri Lanka							
S: China	(3)	CEIEC-408C	Air surv radar	2004		. .	Desig uncertain
USA	2	AN/TPQ-36 Firefinder	Arty locating radar	(2000)	2003–2004	(2)	Deal worth $22 m; status uncertain

Recipient/ supplier (S) or licenser (L)	No. ordered	Weapon designation	Weapon description	Year of order/ licence	Year(s) of deliveries	No. delivered/ produced	Comments
	1	Reliance Class	OPV	2004	2004	1	Ex-US; aid; modernized for $6.9 m before delivery
Sudan							
S: Russia	12	MiG-29S/Fulcrum-C	FGA aircraft	2002	2003–2004	12	Deal worth $120 m; MiG-29SE version; incl 2 MiG-29UB version
Sweden							
S: Finland	63	XA-200	APC	2002	2003–2004	(63)	Deal worth $37 m; XA-2025 version
France	18	NH-90 TTH	Helicopter	2001		. .	Deal worth $660 m (offsets 100% incl production of parts for 200 NH-90 worth $220 m); NH-90TTT version; incl 3 for SAR and 5 for ASW; Swedish desig Hkp-14; most assembled in Finland; option on 7 more delivery 2005–2009
Germany	(250)	IRIS-T	SRAAM	(2003)		. .	Delivery possibly from 2005
Italy	20	A-109K	Light helicopter	2001	2003–2004	(4)	Deal worth €130 m ($113 m; incl components made in South Africa as offsets for South African order for JAS-39 combat aircraft); A-109LUH (A-109M) version; Swedish desig Hkp-15; delivery 2002–2007
USA	(5)	AN/APS-143(V)	MP aircraft radar	2002		. .	Deal worth $7.6 m; for 5 NH-90 helicopters
	(53)	AIM-120C AMRAAM	BVRAAM	2004		. .	Part of deal worth $53 m; AIM-120C-5 version; delivery by 2005
Switzerland							
S: Germany	25	Buffel	ARV	2001	2004	(12)	Deal worth $63–70 m (offsets 10.5%); delivery 2004–2005
	15	PiPz-3 Kodiak	AEV	(2002)		. .	Delivery from 2007
Spain	2	C-295M	Transport aircraft	2004		. .	Deal worth $87 m

Recipient/supplier	No. ordered	Weapon designation	Weapon description	Year of order	Year(s) of deliveries	No. delivered	Comments
UK	(2 000)	Rapier Mk-2	SAM	(2002)	2004	(250)	Assembled in Switzerland; delivery 2004–2007
USA	24	PSTAR-ER	Air surv radar	2003	2004	(24)	Deal worth $24 m
	(222)	AIM-9X Sidewinder	SRAAM	2002		. .	Deal worth SFR104 m ($80 m; offsets 100%); for F/A-18C combat aircraft
L: Sweden	185	CV-9030CH	IFV	2000	2002–2004	(139)	Part of 'Schutzenpanzer-2000' programme worth $424 m; incl 32 CV-9030CH-COM CP version; delivery 2002–2005; option on 124 more
Syria							
S: Russia	(14)	Su-27SK/Flanker-B	FGA aircraft	(1999)		. .	Status uncertain
Taiwan							
S: USA	2	E-2C Hawkeye	AEW&C aircraft	1999		. .	Deal worth $400 m; E-2T/Hawkeye-2000 version; delivery 2005
	54	LVTP-7A1/AAV-7A1	APC	2003		. .	Deal worth $64–156 m; ex-US AAV-7A1 rebuild to AAV-7A1RAM/RS version; incl 4 CP and 2 ARV version; delivery from 2005
	11	AN/FPS-117	Air surv radar	2002	2004	(1)	Incl 4 AN/TPS-117 version
	(449)	AGM-114K Hellfire	Anti-tank missile	(2004)		. .	Deal worth $50 m; AGM-114M version
	. .	AGM-88 HARM	Anti-radar missile	(2001)	2002–2003	(53)	
	182	AIM-9M Sidewinder	SRAAM	2003		. .	Deal worth $17 m; AIM-9M-2 version; delivery by 2006
	290	BGM-71F TOW-2B	Anti-tank missile	2002	2003–2004	(290)	Deal worth $18 m
	360	Javelin	Anti-tank missile	(2002)		. .	Deal worth $51 m incl 40 launchers
	(22)	RGM-84L Harpoon	Anti-ship missile	(2003)		. .	RGM-84L Block-2 version; for Kidd Class destroyers
	(100)	RIM-66M Standard-2	SAM	(2003)		. .	SM-2 Block-3A version; for Kidd Class destroyers
	4	Kidd Class	Destroyer	(2003)		. .	Ex-US; deal worth $740 m; delivery 2005–2007

Recipient/ supplier (S) or licenser (L)	No. ordered	Weapon designation	Weapon description	Year of order/ licence	Year(s) of deliveries	No. delivered/ produced	Comments
L: USA	8	Perry Class	Frigate	1989	1993–2004	8	Taiwanese desig Cheng Kung Class; 'Kwang Hua-1' project; order for last 1 delayed from 1997 to 2001 for financial reasons
Thailand							
S: China	2	OPV-85m Type	OPV	2002		. .	Deal worth $66–88 m; delivery 2005–2006
Italy	2	RAN-30X	Air surv radar	(2002)		. .	For 2 OPV-85m Type OPVs from China
New Zealand	8	CT-4 Airtrainer	Trainer aircraft	2003	2004	8	CT-4E version; Thai desig BF-16
Singapore	7	F-16A	FGA aircraft	2004	2004	7	Ex-Singaporean; aid (in exchange for 15 year access to Thai training areas); inc l 4 F-16B version
UK	2	Super Lynx	ASW helicopter	2001	2004	(1)	Deal worth £25 m ($36 m; offsets 50%)
	22	L-118	Towed gun	2004		. .	L-119 version
USA	30	Bell-205/UH-1H	Helicopter	2001	2002–2004	(30)	Ex-US; aid; modernized to Huey-2 version before delivery for $20–37 m
	(4)	S-70A/UH-60L	Helicopter	2003	2004	2	Deal worth THB3 b ($70 m)
Tunisia							
S: USA	(15)	Bell-205/UH-1H	Helicopter	(2004)		. .	Ex-US; aid; status uncertain
	(30)	M-106 107mm	APC/mortar carrier	(2003)		. .	Ex-US; aid; M-106A2 version; status uncertain
	(92)	M-113	APC	(2003)		. .	Ex-US; aid; M-113A2 version; M-577A2 CP version; status uncertain
Turkey							
S: France	19	Ocean Master	MP aircraft radar	2002		. .	Part of deal worth $400 m; part of 'Meltem' programme; for 9 CN-235MPA and 10 ATR-72MP MP aircraft from Spain and Italy

Germany	6	Frankenthal Class	MCM ship	1999	2003–2004	(2)	Deal worth $625 m; incl 5 assembled/produced in Turkey; Turkish desig Aydin Class; delivery 2003–2007
	1	Kiliç Class	FAC(M)	2000	2004	1	
Israel	(108)	Harpy	Anti-radar UAV	1999	2001–2004	(108)	Deal probably worth $76 m
	(46)	Popeye-1	ASM	(1998)	2002–2004	(46)	Deal worth $90 m; for F-4E-2020 combat aircraft
Italy	10	ATR-72MP	ASW/MP aircraft	(2004)		. .	'Meltem' or 'Uzun Ufuk' programme; contract not yet signed
	4	RAT-31S/L	Air surv radar	2002	2004	(1)	Part 'NATO ACCS' programme; for 'NADGE' air-surveillance network; RAT-31DL version
Netherlands	6	LIROD	Fire control radar	2001	2004	1	For 6 Kilic Class FAC from Germany
	6	MW-08	Air surv radar	2001	2004	1	For 6 Kilic Class FAC from Germany
	6	STING	Fire control radar	2001	2004	1	For 6 Kilic Class FAC from Germany
South Korea	(300)	K-9 Thunder 155mm	Self-propelled gun	2001	2003–2004	(24)	Deal worth $1–1.2 b (incl $60–70 m for first 8–20); majority assembled in Turkey; Turkish desig Firtina; delivery 2003–2013
USA	4	Boeing-737-7ES	AEW&C aircraft	2003		. .	'Peace Eagle' programme worth $1.5 b (offsets worth $500 m); option on 2 more; delivery 2007–2008
	2	S-70A/UH-60L	Helicopter	2003	2004	(2)	Deal worth $27 m; Turkish desig Karaku
	551	AIFV	IFV	2000	2001–2004	(551)	Deal worth $338 m; incl APC and mortar carrier versions; assembled/produced in Turkey
	(140)	Dragoon	APC	(1998)	2002–2004	(140)	Deal worth $45 m; for police
	180	AN/APG-68	Aircraft radar	(2004)		. .	Part of $3.9 b modernization of 218 Turkish F-16C combat aircraft; AN/APG-68(V)9 version
	8	AN/MPQ-64	Air surv radar	2002		. .	For 8 modernized I-HAWK SAM systems; delivery 2005
	8	I-HAWK	SAM system	2002		. .	Ex-US; deal worth $100 m; modernized (partly in Norway) to I-HAWK PIP-3 version before delivery; delivery 2005
	144	AGM-114B Hellfire-2	ASM	2002	2003–2004	(144)	For Bell-209/AH-1W helicopters
	(1 500)	FIM-92C Stinger	Portable SAM	1986	1998–2004	(1 500)	Part of 'European Stinger Production Programme' involving production of components in Germany, Greece, Netherlands and Turkey and final assembly in Germany

Recipient/ supplier (S) or licenser (L)	No. ordered	Weapon designation	Weapon description	Year of order/ licence	Year(s) of deliveries	No. delivered/ produced	Comments
	(175)	MIM-23B HAWK	SAM	(2002)		. .	Ex-US; aid
L: Germany	5	Kiliç Class	FAC(M)	2000		. .	Delivery 2005–2007
	4	Type-209/1400	Submarine	1998	2003–2004	2	Deal worth $556 m; Turkish desig Gur Class; delivery 2003–2007
UK	840	Rapier Mk-2	SAM	1999	2002–2004	(200)	Deal worth $130–150 m; for use with Rapier SAM systems modernized to Rapier B1X (Rapier-2) version; delivery 2002–2010
Turkmenistan							
S: Georgia	. .	Su-25T/Frogfoot	Ground attack ac	(2003)	2004	(1)	Su-25KM version; possibly modernized Turkmeni aircraft; payment for Georgian debts to Turkmenistan
UAE							
S: Denmark	4	SCANTER-2001	Sea surv radar	2004		. .	Part of 'Project Baynunah' worth $500 m; for 4 Baynunah Class corvettes from France;
France	7	AS-365F/565SA Panther	ASW helicopter	1995	1999–2004	(7)	Part of deal worth $230 m; AS-565SB version; for Abu Dhabi
	32	Mirage-2000-5 Mk-2	FGA aircraft	1998	2003–2004	(16)	Deal worth $3.4 b incl modernization of 30 UAE Mirage-2000 to Mirage-2000-9 version; Mirage-2009 version; delivery 2003–2007
	390	Leclerc	Tank	1993	1994–2004	(390)	Part of deal worth $3.4 b (offsets 60%); incl 2 Driver Training Tank version
	46	Leclerc DNG	ARV	1993	1997–2004	(46)	Part of deal worth $3.4 b (offsets 60%)
	24	VBL	Reconnaissance veh	2003	2004	24	
	4	Ocean Master	MP aircraft radar	(2001)		. .	For 4 CN-295MPA MP aircraft from Spain
	(30)	RDY	Aircraft radar	1998		. .	RDY-2 version; for modernization of 30 Mirage-2000 FGA aircraft to Mirage-2009 version

	(1 134)	MICA	BVRAAM	1998	2003–2004	(450)	For Mirage-2000-5 Mk-2 combat aircraft
	(64)	MM-40-3 Exocet	Anti-ship missile	(2004)		. .	Part of 'Project Baynunah' worth $500 m for 4 Baynunah Class corvettes
	500	R-550 Magic-2	SRAAM	(1998)	2003–2004	(200)	For Mirage 2000-5 Mk-2 combat aircraft
	4	Baynunah Class	Corvette	2003		. .	'Project Baynunah' worth $500 m (incl $205 m for French ship producer); incl 3 assembled in UAE; for Abu Dhabi; option on 2 more; delivery from 2008
Italy	4	NA-25XM	Fire control radar	2004		. .	Part of 'Project Baynunah' worth $500 m; for 4 Baynunah Class corvettes from France
Libya	8	CH-47C Chinook	Helicopter	2003		. .	Ex-Libyan; modernized in Italy before delivery in 2006
Romania	10	SA-330 Puma	Helicopter	2001		. .	Deal worth $125 m incl modernization of 15 UAE SA-330; IAR-330SM version; for Abu Dhabi; delivery 2005–2007
Russia	50	96K9 Pantzyr-S1	Mobile SAM system	2000	2004	(10)	Deal worth $734 m; development partly funded by UAE; incl 26 wheeled and 24 armoured tracked version; delivery 2004–2005
	(1 008)	SA-19 Grisom/9M111	SAM	2000	2004	(100)	For 96K9 Pantzyr-S1 SAM systems
Spain	4	C-295MPA	ASW/MP aircraft	2001		. .	'Shaheen-1' programme worth $114–140 m; for Abu Dhabi
Sweden	4	Giraffe AMB-3D	Air surv radar	2004		. .	Part of 'Project Baynunah' worth $500 m; for 4 Baynunah Class corvettes from France
Switzerland	40	M-109A1 155mm	Self-propelled gun	(2001)		. .	Ex-Swiss; deal worth CHF2.3 m ($2 m); M-109A3 version
	180	M-113	APC	2004		. .	Ex-Swiss; M-113A1 version
UK	1	Learjet-35A	Transport aircraft	2004	2004	1	Second-hand
	(600)	Black Shahine	ASM	1998	2003–2004	(110)	For Mirage-2000-5 Mk-2 combat aircraft
USA	80	F-16E	FGA aircraft	2000	2004	(8)	Deal worth $5 b (incl $400 m for engines); incl 25 F-16F version; delivery 2004–2007
	289	AGM-114K Hellfire	Anti-tank missile	(2002)		. .	For modernized AH-64A heliciopters
	(1 163)	AGM-65D Maverick	ASM	(2003)		. .	For F-16E combat aircraft; incl AGM-65G version; contract not yet signed
	159	AGM-88 HARM	Anti-radar missile	2001	2004	(10)	AGM-88C version; for F-16E combat aircraft

Recipient/ supplier (S) or licenser (L)	No. ordered	Weapon designation	Weapon description	Year of order/ licence	Year(s) of deliveries	No. delivered/ produced	Comments
	. .	AIM-120B AMRAAM	BVRAAM	(2003)		. .	For F-16E combat aircraft; contract possibly not yet signed
	(267)	AIM-9M Sidewinder	SRAAM	2002	2004	(25)	For F-16E combat aircraft
	1 000	Javelin	Anti-tank missile	(2004)		. .	Deal worth $135 m incl 100 launchers; contract not yet signed
	52	RGM-84 Harpoon	Anti-ship missile	(2003)		. .	Deal worth $40 m; AGM-84 version for F-16E combat aircraft; contract probably not yet signed
	(237)	RIM-162 ESSM	SAM	(2004)		. .	Deal worth $237 m; for Baynunah Class corvettes and probably for modernized Kortenear Class frigates
Ukraine	1	An-124 Condor	Transport aircraft	2003	2004	1	
UK							
S: Canada	5	BD-700 Global Express	Transport aircraft	1999		. .	Part of deal worth $1.3 b (offsets 100%); for modification to AGS aircraft in USA and UK with ASTOR radars; delivery 2005–2006
Israel	. .	Hermes-180	UAV	(2004)		. .	Part of £800 m ($1.5 b) 'Watchkeeper' programme; assembledIproduced in UK; UK desig WK-180; delivery from 2006
	. .	Hermes-450	UAV	(2004)		. .	Part of £800 m ($1.5 b) 'Watchkeeper' programme; assembled/produced in UK; UK desig WK-450; delivery from 2006
Italy	401	MLV	APC	2003	2004	(3)	'Future Command and Liason Vehicle' (FCLV) programme worth £166 m ($282 m); option on 400 more; delivery 2004–2009
Netherlands	2	Goalkeeper	CIWS	(1996)	2003–2004	(2)	For 2 Albion Class AALS produced in UK
	6	SMART-L	Air/sea surv radar	(2002)		. .	S1850M version; for 6 D Class (Type-45) destroyers produced in UK

South Africa	6	SA-330 Puma	Helicopter	2002	2004	(6)	Ex-South African; SA-330L version; modernized in Romania before delivery
Sweden	108	BvS-10	APC	2000	2001–2004	(74)	Deal worth $86–106 m (armoured parts produced in UK); incl 31 CP and 6 ARV version; UK desig Viking; delivery 2001–2005
	4	ARTHUR	Arty locating radar	2002	2003–2004	(4)	'MAMBA' programme worth $54 m; option on 4 more
USA	7	King Air B200/C12	Light transport ac	(2002)	2003–2004	7	Leased from and operated by civilian company for training of UK pilots
	(1 600)	AGM-114K Hellfire	Anti-tank missile	(1996)	2000–2004	(1 600)	For AH-64D helicopters; assembled in UK
	(150)	AIM-120B AMRAAM	BVRAAM	2004		. .	Deal worth $144 m
	22	BGM-109 Tomahawk	SLCM	2002	2004	(22)	Deal worth $30 m; ex-US UGM-109C version modernized to BGM-109 T-LAM Block-IIIC version; for Swiftsure and Trafalgar Class submarines
	64	BGM-109 Tomahawk	SLCM	2004		. .	Deal worth $47 or $129 m; BGM-109 Tomahawk Block-IV (Tactical Tomahawk) version; for Swiftsure and Trafalgar Class submarines; delivery from 2005
	(100)	FIM-92A Stinger	Portable SAM	2001	2004	(100)	Part of deal worth $89 m for 1007 missiles for Greece, Italy and UK
	(3 871)	Javelin	Anti-tank missile	2003		. .	'LFATGWS' programme worth $459–490 m (offsets 100%); delivery from 2005
	. .	Javelin	Anti-tank missile	2004		. .	Deal worth £100 m ($179 m); delivery from 2007
L: Netherlands	4	Enforcer Type	AALS	2000		. .	Deal worth £320–360 m; UK desig Bay Class; delivery 2005–2006
USA	59	AH-64D Apache	Combat helicopter	1996	2001–2004	(59)	Part of deal worth $2.8–3.95 b (offsets 100%); WAH-64D Apache Mk-1 version

Recipient/ supplier (S) or licenser (L)	No. ordered	Weapon designation	Weapon description	Year of order/ licence	Year(s) of deliveries	No. delivered/ produced	Comments
	5	ASTOR	AGS radar	1999		. .	Part of deal worth $1.3 b (offsets 100%); for modification of 5 BD-700 transport aircraft delivered from Canada to AGS aircraft; delivery 2005–2006
USA							
S: Australia	7	GA-8 Airvan	Light aircraft	2003	2004	(7)	For Auxiliary Civil Air Patrol
Brazil	5	ERJ-145	Transport aircraft	2004		. .	Part of $879 m 'Aerial Common Sensor' programme; modified in USA to ELINT aircraft; delivery from 2005–2006
Canada	(294)	Piranha-3 LPTAG	FSV	2000	2002	8	Part of 'LAV' programme worth $4 b; Stryker MGS version; assembled/produced in USA
	(1 837)	Piranha/LAV-25	IFV	2000	2002–2004	(1 256)	Part of 'LAV' programme worth $4 b; Stryker version; incl APC and mortar carier version; assembled/produced in USA; delivery 2002–2008
France	(69)	MO-120-RT-61 120mm	Mortar	2004		. .	'EFSS' programme
Germany	5	TRS-3D	Air/sea surv radar	2004		. .	For 2 LCS Flight-0 Type frigates, 1 WMSL (MSCL or NSC) Type OPV and 1 land-based site; option on 3 more
Israel	(2)	Aerostar	UAV	2004	2004	(2)	Assembled/produced in USA; for training
	(4)	Kfir C2	FGA aircraft	2002	2002–2004	(4)	Ex-Israeli; modernized before delivery; delivered to civilian company for training of US armed forces
	. .	CARDOM 120mm	Mortar	(2003)	2004	(50)	For Piranha-3 (Stryker) mortar carrier
Italy	2	A-109K	Light helicopter	2003		. .	Lease; for Coast Guard 'Airborne Use of Force' anti-narcotics operations; A-109E Power version; US desig MH-68A Sting Ray

	Spain	2	CN-235MP Persuader	MP aircraft	2004		. .	Deal worth $87 m; part of Coast Guard 'Deepwater-2000' programme; CN-235M-300M/C-235ER version; option on 6 more; assembled/produced in USA; delivery 2006
	Sweden	2	Giraffe AMB-3D	Air surv radar	2002	2004	2	
	Switzerland	32	F-5E Tiger-2	FGA aircraft	2003	2003–2004	(12)	Ex-Swiss; deal worth $19 m; for use as 'enemy' in training; US desig F-5N; delivery 2003–2007
L:	Israel	(250)	Popeye-1/AGM-142	ASM	1998	2000–2004	(210)	US desig AGM-142 Raptor or Have Nap
	Switzerland	(710)	PC-9/T-6A Texan-2	Trainer aircraft	1996	1999–2004	(170)	'JPATS' programme worth $7 b (incl $4.7 b for aircraft only); delivery 1999–2017
	UK	187	Hawk/T-45A Goshawk	Trainer aircraft	1981	1990–2004	(173)	'VTXTS' or 'T-45TS' programme; T-45A and T-45C Goshawk versions; delivery 1990–2006
		(591)	UFH	Towed gun	(2000)	2002–2004	(12)	US desig M-777; delivery 2002–2009
Uganda								
S:	Russia	3	Mi-24P/Mi-35P/Hind-F	Combat helicopter	(2003)	2004	(3)	Desig uncertain; possibly ex-Russian older Mi-24 modernized to Mi-24PN version before delivery
Ukraine								
S:	Macedonia	4	Su-25/Frogfoot-A	Ground attack ac	2004	2004	4	Ex-Macedonian
Unknown country								
S:	Israel	(4)	ATMOS-2000 155mm	Self-propelled gun	2003	2004	(4)	Deal worth $5 m; recipient possibly Botswana
Uruguay								
S:	Spain	2	Descubierta Class	Frigate	2004		. .	Ex-Spanish; deal worth $20 m; contract not yet signed

Recipient/ supplier (S) or licenser (L)	No. ordered	Weapon designation	Weapon description	Year of order/ licence	Year(s) of deliveries	No. delivered/ produced	Comments
Venezuela							
S: Brazil	12	AMX-T	Trainer/combat ac	2002		. .	AMX-ATA version; incl 4 AMX-E EW version; delivery from 2005; status uncertain
France	8	AS-350/550 Fennec	Light helicopter	2003	2004	(4)	Deal worth $50 m; AS-550C2 Fennec version
Israel	12	EL/M-2032	Combat ac radar	(2002)		. .	For 12 AMX-ATA trainer/combat aircraft from Brazil
	(176)	Python-4	BVRAAM	2003	2004	(57)	Deal worth $7.5 m; for F-16A combat aircraft
Russia	(1)	Mi-26/Halo	Helicopter	(2004)		. .	Part of deal worth $120 m; delivery 2005
	(9)	Mi-8/Mi-17/Hip-H	Helicopter	(2004)		. .	Part of deal worth $120 m; Mi-17-1V version; delivery 2005
Viet Nam							
S: Poland	2	An-28/M-28B Bryza-1R	MP aircraft	2003	2004	(1)	
Russia	2	Mi-8/Mi-17/Hip-H	Helicopter	2002	2004	2	Mi-17 version
	4	Su-30MK/Flanker	FGA aircraft	(2003)	2004	4	Deal worth $100–120 m; Su-30MK2V version
	2	SA-10d/S-300PMU-1	SAM system	2003		. .	Part of deal worth $200–380 m; delivery 2005
	(72)	SA-10 Grumble/48N6	SAM	2003		. .	Part of deal worth $200–380 m; for SA-10d/ S-300PMU-1 SAM systems; delivery 2005
	. .	SA-16 Gimlet/Igla-1	Portable SAM	(1996)	2001–2004	(48)	SA-N-10 version for BPS-500 Type (Ho-A Class) and Svetlyak Class FAC
	(32)	SS-N-25/Kh-35 Uran	Anti-ship missile	(1996)	2001–2004	(16)	For BPS-500 Type (Ho-A Class) FAC
	(2)	BPS-500/Type-1241A	FAC(M)	1996	2001	1	Assembled in Viet Nam; Vietnamese desig Ho-A Class
Yemen							
S: Australia	10	Bay Class	Patrol craft	(2003)	2004	(10)	Deal worth $55–69 m
Russia	8	MiG-29SMT Fulcrum	FGA aircraft	2003	2004	(6)	Incl 2 MiG-29UBT version; delivery 2004–2005
	12	Zhuk	Combat ac radar	2003		. .	For modernization of 12 Yemeni MiG-29 combat aircraft to MiG-29SMT version

(176)	AA-11 Archer/R-73	SRAAM	(2001)	2002–2004	(138)	For MiG-29S and MiG-29SMT combat aircraft
(64)	AA-12 Adder/R-77	BVRAAM	(2003)	2004	(32)	For MiG-29SMT combat aircraft
. .	AS-14 Kedge/Kh-29	ASM	(2003)	2004	(25)	For MiG-29SMT combat aircraft

Acronyms and abbreviations

ac	Aircraft
AALS	Amphibious assault landing ship
AAV	Anti-aircraft vehicle
ABL	Armoured bridge-layer
ACV	Air-cushion vessel (hovercraft)
AEV	Armoured engineer vehicle
AEW	Airborne early-warning
AEW&C	Airborne early-warning and control
AFSV	Armoured fire support vehicle
AGS	Airborne ground-surveillance
ALV	Armoured logistic vehicle
AMV	Anti-mine vehicle
APC	Armoured personnel carrier
APC/CP	Armoured personnel carrier/command post
arty	Artillery
ARV	Armoured recovery vehicle
AS	Anti-ship
ASM	Air-to-surface missile
ASW	Anti-submarine warfare
BVRAAM	Beyond visual range air-to-air missile
CIWS	Close-in weapon system
CP	Command post
CSAR	Combat SAR
desig	Designation
ELINT	Electronic intelligence
EU	European Union
FAC	Fast attack craft
FGA	Fighter/ground attack
FMF	Foreign Military Funding (US)
(G)	Gun-armed
IFV	Infantry fighting vehicle
incl	Including/include(s)
LTTE	Liberation Tigers of Tamil Eelam
(M)	Missile-armed
MCM	Mine countermeasures
MLU	Mid-life update
MP	Maritime patrol
MRL	Multiple rocket launcher
NBC	Nuclear, biological and chemical
no.	Number
OPV	Offshore patrol vessel
SAM	Surface-to-air missile
SAR	Search and rescue
SIGINT	Signals intelligence
SLCM	Submarine-launched cruise missile
SRAAM	Short-range air-to-air missile
SSM	Surface-to-surface missile
surv	Surveillance
UAE	United Arab Emirates
UAV	Unmanned air vehicle (drone)
VIP	Very important person

Conventions

. .	Data not available or not applicable
( )	Uncertain data or SIPRI estimate
m	million (10^6)
b	billion (10^9)

'Contract not yet signed' is used in the comments field when sources indicate that preliminary agreements have been signed, but when the final contract has not yet been signed.

'Status uncertain' is used in the comments field when sources are contradictory about the (continued) existence of the reported deal.

'Unknown' is used in cases where it has not been possible to identify a supplier or recipient with an acceptable degree of certainty.

'Multiple sellers' is used in cases where the weapon is a co-production of two or more countries and where it has not been possible to identify the final supplier; the co-producing countries are mentioned in the comments field and the final supplier will be known when actual deliveries will take place.

Appendix 10C. Sources and methods for arms transfers data

SIEMON T. WEZEMAN and MARK BROMLEY

The SIPRI Arms Transfers Project reports on international flows of conventional weapons. Since publicly available information is inadequate for the tracking of all weapons and other military equipment, SIPRI covers only what it terms *major conventional weapons*.[1]

Data are collected from open sources in the SIPRI arms transfers database and presented in a register that identifies the suppliers, recipients and weapon deliveries, and in tables that provide a measure of the trends in the total flow of major weapons and its geographical pattern. SIPRI has developed a unique trend-indicator value system. The figures produced by the system are not comparable to official economic statistics such as gross domestic product, public expenditure and export/import figures.

The database covers the period from 1950. Data collection and analysis are continuous processes. As new data become available the database is updated for all years included in the database.[2]

I. Selection criteria and coverage

Selection criteria

SIPRI uses the term 'transfer' rather than 'trade' since the latter is usually associated with 'sale'. SIPRI covers not only sales of weapons, including manufacturing licences, but also other forms of weapon supply, including aid and gifts.

The weapons transferred must be destined for the armed forces, paramilitary forces or intelligence agencies of another country. Weapons supplied to or from rebel forces in an armed conflict are included as deliveries to or from the individual rebel forces, identified under separate 'recipient' or 'supplier' headings. Supplies to or from international organizations are also included and categorized in the same fashion. In cases where deliveries are identified but where it is not possible to identify either the supplier or the recipient with an acceptable degree of certainty, transfers are registered as coming from 'unknown' suppliers or going to 'unknown' recipients. Suppliers are termed 'multiple' only if there is a transfer agreement for weapons that are produced by two or more cooperating countries and if it is not clear which country will make the delivery.

Weapons must be transferred voluntarily by the supplier. This includes weapons delivered illegally—without proper authorization by the government of the supplier or the recipient country—but excludes captured weapons and weapons obtained from

[1] A complete description of the SIPRI Arms Transfers Project methodology, including a list of the sources used, is available on the SIPRI Internet site at URL <http://www.sipri.se/projects/armstrade/atmethods.html>.

[2] Thus data from several SIPRI Yearbooks or other SIPRI publications cannot be combined or compared. Readers who require time-series trend-indicator value data for periods before the years covered in this Yearbook or who require updated registers should contact SIPRI, preferably via the Internet site at URL <http://projects.sipri.se/armstrade/atrequest.html>.

defectors. Finally, the weapons must have a military purpose. Systems such as aircraft used mainly for other branches of government but registered with and operated by the armed forces are excluded. Weapons supplied for technical or arms procurement evaluation purposes only are not included.

Major conventional weapons: the coverage

SIPRI covers only what it terms *major conventional weapons*, defined as:

1. *Aircraft*: all fixed-wing aircraft and helicopters, including unmanned reconnaissance/surveillance aircraft, with the exception of micro-light aircraft, powered and unpowered gliders and target drones.
2. *Armoured vehicles*: all vehicles with integral armour protection, including all types of tank, tank destroyer, armoured car, armoured personnel carrier, armoured support vehicle and infantry fighting vehicle.
3. *Artillery*: naval, fixed, self-propelled and towed guns, howitzers, multiple rocket launchers and mortars, with a calibre equal to or above 100 millimetres (mm).
4. *Radar systems*: all land-, aircraft- and ship-based active (radar) and passive (e.g., electro-optical) surveillance systems with a range of at least 25 kilometres (km), with the exception of navigation and weather radars, and all fire-control radars, with the exception of range-only radars. In cases where the system is fitted on a platform (vehicle, aircraft or ship), the register only notes those systems that come from a different supplier than the supplier of the platform.
5. *Missiles*: all powered, guided missiles and torpedoes with conventional warheads. Unguided rockets, guided but unpowered shells and bombs, free-fall aerial munitions, anti-submarine rockets and target drones are excluded.
6. *Ships*: all ships with a standard tonnage of 100 tonnes or more, and all ships armed with artillery of 100-mm calibre or more, torpedoes or guided missiles, with the exception of most survey ships, tugs and some transport ships.

The statistics presented refer to transfers of weapons in these six categories only. Transfers of other military equipment—such as small arms/light weapons, trucks, artillery under 100-mm calibre, ammunition, support equipment and components, as well as services or technology transfers—are not included.

II. The SIPRI trend indicator

The SIPRI system for the valuation of arms transfers is designed as a *trend-measuring device*. It permits the measurement of changes in the total flow of major weapons and its geographical pattern. The trends presented in the tables of SIPRI trend-indicator values are based only on *actual deliveries* during the year/years covered in the relevant tables and figures, not on orders signed in a year.

The trend-indicator value system, in which similar weapons have similar values, reflects both the quantity and the quality of the weapons transferred. The value reflects the transfer of *military resources*.

Arms transfers can be measured with several objectives in mind. The two most common objectives are to gain knowledge about the economic factor and about the military implications of arms transfers. However, different goals require different statistical approaches.

The SIPRI values do not reflect the money value of (or payments for) weapons transferred. This is impossible for three reasons. First, in many cases no reliable data on the value of a transfer are available. Second, even if the value of a transfer is known, it is in almost every case the total value of a deal, which may include not only the weapons entered in the SIPRI database but also other items related to these weapons (e.g., spare parts, armament or ammunition) as well as support systems (e.g., specialized vehicles) and items related to the integration of the weapon in the armed forces (e.g., software changes to existing systems or training). Third, even if the value of a transfer is known, there remains the problem that important details about the financial arrangements of the transfer (e.g., credit/loan conditions and discounts) are usually not known.[3]

Measuring the military implications of transfers would require a concentration on the value of the weapons as a military resource. Again, this could be done from the actual money values of the weapons transferred, assuming that these values generally reflect the military capability of the weapon. However, the problems enumerated above would still apply (e.g., a very expensive weapon may be transferred as aid at a 'zero' price, and therefore not show up in financial statistics, but still be a significant transfer of military resources). The SIPRI solution is a system in which military resources are measured by including an evaluation of the technical parameters of the weapons. The tasks and performance of the weapons are evaluated and the weapons are assigned a value in an index. These values reflect the military resource value of the weapon in relation to other weapons. This can be done under the condition that a number of benchmarks or reference points are established by assigning some weapons a fixed place in the index. These are the core of the index, and all other weapons are compared to these *core weapons*.

In short, the process of calculating the SIPRI trend-indicator value for individual weapons is as follows.

For a number of weapon types (noted in the register as the 'weapon designation') it is possible to find the actual average unit acquisition price in open sources. It is assumed that such real prices roughly reflect the military resource value of a system. For example, a combat aircraft bought for $10 million may be assumed to be a resource twice as great as one bought for $5 million, and a submarine bought for $100 million may be assumed to be 10 times the resource a $10 million combat aircraft would represent. Those weapons with a real price are used as the core weapons of the valuation.

Weapons for which a price is not known are compared with core weapons. This comparison is made in the following steps.

1. The description of a weapon is compared with the description of the core weapon. In cases where no core weapon exactly matches the description of the weapon for which a price is to be found, the closest match is sought.

2. Standard characteristics of size and performance (weight, speed, range and payload) are compared with those of a core weapon of a similar description. For example, a 15 000-kg combat aircraft would be compared with a combat aircraft of similar size.

[3] It is possible to present a very rough idea of the economic factors from the financial statistics now available from most arms-exporting countries. However, most of these statistics lack sufficient detail.

3. Other characteristics, such as the type of electronics, loading/unloading arrangements, engine, tracks or wheels, armament and materials, are compared.
4. Weapons are compared with a core weapon from the same period.

Production under licence is included in the arms transfer statistics to reflect the average percentage of licensee-imported components embodied in the weapon (in reality this import share may fluctuate, often gradually decreasing over time). Supplies of sub-systems from other sources than the licenser registered in the database are not included (unless these sub-systems are weapons as defined by SIPRI for the database, in which case a separate record is included in the database with details for these systems).

Weapons delivered in 'second-hand' condition are given a standard value of 40 per cent of the value assigned to the new weapon; second-hand weapons that have been significantly refurbished or modified by the supplier before delivery (and have thereby become a greater military resource) are given a value of 66 per cent of the new value. In reality there may be huge differences in the military resource value of a second-hand weapon depending on its condition after use and the modifications during the years of use.

The SIPRI trend indicator does not measure military value or effectiveness. It does not take into account the conditions under which a weapon is operated (e.g., an F-16 combat aircraft operated by well-balanced, well-trained and well-integrated armed forces has a much greater military value than the same aircraft operated by a developing country; the resource is the same but the effect is very different). The trend indicator also accepts the prices of the core weapons as genuine rather than reflecting costs which, even if officially part of the programme, are not exclusively related to the weapon itself—for example, funds that seem to be part of a programme could be related to optional add-ons and armament or to the development of basic technology that will also be included (free of cost) in other programmes but have for the sake of convenience been put under one programme, and hidden government subsidies to keep industry in being by paying more than the weapon is worth.

III. Sources

The sources for the data presented in the arms transfers register are of a wide variety—newspapers; periodicals and journals; books, monographs and annual reference works; and official national and international documents. The common criterion for all these sources is that they are open—published and available to the general public.

Such open information cannot, however, provide a comprehensive picture of world arms transfers. Published reports often provide only partial information, and substantial disagreement between them is common. Order and delivery dates and exact numbers, or even types, of weapons ordered and delivered, or the identity of suppliers or recipients, may not always be clear from the sources. The exercise of judgement and the making of estimates are therefore important elements in compiling the SIPRI arms transfers database. Estimates are kept at conservatively low levels (and may very well be underestimates).

All sources of data as well as calculations of estimates, while not published by SIPRI, are documented in the SIPRI database.

Part III. Non-proliferation, arms control and disarmament, 2004

Chapter 11. Arms control and non-proliferation: the role of international organizations

Chapter 12. Nuclear arms control and non-proliferation

Chapter 13. Chemical and biological warfare developments and arms control

Chapter 14. Libya's renunciation of nuclear, biological and chemical weapons and ballistic missiles

Chapter 15. Conventional arms control and military confidence building

Chapter 16. International non-proliferation and disarmament assistance

Chapter 17. Transfer controls

Chapter 18. The Proliferation Security Initiative: international law aspects of the Statement of Interdiction Principles

11. Arms control and non-proliferation: the role of international organizations

IAN ANTHONY

I. Introduction

A stable and peaceful international order requires controls on nuclear, biological and chemical (NBC) and other types of weapons and dangerous sensitive materials as well as regulation of the behaviour of both state and non-state actors. For almost a decade, however, there has been little progress in multilateral arms control in general and some processes have suffered severe setbacks. A number of cases have come to light in which states violated their obligations under arms control treaties, which undermined confidence in the value of global arms control agreements as instruments for security building. Given these trends, states have tended not to consider global measures first when contemplating how to make progress in solving particular problems. Instead, efforts to achieve the objectives of arms control have been carried forward mainly through informal political cooperation among small groups of states or through regional processes. However, a number of developments in 2004 suggest that there is a steadily growing momentum behind international efforts to explore how global processes might be strengthened in order to achieve their potential as part of an emerging mosaic of arms control measures.

In April 2004 the United Nations (UN) Security Council unanimously adopted Resolution 1540 on the proliferation of NBC weapons and their means of delivery.[1] Unlike most Security Council resolutions—which respond to developments in a particular location—Resolution 1540 has a preventive character. It was adopted primarily in response to the growing concern that non-state actors would succeed in acquiring NBC weapons. The evidence of an extensive grey market in nuclear and nuclear-related goods and technologies revealed in information released by the Government of Libya[2] and in investigations carried out by the International Atomic Energy Agency (IAEA) was a catalyst for the decision.[3]

In December 2004 UN Secretary-General Kofi Annan released the report of the UN High-level Panel on Threats, Challenges and Change.[4] The report,

[1] UN Security Council Resolution 1540, 28 Apr. 2004; it is reproduced in appendix 11A. See also chapter 17 in this volume.

[2] On Libya's NBC programmes see chapter 14 in this volume.

[3] On nuclear illicit trafficking see chapter 12 in this volume.

[4] United Nations, 'A more secure world: our shared responsibility', Report of the High-level Panel on Threats, Challenges and Change, UN documents A/59/565, 4 Dec. 2004, and A/59/565/Corr.1, 6 Dec. 2004, URL <http://www.un.org/ga/59/documentation/list5.html>. The synopsis and summary of recommendations of the report are reproduced in the appendix to the Introduction in this volume.

approximately one-third of which was devoted to arms control issues, pointed to the urgent need to establish effective controls over nuclear weapons and nuclear materials that can be used to make them. The High-level Panel expressed concern over the lack of progress in two areas of persistent difficulty for multilateral arms control as well as the pressing need for effective measures to reduce the threat of nuclear terrorism. The two areas of concern were: (*a*) how to ensure universal adherence to multilateral agreements intended to establish global norms and rules of behaviour; and (*b*) how to ensure that those states which do adhere to the agreements comply fully with the commitments that they have made.

Section II surveys some of the key developments in arms control and non-proliferation in 2004, which are analysed in detail in other chapters in this Yearbook. Section III addresses the issue of the role of global arms control processes—in particular, the role of the United Nations.

II. Developments in arms control and non-proliferation in 2004

It has increasingly been recognized that the application of a wide range of measures including, but not confined to, multilateral agreements is needed to implement the existing controls on NBC weapons and establish new controls on other types of weapon and on dangerous and sensitive materials and the behaviour of both state and non-state actors.

Nuclear arms control

Since the early 1990s states have been discussing, both formally and informally, the need for an agreement to prohibit the production of fissile materials for use in nuclear weapons. This prohibition is one required element of an effective global nuclear disarmament framework. In 1995 consultations among the members of the UN Conference on Disarmament (CD)[5] led to an agreement that an Ad Hoc Committee on Fissile Material Cut-Off should be established to discuss how such an objective might be achieved. The committee was not formed at that time because of disagreement over the scope of application of measures related to fissile material, in particular whether past production and existing stockpiles should be covered by a treaty or whether measures should focus exclusively on future production. Subsequent efforts to initiate negotiations on a treaty prohibiting the production of fissile material for military purposes have not been fruitful.

In 2003 the Government of China stated its willingness to begin negotiations on a fissile material treaty without requiring a parallel process to negotiate an agreement on the prevention of an arms race in outer space (PAROS), which would limit the military use of space. In 2004 the United States, which

[5] The members of the CD are listed in the glossary in this volume.

had consistently rejected this linkage, restated its commitment to negotiate a treaty banning the future production of fissile material but expressed its opposition to creating a joint system to verify such a ban.[6]

At the meeting of the Preparatory Committee for the 2005 Review Conference of the 1968 Treaty on the Non-Proliferation of Nuclear Weapons (Non-Proliferation Treaty, NPT) the question was raised of how to reconcile the non-proliferation obligations of states with the legitimate requirements of the nuclear power industry, among other users, for items that could be applied in a military programme. A number of states pointed to the need for a new cooperative framework between supplier states and customer states to ensure a reliable supply of items at a reasonable price without undermining non-proliferation objectives.

In 2004, following up a proposal made by its Director General in October 2003, the International Atomic Energy Agency (IAEA) initiated a study of multilateral approaches to the nuclear fuel cycle. The study focused in particular on the parts of the nuclear fuel cycle that are particularly sensitive from a nuclear weapon proliferation perspective, namely, those parts that produce the weapon-usable materials separated plutonium and highly enriched uranium (HEU). The preliminary discussions of the expert group conducting the study took place in September 2004.[7]

The 2004 meeting of the Preparatory Committee did not produce a consensus document and national presentations covered a wide and diverse range of subjects. However, two themes in particular were common to many of the national perspectives.

First, there was widespread support among participants for the strengthened safeguards system developed by the IAEA. The strengthened safeguards combine safeguards applied to all source and special fissionable material in current and future peaceful nuclear activities of a state (so-called full-scope safeguards) with additional measures contained in an Additional Protocol to the bilateral safeguards agreement between a state and the IAEA. There is a growing feeling that these integrated safeguards should be regarded as an international standard as well as a condition for new arrangements for nuclear supply to non-nuclear weapon states. Second, many national presentations showed the concern that the termination of the 1972 Treaty on the Limitation of Anti-Ballistic Missile Systems (ABM Treaty) along with the development of missile defence systems could trigger the development of new advanced missile systems and lead to increases in the number of nuclear weapons held by some states.[8]

[6] Sanders, J. W., Permanent Representative to the Conference on Disarmament and Special Representative of the President for the Nonproliferation of Nuclear Weapons, U.S. proposals to the Conference on Disarmament, 29 July 2004, URL <http://www.reachingcriticalwill.org/political/cd/speeches04/29July US.html>. On progress towards a fissile material treaty see chapter 12 in this volume.

[7] The background to the IAEA study of multilateral approaches to the fuel cycle as well as the activities of the Expert Group are available on the IAEA Internet site at URL <http://www.iaea.org/News Center/Focus/FuelCycle/index.shtml>. See also chapter 12 in this volume.

[8] In the absence of an agreed document the chairman of the meeting, Ambassador Sudjadnan Parnohadinigrat of Indonesia, produced a 'Chairman's Summary', 6 May 2004, URL <http://www.

Against the background of concerns about states violating obligations contained in the NPT or in IAEA safeguards agreements, a number of states emphasized the need to develop additional measures to create confidence about compliance. The appropriate role of export controls in raising confidence about the effectiveness of the non-proliferation regime was prominent among the measures discussed.

The view that effective export controls arc a prerequisite for cooperation on the use of nuclear energy for peaceful purposes has become increasingly widespread, and there is also a demand in some quarters for greater transparency in the development and implementation of export controls. Proposals have also been made to define minimum standards for export controls through an open and inclusive process, perhaps under the auspices of the IAEA, including the identification of international standards for implementation.

The states that participate in two informal cooperation arrangements, the Zangger Committee and the Nuclear Suppliers Group (NSG), have developed export control guidelines that each state implements nationally.[9] The potential role of these arrangements in assisting other participating states to establish effective national export control systems and the extent to which the existing guidelines might be more widely adopted were both discussed following the unanimous adoption of UN Security Council Resolution 1540.

Nuclear export controls focus on controlling those items that are relevant to the development and construction of nuclear explosive devices. However, after the terrorist attacks on the USA in September 2001 concern has grown about the possible use of a radiological dispersal device (RDD), for example in a 'dirty bomb', in a terrorist act. There are international standards and national controls in place to ensure that radiological materials are transported in a safe manner. However, transfers of such materials are not currently assessed to judge the risk of inappropriate or malicious end-use. As an element of the discussion of nuclear security the Group of Eight (G8) industrialized nations has proposed the development of export controls that would require the end-users of listed radiological materials to be assessed prior to any cross-border shipment.[10]

In May 2004 the US Secretary of Energy announced the Global Threat Reduction Initiative (GTRI) in remarks made at the IAEA.[11] The objective of the GTRI is to secure, remove, relocate or dispose of nuclear and radiological

reachingcriticalwill.org/legal/npt/prepcom04/chair.html>. The national presentations at the Preparatory Committee for the 2005 Review Conference of the Parties to the Treaty on the Non-Proliferation of Nuclear Weapons are archived by the UN Department of Disarmament Affairs at URL <http://disarmament.un.org:8080/wmd/npt/2005/PC3-listofdocs.html>. See also chapter 12 in this volume. The text of the ABM Treaty is available at URL <http://www.state.gov/t/np/trty/16332.htm#treaty>; see also annex A in this volume.

[9] The Zangger Committee and the NSG are discussed in chapter 17 in this volume.

[10] The members of the G8 are listed in the glossary in this volume. See also 'Sea Island Summit 2004: G8 Action Plan on Nonproliferation', Sea Island, Ga., 9 June 2004, URL <http://www.g8usa.gov/d_060904d.htm>.

[11] IAEA, 'Remarks prepared for Energy Secretary Spencer Abraham', Vienna, 26 May 2004, URL <http://www.energy.gov/engine/content.do?PUBLIC_ID=15949&BT_CODE=PR_SPEECHES&TT_CODE=PRESSSPEECH>.

materials and equipment considered to be at risk of falling into the hands of users who are planning or contemplating terrorist acts. The GTRI is a US programme that brings together under one roof a number of nuclear security initiatives that the USA had been pursuing for more than a decade. However, in announcing the initiative, the Secretary of Energy was seeking international cooperation and support for the programme as well as highlighting the nuclear security-related activities already undertaken by the IAEA.

While the IAEA was engaged in nuclear security-related programmes during the 1990s, this work accelerated after September 2001. In early 2004 a Code of Conduct on the Safety and Security of Radioactive Sources was published by the IAEA.[12] In 2004 the newly established IAEA International Nuclear Security Advisory Service (INSServ) worked to help states assess their protection of radiological materials and produce recommendations to strengthen nuclear security at the national level.[13]

In September 2004 the IAEA, Russia and the USA organized an international conference in Vienna with four objectives.[14] The objectives were: to build consensus among the widest possible group of states that vulnerable, high-risk nuclear and radiological materials 'pose a threat to our collective security and that all states share the common objective to help reduce this threat'; to stimulate national programmes to identify, secure, recover and facilitate the disposal of such materials; to create international support for practical measures to mitigate the common threat; and to secure the widest possible active participation in implementing these practical measures.[15]

Developments in chemical- and biological weapon-related arms control

The 1993 Chemical Weapons Convention (CWC) is the most critical part of the international framework for chemical weapon disarmament and states parties carry the primary responsibility for meeting their obligations under the convention.[16] In 2003 the parties to the CWC endorsed a collective Action Plan which is intended to ensure that the national implementation measures specified in Article VII of the Convention are in place by late 2005. The Organisation for the Prohibition of Chemical Weapons (OPCW) was created in 1997 as the implementing body of the CWC, and in recent years assisting states with their responsibilities in the field of national implementation has

[12] IAEA, Code of Conduct on the Safety and Security of Radioactive Sources, URL <http://www-ns.iaea.org/tech-areas/radiation-safety/source.htm>.

[13] Nuclear security is discussed further in chapter 12 in this volume.

[14] IAEA, 'Summary of the proceedings and findings of the conference', Global Threat Reduction Initiative International Partners Conference, Vienna, 18–19 Sep. 2004, URL <http://www-pub.iaea.org/MTCD/Meetings/Announcements.asp?ConfID=139>.

[15] The outcome of the conference, in which representatives from over 100 states participated, is summarized in IAEA (note 14).

[16] The corrected text of the Convention on the Prohibition of the Development, Production, Stockpiling and Use of Chemical Weapons and on their Destruction is available at URL <http://projects.sipri.se/cbw/docs/cw-cwc-texts.html>. For complete lists of parties and signatories and non-signatory states see URL <http://projects.sipri.se/cbw/docs/cw-cwc-mainpage.html>. See also annex A and chapter 13 in this volume.

emerged as a critical task for it. Following the endorsement of the Action Plan, one report noted that the OPCW has moved from 'benign lack of interest in CWC national implementing legislation to being fully engaged with the issue'.[17] In the same report the authors note that the development and discussion of the Action Plan has led to 'greater dialogue, organizational change, more intensive reporting and some other concrete outcomes'.

The development of the OPCW Action Plan is an cxample of how states can work with and through an international organization to accelerate the implementation of their treaty obligations and make the implementation more effective. No comparable framework for effective cooperation exists for biological weapon (BW)-related arms control. In the absence of a dedicated international organization, it is more difficult to determine who is responsible for setting common implementation standards, monitoring adherence to them and assisting states when difficulties arise in reaching those standards. In the BW field, these tasks are the subject of discussion in different forums, including global and regional organizations, and in ad hoc processes where clusters of states participate.

Developments in conventional arms control

While no global framework governs the size and structure of the armed forces of states, in Europe there is a well-developed arms control regime covering heavy conventional weapons. Nonetheless, the 1990 Treaty on Conventional Armed Forces in Europe (CFE Treaty) remains entrapped in a prolonged crisis. The 1999 Adaptation Agreement to the CFE Treaty, which is intended to make the treaty better attuned to the security environment in Europe after the enlargement of the North Atlantic Treaty Organization (NATO), has not been implemented.[18] This failure has occurred although all parties agree that implementing the Adaptation Agreement is in their interests. For a number of parties to the CFE Treaty the implementation of the agreement is linked to the status of the 'Istanbul commitments' on Georgia and Moldova, which, in essence, require Russia to end its military presence in Georgia and Moldova by withdrawing forces, equipment and stores from facilities in those countries within a short period. In spite of what has become an entrenched political disagreement between NATO and Russia, however, all parties have continued to comply with their existing commitments under the CFE Treaty. Moreover, the failure to bring the adapted treaty into force did not 'spill over' to undermine the wider NATO–Russia political relations during a second round of NATO enlargement.

[17] Tabassi, L. and Spence, S., 'Improving the CWC implementation: the OPCW Action Plan', ed T. Findlay, Verification Research, Training and Information Centre (VERTIC), *Verification Yearbook 2004* (VERTIC: London 2004), p. 45. See also chapter 13 in this volume.

[18] A consolidated text showing the amended CFE Treaty as adapted in accordance with the Agreement on Adaptation is reproduced in Lachowski, Z., *The Adapted CFE Treaty and the Admission of the Baltic States to NATO*, SIPRI Policy Paper no. 1 (SIPRI: Stockholm, Dec. 2002), URL <http://www.sipri.org/contents/publications/policy_papers.html>. The parties to the CFE Treaty are listed in annex A in this volume. See also chapter 15 in this volume.

Implementation of the EU Strategy against the Proliferation of Weapons of Mass Destruction

In December 2003 the heads of state and government of the European Union (EU) adopted the European Security Strategy (ESS), which identified the proliferation of weapons of mass destruction (WMD) as a key threat confronting the EU.[19] In December 2003 the EU also adopted a Strategy against the Proliferation of Weapons of Mass Destruction (WMD Strategy) setting out measures to be used, ideally, to prevent proliferation from taking place.[20] These documents were intended to place all of the wide-ranging activities being carried out by the various parts of the EU—the European Commission, the Council of the European Union and the member states—in a single framework and thereby increase their coherence and effectiveness.

The WMD Strategy was not adopted in the form of a Common Position, a Joint Action or a Common Strategy—the legal instruments available under the EU Common Foreign and Security Policy (CFSP).[21] The concern that the informal character of the document, in effect a political declaration, would undermine its implementation was offset by the commitment to review implementation regularly and at a high level. In order to satisfy the commitment to conduct regular, high-level scrutiny of implementation, the General Affairs and External Relations Council (GAERC), which is composed of the foreign ministers of the EU member states, will be informed about the actions taken to implement the strategy on a six-monthly basis and is expected to debate the progress of implementation. During 2004 information about implementation was presented to the EU Political and Security Committee (PSC) and to the Permanent Representatives Committee (COREPER) prior to each of the discussions in the GAERC.[22] The measures taken by the EU to implement its WMD Strategy can be grouped under four headings.

1. The first measure is to ensure that the EU itself is a 'model citizen' that does not undermine non-proliferation objectives. A number of companies

[19] Council of the European Union, 'A secure Europe in a better world: European Security Strategy', Brussels, 12 Dec. 2003, URL <http://ue.eu.int/uedocs/cms_data/docs/pressdata/EN/reports/78367.pdf>.

[20] Council of the European Union, 'EU Strategy against Proliferation of Weapons of Mass Destruction', Brussels, 12 Dec. 2003, URL <http://ue.eu.int/cms3_applications/Applications/newsRoom/LoadDocument.asp?directory=en/misc/&filename=78340.pdf>.

[21] Portela, C., 'The EU and the NPT: testing the new European nonproliferation strategy', *Disarmament Diplomacy*, no. 78 (July/Aug. 2004), URL <http://www.acronym.org.uk/dd/dd78/78cp.htm>.

[22] The PSC, composed of political directors from the foreign ministries of all EU member states, is expected to keep track of the international situation in areas falling within the CFSP; help define policies by drawing up opinions for the Council, either at the request of the Council or on its own initiative; and monitor implementation of agreed policies. The Permanent Representatives Committee, known as COREPER, consists of the ambassadors who are the permanent representatives of the member states at the EU. It is responsible for helping the Council of the European Union to deal with the items on its agenda. It also lays down guidelines for, and supervises, the work of the expert groups that report to the Council. Two progress reports have been submitted: Council of the European Union, 'EU Strategy against Proliferation of Weapons of Mass Destruction: draft progress report on the implementation of Chapter III of the Strategy', Brussels, 10 June 2004; and Council of the European Union, 'Implementation of the WMD Strategy', Brussels, 3 Dec. 2004, URL <http://ue.eu.int/cms3_fo/showPage.asp?id=718&lang=en&mode=g>.

located in EU member states were active participants in the 'Khan network' and provided items that contributed to nuclear weapon programmes.[23] From February to July 2004 the national export control systems of member states were scrutinized by teams of officials drawn from other EU states. On the basis of this 'peer review' the EU has recommended concrete actions to improve the efficiency of national systems.[24]

Immediately prior to the enlargement of the EU the then 15 member states completed the ratification of their collective agreements with the IAEA to bring into force an Additional Protocol to their safeguards agreements. The first declarations under the Additional Protocols from these states were submitted to the IAEA in October 2004. As of December 2004, 3 of the 10 states which joined the EU in 2004 (Estonia, Malta and Slovakia) had not completed the process of ratifying an Additional Protocol.[25]

In June 2004, after the adoption of Security Council Resolution 1540, the EU Council invited relevant subsidiary bodies to review the appropriate political and legal instruments, including possible actions in the framework of Justice and Home Affairs, that would further the adoption of concrete steps towards the objective of adopting common policies related to criminal sanctions for the illegal export, brokering and smuggling of WMD-related material.[26] The EU Council Working Group on Non-Proliferation (CONOP) has begun such a review.

2. The second measure was to strengthen global arms control processes in order to stimulate what has been termed 'effective multilateralism'. The EU has continued to provide financial support to conferences and meetings intended to promote the universal ratification of, and adherence to, the NPT, the IAEA safeguards agreements, the 1972 Biological and Toxin Weapons Convention (BTWC)[27] and the Chemical Weapons Convention as well as to bring into force the 1996 Comprehensive Nuclear Test-Ban Treaty (CTBT).[28] The country holding the EU presidency continued to make statements on behalf of the EU at the relevant international meetings and in international organizations.

[23] On the Khan network see chapter 12 in this volume.

[24] On the peer review see chapter 17 in this volume.

[25] IAEA, 'Strengthened safeguard system: status of Additional Protocols', 25 Nov. 2004, URL <http://www.iaea.org/OurWork/SV/Safeguards/sg_protocol.html>. States which have safeguards agreements and Additional Protocol in force are listed in Annex A to this volume.

[26] Council of the European Union, 'Statement by the EU Council on criminal sanctions', EU Council document 10774/04, Brussels, 23 June 2004, URL <http://ue.eu.int/uedocs/cmsUpload/st10774.en04.pdf>.

[27] The Convention on the Prohibition of the Development, Production and Stockpiling of Bacteriological (Biological) and Toxin Weapons and on Their Destruction is available at URL <http://projects.sipri.se/cbw/docs/bw-btwc-text.html>. For complete lists of parties and signatory and non-signatory states see URL <http://projects.sipri.se/cbw/docs/bw-btwc-mainpage.html>. See also annex A and chapter 13 in this volume.

[28] On the CTBT see the Internet site of the Preparatory Commission for the Comprehensive Nuclear-Test-Ban Treaty Organization at URL <http://www.ctbto.org/>. The states which have signed or ratified the CTBT are listed in annex A in this volume.

The EU pledged €1.8 million to finance a number of measures to promote universal participation in the CWC and to assist states parties to the CWC with effective implementation. This financial assistance will support projects carried out by the OPCW.[29] The EU developed an Action Plan on Challenge Inspections in an effort to strengthen the verification of the CWC.[30]

In contrast to the level of engagement in nuclear- and chemical weapon-related arms control processes, the EU has not thus far been particularly active in supporting the strengthening of the BTWC.

In June 2004 the EU member states committed themselves to contribute to the Proliferation Security Initiative (PSI). The EU pledged to 'take the necessary steps in support of interdiction efforts to the extent their national and Community legal authorities permit and consistent with their obligations under international law and frameworks'.[31]

3. The third measure consists of financial support for practical measures to secure weapons and materials of concern. This financial assistance has included contributions by member states as well as contributions from the EU common budget (which can include both Joint Actions under the Council and projects and programmes administered directly by the European Commission).

Historically, the EU has made relatively minor contributions to international non-proliferation and disarmament assistance in comparison with the contribution of the USA. The EU WMD Strategy gives a prominent place to the reinforcement of programmes targeted at disarmament, control and security of sensitive materials, facilities and expertise. However, the new achievements in 2004 in this regard were modest. In addition to the support for the OPCW noted above (only some of which was to be used for practical assistance measures) the EU agreed a Joint Action to support the IAEA in May 2004.[32] Under this Joint Action the EU will provide €3.3 million to support nuclear security projects over a 15-month period. In November 2004 a Joint Action was agreed to support a project for the implementation of physical protection measures at the Bochvar All-Russian Scientific Research Institute of Inorganic Materials of the Russian Federal Agency for Atomic Energy.[33] Under this

[29] Council of the European Union, 'Council Joint Action 2004/797/CFSP of 22 November 2004 on support for OPCW activities in the framework of the implementation of the EU Strategy against Proliferation of Weapons of Mass Destruction', *Official Journal of the European Union*, L349/63 (25 Nov. 2004), pp. 63–69.

[30] Statement by H. E. Ambassador Chris Sanders, Permanent Mission of the Netherlands to the UN on behalf of the European Union, First Committee of the UN General Assembly, 59th session, 'EU Presidency Statement: other weapons of mass destruction', 19 Oct. 2004, URL <http://europa-eu-un.org/articles/en/article_3929_en.htm>.

[31] Council of the European Union, 'Non-proliferation support of the Proliferation Security Initiative (PSI)', document 10052/04, Brussels, 1 June 2004, URL <ue.eu.int/uedocs/cmsUpload/st10052.en04.pdf>. On the PSI see chapter 18 in this volume.

[32] Council of the European Union, 'Council Joint Action 2004/495/CFSP of 17 May 2004 on support for IAEA activities under its Nuclear Security Programme and in the framework of the implementation of the EU Strategy against Proliferation of Weapons of Mass Destruction', *Official Journal of the European Union*, L 182/46 (5 May 2004), pp. 46–50.

[33] Council of the European Union, 'Council Joint Action 2004/796/CFSP of 22 November 2004 for the support of the physical protection of a nuclear site in the Russian Federation', *Official Journal of the European Union*, L 349 (22 Nov. 2004), pp. 57–62.

Joint Action the EU will contribute roughly €8 million to the cost of the project. Nevertheless, overall EU spending is still far short of what is required to meet the financial pledges made in the context of the G8 Global Partnership Against Weapons and Materials of Mass Destruction.[34]

4. The fourth measure consists of the so-called 'mainstreaming' of non-proliferation policies into the wider relations between the EU and its partners, including states and international organizations. Annalisa Giannella, Personal Representative on Weapons of Mass Destruction in the cabinet of the EU High Representative for the CFSP, Javier Solana, has argued that as a result of actions taken in 2004 this process of mainstreaming has given the EU 'real leverage' in negotiations with partners. According to Giannella, 'non-proliferation has now been placed on a similar level to human rights and the fight against terrorism. If you don't meet certain standards it affects your relations with the EU'.[35]

On 19 October 2004 a non-proliferation clause was agreed as part of the Association Agreement between the EU and Syria.[36] The clause has also been included in agreements with Albania and Tajikistan. EU negotiators were discussing how to include the text in inter-regional agreements with the Southern Common Market (MERCOSUR, Mercado Común del Sur),[37] the Gulf Cooperation Council (GCC)[38] and as part of the 2000 Cotonou Agreement.[39]

As part of the European Neighbourhood Policy the Commission, together with partner countries located around the periphery of the enlarged EU, has developed political documents to guide the further development of relations. The Action Plans define a set of agreed priorities in bilateral relations between the EU and the country in question. The Action Plans agreed with Israel, Moldova and Ukraine in 2004 include specific WMD-related objectives.[40] However, the highest-profile case of 'mainstreaming' has been the EU discussion of Iran's nuclear programme.[41]

[34] On the Global Partnership see chapter 17 in this volume. See also Anthony, I., 'Arms control in the new security environment', *SIPRI Yearbook 2003: Armaments, Disarmament and International Security* (Oxford University Press: Oxford, 2003), pp. 567–70; and Anthony, I. and Bauer, S., 'Transfer controls and destruction programmes', *SIPRI Yearbook 2004: Armaments, Disarmament and International Security* (Oxford University Press: Oxford, 2004), pp. 758–61.

[35] Giannella, A., 'The role of export controls in the EU's Strategy for the non-proliferation of WMD', Speech at the Conference on New Challenges and Compliance Strategies, London, 17–19 Nov. 2004.

[36] European Union (EU), 'EU–Syria. Conclusion of the negotiations for an Association Agreement', URL <http://europa.eu.int/comm/external_relations/syria/intro/ip03_1704.htm >.

[37] EU, 'The EU's relations with Mercosur', URL <http://europa.eu.int/comm/external_relations/mercosur/intro/>.

[38] EU, 'The EU & the Gulf Cooperation Council (GCC)', URL <http://europa.eu.int/comm/external_relations/gulf_cooperation/intro/>.

[39] EU, 'Information note on the revision of the Cotonou Agreement', URL <http://europa.eu.int/comm/development/body/cotonou/pdf/negociation_20050407_en.pdf#zoom=100>.

[40] For the texts of the Action Plans see the Internet site of the European Commission External Relations Directorate General, URL <http://europa.eu.int/comm/world/enp/document_en.htm>.

[41] Council of the European Union, 'Fight against the proliferation of weapons of mass destruction: mainstreaming non-proliferation policies into the EU's wider relations with third countries', document14997/03, 19 Nov. 2003, available at URL <http://www.sipri.org/contents/expcon/wmd_mainstreaming.pdf>.

At the end of 2004 the EU resumed its negotiations with Iran on a Trade and Cooperation Agreement after the adoption by the IAEA Board of Governors of a resolution welcoming 'the fact that Iran has decided to continue and extend its suspension of all enrichment related and reprocessing activities'. In addition, in December 2004 three EU members (France, Germany and the United Kingdom) and Iran established a steering committee to launch negotiations on a long-term agreement intended to 'provide objective guarantees that Iran's nuclear programme is exclusively for peaceful purposes. It will equally provide firm guarantees on nuclear, technological and economic cooperation and firm commitments on security issues'. The office of the High Representative for the CFSP plays a supporting role in the steering committee, which has separate working groups on nuclear, economic and technology cooperation, and political and security issues.[42]

III. The United Nations and multilateral arms control

When outlining the context in which Kofi Annan had established the High-level Panel on Threats, Challenges and Change, his advisers explained the challenge to be: can the UN reassert its legitimacy and make itself effective enough to convince nations that it is actually capable of making the world a safer place?[43] Reversing the progressive marginalization of the UN in the sphere of arms control can be regarded as one of the main requirements for meeting this challenge. In bringing about this revitalization of the UN a number of obstacles need to be overcome both within the UN organization and in the way in which the member states use the UN.

Within the UN itself, the past body of decisions, conferences, papers and statements has established a normative basis from which it is difficult for UN staff to depart. This includes the commitment to universal, non-discriminatory measures that emphasize disarmament. However, in current conditions obedience to this canon is not always advantageous. Recently, many of the most important security-related activities have taken place outside institutions—in coalitions of willing, ad hoc processes and regimes, and contact groups. It has been impossible to find practical solutions to security problems within the UN in conditions where the organization is not prepared to recognize the special role of the United States and will not give the USA a special status with enhanced privileges or accommodate the US security policy agenda.

While the capacity of the USA to set the security agenda is strong, UN capacities for strategic planning are weak in this area, as in others, and there is little political support for investment to build this capacity. Moreover, UN arms control decision making is hampered by the lack of clarity about the respective roles of different parts of the disarmament machinery, by a lack of

[42] 'Iran–EU agreement on nuclear programme', 14 Nov. 2004, URL <http://www.globalsecurity.org/wmd/library/news/iran/2004/iran-041114-eu-iran-agreement.htm>. On the EU–Iran dialogue see chapter 12 in this volume.

[43] Turner, M., 'Last year the UN, criticised in the wake of the war in Iraq, commissioned a high-level panel to examine its role', *Financial Times*, 29 Nov. 2004, p. 17.

coherence in the cooperation between different bodies and perhaps by bureaucratic competition between them.

In December 2004 the report of the High-level Panel provided an analysis of future challenges to peace and security. The report had been requested by UN Secretary-General Annan in his address to the UN General Assembly in September 2003. At a time when the question of how the UN should respond to Iraq's non-compliance with Security Council resolutions was beginning to evolve into what became a deep crisis, Annan suggested that the UN had reached what he called 'a fork in the road'. In his speech he suggested that the UN 'must not shy away from questions about the adequacy and effectiveness of the rules and instruments at our disposal'. Annan asserted the necessity to examine whether radical changes are needed to the rules governing international behaviour and the network of institutions set up to help develop and implement those rules—with the United Nations at its centre.

One useful role of the High-level Panel was that of a catalyst for a discussion and analysis of past practice.[44] Implementation of the recommendations might introduce a more realistic view of how to balance commitments and resources. The report could help to establish the cases where the UN can add value and where it can never act but might be able to facilitate actions by others. The report identified six kinds of global threat and asserted that the relationship between these kinds of threat is not hierarchical and that the UN needed to deal with all of them.

The UN must identify its own core competence—what can it offer and how this can be delivered—and, given the limits of that competence, accept non-hierarchical arrangements with other organizations and states, cooperate with them and participate in them. The High-level Panel offers a useful yardstick by pointing out that for the UN the litmus test for any action is the extent to which it helps meet the challenge posed by a virulent threat.[45] Only if the UN acts on the principle of making a useful contribution in a broader overall framework is it likely to be able to market its effectiveness and to shrink the credibility gap that has opened up with some states, notably the USA.

The Secretary-General has pointed to the need to forge a new consensus around the main threats facing the global community.[46] The High-level Panel was asked to identify and focus on threats that could be addressed only through effective collective action and to appraise the role that the UN, including all its principal organs, could play in taking the action considered necessary. The USA, which devotes far more national resources to military security issues than any other state, also allocates far greater financial and human resources to arms control than the rest of the UN members. However, many participants in many multilateral processes have not come to terms with the

[44] The annex to the report indicates that the panel acted as the catalyst for a large number of meetings and consultations on different aspects of global governance, including the sphere of arms control.

[45] United Nations (note 4), p. 77.

[46] United Nations, 'Secretary-General stresses need for global consensus on major threats, policies to address them in New York remarks', Press Release SG/SM/9201, 7 Mar. 2004, URL <http://www.un.org/News/Press/docs/2004/sgsm9201.doc.htm>.

implications of these realities. (Table 11.1 lists the number of parties to select multilateral arms control agreements.) The report of the High-level Panel is useful in that it identifies the need to pay special attention to US concerns and priorities since this is a precondition for effective multilateralism.

One of the types of threat identified was the proliferation of WMD and arms proliferation generally. However, the panellists paid particular attention to the problems associated with nuclear weapons and concluded that the point was now approaching 'at which the erosion of the nuclear regime could become irreversible, and result in a cascade of proliferation'.[47] In the report a prominent place is also given to radiological, chemical and biological weapons. While UN member states are exhorted 'to expedite and conclude negotiations on legally binding agreements on the marking and tracing, as well as the brokering and transfer, of small arms and light weapons', the report does not devote much attention to other types of weapon.[48]

In its report the High-level Panel describes states as 'front-line responders' to threats, and the way in which the member states use the UN is clearly critical to its overall effectiveness. However, the approach to arms control adopted by states in UN processes (based on global norms) is not always easy to reconcile with the approach taken in regional or bilateral discussions, which are often more pragmatic, political and based on a different calculation of national interest. This lack of coherence can be illustrated with examples.

Many states have stressed the need for universal participation in arms control treaties. At present a number of Arab countries do not participate in the CWC and four UN members (India, Israel, North Korea and Pakistan) are not parties to the NPT. The CWC requires the abandonment of all chemical weapons as a condition for participation. It is generally assumed by parties to the NPT that the states joining or rejoining the treaty would do so as non-nuclear weapon states.

At the same time regional and bilateral discussions have not always stressed disarmament but have emphasized the need to create regional stability. In the ongoing dialogue between India and Pakistan, stability is increasingly coming to mean nuclear deterrence combined with elements of conflict prevention and crisis management. Enhanced nuclear security and stable deterrence in South Asia are both desirable objectives but also inconsistent with current global arms control norms.

The growing recognition of a need to correct inconsistencies between global, regional and sub-regional (including bilateral) processes is mirrored by the attempt to address some of the perceived inconsistencies between the approaches followed in global arms control processes and in the closed groupings that cooperate to regulate technology supply. A broad agreement on the basis for a security-related technology assessment has proved elusive. However, there is an emerging consensus that states have a responsibility to

[47] United Nations (note 4), p. 40.

[48] United Nations (note 4), p. 100.

Table 11.1. Participation in select multilateral arms control agreements, as of January 2005

Agreement	Number of signatories	Number of ratifications
BTWC	170	154
CTBT	120	120
CWC	183	167
NPT	189	189

BTWC = Biological and Toxin Weapons Convention, CWC = Chemical Weapons Convention, CTBT = Comprehensive Nuclear Test-Ban Treaty; NPT = Non-Proliferation Treaty

Source: Annex A in this volume.

safeguard against NBC weapon proliferation by a number of means, including the introduction of effective physical protection, material accountancy and export controls.

United Nations Security Council Resolution 1540

In September 2003 US President George W. Bush urged the UN Security Council to adopt an anti-proliferation resolution calling on all members of the UN 'to criminalize the proliferation of weapons of mass destruction, to enact strict export controls consistent with international standards, and to secure any and all sensitive materials within their own borders'.[49]

One of the central arguments for developing an anti-proliferation resolution was the difficulty of adapting traditional approaches to non-proliferation in conditions where non-state actors seek access to technologies in order to misuse them. While, as noted above, the more traditional non-proliferation agenda related to states remains relevant, states have found it difficult to accommodate changes in the strategic context by adapting existing instruments. A number of states (including the USA) have perceived an urgent need to find effective remedies given the growing concern that non-state actors might have the wherewithal to cause mass destruction or mass disruption. In this context, the discovery of the extent of the activities carried out by the Khan network acted as an additional, powerful catalyst for the discussion and adoption of Resolution 1540.

In short, while existing instruments should be preserved and strengthened to help manage security problems arising out of state behaviour, new types of instrument are needed to address the potential threats from non-state actors. As Barry Kellman has expressed this, 'the thesis is a simple one. International

[49] United Nations, 'Address by Mr George W. Bush, President of the United States of America', UN General Assembly document A/58/PV.7, 23 Sep. 2003, URL <http://www.un.org/webcast/ga/58/statements/usaeng030923.htm>.

non-proliferation needs the assistance of international criminal law—including its capabilities of individual deterrence and incapacitation'.[50]

In Resolution 1540 the UN Security Council, acting under Chapter VII of the UN Charter, mandated a number of steps that states should take to establish and enforce legal barriers to the acquisition of NBC, radiological weapons or nuclear explosive devices, whether by terrorists or by states.

Several of the provisions in the resolution took the form of decisions, of which three require member states to take certain actions. States 'shall refrain from providing any form of support to non-State actors that attempt to develop, acquire, manufacture, possess, transport, transfer or use nuclear, chemical or biological weapons and their means of delivery'; 'shall adopt and enforce appropriate effective laws which prohibit any non-state actor to manufacture, acquire, possess, develop, transport, transfer or use nuclear, chemical or biological weapons and their means of delivery, in particular for terrorist purposes, as well as attempts to engage in any of the foregoing activities, participate in them as an accomplice, assist or finance them'; and 'shall take and enforce effective measures to establish domestic controls to prevent the proliferation of nuclear, chemical, or biological weapons and their means of delivery, including by establishing appropriate controls over related materials'.

With regard to the third of these decisions, the resolution further instructs states to put in place specific measures necessary to implement the resolution. Accordingly, states are obliged to 'develop and maintain appropriate effective measures to account for and secure' relevant items 'in production, use, storage or transport'; to 'develop and maintain appropriate effective physical protection measures'; to 'develop and maintain appropriate effective border controls and law enforcement efforts to detect, deter, prevent and combat, including through international cooperation when necessary, the illicit trafficking and brokering in such items in accordance with their national legal authorities and legislation and consistent with international law'; and to 'establish, develop, review and maintain appropriate effective national export and trans-shipment controls over such items, including appropriate laws and regulations to control export, transit, trans-shipment and re-export and controls on providing funds and services related to such export and trans-shipment such as financing, and transporting that would contribute to proliferation, as well as establishing end-user controls; and establishing and enforcing appropriate criminal or civil penalties for violations of such export control laws and regulations'.[51]

Prior to the adoption of Resolution 1540 the Security Council invited all UN member states to an open debate on the draft text of the resolution. The invitation, which was extended after a number of states had communicated their wish to be engaged in the process, was widely taken up and more than one-third of the member states made statements during the debate. In their state-

[50] Kellman, B., 'Bio-criminalization: non-proliferation, law enforcement and counter-smuggling', American Society of International Law Task Force on Terrorism, Task Force Paper, Oct. 2002, URL <http://www.asil.org/resources/terrorism.html>.

[51] UN Security Council Resolution 1540 (note 1).

ments governments generally underlined that they shared the concern of the Security Council members about the potential threat that non-state actors would acquire WMD. However, a number of states expressed their unease about the process by which the resolution was drafted and the implications of a resolution of this kind for the future effectiveness of the Security Council and the overall multilateral arms control process.

In proposing the use of a binding Security Council resolution the co-sponsoring states sidestepped the difficulty of securing universal adherence to multilateral agreements. This approach also meant that a measure could be put in place quickly. The resolution was drafted, discussed and adopted only seven months after President Bush proposed it. However, this procedure had certain controversial aspects.

While accepting the urgent need to address the issue of weapon acquisition by non-state actors, a number of the government representatives questioned whether the Security Council could 'both define the non-proliferation regime and monitor its implementation'.[52] Lack of consultation in establishing the agenda ran the risk of complicating the task of generating the active support and willing cooperation of states where implementing the resolution would require the allocation of new resources. This concern is in essence related to the legitimacy of the Security Council's passing a binding resolution requiring domestic legislation from UN member states without widespread consultation. However, in December 2004 the General Assembly adopted by consensus Resolution 59/80 entitled 'Measures to prevent terrorists from acquiring weapons of mass destruction' that took note of Security Council Resolution 1540 and called on member states to 'support international efforts to prevent terrorists from acquiring weapons of mass destruction and their delivery means'.[53] While similar resolutions had been passed in the two previous years, the 2004 resolution was obviously the first to include reference to Resolution 1540. In introducing Resolution 59/80 the Indian co-sponsor described it as 'an unambiguous statement from a body that is universal and democratic. The representative character of the General Assembly validates and reinforces the commitments we assume as Member States in this regard'.[54]

Several statements questioned the authority of the Security Council to issue the kinds of instructions contained in Resolution 1540 and whether this approach could secure the cooperation that would be needed from states for effective implementation. In this regard, the presentation by Mexico at the debate suggested that the approach proposed by the Security Council 'does not

[52] United Nations, 'Statement by Ambassador V. K. Nambiar on non-proliferation of weapons of mass destruction at the Security Council', 22 Apr. 2004, URL <http://www.un.int/india/ind954.pdf>.

[53] 'Measures to prevent terrorists from acquiring weapons of mass destruction', UN General Assembly Resolution A/RES/59/80, 16 Dec. 2004, URL <http://www.un.org/terrorism/res.htm>.

[54] United Nations, 'Statement by Mr Jayant Prasad, Ambassador & Permanent Representative of India to the Conference on Disarmament, Geneva, on Introduction of the resolution "Measures to prevent terrorists from acquiring weapons of mass destruction" in the First Committee of 59th UNGA on October 22, 2004', 22 Oct. 2004, URL <http://www.un.int/india/ind1017.pdf>.

necessarily create the conditions to reach the desired objective'.[55] A number of concerns exist with regard to the implementation of the resolution.

It is not clear how the Security Council will judge compliance with Resolution 1540. The language of the resolution takes the form of an instruction, but there are no criteria for what constitutes compliance and the process for evaluation is not described. The resolution established a reporting mechanism in the form of a Committee of the Security Council consisting of all members of the Security Council. The committee may also recruit up to six experts to facilitate consideration of national reports submitted by member states. This committee is to report to the Security Council on the implementation of Resolution 1540. In order to facilitate reporting the resolution called on states to inform the so-called 1540 Committee 'no later than six months from the adoption of this resolution' about implementation steps they have taken or intend to take. An additional concern was what would happen if few states submitted a report within the six-month period. The basis on which the 1540 Committee would report on compliance in such circumstances was unclear, as was the manner in which the Security Council could respond to the compliance record of non-reporting states.

In the event, 58 states and one international organization (the EU) submitted reports on or by 28 October 2004 while three other states (Belize, Moldova and South Africa) requested an extension of the deadline. By the beginning of December 2004, the 1540 Committee had received reports from 87 states and the EU.[56]

At the Security Council discussion of the first information presented by the 1540 Committee several of these issues were taken up again. The difficulty of establishing what 'compliance' with the resolution meant in conditions where there was no clear and uniform understanding of what its language was referring to was noted. In this context it was also pointed out that the existing multilateral agreements referred to in Resolution 1540 (the BTWC, the CWC and the NPT) do not have uniform levels of participation and do not provide guidance about a number of matters. In certain areas (such as nuclear security, the physical security of fissile materials and chemical weapon precursors) recognized international standards have been established in the IAEA and the OPCW. In other areas, such as evaluation of what represents an effective export control system, no such standards are recognized outside cooperation arrangements established by groups of states on an informal basis.[57] Resolution 1540 anticipates that states in a position to do so would offer assistance

[55] Permanent Mission of Mexico to the United Nations, 'Statement by Ambassador Enrique Berruga, Permanent Representative of Mexico to the United Nations in the Public Meeting of the Security Council on the issue of the draft resolution on non-proliferation of weapons of mass destruction', 22 Apr. 2004, URL <http://www.un.int/mexico/2004/interv_cs_042204ing.htm>.

[56] 'Letter dated 8 December 2004 from the Chairman of the Security Council Committee established pursuant to Resolution 1540 (2004) to the President of the Security Council', UN Security Council document S/2004/958, 8 Dec. 2004, and S/2004/958/Corr.1, 23 Dec. 2004.

[57] See the intervention by the representative from Pakistan at the Security Council debate on non-proliferation of weapons of mass destruction in UN Security Council document S/PV.5097, 9 Dec. 2004, URL <http://www.un.org/Depts/dhl/resguide/scact2004.htm>.

if requested to do so by states which lack the necessary legal and regulatory infrastructure, implementation experience or resources to meet their obligations. However, the resolution provides little guidance about how this would be managed.

The guidelines for the conduct of its work permit the 1540 Committee to establish arrangements to cooperate with the IAEA and the OPCW and, if deemed appropriate, 'other relevant international, regional, sub-regional bodies and relevant committees established under the Security Council'.[58] In addition, the 1540 Committee is free to invite offers of assistance in response to specific requests received from states that need help with implementation.

The UN Counter-Terrorism Committee (CTC) established in 2001 subsequent to Security Council Resolution 1373 to monitor its implementation by all states and to increase the capability of states to fight terrorism is a potentially important partner of the 1540 Committee.[59] As part of their work the Expert Advisers to the CTC concentrate on the issue of facilitating assistance to states. The CTC maintains a Matrix of Assistance Requests: 'a centralized, comprehensive overview of States' assistance needs, as well as information on any assistance programmes being delivered of which the CTC has been made aware'. The 1540 Committee is following a similar approach.

The 1540 Committee has received specific offers of technical assistance from the IAEA, the NSG, the OPCW and the Zangger Committee. It has also been suggested that the 1540 Committee should schedule regular meetings with representatives of regional organizations and other international organizations.

At the open debate on the draft of Resolution 1540 the idea of increasing the number of Security Council subsidiary bodies in an ad hoc manner was questioned and alternative approaches to strengthening UN capacity were suggested. Japan proposed implementing the resolution under the supervision of the Secretary-General and drawing on existing expertise in, for example, the UN Department of Disarmament Affairs.[60] This proposal would have created an implementation agency that could also have sustained the expertise gained by the UN during its inspection activities in Iraq. A large number of statements underlined the need for the UN to build on the work already undertaken in specialized agencies such as the IAEA and the OPCW in order to avoid duplicating or complicating their efforts by establishing new bodies.

[58] United Nations, 'Security Council Committee established pursuant to Resolution 1540 (2004): guidelines for the conduct of its work', URL <http://disarmament2.un.org/Committee1540/work.html>.

[59] The CTC acts as a clearing house for information supplied by states on the steps taken to implement that resolution. UN Security Council Resolution S/RES/1373, 28 Sep. 2001, URL <http://daccess-ods.un.org/TMP/1021057.html>. In cases where states ask for support to help them implement the resolution, the CTC tries to identify sources of technical and financial assistance. This model was also adopted in Resolution 1540. See the CTC Internet site at URL <http://www.un.org/Docs/sc/committees/1373/index.html>.

[60] Ministry of Foreign Affairs of Japan, 'Statement by H.E. Mr Koichi Haraguchi, Permanent Representative of Japan, at the Security Council Meeting on the Security Council resolution on non-proliferation', 22 Apr. 2004, URL <http://www.mofa.go.jp/announce/speech/un2004/un0404-5.html>.

The 1540 Committee lacks the capacity to diagnose the implementation problems faced by states and has no detailed information about the assistance that potential donors can offer. The 1540 Committee will not be able to make an assistance programme operational, but national '1540 reports' can be a resource for those states and organizations which are interested in being pro-active in offering assistance.

IV. Conclusions

Developments in arms control and non-proliferation in 2004 suggest that it has now become the mainstream view that no single approach, institution or process can establish and enforce rules related to arms and military capabilities. An effective multilateralism must find ways for states, international organizations and informal arrangements to cooperate in pursuit of common objectives.

In 2004 activities outside international organizations continued to have the primary role in setting the international agenda for arms control and non-proliferation. The activities of the G8, the launch of the Global Threat Reduction Initiative and the rapid progress made in the Proliferation Security Initiative can all be highlighted in this respect.

This view, that finding solutions to real world problems should shape the activities of organizations, has implications for those organizations that are or are perceived to be solving yesterday's problems. In the arms control field, as in others, it would appear that the distribution of human and financial resources is no longer well harmonized with the problems of greatest concern. However, mobilizing—and, even more, sustaining—the resources that are needed to address complex problems over a long period of time is very difficult in informal processes since these are likely to reflect political priorities that may change frequently and in unpredictable ways. There is evidence that in 2004 a number of international organizations, most notably the EU and the UN, began to come to grips with the need for change and renewal.

In the United Nations the need for change was reflected in the rapid adoption of Resolution 1540 by the Security Council as well as in the positive response to the report of the High-level Panel on Threats, Challenges and Change. In the European Union the practical need to release resources (intellectual as well as financial) to tackle new security tasks, most of which are outside Europe, was reflected in the implementation of the EU WMD Strategy.

Appendix 11A. United Nations Security Council Resolution 1540

Adopted by the Security Council at its 4956th meeting, on 28 April 2004

The Security Council,

Affirming that proliferation of nuclear, chemical and biological weapons, as well as their means of delivery* constitutes a threat to international peace and security,

Reaffirming, in this context, the Statement of its President adopted at the Council's meeting at the level of Heads of State and Government on 31 January 1992 (S/23500), including the need for all Member States to fulfil their obligations in relation to arms control and disarmament and to prevent proliferation in all its aspects of all weapons of mass destruction,

Recalling also that the Statement underlined the need for all Member States to resolve peacefully in accordance with the Charter any problems in that context threatening or disrupting the maintenance of regional and global stability,

Affirming its resolve to take appropriate and effective actions against any threat to international peace and security caused by the proliferation of nuclear, chemical and biological weapons and their means of delivery, in conformity with its primary responsibilities, as provided for in the United Nations Charter,

Affirming its support for the multilateral treaties whose aim is to eliminate or prevent the proliferation of nuclear, chemical or biological weapons and the importance for all States parties to these treaties to implement them fully in order to promote international stability,

Welcoming efforts in this context by multilateral arrangements which contribute to non-proliferation,

Affirming that prevention of proliferation of nuclear, chemical and biological weapons should not hamper international cooperation in materials, equipment and technology for peaceful purposes while goals of peaceful utilization should not be used as a cover for proliferation,

Gravely concerned by the threat of terrorism and the risk that non-State actors* such as those identified in the United Nations list established and maintained by the Committee established under Security Council resolution 1267 and those to whom resolution 1373 applies, may acquire, develop, traffic in or use nuclear, chemical and biological weapons and their means of delivery,

Gravely concerned by the threat of illicit trafficking in nuclear, chemical, or biological weapons and their means of delivery, and related materials,* which adds a new dimension to the issue of proliferation of such weapons and also poses a threat to international peace and security,

Recognizing the need to enhance coordination of efforts on national, subregional, regional and international levels in order to strengthen a global response to this serious challenge and threat to international security,

Recognizing that most States have undertaken binding legal obligations under treaties to which they are parties, or have made other commitments aimed at preventing the proliferation of nuclear, chemical or biological weapons, and have taken effective measures to account for, secure and physically protect sensitive materials, such as those required by the Convention on the Physical Protection of Nuclear Materials and those recommended by the IAEA Code of Conduct on the Safety and Security of Radioactive Sources,

* Definitions for the purpose of this resolution only:

Means of delivery: missiles, rockets and other unmanned systems capable of delivering nuclear, chemical, or biological weapons, that are specially designed for such use.

Non-State actor: individual or entity, not acting under the lawful authority of any State in conducting activities which come within the scope of this resolution.

Related materials: materials, equipment and technology covered by relevant multilateral treaties and arrangements, or included on national control lists, which could be used for the design, development, production or use of nuclear, chemical and biological weapons and their means of delivery.

Recognizing further the urgent need for all States to take additional effective measures to prevent the proliferation of nuclear, chemical or biological weapons and their means of delivery,

Encouraging all Member States to implement fully the disarmament treaties and agreements to which they are party,

Reaffirming the need to combat by all means, in accordance with the Charter of the United Nations, threats to international peace and security caused by terrorist acts,

Determined to facilitate henceforth an effective response to global threats in the area of non-proliferation,

Acting under Chapter VII of the Charter of the United Nations,

1. *Decides that* all States shall refrain from providing any form of support to non-State actors that attempt to develop, acquire, manufacture, possess, transport, transfer or use nuclear, chemical or biological weapons and their means of delivery;

2. *Decides also* that all States, in accordance with their national procedures, shall adopt and enforce appropriate effective laws which prohibit any non-State actor to manufacture, acquire, possess, develop, transport, transfer or use nuclear, chemical or biological weapons and their means of delivery, in particular for terrorist purposes, as well as attempts to engage in any of the foregoing activities, participate in them as an accomplice, assist or finance them;

3. *Decides also* that all States shall take and enforce effective measures to establish domestic controls to prevent the proliferation of nuclear, chemical, or biological weapons and their means of delivery, including by establishing appropriate controls over related materials and to this end shall:

(*a*) Develop and maintain appropriate effective measures to account for and secure such items in production, use, storage or transport;

(*b*) Develop and maintain appropriate effective physical protection measures;

(*c*) Develop and maintain appropriate effective border controls and law enforcement efforts to detect, deter, prevent and combat, including through international cooperation when necessary, the illicit trafficking and brokering in such items in accordance with their national legal authorities and legislation and consistent with international law;

(*d*) Establish, develop, review and maintain appropriate effective national export and trans-shipment controls over such items, including appropriate laws and regulations to control export, transit, trans-shipment and re-export and controls on providing funds and services related to such export and trans-shipment such as financing, and transporting that would contribute to proliferation, as well as establishing end-user controls; and establishing and enforcing appropriate criminal or civil penalties for violations of such export control laws and regulations;

4. *Decides* to establish, in accordance with rule 28 of its provisional rules of procedure, for a period of no longer than two years, a Committee of the Security Council, consisting of all members of the Council, which will, calling as appropriate on other expertise, report to the Security Council for its examination, on the implementation of this resolution, and to this end calls upon States to present a first report no later than six months from the adoption of this resolution to the Committee on steps they have taken or intend to take to implement this resolution;

5. *Decides* that none of the obligations set forth in this resolution shall be interpreted so as to conflict with or alter the rights and obligations of State Parties to the Nuclear Non-Proliferation Treaty, the Chemical Weapons Convention and the Biological and Toxin Weapons Convention or alter the responsibilities of the International Atomic Energy Agency or the Organization for the Prohibition of Chemical Weapons;

6. *Recognizes* the utility in implementing this resolution of effective national control lists and calls upon all Member States, when necessary, to pursue at the earliest opportunity the development of such lists;

7. *Recognizes* that some States may require assistance in implementing the provisions of this resolution within their territories and invites States in a position to do so to offer assistance as appropriate in response to specific requests to the States lacking the legal and regulatory infrastructure, implementation experience and/or resources for fulfilling the above provisions;

8. *Calls upon* all States:

(*a*) To promote the universal adoption and full implementation, and, where necessary, strengthening of multilateral treaties to which they are parties, whose aim is to prevent the proliferation of nuclear, biological or chemical weapons;

(*b*) To adopt national rules and regulations, where it has not yet been done, to ensure compliance with their commitments under the key multilateral non-proliferation treaties;

(*c*) To renew and fulfil their commitment to multilateral cooperation, in particular within the framework of the International Atomic Energy Agency, the Organization for the Prohibition of Chemical Weapons and the Biological and Toxin Weapons Convention, as important means of pursuing and achieving their common objectives in the area of non-proliferation and of promoting international cooperation for peaceful purposes;

(*d*) To develop appropriate ways to work with and inform industry and the public regarding their obligations under such laws;

9. *Calls upon* all States to promote dialogue and cooperation on non-proliferation so as to address the threat posed by proliferation of nuclear, chemical, or biological weapons, and their means of delivery;

10. Further to counter that threat, *calls upon* all States, in accordance with their national legal authorities and legislation and consistent with international law, to take cooperative action to prevent illicit trafficking in nuclear, chemical or biological weapons, their means of delivery, and related materials;

11. *Expresses* its intention to monitor closely the implementation of this resolution and, at the appropriate level, to take further decisions which may be required to this end;

12. *Decides* to remain seized of the matter.

Source: The United Nations Internet site, URL <http://www.un.org/Docs/sc/unsc_resolutions04.html>.

12. Nuclear arms control and non-proliferation

SHANNON N. KILE

I. Introduction

Developments in 2004 gave urgency to calls for new measures to strengthen the nuclear non-proliferation regime and to reinforce its principal legal foundation, the 1968 Treaty on the Non-Proliferation of Nuclear Weapons (Non-Proliferation Treaty, NPT). Evidence emerged confirming the existence of a clandestine transnational network of middlemen and companies, centred around Pakistan's leading nuclear scientist, that supplied sensitive nuclear technology and expertise to Iran, Libya and possibly other states. This raised concern about the diffusion of nuclear weapon capabilities to non-state as well as state actors, and it spurred new initiatives aimed at preventing the illicit transfer of nuclear technologies and materials. There continued to be controversy over the scope and nature of Iran's nuclear programme, as the International Atomic Energy Agency (IAEA) provided further detail about Iran's repeated failures over many years to declare important nuclear activities, in contravention of its NPT-mandated nuclear safeguards agreement with the IAEA. In addition, little progress was made in the international talks on the future of the nuclear programme of the Democratic People's Republic of Korea (DPRK, or North Korea).

This chapter reviews the principal developments in nuclear arms control and non-proliferation in 2004. Section II describes the discovery of a global black market in nuclear weapon-related technologies and assesses its implications for the non-proliferation regime. Section III summarizes the IAEA's findings about Iran's past and current nuclear activities and describes developments in the country's nuclear programme. Section IV summarizes efforts to resolve the diplomatic impasse over North Korea's nuclear programme and related developments. Section V summarizes the latest findings of the US inspection team that searched for evidence of Iraq's nuclear weapon programme. Section VI describes the IAEA's investigation following the disclosure by the Republic of Korea (South Korea) that it has conducted undeclared nuclear activities in contravention of its safeguards agreement with the IAEA. Section VII reports on the results of the 2004 Preparatory Committee meeting for the 2005 NPT Review Conference. Section VIII discusses the proposals for multilateral arrangements to manage the nuclear fuel cycle and the appointment of an IAEA-sponsored Expert Group to survey the most promising approaches, while section IX examines the opposition in the US Congress to the proposals of the Administration of President George W. Bush to develop new types of nuclear weapons. Section X presents the conclusions.

Appendix 12A provides tables of data on world nuclear forces and on the forces of the United States, Russia, the United Kingdom, France, China, India, Pakistan and Israel.

II. The Khan nuclear network

A series of revelations in 2004 confirmed long-circulating rumours that Pakistan's most prominent nuclear scientist, Abdul Qadeer Khan, was behind an illicit nuclear trafficking network.[1] Khan, who has been called 'the father of Pakistan's bomb', is widely seen as a national hero in Pakistan. As the head of the Khan Research Laboratory for two decades he had considerable autonomy in running the country's nuclear programme.

Although Khan had long been suspected of involvement in the illicit transfer of nuclear technology, evidence of his network's activities began to emerge publicly in October 2003, when Iran admitted to the IAEA that it had secretly imported centrifuge components from Pakistan. Libya's decision in December 2003 to abandon its weapons of mass destruction (WMD) and missile programmes resulted in the disclosure of detailed information about the network's activities and about individual suppliers.[2] Investigators identified foreign intermediaries—based in Germany, Malaysia, South Africa, Switzerland, Turkey, the UK and the United Arab Emirates—who had helped Khan deliver nuclear technology to client states. Among them was Buhary Syed Abu Tahir, a Sri Lankan businessman and Khan confidante based in Dubai, who reportedly oversaw the network's financial operations. Tahir gave Malaysian police detailed information about how the network had arranged for the manufacture and shipment of nuclear-related components to Iran and Libya.[3]

Khan initially denied allegations about his involvement but later confessed to Pakistan's Inter-Services Intelligence agency that he was behind the illicit transfers of nuclear technology.[4] On 5 February 2004 Pakistani President Pervez Musharraf pardoned Khan following Khan's nationally televised confession the previous day. In pardoning Khan, Musharraf insisted that the scientist had acted on his own, without the knowledge or support of the Pakistani Government.[5] This claim was disputed by opposition parties in Pakistan as well as by many outside observers, who doubted that Khan could have cir-

[1] For an overview of the Khan network's activities see Powell, B. and McGirk, T., 'The man who sold the bomb', *Time*, 14 Feb. 2005, pp. 38–42.

[2] On the Libyan decision see chapter 14 in this volume.

[3] Royal Malaysia Police, 'Press release by Inspector General of Police in relation to investigation on the alleged production of components for Libya's uranium enrichment programme', 20 Feb. 2004, URL <http://www.rmp.gov.my/rmp03/040220scomi_eng.htm>.

[4] Khan, K., 'Pakistani exploited nuclear network', *Washington Post* (Internet edn), 28 Jan. 2004, URL <http://www.washingtonpost.com/ac2/wp-dyn/A54334-2004Jan 27>; and Iqbal, N., 'Dr Khan "admits" he transferred N-technology: action to be decided by NCA', *Dawn* (Internet edn), 2 Feb. 2004, URL <http://www.dawn.com/2004/02/02/top2.htm>.

[5] Ziauddin, M., 'Dr A. Q. Khan pardoned: other scientists' fate hangs in the balance', *Dawn* (Internet edn), 6 Feb. 2004, URL <http://www.dawn.com/2004/02/06/top1.htm>; and Akhtar, H., 'Dr Khan not given blanket pardon: investigations continuing—FO', *Dawn* (Internet edn), 10 Feb. 2004, URL <http://www.dawn.com/2004/02/10/top2.htm>.

cumvented security measures for more than a decade without the tacit approval of the government or the military high command.[6] Islamabad pledged that Pakistan would cooperate with the international bodies that were investigating the network, such as the IAEA, but stated repeatedly that these bodies would not be granted direct access to Khan or to other scientists suspected of involvement in the network.[7]

The Khan network's activities

The network's origins are believed to date from the time after Khan quit his job at the European uranium enrichment consortium, Urenco, in the Netherlands. According to Dutch court documents, Khan fled to Pakistan in 1976 with stolen Urenco blueprints for G-1 and G-2 centrifuges; Pakistan's uranium enrichment programme was based on modifications of these designs, called the P-1 and P-2 centrifuges. Khan used his experience and contacts from working at Urenco to build up a clandestine network of suppliers which procured the components needed for Pakistan's centrifuge programme.[8]

As the network's activities expanded, Khan began to sell nuclear technology. This reportedly occurred in the late 1980s, when Khan ordered more centrifuge components from the foreign suppliers than Pakistan's nuclear programme needed and then secretly sold the excess items to other countries.[9] This enabled Khan to sell P-1 centrifuge components to Iran. He later sold complete P-1 assemblies as Pakistan's enrichment programme phased out the P-1 in favour of the more sophisticated P-2 centrifuge. He also eventually provided Iran with P-2 design information.

Khan began to sell technology to Libya in the mid-1990s and continued to do so until 2003. This included centrifuge components and assemblies for Libya's undeclared uranium enrichment programme.[10] According to the IAEA, Libya also received from 'a foreign source' detailed engineering drawings for nuclear weapon components.[11] It has not been publicly con-

[6] See, e.g., Masood, S. and Rhode, D., 'Pakistan opposition charges atomic cover-up', *New York Times* (Internet edn), 17 Feb. 2004, URL <http://www.nytimes.com/2004/02/17/international/asia/17STAN.html>; and Fidler, S. and Burnett, V., 'Pakistan's "rogue nuclear scientist": what did Khan's government know about his deals?', *Financial Times*, 6 Apr. 2004, p. 11.

[7] Ziauddin (note 5); Efron, S., 'Musharraf scorns nuclear probe', *Los Angeles Times*, 6 Dec. 2004, p. A4; and 'Foreigners access to Dr Khan ruled out', *Dawn* (Internet edn), 10 Dec. 2004, URL <http://www.dawn.com/2004/12/11/top1.htm>.

[8] For the history of Pakistan's nuclear weapons programme see Ahmed, S., 'Pakistan's nuclear weapons program: turning points and nuclear choices', *International Security*, vol. 23, no. 4 (spring 1999), pp. 178–204; Albright, D. and Hibbs, M., 'Pakistan's bomb: out of the closet', *Bulletin of the Atomic Scientists*, vol. 48, no. 6 (July/Aug. 1992), pp. 38–43, URL <http://www.thebulletin.org/article.php?art_ ofn=ja92albright>; and Burrows, W. and Windrem, R., *Critical Mass* (Simon & Schuster: New York, 1994), pp. 60–90.

[9] Broad, W., Sanger, D. and Bonner, R., 'A tale of nuclear proliferation: how Pakistani built his network', *New York Times* (Internet edn), 12 Feb. 2004, URL <http://www.nytimes.com/2004/02/12/international/asia/12NUKE.html>.

[10] IAEA, 'Implementation of the NPT safeguards agreement in the Socialist People's Libyan Arab Jamahiriya', Report by the Director General to the IAEA Board of Governors, GOV/2004/12, Vienna, 20 Feb. 2004, p. 5, URL <http://www.iaea.org/Publications/Documents/Board/2004/gov2004-12.pdf>.

[11] IAEA (note 10), pp. 6–7.

firmed that the drawings came from Pakistan, but US officials have indicated that the design was for a uranium implosion weapon that was developed by China in the 1960s and was rumoured to have been transferred to Pakistan.[12] The US Government estimates that Khan's network may have earned as much as $100 million from sales to Libya alone.[13]

The extent to which Khan may have transferred sensitive nuclear technology and expertise to North Korea is unclear from publicly available information. US intelligence officials believe that in 1997–2001 Khan provided North Korea with centrifuge components and design information as well as uranium hexafluoride gas.[14] There have been numerous reports alleging that Pakistan gave North Korea uranium enrichment technology in exchange for missile technology. The Pakistani Government has denied that it made any barter deals with North Korea to obtain missile technology, and both governments have denied reports about the transfer of centrifuge designs and components.[15] In addition to these questions, US officials have indicated that Khan may have shared documentation with North Korea on how to make nuclear warheads that were compact enough to be delivered by ballistic missiles.[16]

The Khan network and proliferation concerns

The revelations during 2004 about Khan's activities heightened concern about the proliferation risks posed by knowledgeable individuals or non-state purveyors of nuclear and missile-related materials and technology, either acting independently or in complicity with government officials. There was particular concern about the nature and scope of the black market activities of the network. IAEA Director General Mohamed ElBaradei described it as a 'Nuclear Wal-Mart'—a reference to the USA's largest retailer.[17] As a source for 'one-stop shopping', Khan's network effectively circumvented many of the legal and regulatory arrangements put into place to prevent state actors from spreading nuclear weapon-relevant technology. These concerns gave impetus to new initiatives, most notably UN Security Council Resolution 1540, aimed at reinforcing the non-proliferation regime by requiring states to

[12] Broad, W. and Sanger, D., 'Warhead blueprints link Libya project to Pakistan figure', *New York Times* (Internet edn), 4 Feb. 2004, URL <http://www.nytimes.com/2004/02/04/politics/04NUKE.html>.

[13] Sanger, D. and Broad, W., 'Pakistani's nuclear earnings: $100 million', *New York Times* (Internet edn), 16 Mar. 2004, URL <http://www.nytimes.com/2004/03/16/international/asia/16NUKE.html>.

[14] Sanger, D., 'US sees more arms ties between Pakistan and Korea', *New York Times* (Internet edn), 14 Mar. 2004, URL <http://www.nytimes.com/2004/03/14/international/asia/14KORE.html>.

[15] Takeishi, E., 'Bhutto: we bought missile technology', Asahi.com, 19 July 2004, URL <http://www.asahi.com/english/world/TKY200407190155.html>.

[16] Squassoni, S., Congressional Research Service (CRS), *Weapons of Mass Destruction: Trade Between North Korea and Pakistan*, CRS Report for Congress RS 31900, updated 11 Mar. 2004, p. 9, URL <http://fpc.state.gov/documents/organization/30781.pdf>.

[17] Landler, M., 'UN official sees a "Wal-Mart" in nuclear trafficking', *New York Times* (Internet edn), 23 Jan. 2004, URL <http://www.nytimes.com/2004/01/23/international/23CND-NUKE.html>.

criminalize black market activities by private actors, enact strict export controls and secure all sensitive materials within their borders.[18]

III. Iran and nuclear proliferation concerns

In 2004 the controversy over the scope and nature of Iran's nuclear programme intensified, as Iran reaffirmed its plans to develop a uranium enrichment capability and to construct a heavy-water research reactor.[19] The controversy arose after evidence began to emerge in 2002 that the Atomic Energy Organization of Iran had engaged in sensitive nuclear fuel cycle activities, including uranium enrichment and plutonium separation, without declaring them in a timely manner to the IAEA, as it was required to do under the terms of its full-scope safeguards agreement.[20] This gave rise to concern in Europe and the USA that Iran was attempting to put into place, under the cover of a civil nuclear energy programme, the fuel cycle facilities needed to produce fissile material—plutonium and enriched uranium—for a clandestine nuclear weapon programme. Iranian officials insisted that the country's ambitious nuclear programme was aimed solely at producing electricity and that any violations of its safeguards agreement were inadvertent and minor in nature and did not constitute non-compliance with that agreement.[21] They also emphasized that Iran was entitled, as a non-nuclear weapon state (NNWS) party to the NPT, to develop nuclear energy for peaceful purposes.[22]

Cooperation between Iran and the IAEA

On 21 May 2004 Iran submitted to the IAEA its initial expanded declaration under the NPT Additional Safeguards Protocol.[23] Iranian officials stressed that

[18] On UN Security Council Resolution 1540 see chapters 11 and 18 in this volume; and for the text of the resolution see appendix 11A.

[19] For a description of the Iranian nuclear controversy see Kile, S. N., 'Nuclear arms control and non-proliferation', *SIPRI Yearbook 2004: Armaments, Disarmament and International Security* (Oxford University Press: Oxford, 2004), pp. 604–12.

[20] For the agreement see IAEA, The text of the agreement between Iran and the agency for the application of safeguards in connection with the Treaty on the Non-proliferation of Nuclear Weapons, INFCIRC/214, 13 Dec. 1974, URL <http://www.iaea.org/Publications/Documents/Infcircs/Others/infcirc214.pdf>.

[21] In 2002 Iran announced plans to construct, over the next 20 years, nuclear power plants with a total capacity of 6000 MW as part of a long-term energy policy to make up for the expected depletion of Iran's extensive fossil fuel reserves. Statement by H.E. Reza Aghazadeh, President of the Atomic Energy Organization of Iran, at the 46th General Conference of the International Atomic Energy Agency, Vienna, 16 Sep. 2002, URL <http://www.iaea.org/About/Policy/GC/GC46/iran.pdf>.

[22] According to Art. IV of the NPT, all parties have an 'inalienable right' to research, produce and use nuclear energy 'for peaceful purposes without discrimination'. Art. IV also mandates that 'Parties to the Treaty in a position to do so' shall cooperate in contributing to the development of nuclear energy for peaceful purposes. For the full text of the NPT see URL <http://www.iaea.org/Publications/Documents/Treaties/npt.html>.

[23] See IAEA, 'Iran signs Additional Protocol on nuclear safeguards', IAEA News Centre, 18 Dec. 2003, URL <http://www.iaea.org/NewsCenter/News/2003/ iranap20031218.html>. For a discussion of the domestic debate surrounding the Iranian Government's decision to sign the Additional Protocol see Balouji, H., 'The process of national security decision making in Iran: the signature of the Additional

the submission of the expanded declaration was a 'voluntary confidence-building measure', since the Majlis (parliament) had not yet ratified the Additional Protocol.[24] They also insisted that all of the IAEA's remaining safeguards compliance questions were being satisfactorily answered and that the IAEA Board of Governors therefore should vote to close the Iranian nuclear file at its next meeting.

In a report sent to the IAEA Board of Governors on 1 June 2004, Director General ElBaradei criticized Iran's cooperation with the agency as having 'fallen far short of what was required' to resolve the agency's safeguards concerns.[25] The report stated that serious questions remained about nearly all aspects of Iran's past and current nuclear fuel cycle activities, especially its uranium enrichment programme. On 18 June the Board adopted a resolution 'deploring' Iran's failure to provide the agency with 'full, timely and proactive co-operation'.[26] Among other measures, the Board's resolution urged Iran to take additional steps to answer questions about its advanced gas centrifuge programme and about the source of enriched uranium particles found in environmental samples taken at three nuclear-related sites. It also urged Iran to fully implement its October 2003 pledge to suspend its uranium enrichment programme by halting all manufacturing and testing of centrifuge components and not proceeding with the planned production of uranium hexafluoride (UF_6) at its conversion facility at Esfahan.[27] At its next meeting, on 18 September, the Board of Governors reiterated its call for Iran to immediately suspend all uranium enrichment activities.[28] Iran promptly rejected this call as a capitulation to pressure from the US Administration, which had been urging the Board to take a tougher approach to the nuclear controversy, including bringing the matter before the UN Security Council.[29] The Board also urged Iran to 'proactively assist the Agency to understand the full extent and nature' of its uranium enrichment programme before the meeting scheduled for the end of November 2004.[30]

Protocol', ed. S. N. Kile, *Europe and Iran: Perspectives on Non-proliferation*, SIPRI Research Report no. 21 (Oxford University Press: Oxford, forthcoming 2005).

[24] 'Iran submits full report on nuclear program to UN nuclear agency', *Tehran Times*, 23 May 2004, pp. 1, 15.

[25] IAEA, 'Implementation of the NPT safeguards agreement in the Islamic Republic of Iran', Report by the Director General to the IAEA Board of Governors, GOV/2004/34, Vienna, 1 June 2004, p. 1, URL <http://www.iaea.org/Publications/Documents/Board/2004/gov2004-34.pdf>.

[26] IAEA, 'Implementation of the NPT safeguards agreement in the Islamic Republic of Iran', Resolution adopted by the IAEA Board of Governors, GOV/2004/49, Vienna, 18 June 2004, p. 2, URL <http://www.iaea.org/Publications/Documents/Board/2004/gov2004-49.pdf>.

[27] IAEA, 'Implementation of the NPT safeguards agreement in the Islamic Republic of Iran', Report by the Director General, GOV/2004/60, Vienna, 1 Sep. 2004, p. 2, URL <http://www.iaea.org/Publications/Documents/Board/2004/gov2004-60.pdf>. UF_6, either alone or in combination with hydrogen or helium, is the feedstock used in most uranium enrichment processes, including gas centrifuges.

[28] IAEA (note 27), p. 2.

[29] Mehr News Agency, 'Tehran will not forgo civilian nuclear program at any cost', *Tehran Times* (Internet edn), 21 Sep. 2004, URL <http://www.tehrantimes.com/archives/description.asp?DA=9/21/2004&Cat=2&Num=009>.

[30] IAEA, 'Implementation of the NPT safeguards agreement in the Islamic Republic of Iran', Resolution adopted by the IAEA Board of Governors, GOV/2004/79, Vienna, 18 Sep. 2004, p. 2, URL <http://www.iaea.org/Publications/Documents/Board/2004/gov2004-79.pdf>.

The IAEA Director General's assessment of Iran's nuclear programme

On 15 November 2004 Director General ElBaradei sent to the IAEA Board of Governors the sixth in a series of written reports on the progress made by the agency in verifying Iran's implementation of its safeguards agreement with the agency.[31] The report came against the background of mounting pressure from Iran and the USA for the Board to make its upcoming meeting a decisive one in terms of either closing the nuclear file, as demanded by Iran, or referring it to the UN Security Council for further action, as urged by the USA. It offered an overall assessment of the IAEA's efforts since the beginning of 2003 to clarify the scope and nature of Iran's nuclear activities and to resolve safeguards-related questions arising from these activities.

According to ElBaradei, prior to October 2003 Iran had pursued a 'policy of concealment' which resulted in many aspects of its nuclear activities and experiments, particularly in the areas of uranium enrichment, uranium conversion and plutonium separation, not being declared to the IAEA.[32] The agency had discovered a number of instances, occurring over an extended period of time, in which Iran had failed to comply with its safeguards obligations with respect to the reporting of the processing, use and storage of nuclear material and the facilities where this took place. The report stated that since October 2003, when Iran issued a revised declaration of its past and current nuclear activities and pledged to cooperate fully with the agency, 'good progress' had been made in correcting these failures.[33] As a result, the IAEA was able to verify that none of the declared nuclear material inside Iran had been diverted to prohibited activities and to confirm certain aspects of Iran's current declarations. ElBaradei's report noted that verifying all aspects of Iran's declaration would probably be a time-consuming process, even with the implementation of the Additional Protocol, in the light of Iran's past pattern of concealment and its failure to declare significant aspects of its nuclear programme.[34] At the same time, it cautioned that the focus of safeguards agreements and Additional Protocols is on nuclear material: in the absence of some connection to nuclear material, the agency's legal authority to pursue the verification of possible nuclear weapons-related activity was limited.

ElBaradei's report included detailed summaries of the agency's findings that Iran had failed to report or declare to the IAEA eight different nuclear activities, including uranium conversion and enrichment experiments, as required under its safeguards agreement. It also included six instances in which Iran had failed to provide in a timely manner design information, or updated information, about nuclear fuel processing, storage and waste handling facilities.[35] In addition, it noted that the agency had not been able to come to a

[31] See IAEA, 'Implementation of the NPT safeguards agreement in the Islamic Republic of Iran', Report by the Director General to the IAEA Board of Governors, GOV/2004/83, 15 Nov. 2004, p. 23, URL <http://www.iaea.org/Publications/Documents/Board/2003/gov2003-75.pdf>.

[32] IAEA (note 31), p. 23.

[33] IAEA (note 31), p. 23.

[34] IAEA (note 31), p. 24.

[35] IAEA (note 31), pp. 22–23.

judgement about explanations provided by Iran for several other nuclear-related activities.[36]

Unresolved safeguards compliance issues

The November 2004 report by ElBaradei identified three outstanding issues which the IAEA was working with Iran to clarify.

1. *The origins of enriched uranium contamination.* In February 2003, in response to IAEA enquiries, Iran acknowledged that two centrifuge enrichment plants were under construction at Natanz: a research-scale facility designed to house 1000 centrifuges; and a commercial-scale plant designed to house 50 000 centrifuges.[37] Iran also admitted that a facility at the Kalaye Electric Company workshop in Tehran had been used for the production of centrifuge components. It initially stated that there had been no testing of centrifuges assembled from these components involving the use of nuclear material, either at that workshop or at any other location in the country. However, in October 2003 Iran acknowledged that in 1999–2002 it had conducted 'a limited number' of tests at the Kalaye workshop using small amounts of imported UF_6, without informing the IAEA.[38] Iran also acknowledged that in 1994–95 it had received engineering plans and components for the centrifuges, based on the Pakistani P-1 design, through a foreign intermediary. This contradicted Iran's previous claim that the centrifuge programme was entirely indigenous.[39]

In verifying Iran's declarations concerning its enrichment activities, the IAEA conducted extensive environmental sampling at locations where Iran had declared that centrifuge components were manufactured and stored. The results of samples taken at the pilot centrifuge plant in Natanz and at the Kalaye workshop and a subsidiary company revealed particles of low enriched uranium (LEU) and highly enriched uranium (HEU).[40] These particles were 'indicative of types of nuclear material' that were not included in Iran's inventory of declared nuclear material.[41] This raised doubts about the correct-

[36] The IAEA discovered that in 1989–93 Iran had conducted experiments to produce polonium-210 (Po-210), a short-lived unstable element which has very few commercial applications but which has been used in the past as a neutron initiator for nuclear weapons. Iran told the IAEA that its experiments with Po-210 were for nuclear batteries for satellites to be used in future Iranian space programmes.

[37] IAEA, 'Introductory Statement by IAEA Director General Mohamed ElBaradei to the Board of Governors', Vienna, 17 Mar. 2003, URL <http://www.iaea.org/NewsCenter/Statements/2003/ebsp2003n008.shtml>.

[38] IAEA, 'Implementation of the NPT safeguards agreement in the Islamic Republic of Iran', Report by the Director General to the IAEA Board of Governors, GOV/2003/75, 10 Nov. 2003, p. 9, URL <http://www.iaea.org/Publications/Documents/Board/2003/gov2003-75.pdf>.

[39] Albright, D., and Hinderstein, C., 'The centrifuge connection', *Bulletin of the Atomic Scientists*, vol. 60, no. 2 (Mar./Apr. 2004), pp. 62–63. A report from the Malaysian Inspector-General of Police stated that centrifuges were shipped from Pakistan to Iran, through a company based in the United Arab Emirates, in the mid-1990s. Royal Malaysia Police (note 3).

[40] HEU is uranium enriched to 20% or above in the isotope uranium-235 (U-235); LEU is uranium enriched to 0.72–20% U-235. Weapons-grade uranium is uranium enriched to more than 90% U-235.

[41] The environmental samples revealed that domestically manufactured components were contaminated mainly with LEU, while imported components showed both LEU and HEU contamination; some

ness and completeness of Iran's declarations to the agency and suggested that Iran might have conducted other undeclared activities or might be concealing nuclear material. Iran attributed the presence of the particles of enriched uranium to contamination from centrifuge components imported through the foreign intermediary and continued to insist that it had not enriched uranium beyond 1.2 per cent in the isotope uranium-235 (U-235).[42]

According to ElBaradei, the IAEA's overall assessment was that the environmental sampling data tended, 'on balance, to support Iran's statement about the origin of much of the contamination'.[43] The agency believed that it was 'plausible' that the HEU contamination found at the Kalaye workshop and at Natanz may not have resulted from the enrichment of uranium there. However, the report added that, while contamination resulting from imported components and equipment was one possible explanation, the agency continued to investigate other explanations, including the possibility that the contamination resulted from undeclared enrichment activities, from undeclared imported enriched uranium or from contaminated equipment imported from an undisclosed supplier. It also noted that, in order for the IAEA inspectors to be able to confirm the actual source of contamination and the correctness of statements made by Iran, they needed to take samples from the centrifuges and centrifuge components 'at relevant locations in the State from which most of the imported components originated'.[44] The report stated that the IAEA was discussing with this state—widely reported to be Pakistan—the modalities for taking the samples.[45]

2. *The design and manufacture of an advanced centrifuge.* The IAEA has questioned Iran's claims about its research and development (R&D) work on the P-2 centrifuge. Iranian officials acknowledged in January 2004 that they had previously failed to report the acquisition of design plans for this more advanced centrifuge. Iran told the IAEA that it received the P-2 plans through a foreign intermediary in 1995; however, because of a 'shortage of professional resources', it did not begin manufacturing work and mechanical testing of the centrifuge's composite rotors until 2002.[46] IAEA investigators questioned this account, citing the investment made by Iran in obtaining the design drawings and the technical capabilities that existed inside the country. They also expressed doubt about the feasibility of carrying out centrifuge tests based on the P-2 design—which required the procurement of magnets, bearings and other parts from abroad as well as the manufacture of casings and centrifuge components—within the stated period of less than a year. According to ElBaradei's report, the IAEA is continuing to investigate Iran's claim that it did not pursue any work on the P-2 centrifuge design in 1995–2002 in

of the imported components, along with associated assembly equipment and work areas, were contaminated with particles of *c.* 36% U-235 and others with *c.* 54% U-235. IAEA (note 31), p. 9.

[42] IAEA (note 31), p. 9.

[43] IAEA (note 31), p. 10.

[44] IAEA (note 31), p. 10.

[45] IAEA (note 31), p. 23.

[46] IAEA (note 31), pp. 10–11.

order to be able to give 'sufficient assurances that there were no related activities carried out during that period'.[47]

3. *Plutonium reprocessing.* The IAEA has been unable to verify Iran's account of the dates of experiments conducted at the Tehran Nuclear Research Center (TNRC) involving the irradiation of uranium dioxide targets and the subsequent separation of a small amount of plutonium. According to Iran, the experiments took place in the period 1988–93; it did not declare the experiment or the plutonium separation to the IAEA.[48] On the basis of samples taken in November 2003, the IAEA concluded that Iran had underestimated the quantities of plutonium that had been separated, and it discovered that the age of the plutonium solution appeared to be less than the declared 12–16 years. Iran subsequently corrected the declared amount of separated plutonium, from microgram to milligram quantities. However, it reiterated previous statements that it had not conducted any plutonium separation experiments after 1993, but the results from samples taken by the IAEA in September 2004 again indicated that the plutonium could have been separated more recently. The IAEA has requested additional clarifications to determine whether Iran might have conducted other undeclared separation experiments.[49]

Other safeguards-related issues

In 2004 the IAEA investigated two Iranian Ministry of Defence (MOD) facilities where undeclared nuclear experiments may have been carried out. The first site, called the Lavizan-Shian Technical Research Center, came to public attention in May 2003 and then in November 2004 following allegations from an Iranian opposition group, the National Council of Resistance of Iran, that it was associated with nuclear weapon research.[50] Iran denied this allegation, saying that a Physics Research Center was established there in 1989 to prepare emergency responses to nuclear attacks or accidents and to provide scientific advice and services to the MOD. The site was razed following its return to the Municipality of Tehran. The results of soil samples taken by the IAEA in June 2004 showed no sign of nuclear activity.[51]

The second site was the Parchin complex, located outside Tehran. This large military complex is dedicated to the R&D and production of ammunition, rockets and high explosives. Within the complex there is an isolated, separately secured site for the testing of high explosives. Some reports have suggested that this could be part of a programme to develop conventional explosives for a nuclear warhead.[52] Although Iran stated that it was under no legal

[47] IAEA (note 31), p. 23.

[48] IAEA (note 38), p. 5.

[49] IAEA (note 31), p. 17.

[50] National Council of Resistance of Iran, 'Disclosing a nuclear site under Ministry of Defence', 17 Nov. 2004, at URL <http://www.globalsecurity.org/wmd/library/report/2004/new-nuke-info.htm>.

[51] IAEA (note 31), p. 22.

[52] E.g., Albright, D. and Hinderstein, C., 'Parchin: possible nuclear weapons-related site in Iran', Institute for Science and International Security (ISIS), *ISIS Issue Brief*, 17 June 2004, URL <http://www.isis-online.org/publications/iran/parchin.html>.

obligation to do so, it nevertheless agreed in early January 2005 to grant IAEA inspectors partial access to the Parchin complex.[53]

The new E3–Iranian suspension agreement

In the autumn of 2004 intense negotiations were held between Iran and France, Germany and the UK (the so-called E3), supported by the High Representative for the European Union Common Foreign and Security Policy, Javier Solana. The main issue was the E3's demand that Iran completely suspend its uranium enrichment programme.

On 21 October 2003 the foreign ministers of Iran and the E3 states had issued a joint declaration in Tehran announcing that Iran agreed to suspend its enrichment programme in exchange for access to advanced European technology.[54] However, in the ensuing months the deal became mired in disputes over the length and scope of application of the moratorium amid allegations of bad faith from both sides. Following the June 2004 IAEA Board of Governors resolution, which strongly criticized Iran, Iran announced that it would resume its production of centrifuges.[55] In August 2004 Iran announced plans to convert 37 tonnes of uranium oxide ('yellowcake') into UF_6 at its Esfahan facility.[56] This led to renewed calls from the US Administration for the E3 to take a tougher approach to resolving the nuclear controversy, including referral of the issue to the UN Security Council.

On 15 November 2004 the E3 reached an agreement with Iran on a new deal, which envisioned several steps.[57] Iran undertook, as a 'voluntary confidence-building measure', to continue to extend the previous suspension of its enrichment programme to include all enrichment-related and reprocessing activities.[58] The suspension would be sustained, under IAEA verification and monitoring, while negotiations proceeded 'on a mutually acceptable agreement on long-term arrangements'. The aim of the long-term agreement was to provide 'objective guarantees' that Iran's nuclear programme was exclusively for peaceful purposes as well as guarantees regarding nuclear, technological and economic cooperation between the EU and Iran and 'firm

[53] Bernstein, R., 'US accuses Iran of deceiving UN inspectors', *New York Times* (Internet edn), 2 Mar. 2005, URL <http://www.nytimes.com/2005/03/02/international/europe/02cnd-nuke.html>.

[54] 'Statement by the Iranian Government and visiting EU foreign ministers', Tehran, 21 Oct. 2003, URL <http://www.iaea.org/NewsCenter/Focus/IaeaIran/statement_iran21102003.shtml>.

[55] Mehr News Agency, 'Nation backs bid by government to resume construction of centrifuges: legislators', *Tehran Times* (Internet edn), 27 June 2004, URL <http://www.tehrantimes.com/archives/description.asp?DA=6/27/2004&Cat=2&Num=031>.

[56] Two non-governmental experts calculated that theoretically this could produce *c.* 100 kg of weapons-grade HEU, or enough for 5 crude nuclear weapons. Albright, D. and Hinderstein, C., 'Iran: countdown to showdown', *Bulletin of the Atomic Scientists*, vol. 60, no. 6 (Nov./Dec. 2004), p. 67.

[57] IAEA, The text of the agreement between Britain, France, Germany and Iran, signed in Paris on 15 Nov. 2004, INFCIRC/637, 26 Nov. 2004, URL <http://www.iaea.org/Publications/Documents/Infcircs/2004/infcirc637.pdf>.

[58] These activities were specified in the agreement as: the manufacture and import of gas centrifuges and their components; the assembly, installation testing or operation of gas centrifuges; work to undertake any plutonium separation, or to construct or operate any plutonium separation installation; and all tests or production at any uranium conversion installation. IAEA (note 57).

commitments on security issues'.[59] On 29 November ElBaradei reported that the IAEA had completed its verification of Iran's suspension of its uranium enrichment-related and plutonium reprocessing activities. This included the application of IAEA containment and surveillance measures at the Esfahan conversion facility and at declared centrifuge component production locations.[60]

The agreement on suspension called for negotiations to be launched by an E3–Iranian steering committee, which was also responsible for setting up working groups on political and security issues, technology and economic cooperation, and nuclear issues. The first meeting of the steering committee, which was attended by Solana, the British, French and German foreign ministers and the head of Iran's Supreme National Security Council, Hassan Rowhani, was held on 13 December 2004.[61] The first meetings of the working groups were held five days later. On 12 January 2005 the EU resumed talks with Iran, suspended for 18 months, on a Trade and Cooperation Agreement (TCA).[62]

Criticism of the suspension agreement

The 2004 E3–Iran suspension agreement has come under criticism, particularly in Israel and the USA.[63] The main complaint is that the deal did not go far enough: Iran's moratorium on enrichment activities was a voluntary measure rather than a legal obligation; and its duration was directly linked to the duration of the negotiations between Iran and the E3 on the broader sets of issues. Iran has repeatedly stated that it will restart its uranium enrichment programme, with appropriate assurances about its peaceful purpose, once the concerns raised by the IAEA have been resolved.[64] The deal has also been criticized for not requiring Iran to halt construction of a heavy water-moderated reactor near the town of Arak.[65] This type of reactor is well suited for producing weapons-grade plutonium. There has been speculation that Israel or the USA might launch pre-emptive military strikes against Iranian

[59] IAEA (note 57).

[60] IAEA, 'Introductory Statement by IAEA Director General Dr. Mohamed ElBaradei', IAEA Board of Governors, DG 25112004, 25 Nov. 2004, URL <http://www.iaea.org/NewsCenter/Statements/2004/ebsp 2004n016.html>. Iran requested an exemption from the suspension, stating that it wanted to 'use up to 20 sets of [centrifuge] components for R&D purposes and provide the Agency with access when requested'. Iran subsequently withdrew this request because of opposition from the E3.

[61] 'European restart talks with Iran', *International Herald Tribune*, 14 Dec. 2004, p. 5.

[62] Hafezi, P., 'Iran says EU nuclear talks going well', Reuters, 16 Jan. 2005, URL <http://uk.news yahoo.com/051116/325/fadpn.html>. The Nov. 2004 agreement stipulated that, once a suspension of Iran's enrichment programme had been verified, the negotiations on the TCA would resume.

[63] Asculai, E. and Kam, E., 'Iran's slippery nuclear slope', *Tel Aviv Notes* (Jaffee Center for Strategic Studies, Tel Aviv University), no. 117 (22 Dec. 2004), pp. 2–3; Reuters, 'EU defends Iran diplomacy after Bush remarks', 18 Jan. 2005, URL <http://www.alernet.org/thenews/newsdesk/L18331811.htm>.

[64] Mehr News Agency, 'Iran's nuclear activities will never be halted–Leader', *Tehran Times* (Internet edn), 30 Nov. 2004, URL <http://www.tehrantimes.com/archives/description.asp?DA=11/30/2004&Cat=2&Num=008>.

[65] Broad, W. and Sciolino, E., 'Iranians retain plutonium plan in nuclear deal', *New York Times* (Internet edn), 25 Nov. 2004, URL <http://www.nytimes.com/2004/11/25/international/middleeast/25NUKE.html>.

nuclear facilities in order to prevent, or at least slow down, Iran's development of a nuclear weapon capability.[66] Neither Israel nor the USA has ruled out the possibility of taking military action against Iran.[67]

The IAEA Board of Governors resolution

On 29 November 2004 the IAEA Board of Governors adopted a much-anticipated resolution on the implementation of safeguards in Iran which noted that 'Iran's practices before October 2003 had resulted in many breaches of its obligations to comply with its safeguards agreement'.[68] It also noted that the 'Agency is not yet in a position to conclude that there are no undeclared nuclear materials or activities in Iran'.[69] At the same time, the resolution acknowledged Iran's corrective measures, as described in ElBaradei's report, and welcomed Iran's decision to continue and extend the suspension of all of its uranium enrichment-related and plutonium reprocessing activities.

While acknowledging Iran's breaches of its NPT safeguards agreement, the Board of Governors did not declare Iran to be in non-compliance with that agreement or with its commitments under the NPT and did not refer the issue to the UN Security Council.[70] Prior to the Board's meeting, the US Administration had pushed for the issue to be moved to the Security Council, over Iran's strong opposition. Many EU member states resisted the US demand to incorporate in the IAEA resolution a 'trigger mechanism' that would automatically require the Board to report Iran to the Security Council if it did not fully resolve outstanding concerns about its nuclear activities.[71] They argued that Iran's recent steps warranted a more conciliatory approach. They also argued that a referral would be premature and possibly counterproductive in that it might spur Iran to disengage altogether from its cooperation with the IAEA or withdraw from the NPT, following the North Korean precedent.

The disagreement between the E3 and the US Administration over a referral to the UN Security Council highlighted fundamental differences over means and modalities in their respective strategies for addressing WMD proliferation

[66] See Hersh, S., 'The coming wars', *New Yorker*, 24–31 Jan. 2005, URL <http://www.newyorker.com/fact/content/?050124fa_fact>.

[67] Reuters, 'Bush won't rule out action against Iran over nukes', ABC News (Internet edn), 17 Jan. 2005, URL <http://abcnews.go.com/International/wireStory?id=420027>; and Penketh, A., 'Israel refuses to rule out attack on Iran', *The Independent*, 27 Jan. 2005, URL <http://news.independent.co.uk/world/middle_east/story.jsp?story=604945>.

[68] IAEA, 'Implementation of the NPT safeguards agreement in the Islamic Republic of Iran', Resolution adopted by the IAEA Board of Governors, GOV/2004/90, Vienna, 29 Nov. 2004, p. 1, URL <http:// www.iaea.org/Publications/Documents/Board/2004/gov2004-90.pdf>.

[69] IAEA (note 68).

[70] According to Article XII.C of the IAEA Statute, the 'Board shall call upon the recipient State or States to remedy forthwith any [safeguards] non-compliance which it finds to have occurred. The Board shall report the non-compliance to all members and to the Security Council and General Assembly of the United Nations.' The full text of the IAEA Statute is available at URL <http://www.iaea.org/About/statute_text.html>.

[71] Reuters, 'US, Iran face off over EU nuclear draft-diplomats', ABC News (Internet edn), 23 Nov. 2004, URL <http://abcnews.go.com/International/print?id=276168>.

risks and challenges.[72] Some analysts have portrayed the issue as posing a crucial test of the credibility of the EU's multifunctional strategy of 'conditional engagement': specifically, whether that strategy—which includes the prospect of improved political and economic ties, but also, if necessary, the imposition of sanctions—can deliver real and sustainable results in addressing concerns about Iran's nuclear activities.[73]

IV. The Six-Party Talks on North Korea's nuclear programme

During 2004 two new rounds were held in the Six-Party Talks between China, Japan, North Korea, South Korea, Russia and the USA aimed at resolving the crisis over North Korea's nuclear programme.[74] The first round had been held on 27–29 August 2003 and ended inconclusively. The next round, held on 25–28 February 2004, resulted in an agreement to establish a working group to prepare for further talks. However, neither North Korea nor the USA showed signs of moving away from their initial negotiating positions.

The principal reason for the impasse was a fundamental difference between the two main protagonists over the timing, or sequencing, of a possible deal. North Korean officials insisted on a multiphase agreement, consisting of step-by-step 'simultaneous actions', under which it would 'clear up all US security concerns' in exchange for the USA's abandoning its 'hostile policy' towards North Korea.[75] Their proposals envisioned a deal similar to the one worked out under the 1994 Agreed Framework between North Korea and the USA.[76] This would involve, in the first phase, the normalization of bilateral relations, including the lifting of US sanctions against North Korea. The USA would resume shipments of heavy fuel oil, which were suspended in November 2003, and pledge not to hinder North Korea's economic cooperation with other countries. In return, North Korea would refreeze activity at its nuclear facilities at Yongbyon. In the next phase, the two sides would conclude a non-aggression treaty; following this, North Korea would begin to dismantle the Yongbyon facilities. This would be completed once the two light-water power reactors promised to North Korea under the 1994 Agreed Framework were

[72] For a discussion of the progress in implementing the Action Plan accompanying the EU's Strategy Against Proliferation of Weapons of Mass Destruction see chapter 11 in this volume.

[73] Everts, S., 'Engaging Iran: a test case for EU foreign policy', Centre for European Reform, Working Paper 513 (Mar. 2004), URL <http://www.cer.org.uk/publications/513.html>; and Eizenstat, S., 'Iran: a test for the European approach', *International Herald Tribune*, 14 Dec. 2004, p. 9.

[74] For a description of the controversy over North Korea's nuclear programme see Kile (note 19), pp. 612–17; and Kile, S. N., 'Nuclear arms control, non-proliferation and ballistic missile defence', *SIPRI Yearbook 2003: Armaments, Disarmament and International Security* (Oxford University Press: Oxford, 2003), pp. 578–92.

[75] See, e.g., KCNA, 'KCNA slams US talk about "early inspection"', 20 Aug. 2003, URL <http://www.kcna.co.jp/item/2003/200308/news08/21.htm>.

[76] The Agreed Framework between the United States of America and the Democratic People's Republic of Korea was signed in Geneva on 21 Oct. 1994. It is reproduced at URL <http://www.kedo.org/pdfs/AgreedFramework.pdf>.

operating, or when the USA provided compensation in the form of 'heavy oil and electricity, etc.' equal to the 2000-MW capacity of the reactors.[77]

The USA insisted that a 'complete, verifiable and irreversible' end to all of North Korea's nuclear activities, including a suspected uranium enrichment programme, was a precondition for beginning serious negotiations. This meant that North Korea first had to declare all its nuclear facilities, including the alleged enrichment facility, and then dismantle them under international supervision. On the issue of non-aggression, the USA indicated that it would be willing to offer written security assurances; however, it continued to rule out concluding a formal treaty.

In the third round of talks, held on 23–26 June 2004, the USA adopted a more flexible approach.[78] This was motivated in part by the concerns of the USA's allies that the US focus on rolling back North Korea's nuclear programme threatened to undermine regional stability. Some analysts have also charged that the US Administration is not interested, for ideological reasons, in holding serious negotiations with North Korea.[79] The new US proposal called for the complete and verified dismantlement of North Korea's nuclear programme, to take place in two stages. During the first, three-month 'preparatory' phase, North Korea would freeze its nuclear programme in return for receiving fuel oil from China, South Korea and Russia. It would also prepare a comprehensive declaration of all the nuclear material, facilities and equipment in the country. In the second phase, North Korea would agree to eliminate these with international verification. US officials presented their North Korean counterparts with a document providing, for the first time, detailed information about what economic and political benefits North Korea might receive in exchange for verifiably dismantling its nuclear programme.[80] Among other benefits, these included a gradual lifting of US sanctions and the normalization of political relations. In addition, the proposal called for the USA and the other parties to conclude a new regional security agreement.

A North Korean foreign ministry spokesman condemned the US proposal for moving away from the 'principle of simultaneous action' by requiring that North Korea complete the unilateral dismantlement of its nuclear programme as a first step.[81] North Korea insisted that the first step should consist of a 'reward for freeze' in which North Korea's agreement to freeze its nuclear programme at Yongbyon would be accompanied by tangible 'rewards' from the USA, the nature of which would determine the duration of the freeze.[82] On

[77] KCNA, 'Keynote speeches made at six-way talks', 30 Aug. 2003, URL <http://www.kcna.co.jp/item/2003/200308/news08/30.htm>; and KCNA, 'Spokesman for DPRK FM on prospect of resumption of Six-Party Talks', 13 Nov. 2004, URL <http://www.kcna.co.jp/item/2004/200411/news11/15.htm>.

[78] Kerr, P., 'US unveils offer at North Korea talks', *Arms Control Today*, vol. 34, no. 6 (July/Aug. 2004), pp. 35–37.

[79] Eckert, P., 'US should renew focus on N. Korea talks—analysts', Reuters, 25 Jan. 2005, URL <http://www.reuters.ch/newsArticle.jhtml?type=reutersEdge&storyID=7429557>.

[80] 'Dealing with North Korea's nuclear programs', Statement of James A. Kelly, Assistant Secretary of State for East Asian and Pacific Affairs, to the Senate Foreign Relations Committee, Washington, DC, 15 July 2004, URL <http://www.senate.gov/~foreign/testimony/2004/KellyTestimony040715.pdf>.

[81] KCNA, 'Spokesman for DPRK FM on prospect of resumption of Six-Party Talks' (note 77).

[82] KCNA, 'Spokesman for DPRK FM on prospect of resumption of Six-Party Talks' (note 77).

16 August North Korea announced that it would not participate in the working group meetings to prepare for the next round of talks, scheduled for September 2004, arguing that the USA's 'hostile attitude' made such meetings pointless.[83] North Korea also cited South Korea's disclosure of several undeclared nuclear experiments in justifying its withdrawal from the talks[84] (see section VI). Throughout the autumn, the state-run media accused the USA of plotting to overthrow the North Korean Government, including making preparations for the use of military force.[85]

International concern about the impasse was heightened when IAEA Director General ElBaradei stated, in November 2004, that he believed that North Korea had separated plutonium from the spent fuel rods which the IAEA had monitored before being expelled from the country in December 2003 and had used it to manufacture four to six nuclear weapons.[86] There has been considerable debate over the question of whether or not North Korea has produced operational nuclear weapons.[87] Although official statements on the subject from Pyongyang are ambiguous, the emerging consensus among governmental and independent experts is that North Korea has probably managed to develop a small number of nuclear weapons.

V. Post-war findings about Iraq's nuclear programme

Iraq's suspected WMD programme remained a focus of international attention during 2004, as inspection teams from the coalition Iraq Survey Group (ISG) failed to discover stockpiles of nuclear, chemical or biological weapons or evidence of recent programmes to manufacture them. This fuelled the controversy over the validity of the rationale given by the British and US governments for the decision to invade Iraq in March 2003. With regard to nuclear weapons, the main question was whether Iraq had engaged in proscribed nuclear weapon-related activities, as alleged in British and US intelligence reports prior to the invasion of the country. The accuracy of these reports—and the process by which they had been put together—came under the scrutiny of parliamentary commissions of inquiry in a number of countries taking part in the occupation of Iraq, including an investigation launched by the US Senate.[88]

[83] KCNA, 'Spokesman for DPRK Foreign Ministry on prospect of Six-Party Talks', 17 Aug. 2004, URL <http://www.kcna.co.jp/item/2004/200408/news08/17.htm>. Many observers believed that North Korea refused to participate because it was awaiting the outcome of the US presidential election.

[84] KCNA, 'US double standards assailed', 20 Sep. 2004, URL <http://www.kcna.co.jp/item/2004/200409/news09/21.htm>.

[85] KCNA, 'Spokesman for DPRK FM on prospect of resumption of Six-Party Talks', 13 Nov. 2004, URL <http://www.kcna.co.jp/item/2004/200411/news11/15.htm>. North Korea cited the Proliferation Security Initiative (PSI) interdiction exercise, which Japan hosted in late Oct. 2004, as evidence of this strategy. On the PSI see chapter 18 in this volume.

[86] Sanger, D. and Broad, W., 'UN atom chief certain North Korea has made fuel for 4 to 6 bombs', *International Herald Tribune*, 7 Dec. 2004, p. 5.

[87] See Kile (note 19), pp. 615–17.

[88] See chapter 13 in this volume.

On 30 September 2004 Charles Duelfer, the head of the ISG, published a new interim report on the inspectors' findings.[89] The report confirmed the main findings of an October 2003 interim report by then ISG head David Kay.[90] It stated that Iraq's WMD capability had been 'essentially destroyed in 1991' and was never reconstituted.[91] Duelfer told the US Congress that he did not 'expect that militarily significant WMD stocks are cached in Iraq'.[92]

With regard to nuclear weapons, the new report confirmed the ISG's previous finding that former Iraqi Presisdent Saddam Hussein had ended the country's nuclear weapon programme in 1991, after the Persian Gulf War, and had not made any 'concerted efforts to restart the program'.[93] It also stated that 'Saddam aspired to develop a nuclear capability in an incremental fashion, irrespective of international pressure' and assigned a 'high value' to retaining the 'nuclear progress and talent that had been developed'.[94] Towards this end, Iraq had taken steps to preserve some technological capability from the pre-1991 programme. These included, for example, hiding in scientists' homes documents and equipment that would have been useful for resuming a uranium enrichment programme. Iraq also transferred many nuclear scientists to related jobs in the Military Industrial Commission (MIC) in order to help them maintain their weapons knowledge. Despite these efforts, the report concluded that, after the nuclear programme was ended in 1991, Iraq's accumulated 'intellectual capital decayed in the succeeding years'.[95] It also concluded that Saddam eventually would have sought to reconstitute the country's WMD programmes but probably intended to give higher priority to ballistic missile and chemical warfare capabilities than to nuclear weapons.[96]

The ISG ended its search for Iraqi non-conventional weapons in December 2004. According to US officials, the group's operations were brought to a close because there was little expectation of finding any substantial new evidence and the hunt could no longer be justified in view of the rising danger to the investigators.[97]

[89] [US Central Intelligence Agency (CIA)], Director of Central Intelligence, *Comprehensive Report of the Special Advisor to the Director of Central Intelligence on Iraq's WMD*, 3 vols, 30 Sep. 2004, URL <http://www.odci.gov/cia/reports/iraq_wmd_2004/index.html>.

[90] See Kile (note 19), pp. 620–21. On the work of the ISG see also chapter 13 in this volume.

[91] CIA, (note 89), vol. 1, 'Key findings', p. 1.

[92] Testimony of Charles Duelfer, Special Advisor to the Director of Central Intelligence for Iraqi Weapons of Mass Destruction, to the Armed Services Committee, US Senate, Washington, DC, 6 Oct. 2004, URL <http://armed-services.senate.gov/statemnt/2004/October/Duelfer%2010-06-04.pdf>.

[93] CIA (note 89), vol. 1, 'Key findings'.

[94] CIA (note 89), vol. 1, 'Key findings', and vol. 2, 'Nuclear', p. 1.

[95] CIA (note 89), vol. 2, 'Nuclear'.

[96] CIA (note 89), vol. 1, 'Key findings'.

[97] Borger, J. and Steele, J., 'US gives up search for Saddam's WMD', *The Guardian*, 13 Jan. 2005, URL <http://www.guardian.co.uk/Iraq/Story/0,2763,1389370,00.html>; and Linzer, D., 'Search for banned arms in Iraq ended last year', *Washington Post*, 12 Jan. 2005, URL <http://www.washingtonpost.com/ac2/wp-dyn/A2129-2005Jan11>.

VI. South Korean safeguards violations

Another safeguards-related controversy arose in September 2004 when South Korea acknowledged that it had conducted uranium enrichment and plutonium separation experiments without reporting them in a timely manner to the IAEA, as required by its full-scope safeguards agreement. Since these activities have direct applications in the development of nuclear weapons, the revelations raised international concern that there was renewed interest in weapon research in South Korea.[98] However, the IAEA's subsequent investigations did not find evidence that South Korea was attempting to reconstitute the nuclear weapon R&D programme which it had abandoned in the 1970s, under strong US pressure.[99] ElBaradei stated in an interview that there were no signs that South Korea had 'any intentions to develop nuclear weapons'.[100]

The uranium enrichment experiments came to light in connection with South Korea's submission to the IAEA Secretariat, on 23 August 2004, of its initial expanded declaration under the NPT Additional Safeguards Protocol.[101] South Korea's Ministry of Science and Technology reported to the IAEA that it had discovered, in June 2004, that scientists at the Korea Atomic Energy Research Institute (KAERI) had conducted laboratory-scale uranium enrichment experiments using the atomic vapour laser isotope separation (AVLIS) method.[102] The experiments had been conducted in 2000 along with unrelated isotope separation experiments.[103] A senior South Korean scientist said that the experiments had not been reported to the IAEA because they were a one-time 'academic test' that had produced a 'miniscule' amount of uranium.[104]

South Korea's failure to report the experiments violated its safeguards agreement, which obliges it to declare to the IAEA the use of nuclear material in enrichment experiments and to provide the agency with information about

[98] Some experts have warned that the protracted crisis over North Korea's nuclear programme might eventually lead South Korea and Japan to re-evaluate their status as NNWSs. Pollack, J. and Reiss, M., 'South Korea: the tyranny of geography and the vexations of history', eds K. Campbell *et al.*, *The Nuclear Tipping Point: Why States Reconsider Their Nuclear Choices* (Brookings Institution Press: Washington, DC, 2004).

[99] For an overview of South Korea's nuclear policies see Feldman, Y. and Boureston, J., 'Country profile 2: South Korea', SIPRI–FirstWatch International Internet site on Countries of Nuclear Strategic Concern, URL <http://projects.sipri.se/nuclear/cnscindex.htm>.

[100] Quoted by Faiola, A., 'IAEA chief doubts S. Korea arms plans', *Washington Post* (Internet edn), 9 Oct. 2004, URL <http://www.washingtonpost.com/wp-dyn/articles/A18674-2004Oct8.html>.

[101] South Korea signed an Additional Protocol on 21 June 1999, which entered into force on 18 June 2004; see IAEA INFCIRC236.Add1, 18 June 2004, URL <http://www.iaea.org/Publications/Documents/Infcircs/2004/infcirc236a1.pdf>.

[102] IAEA, 'Implementation of the NPT safeguards agreement in the Republic of Korea', Report by the Director General to the IAEA Board of Governors, GOV/2004/84, Vienna, 11 Nov. 2004, p. 1, URL <http://www.iaea.org/Publications/Documents/Board/2004/gov2004-84.pdf>.

[103] The experiments used 3.5 kg of natural uranium metal to produce 200 mg of uranium enriched to an average of 10.2% in U-235. The peak level of enrichment produced by the experiments was 77% U-235, which was close to weapons-grade level (90%). Hibbs, M.,'77% U-235 was peak enrichment reported to IAEA by South Korea', *Nuclear Fuel*, vol. 29, no. 30 (27 Sep. 2004), pp. 7–8.

[104] Chang In Soon, President of the Korea Atomic Energy Research Institute, quoted by Brooke, J., 'South Korean scientist calls uranium test "academic"', *New York Times* (Internet edn), 7 Sep. 2004, URL <http://www.nytimes.com/2004/09/07/international/asia/07korea.html>.

the facilities and equipment involved.[105] In the course of verifying South Korea's account of the enrichment experiments, IAEA inspectors learned that KAERI had failed to declare all of its uranium conversion activities. These included the production, in 1982–84, of 154 kg of natural uranium metal—a sample from which was used in the AVLIS laser enrichment experiments.[106]

One week after disclosing the uranium enrichment experiments, South Korean officials acknowledged, in response to press inquiries, that scientists at KAERI had conducted an undeclared plutonium separation experiment.[107] This experiment was already the subject of discussions between South Korea and the IAEA. In 1997 IAEA inspectors had taken environmental samples at a hot cell facility at the TRIGA III research reactor that revealed the presence of slightly irradiated depleted uranium with associated plutonium that was not consistent with any reported activities.[108] In March 2004 South Korea informed the IAEA that its scientists had conducted an undeclared laboratory-scale plutonium separation experiment in 1981–82. The experiment yielded a small amount of plutonium, estimated to be less than 40 mg.[109]

The reaction to the disclosures

The disclosures impeded efforts to restart the Six-Party Talks on North Korea's nuclear weapon programme and complicated South Korea's efforts to engage North Korea in improving inter-Korean relations.[110] According to a North Korean foreign ministry spokesman, the key issue was not the level of uranium enrichment or the amount of separated plutonium; rather, it was that 'South Korea had pursued in secrecy a nuclear weapons program with the connivance of the US' and now had 'full access' to technology for developing a nuclear weapons capability.[111]

The South Korean Government played down the undeclared nuclear activities, describing them as 'isolated laboratory-scale research activities' which a few scientists had conducted on their own initiative without the knowledge of their supervisors or the government.[112] Some observers doubted the plausibility of this explanation, at least with respect to the plutonium separation

[105] In addition, the 1992 Joint Declaration of the Denuclearization of the Korean Peninsula, signed by North Korea and South Korea on 20 Jan. 1992, prohibits the 2 parties from possessing or developing uranium enrichment capabilities. The text of the Joint Declaration is available at URL <http://www.ceip.org/files/projects/npp/resources/koreadenuclearization.htm>.

[106] IAEA (note 102), pp. 4–5.

[107] Faiola, A. and Linzer, D., 'S. Korea admits extracting plutonium', *Washington Post* (Internet edn), 10 Sep. 2004, p. 1, URL <http://www.washingtonpost.com/wp-dyn/articles/A9761-2004Sep9.html>.

[108] IAEA (note 102), p. 5.

[109] IAEA (note 102), p. 5.

[110] 'Seo, H., 'Pyongyang seizes on Seoul's nuclear dabbling', *Asia Times* (Internet edn), 14 Sep. 2004, URL <http://www.atimes.com/atimes/Korea/FI14Dg05.html>.

[111] KCNA, 'Foreign Ministry spokesman demands clarification of S. Korea's nuclear issue', 6 Oct. 2004, URL <http://www.kcna.co.jp/item/2004/200410/news10/07.htm>.

[112] Statement by H.E. Mr Ban Ki-moon, Minister of Foreign Affairs and Trade, Republic of Korea, at the 59th Session of the United Nations General Assembly, New York, 24 Sep. 2004, URL <http://www.un.org/webcast/ga/59/statements/koreng040924.pdf>.

experiment, saying that it was widely known among nuclear specialists and within US intelligence agencies; they also pointed out that the scientists involved should have been aware that the activities had to be reported to the IAEA.[113] The revelations raised concerns about the South Korean Government's regulatory and supervisory capacities with respect to the country's nuclear establishment.[114] On 25 October 2004 the Ministry of Science and Technology announced the creation of a National Nuclear Management and Control Agency to 'monitor nuclear energy-related activities' and assist with national safeguards implementation.[115]

The IAEA Board of Governors took up the issue of South Korea's undeclared nuclear activities at its November 2004 meeting, which concluded that South Korea's failure to declare the experiments was a 'matter of serious concern'.[116] However, the Board noted that the quantities of nuclear material involved had not been significant and that there was no indication that the experiments had continued. It also noted the corrective action taken by South Korea and welcomed the active cooperation it had provided to the agency. The Board requested that the Director General 'report as appropriate' on the safeguards issue but did not discuss whether to refer it to the UN Security Council.[117] Prior to the meeting, there had been speculation that the US Administration intended to push for a referral of the issue to the UN Security Council in order to create a precedent for dealing with what the White House considered to be Iran's more serious safeguards violations.[118]

VII. The NPT Review Conference Preparatory Committee

The third meeting of the Preparatory Committee (PrepCom) for the 2005 NPT Review Conference was held at UN Headquarters in New York on 26 April–7 May 2004.[119] Delegations from 123 states parties to the NPT par-

[113] Kang, J. *et al.*, 'South Korea's nuclear surprise', *Bulletin of the Atomic Scientists*, vol. 61, no. 1 (Jan./Feb. 2005), pp. 40–49.

[114] Pinkston, D., 'South Korea's nuclear experiments', *CNS Research Story*, Center for Nonproliferation Studies, Monterey Institute of International Studies, 9 Nov. 2004, URL <http://cns.miis.edu/pubs/week/041109.htm>; and Kang, *et al.* (note 113).

[115] Fifield, A., 'S. Korea establishes its own nuclear watchdog', *Financial Times* (Internet edn), 25 Oct. 2004, URL <http://www.ransac.org/printerfriendly.asp?doc=1025200493619AM.html>.

[116] IAEA, 'Implementation of the NPT safeguards agreement in the Republic of Korea', Chairman's conclusion on item 4(c): nuclear verification, IAEA Board of Governors, Vienna, 26 Nov. 2004, URL <http://www.iaea.org/NewsCenter/News/2004/south_korea.html>.

[117] IAEA (note 116).

[118] Linzer, D., and Faiola, A., 'US won't report South Korea to UN for nuclear tests', *Washington Post* (Internet edn), 25 Nov. 2004, URL <http://www.washingtonpost.com/wp-dyn/articles/A11256-2004Nov24.html>; and Fifield, A., 'Seoul hopes to escape UN referral over nuclear plans', *Financial Times*, 13–14 Nov. 2004, p. 5.

[119] The 1995 NPT Review and Extension Conference had sought to strengthen the review process by requiring that Preparatory Committee meetings be held in each of the 3 years leading up to the 5-yearly Review Conferences. The purpose of the Preparatory Committee meetings is to 'consider principles, objectives and ways in order to promote the full implementation of the Treaty, as well as its universality, and to make recommendations thereon to the Review Conference'. 'Strengthening the review process for the Treaty', New York, 11 May 1995, NPT/CONF.1995/32 (Part I), URL <http://disarmament2.un.org/wmd/npt/1995dec1.htm>.

ticipated, with Ambassador Sudjadnan Parnohadiningrat, of Indonesia, serving as chairman.[120] Under the 'enhanced', strengthened review process agreed at the 2000 Review Conference, the main purpose of the 2004 PrepCom meeting was to produce consensus recommendations to the upcoming Review Conference on a range of treaty-related issues, taking into account the deliberations and results of the two previous sessions.[121]

The meeting was marked by discord and deep division between the states parties. The PrepCom failed to produce a report containing any substantive recommendations for the conference on treaty implementation issues. It also failed to adopt an agenda for the conference. This was primarily because of opposition from the USA and other nuclear weapon states (NWSs) to a proposal, supported by many NNWSs, to frame the 2005 treaty review in terms of the 13-step programme of action on nuclear disarmament agreed at the 2000 Review Conference.[122] The Committee did manage to adopt the minimum organizational and procedural agreements needed for the Conference to be able to take place.[123]

The 2004 PrepCom meeting highlighted deep differences between the states parties over the issue of responding to suspected or clear-cut cases of non-compliance and the perceived lack of commitment of some parties to fulfilling their treaty obligations.[124] The main division was between the five NPT-defined NWSs—China, France, Russia, the UK and, especially, the USA—and the members of the Non-Aligned Movement (NAM)[125] and other NNWS parties. The former discussed treaty non-compliance primarily in terms of NNWS parties seeking to develop nuclear weapons, in contravention of Articles I and II of the NPT.[126] Many NNWS parties, led by NAM members such as Indonesia, Iran and Malaysia, focused on the obligation of the NWSs, codified in Article VI, to work 'in good faith' towards nuclear disarmament.

[120] 'Third session of Preparatory Committee for 2005 Review Conference of parties to NPT concludes in New York', United Nations Press Release DC/2923, 13 May 2004, URL <http://www.un.org/News/Press/docs/2004/dc2923.doc.htm>.

[121] 'Improving the effectiveness of the strengthened review process for the Treaty', New York, 19 May 2000, NPT/CONF.200/28 (Part I), URL <http://disarmament2.un.org/wmd/npt/finaldoc.html>.

[122] As part of the compromise paving the way for the consensus adoption of a final document at the 2000 Review Conference, the NWSs reaffirmed their commitment to nuclear disarmament, as mandated by Art. VI of the NPT, by agreeing to a specific programme of action to reduce the role of—and eventually eliminate—their nuclear arsenals. 'Review of the operation of the treaty, taking into account the decisions and the resolution adopted by the 1995 Review and Extension Conference', New York, 19 May 2000, NPT/CONF2000.28 (Part I), URL <http://disarmament2.un.org/wmd/npt/finaldoc.html>.

[123] These included decisions setting the conference date for 2–27 May 2005 and selecting Ambassador Sérgio de Queiroz Duarte of Brazil as its president. 'Third session of Preparatory Committee for 2005 Review Conference of parties to NPT concludes in New York' (note 120).

[124] Johnson, R., 'Report on the 2004 NPT PrepCom', *Disarmament Diplomacy*, no. 77 (May/June 2004), URL <http://www.acronym.org.uk/dd/dd77/77npt.htm>; and Boese, W., 'NPT meeting marked by discord', *Arms Control Today*, vol. 34, no. 5 (June 2004), pp. 28–29.

[125] For the members of the NAM see the glossary in this volume.

[126] A US official named 4 NNWS—Iraq, Iran, Libya and North Korea—as suspected or known to have proscribed military nuclear programmes and warned of a 'crisis of NPT noncompliance' that was eroding confidence in the regime. 'The NPT: a crisis of non-compliance', Statement by John R. Bolton, Under Secretary for Arms Control and International Security, to the Third Session of the Preparatory Committee for the 2005 Review Conference on the Treaty on the Non-Proliferation of Nuclear Weapons, New York, 27 Apr. 2004, URL <http://www.state.gov/t/us/rm/ 31848.htm>.

They argued that the failure of the NWSs to make sufficient progress towards complying with their nuclear disarmament obligation posed at least as serious a threat to the vitality of the NPT as 'horizontal' proliferation by NNWS, since disarmament and non-proliferation are interdependent and mutually reinforcing.[127] This view was supported by the seven members of the New Agenda Coalition (NAC), which expressed disappointment over the lack of progress made by the NWS in implementing the practical steps towards disarmament to which they had agreed at the 2000 Review Conference.[128] The NAC was particularly critical of the USA's retreat from its commitment, as part of the 13-step programme of action agreed at the 2000 Review Conference, to seek the early entry into force of the 1996 Comprehensive Nuclear Test-Ban Treaty.

A number of perennially controversial NPT issues surfaced during the third PrepCom meeting. The League of Arab States took the lead in calling for the establishment of a nuclear weapon-free zone in the Middle East.[129] There was considerable debate about proposals for a global treaty on negative security assurances—that is, legally binding promises by the NWSs not to use, or threaten to use, nuclear weapons against NNWS parties to the NPT.[130] There was also debate about proposals to make the Additional Protocol a mandatory condition for suppliers' transfer of nuclear technology and materials to recipient states.[131]

VIII. Internationalization of the nuclear fuel cycle

During 2004 there was new interest in the old idea of establishing multinational or international arrangements for controlling the nuclear fuel cycle activities of greatest proliferation concern—uranium enrichment and plutonium reprocessing; and spent fuel management and waste disposal.[132] This idea had been widely discussed in the late 1970s in connection with the Inter-

[127] See, e.g., 'Working paper submitted by Malaysia on behalf of the Group of Non-Aligned and Other States Parties to the Treaty on the Non-Proliferation of Nuclear Weapons', New York, 5 May 2004, NPT/ CONF.2005/PC.III/WP.24, URL <http://daccess-ods.un.org/TMP/3589686.html>.

[128] 'New Agenda Coalition substantive recommendations to the third session of the Preparatory Committee of the 2005 NPT Review Conference', New York, 26 Apr. 2004, NPT/CONF.2005/PC.III/11, URL <http://daccess-ods.un.org/TMP/7933799.html>. For the members of the NAC see the glossary in this volume.

[129] 'Paper presented on behalf of the States members of the League of Arab States at the third session of the Preparatory Committee for the 2005 Review Conference of the Parties to the Treaty on the Non-Proliferation of Nuclear Weapons, New York, 28 Apr. 2004, NPT/CONF.2005/PC.III/WP.12, URL <http://daccess-ods.un.org/TMP/6450427.html>. For the members of the League of Arab States see the glossary in this volume.

[130] For more detail see du Preez, J., 'Security assurances against the use or threat of use of nuclear weapons: is progress possible at the NPT Prepcom?', Monterey Institute of International Studies, Centre for Nonproliferation Studies, 28 Apr. 2003, URL, <http://cns.miis.edu/research/npt/nptsec.htm>.

[131] Johnson (note 124).

[132] Rauf, T. and Simpson, F., 'The nuclear fuel cycle: is it time for a new approach?', *Arms Control Today*, vol. 34, no. 8 (Dec. 2004), URL <http://www.armscontrol.org/act/2004_12/Rauf.asp>.

national Nuclear Fuel Cycle Evaluation (INFCE) conference.[133] However, the discussions led to few concrete results because of opposition from the nuclear power industry and the unwillingness of some countries with advanced nuclear power programmes to foreclose fuel cycle options.

The resurgence of interest in proposals to internationalize the nuclear fuel cycle has been stimulated by the controversies over the scope and nature of nuclear programmes in Iran and North Korea. These controversies have led some observers to conclude that there is an inherent structural weakness in the NPT: namely, that NPT Article IV, which gives NNWS parties an 'inalienable right' to import and develop materials and technologies for use in civil nuclear energy programmes, opens the possibility that an NNWS can covertly develop a nuclear weapon capability by putting in place, under the cover of a civil nuclear energy programme, the fuel cycle facilities needed to produce weapon-usable nuclear material.[134] This concern has been reinforced by revelations about the existence of a global black market in nuclear technology and expertise. The perceived weaknesses in the NPT regime have led to recent calls for a permanent halt to the construction of new nationally controlled facilities for producing fissile material.[135] The main aim of proposals to internationalize the fuel cycle is to allow states to continue to develop nuclear energy for peaceful purposes, as guaranteed by Article IV, while preventing the diversion of nuclear technologies and material to clandestine weapon programmes.

A number of proposals are currently being discussed that envision new management or control arrangements for limiting the front end of the civilian nuclear fuel cycle.[136] These fall into four general categories: (*a*) the establishment of a more intrusive international inspection and regulatory regime for existing fuel processing and production facilities; (*b*) the creation of new multinational consortia involving the sharing of the ownership and operation of sensitive fuel cycle facilities among a number of nations (the 'Urenco model');[137] (*c*) the creation of multinational enterprises, hosted and operated by a single national authority, having other nations as shareholders (the

[133] The INFCE was an international study initiated by US President Jimmy Carter in Oct. 1977 to assess the comparative economic, technical and political advantages of various nuclear fuel cycles, with particular reference to the use of plutonium for recycling.

[134] See, e.g., ElBaradei, M., 'Towards a safer world', *The Economist*, 18 Oct. 2003, pp. 43–44; Cirincione, J. and Wolfsthal, J., 'North Korea and Iran: test cases for an improved non-proliferation regime?', *Arms Control Today*, vol. 33, no. 10 (Dec. 2003), pp. 11–14; and Levi, M., 'There is no absolute right to nuclear energy', *Financial Times*, 22 Sep. 2004, p. 15.

[135] Allison, G., 'How to stop nuclear terror', *Foreign Affairs*, vol. 83, no. 1 (Jan./Feb. 2004), pp. 64–74; and Campbell, K. and Einhorn, R., 'Avoiding the tipping point: concluding observations', eds Campbell *et al.* (note 98).

[136] The nuclear fuel cycle consists of front-end steps (milling and mining of uranium ore, uranium conversion and enrichment, fuel fabrication) that lead to the preparation of uranium for use as fuel for reactor operation and back-end steps that are necessary to safely manage, prepare and dispose of the highly radioactive spent nuclear fuel.

[137] Urenco is a multinational uranium enrichment enterprise, established by a 1970 treaty between Germany, the Netherlands and the UK, that operates gas centrifuge facilities to provide fuel for commercial nuclear power reactors.

'Eurodif model');[138] and (*d*) the establishment of international nuclear fuel bank, under an international nuclear fuel authority, into which producers would deposit their fuel output to be 'paid out' to end-users.[139] With regard to the back end of the fuel cycle, proposals have been put forward for establishing new multinational programmes for managing and disposing of spent fuel and radioactive waste.

At the June 2004 meeting of the IAEA Board of Governors, ElBaradei announced the appointment of an international Expert Group to consider possible multilateral approaches to sensitive nuclear fuel cycle activities.[140] The Group's mandate is to support decision making in government and industry by providing an initial survey of the most promising institutional and technical approaches, including consideration of relevant economic, legal and security issues.[141] The first meeting of the Group, consisting of 23 experts, took place on 10 September 2004.[142] It is scheduled to submit a report to ElBaradei by March 2005.

IX. New US nuclear weapons

There has been a long-running debate in the US Congress over the building of new types of nuclear weapons. The debate intensified in 2002, when officials of the Bush Administration called for the development of a robust nuclear earth-penetrating (RNEP) weapon. They argued that this nuclear 'bunker buster' was needed for the USA to be able to hold at risk the command-and-control and WMD production facilities that potential adversaries were building deep underground, beyond the reach of current US conventional munitions.[143] The administration also urged the development of new very-low-yield

[138] Eurodif is a uranium enrichment consortium established in 1973 by Belgium, France and Spain, and later joined by Italy, that operates a gaseous diffusion plant at a site in France, under the management of the French Atomic Energy Commission.

[139] See, e.g., 'Statement by Director General Mohamed ElBaradei, at the 47th Regular Session of the General Conference of the International Atomic Energy Agency', Vienna, 15 Sep. 2003, available at URL <http://www.acronym.org.uk/docs/0309/doc26.htm>; and McCombie, C. and Chapman, N., 'Nuclear fuel cycle centres—an old and new idea', Paper presented at World Nuclear Association annual symposium, London, 10 Sep. 2004, URL <http://www.world-nuclear.org/sym/2004/mccombie.htm>.

[140] IAEA, Introductory statement to the Board of Governors by IAEA Director General Dr Mohamed ElBaradei, DG/14062004, Vienna, 14 June 2004, URL <http://www.iaea.org/NewsCenter/Statements/2004/ebsp2004n003.html>.

[141] These include, *inter alia*, questions about ownership, management and control of facilities, financing arrangements, conditions for supplying fuel services, insurance and liability, safety and environmental protection, physical security, and international safeguards arrangements. IAEA Office of External Relations and Policy, 'Multilateral approaches to the nuclear fuel cycle: preliminary views of the IAEA Secretariat for the proposed study', Vienna, 2004, URL <http://www.iaea.org/NewsCenter/Focus/FuelCycle/preliminaryviews.pdf>.

[142] IAEA, 'Expert Group meeting on control of nuclear fuel cycle' IAEA News Centre, Vienna, 10 Sep. 2004, URL <http://www.iaea.org/NewsCenter/News/2004/bettercontrols.html>.

[143] See, e.g., Younger, S., 'Nuclear weapons in the twenty-first century', Los Alamos National Laboratory, Report LAUR-00-2850, 27 June 2000, URL <http://www.fas.org/nuke/guide/usa/doctrine/doe/younger.htm>. Critics have argued that even very-low-yield nuclear weapons detonated deep underground will produce considerable collateral blast damage as well as significant radioactive fallout. Nelson, R., 'Low-yield earth-penetrating nuclear weapons', *FAS Public Interest Report*, vol. 54, no. 1 (Jan./Feb. 2001), URL <http://www.fas.org/faspir/2001/v54n1/weapons.htm>.

nuclear weapons (so-called mini-nukes) to enhance US capabilities to deter 'rogue states' from using, or threatening to use, non-conventional weapons, and even to dissuade them from developing such weapons.[144] In 2003 Congress voted to repeal the 10-year-old Spratt–Furse ban (named after its two congressional sponsors) on research leading to development of nuclear weapons with yields of less than five kilotons.[145] It also approved funding, with some restrictions, for proposals to continue researching new types of nuclear 'bunker busters'.[146] However, it withheld authorization for work on designing, engineering and testing new or modified nuclear weapons.

The debate took a new turn when, on 22 November 2004, the Republican Party-controlled Congress passed an omnibus appropriation bill for financial year (FY) 2005 that eliminated or reduced funding requested by the administration for work on new types of nuclear weapons. The bill deleted the White House's request for $27 million to continue research on modifying two existing nuclear weapons (B-61 and B-83 gravity bombs) for the earth-penetrator role; spending on this programme had been set to rise sharply, to $485 million over five years.[147] The bill also rescinded $9 million that had been previously authorized for work on the Advanced Concepts Initiative, which included research into very-low-yield nuclear weapons. The money was redirected into the Reliable Replacement Warhead programme, which is aimed at improving the reliability and longevity of existing weapons and their components without nuclear explosive testing.[148] In addition, the bill cut funding requested for selecting a site for a $4 billion facility for making new plutonium triggers ('pits') for nuclear warheads.[149]

The vote revealed significant bipartisan opposition to the administration's funding requests for nuclear weapon research and a reinvigorated testing capacity. This opposition stemmed from two main concerns. First, some legislators were worried that new types of low-yield and earth-penetrating nuclear weapons were likely to be viewed as being more usable than existing

[144] The White House, 'National Strategy to Combat Weapons of Mass Destruction', Washington, DC, Dec. 2002, URL <http://www.whitehouse.gov/news/releases/2002/12/WMDStrategy.pdf>; and House Policy Committee, Subcommittee on National Security and Foreign Affairs, *Differentiation and Defense: An Agenda for the Nuclear Weapons Program* (House Policy Committee: Washington, DC, Feb. 2003), URL <http://cox.house.gov/files/nuclear_report.pdf>.

[145] 'US lawmakers agree to end ban on low-yield nuclear weapons research', *Global Security Newswire*, 7 Nov. 2003, URL <http://www.nti.org/d_newswire/issues/print.asp?story_id=B8DDB202-0889-427B-AD35-CDD79E709BB1>. For further detail about the 1994 Spratt–Furse ban (Section 3136 of Public Law 103-160) see Wright, D., 'The Spratt–Furse law on mini-nuke development', Backgrounder, Union of Concerned Scientists, 11 May 2003, URL <http://www.ucsusa.org/global_security/nuclear_weapons/page.cfm?pageID=1182>.

[146] In addition, Congress approved measures to shorten the time required to prepare for a full-scale nuclear test from 24 months to 18 months.

[147] Wald, M., 'Nuclear weapons money is cut from spending bill', *New York Times* (Internet edn), 23 Nov. 2004, URL <http://www.nytimes.com/2004/11/23/politics/23nuke.html>.

[148] Wald (note 147); and 'US nuclear security in the 21st century', Address by Rep. David Hobson to the Arms Control Association, 3 Feb. 2005, URL <http://www.armscontrol.org/events/20050203_hobson_text.asp>.

[149] Opponents of the Modern Pit Facility have argued that, with a planned 50% reduction of the US nuclear stockpile, a small facility currently operating at Los Alamos National Laboratory could produce enough pits for the US arsenal. Fetter, S. and von Hippel, F., 'Does the United States need a new plutonium-pit facility?', *Arms Control Today*, vol. 34, no. 4 (May 2004), pp. 10–14.

weapons, especially as part of the administration's strategy of pre-empting WMD threats, and hence would increase the risk of war.[150] Second, there was concern that the administration's interest in these weapons was undermining broader international efforts to devalue the role of nuclear weapons in military planning and to reduce the incentives for their acquisition.[151] Despite congressional opposition, administration officials indicated that they would make a new effort to secure funding in the FY 2006 and FY 2007 budgets to complete the RNEP study.[152]

X. Conclusions

In 2004 concern about the long-term vitality of the nuclear non-proliferation regime led to new initiatives aimed at strengthening the regime. Revelations about the activities of the clandestine black market network organized by Pakistani nuclear scientist A. Q. Khan highlighted the difficult problem posed by the willingness of some states, or of individual scientists, to sell sensitive nuclear technologies and expertise that can be used to develop nuclear weapons. The discovery of the Khan network gave impetus to new strategies aimed at curbing 'secondary proliferation', in which illegally acquired nuclear technologies and materials are re-exported to other would-be proliferators. It also led to a new legally binding initiative, UN Security Council Resolution 1540, which requires governments to tighten domestic legislation and to take action against private companies or individuals found to be operating outside the law.

During 2004 there continued to be concern about a perceived lacuna in Article IV of the NPT that potentially allowed NNWSs such as Iran to put in place the key fuel cycle facilities for manufacturing nuclear weapons under the cover of civil nuclear energy programmes. This led to growing interest in the idea of limiting civil uranium enrichment and plutonium reprocessing programmes to a handful of fully transparent nuclear fuel cycle facilities, operating under multinational or international control. It reflected a broader concern that the diffusion of sensitive nuclear technology and expertise is undermining the efficacy of traditional regime instruments, including export controls and international safeguards on nationally controlled fuel cycle facilities and nuclear material holdings, in reducing proliferation risks.

The serious weaknesses evident in the non-proliferation regime underscore the urgent need for the international community to work to revitalize and strengthen the regime. This will involve filling gaps in safeguards and export control arrangements as well as closing loopholes that have been exploited in the past by some states. This in turn will require new multifunctional

[150] Pincus, W., 'Funds for atomic bomb research cut from spending bill', *Washington Post* (Internet edn), 23 Nov. 2004, URL <http://www.washingtonpost.com/ac2/wp-dyn/A5554-2004Nov22>.

[151] Ruppe, D., 'Bush nuclear policies undermine nonproliferation, Republican Congressman says', *Global Security Newswire*, 12 Aug. 2004, URL <http://www.nti.org/d_newswire/issues/print.asp?story_id=49C0280E-D749-4916-81AB-1882EC615784>.

[152] Pincus, W., 'Rumsfeld seeks to revive burrowing nuclear bomb', *Washington Post* (Internet edn), 1 Feb. 2005, URL <http://www.washingtonpost.com/ac2/wp-dyn/A52564-2005Jan31>.

approaches to addressing proliferation challenges that make use of the full range of political and economic as well as military instruments that the international community has at its disposal. Above all, it will require a renewed commitment by all states to fully implement their arms control and disarmament commitments within the existing multilateral treaty framework.

Appendix 12A. World nuclear forces, 2005

SHANNON N. KILE and HANS M. KRISTENSEN*

I. Introduction

A decade and a half after the end of the cold war, eight states deploy more than 13 000 operational nuclear weapons (see table 12A.1). If all warheads are counted—operational warheads, spares, and those in both active and inactive storage—the eight states possess a total of roughly 27 600 warheads. In addition to these intact weapons, thousands more plutonium cores (pits) are stored as a strategic reserve. The nuclear arsenals vary in both size and capability, ranging from Russia's 7360 operational weapons to those of India and Pakistan, whose combined arsenal still contains fewer than 100 warheads. Despite their different circumstances, however, all the eight states continue to maintain and modernize their arsenals and insist, publicly or covertly, that nuclear weapons play a crucial and enduring role for their national security.

Both Russia and the United States are in the process of reducing their operational nuclear forces under the terms of the 1991 START I Treaty and the 2002 Strategic Offensive Reductions Treaty (SORT).[1] China, India and Pakistan, on the other hand, may increase their arsenals somewhat over the next decade. France appears to have reached an equilibrium of some sort in the size of its arsenal, while the United Kingdom will soon face a decision about the future of its nuclear arsenal. When the current Russian and US reductions have been completed, in 2012, these eight states (assuming no others have joined the 'nuclear club') will still possess a total of about 14 000 intact nuclear warheads. In the USA, implementation of the decisions of the 2001 Nuclear Posture Review (NPR) has begun, entailing a reduction of almost half the total US stockpile and the development of new ballistic missiles, strategic submarines, long-range bomber aircraft, nuclear weapons, nuclear weapon production facilities, and nuclear command and control systems.[2] Similarly, Russia has announced a plan to reduce its land-based strategic missiles in particular but also to retain for another decade, rather than dismantling, some of its intercontinental-range ballistic missiles equipped with multiple, independently targetable re-entry vehicles (MIRVed ICBMs). It will introduce a new ICBM, a new class of strategic submarines and a new cruise missile. Tables 12A.2 and 12A.3, respectively, show the composition of the US and Russian deployed nuclear forces.

[1] The Treaty on the Reduction and Limitation of Strategic Offensive Arms (START I Treaty) was signed in 1991 by the USA and the USSR; it entered into force on 5 Dec. 1994 for Russia and the USA (under the 1992 Lisbon Protocol, which entered into force on 5 Dec. 1994, Belarus, Kazakhstan and Ukraine also assumed the obligations of the former USSR under the treaty). For the treaty see URL <http://www.state.gov/www/global/arms/starthtm/start/toc.html>. SORT was signed by Russia and the USA in 2002; it entered into force on 1 June 2003 and is available at URL <http://www.state.gov/t/ac/trt/18016.htm>. On the implications of SORT see 'Special Section', *Arms Control Today*, vol. 32, no. 5 (June 2002), pp. 3–23.

[2] See 'Nuclear Posture Review [excerpts], submitted to Congress on 31 December 2001', 8 Jan. 2002, URL <http://www.globalsecurity.org/wmd/library/policy/dod/npr.htm>.

* Vitaly Fedchenko assisted in the research for this appendix.

Table 12A.1. World nuclear forces, by number of deployed warheads, January 2005

Country	Strategic warheads	Non-strategic warheads	Total number of deployed warheads
USA	4 216	680	**4 896**[a]
Russia	3 980	3 380	**7 360**[b]
UK	185	–	**185**
France	348	–	**348**
China	282	120	**~400**
India	–	–	**(30–40)**[c]
Pakistan	–	–	**(30–50)**[c]
Israel	–	–	**(~200)**[c]
Total			**~13 470**

[a] The total US stockpile, including reserves, contains *c.* 10 350 warheads. In addition, 5000 plutonium cores (pits) are in storage as a strategic reserve, while another 7000 pits make up most of the 34 tons of weapon-grade plutonium declared in excess of military needs.

[b] The total Russian stockpile contains *c.* 16 000 warheads, of which *c.* 8800 are in storage or awaiting dismantlement.

[c] The stockpiles of India, Pakistan and Israel are thought to be only partly deployed.

The nuclear arsenals of the UK, France and China are considerably smaller than those of the USA and Russia, but these three states are also modernizing their forces (see tables 12A.5 and 12A.6). The British nuclear weapon stockpile has levelled out at slightly fewer than 200 warheads: the UK is the only one of the five states defined by the 1968 Non-Proliferation Treaty (NPT) as nuclear weapon states (NWSs) that is not known to have new nuclear weapon systems under development (see table 12A.4).[3] Before long, however, the UK will need to make a decision on whether to begin development of a replacement for the Trident system.

France is currently engaged in developing and deploying a new generation of nuclear-powered ballistic-missile submarines (SSBNs), submarine-launched ballistic missiles (SLBMs) and air-launched nuclear weapons, although the number of operational warheads may decrease somewhat when the new SLBM is introduced, in about 2010. China is on the verge of deploying a new generation of strategic missiles, but it remains unclear whether it intends to deploy a significantly larger strategic nuclear force or a more modern force of about the same size.

It is particularly difficult to obtain public information about the nuclear arsenals of the three states that are not parties to the NPT—India, Pakistan and Israel (see tables 12A.7–12A.9). The information that is available is limited and often contradictory. India and Pakistan are both busy creating operational nuclear strike capabilities, while Israel appears to be taking a wait-and-see position, depending on the situation in Iran.

The figures in the tables are estimates based on public information and contain some uncertainties, as reflected in the notes.

[3] On developments in world nuclear forces see Kristensen, H. M., 'World nuclear forces', *SIPRI Yearbook 2004: Armaments, Disarmament and International Security* (Oxford University Press: Oxford, 2004), pp. 628–46, and previous editions of the SIPRI Yearbook. The Treaty on the Non-proliferation of Nuclear Weapons entered into force on 5 Mar. 1970; it was extended indefinitely at the 1995 NPT Review and Extension Conference. For a discussion of the run-up to the 2005 NPT Review Conference see chapter 12, section VII.

II. US nuclear forces

As of January 2005, the USA maintained a stockpile estimated at nearly 5000 operational nuclear warheads, consisting of 4216 strategic and 680 non-strategic warheads. Another 315 warheads are spares. This is a reduction of 2100 operational warheads compared to the estimate for early 2004, owing to a reduction in the number of ballistic missiles, the downloading of warheads on sea-based ballistic missiles, and new information about the number of warheads in the US stockpile. In addition, over 5100 warheads are held in reserve, for a total US stockpile of approximately 10 350 warheads.

In June 2004 the Administration of President George W. Bush approved a new Nuclear Weapons Stockpile Plan that will cut the total stockpile 'almost in half' by 2012. The plan implements the 2001 NPR, which mandated a reduction in the number of 'operationally deployed strategic warheads' to 1700–2200 by the end of 2012. The NPR force level was incorporated in SORT. It is estimated that the new US stockpile plan will involve the retirement of some 4300 warheads and result in a total US stockpile of approximately 6000 warheads by 2012, which is more than twice the number allowed under SORT.[4] The discrepancy is because SORT only counts strategic warheads and only those that are considered to be operationally deployed. Other warheads, whether strategic or non-strategic, are not affected by the treaty, which also fails to address reserve warheads.

No verification regime is associated with SORT, and when the START I Treaty expires in 2009 on-site inspections by US and Russian officials of ICBM silos, submarine facilities and bomber bases will cease. Much as during the cold war, satellite surveillance and human intelligence (spying) will again be the primary means by which the world's two largest nuclear weapon powers monitor each other's nuclear force developments.

Land-based ballistic missiles

The US ICBM force was reduced by 17 missiles in 2004 by the retirement programme for the Peacekeeper (MX) ICBM. Of an initial force of 50 missiles, 10 remained on alert at the beginning of 2005. The 400 W87 warheads from the 40 retired Peacekeeper missiles are being converted to replace W62 warheads on Minuteman ICBMs from financial year (FY) 2006. With a yield of 310 kt, the W87 has nearly twice the explosive power of the W62, and this will broaden the range of hardened targets that can be held at risk by the Minuteman missile force. The W62 warhead will be retired in 2009. During 2004, work continued on modernizing the guidance and propulsion systems of the Minuteman ICBM force.

Following the abandonment of the 1993 START II Treaty in 2002,[5] the USA plans to retain multiple warheads on some of its ICBMs: instead of the goal of 500 war-

[4] Norris, R. S. and Kristensen, H. M., 'What's behind Bush's nuclear cuts', *Arms Control Today*, Dec. 2004, pp. 6–12.

[5] The US–Russian Treaty on Further Reduction and Limitation of Strategic Offensive Arms was ratified by the Russian and US legislatures but did not enter into force. On 14 June 2002, in response to the taking effect on 13 June of the USA's withdrawal from the 1972 Treaty on the Limitation of Anti-Ballistic Missile Systems, Russia declared that it would no longer be bound by the START II Treaty.

heads on 500 missiles by 2007, as planned under START II, the US Department of Defense (DOD) is considering maintaining up to 800 warheads for the ICBM force.[6]

Three ICBMs were test launched in 2004: two Minuteman III ICBMs, each carrying three re-entry vehicles (RVs); and one Peacekeeper ICBM with eight RVs. A test launch was conducted even though the weapon system is being retired. The US Air Force has begun planning for a new ICBM to begin replacing the existing Minuteman III missiles from 2018. Notwithstanding the obligations undertaken by the USA under Article VI of the NPT to pursue nuclear disarmament, the Mission Need Statement for the new ICBM states that nuclear weapons will 'continue to play a unique and indispensable role in US security policy' and that a credible and effective land-based nuclear deterrent force 'beyond 2020' will 'prepare the US for an uncertain future by maintaining US qualitative superiority in nuclear war-fighting capabilities in the 2020–2040 time frame'.[7]

Ballistic missile submarines

In 2004 the US fleet of SSBNs was reduced to 14 boats with the offloading in October of strategic missiles from the USS *Michigan* and USS *Georgia* as part of a programme to convert four older submarines for cruise-missile and special-forces missions. In parallel with the conversion of these four SSBNs to non-nuclear missions, four Trident I (C-4) missile-equipped boats are being modernized to carry the newer, more powerful and more accurate Trident II (D-5) missile. Two have been converted so far (the USS *Alaska* and the USS *Nevada*) and two will be converted in 2005 and 2006 (USS *Henry M. Jackson* and USS *Alabama*, respectively).

The shifting of the emphasis of the US SSBN fleet continued in 2004 with the announcement by the US Navy (USN) in September that two more submarines were to move from Kings Bay, Georgia, to Bangor, Washington. Three SSBNs have changed homeport, in 2002 (USS *Pennsylvania* and USS *Kentucky*) and 2004 (USS *Nebraska*), and two more submarines (USS *Maine* and USS *Louisiana*) will follow in 2005, increasing the US Pacific SSBN fleet to nine submarines. This will temporarily leave only five SSBNs in the Atlantic, the lowest number since US ballistic missile-equipped submarines first deployed to sea in 1961.

The USN purchased five more Trident II (D-5) SLBMs from the FY 2005 budget, and production of the missile has been extended to the end of 2013. The development of a Life Extension modification of the D-5 missiles has begun in order to match the extended service life of the SSBN force until 2040. The USN has also begun planning for a new intermediate-range ballistic missile for future strategic submarines.

[6] Kristensen, H. M., 'To MIRV or not to MIRV', Nuclear Information Project, 2004, URL <http://www.nukestrat.com/us/afn/mirv.htm>; Herbert, A. J., 'The future missile force', *Air Force Magazine*, Oct. 2003, p. 67; and US Department of Defense, Public Affairs, Personal communication with H. Kristensen.

[7] US Department of the Air Force, HQ, Air Force Space Command/Data Records Management, 'Final Mission Need Statement (MNS), AFSPC 001-00: Land-Based Strategic Nuclear Deterrent', Acquisition Category One (ACAT I), 18 Jan. 2002, p. 2.

Table 12A.2. US nuclear forces, January 2005

Type	Designation	No. deployed	Year first deployed	Range (km)[a]	Warheads x yield	Warheads in stockpile
Strategic forces						
Bombers[b]						
B-52H	Stratofortress	93/56	1961	16 000	ALCM 5–150 kt	450[c]
					ACM 5–150 kt	400
B-2	Spirit	21/16	1994	11 000	Bombs	200[d]
Subtotal		*114/72*				*1 050*
ICBMs						
LGM-30G	Minuteman III					
	Mk-12	50	1970	13 000	3 x 170 kt	150
		150			1 x 170 kt[e]	150
	Mk-12A	300	1979	13 000	2–3 x 335 kt	750
LGM-118A	MX/Peacekeeper[f]	10	1986	11 000	10 x 310 kt	100
Subtotal		*510*				*1 150*
SSBNs/SLBMs[g]						
UGM-96A	Trident I (C-4)	48	1979	7 400	6 x 100 kt	288
UGM-133A	Trident II (D-5)	288				
	Mk-4	n.a.	1992	>7 400	6 x 100 kt	1 344
	Mk-5	n.a.	1990	>7 400	6 x 455 kt	384
Subtotal		*360*				*2 016*
Strategic subtotal						*4 216*
Non-strategic forces						
B61-3, -4, -10 bombs		n.a.	1979	n.a.	0.3–170 kt	580[h]
Tomahawk SLCM		320	1984	2 500	1 x 5–150 kt	100[i]
Non-strategic subtotal						*680*
Total						**4 896**[j]

[a] Aircraft range is for illustrative purposes only; actual mission range will vary according to flight profile and weapon loading.

[b] The first figure in the *No. deployed* column is the total number of B-52Hs and B-2s in the inventory, including those for training, test and reserve. The second figure is the primary mission inventory (PMI) aircraft, i.e., the number of operational aircraft assigned for nuclear and conventional wartime missions.

[c] Another 400 ALCMs are in reserve.

[d] Available for both the B-52H and the B-2A bomber.

[e] Each of the 150 Minuteman III missiles of the 90th Space Wing at F.E. Warren Air Force Base have been downloaded from 3 to 1 W62 warhead.

[f] From Oct. 2002 to Dec. 2004, 40 Peacekeeper ICBMs were dismantled; the last 10 will be withdrawn by the end of FY 2005.

[g] Of 8 initial Bangor-based Ohio Class SSBNs, 4 are under conversion to nuclear-powered guided-missile submarines (SSGNs) and 2 have completed Trident II (D-5) refit. Two Atlantic-based D-5 missile-equipped SSBNs were shifted to the Pacific in late 2002 and a third followed in Oct. 2004. The remaining 2 Trident I (C-4) missile-equipped SSBNs will be upgraded with the D-5 in FY 2005 and FY 2006, respectively. According to START I Treaty counting rules, C-4 missiles are counted as carrying no more than 6 warheads. Although D-5 missiles are counted as carrying 8 warheads each, the US Navy has begun downloading them to meet an interim force level by 2006 as part of the implementation of SORT.

[h] Approximately 480 of these are deployed in Europe.

[i] Another 200 W80-0s are in inactive storage. The TLAM/N is no longer deployed with the fleet but is stored on land.

[j] Another 315 warheads are spares, and just over 5100 warheads are kept in the reserve stockpile.

Sources: US Department of Defense, various budget reports; US Department of Energy, various budget reports; US Department of State, START I Treaty MOUs, 1990 through Jan. 2005; US Navy, Personal communication; US Department of Defense, various documents obtained under the Freedom of Information Act; 'NRDC Nuclear Notebook', *Bulletin of the Atomic Scientists*, various issues; US Naval Institute, *Proceedings*, various issues; and Authors' estimates.

Modernization of the W76 RV continues to add surface-burst capability and increased accuracy to the weapon. The modernization programme will significantly enhance the capability of the W76 and add to the types of targets that can be held at risk by the 100-kt warhead. The first delivery to the USN of the surface-burst W76 (designated W76-1/Mk4A) RV is scheduled for 2007, and some 800 warheads will be upgraded by the end of 2012.

Three SLBMs were flight tested in 2003 and two in 2004, one of which was launched at the Pacific Missile Range, the first Pacific SLBM launch in 12 years.

Long-range bombers

The size of the US bomber force remained unchanged in 2004, but the aircraft and their nuclear weapons continued to be upgraded. The US Air Force (USAF) awarded a contract to EMS Technologies in 2004 to develop an Extremely High Frequency satellite communications antenna for the B-2 bomber to ensure secure communication with the Milstar and future Advanced Extremely High Frequency satellites in nuclear missions. The USAF also began applying a new radar-absorbing coat to the B-2: the Alternate High-Frequency Material will improve the stealth of the aircraft and simplify maintenance. Modernization will be completed in 2011.

The USAF began preparations for a ground-based test facility for the Air-Launched Cruise Missile (ALCM) and Advanced Cruise Missile (ACM). Currently, the weapons must be test launched from airborne B-52 bombers, but the USAF plans to begin testing the missiles on the ground. The B-52 is the only carrier of the ALCM/ACM and can also carry gravity bombs.

Non-strategic nuclear weapons

As of January 2005, the USA retained approximately 680 active non-strategic nuclear warheads. These consisted of 580 B61 gravity bombs of three types and 100 W80-0 warheads for Tomahawk Land-Attack Cruise Missiles (TLAM/Ns). Another 1020 non-strategic warheads are in inactive storage. Despite the significant number of warheads, neither the 2001 NPR nor the 2002 SORT Treaty addresses non-strategic nuclear weapons.

The 580 operational B61 non-strategic nuclear bombs are earmarked for delivery by various US aircraft and aircraft assigned to NATO. Another 440 are in reserve. More than 400 of the 580 gravity bombs have been authorized by the president for deployment at eight airbases in six European NATO member states (Belgium, Germany, Italy, the Netherlands, Turkey and the UK) and constitute the only US nuclear weapons that are still forward-deployed (other than SSBNs). The aircraft of non-nuclear weapon state (NNWS) NATO members that are assigned nuclear strike missions with US weapons include Belgian, Dutch and Turkish F-16 aircraft and German and Italian Tornado bombers.[8]

Only 100 W80-0 warheads for the TLAM/N are active, but another 200 are in inactive storage. After deciding in 2003 to retain rather than retire the TLAM/N, the US Navy has begun efforts to extend the service life of the missile. The Department of Energy plans to extend the service life of the W80 warhead. TLAM/Ns can be deployed on select Los Angeles, Improved Los Angeles and Virginia Class attack submarines. The weapon is not deployed at sea under normal circumstances, but it can be redeployed in only 30 days after a decision to do so.

Nuclear warhead stockpile management and modernization

The US stockpile of active weapons includes intact warheads with all components that are either deployed on operational delivery systems or can be so deployed in a relatively short time. The inactive weapons includes warheads that are held in long-term storage as a reserve with their limited life components (tritium) removed. The 2001 NPR defined a new subcategory of active warheads, called the Responsive Force, which consists of intact warheads that have been removed from operational service but could relatively quickly be 'uploaded' back onto ballistic missiles and aircraft. The W87 warheads from dismantled Peacekeeper ICBMs and W76 warheads from non-strategic Trident submarines are held in the Responsive Force. As the decisions of the NPR are implemented over the next decade, there will be roughly three times as many warheads in non-operational categories as there are operationally deployed warheads.

In addition to the total of about 10 350 intact active and inactive warheads, the USA keeps about 5000 plutonium cores in storage at the Pantex Plant in Texas as a strategic reserve. Approximately the same number of canned assemblies (thermonuclear secondaries) is kept at the Oak Ridge Y-12 Plant in Tennessee. Another 7000 pits held at Pantex make up most of the 34 tons of weapon-grade plutonium previously declared in excess of military needs by the Administration of President Bill Clinton. All of these 12 000 pits come from retired warheads. A programme to repackage the 12 000 pits for long-term storage is currently under way at the Pantex facility, and small-scale pit production has resumed at Los Alamos National Laboratory.

In a surprise move in 2004, the US Congress cut funding for design development of a new nuclear-armed earth-penetrating weapon. The cut was a surprise because of the Bush Administration's recent successful effort to repeal a ban from the Clinton era on studying low-yield nuclear weapons. The Congress also cut funding for a new plutonium pit production facility.[9] The Bush Administration is seeking to restore part of the funding in its budget request for FYs 2006 and 2007.

[8] For further background to the history and status of US nuclear weapons in Europe see Kristensen, H. M., 'US nuclear weapons in Europe', Natural Resources Defense Council, Washington, DC, 2005, URL <http://www.nrdc.org/nuclear/default.asp>.

[9] See Wald, M., 'Nuclear weapons money is cut from spending bill', *New York Times* (Internet edn), 23 Nov. 2004, URL <http://www.nytimes.com/2004/11/23/politics/23nuke.html>; and chapter 12, section IX.

III. Russian nuclear forces

In February 2004 the Russian Ministry of Defence (MOD) conducted its largest strategic military exercise since 1982, called 'Bezopasnost 2004' (Security 2004). It involved all the elements of Russia's strategic forces and included test firings of sea- and land-based ballistic missiles and ALCMs, strategic bomber sorties, an early-warning satellite launch, and a test of the Moscow anti-ballistic missile (ABM) system.[10] It was marred by the highly publicized failures of two SLBM test launches. In the view of many analysts, one of the purposes of the exercise was to remind the world, especially the USA, that Russia retained a formidable nuclear arsenal and hence was a power to be reckoned with. Others speculated that the exercise was a political manoeuvre in anticipation of the Russian presidential election in March.

Following the exercise, President Vladimir Putin announced that Russia was developing a new nuclear missile system, which had no counterpart elsewhere in the world, that would be able to defeat any strategic missile defence system. Many observers believe that Putin may have been referring to a new hypersonic manoeuvrable RV for the Topol-M ICBM (see below) that is designed to evade missile interceptors.[11]

ICBMs

The ICBMs assigned to the Russian Strategic Rocket Forces (SRF) have traditionally made up the largest element of the Soviet/Russian strategic nuclear forces. The size of this force will gradually decline over the next 10–15 years, as older ICBMs are retired and replaced by a smaller number of fourth-generation missiles. The SRF currently consist of three missile armies: the 27th Guards Missile Army (headquarters in Vladimir), the 31st Missile Army (Orenburg) and the 33rd Guards Missile Army (Omsk). As of December 2004 the armies included 15 missile divisions with operational missiles. According to the long-term plan for Russia's strategic forces, made public in November–December 2004, the number of missile divisions will be reduced to 10–12. The divisions in Kartaly (SS-18 missiles) and Kostroma (SS-24 missiles) are scheduled to be disbanded in 2005.[12]

The SS-27 (RS-12M2, Topol-M) remains the only ICBM currently in production in Russia. On 16 December 2004 the fourth regiment of silo-based Topol-Ms became operational. The regiment is part of the missile division in Tatishchevo, Saratov oblast, which now has a total of 40 Topol-M missiles.

According to Russian press reports, serial production of the Topol-M had to be stopped twice in 2004 because of delays in funding from the MOD. The director-general of the Moscow Institute for Thermal Technology (MITT), which developed the missile, warned in October that the delays threatened to disrupt deployment plans

[10] 'Russian Defense Ministry to conduct first big military exercise in 25 years', *Pravda* (Internet edn), 4 Feb. 2004, URL <http://english.pravda.ru/main/18/88/351/11962_military.html>.

[11] Ischenko, S., 'Putin prepared a surprise: a new strategic weapon has been created in Russia', *Trud*, 20 Feb. 2004, in 'Commentary on Putin's remark about new weapon systems', Foreign Broadcast Information Service, *Daily Report–Central Eurasia (FBIS-SOV)*, FBIS-SOV-2004-0220, 25 Feb. 2004.

[12] 'Strategic Rocket Forces commander outlines plans for the future', Russian Nuclear Forces Project, 12 Dec. 2004, URL <http://russianforces.org/eng/news/archive/000145.shtml>.

Table 12A.3. Russian nuclear forces, January 2005

Type	NATO designation	No. deployed	Year first deployed	Range (km)[a]	Warheads x yield	Warheads in stockpile
Strategic offensive forces						
Bombers						
Tu-95MS6	Bear-H6	32	1984	6 500–10 500	6 x AS-15A ALCMs, bombs	192
Tu-95MS16	Bear-H16	32	1984	6 500–10 500	16 x AS-15A ALCMs, bombs	512
Tu-160	Blackjack	14	1987	10 500–13 200	12 x AS-15B ALCMs or AS-16 SRAMs, bombs	168
Subtotal		*78*				*872*
ICBMs[b]						
SS-18	Satan	110	1979	11 000–15 000	10 x 500–750 kt	1 100
SS-19	Stiletto	140	1980	10 000	6 x 500–750 kt	840
SS-24 M1	Scalpel	15	1987	10 000	10 x 550 kt	150
SS-25	Sickle	306	1985	10 500	1 x 550 kt	306
SS-27	Topol-M	40	1997	10 500	1 x 550 kt	40
Subtotal		*611*				*2 436*
SLBMs[b]						
SS-N-18 M1	Stingray	96	1978	6 500	3 x 200 kt (MIRV)	288
SS-N-23	Skiff	96	1986	9 000	4 x 100 kt (MIRV)	384
Subtotal		*192*				*672*
Total strategic offensive forces						**3 980**
Strategic defensive forces						
ABMs						
Gorgon/Gazelle		100				100
Grumble[c]		1 100				1 100
Non-strategic forces						
Land-based non-strategic						
Bombers and fighters						
Tu-22M Backfire		105			AS-4 ASM,	
Su-24 Fencer		280			AS-16 SRAM, bombs	
Subtotal		*385*				*1 540*[c]
Naval non-strategic						
Attack aircraft						
Tu-22M Backfire		45			AS-4 ASM, bombs	
Su-24 Fencer		50				
Subtotal		*95*				*190*[d]
SLCMs						
SS-N-9, SS-N-12, SS-N-19, SS-N-21, SS-N-22						240
ASW weapons						
SS-N-15, SS-N-16, torpedoes		n.a.				210
Total defensive and non-strategic						**3 380**
Total						**7 360**

[a] Aircraft range is for illustrative purposes only; actual mission range will vary according to flight profile and weapon loading.

[b] US designations are used in this column for Russian ICBMs and SLBMs.

[c] The SA-10 Grumble is not a dedicated ABM system but may have some capability against some ballistic missiles.

[d] Figure includes warheads for all the land-based and naval aircraft.

Sources: US Department of State, START I Treaty Memoranda of Understanding (MOU), 1990 through Jan. 2005; Podvig, P. L. (ed.), *Russian Strategic Nuclear Forces* (MIT Press: Cambridge, Mass., 2001); US Central Intelligence Agency, National Intelligence Council, 'Foreign missile developments and the ballistic missile threat through 2015' (unclassified summary), Dec. 2001, URL <http://www.cia.gov/nic/pubs/other_products/Unclassified ballisticmissilefinal.pdf>; US Department of Defense, *Proliferation: Threat and Response,* Jan. 2001; US Naval Institute, *Proceedings*, various issues; 'NRDC Nuclear Notebook', *Bulletin of the Atomic Scientists*, various issues; and Authors' estimates.

for the Topol-M and jeopardized the retention of critical skills and manufacturing capabilities at the Votkinsk Machine-Building Plant, where the missiles are built.[13] Under the 2005 State Defence Order, four silo-based Topol-M missiles will be procured, compared to six in 2004.[14] On 24 December 2004 a road-mobile version of the Topol-M was successfully launched from the Plesetsk test site. This was the fourth and final test of the road-mobile Topol-M system prior to its scheduled entry into service beginning in 2006. In 2005 three mobile Topol-Ms will be procured.[15]

On 22 December 2004 Russia successfully test launched an SS-18 Satan (R-36M2 or RS-20V Voevoda) missile as part of its programme to extend the service lives of the Soviet-era ICBMs. The missile, which had been on combat alert for 16 years, was launched from the Dombarovsky missile base in the Orenburg region of Russia; the warhead reached its training target at the Kura test range in Kamchatka. All the previous launches of the SS-18 after the collapse of the Soviet Union in 1991—as well as launches of the Dnepr space launch vehicle (a converted SS-18 missile)—were conducted at the Russian-leased Baikonur cosmodrome in Kazakhstan. Older SS-18 missiles will be retired under the new defence plan, but the service life of about 50 newer SS-18s may be extended for another 10–15 years. Russia was supposed to scrap all of its SS-18 heavy missiles under the now abandoned START II Treaty.[16]

SLBMs

In 2004 the size of the Russian SLBM force changed significantly owing to the withdrawal from operational service of the SS-N-20, which was carried on the Typhoon Class SSBN. This leaves only two types of SLBM in service compared to the six SLBM types in service in the late 1980s. Three submarines of the new Borey Class (Project 955) are under construction at the Severnoye Mashinostroitelnoye Predpriyatiye (Sevmash) shipyard in Severodvinsk in northern Russia. The first of the new SSBNs, *Yuri Dolgoruky*, was laid down in November 1996 and is scheduled to be delivered in 2005; its completion has been delayed by funding problems and a

[13] Litovkin, D., 'Strategic Missile Troops commander Nikolay Solovtsov: "we will have something to show withing next few years"', *Izvestiya* (Moscow), 14 Dec. 2004, p. 6, in FBIS-SOV-2004-1214, 15 Dec. 2004.

[14] Barabanov, M., 'Whole Russian army', *Kommersant Vlast* (in Russian), no. 7 (21 Feb. 2005), p. 69, URL <http://www.kommersant.ru/k-vlast/get_page.asp?_id=2005769-22.htm&show=print>.

[15] Plugatarev, I., '"Topol-M" replaces "Molodets" and "Voevoda"', *Nezavisimoe Voennoe Obozrenie* (in Russian), 28 Jan. 2005, URL <http://nvo.ng.ru/printed/forces/2005-01-28/1_topol.html>.

[16] See note 5.

decision to arm it with a new SLBM. It will be followed in 2008 by a second submarine, *Alexander Nevskiy*, which was laid down in March 2004, and by a third in 2010. Three more submarines are planned for construction after 2010.[17]

In addition to these submarines, the Russian Government has decided to keep six Delta IV Class (Project 667 BDRM Delphin) submarines in service. After service-life extension overhauls and refitting with newly produced SS-N-23 (R-29RM) missiles, the Delta IV submarines may be kept in service until 2015–20. Russia also maintains six Delta III Class (Project 667 BDR Kalmar) submarines in service.

The Borey Class SSBNs will each carry 12 SS-NX-30 (Bulava) SLBMs, which are being developed by the MITT. The Bulava programme is based on MITT's land-based Topol-M ICBM. It is a replacement for the SS-NX-28 (D-19M Bark) SLBM programme, which had been cancelled because of technical problems and rising costs. According to Russian media reports, the Bulava is also experiencing design and engineering problems, which means that it may not be able to carry the originally planned payload of 10 warheads over a distance of 8000 km. On 23 September 2004 an unpowered test launch of a Bulava was carried out from the *Dmitry Donskoy* modified Typhoon Class submarine in the White Sea. The missile is expected to begin flight tests in 2005 and is scheduled to enter into service after 2006.

The year 2004 began inauspiciously for the Russian Navy's SSBN force. On 17 February, during the 'Security 2004' exercises, the *Novomosovsk* Delta 4 Class submarine had to abort the launches of two SS-N-23 SLBMs for technical reasons. The following day, an SS-N-23 (R-29M or RSM-54) missile launched by its sister ship, *Kareliya,* reportedly had to be destroyed in flight after it departed from its planned flight trajectory. The Russian Navy subsequently conducted five successful test launches of SLBMs from submarines in the Barents Sea: on 17 March two SS-N-23s were launched from the *Novomosovsk*; on 29 June an SS-N-23 was launched from the Delta IV Class submarine *Yekaterinburg*; and on 8 September an SS-N-18 (R-29R) and an SS-N-23 were launched from the *Borisoglebsk* and *Yekaterinburg*, respectively, with each missile carrying three dummy warheads. On 2 November an SS-N-18 missile was launched in the Sea of Okhotsk by the *Svyatoy Georgiy Pobedonosets*, one of the four Delta III submarines of the Pacific Fleet.

Aircraft

Russia resumed low-rate production of the Tu-160 Blackjack long-range bomber in 2004. Two aircraft are planned for delivery in 2005, one equipped to carry cruise missiles and the other gravity bombs.[18] Russia may begin to deploy a nuclear-armed version of a new long-range ALCM, known as the Kh-102, for its Blackjack and Tu-95 Bear bombers by the end of 2005.

[17] Plugatarev (note 14).

[18] Litovkin, D., 'Air Force will be flying for twice as long', *Izvestiya* (in Russian), 18 Jan. 2005, p. 6.

Table 12A.4. British nuclear forces, January 2005

Type	Designation	No. deployed	Year first deployed	Range (km)	Warheads x yield	Warheads in stockpile
SLBMs						
D-5	Trident II (D-5)	48	1994	>7 400	1–3 x 100 kt	185

Sources: British Ministry of Defence (MOD), press releases and the MOD Internet site, URL <http://www.mod.uk/issues/sdr/index.htm>; MOD, *Strategic Defence Review* (MOD: London, July 1998); British House of Commons, *Parliamentary Debates (Hansard)*; Ormond, D., 'Nuclear deterrence in a changing world: the view from a UK perspective', *RUSI Journal*, June 1996, pp. 15–22; Norris, R. S. *et al., Nuclear Weapons Databook*, vol. 5, *British, French, and Chinese Nuclear Weapons* (Westview: Boulder, Colo., 1994), p. 9; 'NRDC Nuclear Notebook', *Bulletin of the Atomic Scientists*, various issues; and Authors' estimate.

IV. British nuclear forces

The UK maintains an arsenal of about 185 warheads for use by a fleet of four Vanguard Class Trident SSBNs, consisting of 160 operational warheads and an additional 15 per cent of that number for spares. At any given time one British SSBN will be on patrol, carrying up to 48 warheads on 16 US-produced Trident II (D-5) SLBMs. The second and third SSBNs can be put to sea fairly rapidly, with similar loadings, while the fourth might take longer because of its cycle of overhaul and maintenance. With the end of the cold war, the SSBN on patrol is maintained at a level of reduced readiness with a 'notice to fire' measured in days, and its missiles are de-targeted. There are reports that some patrol coordination takes place between the UK and France.

In January 2005 HMS *Victorious* arrived at the Devonport Naval Base for a major refit, including a refuelling of its nuclear reactor. This leaves three SSBNs in the fleet—*Vanguard, Vigilant* and *Vengeance*—for operational deployment. HMS *Vanguard* emerged from Devonport in December 2004, after undergoing a three-year overhaul.

The 2003 Defence White Paper stated that the UK's nuclear deterrent capability is 'likely to remain a necessary element of our security' and anounced plans to consider in the next parliament whether to replace the current deterrent force, which is based on the Trident SSBN.[19] While the nominal retirement date of the four Vanguard Class submarines is still almost two decades away, the government must make a decision by 2006 on whether to upgrade the ageing warheads or scrap the weapons entirely. Another option would be to adapt the Vanguard Class submarines to launch conventionally armed Tomahawk cruise missiles or use them for special forces operations.

The UK is the only NWS that has publicly assigned its SSBNs 'sub-strategic missions'. According to a former British MOD official, 'A sub-strategic strike would be the limited and highly selective use of nuclear weapons in a manner that fell demonstrably short of a strategic strike, but with a sufficient level of violence to convince an aggressor who had already miscalculated our resolve and attacked us that he should halt his aggression and withdraw or face the prospect of a devastating strategic

[19] British Ministry of Defence, *Delivering Security in a Changing World*, Defence White Paper, Cm 6041-I (Stationery Office: London, Dec. 2003), p. 9, URL <http://www.mod.uk/linked_files/publications/whitepaper2003/volume1.pdf>.

strike'.[20] Much like the doctrines of Russia and the USA, the UK's nuclear doctrine has taken on a new role in deterring, or responding to, attacks by NNWSs using chemical or biological weapons. In 2002, an addendum to the 1998 Strategic Defence Review extended the role of nuclear weapons to include deterring 'leaders of states of concern and terrorist organizations'.[21]

V. French nuclear forces

France maintains an operational arsenal of an estimated 348 nuclear warheads for delivery by strategic submarines, carrier-based strike aircraft and land-based aircraft. France continues to modernize its nuclear forces, including construction of the fourth and final Triomphant Class SSBNs, the M51 SLBM with a new nuclear warhead, the ASMP-A (Air-Sol Moyenne Portée) cruise missile and the Rafale nuclear-capable strike aircraft. According to French press reports, the French MOD allocated €3 billion ($3.75 billion) in the 2004 equipment budget for nuclear systems, a figure which accounts for less than 10 per cent of France's total defence expenditure, compared with 17 per cent in 1990.

Ballistic missiles

The backbone of France's nuclear deterrent force is the Force Océanique Stratégique, which consists of a fleet of four SSBNs of two classes: three of the new Triomphant Class SSBNs; and one L'Inflexible (formerly Redoubtable Class) SSBN. Three of these submarines are maintained in the operational cycle, with one or two normally 'on station' in designated patrol areas at any given time, compared with three in the early 1990s.

On 19 November 2004 the naval procurement directorate of the French armament procurement agency Délégation Générale pour l'Armement (DGA) took delivery of *Le Vigilant* SSBN from the prime contractor, DCN Warships & Systems. The vessel is the third of a planned class of four (originally six) nuclear-powered Sous-marins Nucléaires Lanceurs d'Engins–Nouvelle Génération (SNLE–NG) ballistic missile submarines, also called the Triomphant Class after the lead boat, which was launched in 1997. The second boat, *Le Téméraire*, entered service in December 1999. The fourth and final vessel of the class, *Le Terrible*, is scheduled to enter service in 2010. The delivery of the *Le Vigilant* allowed the French Navy to retire *L'Indomptable*, one of the two remaining L'Inflexible Class SSBNs.

The French Navy's four SSBNs are each armed with 16 Aérospatiale M45 missiles. The missiles can carry up to six TN-75 warheads, each with an estimated yield of 100 kt, as well as penetration aids. The accuracy of the TN-75 warhead is not publicly known but has been estimated at a circular error probable (CEP) of 350 metres. From 2010, beginning with the *Le Terrible*, the first three Triomphant Class SSBNs will be retrofitted with the M51.1/TN-75 SLBM, which is currently

[20] Ormond, D., 'Nuclear deterrence in a changing world: the view from a UK perspective', *RUSI Journal*, June 1996, pp. 15–22.

[21] British Ministry of Defence, *The Strategic Defence Review: A New Chapter*, CM 5566, vol. 1 (Stationery Office: London, July 2002), p. 12, URL <http://www.mod.uk/linked_files/SDR_New_Chapter.pdf>.

Table 12A.5. French nuclear forces, January 2005

Type	No. deployed	Year first deployed	Range (km)[a]	Warheads x yield	Warheads in stockpile
Land-based aircraft					
Mirage 2000N	60	1988	2 750	1 x 300 kt ASMP	50
Carrier-based aircraft					
Super Étendard	24	1978	650	1 x 300 kt ASMP	10
SLBMs [b]					
M45	64	1996	6 000[c]	6 x 100 kt	288
Total					**348**

[a] Range for aircraft assumes combat radius, without in-flight refuelling.

[b] The last M4-equipped SSBN, *L'Indomptable*, was replaced by *Le Vigilant* in Nov. 2004. The fourth and final Triomphant Class SSBN, *Le Terrible*, will replace *L'Inflexible* in 2010 with the M51 SLBM.

[c] The range of M45 is listed as only 4000 km in a 2001 report from the National Defence Commission of the National Assembly.

Sources: National Assembly, 'Bill of Law for the 2003–2008 Military Programme', 2002; French Ministry of Defence, 'Nuclear disarmament and non-proliferation', *Arms Control, Disarmament and Non-Proliferation: French Policy* (La Documentation française: Paris, 2000), chapter 3, pp. 36–56; Norris, R. S. *et al.*, *Nuclear Weapons Databook,* vol. 5, *British, French, and Chinese Nuclear Weapons* (Westview: Boulder, Colo., 1994), p. 10; National Assembly, 'Au Nom de la Commission de la Défense Nationale et des Forces Armées, sur le projet de loi de finances pour 2002 (no. 3262), Tome II, Défense, Dissuasion nucléaire, M. Rene Galy-Dejean (Député)', 11 Oct. 2001, URL <http://www.assemblee-nationale.fr/budget/plf2002/a3323-02.asp>; *Air Actualités*, various issues; *Aviation Week & Space Technology*, various issues; 'NRDC Nuclear Notebook', *Bulletin of the Atomic Scientists*, various issues; and Authors' estimates.

entering the production phase. In 2004 EADS Space Transport signed a contract with the DGA, worth more than €3 billion ($3.75 billion), for series production of the M51 over 10 years. The new missile will have a payload of six warheads and a maximum range of 8000 km, which will permit French SSBNs to significantly expand their patrol zones. From 2015 the French Navy plans to take delivery of the improved M51.2 missile, armed with the new Tête Nucléaire Océanique (TNO) warhead.

Strike aircraft

The air component of the French nuclear force consist of two types of aircraft: approximately 60 Mirage 2000Ns, which equip the three French Air Force squadrons currently with nuclear strike roles; and about 24 Super Étendards deployed on the aircraft carrier *Charles de Gaulle*. Both types of aircraft carry the ASMP cruise missile. The ASMP has been equipped with the 300-kt TN81 warhead since 1987 and has a range, depending on the launch altitude, of 80–250 km. It is estimated that France has about 60 operational ASMPs, but additional missiles may be in inactive storage.

A new nuclear-capable cruise missile, designated the ASMP-A, is under development for deployment with the French Air Force and Navy to replace the ASMP beginning in 2007. The ASMP-A will carry the new Tête Nucléare Aéroportée warhead and has a high level of accuracy—reportedly with a CEP of less than 10 metres at a range of 300–400 km. The ASMP-A was specially designed for the Mirage 2000N and hence will be fitted to this aircraft first, which will be redesignated the Mirage 2000N K3, in 2007. Beginning in 2008, the missile will also be integrated with Rafale air force and navy aircraft. Under current planning, 50 Mirage 2000s, 50 air force Rafales and an unspecified number of navy Rafales will be modified to carry the ASMP-A missile.

VI. Chinese nuclear forces

China is estimated to maintain an arsenal of more than 400 nuclear weapons for delivery by aircraft, land-based ballistic missiles, SLBMs and possibly also non-strategic systems, including artillery. The overall size of the Chinese arsenal appears to have remained largely unchanged since the early 1980s.

According to the latest in a series of US DOD reports on Chinese military developments, China is continuing to gradually modernize and increase its force of nuclear-capable ballistic missiles. The purpose of this modernization programme is to 'improve [China's] nuclear deterrence by increasing the number of warheads that can target the United States and augmenting the nuclear force's operational capabilities for contingencies in East Asia'.[22] The DOD report stated that China could have 30 ICBMs capable of reaching the USA by 2005, and 60 by 2010.

There remains considerable uncertainty about the scope and pace of China's long-term force modernization goals. China is known to have been developing three missiles since the 1980s: the road-mobile DF-31 (Dong Feng, or East Wind) ICBM; a longer-range version of the DF-31, called the DF-31A (or DF-41); and the JL-2 (Julang, or Great Wave) SLBM, the sea-based variant of the DF-31 ICBM. There is widespread speculation that China will deploy multiple re-entry vehicle (MRV) payloads, including a MIRV system, on some or all of these new missiles in order to counter a US missile defence system.[23] According to unconfirmed press reports, in 2002 China successfully conducted its first test of a missile—the medium-range DF-21—carrying multiple dummy warheads. However, US intelligence believes that the size and throw-weight of the DF-5A, an existing ICBM, make it the most likely Chinese missile to be given an MRV or a MIRV capability if China chooses to deploy such a capability.

China continues to develop the DF-31 ICBM: its status is unclear, but some sources indicate that China has begun to operationally deploy the DF-31.[24] There were reports in the Hong Kong press in 2004 that China is developing a rail-mobile version of the DF-31. The system may use technology developed in the Soviet Union for its rail-mobile SS-24 ICBM, which entered service in 1987: Ukraine, where the SS-24 was manufactured, has been identified as the source of the technology.[25]

[22] US Department of Defense, Report to Congress Pursuant to the FY 2000 National Defense Authorization Act, 'Annual Report on the Military Power of the People's Republic of China', 28 May 2004, URL <http://www.dod.gov/pubs/d20040528PRC.pdf>.

[23] An MRV system releases 2 or more RVs along the missile's linear flight path to a single target, which land in a relatively confined area at about the same time. The more sophisticated and flexible MIRV system can manoeuvre multiple RVs to several different release points to provide targeting flexibility against several independent targets over a much wider area and longer period of time.

[24] International Institute for Strategic Studies (IISS), *The Military Balance 2004–2005* (Oxford University Press: Oxford, 2004), p. 170.

[25] 'China develops rail-mobile ICBM', *Jane's Missiles & Rockets*, vol. 9, no. 1 (Jan. 2005) p. 6.

Table 12A.6. Chinese nuclear forces, January 2005

Type	NATO designation	No. deployed	Year first deployed	Range (km)[a]	Warheads x yield	Warheads in stockpile
Aircraft[b]						
H-6	B-6	120	1965	3 100	1–3 bombs	120
Q-5	A-5	30	1970	400	1 x bomb	30
Land-based missiles						
DF-3A	CSS-2	40	1971	2 800	1 x 3.3 Mt	40
DF-4	CSS-3	12	1980	5 500	1 x 3.3 Mt	12
DF-5A	CSS-4	20	1981	13 000	1 x 4–5 Mt	20
DF-21A	CSS-5	48	1985–86	1 800	1 x 200–300 kt	48
DF-31	CSS-X-10	n.a.	2005–2009?	8 000	1 x ?	0
SLBMs						
Julang I	CSS-N-3	12	1986	1 700	1 x 200–300 kt	12
Strategic weapons						*282*
Non-strategic weapons[c]						
Artillery/ADMs, Short-range missiles					Low kt	~120
Total						**~400**

[a] Range for aircraft indicates combat radius, without in-flight refuelling.

[b] All figures for bomber aircraft are for nuclear-configured versions only. Hundreds of aircraft are also deployed in non-nuclear versions. The status of China's air-delivered nuclear capability is uncertain.

[c] Information on Chinese non-strategic nuclear weapons is limited and contradictory. There is no confirmation of their existence from official Chinese sources.

Sources: US Department of Defense (DOD), Report to Congress Pursuant to the FY 2000 National Defense Authorization Act, 'Annual Report on the Military Power of the People's Republic of China', 28 July 2003; US National Intelligence Council, 'Foreign missile developments and the ballistic missile threat through 2015' (unclassified summary), Dec. 2001, URL <http:// www.cia.gov/nic/pubs/other_products/Unclassifiedballisticmissilefinal. pdf>; US DOD, Office of the Secretary of Defense, 'Proliferation: threat and response', Washington, DC, Jan. 2001, URL <http://www.defenselink.mil/pubs/ptr20010110.pdf>; US Central Intelligence Agency, various documents; US DOD, National Air and Space Intelligence Center (NAIC), *Ballistic and Cruise Missile Threat* (NAIC: Wright-Patterson Air Force Base, Ohio, Aug. 2003, revised); Norris, R. S. *et al., Nuclear Weapons Databook,* vol. 5, *British, French, and Chinese Nuclear Weapons* (Westview: Boulder, Colo., 1994); 'NRDC Nuclear Notebook', *Bulletin of the Atomic Scientists*, various issues; and Authors' estimates.

China has had great difficulty in developing a sea-based nuclear deterrent. The single Type 092 (Xia Class) SSBN, armed with the JL-1 SLBM, is not believed to have achieved full operational capability. According to a US press report, in July 2004 China launched its first Type 094 nuclear-powered ballistic missile submarine that had been under development for more than decade.[26] The submarine is in the early stages of being outfitted at the Huludao shipyard, located about 400 km northwest of Beijing, and is believed to be based on Russian nuclear submarine technology. The Type 094 is expected to be significantly quieter than the Type 092 and will have enhanced sensors and a more reliable propulsion system.

[26] Gertz, B., 'China tests ballistic missile submarine', *Washington Times* (Internet edn), 3 Dec. 2004, URL <http://www.washingtontimes.com/functions/print.php?StoryID=20041202-115302-2338r>.

The new submarine is designed to carry 16 JL-2 SLBMs. Some reports suggest that it might be loaded with multiple warheads. Most reports agree that the JL-2 will have a range of about 7500–8000 km. This means that it will have a true intercontinental capability and be able to strike targets throughout the United States from the relative safety of launch points near Chinese waters. The first at-sea test of the JL-2, an unpowered 'pop-up' test, was conducted from a Golf Class trials submarine in January 2001. China reportedly conducted tests of the JL-2 in 2002 and 2003. However, a test that took place in the summer of 2004 was reportedly a failure and may have delayed the development programme. According to the US DOD, the missile is not expected to enter service until the end of the decade.

VII. Indian nuclear forces

It is difficult to estimate the size and composition of India's nuclear arsenal. Published estimates vary widely, ranging from several dozen up to 150 weapons. The cautious estimate presented here is that India's nuclear stockpile contains 30–40 weapons. Some of these weapons may be stored in unassembled form, with the plutonium core kept separately from the non-nuclear ignition components, in accordance with India's no-first-use declaratory policy.

India is widely believed to be working to expand its nuclear weapon stockpile. There have been no official statements specifying the size of the stockpile required for the 'credible minimum deterrence' posture called for in India's nuclear doctrine.

Estimating the inventory

There is considerable uncertainty in published estimates of the total amount of weapon-grade plutonium that India has produced and, hence, in estimates of the number of nuclear weapons that it could have built.[27] A number of factors contribute to the uncertainty in estimating India's inventory of fissile material. First, there are different assessments of the lifetime operating capacity of the CIRUS and Dhruva plutonium production reactors (i.e., of their reliability and efficiency). According to the World Nuclear Association, in the 1990s India's nuclear power reactors had some of the world's lowest operating capacity factors.[28] Second, it is unclear whether India has used all of its available weapon-grade plutonium to fabricate nuclear weapons, as some analysts have assumed. Finally, there are different views on how to take into account the losses and draw-downs of nuclear material that occur during production, processing and testing.

There is also a continuing debate about whether one of the nuclear explosive tests carried out by India in May 1998 used non-weapon-grade plutonium (either in the form of reactor-grade plutonium or a mix of isotopes closer to weapon-grade plu-

[27] One widely cited report estimated that, at the end of 1999, India had an inventory of 240–395 kg of weapon-grade plutonium. This would have been sufficient to manufacture 45–95 nuclear weapons, assuming that each weapon would require 4.5 kg of plutonium. Albright, D., 'India's and Pakistan's fissile material and nuclear weapons inventories, end of 1999', Background Paper, Institute for Science and International Security, 11 Oct. 2000, URL <http://www.isis-online.org/publications/southasia/stocks1000.html>.

[28] World Nuclear Association, 'India and Pakistan', Information and Issues Brief, Nov. 2002, URL <http://www.world-nuclear.org/info/inf53.htm>.

Table 12A.7. Indian nuclear forces, January 2005

Type	Range (km)[a]	Payload (kg)	Status
Ballistic missiles			
Prithvi I (P-I)	150	800	Entered into army service in 1994; may have a nuclear delivery role
Agni I	700	1 000	Missile is 'in process of induction'; third test flight conducted on 4 July 2004
Agni II	>2 000[b]	1 000	Missile is 'in process of induction'; third test flight conducted on 29 Aug. 2004
Aircraft[c]			
Mirage 2000H Vajra	1 850	6 300	Aircraft reportedly has been certified for delivery of nuclear gravity bomb
Jaguar IS Shamsher	1 400	4 760	Some of the 4 squadrons in service may have a nuclear delivery role

[a] Missile payloads may have to be reduced in order to achieve maximum range. Aircraft range is for illustrative purposes only; actual mission range will vary according to flight profile and weapon loading.

[b] The range of the 29 Oct. 2004 test was to 1200 km. An upgraded version currently under development may have a range of 3500 km, possibly with a reduced payload.

[c] Other aircraft in the Indian Air Force's inventory which are potentially suitable for a nuclear role are the MiG-27 and the Su-30MKI.

Sources: Indian Ministry of Defence, annual reports and press releases; Vivek Raghuvanshi, 'India grounds Jaguars; BAE assists review', *Defense News*, 14 June 2004, p. 28 and various other articles; Bharat Rakshak, Consortium of Indian military Internet sites, URL <http://www.bharat-rakshak.com>; Lennox, D. (ed.), *Jane's Strategic Weapon Systems* (Jane's Information Group, Ltd: Coulsdon, 2004); US Department of Defense, National Air and Space Intelligence Center (NAIC), *Ballistic and Cruise Missile Threat* (NAIC: Wright-Patterson Air Force Base, Ohio, Aug. 2003, revised); US Central Intelligence Agency, *Unclassified Report to Congress on the Acquisition of Technology Relating to Weapons of Mass Destruction and Advanced Conventional Munitions*, 1 January through 30 June 2002', Apr. 2003, URL <http://www.cia.gov/cia/publications/bian/bian_apr_2003.htm>; US National Intelligence Council, 'Foreign missile developments and the ballistic missile threat through 2015' (unclassified summary), Dec. 2001, URL <http://www.cia.gov/nic/pubs/other_products/Unclassifiedballisticmissilefinal.pdf>; and Authors' estimates.

tonium). If the test gave confidence that this material could be used for weapons, then India may see the large holdings of plutonium associated with its civilian unsafeguarded power reactors as being a potential part of its military nuclear programme.

India also has a uranium enrichment programme and operates two gas centrifuge facilities: a pilot-scale plant at the Bhabha Atomic Research Centre complex and a larger plant that has reportedly been operating since 1990 at Rattehalli, Karnataka.[29] The primary purpose of the latter facility appears to be to produce highly enriched uranium (HEU) for an indigenous nuclear-powered submarine. HEU can also be fabricated for use in nuclear weapons or as the fission trigger (or 'primary') to aid in initiating a fusion reaction in thermonuclear weapons.

[29] Ramana, M., 'An estimate of India's uranium enrichment capacity', *Science and Global Security*, no. 1–2 (Jan.–Aug. 2004), pp. 115–24.

Indian officials claim that the country has developed both fusion (thermonuclear) and fission nuclear weapons. Many Western experts have questioned whether India has in fact achieved a thermonuclear capability. They point to seismic data which suggest that India's test of a 'thermonuclear device' in May 1998 had a significantly smaller yield than was claimed and probably was not successful.[30] However, the tests may have provided India with the capability to produce 'boosted' fission nuclear weapons.

Strike aircraft

At present, aircraft constitute the core of India's nuclear strike capabilities. The Indian Air Force has reportedly certified the Mirage 2000H for the delivery of nuclear gravity bombs. It is widely speculated that that some of the four squadrons of Jaguar IS fighter-bombers may have a nuclear delivery role. Other aircraft in the Indian Air Force's inventory which are potentially suitable for a nuclear role are the MiG-27 and the Su-30MKI.

Ballistic missiles

India has extensive, largely indigenous development and production infrastructures for both short- and medium-range ballistic missiles. Several missiles are believed to have a nuclear role.

The Prithvi ('Earth') was India's sole ballistic missile for many years before the induction into service of the Agni missile. The Prithvi I is a single-stage, road-mobile ballistic missile capable of delivering an 800-kg warhead to a maximum range of 150 km. Reports suggest that an improved liquid propellant is being developed for the missile to improve its range, and a solid propellant engine is being researched. The missile was first test flown in 1988 and entered into service with the Indian Army in 1994. On 23 January 2004 India announced that it had successfully conducted the twenty-third test launch of the Prithvi I at the Integrated Test Range on Wheeler's Island, in the Bay of Bengal, off the coast of the eastern state of Orissa.

An undisclosed number of Prithvi I missiles have been modified to deliver sub-kiloton nuclear warheads. However, Indian defence sources have indicated that the family of longer-range Agni ballistic missiles has largely taken over the Prithvi's nuclear role.[31]

There are two other versions of the Prithvi missile. Unlike the Prithvi I, these do not have a nuclear role. The Prithvi II, which was developed for the Indian Air Force, has an extended range of 250 km and carries a reduced payload (500–700 kg). It was most recently flight tested on 19 March 2004. A naval version of the Prithvi II, called the Dhanush ('Bow') system, was test fired successfully from a ship, INS *Subhadra*, off the coast of Orissa on 7 November 2004.[32]

[30] 'India has fusion, fission bombs: Abdul Kalam', *The Hindu* (Internet edn), 13 Nov. 2001, URL <http://www.hinduonnet.com/thehindu/2001/11/13/stories/02130001.htm>.

[31] 'Pithvi SRBM', Bharat Rakshak: consortium of Indian military websites, updated 8 Dec. 2004, URL <http://www.bharat-rakshak.com/MISSILES/Prithvi.html>.

[32] Indian Ministry of Defence, 'Dhanush successfully test fired', Press release, New Delhi, 8 Nov. 2004, URL <http://mod.nic.in/pressreleases/content.asp?id=853>; and Indian Ministry of Defence, 'Test of Dhanush', Press release, New Delhi, 8 Dec. 2004, URL <http://mod.nic.in/pressreleases/content.asp?id=882>.

The Prithvi III is a two-stage solid fuel missile which can deliver a 1000-kg payload to a range of 300 km at the Integrated Test Range at Wheeler's Island.[33] A modified naval version, known as the Sagarika, is in development and is intended to be launched from a submerged submarine.[34] It was flight tested for the first time on 27 October 2004, when a missile was launched from a specially constructed underwater platform and canister. It flew 230 km before landing in the Bay of Bengal.[35]

There is considerable confusion in the media and among independent experts about the Agni I missile, which is sometimes reported to exist in a medium-range version and sometimes in a shorter-range version. The original Agni missile was a technology demonstrator that was test flown several times between 1989 and 1994 but was never operationally deployed. The current missile, which has been referred to as the 'Agni Short Range' or 'Agni SR', is designated Agni I by the Indian MOD.[36] It is a single-stage solid-fuel missile that uses the first-stage engine of the Agni II and has a range of 700 km. Like the Agni II, it can be launched from rail or road launchers. On 4 July 2004 India announced that it had successfully test fired an Agni I missile from a mobile launcher at the Integrated Test Range. Many analysts saw the test as India's response to Pakistan's series of ballistic missile tests conducted at the end of June.

The medium-range Agni II has a range exceeding 2000 km and can carry conventional as well as nuclear warheads weighing up to 1000 kg. On 29 August 2004 India announced that it had test launched an Agni II missile, which landed in the designated target area 1200 km away in the Bay of Bengal. It was the third test of an Agni II (the previous tests were conducted in April 1999 and January 2001).

The Agni I and Agni II development programmes have been completed and the missiles have entered into production. During 2004 they were inducted into service with the Indian Army's 334 and 335 Missile Groups, respectively.

The development of the Agni III intermediate-range ballistic missile, with a range exceeding 3200 km, continues to experience enginering and systems integration problems. The missile's maiden flight test was repeatedly postponed in 2004. Indian sources indicate that, because of technical problems, the Defence Research & Development Organization has decided to increase the range of the Agni II missile as an interim measure.[37] The nuclear-capable Agni III will be able to reach targets deep inside China.

There are reports that India is developing an ICBM known as Surya, based on an indigenous space launch vehicle. The missile is believed to be a three-stage design, with the first two stages using solid propellant and the third stage using liquid propellant. The programme's status is unclear from published reports.

[33] Indian Ministry of Defence, 'Prithvi-III test fired', Press release, New Delhi, 27 Oct. 2004, URL <http://mod.nic.in/pressreleases/content. asp?id=838>; and Subramanian, T. S., 'Prithvi III test fired for first time', *The Hindu* (Internet edn), 28 Oct. 2004, URL <http://www.hindu.com/2004/10/28/stories/2004102807641300.htm>.

[34] Indian Defence Ministry sources indicate that Sagarika and Prithvi III are 2 different names for the same missile. United News of India, 'Naval Prithvi testing soon', *The Tribune* (Chandigarh) 7 Sep. 1998, URL <http://www.tribuneindia.com/1998/98sep07/head6.htm>.

[35] 'Prithvi's naval variant is successfully test fired', *Times of India* (Internet edn), 28 Oct. 2004, URL <http://timesofindia.indiatimes.com/articleshow/901642.cms>; and 'India tests Prithvi III and Dhanush', *Jane's Missiles and Rockets*, vol. 8, no. 12 (Dec. 2004), p. 5.

[36] Government of India, Ministry of Defence, *Annual Report 2003–2004*, p. 100, URL <http://mod.nic.in/reports/report04.htm>.

[37] Dikshit, S., 'Step-up of Agni-II range planned', *The Hindu* (Internet edn), 13 Feb. 2005, URL <http://www.hindu.com/2005/02/13/stories/2005021303540900.htm>.

Table 12A.8. Pakistani nuclear forces, January 2005

Type/Designation	Range (km)[a]	Payload (kg)	Status
Aircraft			
F-16A/B	1 600	4 500	32 aircraft, deployed in 3 squadrons; the most likely aircraft in the inventory to have a nuclear delivery role
Ballistic missiles[b]			
Ghaznavi (Hatf-3)	290	500	Entered service with the Pakistani Army on 21 Feb. 2004; test launched on 29 Nov. 2004
Shaheen I (Hatf-4)	>450	750–1 000	Entered service with the Pakistani Army in Mar. 2003
Ghauri I (Hatf-5)	>1 200	700–1 000	Entered service with the Pakistani Army in Jan. 2003; test launched on 12 Oct. 2004

[a] Missile payloads may have to be reduced in order to achieve maximum range. Aircraft range is for illustrative purposes only; actual mission range will vary according to flight profile and weapon loading.

[b] In the 1990s Pakistan received M-11 ballistic missiles from China which are thought to have formed the basis for developing the Hatf-3.

Sources: US Department of Defense, National Air and Space Intelligence Center (NAIC), *Ballistic and Cruise Missile Threat* (NAIC: Wright-Patterson Air Force Base, Ohio, Aug. 2003, revised); US Central Intelligence Agency, *Unclassified Report to Congress on the Acquisition of Technology Relating to Weapons of Mass* Destruction *and Advanced Conventional Munitions*, 1 January through 30 June 2002', Apr. 2003, URL <http://www.cia.gov/cia/publications/bian/bian_apr_2003.htm>; US Central Intelligence Agency, National Intelligence Council, 'Foreign missile developments and the ballistic missile threat through 2015' (unclassified summary), Dec. 2001, URL <http://www.cia.gov/nic/pubs/other_products/Unclassifiedballisticmissilefinal.pdf>; 'NRDC Nuclear Notebook', *Bulletin of the Atomic Scientists*, various issues; and Authors' estimates.

VIII. Pakistani nuclear forces

It is difficult to estimate the size and composition of Pakistan's nuclear arsenal. As is the case with India, a key uncertainty lies in determining how much weapon-usable fissile material Pakistan has produced. It is known that Pakistan has pursued a gas centrifuge uranium-enrichment method to produce the material for its nuclear weapons, at the Kahuta Research Laboratories (also called the Khan Research Laboratories). However, estimates vary as to how much weapon-grade uranium has been produced, in part because of conflicting reports about the number of centrifuges that Pakistan has in operation. In addition, Pakistan may be developing a capability to build plutonium-based nuclear weapons. The unsafeguarded 50-Megawatt thermal heavy water reactor in the Khushab district of Punjab, which became operational in the spring of 1998, has the capability to produce 10–15 kg of weapon-grade plutonium annually. It is also capable of producing tritium, which could be used to 'boost' the explosive yield of fission weapons. In 2004 Pakistan continued to rule out giving the International Atomic Energy Agency (IAEA) or other bodies access to its military nuclear facilities and other sensitive sites.

It is estimated here that Pakistan has manufactured 30–50 nuclear weapons. Some of these weapons are likely to be stored in unassembled form at dispersed locations. In February 2000, Pakistan's military government announced the establishment of a National Command Authority to manage the country's nuclear forces.

Pakistan continues to work to increase the size and sophistication of its nuclear weapon arsenal and associated delivery vehicles. In April 2004 Pakistan's ambassador to the United Nations, Munir Akram, said that, while Pakistan has 'strong support' for non-proliferation, it would also continue to develop nuclear weapons and ballistic missiles in order to 'maintain credible minimum deterrence' with regard to its regional rival, India. This was necessary, according to Akram, because India had 'embarked on major programs for nuclear weapons, missiles, antimissile and conventional arms acquisition and development'.[38]

Ballistic missiles

Pakistan has vigorous research and development and procurement programmes under way for advanced-capability ballistic missiles. Its missile programmes have in the past received considerable technical assistance from China and North Korea. Former Prime Minister Benazir Bhutto acknowledged in July 2004 that Pakistan had purchased missile technology from North Korea, but she denied that it aided North Korea with nuclear technology.[39]

On 21 February 2004 the Ghaznavi (Hatf-3) ballistic missile was formally inducted into service with the Pakistani Army. The Ghaznavi is a nuclear-capable short-range missile that can be transported by road on a modified Scud-B wheeled transporter–erector–launcher (TEL). Its single-stage, solid propellant design is believed to be a domestically produced copy of the Chinese M-11 missile. On 29 November 2004 Pakistan announced that it had successfully test launched a Ghaznavi missile. It had been previously flight tested the missile in October 2003 and twice in 2002.

On 8 December 2004 Pakistan announced that it had successfully test launched a Shaheen I (Hatf-4) medium-range ballistic missile. The Shaheen I, which has been declared to be nuclear-capable, entered into service with the Pakistani Army in March 2003. Analysts remain divided over whether the single-stage solid-fuelled Shaheen I is a version of the Chinese M-9 missile or an improved Chinese M-11 missile. It uses the same wheeled TEL as the Ghaznavi.

Pakistan test fired a new ballistic missile, the Shaheen II (Hatf-6), for the first time on 9 March 2004. The two-stage Shaheen II is believed to use the Shaheen I missile as its second stage and may be able to carry multiple warheads. With a reported range of over 2000 km, it could reach targets in most of India. Following the test, the US State Department issued a statement 'urging Pakistan and other countries in the region to exercise restraint in their nuclear weapon and missile programmes'.[40]

[38] 'Pak not to allow strategic assets' inspection, missiles capability to continue', *Pak Tribune* (Internet edn), 29 Apr. 2004, URL <http://www.paktribune.com/news/index.php?id=63613>.

[39] Takeishi, E., 'Bhutto: we bought missile technology', *Asahi Shimbun* (Internet edn), 19 July 2004, URL <http://www.asahi.com/english/world/TKY200407190155.html>.

[40] US Department of State, 'Pakistan: ballistic missile test', Press release, 2004/245, Office of the Spokesman, Washington, DC, 9 Mar. 2004, URL <http://www.state.gov/r/pa/prs/ps/2004/30302.htm>.

On 29 May 2004 Pakistan conducted a flight test of the nuclear-capable Ghauri I (Hatf-5) medium-range ballistic missile. This was followed by a second Ghauri I test on 4 June. A third test was conducted on 12 October, which coincided with the fifth anniversary of General Pervez Musharraf's seizure of power in a military coup. Senior Pakistani officials emphasized that the launches were part of routine testing and not intended as a political signal to any other country. They also said that Pakistan had given India prior notice of the tests, in accordance with two countries' agreed practice. The Ghauri I missile, with a range exceeding 1200 km, and a longer-range variant, the Ghauri II, are based on North Korea's No-dong 1/2 missile technology and have reportedly been developed with extensive design and engineering assistance from North Korea. It was first successfully test launched in April 1998. Serial production of the Ghauri missile began in late 2002 and that it entered into service in January 2003.

A Ghauri III missile is under development. It has a reported design range of 3500 km, making it the longest-range ballistic missile in Pakistan's inventory. According to a Pakistani press report, a successful test of its liquid-fuel engines took place in September 1999. In May 2004 Pakistani officials indicated that the first test launch of the Ghauri III would be conducted in the near future at a testing range near Nowshera, with the impact point in the Arabia Sea. However, the year ended with no tests having taken place.

Strike aircraft

The aircraft of the Pakistani Air Force (PAF) that is most likely to be used in the nuclear weapon delivery role is the US-manufactured F-16 fighter aircraft. Other aircraft, such as the Mirage V or the Chinese-produced A-5, could also be used.

Pakistan currently maintains 32 F-16s in service, deployed in three squadrons. In 1988–89 Pakistan had contracted to buy 71 F-16s to augment its existing inventory of 40 F-16A/B aircraft, but in October 1990 the US Government announced that it had embargoed any further deliveries to Pakistan in accordance with the Pressler Amendment. (Approved by the US Congress in 1984, the amendment barred military sales to foreign countries unless the president could certify that the country was not pursuing nuclear weapons.) As a result, only 28 of the 71 aircraft were built and none was delivered.

In 2004 senior Pakistani military officials said that the Bush Administration has indicated that it is willing to sell at least 24 F-16 fighter aircraft to Pakistan, pending congressional approval. President Bush had already waived the Pressler Amendment in a Presidential Determination of September 2001.[41]

IX. Israeli nuclear forces

Along with India and Pakistan, Israel is the only UN member state which remains outside the NPT. Israel is widely considered to be a de facto NWS and is estimated to maintain up to about 200 nuclear weapons. Many analysts believe that Israel has a

[41] The White House, 'President waives sanctions on India, Pakistan', Presidential Determination no. 2001-28, 22 Sep. 2001, URL <http://www.whitehouse.gov/news/releases/2001/09/20010922-4.html>.

Table 12A.9. Israeli nuclear forces, January 2005

Type	Range (km)[a]	Payload (kg)	Status
Aircraft[b]			
F-16A/B/C/D/I Falcon	1 600	5 400	205 aircraft in the inventory; some are believed to be certified for nuclear weapon delivery
Ballistic missiles[c]			
Jericho II	1 500–1 800	750–1 000	*c.* 50 missiles; first deployed in 1990; test launched on 27 June 2001
Submarines			
Dolphin	?	?	Rumoured to be equipped with nuclear-capable cruise missiles

[a] Missile payloads may have to be reduced in order to achieve maximum range. Aircraft range is for illustrative purposes only; actual mission range will vary according to flight profile and weapon loading.

[b] Some of Israel's 25 F-15I aircraft may also have a long-range nuclear delivery role.

[c] The Jericho I missile, first deployed in 1973, may no longer be full operational.

Sources: Lennox, D. (ed.), *Jane's Strategic Weapon Systems* (Jane's Information Group, Ltd: Cauldron, 2003); Cohen, A., *Israel and the Bomb* (Columbia University Press: New York, 1998); Albright, D., Berkhout, F. and Walker, W., SIPRI, *Plutonium and Highly Enriched Uranium 1996: World Inventories, Capabilities and Policies* (Oxford University Press: Oxford, 1997); 'NRDC Nuclear Notebook', *Bulletin of the Atomic Scientists*, various issues; and Authors' estimates.

recessed nuclear arsenal (i.e., one that is stored but not armed, requiring some preparation before use); hence, the warheads for Israel's purported nuclear weapon delivery systems may not actually be deployed. These delivery systems are believed to be strike aircraft, land-based ballistic missiles and possibly SLCMs. There is some evidence that Israel may have developed a non-strategic nuclear arsenal, consisting of nuclear artillery shells and atomic demolition munitions (ADMs) or landmines.

Israel continues to maintain its long-standing policy of nuclear ambiguity in which it officially neither confirms nor denies that it possesses nuclear weapons. This policy came under renewed international scrutiny in 2004. At the 2004 Preparatory Committee meeting for the 2005 NPT Review Conference,[42] the League of Arab States and the European Union called for the establishment of a weapons of mass destruction-free zone in the Middle East.[43] In addition, the IAEA reiterated its request that Israel open for inspection its nuclear facility at Dimona. In July 2004, following a visit to Israel by IAEA Director General Mohamad ElBaradei, Israeli Prime Minister Ariel Sharon stated publicly that Israel would consider giving up its 'deterrent

[42] On the work of the Preparatory Committee in 2004 see chapter 12, section VII.

[43] See 'Paper presented on behalf of the States members of the League of Arab States at the third session of the Preparatory Committee for the 2005 Review Conference of the Parties to the Treaty on the Non-Proliferation of Nuclear Weapons, New York, 28 Apr. 2004, NPT/CONF.2005/PC.III/WP.12, URL <http://daccess-ods.un.org/TMP/6450427.html>.

capability' if its neighbours gave up their weapons of mass destruction and fully implemented a comprehensive regional peace agreement.[44]

There continues to be speculation that Israel has developed a sea-based nuclear capability. In December 2004, Germany agreed to permit the sale to Israel of two diesel-powered Dolphin Class submarines in a $700 million deal. The German Government had halted the deal in November 2003, ostensibly because of financing issues. The new vessels, which are to be built by Kiel-based Howaldtswerke-Deutsche Werft AG beginning in 2005, will join the three Dolphin Class submarines that were delivered to the Israeli Navy in 1998–99. The new sale was controversial because there have been unconfirmed media reports—denied by Israeli officials—that Israel has successfully modified US-supplied Harpoon anti-ship cruise missiles to carry nuclear warheads on its submarines. Among other modifications, this may involved reducing the size of the warheads to fit inside the missiles as well as altering the guidance systems so as to be able to hit land-based targets. The missile's 140-km range may also have been extended. Israeli officials have acknowledged that its Dolphin Class submarines carry Harpoon missiles, which are launched through specially designed torpedo tubes. With nuclear-armed missiles deployed at sea, Israel would have a secure nuclear retaliatory capability to offset the potential vulnerability of its aircraft and land-based missiles to a pre-emptive attack.

[44] 'Israel firm on its "deterrent capability"', *Daily Star* (Lebanon), 30 July 2004, URL <http://www.dailystar.com.lb/article.asp?edition_ID=10&article_ID=6772&categ_id=2>.

13. Chemical and biological warfare developments and arms control

RICHARD GUTHRIE, JOHN HART and FRIDA KUHLAU

I. Introduction

In 2004 the states parties to the 1972 Biological and Toxin Weapons Convention (BTWC)[1] held their second annual expert and political meeting, which considered ways to enhance international capabilities for responding to, investigating and mitigating the effects of cases of alleged use of biological or toxin weapons or suspicious outbreaks of disease. The meeting also considered how to strengthen and broaden international institutional efforts and existing mechanisms for the surveillance, detection, diagnosis and combating of infectious diseases affecting humans, animals and plants.

The states parties to the 1993 Chemical Weapons Convention (CWC)[2] approved a request by Libya to convert two former chemical weapon production facilities (CWPFs) to peaceful purposes, after Libya's chemical weapon programme had been dismantled under international supervision, and decided to adopt a new system of budgeting for the operations of the Organisation for the Prohibition of Chemical Weapons (OPCW) starting in 2005.[3]

Activities related to Iraq in 2004 included the publication of an interim report and the effective completion of the inspection and investigation activities by the Iraq Survey Group in its search for nuclear, biological and chemical (NBC) weapons and weapon-related activities in that country. Controversy continued over what had been known about Iraqi activities and capabilities in the years before the military action of 2003, and how what was (and was not) known may have been interpreted or presented. A number of related official inquiries into the handling of intelligence reported in 2004.

In 2004 programmes were implemented in Iraq and Libya in order to redirect the work of former scientists and technicians who were part of the countries' former NBC weapon and longer-range missile programmes.

[1] The Convention on the Prohibition of the Development, Production and Stockpiling of Bacteriological (Biological) and Toxin Weapons and on Their Destruction is reproduced on the SIPRI Chemical and Biological Warfare Project Internet site at URL <http://www.sipri.org/contents/cbwarfare/>. The site includes complete lists of parties and signatory and non-signatory states to the convention. See also annex A in this volume.

[2] The Convention on the Prohibition of the Development, Production, Stockpiling and Use of Chemical Weapons and on their Destruction (corrected version), 8 Aug. 1994, is available on the SIPRI CBW project Internet site (see note 1). The 31 Oct. 1999 amendment to Part VI of the Verification Annex of the CWC is also reproduced there, as are complete lists of parties and signatory and non-signatory states to this convention. See also annex A in this volume.

[3] On Libya see chapter14 in this volume.

On 28 April 2004 the United Nations (UN) Security Council adopted Resolution 1540 by consensus.[4] The resolution calls on UN member states to present, before 28 October, a national report on steps they have taken or intend to take to control materials and technologies that could be used for NBC weapons. Eighty-seven reports had been received by 7 December, plus one by the European Union (EU) collectively, to supplement the national reports by EU member states.[5] Not all of the submitted reports had been published by the end of the year, and because they are not publicly available it is not possible to give a comprehensive analysis of the results. However, it is clear that the process of compiling the reports has led to the identification of gaps in implementation of the key international instruments, particularly as regards issues related to biological weapons.

The key driver behind the adoption of Resolution 1540 was concern about potential terrorist acquisition of NBC materials and technologies. During 2004 attention was also drawn to the potential for raising the barriers to the acquisition of weapons of mass destruction (WMD) by non-state actors through the full implementation of multilateral treaties such as the BTWC and CWC.

Section II of this chapter discusses the results of the 2004 expert and political meetings of the BTWC parties. CWC-related developments are described in section III. Section IV describes developments in relation to Iraq. Section V discusses intelligence issues. Section VI covers other past and present activities and allegations, and section VII presents the conclusions.

II. Biological weapon disarmament

The BTWC entered into force on 26 March 1975.[6] As of 3 December 2004, 153 states were parties to it, and an additional 16 states have signed but not ratified the BTWC.[7] Azerbaijan and Kyrgyzstan[8] acceded to the convention during 2004.

The BTWC is the only global convention prohibiting possession of a class of WMD that has no institutionalized verification and compliance mechanism. Negotiations that had been intended to provide such a mechanism came to an

[4] UN Security Council Resolution 1540, 28 Apr. 2004; it is reproduced in appendix 11A. See also chapters 11 and 17 in this volume.

[5] 'Letter dated 8 December 2004 from the Chairman of the Security Council Committee established pursuant to Resolution 1540 (2004) to the President of the Security Council', UN Security Council document S/2004/958/, 8 Dec. 2004; and S/2004/958/Corr.1, 23 Dec. 2004.

[6] See note 1.

[7] 'List of states parties', BTWC Meeting of States Parties document BWC/MSP/2004/INF.2, 3 Dec. 2004. Unless otherwise noted, all BTWC documents cited in this chapter are available on the UN documents Internet site at URL <http://documents.un.org>.

[8] There has been some confusion about the BTWC status of Kyrgyzstan because it has previously appeared on some lists of states parties and has considered itself bound by the BTWC since becoming an independent state in 1991. The country submitted a confidence-building measures (CBMs) return to the UN Department for Disarmament Affairs on 25 May 1993, an activity that is carried out under the auspices of the BTWC. However, deposit of the instrument of accession with the Russian authorities in Oct. 2004 now puts this matter beyond doubt.

abrupt halt in 2001.[9] During 2004, separate from the formal meetings of the BTWC parties, a number of statements urged that the convention and the broader regime of which it is a key component should be strengthened.

On 2 December the UN High-level Panel on Threats, Challenges and Change published its report.[10] In his introduction to the report, the UN Secretary-General welcomed the panel's 'innovative focus on issues of biological security' and noted its 'attention to the deterioration of our global health system, its vulnerability to new infectious disease; and the promise and peril of advances in biotechnology'.

The panel called for negotiations on a 'credible verification protocol' for the BTWC and on 'a new bio-security protocol to classify dangerous biological agents and establish binding international standards for the export of such agents'. It also suggested that 'the Security Council should avail itself of the Secretary-General's roster of inspectors for biological weapons', who should remain independent and work under UN staff codes. This roster of inspectors should also be available to 'advise the Council and liaise with WHO [World Health Organization] authorities in the event of a suspicious disease outbreak'. The panel also suggested that in the event that a state is unable to adequately quarantine large numbers of potential carriers of disease in an unusual outbreak, the Security Council 'should be prepared to support international action to assist in cordon operations'.

A number of academic studies on the future of the BTWC were published in 2004.[11] One prominent theme was the role of expert advice. For example, on 19 April the Royal Society in the United Kingdom noted: 'It is essential to support international agreements, such as the Biological Weapons Convention, through the formation of international scientific advisory panels to keep up with the rapid pace of technological advance in the relevant sciences'.[12]

The EU in its work on the BTWC under the EU Strategy against Proliferation of Weapons of Mass Destruction suggested that a 'group of experts' could be convened 'in order to develop specific suggestions to strengthen the BTWC, in particular as regards compliance, with a view to the Review Conference' and that this group could be useful in the context of the development of bio-security and bio-safety standards.

International assemblies of parliamentarians adopted resolutions calling for formal compliance mechanisms for the convention, such as the Assembly of

[9] Zanders, J. P., Hart, J. and Kuhlau, F., 'Chemical and biological weapon developments and arms control', *SIPRI Yearbook 2002: Armaments, Disarmament and International Security* (Oxford University Press: Oxford, 2002), p. 665–708.

[10] United Nations, 'A more secure world: our shared responsibility', Report of the High-level Panel on Threats, Challenges and Change, UN documents A/59/565, 4 Dec. 2004, and A/59/565/Corr.1, 6 Dec. 2004, URL <http://www.un.org/ga/59/documentation/list5.html>. The synopsis and summary of recommendations of the report are reproduced in the appendix to the Introduction in this volume.

[11] See, e.g., papers presented to the Weapons of Mass Destruction Commission URL <http://www.wmdcommission.org>.

[12] Royal Society, 'The individual and collective roles scientists can play in strengthening international treaties', Policy document 05/04, 19 Apr. 2004.

the Inter-Parliamentary Union, representing parliamentarians from over 140 countries.[13]

The 2004 BTWC meetings

In 2004 the parties to the BTWC held a Meeting of Experts and a Meeting of States Parties, following on from similar meetings held in 2003.[14] The meetings, which will continue to be held annually until the Sixth Review Conference, scheduled for 2006, are the result of a decision taken by the reconvened Fifth Review Conference of the States Parties to the BTWC in 2002.

The mandate for the 2004 meetings was to 'discuss, and promote common understanding and effective action' on 'enhancing international capabilities for responding to, investigating and mitigating the effects of cases of alleged use of biological or toxin weapons or suspicious outbreaks of disease' and 'strengthening and broadening national and international institutional efforts and existing mechanisms for the surveillance, detection, diagnosis and combating of infectious diseases affecting humans, animals, and plants'.[15]

The significance of the issues was underlined in a working paper submitted by Hungary which noted that since the adoption of the mandate the world has experienced new threats from infectious disease, notably severe acute respiratory syndrome (SARS) and avian influenza. Hungary also stressed that the control of such threats depends on prompt and transparent reporting of cases and on a robust system of global surveillance and response, and that such a system 'will also strengthen protection against a third infectious threat that became prominent in the [northern] autumn of 2001, namely, the risk that biological agents would deliberately be used to cause harm'.[16]

The *Meeting of Experts* was held in Geneva on 19–30 July 2004.[17] Participants from 87 states parties, 4 signatory states, 2 observer states, 4 specialized agencies and intergovernmental organizations (IGOs), and 10 non-governmental organizations (NGOs) attended.[18] The first week was dedicated

[13] 'The Role of Parliaments in Strengthening Multilateral Regimes for Non-Proliferation of Weapons and for Disarmament, in the Light of New Security Challenges', Resolution adopted by the 111th Inter-Parliamentary Assembly, 1 Oct. 2004.

[14] Guthrie, R. *et al.*, 'Chemical and biological warfare developments and arms control', *SIPRI Yearbook 2004: Armaments, Disarmament and International Security* (Oxford University Press: Oxford, 2004), p. 661–67.

[15] 'Final Document of the Fifth Review Conference of the States Parties to the Convention on the Prohibition of the Development, Production and Stockpiling of Bacteriological (Biological) Weapons and on Their Destruction', BTWC Review Conference document BWC/CONF.V/17, para. 18 (a), p. 3, available at URL <http://www.opbw.org/rev_cons/5rc/5rc_conf.htm>.

[16] Hungary, 'Challenges of the second year of the follow-up process', Meeting of Experts document BWC/MSP/2004/MX/WP.83, 6 Aug. 2004.

[17] Pearson, G. S., 'Report from Geneva: the Biological Weapons Convention new process', *CBW Conventions Bulletin*, no. 65 (Sep. 2004), pp. 12–20, URL <http://www.sussex.ac.uk/spru/hsp/cbwcb65.pdf>. Peter Goosen of South Africa was chairman of the meeting.

[18] 'List of participants', BTWC Meeting of Experts document BWC/MSP/2004/MX/INF.5, 30 July 2004. The signatory states were Egypt, Madagascar, Myanmar and the United Arab Emirates; the observer states were Israel and Kazakhstan; and the agencies and IGOs were the Food and Agriculture

to a discussion of surveillance and detection issues and the second week to response issues.

The parties submitted 83 working papers.[19] Unlike the 2003 Meeting of Experts, in which presentations by the states parties were assembled in daily collations and consolidated in Part II of the final report of the meeting, in 2004 the chairman prepared an informal chronological listing of issues raised under each of the topics, and both lists were appended to the report of the meeting.[20]

The *Meeting of States Parties* was held in Geneva on 6–10 December.[21] Participants from 89 states parties, 5 signatory states, 2 observer states, 4 specialized agencies and IGOs, and 15 NGOs attended.[22]

At both sets of meetings there was little controversy over the issues relating to detection and surveillance of disease. The role of international bodies such as the WHO, the Office International des Epizooties (OIE) and the Food and Agriculture Organization (FAO) in dealing with unusual outbreaks of disease was seen as valuable, but concern was expressed that such organizations should not go beyond their general mandates to become involved in investigations of alleged deliberate use.

There was significant disagreement among the states parties on how the international community should proceed in relation to existing mechanisms that could be used to investigate unusual outbreaks of disease that may turn into allegations of biological warfare.

A number of states drew attention to the authority of the UN Secretary-General to investigate the alleged use of biological weapons.[23] Addressing this subject in the BTWC meetings, however, was resisted by other parties. For example, the United States indicated that, as the powers in question derived from UN resolutions citing the 1925 Geneva Protocol,[24] it was not for the parties of the BTWC to review them. A number of parties (including Iran) expressed a concern that the Secretary-General's mechanism was a distraction from preparation of a 'proper' verification system for the convention.

There was a clear divergence of opinion on investigation issues during the preparation of a final report, and this divergence was reflected in the final report itself. It noted: 'the Secretary-General's investigation mechanism, set

Organization, the International Committee of the Red Cross (ICRC), the WHO and the Office International des Epizooties.

[19] For a complete list of documents from the Meeting of Experts see 'Report of the Meeting of Experts', BTWC Meeting of Experts document BWC/MSP/2004/MX/3, 11 Aug. 2004.

[20] 'Report of the Meeting of Experts (note 19).

[21] Pearson, G. S., 'Report from Geneva: the Biological Weapons Convention Meeting of States Parties', *CBW Conventions Bulletin*, no. 66 (Dec. 2004), pp. 21–34, URL <http://www.sussex.ac.uk/spru/hsp/cbwcb66.pdf>. Peter Goosen of South Africa was also chairman of this meeting.

[22] 'List of participants', BTWC States Parties documents BWC/MSP/2004/INF.3, 10 Dec. 2004; and BWC/MSP/2004/INF.3/Add.1, 14 Dec. 2004. The signatory states in attendance were Egypt, Madagascar, Myanmar, Syria and the United Arab Emirates; the observer states were Israel and Kazakhstan; and the agencies and IGOs were the FAO, the ICRC, the WHO and the OIE.

[23] For background to this authority see Lundin, S. J., 'Multilateral and bilateral talks on chemical and biological weapons', *SIPRI Yearbook 1990: World Armaments and Disarmament* (Oxford University Press: Oxford, 1990) pp. 539-40.

[24] On the protocol, its parties and signatories see annex A in this volume.

out in A/44/561 and endorsed by the General Assembly in its resolution A/Res/45/57, represents an international institutional mechanism for investigating cases of alleged use of biological or toxin weapons'.[25] However, on the final day, text which placed the consideration being given by the UN General Assembly to reviewing the Secretary-General's mechanism for investigation of cases of alleged use of biological or toxin weapons in the context of the Sixth BTWC Review Conference was dropped from the draft report because consensus could not be reached.

The meeting decided that the 2005 meetings, which will deal with the issues of codes of conduct, would be held on 13–24 June and 5–9 December. There is still no common understanding of how the outcomes of the series of annual meetings will be handled at the 2006 Review Conference.

III. Chemical weapon disarmament

As of 31 December 2004, 167 states had ratified or acceded to the CWC and a further 16 states had signed but not ratified it,[26] while 11 countries had neither signed nor ratified the convention.[27] The UN General Assembly adopted a resolution which *inter alia* stressed the importance of ensuring that the CWC achieves universal membership and that it be effectively implemented.[28] In November 2004 Austria presented a proposal to the EU for joint efforts on the issue of challenge inspections under the CWC.

The OPCW Action Plans

The OPCW Action Plans on universality and on national implementation made significant progress in 2004.[29] Eight states became parties to the CWC during 2004. As of 31 October 2004, 136 parties (82 per cent) had established or designated a National Authority to the OPCW;[31] 96 parties (58 per cent)

[25] 'Report of the Meeting of States Parties', BTWC Meeting of States Parties document BWC/MSP/2004/3, 14 Dec. 2004

[26] Chad, Libya, Madagascar, Marshall Islands, Saint Kitts and Nevis, Solomon Islands, Sierra Leone and Tuvalu became parties to the CWC in 2004. The states which have signed, but not ratified or acceded to, the CWC are the Bahamas, Bhutan, Cambodia, the Central African Republic, Comoros, Congo, the Democratic Republic of the Congo, Djibouti, the Dominican Republic, Grenada, Guinea-Bissau, Haiti, Honduras, Israel, Liberia and Myanmar. See also annex A in this volume.

[27] The states that had not signed or ratified the CWC as of 31 Dec. 2004 were Angola, Antigua and Barbuda, Barbados, Egypt, Iraq, North Korea, Lebanon, Niue, Somalia, Syria and Vanuatu.

[28] UN General Assembly Resolution A/RES/59/72, 10 Dec. 2004.

[29] The Action Plan on universality aims to bring about global membership of the CWC. The Action Plan on national implementation aims to ensure that all states parties effectively implement their obligations under Article VII (National Implementation Measures) of the CWC, including through the adoption of proper penal legislation. For a more detailed description of this plan see Tabassi, L. and Spence, S., 'Improving CWC implementation: the OPCW Action Plan', Verification Research, Training and Information Centre (VERTIC), *Verification 2004* (VERTIC: London, 2004), pp. 45–64; and Guthrie *et al.* (note 14), p. 670.

[31] The National Authority serves as a focal point for liaison between the OPCW and the states parties. Some states have added additional functions to enhance national implementation of the CWC.

had reported adoption of general domestic legislative or administrative measures to the Technical Secretariat (TS); and 53 parties (32 per cent) had adopted and reported national legislation covering all key enforcement areas required by the CWC.[32]

OPCW Action Plan efforts have received external funding. A number of states have provided cost-free consultants to the OPCW. The Council of the European Union adopted a Joint Action on support for activities by the OPCW in the framework of the EU Strategy against Proliferation of Weapons of Mass Destruction. Under the plan, starting in 2005 the Council will provide €1 841 000 (*c.* $2 465 000) to the OPCW to support programmes in the area of universality, national implementation and international cooperation.[33] Romania and the USA distributed a CWC implementation and assistance programme package.[34]

The Conference of the States Parties to the CWC

The Ninth Session of the Conference of the States Parties (CSP) to the CWC was held on 29 November–2 December.[35] It approved the OPCW 2005 budget of €75 695 000 (*c.* $103 220 000). Of this amount, the CSP estimated that €4 417 600 (*c.* $6 000 000) will be received through Article IV (Chemical weapons) and Article V (CWPFs) reimbursements (see below), and that interest income will comprise €600 000 (*c.* $820 000).[36]

The CSP amended the OPCW Financial Regulations and also took decisions on the Working Capital Fund and on late reimbursements by the states parties to the OPCW for 'direct costs'[37] incurred during inspections carried out under Articles IV and V of the CWC. These costs are to be reimbursed by the inspected state party unless the Executive Council decides otherwise.[38] However, the OPCW has periodically experienced budgetary difficulties partly because some estimates of the amount of money to be reimbursed have been

[32] OPCW, 'Note by the Director-General, report on the OPCW plan of action regarding the implementation of Article VII obligations', OPCW document C-9/DG.7, 23 Nov. 2004 pp. 3–4.

[33] 'Council Joint Action 2004/797/CFSP of 22 November 2004 on support for OPCW activities in the framework of the implementation of the EU Strategy against Proliferation of Weapons of Mass Destruction', *Official Journal of the European Union*, L349/63 (25 Nov. 2004), pp. 63–69. The Joint Action is also published in Council document 14519/04. The OPCW was officially informed of the Joint Action via 'Note by the Kingdom of the Netherlands on behalf of the European Union, joint action on support for OPCW activities in the framework of the EU strategy against proliferation of weapons of mass destruction', OPCW document C-9/NAT.2, 29 Nov. 2004.

[34] US Chemical Weapons Convention Web Site, 'Implementation and Assistance Programme (IAP)', URL <http://www.cwc.gov/Global_Outreach/IAP>.

[35] The CSP was scheduled to end on 3 Dec. but completed its work ahead of schedule.

[36] OPCW, 'Programme and budget of the OPCW for 2005', OPCW document C-9/DEC.14, 2 Dec. 2004.

[37] During the 1993–97 Preparatory Commission period it was agreed that parties that receive inspections carried out under Articles IV and V are to pay the costs of inspection that would not have been incurred had the inspection not occurred (i.e., the 'direct costs' of inspection). This was done in order to avoid the OPCW members having to collectively subsidize the verification of chemical weapon facilities and destruction of stockpiles that are located in a limited number of states.

[38] CWC, Article IV, para. 16.

too high. In addition, the payment of reimbursements has been delayed in some cases because of variation in how the parties' budgeting and payment procedures are structured.[39] The CSP therefore decided to increase the size of the OPCW's Working Capital Fund and to increase the flexibility of the OPCW's Financial Regulations to help address these and related issues.[40]

The CSP also approved the introduction of results-based budgeting (RBB) in 2005[41] as part of an effort to standardize the way in which budgets are formulated and structured by international organizations. The International Atomic Energy Agency (IAEA), the EU and the UN have implemented RBB, reflecting a strong desire by some states for the management model in general. The effect of RBB within the OPCW will probably not be fully known for several years. In addition, complete evaluation of its effectiveness will require detailed understanding of the OPCW's activities at the working level. In principle, RBB should clarify lines of responsibility and therefore improve management in the OPCW, including the question of where policy making ends and its implementation begins. RBB might also highlight the difficulty of assessing important, but rather general, objectives that are hard to quantify such as the 'full and effective national implementation' of the CWC.[42] It will be important to note how the successes or failures of RBB are understood and acted on by the parties. RBB is the third major managerial change at the OPCW in recent years following the removal of the first Director-General in 2002[43] and the introduction of limitations of staff tenure in 2003.[44]

Finally, the CSP agreed an understanding of the term 'captive use', an important chemical industry implementation matter,[45] which has been unre-

[39] Zanders, Hart and Kuhlau (note 9), p. 684.

[40] OPCW, 'Decision, amendments to the financial regulations of the OPCW', OPCW document C-9/DEC.11, 2 Dec. 2004; and OPCW, 'Decision, the Working Capital Fund and late receipt of Article IV and V income', OPCW document C-9/DEC.12, 2 Dec. 2004.

[41] The UN's Programme Planning and Budget Division has defined RBB as 'formulating programmes and budgets that are driven by a number of desired results which are articulated at the outset of the budgetary process and against which actual performance is measured at the end of the biennium'. United Nations, *United Nations: Guide to Results-Based Budgeting* (UN: New York, 23 Oct. 1998), p. 7. Subsequent budgets are formulated partly on the basis of an assessment of the extent to which selected objectives and performance indicators have been fulfilled. In drafting an RBB the results sought are considered first, followed by the activities, resources and the costs necessary to achieve the results. Performance indicators are used to define how performance will be assessed.

[42] For examples of the objectives see OPCW, 'Medium-term plan for the period from 2005 to 2007', OPCW document C-9/5/1, 2 Dec. 2004.

[43] Hart, J., Kuhlau, F. and Simon, J., 'Chemical and biological weapon developments and arms control', *SIPRI Yearbook 2003: Armaments, Disarmament and International Security* (Oxford University Press, Oxford, 2003), pp. 651–52.

[44] See Guthrie *et al.* (note 14), pp. 668–69.

[45] The CSP decided: '(*a*) that the production of a Schedule 2 or Schedule 3 chemical is understood, for declaration purposes, to include intermediates, by-products, or waste products that are produced and consumed within a defined chemical manufacturing sequence, where such intermediates, by-products, or waste products are chemically stable and therefore exist for a sufficient time to make isolation from the manufacturing stream possible, but where, under normal or design operating conditions, isolation does not occur; and (*b*) to request States Parties to take the necessary measures to implement their obligations under Article VII, paragraph 1, of the Convention as soon as possible and in any event no later than 1 January 2005 in respect of Schedule 2 chemicals and 1 January 2006 in respect of Schedule 3 chemicals'. OPCW, 'Decision, understanding of the concept of "captive use" in connection with

solved since the final stages of the CWC negotiations in Geneva in the early 1990s. Captive use has been discussed by the parties in terms of the cost, scope and level of intrusiveness which they believe that the CWC should possess in order to be effective. The term has been defined as 'the case of the production of a chemical [that appears on Schedule 2 or 3 of the CWC's Annex on Chemicals] and its subsequent further conversion without isolation in the same reaction vessel/unit to form another product'.[46] Much of the discussion centred on whether 3-quinuclidinyl benzilate (BZ)—a hallucinogenic compound with potential for hostile use that is also produced as an intermediate in the production of chemicals for peaceful purposes—should be declared. Some parties have declared BZ because it is an intermediate chemical that could be isolated, while other parties have not declared it because the compound is not isolated.[47] (Hydrogen cyanide was the focus of similar discussion.) The agreed understanding of captive use does not require the parties to declare scheduled chemicals that are produced as a by-product where 'under normal or design operating conditions, isolation does not occur'. The effect of the decision (including, for example, the extent to which BZ that is produced as a by-product is declared and inspected) will become clear as it is implemented. Disagreement may remain over what constitutes 'normal or design operating conditions'. In addition, the parties are 'requested' to take the necessary national measures to implement the decision.

Destruction of chemical weapons

The states that declared the possession of chemical weapons at the time the CWC entered into force for them are Albania, India, Libya, Russia, the USA and 'another state party', not identified at its request but widely understood to be South Korea. As of 31 January 2005, of 71 373 agent tonnes of declared chemical weapons, 10 698 agent tonnes had been verifiably destroyed; of 8 671 564 declared items, 2 151 777 munitions and containers had been destroyed;[48] and 12 states had declared past production of chemical weapons.[49]

Albania's chemical weapon stockpile consists of approximately 16 tonnes of agent (reportedly sulphur mustard) filled in canisters, at least a part of which

declarations of production and consumption under Parts VII and VIII of the Verification Annex to the Chemical Weapons Convention', OPCW document C-9/DEC.6, 30 Nov. 2004.

[46] Hart, J., Verification Research, Training and Information Centre (VERTIC), *Chemical Industry Inspections Under the Chemical Weapons Convention*, Verification Matters Research Report no. 1 (VERTIC: London, 2001).

[47] Hart, J., 'The treatment of perfluorisobutylene under the Chemical Weapons Convention', *ASA Newsletter*, no. 88 (28 Feb. 2002), pp. 1, 20–23; and Hart (note 46), pp. 21–22. A related consideration is whether or how the use of temporary chemical storage tanks or 'day tanks' can or should be taken into account.

[48] OPCW, Response to a SIPRI request for information, Feb. 2005.

[49] As of 30 Sep. 2004, 64 CWPFs had been declared by 12 parties. As of the same date, 47 CWPFs had been destroyed or converted. The countries are Bosnia and Herzegovina, China, France, India, Iran, Japan, South Korea, Libya, Russia, Serbia and Montenegro, the UK and the USA. The CWC defines such a facility as any facility that produced chemical weapons at any time since 1 Jan. 1946. CWC, Article II, para. 8.

may have been imported during the 1980s.[50] In early 2003 Albania declared that it had discovered chemical weapons on its territory in November 2002. The CSP approved, in principle, a request by Albania to extend its intermediate deadline for completing the destruction of 1 per cent, 20 per cent and 45 per cent its Category 1 stocks (i.e., weapons containing chemicals listed in Schedule 1 of the CWC's Annex on Chemicals and their parts and components).[51] The Executive Council of the OPCW will determine the destruction deadlines. Albania is obliged to complete the destruction of its stockpile no later than 29 April 2007.[52] In its report to the '1540 Committee' Albania expressed its hope that this deadline would be met.[53]

Official public information on the type and quantity of *India's* chemical weapon stockpile is limited. In 2004 India met its deadline for destroying 45 per cent of its Category 1 stocks[54] and was reported to have completed destruction of 80 per cent of its total stocks.[55]

On 19 December 2003 *Libya* publicly renounced NBC weapons and longer-range missiles and associated programmes and in 2004 additional information became available on those programmes which Libya had pursued.[56] Libya declared *inter alia* approximately 2000 tonnes of precursors not listed in the CWC Annex on Chemicals which had been intended to be used for purposes prohibited by the CWC. Libya thus acknowledged the extent of the CWC's definition of chemical weapons which prohibits all toxic materials and their precursors except where intended for purposes not prohibited by the CWC, a concept also known as the 'general purpose criterion' (GPC).[57] In early 2004 Libya suspended the destruction of chemical weapon air bombs at the request of the OPCW in order to declare the weapons and allow the OPCW to verify their destruction. In March 2004 Libya completed the destruction of its air bombs. In December 2004 the OPCW approved Libya's request to convert two former sulphur mustard production facilities at Rabta into a pharma-

[50] At least some of the canisters reportedly have Chinese markings. 'U.S. to help destroy Albanian weapons', *Chemical & Engineering News*, vol. 82, no. 44 (1 Nov. 2004), p. 19. On Albania see chapter 16 in this volume.

[51] The CWC's 'order of destruction' provisions are provided in CWC, Part IV(A), Verification Annex, paras. 15–19.

[52] OPCW, 'Decision, Request by Albania for extensions of the intermediate deadlines for the destruction of its Category 1 chemical weapons stockpiles', OPCW document C-9/DEC.8, 30 Nov. 2004. The plural 'stockpiles' in the decision's title suggests that Albania has more than 1 storage facility.

[53] Albania's first report to the 1540 Committee is annexed to UN Security Council document S/AC.44/2004/(02)/38, 4 Nov. 2004. On the 1540 Committee see chapter 11 in this volume.

[54] 'UK statement under Agenda item IX', UK delegation statement to the Plenary during the Ninth CSP, The Hague, Netherlands, 28 Nov.–2 Dec. 2004.

[55] Spence, S., 'Progress in The Hague', *CBW Conventions Bulletin*, no 66 (Dec. 2004), p. 8.

[56] There is little, if any, evidence that Libya had an offensive biological weapon programme. On Libya's chemical and biological weapon holdings see chapter 14 in this volume.

[57] CWC, Article II, para. 1. The GPC is the key mechanism by which the CWC can take into account technological and scientific change and ensure that use of other toxic chemicals for chemical warfare purposes is also prohibited. It allows those implementing the CWC to better distinguish between 'offensive' (i.e., prohibited) and 'defensive' (i.e., permitted) chemical warfare programmes. Concern has periodically been expressed that the manner in which the CWC is being implemented is too narrowly focused partly because, since the convention's entry into force on 29 Apr. 1997, declarations and inspections have tended to focus on chemicals listed in the CWC's Annex on Chemicals.

ceutical production facility to produce drugs to treat HIV/AIDS, malaria and tuberculosis.[58] The decision is significant partly because it requires an amendment to the Verification Annex in order to relax the CWC requirement that conversion of any CWPF be completed no later than six years after the CWC enters into force.[59] Such a technical change, which will be enacted by the Executive Council at a later date, has been seen as desirable in order to avoid deterring states that may wish to convert former CWPFs to CWC-permitted purposes from joining the CWC. The CSP approved extensions for Libya to complete the destruction of 1 per cent, 20 per cent and 45 per cent of its Category 1 chemical weapons. The Executive Council will determine the destruction deadlines, but Libya is obliged in any case to complete the destruction of all chemical weapons no later than 29 April 2007.[60]

The declared *Russian* chemical weapon stockpile comprises approximately 40 000 agent tonnes and is stored at seven locations.[61] As of December 2004 Russia had destroyed approximately 2 per cent of its declared chemical weapons.[62] In 2004 destruction operations were carried out at Gorny only; these operations are scheduled to be completed by the end of 2005. Russia's National Authority, the Munitions Agency, was reorganized in 2004 in accordance with a 9 March 2004 Russian presidential decree. The decree folded the agency's functions into the Federal Agency on Industry which, in turn, is subordinate to the Ministry of Industry and Energy of the Russian Federation. Russia's National Authority is currently the Centre for Convention Problems and Programmes of Disarmament Directorate and is headed by Colonel-General Viktor Ivanovich Kholstov.[63]

The *United States*' stockpiled chemical weapons are stored at eight locations.[64] As of 28 December 2004, 33.34 per cent of these stored chemical

[58] OPCW, 'Decision, Request by the Libyan Arab Jamahiriya to use the chemical weapons production facilities Rabta Pharmaceutical Factory 1 and Rabta Pharmaceutical Factory 2 (Phase II) in Rabta, the Libyan Arab Jamahiriya for purposes not prohibited under the Chemical Weapons Convention', OPCW document C-9/DEC.9, 30 Nov. 2004.

[59] CWC, Part V, Verification Annex, para. 72; and CWC, Article XV (Amendments). In Jan. 2005 the Director-General notified all parties that the change had been approved and had entered into force. OPCW, 'Technical change to Chemical Weapons Convention enters into force: provisions for conversion of former chemical weapons production facilities reinforced', Press Release no. 01, 31 Jan. 2005.

[60] OPCW, 'Decision, Request by the Libyan Arab Jamahiriya for extensions of the intermediate deadlines for the destruction of its Category 1 chemical weapons stockpiles', OPCW document C-9/DEC.7, 30 Nov. 2004. On the CWC's 'order of destruction' provisions see CWC, Part IV(A), Verification Annex, paras. 15–19.

[61] See also chapter 16 in this volume, especially table 16.1.

[62] Litovkin, V., 'Russia set to meet chemical weapons destruction deadline', Russian Information Agency (RIA), *Novosti* (Moscow), 17 Nov. 2004. Under the CWC, Russia is obligated to destroy its chemical weapon stockpile no later than 29 Apr. 2012. Russia is still officially committed to meeting this deadline, but intermediate destruction dates provided by Russia's destruction plan have been periodically extended or called into question as a result of official and semi-official Russian Government statements.

[63] 'Struktura: Federal'nikh organov ispolnitel'noi vlasti (utverzhdena Ukazom Prezidenta Rossiiskoi Federatsii ot 9 Marta 2004, no. 314)' [Structure of the federal executive organs (confirmed by decree no. 314 of the President of the Russian Federation)], available on the *Rossiiskya Gazeta* Internet site at URL <http://www.rg.ru/rubricator/index.html>. Kholstov is a deputy head of the Federal Agency on Industry.

[64] The US chemical weapon stockpiles are located at Aberdeen Proving Ground, Md.; Anniston Army Depot, Ala.; Lexington-Blue Grass Army Depot, Ky.; Newport Chemical Depot, Ind.; Pine Bluff

agents had been destroyed as had 42 per cent of US chemical munitions.[65] The US Army's Chemical Materials Agency (CMA) is responsible for overseeing the destruction of the stockpiled chemical weapons, and to achieve this, it is implementing 3 programmes: the Assembled Chemical Weapons Alternatives Program (ACWA), the Alternative Technology and Approaches Program (ATAP) and the Chemical Stockpile Disposal Program (CSDP). The ACWA is tasked to 'test and demonstrate' a minimum of 2 non-incineration-based destruction technologies to be used to destroy the stockpiles located at Pueblo, Colorado, and Richmond, Kentucky. The ATAP is responsible for investigating and developing non-incineration-based destruction technologies to be used to destroy the chemical weapons located at Newport, Indiana, and Edgewood, Maryland. The CSDP is responsible for destroying, using incineration-based technology, the chemical weapon stockpiles at Anniston, Alabama; Pine Bluff, Arkansas; Tooele, Utah; and Umatilla, Oregon. The US Army's Non-Stockpile Chemical Material Programme (NSCMP) is responsible for treating and disposing of materials associated with: (*a*) binary chemical weapons, (*b*) buried chemical warfare matériel, (*c*) former CWPFs, (*d*) miscellaneous chemical warfare matériel (i.e., unfilled munitions and devices and equipment specifically designed for use directly in connection with the employment of chemical munitions), and (*e*) recovered chemical warfare matériel (e.g., chemical agent identification sets).

In 2004 destruction operations were carried out at the Anniston, Edgewood and Tooele facilities. Destruction facilities at Newport, Pine Bluff and Umatilla were essentially completed in 2004, although construction of full-scale CWDFs at Blue Grass and Pueblo had not begun.

Old and abandoned chemical weapons

As of December 2004, three countries had declared that abandoned chemical weapons (ACW) were present on their territories, and 10 countries had declared that they possess old chemical weapons (OCW).[66]

In 2004 further information regarding *Japanese* chemical warfare activities during World War II was made public.[67] Additional World War II-era chem-

Arsenal, Ark.; Pueblo Chemical Depot, Colo.; Deseret Chemical Depot, Utah; and Umatilla Chemical Depot, Oreg.

[65] US Army Chemical Materials Agency, 'One third of the nation's chemical agent now safely destroyed', Press Release 04-14, 28 Dec. 2004. Types and quantities of the US chemical weapon stockpile are given in Zanders, J. P., Eckstein, S. and Hart, J., 'Chemical and biological weapon developments', *SIPRI Yearbook 1997: Armaments, Disarmament and International Security* (Oxford University Press: Oxford, 1997), pp. 449–51.

[66] As of Nov. 2004, the countries that have declared ACW to the OPCW are China, Italy and Panama. The countries that have declared OCW to the OPCW are Australia, Belgium, Canada, France, Germany, Italy, Japan, Slovenia, the UK and the USA. ACWs are defined as those that were abandoned by a state after 1 Jan. 1925 on the territory of another state without the permission of the latter. CWC, Article II, para. 6.

[67] For background see Harris, S., *Factories of Death* (Routledge: London, 1994); Wallace, D. and Williams, P., *Unit 731* (Free Press: New York, 1989); Gold, H., *Unit 731 Testimony* (Yen Books: Tokyo, 1996); and Harris, S., 'The Japanese biological warfare programme: an overview', eds E. Geissler and J. E. van Courtland Moon, *Biological and Toxin Weapons: Research, Development and Use from the*

ical munitions that Japan left in China at the end of World War II were recovered, and in April 2004 China and Japan reportedly agreed to begin construction of a Japanese-funded $2.8 billion CWDF in China.[68] While conducting research at an Australian state archive, a Japanese professor uncovered a 400-page report that contained the record of trials of Japanese prisoners carried out by the Australian military in Hong Kong in 1948. According to the document, a lieutenant and a lieutenant-colonel of the Japanese Imperial Army were sentenced to death for the 1944 killing of two prisoners of war—an Australian Air Force captain and a sergeant in the Dutch East Indies Air Force—by testing cyanide-filled bottles designed for use against tanks on them in order to determine whether the munitions were still usable.[69]

During a press conference in Panama City on 13 November 2004, US Secretary of Defense Donald H. Rumsfeld was asked whether the USA planned to 'clean and decontaminate' San José Island, an island in *Panama* that was used by the USA and a number of its allies for chemical munitions field testing during World War II. The unidentified questioner stated that there were at least 3000, 500-pound (227 kilograms) and 1000-pound (454 kg) 'bombs with chemical warheads, mustard, gas, nerve gas' on the island. In response, Rumsfeld stated: 'I am advised that the status of it [the matter] is that the U.S., apparently, has assumed its obligation under the treaty [CWC] and that the matter is closed'.[70] Panama reportedly declined a US offer to pay to train Panamanians to deal with any chemical munitions recovered and to provide $1.5 million to purchase equipment; as a result, the USA reportedly 'considers that issue closed'.[71] Panama has declared to the OPCW that it has ACW on its territory. However, the nature and extent of any possible ACW and the identity of the abandoning state(s) has not been officially determined.[72]

On 21 June 2004 a number of World War I-era artillery shells, some of which were reportedly filled with chlorine, were uncovered in the village of Toporivka in the Chernovsti region of *Ukraine*.[73]

Middle Ages to 1945, SIPRI Chemical & Biological Warfare Studies no. 18 (Oxford University Press: Oxford, 1999), pp. 127–52.

[68] 'Japan is to put up', AFP (Hong Kong), 21 Aug. 2004, in 'AFP cites Mainichi: Japan to build chemical weapons disposal facility in China', Foreign Broadcast Information Service, *Daily Report–East Asia (FBIS-EAS)*, FBIS-EAS-2004-0821, 21 Aug. 2004.

[69] 'Japan tested chemical weapon on Aussie POW: new evidence', *Japan Times*, 27 July 2004, URL <http://www.japantimes.co.jp/cgi-bin/getarticle.pl5?nn20040727a9.htm>.

[70] US Department of State, 'Rumsfeld praises Panama's role in fighting narco-terrorism: U.S. defense secretary speaks at news conference in Panama', *International Information Programs*, Nov. 2004, URL <http://usinfo.state.gov/gi/Archive/2004/Nov/15-929837.html>.

[71] Seven chemical munitions have reportedly been recovered. Robles, F., 'Panama pushing U.S. to remove its old bombs', *Miami Herald*, 1 Aug. 2004, URL<http://www.miami.com/mld/miamiherald/news/world/americas/9292896.htm?1c>. It is unclear whether the bombs contained chemical warfare agents. Under the CWC a chemical weapon can consist of unfilled munitions and devices that are specifically designed to cause death or other harm through the toxic properties of their chemical fill. CWC, Article II, para. 1.

[72] For background, see Hart, Kuhlau and Simon (note 43), p. 658; and Zanders, Hart and Kuhlau (note 9), p. 695.

[73] 'Workers find poison gas shells at Ukraine construction site', *Deutsche Presse-Agentur*, 21 June 2004. Munitions, mostly dating from World War II, are recovered every month in Ukraine. Daily reports on the recovery of old munitions is provided by the Ministry of Ukraine of Emergencies and Affairs of

IV. Iraq

In 2004 the sole investigative effort in Iraq to uncover its past biological and chemical warfare activities was conducted by the US-led Iraq Survey Group (ISG) because the UN Monitoring, Verification and Inspection Commission (UNMOVIC) remained excluded from Iraq. However, UNMOVIC continued to publish reports and analysis.[74] By the end of 2004, the ISG teams had not discovered any chemical or biological weapons or programmes in Iraq and their inspection activities were essentially finished. While some questions about Iraq's chemical and biological weapon capabilities have been answered to some extent, some may never be resolved.[75] The 'non-discovery' of weapon stockpiles has led to official inquiries into the quality and use of the intelligence information provided before the 2003 invasion of Iraq.

The Iraq Survey Group

The ISG, whose members came from Australia, the UK and the USA, began its work in June 2003. Its primary goal was to uncover and eliminate NBC weapons.[76] On 23 January 2004 the Director of the US Central Intelligence Agency (CIA), George Tenet, announced that Charles A. Duelfer would succeed David Kay as Special Advisor for Strategy regarding Iraqi Weapons of Mass Destruction Programs.[77] Kay's conclusion on leaving his post was that there were no stocks of NBC weapons in Iraq.[78] The ISG comprised approximately 1750 people 750 of whom worked in Iraq; most of the remaining staff worked in Qatar.[79] Owing to the intense violence in Iraq and the absence of new information, the ISG ended its work in Iraq in December 2004.[80]

Population Protection from Consequences of Chernobyl Catastrophe at URL <http://www.mns.gov.ua/daily/showdailyarchive.php?day=22&month=12&year=2004&l=ru>.

[74] UNMOVIC's 16th Quarterly Report is attached as an annex to UN Security Council document S/2004/160, 27 Feb. 2004; the 17th Quarterly report is attached to UN Security Council document S/2004/435, 28 May 2004; the 18th is attached to UN Security Council document S/2004/693, 27 Aug. 2004; and the 19th is attached to UN Security Council document S/2004/924, 26 Nov. 2004. They are available on the UNMOVIC Internet site at URL <http://www.unmovic.org/> and on the UN Internet site at URL <http://documents.un.org>.

[75] The outstanding questions are essentially the same as in 2003. On outstanding questions regarding Iraq's chemical and biological weapons see Guthrie *et al.* (note 14); and UNMOVIC, 19th Quarterly Report, (note 74), para. 27.

[76] On the ISG see Guthrie *et al.* (note 14), pp. 686–88.

[77] Central Intelligence Agency (CIA), 'DCI announces Duelfer to succeed Kay as special advisor', Press Releases and Statements, 23 Jan. 2004, URL <http://www.cia.gov/cia/public_affairs/press_release/2004/pr01232004.html>.

[78] Kay Testimony, Hearing of the Senate Armed Services Committee 'Iraqi weapons of mass destruction programs', 28 Jan. 2004, URL <www.ceip.org/files/projects/ npp/pdf/Iraq/kaytestimony.pdf>.

[79] Iraq Survey Group, 'Statement for the record', Brigadier General Joseph J. McMenamin, US Marine Corps Commander Iraq Survey Group, Oct. 2004, URL <http://www.senate.gov/~armed_services/statemnt/2004/October/McMenamin 10-06-04.pdf>.

[80] Linzer, D., 'Search for banned arms in Iraq ended last month: critical September report to be final word', *Washington Post*, 12 Jan. 2005, p. A01, URL <http://www.washingtonpost.com/ac2/wp_dyn/A2129-2005Jan11>.

Key findings

The ISG produced a short report for the US Congress, which was presented by Duelfer on 30 March 2004.[81] Allegations later surfaced that the CIA and the British Secret Intelligence Service (MI6) had attempted to insert incorrect information into the report, which led to the resignation of a senior Australian member of the ISG, Rod Barton, on 22 March 2004.[82] Rumours circulated that another Australian and a Briton had also resigned from the ISG.

In October the ISG released a substantial unclassified report on its search for chemical and biological weapons.[83] An addendum is scheduled to be released in early 2005, and work continued on revision of the remaining documents and follow-up of any additional discoveries in Iraq.[84]

The report concluded that Iraq's ability to produce chemical and biological weapons had essentially been destroyed in 1991. The report focused on the former regime's *intent* or *capability* to produce new such weapons. However, according to UNMOVIC, the report did not consider the impact of ongoing monitoring and verification (OMV), which was designed to detect the intent to misuse dual-use equipment. The OMV had continued even after the lifting of sanctions.[85] The ISG did not discover any 'formal written' Iraqi strategy for the revival of WMD after the lifting of sanctions.[86]

The ISG estimated that Iraq had unilaterally destroyed the unaccounted for parts of its chemical weapon stockpile in 1991. The Kuwait War crippled the chemical warfare programme and the legitimate chemical industry suffered from sanctions. The ISG also claimed that Iraq had organized the chemical industry after the mid-1990s so as to allow it to preserve the scientific knowledge base needed to restart a chemical warfare programme, conduct a modest amount of dual-use research and partially recover from the decline of its production capability.[87] A small number of pre-1991 abandoned chemical mortar shells were uncovered in Iraq by the ISG and by coalition troops.[88] Analysis of their contents revealed that the chemical fill was decomposed to the extent that

[81] Testimony to the US Congress by Mr Charles Duelfer, Director of Central Intelligence Special Advisor for Strategy regarding Iraqi Weapons of Mass Destruction (WMD) Programs, 30 Mar. 2004, URL <http://www.cia.gov/cia/public_affairs/speeches/2004/tenet_testimony_03302004.html>.

[82] Mangold, T., 'Tomorrow John Scarlett starts his job as boss of MI6', *Mail on Sunday* (London), 1 Aug. 2004, p. 8.

[83] Central Intelligence Agency (CIA), 'Comprehensive Report of the Special Advisor to the DCI on Iraq's WMD', 30 Sep. 2004 (hereafter ISG Report). The report was published in 3 vols, available at URL <http://www.odci.gov/cia/reports/iraq_wmd_2004/index.html>.

[84] The White House, 'Press briefing by Scott McClellan', 12 Jan. 2005, URL <http://www.whitehouse.gov/news/releases/2005/01/20050112-7.html>.

[85] Ember, L. R., 'Assessing Iraq's weapons: Report requested by the President discounts arms threat, undercuts rationale for war', *Chemical and Engineering News*, vol. 82, no. 43 (25 Oct. 2004), pp. 40–44; and UNMOVIC, 19th Quarterly Report, (note 74), Appendix, para. 6.

[86] ISG Report, (note 83), vol. I, 'Key findings', p. 30.

[87] ISG Report, (note 83), vol. III, 'Iraq's chemical warfare program', p. 1.

[88] Global Security, 'Possible Iraqi chemical weapons found—Denmark', 12 Jan 2004, URL <http://www.globalsecurity.org/wmd/library/news/iraq/2004/01/iraq-040112-pla-daily03.htm>; and BBC News, 'Nerve gas bomb' explodes in Iraq', 17 May 2004, URL <http://news.bbc.co.uk/1/hi/world/middle_east/3722255.stm>.

it presented little or no danger.[89] The ISG recovered 53 chemical munitions, which appear to be from pre-Gulf War stocks.[90] The ISG concluded that, because nerve agent produced earlier by Iraq had lacked stability, the intent had been to maintain a 'just-in-time' production capability. Regarding biological weapons, the report concluded that Iraq had destroyed its undeclared stocks and had probably destroyed its remaining bulk biological warfare agent in 1991–92.

The ISG report alleged that the Iraqi Intelligence Service programme possessed a series of chemical and biological laboratories. The scope and nature of the work conducted there has not been established. The laboratories were not declared and were never inspected by the UN Special Commission on Iraq (UNSCOM) or UNMOVIC.[91] It is unclear from the report whether the activity claimed by the ISG to have taken place at these laboratories was related to weapon programmes. It is therefore not certain that they should have been subject to monitoring by UNMOVIC.[92]

Delivery systems and alleged mobile production capabilities

Iraq was accused in 2002 assessments of possessing several unmanned air vehicle (UAV) programmes that were intended to deliver chemical and biological weapons.[93] However, UNMOVIC concluded that there is no evidence that Iraq developed drones, remotely piloted vehicles (RPVs) and UAVs of prohibited ranges or capable of delivering chemical or biological weapons. These systems were more likely intended for 'conventional military purposes such as air defence training, data collection and surveillance'.[94]

This assessment was not shared by the ISG, which claimed in October 2003 that Iraq had tested one of its declared UAVs to a range of 500 kilometre, which is 350 km beyond the permissible limit.[95] Duelfer also concluded that UAVs were tested and 'easily exceeded' the UN limit of 150 km and that a 'very robust' Iraqi programme for delivery systems, not reported to the UN, had been uncovered.[96] However, this original ISG assessment changed and the October 2004 ISG report concluded that the UAV programmes were intended

[89] Manley, R., 'The Butler report: where did Iraq's weapons go?', *Open Democracy*, 21 July 2004, URL <http://www.opendemocracy.net/articles/ViewPopUpArticle.jsp?id=-2&articleId=2015>. Different chemical warfare agents decompose at different rates. Decomposition rates also vary with the original purity of the agent, presence of stabilizers and storage conditions. In general, agents such as sulphur mustard degrade at a slower rate than nerve agents. See also BBC News, ''No blister agent' in Iraq shells', 18 Jan. 2004, URL <http://news.bbc.co.uk/2/hi/middle_east/3407853.stm>.

[90] ISG Report (note 83), vol. III, 'Iraq's chemical warfare program', p. 97.

[91] ISG Report (note 83), vol. III, 'Biological warfare', pp. 1-2.

[92] UNMOVIC, 19th Quarterly Report, (note 74), Appendix, para. 31.

[93] See Guthrie *et al.* (note 14), p. 689.

[94] UNMOVIC, 18th Quarterly Report, (note 74), Appendix II, paras. 12-13.

[95] Central Intelligence Agency, 'Statement by David Kay on the interim progress report on the activities of the Iraq Survey Group (ISG) before the House Permanent Select Committee on Intelligence, the House Committee on Appropriations, Subcommittee on Defense, and the Senate Select Committee on Intelligence', 2 Oct. 2003, URL <http://www.cia.gov/cia/public_affairs/speeches/2003/david_kay_10022003.html>.

[96] Testimony to the US Congress by Mr Charles Duelfer (note 81).

for reconnaissance or electronic warfare; no evidence was found of intent to use UAVs as chemical or biological delivery systems.[97] The report claimed that there were numerous examples of disregard of UN sanctions and resolutions in an effort to improve missile and UAV capabilities.[98]

Unresolved questions regarding Iraq's missile programme remained in 2004. From 1999 until 2002 the Al Samoud-2 and Al Fatah missiles were the key components of Iraq's missile programme.[99] The ISG estimated that 36 Al Samoud-2 and as many as 34 Al Fatah missiles were unaccounted for.[100] At the time UNMOVIC withdrew from Iraq, it was still overseeing the destruction of proscribed Al Samoud-2 missiles and estimated that 25 such missiles remained to be destroyed. According to UNMOVIC, the status of the Al Fatah missiles remained uncertain. UNMOVIC had previously confirmed the existence of 37 complete Al Fatah missiles and 12 such missiles that were still in production.[101]

The ISG found no evidence that Iraq had retained Scud-variant missiles after 1991. It did find evidence of Iraqi interest in developing a long-range missile capability and uncovered plans for three long-range ballistic missiles with 400–1000 km ranges and plans for a 1000-km range cruise missile. However, none of these missiles had progressed to the stage of production.[102]

Alleged mobile biological weapon production units (trailers) constituted part of the coalition's 'evidence' of the presence of NBC weapons in Iraq,[103] but in 2004 the USA acknowledged that the claim was inaccurate.[104] The ISG reached the same conclusion after thorough examination of two trailers that had been found in 2003 and which were the subject of specific CIA allegations in 2003. The ISG stated that they were 'almost certainly' designed for the generation of hydrogen and were not part of a biological warfare programme.[105]

UNMOVIC: status and future

UNMOVIC conducted inspections in Iraq relating to chemical and biological weapons, including at facilities and locations which US intelligence services claimed were used for storing such munitions, until the start of military action

[97] ISG Report (note 83), vol. II, 'Delivery systems', p. 42.

[98] ISG Report (note 83), vol. II, 'Delivery systems', p. 71.

[99] UNMOVIC, 19th Quarterly Report, (note 74), Appendix, para. 33.

[100] ISG Report (note 83), vol. II, 'Delivery systems', pp. 18–28, 95–106.

[101] UNMOVIC's 19th Quarterly Report (note 74), Appendix, para. 34.

[102] ISG Report (note 83), vol. II, 'Delivery systems', pp. 1–2.

[103] The alleged information was used in Feb. 2003 by US Secretary of State Colin L. Powell in his attempt to convince the UN Security Council that Iraq had stockpiles of chemical and biological weapons ready for deployment. US Department of State, 'Remarks to the United Nations Security Council', Statement by US Secretary of State Colin, L. Powell, 5 Feb. 2003, URL <http://www.state.gov/secretary/rm/2003/17300.htm>.

[104] NBC Meet the Press, 'Powell: prewar intel on Iraq labs was 'inaccurate': some information said 'deliberately' misleading', 16 May 2004, URL <http://www.msnbc.msn.com/id/4997766/>. On analysis of UNMOVIC assessments see Guthrie *et al.* (note 14), pp. 688–89.

[105] ISG Report (note 83), vol. III, 'Biological warfare', pp. 3, 79.

in March 2003.[106] Although the UN inspectors have not been allowed back into Iraq their mandate is not terminated and UNMOVIC still exists.[107] The coalition has not requested UNMOVIC's services to resolve the remaining questions about Iraq's chemical and biological weapon capabilities and cooperation between the two has been non-existent. When the ISG report was published, UNMOVIC was not given access to the supporting documentation, interview testimony or details of the inspections conducted by the ISG.[108] Meanwhile, UNMOVIC has *inter alia* begun compiling a compendium to cover several aspects of its findings on Iraq's 'past proscribed' chemical and biological weapons and programmes from the 1960s until 2003.[109] Its staff has been reduced by one-fourth and currently comprises 51 employees.[110] UNMOVIC continues to be financed by revenues from the oil-for-food programme (OFFP)[111] and will have the means to continue to operate until a new UN Security Council resolution terminates its mandate.

UNSCOM and UNMOVIC were both mandated to carry out OMV in Iraq.[112] This mandate is still legally in place, although in practice UNMOVIC has conducted limited monitoring, which mainly involved known equipment and material that now cannot be located.[113] Using commercial satellite images UNMOVIC revealed a systematic looting of items subject to monitoring, which made it difficult to maintain an accurate assessment of Iraq's capabilities. Sites which were part of the main chemical weapon production establishment have been emptied and destroyed without tracking the materials, and sealed structures whose contents were not ascertained may have been breached.[114] Chemical production sites have been looted and destroyed, although biological production sites generally have been left untouched.[115]

The lack of participation by UN weapon inspectors in Iraq after March 2003 has been criticized because it complicates the examination of the role and importance of the constraints, such as inspections and sanctions, imposed on Iraq.[116] The apparent success and effectiveness of UNSCOM's and

[106] Halchin E., L., 'The Coalition Provisional Authority (CPA): origin, characteristics, and institutional authorities', *CRS Report for Congress*, 29 Apr. 2004, URL <www.usembassy.at/en/download/pdf/iraq_cpa.pdf>.

[107] On UNMOVIC's mandate see Zanders, J. P. *et al.*, *Non-compliance with the Chemical Weapons Convention: Lessons from and for Iraq*, SIPRI Policy Paper no. 5, Oct. 2003, URL <http://www.sipri.org/contents/publications/policy_papers.html>.

[108] UNMOVIC 19th Quarterly Report (note 74), para. 3.

[109] UNMOVIC 16th Quarterly Report (note 74), para. 10.

[110] UNMOVIC 19th Quarterly Report (note 74), para. 20.

[111] On 21 Apr. 2004, the UN Security Council authorized an independent inquiry into allegations of corruption and fraud surrounding the OFFP through the passage of Resolution 1538. See the independent Inquiry Committee's official Internet site at URL <http://www.iic-offp.org/>.

[112] The mandate is stipulated in United Nations Security Council Resolution 687, 3 Apr. 1991 and subsequently detailed in United Nations Security Council Resolution 715, 11 Oct. 1991.

[113] UNMOVIC official, interview with F. Kuhlau, 14 Dec. 2004.

[114] UNMOVIC 18th Quarterly Report (note 74), paras 10-11; and UNMOVIC 19th Quarterly Report (note 74), paras 6–12.

[115] UNMOVIC official (note 113).

[116] Cirincione, J. *et al.*, *WMD in Iraq: Evidence and Implications* (Carnegie Endowment for International Peace: Washington, DC, Jan. 2004), URL <http://www.ceip.org/files/pdf/Iraq3FullText.pdf>.

UNMOVIC's unique inspections in curtailing Iraq's biological and chemical weapon programmes prompted discussion of the establishment of a permanent inspection agency. Proposals were made in 2003 to transform UNMOVIC into a permanent UN arms inspectorate, and the Council of the European Union adopted an Action Plan under which 'unique verification and inspection competence' could be retained from UNMOVIC for future use.[117] The discussion continued in 2004. Expertise and institutional memory are important for future inspections specifically relating to biological weapons and missiles where specialized international organizations do not exist, and it has been suggested that UNMOVIC could form the basis for a permanent body operating under the UN Secretary-General.[118] Nuclear issues would generally be addressed by the IAEA and chemical issues by the OPCW.[119] As already noted in the biological context, however, there is influential opposition to this suggestion.[120]

Work programmes to redirect Iraqi weapon scientists and technicians

A number of programmes have been initiated to offer civilian employment to Iraqi scientists, technicians and engineers who previously worked on NBC weapon and missile programmes. Such efforts have been conducted in parallel with a broader international attempt to reduce the threat posed by the proliferation of NBC materials and scientific know-how. In Iraq a limited number of nations focus on this issue. The Iraqi International Center for Science and Industry (IICSI), which was created in December 2003,[121] began operating in June 2004 under the supervision of the US Department of State and was scheduled to operate for two years with an annual budget of approximately $2 million.[122] The Department of State has not requested additional funding for fiscal year 2005.[123] As of January 2005 the programme had engaged about

[117] Guthrie *et al.* (note 14), pp. 690-91.

[118] Carnegie Endowment for International Peace, 'The importance of inspections', Proliferation Brief, vol. 7, no. 11, adapted from remarks by Dr Hans Blix, chairman of the Weapons of Mass Destruction Commission, to the 2004 Carnegie International Non-Proliferation Conference, 21–22 June 2004, URL <http://www.carnegieendowment.org/publications/index.cfm?fa=print&id=1591>; Ifft, E., 'Iraq and the value of on-site inspections', *Arms Control Today*, Nov. 2004, URL <http://www.armscontrol.org/act/2004_11/Ifft.asp?print>; and Findlay, T., 'Preserving UNMOVIC: the institutional possibilities', *Disarmament Diplomacy*, no. 76 (Mar./Apr. 2004), URL <http://www.acronym.org.uk/dd/dd76/76tf.htm>.

[119] Center for Arms Control and Non-Proliferation, 'Arms control experts call for permanent UN body for WMD investigations', 18 Oct. 2004, URL <http://www.armscontrolcenter.org/archives/000895.php>; and Ifft (note 118).

[120] See the section on biological weapon disarmament above.

[121] US Department of State, 'Redirection of Iraqi weapons of mass destruction (WMD) experts', Press Statement, 18 Dec. 2003 <URL http://www.state.gov/r/pa/prs/ps/2003/27408.html>.

[122] Stone, R., 'Coalition throws 11th-hour lifeline to Iraqi weaponeers', *Science*, vol. 304, no. 5679 (25 June 2004), p. 1884.

[123] Roston, M., 'Redirection of WMD Scientists in Iraq and Libya: a status report', *RANSAC: Policy Update*, Apr. 2004, URL <http://www.ransac.org/Publications/Reports%20and%20Publications/Policy%20Updates/index.asp>.

120 scientists in various activities.[124] The Department of State reportedly plans to employ up to 500 Iraqis under the IICSI programme.[125]

On 19 June 2004 the Coalition Provisional Authority (CPA) created the Iraqi Nonproliferation Programs Foundation (INPF) with initial funding of $37.5 million.[126] The programme will fund projects involving Iraqi scientists and technicians who participated in weapon-related activities to work on 'reconstruction projects'.[127] The CPA's 2004 budget included 90 billion new Iraqi dinar (NID) (*c.* $60 million) allocated for 'WMD scientist retention' and 30 billion NID (*c.* $20 million) per year for 2005 and 2006.[128] Another US Government-funded initiative was launched by the Arab Science and Technology Foundation and the Cooperative Monitoring Center at Sandia National Laboratories to identify, contact and engage members of the Iraqi science and technology community.[129]

Implementation of these programmes has been complicated by factors such as lack of funding but primarily by the continued and increasing violence in Iraq since the regime change. Some experts regard the efforts as insufficient to prevent 'brain drain' from occurring.[130] Iraqi scientists have expressed concern that they might be imprisoned or prosecuted after coming forward and that cooperating with the occupation forces puts them at risk of being killed by insurgents.[131] In addition, the whereabouts of many of the scientists and technicians remains unknown.[132]

V. Intelligence issues

The public case for military action in Iraq was based to a large extent on intelligence assessments that it possessed chemical and biological weapons. After several months of fruitless inspections in Iraq the quality and use of the earlier intelligence information were deeply questioned.

The statement by former head of the ISG David Kay that 'we were almost all wrong' in believing Iraq had WMD[133] was reflected in the decisions to conduct official inquiries into the pre-war handling of intelligence in Australia,

[124] US Department of State, 'Daily press briefing', 12 Jan. 2005, URL <http://www.state.gov/r/pa/prs/dpb/2005/40828.htm>.

[125] Stockman, F., 'U.S. finds jobs in Iraq for nuclear scientists: goal is to thwart proliferation threat', *International Herald Tribune*, 16 July 2004, p. 5.

[126] Stone (note 122).

[127] Stone (note 122).

[128] Republic of Iraq, Minister of Finance and Minister of Planning, '2004 budget', Oct. 2003, p. 27, URL <http://www.cpa-iraq.org/budget/NIDmergedfinal-11Oct.pdf>. See the CPA Internet site at URL <http://www.cpa-iraq.org/>.

[129] Alnajjar, A. *et al.*, 'International initiative to engage Iraq's science and technology community: report on the priorities of the Iraqi Science and Technology Community', *Sandia Report*, May 2004.

[130] NTI Global Security Newswire 'US effort to redirect Iraqi scientists stalls', 4 Oct. 2004 URL <http://www.nti.org/d_newswire/issues/2004_10_4.html#18639321>.

[131] Scarborough, R., 'Iraqi arms scientists killed before they can talk', *Washington Times*, 23 Aug. 2004

[132] Stockman (note 125).

[133] Kay Testimony (note 78).

the UK and the USA. The capabilities, limits and selection of intelligence information were frequently discussed, leading to calls for structural changes within intelligence organizations and of the means by which the results are distributed within government and beyond.[134]

National inquiries into pre-war intelligence on Iraq

In *Australia*, the government established an inquiry, headed by Philip Flood, in response to the recommendations in a report by the Parliamentary Joint Committee investigating (and clearing) the government of exaggerating the threat posed by Iraq and WMD.[135]

In the *United Kingdom*, the report of the Hutton Inquiry into the death of Dr David Kelly was published on 28 January 2004 and drew controversy over its findings and the narrow interpretation of its remit.[136] This led to the announcement in the House of Commons[137] of the establishment of an inquiry to be led by Lord Butler to 'investigate the intelligence coverage available in respect of WMD programmes in countries of concern and on the global trade of WMD' and specifically to 'investigate the accuracy of intelligence on Iraqi WMD up to March 2003'.[138]

In the *United States*, an independent inquiry into US intelligence capabilities was established by presidential executive order on 6 February 2004 with a broad remit to examine not only intelligence regarding Iraq but also NBC programmes in countries such as Iran, North Korea, Libya and Afghanistan under the Taliban. The report on its findings is expected by 31 March 2005.[139] On 12 February 2004 the terms of the formal review by the US Senate Select Committee on Intelligence (established in 2003)[140] into the existence of Iraq's

[134] The White House Press, 'Commission on the Intelligence Capabilities of the United States Regarding Weapons of Mass Destruction', 6 Feb. 2004, URL <http://www.whitehouse.gov/news/releases/2004/02/print/20040206-13.html>; and Pullinger, S., 'Lord Butler's Report on UK intelligence', *Disarmament Diplomacy,* no. 78 (July/Aug. 2004), URL <http://www.acronym.org.uk/dd/dd78/78sp.htm>; and Ember, L., 'Intelligence overhaul: proposal would dismantle CIA, move some key Pentagon intelligence agencies', *Chemical and Engineering News,* vol. 82, no. 35 (30 Aug. 2004), p. 5.

[135] Flood, P., 'Report of the inquiry into Australian intelligence agencies' (hereafter 'Flood Report'), 20 July 2004, URL <http://inquiry.dpmc.gov.au/docs/Intelligence_Report.pdf>; and Parliament of the Commonwealth of Australia, Parliamentary Joint Committee on ASIO, ASIS and DSD, 'Intelligence on Iraq's weapons of mass destruction', Dec. 2004 (presented on 1 Mar. 2004), ch. 5, p. 97, URL <http://www.aph.gov.au/house/committee/pjcaad/WMD/report.htm>.

[136] 'Investigation into the Circumstances Surrounding the Death of Dr David Kelly', URL <http://www.the-hutton-inquiry.org.uk>. See also Guthrie *et al.* (note 14), pp. 679–80.

[137] *Hansard*, 3 Feb. 2004, c625-43.

[138] Report of a Committee of Privy Counsellors, 'Review of Intelligence on Weapons of Mass Destruction' (hereafter 'Butler Report'), 14 July 2004, p. 1. See the official Internet site of the inquiry at URL <http://www.butlerreview.org.uk/report/>.

[139] The White House, 'Commission on the Intelligence Capabilities of the United States Regarding Weapons of Mass Destruction', 2 Feb. 2004, URL <http://www.whitehouse.gov/news/releases/2004/02/20040206-10.html>.

[140] United States Senate Select Committee on Intelligence, 'As part of its ongoing oversight of the intelligence community, the Senate Select Committee on Intelligence will conduct a review of intelligence on Iraqi weapons of mass destruction', 4 June 2003, URL <http://intelligence.senate.gov/030604.htm>.

NBC programmes were expanded to include among other things a probe into whether the US Government exaggerated intelligence information. The additional issues will be examined in two phases. The first report was released on 7 July 2004,[141] and the second report is expected in 2005. The official inquiry into the 11 September 2001 attacks in the USA also reported in 2004.[142]

Weaknesses in pre-war intelligence estimates

A common theme of the inquiries detailed above was that pre-war assessments were inaccurate and unsupported by the available sources. The US Senate inquiry concluded that the information in Secretary of State Colin Powell's presentation of evidence to the UN Security Council was 'overstated, misleading or incorrect'.[143] It also considered most key judgements in the 2002 National Intelligence Estimate (NIE)[144] to be overstated or not supported by intelligence.[145]

While the Hutton Report had essentially cleared the British Government of 'sexing up' intelligence in relation to Iraq, the Butler Report criticized British intelligence and the government's failure to provide warnings about the thinness of the evidence. The intelligence material had great weaknesses, but these uncertainties were not noted, leading to the impression that the intelligence was firmer than it was. [146] The report also criticized the Joint Intelligence Committee's findings and concluded that the intelligence on Iraq's biological agent capabilities was 'seriously flawed'.[147] The sources of information were few and not sufficiently checked, and the 2002 dossier on Iraqi WMD[148] should not have included the assertion that Iraq was capable of using WMD within 45 minutes since the limitations to this claim were not made sufficiently clear.[149]

The Flood Report concluded that intelligence on Iraq's alleged weapon capabilities was 'thin, ambiguous and incomplete'.[150] Australia shared the intelligence failure on the key question of WMD stockpiles with its coalition partners, but the overall assessment of Iraqi WMD up to the time of combat

[141] US Senate Select Committee on Intelligence, 'Report on the US intelligence Community's Prewar Intelligence Assessments on Iraq', 7 July 2004, URL <http://intelligence.senate.gov/iraqreport2.pdf>.

[142] 'Final Report of the National Commission on terrorist attacks upon the United States: the 9/11 Commission report', 22 July 2004, URL <http://www.9-11commission.gov/report/index.htm>.

[143] US Senate Select Committee on Intelligence (note 141), p. 253, conclusion 72.

[144] US Central Intelligence Agency, *Iraq's Weapons of Mass Destruction Programs*, 4 Oct. 2002; and US Department of State (note 103).

[145] US Senate Select Committee on Intelligence (note 141), pp. 14–25.

[146] Butler Report (note 138), paras 464–65; and Reynolds, P., 'Devil in the detail', BBC News, 15 July 2004, URL <http://news.bbc.co.uk/1/hi/uk_politics/3894403.stm>.

[147] Butler Report (note 138), para. 409.

[148] UK Government, *Iraq's Weapons of Mass Destruction: the Assessment of the British Government* (Stationery Office: London, 24 Sep. 2002). The strength and reliability of this dossier, and whether Dr David Kelly had been the source of comments to a journalist that the material in it had been 'sexed up' to justify the invasion of Iraq, were at the heart of the inquiry led by Lord Hutton (note 136).

[149] Butler Report (note 138), para. 511.

[150] Flood Report (note 135), p. 34.

operations was considered to have 'reflected reasonably the limited available information and used intelligence sources with appropriate caution'.[151] The Flood Report omitted to note that there was a lack of consensus in the Australian Government's analytical community over this assessment.[152]

The US Senate report claimed that 'the failure of the intelligence community to accurately analyse and describe the intelligence in the NIE was the result of a combination of systemic weaknesses, primarily in analytic trade craft, a lack of information sharing, poor management and inadequate intelligence collection'.[153] It claimed that management had failed to encourage analysts to challenge their assumptions and to consider alternative arguments.[154] The poor intelligence on Iraq was explained as a result of the structure of the intelligence organizations and their procedures and of collective mistakes—referred to both in the British and US reports as 'group think'—rather than as the responsibility of individuals. Ambiguous evidence was interpreted as indicative of NBC weapon stockpiles and programmes, while evidence that Iraq did not have such stockpiles and programmes was ignored or minimized.[155]

Government officials were accused of pressuring the intelligence community to produce intelligence to build a case for war, and the intelligence community was accused of generating inaccurate information. The US Senate committee did not find evidence that pressure or influence from officials was put on analysts to change their judgements.[156] Similarly, in Australia and the UK, the government-initiated inquiries concluded that the intelligence information was not considered to have been distorted in order to exaggerate the threat.[157] The political context in which the pre-war intelligence was gathered and analysed was not considered in the inquiry reports.

UNMOVIC Executive Chairman Hans Blix has noted that pre-war intelligence on Iraq lacked critical thinking and UNMOVIC reports were not taken as seriously as were worst-case scenario intelligence estimates.[158] Questions were raised as to why the negative results of UNMOVIC inspections that had been reported in early 2003 had not led to a re-evaluation of intelligence.[159]

[151] 'Introduction' and 'conclusion', Flood Report (note 135).

[152] This lack of consensus became clear when it was revealed during 2004 that a senior defence scientist had written to the Australian Prime Minister in Mar. 2003 stating there was no 'specific information, or even convincing circumstantial evidence that Iraq 'currently has a substantial usable CBW stockpile'. See Allard, T., 'Weapons expert's fight to warn PM', *Sydney Morning Herald*, 25 Sep. 2004, URL <http://smh.com.au/articles/2004/09/24/1095961864769.html> and 'Letter by R. J. Mathews to Prime Minister John Howard', *Sydney Morning Herald*, 27 Sep. 2004, URL <http://smh.com.au/articles/2004/09/26/1096137098800.html>.

[153] US Senate Select Committee on Intelligence (note 141), p. 15.

[154] US Senate Select Committee on Intelligence (note 141), pp. 14–25.

[155] Cirincione, J., 'Two terrifying reports: the US Senate and the 9/11 Commission on intelligence failures before September 11 and the Iraq war', *Disarmament Diplomacy,* no. 78 (July/Aug. 2004), URL <http://www.acronym.org.uk/dd/dd78/78jc.htm>.

[156] US Senate Select Committee on Intelligence (note 141), p. 284, para. 83.

[157] Flood Report (note 135), p. 176; and Butler Report (note 138), para. 449.

[158] Blix, H., *Disarming Iraq: The Search for Weapons of Mass Destruction* (Bloomsbury Publishing: London, 2004), pp. 260–64.

[159] Butler Report (note 138), paras 362–64.

Of all of the inquiries, that headed by Lord Butler was most involved in comparing the information gathered from national and multinational sources. The Butler report concluded:

> We note that much of what was reliably known about Iraq's unconventional weapons programmes in the mid- and late-1990s was obtained through the reports of the UN Special Commission (UNSCOM) and of the International Atomic Energy Agency (IAEA). These international agencies now appear to have been more effective than was realised at the time in dismantling and inhibiting Iraq's prohibited weapons programmes. The value of such international organisations needs to be recognised and built on for the future, supported by the contribution of intelligence from national agencies.[160]

VI. Other past and present activities and allegations

In 2004 a number of allegations were made about past and present activities in the field of chemical and biological warfare.

Hungary's Ministry of Defence reportedly acknowledged that Hungary possessed a chemical weapon stockpile during the cold war, and Hungary also reported that it had carried out field training exercises with chemical warfare agents in the 1960s and 1970s. Hungary reportedly maintains small quantities of chemical warfare agents—including lewisite, sulphur mustard and nerve agents—as part of a protective programme permitted by the CWC.[161]

It was alleged that *North Korea* had carried out experiments on humans with chemical warfare agents.[162] One set of allegations centred around a set of documents claimed to be evidence of North Korean experiment activities.[163]

Allegations were made in April 2004 that *Sudan* was storing 'WMD components' on behalf of *Syria*. The main allegation centred around press reports, citing Western intelligence sources, which were said to suggest that the government of President Omar Bashir was not informed of the shipments.[164] In September separate allegations were made by a German magazine suggesting that Syrian forces had tested chemical weapons in the Darfur region of Sudan.[165] These latter allegations were denied by Sudan.[166]

[160] Butler Report (note 138), para. 584.

[161] Haszán, Z., 'Hová lettek a magyar vegyi fegyverek?' [Where have the Hungarian chemical weapons disappeared to?], *Népszabadság*, 25 Sep. 2004, pp. 1–2, URL <http://www.nol.hu/>.

[162] See, e.g., 'I saw an entire family being killed. They were put in the gas chamber where they all suffocated. The last to die was the youngest son', *Daily Telegraph*, 1 Feb. 2004; and Demick, B., 'North Korea's use of chemical torture alleged', *Los Angeles Times*, 3 Mar. 2004.

[163] Kim So-young, 'N. Korea tested gases on prisoners', *Korea Herald*, 13 Feb. 2004, URL <http://www.koreaherald.co.kr>.

[164] 'Syria smuggles missiles, WMD to Sudan', Middle East Newsline, 9 Apr. 2004, URL <http://www.menewsline.com/stories/2004/april/04_09_1.html>.

[165] Schuster, J., 'Syrien testet chemische waffen an Sudanern' [Syria tested chemical weapons in Sudan], *Die Welt*, 15 Sep. 2004, URL <http://www.welt.de/data/2004/09/15/332689.html>.

[166] United Nations, Letter dated 8 February 2005 from the Permanent Representatives of the Sudan to the United Nations addressed to the President of the Security Council, UN document S/2005/77, 10 Feb. 2005.

In *Ukraine*, presidential candidate Viktor Yushchenko fell seriously ill on 5 September 2004. Allegations were made that he had been poisoned, but it was not until the end of the year that this was confirmed. Dr Michael Zimpfer, director of Vienna's Rudolfinerhaus clinic, where Yushchenko was treated since falling ill, was quoted as saying: 'There is no doubt about the fact that Mr. Yushchenko's disease is caused by poisoning and that dioxin is one of the agents'. He added, 'We have identified the cause. We suspect involvement of a third party'.[167]

A reopened inquest in *the United Kingdom* into the death of 20-year-old airman Ronald Maddison on 6 May 1953 returned a verdict of 'unlawful killing'. Maddison had been a volunteer in a testing programme at the research establishment at Porton Down. He was exposed to 200 milligrams of sarin (GB) dropped onto cloth on his arm, felt unwell within minutes of the exposure and died within an hour. An initial inquest held in secret in 1953 recorded a verdict of 'misadventure'.[168]

The United States was alleged to have used toxic chemicals in its military action in Fallujah, Iraq, in November 2004.[169] While the allegations have not been confirmed, they highlight one of the difficult areas in implementing the CWC. If riot control agents are employed as a method of warfare, this activity is illegal under the terms of the convention. If the military action is considered to be a law enforcement activity in which the soldiers are acting in support, the use of riot control agents in certain circumstances would not be prohibited under the CWC.

VII. Conclusions

The separate influences of UN Security Council Resolution 1540 and the OPCW Action Plans have highlighted the need for more effective national implementation of multilateral conventions. In modern conditions, the control of chemical and biological weapons cannot be left simply to international organizations. More effective national implementation can substantially strengthen all of the regimes, yet countries cannot solve the problem either without stronger global institutional capacities, not least to set the standards for national implementation. The national and international elements are complementary and are both essential.

The lack of a global institution in the biological field was felt in a number of ways in 2004. Efforts such as the OPCW Action Plans could not have had an equivalent in the biological arena because of the lack of an equivalent institution. In Libya there was international oversight of the dismantling of the country's programmes in the chemical and nuclear fields, but the equivalent

[167] As quoted in Zarakhovich, Y., 'The dirtiest trick', *Time*, 20 Dec. 2004.

[168] Evans, R., 'The past Porton can't hide', *The Guardian*, 6 May 2004; 'Nerve gas death was 'unlawful'', BBC News, 15 Nov. 2004; and Carrell, S., 'Porton Down veterans to sue MoD over gas tests', *Independent on Sunday*, 21 Nov. 2004.

[169] See, e.g., 'US troops reportedly gassing Fallujah', IslamOnline, 10 Nov. 2004, URL <http://www.islamonline.org/English/News/2004-11/10/article05.shtml>.

process for the smaller biological research effort was overseen only by the UK and the USA. By definition this could not bring the same confidence to the international community that inspection by a global organization would have.

The warnings being given by certain governments, supposedly based on intelligence, that recent years have brought a substantially increased threat of large-scale terrorist use of biological and chemical weapons are notably similar to the warnings being given by the same countries a few years ago about the threat posed by Iraqi chemical and biological weapons. Many of the intelligence service reforms prompted by the numerous official inquiries into the incorrect assessments of the Iraqi situation have yet to be implemented, and it is not clear from what is available on the public record whether similar mistakes are being repeated. Another factor is that field officers in law enforcement and intelligence agencies are currently under great pressure to report every little detail up through the chain of command—no officer wants to be later discovered to have had a small but vital piece of information that could have predicted any sort of terror attack. Intelligence assessment of non-state actors can be even more difficult than assessment of states.

If the threat of large-scale attack should prove to have been overstated, does this matter? After all, even if the threat is low, it is still there, and it is worth taking pains to protect modern societies against their many vulnerabilities to novel types of terror attack. The focus on a large-scale biological and chemical threat could, however, prove to be counterproductive. While small-scale use of hazardous materials is within the technical reach of small organizations, large-scale use such as that required to devastate a large part of a city would require greater resources than most groups possess, or might want to commit. Nevertheless, if such groups hear messages in the Western media based on intelligence information that terrorists are pursuing such methods and could use them easily, the incentive to explore them—at the very least—risks being reinforced.

The BTWC meetings in 2004 were just one forum at which the primary importance of good public health measures for reducing the impact of any use of biological weapons was recognized.[170] At one level bio-terrorism is just deliberate disease: and with fears of new 'natural' pandemics currently so high, posterity may have reason to rue policies that divert resources from diseases that would kill millions to the narrower and still imponderable risks of a bio-terror attack.

[170] Njuguna, J., 'The SARS epidemic: the control of infectious diseases and biological weapon threats', *SIPRI Yearbook 2004* (note 14).

14. Libya's renunciation of nuclear, biological and chemical weapons and ballistic missiles

JOHN HART and SHANNON N. KILE

I. Introduction

In a joint statement with the United Kingdom and the United States on 19 December 2003, Libya publicly renounced nuclear, biological and chemical (NBC) weapons and agreed to restrict itself to the possession of ballistic missiles with a range of no more than 300 kilometres. It agreed to adhere to the 1968 Treaty on the Non-Proliferation of Nuclear Weapons (Non-Proliferation Treaty, NPT), the 1972 Biological and Toxin Weapons Convention (BTWC), the 1993 Chemical Weapons Convention (CWC) and the guidelines of the Missile Technology Control Regime (MTCR).[1] Libya also agreed to allow international inspectors to verify its commitments, including the dismantlement of its nuclear weapon programme and the destruction of its chemical weapon (CW) stockpile. In 2004 the remaining sanctions against Libya were lifted and the country took further steps to implement its commitments and to reintegrate itself into the international community.[2]

As information became available on Libya's former programmes, details of an informal nuclear weapon suppliers' network (the so-called Khan network, which sold technology to Libya until 2003[3]) emerged and a new basis was provided for evaluating the proliferation assessments that governments had made in the past. The British and US role in prompting Libya's action intensified debate over the merit of different approaches—national and institutional, foreign and domestic—to addressing concerns about NBC weapons.

Section II provides background to Libya's decision to renounce NBC weapons and its most capable ballistic missiles. Section III describes the trilateral process of negotiation between Libya, the UK and the USA and the subsequent lifting of remaining sanctions. International reaction to Libya's

[1] Libya acceded to the 1925 Geneva Protocol on 29 Dec. 1971 with the reservation that this did not imply recognition of Israel and that Libya would not be bound by Geneva Protocol provisions if other states or their allies did not adhere to those prohibitions. Libya acceded to the CWC on 6 Jan. 2004 and to the BTWC on 19 Jan. 1982. In 1999 Libya began to participate in negotiations on a protocol to strengthen the BTWC. (The negotiations were suspended indefinitely in 2001.) Libya deposited its instrument of ratification to the 1996 Comprehensive Nuclear Test-Ban Treaty on 6 Jan. 2004. On the BTWC and CWC see chapter 13 in this volume. On MTCR see chapter 17 in this volume.

[2] E.g., Williams, F., 'Libya to start talks to end world trading isolation', *Financial Times*, 28 July 2004, p. 6.

[3] On the Khan network see section V and chapter 12 in this volume.

decision is discussed in Section IV. Libya's weapon programmes are described in sections V–VII. The conclusions are presented in section VIII.

II. Background

Until 2004 Libya was subjected to one of the most stringent of all United Nations (UN) sanctions regimes,[4] not for reasons connected with weapon programmes but in consequence of its involvement in a number of violent incidents during the 1980s, for which it subsequently admitted at least partial responsibility.[5] The country was implicated *inter alia* in the 21 December 1988 bombing of the Pan Am airliner which exploded over Lockerbie, Scotland, and the 19 September 1989 bombing of the UTA French airliner which crashed over Niger. In 1992 the UN Security Council passed Resolution 731, which strongly deplored the fact that Libya had not 'responded effectively' to the requests of other governments for help in their criminal investigations and called on it to 'cooperate fully in establishing responsibility for the terrorist acts' against the two aircraft. The resolution requested the UN Secretary-General to 'seek the cooperation' of Libya to provide 'a full and effective response' to the requests.[6] In 1992 the Security Council passed Resolution 748, which imposed an arms and air travel embargo on Libya for failing to comply with Resolution 731.[7] In April 1999 the Security Council suspended its sanctions against Libya after it turned over to a Scottish court two suspects wanted in connection with the Lockerbie bombing. In August 2003 Libya accepted responsibility for the bombing and agreed to pay $2.7 billion in compensation. In 2003 the UN Security Council approved Resolution 1506, which lifted the sanctions imposed in 1992.[8]

III. The trilateral process and the lifting of sanctions

Throughout the 1990s, Libya is reported to have signalled interest in normalizing its relations with Europe and the USA.[9] According to a member of the

[4] For background see Katzman, K., *U.S.–Libyan Relations: An Analytical Compendium of U.S. Policies, Laws & Regulations* (Atlantic Council: Washington, DC, Aug. 2003).

[5] Libya was implicated in supporting the Abu Nidal organization when the group attacked the Rome and Vienna airports on 27 Dec. 1985. Libya was also implicated in the bombing of the La Belle nightclub in Berlin on 5 Apr. 1986. On 13 Nov. 2001 a German court found 4 people guilty of the bombing, including a former employee of the Libyan Embassy to East Germany. US Department of State, 'Background note: Libya', Fact Sheet, Oct. 2004, URL <http://www.state.gov/r/pa/ei/bgn/5425.htm>. On 17 April 1984 Yvonne Fletcher, a British policewoman, was killed outside Libya's embassy in London during a confrontation between pro- and anti-Qadhafi demonstrators. The shooting suspect was afforded diplomatic immunity by Libya and was therefore permitted to leave the UK.

[6] UN Security Council Resolution 731, 21 Jan. 1992.

[7] UN Security Council Resolution 748, 31 Mar. 1992. On 11 Nov. 1993 the Security Council passed Resolution 883 which strengthened UN sanctions against Libya under Chapter VII of the UN Charter, under which military intervention to maintain or restore international peace and security may be invoked.

[8] UN Security Council Resolution 1506, 12 Sep. 2003.

[9] Dunne, M., *Libya: Security is Not Enough*, Policy Brief no. 32 (Carnegie Endowment for International Peace: Washington, DC, Oct. 2004), p. 2.

US National Security Council (NSC), starting in 2002, Libya sent to the USA numerous 'direct and indirect messages' indicating its 'eagerness to resolve differences'.[10] During these contacts, the USA indicated that, in addition to the Lockerbie bombing, two main issues needed to be addressed: (*a*) the verifiable renunciation of Libya's NBC weapon and medium- and long-range missile programmes, and (*b*) an end to Libya's support of terrorism.[11]

In March 2003, while negotiations were being held on the Lockerbie settlement, the head of the Libyan intelligence service reportedly approached officials from the British Secret Intelligence Service (SIS, commonly known as MI6) and expressed Libya's willingness to renounce NBC weapons.[12] Officials from the US Central Intelligence Agency (CIA) were later invited to participate in the discussions. Libya, the UK and the USA then engaged in secret negotiations that resulted in two visits, in October and December 2003, to Libya by CIA and MI6 officials, who interviewed Libyan scientists and were said to be struck by their openness.[13] According to Libya's official news agency, the British and US officials were given information on 'materials, equipment and programmes [for NBC weapons] which led to the manufacture of internationally banned weapons with centrifuges and containers for the transfer of chemical materials'.[14] In addition, Libya reportedly provided the CIA and MI6 with 'exceptional' information on 'hundreds' of Islamic extremists, including those affiliated with al-Qaeda.[15]

A joint public statement issued on 19 December 2003[16] was drafted at a meeting between British and Libyan officials in London on 16 December 2003 and subsequently agreed by Libya, the UK and the USA. Final approval of the document was facilitated by a telephone conversation between British Prime Minister Tony Blair and Libyan President Muammar Qadhafi.[17] In its national press release of 20 December, Libya indicated that it was also committed to working for a Middle East and Africa that are 'free from weapons of mass destruction' (WMD).[18]

[10] Dunne (note 9), footnote 3. Michele Dunne was the NSC member in question.

[11] Dunne (note 9), p. 2.

[12] Fidler, S., Khalaf, R. and Huband, M., 'Return to the fold: how Gaddafi was persuaded to give up his nuclear goals', *Financial Times*, 27 Nov. 2004, p. 11.

[13] Tyler, P. E. and Risen, J., 'Libya arms talks lasted months', *International Herald Tribune*, 22 Dec. 2003, pp. 1, 6.

[14] 'Foreign Liaison Secretary—Statement', Jana, 20 Dec. 2003, URL <http://www.jamahiriyanews.com/>.

[15] Beaumont, P., Bright, M. and Ahmed, K., 'Libya's spies' secret deal to reveal terrorists', *The Observer* (Internet edn), 21 Dec. 2003, URL <http://observer.guardian.co.uk/international/story/0,6903,1111197,00.html>.

[16] 'Foreign Liaison Secretary—Statement' (note14).

[17] Beaumont, P., Ahmed, K. and Bright, M., 'The meeting that brought Libya in from the cold', *The Observer* (Internet edn), 21 Dec. 2003, URL <http://observer.guardian.co.uk/international/story/0,6903,1111161,00.html>.

[18] 'Foreign Liaison Secretary—Statement' (note 14). In Sep. 2004 Libya, the UK and the USA agreed an 'arrangement to discuss any future WMD concerns'. Dunne (note 9), p. 4.

International reaction

International reaction to Libya's commitment was positive. The Organisation for the Prohibition of Chemical Weapons (OPCW), the body which monitors compliance with the CWC, welcomed the Libyan Foreign Minister's announcement that his country would adhere to the convention 'without delay'.[19] The UN Security Council welcomed Libya's decision to abandon its WMD programmes and the means to deliver such weapons. It also reaffirmed 'the need to seek to resolve proliferation problems by peaceful means through political and diplomatic channels'.[20] On 26 June 2004 the US–European Union (EU) Declaration on the Non-proliferation of Weapons of Mass Destruction welcomed 'Libya's decision to abandon, under international verification, its WMD and longer-range missile programs'.[21] The US Administration also welcomed Libya's decision, citing it as a 'powerful precedent that a state can surrender WMD without a regime change'.[22]

Egypt and Syria expressed their support for Libya's decision. However, some government officials in the Middle East reportedly expressed the view that Libya should not have taken what they perceived as a unilateral step without first having secured agreement on verifiably transforming the Middle East into a WMD-free zone and that such a step should only have been taken once Israel had agreed to become a party to the NPT.[23]

The lifting of sanctions

In February 2004 the USA lifted restrictions on travel to Libya and, in April 2004, it ended the applicability of the 1996 Iran–Libya Sanctions Act.[24] The USA re-established direct diplomatic relations with Libya on 28 June 2004.[25] On 20 September US President George W. Bush issued an executive order

[19] Organisation for the Prohibition of Chemical Weapons (OPCW), 'Libya to adhere to the Chemical Weapons Convention', Press Release no. 40, 22 Dec. 2003, URL <http://www.opcw.org/html/global/press_releases/2k3/PR40_2003.prt.html>.

[20] United Nations News Service, 'Security Council welcomes Libya's decision to abandon weapons of mass destruction programmes', Press Release SC/8069, New York, 22 Apr. 2004, URL <http://www.un.org/News/Press/docs/2004/sc8069.doc.htm>.

[21] The White House, 'Fact sheet: U.S.–EU summit: declaration on the nonproliferation of weapons of mass destruction', 26 June 2004, URL <http://www.whitehouse.gov/news/releases/2004/06/20040626-11.html>.

[22] Bolton, J., 'The Bush Administration's forward strategy for nonproliferation', Presentation to the American Enterprise Institute, Washington, DC, 24 June 2004, URL <http://www.state.gov/t/us/rm/33907.htm>; and Mahley, D., 'Dismantling Libyan weapons: lessons learned', *The Arena* (Chemical & Biological Arms Control Institute: Washington, DC, Nov. 2004), available at URL <http://www.cbaci.org>.

[23] Middle East Media Research Institute (MEMRI), 'Arab media reactions to Libya's announcement of WMD dismantlement', Special Dispatch no. 640, 13 Jan. 2004.

[24] 'Travel warning', US Department of State advisory, 29 Dec. 2004, URL <http://travel.state.gov/travel/cis_pa_tw/tw/tw_926.html>; and US Department of Energy, Energy Information Administration, 'Global energy sanctions', URL <http://www.eia.doe.gov/emeu/cabs/sanction.html>.

[25] 'US resumes relations with Libya', BBC News Online, 28 June 2004, URL <http://news.bbc.co.uk/1/hi/world/africa/3848499.stm>.

lifting trade sanctions against Libya that had been in place since 1986.[26] In October 2004 the EU lifted its trade embargo and other sanctions against Libya and removed most of its restrictions on arms sales to the country.[27] UN sanctions were lifted on 12 September 2003.[28]

The rationale for Libya's decision

A number of possible factors have been cited to explain Libya's decision to renounce NBC weapons and medium- and long-range missiles. US Administration officials have portrayed the decision as a vindication of the administration's robust approach to combating the spread of NBC weapons.[29] They noted that Qadhafi had initiated the discussions a few days before the US-led war on Iraq began in March 2003. They also suggested that a US-initiated coalition operation that intercepted, in October 2003, a German-owned freighter carrying a secret shipment of centrifuge parts to Tripoli was an important factor in convincing Libya of the futility of pursuing its NBC weapon programmes.[30]

However, there has been disagreement over whether—or to what extent—the Bush Administration's counter-proliferation strategy should be credited for Libya's decision. Some observers have described it as part of the Qadhafi regime's long-term diplomatic efforts to overcome two decades of political and economic isolation.[31] The stringent international sanctions regime imposed on Libya had caused serious damage to its economy. According to Libya's prime minister, the government concluded that its NBC weapon and missile programmes were consuming scarce resources but would have only limited military and political utility.[32] Other Libyan officials reportedly expressed irritation over the US Administration's efforts to portray the Libyan decision as a vindication of its policies.[33]

[26] 'Executive Order 13357 of September 20, 2004', *Federal Register*, 22 Sep. 2004, pp. 56665–66, URL <http://www.access.gpo.gov/su_docs/aces/fr-cont.html>.

[27] Council of the European Union, 'Press release, 2609th Council meeting', EU Press Release, 11 Oct. 2004, p. 8, para. 7, available at URL <http://www.europa.eu.int>.

[28] United Nations, 'Security Council lifts sanctions against Libya imposed after Lockerbie bombing', UN Press Release, 12 Sep. 2003, URL <http://www.un.org/av/photo/sc/sc091203.htm>.

[29] The White House, Office of the Press Secretary, 'The President's national security strategy to combat WMD: Libya's announcement', Fact Sheet, 19 Dec. 2003, URL <http://www.whitehouse.gov/news/releases/2003/12/20031219-8.html>.

[30] Wright, R., 'Ship incident may have swayed Libya', *Washington Post* (Internet edn), 1 Jan. 2004, URL <http://www.washingtonpost.com/ac2/wp-dyn/A46260-2003Dec31>. The operation marked the first interception of a vessel under the US-organized Proliferation Security Initiative (PSI). On the PSI see chapter 18 in this volume.

[31] Williams, D., 'Possible opening to West stirs hope in Libya', *Washington Post* (Internet edn), 27 Dec. 2003, URL <http://www.washingtonpost.com/wp-dyn/articles/A33259-2003Dec26.html>; and Indyk, M., 'The Iraq War did not force Gaddafi's hand', *Financial Times*, 9 Mar. 2004, URL <http://www.brookings.edu/views/op-ed/indyk/20040309.htm>.

[32] Shukri Ghanem, quoted by Fidler, Khalaf and Huband (note 12).

[33] Referring to the US Government's display to the media of some sensitive nuclear equipment and material it had removed from Libya, an official from the International Atomic Energy Agency reported that Libya was 'quite unhappy with this dog and pony show because it hurts them domestically [and] in the Arab world'. 'Libya upset over US calling disarmament a "victory" for Washington', Channel News Asia, 17 Mar. 2004, distributed via the BioWeapons Prevention Project discussion forum, 19 Mar. 2004.

There has been speculation that Libya may have been motivated by additional considerations. It has been suggested that Qadhafi wished to improve his relations with the West at least in part because he believed that al-Qaeda-affiliated militants were planning to assassinate him.[34] This view is supported by the fact that, in October 1993, Libyan security forces arrested suspected coup plotters, including some members of Libya's military, who were said to have held extreme Islamic views.[35]

In a November 2004 interview Qadhafi described the decision by Libya in the context of its security concerns and regional geopolitical interests.[36] In particular, he noted that Libya's weapon programmes were in line with similar programmes being undertaken elsewhere and that, had Libya succeeded in developing nuclear weapons, it was not clear under what circumstances they might actually have been used. He also stated that Libya's decision was partly the result of 'fear' of such weapons among its neighbouring states. Qadhafi expressed dissatisfaction about the benefits received by his country stating: 'They have not really compensated Libya for its contribution to international peace. If we are not compensated other countries, in turn, are not going to follow our example'. Finally, Qadhafi said that Libya had received neither security guarantees from other countries nor adequate assistance to help transform military programmes for civilian purposes.[37]

Qadhafi has periodically attempted to change his image and his government's policies, at various times emphasizing Libya's geopolitical role as either a part of a pan-Arab Middle East or more oriented towards sub-Saharan Africa. Libya's decision can therefore be seen as an example of another such shift by Qadhafi.

IV. Assessments of Libya's activities

Intelligence information played an important role in the trilateral negotiations on Libya's past weapon programmes and allowed the UK and the USA to compare notes with Libya and to seek clarification of issues of concern partly through carrying out on-site visits and interviews with facility personnel.

Public information about Libya's biological weapon (BW) and nuclear weapon-related activities did not adequately reflect the true situation, while information on its missile programme and, to a lesser extent, its CW programme was more accurate. Until recently, most authoritative or official information on suspected Libyan NBC weapon and missile programmes was contained in status-of-proliferation reports and statements issued by the USA and other states. Some information was also released as a consequence of criminal proceedings against individuals and companies which had violated

[34] For background see US Department of State, 'Appendix C: background information on other terrorist groups', URL <http://www.state.gov/documents/organizations/31947.pdf>.

[35] US Department of State (note 5).

[36] Prier, P., 'Muammar Kadhafi: "Que fait l'armée française en Afrique?"' [Muammar Kadhafi: 'what is the French Army doing in Africa?'], *Le Figaro*, no. 18756 (24 Nov. 2004), p. 2.

[37] Prier (note 36).

the sanctions regime. Notably, a number of nuclear and CW-related prosecutions in Germany in the 1980s resulted in a large number of German investigative press reports and government inquiries.[38] Most other information came from media reports of varying or doubtful quality.

Most of the information produced by the USA is contained in reports and congressional testimony, including annual status-of-proliferation reports that are produced by the CIA.[39] In 1993 Russia's Foreign Intelligence Service (SVR, Sluzhba Vneshnoi Razvedky) issued a report on threats posed by NBC weapons and medium- and long-range missiles that included information on Libya.[40] The language in US assessments from year to year was often identical or very similar but could contain significant omissions: for instance, a 1998 CIA report to Congress did not discuss whether Libya was pursuing a nuclear or a BW programme.[41] In general, the CIA also emphasized Libya's dependence on other countries for equipment, matériel, technology and expertise. While various intelligence services undoubtedly possessed more detailed information, it is reasonable to assume that classified assessments did not reach opposite conclusions from those that were published.

According to the CIA, during the trilateral process Libya 'made significant disclosures' about its 'nuclear, chemical and missile-related activities' and 'minor disclosures about biological-related activities'.[42] Libya's weapon laboratories were characterized by some involved in the trilateral process as 'weak, inefficient and demoralized'.[43] Its NBC and missile programmes were also alleged to have been mismanaged and underfunded.[44]

V. Libya's nuclear weapon programme

Under Qadhafi's leadership, Libya has been a perennial source of concern as regards the proliferation of nuclear weapons and ballistic missile delivery

[38] Wiegele, T. C., *The Clandestine Building of Libya's Chemical Weapons Factory: A Study in International Collusion* (Southern Illinois University Press: Carbondale, Ill., 1992); Lundin, S. J., 'Chemical and biological warfare: developments in 1988', *SIPRI Yearbook 1989: World Armaments and Disarmament* (Oxford University Press: Oxford, 1989), pp. 110–111; and *Händler des Todes: Bundesdeutsche Rüstungs-und Giftgasexporte im Golfkrieg und nach Libyen* [Trade in death: Federal German Republic arms and poison gas exports in the Gulf War and to Libya] (ISP-Verlag: Frankfurt am Main, 1989).

[39] See the US Central Intelligence Agency Internet site at URL <http://www.cia.gov/cia/reports/index.html>.

[40] Russian Foreign Intelligence Service (SVR), *Novy Vyzov posle 'Kholodnoi Voiny': Rasprostranenie Oruzhiya Massovogo Unichtozheniya (Otkryty Doklad SVR za 1993g)* [New challenges after the 'cold war': the proliferation of weapons of mass destruction (SVR open report for 1993)] (SVR: Moscow, 1993), URL <http://svr.gov.ru/material/2-1.html>.

[41] US Central Intelligence Agency, 'Unclassified report to Congress on the acquisition of technology relating to weapons of mass destruction and advanced conventional munitions, 1 January through 30 June 1998', URL <http://www.cia.gov/cia/reports/721_reports/jan_jun1998.html#libya>.

[42] US Central Intelligence Agency, 'Attachment A, Unclassified report to Congress on the acquisition of technology relating to weapons of mass destruction and advanced conventional munitions, 1 July through 31 December 2003', URL <http://www.cia.gov/cia/reports/721_reports/july_dec2003.htm>.

[43] Slevin, P. and Pincus, W., 'Libya made progress in nuclear goal', *Washington Post,* 21 Dec. 2003, p. A01, URL <http://www.washingtonpost.com>.

[44] Beaumont, Ahmed and Bright (note 17).

systems.[45] Libya ratified the NPT in 1975 and concluded a full-scope safeguards agreement with the International Atomic Energy Agency (IAEA) in 1980.[46] Despite these steps, many government analysts and independent experts suspected that the Qadhafi regime was engaged in undeclared nuclear activities as part of a proscribed military programme.[47] There were persistent suspicions, for example, that some installations being built as part of Libya's ambitious Great Man-Made River Project, a water-diversion scheme for irrigation purposes, were connected with NBC weapon-related activities.[48] At the same time, it was generally believed that Libya had not been able to make significant progress towards achieving a nuclear weapon capability owing to a lack of indigenous resources and expertise resulting from the imposition of international sanctions.[49] The 1993 Russian SVR report stated that it had no information that Libya possessed nuclear weapons and that approximately 50 foreign nuclear specialists, none of whom were nuclear weapon experts, were working in Libya on private contracts.[50]

The nuclear infrastructure

Libya has a modest civil nuclear infrastructure, centred on the Tajura Nuclear Research Center (TNRC) near Tripoli. The TNRC is the site of a 10-megawatt (MW) research reactor that was completed with Soviet assistance in 1981 and placed under IAEA safeguards.[51] It encompasses 15 facilities and laboratories, including a critical facility, a neutron generator and a Tokamak fusion reactor. It also is the site of a radiochemical laboratory that supports isotope production activities and a nuclear metallurgy laboratory.[52]

[45] For an overview of Libya's nuclear programme see Feldman, Y. and Mahaffey, C., 'Country profile 6: Libya', in the SIPRI series 'Countries of nuclear strategic concern', URL <http://projects.sipri.se/nuclear/cnsc1lya.htm>; and Federation of American Scientists, 'Libya special weapons', 27 Sep. 2004, URL <http://www.fas.org/nuke/guide/libya>.

[46] Libya concluded a safeguards agreement with the IAEA. IAEA, 'The text of the Agreement of 8 July 1980 between the Libyan Arab Jamahiriya and the Agency for the Application of Safeguards in Connection with the Treaty on the Non-Proliferation of Nuclear Weapons', INFCIRC/282, 13 Oct. 1980, URL <http://www.iaea.org/Publications/Documents/Infcircs/Countries/libya.shtml>. States which have safeguards agreements and Additional Protocols in force are listed in annex A to this volume. Libya is also party to the 1996 African Nuclear-Weapon-Free Zone (Treaty of Pelindaba), which established an African nuclear weapon-free zone. For lists of parties and signatory and non-signatory states see annex A in this volume.

[47] See, e.g., US Department of Defense, *Proliferation: Threat and Response* (Department of Defense: Washington, DC, Jan. 2001), pp. 45–48; and Cirincione, J., Wolfstahl, J. and Rajkumar, M., *Deadly Arsenals: Tracking Weapons of Mass Destruction* (Carnegie Endowment for International Peace: Washington, DC, 2002), pp. 307–12.

[48] See, e.g., Center for Security Policy, 'Great "Man-Made River" project', Decision Brief no. 03-D49, 22 Dec. 2003, URL<http://www.centerforsecuritypolicy.org/index.jsp?section=papers & code=03-D_49>.

[49] Albright, D., Berkhout, F. and Walker, W., SIPRI, *Plutonium and Highly Enriched Uranium 1996* (Oxford University Press: Oxford, 1997), p. 351; and US Department of Defense (note 47), p. 45.

[50] Russian Foreign Intelligence Service (SVR) (note 40).

[51] Feldman and Mahaffey (note 45). The reactor was operated only intermittently by local staff after Soviet technical support was withdrawn in 1991.

[52] Boureston, J. *et al.*, 'Verifying Libya's nuclear disarmament', *Trust & Verify*, no. 112 (Jan./Feb. 2004), p. 1, URL <http://www.vertic.org/assets/TV112.pdf>.

The suspension of UN sanctions in 1999 provided Libya with the opportunity to enhance its nuclear infrastructure through foreign procurement and scientific cooperation. Russia initiated discussions with Libya on resurrecting a controversial Soviet-era proposed deal to construct a nuclear power reactor and offered to assist Libya in modernizing the TNRC.[53] The USA sought to block this and other forms of nuclear energy cooperation, arguing that such civil-sector work could help Libya develop the dual-use infrastructure and technical expertise suitable for a military programme.[54]

Libya received considerable foreign assistance in procuring sensitive nuclear materials, technologies and components. Much of this assistance was provided by a sophisticated clandestine network run by Abdul Qadeer Khan, sometimes referred to as the 'father' of Pakistan's nuclear weapon programme.[55] Beginning in 1997, the Khan network supplied Libya with centrifuges and related components for an undeclared uranium-enrichment programme. It also gave Libya documentation related to designing nuclear weapons.[56] However, the relatively low technical absorption capacity of Libya's scientific–industrial base meant that these 'short cuts' did not bring it appreciably closer to achieving a nuclear weapon capability.

Cooperation with the IAEA

At a meeting on 20 December 2003, Libyan officials informed the IAEA that the country had been engaged for more than a decade in undeclared nuclear activities aimed at producing material for 'internationally proscribed weapons'.[57] On 28 December IAEA Director General Mohamed ElBaradei travelled to Tripoli with a team of senior inspectors to 'initiate an in-depth process of verification of Libya's past and present nuclear activities'.[58] During the visit, ElBaradei was informed by the Libyan authorities that Libya's nuclear programme involved a total of 12 sites, 4 of which were previously undeclared. Some of the sites shown to ElBaradei housed unopened crates of dual-use equipment, including dozens of gas centrifuges for uranium enrichment, provided by foreign manufacturers. Based on these preliminary inspections, the IAEA determined that Libya's military nuclear programme had most likely been 'in the very initial stages of development'.[59]

[53] Federation of American Scientists (note 45).

[54] US Central Intelligence Agency, 'Unclassified report to Congress on the acquisition of technology relating to weapons of mass destruction and advanced conventional munitions, 1 January through 30 June 2002', URL < http://www.cia.gov/cia/reports/721_reports/jan_jun2002.html#6>.

[55] On the Khan network see chapter 12 in this volume.

[56] Tyler, P. and Sanger, D., 'Pakistan called Libyans source of atom design', *New York Times* (Internet edn), 6 Jan. 2004, URL <http://www.nytimes.com/2004/01/06/international/middleeast/06NUKE.html>.

[57] IAEA, 'IAEA Director General to visit Libya', Press Release 2003/14, Vienna, 22 Dec. 2003, URL <http://www.iaea.org/NewsCenter/PressReleases/2003/prn200314.html>.

[58] IAEA (note 57).

[59] 'Libya "not close to nuclear arms"', BBC News Online, 29 Dec. 2003, URL <http://news.bbc.co.uk/2/hi/africa/3355277.stm>; and Koppel, A., 'ElBaradei: Libya nuclear program dismantled',

In February 2004 ElBaradei submitted a report to the IAEA Board of Governors stating that Libya had failed to meet its obligations under its safeguards agreement with the IAEA.[60] The report stated that, beginning in the early 1980s, Libya imported nuclear material and conducted a wide variety of nuclear activities which it had failed to report to the IAEA, as required by its safeguards agreement. It also did not declare the facilities and other locations where the material had been stored and processed.

On 10 March 2004, the IAEA Board of Governors adopted a resolution finding that Libya's past failures to meet the requirements of its safeguards agreement with the agency, as identified by the Director General, 'constituted non-compliance' under Article XII.C of the IAEA Statute.[61] In accordance with the Statute, the resolution requested ElBaradei to report the matter to the UN Security Council. However, it also stated that the report to the Security Council was 'for information purposes only' and commended Libya 'for the actions it has taken to date, and has agreed to take, to remedy the non-compliance'.[62] The Security Council subsequently declined to consider punitive measures against Libya.[63]

On 10 March Libya signed an Additional Protocol to its safeguards agreement with the IAEA.[64] The protocol grants greater authority to IAEA inspectors in verifying that Libya has not diverted safeguarded nuclear materials for proscribed purposes or built undeclared nuclear facilities.[65] Libya announced that it would abide by the protocol's provisions prior to its ratification and entry into force.[66] On 26 May 2004, Libya submitted the initial expanded declaration required under the Additional Protocol.

During the spring and summer of 2004 Libya and the IAEA discussed how to provide a full account of Libya's past nuclear activities and how to clarify a number of safeguards-related issues. On 30 August ElBaradei reported to the Board of Governors that Libya had shown 'good co-operation with the Agency' since December 2003, including providing prompt access to locations and senior personnel requested by the agency; it also had taken 'corrective

CNN International (Internet edn), 29 Dec. 2003, URL <http://edition.cnn.com/2003/WORLD/africa/12/29/libya.nuclear/index.html>.

[60] IAEA, 'Implementation of the NPT safeguards agreement of the Socialist People's Libyan Arab Jamahiriya', Report by the Director General to the IAEA Board of Governors, GOV/2004/12, Vienna, 20 Feb. 2004, pp. 7–8, URL <http://www.iaea.org/Publications/Documents/Board/2004/gov2004-12.pdf>.

[61] IAEA, 'Implementation of the NPT Safeguards Agreement of the Socialist People's Libyan Arab Jamahiriya', Resolution adopted by the IAEA Board of Governors, GOV/2004/18, Vienna, 10 Mar. 2004, p. 2, URL <http://www.iaea.org/Publications/Documents/Board/2004/gov2004-18.pdf>. The IAEA Statute is available at URL <http://www.iaea.org/About/statute_text.html>.

[62] IAEA (note 61), p. 2.

[63] United Nations News Service (note 20).

[64] IAEA, 'IAEA verification of Libya's nuclear programme: Board adopts resolution, Libya signs Additional Protocol', Press Release, 10 Mar. 2004, URL <http://www.iaea.org/NewsCenter/News/2004/libya_ ap1003.html>. Libya has also ratified the CTBT (note 1).

[65] For further detail about the Model Additional Protocol contained in INFCIRC/540, Sep. 1997, see IAEA, 'The safeguards system of the International Atomic Energy Agency', IAEA Department of Safeguards, Vienna, URL <http://www.iaea.org/OurWork/SV/Safeguards/safeg_system.pdf>.

[66] IAEA (note 64). As of 31 Dec. 2004, Libya's Additional Protocol had not entered into force.

actions' to come into compliance with it safeguards agreement.[67] He noted, however, that Libya had not always been able to provide adequate documentation in its account of its nuclear activities, especially those for which the assistance was provided by foreign intermediaries. In these instances, the IAEA's verification activities 'would benefit greatly from the provision of additional information, including from the provider of the weapon design and fabrication information and from those contractors which helped Libya develop some of its dual use infrastructure'.[68]

Safeguards compliance issues

ElBaradei's reports to the IAEA Board in 2004 included detailed descriptions of Libya's nuclear programme and of its failure to comply with its safeguards obligations.

Imports of nuclear materials. In 1985 Libya exported uranium ore concentrate ('yellowcake') to a 'nuclear weapon state', which then processed it and shipped the resulting products, including uranium hexafluoride (UF_6), back to Libya later in the year. Libya acknowledged that it had failed to declare the import of the UF_6 and other uranium compounds subject to safeguards to the IAEA.[69] The materials were intended to serve as samples for a uranium conversion facility but were never used. Libya had also failed to declare the import of three cylinders of UF_6 supplied by another country, through clandestine intermediaries, in September 2000 and February 2001.[70] Pakistan has been identified in some reports as the source of the UF_6.[71] In early 2005 US intelligence agencies concluded, based on the presence of certain isotopes in the UF_6 containers turned over by Libya to the USA, that the material had originated in North Korea.[72]

Uranium conversion. Libya conducted undeclared laboratory- and bench-scale uranium conversion experiments using imported uranium ore between

[67] IAEA, 'Implementation of the NPT safeguards agreement of the Socialist People's Libyan Arab Jamahiriya', Report by the Director General to the IAEA Board of Governors, GOV/2004/59, Vienna, 30 Aug. 2004, p. 7, URL <http://www.iaea.org/Publications/Documents/Board/2004/gov2004-59. pdf>.

[68] IAEA (note 67).

[69] IAEA, 'Implementation of the NPT safeguards agreement of the Socialist People's Libyan Arab Jamahiriya', Report by the Director General to the IAEA Board of Governors, GOV/2004/33, Vienna, 28 May 2004, Annex 1, p. 3, URL <http://www.iaea.org/Publications/Documents/Board/2004/gov 2004-33.pdf>.

[70] IAEA (note 69).

[71] Citing British and US intelligence officials, a report from a police investigation into the involvement of Malaysian firms in the Khan network stated that Pakistan sent uranium hexafluoride to Libya in 2001. Royal Malaysia Police, 'Press release by Inspector General of Police in relation to investigation on the alleged production of components for Libya's uranium enrichment programme', 20 Feb. 2004, URL <http://www.rmp.gov.my/rmp03/040220 scomi_eng.htm>.

[72] However, scientists at the IAEA and some non-governmental experts concluded that the US test results were ambiguous and pointed with equal likelihood to Pakistan as the source of the uranium hexafluoride. Kessler, G., 'North Korea may have sent Libya nuclear material, US tells allies', *Washington Post* (Internet edn.), 2 Feb. 2005, URL <http://www.washingtonpost.com/wp-dyn/articles/A55947-2005Feb2.html>.

1983 and 1989 as well as 'limited' experiments after 1994.[73] Libya failed to provide the IAEA with design information for the facilities at the TNRC where these experiments took place. Libya also failed to provide design information for a pilot-scale uranium conversion facility (UCF) which it ordered, in the form of portable modules, from a 'Far Eastern' manufacturer in 1984.[74] Libyan officials have stated that uranium was never processed at the UCF, which was moved between several locations for security reasons following its assembly in 1998, although some cold tests were conducted in 2002.

Uranium enrichment. Libya had an undeclared uranium enrichment programme under way for two decades. This included a pilot centrifuge facility for which Libya failed to provide to the IAEA design information in a timely manner, as it was obligated to do under its safeguards agreement. In addition, through the Khan network, Libya had ordered what was in effect a 'turnkey' enrichment plant for which the network would provide the centrifuge parts, with final assembly to take place in Libya.[75]

In the early 1980s Libya initiated a research and development (R&D) programme for gas centrifuge uranium enrichment, using a design brought to Libya by a European expert.[76] This did not result in a working centrifuge system but gave Libyan scientists experience in designing and operating centrifuges and related equipment. Following a 1995 decision to reinvigorate its nuclear weapon-related activities, Libya acquired from the Khan network 20 pre-assembled L-1 centrifuges and the components for another 200.[77] Libyan scientists constructed three different enrichment cascades, but only the smallest (using nine centrifuges) was completed. Libya stated that no nuclear material had been used during any of the tests conducted on the L-1 centrifuges.

In 2002 Libya received from the Khan network two centrifuges of a more advanced design (L-2) and placed an order for an additional 10 000 L-2 centrifuges. By late December 2003 a considerable number of centrifuge components, primarily casings, had arrived in Libya. Most of the parts had been manufactured by a Malaysian company—Scomi Precision Engineering (SCOPE)—in a deal arranged by a Sri Lankan business associate of Khan. Several British, German and Swiss citizens were also involved in the deal as technical, manufacturing and trans-shipment experts.[78] It remains unclear,

[73] IAEA (note 60), p. 4; and IAEA (note 69), Annex 1, pp. 3–4.

[74] According to media reports, a Japanese manufacturer sold the conversion facility to Libya, based on Libyan design specifications. Charbonneau, L., Reuters, 'Japanese firm sold Libya uranium conversion plant', 12 Mar. 2004, URL <http://in.news.yahoo.com/040312/137/2byvq.html>; and MSNBC News/Associated Press, 'Japan firm sold Libya key nuclear technology', 12 Mar. 2004, URL <http://msnbc.msn.com/id/4514496>.

[75] Albright, D. and Hinderstein, C., Institute for Science and International Security (ISIS), 'Libya's gas centrifuge procurement: much remains undiscovered', *Issues Brief*, 1 Mar. 2004, URL <http://www.isis-online.org/publications/libya/cent_procure.html>.

[76] IAEA (note 69), Annex 1, p. 5.

[77] The L-1 centrifuge is an IAEA designation for an older design of European origin, also referred to as G-1 or P-1.

[78] Royal Malaysia Police (note 71); Gertz, B., 'Libyan sincerity on arms in doubt', *Washington Times* (Internet edn), 9 Sep. 2004, URL <http://www.washingtontimes.com/functions/print.php?storyID=

however, where the centrifuge rotors were made, leading to concern that they may have been shipped by an as-yet unidentified supplier in the Khan network. A German-owned freighter bound for Tripoli from Dubai that was intercepted in October 2003 had been carrying some of the centrifuge components. According to the IAEA, all centrifuge components found inside Libya were manufactured by foreign companies. The advanced centrifuges procured by Libya were similar to those built by Iran based on designs obtained from Pakistan.[79] Some reports indicate that suppliers from South Africa and Turkey also sold Libya advanced centrifuge components.[80]

Environmental samples taken by the IAEA inspectors found that a number of the L-1 and L-2 centrifuges had been contaminated with traces of highly enriched uranium (HEU) and low-enriched uranium (LEU). Both types of enriched uranium were found in a test facility for the L-1 centrifuges. ElBaradei reported that the IAEA's investigation 'tended to confirm' Libya's assertion that it had not tested the centrifuges with nuclear material and that the components were contaminated when Libya received them.[81]

Reprocessing. In 1984–90 Libya conducted undeclared experiments at the 10-MW research reactor at the TNRC involving the fabrication of several dozen uranium dioxide and uranium metal targets, and their subsequent irradiation to produce fission product radioisotopes. Libya has indicated that small quantities of plutonium were separated from at least two of the targets. Libya did not report either the experiments or the separated plutonium at the time and failed to provide design information for the radiochemical laboratory where the work was carried out.

ElBaradei reported to the IAEA Board that, in late 2001 or early 2002, Libya had received 'from a foreign source' at least one set of design plans for a nuclear weapon.[82] The documents shown to IAEA inspectors by the Libyan authorities included a series of engineering drawings relating to nuclear weapon components and detailed notes on the fabrication of weapon components. According to one report, the bomb designs depicted in the blueprints were for a 10-kiloton implosion-type weapon that China had detonated in its fourth nuclear test, in 1966. The design was notable because it was compact and the first one that China had developed that could easily fit on a ballistic

20040909-121930-9087r>; and 'German held in Libya arms probe', BBC News Online, 16 Nov. 2004, URL <http://news.bbc.co.uk/2/hi/europe/4017789.stm>.

[79] IAEA (note 67), pp. 5–6; and Tyler and Sanger (note 56).

[80] Fidler, S. and Huband, M., 'Turks and South Africans "helped Libya's secret nuclear arms project"', *Financial Times* (Internet edn), 10 June 2004, URL <http://search.ft.com/s03/search/article.html?id=040610001054>.

[81] IAEA (note 69), Annex 1, p. 6. The report emphasized that the cooperation of the 'supplier State' (i.e., Pakistan) was essential for the agency to be able to determine the origins of the contamination.

[82] IAEA (note 60), p. 6.

missile.[83] The plans were believed to have been transferred by China to Pakistan in the 1980s and later sold by the Khan network to Libya.[84]

Libya has stated that the entity in charge of the nuclear weapon programme—the National Board for Scientific Research (NBSR)—did not act on the design information, or even attempt to assess its credibility and practical utility, because it had no national personnel competent to evaluate the data.[85] IAEA experts did not find evidence that any of the inspected facilities which had technical capabilities relevant for a nuclear weapon programme (e.g., laboratories, precision machine tools and other equipment) had been involved in the design, production or testing of the weapon components.[86]

In late January 2004, pursuant to an agreement between the IAEA, the UK and the USA which was reached after reportedly difficult negotiations, all of the documents and drawings related to nuclear weapon design and fabrication were transferred, under IAEA seal, to the USA. In addition, in January–March 2004 Libya shipped to the USA's Oak Ridge National Laboratory all centrifuges, centrifuge components and associated equipment as well as sensitive nuclear materials, including several containers of UF_6, for secure storage and disposal.[87] In March 2004 Russia also removed 13 kilograms of research reactor fuel assemblies containing 80 per cent HEU which it had supplied in the 1980s to the 10-MW research reactor at the TNRC.[88] The reactor will be converted to use LEU fuel.

VI. Libya's biological and chemical weapon programme

Biological weapons

The 1993 Russian SVR report concluded that Libya was conducting preliminary research work in the BW field. The report noted that Libya had shown a marked interest in work carried out with BW agents in other countries and stated that Libyan officials had indicated to other Arab countries that Libya was 'prepared to finance joint biological programmes, including those of an applied military' nature on condition that such work be conducted in Libya.[89]

[83] Sanger, D. and Broad, W., 'As nuclear secrets emerge in Khan inquiry, more are suspected', *New York Times* (Internet edn.), 26 Dec. 2004, URL <http://www.nytimes.com/2004/12/26/international/asia/26.nuke.html>.

[84] Broad, W. and Sanger, D., 'Warhead blueprints link Libya project to Pakistan figure', *New York Times* (Internet edn), 4 Feb. 2004, URL <http://www.nytimes.com/2004/02/04/politics/04nuke.html>; and Warrick, J. and Slevin, P., 'Libyan arms designs traced back to China', *Washington Post* (Internet edn), 15 Feb. 2004, URL <http://www.washingtonpost.com/ac2/wp-dyn/A42692-2004Feb14>.

[85] IAEA (note 69), Annex 1, p. 7.

[86] IAEA (note 69), Annex 1, p. 7.

[87] Warrick, J., 'US displays nuclear parts given by Libya', *Washington Post* (Internet edn), 16 Mar. 2004, URL <http://www.washingtonpost.com/ac2/wp-dyn/A61439-2004Mar15>; and IAEA (note 69), Annex 1, p. 6.

[88] Squassoni, S. and Feickert, A., Congressional Research Service, *Disarming Libya: Weapons of Mass Destruction*, CRS Report for Congress RS 21823, 22 Apr. 2004, p. 5, URL <http://fpc.state.gov/documents/organization/32007.pdf>. On nuclear disarmament see chapter 16 in this volume.

[89] Russian Foreign Intelligence Service (SVR) (note 40).

During the trilateral process 'no concrete evidence of an existing' BW programme was uncovered.[90] The UK and the USA reportedly hold the view that certain agricultural and pharmaceutical facilities 'were established with biological weapons also in mind'.[91] However, without access to internal policy documentation it would probably be impossible to determine whether such a programme was 'defensive' (i.e., permitted by the BTWC) or 'offensive' (i.e., prohibited by the BTWC).[92]

Chemical weapons

The SVR report concluded that Libya possessed a CW stockpile totalling 70–80 tonnes and that it had recently produced phosgene, sarin and sulphur mustard in limited quantities. It stated that Libyan efforts to obtain production technology from Iran and Iraq had been unsuccessful and that, by 1992, the international sanctions had compelled Libya to scale back its CW production capacity and to convert parts of more than one facility for the production of medicines. The report stated that these activities were concentrated at a chemical factory located at Rabta, which had been established to produce sulphur mustard, and that it could not confirm information that CW production equipment and approximately 50 tonnes of sulphur mustard had been destroyed.[93] The SVR report stated that some experts had expressed concern that research might be conducted at a military scientific facility in the Gharyan region where foreign laboratory equipment and 'critical chemical components' were being brought together.[94]

In the early to mid-1990s the USA alleged that Libya was constructing an underground CW production facility at Tarhunah; Libya claimed that the facility was part of the Great Man-Made River Project.[95] During the same period a number of German businessmen were criminally prosecuted for selling Libya dual-use chemical process equipment that could be adapted for the production of nerve agent.[96]

[90] Slevin and Pincus (note 43).

[91] 'Libya and "dual use"', *CBW Conventions Bulletin*, no. 65 (Sep. 2004), p. 1.

[92] Historically, a defensive BW programme could be understood to mean a programme in which BW would be used for retaliatory purposes. Under current international law, however, BW may not be used under any circumstances. A defensive programme is therefore one where BW agents are evaluated for protective or prophylactic purposes only. See Roffey, R., 'Biological weapons and potential indicators of offensive biological weapon activities', *SIPRI Yearbook 2004: Armaments, Disarmament and International Security* (Oxford University Press: Oxford, 2004), pp. 557–71.

[93] Russian Foreign Intelligence Service (SVR) (note 40). The fact that Libya may have destroyed sulphur mustard could indicate that the product had a limited shelf-life. See Perry Robinson, J. and Trapp, R., 'Production and chemistry of mustard gas', ed. S. J. Lundin, *Verification of Dual-use Chemicals under the Chemical Weapons Convention: The Case of Thiodiglycol*, SIPRI Chemical & Biological Warfare Studies no. 13 (Oxford University Press: Oxford, 1991), pp. 4–15.

[94] Russian Foreign Intelligence Service (SVR) (note 40).

[95] See Mark, C., Congressional Research Service, *Libya: Suspected Chemical Weapons Facility at Tarhunah*, Report no. 96–849 F (US Government Printing Office: Washington, DC, 23 Oct. 1996).

[96] Zanders, J. P., Eckstein, S. and Hart, J., 'Chemical and biological weapon developments and arms control', *SIPRI Yearbook: Armaments, Disarmament and International Security* (Oxford University Press: Oxford, 1997), p. 462–63; and Mark (note 95), pp. 1–4.

In mid-2003 the CIA stated that Libya 'appeared to be working towards an offensive [chemical warfare] capability and eventual indigenous production' and 'evidence suggested' that the country was seeking 'dual-use capabilities that could be used to develop and produce BW agents'.[97] Later in 2003 the CIA stated that Libya had shown British and US visitors an unspecified amount of sulphur mustard that had been produced at Pharma 150 near Rabta more than 10 years earlier.[98]

On 20 February 2004 Libya submitted a partial initial declaration to the OPCW, and, on 5 March 2004, following two technical assistance visits to Libya by the OPCW's Technical Secretariat, Libya submitted its full initial declaration on its CW holdings and related activities.[99] It declared 3563 empty CW air bombs, 23.62 tonnes of sulphur mustard and more than 1000 tonnes of a Category 2 chemical,[100] which had been intended for use in the production of Category 1 CW.[101] Libya also declared approximately 2000 tonnes of CW precursors not listed in the CWC Annex on Chemicals; the precursors had been intended to be used for purposes prohibited under the CWC.[102] Libya stated that it had never transferred chemical weapons.[103] It also declared that it possessed an inactivated CW production facility at Rabta as well as two CW storage facilities.[104] In early 2004 Libya suspended the destruction of the empty CW air bombs at the request of the OPCW in order to allow it to verify their destruction. In March 2004 Libya completed the destruction of the bombs. In December 2004 the OPCW approved Libya's request to convert a former sulphur mustard production facility at Rabta into a pharmaceutical production facility to produce pharmaceuticals.[105] It also approved an extension of the intermediate deadline for the destruction of its Category 1 CW.[106]

[97] US Central Intelligence Agency, 'Attachment A, Unclassified report to Congress on the acquisition of technology relating to weapons of mass destruction and advanced conventional munitions, 1 January through 30 June 2003', URL <http://www.cia.gov/cia/reports/721_reports/jan_jun2003.htm>.

[98] US Central Intelligence Agency (note 42).

[99] 'Summary: 36th session of the Executive Council', *Chemical Disarmament Quarterly*, vol. 2, no. 2 (June 2004), p. 16.

[100] Category 2 chemical weapons are defined as CW that are not based on chemicals that appear on Schedule 1 of the CWC's Annex on Chemicals and their parts and components. CWC, Verification Annex, Part IV(A), para. 16.

[101] Category 1 chemical weapons are defined as CW that are based on chemicals that appear on Schedule 1 of the CWC's Annex on Chemicals and their parts and components. CWC, Verification Annex, Part IV(A), para. 16.

[102] 'Summary: 36th session of the Executive Council' (note 99), p. 16; and OPCW, 'Destruction of chemical weapons in Libya commences on 27 February 2004', Press Release no. 6, 26 Feb. 2004.

[103] The OPCW requires that states parties declare whether they have transferred CW at any time since 1 Jan. 1946. CWC, Article III, para.1(a)(iv).

[104] OPCW, 'Initial inspection in Libya completed', Press Release no. 10, 22 Mar. 2004. Some sources indicate that Libya declared 3 CW production facilities. 'Libya and "dual use"' (note 91), p. 2. The Rabta production facility had 2 production lines. Libya also had a mobile CW filling capability based in Tripoli. Spence, S., 'Progress in The Hague: developments in the Organization for the Prohibition of Chemical Weapons, quarterly review no. 48', *CBW Conventions Bulletin*, no. 66 (Dec. 2004), p. 11; and US Government official, Private communication with J. Hart, May 2004.

[105] OPCW, 'Decision, Request by the Libyan Arab Jamahiriya to use the chemical weapons production facilities Rabta Pharmaceutical Factory 1 and Rabta Pharmaceutical Factory 2 (Phase II) in Rabta, the Libyan Arab Jamahiriya for purposes not prohibited under the Chemical Weapons Convention', OPCW document C-9/DEC.9, 30 Nov. 2004. The CWC defines a chemical weapon production facility

It is evident that Libya stockpiled air bombs and sulphur mustard, but the exact nature of work with other agents is less clear. For example, Libya reportedly carried out experimental work with sarin and soman,[107] but no information regarding CW agents other than sulphur mustard appears to have been released by Libya or the OPCW. (Although Libya's declaration to the OPCW was not marked as restricted, the declaration has not been released owing to the OPCW's policy on confidentiality.[108]) Despite allegations dating from the early 1990s that Libya had or was constructing two underground CW production facilities at Sebha and Tarhunah, British and US officials apparently found no such facilities and none was declared to the OPCW.[109] Finally, it is significant that Libya declared chemicals that were not listed in the CWC's Annex on Chemicals but had been meant for use as part of its CW programme. In so doing, Libya was implementing the CWC's general purpose criterion (GPC), which bans all toxic materials and their precursors except where intended for purposes not prohibited by the CWC.[110]

VII. Libya's ballistic missile programme

Libya's programmes to develop ballistic missiles and to obtain ballistic missile-related equipment, materials, technology and expertise from foreign sources have been the focus of international attention for two decades.[111] During the 1980s Libya received missile-related assistance from a West German firm and reportedly approached Brazil for missile assistance.[112] There has been particular concern that Libya was seeking to produce or otherwise acquire ballistic missiles as delivery systems for NBC weapons.

(CWPF) essentially as any facility that produced CW at any time since 1 Jan. 1946. CWC, Article II, para. 8. Under the CWC, a CWPF must either be destroyed, temporarily converted for use as a CW destruction facility or permanently converted for purposes not prohibited by the CWC. If a former CWPF has already been converted for non-prohibited purposes when the CWC enters into force for the state party, it must seek approval for its conversion from the OPCW. CWC, Verification Annex, Part V.

[106] OPCW, 'Decision, Request by the Libyan Arab Jamahiriya for extensions of the intermediate deadlines for the destruction of its Category 1 chemical weapons stockpiles', OPCW document C-9/DEC.7, 30 Nov. 2004. The CWC currently requires that conversion of CWPFs for non-prohibited purposes be completed no later than 6 years after it enters into force (i.e., no later than 19 Apr. 2003). CWC, Verification Annex, Part V, para. 72.

[107] 'Libya and "dual use"' (note 91), p. 1.

[108] See CWC, Annex on the Protection of Confidential Information ('Confidentiality Annex').

[109] 'Libya and "dual use"' (note 91), p. 2.

[110] CWC, Article II, para. 1. The GPC is the key mechanism by which the CWC can take into account technological and scientific change. It also allows those implementing the convention to better distinguish between 'offensive' (prohibited) and 'defensive' (permitted) CW programmes. Concern has periodically been expressed that the manner in which the CWC is being implemented is too narrowly focused partly because, since the convention's entry into force on 29 Apr. 1997, declarations and inspections have been focused on chemicals listed in the CWC's Annex on Chemicals.

[111] See, e.g., US Central Intelligence Agency (note 97).

[112] Federation of American Scientists (note 45); and Nuclear Threat Initiative (NTI), 'Libya: missile chronology, 1969–2004', 3 Dec. 2004, URL <http://www.nti.org/e_research/profiles/Libya/Missile/3840_3841.html>.

The bulk of Libya's ballistic missile inventory consisted of ageing FROG and Scud-B missiles which had been imported from the Soviet Union.[113] In 1989 Libya concluded a deal with North Korea to purchase 60 Scud Mod-C missiles (known in North Korea as the Hwasong-6).[114] Libya received an initial shipment of the missile (with a range of 500–600 km) in 1993–94, despite the existence of a UN arms embargo since March 1992.[115] In 2000 there were reports that Libya had acquired from North Korea a small number of No-dong ballistic missiles (1300-km range) as part of a larger purchase. However, in 2001 the USA concluded that Libya had not received complete missiles and that its operational capability remain limited to Scud missiles.[116]

Libya made little progress in developing an indigenous medium-range ballistic missile or in extending the range of its Scud missiles. These programmes were heavily dependent on foreign assistance.[117] Libya's missile assembly and production facilities were centred at the Al-Rabta and Tarhuna weapon complexes.[118] Throughout the 1990s Libya had a missile with a range of 800–100 km under development, called Al-Fatah. However, the programme was hampered by the imposition of UN sanctions between 1992 and 1999, which restricted the flow of ballistic missile technology to Libya. The Qadhafi regime reportedly had some success in circumventing sanctions and obtaining missile-related components and technology from companies in China, India and the former Yugoslavia.[119] In the 1990s, Libya also maintained cooperation with Iran in developing missile technology and components.[120]

Libya's missile force had only a limited capability to deliver non-conventional warheads. The 1993 Russian SVR report concluded that Libya was not capable of mounting nuclear warheads on its FROG and Scud missiles.[121] Libya is believed to have developed CW warheads for its Scud-C missiles, possibly with Iranian and North Korean assistance, and may have sought to do so for its No-dong missiles.[122] It does not appear that Libya had an active programme under way to develop a missile delivery system for

[113] Bermudez, J., 'Ballistic missile development in Libya', *Jane's Intelligence Review,* vol. 15, no. 1 (Jan. 2003), p. 28; and Global Security.org, 'Libyan missiles', 21 Dec. 2003, URL <http://www.global security.org/wmd/world/libya/missile.htm>.

[114] Bermudez (note 113), p 28

[115] Bermudez (note 113), pp 28; and Nuclear Threat Initiative (NTI), 'Country profiles: Libya', Dec. 2004, URL <http://www.nti.org/e_research/profiles/Libya/index.html>.

[116] Bermudez (note 113), pp. 28–29; and US Central Intelligence Agency, 'Unclassified report to Congress on the acquisition of technology relating to weapons of mass destruction and advanced conventional munitions, 1 July through 31 December 2001', URL <http://www.cia.gov/cia/reports/721_reports/july_ dec2001.htm#6>.

[117] US Central Intelligence Agency, National Intelligence Council, *Foreign Missile Developments and the Ballistic Missile Threat through 2015*, Dec. 2001, URL <http://www.cia.gov/nic/special_missile threat2001.html>; and US Department of Defence (note 47), p. 47.

[118] Bermudez (note 113), p. 31.

[119] US Department of Defence (note 47), p. 47; and Gertz, B., 'Serbia is helping Libya with ballistic missiles, CIA says', *Washington Times* (Internet edn), 12 Nov. 1996, p. A3, URL <http://www.fas.org/news/libya/wt961112.htm>.

[120] Bermudez (note 113), p. 29.

[121] Russian Foreign Intelligence Service (SVR) (note 40).

[122] Bermudez (note 113), pp. 28, 29.

nuclear warheads. The Libyan authorities have told the IAEA that no institutional interaction took place between the NBSR and the organization responsible for missile activities, the Central Organization for Electronic Research (COER).[123]

As part of the announcement made by Libya in December 2003 that it would eliminate all elements of its NBC weapon programmes, it pledged to dismantle all ballistic missiles capable of carrying a 500-kg payload beyond 300 km.[124] In September 2004 the USA announced that its verification of the dismantling of Libya's NBC weapon programmes, including 'MTCR-class missiles', was 'essentially complete'.[125] Libya had turned over to British and US experts its inventory of operational Scud-C missiles as well as partially assembled missiles, missile launchers and related equipment. Libya also pledged to eliminate entirely its arsenal of Scud-B missiles at the end of their operational service. Earlier in 2004 Libya had indicated that it wanted to convert these into shorter-range missiles for defensive purposes.[126] In addition, Libya undertook to sever its military trade ties with Iran, North Korea (including cooperation on developing medium-range ballistic missiles) and Syria. Libya's fulfilment of its December 2003 pledge will leave it primarily with shorter-range cruise missiles.[127]

VIII. Conclusions

Although US officials have cited Libya as an example of the effectiveness of ad hoc approaches and the threat of pre-emptive military action, it is unclear how the Libya 'model' might be applied to other states. No other country of concern has indicated its willingness to submit to a similar process, and it is unclear what additional incentives, in terms of 'carrots' and 'sticks', might be offered to such countries in the current international security environment to cause them to reconsider their strategic choices. Over the long term, a key factor that will determine how both Libya and others will view the merits of its choice is the actual and perceived benefits Libya obtains through *inter alia* resumed international trade and unrestricted relations with outside institutions. For example, in 2004 the cooperative threat reduction model was extended to

[123] IAEA (note 69), Annex 1, p. 7.

[124] These correspond to the performance criteria that define category I items, as set out in the MTCR guidelines regulating the transfer of complete missile systems. The complete guidelines are available at the MTCR Internet site at URL <http://www.mtcr.info/english/ guidelines.html>. On MTCR see chapter 17 in this volume.

[125] US Department of State, 'Completion of verification work in Libya', Paula A. DeSutter, Assistant Secretary for Verification and Compliance, Testimony Before the Subcommittee on International Terrorism, Nonproliferation and Human Rights, Washington, DC, 22 Sep. 2004, URL <http://www.state.gov/t/vc/rls/rm/ 2004/37220.htm>.

[126] Miller, J., 'US says Libya will convert missiles to defensive weapons', *New York Times* (Internet edn), 11 Apr. 2004, URL <http://www.nytimes.com/2004/04/11/international/africa/11LIBY.html>.

[127] Bhattacharjee, A. and Salama, S., 'Libya and nonproliferation', CNS Research Story, Center for Nonproliferation, Monterey Institute of International Studies, 24 Dec. 2003, URL <http://cns.miis.edu/pubs/031223.htm>. Libya will retain the SS-N-2c Styx, Otomat Mk2 and Exocet anti-ship cruise missiles.

include a programme for redirecting the work of former scientists and technicians who were part of Libya's NBC weapon and medium- and long-range missile programmes in Libya.[128]

The case of Libya also demonstrates the 'dual-use' difficulties inherent in efforts to prevent a state from misusing matériel, technology and equipment for developing BW and CW. Determining a state's intent is often the principal difficulty in assessing its compliance with its treaty commitments and the nature of the threat it may pose. Intelligence information on the matter is often ambiguous, and political or ideological disagreements may make it hard for states to be frank with each other about compliance, particularly outside multilateral frameworks. States are reluctant to share with others the intelligence underpinning their concerns, especially with an organization that is open to universal membership. In the Libya case, information on criminal proceedings within the UN framework was more readily shared among states and acted on than corresponding information on possible NBC weapon programmes.

On the other hand, the Libya case also demonstrated the value of having a multilateral body confirm (and in effect legitimize) the country's declarations and treaty compliance status. Libya's commitments regarding nuclear weapons and CW were verified through a system of declarations and on-site inspections carried out by international bodies. In the case of BW, however, the international community will have to essentially rely on information provided to the BTWC parties by Libya, the UK and the USA. This is also true with respect to Libya's missile programme. In addition, the IAEA and the USA appear to have disagreed over what, if any, role US officials should have in the IAEA inspection process.[129]

Concern has been expressed that the UK, the USA and other states may have overlooked other problems—such as human rights, despite the USA's much publicized drive for greater democracy in the Arab world—in granting Libya so many benefits for its renunciation of NBC weapons and advanced-capability missiles. In fact, the UK and the USA have been reported to be pursuing their dialogue with Libya on the country's foreign and domestic policies, including human rights and other matters of concern.[130] As of October 2004 the USA was continuing to review Libya's 'record of support for terrorism'.[131]

[128] For background see Roston, M., *Redirection of WMD Scientists in Iraq and Libya: a Status Report* (Russian American Nuclear Security Advisory Council: Washington, DC, Apr. 2004); and chapter 17 in this volume.

[129] Global Security.org, 'US, Britain to hold talks with IAEA over Libya's nuclear issue', 18 Jan. 2004, URL <http://www.globalsecurity.org/wmd/library/news/libya/2004/libya-040118-pla-daily01.htm>.

[130] Dunne (note 9), p. 4.

[131] E.g., the USA has expressed the view that Libya 'may have some residual contacts with some of its former terrorist clients'. In Oct. 2004 the head of the American Muslim Council, Abdulrahman Alamoudi, was convicted and sent to prison for plotting to assassinate a member of the Saudi royal family, reportedly at the instigation of the Libyan Government. US Department of State (note 5).

15. Conventional arms control and military confidence building

ZDZISLAW LACHOWSKI and PÁL DUNAY

I. Introduction

The year 2004 marked the fifth anniversary of the decisions taken by the participating states of the Organization for Security and Co-operation in Europe (OSCE) at its 1999 Istanbul Summit on 'hard' conventional arms control in Europe.[1] Regrettably, the process remained stalemated in 2004. Seven new members were admitted to the North Atlantic Treaty Organization (NATO) in its second wave of post-cold war enlargement. This increased Russia's concerns about the 1990 Treaty on Conventional Armed Forces in Europe (CFE Treaty), which are related to the fact that Russia considers itself to be at a security disadvantage. The 1999 Agreement on Adaptation of the CFE Treaty did not enter into force because of the refusal of the NATO members and other states to ratify it in the face of Russia's non-compliance with some of its so-called 'Istanbul commitments' related to military pullouts from Georgia and Moldova. Russia nonetheless refrained from taking radical steps, such as withdrawing from the CFE Treaty regime.

In 2004 the OSCE participating states continued to focus on adjusting and further developing certain norm- and standard-setting measures (NSSMs) in order to better respond to risks and challenges facing Europe and its neighbours. Regional arms control developed and functioned smoothly. In this context, the OSCE decided to suspend the operation of the Agreement on Confidence- and Security-Building Measures in Bosnia and Herzegovina from September 2004.[2]

Croatia and Slovenia ratified the 1992 Treaty on Open Skies in 2004.[3] Its February 2005 review conference was preceded by discussion of the relevance of the treaty and its applicability in the current security environment. The

[1] On conventional arms control in Europe before 1999 see the relevant chapters in previous editions of the SIPRI Yearbook. For the text of the CFE Treaty and Protocols see Koulik, S. and Kokoski, R., SIPRI, *Conventional Arms Control: Perspectives on Verification* (Oxford University Press: Oxford, 1994), pp. 211–76; and the OSCE Internet site at URL <http://www.osce.org/docs/english/1990-1999/cfe/cfetreate.htm>. For the text of the Agreement on Adaptation see *SIPRI Yearbook 2000: Armaments, Disarmament and International Security* (Oxford University Press: Oxford, 2000), pp. 627–42; and the OSCE Internet site. A consolidated text showing the amended CFE Treaty as adapted in accordance with the 1999 Agreement on Adaptation is reproduced in Lachowski, Z., *The Adapted CFE Treaty and the Admission of the Baltic States to NATO,* SIPRI Policy Paper no. 1 (SIPRI: Stockholm, Dec. 2002), URL <http://www.sipri.org/contents/publications/policy_papers.html>. The parties to the CFE Treaty and the signatories of the Agreement on Adaptation are listed in annex A in this volume.

[2] Agreement on Confidence- and Security-Building Measures in Bosnia and Herzegovina, signed on 26 Jan. 1996, URL <http://www.oscebih.org/regional_stab/pdf/article2-eng.pdf>.

[3] The parties and signatories of the Open Skies Treaty are listed in annex A in this volume.

problem of inhumane weapons also continues to engage the international community.

This chapter describes the major issues and developments relating to conventional arms control in 2004. Section II deals with the arms control aspects of the second OSCE Annual Security Review Conference (ASRC) and critical elements of the implementation of the CFE Treaty. Efforts to promote confidence and stability in the OSCE area are addressed in section III. Arms control and confidence building in the Balkans and regional military confidence building are addressed in section IV. Section V covers matters related to the Treaty on Open Skies, and the issue of mines is dealt with in section VI. Section VII briefly examines arms control developments in Asia, and section VIII presents the conclusions.

II. European arms control

The CFE Treaty regime for Europe remains the most elaborate conventional arms control regime worldwide. Consistently acclaimed as the 'cornerstone of European security', it has contributed significantly to removing the threat of large-scale military attack and has enhanced confidence, openness and mutual reassurance on the continent. Conventional arms control has become an integral part of an inclusive, cooperative security system that evolves in response to changes taking place in the OSCE area. The CFE Treaty process inspired regional arms control solutions in the Balkans that have functioned since 1996. In recent years, however, there has been a discernible shift from 'hard' to 'soft' arms control arrangements.

In June 2004 the second OSCE Annual Security Review Conference was held in Vienna. In contrast to the first review conference, it addressed not only the politico-military dimension of the OSCE, but also other aspects of the 2003 Strategy to Address Threats to Security and Stability in the 21st Century, with particular emphasis on terrorism, border security and management.[4] This signalled the continued de-prioritization of traditional arms control relative to other security issues on the European agenda. The discussions at the ASRC displayed little new thinking about how to address the crucial problems. They were limited to further strengthening, streamlining and coordinating of the work of existing institutions; reaching out to partners beyond the OSCE area; and exhortations to pursue cooperative measures to better meet the new threats and challenges. Much attention was devoted to further efforts to control the spread of man-portable air defence systems (MANPADS) and small arms and light weapons (SALW).[5]

[4] OSCE, Permanent Council, 2004 Annual Security Review Conference, 23–24 June 2004, Vienna, Chair's Report, OSCE document PC.DEL/651/04. Rev. 1, 29 July 2004, URL <http://www.osce.org/events/conferences/2004asrc/>. The text of the OSCE Strategy to Address Threats to Security and Stability in the 21st Century was adopted at the Maastricht Ministerial Council Meeting on 2 Dec. 2003. It is reproduced at URL <http://www.osce.org/docs/english/mincone.htm>.

[5] For the list of proposals and suggestions made at the 2004 ASRC see OSCE (note 4), pp. 24–31.

The CFE Treaty and related commitments

The CFE Treaty set equal ceilings in the Atlantic-to-the-Urals (ATTU) zone of application on major categories of the heavy conventional armaments and equipment of the two groups of states parties.[6]

The CFE Treaty and the Agreement on Adaptation together constitute the adapted CFE Treaty regime. The Agreement on Adaptation discarded the original, bipolar CFE concept of a balance of forces between NATO and the Warsaw Treaty Organization (WTO); introduced a new regime of arms control based on national and territorial ceilings, codified in the agreement's protocols as binding limits; and opened the adapted CFE Treaty to European states which were not yet parties to the CFE Treaty in 1999. The agreement has not entered into force because of the refusal of the NATO members and other states to ratify it in the face of Russia's non-compliance with the commitments it made at the 1999 OSCE Istanbul Summit.[7] The original CFE Treaty and the associated documents and decisions therefore continue to be binding on all parties. The Joint Consultative Group (JCG) is the body established by the states parties to monitor implementation, resolve issues arising from implementation and consider measures to enhance the viability and effectiveness of the CFE Treaty regime.

By 1 January 2005 more than 63 500 pieces of conventional armaments and equipment within and outside the Atlantic-to-the Urals area of application had been scrapped or converted to civilian or other use by the parties, and many parties had reduced their holdings to lower levels than required.

Treaty adaptation, operation and compliance issues

In 2004 Russia intensified its campaign for reform of the OSCE, which it has argued is necessary to restore the status of the politico-military dimension relative to the (Western) preoccupation with the areas of humanitarian issues and democracy. However, Russia's own record in the politico-military dimension is hardly impeccable.[8]

Both Russia and NATO have repeatedly pledged in their joint declarations to 'work cooperatively' towards ratification of the Agreement on Adaptation of the CFE Treaty. However, Russia's unrelenting policy on its remaining commitments regarding Georgia and Moldova—to resolve the issues of Russian military bases in Georgia and the pull out of Russian troops and ammunition from the breakaway Trans-Dniester region in Moldova—has

[6] For a brief summary of the CFE Treaty see annex A in this volume. See also Lachowski (note 1).

[7] OSCE, Final Act of the Conference of the States Parties to the Treaty on Conventional Armed Forces in Europe, Istanbul, 17 Nov. 1999. The text is reproduced as appendix 10B in *SIPRI Yearbook 2000* (note 1) , pp. 642–46.

[8] At the Maastricht Ministerial Council Meeting in 2003 Russia succeeded by putting pressure on Armenia to prevent the initiation of the end of the year JCG letter to the OSCE Chairperson-in-Office. The JCG letter drafted by Luxembourg at the end of 2004, which mentioned unaccounted for and uncontrolled treaty-limited equipment and Russia's non-compliance related to the Istanbul commitments, was effectively vetoed by Russia. On the OSCE see also appendix 1A in this volume.

made it impossible to move forward.[9] Ratification of the Agreement on Adaptation by the NATO states has also been delayed as a result of Russia's failure to meet its commitments. In 2004 Russia continued to reject the 'artificial and legally unjustifiable' link between ratification of the Agreement on Adaptation and the Istanbul commitments. Several NATO members appeared to sympathize with the Russian position, but for the most part the NATO states presented a united front. Russia holds the view that it has fulfilled its CFE Treaty obligations[10] and that the political commitments it undertook in Istanbul have been delayed by the complex situation in the two former Soviet republics. At the OSCE Sofia Ministerial Council Meeting, the Russian delegation reiterated the Russian view that the link is not legitimate since the Istanbul commitments are bilateral and 'do not imply any obligations for Russia with regard to third countries'.[11]

At the February 2004 Munich Conference on Security Policy, Russian Defence Minister Sergei Ivanov identified the issues related to the CFE Treaty as a serious problem in the relations between Russia and the West. Ivanov criticized the Western countries and proposed an 'escape forward' solution, suggesting that, instead of pressing Russia to fulfil its Istanbul commitments, a broad discussion should begin on a new arms control and confidence-building system. Despite Russian assertions that the CFE Treaty was inadequate and approaching a 'slow death', Russia chose not to undermine the treaty. In 2004 Russian officials also stressed that there is no alternative to the entry into force of the Agreement on Adaptation of the CFE Treaty.

The Russian military, who have shown greater anxiety than Russian diplomats, expressed deep concern about the perceived increasing imbalance of NATO versus other forces as a result of NATO's enlargement in 2004. According to the Russian military, NATO would obtain a certain advantage over Russia in Central Europe and a huge excess in ground forces in the south-western part of the flank region. According to the first deputy chief of the Russian General Staff, while the imbalance would in Central Europe be some 170 artillery pieces in favour of NATO, in the flank zone—after Bulgaria and Romania joined NATO—the West's advantage would be as much as

[9] So far Russia has failed to implement the following Istanbul commitments: (*a*) to close the Gudauta base in Georgia, which it was required to shut down in 2001; (*b*) to set a date for the closure of the Batumi and Akhalkalaki bases in Georgia; (*c*) to withdraw all Russian troops from Moldova's Trans-Dniester region, which it was required to complete by 2002; and (*d*) to eliminate the stocks of ammunition and military equipment in the Trans-Dniester region. See Lachowski, Z., 'Conventional arms control', *SIPRI Yearbook 2000* (note 1), pp. 577–612; Lachowski, Z., 'Conventional arms control', *SIPRI Yearbook 2001: Armaments, Disarmament and International Security* (Oxford University Press: Oxford, 2001), pp. 549–77; Lachowski, Z., 'Conventional arms control', *SIPRI Yearbook 2002: Armaments, Disarmament and International Security* (Oxford University Press: Oxford, 2002), pp. 709–39; Lachowski, Z., 'Conventional arms control in Europe', *SIPRI Yearbook 2003: Armaments, Disarmament and International Security* (Oxford University Press: Oxford, 2003), pp. 691–711, and Lachowski, Z. and Sjögren, M., 'Conventional arms control', *SIPRI Yearbook 2004: Armaments, Disarmament and International Security* (Oxford University Press: Oxford, 2004), pp. 713–36.

[10] In the flank area the Russian holdings remain below the sub-ceilings under the adapted CFE Treaty but exceed the original CFE Treaty limits.

[11] OSCE Ministerial Council, Statement by the delegation of the Russian Federation, OSCE, document MC(12)JOUR/2, 7 Dec. 2004.

2200 battle tanks, 3300 armoured combat vehicles (ACVs) and 2000 artillery pieces.[12]

In the lead-up to the admission of the seven new members to NATO on 29 March 2004 negative comments abounded in Russia and sometimes included tough talk on arms control. On 30 March the State Duma (the lower house of Parliament) passed a resolution urging the president and the government to assess the expediency of Russia's participation in conventional arms control agreements, to consider deploying additional forces in Russia's regions bordering NATO states and to put more emphasis on Russia's nuclear deterrence policy.[13] Nevertheless, Russia officially reaffirmed its 'calmly negative attitude' to NATO enlargement and continued to deal pragmatically with the Western partners.[14]

Two months after the anti-NATO resolution, the Duma held a hearing on the prospects for the Agreement on Adaptation of the CFE Treaty where the necessity of its 'earliest possible' ratification was the common view.[15] Nevertheless, President Vladimir Putin chose not to accept an invitation to attend the June 2004 NATO Summit at Istanbul. NATO's reluctance to ratify the Agreement on Adaptation and to place its new Baltic members under CFE restrictions was given as a major reason for Putin's refusal to attend.[16]

Of the 30 signatories of the CFE Treaty, only Belarus and Kazakhstan have ratified the Agreement on Adaptation and deposited their instruments of ratification with the depositary. Ukraine has ratified the agreement but has not

[12] 'After the eventual breakdown of the treaty's flank construction in the wake of the second NATO "enlargement wave" Russia's conformity with its flank obligations becomes not only absurd, but also an instance of unprecedented discrimination in the history of international arms control'. 'Yuriy Baluyevskiy: Rasshireniye NATO naneset smertelnyi udar po Dogovoru ob obychnykh vooruzhennykh silakh v Evrope' [Yuriy Baluyevskiy: NATO enlargement will deal a fatal blow to the CFE Treaty], *Izvestiya*, 2 Mar. 2004.

[13] 'Duma passes resolution on NATO expansion', *RFE/RL Newsline*, vol. 8, no. 60 (31 Mar. 2004), URL <http://www.rferl.org/newsline/2004/03/1-RUS/rus-310304.asp>. At the same time, Belarus warned that it will be 'compelled . . . to take appropriate measures, and we are taking them'. OSCE, Permanent Council document PC.DEL/268/04, 1 Apr. 2004.

[14] See interview by the Director of the Department of All-European Cooperation, Russian Ministry for Foreign Affairs, A.V. Grushko, 'Otnosheniye Rossii k rasshireniyu NATO—spokoino negativnoye' [Russia's attitude to NATO enlargement—calmly negative], *Vremya Novostei,* 1 Apr. 2004. For a review of responses see, e.g., 'Russia: official line on NATO enlargement "calmly negative"; media, lower-level officials less optimistic', 8 Apr. 2004, Foreign Broadcast Information Service, *Daily Report–Central Eurasia* (*FBIS-SOV*), FBIS-SOV-2004-0409, 12 Apr. 2004.

[15] Russian Ministry of Foreign Affairs, 'On hearings in State Duma of Federal Assembly of Russian Federation on ratification prospects of Agreement on Adaptation of CFE Treaty', Press Release, 3 June 2004, URL <http://www.ln.mid.ru/brp_4.nsf/english?OpenView&Start=2.811&Count=30&Expand=2#2>. According to a high Russian Foreign Ministry official, 'ratification [of the Agreement on Adaptation] by Russia would give a positive signal to European supporters, first and foremost, of the adapted treaty'. As to alleged US motives not to ratify the Agreement, Russia suspected that the real reason was fear that the agreement would constrain US freedom to set up large bases in Central Europe (large-scale transfers and concentration of equipment would require detailed notification). RIA-Novosti (Moscow), 'Russian diplomat urges Duma to ratify revised conventional forces treaty', 1 June 2004, in FBIS-SOV-2004-0601, 2 June 2004 (in Russian).

[16] The issue of linkage between the ratification of the agreement and the Istanbul commitments led the NATO Secretary General to make an embarrassing mistake in citing a 'legal' link between the adapted CFE Treaty and the Istanbul commitments. NATO, Press Conference by NATO Secretary General, Jaap de Hoop Scheffer, after the NATO–Russia Council at Foreign Ministers level, Istanbul, 28 June 2004, URL <http://www.nato.int/docu/speech/2004/s040628i.htm>.

deposited its ratification document. On 25 June, on the eve of the Istanbul NATO Summit, the Duma ratified the Agreement on Adaptation with certain reservations;[17] it was endorsed by the Federation Council on 7 July and signed into federal law by Putin on 19 July. Russia committed itself to be guided by its military restraint commitments, including the obligations deriving from the CFE Treaty, to the extent the other parties are guided by those provisions.[18] Russia's ratification instrument was deposited on 6 December 2004.

Questions relating to the distribution of the costs for inspections and observation visits (to be charged to the inspecting party) remain on the JCG agenda as do the negotiations on the further development of the CFE Protocol on Existing Types of Conventional Armaments and Equipment (POET).[19] In addition, it was proposed to digitalize the exchange of photographs and technical data regarding treaty-limited equipment (TLE).

In June 2004 a dispute arose in the JCG about BRM-1K armoured infantry fighting vehicles (AIFV).[20] On 29 June Russia announced in the JCG that it would no longer account for this type of light-tracked combat vehicle in its equipment data except as an AIFV look-alike (a type of armament not limited by the treaty) in view of the alleged vagueness of definitions in the POET which fail to cover similar Western equipment. The United States and seven other NATO states urged Russia to reconsider this 'fundamental departure from agreed counting rules'.[21]

The problem of unaccounted-for and uncontrolled treaty-limited equipment (UTLE) was not resolved in 2004. In violation of the CFE Treaty, residual amounts of Russian TLE, which should have been destroyed or returned to Russia long ago, were still at the disposal of the self-proclaimed authorities of the Trans-Dniester region (Moldova), Abkhazia and South Ossetia (Georgia). The issue of UTLE in Nagorno-Karabakh, Armenia, also continues to adversely affect the operation of the treaty.

CFE-related consequences of NATO enlargement in Central Europe

Since 1997 Russia has received successive political assurances that NATO will exercise restraint in conventional weapon deployments and capabilities on the territories of its new members.[22] Russian officials, however, continue to express concerns (in contrast to the Russian military's emphasis on the southern flank areas) about the admission to NATO of the three Baltic states

[17] 'Statement by the State Duma concerning the ratification of the Agreement on Adaptation of the Treaty on Conventional Armed Forces in Europe', OSCE document SEC.DEL/125/04, 30 June 2004.

[18] Russian Ministry of Foreign Affairs, 'Transcript of Minister of Foreign Affairs of the Russian Federation Sergey Lavrov interview with Russian media', 28 June 2004, URL <http://www.ln.mid.ru/brp_4.nsf/e78a48070f128a7b43256999005bcbb3/136ce0af26b3e62fc3256ec200422760?OpenDocument>.

[19] The CFE Treaty specifies that POET should be updated periodically. Although this was discussed at the 1996 and 2001 review conferences, the task has not been completed.

[20] BRM-1K is listed in the protocol (POET) to the CFE Treaty.

[21] Joint Consultative Group, 538th plenary meeting, JCG document JCG/JOUR/538, 20 July 2004, annexes 1–8.

[22] See the chapters on developments in conventional arms control since 1997 in SIPRI Yearbooks.

that are not subject to CFE limitations and restraints, Estonia, Latvia and Lithuania. After Defence Minister Sergei Ivanov's warnings and unsuccessful demands at the Munich Security Policy Conference in February 2004, the issue of aerial patrol of the Baltic borders by NATO aircraft came to the fore and was pursued by Russia's Foreign Minister Sergei Lavrov at the first session of the NATO–Russia Council (NRC) in its enlarged format 'at 27' (the 26 NATO members and Russia). While it was hard to construe the fact of four NATO aircraft stationed in Lithuania to patrol the Baltic states' borders as a threat, Russia voiced anxiety that this might be followed by further deployments (e.g., the presence of NATO armed forces and the creation of large NATO–US military bases close to its borders).[23]

In response, at the NRC on 2 April 2004 NATO reiterated its previous pledges regarding the non-deployment of nuclear weapons and substantial conventional armaments on a permanent basis on the territories of the new members, as well as the Baltic states' own promise to demonstrate military restraint and to promptly accede to the adapted treaty regime once it enters into force. This effectively de-emphasized the Baltic states item in the list of Russian–Western disagreements regarding CFE issues.[24]

Russian troops and equipment in Georgia

The issue of the withdrawal of Russian forces from Georgia remained deadlocked in 2004. At the 1999 OSCE Istanbul Summit Russia pledged to reduce the number of its heavy ground weapons deployed on Georgian territory to the agreed levels, which was completed on schedule. The Russian TLE located at Vaziani and Gudauta (Abkhazia) were scheduled to be removed, and those two bases as well as the repair facilities at Tbilisi were to be closed by 1 July 2001. Georgia agreed that Russia could temporarily retain TLE at the Batumi (Adzharia) and Akhalkalaki (southern Georgia) bases.[25] Russia handed over control of its Vaziani base to Georgia in mid-2001 but retained the Gudauta military base, reclassifying its garrison as a 'peacekeeping force' and seeking Georgian and international acceptance of that arrangement.[26] The terms of the Russian withdrawal from the Batumi and Akhalkalaki bases have never been

[23] See interview by Russian Deputy Foreign Minister V. A. Chizhov for Interfax, 31 Mar. 2004 (in Russian), URL <http://www.ln.mid.ru/ns-dvbr.nsf/6786f16f9aa1fc72432569ea0036120e432569d80022 6387c3256e6e002aebea?OpenDocument>; and Ivanov, S., 'As NATO grows, so do Russia's worries', *New York Times*, 7 Apr. 2004. Russia complained that NATO argued that its air patrols were warranted because of alleged terrorist threats.

[24] In the run-up to the commemoration of the 60th anniversary of the end of World War II, Russia reportedly insisted that the 3 Baltic states agree bilaterally to adhere to the CFE Treaty, a move that would decouple them from the NATO and EU policies. Socor, V., 'To attend or not to attend? That's not really a question', *Eurasia Daily Monitor*, vol. 2, issue 29 (10 Feb. 2005), URL <http://www.jamestown.org/edm/article.php?article_id=2369240>.

[25] *SIPRI Yearbook 2000* (note 1), pp. 645–46. The basic temporary deployment is 153 tanks, 241 ACVs and 140 artillery pieces. There are reportedly some 80 tanks and *c.* 2000 Russian personnel stationed in Akhalkalaki and Batumi. *Nezavisimaya Gazeta*, 15 Nov. 2004, pp. 1, 5.

[26] In the spring of 2004 Germany proposed to lead a fact-finding mission to Gudauta in order to facilitate agreement between Georgia and Russia. Later the proposal was put on hold at Georgia's request.

agreed. Georgia insists on a three-year withdrawal period, while Russia has suggested a much longer withdrawal schedule.[27] Despite the clear commitments made in the joint Georgian–Russian statement attached to the 1999 CFE Final Act,[28] Russia now claims that the agreement with Georgia and Moldova did not set deadlines for 'physical action'.[29]

Since 2003 Russia has under various pretexts suspended or stalled talks on Russian withdrawal. In early 2004 the USA unsuccessfully tried to persuade Russia to resume negotiations and accelerate the withdrawal of troops from Georgia, offering financial assistance and a promise not to set up new US military bases, supported by Georgia's declared willingness to ban all third countries from having bases on its territory. Russia continued to insist that additional conditions—not mentioned in the Istanbul commitments—be applied to its withdrawal and refused to talk with Georgia until the latter responded 'constructively' to the Russian demands.[30] At the Sofia OSCE Ministerial Council Meeting in 2004 Russia refused, as it had done in 2003 at the Maastricht OSCE Ministerial Council Meeting, to consent to political declarations and 'regional' statements which *inter alia* would have stressed its Istanbul commitments.

Russian armed forces and ammunition in Moldova

In 2004 not only was there no progress on CFE issues regarding Moldova, but the situation worsened. Under its 1994 constitution, Moldova is permanently neutral and refuses to host foreign forces on its territory. At the 1999 OSCE Istanbul Summit Meeting Russia pledged to withdraw or destroy its TLE in Moldova by the end of 2001 and to remove its troops from Moldova by the end of 2002.[31] Withdrawal of the Russian TLE was completed on time. The failure to arrive at a political settlement of the problem of the separatist Trans-Dniester region in 2002–2004 affected the implementation of Russia's commitments to complete the withdrawal of its forces and dispose of its ammunition and non-CFE-limited equipment.[32] Russia assured the OSCE that

[27] Russia sought a 7- to 11-year extension for the Batumi and Akhalkalaki bases and a bilateral treaty with Georgia that would legalize those bases for the duration. In the spring of 2005 Russian officials reportedly suggested a 3- to 4-year withdrawal scheme. *Atlantic News*, no. 3661 (17 Mar. 2005), p. 3.

[28] OSCE (note 7).

[29] 'Transcript of remarks by Minister of Foreign Affairs of Russia Sergey Lavrov at press conference following Russia–NATO Council session, Istanbul, 28 June 2004', Press Release, URL <http://www.ln.mid.ru/brp_4.nsf/e78a48070f128a7b43256999005bcbb3/f49e7d32324eb164c3256ec3002567be?OpenDocument>. For the text of the Russian–Georgian statement see *SIPRI Yearbook 2000* (note 1), pp. 645–46; it is also available at URL <http://www.osce.org/docs/english/1990-1999/cfe/cfefinact99e.htm>.

[30] Lachowski and Sjögren (note 9), pp. 718–19.

[31] OSCE (note 7), para. 19.

[32] During 2003 several proposals were discussed in an effort to resolve the conflict. In July 2003 the OSCE suggested that the EU could send a peacekeeping contingent to the region. Russia strongly opposed this suggestion, stating that its own 'peacekeepers' were sufficient. In Nov. 2003, Russia proposed another 'federalization', the so-called 'Kozak memorandum' plan.

it would complete the withdrawal of its forces as early as possible—by the end of 2003 'provided necessary conditions are in place'.[33]

The stalemate continued in 2004, and only one train carrying Russian munitions left Moldova during the year. An estimated 40 trainloads of munitions remain to be removed. In April the talks on settlement of the conflict resumed after a long break following the collapse of the Russia-sponsored November 2003 federalization plan for Moldova. In May 2004 Moldova strongly demanded that Russia withdraw its troops from Moldovan territory.[34] On 1 June Moldovan President Vladimir Voronin proposed that the European Union (EU), Romania, Russia, Ukraine and the USA hold a high-level conference on a 'pact' on stability and security for Moldova to *inter alia* guarantee Moldova's permanent strategic neutrality and the settlement of the Trans-Dniester issue.[35] Since then Moldova has sought stronger international support in its settlement talks with Russia.

A denouement came in the autumn in the run-up to the OSCE Ministerial Meeting in Sofia. On 30 November Moldovan Foreign Minister Andrei Stratan delivered a harsh statement to the OSCE Permanent Council[36] decrying the fact that part of Moldovan territory remained 'under the foreign military occupation, that of the Russian Federation'. He stated that the international community was 'facing a group of foreign citizens manipulated from outside' (i.e., Russia) and called for completion of the withdrawal process from Moldova's 'eastern districts' (Trans-Dniester area) in a transparent manner—that is, through the deployment of an OSCE-led international inspection and assessment mission with broadly conceived competences.[37] Stratan denounced the production of unreported military equipment subject to CFE competence by 14 enterprises in the Trans-Dniester region. The armaments handed over to the Trans-Dniester separatist entity by Russia constitute the UTLE. Finally, Stratan warned that full implementation of Russia's Istanbul commitments was a prerequisite for Moldovan ratification of the adapted CFE Treaty.

Moldova reaffirmed its position, albeit in a milder form, at the Sofia Ministerial Council Meeting one week later. Russia's official response to Moldova's demands was to denounce them as 'absurd, irresponsible and obviously unfriendly' and to argue again that the withdrawal problem stemmed from the

[33] OSCE, Ministerial Council, Porto, 2002, Statements by the Ministerial Council, annex 3 (3), OSCE document MC(10)JOUR/2, 7 Dec. 2002.

[34] Infotag (Chisinau), 6 May 2004, in 'Moldova "insists" on Russian withdrawal from Dniester', FBIS-SOV-2004-0506, 7 May 2004 (in Russian).

[35] For more on the pact see Socor, V. 'Moldovan president delivers secret draft on externally guaranteed "neutrality", *Eurasia Daily Monitor*, vol. 1, issue 24 (4 June 2004), URL <http://www.jamestown.org/publications_details.php?volume_id=401&issue_id=2974&article_id=2368048>. The declaration has not been endorsed.

[36] The Permanent Council is the main regular decision-making body of the OSCE. It convenes weekly in Vienna to discuss developments in the OSCE area and to make appropriate decisions.

[37] OSCE, Statement delivered by H. E. Mr Andrei Stratan, the Minister of Foreign Affairs of the Republic of Moldova at the special session of the Permanent Council of the OSCE, Vienna, 30 Nov. 2004, Permanent Council document PC.DEL/1170/04, 30 Nov. 2004. By labelling the Trans-Dniester region as 'eastern districts', Moldova seeks both to stress the Russian minority rule in all 5 districts of the Dniester Left Bank region (except for Tiraspol) and to deny attempts to give it the status of a separate entity.

distrust between Moldova and the Trans-Dniester region because of the failure of the federalization plan.[38]

III. Building confidence and stability in Europe

The OSCE Forum for Security Co-operation (FSC) provides the institutional framework for the implementation and coordination of all OSCE agreements on conventional arms control, ensures their continuity and works out new priorities for future arms control negotiations. Its work derives from three main sources: the Ministerial Council meetings, the ASRCs and the Annual Implementation Assessment Meetings (AIAMs).

The FSC deals with the double task assigned to it by the OSCE Strategy to Address Threats to Security and Stability in the 21st Century: on the one hand, to take responsibility for the complete implementation of the existing politico-military *acquis*; and, on the other hand, to adapt the existing instruments and develop new arms control agreements, confidence- and security-building measures (CSBMs) or other suitable instruments where necessary.

In 2004, with 'hard' arms control still deadlocked, the participating states found it difficult to adapt the existing instruments to a new security environment, although in principle they all perceived this as necessary.

Efforts have been made to make the work of the FSC more efficient. In order to facilitate interaction between the Permanent Council and the FSC, the Chairperson-in-Office (CIO) is represented at the FSC Troika meetings, and the FSC chairperson is represented at the OSCE Troika meetings on matters of FSC concern.[39] Since 2003 special associates—*chefs de file* and coordinators—have been appointed by the FSC chairperson from among the delegations to facilitate the work; to avoid duplication; to ensure a smooth flow of information on discussions in the FSC and the Permanent Council; and to systematize and consolidate tasks, views, ideas and other input by the delegations in the areas addressed by the FSC.[40]

With the growing proliferation of threats, the OSCE has begun to consider possibilities for expanding its norms and commitments to adjacent and other regions, particularly in the context of cooperation with its Asian Partners for

[38] 'Russian MFA Information and Press Department commentary regarding a media question concerning remarks of official Moldovan representatives about Russia's military presence on the territory of Moldova', 15 Dec. 2004, URL <http://www.ln.mid.ru/brp_4.nsf/e78a48070f128a43256999005bcbb3/8a3877d060f1bf4cc3256f6b004399fa?OpenDocument>.

[39] The FSC Troika meets on a weekly basis; it comprises the chairperson and the previous and succeeding chairpersons. It has no formal right to table proposals. The current chairperson issues a schedule of meetings for the subsidiary working bodies based on proposals from delegations. After discussion in the Troika, weekly draft agendas are prepared. The working groups report to the FSC on their activities. Their work is organized on a rolling schedule and additional meetings are convened as necessary. The working groups may also recommend that the FSC hold seminars on specific topics. The OSCE Troika comprises the current CIO and the previous and succeeding CIOs.

[40] In 2003 the *chefs de file* were responsible for 3 key issues: the Annual Security Review Conference (ASRC), development of the OSCE Strategy to Address Threats to Security and Stability in the 21st Century, and the review of the OSCE role in peacekeeping. In 2004, 2 *chefs de file* were appointed for the ASRC and interactions with other international organizations, and 2 coordinators for the projects concerning conventional ammunition and SALW.

Co-operation (Afghanistan, Japan, South Korea and Thailand) and its Mediterranean Partners for Co-operation (Algeria, Egypt, Israel, Jordan, Morocco and Tunisia). The OSCE has encouraged these partner countries to participate in a number of information exchanges and other endeavours within the CSBM framework. In addition, the OSCE declared its intent to explore wider sharing of OSCE norms, principles and commitments with 'adjacent areas'.[41] Since the AIAM of 1998, the Partners for Co-operation have been invited to attend the opening and closing sessions of the meetings. At the AIAM in 2004, representatives of the partner countries were invited for the first time to attend all the working group sessions. Mongolia was granted the status of Partner for Co-operation in December 2004.[42]

Developments in the control of small arms and light weapons

In 2003 the main items on the OSCE agenda relating to SALW were the completion of the Handbook of Best Practices on SALW[43] and MANPADS. In January 2004 a seminar was organized in Vienna to discuss the threat posed by MANPADS to civilian aviation, responses to such threats and strengthening of national capacities.[44] At the seminar, various countermeasures were discussed such as protecting aircraft and patrolling the perimeter of airports, raising awareness of civilian communities in and around airports, introducing variations of landing and take-off patterns, and the like.[45]

In December 2003 the 33 states which participate in the Wassenaar Arrangement on Export Controls for Conventional Arms and Dual-Use Goods and Technologies (WA) agreed to enhance their export controls on MANPADS, institute tougher national legislation regulating arms brokers and exchange information on their exports of small arms. In response, the OSCE states agreed in May 2004 to adopt the principles developed by the WA and incorporate them into their national practices or regulations (i.e., as regards

[41] OSCE, Further dialogue and cooperation with the Partners for Co-operation and exploring the scope for wider sharing of OSCE norms, principles and commitments with others, Permanent Council document PC/DEC/571.Corr.1, 2 Dec. 2003. As a follow-up to that initiative, at the 2004 ASRC Finland presented a 'food-for-thought' paper. Finland, Present state of affairs and potential additional fields of co-operation and interaction with the OSCE Mediterranean and Asian Partners for Co-operation, Permanent Council document PC/DEL/366/04, 5 May 2004. In that context, the FSC chairperson has pointed out: 'Our Chairmanship takes the challenge of "outreach" seriously. . . . However, . . . it takes two to tango; our Partners must demonstrate that they are ready to proceed beyond spectatorship and become active participants in that process'. OSCE, Report by the Chairman of the Forum for Security Cooperation to the Second Annual Security Review Conference, Permanent Council document PC. DEL/571/04, 24 June 2004.

[42] OSCE, Granting of the status of Partner for Co-operation to Mongolia, Permanent Council document PC.DEC.636, 2 Dec. 2004.

[43] OSCE, Handbook of Best Practices on Small Arms and Light Weapons, Vienna, 2003, URL <http://www.osce.org/events/mc/netherlands2003/handbook/salw_all.pdf>. For discussion of small arms issues in 2003 see Lachowski and Sjögren (note 9), pp. 691–11.

[44] On MANPADS see Anthony, I. and Baurer, S., 'Transfer controls and destruction programmes', *SIPRI Yearbook 2004* (note 9), pp. 753–56.

[45] OSCE, Technical Experts Workshop on countering the MANPADS threat to civil aviation security at airports, Workshop Report, Executive Summary. Vienna, OSCE document SEC.GAL/24/04, 4 Feb. 2004.

surface-to-air missile systems, strict control conditions and evaluation criteria).[46] This action essentially doubled the number of nations that have pledged to abide by these controls. The WA participating states will report transfers and retransfers of MANPADS using the 2000 OSCE SALW Document's information exchange requirements.[47] The participating states also agreed to promote the application of these to non-OSCE countries.

Following Belarus' request in 2003 for assistance to destroy surplus SALW and improve stockpile management and security, an assessment visit to Belarus took place at the end of 2004. A similar initial assessment visit was made to Tajikistan in the autumn of 2004.[48] Kazakhstan requested assistance in December 2004.

In 2004 the FSC focused on two aspects of the SALW Document: (*a*) the elaboration of standard elements for end-user certificates (EUCs); and (*b*) the establishment of norms for small arms brokering (verification procedures and principles for the control of brokering in small arms). In November two decisions were adopted. One set out a number of criteria to be included in an EUC prior to the export of SALW or technology for producing them (it included commitments on checking the 'bona fides' of EUCs and ensuring that the same criteria were extended to SALW that were manufactured under United Nations (UN) licence).[49] The second decision, designed to underpin enforcement of OSCE, UN and other provisions against arms brokering, covered such matters as licensing and record-keeping, registration and authorization of arms brokers, exchange of information on brokering activities and adequate sanctions for enforcement.[50] Several states suggested that these measures should be followed by an 'enhancement analysis' of the whole spectrum of SALW control efforts, with the aim of making the OSCE a leading organization in this field as well as curbing illicit trafficking in SALW and increasing the security of those stored in the region.[51]

In a February 2004 decision, the FSC requested that an overview be prepared and an accounting made of the 2002 and 2003 annual submissions for the information exchange on SALW.[52] The result showed that not all participating states had provided information on destruction, import and export of SALW using the templates that were suggested. There are still different national practices of categorizing SALW and reporting the import and export

[46] OSCE, Decision no. 3/04: principles for export controls of man-portable air defence systems (MANPADS), FSC document FSC.DEC/3/04, 26 May 2004. It was endorsed by the Ministerial Council in Dec. 2004. OSCE, Decision no. 8/04: OSCE principles for export controls of man portable air defence systems, Ministerial Council document MC.DEC/8/04, 7 Dec. 2004.

[47] The SALW Document is reproduced in *SIPRI Yearbook 2001* (note 9), pp. 590–98.

[48] The work of the OSCE Mission in Georgia on SALW in South Ossetia was suspended in June 2004 because of the security situation in the region.

[49] OSCE, Decision no. 5: standard elements of end-users and verification procedures for SALW exports, FSC document FSC.DEC/5/04, 17 Nov. 2004.

[50] OSCE, Decision no. 8: OSCE principles on the control of brokering in SALW, FSC document FSC.DEC/8/04, 24 Nov. 2004.

[51] US Mission to the OSCE, ASRC Session 3, Comprehensive Security, as delivered by James H. Cox, chief arms control delegate, Permanent Council document PC.DEL/576/04, 24 June 2004.

[52] OSCE, An overview and an accounting of the 2002 and 2003 annual submissions for the information exchange on SALW, FSC document FSC.DEC/2/04, 18 Feb. 2004.

data. The lack of a general definition of SALW is clearly part of the problem. All in all, more coherent modalities for information exchange are needed to make the data more comparable.[53]

Surplus ammunition and landmines

Under Section VI of the OSCE Document on Stockpiles of Conventional Ammunition any OSCE state that has identified a security risk to its surplus stockpiles and that needs assistance to address such a risk may request the assistance of the international community through the OSCE. Belarus, Kazakhstan, Russia, Tajikistan and Ukraine made such requests in 2004. Furthermore, in 2004 Armenia requested assistance to eliminate liquid rocket fuel components ('mélange'), and Uzbekistan requested similar assistance in January 2005. Numerous questions concerning technical, managerial and financial aspects arose while dealing with the requests and it was proposed that a seminar be held to address such issues.

A special FSC meeting on implementing the OSCE Document on Stockpiles of Conventional Ammunition was held on 29 September 2004. It helped to identify the most common difficulties, which include lack of finance, unequal access to destruction techniques and lack of arrangements to pool and exchange technologies. In order to improve matters, the OSCE would need to seek synergies with other international bodies—the EU, NATO and the UN Development Programme (UNDP)—and do more to mobilize public awareness of the importance and urgency of the problem. In the view of the chairman of the meeting, 'a dedicated but realistic and pragmatic approach' seems advisable.[54] The CPC prepared a survey of suggestions made at the meeting, with a list of practical, organizational and technical guidelines for managing the securing and destruction of surplus ammunition.

Since 1997 the OSCE has also had a programme for information exchange on landmines. In 2004 several states proposed that the programme should be updated and expanded to reflect the fact that 43 OSCE states are now parties to the 1997 Convention on the Prohibition of the Use, Stockpiling, Production and Transfer of Anti-Personnel Mines and on their Destruction (APM Convention), and two more are signatories. In the light of this and the adoption in November 2003 of Protocol V on Explosive Remnants of War of the 1981 Convention on Prohibitions or Restrictions on the Use of Certain Conventional Weapons which may be deemed to be Excessively Injurious or to have Indiscriminate Effects (CCW Convention or 'Inhumane Weapons' Convention), several participating states proposed that the OSCE question-

[53] OSCE, Overview of the 2002 and 2003 annual submissions for the information exchange on SALW, CPC document FSC.GAL/37/04, 24 Mar. 2004.

[54] The FSC Chair summed up the result stating that 'we are navigating in unchartered [*sic*] waters' and 'more questions remain open than have been answered'. Special FSC Meeting on implementing the OSCE Document on Stockpiles of Conventional Ammunition, Closing Session: Concluding Remarks by the FSC Chair, Ambassador H. Werner Ehrlich, FSC document FSC.DEL/420/04, 1 Oct. 2004.

naire be updated.[55] The FSC agreed a new decision in December 2004 which replaced the former landmine questionnaire and supplemented it with a questionnaire on explosive remnants of war (ERW).[56]

IV. Regional arms control and confidence building

The Balkans

Regional arms control is designed to play a major stabilizing role in post-conflict security building in the Balkans.[57] Under the terms of the 1995 General Framework Agreement for Peace in Bosnia and Herzegovina (Dayton Agreement), Annex 1-B, Agreement on Regional Stabilization, agreements have been achieved on CSBMs in Bosnia and Herzegovina (Article II); on arms control in states and entities emerged from the former Yugoslavia (Article IV); and on establishing 'a regional balance in and around the former Yugoslavia' (Article V). The characteristic feature of the agreements is that compliance is monitored and assisted by the international community. The military security of the region is built on a balance of forces among the local powers.

The 1996 *Agreement on Confidence- and Security-Building Measures in Bosnia and Herzegovina* (also known as the Article II Agreement) outlines a set of measures to enhance mutual confidence and reduce the risk of conflict in the country. The parties to the agreement are Bosnia and Herzegovina (BiH) and its two entities, the Muslim–Croat Federation of Bosnia and Herzegovina and the Republika Srpska, which in reality comprises three separate armed forces because two components (the Croats and Bosnian Muslims) of the Federation of Bosnia and Herzegovina have not been fully integrated.[58]

In June 2004 the Personal Representative of the CIO announced that the CSBM Agreement would be formally suspended in September 2004 as a result both of the progress of security sector reform in BiH and of the generally high level of confidence, openness and transparency between the armed forces of the entities.[59] On 28 September the parties to the agreement announced its ter-

[55] OSCE, Delegations of Belarus, Canada, Croatia, Germany, Norway, Poland and the Netherlands, an updated questionnaire on landmines and explosive remnants of war: food for thought, FSC document FSC.DEL/65/04, 3 Mar. 2004. For a list of parties and signatories see the International Campaign to Ban Landmines Internet site at URL <http://www.icbl.org> and the UN Internet site at URL <http://disarmament.un.org:8080/TreatyStatus.nsf/CCWC%20Amended%20Protocol%20II?OpenView>.

[56] OSCE, Decision no. 7/04: updating the OSCE questionnaire on anti-personnel mines and explosive remnants of war, FSC document FSC.DEC/7/04, 24 Nov. 2004.

[57] General Framework Agreement for Peace in Bosnia and Herzegovina (Dayton Agreement), Dayton, Ohio, 14 Dec. 1995, Annex 1-B, Regional Stabilization, URL <http://www.oscebih.org/essentials/gfap/eng/annex1b.asp>. The Agreement on Regional Stabilization is reproduced in *SIPRI Yearbook 1996: Armaments, Disarmament and International Security* (Oxford University Press: Oxford, 1996), pp. 241–43.

[58] See also Caparini, M., 'Security sector reform in the Western Balkans', *SIPRI Yearbook 2004* (note 9), pp. 251–82.

[59] OSCE, 'OSCE announces that confidence- and security-building agreement for Bosnia and Herzegovina will end in September 2004', Press Release, 24 June 2004. See also Annual Report on the Implementation of the Agreement on Confidence- and Security-Building Measures in BiH (Article II, Annex 1-B Dayton Peace Accords) and the Agreement on Sub-Regional Arms Control (Article IV,

mination. That fact does not, however, preclude any party from agreeing to continue voluntary measures previously included or associated with it.

The 1996 *Agreement on Sub-Regional Arms Control* (Florence Agreement, also known as the Article IV Agreement)—signed by BiH and its two entities, and by Croatia and the Federal Republic of Yugoslavia (FRY, now Serbia and Montenegro)—remains the only structural (i.e., dealing with arms reductions and limitations) regional arms control arrangement still operating below the European level.[60] Its distinguishing feature is that compliance is monitored and assisted by the international community. The military security of the sub-region is built on a balance of forces among the local powers.

At the 2004 fourth review conference of the Article IV Agreement, further agreements were reached on the reduction of agreement-limited armaments (ALA) to a maximum 5 per cent of each category by the end of 2004. The Republika Srpska further reduced its ALA declared as decommissioned equipment, and some ACVs belonging to internal security forces were also scrapped. On the whole, the implementation of the Florence Agreement has gone smoothly, including the system of inspections, annual exchange of information and reductions. The process of transferring 'ownership' of the agreement to the parties has been declared to have been achieved, although the international community (through the CIO's Personal Representative) continues to provide guidance, expertise and technical support for better implementation.[61]

Regional confidence building

There are more than 20 regional military confidence-building arrangements in Europe. These measures aim to better address specific security concerns and defuse tensions in, for example, a neighbour-to-neighbour framework; to overcome historical resentments; to substitute for the lack of CFE assurances in areas outside the treaty; to allow participating states to meet NATO and/or EU political and security-related criteria as part of their accession strategy; and to encourage neighbouring states to modify their security policies. The presence of new NATO member states on Russia's border as a result of the 2004 enlargement may lead Russia to request more advanced CSBMs with those states, in addition to CFE confidence-building provisions.[62] Conversely, some of the existing CSBM arrangements involving states which have now been included in NATO may be phased out in coming years.[63]

Annex 1-B Dayton Peace Accords), 1 Jan.-30 Nov. 2004. Brigadier General Claudio Sampaolo (Italian Army), Personal Representative of the OSCE CIO, OSCE document CIO.GAL/124/04, 20 Dec. 2004.

[60] The text of the Florence Agreement is available at URL <http://www.oscebih.org/security_cooperation/?d=4>.

[61] Annual Report (note 59).

[62] In this context, the Russian Minister of Foreign Affairs stated: 'There is a need for additional confidence-building measures, measures of reciprocal control, measures to stave off hazardous military actions'. 'Transcript of remarks by Minister of Foreign Affairs of Russia Sergey Lavrov' (note 29).

[63] On 19 Jan. 2005, the 1998 Hungarian–Slovak CSBM agreement was terminated because the countries had become members of NATO.

Regional CSBMs have been used with success in the arc ranging from North-Eastern (the Baltic Sea states) through Central Eastern to South-Eastern (the Balkans) Europe. In 2004 Belarus and Latvia made a CSBM declaration providing for one additional evaluation visit a year and added information exchanges *inter alia* on the most significant military activity below the thresholds of the 1999 Vienna Document.[64] In 2004 Belarus and Poland exchanged diplomatic notes on a 'set' of complementary military CSBMs for their border zones. An agreement between Poland and Ukraine, signed on 20 July 2004, went further and covers the armed forces and the internal and border units of both states in their respective border areas.[65] Such arrangements are notably lacking, however, along the new NATO–Russia borders between Latvia and Russia and Poland and Russia, respectively.[66]

In 2004 other European CSBM initiatives were suggested or put forward. In June 2004 the OSCE proposed a set of CSBMs drawing both on European and on regional precedents that might be useful for the two sides in the 'frozen conflict' in Moldova. The OSCE mission to Moldova has selected and adapted a package of provisions, including separation of the forces of the two former combatants, reductions in their arms and military personnel, and a range of steps to increase transparency and confidence (e.g., exchange of information, visits, cooperative activities, exercises and training).[67]

After the Greek Cypriots rejected a UN plan to end the island's 30-year division, on 24 April 2004, the Republic of Cyprus put forward a proposal on CBMs in the military field, 'aimed at enhancing a sense of security among Greek Cypriots and Turkish Cypriots'. The proposed measures include opening new crossing points along the ceasefire line, de-mining several minefields within the buffer zone (2 kilometres on either side of the ceasefire line), withdrawing military forces from some sensitive areas and prohibiting military manoeuvres across two ceasefire lines.[68]

Other cases of 'frozen' or low-intensity conflicts involving the Nagorno-Karabakh Armenian separatist entity in Azerbaijan, the secessionist Abkhazian and South Ossetian regions in Georgia, and the self-proclaimed Trans-Dniester republic in Moldova continue to pose a threat to regional security in Europe. Although all of these conflict-ridden regions and areas of instability are formally subject to the Vienna Document regime, more intrusive regimes tailored to the local needs seem advisable at some stage of the post-conflict processes.

[64] OSCE, 'Declaration on additional CSBMs by Belaraus and Latvia', FSC document, FSC.DEL/71/04, 5 Mar. 2004.

[65] Belarus and Ukraine informed the 2001 AIAM of their intention to negotiate a CSBM agreement with Poland. The Belarusian–Polish agreement encountered some obstacles (mainly owing to the negotiated area of application) but was eventually signed on 20 July 2004.

[66] For more on regional CSBMs in Europe see Lachowski, Z., *Confidence- and Security-Building Measures in the New Europe*, SIPRI Research Report no. 18 (Oxford University Press: Oxford, 2004), pp. 129–55.

[67] OSCE, 'OSCE Chairman-in-Office calls for settlement and easing of tension in Moldova', Press Release, 22 June 2004, URL <http://www.osce.org/news/show_news.php?id=4175>.

[68] OSCE, Permanent Mission of the Republic of Cyprus, Note Verbale, FSC document FSC.DEL/365/04, 28 July 2004.

Monitoring on the Georgian–Russian border

Arrangements for monitoring the Georgian–Russian border were drawn into the general Russia–West disagreement over the OSCE in 2004.[69] Monitoring began in 2000 along the Chechen-inhabited part of the Georgian–Russian border following Russian claims that Chechen rebels were crossing it (later it was extended to the Ingush and Dagestani sectors of the border).[70] The duration of the Border Monitoring Operation (BMO) had been extended regularly by the OSCE until 2004. According to Georgia and observers from other countries, the BMO worked well as a CBM[71] and politically helped to shield Georgia from accusations that 'rebels and terrorists' allegedly based in the Pankisi Gorge were operating out of Georgian territory.[72]

Russia, however, had for some time been trying to modify the OSCE's monitoring operations in the Chechen, Ingush and Dagestani sectors of the border, and in 2004 it declared openly that the BMO had been ineffective and too costly to the OSCE budget. At the end of the year Russia changed its tactics and claimed that the operation had fulfilled its mandate and, as of 1 January 2005, should be switched to 'administrative–technical closure mode' and start phasing out its infrastructure. According to Russian authorities, the border can be protected on a bilateral Georgian–Russian basis.[73] The Western attitude so far has been to try to find a more positive compromise in the framework of a wider 'package' which would satisfy at least some of Russia's demands in other areas of OSCE business.

V. The Open Skies Treaty

Some states have worked actively to maintain the viability and relevance of the Open Skies Treaty since its entry into force on 1 January 2002, while others (including the USA) have accepted the status quo and the de facto marginalization of the treaty caused by changes in the political environment. In the view of this latter group of states, regional arms control in Europe is no longer of prime relevance for security building.

[69] For discussion on the OSCE see appendix 1A in this volume.

[70] The monitors were unarmed military officers seconded from some 30 countries. There were *c.* 150 men deployed in summer; in winter the number sank to *c.* 70 men.

[71] The Georgian Foreign Minister Salome Zourabishvili depicted the monitoring as 'one of our Organization's [OSCE's] most successful missions, simultaneously making a tremendous contribution to Georgia's border security along the most volatile and controversial segments of the Georgian–Russian border'. OSCE, Statement by the Delegation of Georgia, Ministerial Council, Sofia 2004, Ministerial Council document MC(12).JOUR/2, 7 Dec. 2004.

[72] Reportedly, the BMO has confirmed that some of the violations of Georgian airspace were committed by Russian military aircraft.

[73] 'Russian MFA Information and Press Department commentary regarding end of OSCE observers' stay on Georgian-Russian border', 31 Dec. 2004, URL <http://www.ln.mid.ru/brp_4.nsf/e78a4807 0f128a7b43256999005bcbb3/74502fb679f8eacfc3256f860022ff4c?OpenDocument>.

During 2004 and in preparation for the first Review Conference of the Open Skies Treaty[74] (scheduled for 14–16 February 2005 in Vienna) discussions and multilateral consultations took place in the framework of two seminars co-organized by the Chair of the review conference, Germany.[75] There were also extensive bilateral consultations between some key players. In the event, the review conference showed wide support for the view that the treaty still has potential to contribute to European security in spite of the changed political and technical conditions. There is much less need for Open Skies to verify arms control agreements between the former blocs, including agreements on the limitation of major armaments. Switching the emphasis to the potential use of aerial monitoring for post-conflict situations in the sub-regional context and to certain non-military uses, such as the monitoring of environmental catastrophes, could provide an answer. Technological conditions have changed because of the availability of satellite imagery similar to or of better resolution than that which Open Skies can provide. However, the Open Skies approach still has certain advantages, such as: (*a*) the ability to fly under the cloud cover higher than 1500 metres and thus provide images when satellite imagery is not available; (*b*) the incomparably better thermal imaging offered by Open Skies;[76] and (*c*) the flexibility to carry out Open Skies flights with a minimum of 72 hours' advance notice.

The review conference did not address one of the most sensitive matters, the modernization of the agreed list of sensors. According to two earlier decisions of the Open Skies Consultative Commission (OSCC),[77] which remain in force until 31 December 2005, the third year after entry into force of the treaty, the OSCC must decide before the end of 2005 whether or not to revise the specifications for the sensor set. This will determine the future capabilities of the sensors and whether they would provide better resolution than satellites. Owing to the technical nature of the matter, the OSCC agreed that it would be addressed at sessions of the Informal Working Group on Sensors rather than at

[74] According to the treaty's article XVI, para. 3 the depositaries shall convene a review conference 'three years after its entry into force . . . and at five-year intervals' thereafter. The Treaty on Open Skies, URL <http://www.osce.org/docs/english/oskiese.htm>.

[75] The OSCC Seminar on the Environmental/Ecological Use of the Open Skies Regime was held in Vienna on 14–15 Oct. 2004. A workshop on the Perspectives for Co-operative Aerial Observation and the Treaty on Open Skies was hosted by SIPRI in Stockholm on 30 Nov.–1 Dec. 2004. The workshop report and workshop papers are available at URL <http://www.sipri.org/contents/director/esdp/report.html> and <http://www.sipri.org/contents/director/esdp/papers.html>, respectively.

[76] Thermal-imaging sensors detect heat radiation that makes it possible to observe, day and night, whether vehicles and equipment are in use. The information thus provided goes beyond that delivered by photographic means.

[77] OSCC, Decision no. 14, Methodology for calculating the minimum height above ground level at which each video camera with real time display installed on an observation aircraft may be operated during an observation flight, OSCC document OSCC/VI/Dec.14, 12 Oct. 1994; and OSCC, Decision no. 15, Methodology for calculating the minimum height above ground level at which each infrared line-scanning device installed on an observation aircraft may be operated during an observation flight, OSCC document OSCC/VI/Dec.15, 12 Oct. 1994. OSCC decisions to the Treaty on Open Skies are available at URL <http://www.osmpf.wpafb.af.mil/Treaty_info/Treaty.htm>.

the review conference.[78] The review conference welcomed the resumption of work on the matter.[79]

The distribution of flight quotas has been a source of concern since the treaty entered into force. In accordance with a gentlemen's agreement among its member states, NATO agreed not to carry out inspections on the territory of the alliance. As the number of NATO members significantly increased, each member state was free to use its active quota to inspect non-members. The most strategically important of the non-members—Belarus, Russia and Ukraine—have been the most 'in demand' for this purpose, and the result is a largely asymmetric pattern of flights. The draft final document of the review conference declared that 'the Open Skies mechanism of quota distribution should reflect the principles of equity, reciprocity and cooperation, and that the OSCC may further review this mechanism after January 2006'. The conference did not adopt the final document (see below) and the same text was included in the chairman's statement. In effect, this amounts, once again, to deferring the substance of a decision.[80]

The review conference welcomed the increasing number of states parties. Since the entry into force of the Open Skies Treaty, six states have completed the accession process.[81] The accessions of Estonia and Lithuania have been approved by the OSCC: their national accession processes have been completed and both states will soon deposit their accession instruments, thereby extending the coverage of the treaty to all of the new NATO members. In this context, there were often heated debates both in the run-up to and during the review conference over whether to discuss the pending accession of the Republic of Cyprus. The Foreign Minister of the Republic of Cyprus had called attention to this issue at the OSCE Ministerial Council: 'We are convinced that a process of normalization will engender further positive developments for all concerned. In this context we hope that Turkey will terminate its opposition towards Cyprus's accession to the Open Skies Treaty'.[82] Turkey, the country that has systematically blocked the accession of Cyprus in the OSCC, in the event opposed such discussion at the review conference although every other state party was in favour of bringing up the issue.[83] For

[78] OSCC, Decision no. 1/05, Work Programme of the Informal Working Group on Sensors, OSCC document OSCC.DEC/1/05, 31 Jan. 2005.

[79] OSCC, Statement by the Chairman of the First Review Conference on the Implementation of the Treaty on Open Skies at the Closing Plenary, 16 Feb. 2005, point 8, OSCC document OSCC.RC/45/05.

[80] See OSCC, Draft Final Document of the First Review Conference on the Implementation of the Treaty on Open Skies, 14–16 Feb. 2005, point 10, OSCC document OSCC.RC/2/04/Rev.6, 10 Feb. 2005; and OSCC, Statement by the Chairman of the First Review Conference on the Implementation of the Treaty on Open Skies at the Closing Plenary' 16 Feb. 2005, point 9, OSCC document OSCC.RC/45/05.

[81] Bosnia and Herzegovina, Croatia, Finland, Latvia, Slovenia and Sweden joined the treaty between 2002 and the end of 2004.

[82] Statement by H. E. the Foreign Minister of Cyprus Mr George Iacovou before the 12th Meeting of the OSCE Ministerial Council Sofia, 6–7 Dec. 2004, p. 2, URL <http://www.osce.org/events/mc/bulgaria2004/documents/files/mc_1102354474_e.pdf>.

[83] Accession requires the consensus of each state party at the OSCC, and each party to the treaty thus is able to veto the accession of the country. This rule does not apply to those successor states of the former Soviet Union which are not signatories. They can accede to the treaty unilaterally in accordance

this reason alone the review conference failed to adopt a final document. Despite heavy pressure on Turkey by the chairmanship country Germany and by other states, it blocked consensus and also attempted to block a statement by the chairman. It was difficult to understand this approach because the draft final document did not refer to Turkey and merely stated that 'the application of Cyprus remains on the agenda of the Open Skies Consultative Commission (OSCC)'.[84]

Regional application of the Open Skies approach has often been viewed as a useful CBM. A bilateral open skies agreement was concluded between Hungary and Romania before the signature of the multilateral Open Skies Treaty.[85] However, because both parties are now members of NATO this agreement is expected to be terminated soon, as was the Hungarian–Slovakian CSBM agreement in 1998.[86]

VI. Mines

The elimination of deployed landmines and reduction of landmine stocks under the 1997 APM Convention continues to be the main success story of global-level conventional arms control. The APM Convention has shown the potential of timely initiatives that are widely supported both by states and popular movements, and it can be viewed as a contribution to 'human' as well as traditional security. In 2004 the First Review Conference of the APM Convention provided a good opportunity to take stock of the achievements, and the balance was overwhelmingly positive. The number of parties to the convention had increased to 144 states by the end of 2004.[87] The rate of new accessions will now inevitably slow, as 8 more countries are signatories, leaving 42 states outside the convention. The non-parties are concentrated mostly in conflict-prone areas, such as Asia, the Middle East and the Commonwealth of Independent States (CIS). It is particularly worrying that some states have begun to deploy mines in areas previously free from them (e.g., in some parts of Central Asia).[88]

The production of landmines has decreased significantly. Thirty-three of the 50 countries which produced landmines before the APM Convention was

with Article XVII, para. 3 of the Treaty on Open Skies, URL <http://www.osce.org/docs/english/oskiese.htm>.

[84] OSCC, Statement by the Chairman of the First Review Conference on the Implementation of the Treaty on Open Skies at the Closing Plenary, 16 Feb. 2005,OSCC document OSCC.RC/45/05.

[85] Agreement Between the Government of the Republic of Hungary and the Government of Romania on the establishment of an Open Skies regime. It is reproduced in Dunay, P. *et al.*, *Open Skies: A Cooperative Approach to Military Transparency and Confidence Building* (UN Institute for Disarmament Research (UNIDIR): Geneva, 2004), pp. 265–90.

[86] See note 63.

[87] Three states (Estonia, Ethiopia and Papua New Guinea) joined the convention in 2004. In 2003, 11 states joined; 8 joined in 2002, and 13 states joined in 2001.

[88] Notably, the laying of APMs was reported on the borders of Uzbekistan with Tajikistan and Kyrgyzstan and on the Kyrgyz–Tajik border by Kyrgyzstan. See *Landmine Monitor Report 2004: Toward a Mine-Free World* (Human Rights Watch–International Campaign to Ban Landmines: Geneva, 2004), p. 10.

opened for signature and ratification in December 1997 are now parties to the convention, and 3 non-parties have announced the end of production. The International Campaign to Ban Landmines (ICBL) is of the view that a number of other states—Egypt, South Korea and the USA—have not produced mines for several years.[89] More strikingly, the trade in landmines has effectively ceased. Most non-parties to the convention have put in place moratoria or bans on the transfer of such weapons, including influential powers such as China, Russia and the USA.[90] The use of landmines has declined sharply.[91]

The declaration adopted at the end of the review conference stated that more than 37 million stockpiled landmines have been destroyed since the entry into force of the APM Convention in 1999. The goal of a mine-free world 10 years after the entry into force of the convention (by late 2009)—as demanded by many campaigners—seems unrealistic, however. The President of the Review Conference recognized this by naming some countries that would face special difficulties and noted that, 'one must not give up five years before the deadline. The closer the goal comes, the greater will be the motivation'.[92] The declaration adopted at the end of the First Review Conference emphasized that '[w]e will strengthen our efforts to clear mined areas and destroy stockpiled anti-personnel mines in accordance with our time-bound obligations'.[93]

Forty-six states parties are still carrying out mine clearance, many of them with weak capacities and limited resources. The clearing of deployed mines is far more demanding than the elimination of stockpiles and may present more of a problem for the success of the APM ban. Although capacity and institution building has been extensive since the convention was opened for signature, further sustained effort is necessary to implement the agreed goals.

Since the end of the cold war most armed conflicts have been intra-state, and the use of landmines by non-state actors presents a problem for the operation of the APM Convention. The number of countries where such use has occurred is on the increase.[94] A humanitarian organization, Geneva Call, has taken steps since 2001 to encourage 'armed non-state actors' to commit themselves not to use landmines,[95] with some success. However, states are often concerned that such contacts with armed non-state actors operating on their

[89] These 3 countries are still identified as producers as they have the right to produce APMs. See *Landmine Monitor Report 2004* (note 88), p. 11; and Final Report, First Review Conference of the States Parties to the Convention on the Prohibition of the Use, Stockpiling, Production and Transfer of Anti-Personnel Mines and on their Destruction, APLC/CONF/2004/5, 8 Dec. 2004, available at URL <http://www.reviewconference.org>.

[90] Final Report (note 89), p. 11.

[91] Apparently, the trend of mine casualties is somewhat more uncertain than that of mine use. There are not accurate data available on mine casualties.

[92] 'Official on chances of implementing total landmine ban by 2009—Austrian daily', BBC Monitoring Service, 29 Nov. 2004.

[93] Small Arms Net, 'Towards a Mine-Free World: the 2004 Nairobi Declaration', URL <http://www.smallarmsnet.org/docs/nairobidecl04.pdf>.

[94] Such use occurred 'in at least 16 countries' according to the *Landmine Monitor Report 2004* (note 88), p. 7.

[95] See Geneva Call, 'Deed of Commitment under Geneva Call for Adherence to a Total Ban on Anti-Personnel Mines and for Cooperation in Mine Action', URL <http://www.genevacall.org/about/testimission/gc-04oct01-deed.htm>.

territory would legitimize the non-state actors. One non-party to the APM Convention, Sri Lanka, has suggested that its accession to the convention may be linked to a commitment to end the use of APMs by an armed non-state actor operating on its territory. Such an approach would raise complex international legal questions and may in effect be an excuse for not acceding to the convention. On the other hand, shutting the door to non-state actors can only prolong the landmine problem in states where the centre does not effectively control the whole territory.

The effort to control, reduce and eliminate landmines is not confined to the APM Convention. Protocol V of the CCW Convention addresses post-conflict remedies for explosive remnants of war[96] and it may gain importance as a complementary instrument.

Work on mines other than anti-personnel mines (MOTAPMs) continued in 2004 in the context of the CCW. Some non-governmental organizations (NGOs) and states advocate the extension of the landmine ban to this category, but the popular pressure that helped overcome the objections of many states to the APM ban is harder to summon up in the case of mines that have less obvious humanitarian impact. On the other hand, unrestricted use of MOTAPMs compounds the problems of post-conflict societies by blocking access to communities and raising the cost of implementing humanitarian projects. Some communities are not even considered for humanitarian assistance because their needs cannot be assessed.[97] A recent study outlines recommendations to address MOTAPMs: (*a*) to prohibit the use of MOTAPMs that are not detectable by commonly available mine detection equipment and that do not provide a response signal equivalent to a signal from 8 grams or more of iron in a single coherent mass; (*b*) to prohibit MOTAPMs that are not detectable by technical mine-detection methods and equipment other than that specified under point (*a*); and (*c*) to prohibit all MOTAPMs.[98]

Countries that have not joined the landmine ban but which also do not need to deploy mines for any major conflict have made efforts to align their policies to the extent possible. China declared that it 'endorses the purposes and objectives of the Ottawa Convention'.[99] Russia, although it uses landmines in Chechnya, ratified the Amended Protocol II to the CCW Convention.[100] The USA has come under particular criticism for not acceding to the APM Convention *inter alia* because of the alibi this provides for 'problem' countries

[96] See Lachowski and Sjögren (note 9), pp. 713–36.

[97] For more details see *Humanitarian Impact from Mines other than Anti-Personnel Mines* (Geneva International Centre for Humanitarian Demining: Geneva, Oct. 2004), URL <http://www.gichd.org/pdf/publications/Humanitarian_Impact_from_MOTAPM.pdf>.

[98] Group of Governmental Experts of the States Parties to the Convention on Prohibitions or Restrictions on the Use of Certain Conventional Weapons which may be Deemed to be Excessively Injurious or to Have Indiscriminate Effects, Working Group on Mines Other Than Anti-Personnel Mines, Proposals and ideas on MOTAPM in the Group of Governmental Experts (GGE) with the purpose to provide a basis for further work, CCW/GGE/VIII/WG.2/1, 11 June 2004, p. 4.

[99] 'Envoy says China endorses objectives of Ottawa Convention on landmines', BBC Monitoring International Reports, 3 Dec. 2004.

[100] Interfax (Moscow), 'Russian Duma ratifies protocol on restriction on military mine usage', 23 Nov. 2004, in FBIS-SOV-2004-1123, 24 Nov. 2004.

also to stay outside the regime. However, in practice US national policy is far more complex than most observers realize. In 2004 the USA declared that it would not use long-lasting or 'persistent' APMs or persistent anti-vehicle mines after 2010; it will no longer have any undetectable landmines in its inventory; and it will increase its budget for global humanitarian mine action programmes.[101] US policy still permits the use of detectable landmines with timing mechanisms that self-destruct the mine in 30 days or less,[102] but in the view of most experts these mines do not pose the same wholesale humanitarian problem that long-lived ones do. It is regrettable that the USA's progress in the limitation of landmines has not positively influenced other states and non-state entities.

VII. Confidence building in Asia

While 'hard' conventional arms control remains a European phenomenon, confidence-building processes are pursued in various other regions worldwide. In 2004 there was a renewed effort in South Asia to arrive at a confidence-building arrangement. In a broader Asian context, the Conference on Interaction and Confidence-Building Measures in Asia (CICA) adopted a catalogue of CBMs.[103]

India–Pakistan

Both India and Pakistan have a history of repeated but unsuccessful endeavours to apply CBMs in their mutual relations.[104] The change of government in India in May 2004 furnished a new incentive for both India and Pakistan to discuss nuclear and conventional CBMs. In mid-2004 they agreed a set of 'nuclear and strategic' CBMs, including the establishment of a hotline, a pledge to notify each other in advance of tests of nuclear-capable missiles and a continuation of the moratorium on tests of nuclear warheads.[105] However, in the following months progress was limited to a list of symbolic agreements and CBMs, while the countries at the same time demonstrated their military prowess through a series of missile tests.

In mid-December the two states held their first, exploratory talks on conventional weapons as part of the so-called 'composite dialogue', which covers

[101] US Department of State, International Information Program, 'Bloomfield details landmine policy changes', 27 Feb. 2004, URL <http://usinfo.state.gov/xarchives/display.html?p=washfile-english>.

[102] Garwin, R.L., 'On land mines, America is a humanitarian leader', *International Herald Tribune,* 20–21 Mar. 2004, p. 6.

[103] Kazakhstan Ministry of Foreign Affairs, Conference on Interaction and Confidence-Building Measures in Asia, 'Catalogue of confidence building measures (CBMs), adopted by the decision of the CICA ministers of foreign affairs meeting, Almaty, 22 Oct. 2004', URL <http://www.mfa.kz/eng/index.php?meeting=1&selected=10>. The members of the CICA are listed in the glossary in this volume.

[104] For texts of selection of Indian–Pakistan military CBMs see Institute for Defence Studies and Analyses, *Strategic Digest* (Delhi), vol. 34, no. 6 (June 2004), pp. 869–74.

[105] 'India and Pakistan set up nuclear hotline', *Financial Times*, 20 June 2004.

eight problem areas including the Kashmir dispute. Having established a hotline between India and Pakistan, the officials discussed a framework for further measures, such as advance notification of military exercises, avoidance of firing incidents across the international border and communication between the military authorities and local commanders in the border zones.[106] Once again, the talks reportedly broke up over the issucs of missiles and a 'strategic restraint regime' proposed by Pakistan.[107] At the end of the year the two foreign ministers agreed to continue to explore further CBMs along the their border and the line of control (LoC).[108]

The Conference on Interaction and Confidence-Building Measures in Asia

On 22–23 October 2004 a meeting of the foreign ministers of the CICA member states was held in Almaty, Kazakhstan. The main outcome of the meeting was the adoption of a Catalogue of Confidence-Building Measures.[109] The list of CBMs is extensive, covering not only politico-military, but also economic, environmental and human dimensions.

Given the diversity of the states to which they apply, the agreed CBMs are not so much a regime as a 'catalogue' of voluntary measures to be applied on a selective (where feasible and appropriate) and gradual basis. Inspired mainly by the European record, the military CBMs envisage the exchange of military information, inviting observers to military exercises, consultations on unexpected and hazardous incidents of a military nature, other forms of cooperation between armed forces, and the exchange of information on the status of states' ratification of or accession to various arms control and disarmament agreements. Information exchanges are also foreseen as measures to combat the new threats of terrorism, extremism and separatism in all their forms, the proliferation of weapons of mass destruction, the fight against crime, illicit trade in small arms and smuggling.

VIII. Conclusions

The prolonged crisis over the adapted CFE Treaty has had a corrosive influence on the political atmosphere and the prospects for a pan-European arms control regime. At the end of 2004 the two main actors on the European scene, NATO and Russia, continued to stick to the unyielding standpoints that have

[106] 'AFP: more on Pakistan, India hold first talks on conventional arms', AFP (Hong Kong), 15 Dec. 2004, in Foreign Broadcast Information Service, *Daily Report–Near East and South Asia* (*FBIS–NES*), FBIS-NES-2004-1215, 15 Dec. 2004.

[107] 'Pakistan: India rejects proposals for CBMs on nuclear, conventional arms', *The News* (Islamabad), 19 Dec. 2004, in Foreign Broadcast Information Service, *Daily Report–China* (*FBIS–CHI*), FBIS-CHI-2004-1219, 19 Dec. 2004.

[108] Indian Ministry of External Affairs, 'India–Pakistan Joint Statement, Meeting between Foreign Secretaries of India and Pakistan', Islamabad, 28 Dec. 2004, URL <http://www.meaindia.nic.in/jshome.htm>.

[109] Kazakhstan Ministry of Foreign Affairs (note 103).

resulted in a stalemate lasting for over five years. Nevertheless, the hard conventional arms control regime successfully weathered the 2004 wave of NATO enlargement and the associated problem of a legal CFE 'black hole' (the fact that the Baltic states are not covered by the treaty) along the new NATO–Russia border. Russia made the conciliatory gesture of ratifying the Agreement on Adaptation, which was intended to encourage positive reciprocation on the part of NATO. The completion by Russia of its ratification process of the Agreement on Adaptation underscores its legal, political and moral duty to terminate its unwanted military presence in Georgia and Moldova. The NATO states continue to call on Russia to abide by its commitments. Significantly, vigorous steps have been taken by Georgia and Moldova to resolve their 'frozen conflicts' where Russia plays the pivotal role. Apart from the issue of the Istanbul commitments, increasing and costly difficulties stem from the constraints that the outdated CFE Treaty places on NATO's operational flexibility, for instance, on its deployments in the south-western parts of the flank zone (Bulgaria and Romania). This intensifies pressure on the West to reassess its attitude to the issue of ratification of the Agreement on Adaptation of the CFE Treaty.

The evolution of European CSBMs and NSSMs is currently directed at sharing these accomplishments with adjacent regions and regions outside the OSCE area; developing measures to ensure stricter controls of SALWs, surplus ammunition, landmines, and the like; and regional application. Regional CSBMs that focus on security and military activities in the vicinity of borders as well as other measures could be applied to stalemated crisis situations.

The prospects for the Open Skies Treaty regime also have regional and possible non-military dimensions. The treaty's review conference in early 2005 demonstrated that many states parties value the achievements of this aspect of European arms control and wish to maintain its relevance. An increase in the number of parties and extension of the open skies regime to countries in potential conflict zones in the Balkans and the eastern part of Europe would help to promote that goal.

In 2004 the major humanitarian and military security frameworks continued to gain support and importance, thereby helping to decrease the scourge of mines worldwide, although the dilemma prevails of a total ban versus restraint in the application of such weapons.

16. International non-proliferation and disarmament assistance

IAN ANTHONY and VITALY FEDCHENKO

I. Introduction

As part of the international anti-proliferation effort, a growing number of countries offer practical help to other countries in order to secure or eliminate nuclear, biological and chemical (NBC) weapons, the missile delivery systems for such weapons and capacities that might contribute to NBC weapon programmes. The provision of international non-proliferation and disarmament assistance (INDA) is steadily evolving from an emergency programme intended to manage the extraordinary circumstances surrounding the break-up of the Soviet Union to a broader international programme involving new donor states, new recipient states and new types of activity.

This chapter surveys the recent activities of key donors and of Russia, the country in which most INDA activities have been carried out—reflecting the scale of the arsenals, infrastructure and knowledge base that was developed during the cold war. It also examines some of the mechanisms used to manage and organize assistance efforts. Section II examines recent decisions and programmes in the United States. Since their summit meeting in Kananaskis, Canada, in 2002 the Group of Eight (G8) industrialized nations has been engaged in a sustained manner in organizing non-proliferation and disarmament assistance. Section III describes the re-design of these efforts that was undertaken in 2004. Section IV examines the efforts by the European Union (EU), including its member states at the national level, to become a more coherent and effective INDA provider as part of the wider effort to further develop and implement the EU Strategy Against the Proliferation of Weapons of Mass Destruction (WMD).[1] External contributions play an important role in helping Russia to manage the consequences of the massive militarization of its economy and society during the cold war. However, the most critical factor in defining and carrying out related projects is actions taken by the Russian Government and entities under its control. Section V examines the impact on INDA projects of the reorganization of the Russian Government undertaken

[1] Council of the European Union, 'Basic Principles for an EU Strategy Against the Proliferation of Weapons of Mass Destruction', document 10352/03, Brussels, 10 June 2003, URL <http://register.consilium.eu.int/pdf/en/03/st10/st10352en03.pdf>; and Council of the European Union, 'Action Plan for the Implementation of the Basic Principles for an EU Strategy Against the Proliferation of Weapons of Mass Destruction', document 10354/03, Brussels, 10 June 2003, URL <http://register.consilium.eu.int/pdf/en/ 03/st10/st10354en03.pdf>. The background to the adoption of this strategy is discussed in Anthony, I., 'Major trends in arms control and non-proliferation', *SIPRI Yearbook 2004: Armaments, Disarmament and International Security* (Oxford University Press: Oxford, 2004), pp. 575–601. Implementation of the strategy in 2004 is described in chapter 17 in this volume.

by President of the Russian Federation Vladimir Putin in 2004. Section VI gives conclusions.

II. Developments in the United States

As part of what US officials have labelled a 'layered nonproliferation defence' the USA has sponsored and supported different types of measures to reduce the risk that state or non-state actors might acquire nuclear weapons, nuclear explosive devices, biological weapons (BW), chemical weapons (CW), radiological dispersal devices (RDDs, or 'dirty bombs'), or delivery systems for any of the above weapons. The measures include: (*a*) multilateral treaties and agreements; (*b*) cooperation in ad hoc groupings to develop shared rules and understandings regarding export controls; (*c*) action taken through the United Nations (UN) to reduce the threat to the USA from state or non-state actors that might acquire nuclear weapons, nuclear explosive devices, BW, CW or RDDs; and (*d*) efforts to intercept and seize weapons or materials during transport to countries of concern and non-state actors.

In addition to these measures the USA has, since the enactment of the 1991 Soviet Nuclear Threat Reduction Act, provided practical technical and financial assistance of different kinds as part of its overall arms control and non-proliferation programme.[2] In the past, most US assistance was provided to Russia and the states that emerged on the territory of the former Soviet Union in order to assist with the implementation of arms control and disarmament treaties. US assistance has been particularly important for implementation of the 1991 Strategic Arms Reduction Treaty (START I) by Russia and the other former-Soviet republics with strategic nuclear forces based on their territories—Belarus, Kazakhstan and Ukraine.[3] Under START I, more than 6500 nuclear warheads were deactivated, over 1700 missile delivery systems were destroyed, and the platforms and silos from which these delivery systems would have been launched were dismantled.[4]

After the enactment of the 1996 Defense Against Weapons of Mass Destruction Act,[5] the functional scope of US non-proliferation and disarmament assistance expanded, facilitating further US financial support for nuclear security projects in the former Soviet Union. This expanded remit also opened the way for assistance targeted at projects to assist with the implementation of CW stockpile destruction commitments under the 1993 Convention on the

[2] Under the framework of the 1991 Soviet Nuclear Threat Reduction Act (also known as the Nunn–Lugar Act after the senators who co-sponsored the original authorizing legislation), the US Department of Defense (DOD) manages the Cooperative Threat Reduction (CTR) programme. The programme has subsequently evolved to encompass a wide range of non-proliferation and demilitarization activities under the auspices of the Department of Commerce, the Department of Energy, the Department of State and the DOD.

[3] For a summary of the main provisions of the START I Treaty see annex A in this volume.

[4] Defense Threat Reduction Agency, Reduction scorecard, URL <http://www.dtra.mil/toolbox/directorates/ctr/scorecard.cfm>.

[5] US Defense Against Weapons of Mass Destruction Act 1996, Public Law 104-201, 23 Sep. 1996, incorporated into the 1997 National Defense Authorization Act, available at URL <http://www.gpoaccess.gov/plaws/search.html>.

Prohibition of the Development, Production, Stockpiling and Use of Chemical Weapons and on their Destruction (Chemical Weapons Convention, CWC) and to address BW-related concerns.

The terrorist attacks on the USA in September 2001 provided further impetus for US programmes to deliver non-proliferation and disarmament assistance. In particular, the USA began to examine how the techniques developed for application in the former Soviet Union might be applied in other countries and regions. The USA has made the largest financial commitment of any nation to international non-proliferation and disarmament assistance. The pledge made by the USA, covering the period 2002–12, in the framework of the G8 Global Partnership Against Weapons and Materials of Mass Destruction (Global Partnership) indicates that the US contribution will be roughly equivalent to those of all other donor states combined. In total, the USA is likely to spend around $2 billion (€1.53 billion) each year on threat reduction projects, of which around half will be spent on international projects.[6]

Delivering this assistance is a task that has engaged a number of different parts of the US Government. The Department of Defense (DOD) and its Defense Threat Reduction Agency (DTRA), the Department of Energy (DOE), the Department of State and the Department of Commerce are all responsible for implementing non-proliferation and disarmament assistance programmes. The relative roles of the different US agencies are changing in line with the different programme priorities. The capacity of the DOE is being strengthened to reflect the strong priority currently given to nuclear security projects, which are likely to be costly and of long duration.[7]

As a result of decisions taken in 2004, the range of non-proliferation and disarmament assistance programmes carried out by the USA will also be expanded to include additional projects to 'improve and expedite efforts to secure and recover at-risk nuclear materials and related equipment from vulnerable facilities around the world, which could be used to make radiological or nuclear bombs'.[8]

Repatriation and down-blending of highly enriched uranium

The September 2001 terrorist attacks in the USA, as well as information gained in subsequent anti-terrorist operations in Afghanistan and elsewhere,

[6] Russian–American Nuclear Security Advisory Council (RANSAC), 'Congress passes far-reaching nuclear security measure', RANSAC press release, 12 Oct. 2004. The remaining money will be used to pay for the destruction of US chemical weapons and the disposal of plutonium and highly enriched uranium released by the decommissioning of US nuclear weapons.

[7] US Department of Energy, National Nuclear Security Administration (NNSA), 'Nonproliferation spending and activities up dramatically in this administration', Fact Sheet, June 2004, URL <http://www.nnsa.doe.gov/page_new.htm>. While spending by the NNSA on non-proliferation will increase, spending by the DOD, which has implemented a number of expensive START I-related projects through its Defense Threat Reduction Agency, is likely to fall. Aggregate annual US financing for INDA is likely to remain stable at roughly $1 billion during the G8 Global Partnership

[8] Russian–American Nuclear Security Advisory Council (note 6). The measures, to be implemented by the DOE, were included in the 2005 National Defense Authorization Act, Section 3132, 'Acceleration of removal or security of fissile materials, radiological materials and related equipment at vulnerable sites worldwide'.

have heightened US concern that a nuclear explosive device might be used in a terrorist attack. A number of technical evaluations have concluded that over a period of time a sophisticated terrorist group would be able to accumulate nuclear fissile material and develop the design and engineering skills required to build such a device.[9] In 2004 the USA increased the tempo of and its financial support for programmes intended to reduce the risk of unauthorized access to weapon-usable fissile materials—plutonium and highly enriched uranium (HEU). Particular attention has been paid to securing stocks of HEU, the material considered most vulnerable to misuse.

To this end, the USA has helped to initiate the Global Threat Reduction Initiative as well as processes being undertaken by the International Atomic Energy Agency (IAEA) and the G8, which are discussed below. In addition to these international activities, the USA has conducted or facilitated specific actions to move identified vulnerable HEU stocks to more secure locations.

In 1999 Russia, the USA and the IAEA launched what is now known as the Tripartite Initiative to focus on the possible management and disposition of fuel of Russian-origin located at research reactors on the territory of the former Soviet Union and around the world, and essentially on its return to Russia. A large part of this fuel contains the HEU. The first shipment under the framework of the Tripartite Initiative took place in September 2003.[10]

Three such activities were carried out under the framework of the Tripartite Initiative in 2004. In early March, a shipment took place from the Tajoura Nuclear Research Centre near Tripoli, Libya. The shipment, consisting of 16 kg of 80 per cent HEU in the form of fresh fuel, was airlifted to a secure facility in Dimitrovgrad, Russia. The $700 000 fuel removal project was funded by the USA.[11] In September, a mission to recover 11 kg of enriched uranium fuel, including HEU, from Uzbekistan was completed.[12] The HEU was airlifted under guard from an airport near Tashkent, Uzbekistan, to the same facility at Dimitrovgrad, where it will be down-blended into low-enriched uranium (LEU). Russia provided special transportation canisters for the material and the action was carried out by technical experts from Russia, the USA and the IAEA. In December, 6 kg of HEU was removed from the

[9] See, e.g., Bremer Maerli, M., Norwegian Atlantic Committee, *Nuclear Terrorism: Threats, Challenges and Response* (Security Policy Library: Oslo, Aug. 2002), URL <http://www.nupi.no/IPS/?module=Articles;action=Article.publicShow;ID=966;nocache=true>.

[10] Goldman, I. N., Adelfang, P. and Ritchie, I. G., International Atomic Energy Agency (IAEA), 'IAEA activities related to research reactor fuel conversion and spent fuel return programs', Nuclear Fuel Cycle and Materials Section, Nuclear Fuel Cycle and Waste Technology Division, URL <www.iaea.org/NewsCenter/News/PDF/sfr_programs.pdf>. In addition, similar activities have been carried out in Bulgaria, Georgia, Kazakhstan, Romania and Serbia and Montenegro.

[11] International Atomic Energy Agency (IAEA), 'Removal of high-enriched Uranium in Libyan Arab Jamahiriya: IAEA, United States, Russia assist Libyan Arab Jamahiriya in removing fissile material', IAEA News Centre, 8 Mar. 2004, URL <http://www.iaea.org/NewsCenter/News/2004/libya_uranium0803.html>.

[12] US Department of Energy, 'Secret mission to recover highly enriched uranium in Uzbekistan successful', Press Release, Washington, DC, 13 Sep. 2004, URL <http://www.energy.gov/engine/content.do?PUBLIC_ID=16642&BT_CODE=PR_PRESSRELEASESTT_CODE=PRESSRELEASE>.

Czech Republic and taken to Dimitrovgrad to be down-blended.[13] In all cases, the HEU was contained in nuclear fuel assemblies originally supplied for use in a Russian-designed research reactor. In the past both Russia and the USA have supplied research reactors to countries around the world. In addition to its cooperation with Russia, the USA intends to repatriate approximately 20 tonnes of spent HEU fuel from research reactors of US origin in more than 40 locations. The USA also plans to convert 105 civilian research reactors of Russian and US origin, which currently use HEU fuel, to use LEU fuel.

Russia and the USA continue to implement the 1993 intergovernmental agreement, also known as the 'Megatons to Megawatts Program', which calls on Russia to convert 500 tonnes of HEU from dismantled nuclear warheads to LEU to be used as fuel to generate electricity. The down-blending of HEU takes place in Russia. The resulting LEU fuel is then purchased by the USA for use in power generation. As of 31 December 2004, 231.5 tonnes of weapon-grade HEU—reportedly equivalent to more than 9000 warheads—had been downblended into 6824 tonnes of LEU.[14]

Down-blending HEU into LEU to eliminate a source of fissile material has been validated from a technical perspective and has been shown to have other advantages as a non-proliferation instrument. For this reason a number of proposals have been put forward in Europe and the USA to accelerate the down-blending process.[15] However, this acceleration has not yet taken place.

Ending the production of plutonium for nuclear weapon production

In June 1994, as part of their commitment to make irreversible and transparent reductions in nuclear arms, Russia and the USA agreed steps to end the production of plutonium for use in nuclear weapons and to progressively reduce their respective plutonium stockpiles.[16] In this context, in 1994 Russia agreed to close three reactors that had been used to produce plutonium for nuclear weapons on the condition that an alternative source of energy could be provided for the cities that depended on them for power. The USA agreed to provide financial support for this project, to be carried out in the closed nuclear cities of Seversk and Zheleznogorsk (formerly known as Tomsk-7 and Krasnoyarsk-26). According to an amended timetable agreed in 2001, two reactors in Seversk will close by the end of 2005 and the reactor in Zheleznogorsk

[13] US International Information Programs, 'Highly enriched uranium repatriated from the Czech Republic to Russia', Press Release, Washington, DC, 23 Dec. 2004, available at URL <http://www.globalsecurity.org/wmd/library/news/russia/2004/russia-041223-usia01.htm>.

[14] US Enrichment Corporation, 'US–Russian Megatons to Megawatts Program: recycling nuclear warheads into electricity', Fact Sheet, 31 Dec. 2004, URL <http://www.usec.com/v2001_02/HTML/megatons_fact.asp>.

[15] Arbman, G. *et al.*, Statens Kärnkraftinspektion (SKI) [Swedish Nuclear Power Inspectorate], *Eliminating Stockpiles of Highly Enriched Uranium: Options for an Action Agenda in Cooperation with the Russian Federation*, Report submitted to the Swedish Ministry for Foreign Affairs, SKI Report 2004:15 (SKI: Stockholm, Apr. 2004), URL <http://www.ski.se/dynamaster/file_archive/040511/4e8cb165a0a960aba648aaf3479fe05e/2004%5f15.pdf>.

[16] US Department of State, Bureau of Public Affairs, 'Gore–Chernomyrdin Commission', Fact Sheet, 21 Sep. 1994.

should close by the end of 2006. In December 2004 US company Washington Group International (WGI) was contracted to carry out the conversion of electricity generating facilities in Seversk.[17] Under the contract, the city of Seversk will be supplied by an existing coal-fired plant, which is to be refurbished as part of the WGI project.

Enhancing the protection, control and accounting of nuclear materials

The US Department of Energy's Nuclear Materials Protection, Control, and Accounting (MPC&A) Program is the largest and most successful international cooperative effort to secure and account for nuclear weapons and materials.[18] The programme ensures that nuclear materials are securely stored in designated facilities and properly accounted for, thereby minimizing the threat of their diversion. The USA has been providing assistance to Russia for more than a decade, focusing primarily on security upgrades for vulnerable sites.

In 2004 the security at three sites was upgraded under the MPC&A Program: the Novosibirsk Chemical Concentrates Plant, the Urals Integrated Electrochemical Plant and the Electrochemical Plant at Zelenogorsk. The DOE estimates that security improvements have now been completed at 12 sites and expects this figure to rise to 14 by the end of 2005. The programme goal—to provide all 18 designated Russian civilian sites with security upgrades—is expected to be achieved in 2008, after which the DOE will provide low levels of support to ensure the long-term maintenance and operability of upgraded systems.[19] The DOE programme to provide physical protection at military sites, specifically those of the Russian Navy and the Strategic Rocket Forces, is also nearing completion.

The emphasis is now likely to shift from physical protection measures to improving the quality of site personnel, which will also help to ensure the sustainability of the security upgrades.[20] In addition, the DOE has been focusing more attention on export control and border security assistance programmes as part of the Second Line of Defense Program.[21]

[17] US Department of Energy, National Nuclear Security Administration, 'US signs contract as part of effort to permanently shut down plutonium production reactors in Russia', Press Release, 20 Dec. 2004, URL <http://www.nnsa.doe.gov/docs/PR_NA-04-34.htm>.

[18] Nuclear Threat Initiative (NTI), 'Securing nuclear warheads and materials: materials protection control and accounting', NTI Research library, URL <http://www.nti.org/e_research/cnwm/securing/mpca.asp>.

[19] National Nuclear Security Administration (NNSA), 'Security upgrades completed at three Russian nuclear facilities: NNSA continues work to keep nuclear material out of the hands of terrorists', Press Release, 10 Dec. 2004, URL <http://www.nnsa.doe.gov/docs/PR-NA-04-33%20%20Security%20upgrades%20completed(12-04).htm>; and NNSA, Office of Material Consolidation and Civilian Sites, URL <http://www.nnsa.doe.gov/na-20/mccs.shtml>.

[20] Khripunov, I. and Holmes, J. (eds), *Nuclear Security Culture: the Case of Russia*, (Center for International Trade and Security: University of Georgia, Dec. 2004), URL <http://www.uga.edu/cits/documents/pdf/Security%20Culture%20Report%2020041118.pdf>.

[21] For more information on the Second Line of Defense Program see the National Nuclear Security Administration Internet site, URL <http://www.nnsa.doe.gov/na-20/sld.shtml>.

Destruction of chemical weapons in Russia

The USA is also a major contributor to the international effort to dispose of 40 000 agent tonnes of CW in Russia. The US DOD is using funds allocated by Congress to (*a*) build the CW destruction facility at Shchuch'ye; (*b*) improve security systems at the Shchuch'ye and the Kizner CW storage sites; and (*c*) demilitarize former Soviet nerve agent production facilities.[22]

The level of US assistance in this area in 2004 ($200 million) was slightly higher than Russia's contribution ($189 million) and equal to those of the other 14 donors combined.[23] The USA has tried to make funding conditional on Russia meeting a variety of unrelated conditions. For example, the USA wants to obtain a sample of a genetically modified strain of *B. anthracis* that is resistant to antibiotic treatment. The USA is also inflexible about how money allocated to CW destruction can be spent—partly because the US Congress has attached the general condition that there should be no funding for infrastructure. The US Congress has never fully appreciated the fact that CW destruction facilities cannot be operated in areas with no proper roads, sewage systems, reliable power supply, and so on. At the operational level, the dividing line between infrastructure support and supporting the construction of a pilot CW destruction facility becomes blurred.

III. Developments in the Group of Eight

The Global Partnership was created at the 2002 G8 Summit in Kananaskis, Canada. It was established to support specific cooperation projects, initially in Russia, that address non-proliferation, disarmament, counter-terrorism and nuclear safety issues. The G8 identified the destruction of CW, the dismantlement of decommissioned nuclear submarines, the permanent disposition of fissile materials and the employment of former weapon scientists as the main immediate project priorities. President Putin subsequently stated that, from a Russian perspective, the destruction of CW and the dismantling of nuclear submarines were particularly important.

The G8 leaders revised the Global Partnership at the 2004 G8 Summit at Sea Island, Georgia. They highlighted the need for a 'long-term strategy' and for 'multi-faceted approaches' in order 'to prevent, contain and roll back proliferation' to supplement the fairly confined 2002 objectives of the programme. In addition to setting more ambitious objectives, the G8 leaders discussed projects with a wider functional scope and a new geographic orientation and announced an Action Plan to reinforce the global non-proliferation regime.[24] The Action Plan contained: (*a*) an endorsement of a US initiative

[22] CSIS, Strengthening the Global Partnership Project, the United States, URL <http://www.sgpproject.org/Donor%20Factsheets/US.html>.

[23] For the list of those donors and further discussion see chapter 13 in this volume; and G8 Sea Island Summit 2004, 'Consolidated Report of Global Partnership Projects', Summit documents. 9 June 2004, URL <http://www.g8usa.gov/pdfs/GPConsolidatedReportofGPProjectsJune2004.pdf>.

[24] G8 Sea Island Summit 2004, 'G8 Action Plan on Nonproliferation', Summit documents, 8 June 2004, URL <http://www.g8usa.gov/d_060904d.htm>.

calling for a one-year ban on the sale of enrichment and reprocessing technologies to any state that does not already possess full-scale, functioning enrichment and reprocessing plants; (*b*) an exhortation to introduce integrated safeguards—or comprehensive safeguards—in cooperation with the IAEA; (*c*) a proposal for a special committee to be created at the IAEA to focus on safeguards and verification; (*d*) a commitment to support the Proliferation Security Initiative (PSI)[25] and a commitment by the G8 to provide resources to help states combat illicit trafficking in WMD-related items; (*e*) measures specific to Iran and North Korea, two countries of proliferation concern, and Libya, a country where proliferation concerns have been addressed;[26] (*f*) support for the implementation of the CWC; (*g*) support for efforts to defend against bio-terrorism, including strengthening security measures for dangerous pathogen collections; (*h*) support for the implementation of a 2003 G8 initiative related to the security of radioactive materials and sources; and (*i*) support for the completion of nuclear safety measures at the Chernobyl nuclear power plant—a programme unconnected with non-proliferation.

The Action Plan also refers back to the original Global Partnership activities and stresses the need to implement past decisions and programmes. The G8 had previously committed itself to raising up to $20 billion (€15.3 billion) to support specific projects over the 10-financial year period 2002–12 in order to finance these activities. This level of funding will be required to cover the programmes launched in 2002. The financial implications of the new commitments made at the Sea Island Summit were not spelled out. Additional funding will be needed and the sums pledged in 2002 should be regarded as a floor for spending on non-proliferation rather than a ceiling.

The reorganization of the Global Partnership

The G8 has become an important forum in which to conduct regular high-level discussions on any aspect of non-proliferation. The way in which G8 INDA activities are now organized reflects this change.

A Senior Officials Group was established in 2002 to coordinate Global Partnership activities. This group was made up of officials from G8 member states. However, in January 2004 the group was replaced with a new Senior Nonproliferation Officials Group made up of officials at the level of deputy minister and open to both G8 and non-G8 members. The new group has three sub-committees—the Nonproliferation Expert Group, the Nuclear Safety and Security Group and the Global Partnership Working Group. The first two are pre-existing groups that have now been brought under the 'umbrella' of the Senior Nonproliferation Officials Group. The Global Partnership Working Group addresses issues related to the implementation of non-proliferation and disarmament projects that fall within the Global Partnership framework.

[25] For a detailed discussion of the PSI see chapter 17 in this volume.

[26] Developments in Libya are discussed in chapter 14 in this volume.

The Global Partnership Working Group meets regularly and is attended by officials from all partnership countries. Since 2002 the Global Partnership has expanded from its original eight partners plus the EU to include an additional 13 states. Eight of these additional states are EU members.[27] At the meetings, officials—who are nearly always diplomats—can address themselves to specific implementation problems and bring these to the attention of the Russian participants, in particular, who come from the Foreign Ministry. The working group does not coordinate project implementation, and neither project managers nor the companies and entities involved in project implementation on the ground usually attend. Reportedly, the working group does not have detailed information on the financial or technical issues involved in particular projects. Given these facts, its main value lies in bringing high-level attention to difficulties encountered when carrying out projects that are designed and implemented in other forums.

At present, projects related to CW destruction and nuclear submarines—the programmes identified by President Putin as his top priority—are making the most rapid progress. These programmes are discussed in section V below. Programmes related to fissile material disposition and the retraining of scientists who participated in Soviet and Russian NBC weapon programmes are also agreed Global Partnership priorities.

In September 2000 Russia and the USA agreed to irreversibly eliminate 34 metric tonnes each of weapon-grade plutonium. The plutonium cores, or 'pits', recovered from deactivated nuclear warheads were the main target of this initiative. At their Summit in 2002, the G8 members agreed to fund a mixed oxide (MOX) fuel programme in Russia to help with the implementation of plutonium disposal by blending it with uranium for use as fuel in nuclear power reactors. However, implementation of this programme is progressing only very slowly. In the 2003 annual report on the Global Partnership, reference is made to the 'initial steps' supporting the design, costing and licensing of the facilities needed for plutonium disposition.[28] With regard to US activities, the report focuses on the replacement of reactors used in the past for plutonium production rather than on the MOX fuel programme.

The main obstacle to the implementation of plans for the disposal of plutonium has been the failure to conclude an agreement specifying liability to make reparations in cases of accidents or acts of sabotage leading to damage or injury in the course of the project. After more than five years of discussion, it is likely that political support for this project will decline unless an agreement can be reached in 2005.

The fourth priority that the G8 leaders identified in 2002 was preventing the spread of the knowledge and expertise necessary to manufacture WMD. To support its massive NBC weapon capabilities the Soviet Union trained a large

[27] These states are Belgium, the Czech Republic, Denmark, Ireland, Finland, the Netherlands, Poland and Sweden.

[28] G8 Senior Officials Group Annual Report, presented at the Annual Summit of the G8 Heads of State and Government, Evian, June 2003, available on the Internet site of the US State Department, URL <http://www.state.gov/t/np/rls/other/34773.html>.

cadre of scientists. With the dissolution of the Soviet Union the future of these scientists became unclear. Immediately after the end of the cold war a number of emergency programmes were put in place to try to ensure that the location and activities of these scientists was known and that they were engaged in peaceful activities. The International Science and Technology Centre (ISTC) in Moscow and the Science and Technology Centre in Ukraine (STCU) in Kyiv were created to help manage and deliver financing to projects involving former weapon scientists.[29]

The projects implemented through the ISTC and the STCU were designed to ensure that former weapon scientists had opportunities to redeploy their skills. Financing for identified projects has been provided by Canada, Japan, South Korea and the USA as well as EU member states—both individually and through the EU budget using Joint Actions and the Technical Assistance for the Commonwealth of Independent States (TACIS) programme. Important initiatives to organize and coordinate projects include the US-sponsored Initiative for Proliferation Prevention (IPP) and the Nuclear Cities Initiative (NCI).

Fifteen years after the break up of the Soviet Union, the body of 'surplus' scientific knowledge that could contribute to proliferation has been reduced in Russia and the other successor states. Russia has identified and consolidated the scientific knowledge necessary to maintain a nuclear deterrent within its nuclear weapon establishment and other scientists have found alternative employment. In these circumstances, a growing share of the projects sponsored by the ISTC and the STCU are non-nuclear in nature. Future projects are expected to emphasize facilitating commercial research in international project teams as a contribution to economic development through the modernization of science. However, verifying the non-proliferation impact of non-nuclear projects is complicated given the 'dual-use' nature of many projects in the fields of chemistry and biology and the lack of information about former Soviet biological weapon programmes in particular. At the same time, the ISTC and the STCU are international organizations with a membership that includes most countries of the former Soviet Union. They have a legal status that permits them to operate in regions and with facilities where access is otherwise restricted—such as the nuclear 'closed cities' in Russia. There is often no obvious alternative to working through the science centres. However, the effectiveness of the ISTC and STCU is currently being evaluated.[30]

[29] The International Science and Technology Center (ISTC) was established in Nov. 1992. See the ISTC Internet site at URL <http://www.istc.ru/>. The Science and Technology Centre in Ukraine (STCU) was established in 1993, more or less in parallel with ISTC. See the STCU Internet site at URL <http://www.stcu.int>.

[30] E.g., 'Redirection of the Russian weapons of mass destruction workforce: new concepts and initiatives', Paper presented by the Landau Network Centro Volta (LNCV), Como, Italy, and the Russian-American Nuclear Security Advisory Council (RANSAC), Washington, DC, at the Non-proliferation and Disarmament Cooperation Initiative (NDCI) meeting, London, 4–5 Mar. 2004; and Ball, D. Y. and Gerber, T. P., 'Will Russian scientists go rogue? A survey on the threat and the impact of Western assistance', PONARS Policy Memo no. 357 (Nov. 2004), URL <http://www.csis.org/ruseura/ponars/policymemos/pm_0357.pdf>

Expanding the geographic coverage of the Global Partnership

The initial focus of the Global Partnership has been Russia. However, at its 2004 Summit the G8 expressed its intention to apply some of the measures in new countries and regions. The G8 has often expressed an interest in carrying out activities in other countries in the former Soviet Union. In 2004 discussions were held between G8 officials and their counterparts from Georgia, Kazakhstan, Ukraine and Uzbekistan. Ukraine joined the Global Partnership in 2004 and by the end of the year detailed discussions were taking place to elaborate specific projects. The retraining of Iraqi and Libyan scientists involved in past WMD programmes was also highlighted as an objective in the Action Plan on non-proliferation.

The G8 has made clear its intention to use the Global Partnership to coordinate efforts made in a number of functional areas that were not given priority in its original decisions taken in 2002. The projects that have been mentioned specifically in this regard are: (*a*) projects to eliminate over time the use of HEU fuel in research reactors worldwide; (*b*) projects to secure and remove fresh and spent HEU fuel; (*c*) projects to control and secure radiation sources; and (*d*) projects to strengthen export controls and border security.

In 2004 the USA also decided to expand its international non-proliferation and disarmament assistance efforts. Albania had notified the Organization for the Prohibition of Chemical Weapons in November 2002 that it had discovered a small stockpile of CW on its territory containing 'very old' mustard agent. In 2003 the US Congress approved the Nunn–Lugar Expansion Act, which allowed the US President to use up to $50 million of funds, initially targeted for non-proliferation and disarmament assistance to the states of the former Soviet Union, in other countries.[31] For the first time, funds provided through the CTR programme are being used outside the former Soviet Union. In April 2004 Switzerland announced that it also plans to assist Albania to destroy its CW.[32] On 22 October 2004 the USA announced that it had secured the stockpile site and that destruction, involving '16 tons (*c*. 14.5 tonnes) of bulk chemical agent', would begin in 2005 and take around two years.

The security of radiological materials

At the 2003 G8 Summit in Evian, France, the G8 leaders announced an initiative to make powerful radioactive sources secure. Through this initiative the G8 pledged to support the completion and subsequent implementation of an IAEA Code of Conduct on the Safety and Security of Radioactive Sources, which was under development at that time and was published in January

[31] US Senate, Richard G. Lugar, US Senator for Indiana, 'Nunn–Lugar to destroy Albania chemical weapons stash: first time Nunn–Lugar used outside former Soviet Union', 21 Oct. 2004, URL <http://lugar.senate.gov/pressapp/record.cfm?id=227616>.

[32] Nartker, M., 'Switzerland to aid Albanian chemical weapon disposal', Nuclear Threat Initiative Global Security Newswire, 26 Apr. 2004, URL <http://www.nti.org/d_newswire/issues/2004_4_26.html#1171ADE3>.

2004.[33] The G8 agreed to finance and participate in measures to secure high-risk stray or inadequately protected radiological sources, so-called 'orphaned' sources of ionizing radiation, including through greater support of IAEA action in this area.[34] France agreed to convene a conference in 2005 to follow-up a 2003 conference on the security of radioactive sources.[35]

While the legal responsibility for ensuring radiological security rests with the states owning the relevant facilities, international cooperation has helped these states to advance their self-interest by securing such sources and to live up to their commitments in this respect. The IAEA Code of Conduct—which was discussed at the IAEA General Conference in September 2003, when its objectives and principles were endorsed—contains enhanced references to the security of radioactive sources.

International efforts to secure radioactive sources were already under way before the terrorist attacks of 11 September 2001. However, since 2001 these efforts have attracted greater attention from political decision makers and the public because of heightened concern about the possible use of an RDD in a terrorist attack. An RDD is a combination of radioactive material and conventional explosives, or some other dispersal agent such as an aerosol, that is used to scatter radioactive debris. Such a device would be unlikely to produce large numbers of fatalities or, if it did, these would occur over a number of years—or even generations.[36]

Although Iraq developed and experimented with an RDD in the 1980s, such devices have generally been considered to have little use on the battlefield. Iraq ended its own RDD programme unilaterally in 1987, presumably for this reason.[37] However, the use of such devices could exert a psychological effect and inflict economic damage by making land or water unusable. In November 1995, a Chechen group led by Shamil Basayev buried a container containing caesium-137 in a Moscow park and then alerted a Russian television network. This incident was one of a number where Chechen groups have threatened

[33] International Atomic Energy Agency (IAEA), Code of Conduct on the Safety and Security of Radioactive Sources, document Codeoc/2004, Jan. 2004, URL <http://www-ns.iaea.org/tech-areas/radiation-safety/default.htm>.

[34] The IAEA defines orphaned sources as radioactive sources that are outside regulatory control. Some sources may not be formally orphaned but control over them may be weak and they therefore might be vulnerable to being mishandled or lost.

[35] G8 Evian Summit 2003, 'Non-proliferation of weapons of mass destruction: securing radioactive sources, a G8 Action Plan', Summit documents, 1–3 June 2003, URL <http://www.g8.fr/evian/english/navigation/2003_g8_summit/summit_documents.html>.

[36] Radioactive substances might be dispersed through the air or used to contaminate water or food. If radioactive material emits penetrating radiation it poses a risk through external exposure. The material also poses a risk if inhaled, eaten or absorbed through the skin. The dispersion of radioactive material could be used to complicate the response to and recovery from a terrorist incident. It could also impose significant economic costs by requiring the decontamination of buildings, land or water or result in the abandonment of land if decontamination was not feasible. United Nations, Office on Drugs and Crime, 'Nuclear and radiological weapons: what's what?', URL <http://www.unodc.org/unodc/terrorism_weapons_mass_destruction_page006.html>.

[37] Nuclear Threat Initiative (NTI), Radiological terrorism tutorial, 'Terrorists and radiological terrorism', NTI research library, URL <http://www.nti.org/h_learnmore/radtutorial/chapter04_01.html>.

either to use an RDD or to attack a Russian nuclear facility, each with an attendant risk of releasing radioactive materials.[38]

The IAEA has maintained a database on incidents of illicit trafficking in nuclear or other radioactive material since the early 1990s.[39] As of November 2004 the IAEA database included around 650 confirmed cases of illicit trafficking, 57 of which were reported in the first six months of 2004. Nearly 80 states have agreed to collect information systematically on trafficking incidents as well as other unauthorized movements of radioactive sources and other radioactive materials, and to share this data with the IAEA for inclusion in the database. Information is submitted to the IAEA using a standardized incident notification form to ensure detailed and uniform entries in the database that allow trend and pattern analyses. The data stored only include confirmed incidents in which information has been verified to the IAEA through official points of contact from the reporting country.[40] The database has become an important resource for law enforcement agencies worldwide.

As part of a nuclear security Action Plan first adopted in 1999 but subsequently revised on several occasions, the IAEA has proposed, as an ultimate objective, the creation of a system to ensure the secure custody and safe use of powerful radioactive sources from 'cradle to grave'.[41] Under the definition applied by the IAEA, nuclear security covers nuclear and radioactive materials and nuclear installations. The focus is on helping states to prevent, detect and respond to terrorist or other malicious acts—such as illegal possession, use, transfer, and trafficking—and to protect nuclear installations and transport against sabotage.

The IAEA Code of Conduct also contributes to achieving the objectives of the Action Plan. In the Code, states are encouraged to establish an adequate system of regulatory control of radioactive sources, applicable from the stage of initial production to their final disposal, and a system to restore control if it has been lost. The Code includes guidelines and elements that should be included in the system of regulatory control as well as recommendations about establishing a national implementing authority, and its responsibilities.

To achieve the objectives of the Action Plan the IAEA has highlighted the need to secure powerful radioactive materials by ensuring that the sites and facilities where they are located have adequate provisions against sabotage,

[38] Bale, J. M., 'Issue brief: Chechen resistance and radiological terrorism', NTI Research Library, Apr. 2004, URL <http://www.nti.org/e_research/e3_47b.html>. Moreover, al-Qaeda is said to be examining the use of radiological devices. Karon, T., 'The "dirty bomb" suspect: lots of questions, few answers', *Time* (online edn), 11 June 2002, URL <http://www.time.com/time/nation/article/0,8599,261119,00.html>.

[39] For an analysis of the longer-term trends see Zarimpas, N., 'The illicit trade in nuclear and radioactive materials', *SIPRI Yearbook 2001: Armaments, Disarmament and International Security* (Oxford University Press: Oxford, 2001), pp 503–11.

[40] Confirmed incidents are incidents where investigations have taken place. They do not necessarily imply a transfer of material.

[41] The background to the Action Plan is explained in International Atomic Energy Agency (IAEA), 'Measures to strengthen international cooperation in nuclear, radiation and transport safety and waste management', Report to the Board of Governors, IAEA General Conference document, GOV/2003/47-GC47/7, 4 Aug. 2003, URL <http://www.iaea.org/About/Policy/GC/GC47/Documents/gc47-7.pdf>.

attack or unauthorized access. In addition, the IAEA has stressed the need to find and recover orphaned radiological sources.

The IAEA has carried out this kind of activity in several countries on request and has also worked with the US DOE and the Russian Ministry for Atomic Energy (Minatom) in a Tripartite Working Group on Securing and Managing Radioactive Sources. In this group, officials have agreed to develop a coordinated and proactive strategy to locate, recover, secure and recycle orphaned sources throughout the former Soviet Union. Fact-finding missions have been carried out to identify and characterize radioactive sources in Armenia, Azerbaijan, Belarus, Kazakhstan and Moldova, and to propose security measures for them. At the end of 2004 additional were also nearing completion in Kyrgyzstan and Tajikistan.

The IAEA provides advisory services to its members that are relevant to nuclear and radiological security. The International Physical Protection Advisory Service (IPPAS) has revised and updated its guidelines on physical protection to introduce modules related to securing radioactive sources.[42] In particular, the issue of how to protect against 'insider threats' at nuclear facilities has been examined. The IAEA has also created a new advisory service, called the International Nuclear Security Advisory Service (INSServ) to help states assess their protection of radioactive materials. INSServ expert recommendations can then form the basis for follow-on assistance, either through the IAEA or bilaterally between states. Azerbaijan, the Democratic Republic of the Congo, the Philippines, Tanzania, Uganda, Uzbekistan and Yemen had each hosted an INSServ mission by the end of 2004.[43]

The IAEA has developed a number of technical resources to help states strengthen security in the light of the heightened consciousness surrounding the possible use of radiological materials in terrorist acts. Radioactive materials and sources take many different physical forms and vary in size. Radioactive sources are used in industry, medicine, agriculture, research and education as well as in military applications such as sonar devices and other sensors. The IAEA has developed a system for classifying radioactive sources and ranking them according to their potential to cause harm to human health.[44] The IAEA has also produced guidelines for the physical storage of radiological sources of different types and recommendations to ensure that radioactive sources are subject to export controls.[45]

[42] IAEA, International Physical Protection Advisory Service (IPPAS), 'Nuclear security: measures to protect against nuclear terrorism', Supplementary Information to GOV/2004/50-GC(48)/6 Part A, Progress in implementing activity areas 1 to 8 as defined in GOV/2002/10, paragraph 3, URL <http://www.iaea.org/About/Policy/GC/GC48/Documents/gc48-6suppl.pdf>.

[43] Sanders, J. W., 'Safe and secure peaceful nuclear programs', Presentation of the Special Representative of the President of the USA for the Non-Proliferation of Nuclear Weapons, at the 3rd Session of the Preparatory Committee for the 2005 Review Conference of the Treaty on the Non-Proliferation of Nuclear Weapons, New York, 4 May 2004.

[44] IAEA, 'Categorization of radioactive sources', IAEA technical document-1344, July 2003.

[45] IAEA, 'Security of radioactive sources: interim guidance for comment', IAEA technical document-1355, June 2003.

IV. Developments in the European Union

Most of the international non-proliferation and disarmament assistance provided by the EU is in the form of bilateral programmes and actions undertaken by member states. These are loosely coordinated and information about them is exchanged in the working group on non-proliferation (CONOP) that meets under the auspices of the Council of the European Union.

Activities of EU member states

Four EU member states—France, Germany, Italy and the United Kingdom—made significant national financial commitments under the Global Partnership.

Germany

In the framework of the Global Partnership, Germany pledged to provide up to \$1.5 billion (€1.15 billion) to support projects to be carried out mainly in Russia. Among EU countries, Germany has had the most sustained and significant engagement in Russia. Since 1993 Germany has been continuously engaged in the construction of a CW destruction facility at Gorny in the Saratov region of Russia. Since 1995 Germany has also carried out projects to enhance nuclear security at several Russian facilities.[46] Russia has expressed appreciation of the German approach to assistance and likes to contrast it to the US approach. Germany has been more flexible on how its money can be spent. In future, German efforts under the Global Partnership are likely to be concentrated in three areas. First, in order to help Russia meet its obligations under the CWC, Germany has agreed to support the development of a CW destruction facility in Kambarka as well as continuing to provide further financing for the facility in Gorny. Second, to support the dismantlement of nuclear-powered submarines, Germany will finance the construction of a facility for the long-term secure storage of radioactive reactors and their surrounding compartments that have been removed from vessels decommissioned by the Russian Navy.[47] Finally, Germany will continue to assist with modernizing the measures for the physical protection of nuclear material at Russian nuclear facilities. In total, Germany has already agreed to support projects in the period to 2009 at a cost of about €800 million.

Germany is expected to play a leading role among EU countries in implementing disarmament assistance projects in Russia. This is partly because of the insights gained through long experience of project management, and partly because Germany has developed a legal and administrative framework for

[46] For a breakdown of the nature and type of CW destruction assistance provided by various countries and the EU see Zanders, J. P., Hart, J. and Kuhlau, F., 'Chemical and biological weapon developments and arms control', *SIPRI Yearbook 2002: Armaments, Disarmament and International Security* (Oxford University Press: Oxford, 2002), pp. 692–93.

[47] German Federal Ministry of Economics and Labour, 'The G8 Global Partnership: German–Russian cooperation', Sherpa-Group, Preparation for the World Economic Summit, 15 May 2004, p. 5, URL <http://www.sgpproject.org/Donor%20Factsheets/German-Russia%20Report%2015%20May%202004.pdf>.

cooperation with Russia in this field that other countries lack. The EU has also used Germany to implement collective projects. In the framework of a 1999 Joint Action on non-proliferation in Russia,[48] the EU contributed roughly €6 million to the construction of the CW destruction facility at Gorny. The money, which was used to pay for part of the air filtration system, was transferred by the European Commission from the EU Common Foreign and Security Policy budget to the German Foreign Ministry, which implemented the project alongside its own much larger project. This model is to be repeated in the context of the project to support the enhancement of physical protection at the Bochvar Institute in Moscow. The institute contains fissile materials that need to be secured from any attempt at diversion. To this end, the EU will finance the construction of a new, reinforced and secure storage facility at the institute equipped with modern, specialized protection measures. The project, valued at roughly €8 million, will be managed by the German Foreign Ministry assisted by the Federal Office for Defence Technology and Procurement. The project will be implemented by the German company Gesellschaft für Anlagen-und Reaktor-Sicherheit mbH (GRS).

This arrangement provides a pragmatic solution to the problem of how to deliver practical assistance from the common EU budget in circumstances where the Commission does not have a legal framework for cooperation with Russia on disarmament and non-proliferation matters.[49] This approach is not, however, without difficulties because it requires the EU member state concerned, which is likely to create a relatively small project management team, to apply EU standards for cash management and financial reporting alongside its national system. For sums of EU aid that are relatively small in the context of the overall costs of a project, this might lead member states to resist using this model too often.

The United Kingdom

In 2002 the UK pledged to spend up to £740 million (€1070 million) on international non-proliferation and disarmament assistance over the period 2003–12. The current spending level for this type of assistance from British sources is approximately £37 million (€54 million) per financial year. The UK has focused its efforts on four areas that closely match the 2002 priorities of the Global Partnership. Enhancing nuclear security and providing secure storage for spent nuclear fuel assemblies taken from decommissioned submarines in north-west Russia are high priorities in the British programme. Assisting Russia to destroy CW and the question of how to retrain and redeploy scien-

[48] Council of the European Union, 'Joint Action 2004/796/CFSP for the support of the physical protection of a nuclear site in the Russian Federation', 22 Nov. 2004, *Official Journal of the European Union*, L349 (25 Nov. 2004), URL <http://europa.eu.int/eur-lex/lex/JOHtml.do?uri=OJ:L:2004:349:SOM:EN:HTML>.

[49] Programmes for technical assistance, where there *is* a legal framework in place for EU–Russian cooperation, may not be used for arms control and disarmament projects because these are still considered to be outside the realm of Community competence by EU member states.

tists and technicians formerly employed in nuclear, BW and CW programmes have also been given high priority.

The UK has developed partnerships with other countries that share an interest in a particular problem area to be addressed. The UK has close relations with Canada, Norway and the USA when implementing nuclear programmes in Russia. To strengthen nuclear security the UK and its partners have emphasized the need to improve physical protection of nuclear and radioactive materials. The UK-led programme helped to complete two submarine dismantlement projects in 2004 and is helping to transfer spent nuclear fuel assemblies currently stored in ships to a dedicated onshore storage facility near Murmansk.

British CW destruction activities are carried out in partnership with Canada, the Czech Republic, Norway and the USA as well as the European Commission. The activities are focused on the destruction facility at Shchuch'ye, where by November 2004 all of the equipment promised under the programme had been delivered to Russian authorities for installation at the facility. Additional projects are being developed to expand the Shchuch'ye facility and its infrastructure. New Zealand is expected to join the group of states implementing infrastructure projects under the British–Russian bilateral agreement.

British projects to redirect the skills of scientists have been concentrated in the Russian closed nuclear cities. Recent emphasis has been placed on how to commercialize projects initiated with foreign assistance in order to make them self-sustaining. Expanding the scope of projects to include not only designers but also engineers and production workers is also being considered.

To meet its pledge under the Global Partnership it is likely that the UK's spending on international non-proliferation and disarmament assistance will increase significantly and that its functional and geographic scope will expand. In its first biological non-proliferation project the UK is supporting the development of civilian projects at a research institute in Georgia where plant health scientists worked as part of the Soviet BW programme. In widening the geographic scope of activities, the UK is examining how to develop and deliver projects in Iraq and Libya.

Italy

Italy has pledged €1 billion to the Global Partnership—the fourth highest pledge and an amount equivanent to the EU pledge. Three priorities have been identified: (*a*) €360 million for submarine dismantlement and the safe management of radioactive waste and spent nuclear fuel in 2004–2013; (*b*) €365 million for CW destruction in 2004–2008; and (*c*) €80 million to be spent on plutonium disposition projects.[50]

Italy and Russia signed two bilateral agreements on 5 November 2003, which were not ratified by the Russian State Duma until the end of 2004. The first agreement is on the dismantlement of nuclear submarines and the storage

[50] CSIS, Strengthening the Global Partnership Project, Italy, URL <http://www.sgpproject.org/Donor%20Factsheets/Italy.html>.

of nuclear fuel. Russia has proposed the following projects to Italy in the naval sphere: (*a*) the dismantlement of three submarines at a cost of €70 million; (*b*) the construction of two radioactive waste processing plants at a cost of €133 million; (*c*) the improvement of physical security measures at seven naval bases in north-west Russia at a cost of €45 million; (*d*) the construction of spent nuclear fuel transport and storage casks at a cost of €30 million; and (*e*) the construction of a ship to carry dismantled submarine parts at a cost of €60 million.[51] The second agreement is for the construction of the CW destruction facility in Pochep. Also in November 2003, Italy announced that it would provide €5 million over two years for infrastructure and energy projects at Shchuch'ye under a bilateral intergovernmental agreement signed in 2000 and an Additional Protocol signed in April 2003.

France

France has been formally engaging with Russia in nuclear cooperative threat reduction since 1992, when the aide au démantèlement (AIDA) programme was launched.[52] It also participated in later EU programmes, including the Joint Action on non-proliferation in Russia and the ISTC. French assistance is focused mainly on the various aspects of nuclear weapon dismantlement and protection, particularly plutonium disposition.

The French Global Partnership pledge of €750 million in 2003–12 can be roughly divided into €500 million for nuclear projects—including plutonium disposition, submarine dismantlement and nuclear safety programmes—and €250 million for CW destruction, bio-safety and bio-security.[53] In 2003–2004 France spent €13.1 million on nuclear safety, €17 million on nuclear submarine dismantlement, €3 million on nuclear MPC&A, €9 million on CW destruction and €5 million on bio-security and bio-safety.[54]

Activities financed by the common EU budget

In addition to activities carried out by EU member states, at the 2002 G8 Summit the EU committed itself to spend €1 billion over a period of 10 years. In the period up to 2006 a number of programmes that are specifically relevant to non-proliferation objectives are being financed from the EU common budget. These programmes include the EU's contribution to Nordic Dimension Environmental Partnership (NDEP) projects carried out in north-west

[51] Center for Nonproliferation Studies, Global Partnership funding commitments, Global Partnership resource page, 7 May 2004, URL <http://cns.miis.edu/research/globpart/funding.htm>.

[52] Facon, I., Maisonneuve, C. and Tertrais, B., 'France', eds R. J. Einhorn and M. A. Flournoy, Center for Strategic and International Studies (CSIS), *Protecting Against the Spread of Nuclear, Biological and Chemical Weapons: An action agenda for the Global Partnership,* vol. 3, *International Responses* (CSIS Press: Washington, DC, Jan. 2003), available at URL <http://www.csis.org/pubs>.

[53] CSIS, Strengthening the Global Partnership Project, France, URL <http://www.sgpproject.org/Donor%20Factsheets/France.html>.

[54] G8 Sea Island Summit 2004, 'Consolidated Report of Global Partnership Projects', Summit documents. 9 June 2004, URL <http://www.g8usa.gov/pdfs/GPConsolidatedReportofGPProjectsJune2004.pdf>.

Russia,[55] nuclear security projects, export control and border security-related projects, and a financial contribution to the ISTC and the STCU. Taken together, the value of these programmes is roughly €150 million in 2004–2006. If funding continues at this level, the EU will not meet its €1 billion Kananaskis commitment. The EU's current spending priorities—valid until 2007, when the next common budget cycle will begin—reflect decisions taken at a time when non-proliferation was a relatively low political priority for the EU. It is likely that the level of spending on non-proliferation projects will be increased in the EU budget covering the period 2007–13.

V. Developments in Russia

As is clear from the sections above, most of the international non-proliferation and disarmament assistance provided so far has gone to Russia and most of the future projects that are planned are also to be carried out in Russia. The actions taken by the Russian authorities are critical to their success.

The administration of INDA in Russia

In 2004 a major reform of the civil service, a process known as 'administrative reform', was launched in Russia. Government departments and agencies, including those closely associated with defining and implementing INDA projects, were reorganized and the relationships between them were changed. On 9 March President Putin issued Presidential Decree 314, which set out a new system of federal executive bodies—federal ministries, federal services and federal agencies.[56] The decree set out the number of these entities, their functions and the hierarchy or relationship between them. The development and implementation of the reform process continued throughout 2004 and a further presidential decree was published on 20 May.[57]

The INDA functions of the Ministry of Foreign Affairs (MOFA) were preserved almost intact, with only minor changes such as the appointment of a new minister and a reduction in the number of his deputies. INDA issues in the MOFA are dealt with by Deputy Minister Sergei Kislyak.[58]

Prior to the administrative reform, the Ministry of Defence (MOD) was already responsible for international cooperation in the field of military issues including: (*a*) preparing regulations and procedures in areas related to nuclear weapons; (*b*) supervising nuclear and radiological security during the entire

[55] For background material on the Nordic Dimension Environmental Partnership see URL <http://europa.eu.int/comm/external_relations/north_dim/ndep/index.htm>.

[56] 'O sisteme i struktury federal'nikh organov ispol'nitel'noi vlasti' [On the system and structure of federal executive bodies], Russian Presidential Decree no. 314, 9 Mar. 2004, Internet site of the President of the Russian Federation (in Russian), URL <http://document.kremlin.ru/doc.asp?ID=021438>.

[57] 'Voprosy struktury federal'nikh organov ispol'nitel'noi vlasti' [Issues of the structure of federal executive bodies], Russian Presidential Decree no. 649, 20 May 2004, Internet site of the President of Russia (in Russian), URL <http://document.kremlin.ru/doc.asp?ID= 22560>.

[58] Organization Chart of the Russian Ministry of Foreign Affairs (MOFA), Internet site of the Russian MOFA, URL <http://www.ln.mid.ru>.

Table 16.1. The programme for eliminating chemical weapon stockpiles in Russia[a]

Facility	Percentage of original declared stockpile stored	Destruction facility operational since	Destruction facility operational until
Gornyi, Saratov region	*2.9*	2002	2005
Shchuch'ye, Kurgan region	*13.6*	2008	2012
Kambarka, Udmurt Republic	*15.9*	2006	2009
Pochep, Bryansk region	*18.8*	2008	2012
Maradykovskiy, Kirov region	*17.4*	2006	2010
Leonidovka, Penza region	*17.2*	2008	2012
Kizner, Udmurt Republic	*14.2*	2009	2012

[a] The time frames for the construction and operation of destruction facilities are subject to change in accordance with periodic Russian Government statements.

Source: Kholstov, V., 'Urgent problems of chemical disarmament in the Russian Federation', Presentation to the Green Cross National Dialogue, Moscow, 10 Nov. 2004. Viktor Kholstov is Deputy Chief of the Federal Agency for Industry.

lifecycle of nuclear weapons and military nuclear facilities; (*c*) military-to-military cooperation; and (*d*) supporting the government in negotiations.[59] In addition, the MOD was officially allocated two further tasks in 2004. The supervision of export control procedures in Russia was allocated to a new Federal Service for Technical and Export Control, which inherited functions and personnel from a corresponding division in the Ministry of Economic Development and Trade.[60] Under Decree 314, the MOD is responsible for overseeing the work of the Federal Agency for Atomic Energy (Rosatom) on issues related to the nuclear weapon complex.

Minatom was transformed into Rosatom by Decree 314 and initially placed under the control of the Ministry of Industry and Energy (MIE). This demotion meant that Rosatom could not participate directly in negotiations on international agreements, including those related to non-proliferation and INDA. This situation was later modified by Decree 649, which subordinated Rosatom directly to the Russian Federal Government,[61] allowing Rosatom to participate in international negotiations. Three of the four Global Partnership priorities agreed at the 2002 G8 Summit—the dismantling of decommissioned nuclear submarines, the disposition of fissile materials and the employment of former weapon scientists—remain the responsibility of Rosatom, and it is still the major recipient of INDA.

[59] Statute of the Russian Ministry of Defence, Chapter 2, Article 6, paragraph 11; Chapter 3, Article 7, paragraphs 14, 34, 36, 37; and Chapter 4, Article 11, paragraphs 6 and 32 (in Russian), URL <http://www.government.ru/data/static_text.html?st_id=7518&he_id=671>.

[60] 'Putin naznachil Sergeya Yakimova zamdirektora Federal'noi sluzhby po tekhnicheskomu i eksportnomu kontrolyu' [Putin appoints Sergey Yakimov as the Deputy Director of the Federal Service for Technical and Export Control], *RIA Novosti*, 22 Oct. 2004 (in Russian), URL <http://www.rian.ru/rian/intro.cfm?nws_id=713660>.

[61] Russian Presidential Decree no. 649 (note 57), p. 2.

GosAtomNadzor (GAN), which was responsible for the control and inspection of security in the use of atomic energy on Russian territory, was abolished in 2004. A new Federal Service for Atomic Inspection (FSAI) was created to take over its responsibilities.[62] The FSAI survived only a few months, however, before Presidential Decree 649 created the 'Federal Service for Ecological, Technological and Atomic Inspection', which combined the FSAI with entities unrelated to INDA.[63]

The Russian Munitions Agency (Rosboepripasy) had been responsible for the fourth Global Partnership priority—the destruction of the CW stockpiles. This agency was abolished by Decree 314 and its functions were divided between the MIE and its subordinate Federal Agency for Industry (FAI). The MIE is empowered to elaborate state policy and laws, and to participate in international negotiations on CW destruction.[64] Government Decree 190 gives the FAI the task of meeting Russia's obligations under the CWC and the 1972 Biological and Toxin Weapons Convention (BTWC).[65]

Major INDA projects under way in Russia

As noted above, President Putin has identified CW destruction and dismantling nuclear submarines as the two most important priorities for Russia among the range of projects for which international non-proliferation and disarmament assistance could be used.[66] Thus far, the funds that Russia itself has earmarked under the Global Partnership are being spent almost exclusively on these two areas.[67]

In the area of *CW destruction*, Russia has continued to fulfil its obligations under the CWC. The first agreed deadline, eliminating 1 per cent of Russia's CW stockpile of 40 000 agent tonnes by the end of 2003, has been met.[68]

[62] 'Voprosy Federal'noi sluzhby po atomnomu nadzoru' [Issues for the Federal Service for Atomic Inspection], Russian Government Decree no. 192, 7 Apr. 2004, Internet site of the Government of Russia (in Russian), URL <http://npa-gov.garweb.ru:8080/public/default.asp?no=86943>.

[63] 'O Federal'noi sluzhbe po ekologicheskomu, tekhnologicheskomu i atomnomu nadzoru' [On the Federal Service for Environmental, Technological and Atomic Inspection], Russian Government Decree no. 401, 30 July 2004, Internet site of the Government of Russia (In Russian), URL <http://npa-gov.garweb.ru:8080/public/default.asp?no= 12036495>.

[64] 'Ob utverzhdenii Polozheniya o Ministerstve promyshlennosi i energetiki Rossi'iskoi' Federatsii' [On the adoption of the Statute of the Ministry of Industry and Energy of the Russian Federation], Russian Government Decree no. 284, 16 June 2004 (as amended on 10 Sep. 2004), Internet site of the Government of Russia (in Russian), URL <http://npa-gov.garweb.ru:8080/public/default.asp?no=87118>.

[65] 'Voprosy Federal'nogo agentstva po promyshlennosti' [Issues for the Federal Agency for Industry], Russian Government Decree no. 190, Government of the Russian Federation, 8 Apr. 2004, Internet site of the Government of Russia (in Russian), URL <http://npa-gov.garweb.ru:8080/public/default.asp?no=86941>. For a discussion of the CWC and the BTWC in 2004 see chapter 13 in this volume.

[66] 'Zayavleniya dlya pressy po okonchanii sammita 'Bol'shoi vos'merki' [Comments to the press after the G8 summit], Internet site of the President of Russia, 27 June 2002 (in Russian), <http://www.kremlin.ru/appears/2002/06/27/2300_type63380_29029.shtml>.

[67] G8, Sea Island Summit 2004, 'Consolidated report of Global Partnership projects', Summit documents 9 June 2004, URL <http://www.g8usa.gov/pdfs/GPConsolidatedReportofGPProjectsJune2004.pdf>.

[68] 'Na obekte UKhO v p. Gorny Saratovskoi oblasti unichtozhen iprit', [Yperite is destroyed at chemical weapon destruction facility in Gorny settlement, Saratov oblast], *IA Regnum*, 16 Nov. 2003 (in

Russia is working to meet the second deadline—the elimination of 20 per cent of its stockpile by 29 April 2007.[69] Under its CWC obligations, Russia should go on to eliminate 45 per cent of its stockpile by 2009 and its entire stockpile by 2012. By the end of November 2004, over 740 agent tonnes had been eliminated at the facility in Gorny.[70]

The extent to which foreign assistance might support the Russian destruction programme continued to be debated.[71] Russia has reportedly signed 28 intergovernmental and interdepartmental agreements with international donors which could result in just over $1 billion in funding being provided by 2009.[72] In 2004 Victor Kholstov, Deputy Chief of the Federal Agency for Industry, estimated that foreign destruction assistance had accounted for approximately 7 per cent ($217 million) of the total amount of money spent on chemical weapon destruction in Russia.[73] In 2004 further international assistance for destruction of Russia's stockpile was agreed to be provided by Canada, the Czech Republic, the EU, Finland, France, Germany, Italy, Japan, New Zealand, the Netherlands, Norway, Poland, Sweden, Switzerland, the UK and the USA.[74]

Russia has set a goal of dismantling all its *decommissioned submarines* by 2010.[75] Since the Soviet Union commissioned its first nuclear submarine in 1958, around 250 have been built. At the end of 2004, 83 Russian nuclear-powered submarines still await dismantlement—41 in the Northern Fleet and 42 in the Pacific Fleet. Russian facilities have the capacity to dismantle about 20 submarines annually but the funds to dismantle only about 15. To achieve

Russian), URL <http://www.regnum.ru/expnews/180620.html>. The declared Russian stockpile is held in the 7 storage sites identified in table 16.1.

69 'V 2005 godu predusmatrivaetsya uvelichenie finansirovaniya programmy po stroitel'stvu obektov dlya unichtozheniya khimoruzhiya' [Increase in funding for the construction of chemical weapon destruction facilities is envisaged for 2005], *RIA Novosti* 10 Nov. 2004 (in Russian), URL <http://www.rian.ru/rian/intro.cfm?nws_id=729450>; and Organisation for the Prohibition of Chemical Weapons (OPCW), 'Decision: extension of the intermediate and final deadlines for the destruction by the Russian Federation of its Category 1 chemical weapons', OPCW document C-8/DEC.13, 24 Oct. 2003.

70 'Unichtozhenie pod kontrolem' [Destruction under control], *Nezavisimoe Voennoe Obozrenie.* 12 Nov. 2004 (in Russian), URL <http://nvo.ng.ru/printed/forces/2004-11-12/1_korotko.html>; and 'Statement by Anatoliy Antonov: Head of the Russian delegation to the 9th Session of the Conference of the States Parties to the Convention on the Prohibition of Chemical Weapons', The Hague, the Netherlands, 29 Nov.–2 Dec. 2004, p. 1.

71 On problems associated with Russia's implementation of the CWC see Hart, J. and Miller, C. D. (eds), *Chemical Weapon Destruction in Russia: Political, Legal and Technical Aspects*, SIPRI Chemical and Biological Warfare Studies no. 17 (Oxford University Press: Oxford, 1998); and Foreign Intelligence Service of Russia, *Problemy Ratifikatsii Konventsii o Zapreshchenii i Unichtozhenii Khimicheskogo Oruzhiya (otkrity doklad SVR za 1996 god)* [Problems of ratification of the convention on the prohibition and destruction of chemical weapons (open report of the SVR for 1996)] (SVR: Moscow, 1996), URL <http://svr.gov.ru/material/1-0.html>.

72 'Some $217 million . . .', Agentstvo Voyennykh Novostey [Military News Agency] (Moscow), 10 Nov. 2004, in 'Russia: $217 million in foreign aid spent for destruction of chemical weapons', Foreign Broadcast Information Service, *Daily Report–Central Eurasia (FBIS-SOV)*, FBIS-SOV-2004-1110, 10 Nov. 2004.

73 'Some $217 million . . .' (note 72).

74 'Statement by Anatoliy Antonov' (note 70).

75 'Rossiya zavershit k 2010 g utilizatsiyu spisannikh atomnikh podlodok' [Russia will complete the dismantlement of decommissioned nuclear submarines by 2010], *Regions Ru*, 27 Apr. 2004 (in Russian), URL <http://www.regions.ru/article/any/id/1493029.html>.

its own deadline, Russia should dismantle 15–18 vessels each year. In 2004 Russia dismantled 17 nuclear submarines, 5 using funds provided by foreign donors in the framework of Global Partnership.[76]

Nuclear-powered submarines must be dismantled in a manner that is safe and secure from an environmental perspective. Three main challenges have been identified in this respect: (*a*) the safe transportation of a retired submarine to the dismantling shipyard; (*b*) insufficient funding in the Russian budget; and (*c*) the 'clean-up' of nuclear sites (ex-naval bases) to prepare them for alternative use.[77] The submarines do not present a proliferation risk and the process of dismantling them must not create new proliferation risks or vulnerabilities that could be exploited by terrorist groups. In order to address these problems systematically, the Russian Government published a 'strategic master-plan on submarine dismantlement' in 2004.[78] In a number of cases donor countries have identified obstacles to safe, secure and proliferation resistant dismantlement. The masterplan was designed to integrate and coordinate the efforts of all donors and the Russian authorities, and to systematically assess all programmes and projects that still need to be implemented in order to complete the process of dismantlement. Rosatom has estimated that the total cost of the submarine dismantlement programme will be $4 billion (€3 billion).[79] Another 17 submarines are scheduled to be dismantled in 2005.[80]

VI. Conclusions

International non-proliferation and disarmament assistance continues to be a critical element in helping states to implement their disarmament obligations. In addition, INDA is increasingly establishing itself as a significant element of the wider anti-proliferation effort. The geographic and functional scope of assistance is expanding and this expansion is likely to continue for the foreseeable future. At present, the most important initiatives continue to be bilateral. However, some of the programmes currently being evaluated—such as

[76] Rybachenkov, V., 'Prospects for Russian Nuclear-powered submarine dismantlement', Presentation to the conference 'Prospects for Russian nuclear-powered submarine dismantlement: a discussion of current programs, progress and challenges', Washington, DC, 27 Jan. 2005.

[77] IAEA, Minutes of the 18th CEG [IAEA Contact Expert Group for International Radioactive Waste Projects in the Russian Federation] Meeting, Moscow, 13–15 Oct. 2004, URL <http://www.iaea.org/OurWork/ST/NE/NEFW/CEG/documents/Minutes18fin.pdf>.

[78] Northern Dimension Environmental Partnership (NDEP), 'Nuclear Operating Committee discusses Strategic Master Plan', NDEP News, no. 6 (Dec. 2004), p. 2, URL <http://www.ndep.org/files/uploaded/NDEP%20News%20issue%206.pdf>. For background on nuclear submarine dismantlement see Chuen, C., 'Russian submarine dismantlement issues', Monterey Institute of International Studies, Center for Nonproliferation Studies, 3 Dec. 2003, URL <http://cns.miis.edu/pubs/week/031203.htm>.

[79] Obshchestvennosti garantiriyut otkrytost vsekh meropriyatii Strategicheskogo master-plana po kompleksnoi utilizatsii APL [The openness of the Strategic master-plan on submarine dismantlement is guaranteed to the public], Official Rosatom nuclear submarine Internet site, 1 Dec. 2004 (in Russian), URL <http://www.a-submarine.ru/News/Main/view?id=9599&idChannel=105>.

[80] 'Podderzhka ot bol'shoi vos'merki' [Assistance from the G8], *Zvezdochka* [local newspaper of Severodvinsk, Arkhangelsk region], 26 Oct. 2004 (in Russian), available at URL <http://www.shipbuilding.ru/rus/news/russian/2004/10/26/magate/print.phtml>.

the development of a comprehensive approach to securing powerful radiological sources—are too costly and complicated to be undertaken on a bilateral basis. As new countries become engaged in the overall effort, questions continue to arise about how the delivery of assistance can be organized, financed and coordinated in the most effective manner. The relationship between bilateral efforts, informal coordination mechanisms and the activities of international organizations, in particular the IAEA, is continuing to develop in this field.

The anticipated expansion in the geographic and functional scope of INDA may bring forward the 'moment of truth' for a number of long-standing projects, such as plutonium disposition and scientist redirection projects, which have so far proved impossible to implement in spite of the fact that their clear non-proliferation significance is clear.

17. Transfer controls

IAN ANTHONY and SIBYLLE BAUER

I. Introduction

In 2004 evidence continued to accumulate that more countries recognize the strong self-interest in maintaining modern and effective national transfer controls.

In 2004 the international community was digesting the consequences of the war in Iraq where, as one author has noted, 'it has become abundantly clear through revelations in the last decade that the lax export control standards of both national and multilateral regulatory frameworks contributed significantly to the development of the clandestine Iraqi WMD [weapons of mass destruction] programme, which has been a primary cause of two multinational wars in 12 years'.[1] Concern about new suppliers of technologies that are relevant to the development or production of nuclear, biological and chemical (NBC) weapons was heightened by the public disclosure of the activities of a network of 'knowledgeable individuals' led by Pakistani nuclear scientist Abdul Qadeer Khan, which had been working for more than a decade to supply weapon-relevant materials and technology to Iran, North Korea and Libya, perhaps without the knowledge of the Government of Pakistan.[2] Khan's global network of collaborators included a number of participants located in and operating from countries that participate in the relevant export control group, the Nuclear Suppliers Group (NSG).

This chapter surveys the main efforts to strengthen multilateral export control cooperation in 2004, both in informal arrangements and in the European Union (EU). Section II focuses on the Australia Group (AG), the Missile Technology Control Regime (MTCR) and the Wassenaar Arrangement on Export Controls for Conventional Arms and Dual-Use Goods and Technologies (WA). Section III examines developments in the NSG and the Zangger Committee. Supply-side measures in the EU, including both dual-use and defence items, are discussed in section IV. The conclusions are presented in section V. Appendix 17A addresses export controls in the United States.

[1] Joyner, D. H., 'Restructuring the multilateral export control regime system', *Journal of Conflict and Security Law*, vol. 9, no. 2 (summer 2004), p. 182.

[2] In Feb. 2004 Dr Khan, a central figure in the Pakistani nuclear weapon programme, appeared on Pakistani television and acknowledged that after 1992 he had arranged and coordinated supplies of nuclear materials, know-how and equipment to North Korea. The Khan network is described in chapter 12 in this volume. See also Braun, C. and Chyba, C. F., 'Proliferation rings: new challenges to the nuclear nonproliferation regime', *International Security*, vol. 29, no. 2 (fall 2004), pp. 5–49.

Table 17.1. Membership of multilateral weapon and technology transfer control regimes, as of 1 January 2005

State	Zangger Committee[a] 1974	NSG[b] 1978	Australia Group[a] 1985	MTCR[c] 1987	Wassenaar Arrangement 1996
Argentina	x	x	x	x	x
Australia	x	x	x	x	x
Austria	x	x	x	x	x
Belarus		x			
Belgium	x	x	x	x	x
Brazil		x		x	
Bulgaria	x	x	x	x[d]	x
Canada	x	x	x	x	x
China	x	x[d]			
Cyprus		x	x		
Czech Republic	x	x	x	x	x
Denmark	x	x	x	x	x
Estonia		x[d]	x[d]		
Finland	x	x	x	x	x
France	x	x	x	x	x
Germany	x	x	x	x	x
Greece	x	x	x	x	x
Hungary	x	x	x	x	x
Iceland			x	x	
Ireland	x	x	x	x	x
Italy	x	x	x	x	x
Japan	x	x	x	x	x
Kazakhstan		x			
Korea, South	x	x	x	x	x
Latvia		x	x[d]		
Lithuania		x[d]	x[d]		
Luxembourg	x	x	x	x	x
Malta		x[d]	x[d]		
Netherlands	x	x	x	x	x
New Zealand		x	x	x	x
Norway	x	x	x	x	x
Poland	x	x	x	x	x
Portugal	x	x	x	x	x
Romania	x	x	x		x
Russia	x	x		x	x
Slovakia	x	x	x		x
Slovenia	x	x	x[d]		x[d]
South Africa	x	x		x	
Spain	x	x	x	x	x
Sweden	x	x	x	x	x
Switzerland	x	x	x	x	x
Turkey	x	x	x	x	x
UK	x	x	x	x	x
Ukraine	x	x		x	x
USA	x	x	x	x	x
Total	**35**	**44**	**38**	**34**	**34**

Note: The years in the column headings indicate when the export control regime was formally established, although the groups may have met on an informal basis before then.

[a] The European Commission participates in this regime.

[b] The Nuclear Suppliers Group. The European Commission is an observer in this regime.
[c] The Missile Technology Control Regime.
[d] Joined in 2004.

II. The main developments in multilateral transfer control regimes in 2004

In 2004 a number of proposals were put forward that suggest the need to develop a new legal framework for multilateral export control cooperation.

In May 2004 Mohamed ElBaradei, the Director General of the International Atomic Energy Agency (IAEA), asserted that the existing export control mechanisms 'are completely busted right now. There [are] a lot of countries [which] are able to export [that] are not part of the regime—India, Pakistan, Malaysia, Israel. You cannot just pretend they do not exist. We need to have everybody as part of the export control regime'.[3] Previously, immediately after A. Q. Khan had confessed to his proliferation activities, ElBaradei had observed that the current export control cooperation:

> relies on a gentlemen's agreement that is not only non-binding, but also limited in its membership: it does not include many countries with growing industrial capacity. And even some members fail to control the exports of companies unaffiliated with government enterprise. We must universalize the export control system, remove these loopholes, and enact binding, treaty-based controls—while preserving the rights of all States to peaceful nuclear technology.[4]

The widespread belief that a stronger legal basis may be required for effective national action to be taken against non-state actors was reflected in the adoption, on 28 April 2004, of United Nations (UN) Security Council Resolution 1540 by a unanimous vote. The resolution, passed under Chapter VII of the UN Charter and therefore binding on UN member states, called for a strengthening of national export controls, among other measures.[5]

More generally, there have been increasing calls to strengthen the international legal basis for controls on transfers of military items. Several non-governmental organizations (NGOs) have argued that an international treaty should be negotiated to provide a set of common minimum standards for the control of arms transfers and to ensure a workable operative mechanism for the application of these standards.[6] This idea has also been espoused by governments. In September 2004 the British Foreign Minister, in a speech to the Labour Party Annual Conference, stated that the United Kingdom would 'start work soon with international partners, drawing on experience from the EU, to

[3] 'The challenges facing non-proliferation', Remarks of Mohamed ElBaradei at the Council on Foreign Relations, New York, 14 May 2004, URL <http://www.cfr.org/pub7032/graham_t_allison_mohamed_elbaradei/the_challenges_facing_nonproliferation.php>.

[4] ElBaradei, M., 'Saving ourselves from destruction', *New York Times*, 12 Feb. 2004.

[5] UN Security Council Resolution 1540, 28 Apr. 2004. It is discussed in chapters 11 and 18 in this volume and reproduced as appendix 11A.

[6] Information on the draft treaty is available on the Internet site of the International Action Network on Small Arms at URL <http://www.iansa.org/action/new_york/arms_trade_treaty.htm>.

build support for an International Arms Trade Treaty, further to extend the international rule of law'.[7] Commenting on the speech, an unnamed British official noted that the UK could use its presidency of the EU Council of Ministers in the second half of 2005 to initiate a dialogue about the treaty.[8]

The calls for strengthening international legal controls notwithstanding, the main cooperative efforts to improve the effectiveness of export controls have been carried out in ad hoc groups with limited membership. The Australia Group, the Missile Technology Control Regime, the Nuclear Suppliers Group and the Wassenaar Arrangement are informal groupings in which states seek to improve the effectiveness of their national export controls by agreeing common rules and exchanging information about a range of issues. The participating states in these arrangements as well as the Zangger Committee (discussed below) are identified in table 17.1.

The Australia Group

The Australia Group was established in 1985 following international concern about the use of chemical weapons (CW) in the 1980–88 Iraq–Iran War.[9] The participating states of this informal group initially cooperated to maintain and develop their national export controls to prevent the further spread of chemical exports that may be used for, or diverted to, CW programmes. The participating states seek to prevent the intentional or inadvertent supply by their nationals of materials or equipment to CW or biological weapon (BW) programmes. The AG is currently also developing measures that seek to prevent the acquisition of BW or CW by non-state actors, with a particular focus on measures aimed at individuals or groups planning to carry out terrorist attacks.

In 2004 the AG expanded to 38 states. The European Commission also participates. Five states participated in the group for the first time in 2004: Estonia, Latvia, Lithuania, Malta and Slovenia.

The AG has agreed a series of lists that define dual-use precursor chemicals, biological agents, chemical and biological equipment and related technology, and animal and plant pathogens.[10] The participating states are informally committed to ensure that these items are subject to national export controls, and they have agreed a set of guidelines to consider when assessing export licence applications. In 2004 the AG added three bacteria and two new viruses to the list of controlled biological agents.

In 2004 the Australia Group participating states agreed to consider whether brokering controls should be introduced to help curtail the activities of front companies and intermediaries. A front company works on behalf of a client in

[7] 'Delivering progressive values to the wider world', Speech by Jack Straw, Foreign Secretary, Labour Party Annual Conference, Brighton Centre, 30 Sep. 2004, URL <http://www.labour.org.uk/ac2004news?ux_news_id=ac04js>.

[8] Boese, W., 'British call for arms trade treaty', *Arms Control Today*, Nov. 2004, URL <http://www.armscontrol.org/act/2004_11/British.asp>.

[9] See the AG Internet site at URL <http://www.australiagroup.net>.

[10] Australia Group, 'AG common control lists', URL <http://www.australiagroup.net/en/agcomcon.htm>.

order to hide the identity of the true end-user of a controlled item. The front company—which might or might not be based in the same country as the true end-user—acquires a particular item (apparently legally) and then diverts or re-exports it to another recipient. In this way the true end-user avoids being scrutinized by export control authorities. The heightened concern with brokering and front companies is the result of the increasing sophistication of procurement efforts by proliferants.[11] The 2004 plenary meeting also sought to develop controls for the proliferation threat posed by non-state actors.

The Missile Technology Control Regime

The MTCR is an informal arrangement in which countries that share the goal of non-proliferation of unmanned delivery systems for NBC weapons cooperate to exchange information and coordinate their national export licensing processes.[12]

The MTCR was formed in 1987, at which time the primary focus of its activities was on ballistic missiles able to deliver a payload weighing 500 kilograms to a range of 300 kilometres. These technical parameters were considered to be consistent with missiles likely to be used to deliver first-generation nuclear weapons. The MTCR participating states have subsequently expanded the scope of their activities to include any unmanned air vehicles (UAVs)—a category that includes cruise missiles—capable of delivering NBC weapons.

The role of export controls in combating terrorism continues to be discussed in the MTCR as in other export control cooperation arrangements. One important issue in this context is how to share information and intelligence—an activity that normally takes place on a bilateral basis—more effectively in order to provide the most critical information to the people who need it in real time.

At their annual plenary meetings the MTCR participating states make a general assessment of proliferation risks, including a discussion of missile programmes of concern to the regime. However, the participating states have stressed that the MTCR Guidelines are for general application and do not 'target' particular states. In line with this approach, the MTCR public documents have not, in the past, named particular countries. In 2004 the press statement agreed at the MTCR plenary meeting drew attention to 'serious concern' over missile proliferation in North-East Asia, South Asia and the Middle East. However, the MTCR stopped short of naming particular countries of missile proliferation concern.

The press statement drew attention to the 'exemplary decision' of Libya to give up its WMD and ballistic missile programmes. European Union countries

[11] E.g, in his annual report to the US Congress, the Director of the Central Intelligence Agency noted the increasing prevalence of front companies in the acquisition of WMD components. US Central Intelligence Agency, 'Attachment A, Unclassified report to Congress on the acquisition of technology relating to weapons of mass destruction and advanced conventional munitions, 1 July through 31 December 2003', URL <http://www.cia.gov/cia/reports/721_reports/july_dec2003.htm>.

[12] See the MTCR Internet site at URL <http://www.mtcr.info/english/>.

were keen to have a statement encouraging Syria to strengthen its national export control system.[13]

On the basis of an analysis of illicit trafficking by companies located in Dubai, the MTCR discussed the issues of strengthening controls on goods destined for trans-shipment centres and the activities of front companies.

Participation

In 2004 Bulgaria joined the MTCR, bringing the number of participating states to 34.[14] However, decisions were deferred regarding the participation of a number of other applicant states. Applications are pending from states that have become members of the EU but that do not participate in the MTCR, from several countries that are located on the territory of the former Soviet Union, and from China.

As with the other export control regimes, the decision to expand the MTCR participation is taken by consensus among the existing participants and is based on an assessment of a number of criteria: whether the applicant has demonstrated a sustained and sustainable commitment to non-proliferation; whether the country has a legally based and effective export control system that can put into effect the MTCR Guidelines and procedures and administer them; and whether that control system is enforced effectively. The MTCR does not have an observer category.[15]

In 2003 the Chinese Government sent a letter to the Chairman of the MTCR indicating that China would have no difficulty in participating in the regime in the light of recent changes in its national export control regulations.[16] The letter was interpreted as an application to join the MTCR and the idea was subsequently discussed, although no decision was taken in 2004.

On 10–11 February 2004, the Chairman of the MTCR and a delegation of diplomats and experts from 15 MTCR participating states conducted in-depth talks with a high-level delegation from China. At that meeting the documents presented by China on its national export control system were reviewed and agreed to be consistent with international standards. However, the imple-

[13] In Oct. 2004 the EU and Syria agreed on a trade and cooperation agreement that included a so-called 'non-proliferation clause' under which they agreed to contribute to countering the proliferation of WMD and their means of delivery through full compliance with and national implementation of their existing obligations under international disarmament and non-proliferation treaties and agreements and other relevant international obligations. This issue is discussed further below. On Libya see chapter 14 in this volume.

[14] Plenary Meeting of the Missile Technology Control Regime, Seoul, 6–8 Oct. 2004, Press Statement, 8 Oct. 2004, URL <http://www.sipri.org/contents/expcon/mtcr04.html>.

[15] The issue of participation in the export control regimes by EU member states is discussed in section IV of this chapter.

[16] In Aug. 2002 China introduced strengthened regulations on export control of missiles and missile-related items and technologies as well as an updated control list. The regulations and the control list conform closely to the MTCR documents. In Dec. 2003 the State Council of the People's Republic of China published a White Paper which stated that China 'adopts a positive and open attitude toward all international proposals for strengthening the missile non-proliferation regime'. *China's Non-Proliferation Policy and Measures* (Information Office of the State Council of the People's Republic of China: Beijing, Dec. 2003), p. 7, URL <http://www.gcdd.net/TX=2003/TX.031=2003.12.03.China.English.pdf>.

mentation and enforcement aspects of Chinese controls continue to be discussed and some questions remain unresolved. The difficulty is believed to relate to the continued cooperation between Chinese enterprises and missile programmes of concern, including programmes in Iran. This cooperation raises questions for some participating states, including the USA, about how Chinese authorities interpret the MTCR Guidelines when making licensing decisions and about how export controls are enforced.

Outreach activities

A country can choose to adhere to the MTCR Guidelines,[17] which is a public document, without participating in the regime. A number of countries, such as Israel, have done so, and the MTCR participating states have encouraged all non-participating countries to take this approach. In order to further this objective the MTCR participating states have carried out a broad dialogue on missile proliferation issues with a range of different countries.

The Chairman carries the main responsibility for outreach and the participating states have discussed how to coordinate and carry out this activity. In 2004 the MTCR Chairman was not received in two countries (Iran and Pakistan) and alternative ways of interacting with these countries need to be found.

In 2004 outreach activities included a visit to Libya at the invitation of the Libyan Government. Libya explained its decision to give up its programme to acquire ballistic missiles that exceed the MTCR Category I range and payload parameters, and the MTCR team visited a number of sites of interest. During the visit the issue of Libyan adherence to the MTCR Guidelines was raised, and it was agreed that the MTCR participating states would assist Libya to put in place efficient export control procedures.

The Wassenaar Arrangement

The decision to establish the WA was taken by 33 states in December 1995 at a meeting in Wassenaar, the Netherlands. The objective of the WA is to promote transparency, exchange of information and exchange of views on transfers of an agreed range of items with a view to promoting responsibility in transfers of conventional arms and dual-use goods and technologies and to preventing 'destabilizing accumulations' of such items.

The participating states held the second WA assessment in 2003,[18] which brought about the first substantial changes in the way in which the WA functions. The participating states agreed on major revisions of the founding document, the Initial Elements (e.g., to extend the arms transfer notification

[17] MTCR 'Guidelines for sensitive missile-relevant transfers', URL <http://www.mtcr.info/english/guidetext.htm>.

[18] At its creation the participating states recognized that the WA would need to develop additional elements if it was to achieve its stated objectives. This was reflected in the decision to call the founding document Initial Elements and to conduct a review of the WA in 1999. Following the second assessment, in 2003, the participating states decided to review their activities regularly—the next time in 2007. See the WA Internet site at URL <http://www.wassenaar.org>.

requirement also to small arms and light weapons, SALW) and adopted three documents aimed at tightening export controls on man-portable air defence systems (MANPADS), brokering and unlisted equipment. For the first time, a Ministerial Statement affirmed the commitment of the participating states to the WA.[19]

In 2004 much of the work in the WA focused on the implementation of decisions reached in 2003, in particular with regard to export control measures to counter terrorism. A noteworthy result of the 2004 plenary meeting was the admission of Slovenia to the WA. This was the first enlargement of the WA since its establishment. Previously, consensus on the admission of new members could not be reached.[20] The decision to expand WA participation is taken by consensus among existing participants and is based on an assessment of various criteria: whether the applicant state 'is a producer/exporter of arms or industrial equipment respectively'; whether the country adheres to 'fully effective export controls'; and whether the country has 'non-proliferation policies and appropriate national policies'. At the 2003 assessment an additional criterion was agreed which takes into account whether a country has adopted the WA control lists as a reference in its national export controls.[21]

In the 2004 plenary meeting's Public Statement, the participating states 'in a position to do so' committed themselves to providing 'assistance on the development of effective export controls to those States that request it'.[22] This commitment was explicitly put into the context of UN Security Council Resolution 1540, which requires all states to establish, develop and maintain effective export and trans-shipment controls.

The working method of inter-sessional activities conducted by task forces and working groups, which had proven useful in 2003, was continued in 2004. The task forces are composed of several participating states of which one or more acts as chairman. In 2004 task forces worked on criteria for the selection of dual-use items, the dual-use list review and best-practice guidelines on licensing mechanisms. In addition, an ad hoc working group on export control documentation was established.

Much of the work of the outreach group focused on the preparation of the regime's first outreach seminar, which was held in Vienna on 19 October 2004. Representatives of non-participating governments (Belarus, China, Croatia, Cyprus, Estonia, Israel, Latvia, Lithuania, Malta, Slovenia[23] and South Africa), NGOs, academia, industry and the media participated. The aim

[19] On the 2003 assessment plenary see Anthony, I. and Bauer, S., 'Transfer controls and destruction programmes', *SIPRI Yearbook 2004: Armaments, Disarmament and International Security* (Oxford University Press: Oxford, 2004), pp. 737–62. The plenaray documents are available at URL <http://www.wassenaar.org>.

[20] See the section on 'Export control elements of the WMD Action Plan' in this chapter.

[21] Wassenaar Arrangement (WA), 'Purposes, Guidelines & Procedures, including the Initial Elements, as adopted and amended by the Plenary of December 2003', URL <http://www.wassenaar.org/2003Plenary/2003PlenaryDocs.htm>.

[22] WA, 'Public Statement, 2004 Plenary Meeting of the Wassenaar Arrangement on Export Controls for Conventional Arms and Dual-Use Goods and Technologies', URL <http://www.wassenaar.org/docs/docindex.html>.

[23] At this stage Slovenia was a non-participating country.

of the seminar was to 'raise awareness of the positive contribution that the Wassenaar Arrangement makes to responsible transfers of conventional arms and dual-use goods and technologies'.[24] The presentations explained the WA's purpose, history, working methods, activities and areas of ongoing negotiation. Speakers also addressed a range of policy areas of particular interest to the WA, including brokering, small arms and light weapons, and MANPADS. Follow-up events are planned for future years, and outreach to industry will be one of the priorities for such activities. In late 2003 the WA initiated contact with China to establish a mechanism for bilateral dialogue. This led to two days of talks in Beijing in April 2004. A WA outreach visit to South Africa took place in early 2005.

At the 2004 plenary session, the participating states also exchanged information on national measures taken to implement the 2003 decision to tighten controls on the export of MANPADS.

As a matter of routine, the WA control lists were amended to take into account technical and security developments. Particular attention was paid to items which may be used for terrorist purposes. Changes to the WA list are prepared through technical meetings during the year and formally approved at the December plenary session.

The growing attention to national export controls

As noted above, UN Security Council Resolution 1540 *inter alia* requires states to put in place effective national export control systems. States are requested to report on the measures currently in place in order to ensure that sensitive items that could contribute to NBC weapons or missile delivery systems for such weapons are not exported without prior assessment. The response by states to the resolution indicated that a large number of them accept that there is a need for effective export controls.[25] In 2004 three states whose capacity and technical expertise are of direct concern in this regard, and that remain outside the 1968 Treaty on the Non-proliferation of Nuclear Weapons (Non-Proliferation Treaty, NPT), took action to strengthen their national export controls.

In April 2004 *Israel* adopted a new Export Control Order, which entered into force in July 2004. The order strengthened government control over transfers of NBC items. It includes a list of items that cannot be exported without specific authorization and incorporates the control lists developed by the AG and the NSG. However, the order also includes a 'catch-all' or end-use control which prohibits the export of any items (whether they are included on any control list or not) to NBC weapon programmes and criminalizes such exports should they occur. The authorization to export controlled items is given by the

[24] WA, 'Outreach seminar 19 October 2004', Press Statement, 21 Oct. 2004, URL <http://www.wassenaar.org/docs/Seminar_press_statement.htm>.

[25] See the Internet site of the SIPRI Non-proliferation and export control project at URL <http://www.sipri.org/contents/expcon/>.

Minister of Industry, Trade and Labour but only after consultation with and approval by the Ministry of Foreign Affairs and the Ministry of Defence.

In 2004 *India* evaluated changes to its export control system. India has been engaged in a dialogue with the USA on export control issues since the meeting between President George W. Bush and Prime Minister Atal Bihari Vajpayee in November 2001. After that meeting the 'next steps in strategic partnership' were defined, including a dialogue on a range of non-proliferation issues, such as export control. The USA agreed to consider options for expanded Indian–US technical cooperation in the areas of civil nuclear and space applications and to examine the possibilities for expanding high-technology commerce. India has agreed to take concrete steps to address what the USA considers to be shortfalls in the Indian export control system.

India currently controls exports using a complicated patchwork of at least nine different pieces of primary legislation, some of which date from the 1960s. This is supplemented by secondary legislation (in the form of Public Orders) on specific technical matters. In 1993 the Indian Government established the Small Group on Strategic Export Controls as an inter-agency effort to review and coordinate the list of items subject to control. In particular, this exercise was intended to develop the content of a control list attached to the 1992 Foreign Trade Development and Regulation Act, which aims to catch any items not already subject to control under existing legislation.[26]

The USA has urged India to provide government-to-government assurances that items supplied by US companies will not be used for unauthorized purposes in facilities owned and operated by the Indian Government. To this end the Indian Government is also being asked to agree to facilitate on-site visits by US officials at facilities where US-origin items are located. The USA has also requested that a system be put in place to prevent the transfer of US-origin items to India's ballistic missile programme, to unsafeguarded nuclear facilities and to third countries.

The USA has urged India to apply the MTCR and the NSG guidelines in its national export licence assessments. It asked India to harmonize its lists of items which require a licence before export with the control lists that have been developed in the multilateral export control regimes. India is considering these requests and is reviewing the introduction of controls on intangible technology transfer and on brokering.

In 2004 *Pakistan* enacted the Export Control on Goods, Technologies, Material and Equipment Related to Nuclear and Biological Weapons and Their Delivery Systems Act 2004, which entered into force in September 2004. The new law supplemented legislation related to chemical weapons that was enacted in 2000. The act commits Pakistan to prevent the proliferation of biological and nuclear weapons and missile delivery systems for both types of weapon. Pakistan controls the export of items of relevance to the production of

[26] Ramachandran, R., 'For a controls regime', *Frontline*, 1–14 Jan. 2005, URL <http://flonet.com/fl2201/20050114002404800.htm>.

CW by using the national implementing legislation for the 1993 Chemical Weapons Convention.[27]

III. The Nuclear Suppliers Group

The aim of the NSG is to prevent the proliferation of nuclear weapons through controls on the export of nuclear and nuclear-related material, equipment, software and technology. The export controls, which are implemented by the participating states through national legislation and procedures, are not intended to prevent or hinder international cooperation on peaceful uses of nuclear energy.[28]

At the 2004 plenary meeting of the NSG the participating states, which operate by consensus, agreed that four new states—China, Estonia, Lithuania and Malta—would participate in the activities of the group from 10 June 2004. With the accession of these states, the NSG now includes 44 countries.[29]

The NSG participating states have agreed two sets of guidelines which they apply when assessing applications to export controlled items. One set of guidelines is applied to items that were specially designed or developed for nuclear use, while the other set of guidelines is applied to exports of nuclear dual-use items. The NSG participating states include states in which the main exporters of nuclear technology are located, and the group recognizes that peaceful nuclear cooperation is both legitimate and necessary. The participating states share the view that its guidelines 'facilitate the development of trade' by 'providing the means whereby obligations to facilitate peaceful nuclear cooperation can be implemented in a manner consistent with international nuclear non-proliferation norms'.[30]

The obligation to facilitate peaceful nuclear cooperation is codified in Article IV of the NPT. This article states that nothing in the treaty shall be interpreted as affecting 'the inalienable right of all the Parties to the Treaty to develop research, production and use of nuclear energy for peaceful purposes'. Moreover, under Article IV all the parties to the treaty 'undertake to facilitate, and have the right to participate in, the fullest possible exchange of equipment, materials and scientific and technological information for the peaceful uses of nuclear energy'.

In order to ensure that transfers are exclusively for peaceful purposes the non-nuclear weapon states which are parties to the NPT commit themselves, in Article III, to accept safeguards contained in bilateral agreements with the International Atomic Energy Agency. The IAEA has developed a safeguards

[27] See chapter 13 in this volume.

[28] See the NSG Internet site at URL <http://www.nsg-online.org/>.

[29] Nuclear Suppliers Group (NSG), 'Press Statement from the 2004 Plenary Meeting of the Nuclear Suppliers Group', Gothenburg, Sweden, 27–28 May 2004, URL <http://www.nuclearsuppliersgroup.org/public.htm>.

[30] The latest versions of the NSG Guidelines as well as a statement on how they are to be applied are available at URL <http://www.nuclearsuppliersgroup.org/guide.htm>.

system based on nuclear material accountancy to detect any diversion of declared nuclear materials for proscribed purposes.

On a number of occasions the IAEA has found that states have violated the terms of their safeguards agreements. In recent years the NSG has discussed what impact these violations should have on nuclear supply policies. The NSG has discussed the proposal to suspend the supply of items that were specially designed and developed for nuclear use to any state that the IAEA Board of Governors finds to be in non-compliance with its safeguards obligations. As of the end of 2004 no decision had been taken on this proposal.

The NSG has also discussed whether existing guidelines ought to be supplemented or revised to reflect concerns about the transfer of equipment and technology for parts of the nuclear fuel cycle that are considered particularly sensitive from a proliferation perspective. The sensitive parts of the fuel cycle are those that can produce the fissile materials (certain isotopes of highly enriched uranium and plutonium) that are essential parts of a nuclear weapon. In particular, the NSG has discussed whether specific criteria should apply to assessments of applications to export the equipment and technology that are required to enrich natural uranium and to reprocess spent fuel in order to extract plutonium.

As noted above, the IAEA has developed a set of safeguards to detect the diversion of nuclear material to unauthorized uses. The recognition that the comprehensive or 'full-scope' safeguards had been violated by Iraq without prompt detection led the IAEA to develop a model Additional Protocol that would supplement existing arrangements by increasing the transparency of the nuclear sector in states and by providing the agency with new rights of access and a new right to information.[31]

The NSG has discussed the proposal that the Additional Protocol should become an essential condition of nuclear supply and has examined how the existing guidelines would have to be modified to that end. As of the end of 2004 agreement had not been reached on what kinds of change would be required.

At the Group of Eight (G8) Summit in Sea Island, Georgia, in June 2004 it was proposed that 'sensitive nuclear items with proliferation potential will not be exported to states that may seek to use them for weapons purposes, or allow them to fall into terrorist hands'.[32] The G8 leaders set the objective of amending the NSG guidelines to reflect this proposal by the time of the June 2005 G8 Summit in the UK. In the interim, the G8 leaders agreed that they would not sanction new transfers of enrichment and reprocessing equipment and technologies, except to states that already possess such items. In the face of opposition from a number of NSG states and the European Commission to this ban, the G8 are now discussing a set of restrictive guidelines for transfers of the most sensitive technologies.

[31] States which have safeguards agreements and Additional Protocols in force are listed in annex A to this volume.

[32] 'Sea Island Summit 2004: G8 Action Plan on Nonproliferation', Sea Island, Ga., 9 June 2004, URL <http://www.g8usa.gov/d_060904d.htm>.

The G8 leaders also agreed to cooperate to complement export controls by developing new measures to ensure that all states would have 'reliable access to nuclear materials, equipment, and technology, including nuclear fuel and related services, at market conditions, for all states, consistent with maintaining nonproliferation commitments and standards'.[33] To this end the IAEA established an independent expert group to examine alternatives to national controls on uranium enrichment and plutonium separation as well as the storage and disposal of spent nuclear fuel.[34]

The Zangger Committee

The Zangger Committee is not formally a part of the NPT regime, but its participants seek to take account of the effect of changing security aspects on the NPT and to adapt export control conditions and criteria in that light. The Zangger Committee is an informal group of states that meet to discuss how to interpret their obligations under Article 3.2 of the NPT. According to Article 3.2 each party to the treaty 'undertakes not to provide: (*a*) source or special fissionable material, or (*b*) equipment or material especially designed or prepared for the processing, use or production of special fissionable material, to any non-nuclear-weapon State for peaceful purposes' unless the material is subject to IAEA safeguards. The Zangger Committee was established to help its members define exactly what constitutes 'equipment or material especially designed or prepared for the processing, use or production of special fissile material' and to examine the conditions and procedures that would govern exports of such material.[35] The committee has agreed a so-called Trigger List containing items whose export would 'trigger' a need for safeguards to be put in place. In 2004 the Zangger Committee discussed the need for a review of the conditions that a recipient state must satisfy to be eligible to receive items on the Trigger List.

IV. Supply-side measures in the European Union

The first major review of the 1998 EU Code of Conduct on Arms Exports and the peer review of the implementation of Council Regulation 1504/2004[36] by

[33] Sea Island Summit 2004 (note 32).

[34] The proposals to place certain parts of the nuclear fuel cycle under international control are discussed in chapter 12 in this volume.

[35] On the Zangger Committee see URL <http://www.sipri.org/contents/expcon/NSG_documents.html>, and the Zangger Committee Internet site at URL <www.zanggercommittee.org/Zangger/default.htm>.

[36] 'Council Regulation (EC) no. 1334/2000 of 22 June 2000 setting up a Community regime for the control of exports of dual-use items and technologies', *Official Journal of the European Communities*, L159 (30 June 2000). It has been updated and amended regularly and was reissued in 2004 to adapt it to enlargement. 'Council Regulation (EC) no. 1504/2004 of 19 July 2004 amending and updating Regulation (EC) no. 1334/2000 setting up a Community regime for the control of exports of dual-use items and technology', *Official Journal of the European Union*, L281 (31 Aug. 2004), pp. 1–225. For an overview of national implementation efforts see 'Report to Parliament and the Council on the implementation of Council Regulation (EC) no. 1334/2000 setting up a Community regime for the control of exports of

the member states were at the centre of the EU's export control activities in 2004. The regulation forms a common and uniform legislative basis for dual-use export control in all member states. Like all other EU activities in 2004, these initiatives have to be seen against the political and institutional background of the admission of 10 new member states on 1 May 2004.

Export control elements of the WMD Action Plan

The EU's Action Plan for the Implementation of the Basic Principles for an EU Strategy against Proliferation of Weapons of Mass Destruction of June 2003[37] contains a number of action points in the area of export controls. Several of these points have been taken forward,[38] the most visible being the role of the EU in the export control regimes. In 2004, for the first time, the member states systematically coordinated their positions before and during the meetings of the export control regimes and presented agreed EU positions through the EU Presidency. This is the EU's established practice in the UN, but it had not been employed systematically in these regimes until then. In export control regimes where the European Commission and the Council Secretariat do not have observer or participant status (i.e., the MTCR and the WA), both attended the meetings in their capacity as part of the presidency delegation. Although the Commission had previously been invited to join the presidency delegation to the WA plenary meetings, in 2004 the Commission also attended the working group meetings.

The incomplete nature of the participation of the EU member states in export control regimes remains a challenge to the effective and consistent implementation of the EU dual-use regulation.[39] The regulation obliges the member states to apply the rules agreed in export control cooperation arrangements in licensing assessments. Most dual-use items that have both military and civilian applications move freely within the single market of the European Union, and any member state can issue an export licence which authorizes their export (including for items that are physically located elsewhere in the EU). In these circumstances, the EU has argued that each national authority must have a clear understanding of its commitments and access to the information that will allow it to make an informed decision when an application is being considered. The new EU member states that do not participate in the regimes also do not participate in the denial notification procedures, the technical discussions updating the lists of controlled items, the exchange of views

dual-use items and technology, October 2000 to May 2004', URL <http://trade-info.cec.eu.int/doclib/html/118993.htm>.

[37] Council of the European Union, 'Action Plan for the Implementation of the Basic Principles for an EU Strategy against Proliferation of Weapons of Mass Destruction of June 2003', document 10354/1/03 REV 1, Brussels, 13 June 2003.

[38] Council of the European Union, 'Progress Report on the implementation of Chapter III of the EU Strategy against the Proliferation of Weapons of Mass Destruction', document 15246/04, Brussels, 3 Dec. 2004.

[39] See note 36.

and information considered relevant to the purposes of the regimes, and the informal networking between officials at meetings.

All EU member states now participate in the Australia Group and the Nuclear Suppliers Group, but the Czech Republic, Hungary and Poland are the only new member states that participate in all four export control regimes. The involvement of non-participating EU members therefore remains a key question to address in 2005.

In the MTCR—in which Cyprus, Estonia, Latvia, Lithuania, Malta, Slovakia and Slovenia do not currently participate—it has not proved possible to expand participation because of objections by Russia and Turkey. Together with Belarus, Kazakhstan and Ukraine, Russia is negotiating to create a Common Economic Area which would allow the free movement of goods within one joint customs zone. However, the USA has not yet agreed to the participation of Kazakhstan in the MTCR, and the Russian objection to expansion to include EU member states is believed to be part of a campaign to gain US acceptance of Kazakhstan. Turkey, while not arguing against the idea of participation by EU member states per se, currently does not support the participation of Cyprus in the MTCR.

Consideration of expanded participation in the WA will be carried out on a country-by-country basis. The applicants will be considered in the order of their date of application, which will require the WA participating countries to state specific objections to the participation of the country in question. The 2004 WA plenary meeting did not extend membership to the other EU acceding countries, Cyprus, Estonia, Latvia, Lithuania and Malta, or to the candidate country Croatia—all of which had submitted applications to join.[40]

The EU's WMD Action Plan included an assistance programme for states in need of technical knowledge in the field of export control. A Technical Assistance to the Commonwealth of Independent States (TACIS) project for Russia to support the development of effective dual-use export controls is being developed. The December 2004 progress report on the WMD Action Plan proposed providing assistance to and cooperation with third countries: the team of experts set up for the peer review could coordinate and participate in assistance programmes in the Balkans and the European Neighbourhood Policy (ENP) countries in Eastern Europe, the Middle East and North Africa; 'administrative twinning' programmes could be established between ENP countries and one or two EU member states; existing community programmes on border management could be expanded to include export control elements; and ad hoc meetings could be held with China on export controls and exchange of best practice, which could include an offer to train Chinese export control officials. To this end, national expertise and the Common Foreign and Security Policy (CFSP), TACIS, MEDA[41] and Community Assistance for Reconstruction, Development and Stabilisation (CARDS) programmes would be used, as appropriate. In the context of the Euro-Mediterranean Partnership (Barcelona

[40] As a result of inter-sessional consultations in the spring of 2005, Estonia, Latvia, Lithuania and Malta were admitted.

[41] MEDA is the financial instrument for implementation of the Barcelona Process.

Process),[42] it was recommended that export control and border management assistance in the MEDA programme be expanded. It was proposed that up to €5 million be made available to both India and Pakistan for nuclear material accountancy and export control assistance.[43]

The peer review

In 2004 the first stage of a peer review of the export control systems of EU member states and accession countries as regards dual-use items was conducted. The peer review aims to strengthen the coordination of the dual-use export control activities of member states and to provide opportunities for mutual learning in order to enhance the effectiveness of implementation of Council Regulation 1504/2004 in an enlarged EU. The rationale behind the peer review is that the EU dual-use system is only as strong as its weakest link since illicit exports are likely to take the path of least resistance.

A peer review task force was set up in September 2003, consisting of representatives from the Council Secretariat, the European Commission and Finland.

The review process was organized around clusters of countries, comprising two member states and one acceding country. Some member states were represented in more than one cluster. For example, the UK was grouped together with Ireland and Malta, and also with Greece and Cyprus. Experts from member states visited the acceding country, which in turn made return visits. The visits were held between February and July 2004. Discussions were structured around 20 fundamental issues relevant to licensing, enforcement, industry awareness programmes and control of technical assistance.

The peer review revealed discrepancies regarding implementing legislation, industrial awareness programmes, the technical capacities available to national authorities to evaluate licence applications and classify items, and as regards the intelligence infrastructure. The review also found that the application of the dual-use regulation differed with regard to *inter alia* the use of the catch-all clause, the implementation of denial exchanges, intangible technology transfer controls, and transit and trans-shipment controls.

Future peer review activities will be based on the results of these visits, which were summarized in country reports. Each cluster subsequently summarized the main conclusions in a cluster report. On the basis of these reports, the peer review task force produced a report and recommendations for future action. The General Affairs Council of 13–14 December 2004 decided that these recommendations should be 'acted upon without delay'.[44]

In order to 'further improve EU export controls and thereby enhance Member States' capabilities to prevent access by undesirable end-users, including

[42] See the Euro-Mediterranean Partnership/Barcelona Process Internet site at <http://europa.eu.int/comm/external_relations/euromed/>.

[43] Council of the European Union (note 38).

[44] Council of the European Union, 2630th Council Meeting General Affairs and External Relations, Brussels, General Affairs, Press Release no. 15460/04 (Presse 343), 13 Dec. 2004, URL <http://www.consilium.eu.int>.

terrorists in third countries, to dual-use items relevant for WMD purposes', it was decided that actions should be taken to: (*a*) 'ensure transparency and awareness of legislation implementing the EU system'; (*b*) 'minimise any significant divergence in practices amongst Member States'; (*c*) 'investigate the possibilities for adding controls on transit and transhipment'; (*d*) 'provide assistance in recognition of dual-use items subject to control'; (*e*) 'improve exchanges of information on denials, and consider the creation of a data base to exchange sensitive information'; (f) 'agree best practices for the enforcement of controls'; (*g*) 'improve transparency to facilitate harmonisation of implementation of controls on nonlisted items (catch-all)'; (*h*) 'enhance interaction with exporters'; and (*i*) 'agree best practices for controlling intangible transfers of technology'.[45]

The peer review is likely to lead to substantive changes to the dual-use export control systems of countries and to a review of Council Regulation 1504/2004 in order to strengthen controls and increase the consistency of practice throughout the EU.

The European Union Code of Conduct on Arms Exports

The EU Code of Conduct on Arms Exports was adopted in June 1998. The countries which acceded to the EU in May 2004, the European Free Trade Association (EFTA) countries which are members of the European Economic Area (EEA)—Iceland, Liechtenstein and Norway—and Bulgaria, Canada, Croatia, Romania and Turkey have aligned themselves with its principles. Although it is not legally binding, the Code of Conduct contains political commitments: eight criteria for export licensing and operative provisions, which outline reporting procedures and mechanisms for intergovernmental denial notification and consultation. In 2000 the EU member states agreed a list of military equipment to which the Code is applied, and that list was revised in 2003.[46]

In 2004 the EU Code of Conduct was formally reviewed. The review process coincided with the full integration of the 10 new EU states into the information and consultation procedures of the Code of Conduct. Conclusion of the review is now anticipated by mid-2005. A central database of notifications of both export licence and brokering licence denials, where these exist, was created in 2004 (the decision was taken in 2003 and announced in the 2003 User's Guide).

In addition to the review process, in 2004 the Conventional Arms Exports Working Group (COARM) took a number of other decisions, which were announced in its Sixth Annual Report. The EU member states agreed that they

[45] Council of the European Union (note 44).

[46] 'Common Military List of the European Union (equipment covered by the European Union Code of Conduct on Arms Exports) adopted by the Council on 17 November 2003 (updating and replacing the Common List of military equipment covered by the European Union Code of Conduct on Arms Exports adopted by the Council on 13 June 2000)', *Official Journal of the European Union*, C 314 (23 Dec. 2003), pp. 1–26.

will 'fully apply the Code of Conduct to licence applications where it is understood that the goods are to be incorporated into products for re-exports'.[47] In assessing such applications, they will also take into account five other criteria, which are identical to the additional criteria for incorporation purposes announced by the British Government[48] in 2002: (*a*) 'the export control policies and effectiveness of the export control system of the incorporating country'; (*b*) 'the importance of their defence and security relationship with that country'; (*c*) 'the materiality and significance of the goods in relation to the goods into which they are to be incorporated, and in relation to any end-use of the finished products which might give rise to concern'; (*d*) 'the ease with which the goods, or significant parts of them, could be removed from the goods into which they are to be incorporated'; and (*e*) 'the standing entity to which the goods are to be exported'.[49]

In 2003 COARM agreed 'in principle to share information on denials on an aggregate basis, without indicating which Member States issued the denials, with selected non-member countries whose export control legislation and policy meet the high standards set by Member States for themselves'.[50] Each decision is taken on a case-by-case basis. The first such agreement was reached with Norway, and the exchange of information on denials between the EU and Norway began in November 2004.

Developing a dialogue with the European Parliament was one of the priorities for future action outlined in 2003, and in 2004, for the first time, the dialogue contained elements going beyond a presidency briefing to the European Parliament Foreign Affairs Committee. In addition to an 'exchange of views' at the Foreign Affairs Committee's Sub-committee on Security and Disarmament on the issue of the review of the Code of Conduct, the Netherlands Presidency invited the European Parliament's rapporteur on the EU Code of Conduct[51] to brief a COARM meeting and to speak at an informal meeting on the EU Code review that was held in The Hague.

Among COARM's priorities for 2004 was the harmonization of reporting. To this end, the Netherlands Presidency and SIPRI organized a meeting of national experts from EU member states to discuss data collection and reporting methods in the EU and ways to improve the comparability and comprehensiveness of the annual reports on implementation of the EU Code of Conduct.[52]

[47] 'Sixth annual report according to operative provision 8 of the European Union Code of Conduct on arms exports', *Official Journal of the European Communities*, C 316 (21 Dec. 2004), pp. 1–215.

[48] British Foreign and Commonwealth Office, 'Foreign Secretary's statement on incorporation issues', 8 July 2002, URL <http://www.fco.gov.uk/Files/kfile/Incorporation.pdf>.

[49] 'Sixth annual report according to operative provision 8 of the European Union Code of Conduct on arms exports' (note 47).

[50] 'Sixth annual report according to operative provision 8 of the European Union Code of Conduct on arms exports' (note 47).

[51] The European Parliament's reports on the EU Code of Conduct are available at URL <http://www.sipri.org/contents/expcon/euparl.html>.

[52] SIPRI published a study which analyses the data collection and reporting methods in EU member states, evaluates the utility of existing data for drawing meaningful conclusions about the implementation of the EU Code of Conduct, and makes recommendations for improving the comprehensiveness,

The EU Code of Conduct review

Much of the review focused on the codification of decisions that have been taken piecemeal since 1998 without formal modification to the Code's text. Since 2002 the annual report on the implementation of the Code of Conduct has included a compendium of decisions taken each year. In addition, a User's Guide to the EU Code was published in November 2003 which further defines and interprets the terms and procedures outlined in the 1998 Code of Conduct.[53] An updated version of the User's Guide was published in December 2004.[54] The development of a 'handbook' for use at working level has made the Code of Conduct an instrument whose impact on export controls has gone considerably beyond its original scope. The revised Code, as agreed by COARM,[55] includes an obligation to apply the most recent version of the User's Guide.

Most amendments to the Code affect its operative provisions (i.e., its procedures for implementation) and therefore the licensing procedures. The scope of the Code was clarified and amended to make clear that licence applications for licensed production overseas, brokering, trans-shipment and intangible technology transfers should be assessed against the criteria of the Code in the same way as licence applications for physical transfers. The modifications also strengthen the requirement for end-use certification and introduce a requirement that member states publish national reports on arms exports.

With regard to the Code's export criteria, a reference to international humanitarian law was added to the human rights criterion (criterion 2). As a result, the assessment of a recipient country's attitude towards international humanitarian law may lead to the denial of an export licence. Criterion 7, on the risk of diversion within the recipient country or re-export under undesirable conditions, was modified to take into account the risk of reverse engineering, the record of the recipient country in respecting re-export provisions imposed by the exporter and the risk of diversion to terrorists. The governments of the EU member states are also elaborating guidelines for the application of criterion 8 for inclusion in the User's Guide. Criterion 8 considers the impact of an export on the technical and economic capacity of the recipient country. Guidelines for the application of other criteria may be added over time.

The governments of the EU member states also considered changing the status of the Code of Conduct from a Council Declaration to a Common Position, but they have not reached consensus on this issue. Unlike a Council Declaration, a Common Position is an instrument of the CFSP referred to in

usefulness and comparability of the annual reports. Bauer, S. and Bromley, M., *The European Union Code of Conduct on Arms Exports: Improving the Annual Report*, SIPRI Policy Paper no. 8 (SIPRI: Stockholm, Nov. 2004, URL <http://www.sipri.org/contents/publications/policy_papers.html>.

[53] Council of the European Union 'User's Guide to the European Union Code of Conduct on Arms Exports', document 1428/03, Brussels, 6 Nov. 2003.

[54] Council of the European Union 'User's Guide to the European Union Code of Conduct on Arms Exports', document 16133/1/04, rev.1, Brussels, 23 Dec. 2004.

[55] At the time of writing, the document was awaiting formal approval by the foreign ministers of the EU member states.

the 1992 Treaty on European Union,[56] which politically obliges member states to bring their legislation and policies in line with the agreed Common Position. While a Common Position would not transform the Code of Conduct into European law or make it subject to the jurisdiction of the European Court of Justice, a Common Position has national legal implications for some member states.

The review negotiations should be considered in the context of the discussion of lifting the EU arms embargo on China. At the December 2004 China–EU Summit, the Netherlands Presidency made clear that the embargo would not be lifted until a strengthened Code of Conduct was agreed.[57] In addition, a post-embargo 'toolbox' (temporary measures) would be agreed to address the concerns of some EU members, as well as the USA, that the lifting of the embargo may lead to an increase in arms exports to China.[58] Future agreement of a post-embargo toolbox had already been announced when the embargo on Libya was lifted. The elements of the toolbox include the sharing of information on equipment licensed in the past five years. In the case of China, this is intended to enable the EU governments to monitor that the commitment made at the December 2004 summit not to increase arms exports to China in qualitative or quantitative terms is being respected. The toolbox will also provide for: a quarterly exchange of detailed information on licences granted for exports of EU Common Military List items to countries that were formerly subject to arms embargo, specifying the type of military equipment, the quantity, the end-use and the end-user; regular consultations about the destination of such exports; discussions at Council level in the event of major national policy changes by one or more member states; and a review of denial notifications issued over the past three years to see if they remain valid.

V. Conclusions

The states that participate in informal multilateral groups to enhance the effectiveness of their national export controls continue to acknowledge that additional efforts are needed to combat and, if possible, reverse the proliferation of weapons of mass destruction and their delivery systems.

A number of processes have been proposed for strengthening the international legal framework for export controls as one important way of enhancing the wider non-proliferation regime. The growing number of states that accept the need for effective national export controls indicates that the environment for such international initiatives may currently be favourable.

In 2004 the need for well-funded and targeted assistance programmes to help countries put in place modern and effective national export controls

[56] The text of the Treaty on European Union (Maastricht Treaty) is available at URL <http://europa.eu.int/en/record/mt/top.html>.

[57] 'EU/China: relations between EU and China move forward—lifting of arms embargo may be envisaged', *Atlantic News*, no. 3635 (11 Dec. 2004), p. 4.

[58] On the embargo and European arms exports to China see chapter 10 in this volume.

emerged as a theme in the EU, the G8, the UN and the WA.[59] This implies that the scale of such assistance may grow in future and that there may be a need to strengthen the coordination of such programmes.

For the European Union, effectiveness will require better coordination between the parts of the EU which are responsible for different functions (e.g., border control, dual-use export control and external relations activities). One of the lessons of EU enlargement is that cooperation and assistance at an early stage facilitate compliance with the EU's export control rules and regulations. This lesson should be applied in candidate countries (currently Bulgaria, Croatia, Romania and Turkey) and to prospective applicants such as Serbia and Montenegro. Cooperation in the fight against WMD proliferation is also one of the elements of the European Neighbourhood Policy Strategy,[60] and export control assistance programmes ought to be an integral part of the ENP.

One way to enhance the consistency of export controls for dual-use and defence items across the EU would be to develop structures to pool technical capacities and intelligence on end-use, and to establish joint training of licensing and enforcement officers in the EU. Such a training capacity could also be used for outreach activities and in assistance programmes.

In addition to assisting the EU countries which are not members of all the export control regimes to prepare for and obtain membership, other EU members may need to develop interim structures and methods to ensure that sufficient and timely information is available to licensing and enforcement officers. This would enhance the consistent application of the dual-use regulation throughout the European Union.

[59] Assistance programmes were also on the agenda of the Sixth Oxford Conference, an annual, informal gathering of export control experts. It includes countries such as China, which participates in 1 export control regime, and Israel and Serbia, which do not participate in any. The 2004 conference was held in London on 8–10 Nov. 2004. Some presentations are available at URL <http://www.exportcontrol.org/index.php/pagetype/pastconferences/id/1379/itemid/2145.html>.

[60] European Commission, 'Communication from the Commission: European Neighbourhood Policy Strategy Paper', document no. COM(2004) 373 final, Brussels, 12 May 2004, URL <http://www.europa.eu.int/comm/world/enp/document_en.htm>.

Appendix 17A. US export controls

MATTHEW SCHROEDER and RACHEL STOHL

I. Introduction

The United States is the world's largest arms exporter, claiming nearly 57 per cent of the global arms market in 2003.[1] The USA has considerable influence over the global arms trade because of the size of its market share and its diplomatic, military and economic resources. It is therefore important to understand the US arms export control system. This appendix describes US arms export controls, summarizes recent changes to these controls and outlines key issues and debates.

Section II sets out the legislative and regulatory foundation of US arms export programmes and explains how these programmes are administered by the departments of State, Defense and Homeland Security. Particular attention is given to the processes used to review requests for arms sales. Section III describes US end-use monitoring policies and programmes. Section IV highlights the importance of oversight and transparency in arms export programmes through a brief overview of the roles played by the US Congress, civil society and the Government Accountability Office (GAO). Section V examines two particularly significant developments in US defence trade policy—International Traffic in Arms Regulations (ITAR) licensing exemptions and the 'global war on terrorism' launched by the Administration of President George W. Bush. Section VI discusses the future of US defence trade policy and export controls.

II. Controlling exports of defence items and services

There are five main mechanisms through which US arms are transferred to other countries. The two most common are Foreign Military Sales (FMS), which are government-to-government deals, and Direct Commercial Sales (DCS), which are sales negotiated directly between US companies and foreign buyers. The other three are leases of military equipment, the transfer of excess defence items and emergency drawdowns of Department of Defense (DOD) stocks. The USA exports around $20 billion in defence items and services through these five avenues each year.[2]

Legislation, regulations and presidential directives

Most US arms sales are governed by the 1976 Arms Export Control Act and the 1961 Foreign Assistance Act.[3] The Arms Export Control Act authorizes the president to

[1] Grimmett, R. F., US Congress, Congressional Research Service (CRS), *Conventional Arms Transfers to Developing Nations 1996–2003*, CRS Report for Congress RL32547 (US Government Printing Office: Washington, DC, 26 Aug. 2004).

[2] Grimmett (note 1). The five-year moving average for US deliveries in 1999–2003 is $20 billion.

[3] The 1961 Foreign Assistance Act (PL87-195) is available on the Internet site of the Federation of American Scientists at URL <http://www.fas.org/asmp/resources/govern/faa01.pdf>. The 1976 Arms Export Control Act (PL90-629) is available on the Internet site of the Federation of American Scientists at URL <http://www.fas.org/asmp/resources/govern/aeca01.pdf>.

sell and lease defence items, establishes limitations on the use of these items, prohibits their export to certain end-users and requires the establishment of export controls. It also contains several congressional reporting requirements, including a requirement to notify Congress in advance of any major arms sale.[4] Through Executive Order 11958,[5] the president delegates most of these functions to the Department of State and the DOD. The departments of Commerce and the Treasury are also given roles.

The Foreign Assistance Act sets out the processes and procedures for providing foreign aid, including military assistance, to foreign countries. Particularly relevant to arms exports are sections 502, 503, 506 and 516. Section 502 specifies the purposes for which defence items and services may be provided and prohibits their distribution to governments that engage in 'consistent pattern[s] of gross violations of internationally recognized human rights'. Section 503 authorizes the president to provide military assistance to foreign countries, including loans and grants for the procurement of defence items and services. Sections 506 and 516 authorize two of the five major categories of US arms transfers—drawdowns and excess defence items.[6]

International Traffic in Arms Regulations

Transfers of defence items and services are regulated by the International Traffic in Arms Regulations. The ITAR implement existing US laws, including the Arms Export Control Act. It lays out the rules, requirements and procedures for (*a*) registering manufacturers, exporters and brokers of defence items; (*b*) licensing the import and export of defence items, including technical data and classified defence items; and (*c*) manufacturing defence items abroad. The ITAR sets out the penalties for violating its rules and requirements, and identifies the countries and other entities that are prohibited from receiving US defence items and services. It also contains the US Munitions List (USML).

The USML identifies those items and services that are specifically designed or modified for a military application and that: (*a*) have no predominantly civil applications; or (*b*) have civil applications but also have 'significant military or intelligence applicability'. Items with both military and civilian uses are controlled by the Department of Commerce.[7] The Department of State, with input from the DOD, determines which items are on the USML. All USML items are subject to the ITAR, and all commercial sales of these items—with a handful of exceptions—require an export licence from the State Department. The US Congress has an oversight role in that relevant congressional committees must be notified at least 30 days in advance of the removal of any item from the USML.

Questions about whether items are covered by the USML, and requests by US companies to have an item transferred from the USML to the Department of Com-

[4] For more information see Lumpe, L. and Donarski, J., *The Arms Trade Revealed: A Guide for Investigators and Activists* (Federation of American Scientists Arms Sales Monitoring Project: Washington, DC, 1998).

[5] Executive Order 11958 is available on the Internet site of the Federation of American Scientists at URL <http://www.fas.org/asmp/resources/govern/eo-11958.htm>.

[6] The 1961 Foreign Assistance Act (note 3).

[7] These items were formerly regulated by the Export Administration Act (EAA), administered by the Bureau of Industry and Security at the Department of Commerce. Since the EAA expired in 1994, dual-use items have been regulated by the International Emergency Economic Powers Act, which gives the president 'temporary authority to continue controls and most enforcement activities'. Attempts to pass an updated version of the EAA in the first term of the Bush Administration failed.

merce's Commerce Control List (CCL), are settled by the Commodity Jurisdiction Procedure laid out in the ITAR. The State Department coordinates the determinations, which are made in consultation with the Department of Commerce, the DOD, other government agencies and the defence industry. State Department officials have the final say in any dispute, and only they can change the jurisdiction of an item.[8]

Over the past several years, defence industry groups and others have pushed for changes to the USML and the Commodity Jurisdiction Procedure in an attempt to expedite—or perhaps bypass—the State Department's licensing and review processes. Some analysts fear that these efforts will result in the deregulation of significant USML items but, thus far, changes to the USML have been minimal. The State Department's Directorate of Defense Trade Controls (DDTC) has published the results of its review of nine USML categories and only a handful of items have been removed.[9] However, revisions to several categories—including those categories of greatest concern to arms control analysts—have not yet been made public.

Presidential directives

In addition to the abovementioned laws and regulations, the White House makes and amends defence trade policy through presidential directives. Executive Order 11958 delegated presidential authority over arms exports to the Departments of Defense, State, Commerce and Treasury. Presidential Decision Directive 34 set out President Bill Clinton's conventional arms export policy, which added commercial concerns ('[t]he impact on US industry and the defense industrial base') to the list of criteria used to guide decision making about arms exports.[10] Most recently, directives issued by the Bush Administration waived sanctions against India and Pakistan[11]—paving the way for hundreds of millions of dollars in arms sales to both countries—and authorized President Bush's comprehensive review of defence trade controls.[12]

The Department of State

The State Department administers and regulates the export and temporary import of US defence items and services through its Political–Military Affairs Bureau. The Bureau's 130-person DDTC registers arms manufacturers, brokers and exporters; conducts individual reviews of over 50 000 requests for arms export licences that it

[8] US General Accounting Office (GAO), *Export Controls: Processes for Determining Proper Control of Defense-Related Items Need Improvement*, GAO-02-996 (GAO: Washington, DC, 20 Sep. 2002), p. 4. GAO reports are available in a searchable database at URL <http://www.gao.gov/docsearch/repandtest.html>. The GAO became the Government Accountability Office in July 2004.

[9] Amendments to the USML are published in the *Federal Register*, URL <http://www.gpoaccess.gov/fr/index.html>.

[10] The White House, Office of the Press Secretary, 'Fact sheet: criteria for decision-making on US arms exports', Washington, DC, 17 Feb. 1995, available at URL <http://www.fas.org/asmp/resources/govern/whcrit.html>. Presidential Decision Directive 34 remains US conventional arms policy because the Bush Administration has not published a new directive.

[11] See White House, Office of the Press Secretary, 'White House memo for the Secretary of State on waiver of nuclear-related sanctions on India and Pakistan,' 23 Sep. 2001, URL <http://www.fas.org/terrorism/at/docs/2001/Ind-PakWaiver.htm> and US Department of State, Office of the Spokesman, 'Fact sheet: sanctions on Pakistan and India', 28 Sep. 2001, URL <http://www.fas.org/terrorism/at/docs/2001/Ind-PakSanctions.htm>.

[12] The White House, Office of the Press Secretary, 'Fact sheet: Bush Administration review of defense trade export policy and national security', 21 Nov. 2002, URL<http://www.fas.org/asmp/campaigns/control/DTPolicyReview%20-%20Revised.htm>.

receives annually; and monitors the end-use of defence items licensed for export.[13] It also maintains the USML and enforces US and United Nations (UN) arms embargoes. The Office of Regional Security and Arms Transfers works with the DOD to review requests for government-to-government sales.

Companies that wish to export arms through the Direct Commercial Sales programme must first register with the DDTC. Even after a company has registered, it must still submit an individual licence application for most commercial sales. When the application is received by the DDTC, it is assigned to a licensing officer. The licensing officer checks to see if the applicant or other parties to the sale are on a watch list of debarred parties or other Arms Export Control Act violators and determines if an inter-agency review of the application is required. Cases that require inter-agency review (so-called staffed cases) are distributed to the relevant stakeholders, such as the DOD and the State Department regional bureaux, each of which provides feedback based on its expertise and unique perspective. Congress must also be notified if the application is for a major arms sale (i.e., a sale that exceeds specific dollar-value thresholds).[14] After input from the DOD and other State Department offices is received—and provided that Congress has raised no objections—the licensing officer reviews the sale once more:

> in light of these comments to determine whether it is consistent with the foreign policy and national security interests of the United States and then approves or disapproves the request. Many exports are approved subject to specific provisions (called provisos). All exports of defence articles or services are subject to a requirement that the recipient not retransfer the item or change its end-use without the prior written consent of the United States Government.[15]

Issues and recent developments

The most significant set of changes to US arms export policy since the end of the cold war is the Defense Trade Security Initiative (DTSI)—a collection of 17 proposals launched by the Clinton Administration in May 2000. The proposals are aimed at streamlining the licensing process and reducing the time needed to export defence items and services to some of the USA's closest allies (Australia, Japan, Sweden and the member states of the North Atlantic Treaty Organization, NATO). The DOD and the State Department argued that the changes would help 'make allied military forces more capable and interoperable with US forces' by eliminating some of the barriers to cooperative defence projects.[16] Proposals include the creation of a 'single, comprehensive export authorization to permit qualified US defence companies to exchange a broad set of technical data necessary for team arrangements, joint ventures, mergers, acquisitions, or similar arrangements with qualified foreign firms from NATO, Japan

[13] US Department of State, 'End-use monitoring of defense articles and defense services: commercial exports', Washington, DC, available at URL <http://www.pmdtc.org/docs/End_Use_FY2003.pdf>.

[14] The dollar-value threshold for notifications of major defence equipment is currently $14 million and thresholds for other sales are currently $50 million. Major defense equipment is defined in the Arms Export Control Act as any item of significant military equipment on the US Munitions List having a non-recurring research and development cost of more than $200 million.

[15] Senior State Department official, Correspondence with the authors, 26 Jan. 2005.

[16] Senior State Department official, Correspondence with the authors, 26 Jan. 2005.

or Australia',[17] and proposal no. 7, which expedites the review of licence applications for exports related to NATO's Defense Capabilities Initiative (DCI).

Several of the DTSI proposals have already been implemented and others are in progress. The State Department has implemented proposal no. 17, which calls for four-year reviews of the USML. In 2002 the department also approved the first use of a Global Project Authorization (GPA). The GPA, which was approved for the Joint Strike Fighter programme, allowed more than 400 defence companies in eight countries, including the USA, to cooperate on specific technologies based on a single authorization.[18] Progress on other proposals has been much slower. Efforts by the State Department to extend arms export licensing waivers to Australia and the United Kingdom have been blocked by opposition from Congress (see section VI below).

Promises to reform export controls were set aside by the Bush Administration after the 11 September 2001 terrorist attacks on the USA.[19] Only sporadic progress was made on defence trade initiatives during the rest of the first Bush term. The Bush Administration did launch a comprehensive review of defence trade controls—commonly referred to as NSPD-19 after the presidential order authorizing it. However, shortly after the review was announced, staffing and other resources were diverted to preparations for the invasion of Iraq. The administration reportedly presented preliminary results of the review to key congressional staff in the spring of 2004 but the results have yet to be made public.

The most important accomplishment of the Bush Administration during its first term was the organizational overhaul of the State Department's Office of Defense Trade Controls. The new Directorate of Defense Trade Controls: (*a*) created four new Offices (Policy, Licensing, Compliance, and Management); (*b*) doubled the number of licensing officers; (*c*) increased resources for compliance; and (*d*) introduced a new system for processing licences that imposes deadlines on licensing officers and a public outreach team to address industry complaints about transparency.[20] The DDTC is also completing work on a new electronic licensing system (D-Trade), which automatically checks all entities associated with an export against the watchlist and 'will allow staff to spend more time on the case rather than the case spending time in the mail room'.[21] Average processing times for staffed licence requests have dropped to within a few days of the 45-day target proposed by the Aerospace Industry Association—one of the most vocal critics of the licensing system.[22] State Department officials predict that full implementation of D-Trade will reduce processing times even further.[23]

[17] Stohl, R., Centre for Defence Information, 'US changes arms export policy', *Weekly Defense Monitor*, 1 June 2000.

[18] Armitage, R., 'Security cooperation in a post 9-11 world', Remarks at the 2002 Defense Security Cooperation Agency Conference, 17 Oct. 2002, Washington, DC, available at URL <http://fas.org/asmp/campaigns/control/Armitage-DSCA-17oct02.html>; and Senior State Department official, Correspondence with the authors, 26 Jan. 2005.

[19] Matthews, W., 'Powell leaves scant export-control legacy', *Defense News*, 22 Nov. 2004.

[20] Senior State Department official, Correspondence with the authors, 26 Jan. 2005.

[21] Senior State Department official, Interview with the authors, 10 Nov. 2004.

[22] Aerospace Industries Association, 'Proposed changes to the export control system', 25 July 2001, available at URL <http://www.aia-aerospace.org/issues/subject/export_control_changes.pdf>.

[23] See US Department of State, Defense Trade Advisory Group, 'Minutes of the December 2003 plenary session of the Defense Trade Advisory Group', 17 Dec. 2003, URL <http://pmdtc.org/dtag_index.htm>.

The Department of Defense

The DOD plays several important roles in the export control process. It assists with the development of export control procedures and regulations for the State and Commerce departments' licensing review programmes, provides the State and Commerce departments with technical assessments of licensing requests and Commodity Jurisdiction Determinations, and participates in the four-year review of the USML. The DOD's biggest role, however, is to administer and implement Security Assistance Programs, including the FMS programme.

The Foreign Military Sales programme

The FMS programme allows foreign governments and international institutions to acquire US defence items and services directly from the US Government, either from DOD stocks or under DOD-awarded contracts. The DOD uses a 'total package approach' to ensure that FMS purchasers can obtain the support items and services needed to integrate and maintain equipment.

Before a country can participate in the FMS programme, the president must certify that the prospective purchaser is eligible. The US Arms Export Control Act limits arms sales to countries where such a transfer would strengthen US national security. Potential recipients must also agree to: (*a*) use items only for authorized purposes; (*b*) provide security for the item that is comparable to that which it would receive in the USA; and (*c*) seek US permission before re-transferring the items. The US Government could suspend or terminate participation in the FMS programme if a country violates these requirements.[24]

Individual FMS transfers begin with a written request from an official representative of the purchaser government, a letter of request (LOR), for a specific defence item or service or for information about a potential purchase (e.g. the price and availability of US defence items or services). LORs are sent to the appropriate Military Department (MILDEP) or defense agency and copies are sent to various offices and agencies in the DOD and the State Department.

On receiving the LOR, the MILDEP or the Defense Agency becomes the implementing agency (IA) and begins shepherding the request through the FMS system. The IA checks to make sure that the potential recipient is eligible to receive the requested items and enters it as a Customer Request into the Defense Security Assistance Management System. The IA then compiles the information used to write a letter of offer and acceptance (LOA). The LOA is a government-to-government agreement and contains terms and conditions limiting the use and transfer of the items and services to be sold.

After the IA has drafted the LOA, it is normally sent to the Defense Security Cooperation Agency (DSCA). Final approval by the State Department is also sought at this point. After the State Department approves the sale, DSCA electronically countersigns the LOA and forwards it to the IA, which signs it and sends it to the purchaser. The authorization process is complete when the purchaser signs the LOA. The length of time taken to deliver the requested items and services depends on their

[24] Actions that can result in the suspension or termination of FMS programme eligibility include: (*a*) diverting economic aid to military spending; (*b*) aiding or abetting terrorists; (*c*) failing to combat narcotics trafficking; and (*d*) violating the terms of FMS agreements. For more information see US Department of Defense, 'Security Assistance Management Manual', DOD 5105.38-M, 3 Oct. 2003 (incorporating e-changes 18–23 Oct. 2004), chapter 4.2.4, URL <http://www.dsca.mil/samm>.

availability and complexity. Weapon systems and platforms that must be manufactured usually take the longest to be delivered.

Certain FMS requests are subjected to greater scrutiny. Requests for major defence equipment[25] require the preparation of a 'Country Team Assessment', whereby officials from the local embassy and Security Assistance Office (SAO) determine whether a potential sale is consistent with the purposes of the Arms Export Control Act and other export criteria. The assessment must also include an end-use monitoring and verification plan for 'sensitive and advanced war-fighting technology' and—if the request would introduce new military technology into the country or region—an assessment from the Combatant Commander concurring with the proposed sale.[26]

FMS requests that require Congressional notifications are also subjected to special scrutiny. DSCA must notify Congress of major arms sales up to 30 days in advance of signing the LOA, and Congress can block the sale by passing a joint resolution of disapproval (see section IV below). Sales that require congressional notification are subjected to intense review by the State Department as well. Before the request is forwarded to Congress, it is reviewed by officials from the State Department Legislative Affairs Office; the Office of the Undersecretary for Arms Control and International Security; the relevant regional bureau; the Bureau of Democracy, Human Rights and Labor Affairs, one of the four bureaux that comprise the Office of the Under Secretary for Global Affairs; and the office of the Undersecretary for Political Affairs. When applicable, the bureaux of Nonproliferation, Arms Control, and International Narcotics Control and Law Enforcement; and the National Security Council also review these requests.[27]

Issues and recent developments

Since 1998, most significant changes to the FMS process have stemmed from former Deputy Secretary of Defense John Hamre's 'FMS Reinvention', the primary aim of which was to reform administrative and financial processes. Nonetheless, the DOD has enacted several regulatory changes to the FMS process that have strengthened export controls. For example, it sought to improve compliance with the Missile Technology Control Regime (MTCR) by: (*a*) requiring technical reviews of each LOA to identify items controlled by the MTCR; (*b*) developing a course on MTCR guidelines for personnel who draft and review LOAs; and (*c*) adding several items—such as aerosol-dispensing unmanned air vehicles (UAVs)—to the MTCR technical annex.[28]

[25] See note 14.

[26] US Department of Defense (note 24), table C5. T1. Combatant Commanders are the commanders of the 10 unified combatant commands that are assigned operational control over US combat forces.

[27] There are additional reviews and use limitations that are too numerous to summarize adequately in this appendix. For more information see chapter 4 of the Security Assistance Management Manual (note 24).

[28] See Rimpo, B., 'Foreign military sales and the Missile Technology Control Regime: a new focus for the future', *DISAM Journal*, vol. 24, no. 4 (summer 2002), p. 156; and 'Nonproliferation: assessing missile technology export controls', Testimony of Lisa Bronson, Deputy Under Secretary of Defense for Technology Security Policy and Counterproliferation, before the Committee on Government Reform, Subcommittee on National Security, Emerging Threats and International Relations, House of Representatives, 108th Congress, 9 Mar. 2004, URL <http://fas.org/asmp/campaigns/control/BronsonTestimony9march04.pdf>. For a discussion of the MTCR see chapter 17.

Other departments

In addition to the DOD and the Department of State, several other departments and agencies play various roles in the control of US arms exports. The intelligence community provides input on alleged diversions and unauthorized transfers. Similarly, the US Department of Justice and the US Attorneys prepare court cases against violators of arms export laws.[29] The Department of Homeland Security monitors arms shipments at the border and works closely with the State Department to enforce the Arms Export Control Act. Its agents collect and check export documents at the point of departure, inspect outgoing shipments of USML items, seize and detain unauthorized exports, and investigate possible violations of US export controls.[30] In 2004 the Department of Homeland Security's Immigration and Customs Enforcement (ICE), which is the lead investigative agency on violations of US arms export laws, worked on over 2500 investigations, brought 102 indictments and made 146 arrests.[31]

One of the most important recent initiatives by the Department of Homeland Security is 'Project Shield America', through which the department has stepped up investigations and prosecutions of illegal shipments of arms and dual-use items, compiled a list of weapons and other sensitive items of particular interest to terrorists and engaged in extensive outreach to US manufacturers and distributors of such items. ICE officials educate these firms about US export controls and teach them how to spot attempts by potential terrorists to acquire their products. Since 2001, ICE has completed more than 10 000 industry outreach visits.[32]

III. End-use monitoring

The GAO defines end-use monitoring (EUM) as 'the procedures used to verify that foreign governments are using and controlling US defence items and services in accordance with US terms and conditions of the transfer'.[33] Like arms export licensing, end-use monitoring is implemented by numerous government agencies.

The Department of State

The State Department is responsible for monitoring the end-use of commercial exports, which it accomplishes through: (*a*) registering arms exporters and reviewing requests for arms export licences, as described above; (*b*) outreach to defence companies;[34] and (*c*) the Blue Lantern Program.

[29] US Department of State, Directorate of Defense Trade Controls, 'The Directorate of Defense Trade Controls and the defense trade function: an overview', URL <http://pmdtc.org/docs/ddtc_overview.doc>.

[30] US Department of State, Directorate of Defense Trade Controls, International Traffic in Arms Regulations, Part 127, Section 127.4, URL <http://pmdtc.org/reference.htm>.

[31] US Department of State, Immigration and Customs Enforcement, 'Fact sheet: select ICE arms and strategic technology investigations', Washington, DC, Dec. 2004.

[32] US Department of Homeland Security, US Customs and Border Protection, Remarks of Commissioner Robert C. Bonner: Safeguarding America, Washington, DC, 3 June 2002, URL <http://www.customs.ustreas.gov/xp/cgov/newsroom/commissioner/speeches_statements/jun032002.xml>.

[33] US General Accounting Office (GAO), *Foreign Military Sales: Changes Needed to Correct Weaknesses in End-Use Monitoring Program*, GAO/NSIAD-00-208 (GAO: Washington, DC, Aug. 2000), p. 3 (see note 8).

[34] Recognizing that arms exporters are the 'first line of defense against illicit exports', the State Department developed and disseminated a set of 20 warning flags to be used by companies to spot

The Blue Lantern Program, which was established in 1990, consists of various end-use checks that State Department compliance and licensing officers can initiate in response to suspicious licence requests or reports of end-use violations. The checks are usually performed by personnel assigned to US consular and diplomatic posts with the assistance of host government officials.[35] There are two primary categories of Blue Lantern checks: (*a*) pre-licence checks and (*b*) post-shipment verifications. Each category contains three levels of checks.

Pre-licence checks

Pre-licence checks are used to check the reliability of the end-user and that the end-user will abide by end-use and retransfer provisions. These checks are divided into three levels:

1. A *level one check* is usually conducted in response to reliable information that a diversion may occur. A weapon's sensitivity or military value may also trigger this kind of check, which is often completed with the help of officials from foreign governments.
2. A *level two check* is carried out when significant reasons exist to undertake a check, usually because of past company violations or other reports.
3. A *level three check*, the least serious, is initiated in order to verify the bona fides of a given transaction, and is completed either by government officials or the companies involved in the export. Usually, the purpose is to check the reputation of the recipient company and the legality of it importing the defence item.[36]

Post-shipment verifications

Post-shipment verifications help to ensure that defence items are received by the authorized end-user and are being used in accordance with the provisions in the licence. Post-shipment verifications have three levels of priority:

1. A *level one check* is extremely rare and is initiated in cases where diversion or misuse has probably occurred. This type of check would be very complex and might involve US personnel in various countries.
2. The DDTC places the highest priority on *level two checks*, which are frequently based on information received after the issuance of a licence. Situations that might trigger level two checks include if end-use checks on previous licences issued by the DDTC established that a foreign recipient had been involved in illegal transactions, or if reports of diversions had been received. This type of check may also entail a visual inspection.
3. The most common post-shipment end-use checks, *level three checks,* are conducted when there are questions about an export but the concerns are not serious enough to deny the licence request. This concern could be because a company or entity named may not have been a party to a previous transaction, because the

potentially risky transfers. Burke, F., *How Little is Enough? US End-Use Monitoring and Oversight of the Weapons Trade* (Centre for Defence Information: Washington, DC, Jan. 2002).

[35] Burke (note 34).

[36] Burke (note 34), p. 53

defence item is particularly sensitive or because the item has been sent to a country where the potential for diversion is relatively high.[37]

Of the approximately 500 Blue Lantern checks performed each year, several dozen result in 'unfavourable determinations', that is, evidence of end-use violations. Penalties for such violations include denials or revocations of licences, hefty fines and debarment (i.e., ineligibility to export defence items).[38] In fiscal year (FY) 2004 the State Department performed 530 Blue Lantern checks, resulting in an unprecedented 93 unfavourable determinations.[39] Half the checks in FY 2004 were on exports destined for the western hemisphere and Europe, while East and South Asia accounted for 49 per cent of the unfavourable determinations.[40]

Issues and recent developments

In January 2004, the GAO released a report critical of State Department end-use monitoring of cruise missile and UAV exports. The GAO determined that no post-shipment verifications had been conducted on the 480 licences for cruise missiles, UAVs or related items issued between FYs 1998 and 2002, and that only 4 post-shipment verifications were conducted on licences without conditions limiting how the export could be used. Of those four checks, three had resulted in unfavourable determinations.[41] The State Department argued that so few checks were conducted because the items were exported to friendly governments for their own defence forces. However, according to the GAO, the countries were also potential proliferation risks—'129 of the 786 licences authorized the transfer of cruise missile and UAV-related items to countries such as Egypt, Israel, and India. These countries are not MTCR members, which indicates that they might pose a higher risk of diversion'.[42]

The State Department criticized the GAO report for downplaying the importance of the 'licensing process as a whole' in preventing diversions and unauthorized retransfers. The State Department argued that the report's analysis was 'flawed' because it 'took a snapshot of Blue Lantern activity without regard to past reviews of the parties to these exports and without regard to other checks performed during the license process'.[43] The GAO agreed with the State Department about the importance of pre-licence checks but also stressed their limitations. Pre-licence checks can confirm neither that the intended recipient received the export nor that the recipient complied with limitations on their use. The GAO further argued that the State Department performed few pre-licence checks on UAV and Cruise missile exports.

During a congressional hearing held shortly after the release of the GAO report, State Department official Robert Maggi called attention to recent steps taken by the USA to address the cruise missile proliferation threat. According to Maggi, the State Department clarified its controls on UAVs, updated US regulations to conform with

[37] Burke (note 34), pp. 54–55.

[38] Senior State Department official, Correspondence with the authors, 26 Jan. 2005.

[39] Senior State Department official, Correspondence with the authors, 28 Jan. 2005.

[40] Senior State Department official, Correspondence with the authors, 26 Jan. 2005.

[41] US General Accounting Office (GAO), *Nonproliferation: Improvements Needed to Better Control Technology Exports for Cruise Missiles and Unmanned Aerial Vehicles*, GAO-04-175 (GAO: Washington, DC, 23 Jan. 2004), p. 28 (see note 8).

[42] US General Accounting Office (note 41), p. 29.

[43] US General Accounting Office (note 41), p. 54.

the MTCR's range and payload parameters for UAVs,[44] and initiated 18 Blue Lantern checks on UAV-related cases in FY 2004.[45]

The Department of Defense

The DOD's EUM activities cover exported items throughout their life cycle—from 'cradle to grave'. These activities can be divided into three categories—pre-sale, in-transit and post-transfer.

Pre-sale processes

The DOD's first line of defence against unauthorized use or retransfer of items exported via the FMS programme is the pre-sale system of certifications, checks and notifications summarized in Section II. DOD officials interviewed for this appendix repeatedly underlined the importance of pre-sale processes for preventing unauthorized end-use. In the words of one official, 'before [the] LOA has even been signed, there is an enormous amount of upfront work that is done to take a look at what the article is, whose going to get it [and] why they want it'.[46]

In-transit processes

The risk of in-transit diversion is addressed through regulations on the transportation of FMS items. In all cases, the mode of shipment must be identified in the LOA and, if the recipient uses a freight forwarder,[47] the freight forwarder must be licensed and registered with the State Department.[48] Special requirements apply to the shipment of classified items and sensitive arms, ammunition and explosives (AA&E).[49] For example, shipments of certain sensitive AA&E must be: (*a*) transported in special containers that are checked, locked and sealed by two agents of the shipper; (*b*) inspected in transit; and (*c*) processed through military-operated or DOD-approved air and ocean terminals.[50]

[44] Statement by Robert W. Maggi, Directorate of Defence Trade Controls, US Department of State before the Subcommittee on National Security, Emerging Threats, and International Relations, Committee on Government Reform, House of Representatives, 9 Mar. 2004, available at URL <http://fas.org/asmp/campaigns/control/MaggiTestimony 9march04.pdf>.

[45] Senior State Department official, Correspondence with the authors, 28 Jan. 2005.

[46] Department of Defense officials, Interviews with the authors, 28 Oct. 2004.

[47] The US Defense Logistics Management Standards Office defines a freight forwarder as '[a]ny agent designated by a foreign country to receive, process and transship security assistance program matériel/documentation'. US Department of Defense, Military Assistance Program Address Directory (MAPAD), report no. DoD 4000.25-8-M, URL <http://www.dla.mil/j-6/dlmso/eLibrary/Manuals/MAPAD/mapad.asp>.

[48] Written Statement of Lt. Gen. Tome H. Walters Jr, USAF Director, Defense Security Cooperation Agency before the Committee on Government Reform, Subcommittee on National Security, Emerging Threats, and International Relations, House of Representatives, 9 Mar. 2004, URL <http://fas.org/asmp/campaigns/control/WaltersTestimony9march04.pdf>.

[49] Sensitive arms, ammunition and explosives include certain small arms and light weapons, ammunition, explosives and other items such as night vision goggles that 'pose a special danger to the public if they fall into the wrong hands'.

[50] US Department of Defense, Assistant Secretary of Defense for Command, Control, Communications and Intelligence, 'Physical security of sensitive conventional arms, ammunition, and explosives', 12 Aug. 2000, pp. 35–36, available at URL <http://www.dtic.mil/whs/directives/corres/pdf/510076m_0800/p51007m.pdf>.

Post-shipment processes

Ensuring that recipients comply with use and retransfer terms after they take possession of defence items is accomplished through the Golden Sentry end-use monitoring programme. Golden Sentry officials work with the Combatant Commands, SAOs and foreign governments to establish inventory and reporting procedures, monitor compliance with end-use requirements and investigate possible end-use violations. There are two levels of end-use monitoring: 'routine' and 'enhanced'. Routine EUM is performed when the recipient is a 'presupposed trusted partner' and is completed in conjunction with other activities. Enhanced EUM is reserved for particularly sensitive items (e.g., communication security equipment, night vision devices, cruise missile and UAV technologies as well as STINGER, AIM-120, JAVELIN, and TOW II-B missiles), defence items provided through grant assistance programmes and transfers of defence items in 'sensitive political situations'.[51]

A cornerstone of the Golden Sentry programme is the system of in-country visits used to 'assess and evaluate' EUM compliance. These visits are divided into three categories: (*a*) EUM familiarization visits; (*b*) EUM Tiger Team visits; and (*c*) EUM investigation visits. DSCA uses familiarization visits to help host nations and the US officials working with them to develop EUM compliance plans and to lay the groundwork for Tiger Team visits. Tiger Team visits are used to assess compliance by SAOs and host nations with end-use requirements. Investigation visits are conducted in response to possible or actual violations of US end-use laws.[52]

Finally, the DOD works with host governments to develop plans for the disposal of defence items at the end of their life cycle. US personnel monitor the disposal to ensure that it complies with US Government standards—and are required to report any failures to comply with these standards.

Issues and recent developments

The DOD end-use monitoring system has changed significantly over the past five years. The most notable development is the establishment of the Golden Sentry programme, which is expanding its size and activities each year. Since DSCA hired the programme's first full time staff member in June 2002, Golden Sentry has added a full time contractor and another full time civilian employee, and has allocated funding for three more civilian employees in 2005. Five Tiger Team assessment visits have been conducted—two in 2003 and three in 2004. There were also five familiarization visits in 2004, including three visits that were supported by the Defense Threat Reduction Agency's On-Site Inspection Directorate. A Golden Sentry handbook is being produced, and upgrades to DSCA's Security Cooperation Information 'Portal' will reportedly allow officials to track sensitive items from initial shipment to final disposal. Also noteworthy is a recent policy memorandum that provides—in great detail—deadlines, checklists and other guidance for Tiger Team inspections. The procedures for inspecting Stinger missiles are particularly detailed.[53]

[51] US Department of Defense, Defense Security Cooperation Agency, 'End use monitoring responsibilities in support of the Department of Defense Golden Sentry EUM Program', Policy Memorandum no. 02-43, Washington, DC, 4 Dec. 2002.

[52] For more information on the 3 types of visits see US Department of Defense, Defense Security Cooperation Agency, 'Golden Sentry end-use monitoring (EUM) visit policy', Policy Memorandum no. 04-11, Washington, DC, 2 Apr. 2004.

[53] 'Our goal is to establish similar standards for all defence articles that encompass the Enhanced EUM category'. Senior defense official, Communication with the authors, 4 Nov. 2004.

Despite these and other accomplishments, the DOD is, in the words of former DSCA Director Tome Walters, 'still in the process of fully putting [Golden Sentry] procedures in place throughout the Security Assistance Community'.[54] Two studies conducted by the GAO in 2004 highlight some of the challenges that still confront the programme. The first study, which focuses on US efforts to control US missile technology exports, found no evidence of DOD end-use checks, 'routine or otherwise', on the 500 cruise missiles and related items approved for export between 1998 and 2002.[55] The second report revealed problems with record keeping and inventory inspections of exported Stinger missiles.[56] DSCA has taken steps to implement the GAO's recommendations, including adding cruise missiles and UAVs to the list of exports subject to enhanced EUM, creating a course on the requirements of the MTCR as it applies to US missile and UAV exports, and working towards the establishment of a centralized electronic database for tracking Stinger and other enhanced EUM items throughout their lifecycle.[57]

IV. Oversight and transparency

The role of the US Congress

The Arms Export Control Act assigns Congress the task of overseeing defence export controls and the licensing process. Of particular importance is Section 36, which requires the DOD and the Department of State to formally notify Congress of potential arms sales that exceed certain dollar-value thresholds.[58] The Arms Export Control Act also gives Congress the power to block a proposed sale, although the barriers to doing so are nearly insurmountable. According to David Fite, a veteran staff member of the US House of Representatives Committee on International Relations:

> [I]t is extremely difficult for Congress to legally prevent any sale. In order to do so, both chambers must pass identical joint resolutions of disapproval within the specified time periods. . . . In the Senate, a resolution of disapproval must come to the Senate floor for consideration, and will automatically be discharged from the SFRC [Senate Foreign Relations Committee] within five days, whether or not the SFRC acts upon it. In the House, however, a resolution of disapproval may never be brought up for consideration, as there is no procedure in the Arms Export Control Act for automatic discharge from the International Relations Committee to the House floor. If such a resolution were reported out of the International Relations Committee, it would proceed quickly to consideration by the House as a privileged matter. In any case, simple majority passage by both chambers would be insufficient to disapprove a sale. The joint resolution . . . must be signed into law by the president—whose administration is proposing the sale in the first place. Therefore, a resolution of disapproval

[54] Written Statement of Lt. Gen. Tome H. Walters Jr (note 48).

[55] According to the General Accounting Office, 'the [Golden Sentry] program director stated that he was unaware of any end-use monitoring checks, routine or otherwise, for transferred US cruise missiles over the period of our review'. US General Accounting Office (note 41), p. 27.

[56] US General Accounting Office (GAO), *Further Improvements needed in US Efforts to Counter Threats from Man-Portable Air Defense Systems*, GAO-04-519 (GAO: Washington, DC, 13 May 2004), see note 8.

[57] Written Statement of Lt. Gen. Tome H. Walters, Jr (note 48).

[58] State Department official, Correspondence with authors, 1 Feb. 2005. Relevant House and Senate Committees are given an indefinite period of time in pre-official notification consultations to review the sale and ask questions.

must pass both chambers, within 15 or 30 days, by two-thirds majority to be able to override an expected presidential veto.[59]

Nonetheless, if Congress has serious objections to a sale, the administration rarely pursues it.[60] According to Fite, 'Congress' real oversight authority for arms sales lies in its ability to pass legislation affecting the manner by which new sales are considered and to take actions that will raise the political cost of the sale itself'.[61] There are many recent examples of Congress prohibiting potentially problematic arms sales, and publicizing the executive branch proposals. Throughout the 1990s, Congress inserted a provision in the annual foreign affairs appropriations legislation that prohibited the transfer of Stinger Missiles to the Gulf States, except to replace old missiles. Congress can also deter through the threat of punishment, as exemplified by House of Representatives Chairman Henry Hyde's use of Committee hearings to thwart the Bush Administration's arms export reform initiatives (see section V).

Public reporting of arms transfers

Each year, the State Department, DOD and the Library of Congress compile detailed reports on US arms transfers and arms export programmes. Many of these reports are made available to the public through the issuing agencies' Internet sites. Others are acquired by non-governmental organizations (NGOs), either informally—through their government contacts—or under the Freedom of Information Act. Data provided in these reports are supplemented by the dozens of congressional notifications of major arms sales issued each year.

Together, government reports and congressional notifications provide a solid overview of US defence exports. Using the DOD's FMS Facts Book, for example, it is possible to determine the dollar value of all FMS sales worldwide, regionally and to individual countries in a given year. The annual '655 report' provides a summary—broken down by USML category—of defence items and services exported (or licensed for export) to each country.[62] Congressional notifications provide the most detailed snapshot of individual arms transfers, but only for the small percentage of sales that exceed the dollar-value thresholds.

Issues and recent developments

Since 2000, most significant changes to reporting requirements have come in the form of adjustments to the dollar-value thresholds for congressional notifications of major arms sales. As mentioned above, these notifications are among the most detailed public sources of government information on FMS and direct commercial

[59] Fite, D., 'A View from Congress', eds. T. Gabelnick and R. Stohl, *Challenging Conventional Wisdom: Debunking the Myths and Exposing the Risks of Arms Export Reform* (Federation of American Scientists and Centre for Defence Information: Washington, DC, 2003), p. 155.

[60] State Department official, Correspondence with the authors, 1 Feb. 2005.

[61] Fite (note 59), p. 155.

[62] The US administration is required by Congress to prepare an annual report on military assistance, military exports and military imports known as the 'Section 655' report—after the section of the Foreign Assistance Act which contains the requirement. The report provides the most detailed official accounting available of specific US weapon systems exported or licensed for export to governments or private buyers around the world. The DOD and the State Department each prepare their own portion of the 655 report. See US Department of State, Report by the Department of State Pursuant to Sec. 655 of the Foreign Assistance Act, available on the Internet site of the Federation of American Scientists, URL <http://www.fas.org/asmp/profiles/worldfms.html#655reps>.

sales—the two largest US arms transfer programmes. The notifications process itself, however, is viewed by some as an impediment to the expeditious and predictable delivery of US defence items. In response to such complaints, Congress increased the dollar-value threshold for notifications of sales to NATO members, Australia, Japan and New Zealand in 2002.[63] In 2003 the SFRC tried unsuccessfully to raise thresholds for notifications to all countries.

Had the Committee's proposal been enacted into law, notification thresholds for all countries would have increased from $14 million to $50 million for major defence equipment, and from $50 million to $100 million for other sales.[64] Had the Senate's proposed thresholds been in place in 2001, Congress would not have been notified of the 2001 sale to Jordan of 110 Javelin anti-tank missile systems—a weapon system that the DOD has singled out for special end-use monitoring. Like the ITAR licensing waivers (see below), opposition from the House of Representatives to the Senate-backed changes is probably sufficient to sideline them for the foreseeable future.

Also notable are the findings of a January 2005 report from the Government Accountability Office on data reliability problems with the State Department's section of the annual 655 report. The problems were discovered during a GAO inquiry into reports that Stinger missiles—which may only be sold through the FMS programme—had been licensed for commercial export by the State Department. The GAO found no evidence of commercial sales of Stinger missile systems. Instead, it concluded that State Department data entry employees had erroneously coded licences for Stinger components (which can be sold commercially) as licences for complete missile systems into the State Department's licensing database.[65] According to the GAO, the errors highlight database design problems, inaccurate reporting practices and miscoding practices that 'call into question the overall reliability of the commercial licensing data in the Section 655 report'.[66]

The State Department disputes GAO claims that the errors were indicative of broader problems with the data. Nonetheless, State Department officials claim that their new D-Trade electronic licensing system addresses many GAO concerns, particularly those related to miscoding. D-Trade may improve transparency in other ways as well. State Department officials claim that by linking D-Trade to the US Customs Service, which collects data on arms transfers at the time of shipment, the department will 'greatly enhance [its] knowledge of what defense goods are actually being exported'.[67] If they are able to convert this improved awareness of commercial

[63] The 2002 Security Assistance Act, Foreign Relations Authorization Act, Fiscal Year 2003, PL 107—228, 107th Congress, 2nd Session, 30 Sept. 2003, URL <http://fas.org/asmp/resources/govern/107th_hr1646pl.pdf>.

[64] Foreign Assistance Authorization Act, Fiscal Year 2004, Section 1161, 108th Congress, 1st Session, 29 May 2003, URL <http://fas.org/asmp/resources/govern/108th/s1161rs.htm>.

[65] The State Department acknowledged the data entry errors for Stinger missiles but claimed that they 'were not numerically significant enough to undermine the overall data reliability in the [655] report.' The Government Accountability Office (GAO) countered that the records for the 200 000 other license applications received for the years reviewed were 'subject to the same opportunity for miscoding and misreporting'. US GAO, *State Department Needs to Resolve Data Reliability Problems that Led to Inaccurate Reporting to Congress on Foreign Arms Sales*, GAO-05-156R (GAO: Washington, DC, 28 Jan. 2005).

[66] US Department of State (note 62), p. 7.

[67] US Department of State, Directorate of Defense Trade Controls, 'Status of US interagency review of US export licensing and technology transfer policy', Remarks by Lincoln P. Bloomfield Jnr, Assistant Secretary for Political–Military Affairs, to the Conference on 'transatlantic defense industrial cooperation: challenges and prospects', Brussels, Belgium, 18 July 2003, URL <http://pmdtc.org/speech_inter_review.htm>.

arms shipments into data on *deliveries* of commercial sales, their annual report on commercial arms transfers would be much improved.

Finally, Congress enacted two new reporting requirements for exports of small arms and light weapons (SALW). The first requires the State Department to include a summary of commercial sales of semi-automatic weapons in the annual Congressional Budget Justification for Foreign Operations. The second is an amendment to the Arms Export Control Act that requires congressional notifications for commercial sales of firearms valued at $1 million or more.

The role of the Government Accountability Office

No organization is more essential to the preservation of transparency and accountability in US arms transfer programmes than the Government Accountability Office. The GAO is an independent, non-partisan agency that investigates and reports on congressional and executive branch agencies and processes. Its 3300 employees publish approximately 1000 reports each year that contain several thousand recommendations for strengthening and reforming the government process.[68] The GAO claims that 83 per cent of the recommendations it has made over the past four years have been implemented,[69] some with dramatic results. Recommendations contained in an August 2000 report, for example, helped prompt DSCA to establish the Golden Sentry EUM programme.[70]

The GAO is often the only source of timely, in-depth analysis on critically important but highly technical defence trade issues—issues that are unlikely to be adequately researched by other government agencies or civil society. The GAO is uniquely suited for this role because of its access to government data and personnel, its large staff and budget, and its mandate to engage in research that is too resource-intensive and esoteric for most journalists and private researchers. It is hard to imagine, for example, a newspaper editor approving a request by a reporter to spend 11 months studying the differences in processing times for export licences between the Commerce and State departments. The GAO report on this topic debunked myths about the State Department's licensing system, thereby helping to balance a largely one-sided debate on export control reform.[71]

The role of civil society

US data on arms are among the most transparent and most widely available in the world. Thousands of pages of data and information on all aspects of the US arms export process are available online to anyone with Internet access. However, only a handful of US academics and NGOs have adopted the arms trade as a key component of their work. These individuals and organizations provide an essential public service. They provide journalists, policy makers and the general public with clear and succinct explanations of defence trade policy and arms export data. They also educate

[68] US General Accounting Office (GAO), *Performance Plan: Fiscal Year 2005*, GAO-04-776SP (GAO: Washington, DC, May 2004), URL <http://www.gao.gov/sp.html>.

[69] US Government Accountability Office, 'GAO at a Glance', URL <http://www.gao.gov/about/gglance.html>.

[70] GAO official, Interview with the authors, Nov. 2004.

[71] US General Accounting Office (GAO), *Export Controls: State and Commerce Department License Review Times are Similar*, GAO-01-528 (GAO: Washington, DC, 1 June 2001), see note 8.

policy makers about the human rights, security and economic implications of US arms export policies.

One of the largest US NGO efforts on the arms trade in recent years was the campaign, led by the Council for a Livable World, Demilitarization for Democracy, the Federation of American Scientists and the Friends Committee on National Legislation, to enact a US arms trade code of conduct. It was intended that the code would prevent US arms being exported to governments that are undemocratic, abuse citizens' human rights, engage in armed aggression or fail to contribute data to the UN Register of Conventional Arms.[72] Several years of sustained effort culminated in the passage of the 1999 International Arms Sales Code of Conduct Act. This provision—which was passed as part of an appropriations bill—required the president to enter into negotiations on an international code of conduct on arms sales within 120 days of the bill's enactment. However, little has been done to implement the requirement.

Since the code of conduct campaign, civil society has focused primarily on media outreach, data gathering and dissemination and, in the parlance of Washington insiders, 'under-the-radar-screen tinkering' with arms export laws, regulations and policies. Examples include consultation and advocacy on behalf of small arms export control legislation, drawing congressional attention to potentially problematic arms sales, exposing behind the scenes policy reforms and ensuring that publicly available reports continue to be produced and to remain unclassified.

V. Current issues in US defence trade policy and arms export controls

The ITAR waivers process and debate

Since 2000, policy makers have proposed several significant changes to the arms export licensing system—many of which are linked to the Clinton Administration's Defense Trade Security Initiative. None of these proposals has generated more controversy or political friction than the extension of ITAR licensing waivers to Australia and the UK. The battle over the waivers illustrates the capacity of individual congressional leaders to thwart policy proposals that they strongly oppose.

ITAR licensing waivers allow persons or entities in the USA that are registered with the State Department to export certain defence items licence-free to countries with which the USA has negotiated bilateral agreements. In order to qualify, US law requires that the country's export controls be 'at least comparable' to US controls in several specific ways. Australia and the UK were selected to be the initial participants in the arrangement because of the general compatibility of their foreign policy and the perceived comparability of their export controls with those of the USA.

In 2003 the State Department completed three years of negotiations on the arrangements with the Australian and British Governments. The resulting agreements permitted US firms to ship certain defence items licence-free to a list of vetted Australian and British companies. In exchange, Australia and the UK agreed to make adjustments to their export controls. The agreements did not fully comply with US law, however, and the State Department sought 'legislative relief' from Congress in the form of a new law that would have amended the Arms Export Control Act to exempt both countries from US requirements. Initial attempts to pass the amendment

[72] For more information on the campaign see Lumpe and Donarski (note 4).

were thwarted by two powerful Congressmen who outflanked the Bush Administration in a high stakes game of election year political chicken.

In early 2003, Richard Lugar, chair of the SFRC, led the first attempt to provide the legislative relief sought by the Bush Administration. His committee's version of the 2003 foreign aid authorization bill contained language that exempted Australia from the ITAR licensing waiver requirements. Smooth passage of the bill required that Senator Lugar's counterpart in the House of Representatives, Henry Hyde, include similar language in his committee's version of the bill. Hyde's version of the bill was silent on the ITAR waivers, requiring mandatory expedited processing of licence requests for Australia and the UK instead. A showdown between the House and the Senate over the differences in the two bills was avoided only because the full Senate failed to pass Lugar's bill.

In 2004 the argument over licensing exemptions reached fever pitch as all sides turned up the rhetorical and political heat.[73] In an unusual move, Senate Committee on Armed Services Chairman John Warner inserted the ITAR waivers amendment language into the DOD authorization bill—a bill over which Hyde had no immediate jurisdiction. However, Duncan Hunter, Senator Warner's counterpart in the House of Representatives, effectively blocked the passage of Warner's amendment by inserting a blanket prohibition on licensing exemptions for significant military equipment into his committee's version of the bill. Hyde, Hunter and Congressman Tom Lantos also released a scathing critique of the licensing exemptions that caught the attention of the media and angered proponents of licensing exemption agreements. The trade journal *Defense News* published an unusually acerbic commentary piece in which they attacked Hunter, Hyde and two of Hyde's staffers by name.[74] Shortly afterwards, the British Government sent a 'stinging' letter to Secretary of Defense Donald Rumsfeld that reportedly threatened to limit US firms' access to British markets if the ITAR exemptions were not granted.[75]

Ultimately, however, Hyde had the better election-year hand. In July, he and Hunter scheduled a joint hearing on 'the Role of Arms Export Policy in the Global War on Terror'. The threat of a 'public hammering of the Pentagon and other officials at the hands of senior members of their own party during an election year'[76] proved too much for the White House and, hours before the hearing was scheduled to begin, the administration agreed to temporarily shelve the ITAR exemptions and other defence trade initiatives if Hyde and Hunter would cancel the hearing.[77]

Proponents of the ITAR waivers agreements with Australia and the UK—and legislative relief from Arms Export Control Act requirements—argue that the exemptions would strengthen export controls by allowing State Department licensing officers to 'concentrate more on high-risk exports' and by prompting foreign governments to strengthen their export controls on US items. An example of the latter is the British Government's commitment to require proof of US Government retransfer consent before allowing British companies to retransfer defence items containing US

[73] Commenting on the intensity of the battle over the exemptions, one analyst said 'I've never seen such bad blood between the White House, the State Department and the House in this all-Republican crowd. If one says "black", the other is going to say "white"'. Donnelly, J., 'GOP splits over liberalization of military technology rules', *Congressional Quarterly*, 25 Oct. 2004.

[74] 'A very low blow', *Defence News*, 14 June 2004, p. 50.

[75] Matthews, W., 'Waffling on trade waivers for the UK', *Defence News*, 2 Aug. 2004, p. 8.

[76] Matthews (note 75).

[77] Matthews (note 75).

components.[78] ITAR waiver proponents also claim that continued failure to grant the exemptions would be diplomatically, militarily and financially damaging. Commenting on the European attitude to the battle over the British ITAR exemptions, the editorial staff at *Defense News* observed that '[o]fficials from across the world said they were closely watching the US stance toward Britain. If Washington is unwilling to treat its closest ally with respect, it is best to keep America at arm's length'.[79]

Critics of the waiver agreements claim that they only increase the risk of arms export diversions and send the wrong message to US allies and the rest of the world. Routine State Department checks on parties to a transfer, which are part of the licensing process, are not performed on exports shipped under the waivers. While recipients would be limited to Australian and British companies vetted by the US Government, other parties to the deal (e.g., freight forwarders and intermediate consignees)[80] would no longer be reviewed by a trained licensing officer prior to shipment.[81] This reduction in US Government scrutiny, critics argue, 'will almost certainly enlarge risks of diversion'.[82] Furthermore, the Australian and British ITAR waiver agreements do not deliver all of the improvements to their export controls required by US law. Hyde bemoaned the absence of legally binding government-to-government commitments on re-export controls, which his office called a 'sine qua non for the benefit of a licensing exemption'.[83] Finally, critics charge that the exemption agreements—the 'single largest deregulatory measure related to armaments involving any country in modern history'—could be used by other arms exporters as a 'pretext for relaxation of control over their sensitive exports'.[84]

The role of arms sales and export controls in the war on terrorism

Since 11 September 2001, the Bush Administration has made extensive use of both arms exports and arms export controls in its global war on terrorism. This approach has resulted in dramatic increases in arms transfers to particular countries and significant national and international efforts to curb the availability and utility of weapon systems sought by terrorists.

In the past three years, military aid and arms sales to the so-called frontline states in the Bush Administration's war on terrorism have increased by several orders of magnitude. The biggest beneficiary has been the Pakistani Government. Prior to 11 September 2001, arms exports and military aid to Pakistan were prohibited by nuclear non-proliferation and anti-military coup provisions in US law. President Bush waived these sanctions in exchange for Pakistan's cooperation in the war against the Taliban and the hunt for Osama bin Laden. Since 2001, Congress has appropriated $1 billion dollars for Pakistan in Foreign Military Financing—funds provided specifi-

[78] US House of Representatives, Committee on International Relations, *US Weapons Technology at Risk: the State Department's Proposal to Relax Arms Export Controls to Other Countries* (US Government Printing Office: Washingon, DC, 2004), pp. 104, 110–11.

[79] 'Don't take UK for granted', *Defence News*, 26 July 2004.

[80] The US Census Bureau defines an intermediate consignee as 'the party in a foreign country who receives and then delivers the merchandise to the ultimate consignee'. US Census Bureau, Foreign Trade Division, Questions & answers relating to the shipper's export declaration, URL <http://www.census.gov/foreign-trade/regulations/forms/qna.html>.

[81] For a more detailed synopsis of Hyde's argument, see his 10 Feb. 2004 letter to Secretary of State Colin Powell in US House of Representatives (note 78), appendix 16.

[82] US House of Representatives (note 78), p. 18.

[83] US House of Representatives (note 78), p. 160.

[84] US House of Representatives (note 78), p. 9.

cally for the purchase US defence items and services.[85] Pakistan has used these funds to buy hundreds of millions of dollars' worth of US weaponry, including Phalanx anti-ship missile systems, surveillance and military transport aircraft, radar, TOW-2A anti-tank missiles and riot control equipment.[86] The connection between these weapons and anti-terrorism is often unclear. The US weapon that Pakistan covets most, however, is the F-16 combat aircraft. The USA sold 28 of these aircraft to Pakistan in the 1980s and was scheduled to deliver 71 more when President George H. W. Bush cut off arms transfers in 1990 in response to Pakistan's ongoing efforts to develop nuclear weapons. Pakistani requests for the aircraft, which have been incessant since the resumption of arms sales in 2001, had been rebuffed by the Bush Administration. However, an F-16 sale to Pakistan was confirmed in March 2005, when it was also announced that F-16s would be supplied to India.[87]

While Pakistan is the largest recipient of war on terrorism-related military aid, other countries have also benefited. Since the ban on arms transfers to India was lifted, India has entered into contracts for US defence items and services worth over $200 million.[88] Several other frontline states, including Djibouti, Kenya and the Philippines, have seen huge increases in their foreign military financing.[89] This aid—and the arms sales it funds—has both immediate and long term benefits for the DOD and US companies. It serves the immediate goal of bolstering the recipient country's capacity to engage in counter-terrorism activities. Foreign Military Financing for Djibouti, for example, was appropriated specifically for the purchase of 'vehicles, small craft and patrol vessels, communications equipment, fencing, guard towers, and night vision goggles . . . [to] help Djibouti secure its borders and coastline from the increased threat of terrorism'.[90] Many weapon systems, particularly sophisticated platforms such as aircraft, require regular investment in new parts, maintenance, and upgrades. These requirements tether the purchaser to the US defence-industrial complex—creating opportunities for the DOD to expand defence cooperation with the recipient and generating years of revenue for US companies.

Since 11 September 2001, the USA has taken several important steps to improve controls on weapons that are particularly deadly in the hands of terrorists. These steps include banning commercial sales of 12.7 mm sniper rifles,[91] and improving export controls on components for UAVs.[92] However, the weapons that have received the most attention from policymakers are shoulder-fired surface-to-air missiles (i.e. man-portable air defence systems, MANPADS).[93] The spectre of a successful attack on

[85] US Department of State (note 13).

[86] Prosser, A. and Stohl, R., 'The need for arms transfer restraint', *Defense News*, 29 Nov. 2004, URL <http://www.defensenews.com/story.php?F=524118&C=commentary>.

[87] Baker, P., 'Bush: US to sell F-16s to Pakistan, reversal, decried by India, is coupled with fighter-jet promise to New Delhi', Washington Post (Online edn), 26 Mar. 2005, p. A01, URL <http://www.washingtonpost.com/wp-dyn/articles/A800-2005Mar25.html>.

[88] US Department of Defense, Defense Security Cooperation Agency, 'Foreign military sales, foreign military construction sales and military assistance: facts as of September 30 2003,' available on the Internet site of the Federation of American Scientists at URL <http://www.fas.org/asmp/profiles/facts_book_2003.pdf>.

[89] For a more complete overview of war on terrorism-related US arms sale trends, including data on over 20 countries, see the Centre for Defence Information's arms trade series, available at URL <http://www.cdi.org>.

[90] US Department of State (note 13), p. 239.

[91] Federation of American Scientists, 'America's war on terrorism: arms transfers', URL <http://fas.org/terrorism/at/index.html>.

[92] Written Statement of Lt. Gen. Tome H. Walters, Jr (note 48).

[93] US General Accounting Office (note 56).

commercial aircraft by terrorists wielding these weapons has resulted in one of the largest and most comprehensive US campaigns to strengthen national and international controls on a particular weapon system in history.

At the international level, the USA has spearheaded intergovernmental efforts to tighten controls on the export of MANPADS, improve stockpile security and increase cooperation between national law enforcement agencies. These efforts have resulted in agreements of various kinds among members of the Asia–Pacific Economic Cooperation, the Group of Eight, the Organization for Security and Co-operation in Europe and the Wassenaar Arrangement.[94] The USA has also worked with several countries on a bilateral basis to secure MANPADS storage facilities and destroy nearly 10 000 surplus missiles. Finally, the USA has strengthened its own end-use monitoring of exported Stinger missile systems, and is exploring the possibility of equipping US commercial aircraft with infra-red countermeasures—a programme that could cost billions of dollars.[95] The significance of these actions extends beyond their impact on the availability of MANPADS to terrorists. By increasing the awareness of the threat from SALW more generally, US MANPADS threat reduction efforts are laying the groundwork for policy initiatives with the potential to curb the illicit trafficking in other forms of SALW.

VI. The future of US defence trade controls

Shortly after the events of 11 September 2001, the Bush Administration asked Congress to approve section 505 of the 2001 Anti-Terrorism Act[96]—one of the most brazen challenges to congressional oversight of the arms trade in decades. The provision would have allowed the president to export arms to any country—even those countries that were otherwise ineligible—if doing so would further the war on terrorism. Even though the administration ultimately withdrew the provision just days after sending it to Congress, arms control advocates feared that it portended a significant shift in US defence trade policy.[97] Since then, however, there have been only a small number of significant changes. The speed with which the policy system regained its equilibrium after 11 September 2001 is a testament to the vitality and durability of the 'checks and balances' in the US federal government. The same checks and balances that prevented executive branch overreach in 2001—fiercely independent congressional leaders, an energetic civil society and an attentive media—are probably sufficient to prevent dramatic changes to US arms export controls in the near future.

This is not to rule out the possibility of changes to the current system. There are major policy initiatives in the pipeline that could result in significant legislative or regulatory adjustments. However, any significant changes will be hard won, achieved incrementally and limited to areas in which there is consensus among the various players in the policy-making community. Thus, paradigmatic shifts in defence trade policy and the arms export control system are unlikely.

[94] For details of the G8, the Organization for Security and Co-operation in Europe and the Wassenaar Arrangement, and a list of their members, see the glossary in this volume.

[95] Federation of American Scientists, 'Issue brief 1: MANPADS proliferation', URL <http://fas.org/asmp/campaigns/MANPADS/MANPADS.html>.

[96] 2001 Anti-Terrorism Act, HR 2975, 107th Congress, 1st Session, URL <http://www.epic.org/privacy/terrorism/ata2001_text.pdf>.

[97] Arms Transfers Working Group, 'Waivers of arms sales restrictions', Letter to Congress, 28 Sep. 2001, available at URL <http://fas.org/asmp/atwg/letters/ATWG-terrorism.htm>.

18. The Proliferation Security Initiative: international law aspects of the Statement of Interdiction Principles

CHRISTER AHLSTRÖM

I. Introduction

On 9 December 2002 the Spanish frigate *Navarra* intercepted the freighter *So San* in international waters in the Arabian Sea. The freighter was registered in Cambodia, although sources differ as to whether or not the vessel was flying a Cambodian flag at the time of the interception.[1] On board the ship, underneath sacks of cement, the boarding party found hidden 15 short-range ballistic missiles of North Korean origin armed with conventional warheads and 23 containers of nitric acid, an oxidizer for rocket engines. The freighter was handed over to the US authorities and was escorted towards the US military base at Diego Garcia in the Indian Ocean for further investigation.[2] Soon thereafter Yemen sent a letter to the United States formally protesting against the interception of the *So San.* The Yemeni authorities declared that they were the intended recipients of the shipment, part of a long-standing order from North Korea, and demanded that the missiles be returned to Yemen.[3] This turn of events prompted a shift in focus on the interdiction of the freighter. Questions were raised as to the authority under which Spain and the USA had stopped, searched and seized the *So San*.

On 11 December 2002, the USA decided to release the freighter and allow it to proceed to Yemen with the ballistic missiles and nitric acid still on board. At a White House press briefing, a spokesperson gave the following explanation for the US decision: 'There is no provision under international law prohibiting Yemen from accepting delivery of missiles from North Korea. While there is authority to stop and search, in this instance *there is no clear authority to seize the shipment of Scud missiles* from North Korea to Yemen. And therefore, the merchant vessel is being released'.[4]

This about-face caused the USA considerable embarrassment and, furthermore, confounded the Spanish authorities, who apparently believed that the fact that the cargo manifest listed neither the ballistic missiles nor the nitric

[1] 'Spanish official details high seas drama', CNN.com, 11 Dec. 2002, URL <http://www.cnn.com/2002/WORLD/europe/12/11/missile.ship.spain/index.html>.

[2] *Keesing's Record of World Events*, vol. 48 (2002), p. 45139.

[3] 'Scud missiles are ours, says Yemen', CNN.com, 11 Dec. 2002, URL <http://archives.cnn.com/2002/WORLD/asiapcf/east/12/11/scud.ship/>; and 'Yemen protests over Scud seizure', BBC News World Edition, 11 Dec. 2002, URL <http://news.bbc.co.uk/2/hi/middle_east/2566207.stm>.

[4] Press Briefing by Ari Fleischer, The White House, Office of the Press Secretary, 11 Dec. 2002, URL <http://www.whitehouse.gov/news/releases/2002/12/20021211-5.html>. Emphasis added.

acid constituted a reason for holding the ship.[5] On 13 December 2002 the North Korean Ministry for Foreign Affairs issued a statement condemning the incident as an act of piracy.[6] The statement declared that the interdiction 'had no legal ground' and constituted 'an unpardonable piracy that wantonly encroached upon the sovereignty of the DPRK'.[7] It also called on the USA to 'apologize for its high-handed piracy committed against the DPRK's trading ship and duly compensate for all the mental and material damage done to the ship and its crew'.[8]

The day before the US authorities decided to release the freighter, the White House had released the US National Strategy to Combat Weapons of Mass Destruction (WMD).[9] A significant aspect of this strategy was that, in contrast to more traditional non-proliferation efforts, it strongly emphasized counter-proliferation.[10] In particular, it highlighted that 'effective interdiction is a critical part of the U.S. strategy to combat WMD and their delivery means'.[11] Given this clear policy statement, it was noteworthy that the White House had to admit the very next day not only that it lacked a clear legal authority to seize the missiles but also that there was no provision under international law prohibiting the delivery of such missiles. The *So San* incident seemed to demonstrate the limits of counter-proliferation policy in the light of existing international law. It thus provided an important impetus for the US authorities to formulate a policy response that would pave the way for more robust action against proliferators in future.[12]

Almost six months after the *So San* incident, on 31 May 2003, President George W. Bush announced a new multilateral initiative focusing on law enforcement cooperation for the interdiction and seizure of 'illegal weapons or missile technologies'. This initiative became known as the Proliferation

[5] 'Official: Spain perplexed by Scud decision', CNN.com, 11 Dec. 2002, URL <http://archives.cnn.com/2002/WORLD/europe/12/11/spain.ship.reax/>.

[6] Korean Central News Agency (KCNA), 'DPRK Foreign Ministry condemns U.S. piracy', 13 Dec. 2002, URL <http://www.kcna.co.jp/item/2002/200212/news12/14.htm#10>. See also Kerr, P., 'U.S. stops then releases shipment of N. Korean missiles', *Arms Control Today*, vol. 33, no. 1 (Jan./Feb. 2003), p. 25, URL <http://www.armscontrol.org/act/2003_01-02/yemen_janfeb03.asp>.

[7] KCNA (note 6).

[8] KCNA (note 6).

[9] The White House, 'National Strategy to Combat Weapons of Mass Destruction', Washington, DC, Dec. 2002, URL <http://www.state.gov/documents/organization/16092.pdf>. See also Boese, W., 'Bush Administration releases strategy on WMD threats', *Arms Control Today*, vol. 33, no. 1 (Jan./Feb. 2003), p. 22, URL <http://www.armscontrol.org/act/2003_01-02/wmdstrategy_janfeb03.asp>.

[10] The current US focus on counter-proliferation activities (in the sense of anticipatory use of offensive military force in order to eliminate WMD capabilities) predates the 2002 National Strategy to Combat Weapons of Mass Destruction. For a conceptual discussion of the different meanings of the notion of counter-proliferation see, e.g., Müller, H. and Reiss, M., 'Counterproliferation: putting new wine in old bottles', ed. B. Roberts, *Weapons Proliferation in the 1990s* (MIT Press: Cambridge, Mass., 1995), pp. 139–50.

[11] The White House (note 9).

[12] Arms Control Association, 'The new Proliferation Security Initiative: an interview with John Bolton', Washington, DC, 4 Nov. 2003, URL <http://www.armscontrol.org/aca/midmonth/November/Bolton.asp?print>. See also Joyner, D. H., 'The Proliferation Security Initiative and international law', CITS Brief 1 (Center for International Trade and Security (CITS), University of Georgia, Atlanta, Ga., 22 June 2004), URL <http://www.uga.edu/cits/documents/pdf/Briefs/CITSBrief_001.pdf>; and Byers, M., 'Policing the high seas: the Proliferation Security Initiative', *American Journal of International Law*, vol. 98, no. 3 (July 2004), pp. 526–45, at p. 527.

Security Initiative (PSI).[13] Thus far, only a limited number of states participate in the 'core group' of this initiative, while a significant number of states have expressed support for the interdiction principles that have been developed within its framework. However, some states—notably China—have expressed concerns that the PSI may involve activities that do not conform with, or at least are not authorized by, the rules and principles of international law.[14] Scholars and other commentators have voiced similar concerns.[15]

Section II of this chapter describes the rather rapid development of the PSI during 2003 and 2004.[16] Section III analyses the PSI's main output thus far—the Statement of Interdiction Principles (SOP), reproduced in appendix 18A. The task here is to compare the interdiction principles enshrined in the SOP with rules and principles of international law on enforcement jurisdiction at sea, in the air and on land, in order to discuss possible contradictions between the SOP and international law. State jurisdiction is a complex legal matter, however, and this chapter outlines only the main rules and principles.

One of the PSI's goals was to establish a new normative situation in order to avoid a repetition of the outcome of the *So San* incident. To assess whether this goal has been met, the legal impact of the PSI itself must be addressed. The chapter concludes with an assessment of the PSI and some final observations in section IV.

II. Development of the Proliferation Security Initiative

On 31 May 2003 President Bush delivered a speech in Krakow, Poland, in which he declared that the 'greatest threat to peace is the spread of nuclear, chemical and biological weapons' and announced the Proliferation Security Initiative.[17]

When weapons of mass destruction or their components are in transit, we must have the means and authority to seize them. So today I announce a new effort to fight pro-

[13] For information and documents see the PSI Internet site of the US Department of State, Bureau of Nonproliferation, at URL <http://www.state.gov/t/np/c10390.htm>.

[14] See Ru'an, Y., 'The PSI: Chinese thinking and concern', *The Monitor*, vol. 10, no. 1 (spring 2004), p. 22; and Su Wei, 'China's views on PSI', in 'Countering the spread of weapons of mass destruction: the role of the Proliferation Security Initiative', *Issues & Insights*, vol. 4, no. 5 (July 2004), p. 31.

[15] See *The Proliferation Security Initiative: The Legal Challenge*, Bipartisan Security Group Policy Brief (Bipartisan Security Group: Washington, DC, 2003), URL <http://www.gsinstitute.org/gsi/pubs/09_03_psi_brief.pdf>; Persbo, A. 'The Proliferation Security Initiative: dead in the water or steaming ahead?', *BASIC Notes*, 12 Dec. 2003, URL <http://www.basicint.org/pubs/Notes/BN031212.htm>; and Persbo, A. and Davis, I., *Sailing into Uncharted Waters? The Proliferation Security Initiative and the Law of the Sea*, BASIC Research Report 2004.2 (BASIC: London/Washington, DC, June 2004), URL <http://www.basicint.org/pubs/Research/04PSI.htm>.

[16] See Anthony, I., 'Major trends in arms control and non-proliferation', *SIPRI Yearbook 2004: Armaments, Disarmament and International Security* (Oxford University Press: Oxford, 2004), pp. 575–601, for a description of activities in 2003.

[17] The White House, Office of the Press Secretary, 'Remarks by the President to the people of Poland', Krakow, Poland, 31 May 2003, URL <http://www.whitehouse.gov/news/releases/2003/05/print/20030531-3.html>.

liferation called the Proliferation Security Initiative. The United States and a number of our close allies, including Poland, have begun working on new agreements to search planes and ships carrying suspect cargo and to seize illegal weapons or missile technologies. Over time, we will extend this partnership as broadly as possible to keep the world's most destructive weapons away from our shores and out of the hands of our common enemies.[18]

The *goal* of the initiative was to acquire the 'means and authority' to seize illegal WMD, missiles and components in transit. The *means* to achieve this goal would be a series of 'new agreements', initially to be worked out by the USA and some close allies but later to be opened for participation on a broad basis. The proposal thus acknowledged that the necessary means and authorities had yet to be developed. The proposal was ambiguous in that it did not define the terms 'suspect cargo' or 'illegal weapons and missile technologies'. Furthermore, the geographical scope was ambiguous: could such goods and technologies be seized wherever they are in transit?

The first PSI meeting at the policy level took place in Madrid on 12 June 2003. At this meeting a 'core group' of 11 countries discussed more active measures to stop the flow of WMD and missiles to and from states and non-state actors of proliferation concern.[19] Practical recommendations on how to achieve this goal were minimal: the first meeting resulted in only the broad statement that the participants should 'assess existing national authorities under which such practical measures could be pursued, and . . . encourage the various export control regimes to take this initiative into account in strengthening the regimes'. The outcome of the Madrid meeting must therefore be seen as preliminary. The task of the participants was to assess the fulfilment of the initiative's goal under existing domestic legislation. Furthermore, the public documents from the meeting do not clarify how the participating states foresaw the continuation of the PSI.

The next phase in the development of the PSI was the meeting in Brisbane, Australia, on 10 July 2003. Noting the preliminary nature of the Madrid meeting, the Brisbane meeting built on its results and 'moved forward in translating the collective political commitment of PSI members into practical measures'.[20] The meeting focused on defining actions necessary to interdict shipments at sea, in the air and on land. Participants emphasized their willingness to take robust and creative steps to prevent trafficking in such items, while 'reiterating that actions taken would be consistent with existing domestic and international legal frameworks'. The meeting also stressed the importance of sharing information and agreed to 'strengthen and improve capabilities for the exchange of information and analysis between participants as a basis for cooperative action to impede WMD and missile trade'. Furthermore,

[18] The White House (note 17).

[19] Proliferation Security Initiative, 'Chairman's statement at the first meeting', Madrid, Spain, 12 June 2003, URL <http://www.state.gov/t/np/rls/other/25382.htm>. The core group countries were Australia, France, Germany, Italy, Japan, the Netherlands, Poland, Portugal, Spain, the UK and the USA.

[20] Proliferation Security Initiative, 'Chairman's statement at the second meeting', Brisbane, Australia, 10 July 2003, URL <http://www.state.gov/t/np/rls/other/25377.htm>.

the participants agreed to organize interdiction exercises involving both military and civilian assets.

Perhaps in order to allay concerns about the PSI's relationship to other elements of the non-proliferation regimes, the Brisbane meeting expressed strong support for the 'strengthening of the existing framework of national laws and export controls, multilateral treaties and other tools which remain the international community's main means for preventing the spread of WMD and missiles'. It was also emphasized that the increasing ability of proliferators to circumvent or thwart existing non-proliferation mechanisms warranted 'new and stronger enforcement action by law-abiding nations'.[21]

The third PSI meeting was held in Paris on 3–4 September 2003. The chairman's statement notes that the PSI 'is an initiative to develop political commitments and practical cooperation to help impede and stop the flow of WMD . . ., their delivery systems, and related materials to and from states and non-State actors of proliferation concern'.[22] The substantial output from the Paris meeting was a Statement of Interdiction Principles that identified concrete actions to collectively or individually interdict shipments of WMD, their delivery systems and related materials (see section III below).

The fourth meeting, held in London on 9–10 October 2003, had been preceded by outreach activities with non-participants of the SOP. It was noted that the initiative had been 'well received. Over 50 non-participating countries had already expressed support for the Statement of Principles'. [23] The London meeting focused on participation in the PSI, described as 'a global initiative with an inclusive mission'. States recognized that, in order for interdiction to be effective, participation in the PSI had to be expanded. The question of establishing international authority for the initiative was also raised. The chairman's statement noted that the participants were considering some form of international recognition of their work: 'recalling the 1992 UN Security Council Presidential Declaration on the proliferation of WMD, the meeting noted the value of securing an expression of support in relevant international fora for greater international co-operation against trafficking in WMD, their delivery systems and related materials'. Finally, the participants agreed that, in the light of the rapid development of the PSI, the high-level meetings need not be held as frequently in the future.

The fifth PSI plenary meeting took place in Lisbon on 4–5 March 2004. Canada, Norway and Singapore had joined the initiative, bringing the total number of participants to 14. [24] President Bush had presented new measures to counter the threat of WMD in a speech at the National Defense University in

[21] Proliferation Security Initiative (note 20).

[22] Proliferation Security Initiative, 'Chairman's statement at the third meeting', Paris, 3–4 Sep. 2003, URL <http://www.state.gov/t/np/rls/other/25425.htm>.

[23] Proliferation Security Initiative, 'Chairman's statement at the fourth meeting', London, 9–10 Oct. 2003, URL <http://www.state.gov/t/np/rls/other/25373.htm>.

[24] Proliferation Security Initiative, 'Chairman's statement at the fifth meeting', Lisbon, 4–5 Mar. 2004, URL <http://www.state.gov/t/np/rls/other/30960.htm>.

Washington, DC on 11 February 2004.[25] He proposed that the PSI should not focus only on shipments and transfers: 'PSI participants and other willing nations should use Interpol and all other means to bring to justice those who traffic in deadly weapons, to shut down their labs, to seize their materials, to freeze their assets'. This proposal received general support among the core group at the Lisbon meeting: they pledged to cooperate in 'preventing WMD proliferation facilitators (i.e. individuals, companies, and other entities) from engaging in this deadly trade. . . . Participants agreed to pursue greater cooperation through military and intelligence services and law enforcement to shut down proliferation facilitators and bring them to justice'.[26] More specifically, PSI participants agreed to begin examining the steps necessary for this expanded role. As of the end of December 2004, this work had not yet resulted in any tangible result similar to the SOP.

The question of widening international support for the PSI and the SOP was also raised at the Lisbon meeting. Participants agreed that it was essential to continue broadening international consensus in favour of the non-proliferation of WMD, their delivery systems and related materials. It was also deemed essential to widen the 'international political and operational support for PSI aims and actions'. Apart from outreach activities, it was recognized that this could be achieved by 'concluding bilateral agreements with interested States, notably in view of obtaining their consent for expeditious procedures for the boarding of vessels flying their flag, as required'.[27]

The Lisbon meeting also outlined in more detail the practical steps to be taken in order to lay the foundation for involvement in PSI activities. Prospective participants should: (*a*) formally commit to and publicly endorse the PSI and the SOP and indicate their willingness to take all available steps to support PSI efforts; (*b*) undertake a review and provide information on current national legal authorities to undertake interdictions at sea, in the air or on land and indicate their willingness to strengthen authorities where appropriate; (*c*) identify specific national assets that might contribute to PSI efforts (e.g., information sharing and military and/or law enforcement assets); (*d*) provide points of contact for PSI interdiction requests and other operational activities and establish appropriate internal government processes to coordinate PSI response efforts; (*e*) be willing to actively participate in PSI interdiction training exercises and actual operations as opportunities arise; and (*f*) be willing to consider signing relevant agreements (e.g., boarding agreements) or otherwise establish a concrete basis for cooperation with PSI efforts (e.g., memoranda of understanding on overflight denial).

Regarding the development of the initiative, the participants noted that the PSI had become 'operationally active' and that it had established itself as a 'crucial instrument to respond effectively to some of the most serious security

[25] The White House, Office of the Press Secretary, 'President announces new measures to counter the threat of WMD', 11 Feb. 2004, URL <http://www.whitehouse.gov/news/releases/2004/02/print/20040211-4.html>.

[26] Proliferation Security Initiative (note 24).

[27] Proliferation Security Initiative (note 24).

challenges of the XXI century'. As for its future, participants noted that 'the main lines of the PSI are now well established and that several directions of action can be pursued separately but still in a mutually reinforcing mode'. [28]

The meeting to mark the first anniversary of the PSI was held in Krakow on 31 May–1 June 2004, with representatives from over 60 countries.[29] The main purpose of the meeting was apparently to demonstrate the international support that the initiative had received over the past year, and the main development was the announcement on 31 May that Russia was to become a member of the 'core group'.[30] Like China, Russia had previously raised concerns about the legality of the interdiction measures envisaged under the PSI. A press statement issued by the Russian Ministry for Foreign Affairs noted that '[t]he Russian side intends to make its contribution to implementing the PSI with consideration for the compatibility of the actions with the rules of international law, for their conformance to national legislation and for the commonality of non-proliferation interests with the partners'.[31] The adoption of UN Security Council Resolution 1540 in April 2004 was also reflected in the chairman's statement, which noted that the PSI was consistent with the resolution's call for all states 'to take cooperative actions to prevent illicit trafficking in nuclear, chemical or biological weapons, their means of delivery and related materials'.[32]

In addition to these policy-level meetings, PSI participating states have held nine so-called Operational Experts Meetings, dealing *inter alia* with the planning of interdiction training exercises.[33] As of 31 December 2004, the participating states had held 13 interdiction exercises, of which seven were devoted to maritime interdiction. Two of the exercises involved interdiction of WMD and related goods on land, and three (including a so-called table-top exercise) involved the interdiction of aircraft. If the pattern of exercises is any indication of the intended activities, it is that the PSI is focusing primarily on maritime interdictions and giving less attention to interdictions on land and of aircraft in flight.

[28] Proliferation Security Initiative (note 24).

[29] Proliferation Security Initiative, 'Chairman's statement at the first anniversary Proliferation Security Initiative meeting', Krakow, Poland, 1 June 2004, URL <http://www.state.gov/t/np/rls/other/33208.htm>. See also *Cracow Initiative: Proceedings of the Conference*, First Anniversary Proliferation Security Initiative Meeting, Krakow, 31 May–1 June 2004 (Polish Ministry for Foreign Affairs: Warsaw, 2004).

[30] The number of 'founding members' of the PSI has risen from 11 to 17 countries, but 2 of these founding members (Denmark and Turkey) are apparently not considered to be 'core members' of the initiative. Squassoni, S., *Proliferation Security Initiative (PSI)*, (Library of Congress, Congressional Resarch Service: Washington, DC, 14 Jan. 2005), p. 2.

[31] 'Press release on Russia's participation in Proliferation Security Initiative (PSI)', No. 1224-31-05-2004, unofficial translation from Russian, Ministry of Foreign Affairs of the Russian Federation, Moscow, 1 June 2004, URL <http://www.ln.mid.ru/bl.nsf/0/2e1470910be746b6c3256ea600359aef?OpenDocument>.

[32] Proliferation Security Initiative (note 29). On US Security Council Resolution 1540, see also section III of this chapter and chapter 11 in this volume; the resolution is reproduced in appendix 11A.

[33] See US Department of State, Bureau of Nonproliferation, 'Calendar of events', URL <http://www.state.gov/t/np/c12684.htm>. See also the PSI Internet site maintained by the Canadian Government at URL <http://www.proliferationsecurity.info>.

Regarding actual interdictions, the PSI participants have adopted a policy of opacity. Participating states will not make public interdictions undertaken within the PSI framework.[34] One interdiction that has been credited to the cooperation within the PSI was the October 2003 seizure of uranium enrichment technology bound for Libya on board the *BBC China*. The *BBC China* was owned by a German shipping company and was flying a flag of convenience (Antigua and Barbuda). The British and US authorities suspected that it was carrying nuclear equipment to Libya. When the ship entered the Mediterranean Sea, the British and US authorities asked the German authorities for assistance. The German authorities asked the shipping company to voluntarily divert the vessel to an Italian port, where it was searched. The centrifuge equipment found on board was not listed on the ship's manifest and was subsequently confiscated.[35] No interdictions were reported in the public domain during 2004. In the light of this policy of opacity, it is difficult to make an independent assessment of the impact or success of the initiative.

III. The Statement of Interdiction Principles

State jurisdiction and the interdiction and seizure of weapons of mass destruction

The purpose of the PSI is to establish the necessary authority to 'interdict' and 'seize' illegal WMD, missile technology and related materials when in transit on land, in the air or at sea to prevent them from falling into the hands of states, or non-state actors, of proliferation concern. The term 'interdiction' is normally used to describe the obstruction of an activity that should not be allowed to proceed, while 'seize' denotes the forcible taking into possession of items (typically in relation to a criminal act) that may be subject to confiscation. Interdiction, seizure and confiscation are acts of physical interference undertaken by the executive of a state, and the authority to undertake such measures should be assessed in relation to the rules and principles of international law pertaining to state jurisdiction. International law gives states the authority to exercise jurisdiction, but also sets limits on that authority.[36]

To assess a state's jurisdictional competences, it is important to take into account both the geographical location in which the physical interference takes place and the nationality of the interdicted vessel. The circumstances in which a state may seize and confiscate goods on a vessel with a different nationality are discussed below.

[34] Arms Control Association (note 12).

[35] See Persbo and Davis (note 15), p. 37.

[36] See, e.g., Brownlie, I., *Principles of Public International Law*, 4th edn (Clarendon Press: Oxford, 1990), pp. 298 ff; and Elsea, J. K., *Weapons of Mass Destruction Counterproliferation: Legal Issues for Ships and Aircraft* (Library of Congress, Congressional Research Service: Washington, DC, 1 Oct. 2003).

Land territory

The authority of a state to exercise jurisdiction is strongest when it comes to its land territory. Few legal limits exist on a state's power to enact legislation that controls the import and export of weapons and dual-use goods. It may be necessary, however, to take account of existing international agreements governing trade (e.g., trade-related agreements on the movement of goods within the European Community).[37] Limits may also exist when it comes to the exercise of enforcement jurisdiction in the light of international agreements, for example, those on state and diplomatic immunity. In most situations, however, international law would not hinder the enactment and enforcement of laws and regulations on the interdiction and seizure of WMD-related goods on the land territory of a state.

There are many cases in which a state has seized goods and technologies destined for export but lacking the necessary licences. Often the domestic export control and customs legislation of a state stipulates that goods seized in such cases may be forfeited.

Airspace

Under the 1944 Convention on International Civil Aviation (Chicago Convention), a state possesses complete and exclusive sovereignty over the airspace above its land territory (which also includes the airspace over its territorial sea; Articles 1 and 2).[38] A *state-operated* aircraft enjoys immunity if it traverses the airspace of another state with prior approval from that state (Article 3:c). In contrast to the legal regime governing the territorial sea (see below), states do not have the right to 'innocent passage' through the airspace above another state. If a state receives a request for overflight and suspects that the state aircraft in question will carry prohibited goods, the state receiving the request may legally deny the overflight. The legal situation regarding *civil* aircraft is different. Non-scheduled flights have a right to fly into and transit a state without obtaining prior permission, but they must land if requested to do so by the territorial state. Scheduled air services are required to obtain special permission or other authorization from the territorial state. Such an authorization may include special terms defined by the territorial state.

There are also important limitations on the actions that may be taken against civilian aircraft. In 1984, after the downing of the South Korean KAL 007

[37] Examples of such international trade agreements are the 1956 Convention on the Contract for the International Carriage of Goods by Road (CMR), URL <http://www.unece.org/trans/conventn/cmr_e.pdf>; and the regional 1975 Customs Convention on the International Transport of Goods Under Cover of TIR ('Transports Internationaux Routiers') Carnets, URL <http://www.unece.org/trans/bcf/tir/handbook/english/newtirhand/10.pdf>.

[38] The Convention on International Civil Aviation was signed at Chicago on 7 Dec. 1944. See *United Nations Treaty Series*, vol. 15 (1948), p. 295, and URL <http://www.iasl.mcgill.ca/airlaw/public/chicago/chicago1944a.pdf>. The international carriage of goods by air is governed by the 1929 Warsaw Convention as subsequently amended. The Convention for the Unification of Certain Rules Relating to International Carriage by Air (Warsaw Convention), signed at Warsaw on 12 Oct. 1929, URL <http://www.jus.uio.no/lm/air.carriage.warsaw.convention.1929/doc.html>.

civilian aircraft by a Soviet warplane, the following amendment was made to the Chicago Convention: 'every State must refrain from resorting to the use of weapons against civil aircraft in flight and . . . in case of interception, the lives of persons on board and the safety of aircraft must not be endangered' (Article 3 *bis*).[39]

There is little information in the public domain on interdictions in flight of civilian aircraft suspected of carrying dual-use goods over the territory of states. For practical purposes, most seizures of dual-use goods destined to be transported by air would occur during customs procedures before the aircraft departs.

Water areas

The international law of the sea contains important provisions on the exercise of state jurisdiction in water areas. While the law of the sea is codified in several international treaties, the 1982 United Nations Convention on the Law of the Sea (UNCLOS) is the most comprehensive and modern instrument.[40]

When a foreign vessel enters the port of a state, it subjects itself to the territorial jurisdiction of that state. This signifies that the coastal state 'is entitled to enforce its laws against the ship and those on board'.[41] State practice includes several interdictions that have been carried out by local authorities when merchant vessels have entered the ports of other states. Such interdictions have also resulted in the seizure of goods—often because the goods in question were not listed on the ship's manifest.[42] One example of such an interdiction was the 1999 *Ku Wol San* incident, in which Indian authorities boarded and searched a North Korean freighter that had called at an Indian port. The authorities found on board ballistic missile-related goods and technologies that were apparently destined for Pakistan and were subsequently confiscated on the grounds that they had not been declared.[43] The Indian authorities later made clear that they would not have seized the goods if they

[39] The Protocol Relating to an Amendment to the Convention on International Civil Aviation was signed at Montreal on 10 May 1984 and entered into force on 1 Oct. 1998. As of 31 Dec. 2004, 128 states were party to the Protocol, including a majority of PSI participants but excluding the USA.

[40] The UN Convention on the Law of the Sea was opened for signature at Montego Bay, Jamaica, on 10 Dec. 1982 and entered into force on 16 Nov. 1994; it is reproduced in *The Law of the Sea: United Nations Convention on the Law of the Sea* (United Nations: New York, 1983) and at URL <http://www.un.org/Depts/los/index.htm>. A UN Conference on the Law of the Sea was held in Geneva in 1958: it resulted in the adoption of 4 conventions, among them the Convention on the Territorial Sea and the Contiguous Zone; and the Convention on the High Seas. UNCLOS reiterates much of these 2 conventions. The USA is not among the 147 parties to UNCLOS as of 5 Jan. 2005, but it ratified the 1958 conventions in 1961. However, the USA considers parts of UNCLOS to reflect customary international law of the sea; see *Department of State Bulletin* vol. 83, no. 2075 (1983), pp. 70–71.

[41] Churchill, R. R. and Lowe, A. V., *The Law of the Sea*, 2nd edn (Manchester University Press: Manchester, 1988), p. 54.

[42] The ship's manifest should contain details on the complete cargo of the vessel. It should be produced when calling on a port and shown to custom authorities. See Schmitthoff, C. M., *Schmitthoff's International Trade: The Law and Practice of International Trade*, 9th edn (Stevens & Sons: London, 1990), p. 543. See also the 1924 Convention for the Unification of Certain Rules Relating to Bills of Lading, as amended in 1968 (the 'Hague–Visby Rules'), available at URL <http://www.jus.uio.no/lm/sea.carriage.hague.visby.rules.1968/doc.html>.

[43] Persbo and Davies (note 15), p. 28.

had been properly declared, as the mere transit of war material to another country would not be sufficient grounds for a seizure.[44]

The sovereignty of a coastal state extends beyond its land territory and internal waters to the 'territorial sea'. The breadth of the territorial sea should not exceed 12 nautical miles from the coastal state's base-lines. Within the territorial sea, however, ships from all states enjoy a right of 'innocent passage'—that is, continuous and expeditious navigation through the territorial sea to either traverse the sea without entering internal waters or to proceed to and from internal waters. So long as such passage remains innocent, there are important limitations on what action a coastal state may take against the vessel. A passage should be deemed to be innocent so long as it is not prejudicial to the peace and good order of the coastal state. UNCLOS defines the circumstances in which a passage should not be seen as innocent (Article 19): the list does not specifically include the transfer of WMD, their delivery systems or components thereof, so long as they are not intended to be used against the coastal state. In fact, the USA itself previously stated (in another context) that Article 19 contains an exhaustive list of activities that would render a passage not innocent and that the right to innocent passage may be exercised irrespective of the cargo or armament of a vessel.[45] The mere fact that a ship is carrying dangerous goods should not in itself be seen as a circumstance that would render the passage non-innocent (Article 23). UNCLOS acknowledges that a coastal state may adopt laws and regulations relating to innocent passage through the territorial sea, and it defines the subject matter of such domestic legislation (Article 21). However, this permitted legislation should pertain to either safety of navigation or to conservation of the sea's living resources, not to extraneous issues such as the non-proliferation of WMD. Furthermore, such legislation may not be discriminatory against the ships of any state or against ships carrying cargoes to, from or on behalf of any state (Article 24).

The general rule of UNCLOS is that a coastal state's criminal jurisdiction should not be exercised on board a foreign ship passing through the territorial sea if the state's intention is to arrest any person or to conduct any investigation in connection with any crime committed on board the ship during its passage. However, there are four exceptions to this general rule: (*a*) if the consequences of the crime extend to the coastal state; (*b*) if the crime disturbs the peace of the country or the good order of the territorial sea; (*c*) if assistance from local authorities has been requested by the ship's master or by a diplomatic or consular agent of the flag state; or (*d*) if such measures are necessary for the suppression of illicit trafficking in narcotics or psychotropic substances. Again, the authority in UNCLOS for the exercise of criminal jurisdiction is not designed for combating the illicit trafficking of WMD-

[44] Persbo and Davies (note 15).

[45] The US–Soviet Joint Statement, with attached uniform interpretation of rules of international law governing innocent passage, was signed at Jackson Hole, Wyo., on 23 Sep. 1989. See *International Legal Materials*, vol. 28 (1989), p. 1444.

related goods and technologies. The explicit provision on the suppression of illicit trafficking refers solely to narcotics or psychotropic substances.

Under Article 33 of UNCLOS, a coastal state may declare a 'contiguous zone' outside its territorial sea. Such a contiguous zone must not extend beyond 24 nautical miles from the baselines from which the territorial sea is measured. In such a zone, the coastal state is authorized to exercise control to: (*a*) prevent infringements of its customs, fiscal, immigration or sanitary laws and regulations within its territory or territorial sea; and (*b*) punish infringements on such laws and regulations committed within its territory and territorial waters. The control to be exercised by the coastal state is first of all confined to the four types of laws and regulations defined, but also with a view to their application and enforcement within the territory or the territorial sea.[46] A coastal state is authorized to exercise enforcement jurisdiction only in relation to infringements committed within its territory or territorial waters. Hence, under the legal regime governing a contiguous zone, the coastal state may exercise preventative or protective control concerning customs regulations in order to prevent attempted infringements of its customs regulations within its territory or territorial sea. However, the authority may not be exercised when there is no attempted infringement of the state's customs regulations—for example, when a ship is traversing a contiguous zone in order to exercise its right to innocent passage in the territorial sea without discharging any goods.

The sea area beyond and adjacent to the territorial sea may, according to UNCLOS Article 55, be claimed by a coastal state as an 'exclusive economic zone' (EEZ). Such a zone shall not extend beyond 200 nautical miles from the baselines from which the territorial sea is measured. In an EEZ the coastal state has sovereign rights over natural resources. For navigation in such a zone, Article 58 declares that, in essence, the regime of freedom of navigation will apply. In other words, the jurisdictional competence accorded to a coastal state under the regime of EEZ does not apply to combating illicit trafficking in WMD and related goods.

All parts of the sea that are not included in the EEZ, the territorial sea or the internal waters of a state are part of the 'high seas'. Ships from all states enjoy several freedoms on the high seas. One is the 'freedom of navigation' (Article 87), expressed in the right for all states to sail ships flying their flag on the high seas (Article 90). A ship navigating the high seas should fly the flag of a state in order to demonstrate its nationality (Article 91). The general rule is that only the flag state may exercise legislative and enforcement jurisdiction on vessels flying its flag:[47] 'Ships shall sail under the flag of one State only and, save in exceptional cases expressly provided for in international treaties or in this Convention, shall be subject to its exclusive jurisdiction on the high seas' (Article 92). UNCLOS itself defines several such exceptional cases in which third states are entitled to exercise jurisdiction: piracy (Articles 100–107), unauthorized broadcasting (Article 109), the slave

[46] Jennings, R. and Watts, A. (eds), *Oppenheim's International Law,* vol. 1, *Peace*, 9th edn (Longman: London, 1996), p. 625.

[47] Churchill and Lowe (note 41), p. 168.

trade (Article 99) and illicit trafficking in narcotics or psychotropic substances (Article 108). These exceptions should be read in conjunction with Article 110, which gives warships the 'right of visit'. A warship which encounters a foreign ship (not enjoying immunity) on the high seas is not justified in boarding the ship unless there are reasonable grounds to suspect that the ship: (*a*) is engaged in piracy, (*b*) is engaged in the slave trade, (*c*) is engaged in unauthorized broadcasting, (*d*) is without nationality, or (*e*) although flying a foreign flag or refusing to show its flag, the ship is of the same nationality as the warship. These are defined exceptions to the general rule of exclusive flag state jurisdiction, and as such they should not be subject to wide interpretation. Trafficking in WMD and related goods does not fall within the scope of the recognized exceptions to the general rule.

Self-defence has also been cited as a legitimate justification for interfering with foreign ships on the high seas.[48] In the late 1950s and 1960s, on the basis of its right to self-defence under Article 51 of the United Nations Charter, France asserted its right to visit and search ships on the high seas that were suspected of carrying arms to Algeria. However, France's actions were strongly criticized by the flag states of the interdicted vessels.[49] Another example was the January 2002 interdiction by Israeli authorities of the freighter *Karine A* in the Red Sea.[50] The freighter was carrying significant quantities of conventional weapons, and Israel maintained that the cargo was destined for the Palestinian Authority. Israel argued that its action amounted to an exercise of self-defence against an imminent threat.[51] States have also invoked provisions of regional organizations in support of interdictions at sea, like the 1962 Cuban quarantine.[52]

Article 51 of the UN Charter gives states the right to use military force in self-defence 'if an armed attack occurs'. However, state practice has included cases in which states have used armed force outside the context of a direct response to an imminent threat—so-called 'anticipatory self-defence'.[53] The notion of anticipatory self-defence remains highly controversial, however, and the International Court of Justice (ICJ) has stressed that the right to use force in self-defence is limited by necessity.[54]

[48] Fidler, D. P., 'Weapons of mass destruction and international law', *ASIL Insights*, Feb. 2003, URL <http://www.asil.org/insights/insigh97.htm>.

[49] Churchill and Lowe (note 41), p. 174.

[50] Israel Defense Forces, 'A briefing following the seizure of *Karin A*, a Palestinian weapons ship', 19 Oct. 2004, URL <http://www1.idf.il/DOVER/site/mainpage.asp?clr=1&sl=EN&id=7&docid=34484>.

[51] Byers (note 12), p. 533.

[52] On the legal argument in support of the Cuban quarantine see Henkin, L., *How Nations Behave: Law and Foreign Policy*, 2nd edn (Columbia University Press: New York, 1979), p. 290.

[53] One prominent example with a direct bearing on WMD was the 1981 Israeli attack against the Osirak nuclear reactor in Iraq. Israel claimed that it had used force in order to prevent Iraq from acquiring plutonium for a nuclear weapon that would probably be used against it. However, the UN Security Council did not accept the Israeli argument and condemned the attack as a 'clear violation of the Charter of the United Nations and the norms of international conduct'. United Nations Security Council Resolution 487, 19 June 1981, URL <http://www.un.org/Docs/scres/1981/scres81.htm>.

[54] See International Court of Justice (ICJ), *Military and Paramilitary Activities in and Against Nicaragua* (Nicaragua *v.* United States of America), *ICJ Reports 1986*, p. 14, para. 176; *Legality of the*

The right of visit on the basis of powers explicitly conferred by a treaty is also recognized as grounds for interference with a foreign vessel on the high seas (UNCLOS Article 110). State practice includes several examples of treaties—bilateral as well as multilateral—that confer on the parties the right of visit to ships of other flag states in order to uphold their material provisions. One multilateral example is Article 17 of the 1988 UN Convention Against Illicit Traffic in Narcotic Drugs and Psychotropic Substances.[55] Another is Article 8:2 of the 2000 Protocol Against the Smuggling of Migrants by Land, Sea and Air, supplementing the 2000 UN Convention Against Transnational Organized Crime.[56] Treaties explicitly conferring the right of visit need not be multilateral. The USA has concluded several such agreements bilaterally with other states for the purpose of combating illicit trafficking in narcotics.[57]

Seizure and confiscation of goods

Domestic legislation often includes provisions for the seizure and confiscation of goods that have been used in connection with a crime. Dual-use goods discovered in customs checks without proper licences are usually confiscated. Such measures undertaken against activities on a state's own territory, or vessels with its own nationality, would normally not raise questions from the perspective of international law. The seizure of goods carried on vessels of another nationality is a different matter, however. It is typically an international treaty that endows a state with the necessary authority to take action against foreign vessels outside its own territory.[58] Examples are found in international agreements on mutual legal assistance in relation to certain defined offences. One is the above-mentioned UN Convention Against Illicit Traffic in Narcotic Drugs and Psychotropic Substances: the parties are obliged to adopt such measures as may be necessary in their domestic legislation to enable the confiscation of narcotic drugs and related materials and equipment (Article 5). They should also afford other parties the widest possible measure of mutual legal assistance, *inter alia* by seizing property under their jurisdiction that is

Threat or Use of Nuclear Weapons, Advisory Opinion, *ICJ Reports 1996*, p. 26, para. 41; and Gray, C., *International Law and the Use of Force* (Oxford University Press: Oxford, 2000), p. 106.

[55] The UN Convention Against Illicit Traffic in Narcotic Drugs and Psychotropic Substances, signed at Vienna on 20 Dec. 1988, is reproduced at URL <http://www.incb.org/e/conv/1988/index.htm>.

[56] The Protocol Against the Smuggling of Migrants by Land, Sea and Air, supplementing the 2000 UN Convention against Transnational Organized Crime, is reproduced in UN General Assembly Resolution A/RES/55/25, 8 Jan. 2001, Annex III.

[57] Byers (note 12), p. 538.

[58] The argument that the ballistic missiles on board the *So San* should have been seized as 'contraband' has been discarded by legal experts. See Kirgis, F. L., 'Boarding of North Korean vessel on the high seas', *ASIL Insights*, 12 Dec. 2002, URL <http://www.asil.org/insights/insigh94.htm>. Contraband is a concept under the law of naval warfare specifying which goods a state may interdict and seize if the goods are destined for territory belonging to or occupied by an enemy state. The concept of contraband is, however, inadequate in relation to the non-proliferation of WMD. First, it only applies to wartime situations and, second, the definition of contraband is hopelessly outdated. See 'Declaration Concerning the Laws of Naval War', London, 26 Feb. 1909, reprinted in Schindler, D. and Toman, J., *The Laws of Armed Conflicts: A Collection of Conventions, Resolutions and Other Documents* (Martinus Nijhoff: Dordrecht, 1988), p. 843. See also Doswald-Beck, L. (ed.), *San Remo Manual on International Law Applicable to Armed Conflicts at Sea* (Cambridge University Press: Cambridge, 1995).

the object of a criminal investigation in another state party (Article 7). Similar provisions are found in the above-mentioned UN Convention Against Transnational Organized Crime: Article 12 states that the parties should adopt within their domestic legal systems such measures as may be necessary to enable the confiscation of 'property, equipment or other instrumentalities used in or destined for use in offences covered by this Convention'. The convention also provides for international cooperation on confiscation (Article 13). A common denominator in these two instances is that seizure and confiscation are identified as measures to be undertaken in accordance with domestic laws and procedures in relation to offences defined in multilateral instruments. What is the position of the formal instruments dealing with the non-proliferation of WMD—do they provide for mutual legal assistance, seizure and confiscation of WMD and related equipment?

The 1993 Chemical Weapons Convention (CWC) established a general obligation that the parties 'shall cooperate with other States Parties and afford the appropriate form of legal assistance to facilitate the implementation of the obligations' of the treaty (Article VII:2).[59] However, both the 1968 Treaty on the Non-Proliferation of Nuclear Weapons (Non-Proliferation Treaty, NPT)[60] and the 1972 Biological and Toxin Weapons Convention (BTWC)[61] are silent on the matter of legal assistance. Furthermore, the shipment of goods and materials that may be used for the production of WMD (so-called 'dual-use' goods) is not necessarily a violation of the treaties in question. In fact, all three treaties provide for the right to transfer dual-use goods for peaceful purposes.

Bilateral ship-boarding agreements

The USA has concluded three bilateral agreements on cooperation to combat the proliferation of WMD: with Liberia,[62] the Marshall Islands[63] and Pan-

[59] The Convention on the Prohibition of the Development, Production, Stockpiling and Use of Chemical Weapons and on their Destruction is reproduced in *International Legal Materials*, vol. 32 (1993), p. 800, and is available on the SIPRI Internet site at URL <http://www.sipri.org/contents/cbwarfare/cbw_research_doc/cbw-resdoc.html>. See also Yepes-Enríquez, R. and Tabassi, L., *Treaty Enforcement and International Cooperation in Criminal Matters: With Special Reference to the Organisation for the Prohibition of Chemical Weapons, Chemical Weapons Convention* (T. M. C. Asser Press: The Hague, 2002). For the parties to the CWC see annex A in this volume.

[60] The Treaty on the Non-proliferation of Nuclear Weapons is reproduced in *United Nations Treaty Series* vol. 729 (1970), p. 161, and is available at URL < http://www.iaea.org/Publications/Documents/Treaties/npt.html>. For the parties to the NPT see annex A in this volume.

[61] The Convention on the Prohibition of the Development, Production and Stockpiling of Bacteriological (Biological) and Toxin Weapons and on their Destruction is reproduced in *United Nations Treaty Series* vol. 1015 (1976), p. 163, and is available on the SIPRI Internet site at URL <http://www.sipri.org/contents/cbwarfare/cbw_research_doc/cbw-resdoc.html>. For the parties to the BTWC see annex A in this volume.

[62] The US–Liberian Agreement Concerning Cooperation to Suppress the Proliferation of Weapons of Mass Destruction, Their Delivery Systems, and Related Materials by Sea was signed on 11 Feb. 2004 and entered into force on 9 Dec. 2004. See URL <http://www.state.gov/t/np/trty/32403.htm>.

[63] The US–Marshall Islands Agreement Concerning Cooperation to Suppress the Proliferation of Weapons of Mass Destruction, Their Delivery Systems, and Related Materials by Sea was signed on 13 Aug. 2004 and entered into force on 24 Nov. 2004. See URL <http://www.state.gov/t/np/trty/35237.htm>.

ama.[64] The agreement with Panama is an amendment of the 2002 US–Panama Supplementary Arrangement on US Coast Guard Assistance.[65]

The agreements with Liberia and the Marshall Islands are almost identical in substance. They deal with the boarding in international waters of suspect vessels claiming the nationality of a party to the bilateral agreement. A party encountering a suspect vessel should request authority from the other party to: (*a*) confirm the claim of nationality of the suspect vessel, and (*b*) if the claim of nationality is confirmed, to board and search the vessel and, if evidence of WMD proliferation is found, detain the vessel, its crew and the goods. However, this is not an absolute right conferred under the agreements. The other party may decide to conduct the boarding and search of the vessel with its own personnel. It may also deny permission to board and search. Authorization may, however, be presumed if two hours (in the cases of the agreements with Liberia and Panama) or four hours (in the case of the Marshall Islands) have elapsed since receipt of the request to board and search was acknowledged. The agreements stipulate that the flag state has 'the primary right to exercise jurisdiction over a detained vessel, cargo or other items and persons on board (including seizure, forfeiture, arrest and prosecution)'. The flag state may, however, waive this right. The boarding party is accorded the primary right to exercise jurisdiction in a contiguous zone, except in the case of 'hot pursuit' (i.e., a case in which a vessel involved in a crime committed in territorial waters is pursued into international waters). The agreements also state that they may be used as a model for agreements with third states (this presumably refers to other PSI participants).

In the spring of 2004 the USA put forward the Regional Maritime Security Initiative (RMSI) for South-East Asia (with a particular focus on the Malacca Strait) as an extension of the PSI. The initiative proposed the use of US special forces to police sea traffic in the strait. However, this initiative was not acceptable to Indonesia and Malaysia,[66] although it appears that the USA is still pursuing the idea of an RMSI in South-East Asia.

[64] The Amendment to the Supplementary Arrangement between the Government of the United States of America and the Government of the Republic of Panama to the Arrangement between the Government of the United States of America and the Government of Panama for Support and Assistance from the United States Coast Guard for the National Maritime Service of the Ministry of Government and Justice was signed on 12 May 2004 and entered into force on 1 Dec. 2004. See URL <http://www.state.gov/t/np/trty/32858.htm>.

[65] The Supplementary Arrangement Between the Government of the United States of America and the Government of the Republic of Panama to the Arrangement Between the Government of the United States of America and the Government of Panama for Support and Assistance from the United States Coast Guard for the National Maritime Service of the Ministry of Government and Justice was signed at Panama City, Panama, on 5 Feb. 2002 and entered into force on the same day. See URL <http://www.state.gov/t/np/trty/32859.htm>.

[66] Shie, T. R., 'Ports in a storm?: the nexus between counterterrorism, counterproliferation, and maritime security in Southeast Asia', *Issues & Insights*, vol. 4, no. 4 (June 2004), p. 23, URL <http://www.csis.org/pacfor/issues/v04n04_pdf.pdf>.

The substance of the Statement of Interdiction Principles

The SOP constitutes the most concrete result of the PSI thus far in that it outlines the actions to be taken by the participants (see appendix 18A). The SOP notes that PSI participants 'are committed to the following interdiction principles to establish a more coordinated and effective basis through which to impede and stop shipments of WMD, delivery systems, and related materials flowing to and from states and non-state actors of proliferation concern, consistent with national legal authorities and relevant international law and frameworks, including the UN Security Council'. The interdiction principles are thus based on a correspondence between the various national legal authorities of the PSI participating states and relevant international law and frameworks, including the UN Security Council. It may seem obvious that 'relevant' international law should be considered, but the modifier 'relevant' may be interpreted by outsiders as an indication that PSI participating states have reserved for themselves the authority to decide which international law may be deemed relevant for the interdiction of WMD. It goes without saying that such an assumption of interpretative powers in relation to multilateral frameworks could raise legitimate concerns among other states.

In the first paragraph of the SOP, the participants commit themselves to taking 'effective measures' to interdict trafficking in WMD, their delivery systems, and related materials to and from 'states and non-state actors of proliferation concern'. 'States of proliferation concern' are not defined by the PSI states collectively. Rather, it is up to those 'involved' in the interdiction effort to determine which states are of concern. Furthermore, the formulation 'to and from' would seem to limit PSI activities to cases in which both the exporter and the recipient are entities 'of proliferation concern'. However, since other provisions of the SOP contain the formulation 'to or from', it appears that this formulation is merely a drafting oversight. The material field of application of the SOP is also vague in that it does not provide a more specific definition of 'WMD, their delivery systems, and related materials'.

More importantly, the definition of 'states and non-state actors of proliferation concern' does not take into consideration the treaty obligations of the entity in question—that is, the question of whether or not efforts to develop or acquire chemical, biological or nuclear weapons and their associated delivery systems would violate the entity's international obligations. The ICJ has stated that, regarding limitations on the armaments of states, it is important to consider the limitations that states have accepted.[67] However, some states are not party to all the treaties relevant to arms limitations. Furthermore, while the non-proliferation obligations in these treaties prohibit the transfer of the weapons themselves, they do not prohibit the transfer of 'related materials' (i.e., dual-use goods). Rather, the opposite applies—the parties have the right

[67] See International Court of Justice (ICJ), *Military and Paramilitary Activities in and Against Nicaragua* (Nicaragua *v.* United States of America), *ICJ Reports 1986*, p. 14, para. 269.

to participate in the widest possible sharing of such goods so long as they are intended for peaceful purposes.[68]

Paragraph 2 of the SOP focuses first on information exchanges on proliferation activities. The participants have agreed to adopt 'streamlined procedures' for the rapid exchange of such information and have committed themselves to protecting the confidential nature of this information when it is provided by other PSI participants. They will also 'dedicate appropriate resources and efforts' to interdiction operations and maximize coordination among themselves in interdiction efforts.

In paragraph 3 the participants commit themselves to reviewing and strengthening their 'relevant national legal authorities' where deemed necessary to accomplish the goals of the PSI. They have assumed a similar commitment to work to strengthen, where deemed necessary, 'relevant international law and frameworks in appropriate ways' to support the SOP commitments. The level of commitment is therefore relatively low. The participants should first review their national legal authorities—and if these are found to be wanting, they are committed merely to 'working' to strengthen them. In other words, the SOP includes no clear obligation to produce a tangible result. This also applies to the development of international law. It is noteworthy that the participants have committed themselves to work for the strengthening of international legal frameworks 'in appropriate ways'—which must be understood to mean that amendments should be in accordance with the procedures prescribed by international law.

Paragraph 4 is more specific, outlining specific action to be taken in support of interdiction efforts regarding 'cargoes of WMD, their delivery systems or related materials'. However, it includes an important qualification: specific actions are to be taken 'to the extent their national legal authorities permit and consistent with their obligations under international law and frameworks'. This formulation is important for two reasons: first, no new authority is envisaged under domestic or international law; and second, the subjection of the activities to pre-existing domestic legislation is used here, as in other cases, to indicate that there is no intent for the commitments to become legally binding under international law.

In subparagraph 4:a the participants commit themselves not to 'transport or assist in the transport of any such cargoes to or from states or non-state actors of proliferation concern, and not to allow any persons subject to their jurisdiction to do so'. This commitment should not be difficult for the participating governments to implement, since they are under no obligation to facilitate or participate in such transports. However, the participants also commit themselves to preventing any persons subject to their jurisdiction from doing so. Such a prohibition on individuals would normally be implemented by domestic legislation binding on subjects under the national legal system. The potential problem here is that the related materials are not adequately defined. While WMD and delivery systems can be defined in general terms, the same

[68] See Article IV of the NPT, Article X of the BTWC and Article XI of the CWC.

does not apply for 'related materials'.[69] Given the relatively large number of goods and technologies that may have implications for the manufacture of WMD, and the manifest dual-use nature of several of these, an effective prohibition on transport by individuals requires more precision. One way to resolve this issue would be to base domestic legislation on the lists of dual-use goods developed within the framework of multilateral export control regimes such as the Australia Group, the Missile Technology Control Regime and the Nuclear Suppliers Group.[70] However, it must be borne in mind that these lists were developed with a different purpose—to control exports, not to prohibit them.

Subparagraph 4:b commits the participants, at their own initiative or at the request and good cause shown by another state, to take action to 'board and search any vessel flying their flag in their internal waters or territorial seas, or areas beyond the territorial seas of any other state, that is reasonably suspected of transporting such cargoes to or from states or non-state actors of proliferation concern, and to seize such cargoes that are identified'. The commitment accurately reflects what is to be seen as the present state of international law under UNCLOS. It focuses on the flag state as the country taking the action against the suspected vessel and therefore follows the legal principle of flag state jurisdiction. The commitment does not add anything to the present legal situation.

A common factor between the SOP and the present state of international law under UNCLOS is also evident in subparagraph 4:c. Under this provision, each participant should 'seriously consider providing consent under the appropriate circumstances to the boarding and searching of its own flag vessels by other states, and to the seizure of such WMD-related cargoes in such vessels that may be identified by such states'. The boarding and searching of another participant's vessel are contingent on that participant's prior consent, however. As noted above, UNCLOS provides for an extension of the right of visit by means of a treaty conferring such powers (Article 110). The SOP does not in itself qualify as an instrument that confers a right of visit to other participants: first, the participants commit themselves only to 'seriously considering' such an act; and second, as apparent from the discussion below, the SOP hardly qualifies in itself as the legal transaction (i.e., a treaty) that UNCLOS requires.

Subparagraph 4:d gives rise to more legal questions. Unlike the previous two subparagraphs, this provision does not address a situation in which a state undertakes enforcement measures against vessels carrying its own flag or a case in which the flag state has given prior approval to board and search the

[69] In this context it should also be noted that this issue would also arise in relation to the national implementation of UN Security Council 1540, which provides the following general definition of 'related materials': 'materials, equipment and technology covered by relevant multilateral treaties and arrangements, or included on national control lists, which could be used for the design, development, production or use of nuclear, chemical and biological weapons and their means of delivery'. See appendix 18A.

[70] The control lists of the export control regimes are available on the SIPRI Internet site at URL <http://www.sipri.org/contents/expcon/expcon.html>; see also chapter 17 in this volume.

vessel. The provision also bundles together three distinct geographical areas with equally distinct legal regimes. The use of the qualification 'appropriate' is important, as it must be interpreted as 'appropriate' under both domestic and international legal authorities. As noted above, a vessel that enters the internal waters of a state and is not entitled to immunity subjects itself to the enforcement jurisdiction of the coastal state: that state may board and search the vessel and seize goods that are being smuggled into the country. Such actions would typically not raise questions in relation to the law of the sea. This is not the case, however, in the territorial sea, where there are limits on what actions a state may take against a vessel exercising its right to innocent passage. Limits also exist on what actions a coastal state may take in a contiguous zone. It is significant that the provision does not refer to interdictions on the high seas. This could be interpreted as an indication that the PSI participating states have realized that, at present, the legal authority for such measures in a non-cooperative setting is simply too weak.

Subparagraph 4:e deals with interdiction of aircraft. PSI participants should at their own initiative or on the request and good cause shown by another state require aircraft to land for inspection if they are reasonably suspected of carrying cargoes of WMD, their delivery systems or related materials to or from states or non-state actors of proliferation concern and that are transiting their airspace. States should then seize any such cargoes that are identified. Alternatively, PSI participating states could deny aircraft reasonably suspected of carrying such cargoes transit rights through their airspace in advance of such flights.

The final subparagraph deals with trans-shipments of WMD, their delivery systems or related materials to or from countries of proliferation concern. If a PSI participant has ports or airfields that are used as trans-shipment points for shipments of such cargoes to or from states or non-state actors of proliferation concern, it must inspect vessels reasonably suspected of carrying such cargoes and seize such cargoes that are identified.

Overall, the SOP complies with the current state of international law as reflected in multilateral instruments. However, it also contains interdiction principles whose application could come into conflict with the legal regime governing 'innocent passage' in the territorial sea as well as the limits on authority of a coastal state in the contiguous zone.

The legal status of the SOP and the question of legal authority

The development of the PSI has brought to the fore the challenge of reconciling two interests that, at least prima facie, appear difficult to reconcile: the interest in taking robust and creative steps to prevent the proliferation of WMD (which would require changes and new developments in the existing rules and principles of international law); and the apparent preference of most concerned governments to take these measures within existing domestic and international legal frameworks (which, as exemplified by the *So San* incident, might not support overly robust and creative steps). The process of developing the initiative seems to have resulted in a shift in emphasis—from the recognition of a need to change the law to a focus on what actions may legally be taken under existing international and domestic legislation. Because the issue of the legality of interdiction measures was raised at an early stage in the development of the PSI, the participants have devoted some effort to the question of what legal authority they have. The formal status of the PSI and the SOP should also be addressed: do they establish legally binding obligations under international law, or do they reflect a non-legally binding commitment?[71]

It has been recognized in international legal scholarship that not every agreement concluded between states should necessarily be considered binding under international law,[72] but less attention has been devoted to the question of how to differentiate non-legally binding agreements from treaties.[73] It should first be noted that the process of concluding legally binding agreements under international law is a markedly informal process. There are few requirements regarding the form of the act in order for it to have binding effects under the law of treaties. The conclusion of a treaty normally evinces a number of formal indicators of a legally binding undertaking, such as its existence in written form; its use of stringent language (formulating rights, obligations and entitlements); and the processes of signature, ratification and registration in national and multilateral treaty registers. However, many of these formal acts are technically not required for an agreement to be legally binding. The key aspect for the distinction between what is legally binding and what is not is the subjective intentions of the parties to enter into a legally binding relationship. While the language and the context of an ambiguous arrangement may be useful for assessing its normative status, the profound diversity of state practice renders it difficult to accord any of these elements a decisive importance. Thus, an external assessment of whether or not an ambiguous agreement amounts to a legally binding treaty is indeed a complicated task. It essentially requires knowing the subjective intentions of the parties—a task which cannot realistically be carried out—rather than an analysis of the formal appearance of the instrument that records the agreement.

There seems to be no specific statement from the participants in the 'core group' regarding the formal status of the PSI and the SOP. The status of the cooperation has generally been couched in startlingly vague terms. The PSI has been described by its participants as a 'collective political commitment' (at the Brisbane meeting) and as an 'initiative to develop political commit-

[71] For a discussion of the distinction between legally and non-legally binding agreements in international cooperation generally, see Ahlström, C., *The Status of Multilateral Export Control Regimes: An Examination of Legal and Non-Legal Agreements in International Co-operation* (Iustus Förlag: Uppsala, 1999).

[72] See, e.g., Aust, A., *Modern Treaty Law and Practice* (Cambridge University Press: Cambridge, 2000); and Shelton, D. (ed.), *Commitment and Compliance: The Role of Non-Binding Norms in the International Legal System* (Oxford University Press: Oxford, 2003).

[73] See Widdows, K., 'What is an agreement in international law?', *British Yearbook on International Law*, vol. 50 (1979), pp. 117–49.

ments' (at Paris).[74] It has also been said that the PSI 'is an activity, not an organization'.[75] A variation on this theme is that the 'PSI is not a formal institution, nor is it a treaty organization. It is a statement of purpose'.[76] The documentation from the various meetings at the political level has a distinct character of *punctationes*—it lists what the chairman deems to have been the main points of agreement during the meeting. There is nothing to indicate that the participants intended to accept the points as legally binding. Hence, the nature of the cooperation within the PSI may be described as informal and not based on a legally binding agreement.

Although the SOP is formulated along the lines of an agreement, its hortatory language and consistent use of 'commitments'—rather than 'obligations'—indicate that the PSI participants did not believe that they were setting out legally binding obligations for themselves in the document. The main reason why the PSI core group did not use legally binding agreements as the basis for its cooperation was probably that the participating states wanted to reach a quick resolution to their discussions. Negotiations on legally binding agreements often become time-consuming. The group may also have sought to avoid the delays involved in getting the imprimatur of their respective parliamentary bodies in cases where they shared treaty-making powers under constitutional law.

Despite the fact that the PSI core group has opted for informal cooperation, it has devoted significant attention to the legal framework for its activities. As noted above, the question of the legal authority for the group's engagement in interdiction arose early in the process of developing the initiative. The first attempt to argue for the existence of such authority fell somewhat short. The chairman's conclusions from the Paris meeting noted that:

> the PSI is consistent with and a step in the implementation of the UN Security Council Presidential statement of 31 January 1992, which states that the proliferation of all WMD constitutes a threat to international peace and security, and underlines the need to prevent proliferation. It is also in line with the Kananaskis and Evian G-8 Summit declarations as well as recent EU (European Union) statements, establishing that more coherent and concerted efforts are needed to prevent the proliferation of WMD, their delivery systems, and related materials.[77]

While the 1992 UN Security Council presidential statement[78] carries significant *political* value, the *legal* impact of such a statement is limited, as it was not adopted in the form of a binding resolution under Chapter VII of the UN Charter. The fact that the PSI is in line with declarations of the Kananaskis and Evian summit meetings of the Group of Eight (G8) industri-

[74] See Proliferation Security Initiative (notes 20 and 22).

[75] US Department of State, 'Proliferation Security Initiative Frequently Asked Questions', Fact Sheet, Bureau of Nonproliferation, Washington DC, 11 Jan. 2005, URL <http://www.state.gov/t/np/rls/fs/32725.htm>.

[76] See URL <http://www.proliferationsecurity.info/introduction.php>.

[77] Proliferation Security Initiative (note 22).

[78] Note by the President of the UN Security Council, UN Security Council document S/23500, 31 Jan. 1992, reproduced in *International Legal Materials*, vol. 31 (1992), p. 762.

alized nations and with statements of the European Union does not provide much authority since, whatever legal significance such declarations and statements may carry, it would only apply in relation to the limited number of members of the G8 and the EU.

The question of international authority should also be seen in connection with developments within the UN. In his speech before the General Assembly on 23 September 2003, President Bush urged the Security Council to adopt a new 'anti-proliferation' resolution that would call on UN member states to criminalize the proliferation of WMD.[79] After seven months of negotiations, UN Security Council Resolution 1540 was adopted by consensus on 28 April 2004. The resolution was adopted under Chapter VII of the UN Charter—and is legally binding on the members of the organization (Article 25). It 'calls upon all States, in accordance with their national legal authorities and legislation and consistent with international law, to take cooperative action to prevent illicit trafficking in nuclear, chemical or biological weapons, their means of delivery, and related materials'.[80]

The USA had sought to include a formulation in the draft resolution that would have provided authority for the interdiction of suspect vessels. However, this proposal met resistance within the UN Security Council (notably from China) and was ultimately withdrawn in order to achieve consensus. As discussed above, the chairman's statement at the anniversary meeting in Krakow noted that the PSI is consistent with Resolution 1540. However, that resolution also clearly states that the cooperation must be 'in accordance with their national legal authorities and legislation and consistent with international law'. This signifies that Resolution 1540 does not provide any authority where none already exists under international law. It also implies that the PSI has not yet been endowed with any legal authority that would override the applicable international agreements.

In an effort to strengthen the legal authority for interdiction activities, the PSI participating states have also discussed proposed amendments to the 1988 Convention for the Suppression of Unlawful Acts against the Safety of Maritime Navigation (SUA Convention).[81] The main purpose of the SUA Convention is to ensure that appropriate action is taken against persons committing unlawful acts against ships. The convention requires that the parties either extradite or prosecute alleged offenders. The proposed amendments aim to expand the SUA Convention by criminalizing the transport of WMD, their delivery systems and related materials on commercial vessels at sea and to provide a treaty-based right to board vessels suspected of involvement in such acts. However, objections have been raised regarding these proposed amendments: *inter alia*, that they are not specific enough; that they may hamper

[79] The White House, Office of the Press Secretary, 'President Bush addresses United Nations General Assembly', 23 Sep. 2003, URL <http://www.whitehouse.gov/news/releases/2003/09/20030923-4.html>.

[80] For the resolution see appendix 11A in this volume.

[81] The Convention on the Suppression of Unlawful Acts against the Safety of Maritime Navigation, was adopted by the International Maritime Organization (IMO) on 10 Mar. 1988 and entered into force on 1 Mar. 1992; the convention is reproduced in *International Legal Materials*, vol. 27 (1988), p. 668. See also the IMO Internet site at URL <http://www.imo.org>.

legitimate trade; and that the International Maritime Organization (IMO) is not the correct forum in which to discuss these matters.[82] Furthermore, the question of the relationship between an amended SUA Convention and UNCLOS has also been discussed, particularly the need to avoid infringing the principles contained in that treaty (e.g., on flag state jurisdiction and freedom of navigation).

The IMO will convene a diplomatic conference in 2005 to consider the adoption of two protocols incorporating amendments intended to strengthen the SUA Convention in response to the increasing risks posed to maritime navigation by international terrorism. Proposed amendments to the treaties in the revised draft Protocols include a substantial broadening of the range of offences (Article 3 *bis*) and the introduction of provisions for boarding vessels suspected of being involved in terrorist activities (Article 8 *bis*). The SUA amendments are intended to complement the 2004 International Ship and Port Facilities Security (ISPS) Code. The ISPS Code was signed in 2002 together with amendments to the 1974 International Convention for the Safety of Life at Sea (SOLAS).[83] The ISPS Code entered into force on 1 July 2004. The purpose of the Code is to provide a framework for the assessment of security risks to ships and to enhance maritime security.[84]

IV. Conclusions

This chapter shows that the law of the sea establishes important limitations on states' authority to exercise enforcement jurisdiction against vessels suspected of carrying WMD and related goods. This has been seen by some commentators as a serious defect in the law of the sea.[85] However, such criticism fails to acknowledge the fact that the legal rules and principles on 'innocent passage', 'flag-state jurisdiction' and 'freedom of navigation on the high seas' have evolved over hundreds of years in order to serve important interests that the international community considers legitimate and worthy of protection—primarily to facilitate interaction and trade between states and to avoid friction and conflict. Over the years, the law of the sea has been adapted to changed priorities. Today, the general rule of flag-state jurisdiction has yielded to the universal interest of combating the slave trade, piracy and drug

[82] See Cirincione, J., 'A new, effective non-proliferation strategy for the United States', Testimony before the Committee on International Relations, US House of Representatives, 30 Mar. 2004, URL <http://wwwc.house.gov/international_relations/108/ciri033004.htm>.

[83] The SOLAS convention entered into force on 25 May 1980; it is reproduced at URL <http://www.imo.org/Conventions/contents.asp?topic_id=257&doc_id=647>.

[84] The code is available on the IMO Internet site at URL <http://www.imo.org>.

[85] Lehrman concludes that 'international maritime law and its traditional interpretations have failed to provide a clear justification for interdicting foreign flag ships reasonably suspected of transporting WMD on the high seas. Traditional legal principles such as freedom of the seas and the right of innocent passage have created an environment in which rogue states and non-state actors face relatively few obstacles to the transport of WMD-related technology'. Lehrman, T. D., 'Rethinking interdiction: the future of the Proliferation Security Initiative', *Nonproliferation Review*, vol. 11, no. 2 (summer 2004), pp. 1–45, at p. 1.

trafficking. In future, the non-proliferation of WMD may also be added to this list.

The PSI participating states have tried to remedy their lack of legal authority by means of quick fixes (such as UN Security Council resolutions) or 'out-flanking', as in the case of amendments to conventions that do not directly deal with the fundamental rules and principles of the law of the sea (such as the SUA Convention). In order to gain legitimacy, however, the process should be more inclusive as regards participation.[86] Furthermore, the process should directly focus on the most relevant treaty—UNCLOS.

[86] The UN High-level Panel on Threats, Challenges and Change recommended that 'all States should be encouraged to join this voluntary initiative'. United Nations High-level Panel on Threats, Challenges and Change, *A More Secure World: Our Shared Responsibility, Report of the UN High-level Panel on Threats, Challenges and Change*, reproduced in UN General Assembly document A/59/565, 2 Dec. 2004, p. 43, and at URL <http://www.un.org/secureworld/>.

Appendix 18A. The PSI Statement of Interdiction Principles

Issued at Paris on 4 September 2003

The Proliferation Security Initiative (PSI) is a response to the growing challenge posed by the proliferation of weapons of mass destruction (WMD), their delivery systems, and related materials worldwide. The PSI builds on efforts by the international community to prevent proliferation of such items, including existing treaties and regimes. It is consistent with and a step in the implementation of the UN Security Council Presidential Statement of January 1992, which states that the proliferation of all WMD constitutes a threat to international peace and security, and underlines the need for member states of the UN to prevent proliferation. The PSI is also consistent with recent statements of the G8 and the European Union, establishing that more coherent and concerted efforts are needed to prevent the proliferation of WMD, their delivery systems, and related materials. PSI participants are deeply concerned about this threat and of the danger that these items could fall into the hands of terrorists, and are committed to working together to stop the flow of these items to and from states and non-state actors of proliferation concern.

The PSI seeks to involve in some capacity all states that have a stake in nonproliferation and the ability and willingness to take steps to stop the flow of such items at sea, in the air, or on land. The PSI also seeks cooperation from any state whose vessels, flags, ports, territorial waters, airspace, or land might be used for proliferation purposes by states and non-state actors of proliferation concern. The increasingly aggressive efforts by proliferators to stand outside or to circumvent existing non-proliferation norms, and to profit from such trade, requires new and stronger actions by the international community. We look forward to working with all concerned states on measures they are able and willing to take in support of the PSI, as outlined in the following set of 'Interdiction Principles.'

Interdiction Principles for the Proliferation Security Initiative

PSI participants are committed to the following interdiction principles to establish a more coordinated and effective basis through which to impede and stop shipments of WMD, delivery systems, and related materials flowing to and from states and non-state actors of proliferation concern, consistent with national legal authorities and relevant international law and frameworks, including the UN Security Council. They call on all states concerned with this threat to international peace and security to join in similarly committing to:

1. Undertake effective measures, either alone or in concert with other states, for interdicting the transfer or transport of WMD, their delivery systems, and related materials to and from states and non-state actors of proliferation concern. 'States or non-state actors of proliferation concern' generally refers to those countries or entities that the PSI participants involved establish should be subject to interdiction activities because they are engaged in proliferation through: (a) efforts to develop or acquire chemical, biological, or nuclear weapons and associated delivery systems; or (b) transfers (either selling, receiving, or facilitating) of WMD, their delivery systems, or related materials.

2. Adopt streamlined procedures for rapid exchange of relevant information concerning suspected proliferation activity, protecting the confidential character of classified information provided by other states as part of this initiative, dedicate appropriate resources and efforts to interdiction operations and capabilities, and maximize coordination among participants in interdiction efforts.

3. Review and work to strengthen their relevant national legal authorities where necessary to accomplish these objectives, and work to strengthen when necessary relevant international laws and frameworks in appropriate ways to support these commitments.

4. Take specific actions in support of interdiction efforts regarding cargoes of WMD, their delivery systems, or related materials, to the extent their national legal authorities permit and consistent with their obligations under international law and frameworks, to include:

a. Not to transport or assist in the transport of any such cargoes to or from states or non-state actors of proliferation concern, and not to allow any persons subject to their jurisdiction to do so.

b. At their own initiative, or at the request and good cause shown by another state, to take action to board and search any vessel flying their flag in their internal waters or territorial seas or areas beyond the territorial seas of any other state that is reasonably suspected of transporting such cargoes to or from states or non-state actors of proliferation concerns, and to seize such cargoes that are identified.

c. To seriously consider providing consent under the appropriate circumstances to the boarding and searching of its own flag vessels by other states and to the seizure of such WMD-related cargoes in such vessels that may be identified by such states.

d. To take appropriate actions to (1) stop and/or search in their internal waters, territorial seas, or contiguous zones (when declared) vessels that are reasonably suspected of carrying such cargoes to or from states or non-state actors of proliferation concern and to seize such cargoes that are identified; and (2) to enforce conditions on vessels entering or leaving their ports, internal waters or territorial seas that are reasonably suspected of carrying such cargoes, such as requiring that such vessels be subject to boarding, search, and seizure of such cargoes prior to entry.

e. At their own initiative or upon the request and good cause shown by another state, to (1) require aircraft that are reasonably suspected of carrying such cargoes to or from states or non-state actors of proliferation concern and that are transiting their airspace to land for inspection and seize any such cargoes that are identified; and/or (2) deny aircraft reasonably suspected of carrying such cargoes transit rights through their airspace in advance of such flights.

f. If their ports, airfields, or other facilities are used as transshipment points for shipment of such cargoes to or from states or non-state actors of proliferation concern, to inspect vessels, aircraft, or other modes of transport reasonably suspected of carrying such cargoes, and to seize such cargoes that are identified.

Source: US Department of State, Bureau of Nonproliferation, Proliferation Security Initiative, at URL <http://www.state.gov/t/np/c10390.htm>.

Annexes

Annex A. Arms control and disarmament agreements

Annex B. Chronology 2004

Annex A. Arms control and disarmament agreements

NENNE BODELL

Notes

1. The agreements are listed in the order of the date on which they were adopted, signed or opened for signature (multilateral agreements) or signed (bilateral agreements); the date on which they entered into force and the depositary for multilateral treaties are also given. Information is as of 1 January 2005 unless otherwise indicated: where confirmed information became available in early 2005, states are shown in italics, followed by notes which provide the dates of their signature, ratification or accession.

2. The main source of information is the lists of signatories and parties provided by the depositaries of the treaties.

3. For a few major treaties, the substantive parts of the most important reservations, declarations and/or interpretive statements made in connection with a state's signature, ratification, accession or succession are given in footnotes below the lists.

4. States listed as parties have ratified, acceded or succeeded to the agreements. Former non-self-governing territories, upon attaining independence, sometimes make general statements of continuity to all agreements concluded by the former colonial power. This annex lists as parties only those new states which have made an uncontested declaration on continuity or have notified the depositary about their succession.

5. Taiwan, while not recognized as a sovereign state by some nations, is listed as a party to those agreements which it has ratified.

6. The Russian Federation confirmed the continuity of international obligations assumed by the USSR.

7. Unless stated otherwise, the multilateral agreements listed in this annex are open to all states for signature, ratification, accession or succession.

8. A complete list of UN member states, with the year in which they became members, appears in the glossary at the front of this volume. Not all the signatories and parties listed in this annex are UN members.

Protocol for the Prohibition of the Use in War of Asphyxiating, Poisonous or Other Gases, and of Bacteriological Methods of Warfare (1925 Geneva Protocol)

Signed at Geneva on 17 June 1925; entered into force on 8 February 1928; depositary French Government

The protocol declares that the parties agree to be bound by the prohibition on the use of these weapons in war.

Parties (134): Afghanistan, Albania, Algeria[1], Angola[1], Antigua and Barbuda, Argentina, Australia, Austria, Bahrain[1], Bangladesh[1], Barbados, Belarus, Belgium, Benin, Bhutan, Bolivia, Brazil, Bulgaria, Burkina Faso, Cambodia[1], Cameroon, Canada, Cape Verde, Central African Republic, Chile, China[1], Côte d'Ivoire, Cuba, Cyprus, Czech Republic, Denmark, Dominican Republic, Ecuador, Egypt, Equatorial Guinea, Estonia, Ethiopia, Fiji[1], Finland, France, Gambia, Germany, Ghana, Greece, Grenada, Guatemala, Guinea-Bissau, Holy See, Hungary, Iceland, India[1], Indonesia, Iran, Iraq[1], Ireland, Israel[2], Italy, Jamaica, Japan, Jordan[3], Kenya, Korea (North)[1], Korea (South)[1], Kuwait[1], Laos, Latvia, Lebanon, Lesotho, Liberia, Libya[1], Liechtenstein, Lithuania, Luxembourg, Madagascar, Malawi, Malaysia, Maldives, Malta, Mauritius, Mexico, Monaco, Mongolia, Morocco, Nepal, Netherlands, New Zealand, Nicaragua, Niger, Nigeria[1], Norway, Pakistan[1], Panama, Papua New Guinea[1], Paraguay, Peru, Philippines, Poland, Portugal[1], Qatar, Romania, Russia, Rwanda, Saint Kitts and Nevis, Saint Lucia, Saint Vincent and the Grenadines, Saudi Arabia, Senegal, Serbia and Montenegro[1], Sierra Leone, Slovakia, Solomon Islands, South Africa, Spain, Sri Lanka, Sudan, Swaziland, Sweden, Switzerland, Syria, Tanzania, Thailand, Togo, Tonga, Trinidad and Tobago, Tunisia, Turkey, Uganda, UK[4], Ukraine, Uruguay, USA[4], Venezuela, Viet Nam[1], Yemen

[1] The protocol is binding on this state only as regards states which have signed and ratified or acceded to it. The protocol will cease to be binding on this state in regard to any enemy state whose armed forces or whose allies fail to respect the prohibitions laid down in it.

[2] The protocol is binding on Israel only as regards states which have signed and ratified or acceded to it. The protocol shall cease to be binding on Israel in regard to any enemy state whose armed forces, or the armed forces of whose allies, or the regular or irregular forces, or groups or individuals operating from its territory, fail to respect the prohibitions which are the object of the protocol.

[3] Jordan undertakes to respect the obligations contained in the protocol with regard to states which have undertaken similar commitments. It is not bound by the protocol as regards states whose armed forces, regular or irregular, do not respect the provisions of the protocol.

[4] The protocol shall cease to be binding on this state with respect to use in war of asphyxiating, poisonous or other gases, and of all analogous liquids, materials or devices, in regard to any enemy state if such state or any of its allies fails to respect the prohibitions laid down in the protocol.

Signed but not ratified: El Salvador

Treaty for Collaboration in Economic, Social and Cultural Matters and for Collective Self-defence among Western European states (Brussels Treaty)

Signed at Brussels on 17 March 1948; entered into force on 25 August 1948; depositary Belgian Government

The treaty provides for close cooperation of the parties in the military, economic and political fields.

Parties (7): *Original parties:* Belgium, France, Luxembourg, Netherlands, UK

Germany and Italy acceded through the Protocols of 1954.

See also Modified Brussels Treaty and Protocols of 1954.

Convention on the Prevention and Punishment of the Crime of Genocide (Genocide Convention)

Adopted at Paris by the UN General Assembly on 9 December 1948; entered into force on 12 January 1951; depositary UN Secretary-General

Under the convention any commission of acts intended to destroy, in whole or in part, a national, ethnic, racial or religious group as such is declared to be a crime punishable under international law.

Parties (136): Afghanistan, Albania*, Algeria*, Antigua and Barbuda, Argentina*, Armenia, Australia, Austria, Azerbaijan, Bahamas, Bahrain*, Bangladesh*, Barbados, Belarus*, Belgium, Belize, Bosnia and Herzegovina, Brazil, Bulgaria*, Burkina Faso, Burundi, Cambodia, Canada, Chile, China*, Colombia, Comoros, Congo (Democratic Republic of the), Costa Rica, Côte d'Ivoire, Croatia, Cuba, Cyprus, Czech Republic, Denmark, Ecuador, Egypt, El Salvador, Estonia, Ethiopia, Fiji, Finland, France, Gabon, Gambia, Georgia, Germany, Ghana, Greece, Guatemala, Guinea, Haiti, Honduras, Hungary*, Iceland, India*, Iran, Iraq, Ireland, Israel, Italy, Jamaica, Jordan, Kazakhstan, Korea (North), Korea (South), Kuwait, Kyrgyzstan, Laos, Latvia, Lebanon, Lesotho, Liberia, Libya, Liechtenstein, Lithuania, Luxembourg, Macedonia (Former Yugoslav Republic of), Malaysia*, Maldives, Mali, Mexico, Moldova, Monaco, Mongolia*, Morocco*, Mozambique, Myanmar (Burma)*, Namibia, Nepal, Netherlands, New Zealand, Nicaragua, Norway, Pakistan, Panama, Papua New Guinea, Paraguay, Peru, Philippines*, Poland*, Portugal*, Romania*, Russia*, Rwanda*, Saint Vincent and the Grenadines, Saudi Arabia, Senegal, Serbia and Montenegro*, Seychelles, Singapore*, Slovakia, Slovenia, South Africa, Spain*, Sri Lanka, Sudan, Sweden, Switzerland, Syria, Tanzania, Togo, Tonga, Trinidad and Tobago, Tunisia, Turkey, Uganda, UK, Ukraine*, Uruguay, USA*, Uzbekistan, Venezuela*, Viet Nam*, Yemen*, Zimbabwe

* With reservation and/or declaration.

Signed but not ratified: Bolivia, Dominican Republic

Geneva Convention (IV) Relative to the Protection of Civilian Persons in Time of War

Signed at Geneva on 12 August 1949; entered into force on 21 October 1950; depositary Swiss Federal Council

Geneva Convention (IV) establishes rules for the protection of civilians in areas covered by war and on occupied territories. This convention was worked out at the Diplomatic Conference held from 21 April to 12 August 1949. (Other conventions adopted at the same time: Convention (I) for the Amelioration of the Condition of the Wounded and Sick in Armed Forces in the Field; Convention (II) for the Amelioration of the Condition of the Wounded, Sick and Shipwrecked Members of Armed Forces at Sea; and Convention (III) Relative to the Treatment of Prisoners of War.)

Parties (192): Afghanistan, Albania*, Algeria, Andorra, Angola*, Antigua and Barbuda, Argentina, Armenia, Australia*, Austria, Azerbaijan, Bahamas, Bahrain, Bangladesh, Barbados*, Belarus*, Belgium, Belize, Benin, Bhutan, Bolivia, Bosnia and Herzegovina, Botswana, Brazil, Brunei Darussalam, Bulgaria*, Burkina Faso, Burundi, Cambodia, Cameroon, Canada, Cape Verde, Central African Republic, Chad, Chile, China*, Colombia, Comoros, Congo (Democratic Republic of the), Congo (Republic of), Cook Islands, Costa Rica, Côte d'Ivoire, Croatia, Cuba, Cyprus, Czech Republic*, Denmark, Djibouti, Dominica, Dominican Republic,

Ecuador, Egypt, El Salvador, Equatorial Guinea, Estonia, Eritrea, Ethiopia, Fiji, Finland, France, Gabon, Gambia, Georgia, Germany*, Ghana, Greece, Grenada, Guatemala, Guinea, Guinea-Bissau*, Guyana, Haiti, Holy See, Honduras, Hungary*, Iceland, India, Indonesia, Iran*, Iraq, Ireland, Israel*, Italy, Jamaica, Japan, Jordan, Kazakhstan, Kenya, Kiribati, Korea (North)*, Korea (South)*, Kuwait*, Kyrgyzstan, Laos, Latvia, Lebanon, Lesotho, Liberia, Libya, Liechtenstein, Lithuania, Luxembourg, Macedonia (Former Yugoslav Republic of)*, Madagascar, Malawi, Malaysia, Maldives, Mali, Malta, Marshall Islands, Mauritania, Mauritius, Mexico, Micronesia, Moldova, Monaco, Mongolia, Morocco, Mozambique, Myanmar (Burma), Namibia, Nepal, Netherlands, New Zealand, Nicaragua, Niger, Nigeria, Norway, Oman, Pakistan*, Palau, Panama, Papua New Guinea, Paraguay, Peru, Philippines, Poland*, Portugal*, Qatar, Romania*, Russia*, Rwanda, Saint Kitts and Nevis, Saint Lucia, Saint Vincent and the Grenadines, Samoa (Western), San Marino, Sao Tome and Principe, Saudi Arabia, Senegal, Serbia and Montenegro*, Seychelles, Sierra Leone, Singapore*, Slovakia*, Slovenia, Solomon Islands, Somalia, South Africa, Spain, Sri Lanka, Sudan, Suriname*, Swaziland, Sweden, Switzerland, Syria, Tajikistan, Tanzania, Thailand, Timor-Leste, Togo, Tonga, Trinidad and Tobago, Tunisia, Turkey, Turkmenistan, Tuvalu, Uganda, UK, Ukraine*, United Arab Emirates, Uruguay*, USA*, Uzbekistan, Vanuatu, Venezuela, Viet Nam*, Yemen*, Zambia, Zimbabwe

* With reservation and/or declaration.

In 1989 the Palestine Liberation Organization (PLO) informed the depositary that it had decided to adhere to the four Geneva Conventions and the two Protocols of 1977.

See also Protocols I and II of 1977.

Treaty of Economic, Social and Cultural Collaboration and Collective Self-defence among Western European States (Modified Brussels Treaty); Protocols to the 1948 Brussels Treaty (Paris Agreements)

Signed at Paris on 23 October 1954; entered into force on 6 May 1955; depositary Belgian Government

The 1948 Brussels Treaty was modified by four protocols which amended the original text to take account of political and military developments in Europe, allowing the Federal Republic of Germany (West Germany) and Italy to become parties in return for controls over German armaments and force levels (annulled, except for weapons of mass destruction, in 1984). The Western European Union (WEU) was created through the Modified Brussels Treaty. The treaty contains an obligation for collective defence of its members.

Members of the WEU: Belgium, France, Germany, Greece, Italy, Luxembourg, Netherlands, Portugal, Spain, UK

Antarctic Treaty

Signed at Washington, DC, on 1 December 1959; entered into force on 23 June 1961; depositary US Government

Declares the Antarctic an area to be used exclusively for peaceful purposes. Prohibits any measure of a military nature in the Antarctic, such as the establishment of military bases and fortifications, and the carrying out of military manoeuvres or the testing of any type of weapon. The treaty bans any nuclear explosion as well as the disposal of radioactive waste material in Antarctica.

In accordance with Article IX, consultative meetings are convened at regular intervals to exchange information and hold consultations on matters pertaining to Antarctica, as well as to recommend to the governments measures in furtherance of the principles and objectives of the treaty.

The treaty is subject to ratification by the signatories and is open for accession by UN members or by other states invited to accede with the consent of all the parties entitled to participate in the consultative meetings provided for in Article IX.

Parties (45): Argentina†, Australia†, Austria, Belgium†, Brazil†, Bulgaria, Canada, Chile†, China†, Colombia, Cuba, Czech Republic, Denmark, Ecuador†, Estonia, Finland†, France†, Germany†, Greece, Guatemala, Hungary, India†, Italy†, Japan†, Korea (North), Korea (South)†, Netherlands†, New Zealand†, Norway†, Papua New Guinea, Peru†, Poland†, Romania, Russia†, Slovakia, South Africa†, Spain†, Sweden†, Switzerland, Turkey, UK†, Ukraine, Uruguay†, USA†, Venezuela†

† Consultative members under Article IX of the treaty.

The Protocol on Environmental Protection to the Antarctic Treaty (**1991 Madrid Protocol**) entered into force on 14 January 1998.

Treaty Banning Nuclear Weapon Tests in the Atmosphere, in Outer Space and Under Water (Partial Test Ban Treaty, PTBT)

Signed at Moscow by three original parties on 5 August 1963 and opened for signature by other states at London, Moscow and Washington, DC, on 8 August 1963; entered into force on 10 October 1963; depositaries British, US and Russian governments

The treaty prohibits the carrying out of any nuclear weapon test explosion or any other nuclear explosion: (*a*) in the atmosphere, beyond its limits, including outer space, or under water, including territorial waters or high seas; and (*b*) in any other environment if such explosion causes radioactive debris to be present outside the territorial limits of the state under whose jurisdiction or control the explosion is conducted.

Parties (125): Afghanistan, Antigua and Barbuda, Argentina, Armenia, Australia, Austria, Bahamas, Bangladesh, Belarus, Belgium, Benin, Bhutan, Bolivia, Bosnia and Herzegovina, Botswana, Brazil, Bulgaria, Canada, Cape Verde, Central African Republic, Chad, Chile, Colombia, Congo (Democratic Republic of the), Costa Rica, Côte d'Ivoire, Croatia, Cyprus, Czech Republic, Denmark, Dominican Republic, Ecuador, Egypt, El Salvador, Equatorial Guinea, Fiji, Finland, Gabon, Gambia, Germany, Ghana, Greece, Guatemala, Guinea-Bissau, Honduras, Hungary, Iceland, India, Indonesia, Iran, Iraq, Ireland, Israel, Italy, Jamaica, Japan, Jordan, Kenya, Korea (South), Kuwait, Laos, Lebanon, Liberia, Libya, Luxembourg, Madagascar, Malawi, Malaysia, Malta, Mauritania, Mauritius, Mexico, Mongolia, Morocco, Myanmar (Burma), Nepal, Netherlands, New Zealand, Nicaragua, Niger, Nigeria, Norway, Pakistan, Panama, Papua New Guinea, Peru, Philippines, Poland, Romania, Russia, Rwanda, Samoa (Western), San Marino, Senegal, Serbia and Montenegro, Seychelles, Sierra Leone, Singapore, Slovakia, Slovenia, South Africa, Spain, Sri Lanka, Sudan, Suriname, Swaziland, Sweden, Switzerland, Syria, Taiwan, Tanzania, Thailand, Togo, Tonga, Trinidad and Tobago, Tunisia, Turkey, Uganda, UK, Ukraine, Uruguay, USA, Venezuela, Yemen, Zambia

Signed but not ratified: Algeria, Burkina Faso, Burundi, Cameroon, Ethiopia, Haiti, Mali, Paraguay, Portugal, Somalia

Treaty on Principles Governing the Activities of States in the Exploration and Use of Outer Space, Including the Moon and Other Celestial Bodies (Outer Space Treaty)

Opened for signature at London, Moscow and Washington, DC, on 27 January 1967; entered into force on 10 October 1967; depositaries British, Russian and US governments

The treaty prohibits the placing into orbit around the earth of any objects carrying nuclear weapons or any other kinds of weapons of mass destruction, the installation of such weapons on celestial bodies, or the stationing of them in outer space in any other manner. The establishment of military bases, installations and fortifications, the testing of any type of weapons and the conduct of military manoeuvres on celestial bodies are also forbidden.

Parties (103): Afghanistan, Algeria, Antigua and Barbuda, Argentina, Australia, Austria, Bahamas, Bangladesh, Barbados, Belarus, Belgium, Benin, Brazil, Brunei Darussalam, Bulgaria, Burkina Faso, Canada, Chile, China, Cuba, Cyprus, Czech Republic, Denmark, Dominican Republic, Ecuador, Egypt, El Salvador, Equatorial Guinea, Fiji, Finland, France, Germany, Greece, Guinea-Bissau, Hungary, Iceland, India, Indonesia, Iraq, Ireland, Israel, Italy, Jamaica, Japan, Kazakhstan, Kenya, Korea (South), Kuwait, Laos, Lebanon, Libya, Madagascar, Mali, Mauritius, Mexico, Mongolia, Morocco, Myanmar (Burma), Nepal, Netherlands, New Zealand, Niger, Nigeria, Norway, Pakistan, Papua New Guinea, Peru, Poland, Portugal, Romania, Russia, Saint Kitts and Nevis, Saint Lucia, Saint Vincent and the Grenadines, San Marino, Saudi Arabia, Seychelles, Sierra Leone, Singapore, Slovakia, Solomon Islands, South Africa, Spain, Sri Lanka, Sweden, Swaziland, Switzerland, Syria, Taiwan, Thailand, Togo, Tonga, Tunisia, Turkey, Uganda, UK, Ukraine, Uruguay, USA, Venezuela, Viet Nam, Yemen, Zambia

Signed but not ratified: Bolivia, Botswana, Burundi, Cameroon, Central African Republic, Colombia, Congo (Democratic Republic of the), Ethiopia, Gambia, Ghana, Guyana, Haiti, Holy See, Honduras, Iran, Jordan, Lesotho, Luxembourg, Malaysia, Nicaragua, Panama, Philippines, Rwanda, Serbia and Montenegro, Somalia, Trinidad and Tobago

Treaty for the Prohibition of Nuclear Weapons in Latin America and the Caribbean (Treaty of Tlatelolco)

Original treaty opened for signature at Mexico, Distrito Federal, on 14 February 1967; entered into force on 22 April 1968. The treaty was amended in 1990, 1991 and 1992; depositary Mexican Government

The treaty prohibits the testing, use, manufacture, production or acquisition by any means, as well as the receipt, storage, installation, deployment and any form of possession of any nuclear weapons by Latin American and Caribbean countries.

The parties should conclude agreements with the IAEA for the application of safeguards to their nuclear activities. The IAEA has the exclusive power to carry out special inspections.

The treaty is open for signature by all the independent states of the region.

Under *Additional Protocol I* states with territories within the zone (France, the Netherlands, the UK and the USA) undertake to apply the statute of military denuclearization to these territories.

Under *Additional Protocol II* the recognized nuclear weapon states—China, France, Russia (at the time of signing, the USSR), the UK and the USA—undertake to respect the statute of military denuclearization of Latin America and not to contribute to acts involving a violation of the treaty, nor to use or threaten to use nuclear weapons against the parties to the treaty.

Parties to the original treaty (33): Antigua and Barbuda, Argentina, Bahamas, Barbados, Belize, Bolivia, Brazil, Chile, Colombia, Costa Rica, Cuba, Dominica, Dominican Republic, Ecuador, El Salvador, Grenada, Guatemala, Guyana, Haiti, Honduras, Jamaica, Mexico, Nicaragua, Panama, Paraguay, Peru, Saint Kitts and Nevis, Saint Lucia, Saint Vincent and the Grenadines, Suriname, Trinidad and Tobago, Uruguay, Venezuela

Amendments ratified by: Argentina, Barbados, Belize, Brazil, Chile, Colombia, Costa Rica, Cuba, Dominican Republic, Ecuador, El Salvador, Grenada, Guatemala, Guyana, Jamaica, Mexico, Panama, Paraguay, Peru, Suriname, Uruguay, Venezuela

Note: Not all the countries listed had ratified all three amendments by 1 Jan. 2005.

Parties to Additional Protocol I: France[1], Netherlands, UK[2], USA[3]

Parties to Additional Protocol II: China[4], France[5], Russia[6], UK[2], USA[7]

[1] France declared that Protocol I shall not apply to transit across French territories situated within the zone of the treaty, and destined for other French territories. The protocol shall not limit the participation of the populations of the French territories in the activities mentioned in Article 1 of the treaty, and in efforts connected with the national defence of France. France does not consider the zone described in the treaty as established in accordance with international law; it cannot, therefore, agree that the treaty should apply to that zone.

[2] When signing and ratifying Protocols I and II, the UK made the following declarations of understanding: The signing and ratification by the UK could not be regarded as affecting in any way the legal status of any territory for the international relations of which the UK is responsible, lying within the limits of the geographical zone established by the treaty. Should any party to the treaty carry out any act of aggression with the support of a nuclear weapon state, the UK would be free to reconsider the extent to which it could be regarded as bound by the provisions of Protocol II.

[3] The USA ratified Protocol I with the following understandings: The provisions of the treaty do not affect the exclusive power and legal competence under international law of a state adhering to this Protocol to grant or deny transit and transport privileges to its own or any other vessels or aircraft irrespective of cargo or armaments; the provisions do not affect rights under international law of a state adhering to this protocol regarding the exercise of the freedom of the seas, or regarding passage through or over waters subject to the sovereignty of a state. The declarations attached by the USA to its ratification of Protocol II apply also to Protocol I.

[4] China declared that it will never send its means of transportation and delivery carrying nuclear weapons to cross the territory, territorial sea or airspace of Latin American countries.

[5] France stated that it interprets the undertaking contained in Article 3 of Protocol II to mean that it presents no obstacle to the full exercise of the right of self-defence enshrined in Article 51 of the UN Charter; it takes note of the interpretation by the Preparatory Commission for the Denuclearization of Latin America according to which the treaty does not apply to transit, the granting or denying of which lies within the exclusive competence of each state party in accordance with international law. In 1974, France made a supplementary statement to the effect that it was prepared to consider its obligations under Protocol II as applying not only to the signatories of the treaty, but also to the territories for which the statute of denuclearization was in force in conformity with Protocol I.

[6] On signing and ratifying Protocol II, the USSR stated that it assumed that the effect of Article 1 of the treaty extends to any nuclear explosive device and that, accordingly, the carrying out by any party of nuclear explosions for peaceful purposes would be a violation of its obligations under Article 1 and would be incompatible with its non-nuclear weapon status. For states parties to the treaty, a solution to the problem of peaceful nuclear explosions can be found in accordance with the provisions of Article V of the NPT and within the framework of the international procedures of the IAEA. It declared that authorizing the transit of nuclear weapons in any form would be contrary to the objectives of the treaty.

Any actions undertaken by a state or states parties to the treaty which are not compatible with their non-nuclear weapon status, and also the commission by one or more states parties to the treaty of an act of aggression with the support of a state which is in possession of nuclear weapons or together with such a state, will be regarded by the USSR as incompatible with the obligations of those countries under the treaty. In such cases it would reserve the right to reconsider its obligations under Protocol II. It further reserves the right to reconsider its attitude to this protocol in the event of any actions on the part of other states possessing nuclear weapons which are incompatible with their obligations under the said protocol.

[7] The USA signed and ratified Protocol II with the following declarations and understandings: Each of the parties retains exclusive power and legal competence, to grant or deny non-parties transit and transport privileges. As regards the undertaking not to use or threaten to use nuclear weapons against the parties, the USA would consider that an armed attack by a party, in which it was assisted by a nuclear weapon state, would be incompatible with the treaty.

Treaty on the Non-proliferation of Nuclear Weapons (Non-Proliferation Treaty, NPT)

Opened for signature at London, Moscow and Washington, DC, on 1 July 1968; entered into force on 5 March 1970; depositaries British, Russian and US governments

The treaty prohibits the transfer by nuclear weapon states (defined in the treaty as those which have manufactured and exploded a nuclear weapon or other nuclear explosive device prior to 1 January 1967) to any recipient whatsoever, of nuclear weapons or other nuclear explosive devices or of control over them, as well as the assistance, encouragement or inducement of any non-nuclear weapon state to manufacture or otherwise acquire such weapons or devices. It also prohibits the receipt by non-nuclear weapon states from any transferor whatsoever, as well as the manufacture or other acquisition by those states, of nuclear weapons or other nuclear explosive devices.

The parties undertake to facilitate the exchange of equipment, materials and scientific and technological information for the peaceful uses of nuclear energy and to ensure that potential benefits from peaceful applications of nuclear explosions will be made available to non-nuclear weapon parties to the treaty. They also undertake to pursue negotiations in good faith on effective measures relating to cessation of the nuclear arms race at an early date and to nuclear disarmament, and on a treaty on general and complete disarmament.

Non-nuclear weapon states undertake to conclude safeguard agreements with the International Atomic Energy Agency (IAEA) with a view to preventing diversion of nuclear energy from peaceful uses to nuclear weapons or other nuclear explosive devices. A Model Protocol Additional to the Safeguards Agreements, strengthening the measures, was approved in 1997; such Additional Safeguards Protocols are signed by states individually with the IAEA.

A Review and Extension Conference, convened in 1995 in accordance with the treaty, decided that the treaty should remain in force indefinitely.

Parties (189): Afghanistan†, Albania†, Algeria†, Andorra, Angola, Antigua and Barbuda†, Argentina†, Armenia†, Australia†, Austria†, Azerbaijan†, Bahamas†, Bahrain, Bangladesh†, Barbados†, Belarus†, Belgium†, Belize†, Benin, Bhutan†, Bolivia†, Bosnia and Herzegovina†, Botswana, Brazil†, Brunei Darussalam†, Bulgaria†, Burkina Faso†, Burundi, Cambodia†, Cameroon†, Canada†, Cape Verde, Central African Republic, Chad, Chile†, China†, Colombia, Comoros, Congo (Democratic Republic of the)†, Congo (Republic of), Costa Rica†, Côte d'Ivoire†, Croatia†, Cuba†, Cyprus†, Czech Republic†, Denmark†, Djibouti, Dominica†, Dominican Republic†, Ecuador†, Egypt†, El Salvador†, Equatorial Guinea, Eritrea, Estonia†, Ethiopia†, Fiji†, Finland†, France†, Gabon, Gambia†, Georgia, Germany†, Ghana†, Greece†, Grenada†, Guatemala†, Guinea, Guinea-Bissau, Guyana†, Haiti, Holy See†,

Honduras†, Hungary†, Iceland†, Indonesia†, Iran†, Iraq†, Ireland†, Italy†, Jamaica†, Japan†, Jordan†, Kazakhstan†, Kenya, Kiribati†, Korea (South)†, Kuwait†, Kyrgyzstan†, Laos†, Latvia†, Lebanon†, Lesotho†, Liberia, Libya†, Liechtenstein†, Lithuania†, Luxembourg†, Macedonia† (Former Yugoslav Republic of), Madagascar†, Malawi†, Malaysia†, Maldives†, Mali†, Malta†, Marshall Islands, Mauritania, Mauritius†, Mexico†, Micronesia, Moldova, Monaco†, Mongolia†, Morocco†, Mozambique, Myanmar (Burma)†, Namibia†, Nauru†, Nepal†, Netherlands†, New Zealand†, Nicaragua†, Niger, Nigeria†, Norway†, Oman, Palau, Panama, Papua New Guinea†, Paraguay†, Peru†, Philippines†, Poland†, Portugal†, Qatar, Romania†, Russia†, Rwanda, Saint Kitts and Nevis†, Saint Lucia†, Saint Vincent and the Grenadines†, Samoa (Western)†, San Marino†, Sao Tome and Principe, Saudi Arabia, Senegal†, Serbia and Montenegro†, Seychelles†, Sierra Leone, Singapore†, Slovakia†, Slovenia†, Solomon Islands†, Somalia, South Africa†, Spain†, Sri Lanka†, Sudan†, Suriname†, Swaziland†, Sweden†, Switzerland†, Syria†, Taiwan, Tajikistan†, Tanzania†, Thailand†, Togo, Timor-Leste, Tonga†, Trinidad and Tobago†, Tunisia†, Turkey†, Turkmenistan, Tuvalu†, Uganda, UK†, Ukraine†, United Arab Emirates†, Uruguay†, USA†, Uzbekistan†, Vanuatu, Venezuela†, Viet Nam†, Yemen†, Zambia†, Zimbabwe†

† Party with safeguards agreements in force with the International Atomic Energy Agency (IAEA), as required by the treaty, or concluded by a nuclear weapon state on a voluntary basis.

65 Additional Safeguards Protocols in force: Armenia, Australia, Austria, Azerbaijan, Bangladesh, Belgium, Bulgaria, Burkina Faso, Canada, Chile, China, Congo (Democratic Republic of the), Croatia, Cuba, Cyprus, Czech Republic, Denmark, Ecuador, El Salvador, Finland, France, Georgia, Germany, Ghana, Greece, Holy See, Hungary, Iceland, Indonesia, Ireland, Italy, Jamaica, Japan, Jordan, Korea (South), Kuwait, Latvia, Lithuania, Luxembourg, Madagascar, Mali, Monaco, Mongolia, Netherlands, New Zealand, *Nicaragua*, Norway, Panama, Paraguay, Peru, Poland, Portugal, Romania, Seychelles, Slovenia, South Africa, Spain, Sweden, *Switzerland*, Tajikistan, *Tanzania*, Turkey, UK, Uruguay and Uzbekistan

Note: Additional Safeguards Protocols entered into force for Switzerland on 1 Feb. 2005, for Tanzania on 7 Feb. 2005 and for Nicaragua on 18 Feb. 2005. Iran and Libya have pledged to apply their Additional Safeguards Protocols pending their entry into force. Taiwan, although it has not concluded a safeguards agreement, has agreed to apply the measures contained in the 1997 Model Additional Safeguards Protocol.

Treaty on the Prohibition of the Emplacement of Nuclear Weapons and other Weapons of Mass Destruction on the Seabed and the Ocean Floor and in the Subsoil thereof (Seabed Treaty)

Opened for signature at London, Moscow and Washington, DC, on 11 February 1971; entered into force on 18 May 1972; depositaries British, Russian and US governments

The treaty prohibits implanting or emplacing on the seabed and the ocean floor and in the subsoil thereof beyond the outer limit of a 12-mile seabed zone any nuclear weapons or any other types of weapons of mass destruction as well as structures, launching installations or any other facilities specifically designed for storing, testing or using such weapons.

Parties (94): Afghanistan, Algeria, Antigua and Barbuda, Argentina[1], Australia, Austria, Bahamas, Belarus, Belgium, Benin, Bosnia and Herzegovina, Botswana, Brazil[2], Bulgaria, Canada[3], Cape Verde, Central African Republic, China, Congo (Republic of), Côte d'Ivoire, Croatia, Cuba, Cyprus, Czech Republic, Denmark, Dominican Republic, Ethiopia, Finland,

Germany, Ghana, Greece, Guatemala, Guinea-Bissau, Hungary, Iceland, India[4], Iran, Iraq, Ireland, Italy[5], Jamaica, Japan, Jordan, Korea (South), Laos, Latvia, Lesotho, Libya, Liechtenstein, Luxembourg, Malaysia, Malta, Mauritius, Mexico[6], Mongolia, Morocco, Nepal, Netherlands, New Zealand, Nicaragua, Niger, Norway, Panama, Philippines, Poland, Portugal, Qatar, Romania, Russia, Rwanda, Saint Vincent and the Grenadines, Sao Tome and Principe, Saudi Arabia, Serbia and Montenegro[7], Seychelles, Singapore, Slovakia, Slovenia, Solomon Islands, South Africa, Spain, Swaziland, Sweden, Switzerland, Taiwan, Togo, Tunisia, Turkey[8], UK, Ukraine, USA, Viet Nam[9], Yemen, Zambia

[1] Argentina precludes any possibility of strengthening, through this treaty, certain positions concerning continental shelves to the detriment of others based on different criteria.

[2] Brazil stated that nothing in the treaty shall be interpreted as prejudicing in any way the sovereign rights of Brazil in the area of the sea, the seabed and the subsoil thereof adjacent to its coasts. It is the understanding of Brazil that the word 'observation', as it appears in para. 1 of Article III of the treaty, refers only to observation that is incidental to the normal course of navigation in accordance with international law.

[3] Canada declared that Article I, para. 1, cannot be interpreted as indicating that any state has a right to implant or emplace any weapons not prohibited under Article I, para. 1, on the seabed and ocean floor, and in the subsoil thereof, beyond the limits of national jurisdiction, or as constituting any limitation on the principle that this area of the seabed and ocean floor and the subsoil thereof shall be reserved for exclusively peaceful purposes. Articles I, II and III cannot be interpreted as indicating that any state but the coastal state has any right to implant or emplace any weapon not prohibited under Article I, para. 1 on the continental shelf, or the subsoil thereof, appertaining to that coastal state, beyond the outer limit of the seabed zone referred to in Article I and defined in Article II. Article III cannot be interpreted as indicating any restrictions or limitation upon the rights of the coastal state, consistent with its exclusive sovereign rights with respect to the continental shelf, to verify, inspect or effect the removal of any weapon, structure, installation, facility or device implanted or emplaced on the continental shelf, or the subsoil thereof, appertaining to that coastal state, beyond the outer limit of the seabed zone referred to in Article I and defined in Article II.

[4] The accession by India is based on its position that it has full and exclusive rights over the continental shelf adjoining its territory and beyond its territorial waters and the subsoil thereof. There cannot, therefore, be any restriction on, or limitation of, the sovereign right of India as a coastal state to verify, inspect, remove or destroy any weapon, device, structure, installation or facility, which might be implanted or emplaced on or beneath its continental shelf by any other country, or to take such other steps as may be considered necessary to safeguard its security.

[5] Italy stated, *inter alia*, that in the case of agreements on further measures in the field of disarmament to prevent an arms race on the seabed and ocean floor and in their subsoil, the question of the delimitation of the area within which these measures would find application shall have to be examined and solved in each instance in accordance with the nature of the measures to be adopted.

[6] Mexico declared that the treaty cannot be interpreted to mean that a state has the right to emplace weapons of mass destruction, or arms or military equipment of any type, on the continental shelf of Mexico. It reserves the right to verify, inspect, remove or destroy any weapon, structure, installation, device or equipment placed on its continental shelf, including nuclear weapons or other weapons of mass destruction.

[7] In 1974, the Ambassador of Yugoslavia transmitted to the US Secretary of State a note stating that in the view of the Yugoslav Government, Article III, para. 1, of the treaty should be interpreted in such a way that a state exercising its right under this article shall be obliged to notify in advance the coastal state, in so far as its observations are to be carried out 'within the stretch of the sea extending above the continental shelf of the said state'. The USA objected to the Yugoslav reservation, which it considered incompatible with the object and purpose of the treaty.

[8] Turkey declared that the provisions of Article II cannot be used by a state party in support of claims other than those related to disarmament. Hence, Article II cannot be interpreted as establishing a link with the UN Convention on the Law of the Sea. Furthermore, no provision of the Seabed Treaty confers on parties the right to militarize zones which have been demilitarized by other international instruments. Nor can it be interpreted as conferring on either the coastal states or other states the right to emplace nuclear weapons or other weapons of mass destruction on the continental shelf of a demilitarized territory.

[9] Viet Nam stated that no provision of the treaty should be interpreted in a way that would contradict the rights of the coastal states with regard to their continental shelf, including the right to take measures to ensure their security.

Signed but not ratified: Bolivia, Burundi, Cambodia, Cameroon, Colombia, Costa Rica, Equatorial Guinea, Gambia, Guinea, Honduras, Lebanon, Liberia, Madagascar, Mali, Myanmar (Burma), Paraguay, Senegal, Sierra Leone, Sudan, Tanzania, Uruguay

Convention on the Prohibition of the Development, Production and Stockpiling of Bacteriological (Biological) and Toxin Weapons and on their Destruction (Biological and Toxin Weapons Convention, BTWC)

Opened for signature at London, Moscow and Washington, DC, on 10 April 1972; entered into force on 26 March 1975; depositaries British, Russian and US governments

The convention prohibits the development, production, stockpiling or acquisition by other means or retention of microbial or other biological agents, or toxins whatever their origin or method of production, of types and in quantities that have no justification of prophylactic, protective or other peaceful purposes, as well as weapons, equipment or means of delivery designed to use such agents or toxins for hostile purposes or in armed conflict. The destruction of the agents, toxins, weapons, equipment and means of delivery in the possession of the parties, or their diversion to peaceful purposes, should be effected not later than nine months after the entry into force of the convention for each country. According to a mandate from the 1996 BTWC Review Conference, verification and other measures to strengthen the convention are being discussed and considered in an Ad Hoc Group.

Parties (154): Afghanistan, Albania, Algeria, Antigua and Barbuda, Argentina, Armenia, Australia, Austria, Azerbaijan, Bahamas, Bahrain, Bangladesh, Barbados, Belarus, Belgium, Belize, Benin, Bhutan, Bolivia, Bosnia and Herzegovina, Botswana, Brazil, Brunei Darussalam, Bulgaria, Burkina Faso, Cambodia, Canada, Cape Verde, Chile, China, Colombia, Congo (Democratic Republic of the), Congo (Republic of), Costa Rica, Croatia, Cuba, Cyprus, Czech Republic, Denmark, Dominica, Dominican Republic, Ecuador, El Salvador, Equatorial Guinea, Estonia, Ethiopia, Fiji, Finland, France, Gambia, Georgia, Germany, Ghana, Greece, Grenada, Guatemala, Guinea-Bissau, Holy See, Honduras, Hungary, Iceland, India, Indonesia, Iran, Iraq, Ireland, Italy, Jamaica, Japan, Jordan, Kenya, Korea (North), Korea (South), Kuwait, Kyrgyzstan, Laos, Latvia, Lebanon, Lesotho, Libya, Liechtenstein, Lithuania, Luxembourg, Macedonia (Former Yugoslav Republic of), Malaysia, Maldives, Mali, Malta, Mauritius, Mexico, Monaco, Mongolia, Morocco, Netherlands, New Zealand, Nicaragua, Niger, Nigeria, Norway, Oman, Pakistan, Palau, Panama, Papua New Guinea, Paraguay, Peru, Philippines, Poland, Portugal, Qatar, Romania, Russia, Rwanda, Saint Kitts and Nevis, Saint Lucia, Saint Vincent and the Grenadines, San Marino, Sao Tome and Principe, Saudi Arabia, Senegal, Serbia and Montenegro, Seychelles, Sierra Leone, Singapore, Slovakia, Slovenia, Solomon Islands, South Africa, Spain, Sri Lanka, Sudan, Suriname, Swaziland, Sweden, Switzerland*, Taiwan, Thailand, Timor-Leste, Togo, Tonga, Tunisia, Turkey, Turkmenistan, Uganda, UK, Ukraine, Uruguay, USA, Uzbekistan, Vanuatu, Venezuela, Viet Nam, Yemen, Zimbabwe

* With reservation.

Signed but not ratified: Burundi, Central African Republic, Côte d'Ivoire, Egypt, Gabon, Guyana, Haiti, Liberia, Madagascar, Malawi, Myanmar (Burma), Nepal, Somalia, Syria, Tanzania, United Arab Emirates

Treaty on the Limitation of Anti-Ballistic Missile Systems (ABM Treaty)

Signed by the USA and the USSR at Moscow on 26 May 1972; entered into force on 3 October 1972; no longer in force as of 13 June 2002

The parties undertook not to build nationwide defences against ballistic missile attack and limited the development and deployment of permitted strategic missile defences. The treaty prohibited the parties from giving air defence missiles, radars or launchers the technical ability to counter strategic ballistic missiles and from testing them in a strategic ABM mode.

The **1974 Protocol** to the ABM Treaty introduced further numerical restrictions on permitted ballistic missile defences.

In 1997 Russia and the USA signed a set of Agreed Statements, specifying the demarcation line between strategic missile defences, which are not permitted under the treaty, and non-strategic or theatre missile defences (TMD), which are permitted under the treaty. The set of 1997 agreements on anti-missile defence were ratified by Russia in April 2000, but because the USA did not ratify them they did not enter into force. On 13 December 2001 the USA announced its withdrawal from the ABM Treaty, which entered into effect on 13 June 2002.

Treaty on the Limitation of Underground Nuclear Weapon Tests (Threshold Test Ban Treaty, TTBT)

Signed by the USA and the USSR at Moscow on 3 July 1974; entered into force on 11 December 1990

The parties undertake not to carry out any underground nuclear weapon test having a yield exceeding 150 kilotons.

Treaty on Underground Nuclear Explosions for Peaceful Purposes (Peaceful Nuclear Explosions Treaty, PNET)

Signed by the USA and the USSR at Moscow and Washington, DC, on 28 May 1976; entered into force on 11 December 1990

The parties undertake not to carry out any underground nuclear explosion for peaceful purposes having a yield exceeding 150 kilotons or any group explosion having an aggregate yield exceeding 150 kilotons.

Convention on the Prohibition of Military or Any Other Hostile Use of Environmental Modification Techniques (Enmod Convention)

Opened for signature at Geneva on 18 May 1977; entered into force on 5 October 1978; depositary UN Secretary-General

The convention prohibits military or any other hostile use of environmental modification techniques having widespread, long-lasting or severe effects as the means of destruction, damage or injury to states party to the convention. The term 'environmental modification techniques' refers to any technique for changing—through the deliberate manipulation of natural processes—the dynamics, composition or structure of the earth, including its biota, lithosphere, hydrosphere and atmosphere, or of outer space. The understandings reached during the negotiations, but not written into the convention, define the terms 'widespread', 'long-lasting' and 'severe'.

Parties (69): Afghanistan, Algeria, Antigua and Barbuda, Argentina, Armenia, Australia, Austria, Bangladesh, Belarus, Belgium, Benin, Brazil, Bulgaria, Canada, Cape Verde, Chile, Costa Rica, Cuba, Cyprus, Czech Republic, Denmark, Dominica, Egypt, Finland, Germany, Ghana, Greece, Guatemala, Hungary, India, Ireland, Italy, Japan, Korea (North), Korea (South)*, Kuwait, Lithuania, Laos, Malawi, Mauritius, Mongolia, Netherlands*, New Zealand, Niger, Norway, Pakistan, Panama, Papua New Guinea, Poland, Romania, Russia, Saint Lucia, Saint Vincent and the Grenadines, Sao Tome and Principe, Slovakia, Solomon Islands, Spain, Sri Lanka, Sweden, Switzerland, Tajikistan, Tunisia, UK, Ukraine, Uruguay, USA, Uzbekistan, Viet Nam, Yemen

* With declaration.

Signed but not ratified: Bolivia, Congo (Democratic Republic of the), Ethiopia, Holy See, Iceland, Iran, Iraq, Lebanon, Liberia, Luxembourg, Morocco, Nicaragua, Portugal, Sierra Leone, Syria, Turkey, Uganda

Protocol I Additional to the 1949 Geneva Conventions, and Relating to the Protection of Victims of International Armed Conflicts

Protocol II Additional to the 1949 Geneva Conventions, and Relating to the Protection of Victims of Non-International Armed Conflicts

Opened for signature at Bern on 12 December 1977; entered into force on 7 December 1978; depositary Swiss Federal Council

The protocols confirm that the right of the parties to international or non-international armed conflicts to choose methods or means of warfare is not unlimited and that it is prohibited to use weapons or means of warfare which cause superfluous injury or unnecessary suffering.

Parties to Protocol I (162) and Protocol II (157): Albania, Algeria*, Angola[1]*, Antigua and Barbuda, Argentina*, Armenia, Australia*, Austria*, Bahamas, Bahrain, Bangladesh, Barbados, Belarus, Belgium*, Belize, Benin, Bolivia, Bosnia and Herzegovina, Botswana, Brazil, Brunei Darussalam, Bulgaria, Burkina Faso, Burundi, Cambodia, Cameroon, Canada*, Cape Verde, Central African Republic, Chad, Chile, China*, Colombia, Comoros, Congo (Democratic Republic of the), Congo (Republic of), Cook Islands, Costa Rica, Côte d'Ivoire, Croatia, Cuba, Cyprus, Czech Republic, Denmark*, Djibouti, Dominica, Dominican Republic, Ecuador, Egypt*, El Salvador, Equatorial Guinea, Estonia, Ethiopia, Finland*, France*, Gabon, Gambia, Georgia, Germany*, Ghana, Greece, Grenada, Guatemala, Guinea, Guinea-Bissau, Guyana, Holy See, Honduras, Hungary, Iceland*, Ireland, Italy*, Jamaica, Japan*, Jordan, Kazakhstan, Kenya, Korea (North)[1], Korea (South)*, Kuwait, Kyrgyzstan, Laos, Latvia, Lebanon, Lesotho, Liberia, Libya, Liechtenstein*, Lithuania, Luxembourg, Macedonia (Former Yugoslav Republic of), Madagascar, Malawi, Maldives, Mali, Malta*, Mauritania, Mauritius, Mexico[1], Micronesia, Moldova, Monaco, Mongolia, Mozambique, Namibia, Netherlands*, New Zealand*, Nicaragua, Niger, Nigeria, Norway, Oman, Palau, Panama, Paraguay, Peru, Philippines[2], Poland, Portugal, Qatar*[1], Romania, Russia*, Rwanda, Saint Kitts and Nevis, Saint Lucia, Saint Vincent and the Grenadines, Samoa (Western), San Marino, Sao Tome and Principe, Saudi Arabia*, Senegal, Serbia and Montenegro*, Seychelles, Sierra Leone, Slovakia, Slovenia, Solomon Islands, South Africa, Spain*, Suriname, Swaziland, Sweden*, Switzerland*, Syria*[1], Tajikistan, Tanzania, Togo, Tonga,

Trinidad and Tobago*, Tunisia, Turkmenistan, Uganda, UK, Ukraine, United Arab Emirates*, Uruguay, Uzbekistan, Vanuatu, Venezuela, Viet Nam[1], Yemen, Zambia, Zimbabwe

* With reservation and/or declaration.

[1] Party only to Protocol I.
[2] Party only to Protocol II.

In 1989 the Palestine Liberation Organization (PLO) informed the depositary that it had decided to adhere to the four Geneva Conventions and the two Protocols.

Convention on the Physical Protection of Nuclear Material

Opened for signature at Vienna and New York on 3 March 1980; entered into force on 8 February 1987; depositary IAEA Director General

The convention obligates the parties to protect nuclear material for peaceful purposes while in international transport.

Parties (111): Afghanistan, Albania, Algeria*, Antigua and Barbuda, Argentina*, Armenia, Australia, Austria, Azerbaijan*, Belarus, Belgium, Bolivia, Bosnia and Herzegovina, Botswana, Brazil, Bulgaria, Burkina Faso, Cameroon, Canada, Chile, China*, Colombia, Congo (Democratic Republic of the), Costa Rica, Croatia, Cuba, Cyprus, Czech Republic, Denmark, Djibouti, Dominica, Ecuador, Equatorial Guinea, Estonia, Euratom*, Finland, France*, Germany, Ghana, Greece, Grenada, Guatemala, Honduras, Hungary, Iceland, India*, Indonesia*, Ireland, Israel*, Italy, Japan, Kenya, Korea (South)*, Kuwait*, Latvia, Lebanon, Liechtenstein, Libya, Lithuania, Luxembourg, Macedonia (Former Yugoslav Republic of), Madagascar, Mali, Malta, Marshall Islands, Mexico, Moldova, Monaco, Mongolia*, Morocco, Mozambique*, Namibia, Netherlands*, New Zealand, Nicaragua, Niger, Norway, Oman*, Panama, Pakistan*, Paraguay, Peru*, Philippines, Poland*, Portugal*, Qatar*, Romania, Russia*, Senegal, Serbia and Montenegro, Seychelles, Slovakia, Slovenia, Spain*, Sudan, Swaziland, Sweden, Switzerland, Tajikistan, Tonga, Trinidad and Tobago, Tunisia, Turkey*, *Turkmenistan*, Uganda, UK, Ukraine, United Arab Emirates, Uruguay, USA, Uzbekistan

* With reservation and/or declaration.

Note: Turkmenistan ratified the convention on 8 Jan. 2005.

Signed but not ratified: Dominican Republic, Haiti, Niger, South Africa

Convention on Prohibitions or Restrictions on the Use of Certain Conventional Weapons which may be Deemed to be Excessively Injurious or to have Indiscriminate Effects (CCW Convention, or 'Inhumane Weapons' Convention)

The convention, with protocols I, II and III, was opened for signature at New York on 10 April 1981; entered into force on 2 December 1983; depositary UN Secretary-General

The convention is an 'umbrella treaty', under which specific agreements can be concluded in the form of protocols. To become a party to the convention a state must ratify a minimum of two of the protocols.

The amendment to Article I of the original, 1981 convention was opened for signature at Geneva on 21 November 2001. It expands the scope of application to non-international armed conflicts. The Amended Convention entered into force on 18 May 2004.

Protocol I prohibits the use of weapons intended to injure by fragments which are not detectable in the human body by X-rays.

Protocol II prohibits or restricts the use of mines, booby-traps and other devices.

Amended Protocol II, which entered into force on 3 December 1998, reinforces the constraints regarding landmines.

Protocol III restricts the use of incendiary weapons.

Protocol IV, which entered into force on 30 July 1998, prohibits the employment of laser weapons specifically designed to cause permanent blindness to unenhanced vision.

Protocol V on Explosive Remnants of War, adopted in Geneva on 28 November 2003, recognizes the need for measures of a generic nature to minimize the risks and effects of explosive remnants of war. It will enter into force after the 20th deposit of the instruments of ratification.

Parties to the 1981 convention and original protocols (99): Albania, Argentina*, Australia, Austria, Bangladesh, Belarus, Belgium, Benin[1], Bolivia, Bosnia and Herzegovina, Brazil, Bulgaria, Burkina Faso, Cambodia, Canada, Cape Verde, Chile[1], China, Colombia, Costa Rica, Croatia, Cuba, Cyprus*, Czech Republic, Denmark, Djibouti, Ecuador, El Salvador, Estonia[1], Finland, France*, Georgia, Germany, Greece, Guatemala, Holy See, Honduras, Hungary, India, Ireland, Israel[2], Italy, Japan, Jordan[1], Korea (South)[3], Laos, Latvia, Lesotho, Liechtenstein, Lithuania[1], Luxembourg, Macedonia (Former Yugoslav Republic of), Maldives[1], Mali, Malta, Mauritius, Mexico, Moldova, Monaco[3], Mongolia, Morocco[4], Nauru, Netherlands*, New Zealand, Nicaragua[1], Niger, Norway, Pakistan, Panama, Paraguay, Peru[1], Philippines, Poland, Portugal, Romania, Russia, Senegal[5], Serbia and Montenegro, Seychelles, Sierra Leone, Slovakia, Slovenia, South Africa, Spain, Sri Lanka, Sweden, Switzerland, Tajikistan, Togo, Tunisia, *Turkey*[3], Turkmenistan[2], Uganda, UK, Ukraine, Uruguay, USA[2], Uzbekistan, *Venezuela*

* With reservation and/or declaration.

[1] Party only to 1981 Protocols I and III.
[2] Party only to 1981 Protocols I and II.
[3] Party only to 1981 Protocol I.
[4] Party only to 1981 Protocol II.
[5] Party only to 1981 Protocol III.

Note: Turkey ratified the convention on 2 Mar. and Venezuela acceded on 19 Apr. 2005.

Signed but not ratified the 1981 convention and original protocols: Afghanistan, Egypt, Iceland, Nigeria, Sudan, Viet Nam

Parties to the Amended Convention and original protocols (40): Argentina, Australia, Austria, Belgium, Bulgaria, Burkina Faso, Canada, China*, Croatia, Denmark, Estonia, Finland, France, *Germany*, Greece, Holy See*, Hungary, Italy, Japan, Korea (South), Latvia, Liechtenstein, Lithuania, Malta, Mexico*, *Moldova*, Netherlands, Norway, Panama, *Peru*, Romania, Serbia and Montenegro, Sierra Leone, Slovakia, Spain, Sri Lanka, Sweden, Switzerland, *Turkey*, UK

* With reservation and/or declaration.

Note: Moldova acceded to the Amended Convention on 5 Jan., Germany accepted it on 26 Jan., Peru ratified it on 14 Feb., and Turkey ratified it on 2 Mar. 2005.

Parties to Amended Protocol II (83): Albania, Argentina, Australia, Austria, Bangladesh, Belarus, Belgium, Bolivia, Bosnia and Herzegovina, Brazil, Bulgaria, Burkina Faso,

Cambodia, Canada, Cape Verde, Chile, China, Colombia, Costa Rica, Croatia, Cyprus, Czech Republic, Denmark, Ecuador, El Salvador, Estonia, Finland, France, Germany, Greece, Guatemala, Holy See, Honduras, Hungary, India, Ireland, Israel, Italy, Japan, Jordan, Korea (South), Latvia, Liechtenstein, Lithuania, Luxembourg, Maldives, Mali, Malta, Moldova, Monaco, Morocco, Nauru, Netherlands, New Zealand, Nicaragua, Norway, Pakistan, Panama, Paraguay, Peru, Philippines, Poland, Portugal, Romania, *Russia*, Senegal, Seychelles, Sierra Leone, Slovakia, Slovenia, South Africa, Spain, Sri Lanka, Sweden, Switzerland, Tajikistan, *Turkey*, Turkmenistan, UK, Ukraine, Uruguay, USA, *Venezuela*

Note: Russia and Turkey ratified Amended Protocol II on 2 Mar. and Venezuela on 19 Apr. 2005.

Parties to Protocol IV (80): Albania, Argentina, Australia, Austria, Bangladesh, Belarus, Belgium, Bolivia, Bosnia and Herzegovina, Brazil, Bulgaria, Burkina Faso, Cambodia, Canada, Cape Verde, Chile, China, Colombia, Costa Rica, Croatia, Cyprus, Czech Republic, Denmark, Ecuador, El Salvador, Estonia, Finland, France, Germany, Greece, Guatemala, Holy See, Honduras, Hungary, India, Ireland, Israel, Italy, Japan, Latvia, Liechtenstein, Lithuania, Luxembourg, Maldives, Mali, Malta, Mauritius, Mexico, Moldova, Mongolia, Morocco, Nauru, Netherlands, New Zealand, Nicaragua, Norway, Pakistan, Panama, Peru, Philippines, Poland, Portugal, Romania, Russia, Serbia and Montenegro, Seychelles, Sierra Leone, Slovakia, Slovenia, South Africa, Spain, Sri Lanka, Sweden, Switzerland, Tajikistan, *Turkey*, UK, Ukraine, Uruguay, Uzbekistan

Note: Turkey ratified Protocol IV on 2 Mar. 2005.

6 ratifications deposited: *Croatia*, *Finland*, *Germany*, Lithuania, Sierra Leone, Sweden

Note: Croatia ratified Protocol V on 7 Feb., Germany on 3 Mar. and Finland on 23 Mar. 2005.

South Pacific Nuclear Free Zone Treaty (Treaty of Rarotonga)

Opened for signature at Rarotonga, Cook Islands, on 6 August 1985; entered into force on 11 December 1986; depositary Director of the Pacific Islands Forum Secretariat

The treaty prohibits the manufacture or acquisition by other means of any nuclear explosive device, as well as possession or control over such device by the parties anywhere inside or outside the zone area described in an annex. The parties also undertake not to supply nuclear material or equipment, unless subject to IAEA safeguards, and to prevent in their territories the stationing as well as the testing of any nuclear explosive device and undertake not to dump, and to prevent the dumping of, radioactive wastes and other radioactive matter at sea anywhere within the zone. Each party remains free to allow visits, as well as transit, by foreign ships and aircraft.

The treaty is open for signature by the members of the Pacific Islands Forum.

Under *Protocol 1* France, the UK and the USA undertake to apply the treaty prohibitions relating to the manufacture, stationing and testing of nuclear explosive devices in the territories situated within the zone, for which they are internationally responsible.

Under *Protocol 2* China, France, Russia, the UK and the USA undertake not to use or threaten to use a nuclear explosive device against the parties to the treaty or against any territory within the zone for which a party to Protocol 1 is internationally responsible.

Under *Protocol 3* China, France, the UK, the USA and Russia undertake not to test any nuclear explosive device anywhere within the zone.

Parties (13): Australia, Cook Islands, Fiji, Kiribati, Nauru, New Zealand, Niue, Papua New Guinea, Samoa (Western), Solomon Islands, Tonga, Tuvalu, Vanuatu

Parties to Protocol 1: France, UK; **signed but not ratified:** USA

Parties to Protocol 2: China, France[1], Russia, UK[2]; **signed but not ratified:** USA

Parties to Protocol 3: China, France, Russia, UK; **signed but not ratified:** USA

[1] France declared that the negative security guarantees set out in Protocol 2 are the same as the CD declaration of 6 Apr. 1995 referred to in UN Security Council Resolution 984 of 11 Apr. 1995.

[2] On ratifying Protocol 2 in 1997, the UK declared that nothing in the treaty affects the rights under international law with regard to transit of the zone or visits to ports and airfields within the zone by ships and aircraft. The UK will not be bound by the undertakings in Protocol 2 in case of an invasion or any other attack on the UK, its territories, its armed forces or its allies, carried out or sustained by a party to the treaty in association or alliance with a nuclear weapon state or if a party violates its non-proliferation obligations under the treaty.

Treaty on the Elimination of Intermediate-Range and Shorter-Range Missiles (INF Treaty)

Signed by the USA and the USSR at Washington, DC, on 8 December 1987; entered into force on 1 June 1988

The treaty obligates the parties to destroy all land-based missiles with a range of 500–5500 km (intermediate-range, 1000–5500 km; and shorter-range, 500–1000 km) and their launchers by 1 June 1991. The treaty was implemented by the two parties before this date.

Treaty on Conventional Armed Forces in Europe (CFE Treaty)

Original treaty signed at Paris on 19 November 1990; entered into force on 9 November 1992; depositary Netherlands Government

The treaty sets ceilings on five categories of treaty-limited equipment (TLE)—battle tanks, armoured combat vehicles, artillery of at least 100-mm calibre, combat aircraft and attack helicopters—in an area stretching from the Atlantic Ocean to the Ural Mountains (the Atlantic-to-the-Urals, ATTU, zone).

The treaty was negotiated and signed by the member states of the Warsaw Treaty Organization and NATO within the framework of the Conference on Security and Co-operation in Europe (from 1995 the Organization for Security and Co-operation in Europe, OSCE).

The **1992 Tashkent Agreement**, adopted by the former Soviet republics (with the exception of the three Baltic states) with territories within the ATTU zone, and the **1992 Oslo Document** (Final Document of the Extraordinary Conference of the States Parties to the CFE Treaty) introduced modifications to the treaty required because of the emergence of new states after the break-up of the USSR.

Parties (30): Armenia, Azerbaijan, Belarus, Belgium, Bulgaria, Canada, Czech Republic, Denmark, France, Georgia, Germany, Greece, Hungary, Iceland, Italy, Kazakhstan, Luxembourg, Moldova, Netherlands, Norway, Poland, Portugal, Romania, Russia, Slovakia, Spain, Turkey, UK, Ukraine, USA

The first Review Conference of the CFE Treaty adopted the **1996 Flank Document**, which reorganized the flank areas geographically and numerically, allowing Russia and Ukraine to deploy more TLE.

The **1999 Agreement on Adaptation of the CFE Treaty** replaces the CFE Treaty bloc-to-bloc military balance with individual state limits on TLE holdings and provides for a new structure of limitations and new military flexibility mechanisms, flank sub-limits and enhanced transparency; it opens the CFE regime to all the other European states. It will enter into force when it has been ratified by all the signatories. The **1999 Final Act**, with annexes, contains politically binding arrangements with regard to the North Caucasus and Central and Eastern Europe, and withdrawals of armed forces from foreign territories.

3 ratifications of the Agreement on Adaptation deposited: Belarus, Kazakhstan, Russia*

* With reservation and/or declaration.

Concluding Act of the Negotiation on Personnel Strength of Conventional Armed Forces in Europe (CFE-1A Agreement)

Signed by the parties to the CFE Treaty at Helsinki on 10 July 1992; entered into force simultaneously with the CFE Treaty; depositary Netherlands Government

The agreement limits the personnel of the conventional land-based armed forces of the parties within the ATTU zone.

Treaty on the Reduction and Limitation of Strategic Offensive Arms (START I Treaty)

Signed by the USA and the USSR at Moscow on 31 July 1991; entered into force on 5 December 1994

The treaty obligates the parties to make phased reductions in their offensive strategic nuclear forces over a seven-year period. It sets numerical limits on deployed strategic nuclear delivery vehicles (SNDVs)—ICBMs, SLBMs and heavy bombers—and the nuclear warheads they carry. In the Protocol to Facilitate the Implementation of the START Treaty (**1992 Lisbon Protocol**), which entered into force on 5 December 1994, Belarus, Kazakhstan and Ukraine also assumed the obligations of the former USSR under the treaty.

Treaty on Open Skies

Opened for signature at Helsinki on 24 March 1992; entered into force on 1 January 2002; depositaries Canadian and Hungarian governments

The treaty obligates the parties to submit their territories to short-notice unarmed surveillance flights. The area of application stretches from Vancouver, Canada, eastward to Vladivostok, Russia.

The treaty was negotiated between the member states of the Warsaw Treaty Organization and NATO. It was opened for signature by the NATO states, the states of the former Warsaw Treaty Organization and the states of the former Soviet Union (except the three Baltic states). For six months after entry into force of the treaty, any other participating state of the Organization for Security and Co-operation in Europe could apply for accession to the treaty, and from 1 July 2002 any state can apply to accede to the treaty.

Parties (35): Belarus, Belgium, Bosnia and Herzegovina, Bulgaria, Canada, Croatia, Czech Republic, Denmark, *Estonia,* Finland, France, Georgia, Germany, Greece, Hungary, Iceland, Italy, Latvia, *Lithuania*, Luxembourg, Netherlands, Norway, Poland, Portugal, Romania, Russia, Slovakia, Slovenia, Spain, Russia, Sweden, Turkey, UK, Ukraine, USA

Note: Estonia ratified the treaty on 24 Mar. 2005 and Lithuania ratified it on 9 May 2005.

Signed but not ratified: Kyrgyzstan

Treaty on Further Reduction and Limitation of Strategic Offensive Arms (START II Treaty)

Signed by the USA and Russia at Moscow on 3 January 1993; not in force

The treaty obligated the parties to eliminate their MIRVed ICBMs and reduce the number of their deployed strategic nuclear warheads to no more than 3000–3500 each (of which no more than 1750 may be deployed on SLBMs) by 1 January 2003. On 26 September 1997 the two parties signed a *Protocol* to the treaty providing for the extension until the end of 2007 of the period of implementation of the treaty.

Note: The START II Treaty was ratified by the US Senate and the Russian Duma and Federation Council, but the two parties never exchanged the instruments of ratification. Hence the treaty never entered into force. On 14 June 2002, as a response to the taking effect on 13 June of the USA's withdrawal from the ABM Treaty, Russia declared that it will no longer be bound by the START II Treaty.

Convention on the Prohibition of the Development, Production, Stockpiling and Use of Chemical Weapons and on their Destruction (Chemical Weapons Convention, CWC)

Opened for signature at Paris on 13 January 1993; entered into force on 29 April 1997; depositary UN Secretary-General

The convention prohibits the use, development, production, acquisition, transfer and stockpiling of chemical weapons. Each party undertakes to destroy its chemical weapons and production facilities within 10 years of the entry into force of the treaty.

Parties (168): Afghanistan, Albania, Algeria, Andorra, Argentina, Armenia, Australia, Austria, Azerbaijan, Bahrain, Bangladesh, Belarus, Belgium, Belize, Benin, Bolivia, Bosnia and Herzegovina, Botswana, Brazil, Brunei Darussalam, Bulgaria, Burkina Faso, Burundi, Cameroon, Canada, Cape Verde, Chad, Chile, China, Colombia, Cook Islands, Costa Rica, Côte d'Ivoire, Croatia, Cuba, Cyprus, Czech Republic, Denmark, Dominica, Ecuador, El Salvador, Equatorial Guinea, Eritrea, Estonia, Ethiopia, Fiji, Finland, France, Gabon, Gambia, Georgia, Germany, Ghana, Greece, Guatemala, Guinea, Guyana, Holy See, Hungary, Iceland, India, Indonesia, Iran, Ireland, Italy, Jamaica, Japan, Jordan, Kazakhstan, Kenya, Kiribati, Korea (South), Kuwait, Kyrgyzstan, Laos, Latvia, Lesotho, Libya, Liechtenstein, Lithuania, Luxembourg, Macedonia (Former Yugoslav Republic of), Madagascar, Malawi, Malaysia, Maldives, Mali, Malta, Marshall Islands, Mauritania, Mauritius, Mexico, Micronesia, Moldova, Monaco, Mongolia, Morocco, Mozambique, Namibia, Nauru, Nepal, Netherlands, New Zealand, Nicaragua, Niger, Nigeria, *Niue*, Norway, Oman, Pakistan, Palau, Panama, Papua New Guinea, Paraguay, Peru, Philippines, Poland,

Portugal, Qatar, Romania, Russia, Rwanda, Saint Kitts and Nevis, Saint Lucia, Saint Vincent and the Grenadines, Samoa (Western), San Marino, Sao Tome and Principe, Saudi Arabia, Senegal, Serbia and Montenegro, Seychelles, Sierra Leone, Singapore, Slovakia, Slovenia, Solomon Islands, South Africa, Spain, Sri Lanka, Sudan, Suriname, Swaziland, Sweden, Switzerland, Tajikistan, Tanzania, Thailand, Timor-Leste, Togo, Tonga, Trinidad and Tobago, Tunisia, Turkey, Turkmenistan, Tuvalu, Uganda, UK, Ukraine, United Arab Emirates, Uruguay, USA, Uzbekistan, Venezuela, Viet Nam, Yemen, Zambia, Zimbabwe

Note: Niue acceded to the convention on 21 Apr. 2005.

Signed but not ratified: Bahamas, Bhutan, Cambodia, Central African Republic, Comoros, Congo (Democratic Republic of the), Congo (Republic of), Djibouti, Dominican Republic, Grenada, Guinea-Bissau, Haiti, Honduras, Israel, Liberia, Myanmar (Burma)

Treaty on the Southeast Asia Nuclear Weapon-Free Zone (Treaty of Bangkok)

Signed at Bangkok on 15 December 1995; entered into force on 27 March 1997; depositary Government of Thailand

The treaty prohibits the development, manufacture, acquisition or testing of nuclear weapons inside or outside the zone area as well as the stationing and transport of nuclear weapons in or through the zone. Each state party may decide for itself whether to allow visits and transit by foreign ships and aircraft. The parties undertake not to dump at sea or discharge into the atmosphere anywhere within the zone any radioactive material or wastes or dispose of radioactive material on land. The parties should conclude an agreement with the IAEA for the application of full-scope safeguards to their peaceful nuclear activities.

The zone includes not only the territories but also the continental shelves and exclusive economic zones of the states parties.

The treaty is open for all 10 states of South-East Asia.

Under a *Protocol* to the treaty China, France, Russia, the UK and the USA are to undertake not to use or threaten to use nuclear weapons against any state party to the treaty. They should further undertake not to use nuclear weapons within the Southeast Asia nuclear weapon-free zone. The protocol will enter into force for each state party on the date of its deposit of the instrument of ratification.

Parties (10): Brunei Darussalam, Cambodia, Indonesia, Laos, Malaysia, Myanmar (Burma), Philippines, Singapore, Thailand, Viet Nam

Protocol: no signatures, no parties

Agreement on Confidence- and Security-Building Measures in Bosnia and Herzegovina between Bosnia and Herzegovina, the Federation of Bosnia and Herzegovina and the Republika Srpska

Signed at Vienna on 26 January 1996; entered into force on 26 January 1996

The agreement is based largely on the 1994 Vienna Document on Confidence- and Security-Building Measures but includes additional restrictions and restraints on military movements, deployments and exercises and provides for exchange of information and data relating to major weapon systems.

African Nuclear-Weapon-Free Zone Treaty (Treaty of Pelindaba)

Signed at Cairo on 11 April 1996; not in force as of 1 January 2005; depositary Secretary-General of the African Union

The treaty prohibits the research, development, manufacture and acquisition of nuclear explosive devices and the testing or stationing of any nuclear explosive device. Each party remains free to allow visits, as well as transit by foreign ships and aircraft. The treaty also prohibits any attack against nuclear installations. The parties undertake not to dump or permit the dumping of radioactive wastes and other radioactive matter anywhere within the zone. The parties should conclude an agreement with the IAEA for the application of comprehensive safeguards to their peaceful nuclear activities.

The zone includes the territory of the continent of Africa, island states members of the African Union (AU) and all islands considered by the AU to be part of Africa.

The treaty is open for signature by all the states of Africa. It will enter into force upon the 28th ratification.

Under *Protocol I* China, France, Russia, the UK and the USA are to undertake not to use or threaten to use a nuclear explosive device against the parties to the treaty.

Under *Protocol II* China, France, Russia, the UK and the USA are to undertake not to test nuclear explosive devices anywhere within the zone.

Under *Protocol III* states with territories within the zone for which they are internationally responsible are to undertake to observe certain provisions of the treaty with respect to these territories. This protocol is open for signature by France and Spain.

The protocols will enter into force simultaneously with the treaty for those protocol signatories that have deposited their instruments of ratification.

19 ratifications deposited: Algeria, Botswana, Burkina Faso, Côte d'Ivoire, Equatorial Guinea, Gambia, Guinea, Kenya, Lesotho, Madagascar, Mali, Mauritania, Mauritius, Nigeria, South Africa, Swaziland, Tanzania, Togo, Zimbabwe

Signed but not ratified: Angola, Benin, Burundi, Cameroon, Cape Verde, Central African Republic, Chad, Comoros, Congo (Democratic Republic of the), Congo (Republic of), Djibouti, Egypt, Eritrea, Ethiopia, Gabon, Ghana, Guinea-Bissau, Liberia, Libya, Malawi, Morocco, Mozambique, Namibia, Niger, Rwanda, Sao Tome and Principe, Senegal, Seychelles, Sierra Leone, Sudan, Tunisia, Uganda, Zambia

Protocol I: ratifications deposited: China, France[1], UK[3]; **signed but not ratified:** Russia[2], USA[4]

Protocol II: ratifications deposited: China, France, UK[3]; **signed but not ratified:** Russia[2], USA[4]

Protocol III: ratifications deposited: France

[1] France stated that the Protocols did not affect its right to self-defence, as stipulated in Article 51 of the UN Charter. It clarified that its commitment under Article 1 of Protocol I was equivalent to the negative security assurances given by France to non-nuclear weapon states parties to the NPT, as confirmed in its declaration made on 6 Apr. 1995 at the Conference on Disarmament, and as referred to in UN Security Council Resolution 984.

[2] Russia stated that as long as a military base of a nuclear state was located on the islands of the Chagos archipelago these islands could not be regarded as fulfilling the requirements put forward by the Treaty for nuclear-weapon-free territories. Moreover, since certain states declared that they would consider themselves free from the obligations under the Protocols with regard to the mentioned territories,

Russia could not consider itself to be bound by the obligations under Protocol I in respect to the same territories. Russia interpreted its obligations under Article 1 of Protocol I as follows: It would not use nuclear weapons against a state party to the Treaty, except in the case of invasion or any other armed attack on Russia, its territory, its armed forces or other troops, its allies or a state towards which it had a security commitment, carried out or sustained by a non-nuclear-weapon state party to the treaty, in association or alliance with a nuclear-weapon state.

[3] The UK stated that it did not accept the inclusion of the British Indian Ocean Territory within the African nuclear weapon-free zone without its consent, and did not accept, by its adherence to Protocols I and II, any legal obligations in respect of that territory. Moreover, it would not be bound by its undertaking under Article 1 of Protocol I in case of an invasion or any other attack on the United Kingdom, its dependent territories, its armed forces or other troops, its allies or a state towards which it had security commitment, carried out or sustained by a party to the treaty in association or alliance with a nuclear-weapon state, or if any party to the treaty was in material breach of its own non-proliferation obligations under the treaty.

[4] The USA stated, with respect to Protocol I, that it would consider an invasion or any other attack on the USA, its territories, its armed forces or other troops, its allies or on a state toward which it had a security commitment, carried out or sustained by a party to the treaty in association or alliance with a nuclear-weapon state, to be incompatible with the treaty party's corresponding obligations. The USA also stated that neither the treaty nor Protocol II would apply to the activities of the UK, the USA or any other state not party to the treaty on the island of Diego Garcia or elsewhere in the British Indian Ocean Territories. No change was, therefore, required in US armed forces operations in Diego Garcia and elsewhere in these territories.

Agreement on Sub-Regional Arms Control concerning Yugoslavia (Serbia and Montenegro), Bosnia and Herzegovina, and Croatia (Florence Agreement)

Adopted at Florence and entered into force on 14 June 1996

The agreement was negotiated under the auspices of the OSCE in accordance with the mandate in the 1995 General Framework Agreement for Peace in Bosnia and Herzegovina (Dayton Agreement). It sets numerical ceilings on armaments of the former warring parties: Bosnia and Herzegovina and its two entities, Croatia and the Federal Republic of Yugoslavia. Five categories of heavy conventional weapons are included: battle tanks, armoured combat vehicles, heavy artillery (75 mm and above), combat aircraft and attack helicopters. The reductions were completed by 31 October 1997. It is confirmed that 6580 weapon items were destroyed by that date.

Comprehensive Nuclear Test-Ban Treaty (CTBT)

Opened for signature at New York on 24 September 1996; not in force as of 1 January 2005; depositary UN Secretary-General

The treaty prohibits the carrying out of any nuclear weapon test explosion or any other nuclear explosion, and urges each party to prevent any such nuclear explosion at any place under its jurisdiction or control and refrain from causing, encouraging, or in any way participating in the carrying out of any nuclear weapon test explosion or any other nuclear explosion.

The treaty will enter into force 180 days after the date of the deposit of the instruments of ratification of the 44 states listed in an annex to the treaty. All the 44 states possess nuclear power reactors and/or nuclear research reactors.

The 44 states whose ratification is required for entry into force are: Algeria, Argentina, Australia, Austria, Bangladesh, Belgium, Brazil, Bulgaria, Canada, Chile, China*, Colombia*, Congo (Democratic Republic of the), Egypt*, Finland, France, Germany, Hungary, India*, Indonesia*, Iran*, Israel*, Italy, Japan, Korea (North)*, Korea (South), Mexico, Netherlands, Norway, Pakistan*, Peru, Poland, Romania, Russia, Slovakia, South Africa, Spain, Sweden, Switzerland, Turkey, UK, Ukraine, USA* and Viet Nam*.

* States which as of 1 Jan. 2005 had not ratified the treaty.

121 ratifications deposited: Afghanistan, Albania, Algeria, Argentina, Australia, Austria, Azerbaijan, Bahrain, Bangladesh, Belarus, Belgium, Belize, Benin, Bolivia, Botswana, Brazil, Bulgaria, Burkina Faso, Cambodia, Canada, Chile, Congo (Democratic Republic of the), Costa Rica, Côte d'Ivoire, Croatia, Cyprus, Czech Republic, Denmark, Ecuador, El Salvador, Eritrea, Estonia, Fiji, Finland, France, Gabon, Georgia, Germany, Greece, Grenada, Guyana, Holy See, Honduras, Hungary, Iceland, Ireland, Italy, Jamaica, Japan, Jordan, Kazakhstan, Kenya, Kiribati, Korea (South), Kuwait, Kyrgyzstan, Laos, Latvia, Lesotho, Libya, Liechtenstein, Lithuania, Luxembourg, Macedonia (Former Yugoslav Republic of), Maldives, Mali, Malta, Mauritania, Mexico, Micronesia, Monaco, Mongolia, Morocco, Namibia, Nauru, Netherlands, New Zealand, Nicaragua, Niger, Nigeria, Norway, Oman, Panama, Paraguay, Peru, Philippines, Poland, Portugal, Qatar, Romania, Russia, Rwanda, *Saint Kitts and Nevis*, Saint Lucia, Samoa (Western), San Marino, Senegal, Serbia and Montenegro, Seychelles, Sierra Leone, Singapore, Slovakia, Slovenia, South Africa, Spain, Sudan, Sweden, Switzerland, Tajikistan, Tanzania, Togo, Tunisia, Turkey, Turkmenistan, Uganda, UK, Ukraine, United Arab Emirates, Uruguay, Uzbekistan, Venezuela

Note: Saint Kitts and Nevis deposited its instrument of ratification on 27 Apr. 2005.

Signed but not ratified: Andorra, Angola, Antigua and Barbuda, Armenia, Bosnia and Herzegovina, Brunei Darussalam, Burkina Faso, Burundi, Cameroon, Cape Verde, Central African Republic, Chad, China, Colombia, Comoros, Congo (Republic of), Cook Islands, Djibouti, Dominican Republic, Egypt, Equatorial Guinea, Ethiopia, Gambia, Ghana, Guatemala, Guinea, Guinea-Bissau, Haiti, Indonesia, Iran, Israel, Liberia, Madagascar, Malawi, Malaysia, Marshall Islands, Moldova, Mozambique, Myanmar (Burma), Nepal, Palau, Papua New Guinea, Sao Tome and Principe, Solomon Islands, Sri Lanka, Suriname, Swaziland, Thailand, USA, Vanuatu, Viet Nam, Yemen, Zambia, Zimbabwe

Inter-American Convention Against the Illicit Manufacturing of and Trafficking in Firearms, Ammunition, Explosives, and Other Related Materials

Adopted at Washington, DC, on 13 November 1997; opened for signature at Washington, DC, on 14 November 1997; entered into force on 1 July 1998; depositary General Secretariat of the Organization of American States

The purpose of the convention is to prevent, combat and eradicate the illicit manufacturing of and trafficking in firearms, ammunition, explosives and other related materials; and to promote and facilitate cooperation and the exchange of information and experience among the parties.

Parties (26): Antigua and Barbuda, Argentina*, Bahamas, Barbados, Belize, Bolivia, Brazil, Chile, Colombia, Costa Rica, Dominica, Ecuador*, El Salvador, Grenada, Guatemala, Honduras, Mexico, Nicaragua, Panama, Paraguay, Peru, Saint Kitts and Nevis, Saint Lucia, Trinidad and Tobago, Uruguay*, Venezuela

* With reservation.

Signed but not ratified: Canada, Dominican Republic, Guyana, Haiti, Jamaica, Saint Vincent and the Grenadines, Suriname, USA

Convention on the Prohibition of the Use, Stockpiling, Production and Transfer of Anti-Personnel Mines and on their Destruction (APM Convention)

Opened for signature at Ottawa on 3–4 December 1997 and at New York on 5 December 1997; entered into force on 1 March 1999; depositary UN Secretary-General

The convention prohibits anti-personnel mines, which are defined as mines designed to be exploded by the presence, proximity or contact of a person and which will incapacitate, injure or kill one or more persons.

Each party undertakes to destroy all its stockpiled anti-personnel mines as soon as possible but not later that four years after the entry into force of the convention for that state party. Each party also undertakes to destroy all anti-personnel mines in mined areas under its jurisdiction or control not later than 10 years after the entry into force of the convention for that state party.

Parties (144): Afghanistan, Albania, Algeria, Andorra, Angola, Antigua and Barbuda, Argentina, Australia, Austria, Bahamas, Bangladesh, Barbados, Belarus, Belgium, Belize, Benin, Bolivia, Bosnia and Herzegovina, Botswana, Brazil, Bulgaria, Burkina Faso, Burundi, Cambodia, Cameroon, Canada, Cape Verde, Central African Republic, Chad, Chile, Colombia, Comoros, Congo (Democratic Republic of the), Congo (Republic of), Costa Rica, Côte d'Ivoire, Croatia, Cyprus, Czech Republic, Denmark, Djibouti, Dominica, Dominican Republic, Ecuador, El Salvador, Equatorial Guinea, Eritrea, Estonia, Ethiopia, Fiji, France, Gabon, Gambia, Germany, Ghana, Greece, Grenada, Guatemala, Guinea, Guinea-Bissau, Guyana, Holy See, Honduras, Hungary, Iceland, Ireland, Italy, Jamaica, Japan, Jordan, Kenya, Kiribati, Lesotho, Liberia, Liechtenstein, Lithuania, Luxembourg, Macedonia (Former Yugoslav Republic of), Madagascar, Malawi, Malaysia, Maldives, Mali, Malta, Mauritania, Mauritius, Mexico, Moldova, Monaco, Mozambique, Namibia, Nauru, Netherlands, New Zealand, Nicaragua, Niger, Nigeria, Niue, Norway, Panama, Papua New Guinea, Paraguay, Peru, Philippines, Portugal, Qatar, Romania, Rwanda, Saint Kitts and Nevis, Saint Lucia, Saint Vincent and the Grenadines, Samoa (Western), San Marino, Sao Tome and Principe, Senegal, Serbia and Montenegro, Seychelles, Sierra Leone, Slovakia, Slovenia, Solomon Islands, South Africa, Spain, Sudan, Suriname, Swaziland, Sweden, Switzerland, Tajikistan, Tanzania, Thailand, Timor-Leste, Togo, Trinidad and Tobago, Tunisia, Turkey, Turkmenistan, Uganda, UK, Uruguay, Venezuela, Yemen, Zambia, Zimbabwe

Signed but not ratified: Brunei Darussalam, Cook Islands, Haiti, Indonesia, Marshall Islands, Poland, Ukraine, Vanuatu

Inter-American Convention on Transparency in Conventional Weapons Acquisitions

Adopted at Guatemala City on 7 June 1999; entered into force on 21 November 2002; depositary General Secretariat of the Organization of American States

The objective of the convention is to contribute more fully to regional openness and transparency in the acquisition of conventional weapons by exchanging information regarding such acquisitions, for the purpose of promoting confidence among states in the Americas.

Parties (9): Argentina, Canada, Ecuador, El Salvador, Guatemala, Nicaragua, Paraguay, Peru, Uruguay

Signed but not ratified: Bolivia, Brazil, Chile, Colombia, Costa Rica, Dominica, Haiti, Honduras, Mexico, USA, Venezuela

Vienna Document 1999 on Confidence- and Security-Building Measures

Adopted by the participating states of the Organization for Security and Co-operation in Europe at Istanbul on 16 November 1999; entered into force on 1 January 2000

The Vienna Document 1999 builds on the 1986 Stockholm Document on Confidence- and Security-Building Measures (CSBMs) and Disarmament in Europe and previous Vienna Documents (1990, 1992 and 1994). The Vienna Document 1990 provided for military budget exchange, risk reduction procedures, a communication network and an annual CSBM implementation assessment. The Vienna Documents 1992 and 1994 introduced new mechanisms and parameters for military activities, defence planning and military contacts.

The Vienna Document 1999 introduces regional measures aimed at increasing transparency and confidence in a bilateral, multilateral and regional context and some improvements, in particular regarding the constraining measures.

Treaty on Strategic Offensive Reductions (SORT)

Signed by the USA and Russia at Moscow on 24 May 2002; entered into force on 1 June 2003

The treaty obligates the parties to reduce the number of their operationally deployed strategic nuclear warheads so that the aggregate numbers do not exceed 1700–2200 for each party by 31 December 2012.

Annex B. Chronology 2004

NENNE BODELL

For the convenience of the reader, key words are indicated in the right-hand column, opposite each entry. The dates are according to local time.

2 Jan.	North Korea invites US experts to visit its nuclear facility at Yongbyon for the first time since International Atomic Energy Agency (IAEA) inspectors were forced to leave North Korea on 31 Dec. 2002. On 6 Jan., when the US experts arrive, the North Korean Government issues a statement in which it offers to suspend the testing and production of nuclear weapons and to freeze its nuclear industry.	USA; North Korea; Nuclear weapons
6 Jan.	At the South Asian Association for Regional Co-operation (SAARC) summit meeting, held in Islamabad, Pakistani President Pervez Musharraf and Indian Prime Minister Atal Behari Vajpayee issue a joint statement on their agreement to hold discussions on the Jammu and Kashmir dispute (see also *16–18 Feb.*).	India/Pakistan
7 Jan.	Meeting in Naivasha, Kenya, representatives of the Sudanese Government and the Sudan People's Liberation Movement/ Sudan People's Liberation Army (SPLM/A) sign the Agreement on Wealth Sharing During the Pre-Interim and Interim Period. Under the agreement the oil revenues of Sudan will be divided equally between the parties and a presidential commission will be set up to oversee the management of the oil contracts.	Sudan
12 Jan.	Meeting in Beijing, the US Secretary of Energy, Spencer Abraham, and the Chairman of the China Atomic Energy Authority (CAEA), Zhang Huazu, sign a Statement of Intent establishing a process for cooperation and collaboration with the International Atomic Energy Agency (IAEA) on nuclear non-proliferation.	China; USA; IAEA; Non-proliferation
16 Jan.	Japan sends peacekeeping forces to Iraq. This is the first time since World War II that Japan sends troops to a combat zone.	Japan; Peacekeeping
28 Jan.	Lord Hutton delivers his report on the 'Investigation into the Circumstances Surrounding the Death of Dr David Kelly' (Hutton Inquiry). The investigation finds that the BBC reports claiming that the British Government had 'sexed up' its dossier of Sep. 2002 on Iraq's weapons of mass destruction were unfounded.	UK; Iraq; WMD
29 Jan.	Ugandan President Yoweri Museveni requests the International Criminal Court (ICC) to investigate possible crimes against humanity committed by the rebel group Lord's Resistance Army in the northern parts of Uganda. The ICC investigation is opened on 29 July.	Uganda; ICC

2 Feb.	In an interview with *Haaretz,* Israeli Prime Minister Ariel Sharon states that he has ordered a plan for the evacuation of 17 Jewish settlements in the Gaza Strip. No timetable for the withdrawal is given. On 5 Apr. Sharon confirms his plan and states that 'in the unilateral plan, there is no Palestinian state'.	Israel/ Palestinians
3 Feb.	The British Government announces the establishment of the Committee to Review Intelligence on Weapons of Mass Destruction (Butler Inquiry). The Commission presents its report on the intelligence used to justify the war against Iraq on 14 July.	UK; WMD
6 Feb.	US President George W. Bush establishes the Commission on the Intelligence Capabilities of the United States Regarding Weapons of Mass Destruction. (The Commission reports its findings and recommendations to the President on 31 Mar. 2005.)	USA; WMD
6–29 Feb.	In an outbreak of political violence against Haitian President Jean-Bertrand Aristide, a rebel group, Revolutionary Artibonite Resistance Front, takes control of the city of Gonaives. The uprising spreads throughout the country and on 29 Feb., after the rebel groups reach Port-au-Prince, Aristide relinquishes power and flees the country. The UN Security Council unanimously adopts Resolution 1529, authorizing the deployment of a Multinational Interim Force (MIF) to restore security and stability in Haiti (see also *30 Apr.*). Aristide claims from his exile in the Central African Republic that he was forced to leave Haiti.	Haiti; UN
11 Feb.	US President George W. Bush proposes steps to help combat the development and spread of weapons of mass destruction; to strengthen the laws and international controls on proliferation; to restrict the sale and transport of nuclear technologies; to close a loophole in the nuclear non-proliferation regimes that allow states to pursue WMD under false pretext; and to expand efforts to secure and destroy nuclear weapons and materials.	USA; WMD
16–18 Feb.	Meeting in Islamabad, representatives of the Indian and Pakistani foreign ministries start the Composite Dialogue and agree on a 'road map' for peace in Jammu and Kashmir, beginning with high-level talks on 27 June.	India/Pakistan
23 Feb.	At the request of the UN General Assembly, the International Court of Justice (ICJ) starts the hearings on the legality of Israel's controversial West Bank barrier. Israel boycotts the hearings. The ICJ issues its advisory opinion on 9 July (see also *20 July*).	Israel/ Palestinians; ICJ
25 Feb.	Meeting in Beijing, delegates from China, Japan, North Korea, South Korea, Russia and the USA resume the Six-Party Talks of Aug. 2003 on North Korea's nuclear programme. On 26 Feb. North Korea offers to halt its nuclear activities in return for 'corresponding measures' from the USA.	North Korea; Nuclear programme

27 Feb.	The UN Security Council unanimously adopts Resolution 1528, establishing the United Nations Operation in Côte d'Ivoire (UNOCI) as of 4 Apr. 2004.	Côte d'Ivoire; UN; Peacekeeping
27 Feb.	The USA announces a new policy regarding landmines, containing four key elements: the USA will after 2010 not use persistent landmines of any type; within one year the USA will no longer have any non-detectable mine of any type in its arsenal; concerted efforts will be directed to the development of alternatives to the current persistent landmines; and the president will request a 50% increase in the Department of State budget for worldwide humanitarian mine-action programmes.	USA; Mines
28 Feb.	Meeting in Sirte, Libya, the Assembly of the African Union (AU) adopts the Solemn Declaration on a Common African Defence and Security Policy, establishing an African Standby Force, under the authority of the AU Peace and Security Council, for the intervention to end civil wars on the African continent.	AU
10 Mar.	Libya signs an NPT Additional Safeguards Protocol with the IAEA.	Libya; IAEA; Safeguards
11 Mar.	In a series of explosions at train stations in Madrid, 191 people are killed and over 1400 wounded. Spanish officials blame the attack on the Basque separatist group Euzkadi ta Azkatasuna (ETA, Basque Fatherland and Liberty). The UN Security Council unanimously adopts Resolution 1530, condemning the ETA for the attacks. (No links to the ETA are found.) The London-based Arabic newspaper *al-Quds* receives a message from the Abu Hafs al-Masr Brigades, a group linked to al-Qaeda, claiming responsibility for the attacks.	Spain; Terrorism
12 Mar.	The UN Security Council unanimously adopts Resolution 1533, establishing a committee to monitor the arms embargo imposed by Security Council Resolution 1493 (2003), against all armed groups operating in the eastern region of the Democratic Republic of the Congo (DRC). The resolution also condemns the illicit flow of weapons into the DRC.	DRC; UN; Arms embargoes
22 Mar.	Sheikh Ahmed Yassin, the spiritual leader and founder of the Harakat al-Muqawama al-Islamiyya (Hamas), is killed in an Israeli air strike in Gaza City.	Israel/ Palestinians
25 Mar.	The Brussels European Council adopts the Declaration on Combating Terrorism and appoints Gijs de Vries as the EU Counter-Terrorism Coordinator.	EU; Terrorism
29 Mar.	At a ceremony in Washington, DC, NATO formally admits seven new members—Bulgaria, Estonia, Latvia, Lithuania, Romania, Slovakia and Slovenia. Their instruments of accession are deposited with the US Government.	NATO

31 Mar.	UN Secretary-General Kofi Annan presents, in Bürgenstock, Switzerland, a final plan for the reunification of Cyprus. The UN plan envisages a federation of two states with a loose central government, based on the Swiss model, and will be put to both the Greek and the Turkish parts of Cyprus in referenda on 24 Apr.	Cyprus; UN
31 Mar.	Special Representative of the UN Secretary-General for Kosovo, Harri Holkeri, presents, in Pristina, Kosovo's Standards Implementation Plan, drawn up by the UN Interim Administrative Mission in Kosovo (UNMIK) and the government of the province of Kosovo. The plan envisages the creation of functioning democratic institutions and the continuation of the dialogue between the Government of Serbia and Montenegro and the Kosovo Provisional Institutions of Self-Government, initiated in Oct. 2003.	Kosovo; Serbia and Montenegro; UN
4–7 Apr.	As a response to an uprising of Iraqi Shia Muslims led by Muqtada al-Sadr, the US-led coalition forces launch their largest offensive since the formal ending of the Iraq war in May 2003. Coalition forces attack Sadr City and begin a month-long siege of the city of Falluja.	Iraq; USA
17 Apr.	The head of the Harakat al-Muqawama al-Islamiyya (Hamas), Abdel Aziz al-Rantissi, is killed in Gaza in an Israeli missile strike targeted at his automobile. On 18 Apr. UN Secretary-General Kofi Annan condemns the action and calls on Israel to end its practice of extrajudicial killings, in violation of international law.	Israel/ Palestinians; UN
21 Apr.	Meeting in Nairobi, Kenya, officials from Burundi, the Democratic Republic of the Congo, Djibouti, Ethiopia, Eritrea, Kenya, Rwanda, the Seychelles, Sudan, Tanzania and Uganda adopt the Nairobi Protocol for the Prevention, Control and Reduction of Small Arms and Light Weapons in the Great Lakes region and the Horn of Africa, obliging the governments to address the problem of internal conflicts and to curb the circulation of small arms and light weapons (SALW) in the region.	Africa; SALW
24 Apr.	Cyprus holds a referendum on the reunification plan proposed by UN Secretary-General Kofi Annan on 31 Mar. The Greek Cypriots vote against the plan, while the Turkish Cypriots endorse it. As a result, only the Greek part of Cyprus becomes a member of the EU on 1 May.	Cyprus; EU
28 Apr.	The UN Security Council unanimously adopts Resolution 1540, deciding that all states shall refrain from providing any form of support to non-state actors that attempt to develop, acquire, manufacture, possess, transport, transfer or use weapons of mass destruction and their means of delivery.	UN; WMD; Terrorism
30 Apr.	The UN Security Council unanimously adopts Resolution 1542, establishing the United Nations Stabilization Mission in Haiti (MINUSTAH), which will replace the Multinational Interim Force (MIF) on 1 June.	Haiti; UN

1 May	The EU formally admits 10 new members—Cyprus, the Czech Republic, Estonia, Hungary, Latvia, Lithuania, Malta, Poland, Slovakia and Slovenia.	EU
9 May	Chechen President Akhmad Kadyrov and up to 30 other people are killed in a bomb attack in Grozny. Chechen rebels are blamed for the attack.	Chechnya
17 May	The head of the Iraqi Governing Council (IGC), Ezzedine Salim, and several several other people are killed in a car bomb explosion close to the US-led coalition headquarters in Baghdad.	Iraq
17–25 May	Following the killing of five Israeli soldiers in Gaza City on 11 May, the Israeli Army launches a military offensive with tanks and bulldozers, destroying houses in the Palestinian Rafah refugee camp in the Gaza Strip. Several people are killed and wounded, and about 100 houses are destroyed. Israeli officials claim that the camp is a base for the smuggling of weapons from Egypt into the Gaza Strip. On 25 May Israel announces a pause in the operation and withdraws from Rafah.	Israel/ Palestinians
19 May	The UN Security Council adopts, by a vote of 14–0, with 1 abstention (the USA), Resolution 1544, calling on Israel to stop the demolition of Palestinian homes in the Rafah refugee camp in the Gaza Strip.	UN; Israel/ Palestinians
22 May	At the meeting of the Commonwealth of Nations in London, the suspension of Pakistan from the Council of the organization is lifted. (Pakistan was suspended in 1999 after a military coup led by General Pervez Musharraf.)	Pakistan; Commonwealth of Nations
25 May	Meeting in Addis Ababa, the African Union (AU) officially inaugurates the AU Peace and Security Council.	AU
26 May	Meeting in Naivasha, Kenya, representatives of the Sudanese Government and the Sudan People's Liberation Movement/ Sudan People's Liberation Army (SPLM/A) sign three protocols on: Power Sharing; the Resolution of the Conflict in Abyei Area; and the Resolution of the Conflict in the Nuba Mountains and the Blue Nile Area. Together with three previous agreements—the 2002 Machakos Protocol, the 2003 Agreement on Security Arrangements, and the 2004 Agreement on Wealth Sharing (see also *7 Jan.*)—the new protocols will constitute a part of the Comprehensive Peace Agreement (see also *31 Dec.*).	Sudan
26 May	US Secretary of Energy Spencer Abraham announces the Global Threat Reduction Initiative, aiming at the removal of and/or securing of high-risk nuclear and radiological materials and equipment that poses a threat to the USA and the international community.	USA; Nuclear arms control
1 June	The Iraqi Governing Council decides to dissolve itself with immediate effect and the Iraqi Interim Government is sworn in. Ghazi Yawer is appointed president and Ayad Allawi prime minister. The new government will focus on implementing the special arrangements to transfer full sovereignty to Iraq.	Iraq

5 June	Meeting in Nairobi, Kenya, representatives of the Sudanese Government and the Sudan People's Liberation Movement/Sudan People's Liberation Army (SPLM/A) issue the Nairobi Declaration on the Final Phase of Peace in the Sudan, reconfirming their agreements of 26 May.	Sudan
8 June	The UN Security Council unanimously adopts Resolution 1546, endorsing the formation of the Iraqi Interim Government and the holding of democratic elections by Jan. 2005. It welcomes the end of the occupation by 30 June and determines the status of the Multinational Force, its relationship with the Iraqi Government and the role of the UN in the political transition.	Iraq; UN
8–10 June	The leaders of the Group of Eight (G8) industrialized nations, meeting in Sea Island, Georgia, USA, adopt the Action Plan on Non-proliferation, to counter the proliferation of weapons of mass destruction, and the Action Plan on Expanding Global Capability for Peace Support Operations.	G8; WMD; Peacekeeping
23–26 June	Meeting in Beijing, delegates from China, Japan, North Korea, South Korea, Russia and the USA continue the Six-Party Talks on North Korea's nuclear weapons programme.	North Korea; Nuclear programme
26 June	At a Summit Meeting, Dromoland Castle, Ireland, the EU and the USA adopt the EU–US Declaration on the Non-proliferation of Weapons of Mass Destruction.	EU; USA; WMD
27–28 June	Meeting in New Delhi, the Indian and Pakistani foreign secretaries continue the Composite Dialogue, started on 16 Feb., on peace and security including confidence-building measures and on the disputed area of Jammu and Kashmir.	India/Pakistan
28 June	At a ceremony in Baghdad, the Coalition Provisional Authority formally hands over sovereignty to the Iraqi Interim Government.	Iraq
28 June	Meeting in Istanbul, the heads of state and government of the NATO member states issue a Statement on Iraq, the Istanbul Declaration—Our Security in a New Era, and the Istanbul Summit Communiqué.	NATO; Iraq
30 June	Former Iraqi President Saddam Hussein is handed over to Iraqi legal custody by the US forces. On 1 July he is brought to the Iraqi Special Tribunal to hear the charges against him, including genocide against Kurds in Iraq and the 1990 invasion of Kuwait.	Iraq
12 July	Meeting in Brussels, the EU General Affairs and External Relations Council adopts the Joint Action establishing the European Defence Agency in the field of defence capabilities development, research, acquisition and armaments; and the Joint Action on the European Union Military Operation in Bosnia and Herzegovina, to replace by 2 Dec. 2004 the NATO Stabilization Force (SFOR) with the EUFOR ALTHEA.	EU; NATO; Bosnia and Herzegovina

20 July	The UN General Assembly Emergency Special Session adopts, by a vote of 150–6 (Australia, Israel, Marshall Islands, Micronesia, Palau and the USA voting against) and 10 abstentions, Resolution ES-10/15, calling on Israel to comply with the International Court of Justice (ICJ) advisory opinion to halt the construction of its security barrier in the West Bank.	Israel/ Palestinians; UN; ICJ
22 July	The National Commission on Terrorist Attacks upon the United States (9/11 Commission) releases its final report with a full and complete account of the circumstances surrounding the 11 Sep. 2001 terrorist attacks on the USA, including the preparedness for and immediate response to the attacks.	USA; Terrorism
27 July	The UN Security Council unanimously adopts Resolution 1552, renewing until 31 July 2005 the arms embargo, contained in Security Council Resolutions 1493 (2003) and 1533 (2004), against all armed groups operating in the eastern region of the Democratic Republic of the Congo (DRC). It also renewed provisions for the establishment of a sanctions committee contained in Security Council Resolution 1533.	DRC; UN; Arms embargoes
30 July	The UN Security Council adopts, by a vote of 13–0, with 2 abstentions (China and Pakistan), Resolution 1556, calling on the Sudanese Government to halt the atrocities committed by the Arab militias in the Darfur region within 30 days or face further action, including an arms embargo on all Sudanese non-governmental groups. The Darfur conflict and the following humanitarian crisis, with over 100 000 killed and over 1 million refugees, started in 2003 after rebel groups began attacking government targets, claiming that the region was being neglected by the Sudanese Government.	Sudan; UN; Arms embargoes
30 July	Meeting in Accra, Ghana, under the auspices of the African Union (AU) and the UN, the President of Côte d'Ivoire, Laurent Gbagbo, the Prime Minister of the Government of National Reconciliation, Seydou Elimane Diarra, and representatives of all the political forces of Côte d'Ivoire sign the Accra III Agreement, consolidating implementation of the peace process agreed in the 2003 Linas–Marcoussis Agreement.	Côte d'Ivoire; AU; UN
1–3 Sep.	Armed attackers, claimed to be Chechen rebels, seize a secondary school in Beslan, North Ossetian region, Russia, taking around 1000 people, mostly children, as hostage. On 3 Sep., after bomb blasts inside the school, Russian security forces storm the building. In the fighting between the hostage-takers and the soldiers there are several hundred casualties.	Russia; Terrorism
2 Sep.	The UN Security Council adopts, by a vote of 9–0, with 6 abstentions (Algeria, Brazil, China, Pakistan, Philippines and Russia), Resolution 1559, calling on all remaining foreign forces to withdraw from Lebanon; for the disbanding and disarming of all Lebanese and non-Lebanese militias in Lebanon; and for support of the extension of the control of the Government of Lebanon over all Lebanese territory.	Lebanon; UN

5 Sep.	Israel starts building the southern section of the controversial barrier and sophisticated security system along the entire border of the West Bank with the aim of protecting Israel from Palestinian intrusion. (The first part of the barrier was erected in 2002.)	Israel/ Palestinians
5–6 Sep.	Meeting in New Delhi, the Indian and Pakistani foreign ministers begin the first official meeting at ministerial level since 2001 over the disputed area of Kashmir.	India/Pakistan
16–17 Sep.	EU defence ministers, meeting in Noordwijk, the Netherlands, agree to create 'EU Battle Groups', with initial operational capability in 2005.	EU; ESDP
16–17 Sep.	Meeting in Noordwijk, the Netherlands, the defence ministers of France, Italy, Portugal, Spain and the Netherlands sign the Declaration of Intent for a European Gendarmerie Force, creating a police force with military status to be deployed at short notice for peacekeeping missions.	EU; ESDP
18 Sep.	The UN Security Council adopts, by a vote of 11–0, with 4 abstentions (Algeria, China, Pakistan and Russia), Resolution 1564, calling on the Sudanese Government and the rebel groups in Darfur—the Justice and Equality Movement (JEM) and the Sudan People's Liberation Movement/Sudan People's Liberation Army (SPLM/A)—to work together under the auspices of the African Union (AU) to reach 'a political solution'. The resolution also declares the 'grave concern' that the Government of Sudan has not fully met its obligations noted in Resolution 1556 (see also *30 July*).	Sudan; UN; AU
18 Sep.	The International Atomic Energy Agency (IAEA) Board of Governors approves Resolution GOV/2004/79, demanding that Iran suspend all its activities relating to the enrichment of uranium. Iran responds to the resolution by saying that it would not accept any obligation attached to its uranium enrichment and that 'no international body can force Iran to do so'.	Iran; IAEA; Nuclear programme
20 Sep.	US President George W. Bush issues an executive order lifting the US sanctions against Libya in place since 1986, except the arms embargo, and lifting the sanctions from 1992.	Libya; USA; Sanctions
6 Oct.	The head of the US Iraq Survey Group (ISG), Charles Duelfer, presents the ISG final report, stating that Iraq had no stockpiles of biological, chemical or nuclear weapons at the time of the US-led invasion in Mar. 2003.	Iraq; USA; WMD
11 Oct.	Meeting in Luxembourg, the EU General Affairs and External Relations Council agrees to end the EU sanctions against Libya, in place since 1992, including the arms embargo imposed in 1986.	Libya; EU; Sanctions
29 Oct.	Meeting in Rome, representatives of the governments of the 25 EU member states sign the Treaty Establishing a Constitution for Europe. (The treaty will not enter into force until all the EU governments have ratified it, by a parliamentary vote or a referendum.)	EU

11 Nov.	Palestinian President Yasser Arafat dies in a hospital in Paris, France.	Palestinians
11 Nov.	Indian Prime Minister Manmohan Singh issues a statement announcing the reduction of Indian forces deployed in the state of Jammu and Kashmir, which begins on 17 Nov. when Singh pays his first visit to Kashmir.	India; Kashmir
14 Nov.	To resolve the dispute over its nuclear programme, Iran agrees to suspend most of its uranium enrichment programme, as part of a deal with the EU. The suspension will last for an unspecified period of time while Iran and the EU negotiate a larger package of economic and political benefits for Iran. On 22 Nov. Iran states that it has suspended its enrichment programme, meeting the deadline agreed with the EU.	Iran; EU; Nuclear programme
15 Nov.	Following attacks on French peacekeeping forces on 6–9 Nov., the UN Security Council unanimously adopts Resolution 1572, imposing an immediate 13-month arms embargo on Côte d'Ivoire. Additional sanctions, including a travel ban and the freezing of assets for the warring parties, will take effect on 15 Dec., unless the implementation of the 2003 Linas–Marcoussis Agreement and the Accra III Agreement is revived (see also *30 July*).	Côte d'Ivoire; UN; Arms embargoes
21 Nov.	The official results of the presidential elections in Ukraine declare Prime Minister Viktor Yanukovuch the winner against the opposition candidate, Viktor Yushchenko, sparking political tension and large demonstrations. Independent observers declare the elections flawed. On 25 Nov. the Ukrainian Supreme Court suspends publication of the results and on 27 Nov. the parliament declares the election invalid.	Ukraine
22 Nov.	Meeting in Brussels, the EU General Affairs and External Relations Council (GAERC) endorses the Declaration on European Military Capabilities, committing the EU member states to further improvement of their military capabilities and to offer contributions to the EU Battle Groups. The GAERC also endorses the Ministerial Declaration of the Civilian Capabilities Commitment Conference, establishing operational planning and European Security and Defence Policy (ESDP) mission support within the Council Secretariat, ensuring the EU's ability to conduct and plan several civilian crisis management operations simultaneously.	EU; ESDP
29 Nov.	The International Atomic Energy Agency (IAEA) Board of Governors approves Resolution GOV/2004/90 on the Implementation of the NPT Safeguards Agreement in the Islamic Republic of Iran, stating that the IAEA has been able to complete its verification of Iran's suspension of its uranium enrichment and reprocessing activities.	Iran; IAEA; Safeguards
1 Dec.	The High-level Panel on Threats, Challenges and Change, established by UN Secretary-General Kofi Annan in Nov. 2003, presents its report 'A more secure world: our shared responsibility'.	UN

2 Dec.	The EU Military Operation in Bosnia and Herzegovina, (EUFOR ALTHEA), replaces the NATO Stabilization Force (SFOR) (see also *12 July*).	EU; NATO; Bosnia and Herzegovina
3 Dec.	The UN General Assembly unanimously adopts Resolution 59/80, 'Measures to prevent terrorists from acquiring weapons of mass destruction', taking note of UN Security Council Resolution 1540 on the non-proliferation of weapons of mass destruction (see also *28 Apr.*).	UN; WMD; Terrorism
9 Dec.	The NATO–Russia Council agrees the Action Plan against Terrorism. The plan outlines measures to enhance the capabilities of NATO and Russia to act, individually and jointly, in three critical areas: preventing terrorism; combating terrorist activities; and managing the consequences of terrorist acts.	NATO; Russia; Terrorism
9 Dec.	Meeting in Brussels, the EU General Affairs and External Relations Council agrees on the creation of the European Union Police Mission in Kinshasa (EUPOL-Kinshasa) in the Democratic Republic of the Congo (DRC).	EU; DRC
26 Dec.	A re-run of the invalid presidential election of 21 Nov. is held in Ukraine and the opposition candidate, Viktor Yushchenko, is declared the winner. International observers from the Organization for Security and Co-operation in Europe (OSCE), declare the re-run fairer than earlier rounds.	Ukraine; OSCE
26 Dec.	An earthquake registered in the Indian Ocean west of Aceh province, Indonesia, unleashes a series of massive tsunamis, causing devastation and massive loss of life in 12 countries around the rim of the Indian Ocean. By 30 Dec. the total death count was 124 000.	Indian Ocean
30 Dec.	The Government of Senegal and the Mouvement des Forces Démocratiques du le Casamance (MFDC, Movement of the Democractic Forces of Casamance) sign a peace agreement in Ziguinchor, Senegal.	Senegal
31 Dec.	Meeting in Naivasha, Kenya, representatives of the Sudanese Government and the Sudan People's Liberation Movement/ Sudan People's Liberation Army (SPLM/A) sign the Agreement on the Permanent Ceasefire and Security Agreements Implementation Modalities, and the Agreement on the Implementation Modalities of the Protocols and Agreements (see also *7 Jan.* and *26 May*). These agreements constitute an integral part of the Comprehensive Peace Agreement, which does not cover the conflict in the Darfur region.	Sudan

About the authors

Dr Christer Ahlström (Sweden) has been Deputy Director of SIPRI since August 2002. Previously, he served as a Deputy Director in the Swedish Ministry for Foreign Affairs on issues related to disarmament and non-proliferation of weapons of mass destruction. He contributed to the SIPRI Yearbook in 2003 and 2004.

Dr Ian Anthony (United Kingdom) is SIPRI Research Coordinator and the Leader of the SIPRI Non-proliferation and Export Controls Project. In 1992–98 he was Leader of the SIPRI Arms Transfers Project. His most recent publication for SIPRI is *Reducing Threats at the Source: A European Perspective on Cooperative Threat Reduction*, SIPRI Research Report no. 19 (2004). He is also editor of the SIPRI volumes *Russia and the Arms Trade* (1998), *Arms Export Regulations* (1991) and *The Future of Defence Industries in Central and Eastern Europe*, SIPRI Research Report no. 7 (1994), and author of the SIPRI volume *The Naval Arms Trade* (1990) and *The Arms Trade and Medium Powers: Case Studies of India and Pakistan 1947–90* (Harvester Wheatsheaf, 1992). He has written or co-authored chapters for the SIPRI Yearbook since 1988.

Alyson J. K. Bailes (United Kingdom) has been Director of SIPRI since July 2002. She was previously a member of the British Diplomatic Service for 33 years, ending as British Ambassador to Finland in 2000–2002. Her other diplomatic postings include Budapest, the British Delegation to NATO, Bonn, Beijing and Oslo, and she spent several periods on detachment outside the Service, including two academic sabbaticals, a two-year period with the British Ministry of Defence, and assignments to the European Union and Western European Union. Her main analytical interests are politico-military affairs, European integration and Central European affairs. She has published a large number of articles in international journals on these subjects as well as on Chinese foreign policy. She is a co-author of *Armament and Disarmament in the Caucasus and Central Asia*, SIPRI Policy Paper no. 3 (July 2003) and author of *The European Security Strategy: An Evolutionary History*, SIPRI Policy Paper no. 10 (Feb. 2005), and has contributed to the SIPRI Yearbook since 2003.

Dr Sibylle Bauer (Germany) is a Researcher with the SIPRI Non-proliferation and Export Controls Project. Previously, she was a researcher with the Institute for European Studies in Brussels. She has published widely on European export control and armaments issues, including chapters in *The Restructuring of the European Defence Industry* (Office for Official Publications of the European Communities, 2001), *Annuaire Français de Relations Internationales* [French Yearbook of International Relations] (Bruylant, 2001) and *The Path to European Defence* (Maklu, 2003). She co-authored two chapters in the *SIPRI Yearbook 2004*; is a co-author of *The European Union Code of Conduct on Arms Exports: Improving the Annual Report*, SIPRI Policy Paper no. 8 (Nov. 2004); and is the author of the SIPRI volume *European Arms Export Policies and Democratic Accountability* (forthcoming).

Nenne Bodell (Sweden) is Head of the SIPRI Library and Documentation Department and of the SIPRI Arms Control and Disarmament Documentary Survey Project. She contributed to the SIPRI Yearbook in 2003 and 2004.

Dr Hans Born (Netherlands) is a Senior Fellow in democratic governance of the security sector at the Geneva Centre for Democratic Control of the Armed Forces (DCAF). In this capacity, he leads DCAF's working groups on parliamentary accountability of the security sector as well as legal aspects of security sector governance. He is a guest lecturer on civil–military relations at the Federal Institute of Technology in Zürich. His recent publications include, with I. Leigh, *Making Intelligence Accountable: Legal Standards and Best Practice for Oversight of Intelligence Agencies* (Norwegian Parliament, 2005) and, co-edited with H. Hänggi, *The 'Double Democratic Deficit': Parliamentary Accountability and the Use of Force under International Auspices* (Ashgate, 2004). He was lead author of *Parliamentary Oversight of the Security Sector: Principles, Mechanisms and Practices* (Inter-Parliamentary Union/DCAF, 2003).

Mark Bromley (United Kingdom) is a Research Associate on the SIPRI Arms Transfers Project. Previously, he was a Policy Analyst for the British American Security Information Council (BASIC) in London. While at BASIC he authored or co-authored a number of research reports and papers, including the BASIC Research Report, *Secrecy and Dependence: The UK Trident System in the 21st Century* (2001) and the BASIC Paper, *European Missile Defence: New Emphasis, New Roles* (May 2001). He is a co-author of *The European Union Code of Conduct on Arms Exports: Improving the Annual Report*, SIPRI Policy Paper no. 8 (Nov. 2004) and contributed to the SIPRI Yearbook in 2004.

Dr Pál Dunay (Hungary) is a Senior Researcher at SIPRI while on a leave of absence from the Geneva Centre for Security Policy, where he was course director of the International Training Course in Security Policy. He is co-author of *Ungarns Aussenpolitik 1990–1997: zwischen Westintegration, Nachbarschafts- und Minderheitenpolitik* [Hungarian foreign policy 1990–1997: at the crossroads of Western integration, neighbourhood and minority policy] (Nomos Verlag, 1998); and *Open Skies: A Cooperative Approach to Military Transparency and Confidence Building* (UNIDIR, 2004). He contributed to the SIPRI Yearbook in 2004.

Dr Renata Dwan (Ireland) is Leader of the SIPRI Programme on Armed Conflict and Conflict Management. Prior to joining SIPRI in 1999 she was Deputy Director of the EastWest Institute (EWI) European Security Programme at the EWI Budapest Centre. In 2002–2003 she served as Special Adviser to the EU Police Mission in Bosnia and Herzegovina, in the Secretariat of the Council of the European Union, and she participated as an expert in the EU joint fact-finding mission to Iraq and Jordan in October 2004. She has published widely in the areas of conflict prevention, international peace operations and civilian aspects of peacekeeping. She is a former visiting fellow at the EU Institute for Security Studies. She has contributed to the SIPRI Yearbook since 2000 and is currently on leave from the Institute to serve in the UN Department of Peacekeeping Operations.

Vitaly Fedchenko (Russia) joined SIPRI in 2005 as a researcher on reinforcing EU Cooperative Threat Reduction Programmes and actions required to support the EU Strategy Against Proliferation of Weapons of Mass Destruction, with responsibility for nuclear security issues and EU–Russian relations. Previously, he was a visiting researcher at SIPRI; a Researcher and Project Coordinator at the Center for Policy Studies in Russia; and a Research Fellow at the Institute for Applied International Research in Moscow. He is the author or co-author of a number of publications on international non-proliferation and disarmament assistance and Russian nuclear exports.

Richard Guthrie (United Kingdom) is the Leader of the SIPRI Chemical and Biological Warfare Project and editor of the SIPRI Chemical & Biological Warfare Studies series. Previously, he was an independent consultant dealing with defence and security issues with a specialization in the control of materials and technologies used to make nuclear, biological and chemical weapons. He has worked extensively with inter-governmental bodies, governments, non-governmental organizations and academic departments. He was involved in a long-term collaboration with the Harvard Sussex Program (1988–2003), where he was responsible for production of *The CBW Conventions Bulletin* and for managing certain data resources. He edited or co-edited seven volumes of the Verification Research, Training and Information Centre (VERTIC) Yearbook (1991–97) and the VERTIC newsletter *Trust and Verify* (1992–97). He was also responsible for production of the Programme for Promoting Nuclear Non-proliferation Newsbrief (1989–2001). He was retained as a paid adviser to British Members of Parliament (1986–2003). He is co-author of *Non-Compliance with the Chemical Weapons Convention: Lessons from and for Iraq*, SIPRI Policy Paper no. 5 (Oct. 2003) and a chapter in the *SIPRI Yearbook 2004*.

Lotta Harbom (Sweden) is a Research Assistant with the Uppsala Conflict Data Program at the Department of Peace and Conflict Research, Uppsala University. She is currently working on both the Uppsala Conflict Data Program and a project on conflicts and conflict resolution in the context of Africa's weak states.

John Hart (United States) has been a researcher with the SIPRI Chemical and Biological Warfare (CBW) Project since 2001. Previously, he worked as an On-Site Inspection Researcher at the London-based Verification Research, Training and Information Centre and as a Research Associate at the Center for Nonproliferation Studies at the Monterey Institute of International Studies. In 1996–97 he worked as a Research Assistant on the SIPRI CBW Project. He is co-author of the SIPRI Fact Sheets 'The Chemical Weapons Convention' (1997); 'Biotechnology and the future of the Biological and Toxin Weapons Convention' (2001); and 'Maintaining the effectiveness of the Chemical Weapons Convention' (2002). He co-edited *Chemical Weapon Destruction in Russia: Political, Legal and Technical Aspects*, SIPRI Chemical & Biological Warfare studies no. 17 (1998) and is a co-author of *Non-Compliance with the Chemical Weapons Convention: Lessons from and for Iraq*, SIPRI Policy Paper no. 5 (Oct. 2003). He contributed to *Weapons of Mass Destruction: An Encyclopedia of Worldwide Policy, Technology and History*, 2 vols (ABC-CLIO, 2004) and the SIPRI Yearbook in 1997–1998 and 2002–2004.

Dr Rosemary Hollis is Director of Research at the Royal Institute of International Affairs, London, responsible for 10 research programmes and the Institute's publications. She assumed this post in April 2005, after 10 years as Head of the Middle East Programme at the Royal Institute of International Affairs, and five years in the same capacity at the Royal United Services Institute for Defence Studies. In 1980–89 she was a lecturer in Political Science and International Affairs at George Washington University in Washington, DC. Among her most recent publications are 'The Middle East security agenda' in *Strategic Yearbook 2005* (Swedish Defence College, 2005); 'Europe in the Middle East' in *The International Relations of the Middle East* (Oxford University Press, 2005); and 'The US role: helpful or harmful?' in *Unfinished Business: Iran, Iraq and the Aftermath of War* (Palgrave, 2004).

Caroline Holmqvist (Sweden) is a Research Assistant with the SIPRI Armed Conflict and Conflict Management Programme. Previously, she held an internship with the Risk and Security Programme at the Foreign Policy Centre, London. She is the author of *Private Security Companies: The Case for Regulation*, SIPRI Policy Paper no. 9 (Jan. 2005).

Dr Heiner Hänggi (Switzerland) is Assistant Director and Head of Research at the Geneva Centre for the Democratic Control of Armed Forces. He also teaches the Master of Arts in International Affairs and Governance programme at the University of St Gallen, Switzerland. His recent publications include, as co-editor with R. Roloff and J. Rüland, *Inter-regionalism and International Relations* (Routledge, 2005); as co-editor with A. Bryden, *Reform and Reconstruction of the Security Sector* (Transaction, 2004); and, as co-editor with H. Born, *The 'Double Democratic Deficit': Parliamentary Accountability and the Use of Force under International Auspices* (Ashgate, 2004).

Shannon N. Kile (United States) is a Researcher with the SIPRI Non-proliferation and Export Controls Project, focusing on nuclear arms control and non-proliferation issues. He is the editor of *Iran and Europe: Perspectives on Non-proliferation*, SIPRI Research Report no. 21 (forthcoming). He has contributed to numerous SIPRI publications, including chapters on nuclear arms control and non-proliferation for the SIPRI Yearbook since 1995. His recent work has concentrated on nuclear proliferation issues related to Iran and North Korea.

Hans M. Kristensen (Denmark) is a nuclear weapons policy analyst and a consultant to the nuclear programme of the Natural Resources Defense Council (NRDC). He is co-author of the NRDC Nuclear Notebook column in *Bulletin of the Atomic Scientists*. His recent publications include *US Nuclear Weapons in Europe* (NRDC, Feb. 2005); 'What's behind Bush's nuclear cuts?', *Arms Control Today* (Oct. 2004); 'The protection paradox', *Bulletin of the Atomic Scientists* (Mar./Apr. 2004); *The Matrix of Deterrence: US Strategic Command Force Structure Studies* (Nautilus Institute, May 2001); and, with W. Arkin, *The Post Cold War SIOP and Nuclear Warfare Planning: A Glossary, Abbreviations, and Acronyms* (NRDC, 1999). He manages the Nuclear Information Project (URL <http://www.nukestrat.com>) and has contributed to the SIPRI Yearbook since 2001.

Frida Kuhlau (Sweden) is a Research Associate with the SIPRI Chemical and Biological Warfare Project. She is a co-author, with John Hart and Jean Pascal Zanders, of the SIPRI Fact Sheets 'Biotechnology and the future of the Biological and Toxin Weapons Convention' (2001) and 'Maintaining the effectiveness of the Chemical Weapons Convention' (2002) and is a co-author of *Non-Compliance with the Chemical Weapons Convention: Lessons from and for Iraq*, SIPRI Policy Paper no. 5 (Oct. 2003). She has contributed to the SIPRI Yearbook since 2002.

Dr Zdzislaw Lachowski (Poland) is Senior Researcher with the SIPRI Euro-Atlantic, Global and Regional Security Project. Previously, he worked at the Polish Institute of International Affairs in Warsaw. He has published extensively on the problems of European military security and arms control as well as on European politico-military integration. He is the author of *The Adapted CFE Treaty and the Admission of the Baltic States to NATO*, SIPRI Policy Paper no. 1 (Dec. 2002) and a contributor to *Armament and Disarmament in the Caucasus and Central Asia*, SIPRI Policy Paper no. 3 (July 2003). He is the co-editor of *International Security in a Time of Change: Threats–Concepts–Institutions* (Nomos Verlags Gesellschaff, 2004) and author of *Confidence- and Security-Building Measures in the New Europe*, SIPRI Research Report no. 18 (2004). He has contributed to the SIPRI Yearbook since 1992.

Natasza Nazet (France/Poland) joined SIPRI in 2003 and is Project Secretary for the Military Expenditure and Arms Production Project and the Arms Transfers Project. She maintains the Arms Transfers Project's archives and its Internet site, and the SIPRI reporting system for military expenditure. She contributed to the SIPRI Yearbook in 2003 and 2004.

Wuyi Omitoogun (Nigeria) is a Researcher with the SIPRI Military Expenditure and Arms Production Project and is the coordinator of the SIPRI project on the Defence Budgeting Process in Africa. He is the author of 'Arms control and conflict in Africa' in *Arms Control and Disarmament: A New Conceptual Approach* (UN Department for Disarmament Affairs, 2000) and *Military Expenditure Data in Africa: A Survey of Cameroon, Ethiopia, Ghana, Kenya, Nigeria and Uganda*, SIPRI Research Report no. 17 (2003), and is a co-editor and an author of the SIPRI volume *Budgeting for the Military Sector in Africa* (forthcoming 2005). He has contributed to the SIPRI Yearbook since 2000.

Catalina Perdomo (Colombia) is a Research Assistant with the SIPRI Military Expenditure and Arms Production Project. She is responsible for monitoring military expenditure in Latin America and Asia. Previously, she worked at the Inter-American Development Bank in Washington, DC, and at the Washington office of the Fundación Ideas para la Paz of Colombia. She contributed to the SIPRI Yearbook in 2004.

Professor Maria Cristína Rosas (Mexico) has been a full-time professor and researcher at the Faculty of Social and Political Sciences, National Autonomous University of Mexico (UNAM), since 1987. She has worked as a consultant on trade and international security issues to the Mexican Government, the private sector and international organizations. Her most recent publications are *The Political Economy of International Security: Sanctions, Carrots and Sticks* (UNAM, 2003) and *Iraq: The*

Year of Living Dangerously (UNAM/Quimera, 2004). She edited and co-authored *United Nations Peacekeeping Operations: Lessons for Mexico* (UNAM/Folke Bernadotte Academy, 2005).

Matthew Schroeder (United States) is the Project Manager of the Arms Sales Monitoring Project at the Federation of American Scientists in Washington, DC. He has written on US arms export policy and the illicit transfers of small arms and light weapons. He is the co-author of a forthcoming book on small arms proliferation.

Elisabeth Sköns (Sweden) is the Leader of the SIPRI Military Expenditure and Arms Production Project. Her most recent publications outside SIPRI include a chapter on military expenditure in *New Millennium, New Perspectives: The United Nations, Security and Governance* (UN University, 2000), a chapter on defence offsets in *Arms Trade and Economic Development: Theory and Policy in Offsets* (Routledge, 2004) and two papers for the International Task Force on Global Public Goods (2004). She is also the author of a chapter on the internationalization of the arms industry for the SIPRI volume *Arms Industry Limited* (1993). She has contributed to most editions of the SIPRI Yearbook since 1983.

Rachel Stohl (United States) is Senior Analyst at the Center for Defense Information (CDI) in Washington, DC. Her 10 years of experience are in the areas of the international arms trade, small arms and light weapons, landmines, failed states and children in armed conflict. She has written extensively on US arms export policy and is co-editor of *Challenging Conventional Wisdom: Debunking the Myths and Exposing the Risks of Arms Export Reform* (Federation of American Scientists, 2003). She is also co-author of a forthcoming book on small arms proliferation. Prior to joining CDI, she was a Fellow at the British American Security Information Council and worked at the UN Center for Disarmament Affairs and the Program for Arms Control, Disarmament, and Conversion.

Petter Stålenheim (Sweden) is a Researcher with the SIPRI Military Expenditure and Arms Production Project and Head of the Sub-Project on Military Expenditure Data. He is responsible for monitoring data on military expenditure, with a special focus on Europe and Central Asia, and for the maintenance of the SIPRI Military Expenditure Database. He has worked as a consultant to the International Institute for Democracy and Electoral Assistance in Stockholm and lectured at the George C. Marshall Center in Germany. He is a co-author of *Armament and Disarmament in the Caucasus and Central Asia*, SIPRI Policy Paper no. 3 (July 2003) and has contributed to the SIPRI Yearbook since 1998.

Eamon Surry (Australia) is a Research Assistant with the SIPRI Military Expenditure and Arms Production Project. He is responsible for maintaining the project databases and Internet site. Prior to joining SIPRI, he worked as a researcher at a broadcast media consultancy in London. He contributed to the *SIPRI Yearbook 2004*.

Connie Wall (United States) is Head of the SIPRI Editorial and Publications Department. She has edited or contributed to the SIPRI Yearbook since 1970.

Professor Peter Wallensteen (Sweden) has held the Dag Hammarskjöld Chair in Peace and Conflict Research since 1985 and was Head of the Department of Peace and Conflict Research, Uppsala University, in 1972–99. He directs the Uppsala Conflict Data Program and the Stockholm Process on Targeted Sanctions. His publications include *Understanding Conflict Resolution: War, Peace and the Global System* (SAGE, 2002) and, with C. Staibano and M. Eriksson, *Making Targeted Sanctions Effective: Guidelines for the Implementation of UN Policy Options* (Uppsala, 2003). Most recently, he co-edited, with C. Staibano, *International Sanctions*: *Between Words and Wars in the Global System* (Frank Cass, 2005). He has contributed to the SIPRI Yearbook since 1988.

Siemon T. Wezeman (Netherlands) is a Researcher with the SIPRI Arms Transfers Project. Among his publications are several relating to international transparency on arms transfers. His most recent publication is *The Future of the United Nations Register of Conventional Arms*, SIPRI Policy Paper no. 4 (Aug. 2003). He has contributed to the SIPRI Yearbook since 1993.

Sharon Wiharta (Indonesia) is a Research Associate with the SIPRI Armed Conflict and Conflict Management Programme, working on peacekeeping issues and on the role of post-conflict justice in peacebuilding, in particular the need for a multi-layered approach to deliver justice. Previously, she worked at the Center for International Affairs at the University of Washington, Seattle. She has contributed to the SIPRI Yearbook since 2002.

SIPRI Yearbook 2005: Armaments, Disarmament and International Security

Oxford University Press, Oxford, 2005, 853 pp.
(Stockholm International Peace Research Institute)
ISBN 0-19-928401-6 and 978-0-19-928401-6

ABSTRACTS

BAILES, A. J. K., 'Introduction. Global security governance: a world of change and challenge', in *SIPRI Yearbook 2005*, pp. 1–27.

The world cannot be secure without security for all, yet the events of recent years have done little to bring global solutions closer. The UN's High-level Panel on Threats, Challenges and Change identified many of the challenges to security; indeed, the UN stands at the centre of many of them. Enhancing its role offers advantages to the strong as well as the weak. Yet the UN does not govern all (e.g., monetary and economic) dimensions of global action relevant to security. All actors with the power to respond to the proposals of the High-level Panel have a shared responsibility to help realize them.

DUNAY, P. and LACHOWSKI, Z., 'Euro-Atlantic security and institutions', in *SIPRI Yearbook 2005*, pp. 43–75.

International politics continued to be dominated by efforts to rebuild transatlantic relations, which gained new impetus after the re-election of US President Bush. The USA has continued to develop an inclusive security structure to obtain the international support necessary to fight terrorism, 'export' homeland security functions and gain more effective intelligence. The USA has increasingly recognized that the EU is its indispensable partner in these areas. NATO's struggle to be regarded as more than a forum for operational decisions continued, as did the EU's development of its capacity to become a credible security actor. A new divide seems to be emerging along the eastern boundaries of Europe as the leaders of some East European and Central Asian countries are increasingly resentful of the spread of democracy and regard it as a challenge to the long-term survival of their regimes. Hampering democracy may make internal dynamics less stable and eventual changes more violent. The situation may result in a limited, non-systemic West–East conflict in the years to come.

DUNAY, P., 'The Organization for Security and Co-operation in Europe: constant adaptation but enduring problems', in *SIPRI Yearbook 2005*, pp. 76–82.

None of the key features that distinguished the OSCE from other European institutions—complete participation of the Euro-Atlantic states, legitimacy to address domestic issues, a focus on the whole conflict cycle, inclusion of nations outside the main security structures and a relatively non-constraining institutional structure—any longer provides a unique advantage. Either the OSCE agenda cannot increase its relevance or important issues have been taken over by other organizations that want to deal with them more effectively. This situation is aggravated by the criticism from several post-Soviet countries. These factors taken together give the impression of crisis in the organization.

DWAN, R. and HOLMQVIST, C., 'Major armed conflicts', in *SIPRI Yearbook 2005*, pp. 83–120.

All major armed conflicts in 2004 took place within, rather than between, states. Developments in the Kashmir and Israeli–Palestinian conflicts demonstrated the internationalization of certain intra-state conflicts. The conflicts in Burundi, Colombia and Sudan were characterized by a multiplicity of actors and grievances, while the conflicts in Nepal and Uganda illustrated the frequent targeting of civilians and the use of asymmetric tactics. Attempts to isolate or contain intra-state conflicts were largely unsuccessful, as illustrated by conflicts in Russia (Chechnya), Indonesia (Aceh) and the Democratic Republic of the Congo. The conflict in Iraq between the government (supported by coalition forces) and various insurgent groups was further testimony to the complexities of contemporary intra-state conflict.

HARBOM, L. and WALLENSTEEN, P., 'Patterns of major armed conflicts, 1990–2004', in *SIPRI Yearbook 2005*, pp. 121–37.

There were 19 major armed conflicts in 17 locations worldwide in 2004. The number of major armed conflicts and the number of conflict locations were slightly lower in 2004 than in 2003, when there were 20 major armed conflicts in 18 locations. No interstate conflicts were active in 2004. The majority of the conflicts in 2004 occurred in Africa and in Asia. In the 15-year post-cold war period, there were 57 different major armed conflicts. The number of major armed conflicts in 2004 was the lowest for the entire period, equalling the number in 1997.

DWAN, R. and WIHARTA, S., 'Multilateral peace missions: challenges of peace-building', in *SIPRI Yearbook 2005*, pp. 139–98.

Post-conflict peace-building—a process that addresses the political, social and economic development of a post-conflict society—was brought to the top of the international policy agenda in 2004 with the substantial treatment of the topic in the report of the UN High-level Panel on Threats, Challenges and Change. Peace-building is an increasingly important part of multilateral peace missions: 17 of the UN missions launched since 1999 have peace-building tasks included in their mandates. Events in Afghanistan, Côte d'Ivoire, Haiti, Iraq and Liberia in 2004 underscored how the challenges of magnitude and legitimacy (both international and local) intersect to make the practical tasks of peace-building difficult to address, particularly in the areas of disarmament, demobilization and reintegration; the rule of law; economic reconstruction; and elections.

BORN, H. and HÄNGGI, H., 'Governing the use of force under international auspices: deficits in parliamentary accountability', in *SIPRI Yearbook 2005*, pp. 199–222.

The use of force under international auspices has increased substantially in the past decade, but the same cannot be said of its democratic accountability. Standards of parliamentary accountability for the use of force under international auspices illustrate the national and international dimensions of what can be termed a 'double democratic deficit'. The basic question is what rights parliaments should have, but their near exclusion from the sensitive judgements surrounding intervention seems incongruous in a democratic age. Modest improvements could be sought by more networking among national parliaments, enhanced procedural rights and information-handling methods, and—at the international level—more reporting to parliamentary bodies and a greater role both for the European Parliament and national assemblies in scrutinizing the EU's security and defence policy.

HOLLIS, R., 'The greater Middle East', in *SIPRI Yearbook 2005*, pp. 223–50.

The greater Middle East is only partially penetrated by globalization and is highly prone to 'new-style' transnational threats as well as older-style interstate tensions. Cutting across national and bilateral agendas are four issues with region-wide impact: the USA's military presence and security ambitions; the conflict between Israel and the Palestinians; the regional fallout of the Iraqi conflict; and terrorism. Military expenditure by the region's states is high and shows a rising trend since 1996, but it is developments related to weapons of mass destruction that grab international attention. The number of multilateral initiatives focused on the region—from the EU, the G8 and NATO—has grown recently, while the level of home-bred regionalism remains modest. Experience suggests that the impact on the greater Middle East of the EU's 'soft power' is still inferior to that of the USA's 'hard power'. Open questions remain about the interstate order in this region: whether and how a Palestinian state will take root, and the fate of Iraq. The risk of the whole order collapsing may be small but a zero-sum approach to coexistence and competition seems set to continue.

ROSAS, M. C., 'Latin America and the Caribbean: security and defence in the post-cold war era', in *SIPRI Yearbook 2005*, pp. 251–82.

Since the 1980s, the introduction of a more open economic model in most states of Latin America and the Caribbean has been accompanied by the growth and democratization of new regional structures, the dying out of interstate conflicts and a reduction in intra-state conflicts, although levels of domestic violence remain high. The latest developments in the agendas of regional organizations show some effort by local states to assert their own concerns, for example, on aspects of security where the USA is currently less engaged. The area's most fundamental problems may be those of economic vulnerability and unequal development, which in turn feed internal unrest and violence. With or without the USA, only a stronger common political will among the region's states can offer hope of mastering these challenges.

SKÖNS, E., 'Financing security in a global context', in *SIPRI Yearbook 2005*, pp. 285–306.

In the current security environment—in which focus has shifted from state territorial security to broader and deeper security dimensions and towards greater global security interdependence—there is an increased perception of the ineffectiveness and growing irrelevance of military means to address security threats and challenges. Furthermore, there is a growing recognition of the need for global action to address such issues. However, the pattern of security financing still appears to be strongly focused on traditional national military security objectives. Government accounts are not currently structured to show the amount of total government expenditure for international or non-military means of security provision. It is therefore impossible to monitor the extent to which countries are adapting to the requirements to shift the balance from military to non-military means of addressing security problems.

SKÖNS, E., OMITOOGUN, W., PERDOMO, C. and STÅLENHEIM, P., 'Military expenditure', in *SIPRI Yearbook 2005*, pp. 307–43.

World military expenditure in 2004 is estimated to have been $975 billion at constant (2003) prices, or $1035 billion in current dollars, just 6 per cent lower in real terms than the peak of cold war military spending. The high rate of growth during the period 2002–2004—at an average of 6 per cent per year in real terms—is largely determined by the trend in US military expenditure, accounting for 47 per cent of the world total. It has increased as a result of massive budgetary allocations for the USA's 'global war on terrorism'; in 2003–2005 it exceeded the combined military spending of the developing world in 2004. The contribution of military spending to the USA's growing budget deficit has raised questions about its impact on economic growth and the crowding out of non-military government spending. Growing recognition in donor countries that security is a prerequisite for development has led to a debate on how they can support security in developing countries in or at risk of conflict. The examples of US assistance to Colombia and British assistance to Sierra Leone illustrate two different approaches to supporting security.

SKÖNS, E. and SURRY, E., 'Arms production', in *SIPRI Yearbook 2005*, pp. 383–403.

The combined arms sales of the top 100 companies in the world (excluding China) in 2003 was $236 billion. Of the 100 companies, 38 are USA-based and 1 is Canadian, and together these accounted for 63 per cent of arms sales by the top 100; 42 European companies (including 6 from Russia) accounted for 31 per cent of sales. Ten companies are located in 3 other OECD countries and 9 in 4 non-OECD countries. The combined arms sales of the top 100 companies in 2003 was 25 per cent higher than in 2002 in current dollars. The process of adaptation to the new security environment continues. In the USA the industry is adjusting to the new demands created by the ongoing transformation of the armed forces, the privatization of military services and the increasing importance of the homeland security sector. In Europe the emphasis is on intra-European consolidation and access to contracts from the expanding US Government arms procurement budget.

WEZEMAN, S. T. and BROMLEY, M., 'International arms transfers', in *SIPRI Yearbook 2005*, pp. 417–48.

The trend in major arms transfers appears to be changing from stable for 2000–2002 to slightly upwards in 2003–2004. Russia replaced the USA as the largest supplier, but even Russian officials expect a decline in Russian transfers in the near future. China and India are the two main recipients. China is almost completely dependent on Russia for its arms imports. India is also a major Russian client, but here Russia faces strong competition. US–EU relations became strained in 2004 over the issues of technology transfers and more so over EU plans to lift its arms embargo against China. The USA wishes to retain the embargo to prevent a Chinese military build-up. Transparency in arms transfers increased again slightly, mainly because the 10 new EU members are now obliged to report under the EU Code of Conduct on Arms Exports.

ANTHONY, I., 'Arms control and non-proliferation: the role of international organizations', in *SIPRI Yearbook 2005*, pp. 529–47.

The divisions over the military action in Iraq and its aftermath underlined that controls on nuclear, biological and chemical (NBC) weapons are essential for a stable and peaceful international order. A failure to negotiate effective controls—on NBC and other types of weapon; on dangerous and sensitive materials; and on both state and non-state actors—could lead to conflict in the future. Little progress has been made in multilateral arms control and cases have come to light of states violating their obligations under existing treaties, undermining confidence in global arms control agreements. States have tended not to consider global measures when trying to make progress on particular problems. Instead, there has been informal cooperation among groups of states. However, in 2004 some new international efforts were made to strengthen global processes as part of an emerging mosaic of arms control measures: UN Security Council Resolution 1540 on the proliferation of NBC weapons and their means of delivery; and the report of the UN High-level Panel on Threats, Challenges and Change. In response to the report, the UN Secretary-General stated that the global nuclear non-proliferation regime was in a precarious state and requested urgent action on the report's recommendations.

KILE, S. N., 'Nuclear arms control and non-proliferation', in *SIPRI Yearbook 2005*, pp. 551–77.

In 2004 the nuclear non-proliferation regime continued to face serious challenges. Evidence emerged confirming the existence of a clandestine transnational nuclear network of companies and middlemen, centred around A. Q. Khan, Pakistan's leading nuclear scientist, that supplied sensitive nuclear technology and expertise to Iran and Libya. There continued to be controversy over the nature of Iran's nuclear programme, as the IAEA provided further detail about Iran's failure to declare important nuclear activities as required by its safeguards agreement with the agency. In addition, little progress was made in the international talks on the future of North Korea's nuclear programme. In the light of these challenges, there was renewed interest in multinational approaches to managing the global nuclear fuel cycle.

GUTHRIE, R., HART, J. and KUHLAU, F., 'Chemical and biological warfare developments and arms control', in *SIPRI Yearbook 2005*, pp. 603–28.

In 2004 the states parties to the 1972 Biological and Toxin Weapons Convention met to consider ways to enhance international capabilities for responding to cases of alleged use of such weapons or suspicious outbreaks of disease and how to enhance existing mechanisms for monitoring and dealing with infectious diseases affecting humans, animals and plants. The states parties to the 1993 Chemical Weapons Convention approved a request by Libya to convert two former chemical weapon production facilities to peaceful purposes, after that country's chemical weapon programme had been dismantled under international supervision. Inspection activities were essentially completed by the Iraq Survey Group and the release of a substantial unclassified report on the search for nuclear, biological and chemical weapons. Official inquiries into the handling of intelligence relating to Iraq published reports during the year.

HART, J. and KILE, S. N., 'Libya's renunciation of nuclear, biological and chemical weapons and ballistic missiles', in *SIPRI Yearbook 2005*, pp. 629–48.

On 19 December 2003 Libya announced that it would verifiably abandon and dismantle, under international inspection, its nuclear, biological and chemical (NBC) weapon programmes and would restrict itself to the possession of ballistic missiles with a range of no more than 300 km. In 2004 the remaining international sanctions against Libya were lifted and the country took further steps to reintegrate itself into the international community. The new information on Libya's NBC weapon programmes that came to light provided a basis for evaluating earlier assessments of these programmes. The British and US roles in prompting Libya's action intensified debate over the merit of different approaches—national and institutional—to addressing concerns about the proliferation of NBC weapons.

LACHOWSKI, Z. and DUNAY, P., 'Conventional arms control and military confidence building', in *SIPRI Yearbook 2005*, pp. 649–73.

In 2004 the 1999 Agreement on Adaptation of the 1990 Treaty on Conventional Armed Forces in Europe was still held hostage to Russia's non-compliance with its commitment to military pullouts from Georgia and Moldova. Expecting reciprocation on the part of NATO, Russia ratified the agreement. The success of the 1996 Agreement on Confidence- and Security-Building Measures in Bosnia and Herzegovina meant that it could be suspended. European arms control currently aims at: sharing its experience with regions outside the OSCE area; ensuring stricter controls of small arms, surplus ammunition, and the like; and regional and subregional application. The prospects for the 1992 Treaty on Open Skies regime also have regional and possible non-military dimensions. Its review conference in early 2005 demonstrated that the states parties wish to maintain its relevance. The major humanitarian and security frameworks gained support in 2004, thereby helping to decrease the scourge of mines worldwide.

ANTHONY, I. and FEDCHENKO, V., 'International non-proliferation and disarmament assistance', in *SIPRI Yearbook 2005*, pp. 675–98.

The number of countries offering assistance in containing the threat from nuclear, biological and chemical (NBC) weapons is growing. International non-proliferation and disarmament assistance (INDA) is evolving from an emergency programme dealing with the break-up of the Soviet Union into a worldwide tool for building security. The geographic and functional scope of INDA is expanding. While the USA remains the biggest assistance provider, other states, mostly G8 members, also make important contributions, albeit bilaterally and with loose coordination. Most INDA activities were carried out in Russia and still contribute successfully to its security, to meeting its disarmament commitments, and to reducing significantly the global risk of catastrophic terrorism, in spite of the fact that in 2004 the INDA administration system in Russia was reorganized, causing delays in implementation.

ANTHONY, I. and BAUER, S., 'Transfer controls', in *SIPRI Yearbook 2005*, pp. 699–719.

In 2004 more countries recognized the self-interest in maintaining modern and effective national transfer controls. The failure of states to put in place such controls was a factor that contributed to the development of Iraqi weapon programmes in the past. Concern about the emergence of new suppliers of technology was heightened by the disclosure of the network led by Pakistani nuclear scientist A. Q. Khan, which had been working to supply weapon-relevant materials and technology to Iran, North Korea and Libya. The EU member states reviewed the national implementation of the common legal basis for controlling exports of dual-use items. The EU also reviewed its Code of Conduct on Arms Exports: changes will be made in 2005. In 2004 well-funded and targeted assistance programmes to help countries establish export controls emerged as a theme in the EU, the G8, the UN and the Wassenaar Arrangement.

SCHROEDER, M. and STOHL, R., 'US export controls', in *SIPRI Yearbook 2005*, pp. 720–40.

The USA is the world's largest arms exporter and has great influence over the global arms trade. Arms transfers from the USA—through various avenues—are governed by a combination of legislation, regulations and presidential directives and are administered by the departments of State and Defense, which are also responsible for end-use monitoring. Oversight is undertaken by the US Congress and the Government Accountability Office. A January 2004 GAO report criticized the State Department's end-use monitoring of exports of cruise missiles and unmanned air vehicles. Recent controversies include the proposed waiving of licence requirements for certain British and Australian companies and the role of arms sales in the war on terrorism.

AHLSTRÖM, C., 'The Proliferation Security Initiative: international law aspects of the Statement of Interdiction Principles', in *SIPRI Yearbook 2005*, pp. 741–65.

The post-11 September 2001 focus on proliferation of weapons of mass destruction (WMD)—to state as well as non-state actors—has highlighted the need to take more robust measures against proliferators. In May 2003 US President Bush announced a new multilateral initiative on law enforcement cooperation for the interdiction and seizure of illegal weapons and missile technologies: the Proliferation Security Initiative (PSI). Thus far, only a 'core group' of states participate in this initiative. The PSI developed rapidly during 2003 and 2004. Its main output is the Statement of Interdiction Principles (SOP), which establishes limitations on a state's authority to exercise enforcement jurisdiction against vessels suspected of carrying WMD and related goods. The majority of the SOP complies with existing international law. The process of developing the PSI has resulted in a shift in emphasis—from the recognition of a need to change the law to a focus on what actions may legally be taken under existing law.

Erratum

SIPRI Yearbook 2004: Armaments, Disarmament and International Security

Page 170, table 4.3:	*For the Multinational Force in Iraq, the figure in the last column, 'Cost ($m)', should read:* 575 623.0.

Index